Sears List of
Subject Headings

Sears List
of
Subject
Headings

15th Edition

Edited by

JOSEPH MILLER

New York

The H. W. Wilson Company

1994

Printed in the United States of America

97 96 95 94   5 4 3 2 1

Library of Congress Cataloging-in-Publication Data

Sears, Minnie Earl, 1873-1933
    Sears list of subject headings / edited by Joseph Miller. — 15th ed.
      p. cm.
    Includes bibliographical references.
    ISBN 0-8242-0858-7 (lib. bdg. : alk. paper)
    1. Subject headings. I. Miller, Joseph, 1946- . II. Title.
Z695.Z8S43   1994   94-16705
025.4′9—dc20   CIP

Contents

Preface

For over seven decades the *Sears List of Subject Headings* has served the needs of small and medium-sized libraries, suggesting headings appropriate for use in their collections and providing patterns and instructions for adding new headings as they are required. The successive editors of the List have faced the need to accommodate change while maintaining a sound continuity. The new and revised headings in each edition reflect developments in the world and in the use of the English language, while the changes in the form of the headings and in the structure and display of the List reflect shifts in the prevailing philosophy of subject cataloging.

With this fifteenth edition the interval between publication of editions has been shortened to provide more timely updating of terminology. In keeping with current thinking in the field of library and information science, all inverted headings have been canceled in favor of the uninverted form. Likewise, the display of the List on the page is entirely new. While Sears remains a list of subject headings and not a true thesaurus, the display now conforms to the NISO standards for thesauri approved in 1993 and labels the references BT, NT, RT, SA, and UF for broader terms, narrower terms, related terms, See Also, and Used for. The new format does not in any way alter the essential information of the List, but only makes it more accessible to catalogers and other users. Similarly, it does not call for any change in the way headings and cross references are represented in a public catalog.

Other features that are new with this edition are a list of canceled and replacement headings to facilitate the updating of catalogs; the use of the legend "[Former heading]" within the List to identify earlier forms of headings; and a new emphasis, in the "Principles of the Sears List" and in the rewording of the general reference notes, on the expandable nature of the List. It is only by being flexible and expandable that Sears has been able over the years to fill the needs of various kinds of libraries.

History and Scope

Minnie Earl Sears prepared the first edition of this work in response to demands for a list of subject headings that was better suited to the needs of the small library than the existing American Library Association and Library of Congress lists. Published in 1923, the *List of Subject Headings for Small Libraries* was based on the headings used by nine small libraries that were known to be well cataloged. Minnie Sears used only *See* and "refer from" references in the first edition. In the second edition (1926) she added *See also* references at the request of teachers of cataloging who were using the List as a textbook. To make the List more useful for that purpose, she wrote a chapter on "Practical Suggestions for the Beginner in Subject Heading Work" for the third edition (1933).

Isabel Stevenson Monro edited the fourth (1939) and fifth (1944) editions. A new feature of the fourth edition was the inclusion of Dewey Decimal Classification numbers as applied in the *Standard Catalog for Public Libraries*. The new subjects added to the List were based on those used in the Standard Catalog Series and on the catalog cards issued by The H.W. Wilson Company. Therefore, the original subtitle "Compiled from Lists used in Nine Representative Small Libraries" was dropped. Another new feature was the printing in italics of those subdivisions that had a general application.

The sixth (1950), seventh (1954), and eighth (1959) editions were prepared by Bertha M. Frick. In recognition of the pioneering and fundamental contributions made by

Minnie Sears the title was changed to *Sears List of Subject Headings* with the sixth edition. Since the List was being used by medium-sized libraries as well as small ones, the phrase "for Small Libraries" was deleted from the title. The symbols *x* and *xx* were substituted for the "Refer from (see ref.)" and "Refer from (see also ref.)" phrases to conform to the format adopted by the Library of Congress.

The ninth edition (1965), the first to be prepared by Barbara M. Westby, continued the policies of the earlier editions, with the one major exception that the Dewey Decimal Classification numbers were dropped. Many users of Sears had expressed the opinion that the inclusion of numbers often led to a misuse of the publication owing to a misunderstanding of the relationship between subject headings and classification. The tenth edition (1972) also omitted the Dewey numbers, but they were reintroduced in the eleventh edition (1977), largely in response to the needs of librarians in many small libraries who had been left with little or no assistance in the classification of their collections.

With the eleventh edition, the "Practical Suggestions for the Beginner in Subject Heading Work" was retitled "Principles of the Sears List of Subject Headings" to emphasize "principles," and a section dealing with nonbook materials was added. The "Principles" have been revised for this edition to incorporate instructions for translating the new labels for references to display in a public catalog.

The thirteenth edition (1986), prepared by Carmen Rovira and Caroline Reyes, was the first to be created as an online database and to take advantage of computer validation capabilities. It also responded to changing theory in subject analysis occasioned by the development of online public access catalogs. This effort was taken further in the fourteenth edition (1991) under the editorship of Martha T. Mooney, who reduced the number of compound terms, simplified many subdivisions, and advanced the work of uninverting inverted headings.

In accord with a suggestion of the Cataloging of Children's Materials Committee of the American Library Association, the headings from *Subject Headings for Children's Literature* (Library of Congress) were incorporated into the Sears List with the thirteenth edition. Some headings were excluded because they fell into the category of headings that can be added to Sears as needed; others were omitted because they already existed in Sears in a slightly different form. Since the Sears List is intended for both adult and juvenile collections, wherever the Library of Congress has two different headings for adult and juvenile approaches to a single subject, a choice was made for Sears. In cases where the Sears List uses the adult form, the cataloger of children's materials may prefer to use the form found in *Subject Headings for Children's Literature.*

Addition of New Headings

The new terms in the present edition represent developments in many different areas, especially business and technology, health and environment, personal relations, and popular culture. Among the new headings are **Codependency; Computer security; Creationism; Multiculturalism; Pacific rim; Performance art;** and **Technology transfer.** At the heading **Soviet Union** in the List an explanation is offered for all the changes occasioned by political developments in the Soviet Union and related countries. One of the notable additions to this edition is the subject heading **African Americans** as a narrower term than **Blacks** and a number of headings derived from **African Americans** as narrower than the parallel terms derived from **Blacks.** For example, the Sears List now has **African American athletes** as well as **Black athletes.**

Approximately 120 headings have been added to enhance subject and genre access to individual works of fiction, poetry, drama, and other imaginative works, such as films and radio and television programs. These headings are based on the *Guidelines on Subject Access to Individual Works of Fiction, Drama, etc.* prepared by a subcommittee of the

Subject Analysis Committee of the ALA in June 1989 and endorsed and recommended by the Subject Analysis Committee in 1990. They include such headings as **Biographical films; Didactic poetry; Horror films; Medical novels;** and **Science fiction television programs.**

Many of the headings new to this edition were suggested by librarians representing various sizes and types of libraries, by commercial vendors of bibliographic records, and by the catalogers and indexers at The H.W. Wilson Company who are responsible for the headings in the Standard Catalog Series, *Book Review Digest,* and such periodical indexes as *Readers' Guide to Periodical Literature.* In addition, *Library of Congress Subject Headings* and the *HCL [Hennepin County Library] Cataloging Bulletin* were consulted.

No list can possibly provide a heading for every idea, object, process, or relationship. What Sears hopes to offer is a basic list that incorporates patterns and examples that will guide the cataloger in adding new headings as needed. Sources for establishing the wording of new headings are discussed in the Principles of the Sears List.

Revision of Headings

At the same time as new headings are added to the List, revision and updating of existing headings continues. Some terms have been changed to reflect current usage; for example, **Cooking** replaces the old-fashioned **Cookery; Exploration** replaces **Discoveries (in geography); Linguistics** replaces **Philology, Comparative;** and **Steel construction** replaces **Building, Iron and steel.** Other headings of decreasing interest, such as **Milling machines** and **Stokers, Mechanical,** have been removed from the List.

In recent years the Library of Congress has increased the rate of revision and modernization of some of its long-standing subject headings. This edition of Sears, like the previous ones, has incorporated many of the changes, such as **Child sexual abuse** instead of **Child molesting; Stamp collecting** instead of **Postage stamps—Collectors and collecting;** and **Traditional medicine** instead of **Folk medicine.**

Form of Headings

It was the policy of Minnie Earl Sears to use the Library of Congress form of subject headings with some modifications, such as the simplification of phrasing and, in some cases, the broadening of a heading. The Sears List still conforms to the usage of the Library of Congress unless there is some compelling reason to vary, but those instances of variation have become numerous over the years.

Beginning with the thirteenth edition of Sears, the direct form of entry has been preferred to the inverted form, both in new headings and in the revision of those already established, on the theory that most library users search for multiple-word terms in the order in which they occur naturally in the language. That effort has been completed in this edition. With a few exceptions, all the remaining inverted headings in the Sears List have now been uninverted. For example, **American satire** replaces **Satire, American; Organic chemistry** replaces **Chemistry, Organic;** and **Islamic art** replaces **Art, Islamic.** The exceptions are the names of battles and massacres and **State, The,** which remain in the inverted form. For the sake of simplicity and uniformity Sears has gone further than the Library of Congress in uninverting inverted headings. In all cases cross references have been made from the inverted form and from the Library of Congress form where it otherwise varies.

Expandability of the List

The degree or level of specificity required for a collection depends on its size, its function, its nature, and the group of users it serves. Practicality rather than theory should determine the degree of specificity, and a balanced blend of theory and practice has been the philosophy of Sears. In a small collection the use of too many specific headings can result in the scattering of like materials. Over 500 places are indicated in the Sears List where headings of greater specificity may be added by the cataloger as needed.

The use of subdivisions also creates greater specificity. The Sears List has two ways of suggesting suitable subdivisions for terms. The first is a list of seven "key" headings for which numerous subdivisions are provided. These are intended as patterns for subdividing similar terms whenever the quantity of materials warrants. The list of "key" headings is found on p xxxix. The second is a "List of Commonly Used Subdivisions," found on p xli. Most of these subdivisions also appear in the alphabetical list as general references, with instructions and examples of how they can be applied to various subjects. The general references, which are attached both to subject headings and to the entries for free-floating subdivisions, increase considerably the coverage of the List and its usefulness. In this edition all the general reference notes have been revised, with the words "to be added as needed" included, to emphasize the expandable nature of the List and to remind the cataloger that headings for types of things and examples of things can always be added to the List.

Scope Notes

The number of scope notes, which are intended either to clarify the use of a term or to distinguish between terms, has once more been increased in this edition. Scope notes have also been added to identify any headings that may be assigned to individual works of drama, fiction, poetry, etc.

Classification

The classification numbers in this edition of Sears are taken from the twelfth edition of the *Abridged Dewey Decimal Classification* and its periodic supplements. The alphabetic notation of B for biographical materials is occasionally provided in addition to Dewey classification numbers for the benefit of libraries using such notation in shelving these materials. In most cases only one number is assigned to a subject heading. There are instances, however, when a given subject is susceptible to more than one point of view, and one number is consequently inadequate for the subject heading. In the example **Chemical industry 338.4; 660,** the numbers represent possible classification numbers for materials dealing with the chemical industry from the viewpoints of economics and technology respectively. Classification numbers are not assigned to some very general subject headings, such as **Charters, Exhibitions, Gifts, Hallmarks, Identification,** and **National characteristics.** These headings cannot be classified unless a specific application is identified.

Few of the Dewey numbers are carried out more than four places beyond the decimal point. Except for libraries with large collections, where more detailed numbers may be required, the numbers in this edition of Sears should be adequate. The need for more detailed classification can often be satisfied by the addition of form and geographic subdivisions, as given in the Dewey tables. To demonstrate the building of these numbers, the Dewey number has been carried out when an example of a form or geographic subdivision is provided in the List, e.g., **Antiques—United States** is given the Dewey number **745.10973.** A library preferring broad classification might elect to use the number found at the unsubdivided **Antiques,** that is, **745.1.** Libraries for whom even relatively brief numbers are too long should consult the section entitled "Close and Broad Classification" (p 24) in the Introduction to the Dewey volume.

Style, Filing, Etc.

For spelling and definition the editor consulted *Webster's Third New International Dictionary of the English Language, Unabridged* (1961) and *Webster's Tenth New*

Collegiate Dictionary (1993). *Random House Dictionary of the English Language,* 2nd ed., Unabridged (1987) was used for technical terms and some other terms not present in either Webster's. In an effort to make the List more useful with online public access catalogs, the use of the hyphen has been restricted to proper nouns or to topical terms where the absence of a hyphen could alter the meaning. Capitalization and the forms of corporate entries and geographic names used as examples are based on the *Anglo-American Cataloguing Rules,* Second edition, 1988 revision.

Since the thirteenth edition of Sears, the filing of entries has followed the *ALA Filing Rules* (1980) without the exception made in previous editions—that is, all headings are now interfiled regardless of any punctuation. Headings with parenthetical modifiers and phrase headings appear interfiled with those with dashes and commas.

Every term in the List that may be used as a subject headings is printed in boldface type whether it is a main term; a term in a USE reference; a broader, narrower, or related term; or an example in a scope note or general reference. If a term is not printed in boldface type, it is not used as a heading. Earlier forms of revised headings and terms that were once subject headings and are no longer, are found after the UF (used for) label with the legend "[Former heading]."

The display of the List on the page has been changed with this edition. It is expected that the new thesaurus-like format with labels for broader, narrower, and related terms will greatly clarify the relationships among terms both for the cataloger and for the users of the public catalog, if a copy of the List is made available to them. As mentioned earlier, this new display on the page does not in any way affect the essential information of the List, nor does it occasion any change in the way headings and cross references are displayed in the public catalog. For a full explanation of how the information in the new format is translated into cross references in the public catalog, see pp xxviii-xxxiii.

Acknowledgments

The editor wishes to acknowledge with gratitude the contributions to this edition of the individual catalogers, reference librarians, and vendors of cataloging services who have offered suggestions for headings to be added to the List. The Cataloging of Children's Materials Committee of the American Library Association has been an invaluable source of advice. Special appreciation is owed to Fran Corcoran, recently retired as Coordinator of Library Services, Community Consolidated School District 62, Des Plaines, Illinois, who has made her experience available to the editors of the List over several editions. Gregory R. New, Assistant Editor, Dewey Decimal Classification, provided advice on the application of Dewey numbers to the Sears headings. Thanks are extended to the editors and catalogers of The H.W. Wilson Company; to Patricia Kuhr, Editor, Subject Authority Files, for her assistance in formulating subjects; to Martha T. Mooney, Editor of *Book Review Digest,* who edited the fourteenth edition of the Sears List, for her day-by-day, sometimes hour-by-hour, help and encouragement; and to Ann Case, Associate Director of Indexing Services.

The classification numbers have been reproduced from the *Abridged Dewey Decimal Classification Edition 12,* published in 1990, by permission of OCLC Forest Press, a division of OCLC Online Computer Library Center, owner of copyright.

The Sears List has been the work of many hands over the years. The editor hopes that this edition represents the best of the previous editions, adapted to accommodate the most significant developments both in library technique and in the changing world. The editor sincerely invites comments from the users of this volume. All suggestions will be valued and given thoughtful consideration.

Joseph Miller

May 1994

Principles of the Sears List of Subject Headings

Certain principles and practices of subject cataloging should be understood before an attempt is made to assign subject headings to library materials. The discussion that follows makes reference to the Sears List of Subject Headings, but the principles are applicable to other lists of subject headings as well.

Purpose of Subject Cataloging

The purpose of subject cataloging is to list under one uniform word or phrase all of the materials on a given subject that a library has in its collection. A subject is the topic treated in a book, videotape, or other work. A subject heading is the word or phrase used in the library catalog to express this topic. A subject entry is usually displayed at the top of the catalog record, above the main entry, regardless of the format of the catalog (card, book, microform, or online).

Library materials are given subject entries in the catalog in order to show what information the library has on a given subject, just as author entries are made to show the works that the library has by a given author. Properly made, the subject entry is a very important supplement to the reference tools in the library because it may enable the reader or librarian to identify rapidly and surely the material needed to provide information about a topic. Subject entries are sometimes also useful in locating a particular book. Ordinarily one consults the author entry for a specific work, but if there is uncertainty about the author's name, one may find the individual item more readily by searching under subject. Smith's *Basic Mathematics* would be difficult to find quickly if one did not know the author's first name and had to consult all the entries in the catalog under Smith. What if the author's name were really spelled Smyth? In either case, the book could be discovered under the subject **Mathematics.**

A printed list of subject headings, such as the Sears List, incorporates the thought and experience of many librarians in various types of libraries. By using the List as a basis for establishing headings, the cataloger has a standard on which to rely. Consistency in both the level of specificity and the form of subject headings is attained by working from an accepted list where the choice among possible wordings has been made and recorded. By following the patterns of headings printed in the List, the cataloger will also be able to add new headings that will be compatible and to establish useful cross references.

Determining the Subject of the Work

The first step in subject cataloging is to ascertain the true subject of the material and the purpose for which it was produced. Sometimes this is readily determined. **Butterflies** is obviously the subject of the book titled *Butterfly Book.* In others cases, the subject is not so easy to discern because it may be a complex one or the author may not express it in a manner clear to someone unfamiliar with the subject. The subject of a work cannot always be determined from the title alone, which is often uninformative or misleading, and undue dependence on it can result in error. A book entitled *Great Masters in Art* immediately suggests the subject **Artists,** but closer examination reveals the book to be about painters specifically, not artists in general. Therefore, the more exact subject is **Painters,** not **Artists.** Another illustration is "Fundamentals of Instrumentation," part 1 of a *Manual of Instrumentation.* This title may suggest a treatise on musical instruments or music, but actually it is a book about engineering instruments.

The steps to follow in determining the subject of a work are the same whether one is considering its value for a reader, classifying it, or assigning subject headings to it. In the case of a book, after reading the title page, examine the table of contents and skim the preface and introduction. Then, if the subject is still not clear, examine the text carefully and read parts of it, if necessary. For nonbook materials examine the container, the label, any accompanying guides, etc., and view or listen to the contents if possible. The cataloger will be in a position to determine the subject of the item in hand only after this preliminary examination has been made. If the meaning of a subject is not clearly understood, one should consult reference sources, not only an unabridged dictionary and general encyclopedia, but specialized reference books as well. Only when the cataloger has decided on the subject content of the work and identified it with explicit words, can the Sears List be used to advantage. The cataloger's own phrasing of the subject must next be adapted to the terminology of the List. The library catalog will be more useful if the cataloger considers materials from the reader's point of view. The reader's profile depends on age, background, education, occupation and geographical location, and takes into account the type of library—school, public, university, or special—as well. When examining a work the cataloger should ask "If I wanted material on this subject, under what words would I look in the catalog?" Then the List is consulted to insure uniformity in choice and form of the words. Local terminology may be used as references to the words in the List. In choosing these words, that is, assigning the proper subject headings, there are certain principles that should be followed. These are considered in the next five sections: Specific and Direct Entry; Common Usage; Uniformity; Form Headings; and Classification and Subject Headings.

Specific and Direct Entry

The principle of specific entry is fundamental both in using and in making a modern subject catalog. The rule of specific and direct entry is to enter a work directly under the most specific term (i.e., subject heading) that accurately and precisely represents its content. This term serves as a succinct abstract of the work.

The principle of specific entry holds that a work is entered under a specific term rather than under a broader heading. If a work is about penguins, it should be entered directly under the most specific heading available, that is, **Penguins.** It should not be listed under the heading **Birds** or even under **Water birds.** If it were, a reader would have to look through many entries to find information on penguins. The principle of direct entry holds that a topic is formulated as a specific term, rather than as a subdivision of a broader heading. If the reader wants information about bridges, the direct approach is to consult the catalog under the heading **Bridges,** not under the broader subject **Engineering** subdivided by the topic *Bridges*. In other words, make direct entry under **Bridges,** not indirectly under Engineering—Bridges or Engineering—Civil engineering— Bridges. Note that **Penguins, Bridges,** Engineering—Bridges, and Engineering—Civil engineering—Bridges are all specific headings, but only **Penguins** and **Bridges** are both specific and direct.

Having found the most specific entry that will fit the item, the cataloger should not then make a duplicate entry under a general subject heading. A work with the title *Birds of the Ocean* should not be entered under both **Birds** and **Water birds** but only under **Water birds.** To eliminate this duplication, a network of "See also" references in the catalog direct the reader from the broader subject headings to the more specific ones, e.g. "**Birds. See also Water birds;** and names of specific birds. . . ." In many cases the most specific entry will be a general subject. *Birds of the World* would have the subject heading **Birds.** The specific term, as can be seen, refers to the exact word or phrase that comprehends the subject content of the work. The heading should be as specific as possible for the topic it is intended to cover.

If the name of a specific subject is not found in the List, the name of the larger group to which it belongs should be consulted. For example, in assigning subject headings to a work discussing elm and ash trees, the cataloger would find neither **Elm** nor **Ash** listed. However, under the broader subject, **Trees,** the following general reference is given: "SA [see also] names of trees, e.g. **Oak**; to be added as needed, in the singular form." The cataloger thus has the authority to use the two headings, **Elm** and **Ash.** (Further directions for adding headings can be found on p. xxxvii).

Common Usage

The word or words used to express a subject must represent common usage. In American libraries this means current American spelling and terminology: **Labor** not Labour; **Color** not Colour; **Elevators** not Lifts. In British libraries these choices would be reversed. Foreign terms such as Laissez faire are not used unless they have been incorporated into the English language. By the same token contemporary words are to be used: **Home economics** not Domestic economy. Today a more current term might be Homemaking, or Household management, but changing a heading is not always simple. Terminology evolves slowly, and in the case of **Home economics,** the term is still being used and newer usage may not have stabilized.

A general rule is to use a popular or common rather than a scientific or technical word where there is a choice. Subject headings are chosen to fit the needs of the people who are likely to use the catalog. A reader in a small public library will look under **Birds,** not Ornithology. In a scientific library Ornithology might be more appropriate. After deciding on the common name as the heading, the cataloger should make a reference from the scientific name to the form used. Such references will be discussed later.

Uniformity

Another very important factor to be considered is that of uniformity. One uniform term must be selected from several synonyms, and this term must be applied consistently to all works on the topic. Materials on China, Chinaware, and Porcelain are all entered under **Porcelain.** This example also illustrates the fact that the subject heading must be inclusive and cover the topic. The heading chosen must also be unambiguous. If several meanings attach to one word, that word must be qualified: **Masks (Facial); Masks (Plays); Masks (Sculpture).** When variant spellings are in use, one must be selected and uniformly applied: **Sulphur** not Sulfur. A decision also must be made whether the heading is to be in the singular or plural form. The choice of singular or plural will be further discussed under "Grammar of Subject Headings" below.

Some descriptive words also carry various connotations, as with Arab, Arabian, and Arabic. It may seem inconsistent to use all three forms, but they are used consistently in the following ways: Arab relating to the people; Arabian referring to the geographical area; and Arabic for the language, script, or literature. In subject headings such words should be used consistently, with distinction being made among ethnic, geographical, and linguistic terms.

Materials should be considered in categories. The word or phrase chosen as a subject must fit not only the item being cataloged but also apply to a group of items on the same subject. The cataloger must consider not only the one item in hand but also the other book and nonbook materials that discuss the same subject, albeit under different titles, in order to select a subject heading that will serve the entire group with relation to other groups in the catalog. In cataloging *Everybody's Cook Book* the inexperienced cataloger might think first of Cookbooks as the term that will give the best description. But there are two other works that belong in the same group: *How's and Why's of Cooking* and *Cooking for Profit.* These contain not only recipes but also other material on cooking. **Cooking** fits the three closely related items better than Cookbooks, and it also fits well with the related subject **Cooking for the sick.** Terminology for a subject must be uniform to fit many similar works.

Form Headings

In addition to the subject headings that interpret the content of various materials, there are headings of another kind, usually known as form headings, or form subject headings, that have the same appearance as topical subject headings but refer to the literary or artistic form of a work and not to its subject matter, among them **Essays, Poetry, Fiction, Hymns,** and **Songs.** Headings for the major literary forms, such as **Fiction, Poetry, Drama,** and **Essays,** are usually used for collections only rather than for works of an individual. For example, the form heading **Essays** is used not for works of an individual author but for collections of essays by authors of various nationalities. If the collection includes essays only by American authors, then the more specific heading **American essays** would be used. While the use of form entries for works of individual authors might be helpful, the result in most libraries is not considered to be worth the effort. The proliferation of entries is an extra cost and increases the size of the catalog unnecessarily. Materials of this type are generally classified and arranged on the shelves according to their literary forms, and the reader often has access to the shelves or to the shelf list. Ordinarily individual works of literature are remembered in association with an author, and a reader consults the author or title entry in the catalog for such works.

In recent years, however, there has been a greatly increased demand for subject and genre access to individual works of literature as well as to individual nonbook materials, such as films, videos, and sound recordings. Subject access to individual works of fiction, poetry, and drama can be expressed with the subdivisions *Fiction, Poetry,* and *Drama* attached to any appropriate subject heading from the List, for example **Slavery—United States—Fiction.** Subject access to such materials is also available in reference sources such as *Short Story Index, Play Index, Essay and General Literature Index,* etc. Unlike the major literary forms, minor literary forms and genres such as **Fantasy fiction; Pastoral poetry; Science fiction plays;** etc., are not identifiable by the classification numbers. Libraries that want to provide access to these kinds of materials may assign the appropriate form or genre headings to individual works as well as to collections and materials about the form or genre. The matter of subject and genre access to individual literary works will be further discussed under "Language and Literature" below.

Apart from literary works themselves there are also many kinds of library materials about literary forms that require subject headings. For a work about the essay as a literary form—for example, the appreciation of the essay or how to write it—the heading **Essay** represents a true subject and not a form heading. The distinction between form headings and topical subject headings can sometimes be made by using the singular form for the topical heading and the plural for the form heading, e.g. **Short story; Short stories.** But the peculiarities of language do not always permit this. For example, the heading **English poetry** is used for a book about English poetry, but in order to show that a book is a collection of poetry by several English authors, the subdivision *Collections* is added: **English poetry—Collections.** The headings for minor literary forms and genres may be used unsubdivided both for literary works and for materials about the form or genre, but if the amount of the latter material in a library warrants, subdivisions may be used to create such headings as **Fantasy fiction—History and criticism; Fantasy fiction—Bibliography;** etc.

In addition to the literary form headings there are some other useful form headings that are determined by the general format of the material and the purpose of the work, such as **Almanacs; Encyclopedias and dictionaries;** and **Gazetteers.** These headings are customarily assigned to individual works as well as to materials about such forms.

Classification and Subject Headings

The cataloger should recognize a fundamental difference between classification and subject headings for the dictionary catalog. In a system of classification, which determines the arrangement of works on the shelves, a work can obviously have only one class number and stand in only one place, but in a catalog entries representing the work can appear, if necessary, under more than one subject. The cataloger does not have to decide on one subject to the exclusion of all others, but can make the work accessible with entries for as many different points of entry as there are distinct subjects in the work (usually, however, not more than three). Classification is used to gather in one numerical place on the shelf works that give similar treatment to a subject. Subject headings gather in one alphabetical place in a catalog all treatments of a subject regardless of shelf location.

Theoretically there is no limit to the number of subject entries that could be made for one work, but practically an excess of entries is not only expensive but also inefficient for the user of the catalog. For many works, a single subject heading will represent the contents accurately. A book such as *Guide to the Trees* is fully and specifically covered by the subject heading **Trees.** Frequently two headings are necessary; occasionally three are required to do justice to the work. More than three should be considered very carefully. The need for more than three may be due to the cataloger's inability to identify precisely the single heading that would cover all the topics in the work. Similarly, a subject heading should not be assigned for a topic that comprises less than one third of a work.

The commonest practice may be stated as follows: As many as three specific subject headings in a given area may be assigned, but if a work treats of more than three, then the next larger inclusive heading is adopted and the specific headings are omitted. A work about lemons and oranges would be entered under **Lemon** and **Orange.** If the work also included material on grapefruits, a third entry with the heading **Grapefruit** would be made for the catalog. But if the work discussed limes and citron as well, the only subject heading assigned would be **Citrus fruit.** As mentioned above under the principle of specific entry, it is not advisable to assign both a general heading and one of its specific aspects to the same work. The work about citrus fruit in the example may have discussed the orange in somewhat more detail than the other fruits, but **Citrus fruit** and **Orange** would not both be assigned.

The cataloger is now aware of another difference between classification and subject cataloging, and one particularly significant for small libraries: classification is frequently less precise than the subject entries for the catalog. Material on floriculture in general as well as on specific kinds of garden flowers are classed together in **635.9.** A book on flower gardening, one on perennial gardening, and one on rose gardening will all three be classified in one number in a library, while in the catalog each book will have its own specific subject heading: **Flower gardening; Perennials; Roses.**

It is well to remember that books are classified by discipline, not by subject. A single subject may be dealt with in many disciplines. The Dewey classification numbers given with a heading in the Sears List are intended only to direct the cataloger to the disciplines where that subject is most likely to be discussed. They are not meant to be absolute or cover all possibilities. The cataloger must examine the book at hand and determine the discipline in which the author is writing. On the basis of that decision the cataloger classifies the book, not the subject of the book.

Subject headings are used for materials that have definite, definable subjects. There are always, however, a few works in which the subject is so indefinite that it is better not to assign a heading. Such a work might be a collection of materials produced by several individuals on a variety of topics or one person's meandering thoughts and ideas. If a cataloger cannot determine a definite subject, the reader is unlikely to find the item under a makeshift or general heading. Vague terms are a disservice to the reader. The headings

Human behavior and **Happiness** assigned to a book titled *Appreciation* are misleading for what is a personal account of the sources of the author's pleasure in life. The book has no specific subject.

Now that certain principles of assigning subject heading are understood, the cataloger should consider the structure of subject headings.

Grammar of Subject Headings

Single Noun

A single noun is the ideal type of subject heading when the language supplies it. Such terms are not only the simplest in form but often the easiest to comprehend. Most of the large fields of knowledge can be expressed by single words (**Art; Agriculture; Education; Religion**) as can many specific objects (**Apple; Chairs; Pottery; Trees; Violins**). Many words, however, have synonyms from which a choice has to be made. For others there is a choice in the spelling. A further consideration is the use of the singular or plural form. For example, in the case of **Pottery,** other words that might be used are Crockery, Dishes, Earthenware, Faience, and Stoneware. In the Sears List, the term chosen is **Pottery** and references are made from the other terms. On the other hand, there are many words that have two or more quite different meanings. The word Date may mean a fruit, an historical period, or a social engagement; File may refer to an arrangement of material, to a computer document, or to a tool; Forging may mean counterfeiting or metalwork. If possible these various meanings should be formulated into headings in ways that are not ambiguous and that bring out the specific meaning of each heading. Hence Depression can mean either an economic or a mental state, but one is formulated **Economic depressions** and the other **Depression (Psychology).** Stress can mean either stress on materials or stress of mind, and the two headings are **Strength of materials** and **Stress (Psychology).** Notice that the ambiguous word is qualified even when the other meaning is expressed in other words. Furthermore, an ambiguous term such as Feedback should be qualified, **Feedback (Psychology),** even when the other meaning, **Feedback (Electronics),** does not exist in the catalog. Whenever identical words with different meanings are used in the catalog, both require parenthetical qualifiers, usually either a broader term or a discipline of study. In the example of the book on lemons and oranges, if the work also included materials on limes, a third heading would be created. Lime (the singular form, as Sears stipulates for all fruits and trees) is an ambiguous term; hence **Lime (Fruit)** is created to distinguish it from **Lime (Mineral).** Since **Seals (Animals)** and **Seals (Numismatics)** are already in the List, any subject that is added to the List but uses the same word must be qualified: **Seals (Christmas, etc.)** or **Seals (Law).**

A choice must be made between the singular and plural form of a term. The plural is the more common, but in practice both are used. Abstract ideas are usually stated in the singular. A concept or action is singular (**Theater**), whereas objects and things are plural (**Theaters**). The names of trees are stated in the singular so that they can represent either the tree or the wood or the fruit of the tree. In this case, the singular is more inclusive than the plural. In other cases, the plural will have the broader coverage (**Art; Arts**).

Compound Headings

Using two nouns joined by "and" usually groups together under one heading closely related materials that cannot easily be separated in concept and are usually treated together (**Bow and arrow; Cities and towns; Publishers and publishing**), or two different subjects that are treated in their relation to each other (**Aeronautics and civilization; Religion and science; Television and children**), or two subjects that are opposites but are usually discussed together (**Belief and doubt; Good and evil; Joy and sorrow**).

A problem in forming such headings is word order. There is no rule to cover all situations, although catalogers have been prone to follow the alphabetic order when there is no common usage. Whichever order is chosen, reference must be made from the opposite order.

The current trend toward simplification of subject access, influenced by the development of electronic information retrieval systems, argues for limiting compound headings when possible. Subject headings that treat the relationship between two broad subjects from the perspective of each, as with **Religion and science,** are clear exceptions to this.

Adjective with Noun

Often a specific concept is best expressed by qualifying the noun with an adjective (**American literature; Electric engineering; Tropical fish**). In the past the expression was frequently inverted (**Psychology, Religious; Art, Municipal**). The reasons for inversion were two-fold: 1) an assumption was made that the searcher would think first of the noun; or 2) the noun was placed first in order to keep all aspects of a broad subject together. In recent years these arguments have been abandoned in favor of the direct order of natural language. (A few exceptions remain, such as the names of battles and massacres, and **State, The.**) When inverted headings have been uninverted, a reference from the older inverted form is usually added if it seems useful in sending the user to the uninverted form.

Phrase Headings

Some concepts that involve two areas of knowledge can be expressed only by more or less complex phrases. These are the least satisfactory headings as they offer the greatest variation in wording, are often the longest, and may not be thought of readily by either the maker or the user of the catalog, but for many topics the English language seems to offer no more compact terminology. Examples are **Bible as literature** and **Freedom of information.**

Subdivisions

The scope of the List can be enlarged far beyond the actual headings printed through the use of subdivisions. The principle of specific entry can be achieved in some cases only by subdividing a general subject:

Birds	**Food**	**Music**
Birds—Eggs and nests	**Food—Analysis**	**Music—Acoustics and**
Birds—Migration	**Food—Fiber content**	**physics**
Birds—Protection	**Food—Sodium content**	**Music—Theory**

Under each of the subject headings **Birds; Food;** and **Music** above, the subdivisions used are appropriate to the one heading and are not applicable to the other two. The subdivision *Analysis,* however, would be applicable to a number of other topics besides **Food,** such as **Blood; Coal; Plants;** etc. Some terms or phrases used as subdivisions are applicable to so many different topics that the subdivisions are not printed in the List under all possible headings. Some are given in their alphabetic places in the List with instructions for their use. They vary in kind and in value to an individual library and should be used at the discretion of the cataloger or according to local policy.

Subdivisions by Physical Form

Some materials present a subject not in expository or narrative form but as lists, outlines, or tables; or, graphically as maps, pictures, or filmstrips. The work may be a directory of chemists, a bibliography of children's literature, a dictionary of psychology, a collection of geological maps, a Bible picture book. In such cases, it is important to show the user of the catalog that these works are not expository treatises on chemists, or children's literature, or psychology, or geology, or the Bible, respectively. It is equally important to be able to locate a bibliography, a dictionary, maps, or pictures directly without having to read through all the entries under the main heading. Standard terms known as "form divisions" are the most common subdivisions and may be used whenever appropriate. Since they show what the material is, rather than what it is about, they are as necessary for a small library as for a large one. Following are examples of form divisions:

Bibliography	*Gazetteers*	*Pictorial works*
Catalogs	*Handbooks, manuals, etc.*	*Portraits*
Dictionaries	*Indexes*	*Registers*
Directories	*Maps*	*Statistics*

Most of these terms may also stand alone as actual subject headings, or form headings, whenever there is material about the form. In either case, each of these terms is listed in its alphabetic place in the List with directions for its use or as a reference to another term together with an explanation of its use as a subdivision. For example:

Bibliography
>SA [see also] subjects and names of persons and places with the subdivision *Bibliography,* to be added as needed.

Dictionaries
>USE **Encyclopedias and dictionaries**
>>and names of languages and subjects with the subdivision *Dictionaries,* e.g. **English language—Dictionaries; Biography—Dictionaries;** etc., to be added as needed.

Comparable statements are included under each of the other form headings. Applying these directions to the types of materials mentioned above, the headings created would be these:

Chemists—Directories	**Geology—Maps**
Children's literature—Bibliography	**Bible—Pictorial works**
Psychology—Dictionaries	

These heading-subdivision combinations are not printed in the List except for isolated examples. As the references indicate, such subdivided headings are to be created as needed.

Form subdivisions are particularly valuable under headings for the large fields of knowledge that are represented by many entries in the catalog. The cataloger must be guided by the character of an item's content, not by the title. Many works whose titles begin with such expressions as "Outline of," "Handbook of," or "Manual of" are in fact comprehensive works. For example, H. G. Wells's *Outline of History* and H. J. Rose's *Handbook of Latin Literature* are comprehensive, lengthy treatises, and to use the form divisions that the titles suggest would be inaccurate. Other so-titled "Outlines" or "Manuals" or "Handbooks" may prove to be bibliographies, dictionaries, or statistics of the subject.

Subdivisions That Show Special Aspects or Topics

A subject may be presented from a particular point of view. The work may be a history of the subject (the most common of the special aspects) or it may deal with the philosophy of the subject, research in the field, the laws about it, or how to study and teach it. These concepts applied to general subjects are expressed by such headings as the following:

Education—History   **Radio—Law and legislation**
Religion—Philosophy   **Mathematics—Study and teaching**
Aeronautics—Research

Subdivisions That Show Chronology

In any catalog, large or small, there will be many works on American history. If they are all entered under the general heading, the library user must look through many entries to find a specific era. However, with chronological subdivisions corresponding to generally accepted periods of a country's history or to the spans of time most frequently treated in materials, a search can be narrowed to **United States—History—1945-1953,** etc. If a chronological era has been given a specific name, this is included in the heading with dates. The current trend is to use dates rather than names. This facilitates filing both in the manual and machine modes. In fact, the computer needs very explicit instructions in order to create a chronological file if it must ignore a word or phrase preceding a date. Therefore, the Subject Analysis Committee of the American Library Association has recommended that dates precede phrases, as in **United States—History— 1775-1783, Revolution.** It has recommended further that century subdivisions be defined to insure correct numerical filing position, that 19th century, for example, be changed to **1800-1899 (19th century);** and that indefinite subdivisions be written as filed, that To 1500, for example, be changed to **0-1500.** These recommendations were adopted in the twelfth edition of Sears.

The List includes chronological subdivisions only for those countries for which a library is apt to acquire so many works about their history (United States, Great Britain, France, Germany, Italy and a few others) that it is necessary to separate them into groups according to the period treated, or for contemporary events that have produced a considerable amount of literature, for example, **Lebanon—History—1982-1984, Israeli intervention.** Although some countries have a longer history than any of these, period subdivisions are not needed because the library acquires so little material about them. In such cases all the material, regardless of the period treated, would be assigned the general heading, e.g., **India—History.** Libraries that have larger than ordinary collections in the history of a particular country or region will want to establish period subdivisions and with them subdivide the material further than is spelled out in the Sears List.

Some of the topical and form subdivisions that are applicable to a considerable number of subjects are listed in their alphabetic places in the List and are also gathered together in the "List of Commonly Used Subdivisions" on p xli. History subdivisions, however, are different for each country and so cannot be listed in one place. For these the cataloger may wish to consult *LC Period Subdivisions under Names of Places,* 4th ed. 1990.

Subdivisions That Show Place

Subdivision by names of places is discussed below under "Geographic Names: Subjects Subdivided by Place."

Geographic Names

Many works limit the discussion of an otherwise general subject to a specific country, state, city, or region. This is such a common practice that the List has provided directions for many subjects that may be so treated. Other subjects not so identified can be subdivided by the cataloger if this is needed or is desirable. Suggested reference sources to be used in researching and establishing geographic names are the most current editions of *The Columbia-Lippincott Gazetteer of the World, National Geographic Atlas of the World, Statesman's Year-book, Times Atlas of the World,* and *Webster's New Geographical Dictionary.*

Subjects Subdivided by Place

Various subject headings, especially in the fields of science, technology, and economics, are followed by a parenthetic statement giving permission to subdivide the heading geographically, such as **"Agriculture** (May subdiv. geog.)." In application this means that if the work in hand deals with agriculture in general, only the heading **Agriculture** is used; but if it deals with agriculture in Iowa or in France, for example, then the cataloger may assign the heading **Agriculture—Iowa** or **Agriculture—France.**

The unit used as a subdivision may be the name of a country, state, city, or other political or geographic area, depending on the nature of the subject and its treatment in the work. There are, however, some topics that would not apply to cities, in which case the note might read: "(May subdiv. geog. country or state)."

Some subjects, such as art and music, have general references that read: "SA [see also] art of particular countries or regions, e.g. **Greek art."** For these headings the geographic qualification is conveyed by a modifying adjective rather than by a subdivision.

Observe that the parenthetic note is permissive, not mandatory. If the library has only a few works on a subject for which geographic treatment is suggested, perhaps it would be easier for the user of the catalog to find these under the main heading without geographic subdivision. Some small libraries limit the use of geographic subdivision to countries other than the United States and to nationalities other than American since most of their material will be concerned with the United States. Furthermore, if a library prefers geographic subdivisions for subjects that are not so indicated in Sears, the library should feel free to add them. The Sears List historically has never distinguished between French art or Art in France (which is not necessarily French). Should a library have sufficient material to warrant such a distinction, **Art—France** could be established in addition to **French art,** which is suggested, and the art of particular countries could also be subdivided by other countries, e.g., **Italian art—Great Britain.** One of the fundamentals of cataloging is to use one's judgment based on the materials at hand and the purpose and needs of the library.

Geographic subdivisions can be either direct or indirect. The Sears List prefers direct subdivision as the most useful to the reader. In the direct form the name of the place discussed in the work is used as the subdivision, e.g., **Theater—Paris (France)** or **Agriculture—Iowa.** The indirect form of subdivision interposes the name of the country (the larger geographic area) between the subject and the smaller area that is covered in the work, e.g., Theater—France—Paris and Agriculture—United States—Iowa.

Names of Places Subdivided by Subject

A different procedure is followed for most topics in the fields of history, geography, and politics, which are treated from a regional point of view. In works discussing the history of California, a census of Peru, the government of Italy, the boundaries of Bolivia, the population of Paris, or the climate of Alaska, the area treated is the unique factor and its name with the appropriate topical subdivision is the most specific heading for the work. Directions for formulating such headings are given under appropriate subjects, for example:

Census

SA [See also] names of countries, cities, etc., with the subdivision *Census,* to be added as needed.

The SA label introduces a direction to the cataloger to formulate headings as needed for specific areas, and the example, which appears in the NT [narrower term] field under **Census,** is **United States—Census.** Similar directions appear under **Boundaries; Climate; Population,** etc., which, applied to the works cited above, would result in the following headings:

California—History   Bolivia—Boundaries
Peru—Census   Paris (France)—Population
Italy—Politics and government   Alaska—Climate

Some topical subdivisions may be used under the name of any country, state, city, or other area. Some topics are applicable to countries only (e.g., *Commercial policy; Diplomatic and consular service*); and others are used only under names of cities (e.g., *Suburbs and environs*). Instructions for application are explicit, for example, "Foreign policy. USE names of countries with the subdivision *Foreign relations,* e.g. **United States—Foreign relations;** to be added as needed."

A list of suggested subject subdivisions that may be used under the name of any city is given in the List under **Chicago (Ill.);** those that may be used under the name of any state are listed under **Ohio;** and those that may be used under the name of any country or region, except for chronological subdivisions, are given under **United States.** Since each country's history is unique, the period subdivisions for its history are also unique.

Local materials are an exception to these rules for establishing headings for geographic names. If the library wishes to keep community area materials together, then the discussion regarding subjects subdivided by place can be ignored, and all materials entered under the name of the locality with all aspects as subdivisions.

Note that there are no definite rules on whether to subdivide by place or by subject. In general, subject headings in the fields of science, technology, economics, education, and the arts are subdivided by place, while aspects of history, geography, and politics are subdivisions under place. In many of the social sciences, the aspect of the subject that is most important or has the primary focus is the criterion for decision. A work on social life and customs, for example, is likely to be about the social life and customs of a particular place, e.g., **United States—Social life and customs. Single parent family,** on the other hand, is a subject of general interest and is only secondarily about single parent families in a particular place. (Even though it is not subdivided by place in Sears, **Single parent family** may nonetheless be subdivided geographically if the material in a given library warrants.)

In summary, the cataloger should enter under place and subdivide by subject those topics whose predominant interest is focused on an area or people, such as history, geography, or government. One should enter under subject and subdivide by place those topics that are primarily of interest for the subject matter regardless of place. In the social sciences the decision must be made in each instance on the element of predominance, because no general rule applies.

Some headings in the subject areas of biography, language, and literature require subdivisions relevant to their areas, but others do not. Since knowing when not to subdivide is as important as when to use subdivisions, these areas are treated in some detail below.

Biography

Works in the field of biography fall into two categories: those in which biography as a form of writing is discussed, a relatively small class covered adequately by the subject heading **Biography (as a literary form),** and lives of persons, a very large class that must be considered in two groups—individual biography and collective biography.

Individual Biography

Usually the only subject heading needed for the life of an individual is the name of the person, established in the same way as an author entry. If the work is an autobiography, some catalogers do not make a subject entry for it since the author and the subject are the same. However, since readers have been trained to look under subject entries it seems reasonable to make both an author and a subject heading, especially if there are many other entries as author, if there are subject entries by other authors, or if the library has a divided catalog.

Occasionally a biography will include so much material about the field in which the individual was working that a second subject heading is required in addition to the personal name. A life of Mary Baker Eddy, for example, may include a valuable account of the development of Christian Science that would require the subject heading, **Christian Science—History.** It must be emphasized that such additional subject headings should be used only when there is a substantial amount of material included in addition to the subject's personal life. They are not used simply because the biographee was prominent in the field.

There are a few individuals about whom a large amount of material exists that is other than biographical, such as works about their writings or other activities. In such cases, subdivisions are added to the person's name to specify various aspects treated, among them *Biography.* Two such examples are Jesus Christ and William Shakespeare. The List includes these names with subdivisions appropriate to material written about them. The subdivisions listed under Shakespeare may also be used, if needed, under the names of other individuals about whom there is a large amount of varied literature. Subdivisions listed under **Presidents—United States** are to be used where appropriate under the name of any president, or other ruler, if applicable. It must be noted that this represents the exceptional, not the usual, treatment. For most individual biographies only the name is needed.

Collective Biography

Collective biographies are works containing biographies of more than three persons. If there are no more than three, each subject is given a heading consisting of the person's name, as in individual biography. (Some catalogers will treat even larger collections as a group of individual biographies. If they do this, they are analyzing the work, i.e., they are making analytic entries.) There are several varieties of collective biography, each requiring a separate kind of treatment.

General. Collective biographies not limited to any area or to any class of persons are assigned the heading **Biography.** Sometimes the work includes many individuals, such as *International Who's Who;* sometimes a small group, such as *Ten Biographies of Famous Men and Women.*

Local Biography. Very common are the biographies devoted to persons of a particular area, such as *Who's Who in Asia, Who's Who in the Arab World, Dictionary of American Biography, Eminent Californians, Leaders in London;* or to ethnic groups, such as *Who's Who among Hispanic Americans.* In such works the subject heading is the name of the area or ethnic group with the subdivision *Biography:*

Asia—Biography	**California—Biography**
Arab countries—Biography	**London (England)—Biography**
United States—Biography	**Hispanic Americans—Biography**

If there are many entries under any such heading, the literary works (i.e., those designed for continuous reading) may be separated from the reference works, which list a large number of names in alphabetic order, by adding to the heading for the latter the subdivision *Dictionaries.* The heading for such a work as *Who's Who in America* may be, therefore, **United States—Biography— Dictionaries.**

Classes of Persons. Collective biographies that are devoted to lives of persons of a particular occupation or profession are entered under the term applied to its members, such as **Artists; Authors; Engineers; Librarians; Musicians; Poets; Radiologists; Scientists;** etc., with the subdivision *Biography.*

In a field where there is no adequate term to express its members, or when the name of the class or group refers to the subject in general, not to individuals, the heading used for the specific field is subdivided by the term *Biography:*

Catholic Church—Biography	**United States—History—1861-1865,**
Religions—Biography	**Civil War—Biography**
	Women—Biography

Observe that the headings for areas, classes, and groups are used for collective biographies only and not for the life of an individual artist, author, woman, etc. However, a general reference to names of individuals should be made in the catalog under the class names, for example: "Artists. See also names of individual artists."

Language and Literature

Language and literature are closely related, but they differ considerably in their treatment in the catalog. In both fields the major interest is not in the general treatment but in the national aspect, that is, French language, English literature, German grammar, or Italian drama, but the fields differ in the way particular aspects or forms are expressed.

Language

The subject heading for a general work about a specific language is the direct phrase: **English language; French language; German language.** If the work deals with a particular aspect or form of that language, a term representing the aspect or form is used as a subdivision of the name of the language:

English language—Etymology	**German language—Grammar**
French language—Dictionaries	**Spanish language—Terms and phrases**

Many of the general form and topical subdivisions discussed previously will also be needed under names of languages, for example, **Italian language—History.** Names of some languages are included in the List (and others are to be added as needed), but customarily no subdivisions are listed except under **English language.** This serves as a guide or "key" to the subdivisions that may be used under the name of any language.

Literature

The field of literature includes two classes of material that must be distinguished carefully: (1) works about literature, a relatively small group; and (2) examples of literature, that is the literature itself, a very large group. In the first we are dealing with actual subjects; in the second with literary forms, not subjects.

Works about Literature. The subject headings for works about the various literary forms are their specific names, e.g., **Drama; Essay; Fiction; Poetry.** Works about the major literary forms of national literatures are entered under the direct phrase, e.g., **Irish drama; Italian poetry; Russian fiction.** Specific aspects or forms are expressed by subdivisions, as for other subjects; e.g., **Drama—Technique; English literature— Dictionaries; Short story—Congresses; American literature—History and criticism.** It should be noted that the subdivision *History and criticism* is always used in its entirety and corresponds to the subdivision *History* used with subjects other than literature, motion pictures, or music.

Names of some national literatures are included in the List (and others are to be added as needed), but a suggested list of subdivisions appears only under **English literature,** which thus serves as the "key" to subdivisions that may be used under the name of any national literature. Likewise, subject headings for works about the major literary forms may be formulated for any national literature by substituting its name for the word "English."

Examples of Literature, i.e. Belles Lettres. This large class of material must be separated into two categories whose treatment is entirely different: individual authors and collections of several authors.

Individual Authors. In general, the literary works of individual authors receive no subject entry. Literature is best known by author and title, and readers usually want a specific novel or play, or poetry by a specific author—material that can be located in the catalog by author and title entries.

There are, however, many libraries where access by subject and genre to individual works of imaginative literature is thought desirable. Subject access is provided by using any applicable subject heading from the List with the subdivision *Fiction, Drama,* or *Poetry.* Hence a novel about the clergy could be assigned the heading **Clergy—Fiction;** a play in which Napoleon is a character could be assigned the heading **Napoleon I, Emperor of the French, 1769-1821—Drama;** and a single poem or volume of poems by a single author all on the theme of baseball could be assigned the heading **Baseball—Poetry.** This is the most common way of providing subject access to individual works. Personal and corporate names can always be added to the List in order to be used with the subdivisions *Fiction, Drama,* and *Poetry* to provide subject access to individual literary works that deal with real persons or corporate entities. Subjects can also be added to the List for this purpose, but it is not useful to devise very specific categories to describe the characters or situations of individual literary works. The purpose of subject headings is to draw similar works together rather than to describe each one individually.

Headings describing the major genres of literature, e.g. **Drama; Essays; Fiction;** and **Poetry;** and the headings describing the major genres of a national literature, e.g. **Irish drama; American essays; Russian fiction;** and **Italian poetry,** are never assigned to an individual work or to a collection by a single author. The genre and national origin of such a work are expressed in the classification. Headings for more specific forms and sub-genres, however, such as **Fantasy fiction; Epic poetry;** and **Science fiction plays,** which are not expressed in the classification, can be applied to individual works, to collections by one or several authors, or to materials about such works or about the form or sub-genre. In the Sears List these headings are identified in the scope notes as applicable to individual works as well as to material about the topic. If there is no scope note indicating that a literature heading can be applied to an individual work, it can be assumed that it is not intended to be so applied. This policy is in accordance with the *Guidelines on Subject Access to Individual Works of Fiction, Drama, etc.* prepared by the Subcommittee on Subject Access to Individual Works of Fiction, Drama, etc., of the ALA Subject Analysis Committee (ALA, 1990). It varies from the usage of the Library of Congress *Subject Cataloging Manual* in that it allows form and genre as well as subject access to certain kinds of literary works that are often requested in libraries.

Collections of Several Authors. Collections consisting of works of several authors are usually entered in the catalog under the title of the collection. Therefore, as an aid to their location in the catalog, these materials are given a heading that represents the form of literature included in the collection. Since such headings are used also for topical treatment of the subject, distinction must be made between the subject headings for works about a particular literary form and the form headings for collections of literature in a particular literary form. The singular form is used as a topical subject heading. If it has an acceptable plural, this can be used to represent the form heading for collections, but if there is no true plural then the subdivision *Collections* is added to the name of the literary form:

Topical Heading	*Form Heading for Collections*
Essay	**Essays; American essays;** etc.
Parody	**Parodies**
Short story	**Short stories**
Drama	**Drama—Collections**
French drama	**French drama—Collections**
Fiction	**Fiction—Collections**
Russian fiction	**Russian fiction—Collections**
Literature	**Literature—Collections**
German literature	**German literature—Collections**
Poetry	**Poetry—Collections**
Japanese poetry	**Japanese poetry—Collections**

Minor literary forms, such as ballads, fables, fairy tales, parodies, satire, sermons, and short stories, can also be given national adjectives, e.g., **American satire.** These headings are used not only for collections by several authors but also for works of individual authors and for works about such forms. Sub-genres, such as **Fantasy fiction** or **Epic poetry,** can likewise be used for individual works, collections, or works about the sub-genre, but they are not ordinarily given national adjectives. If the number of books for any of these form and genre headings is large, the heading may be subdivided to separate the works about them from the literature itself, e.g., **English satire—History and criticism.** They can also be subdivided as needed by any other subdivisions found under **English Literature,** e.g., **Fantasy fiction—Bibliography.**

In concluding this discussion on subdivision, another fact should be noted: a subdivided subject can be further subdivided, more than once if necessary. As seen in an example above, **United States—Biography—Dictionaries** was the subject for *Who's Who in America.* For a bibliography of the history of education in the United States, the heading would be **Education—United States—History—Bibliography.** The general pattern of order for multiple subdivisions under topical headings is normally topic—place—chronology—form, although considerable variation exists. The use of multiple subdivisions is not the same thing as indirect entry, where the last element alone is the true subject. A subject heading and its subdivisions taken together constitute a single subject as specific as needed for the work being cataloged.

Nonbook Materials

The assignment of subject headings for audiovisual and special instructional materials should follow the same principles that are applied to books. The heading most specifically describing the contents of the material should be used, and the same headings should be applied to book and nonbook materials alike. This is especially important if the catalog integrates all media. One integrated catalog would seem to be preferable because this would bring all materials on one subject together regardless of format. In the thirteenth edition of the List many of the subjects and subdivisions that included the word "book" were changed to make them applicable to all materials. Among the exceptions remaining are the subject **School yearbooks** and the subdivision *Handbooks, manuals, etc.*

Because nonbook materials often concentrate on very small aspects of larger subjects, the cataloger may not find in the List the specific heading that should be used. In such instances the cataloger should be generous in adding new subjects (see p xxxiv). In this edition there are many new form and genre headings that apply equally to nonbook materials and to books about such materials, e.g., **Biographical films, Comedy television programs;** and **Science fiction comic books, strips, etc.**

Subject headings for nonbook materials should not include form subdivisions to describe physical format, i.e., motion pictures, slides, sound recordings, music, etc. Some libraries may choose to maintain a separate catalog for each format; others may choose to list all materials in an omnimedia catalog. For libraries using omnimedia catalogs, AACR2 provides the option of using general materials designations (GMD), which are placed at the end of the title proper and alert users to the general class to which an item belongs. The appropriate GMD is selected from either the North American list or the British list. Additional information on this aspect of descriptive cataloging can be found in the *Anglo-American Cataloguing Rules,* 2nd edition, 1988 revision, supplemented by *1993 Amendments,* and in Rosalind E. Miller and Jane C. Terwilligar's *Commonsense Cataloging.*

Terminology

The subject headings for established fields of knowledge and for concrete objects are simple to comprehend, but terms for new or abstract ideas may offer some difficulty. By looking through the broader, narrower, and related terms (BT, NT, and RT) under a given heading, or noting the UF [Used for] references to it, a cataloger may often determine how the term is used.

Sometimes two or more terms may seem to cover the same subject, unless the exact meaning and limitations of each is appreciated. Many headings in the List are accompanied by a scope note explaining their application as an aid to differentiating among related subjects. For example, the headings **Alcoholism; Drinking of alcoholic beverages; Liquor industry; Prohibition; Temperance** overlap to a certain degree, but because of distinctions in their definition one should not assign all of them for any one work. By means of the scope notes included with these terms, it is understood that **Alcoholism** is used for medical materials, including works on drunkenness; **Drinking of alcoholic beverages** includes works on drinking in its social aspects and as a social problem; **Liquor industry** is used for works on the liquor industry and trade; **Prohibition** for works dealing with the legal prohibition of liquor traffic and liquor manufacture; and **Temperance** is used for general works on the temperance question and the temperance movement.

A cataloger must consult the library's own catalog in order to see how a subject heading has been used. Printed catalogs such as the *Cumulative Book Index* and the "Standard Catalog Series" are also of value in order to see what kind of works are included under a given subject. Other cataloging aids are the *American Book Publishing Record, Subject Guide to Books in Print,* and the *National Union Catalog: Books* fiche. The *Readers' Guide to Periodical Literature* and other indexes are also useful. Aid in interpreting the scope and meaning of a subject heading may also be obtained by looking up its classification number in the *Dewey Decimal Classification.* There the topic can be studied in its relation to other topics, a development usually impossible to see directly in an alphabetic arrangement.

Each cataloger will have individual problems in the interpretation of subject headings. Whenever a decision has been made on the scope of a term about which there has been doubt, a definition or explanation should be recorded for future use. Such notes may be helpful to users of the catalog as well as to the cataloger. Whenever it is felt that such a note, either taken from the List or devised by the cataloger, would be of general value, it may be entered in the catalog preceding the entries under the subject heading.

References

After an item has been assigned a subject heading, attention must be directed to insuring that the reader who is searching for this material will not fail to find it because of insufficient references to the proper heading. References direct the user from terms not used as headings to the term that is used, and from broader and related topics to the heading chosen to represent a given subject. The information needed to make these references is given in the List.

With this edition the Sears List has adopted the symbols used in most thesauri to label the terms associated with a heading. The Lisʳ remains an alphabetical subject heading list and not a true thesaurus, but the thesaurus format should be useful nonetheless in helping the cataloger to distinguish relationships among terms and to establish appropriate references in the public catalog based upon these relationships. Below is a sample heading from the List followed by an explanation of the labels and a summary of the types, methods of formulation, and use of references derived from the various terms listed under a heading.

Card games 795.4
> UF   Cards, Playing
>   Playing cards
> SA   names of card games, to be added as needed
> BT   **Games**
> NT   **Bridge (Game)**
>   **Canasta (Game)**
>   **Card tricks**
>   **Solitaire (Game)**
>   **Tarot**
> RT   **Gambling**

Specific "SEE" References

The UF label stands for "Used for," and it designates those unpreferred terms or phrases for which the subject heading is used instead. Tracings from these unpreferred terms are absolutely essential to the success of a catalog. The reader must be directed from variant spellings and terminology to the one word or phrase that has been selected to represent the subject. Such words and phrases might include the following:

(1) synonyms or terms so nearly synonymous that they would cover the same material. For example, **Instructional materials centers** requires a reference from School media centers.

(2) the second part of compound headings. For example, **Desertion and nonsupport** requires a reference from Nonsupport.

(3) the inverted form of a heading, when the noun is preceded by an adjective. For example, **Adult education** requires a reference from Education, Adult.

(4) variant spellings. For example, **Color** requires a reference from Colour.

(5) the opposite of a term, when it is included in the meaning of a term without being specifically mentioned. For example, **Temperance** requires a reference from Intemperance.

(6) the singular of a plural term, when the two forms would not file together in the catalog. For example, **Mice** requires a reference from Mouse, and **Cats** requires a reference from Cat. (Note the long list of headings between Cat and **Cats.**)

The two terms following the UF label in the **Card games** example above indicate that references exist in the "C" and "P" sections of the List as follows:

Cards, Playing
> USE   **Card games**

Playing cards
> USE   **Card games**

In the public catalog these become specific "SEE" references, as follows:

Cards, Playing
>   SEE   **Card games**

Playing cards
>   SEE   **Card games**

When the heading **Card games** is assigned for the first time to a work in the collection, these SEE references will be entered in the catalog. They will be entered only once, no matter how many times the heading **Card games** is assigned, and the terms "Cards, Playing" and "Playing cards" are not to be assigned as headings.

Specific "See also" references

Following the BT label is a term that is broader in application than the main heading term. As a rule, a term has only one broader term, unless the term is an example or aspect of two or more things. For example **Collies** has only one broader term **Dogs,** not **Dogs** and **Mammals. Dogs,** however, has three broader terms: **Mammals, Pets,** and **Domestic animals.** All three terms are broader than **Dogs** by only one level of specificity.

The broader term serves two functions in the List. The first is to aid the cataloger in finding the best term to assign to a work. If the work being cataloged is about card games but also about various other games, the cataloger would realize that **Card games** is too narrow and assign the broader term **Games** to the work.

The second function is to indicate where specific "See also" references should be made. In the public catalog a "See also" reference is made from a broader term to a narrower term, but not from a narrower term to a broader term. When the heading **Card games** is assigned for the first time to a work in the collection, a reference is made at **Games** "See also **Cards games.**" If **Games** has never been assigned to a work in the collection, it is entered in the catalog and the reference "See also **Card games**" is made.

Following the NT label are terms that are narrower than the main heading. If a work about **Card games** is really about Bridge and Canasta only, the cataloger will know to forgo the term **Card games** in favor of the two more specific headings **Bridge (Game)** and **Canasta (Game).** As a rule, the narrower terms listed after the NT label are narrower than the main term by only one level of specificity. Hence, **Science** has the narrower term **Mathematics; Mathematics** has the narrower term **Arithmetic;** and **Arithmetic** has the narrower term **Mental arithmetic.**

In the public catalog "See also" references are made from a main term to its narrower terms only when the narrower term is assigned for the first time to a work in the collection. A reference at **Card games** "See also **Solitaire (Game)**" would be considered a blind reference if there were no work in the collection assigned the heading **Solitaire (Game).** Blind references are to be avoided.

Following the RT label are terms related to the main term, on similar or associated subjects. Related terms are of more or less equal specificity, neither broader nor narrower. The term **Card games** is related to **Gambling** because not all card games involve gambling and not all gambling involves card games. Each term has the other as a related term in its listing because a cataloger or user may easily look first to one term only to realize that the other is the more precise term for the material being cataloged or being sought.

In the public catalog references between related terms are reciprocal. When the term **Card games** is assigned for the first time to a work in the collection, a reference is made at **Gambling** "See also **Card games.**" If **Gambling** has never been assigned to a work in the collection, it is entered in the catalog with the reference to **Card games.** If **Gambling** has been assigned to a work in the collection, and only if it has been assigned, is the reference made at **Card games** "See also **Gambling.**"

In displaying references to related terms in the public catalog, only knowledge of the library's collection can determine what references should be made. For example, a work that discusses both wages and prices will be assigned the headings **Wages** and **Prices.** Because **Wages** and **Prices** are given as related terms, the List suggests the reference at **Wages** "See also **Prices,**" but this reference should not be made if the only material that is found in the catalog under **Prices** is the same work that is already listed under **Wages.**

General References

The SA stands for "See also" and introduces a "General Reference," not to a specific heading but to a general group or category of things that may be established as needed. In the example of **Card games** given above, the SA label introduces the general reference to "names of card games, to be added as needed." This is a reminder to the cataloger not to be limited to the examples of card games given in the List. In the List there happen to be three card games, **Bridge (Game), Canasta (Game),** and **Solitaire (Game),** which appear in the NT field under **Card games,** but if the library acquires a work devoted to the card game Rummy, it only makes sense for the cataloger to establish a heading **Rummy (Game)** and make references to and from it similar to those for the other card games.

Following are the most common types of headings from which general references are made, along with an example of each:

(1) Common names of various species of a class

> **Flowers**
> SA names of flowers, e.g. **Roses;** to be added as needed

(2) Names of individual persons, etc.

> **Scientists**
> SA types of scientists and names of individual scientists, to be added as needed

(3) Names of particular institutions, buildings, societies, etc.

> **Churches**
> SA names of individual churches, e.g. **Westminster Abbey;** to be added as needed

> **Labor unions**
> SA types of unions and names of individual labor unions, to be added as needed

(4) Names of particular geographic features

> **Mountains**
> SA names of mountain ranges and of individual mountains, to be added as needed

(5) Names of places subdivided by subject

> **Population**
> SA names of countries, cities, etc., with the subdivision *Population,* to be added as needed

(6) Subjects followed by form subdivisions

> Dictionaries
>> USE names of languages or subjects with the subdivision *Dictionaries,* e.g. **English language—Dictionaries; Biography—Dictionaries;** etc., to be added as needed

(7) Subjects with national adjectives

> **Historians**
>> SA historians of particular countries, e.g. **American historians;** to be added as needed

There are two alternative ways of displaying general references in a public catalog. One way is to specify after "See also" only those narrower terms not covered by the general reference and follow these specific terms with a formulation of the general reference from the List (omitting, of course, the words "to be added as needed," which are addressed only to the cataloger). Such a display would read as follows:

Card games
> *See also*
>> **Card tricks**
>> **Gambling**
>> **Tarot**
> and names of card games

A second way of displaying the same information is to expand the general reference and specify after "See also" all the narrower and related terms that have been assigned to works in the collection, whether those terms were from the List or added as needed. For the example **Card games,** given that all the terms had been assigned to works in the collection, an expanded general reference would read as follows:

Card games
> *See also*
>> **Bridge (Game)**
>> **Canasta (Game)**
>> **Card tricks**
>> **Gambling**
>> **Rummy (Game)**
>> **Solitaire (Game)**
>> **Tarot**

The directions and scope notes printed in the List for the guidance of the cataloger should be modified for the catalog if the cataloger feels that a note is needed for the public. Following is an example of a rewording.

As it appears in the List for the cataloger:

> **Space ships   629.45**
>> Use for materials limited to space vehicles with people on board. Comprehensive materials on spacecraft are entered under **Space vehicles.**

As it appears in the catalog for the reader:

Space ships

> Here are listed materials limited to space vehicles with people on board.

> Comprehensive materials on spacecraft are entered under **Space vehicles.**

New Terminology for Existing Subjects

The English language is changing constantly so that from time to time new terms appear for subjects that are not new. Through the years many changes have had to be made: **Child welfare** was formerly *Children—Charities, protection, etc.;* **Radio advertising** started out as *Radio broadcasting—Business applications;* and *Space vehicles, Reusable* was replaced by **Space shuttles.**

It is impossible for the subject headings to reflect all the newest language usage, particularly in fields whose terminology fluctuates frequently. A term that is current today may soon be superseded by another, or a term considered passé may return to favor. But at least new terms can be represented in the catalog by *See* references to the heading used.

If a heading is found to be incorrect or obsolete, or suddenly assumes a pejorative or biased connotation, changes must be made. Likewise, new ideas in information science can prompt changes in the form of headings, as from the inverted to the direct word order. The adoption of a revised term means changing not only all the old entries to the new form but also the various references to and from it. If a change is considered desirable but the number of entries to be revised is prohibitive, one can accomplish the change by providing a history note. Using one of the aforementioned changes as an example, the cataloger would make the following entry substituting for (date) the calendar year in which the change is made:

Space vehicles, Reusable

> For materials issued after (date) consult the following heading

> **Space shuttles**

Space shuttles

> For materials issued before (date) consult the following heading

> **Space vehicles, Reusable**

These references could also assume the following format for a card catalog. A guide card that protrudes above the other cards in the tray is more readily seen by the user.

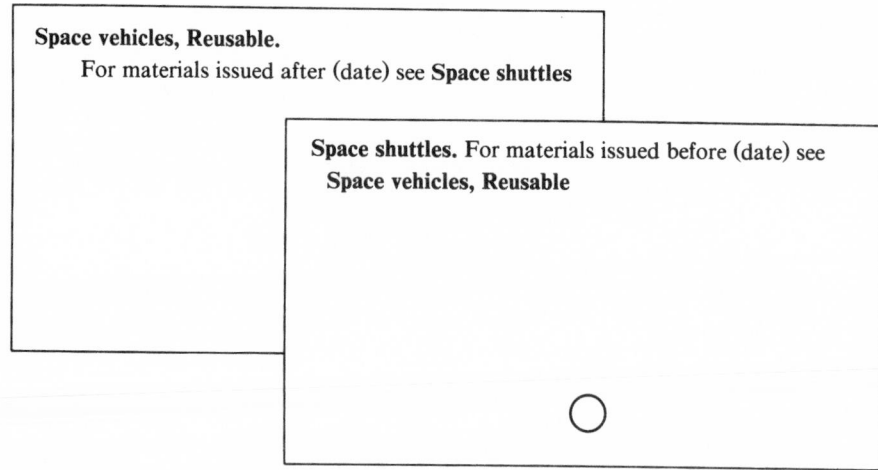

Space vehicles, Reusable.
    For materials issued after (date) see **Space shuttles**

Space shuttles. For materials issued before (date) see
    Space vehicles, Reusable

New Subjects

No printed list of subject headings can be entirely up to date. There are constantly new ideas, new inventions, or new countries being created. The Sears List is not meant to be complete or final. New subjects, when it is determined that they are in fact new subjects and not just varying terminology for old subjects, should be added to the List by the cataloger as needed. New subject headings and the associated references should be constructed in the same way as other subject headings already in the List: with synonymous terms that the heading is used for; with broader, narrower, and related terms; and with *See* and *See also* references in the public catalog. Guides for the wording of new headings may be found in the works themselves as well as in periodical literature and indexes. Although daily newspaper terminology may be too colloquial for use as headings, it does provide a clue to the way in which a user may ask for materials, and also suggests terms to be used as cross references. First aid is supplied by the periodical indexes, such as the *Readers' Guide to Periodical Literature, Applied Science & Technology Index,* etc., since their editors must assign subject headings to material as soon as it appears in the periodical literature. As the new subject develops, some change in the heading may be made in succeeding issues of the index. By the time a book is written about a new subject, the terminology may have become stabilized since the first periodical article on the subject was indexed. Therefore, bibliographies of new works such as *Booklist, Cumulative Book Index,* and *Book Review Digest* are valuable aids. The Library of Congress issues *LC Subject Headings Weekly List* and includes new "subject headings of current interest" in its quarterly *Cataloging Service Bulletin.* Through the Cataloging in Publication program, Library of Congress cataloging information including suggested subject headings will usually appear on the verso of the title page in books of those publishers cooperating in the program.

It is not always possible to decide at once on the permanent form for a new subject heading, but the cataloger cannot necessarily wait for the subject to develop before giving headings to new material. Tentative headings can be assigned and used until the terminology becomes standardized. A list of these tentative headings should be kept (it will never be long) so that they can be reconsidered later and either adopted permanently or changed, as the case may be, and added to the List. One must be sure, of course, that the new term is not merely a new name or a colloquialism for a subject already in the catalog.

Recording Headings and References

The cataloger should keep a record of subject headings used and references made for them. This may be kept on cards or as an electronic file, or a copy of the Sears List may be checked whenever a heading is used for the first time. Additions to the List should be entered and references should be recorded as needed. Detailed directions for checking the List and a sample page illustrating them will be found on pp xliv-xlv.

Bibliography

The bibliography that follows lists those works that were the basis of the original version of the "Principles of the Sears List of Subject Headings" together with more recent scholarship in the field of subject cataloging.

Akers, Susan Grey. *Akers' Simple Library Cataloging.* 7th ed. Completely revised and rewritten by Arthur Curley and Jana Varlejs. Metuchen, N.J.: Scarecrow Press, 1984. (Chapter 2)

American Library Association. Filing Committee. *ALA Filing Rules.* Chicago: American Library Association, 1980.

Association for Library Collections and Technical Services. Subject Analysis Committee. *Guidelines on Subject Access to Individual Works of Fiction, Drama, etc.* Chicago: American Library Association, 1990.

Bakewell, K. G. B. *A Manual on Cataloging Practice.* New York: Pergamon Press, 1972. (Chapter 5)

Chan, Lois Mai. *Cataloging and Classification: an Introduction.* 2nd ed. New York: McGraw-Hill, 1994.

Chan, Lois Mai. *Library of Congress Subject Headings: Principles and Application.* 2nd ed. Littleton, Colo.: Libraries Unlimited, 1986.

Clack, Doris H. *Authority Control: Principles, Applications, and Instructions.* Chicago: American Library Association, 1990.

Coates, Eric. *Subject Catalogues: Headings and Structure.* repr. with new preface. London: Library Association, 1988.

Congress of Librarians (1991: St. John's University). *Cataloging Heresy: Challenging the Standard Bibliographic Product.* Edited by Bella Hass Weinberg. Medford, N.J.: Learned Information, 1992.

Dewey, Harry. *An Introduction to Library Cataloging and Classification.* 4th ed. rev. and enl. Madison, Wis.: Capital Press, 1957. (Chapters 10-13 and 15)

Dewey, Melvil. *Abridged Dewey Decimal Classification and Relative Index.* 12th ed. Edited by John P. Comaromi, et al. Albany, N.Y.: Forest Press, 1990.

Dunkin, Paul S. *Cataloging U. S. A.* Chicago: American Library Association, 1969. (Chapter 5)

Eaton, Thelma. *Cataloging and Classification: an Introductory Manual.* 4th ed. Ann Arbor, Mich.: Edwards Brothers, 1967. (Chapters 5-6)

Elrod, J. McRee. *Choice of Subject Headings.* [programmed text] 3rd ed. Metuchen, N.J.: Scarecrow Press, 1980.

Ferl, Terry Ellen, and Larry Millsap. *Subject Cataloging: a How-to-do-it Workbook.* New York: Neal-Schuman, 1991.

Foskett, A. C. *The Subject Approach to Information.* 4th ed. Hamden, Conn.: Linnet Books, 1982.

Haykin, David Judson. *Subject Headings: a Practical Guide.* Washington: U.S. Government Printing Office, 1951. Reprint. New York: Gordon Press, 1978.

Hennepin County Library (Minn.). *HCL Cataloging Bulletin.* Edina, Minn.

Hennepin County Library (Minn.) *Unreal!: Hennepin County Library Subject Headings for Fictional Characters and Places.* 2nd ed. Jefferson, N.C.: McFarland & Co., 1992.

Intner, Sheila S., and Jean Riddle Weihs. *Standard Cataloging for School and Public Libraries.* Englewood, Colo.: Libraries Unlimited, 1990.

Lancaster, F. W. *Vocabulary Control for Information Retrieval.* 2nd ed. Arlington, Va.: Information Resources Press, 1986.

Library Literature: an Index to Library and Information Science. New York: The H. W. Wilson Co., 1921-

Library of Congress. Office for Subject Cataloging Policy. *LC Period Subdivisions under Names of Places.* 4th ed. Washington, D.C.: Library of Congress, 1990.

Library of Congress. Office for Subject Cataloging Policy. *Subject Cataloging Manual: Subject Headings.* 4th ed. Washington, D.C.: Library of Congress, 1991-

Lighthall, Lynne. *Sears List of Subject Headings: Canadian Companion.* 4th ed. New York: The H. W. Wilson Co., 1992.

Manheimer, Martha L. *Manheimer's Cataloging and Classification: a Workbook.* 3rd ed. Revised and expanded by Jerry D. Saye with Desretta V. McAllister-Harper. New York: Dekker, 1991.

Mann, Margaret. *Introduction to Cataloging and the Classification of Books.* 2nd ed. Chicago: American Library Association, 1943. (Chapters 9-10)

Miksa, Francis L. *The Subject in the Dictionary Catalog from Cutter to the Present.* Chicago: American Library Association, 1983.

Miller, Rosalind E., and Jane C. Terwillegar. *Commonsense Cataloging: a Cataloger's Manual.* 4th ed. rev. New York: The H. W. Wilson Co., 1990. (Chapters 7-9)

Milstead, Jessica L. *Subject Access Systems: Alternatives in Design.* San Diego: Academic Press, 1984.

Studwell, William E., and David V. Loertscher. *Cataloging Books. A Workbook of Examples.* Englewood, Colo.: Libraries Unlimited, 1989.

Tauber, Maurice Falcolm. *Technical Services in Libraries; Acquisitions, Cataloging, Classification, Binding, Photographic Reproduction, and Circulation Operations.* New York: Columbia University Press, 1954. (Chapters 10-11)

Taylor, Arlene G. *Cataloging with Copy: a Decision-Maker's Handbook.* 2nd ed. Englewood, Colo.: Libraries Unlimited, 1988. (pp. 135-169)

Theory of Subject Analysis: a Sourcebook. Edited by Lois Mai Chan, Phyllis A. Richmond, and Elaine Svenonius. Englewood, Colo.: Libraries Unlimited, 1985.

Wynar, Bohdan S. *Introduction to Cataloging and Classification.* 8th ed. by Arlene G. Taylor. Englewood, Colo.: Libraries Unlimited, 1992.

Headings to be Added by the Cataloger

It is neither possible nor necessary to enter all proper and common nouns in a subject heading list such as Sears. If a specific name is not included in the List, the cataloger must establish a heading for it, using available reference sources. Headings may be created for the kinds of names cited below. Note that wherever a term in the List has a general reference, the specific heading may be added even though the term in the List is not represented among the categories below. Furthermore, types of things and names of individual examples of things can always be added to the List even when there is no general reference in the List instructing the cataloger to do so. General references are given only for those terms considered most likely to represent many possible narrower terms or examples, but no attempt is made to cover all possibilities. New headings that are types or names of things are always entered as narrower terms in the NT field under the parent term.

A. PROPER NAMES
   1. Names of persons
   2. Names of families
   3. Names of places
      a. Political units: countries, states, cities, provinces, counties, etc.
      b. Groups of states or countries: e.g. **Southern States; Baltic States;** etc.
      c. Geographic features: mountain ranges and individual mountains; island groups and individual islands; river valleys and individual rivers; regions; oceans; lakes; etc.
   4. Names of nationalities
   5. Names of national languages and literatures
   6. Names of wars and battles
   7. Names of treaties
   8. Names of Indian peoples
   9. Names of corporate bodies
      a. Names of associations, societies, clubs, etc.
      b. Names of institutions: colleges, libraries, hospitals, etc.
      c. Names of religious denominations
      d. Names of government bodies
      e. Names of hotels, retail stores, ships, etc.

B. COMMON NAMES
   1. Names from such categories as:

animals	fruits	sports
birds	games	tools
fishes	musical	trees
flowers	instruments	vegetables
foods	nuts	

   2. Names of diseases
   3. Names of organs and regions of the body
   4. Names of chemicals
   5. Names of minerals

"Key" Headings

To enable the cataloger to see the full display of possible subdivisions that may be used with some of the most popular categories, the editor has provided certain headings in the List to serve as models or "keys." Note that the subdivisions under the "Keys" are illustrative, not exclusive.

Persons:

Presidents—United States (to illustrate subdivisions that may be used under presidents, prime ministers and other rulers)

Shakespeare, William, 1564-1616 (to illustrate subdivisions that may be used under any voluminous author)

Peoples:

Indians of North America (to illustrate subdivisions that may be used under names of peoples and linguistic families)

Places:

United States; Ohio; Chicago (Ill.) (to illustrate subdivisions—except for historical periods—under geographic names)

Languages and Literatures:

English language (to illustrate subdivisions that may be used with any language)

English literature (to illustrate subdivisions that may be used with any literature)

Wars:

World War, 1939-1945 (to illustrate subdivisions that may be used under any war or battle)

List of Commonly Used Subdivisions

In addition to the subdivisions listed under the "keys" mentioned on the preceding page, a large number of form or topical subdivisions may be used under subjects as needed. The following list is not all-inclusive. The subdivisions that appear under the "key" headings are not repeated here, except when they may also be used under other subjects.

Accidents
Accounting
Administration
Air conditioning
Alcohol use
Analysis
Anatomy
Anecdotes
Antiquities
Assassination
Atlases
Attitudes
Audiovisual aids
Automation
Behavior
Bibliography
Bio-bibliography
Biography
Books and reading
Buildings
Care
Care and hygiene
Cartoons and caricatures
Case studies
Catalogs
Censorship
Chronology
Citizen participation
Civil rights
Collectibles
Collection and preservation
Collections
Collectors and collecting
Colonies
Color
Communication systems
Competitions
Composition
Computer assisted instruction
Computer programs

Concordances
Congresses
Conservation and restoration
Contracts and specifications
Control
Correspondence
Corrupt practices
Costs
Costume
Curricula
Data processing
Description
Desertions
Design
Design and construction
Designs and plans
Dictionaries
Diet therapy
Directories
Discography
Diseases
Diseases and pests
Documentation
Drama
Drug therapy
Drug use
Economic aspects
Economic conditions
Education
Employment
Entrance requirements
Environmental aspects
Equipment and supplies
Estimates
Examinations
Exhibitions
Experiments
Fiction
Filmography
Finance

Fire and fire prevention
Folklore
Fuel consumption
Gazeteers
Genetic aspects
Geographical distribution
Government policy
Growth
Guidebooks
Handbooks, manuals, etc.
Health and hygiene
Heating and ventilation
Historiography
History (for all works except
   literature, film, and music)
History and criticism (for literature,
   film, and music)
Home care
Housing
Humor
Identification
In-service training
Indexes
Industrial applications
Insignia
Inspection
Institutional care
Integration
Intellectual life
International cooperation
Jargon
Juvenile literature
Kings, queens, rulers, etc.
Labeling
Labor productivity
Laboratory manuals
Language
Law and legislation
Lighting
Maintenance and repair
Malpractice
Management
Maps
Marketing
Materials
Mathematical models
Mathematics
Measurement
Medals, badges, decorations, etc.
Medical care
Methodology
Miscellanea
Models
Moral and religious aspects

Museums
Music
Noise
Nursing
Nutrition
Officials and employees
Origin
Outlines, syllabi, etc.
Patterns
Periodicals
Philosophy
Photographs from space
Physiological effect
Pictorial works
Poetry
Political activity
Portraits
Practice
Preservation
Prevention
Prices
Problems, exercises, etc.
Production standards
Professional ethics
Programmed instruction
Prophecies
Protection
Protests, demonstrations, etc.
Psychological aspects
Psychology
Public opinion
Quality control
Quotations
Rating
Recreation
Recruiting
Recycling
Registers
Rehabilitation
Religion
Religious life
Remodeling
Repairing
Research
Reviews
Safety appliances
Safety measures
Security measures
Segregation
Sexual behavior
Social aspects
Social conditions
Social life and customs
Societies

Songs
Sources
Statistics
Stories, plots, etc.
Study and teaching
Suffrage
Surgery
Tables
Taxation
Technique
Telephone directories

Terminology
Testing
Texts
Therapeutic use
Thermodynamics
Tournaments
Toxicology
Training
Transplantation
Transportation
Vocational guidance
Voyages and travels

Checking and Adding Headings
See Sample Page opposite

1. *Check the subject heading used.* When the subject heading **Birds** is used for the first time, the cataloger places a check mark in front of it.

2. *Make and check "See" references to the heading.* The UF terms under **Birds** are considered and the cataloger decides to make a reference from Bird and from Ornithology as suggested. Cards are made for the catalog reading: "Bird. See Birds" and "Ornithology. See Birds." The terms Bird and Ornithology are then checked in the List both in their alphabetic places and in the UF field under **Birds.**

3. *Make and check "See also" references to the heading.* The BT and RT headings given under **Birds** are examined to see whether they have been used in the catalog. The heading **Vertebrates** has a check mark beside it showing that it has been used. The cataloger decides to place a reference in the catalog reading: "Vertebrates. See also Birds." It is recorded in the List as follows:

   under **Birds,** in the BT field, **Vertebrates** is checked

   under **Vertebrates,** in the NT field, **Birds** is checked

   For purposes of this explanation, the assumption is made that **Zoology** has not yet been used.

4. *Adding headings to the List.* The library acquires material about ostriches. The term is not in the List, but the directions given in the note under **Birds** tell the cataloger that the names of specific birds may be added. **Ostriches** is written in the margin in its alphabetic place in the List and checked. If the practice is to trace all narrower terms, then the reference: "Birds. See also Ostriches" is added to the public catalog. It is recorded in the List as follows:

   under **Birds, Ostriches** is added to the NT field and checked

   under **Ostriches, Birds** is added in a BT field and checked

   The library acquires material on birds in Maine. Following the permission given with the heading **Birds,** "(May subdiv. geog.)," the cataloger uses the heading **Birds—Maine,** writing it in the margin in its alphabetic place and checking it. Since the library has very little material about this region, it is decided to make a reference for the catalog reading, "Maine—Birds. See Birds—Maine." This reference is also added in its alphabetical place in the List as "Maine—Birds. Use **Birds—Maine,**" and checked. The reference is traced under the new heading by writing "Maine—Birds" in a UF field under **Birds—Maine,** and checking it there.

5. *Canceled subjects* If all entries for a subject are withdrawn from the catalog, turn to the subject heading in the List and remove the check mark from that heading. Then examine the terms in the UF, BT, NT, and RT fields below that heading. Where those terms appear in the alphabetic list the check marks are removed unless those terms are also references to other active terms or are themselves assigned to materials contained in the library. For example, if the book on ostriches is lost or discarded, the heading **Ostriches** is canceled from the List and **Ostriches** is removed from the NT field under **Birds,** provided that there are no other books on ostriches in the library. The heading **Birds** remains checked, however, because there are other materials on birds.

xliv

Sample Page of Checking

Abbreviated entries taken from various pages of the Sears List. A check (✓) indicates that the heading or reference has been used in the library's catalog. The marginal notes show how subjects may be added when needed.

✓ Bird
   USE   **Birds**
✓ **Birds** (May subdiv. geog.) **598**
   UF ✓ Bird
     ✓ Ornithology
   SA   classes of birds, e.g. **Birds of prey**; and names of specific birds, e.g. **Canaries**; to be added as needed
   BT ✓ **Vertebrates**
     Zoology
   NT   **Birds of prey**
     Cage birds
     Canaries
     <u>**Game and game birds**</u> ✓ Ostriches
     Peacocks
     Robins
     State birds
     Water birds
Birds—Habits and behavior
   USE   **Birds—Behavior**
Birds in literature 809
   BT   **Animals in literature**
     Nature in literature
   NT   **Bible—Natural history**
<u>Birds—Marking</u>   ✓ Birds—Maine
   USE   **Birdbanding**   UF ✓ Maine—Birds
Birds—Migration 598.252
   UF   Migration of birds
   BT   **Animals—Migration**
Mail-order business 658.8; 659.13
   BT   **Business**
     Direct selling
     Selling
Mail service
   USE   **Postal service**
Mail systems, Electronic
   <u>USE   **Electronic mail systems**</u> ✓ Maine—Birds
<u>**Mainstreaming in education 371.9**</u> USE Birds—Maine
   BT   **Education**
     Exceptional children
     Handicapped children
   RT   **Special education**

Ornamental plants 635.9; 715
   UF   Plants, Ornamental *[Former heading]*
   BT   **Cultivated plants**
     Flower gardening
     Landscape gardening
   RT   **Shrubs**
✓ Ornithology
   USE   **Birds**
Orphan drugs 615
   Use for materials on drugs that appear to be useful for the treatment of rare disorders but owing to their limited commercial value have difficulty in finding funding for research and marketing.
   UF   Drugs, Orphan
     Nonprofitable drugs
   BT   **Drugs**
Osteopathy 610; 615.5
   BT   **Alternative medicine**
   NT   **Chiropractic**
   <u>RT   **Massage**</u>   ✓ Ostriches
Ostrogoths   BT ✓ Birds
   USE   **Teutonic peoples**
Out-of-doors education
   USE   **Outdoor education**
Versification 808.1
   UF   English language— Versification
     Meter
     Prosody
   BT   **Authorship**
     Poetics
     Rhythm
   NT   **Rhyme**
✓ **Vertebrates 596**
   BT   **Animals**
     Zoology
   NT   **Amphibians**
     ✓ **Birds**
     Fishes
     Mammals
     Reptiles

List of Canceled and Replacement Headings

CANCELED HEADINGS	REPLACEMENT HEADINGS
Actors, American	American actors
Adventure and adventurers—Fiction	Adventure fiction
Aerodynamics, Supersonic	Supersonic aerodynamics
Aeronautics, Commercial	Commercial aeronautics
Aeronautics, Commercial—Chartering	Airlines—Chartering
Aeronautics, Military	Military aeronautics
Agriculture, Cooperative	Cooperative agriculture
Airlines—Flight attendants	Flight attendants
Airplanes—Engines	Airplane engines
Airplanes, Military	Military airplanes
Alcohol, Denatured	Denatured alcohol
Algebra, Boolean	Boolean algebra
Algebras, Linear	Linear algebra
Alpine animals	Mountain animals
Alpine plants	Mountain plants
American literature—Black authors	American literature—African American authors
American poetry—Black authors	American poetry—African American authors
Anatomy, Artistic	Artistic anatomy
Anatomy, Comparative	Comparative anatomy
Animals—Behavior	Animal behavior
Animals—Hibernation	Hibernation
Animals—Infancy	Animal babies
Arbitration, Industrial	Industrial arbitration
Arbitration, International	International arbitration
Architecture, American	American architecture
Architecture, Ancient	Ancient architecture
Architecture, Asian	Asian architecture
Architecture, Baroque	Baroque architecture
Architecture, Byzantine	Byzantine architecture
Architecture, Colonial	Colonial architecture
Architecture, Domestic	Domestic architecture
Architecture, Gothic	Gothic architecture
Architecture, Greek	Greek architecture
Architecture, Medieval	Medieval architecture
Architecture, Modern	Modern architecture
Architecture, Renaissance	Renaissance architecture
Architecture, Roman	Roman architecture
Architecture, Romanesque	Romanesque architecture
Arithmetic, Mental	Mental arithmetic
Armaments	Military readiness
	Military weapons
Arms and armor	Armor
	Weapons
Art, Abstract	Abstract art
Art, American	American art
Art, Ancient	Ancient art
Art, Asian	Asian art
Art, Baroque	Baroque art
Art, Buddhist	Buddhist art
Art, Byzantine	Byzantine art
Art, Greek	Greek art
Art, Islamic	Islamic art
Art, Medieval	Medieval art
Art, Modern	Modern art
Art, Municipal	Municipal art
Art—Museums	Art museums
Art, Prehistoric	Prehistoric art
Art, Renaissance	Renaissance art

CANCELED HEADINGS	REPLACEMENT HEADINGS
Art, Roman	Roman art
Art, Romanesque	Romanesque art
Artificial insemination, Human	Human artificial insemination
Artificial satellites, American	American artificial satellites
Artificial satellites, Soviet	Soviet artificial satellites
Artists, American	American artists
Arts, American	American arts
Assessment	Tax assessment
Atlases, Historical	Historical atlases
Automobile drivers—Education	Automobile driver education
Automobile service stations	Service stations
Automobiles—Design and construction	Automobiles—Design
Automobiles—Engines	Automobile engines
Automobiles—Parts	Automobile parts
Automobiles—Road guides	Automobile travel—Guidebooks
Automobiles—Touring	Automobile travel
Automobiles—Trailers	Travel trailers and campers
Authors, American	American authors
Authors, English	English authors
Ballads, American	American ballads
Ballets	Ballet
Bandages and bandaging	Bandages
Banks and banking, Cooperative	Cooperative banks
Barbecue cookery	Barbecue cooking
Bashfulness	Shyness
Bible—Drama	Bible plays
Bible—History of biblical events—Fiction	Bible fiction
Bible—Study	Bible—Study and teaching
Bicycles and bicycling	Bicycles
	Cycling
Biography (as a literary form)	Biography as a literary form
Birdsong	Birdsongs
Blacks—Arkansas	[No replacement]
Blacks—Chicago (Ill.)	African Americans—Chicago (Ill.)
Blacks—Songs and music	Black music
Blacks—Southern States	African Americans—Southern States
Botany—Anatomy	Plants—Anatomy
Botany—Ecology	Plants—Ecology
Botany, Economic	Economic botany
Botany, Medical	Medical botany
Boycott	Boycotts
Budgets, Business	Business budgets
Budgets, Household	Household budgets
Building, Iron and steel	Steel construction
Business arithmetic	Business mathematics
Cabinet work	Cabinetwork
Cables, Submarine	Submarine cables
Caldecott Medal books	Caldecott Medal
Camps (Military)	Military camps
Canada—History—1763-1791	Canada—History—1763-1867
Carpentry—Tools	Carpentry tools
Catalogs, Book	Book catalogs
Catalogs, Booksellers'	Booksellers' catalogs
Catalogs, Card	Card catalogs
Catalogs, Classified	Classified catalogs
Catalogs, Publishers'	Publishers' catalogs
Catalogs, Subject	Subject catalogs
Caterers and catering	Catering
Catholic Church—Relations (Diplomatic)	Catholic Church—Foreign relations
Catholic converts	Converts to Catholicism
Charities, Medical	Medical charities
Cheers and cheerleading	Cheerleading
Chemistry, Analytic	Analytic chemistry
Chemistry, Inorganic	Inorganic chemistry

CANCELED HEADINGS	REPLACEMENT HEADINGS
Chemistry, Organic	Organic chemistry
Chemistry, Physical and theoretical	Physical chemistry
Chemistry, Technical	Industrial chemistry
Chemotherapy	Cancer—Chemotherapy
	Drug therapy
Chicago (Ill.)—Description—Guidebooks	Chicago (Ill.)—Guidebooks
Chicago (Ill.)—Description—Views	Chicago (Ill.)—Pictorial works
Chicago (Ill.)—Government publications	Government publications—Chicago (Ill.)
Chicago (Ill.)—Popular culture	Popular culture—Chicago (Ill.)
Child care centers	Day care centers
Child molesting	Child sexual abuse
Christmas—Drama	Christmas plays
Christmas—Poetry	Christmas poetry
Chronology, Historical	Historical chronology
Church—Government policy	Church and state
Church history—30 (ca.)-600, Early church	Church history—30-600, Early church
Cities and towns, ruined, extinct, etc.	Extinct cities
Civilization, African	African civilization
Civilization, American	American civilization
Civilization, Ancient	Ancient civilization
Civilization, Arab	Arab civilization
Civilization, Asian	Asian civilization
Civilization, Christian	Christian civilization
Civilization, Greek	Greek civilization
Civilization, Medieval	Medieval civilization
Civilization, Modern	Modern civilization
Civilization, Occidental	Western civilization
Civilization, Scandinavian	Scandinavian civilization
Clothing trade	Clothing industry
Color prints, American	American color prints
Color prints, Japanese	Japanese color prints
Commonwealth of Nations	Commonwealth countries
Composers, American	American composers
Computer programs	Computer software
Concertos	Concerto
Cookery	Cooking
Cookery for the sick	Cooking for the sick
Cookery, French	French cooking
Corruption in politics	Political corruption
Cowhands—Songs and music	Cowhands—Songs
Criminal justice, Administration of	Administration of criminal justice
Czechoslovakia—History—1989-	Czechoslovakia—History—1989-1992
Decoration and ornament, American	American decoration and ornament
Decoration and ornament, Architectural	Architectural decoration and ornament
Delphi (Ancient city)	Delphi (Extinct city)
Depression, Mental	Depression (Psychology)
Depressions, Economic	Economic depressions
Detergent pollution of rivers, lakes, etc.	Water pollution
Detergents, Synthetic	Detergents
Dinners and dining	Dining
	Dinners
Discoveries (in geography)	Exploration
Dissertations, Academic	Dissertations
Diving, Submarine	Submarine diving
DNA Fingerprints	DNA fingerprints
Drainage, House	House drainage
Dramatists, American	American dramatists
Drawing, American	American drawing
Drill (Nonmilitary)	Marching drills
Drugs—Adulteration and analysis	Pharmacology
Drum	Drums
Eclipses, Lunar	Lunar eclipses
Eclipses, Solar	Solar eclipses
Economic assistance, American	American economic assistance

CANCELED HEADINGS	REPLACEMENT HEADINGS
Economic assistance, Domestic	Domestic economic assistance
Efficiency, Industrial	Industrial efficiency
Electric currents, Alternating	Alternating electric currents
Electron microscope and microscopy	Electron microscopes
Employees—Labor productivity	[No replacement]
Employees—Production standards	[No replacement]
Engraving, American	American engraving
Environment—Government policy	Environmental policy
Espionage, American	American espionage
Ethics, American	American ethics
Europe—History—1914-1945	Europe—History—1918-1945
European Economic Community	European Union
Fantastic fiction	Fantasy fiction
Farm engines	Agricultural machinery
Fasts and feasts	Religious holidays
Fasts and feasts—Judaism	Jewish holidays
Fertility, Human	Human fertility
Flute	Flutes
Folk art, American	American folk art
Folk dancing, American	American folk dancing
Folk medicine	Traditional medicine
Folk songs, French	French folk songs
Forgery of works of art	Art forgeries
Free speech	Freedom of speech
Freight and freightage	Freight
French Canadian literature	Canadian literature (French)
Furniture, American	American furniture
Game preserves	Game reserves
Gardens—Design	Garden design
Gardens, Miniature	Miniature gardens
Gas and oil engines	Internal combustion engines
Gay women	Lesbians
Genetic engineering, Automated	Genetic engineering
Geography, Ancient	Ancient geography
Geography, Commercial	Commercial geography
Geography, Historical	Historical geography
Geology, Economic	Economic geology
Geology, Stratigraphic	Stratigraphic geology
Geometry, Analytic	Analytic geometry
Geometry, Descriptive	Descriptive geometry
Geometry, Projective	Projective geometry
Ghosts—Fiction	Ghost stories
Gothic fiction	Gothic novels
Government, Resistance to	Resistance to government
Graduate record examination	Graduate Record Examination
Graphic arts, American	Graphic arts—United States
Greek language, Modern	Modern Greek language
Greek literature, Modern	Modern Greek literature
Guitar	Guitars
Hair and hairdressing	Hair
Health resorts, spas, etc.	Health resorts
Heart—Diseases	Heart diseases
Historians, American	American historians
History, Ancient	Ancient history
History, Modern	Modern history
Holocaust, Jewish (1933-1945)	Jewish holocaust (1933-1945)
Homeless people	Homeless persons
Horror—Fiction	Horror fiction
Hostages, American	American hostages
Hotels, motels, etc.	Hotels and motels
Household appliances, Electric	Electric household appliances
Hull House	Hull House (Chicago, Ill.)
Humanism—1900-1999 (20th century)	Secularism
Humorous stories	Humorous fiction

CANCELED HEADINGS	REPLACEMENT HEADINGS
Ice hockey	Hockey
Illustrators, American	American illustrators
Indians of North American—Costume and adornment	Indians of North America—Costume
Indians of North America—Government policy	Indians of North America—Government relations
Indians of North America—Missions, Christian	Indians of North America—Christian missions
Indians of North America—Songs and music	Indians of North America—Music
Industrial management	Management
Intercultural education	Multicultural education
Iran-Contra Affair, 1985-	Iran-Contra Affair, 1985-1990
Jews—Civilization	Jewish civilization
Journalism, Scientific	Scientific journalism
Justice, Administration of	Administration of justice
Knowledge, Theory of	Theory of knowledge
Languages, Modern	Modern languages
Learning, Psychology of	Psychology of learning
Legends, Celtic	Celtic legends
Legends, Jewish	Jewish legends
Legends, Norse	Norse legends
Library instruction	Bibliographic instruction
Lime	Lime (Mineral)
Liquors and liqueurs	Liquors
Literature, Comparative	Comparative literature
Literature, Medieval	Medieval literature
Little league baseball	Little League baseball
Lobbying and lobbyists	Lobbying
Logic, Symbolic and mathematical	Symbolic logic
Machinery—Design and construction	Machine design
Makeup, Theatrical	Theatrical makeup
Mammals, Fossil	Fossil mammals
Man—Color	[No replacement]
Man—Influence of environment	Environmental influence on humans
Man—Influence on nature	Human influence on nature
Man—Origin	Human origins
MARC system	MARC formats
Medicine, Military	Military medicine
Medicine, Popular	Popular medicine
Medicine, Psychosomatic	Psychosomatic medicine
Medicine, State	State medicine
Men's liberation movement	Men's movement
Mental tests	Intelligence tests
	Psychological tests
Microscope and microscopy	Microscopes
Microwave cookery	Microwave cooking
Migration, Internal	Internal migration
Military assistance, American	American military assistance
Military posts	Military bases
Military service, Voluntary	Voluntary military service
Mills and millwork	Mills
Ministry, Christian	Christian ministry
Missionaries, Christian	Christian missionaries
Missions, Christian	Christian missions
Missions, Medical	Medical missions
Models, Fashion	Fashion models
Modernism	Modernism (Theology)
Molds (Botany)	Molds (Fungi)
Motion picture photography	Cinematography
Moving, Household	Moving
Munitions	Defense industries
	Military weapons
Music, American	American music
Music—Analysis, appreciation	Music appreciation
	Music—History and criticism

CANCELED HEADINGS	REPLACEMENT HEADINGS
Music box	Music boxes
Musical instruments, Electronic	Electronic musical instruments
Musical instruments, Mechanical	Mechanical musical instruments
Musicians, American	American musicians
Mystery and detective stories	Mystery fiction
Mythology, Classical	Classical mythology
National book week	National Book Week
National characteristics, American	American national characteristics
National songs, American	National songs—United States
Neutron bombs	Neutron bomb
Newbery Medal books	Newbery Medal
Nobel prizes	Nobel Prizes
Northwest, Canadian	Canadian Northwest
Northwest coast of North America	Northwest Coast of North America
Novelists, American	American novelists
Numeration	Numbers
Office employees	Office workers
Ohio—Description—Guidebooks	Ohio—Guidebooks
Ohio—Description—Views	Ohio—Pictorial works
Ohio—Government publication	Government publications—Ohio
Ohio—History, Local	Ohio—Local history
Ohio—Public lands	Public lands—Ohio
Oil pollution of rivers, harbors, etc.	Oil pollution of water
Oil well drilling, Submarine	Offshore oil well drilling
Operas	Opera
Operas—Librettos	Opera librettos
Oratorios	Oratorio
Organ	Organs (Musical instruments)
Organiculture	Organic farming
	Organic gardening
Orthodox Eastern Church, Russian	Russian Orthodox Church
Outdoor cookery	Outdoor cooking
Painters, American	American painters
Painting, American	American painting
Painting, Industrial	Industrial painting
Painting, Modern	Modern painting
Painting, Romanesque	Romanesque painting
Paper hanging	Paperhanging
Paraprofessions and paraprofessionals	Paraprofessionals
Parenting, Part-time	Part-time parenting
Pensions, Military	Military pensions
Personal names, Scottish	Scottish personal names
Pests—Biological control	Pest control
Pests—Control	Pest control
Petroleum—Pipelines	Petroleum pipelines
Philology, Comparative	Linguistics
Philosophers, American	American philosophers
Philosophy, American	American philosophy
Philosophy, Ancient	Ancient philosophy
Philosophy, Hindu	Hindu philosophy
Philosophy, Medieval	Medieval philosophy
Philosophy, Modern	Modern philosophy
Photography, Artistic	Artistic photography
Photography—Portraits	Portrait Photography
Physiology, Comparative	Comparative physiology
Piano	Pianos
Plant names, Popular	Popular plant names
Plants, Cultivated	Cultivated plants
Plants—Effect of poisons on	Herbicides
Plants, Fossil	Fossil plants
Poets, American	American poets
Police—Complaints against	Police brutality
	Police corruption
Police—Corrupt practices	Police corruption

CANCELED HEADINGS	REPLACEMENT HEADINGS
Politics, Practical	Politics
Polymers and polymerization	Polymers
Postage stamps—Collectors and collecting	Stamp collecting
Pottery, American	American pottery
Prints, American	American prints
Prisoners of war, American	American prisoners of war
Problem solving, Group	Group problem solving
Propaganda, American	American propaganda
Propellers, Aerial	Aerial propellers
Prophecies (Occult sciences)	Prophecies (Occultism)
Psychology, Applied	Applied psychology
Psychology, Comparative	Comparative psychology
Psychology, Pastoral	Pastoral psychology
Psychology, Pathological	Abnormal psychology
Psychology, Religious	Psychology of religion
Public schools, Endowed (Great Britain)	English public schools
Puns and punning	Puns
Quantity cookery	Quantity cooking
Quick and easy cookery	Quick and easy cooking
Radicals and radicalism	Radicalism
Reader services (Libraries)	Library services
Readings and recitations	Recitations
Recycling (Waste, etc.)	Recycling
Refugees, Arab	Arab refugees
Refugees, Vietnamese	Vietnamese refugees
Religious orders for men, Catholic	Catholic religious orders for men
Religious orders for women, Catholic	Catholic religious orders for women
Reptiles, Fossil	Fossil reptiles
Restaurants, bars, etc.	Bars
	Restaurants
Rewards (Prizes, etc.)	Awards
Robbers and outlaws	Thieves
Salvage (Waste, etc.)	Salvage
Sanitation, Household	Household sanitation
Satire, American	American satire
Satire, English	English satire
Scholarships, fellowships, etc.	Scholarships
Sculptors, American	American sculptors
Sculpture, American	American sculpture
Sculpture, Greek	Greek sculpture
Sculpture, Modern	Modern sculpture
Security, International	International security
Self-culture	Self-improvement
	Self-instruction
Self-respect	Self-esteem
Shakespeare, William, 1564-1616—Biography —Psychology	Shakespeare, William, 1564-1616—Psychology
Shakespeare, William, 1564-1616—Drama	[No replacement]
Shakespeare, William, 1564-1616—Fiction	[No replacement]
Shakespeare, William, 1564-1616—Poetry	[No replacement]
Shakespeare, William, 1564-1616—Songs and music	[No replacement]
Skis and skiing	Skiing
Sleds and sledding	Sledding
Sociology, Christian	Christian sociology
Sociology, Rural	Rural sociology
Sociology, Urban	Urban sociology
Solder and soldering	Soldering
Sonatas	Sonata
Songs, African	African songs
Songs, American	American songs
Soviet Union—History—1905, Revolution	Russia—History—1905, Revolution
Soviet Union—History—1917-	Soviet Union—History
Soviet Union—History—1953-	Soviet Union—History—1953-1991

CANCELED HEADINGS	REPLACEMENT HEADINGS
Soviet Union—History—1985-	Soviet Union—History—1985-1991
Soviet Union—Literatures	Soviet literature
Speeches, addresses, etc.	Speeches
Speeches, addresses, etc., American	American speeches
Speeches, addresses, etc., English	English speeches
States, New	New states
Steel, Structural	Structural steel
Stokers, Mechanical	[No replacement]
Strikes and lockouts	Strikes
Structures, Theory of	Theory of structures
Stunt men and women	Stunt performers
Style, Literary	Literary style
Suites	Suite (Music)
Summer schools, Religious	Religious summer schools
Surfing—Songs and music	Surfing—Songs
Survival (after airplane accidents, shipwrecks, etc.)	Survival after airplane accidents, shipwrecks, etc.
Sympathy	Bereavement
	Consolation
Symphonies	Symphony
Synthesizer (Musical instrument)	Synthesizers (Musical instruments)
Tanks (Military science)	Military tanks
Technical assistance, American	American technical assistance
Telescope	Telescopes
Therapeutics, Suggestive	Suggestive therapeutics
Transportation, Highway	Highway transportation
Transportation, Military	Military transportation
Travelers, American	American travelers
Trusts, Industrial	Industrial trusts
Underground literature	Alternative press
Underground press	Alternative press
Uniforms, Military	Military uniforms
United States. Army—Ordnance and ordnance stores	United States. Army—Ordnance
United States. Army—Songs and music	United States. Army—Songs
United States—Colonies	United States—Territories and possessions
United States—Description—Guidebooks	United States—Guidebooks
United States—Description—Views	United States—Pictorial works
United States—Foreign opinion, French	United States—Foreign opinion—France
United States—Government publications	Government publications—United States
United States—History—1845-1848, War with Mexico	Mexican War, 1846-1848
United States—History—1898, War of 1898	Spanish-American War, 1898
United States—History—Historiography	United States—Historiography
United States—History, Local	United States—Local history
United States—History, Military	United States—Military history
United States—History, Naval	United States—Naval history
United States Military Academy—Songs and music	United States Military Academy—Songs
United States—Popular culture	Popular culture—United States
United States—Public lands	Public lands—United States
Vegetarian cookery	Vegetarian cooking
Vehicles, Military	Military vehicles
Videotape recorders and recording	Video recording
Violin	Violins
Violoncello	Violoncellos
Wages—Annual wage	[No replacement]
Wages—Minimum wage	Minimum wage
Water—Purification	Water purification
Women—Civil rights	Women's rights
Words, New	New words
Work ethics	Work ethic

CANCELED HEADINGS	REPLACEMENT HEADINGS
World War, 1939-1945—Songs and music	World War, 1939-1945—Songs
Zoology, Economic	Economic zoology

Symbols Used

UF = Used for

SA = See also

BT = Broader term

NT = Narrower term

RT = Related term

[Former heading] = Term that was once used as a
  heading and is no longer

(May subdiv. geog.) = Heading that may be subdivided by name of place

See pp xxviii-xxxiii for further explanation of how these symbols may be translated into cross references in the public catalog.

Sears List of Subject Headings

3-D photography
    USE   **Three dimensional photography**
3 mile limit
    USE   **Territorial waters**
3D photography
    USE   **Three dimensional photography**
4-H clubs 630.6
    UF   Boys' agricultural clubs
         Four-H clubs
         Girls' agricultural clubs
    BT   **Agriculture—Societies**
         Boys' clubs
         Girls' clubs
4th of July
    USE   **Fourth of July**
17 year locusts
    USE   **Cicadas**
100 years' war
    USE   **Hundred Years' War, 1339-1453**
200 mile limit
    USE   **Territorial waters**
1200-1299 (13th century)
    USE   **Thirteenth century**
1300-1399 (14th century)
    USE   **Fourteenth century**
1400-1499 (15th century)
    USE   **Fifteenth century**
1500-1599 (16th century)
    USE   **Sixteenth century**
1600-1699 (17th century)
    USE   **Seventeenth century**
1700-1799 (18th century)
    USE   **Eighteenth century**
1800-1899 (19th century)
    USE   **Nineteenth century**
1900-1999 (20th century)
    USE   **Twentieth century**
2000-2099 (21st century)
    USE   **Twenty-first century**
A.B.C.'s
    USE   **Alphabet**

A.B.M.'s
    USE   **Antimissile missiles**
A-bomb victims
    USE   **Atomic bomb victims**
A.C.O.A.s
    USE   **Adult children of alcoholics**
A.D.C.
    USE   **Child welfare**
A.I.D.S. (Disease)
    USE   **AIDS (Disease)**
A.T.V.'s
    USE   **All terrain vehicles**
Abacus 513.028
    BT   **Calculators**
Abandoned children 362.7
    UF   Children, Abandoned
    BT   **Child welfare**
         Children
    RT   **Orphans**
Abandoned towns
    USE   **Extinct cities**
         Ghost towns
Abandonment of family
    USE   **Desertion and nonsupport**
Abbeys 271; 726
    SA   names of individual abbeys, to be added as needed
    BT   **Church architecture**
         Church history
    NT   **Westminster Abbey**
    RT   **Cathedrals**
         Convents
         Monasteries
Abbreviations 411; 413; 421, etc.; 423, etc.
    UF   Contractions
         Symbols
    BT   **Writing**
    NT   **Acronyms**
         Code names
    RT   **Ciphers**
         Shorthand

Abbreviations—*Continued*
　　Signs and symbols
ABCs
　USE　**Alphabet**
Abduction
　USE　**Kidnapping**
Ability 153.9
　SA　types of ability, to be added
　　　　as needed
　NT　**Creative ability**
　　　Executive ability
　　　Leadership
　　　Musical ability
　RT　**Success**
Ability grouping in education 371.2
　UF　Grouping by ability
　BT　**Grading and marking (Educa-**
　　　tion)
　NT　**Nongraded schools**
Ability—Testing 153.9; 371.2
　UF　Aptitude testing
　BT　**Educational tests and mea-**
　　　surements
　　　Intelligence tests
　　　Psychological tests
ABMs
　USE　**Antimissile missiles**
Abnormal children
　USE　**Exceptional children**
　　　Handicapped children
Abnormal growth
　USE　**Growth disorders**
Abnormal psychology 616.89
　Use for systematic descriptions of men-
　tal disorders. Materials on clinical aspects
　of mental disorders, including therapy, are
　entered under **Psychiatry**. Popular materi-
　als and materials on regional or social as-
　pects of mental disorders are entered
　under **Mental illness**.
　UF　Diseases, Mental
　　　Mental diseases
　　　Pathological psychology
　　　Psychology, Abnormal
　　　Psychology, Medical
　　　Psychology, Pathological *[For-*
　　　　mer heading]
　　　Psychopathology
　　　Psychopathy
　BT　**Mental health**
　　　Mind and body

　　　Nervous system
　NT　**Codependency**
　　　Compulsive behavior
　　　Depression (Psychology)
　　　Eating disorders
　　　Hallucinations and illusions
　　　Mental illness
　　　Multiple personality
　　　Neuroses
　　　Personality disorders
　　　Psychosomatic medicine
　RT　**Criminal psychology**
　　　Psychiatry
　　　Psychoanalysis
Abnormalities, Human
　USE　**Birth defects**
　　　Growth disorders
Abolition of capital punishment
　USE　**Capital punishment**
Abolition of slavery
　USE　**Abolitionists**
　　　Slavery
Abolitionists 326; 920
　UF　Abolition of slavery
　BT　**Slavery—United States**
Abominable snowman
　USE　**Yeti**
Aborigines
　USE　**Ethnology**
Aborigines, Australian
　USE　**Australian aborigines**
Abortion 179; 344; 363.4; 618.8
　UF　Fetal death
　　　Pregnancy, Termination of
　　　Termination of pregnancy
　BT　**Birth control**
Abortion—Catholic Church 241
　BT　**Catholic Church**
Abortion—Moral and religious aspects
　　　179; 241; 291.5
　NT　**Pro-choice movement**
　　　Pro-life movement
Abortion rights movement
　USE　**Pro-choice movement**
Abortion, Spontaneous
　USE　**Miscarriage**
Abrasives 553.6
　BT　**Ceramics**
Absence from school
　USE　**School attendance**

BT = Broader Term　　NT = Narrower Term　　RT = Related Term　　SA = See Also　　UF = Used For

2

Absenteeism (Labor) 331.25; 658.3
  UF Employee absenteeism
        Labor absenteeism
  BT **Hours of labor**
        Personnel management
  RT **Employee morale**
Absenteeism (School)
  USE **School attendance**
Abstinence
  USE **Fasting**
        Temperance
Abstinence, Sexual
  USE **Sexual abstinence**
Abstract art 709.04
  UF Art, Abstract *[Former heading]*
        Art, Geometric
        Art, Nonobjective
        Art, Organic
        Geometric art
        Nonobjective art
        Organic art
        Painting, Abstract
  BT **Modern art—1900-1999 (20th century)**
  NT **Cubism**
Abuse of animals
  USE **Animal welfare**
Abuse of children
  USE **Child abuse**
Abuse of husbands
  USE **Husband abuse**
Abuse of persons
  USE **Offenses against the person**
Abuse of substances
  USE **Substance abuse**
Abuse of the elderly
  USE **Elderly abuse**
Abuse of wives
  USE **Wife abuse**
Abuse, Verbal
  USE **Invective**
Abused aged
  USE **Elderly abuse**
Abused wives
  USE **Abused women**
Abused women 362.82
  UF Abused wives
        Battered wives
        Battered women

  BT **Victims of crime**
        Women
  RT **Wife abuse**
Academic achievement 370.1; 371.2
  UF Academic anxiety
        Academic failure
        Achievement, Academic
        Educational achievement
        Scholastic achievement
  BT **Success**
Academic advising
  USE **Educational counseling**
Academic anxiety
  USE **Academic achievement**
Academic degrees 378.2
  UF College degrees
        Degrees, Academic *[Former heading]*
        Doctors' degrees
        Honorary degrees
        University degrees
  BT **Colleges and universities**
Academic dissertations
  USE **Dissertations**
Academic failure
  USE **Academic achievement**
Academic freedom (May subdiv. geog.) **371.1; 378.1**
  Use for materials on the freedom of teachers and students to teach, discuss, or investigate controversial subjects without penalty or restraint from officials, governments, or organized groups.
  UF Educational freedom
        Freedom, Academic
        Freedom of teaching
        Teaching, Freedom of
  BT **Censorship**
        Civil rights
        Freedom
        Intellectual freedom
        Toleration
  RT **Church and education**
Academic libraries 027.7
  UF College and university libraries
        Libraries, College
        Libraries, University
        University libraries
  BT **Colleges and universities**
        Libraries

Accelerated reading
   USE   **Rapid reading**
Accident insurance 368.3
   UF   Disability insurance
         Insurance, Accident *[Former heading]*
         Insurance, Disability
   BT   **Casualty insurance**
   NT   **Workers' compensation**
Accidents 363.1
   UF   Emergencies
         Injuries
   SA   subjects with the subdivision *Accidents,* to be added as needed
   NT   **Aeronautics—Accidents**
         Explosions
         Fires
         Home accidents
         Labor—Accidents
         Poisons and poisoning
         Railroads—Accidents
         Shipwrecks
         Traffic accidents
         Wounds and injuries
   RT   **Disasters**
         First aid
Accidents—Prevention 363.1; 658.3
   UF   Prevention of accidents
         Safety measures
   SA   subjects with the subdivision *Safety appliances* or *Safety measures,* to be added as needed
   NT   **Aeronautics—Safety measures**
         Railroads—Safety appliances
         Safety education
   RT   **Safety appliances**
Accidents, Spacecraft
   USE   **Astronautics—Accidents**
Acclimatization
   USE   **Adaptation (Biology)**
         Environmental influence on humans
         Plant introduction
Accompaniment, Musical
   USE   **Musical accompaniment**
Accountability
   USE   **Liability (Law)**
Accountants 657.092; 920
   UF   Bookkeepers

         Certified public accountants
   RT   **Accounting**
Accounting 657
   UF   Financial accounting
   SA   names of industries, professions, etc., with the subdivision *Accounting,* to be added as needed
   BT   **Business**
         Business education
         Business mathematics
   NT   **Corporations—Accounting**
         Cost accounting
   RT   **Accountants**
         Auditing
         Bookkeeping
Accounting machines
   USE   **Calculators**
Accounts, Collecting of
   USE   **Collecting of accounts**
Acculturation 303.48
   UF   Culture contact
   BT   **Anthropology**
         Civilization
         Culture
         Ethnology
   NT   **Ethnic relations**
         Multicultural education
         Race relations
         Socialization
   RT   **East and West**
Acetate silk
   USE   **Rayon**
Achievement, Academic
   USE   **Academic achievement**
Achievement tests
   USE   **Examinations**
Acid precipitation
   USE   **Acid rain**
Acid rain 363.73; 628.5
   UF   Acid precipitation
         Rain, Acid
   BT   **Rain**
         Water pollution
Acids 546; 661
   SA   names of acids, to be added as needed
   BT   **Chemicals**
         Chemistry
   NT   **Carbolic acid**

Acne 616.5
  UF   Blackheads (Acne)
       Pimples (Acne)
  BT   Skin—Diseases
ACOAs
  USE Adult children of alcoholics
Acoustics
  USE Architectural acoustics
       Hearing
       Music—Acoustics and physics
       Sound
Acquaintance rape
  USE Date rape
Acquired immune deficiency syndrome
  USE AIDS (Disease)
Acquisition of corporations
  USE Corporate mergers and acqui-
       sitions
Acquisitions (Libraries)
  USE Libraries—Acquisitions
Acrobats and acrobatics 791.3; 796.47
  SA   names of acrobatic feats, e.g.
       Tumbling; to be added as
       needed
  BT   Circus
  NT   Tumbling
  RT   Gymnastics
Acronyms 411; 421, etc.
  UF   English language—Acronyms
       Initialisms
  BT   Abbreviations
       Code names
Acting 791.4; 792
    Use for materials on the art and tech-
  nique of acting in any medium (stage, tele-
  vision, etc.) and on acting as a profession.
  Materials limited to the presentation of
  plays are entered under Amateur theater
  or Theater—Production and direction. Ma-
  terials about members of the profession
  are entered under Actors.
  UF   Dramatic art
       Histrionics
       Stage
  BT   Drama
       Public speaking
  NT   Mime
       Pageants
       Pantomimes
  RT   Actors
       Amateur theater
       Drama in education

       Theater
Acting—Costume
  USE Costume
Action, Social
  USE Social action
Actions and defenses
  USE Litigation
Activism, Social
  USE Social action
Activities curriculum
  USE Creative activities
Activity schools
  USE Education—Experimental
       methods
Actors 791.4; 792; 920
    Use for materials on several persons of
  the acting profession, whether male or fe-
  male. Materials on female actors that em-
  phasize their identity as women are
  entered under Actresses. Materials on
  male actors that emphasize their identity
  as men are entered under Men actors.
  UF   Actors and actresses [Former
       heading]
       Motion picture actors
       Stage
       Television actors
  SA   actors of particular countries,
       e.g. American actors; and
       names of individual actors,
       to be added as needed
  BT   Celebrities
       Entertainers
  NT   Actresses
       African American actors
       American actors
       Black actors
       Comedians
       Men actors
       Stunt performers
  RT   Acting
       Theater
Actors, African American
  USE African American actors
Actors, American
  USE American actors
Actors and actresses
  USE Actors
Actors and actresses, American
  USE American actors
Actors, Black
  USE Black actors

BT = Broader Term   NT = Narrower Term   RT = Related Term   SA = See Also   UF = Used For

Actors, Female
  USE **Actresses**
Actors, Male
  USE **Men actors**
Actresses 791.4; 792; 920
  Use for materials on female actors that emphasize their identity as women. General materials on persons of the acting profession, whether male or female, are entered under **Actors.**
  UF Actors, Female
       Female actors
       Women actors
  BT **Actors**
Acupressure 615.8
  UF Finger pressure therapy
       Myotherapy
  BT **Alternative medicine**
       Massage
  RT **Acupuncture**
Acupuncture 615.8
  BT **Alternative medicine**
  RT **Acupressure**
Adages
  USE **Proverbs**
Adaptability (Psychology)
  USE **Adjustment (Psychology)**
Adaptation (Biology) 574.5; 581.5; 591.5
  UF Acclimatization
  BT **Biology**
       Ecology
       Genetics
       Variation (Biology)
  NT **Environmental influence on**
       humans
       Stress (Physiology)
Adaptation (Psychology)
  USE **Adjustment (Psychology)**
Adaptations
  USE **Film adaptations**
       Television adaptations
       and names of authors or individual works entered under title with the subdivision *Adaptations* for criticism and interpretation of literary, cinematic, video, or television adaptations, e.g., **Beowulf—Adaptations; Shakespeare, William—Adaptations;** etc., to be added as needed

Adaptations, Film
  USE **Film adaptations**
Adaptations, Television
  USE **Television adaptations**
Addiction
  USE **Substance abuse**
       and types of addiction, e.g. **Alcoholism; Drug addiction;** etc., to be added as needed
Addiction to alcohol
  USE **Alcoholism**
Addiction to drugs
  USE **Drug addiction**
Addiction to exercise
  USE **Exercise addiction**
Addiction to gambling
  USE **Compulsive gambling**
Addiction to hard drugs
  USE **Drug addiction**
Addiction to substances
  USE **Substance abuse**
Addiction to tobacco
  USE **Tobacco habit**
Addiction to work
  USE **Workaholism**
Addictive behavior
  USE **Compulsive behavior**
       Substance abuse
       and types of addictions and compulsive behaviors, e.g. **Alcoholism; Drug addiction; Compulsive gambling; Workaholism;** etc., to be added as needed
Addicts, Drug
  USE **Drug addicts**
Adding machines
  USE **Calculators**
Additives, Food
  USE **Food additives**
Addresses
  USE **Lectures and lecturing**
       Speeches
Adhesives 620.1; 668; 691
  SA types of adhesives, to be added as needed
  NT **Cement**
       Glue
       Mortar
Adjustment (Psychology) 155.2
  UF Adaptability (Psychology)

Adjustment (Psychology)—*Continued*
    Adaptation (Psychology)
    Coping behavior
    Maladjustment (Psychology)
  BT **Psychology**
Adjustment, Social
  USE **Social adjustment**
Administration
  USE **Civil service**
    Management
    Political science
    Public administration
    State, The
    and types of institutions and
    names of individual institu-
    tions with the subdivision
    Administration, e.g.
    Libraries—Administration;
    Schools—Administration;
    etc.; and names of coun-
    tries, cities, etc., with the
    subdivision *Politics and*
    government, e.g. **United**
    States—Politics and govern-
    ment; to be added as need-
    ed

Administration of criminal justice 345
  UF Criminal justice, Administra-
    tion of *[Former heading]*
  BT **Administration of justice**
    Criminal law
  NT **Amnesty**
    Corrections
    Crime
    Law enforcement
    Pardon
    Parole
    Police
    Prisons
    Punishment
Administration of justice 351.8
  UF Justice, Administration of
    [Former heading]
  BT **Law**
  NT **Administration of criminal**
    justice
    Due process of law
    Governmental investigations
    Impeachments
  RT **Courts**

Administrative ability
  USE **Executive ability**
Administrative agencies—
    Reorganization
  USE **United States—Executive**
    departments—
    Reorganization
Administrative law 342
  UF Law, Administrative
  BT **Law**
  NT **Civil service**
    Local government
    Ombudsman
  RT **Constitutional law**
    Public administration
Administrators and executors
  USE **Executors and administrators**
Admirals 359.0092; 920
  BT **Military personnel**
    Navies
Admissions applications
  USE **College applications**
Admissions essays
  USE **College applications**
Adolescence 155.5; 305.23
    Use for materials on the process or the
state of growing to maturity. Materials on
the time of life between thirteen and twen-
ty-five years, and on people in this general
age range, are entered under **Youth.** Mate-
rials limited to teen youth are entered un-
der **Teenagers.** Materials limited to
people in the general age range of eighteen
through twenty-five years are entered un-
der **Young men** or **Young women.**
  UF Teen age
    Teenagers—Development
  BT **Age**
  RT **Youth**
Adolescence—Psychology
  USE **Adolescent psychology**
Adolescent fathers
  USE **Teenage fathers**
Adolescent mothers
  USE **Teenage mothers**
Adolescent pregnancy
  USE **Teenage pregnancy**
Adolescent prostitution
  USE **Juvenile prostitution**
Adolescent psychiatry 616.89
  UF Psychiatry, Adolescent
    Teenagers, Psychiatry of

BT = Broader Term   NT = Narrower Term   RT = Related Term   SA = See Also   UF = Used For

Adolescent psychiatry—*Continued*
  BT **Psychiatry**
Adolescent psychology 155.5
  UF Adolescence—Psychology
      Psychology, Adolescent
      Teenagers—Psychology
  BT **Psychology**
Adolescents
  USE **Teenagers**
Adopted children 306.87; 362.82
  UF Children, Adopted *[Former
      heading]*
  BT **Adoptees**
      Adoption
  RT **Orphans**
Adoptees 346.01; 362.7
    Use for materials on anyone formally
  adopted as a dependent.
  UF Adult adoptees
  BT **Adoption**
  NT **Adopted children**
  RT **Birthparents**
Adoption 346.01; 362.7
  UF Child placing
      Children—Adoption
      Children—Placing out
  BT **Parent and child**
  NT **Adopted children**
      Adoptees
      Interracial adoption
  RT **Foster home care**
Adoption—Corrupt practices 364.1
  UF Black market children
      Infants, Sale of
      Sale of infants
      Selling of infants
  BT **Criminal law**
Adoption, Interracial
  USE **Interracial adoption**
Adult adoptees
  USE **Adoptees**
Adult children of alcoholics 362.29
  UF A.C.O.A.s
      ACOAs
      Alcoholic parents
      Alcoholics' adult children
  BT **Alcoholics**
      Alcoholism
      Children of alcoholics
      Parent and child

Adult education 374
  UF Education, Adult
      Education of adults
      Lifelong education
  BT **Education**
      Higher education
      Secondary education
      University extension
  NT **Agricultural extension work**
      Prisoners—Education
  RT **Continuing education**
      **Evening and continuation
        schools**
Adult fiction
  USE **Erotic fiction**
Adult films
  USE **Erotic films**
Adulteration of food
  USE **Food adulteration and inspec-
        tion**
Adultery 176; 306.73; 363.4
  UF Extramarital relationships
      Infidelity, Marital
      Marital infidelity
  BT **Sexual ethics**
Adults and children
  USE **Children and adults**
Adults, Runaway
  USE **Runaway adults**
**Adventure and adventurers 904;
        904.092; 910.4; 920**
  NT **Escapes**
      Exploration
      Explorers
      Frontier and pioneer life
      Heroes and heroines
      Sea stories
      Seafaring life
      Shipwrecks
      Underwater exploration
  RT **Voyages and travels**
Adventure and adventurers—Fiction
  USE **Adventure fiction**
Adventure fiction 808.83; 813, etc
    May be used for individual works, col-
  lections, or materials about adventure fic-
  tion.
  UF Adventure and adventurers—
      Fiction *[Former heading]*
      Adventure stories

Adventure fiction—*Continued*
  Suspense novels
  Swashbucklers
  Thrillers
BT Fiction
NT Robinsonades
  Romantic suspense novels
  Science fiction
  Sea stories
  Spy stories
  Western stories

Adventure films 791.43

May be used for individual works, collections, or materials about adventure films.

UF Suspense films
  Swashbucklers
  Thrillers
BT Motion pictures
NT Superhero films
  Western films
RT Adventure television programs

Adventure radio programs 791.44

May be used for individual works, collections, or materials about adventure radio programs.

BT Radio programs
NT Superhero radio programs

Adventure stories
USE Adventure fiction

Adventure television programs 791.45

May be used for individual works, collections, or materials about adventure television programs.

BT Television programs
NT Superhero television programs
RT Adventure films

Advertisement writing
USE Advertising copy

Advertising 659.1

May be subdivided by topic, e.g. **Advertising—Libraries;** to specify the thing advertised.

BT Business
  Retail trade
NT Advertising and children
  Advertising copy
  Advertising layout and typography
  Commercial art
  Coupons (Retail trade)
  Electric signs

Fashion models
Market surveys
Packaging
Posters
Printing—Specimens
Radio advertising
Show windows
Sign painting
Signs and signboards
Television advertising
RT Marketing
  Propaganda
  Public relations
  Publicity
  Selling

Advertising and children 659.1

UF Children and advertising
BT Advertising
  Children

Advertising art
USE Commercial art

Advertising copy 659.13

UF Advertisement writing
  Copy writing
BT Advertising
  Authorship

Advertising, Fraudulent
USE Deceptive advertising

Advertising layout and typography 659.13

BT Advertising
  Printing
  Type and type founding

Advertising—Libraries 021.7

UF Libraries—Advertising
  Library advertising

Advertising, Newspaper
USE Newspaper advertising

Advertising—Newspapers 659.1

Use for materials on the advertising of newspapers. Materials on advertising in newspapers are entered under **Newspaper advertising.**

UF Newspapers—Advertising

Advertising, Pictorial
USE Commercial art
  Posters

Advertising, Radio
USE Radio advertising

Advertising, Television
USE Television advertising

BT = Broader Term   NT = Narrower Term   RT = Related Term   SA = See Also   UF = Used For

Advisors
USE **Consultants**
Aerial bombs
USE **Bombs**
Aerial navigation
USE **Navigation (Aeronautics)**
Aerial photography 778.3
   Use for materials on photography from airplanes, balloons, high buildings, etc.
UF Photography, Aerial *[Former heading]*
BT **Photography**
NT **Remote sensing**
Aerial propellers 629.134
UF Airplanes—Propellers
Propellers, Aerial *[Former heading]*
BT **Airplanes**
Aerial reconnaissance 355.4; 358.4
UF Reconnaissance, Aerial
BT **Military aeronautics**
Remote sensing
Aerial rockets
USE **Rockets (Aeronautics)**
Aerial spraying and dusting
USE **Aeronautics in agriculture**
Aerobatic flying
USE **Stunt flying**
Aerobatics
USE **Stunt flying**
Aerobic dancing
USE **Aerobics**
Aerobic exercises
USE **Aerobics**
Aerobics 613.7
UF Aerobic dancing
Aerobic exercises
Dancing, Aerobic
Exercises, Aerobic
BT **Dancing**
Exercise
Respiration
Aerobiology
USE **Air—Microbiology**
Aerodromes
USE **Airports**
Aerodynamics 533; 629.132
UF Streamlining
BT **Air**
Dynamics

Pneumatics
NT **Ground cushion phenomena**
RT **Aeronautics**
Aerodynamics, Supersonic
USE **Supersonic aerodynamics**
Aeronautical instruments 629.135
UF Airplanes—Instruments
Instruments, Aeronautical
SA names of specific instruments, e.g. **Gyroscope;** to be added as needed
BT **Scientific apparatus and instruments**
NT **Airplanes—Electric equipment**
Gyroscope
Instrument flying
Aeronautical sports 797.5
SA names of specific sports, to be added as needed
BT **Aeronautics**
Sports
NT **Airplane racing**
Skydiving
Aeronautics 629.13
   Use for materials on the scientific aspects of aircraft and their construction and operation; or for materials dealing collectively with various types of aircraft.
UF Aviation
SA aeronautics in particular industries or fields of endeavor, e.g. **Aeronautics in agriculture;** to be added as needed
BT **Engineering**
Locomotion
NT **Aeronautical sports**
Aeronautics in agriculture
Air pilots
Airplanes
Airways
Astronautics
Gliders (Aeronautics)
Gliding and soaring
Helicopters
High speed aeronautics
Kites
Lasers in aeronautics
Meteorology in aeronautics
Military aeronautics

BT = Broader Term   NT = Narrower Term   RT = Related Term   SA = See Also   UF = Used For

Aeronautics—*Continued*
>> Navigation (Aeronautics)
>> Parachutes
>> Radio in aeronautics
>> Rocketry
>> Rockets (Aeronautics)
>> Unidentified flying objects
> RT Aerodynamics
>> Airships
>> Balloons
>> Flight

Aeronautics—Accidents 363.12; 629.13
> UF Air crashes
>> Airplane accidents
>> Airplane collisions
>> Airplanes—Accidents
> BT Accidents
> NT Survival after airplane accidents, shipwrecks, etc.

Aeronautics and civilization 306
> UF Civilization and aeronautics
> BT Civilization
> NT Astronautics and civilization

Aeronautics, Commercial
> USE Commercial aeronautics

Aeronautics, Commercial—Chartering
> USE Airlines—Chartering

Aeronautics—Flights 387.7; 629.13
> UF Aeronautics—Voyages
>> Flights around the world
>> Transatlantic flights
> BT Voyages and travels
> NT Space flight

Aeronautics, High speed
> USE High speed aeronautics

Aeronautics in agriculture 631.3
> UF Aerial spraying and dusting
>> Airplanes in agriculture
>> Crop dusting
>> Crop spraying
> BT Aeronautics
>> Agricultural pests
>> Agriculture
>> Spraying and dusting
> RT Insect pests

Aeronautics—Medical aspects
> USE Aviation medicine

Aeronautics, Meteorology in
> USE Meteorology in aeronautics

Aeronautics, Military
> USE Military aeronautics

Aeronautics, Naval
> USE Military aeronautics

Aeronautics—Navigation
> USE Navigation (Aeronautics)

Aeronautics—Piloting
> USE Airplanes—Piloting

Aeronautics—Safety measures 387.7; 629.134
> BT Accidents—Prevention
> NT Air traffic control

Aeronautics—Study and teaching 629.1307
> UF Flight training
> NT Airplanes—Piloting

Aeronautics—Voyages
> USE Aeronautics—Flights

Aeroplanes
> USE Airplanes

Aeroponics 631.5
> UF Agriculture, Soilless
>> Gardening in space
>> Plants—Soilless culture
>> Soilless agriculture
>> Space gardening
> BT Horticulture

Aerosol sniffing
> USE Solvent abuse

Aerosols 541.3; 551.5; 660
> BT Air pollution

Aerospace industries 338.4
> UF Aircraft production
> BT Industry
> NT Airplane industry

Aerospace law
> USE Space law

Aerospace medicine
> USE Aviation medicine
>> Space medicine

Aerothermodynamics 629.132; 629.4
> UF Thermoaerodynamics
> BT Astronautics
>> High speed aeronautics
>> Supersonic aerodynamics
>> Thermodynamics

Aesthetics 111; 701; 801
> UF Beauty
>> Esthetics *[Former heading]*
>> Taste (Aesthetics)

BT = Broader Term   NT = Narrower Term   RT = Related Term   SA = See Also   UF = Used For

Aesthetics—*Continued*
  SA   styles and movements in the
         arts, e.g. **Classicism; Post-
         modernism;** etc., to be add-
         ed as needed
  BT   **Art**
        Arts
  NT   **Art appreciation**
        Classicism
        Color
        Criticism
        Modernism (Arts)
        Poetry
        Postmodernism
        Rhythm
        Romanticism
        Values
Affection
  USE **Friendship**
        Love
**Affirmative action programs 331.13;
     658.3**
  BT   **Discrimination in employment**
        Personnel management
Affliction
  USE **Joy and sorrow**
        Suffering
Africa 960
  NT   **Africans**
        Central Africa
        East Africa
        North Africa
        Northeast Africa
        Northwest Africa
        Pan-Africanism
        South Africa
        Southern Africa
        Sub-Saharan Africa
        West Africa
Africa, Central
  USE **Central Africa**
Africa, East
  USE **East Africa**
Africa, Eastern
  USE **East Africa**
Africa, French-speaking Equatorial
  USE **French-speaking Equatorial
        Africa**
Africa, French-speaking West
  USE **French-speaking West Africa**

Africa—History 960
Africa—History—1960- 960.3
Africa, North
  USE **North Africa**
Africa, Northeast
  USE **Northeast Africa**
Africa, Northwest
  USE **Northwest Africa**
Africa, South
  USE **South Africa**
Africa, Southern
  USE **Southern Africa**
Africa—Study and teaching 960.07
  UF   African studies
  BT   **Area studies**
Africa, Sub-Saharan
  USE **Sub-Saharan Africa**
Africa, West
  USE **West Africa**
**African American actors 791.4; 792;
     920**
  UF   Actors, African American
        African American actors and
        actresses
        Afro-American actors
  BT   **Actors**
        Black actors
African American actors and actresses
  USE **African American actors**
African American art 704
    Use for materials on works of art by
  several African American artists. Materials
  on African Americans depicted in works
  of art are entered under **African Ameri-
  cans in art.**
  UF   African Americans—Art
        Afro-American art
        Art, African American
  BT   **Art**
        Black art
  NT   **Harlem Renaissance**
  RT   **African American artists**
African American artists 709.2; 920
    Use for materials on several African
  Americans artists.
  UF   Afro-American artists
        Artists, African American
  BT   **Artists**
        Black artists
  RT   **African American art**
African American athletes 796.092; 920
  UF   Afro-American athletes

African American athletes—*Continued*
Athletes, African American
BT   Athletes
Black athletes
African American authors 810.9; 920
Use for materials on several African American authors.
UF   Afro-American authors
Authors, African American
SA   particular forms of American literature with the subdivision *African American authors,* e.g. **American poetry—African American authors;** etc., to be added as needed
BT   Authors
Black authors
RT   American literature—African American authors
African American business people 338.092; 658.0092; 920
UF   Afro-American business people
Afro-Americans in business
Business people, African American
BT   African Americans—Employment
Black business people
Business people
African American children 305.23
UF   African Americans—Children
Afro-American children
Children, African American
BT   Black children
Children
African American elderly 305.26
BT   Elderly
African American folklore
USE   African Americans—Folklore
African American librarians 020.92; 920
UF   Afro-American librarians
Librarians, African American
BT   Black librarians
Librarians
African American literature
USE   American literature—African American authors

African American music (May subdiv. geog.) 780.089
Use for materials on the music of African Americans. Materials on the music of Blacks not limitied to the United States are entered under **Black music.**
UF   African American songs
African Americans—Music
Afro-American music
Afro-American songs
Music, African American
Songs, African American
BT   Black music
Music
NT   Blues music
Gospel music
Harlem Renaissance
Rap music
RT   African American musicians
Spirituals (Songs)
African American musicians 780.92; 920
UF   Afro-American musicians
Musicians, African American
BT   Black musicians
Musicians
RT   African American music
African American poetry
USE   American poetry—African American authors
African American songs
USE   African American music
African American suffrage
USE   African Americans—Suffrage
African American women 305.48
UF   Afro-American women
Women, African American
BT   Black women
Women
African American youth 305.23; 970.004
BT   Youth
African Americans (May subdiv. geog. by cities, states, or regions of the U.S.) 305.896; 973
Use for materials dealing collectively with Blacks in the United States. General materials and materials on Blacks in places other than the United States are entered under **Blacks.**
UF   Afro-Americans
Black Americans
Blacks—United States
Negroes

BT = Broader Term   NT = Narrower Term   RT = Related Term   SA = See Also   UF = Used For

African Americans—*Continued*
SA African Americans in various
occupations and profes-
sions, e.g. **African American
artists; African American li-
brarians;** etc., to be added
as needed
BT **Blacks**
NT **Libraries and African Ameri-
cans**
RT **Slavery—United States**
African Americans and libraries
USE **Libraries and African Ameri-
cans**
African Americans—Art
USE **African American art**
African Americans—Biography 920
UF Afro-Americans—Biography
BT **Blacks—Biography**
**African Americans—Chicago (Ill.)
305.896; 977.3**
UF Chicago (Ill.)—African Ameri-
cans
African Americans—Children
USE **African American children**
**African Americans—Civil rights 323.1;
342**
UF Demonstrations for Black civ-
il rights—United States
Freedom marches—United
States
Marches for Black civil
rights—United States
BT **Blacks—Civil rights
Civil rights**
NT **African Americans—Suffrage
Black power**
African Americans—Economic condi-
tions 330.973
UF Afro-Americans—Economic
conditions
BT **Blacks—Economic conditions
Economic conditions**
NT **Black power**
African Americans—Education 370.19
UF Afro-Americans—Education
BT **Blacks—Education
Education**
NT **School integration
Segregation in education**

African Americans—Employment 331.6
UF African Americans—
Occupations
BT **Blacks—Employment
Discrimination in employment
Employment**
NT **African American business
people**
African Americans—Folklore 398
UF African American folklore
Folklore, African American
BT **Blacks—Folklore
Folklore**
**African Americans—Housing 307.3;
363.5**
UF Afro-Americans—Housing
Housing, African American
BT **Blacks—Housing
Housing**
African Americans in art 704.9
Use for materials on African Americans
depicted in works of art. Materials on the
attainments of several African Americans
in the area of art are entered under **Afri-
can American artists.** Materials on works
of art by several African American artists
are entered under **African American art.**
UF Afro-Americans in art
BT **Art
Blacks in art**
African Americans in literature 809
Use for materials on the theme of African Americans in works of literature. Materials on several African American
authors are entered under **African American authors.** Materials on works of literature by several African American authors
are entered under **American literature—
African American authors** and the various
forms of American literature with the sub-
division *African American authors,* e.g.
**American poetry—African American au-
thors.**
UF Afro-Americans in literature
BT **Blacks in literature
Characters and characteristics
in literature**
**African Americans in motion pictures
791.43**
Use for materials on the depiction of
African Americans in motion pictures.
Materials on several African American ac-
tors are entered under **African American
actors.** Materials discussing all aspects of
African Americans' involvement in mo-
tion pictures are entered under **African
Americans in the motion picture industry.**

BT = Broader Term   NT = Narrower Term   RT = Related Term   SA = See Also   UF = Used For

African Americans in motion pictures—
Continued
   BT   **Blacks in motion pictures**
         Motion pictures
African Americans in the motion picture
     industry 791.43092
   Use for materials on all aspects of Afri-
can Americans' involvement in motion
pictures. Materials on the depiction of Af-
rican Americans in motion pictures are
entered under **African Americans in mo-
tion pictures.**
   BT   **Blacks in the motion picture
         industry**
         Motion picture industry
African Americans—Integration 305.896
   UF   Integration, Racial
   BT   **Blacks—Integration**
   NT   **School integration**
African Americans—Intellectual life
     305.896
   BT   **Blacks—Intellectual life**
         Intellectual life
African Americans—Music
   USE **African American music**
African Americans—Occupations
   USE **African Americans—
         Employment**
African Americans—Ohio 305.896;
     977.1
   UF   Ohio—African Americans
African Americans—Political activity
     322.4; 324
   BT   **Blacks—Political activity**
   NT   **Black nationalism**
         Black power
African Americans—Race identity
     305.896
   BT   **Blacks—Race identity**
         Race awareness
   NT   **Black nationalism**
African Americans—Religion 270.089;
     299; 305.896
   BT   **Blacks—Religion**
         Religion
   NT   **Black Muslims**
African Americans—Segregation
     305.896
   BT   **Blacks—Segregation**
         Segregation
   NT   **Segregation in education**

African Americans—Social conditions
     305.896
   BT   **Blacks—Social conditions**
         Social conditions
African Americans—Social life and cus-
     toms 305.896
   BT   **Blacks—Social life and cus-
         toms**
African Americans—Southern States
     305.896; 975
   UF   Southern States—African
         Americans
African Americans—Suffrage 324.6
   UF   African American suffrage
   BT   **African Americans—Civil
         rights**
         Blacks—Suffrage
         Suffrage
African civilization 306.096; 960
   UF   Civilization, African *[Former
         heading]*
   BT   **Civilization**
African literature (English) 820
   UF   English literature—African au-
         thors
   BT   **Literature**
African peoples
   USE **Africans**
African relations
   USE **Pan-Africanism**
African songs 782.42096
   UF   Folk songs, African
         Folk songs, Black (African)
         Songs, African *[Former head-
         ing]*
   BT   **Songs**
African studies
   USE **Africa—Study and teaching**
Africans 305.896; 960
   UF   African peoples
   SA   names of African peoples, e.g.
         Yoruba (African people); to
         be added as needed
   BT   **Africa**
   NT   **Blacks—Africa**
         Yoruba (African people)
Afrikaaners
   USE **Afrikaners**
Afrikaners 305.83; 968
   UF   Afrikaaners

BT = Broader Term   NT = Narrower Term   RT = Related Term   SA = See Also   UF = Used For

Afrikaners—*Continued*
    Boers
    South African Dutch
    South Africans, Afrikaans-
       speaking
Afro-American actors
  USE **African American actors**
Afro-American art
  USE **African American art**
Afro-American artists
  USE **African American artists**
Afro-American athletes
  USE **African American athletes**
Afro-American authors
  USE **African American authors**
Afro-American business people
  USE **African American business
       people**
Afro-American children
  USE **African American children**
Afro-American librarians
  USE **African American librarians**
Afro-American music
  USE **African American music**
Afro-American musicians
  USE **African American musicians**
Afro-American songs
  USE **African American music**
Afro-American women
  USE **African American women**
Afro-Americans
  USE **African Americans**
Afro-Americans and libraries
  USE **Libraries and African Ameri-
       cans**
Afro-Americans—Biography
  USE **African Americans—Biography**
Afro-Americans—Economic conditions
  USE **African Americans—Economic
       conditions**
Afro-Americans—Education
  USE **African Americans—Education**
Afro-Americans—Housing
  USE **African Americans—Housing**
Afro-Americans in art
  USE **African Americans in art**
Afro-Americans in business
  USE **African American business
       people**

Afro-Americans in literature
  USE **African Americans in litera-
       ture**
After dinner speeches 808.5; 808.85
  BT **Speeches**
  RT **Toasts**
After school day care
  USE **After school programs**
After school programs 362.7; 372.12
  UF After school day care
  BT **Student activities**
Afterlife
  USE **Future life**
Afternoon teas
  USE **Tea**
Age 305.2
  UF Age groups
  NT **Adolescence**
       Aging
       Children
       Drinking age
       Elderly
       Longevity
       Middle age
       Middle aged persons
       Old age
       Teenagers
       Youth
Age and employment 331.3
  UF Employment and age
  BT **Discrimination in employment**
       Middle age
       Old age
  NT **Career changes**
       Children—Employment
       Teenagers—Employment
       Youth—Employment
  RT **Age discrimination**
Age discrimination 305.2
  BT **Discrimination**
  RT **Age and employment**
Age groups
  USE **Age**
Age—Physiological effect
  USE **Aging**
Aged
  USE **Elderly**
Aged men
  USE **Elderly men**
Aged parents
  USE **Aging parents**

Aged women
USE   **Elderly women**
Ageing
USE   **Aging**
Agent Orange 363.17; 615.9
BT   **Herbicides**
Agents, Sales
USE   **Sales personnel**
Aggregates
USE   **Set theory**
Aggressive behavior
USE   **Aggressiveness (Psychology)**
Aggressiveness (Psychology) 152.4;
       155.2
UF   Aggressive behavior
BT   **Human behavior**
       Psychology
NT   **Assertiveness (Psychology)**
       Violence
Aging 574.3; 612.6
UF   Age—Physiological effect
       Ageing
       Senescence
BT   **Age**
       Elderly
       Gerontology
       Longevity
       Middle age
       Old age
NT   **Male climacteric**
       Menopause
Aging parents 306.874
UF   Aged parents
       Elderly parents
       Parents, Aging
BT   **Elderly**
       Family life
Aging persons
USE   **Elderly**
Agnosticism 149; 211
BT   **Free thought**
       Religion
       Truth
RT   **Atheism**
       Belief and doubt
       Faith
       Positivism
       Rationalism
       Skepticism
Agrarian question
USE   **Agriculture—Economic aspects**

Agriculture—Government poli-
       cy
       Land tenure
Agrarian reform
USE   **Land reform**
Agreements
USE   **Contracts**
       Covenants
Agribusiness
USE   **Agricultural industries**
Agricultural bacteriology 630.2
UF   Bacteriology, Agricultural
       [Former heading]
       Diseases and pests
SA   names of crops, etc., with the
       subdivision *Diseases and*
       pests, to be added as need-
       ed
NT   **Fruit—Diseases and pests**
RT   **Soils—Bacteriology**
Agricultural botany
USE   **Economic botany**
Agricultural chemicals 631.8; 668
SA   types of agricultural chemicals
       and names of individual
       chemicals, to be added as
       needed
BT   **Agricultural chemistry**
       Chemicals
NT   **Fertilizers and manures**
       Herbicides
       Insecticides
       Pesticides
Agricultural chemistry 630.2
UF   Chemistry, Agricultural
BT   **Chemistry**
NT   **Agricultural chemicals**
RT   **Soils**
Agricultural clubs
USE   **Agriculture—Societies**
Agricultural cooperation
USE   **Cooperative agriculture**
Agricultural credit 332.7
UF   Credit, Agricultural
       Farm credit
       Rural credit
BT   **Agriculture—Economic aspects**
       Banks and banking
       Credit
       Mortgages

Agricultural economics
    USE   **Agriculture—Economic aspects**
Agricultural education
    USE   **Agriculture—Study and teaching**
Agricultural engineering 630
    UF   Agricultural mechanics
          Bioengineering
          Farm mechanics
    BT   **Agricultural machinery**
          Engineering
    NT   **Drainage**
          Electricity in agriculture
          Irrigation
Agricultural experiment stations 630.7
    UF   Experimental farms
          Farms, Experimental
    BT   **Agriculture—Government policy**
          Agriculture—Research
          Agriculture—Study and teaching
    NT   **Agricultural extension work**
Agricultural extension work (May subdiv. geog.) **630.7**
    UF   Extension work, Agricultural
    BT   **Adult education**
          Agricultural experiment stations
          Agriculture—Government policy
    NT   **County agricultural agents**
    RT   **Agriculture—Study and teaching**
          Community development
Agricultural industries 338.1
    UF   Agribusiness
    BT   **Agriculture—Economic aspects**
Agricultural laborers 331.7
    UF   Farm laborers
    BT   **Labor**
    RT   **Migrant labor**
          Peasantry
Agricultural machinery 631.3
    UF   Agricultural tools
          Farm engines *[Former heading]*
          Farm equipment
          Farm implements
          Farm machinery

          Farm mechanics
          Implements, utensils, etc.
    SA   types of farm machinery, to be added as needed
    BT   **Machinery**
          Tools
    NT   **Agricultural engineering**
          Electricity in agriculture
          Harvesting machinery
          Plows
          Tractors
Agricultural mechanics
    USE   **Agricultural engineering**
Agricultural pests 632
    UF   Diseases and pests
          Garden pests
    SA   names of crops, etc., with the subdivision *Diseases and pests,* to be added as needed
    BT   **Economic zoology**
          Pests
    NT   **Aeronautics in agriculture**
          Fruit—Diseases and pests
          Fungi
          Pest control
          Plant diseases
          Spraying and dusting
          Weeds
    RT   **Insect pests**
Agricultural policy
    USE   **Agriculture—Government policy**
Agricultural products
    USE   **Farm produce**
Agricultural research
    USE   **Agriculture—Research**
Agricultural societies
    USE   **Agriculture—Societies**
Agricultural subsidies 338.9
    UF   Agriculture and state
          Farm subsidies
          State and agriculture
          Subsidies, Agricultural
          Subsidies, Farm
    BT   **Subsidies**
    RT   **Agriculture—Government policy**
Agricultural tools
    USE   **Agricultural machinery**

BT = Broader Term   NT = Narrower Term   RT = Related Term   SA = See Also   UF = Used For

Agriculture (May subdiv. geog.) **630**
  UF Agronomy
        Farming
        Planting
  SA names of agricultural prod-
        ucts, e.g. **Corn;** to be added
        as needed
  BT **Life sciences**
  NT **Aeronautics in agriculture**
        Aquaculture
        Cooperative agriculture
        Crop rotation
        Cultivated plants
        Dairying
        Dry farming
        Economic botany
        Farmers
        Forests and forestry
        Fruit culture
        Gardening
        Horticulture
        Land use
        Organic farming
        Pastures
        Plant breeding
        Reclamation of land
        Soils
  RT **Farms**
        Food supply
Agriculture and state
  USE **Agricultural subsidies**
        **Agriculture—Government poli-
cy**
Agriculture—Bibliography 016.63
  BT **Bibliography**
Agriculture, Cooperative
  USE **Cooperative agriculture**
Agriculture—Documentation 025
  BT **Documentation**
Agriculture—Economic aspects 338.1
  UF Agrarian question
        Agricultural economics
  BT **Economics**
  NT **Agricultural credit**
        Agricultural industries
        Land tenure
  RT **Farm management**
        Farm produce—Marketing
Agriculture—Government policy 338.9
  UF Agrarian question

Agricultural policy
        Agriculture and state
        State and agriculture
  BT **Industry—Government policy**
  NT **Agricultural experiment sta-
tions**
        Agricultural extension work
  RT **Agricultural subsidies**
        Land reform
Agriculture—Research 630.7
  UF Agricultural research
  BT **Research**
  NT **Agricultural experiment sta-
tions**
Agriculture—Societies 630.6
  UF Agricultural clubs
        Agricultural societies
        Boys' agricultural clubs
        Girls' agricultural clubs
  SA names of agricultural societies,
        to be added as needed
  BT **Associations**
        Country life
        Societies
  NT **4-H clubs**
        Grange
Agriculture, Soilless
  USE **Aeroponics**
        Hydroponics
Agriculture—Statistics 338.1; 630.2
  UF Crop reports
  BT **Statistics**
Agriculture—Study and teaching 630.7
  UF Agricultural education
  BT **Vocational education**
  NT **Agricultural experiment sta-
tions**
        County agricultural agents
  RT **Agricultural extension work**
Agriculture—Tenant farming
  USE **Farm tenancy**
Agriculture—Tropics 630.913
  BT **Tropics**
Agriculture—United States 630.973
  UF United States—Agriculture
Agronomy
  USE **Agriculture**
Ague
  USE **Malaria**
AI (Artificial intelligence)
  USE **Artificial intelligence**

Aid to dependent children
    USE **Child welfare**
Aid to developing areas
    USE **Economic assistance**
           Technical assistance
AIDS (Disease) 616.97
    UF A.I.D.S. (Disease)
         Acquired immune deficiency
           syndrome
         HIV disease
    BT **Communicable diseases**
         Diseases
         Sexually transmitted diseases
AIDS (Disease)—Prevention 616.97
    NT **Safe sex in AIDS prevention**
    RT **Sexual hygiene**
Aids (Disease)—Treatment 615.5
    BT **Therapeutics**
Air 533; 546
    Use for materials dealing with air in general and with its chemical and physical properties. Materials on the body of air surrounding the earth are entered under **Atmosphere.**
    BT **Meteorology**
    NT **Aerodynamics**
         Ventilation
    RT **Atmosphere**
Air bases 358.4
    UF Air stations, Military
         Air stations, Naval
         Military air bases
         Naval air bases
    BT **Airports**
         Military aeronautics
Air bearing lift
    USE **Ground cushion phenomena**
Air bearing vehicles
    USE **Ground effect machines**
Air cargo
    USE **Commercial aeronautics**
Air carriers
    USE **Airlines**
Air charters
    USE **Airlines—Chartering**
Air, Compressed
    USE **Compressed air**
Air conditioning 644; 697.9
    SA subjects with the subdivision
         Air conditioning, to be added as needed

    NT **Automobiles—Air conditioning**
    RT **Refrigeration**
         Ventilation
Air crashes
    USE **Aeronautics—Accidents**
Air cushion vehicles
    USE **Ground effect machines**
Air defenses 363.3
    Use for materials on civilian or military defense against air attack. General materials on civilian defense are entered under **Civil defense.**
    UF Air defenses, Civil
         Air defenses, Military
         Air raid defensive measures
         Air warfare
         Defenses, Air
    BT **Civil defense**
         Military aeronautics
    NT **Air raid shelters**
         Ballistic missile early warning system
         Radar defense networks
Air defenses, Civil
    USE **Air defenses**
Air defenses, Military
    USE **Air defenses**
Air freight
    USE **Commercial aeronautics**
Air hostesses
    USE **Flight attendants**
Air lines
    USE **Airlines**
Air mail service 383
    BT **Commercial aeronautics**
         Postal service
Air—Microbiology 576
    UF Aerobiology
    BT **Microbiology**
Air, Moisture of
    USE **Humidity**
Air navigation
    USE **Navigation (Aeronautics)**
Air pilots 629.13092; 920
    UF Airplane pilots
         Airplanes—Pilots
         Aviators
         Pilots, Airplane
         Test pilots
    BT **Aeronautics**

Air pilots—*Continued*
NT   **Astronauts**
    Women air pilots
Air piracy
USE   **Hijacking of airplanes**
Air planes
USE   **Airplanes**
Air pollution (May subdiv. geog.)
    363.73; 628.5
UF   Atmosphere—Pollution
    Pollution of air
BT   **Environmental health**
    Pollution
NT   **Aerosols**
Air pollution—Measurement 363.73;
    628.5
BT   **Measurement**
Air pollution—United States 363.73;
    628.5
UF   United States—Air pollution
Air ports
USE   **Airports**
Air power 358.4
BT   **Military aeronautics**
Air raid defensive measures
USE   **Air defenses**
    Military aeronautics
Air raid shelters 363.3
UF   Blast shelters
    Bomb shelters
    Fallout shelters
    Nuclear bomb shelters
    Public shelters
    Shelters, Air raid
BT   **Air defenses**
    Civil defense
Air rights law
USE   **Airspace law**
Air routes
USE   **Airways**
Air-ships
USE   **Airships**
Air space law
USE   **Airspace law**
Air stations, Military
USE   **Air bases**
Air stations, Naval
USE   **Air bases**
Air stewardesses
USE   **Flight attendants**

Air stewards
USE   **Flight attendants**
Air surfing
USE   **Gliding and soaring**
Air terminals
USE   **Airports**
Air traffic control 387.7
UF   Airports—Traffic control
BT   **Aeronautics—Safety measures**
Air transport
USE   **Commercial aeronautics**
Air warfare
USE   **Air defenses**
    Military aeronautics
    Military airplanes
    and names of wars with the
      subdivision *Aerial opera-*
      tions, e.g. **World War,**
      1939-1945—Aerial opera-
      tions; to be added as need-
      ed
Aircraft
USE   **Airplanes**
    Airships
    Gliders (Aeronautics)
    Helicopters
Aircraft carriers 359.9; 623
UF   Airplane carriers
    Carriers, Aircraft
BT   **Military aeronautics**
    Warships
Aircraft production
USE   **Aerospace industries**
    Airplane industry
Airdromes
USE   **Airports**
Airline hostesses
USE   **Flight attendants**
Airline stewardesses
USE   **Flight attendants**
Airline stewards
USE   **Flight attendants**
Airlines 387.7
    Use for materials on companies engaged
in aerial transportation. Materials on the
routes along which the airplanes are flown
are entered under **Airways.**
UF   Air carriers
    Air lines
BT   **Commercial aeronautics**

Airlines—*Continued*
  NT **Flight attendants**
  RT **Airways**
Airlines—Chartering 387.7
  UF Aeronautics, Commercial—
        Chartering *[Former heading]*
      Air charters
      Airplanes—Chartering
      Charter flights
Airlines—Flight attendants
  USE **Flight attendants**
Airlines—Hijacking
  USE **Hijacking of airplanes**
Airlines—Hostesses
  USE **Flight attendants**
Airplane accidents
  USE **Aeronautics—Accidents**
Airplane carriers
  USE **Aircraft carriers**
Airplane collisions
  USE **Aeronautics—Accidents**
Airplane engines 629.134
  UF Airplane motors
      Airplanes—Engines *[Former
        heading]*
      Airplanes—Motors
  BT **Engines**
  NT **Jet propulsion**
Airplane hijacking
  USE **Hijacking of airplanes**
Airplane industry 338.4; 387.7
  UF Aircraft production
  BT **Aerospace industries**
      Commercial aeronautics
Airplane motors
  USE **Airplane engines**
Airplane pilots
  USE **Air pilots**
Airplane racing 797.5
  UF Airplanes—Racing
  BT **Aeronautical sports**
      Racing
Airplane spotting
  USE **Airplanes—Identification**
Airplanes 387.7; 629.133
  UF Aeroplanes
      Air planes
      Aircraft
  SA types of airplanes and specific
      makes of airplanes, to be
      added as needed

  BT **Aeronautics**
  NT **Aerial propellers**
      Bombers
      Gliders (Aeronautics)
      Helicopters
      Jet planes
      Vertically rising airplanes
Airplanes—Accidents
  USE **Aeronautics—Accidents**
Airplanes—Chartering
  USE **Airlines—Chartering**
Airplanes—Design and construction
        629.134
Airplanes—Electric equipment 629.135
  UF Airplanes—Instruments
  BT **Aeronautical instruments**
Airplanes—Engines
  USE **Airplane engines**
Airplanes—Flight testing
  USE **Airplanes—Testing**
Airplanes—Hijacking
  USE **Hijacking of airplanes**
Airplanes—Identification 623.7; 629.133
  UF Airplane spotting
      Airplanes—Recognition
  BT **Identification**
Airplanes in agriculture
  USE **Aeronautics in agriculture**
Airplanes—Inspection 387.7; 629.134
Airplanes—Instruments
  USE **Aeronautical instruments**
      Airplanes—Electric equipment
Airplanes, Jet propelled
  USE **Jet planes**
Airplanes—Maintenance and repair
        629.134
  UF Airplanes—Repair
Airplanes—Materials 629.134
  BT **Materials**
Airplanes, Military
  USE **Military airplanes**
Airplanes—Models 629.133
  UF Model airplanes
      Paper airplanes
  BT **Machinery—Models**
      Models and model making
Airplanes—Motors
  USE **Airplane engines**
Airplanes, Naval
  USE **Military airplanes**

BT = Broader Term NT = Narrower Term RT = Related Term SA = See Also UF = Used For

Airplanes—Noise 629.132
BT Noise
Noise pollution
Airplanes—Operation
USE **Airplanes—Piloting**
Airplanes—Piloting 629.132
Use for materials on the navigation of airplanes and on instruction in the mechanics of flying.
UF Aeronautics—Piloting
Airplanes—Operation
Flight training
SA types and names of airplanes with the subdivision *Piloting,* to be added as needed
BT **Aeronautics—Study and teaching**
Navigation (Aeronautics)
NT **Helicopters—Piloting**
Instrument flying
Stunt flying
Airplanes—Pilots
USE **Air pilots**
Airplanes—Propellers
USE **Aerial propellers**
Airplanes—Racing
USE **Airplane racing**
Airplanes—Recognition
USE **Airplanes—Identification**
Airplanes—Repair
USE **Airplanes—Maintenance and repair**
Airplanes, Rocket propelled
USE **Rocket planes**
Airplanes—Testing 629.134
UF Airplanes—Flight testing
Test pilots
Airplanes, Vertically rising
USE **Vertically rising airplanes**
Airports (May subdiv. geog.) 387.7; 629.136
UF Aerodromes
Air ports
Air terminals
Airdromes
SA names of individual airports, to be added as needed
NT **Air bases**
Heliports
Airports—Traffic control
USE **Air traffic control**

Airships 629.133
Use for materials on self-propelled aircraft that are lighter than air and can be steered.
UF Air-ships
Aircraft
Balloons, Dirigible
Blimps
Dirigible balloons
Zeppelins
BT **Balloons**
RT **Aeronautics**
Airspace law 341.4
UF Air rights law
Air space law
BT **Property**
Airways 387.7
Use for materials on the routes along which airplanes are flown and where aids to navigation are maintained, such as landing fields, beacons, etc. Materials on the companies engaged in aerial transportation are entered under **Airlines.**
UF Air routes
BT **Aeronautics**
RT **Airlines**
Alaska Highway (Alaska and Canada) 388.1; 979.8
Alchemy 540.1
Use for materials on medieval attempts to change base metals into gold. Materials on the transmutation of metals in nuclear physics are entered under **Transmutation (Chemistry).**
UF Hermetic art and philosophy
Metals, Transmutation of
Philosophers' stone
Transmutation of metals
BT **Chemistry**
Occultism
Superstition
RT **Transmutation (Chemistry)**
Alcohol 547; 661
UF Intoxicants
BT **Chemicals**
Drugs
NT **Alcohol as fuel**
Alcoholic beverages
Alcoholism
Denatured alcohol
Liquors
RT **Distillation**
Alcohol and employees
USE **Employees—Alcohol use**

Alcohol and teenagers
  USE   Teenagers—Alcohol use
Alcohol and youth
  USE   Youth—Alcohol use
Alcohol as fuel 662
  UF   Alcohol fuel
        Ethanol
        Ethyl alcohol fuel
  SA   types of alcohol fuels, e.g.
        Gasohol; to be added as
        needed
  BT   Alcohol
        Fuel
  NT   Gasohol
Alcohol consumption
  USE   Drinking of alcoholic bever-
        ages
Alcohol, Denatured
  USE   Denatured alcohol
Alcohol fuel
  USE   Alcohol as fuel
Alcohol in the workplace
  USE   Employees—Alcohol use
Alcohol, Industrial
  USE   Denatured alcohol
Alcohol—Physiological effect 615
  BT   Alcoholism
        Temperance
Alcohol use
  USE   classes of persons with the
        subdivision Alcohol use, e.g.
        Employees—Alcohol use;
        Youth—Alcohol use; etc., to
        be added as needed
Alcoholic beverage consumption
  USE   Drinking of alcoholic bever-
        ages
Alcoholic beverages 641.2
  UF   Drinks
        Intoxicants
  BT   Alcohol
        Beverages
  NT   Drinking of alcoholic bever-
        ages
        Liquors
        Wine and wine making
Alcoholic parents
  USE   Adult children of alcoholics
        Children of alcoholics
Alcoholics 362.29; 616.86
  UF   Drunkards

        Inebriates
  BT   Alcoholism
  NT   Adult children of alcoholics
        Children of alcoholics
Alcoholics' adult children
  USE   Adult children of alcoholics
Alcoholics' children
  USE   Children of alcoholics
Alcoholism 362.29; 616.86
  UF   Addiction to alcohol
        Dipsomania
        Drinking problem
        Drunkenness
        Intemperance
        Intoxication
        Liquor problem
        Problem drinking
  SA   classes of persons with the
        subdivision Alcohol use, e.g.
        Employees—Alcohol use;
        Youth—Alcohol use; etc., to
        be added as needed
  BT   Alcohol
        Drug abuse
        Substance abuse
  NT   Adult children of alcoholics
        Alcohol—Physiological effect
        Alcoholics
        Children of alcoholics
  RT   Drinking of alcoholic bever-
        ages
        Temperance
        Twelve-step programs
Alfalfa 633.3
  BT   Hay
Algae 561; 589.3
  UF   Sea mosses
        Seaweeds
  BT   Marine plants
Algebra 512
  BT   Mathematical analysis
        Mathematics
  NT   Graph theory
        Group theory
        Linear algebra
        Logarithms
        Number theory
        Probabilities
        Sequences (Mathematics)

Algebra, Boolean
USE **Boolean algebra**
Algebras, Linear
USE **Linear algebra**
Alienation (Social psychology) 302.5
UF Estrangement (Social psychology)
Rebels (Social psychology)
Social alienation
BT **Social psychology**
Aliens 323.6
UF Foreigners
Noncitizens
Nonnationals
SA national groups with the appropriate subdivision for the country of their residence, e.g. **Mexicans—United States;** to be added as needed
BT **Immigration and emigration**
International law
NT **Illegal aliens**
Mexicans—United States
Refugees
RT **Citizenship**
Immigrants
Naturalization
Aliens from outer space
USE **Extraterrestrial beings**
Aliens, Illegal
USE **Illegal aliens**
Alkoran
USE **Koran**
All Fools' Day
USE **April Fools' Day**
All Hallows' Eve
USE **Halloween**
All terrain bicycles
USE **Mountain bikes**
All terrain vehicles 629.22
UF A.T.V.'s
ATVs
SA types of vehicles, e.g. **Snowmobiles;** to be added as needed
BT **Vehicles**
NT **Mountain bikes**
Snowmobiles

Allegories 808.88; 810.8, etc.
May be used for individual works or for collections of allegories. Materials on allegory as a literary form or on allegory in the fine and decorative arts are entered under **Allegory.**
BT **Fiction**
RT **Fables**
Parables
Allegory 704.9; 808
Use for materials on allegory as a literary form as well as for allegory in the fine and decorative arts. Individual allegories and collections of allegories are entered under **Allegories.**
BT **Arts**
Fiction
RT **Symbolism in literature**
Allergies
USE **Allergy**
Allergies, Food
USE **Food allergy**
Allergy 616.97
UF Allergies
SA types of allergies, to be added as needed
BT **Immunity**
NT **Food allergy**
Hay fever
Allergy, Food
USE **Food allergy**
Alleys
USE **Streets**
Allied health personnel 610.69
UF Paramedical personnel
SA types of allied health personnel, to be added as needed
NT **Emergency medical technicians**
Medical technologists
Nurse practitioners
Alligators 597.98
BT **Reptiles**
RT **Crocodiles**
Allocation of time
USE **Time management**
Allowances, Children's
USE **Children's allowances**
Alloys 669
SA types of alloys, to be added as needed
BT **Industrial chemistry**

BT = Broader Term   NT = Narrower Term   RT = Related Term   SA = See Also   UF = Used For

Alloys—*Continued*
>   Metals
> NT   Aluminum alloys
>   Brass
>   Pewter
> RT   Metallurgy

Allusions 031.02; 803
> BT   English language—Terms and
>   phrases

Almanacs 030
> UF   Annuals
> BT   Serial publications
> NT   Nautical almanacs
> RT   Calendars
>   Chronology

Alphabet 411

Use for materials on the series of characters that form the elements of a written language and for materials to be used in teaching children the ABCs. Materials on the styles of alphabets used by artists, etc., are entered under **Alphabets.**

> UF   A.B.C.'s
>   ABCs
>   Alphabet books
>   Letters of the alphabet
> NT   Alphabets
> RT   Writing

Alphabet books
> USE   Alphabet

Alphabetizing
> USE   Files and filing

Alphabets 745.6

Use for materials on the styles of alphabets used by artists, etc. Materials on the series of characters that form the elements of a written language and for materials to be used in teaching children the ABCs are entered under **Alphabet.**

> BT   Alphabet
>   Sign painting
> NT   Illumination of books and
>   manuscripts
>   Monograms
> RT   Initials
>   Lettering

Alpine animals
> USE   Mountain animals

Alpine fauna
> USE   Mountain animals

Alpine flora
> USE   Mountain plants

Alpine plants
> USE   Mountain plants

Alternate energy resources
> USE   **Renewable energy resources**

Alternate work sites
> USE   **Telecommuting**

Alternating current machinery
> USE   **Electric machinery—**
>   **Alternating current**

Alternating currents
> USE   **Alternating electric currents**

Alternating electric currents 621.31
> UF   Alternating currents
>   Currents, Alternating
>   Electric currents, Alternating
>   *[Former heading]*
> BT   **Electric currents**

Alternative energy resources
> USE   **Renewable energy resources**

Alternative histories 808.3; 813, etc.

May be used for individual works, collections, or materials about imaginative works featuring key changes in historical facts.

> BT   **Fantasy fiction**

Alternative lifestyle
> USE   **Counter culture**
>   **Lifestyles**

Alternative medicine 610; 613; 615.5
> UF   Therapeutic systems
> SA   types of alternative medicine,
>   to be added as needed
> BT   **Medicine**
> NT   **Acupressure**
>   **Acupuncture**
>   **Chiropractic**
>   **Health self-care**
>   **Holistic medicine**
>   **Homeopathy**
>   **Mental healing**
>   **Naturopathy**
>   **Osteopathy**

Alternative press (May subdiv. geog.)
070.4; 071, etc.

Use for materials about publications issued clandestinely and contrary to government regulation and for materials about publications issued legally (and usually serially) and produced by radical, anti-establishment, or counter-culture groups.

> UF   Press, Alternative
>   Press, Underground
>   Underground literature *[Former heading]*

Alternative press—*Continued*
    Underground press *[Former heading]*
  BT **Press**
Alternative schools
  USE **Experimental schools**
Alternative universities
  USE **Free universities**
Alternative work schedules
  USE **Hours of labor**
       Part-time employment
Altitude, Influence of
  USE **Environmental influence on humans**
Altruists
  USE **Philanthropists**
Aluminum 669; 673
  BT **Metals**
  NT **Aluminum foil**
Aluminum alloys 669; 673
  BT **Alloys**
Aluminum foil 673
  BT **Aluminum**
       Packaging
Aluminum—Recycling 628.4; 673
  BT **Recycling**
Alzheimer's disease 616.8
  BT **Brain—Diseases**
Amateur films 778.5; 791.43
  May be used for individual works, collections, or materials about amateur films.

  UF Amateur motion pictures
       [Former heading]
       Films, Amateur
       Home movies
       Home video movies
       Motion pictures, Amateur
       Personal films
  BT **Motion pictures**
  RT **Camcorders**
       Motion picture cameras
Amateur motion pictures
  USE **Amateur films**
Amateur radio stations 621.3841
  UF Ham radio stations
       Radio stations, Amateur
  BT **Shortwave radio**

Amateur theater 792
  Use for materials on the production of plays, skits, recitations, etc., by nonprofessional groups. Collections of plays for such groups are entered under **Drama—Collections; American drama—Collections;** etc.
  UF Play production
       Private theater
       Theater, Amateur
  BT **Amusements**
       Theater
  NT **Charades**
       Children's plays
       College and school drama
       Little theater movement
       One act plays
       Pantomimes
       Readers' theater
       Shadow pantomimes and plays
  RT **Acting**
       Drama in education
Ambassadors
  USE **Diplomats**
Amendments, Equal rights
  USE **Equal rights amendments**
America 970
  Use for general materials on the Western Hemisphere.
  SA names of individual countries of the Western Hemisphere, to be added as needed
  NT **Central America**
       Latin America
       North America
       South America
America—Antiquities 970.01
America—Discovery and exploration
  USE **America—Exploration**
America—Exploration 970.01
  UF America—Discovery and exploration
  BT **Exploration**
  NT **Northwest Passage**
       United States—Exploration
America—History 970
  UF American history
America—Politics and government 970
  RT **Pan-Americanism**
American actors 791.4; 792; 920
  UF Actors, American *[Former heading]*

American actors—*Continued*

      Actors and actresses, American *[Former heading]*

      American actors and actresses

  BT **Actors**

American actors and actresses

  USE **American actors**

American architecture 720.973

  UF Architecture, American *[Former heading]*

      United States—Architecture

  BT **Architecture**

American art 709.73

  UF Art, American *[Former heading]*

      United States—Art

  BT **Art**

  NT **American folk art**

American artificial satellites 629.43; 629.46

  UF Artificial satellites, American *[Former heading]*

      United States—Artificial satellites

  BT **Artificial satellites**

American artists 709.2; 920

  UF Artists, American *[Former heading]*

      United States—Artists

  BT **Artists**

American arts 700.973

  UF Arts, American *[Former heading]*

  BT **Arts**

American authors 810.9; 920

  UF Authors, American *[Former heading]*

      United States—Authors

  BT **American literature**

American ballads 811, etc.

  UF Ballads, American *[Former heading]*

      United States—Ballads

  BT **American poetry**

American Bicentennial

  USE **American Revolution Bicentennial, 1776-1976**

American bison

  USE **Bison**

American characteristics

  USE **American national characteristics**

American Civil War

  USE **United States—History— 1861-1865, Civil War**

American civilization 306.097; 306.098; 970; 980

    Use for general materials on the civilization of the Western Hemisphere and on ancient American civilizations. Materials limited to the civilization of the United States are entered under **United States— Civilization.**

  UF Civilization, American *[Former heading]*

  BT **Civilization**

American colleges

  USE **Colleges and universities— United States**

American colonies

  USE **United States—History— 1600-1775, Colonial period**

American color prints 769.973

  UF Color prints, American *[Former heading]*

  BT **Color prints**

American composers 780.92; 920

  UF Composers, American *[Former heading]*

      United States—Composers

  BT **Composers**

American Constitution

  USE **United States—Constitution**

American decoration and ornament 745.4

  UF Decoration and ornament, American *[Former heading]*

      United States—Decoration and ornament

  BT **Decoration and ornament**

American diaries 809; 920

    Use for collections of American diaries and for materials about American diaries.

  UF American journals (Diaries)

      Diaries, American

  BT **Diaries**

American drama 812

    Use for general materials about American drama, not for individual works.

  BT **American literature**

      Drama

American drama—Collections 812.008
   BT   Drama—Collections
American drama—History and criticism
     812.009
   BT   Drama—History and criticism
American dramatists 812.009; 920
   UF   Dramatists, American [Former
       heading]
       United States—Dramatists
   BT   Dramatists
American drawing 741.973
   UF   Drawing, American [Former
       heading]
       United States—Drawing
   BT   Drawing
American economic assistance 338.91;
     361.6
   UF   Economic assistance, Ameri-
       can [Former heading]
       United States—Economic as-
       sistance
   BT   Economic assistance
American engraving 760; 769
   UF   Engraving, American [Former
       heading]
       United States—Engraving
   BT   Engraving
American environmental policy
   USE   Environmental policy—United
       States
American espionage 327.1273; 355.3
   UF   Espionage, American [Former
       heading]
   BT   Espionage
American essays 814; 814.008
   BT   American literature
       Essays
American ethics 170.973
   UF   Ethics, American [Former
       heading]
       United States—Ethics
   BT   Ethics
American exploring expeditions
   USE   United States—Exploring ex-
       peditions
American fiction 813
    May be used for collections or materials
about American fiction, not for individual
works.
   UF   Fiction, American

   BT   American literature
       Fiction
American films
   USE   Motion pictures—United
       States
American flag
   USE   Flags—United States
American folk art 745.0973
   UF   Folk art, American [Former
       heading]
       United States—Folk art
   BT   American art
       Folk art
American folk dancing 793.3
   UF   Folk dancing, American [For-
       mer heading]
       United States—Folk dancing
   BT   Dancing—United States
       Folk dancing
American folk music
   USE   Folk music—United States
American folk songs
   USE   Folk songs—United States
American furniture 684.100973; 749.213
   UF   Colonial furniture (U.S.)
       Furniture, American [Former
       heading]
       Furniture, Colonial
       United States—Furniture
   BT   Furniture
American government
   USE   United States—Politics and
       government
American graphic arts
   USE   Graphic arts—United States
American historians 907; 920
   UF   Historians, American [Former
       heading]
       United States—Historians
   BT   Historians
American history
   USE   America—History
       United States—History
American hostages (May subdiv. geog.
     except U.S.) 920
   UF   Hostages, American [Former
       heading]
       United States—Hostages
   BT   Hostages

American hostages—Iran 920
UF   Hostages, American—Iran
        [Former heading]
NT   **Iran hostage crisis, 1979-1981**
American illustrators 741.6092; 920
UF   Illustrators, American *[Former
        heading]*
        United States—Illustrators
BT   **Illustrators**
American Indians
USE   **Indians**
        Indians of Central America
        Indians of Mexico
        Indians of North America
        Indians of South America
        Indians of the West Indies
American journals (Diaries)
USE   **American diaries**
American labor unions
USE   **Labor unions—United States**
American letters 816; 816.008
BT   **American literature**
        Letters
American literature (May subdiv. geog.
        by the names of states or
        regions for works by or
        about more than one au-
        thor from a state or region
        or writing about a state or
        region, e.g. **American
        literature—Massachusetts;
        American literature—
        Southern States;** etc.) 810
  May be subdivided by the topical subdivi-
sions and literary forms used under
English literature.
UF   United States—Literature
SA   various forms of American
        literature, e.g. **American po-
        etry; American satire;** etc.,
        to be added as needed
BT   **Literature**
NT   **American authors**
        American drama
        American essays
        American fiction
        American letters
        American literature (Spanish)
        American poetry
        American prose literature

American satire
American speeches
American wit and humor
American literature—African American
        authors 810.8; 810.9
  May be used for collections or materials
about American literature by several African American authors, not for individual
works. Use same pattern for literatures
and literary forms written by other ethnic
groups or classes of authors.

UF   African American literature
        American literature—
        Afro-American authors
        American literature—Black
        authors *[Former heading]*
        Black literature (American)

SA   particular forms of American
        literature with the subdivi-
        sion *African American au-
        thors;* e.g., **American
        poetry—African American
        authors;** to be added as
        needed

NT   **Harlem Renaissance**
RT   **African American authors**

American literature—Afro-American au-
        thors
USE   **American literature—African
        American authors**

American literature—American Indian
        authors 810.8; 810.9
  May be used for collections or materials
about American literature written in English by several American Indian authors,
not for individual works. Collections or
materials about literature written in Indian languages by several American Indian
authors are entered under **Indians of
North America—Literature.**

UF   Indian literature (American)

American literature—Black authors
USE   **American literature—African
        American authors**

American literature—Collections 810.8
  Use for collections of both poetry and
prose by several American authors. Collections consisting of prose only are entered under **American prose literature;**
collections of poetry are entered under
American poetry—Collections.

BT = Broader Term   NT = Narrower Term   RT = Related Term   SA = See Also   UF = Used For

American literature—Hispanic American authors 810

Use for materials on American literature in English written by American authors of Spanish or Latin American origins. Materials on American literature written in Spanish are entered under **American literature (Spanish).**

   UF   American literature—Latin American authors

         Hispanic American literature (English)

   SA   genres of American literature with the subdivision *Hispanic American authors;* and **American literature** and genres of American literature with subdivisions for specific groups of Hispanic American authors, e.g. **American literature—Mexican American authors;** to be added as needed

   NT   **American literature—Mexican American authors**

American literature—Latin American authors

   USE **American literature—Hispanic American authors**

American literature—Massachusetts 810

American literature—Mexican American authors 810

Use for materials on American literature written in English by American authors of Mexican origins.

   UF   Chicano literature (English)

         Mexican American literature (English)

   SA   genres of American literature with the subdivision *Mexican American authors,* to be added as needed

   BT   **American literature—Hispanic American authors**

American literature—Southern States 810

   UF   Southern literature

American literature (Spanish) 860

Use for materials on American literature written in Spanish. Materials on American literature in English written by American authors of Spanish or Latin American origins are entered under **American literature—Hispanic American authors.**

   UF   Hispanic American literature (Spanish)

         Spanish American literature

         Spanish literature—Hispanic American authors

   SA   genres of American literature with the qualifier (Spanish), to be added as needed

   BT   **American literature**

American literature—Women authors 810.8; 810.9

May be used for collections or for materials about several American women authors.

   BT   **Women authors**

American Loyalists 973.3

   UF   Loyalists, American

         Tories, American

   BT   **United States—History—1775-1783, Revolution**

American military assistance 355

   UF   Military assistance, American *[Former heading]*

   BT   **Military assistance**

   NT   **Iran-Contra Affair, 1985-1990**

American motion pictures

   USE **Motion pictures—United States**

American music 780.973

   UF   Music, American *[Former heading]*

         United States—Music

   BT   **Music**

American musicians 780.92; 920

   UF   Musicians, American *[Former heading]*

         United States—Musicians

   BT   **Musicians**

American national characteristics 306.0973; 973

   UF   American characteristics

         National characteristics, American *[Former heading]*

         United States—National characteristics

   BT   **National characteristics**

American national songs

   USE **National songs—United States**

American newspapers 071

   BT   **Newspapers**

American novelists 813.009; 920
    UF   Novelists, American *[Former heading]*
         United States—Novelists
    BT   **Novelists**
American orations
    USE   **American speeches**
American painters 759.13; 920
    UF   Painters, American *[Former heading]*
         United States—Painters
    BT   **Painters**
American painting 759.13
    UF   Painting, American *[Former heading]*
         United States—Painting
    BT   **Painting**
American periodicals 051
    BT   **Periodicals**
American personal names
    USE   **Personal names—United States**
American philosophers 191; 920
    UF   Philosophers, American *[Former heading]*
         United States—Philosophers
    BT   **Philosophers**
American philosophy 191
    UF   Philosophy, American *[Former heading]*
         United States—Philosophy
    BT   **Philosophy**
American poetry 811
    Use for general materials about American poetry, not for individual works.
    BT   **American literature**
         Poetry
    NT   **American ballads**
American poetry—African American authors 811, etc.
    May be used for collections or materials about American poetry by several African American authors, not for individual works.
    UF   African American poetry
         American poetry—Afro-American authors
         American poetry—Black authors *[Former heading]*
         Black poetry (American)

American poetry—Afro-American authors
    USE   **American poetry—African American authors**
American poetry—Black authors
    USE   **American poetry—African American authors**
American poetry—Collections 811.008
    BT   **Poetry—Collections**
American poetry—History and criticism 811.009
    BT   **Poetry—History and criticism**
American poets 811.009; 920
    UF   Poets, American *[Former heading]*
         United States—Poets
    BT   **Poets**
American politicians
    USE   **Politicians—United States**
American politics
    USE   **United States—Politics and government**
American pottery 738.0973
    UF   Pottery, American *[Former heading]*
         United States—Pottery
    BT   **Pottery**
American prints 769.973
    UF   Prints, American *[Former heading]*
         United States—Prints
    BT   **Prints**
American prisoners of war 341.6; 355.7
    UF   Prisoners of war, American *[Former heading]*
    BT   **Prisoners of war**
American propaganda 303.3; 327.1
    UF   Propaganda, American *[Former heading]*
         United States—Propaganda
    BT   **Propaganda**
American prose literature 818
    Use for collections of prose writings by several American authors that may include a variety of literary forms, such as essays, fiction, orations, etc. May also be used for general materials about such prose writings.
    UF   Prose literature, American
    BT   **American literature**

American Revolution
  USE **United States—History—**
        1775-1783, Revolution
American Revolution Bicentennial,
        1776-1976 973.3
  UF American Bicentennial
        Bicentennial celebrations—
          United States—1976
        United States—Bicentennial
          celebrations
        United States—History—
          1775-1783, Revolution—
          Centennial celebrations, etc.
  BT **United States—Centennial cel-**
        ebrations, etc.
American Revolution Bicentennial,
        1776-1976—Collectibles
        973.3075
  BT **Collectors and collecting**
American satire 817; 817.008
  UF Satire, American [Former
        heading]
  BT **American literature**
        Satire
American science
  USE **Science—United States**
American sculptors 730.92; 920
  UF Sculptors, American [Former
        heading]
        United States—Sculptors
  BT **Sculptors**
American sculpture 730.973
  UF Sculpture, American [Former
        heading]
        United States—Sculpture
  BT **Sculpture**
American songs 782.420973
  UF Songs, American [Former
        heading]
        United States—Songs
  BT **Songs**
  NT **Folk songs—United States**
        National songs—United States
        Spirituals (Songs)
American-Spanish War, 1898
  USE **Spanish-American War, 1898**
American speeches 815; 815.008
  UF American orations
        Speeches, addresses, etc.,
          American [Former heading]

  BT **American literature**
        Speeches
American technical assistance 338.91;
        361.6
  UF Technical assistance, Ameri-
        can [Former heading]
        United States—Technical as-
          sistance
  BT **Technical assistance**
American teenagers
  USE **Teenagers—United States**
American tourists
  USE **American travelers**
American travelers 910.92; 920
  UF American tourists
        Travelers, American [Former
          heading]
        United States—Travelers
  BT **Travelers**
American wit and humor 817; 817.008;
        817.009
    Use for collections by several authors or
  for materials about American wit and hu-
  mor. Individual works by American hu-
  morists are entered under **Wit and humor.**
  BT **American literature**
        Wit and humor
American youth
  USE **Youth—United States**
Americana 069; 973
    Use for general materials about Ameri-
  can objects of interest to collectors, such
  as historical documents, relics, etc., as well
  as items of little intrinsic value. Materials
  on old American objects that have aes-
  thetic or historical importance and finan-
  cial value are entered under **Antiques—**
  United States.
  BT **Collectors and collecting**
        Popular culture—United
          States
        United States—Civilization
        United States—History
  RT **Antiques—United States**
Americanisms 427
    Use for materials on words and expres-
  sions peculiar to the United States.
  UF English language—
        Americanisms
  BT **English language—Dialects**
Americanization 305.813; 306.0973
  BT **Socialization**
  NT **United States—Foreign popu-**
        lation

Americanization—*Continued*
    United States—Immigration
        and emigration
  RT Immigration and emigration
      Naturalization
Americans (May subdiv. geog. except
        U.S.) **305.813; 920; 973**
  Use for materials on citizens of the
United States.
  BT Ethnology—United States
      United States
Americans—Greece 305.813
Amerindians
  USE Indians
       Indians of Central America
       Indians of Mexico
       Indians of North America
       Indians of South America
       Indians of the West Indies
Amish 289.7
  BT Christian sects
      Mennonites
Ammunition 623.4
  SA types of ammunition, e.g.
      Bombs; to be added as
      needed
  BT Explosives
      Ordnance
      Projectiles
  NT Bombs
  RT Firearms
      Gunpowder
Amnesty 364.6
  BT Administration of criminal
        justice
      Executive power
  RT Forgiveness
      Pardon
Amniocentesis 618.3
  BT Prenatal diagnosis
Amphetamines 615
  UF Pep pills
  SA names of amphetamines, e.g.
      Methamphetamine; to be
      added as needed
  BT Stimulants
  NT Methamphetamine
Amphibians 567; 597.6
  UF Batrachia
  SA names of amphibians, to be
      added as needed

  BT Vertebrates
  NT Frogs
      Salamanders
Amplifiers (Electronics) 621.3815
  SA types of amplifiers, to be add-
        ed as needed
  BT Electronics
  NT Masers
      Transistor amplifiers
Amplifiers, Transistor
  USE Transistor amplifiers
Amusement parks 791.06
  UF Theme parks
  SA names of specific parks, to be
        added as needed
  BT Parks
  NT Walt Disney World (Fla.)
  RT Carnivals
Amusements (May subdiv. geog.) **790**
  UF Entertainments
      Pastimes
  SA types of amusements, e.g.
        Carnivals; to be added as
        needed
  NT Amateur theater
      Carnivals
      Charades
      Children's parties
      Christmas entertainments
      Church entertainments
      Circus
      Concerts
      Creative activities
      Dancing
      Fireworks
      Fortune telling
      Hobbies
      Juggling
      Literary recreations
      Magic tricks
      Mathematical recreations
      Motion pictures
      Puzzles
      Riddles
      Scientific recreations
      Shadow pictures
      Skits
      Theater
      Toys
      Tricks

Amusements—*Continued*
>> Vaudeville
>> Ventriloquism
> RT Entertaining
>> Games
>> Indoor games
>> Play
>> Recreation
>> Sports

Anabolic steroids
> USE Steroids

Anaesthetics
> USE Anesthetics

Analysis (Chemistry)
> USE Analytical chemistry
>> and names of substances with
>> the subdivision *Analysis,*
>> e.g. Food—Analysis; to be
>> added as needed

Analysis (Mathematics)
> USE Calculus
>> Mathematical analysis

Analysis, Microscopic
> USE Metallography
>> Microscopes

Analysis of food
> USE Food adulteration and inspec-
>> tion
>> Food—Analysis

Analysis situs
> USE Topology

Analysis, Spectrum
> USE Spectrum analysis

Analytic geometry 516.3
> UF Geometry, Analytic *[Former
>> heading]*
> BT Geometry

Analytical chemistry 543
> UF Analysis (Chemistry)
>> Chemical analysis
>> Chemistry, Analytic *[Former
>> heading]*
>> Qualitative analysis
>> Quantitative analysis
> SA names of substances with the
>> subdivision *Analysis,* e.g.
>> Water—Analysis; to be
>> added as needed
> BT Chemistry
> NT Distillation

>> Water—Analysis

Anarchism and anarchists 320.5; 335
> BT Freedom
>> Political crimes and offenses
>> Political science
> RT Terrorism

Anatomical gifts
> USE Donation of organs, tissues,
>> etc.

Anatomy 574.4; 611
> UF Morphology
> SA names of organs and regions
>> of the body, e.g. Heart; and
>> subjects with the subdivi-
>> sion *Anatomy,* e.g. Birds—
>> Anatomy; to be added as
>> needed
> BT Biology
>> Medicine
> NT Animals—Anatomy
>> Artistic anatomy
>> Birds—Anatomy
>> Cardiovascular system
>> Comparative anatomy
>> Foot
>> Glands
>> Head
>> Human anatomy
>> Musculoskeletal system
>> Nervous system
>> Plants—Anatomy
>> Reproductive system
>> Respiratory system
>> Skin
>> Stomach
>> Throat
> RT Physiology

Anatomy, Animal
> USE Animals—Anatomy

Anatomy, Artistic
> USE Artistic anatomy

Anatomy, Comparative
> USE Comparative anatomy

Anatomy, Dental
> USE Teeth

Anatomy, Human
> USE Human anatomy

Anatomy of animals
> USE Animals—Anatomy

Anatomy of plants
> USE Plants—Anatomy

BT = Broader Term   NT = Narrower Term   RT = Related Term   SA = See Also   UF = Used For

Anatomy, Vegetable
    USE **Plants—Anatomy**

Ancestor worship 291.2; 291.3
    UF Dead, Worship of the
          Worship of the dead
    BT **Religion**
    RT **Shinto**

Ancestry
    USE **Genealogy**
           Heredity

Ancient architecture 722
    UF Architecture, Ancient *[Former*
           heading]
    BT **Archeology**
         Architecture
    NT **Byzantine architecture**
         Greek architecture
         Pyramids
         Roman architecture
         Temples

Ancient art 709.01
    UF Art, Ancient *[Former heading]*
    BT **Art**
    NT **Byzantine art**
         Classical antiquities
         Greek art
         Roman art

Ancient civilization 306.093; 930
    UF Civilization, Ancient *[Former*
           heading]
    BT **Ancient history**
         Civilization
    NT **Prehistoric man**

Ancient geography 913
   Use for materials on the geography of
the ancient world in general.
    UF Classical geography
         Geography, Ancient *[Former*
           heading]
    SA names of modern countries
         with the subdivision *Histor-*
         ical geography, e.g.
         Greece—Historical geogra-
         phy; and names of coun-
         tries of antiquity with the
         subdivision *Geography,* e.g.
         Rome—Geography; to be
         added as needed
    BT **Ancient history**
         Historical geography

    NT **Greece—Historical geography**
         Rome—Geography

Ancient Greece
    USE **Greece—History—0-323**

Ancient Greece—Description
    USE **Greece—Description—0-323**

Ancient history 930
    UF History, Ancient *[Former*
           heading]
    SA names of ancient peoples, e.g.
         Hittites; and names of
         countries of antiquity, to be
         added as needed
    BT **History**
         World history
    NT **Ancient civilization**
         Ancient geography
         Bible
         Classical dictionaries
         Hittites
         Inscriptions
         Numismatics

Ancient philosophy 180
    UF Greek philosophy
         Philosophy, Ancient *[Former*
           heading]
         Philosophy, Greek
         Philosophy, Roman
         Roman philosophy
    BT **Philosophy**
    NT **Stoics**

Androgyny 155.3; 305.3
   Use for materials on the integration of
male and female characteristics, including
biological traits, personality traits, behavior, roles, etc.
    UF Unisexuality
    BT **Sex (Biology)**
         Sexual behavior
    RT **Sex differences (Psychology)**
         Sex role

Androids
    USE **Robots**

Anecdotes 808.88; 818.008, etc.
   May be used for collections of anecdotes
and for materials about anecdotes.
    UF Facetiae
         Stories
    SA subjects with the subdivision
         Anecdotes, to be added as
         needed

Anecdotes—*Continued*
   NT   Music—Anecdotes
   RT   Wit and humor
Anesthetics 615; 617.9
   UF   Anaesthetics
   BT   Materia medica
         Pain
         Surgery
Angels 235
   UF   Spirits
   BT   Heaven
Angina pectoris 616.1
   BT   Heart diseases
Anglican Church
   USE   Church of England
Angling
   USE   Fishing
Anglo-French intervention in Egypt,
       1956
   USE   Sinai Campaign, 1956
Anglo-Saxon language 429
   UF   English language—0-1100
         English language—Old English
         Old English language
   BT   Language and languages
   RT   English language
Anglo-Saxon literature 829
   UF   English literature—0-1100
         English literature—Old Eng-
          lish
         Old English literature
   BT   Literature
   RT   English literature
Anglo-Saxons 305.82; 941.01
   UF   Saxons
   BT   Great Britain—History—
          0-1066
         Teutonic peoples
Animal abuse
   USE   Animal welfare
Animal attacks 591.6
   UF   Attacks by animals
   BT   Dangerous animals
Animal babies 591.3
   UF   Animals—Infancy *[Former
          heading]*
         Baby animals
   SA   types of baby animals, e.g.
          Kittens; to be added as
          needed

   BT   Animals
   NT   Kittens
         Lambs
         Puppies
Animal behavior 591.51
   UF   Animals—Behavior *[Former
          heading]*
         Animals, Habits and behavior
          of
         Behavior
         Habits of animals
   SA   types of specific behavior, e.g.
          **Animals—Migration; Hiber-
          nation; Sexual behavior in
          animals;** etc.; and names of
          animals with the subdivi-
          sion *Behavior,* to be added
          as needed
   BT   Animals
         Zoology
   NT   Animal communication
         Animal courtship
         Animal defenses
         Animal sounds
         Animals—Food
         Animals—Migration
         Hibernation
         Instinct
         Monkeys—Behavior
         Primates—Behavior
         Sexual behavior in animals
   RT   Animal intelligence
         Nature study
         Tracking and trailing
Animal camouflage
   USE   Camouflage (Biology)
Animal communication 591.59
   UF   Animal language
         Animals—Language
         Communication among ani-
          mals
   BT   Animal behavior
   RT   Animal sounds
Animal courtship 591.56
   UF   Animals—Courtship *[Former
          heading]*
         Courtship (Animal behavior)
         Courtship of animals
         Mate selection in animals
         Mating behavior

Animal courtship—*Continued*
  BT **Animal behavior**
      Sexual behavior in animals
Animal defenses 591.57
  UF Defense mechanisms (Zoology)
      Self-defense in animals
      Self-protection in animals
  BT **Animal behavior**
  NT **Camouflage (Biology)**
Animal drawing
  USE **Animal painting and illustration**
Animal embryos, Frozen
  USE **Frozen embryos**
Animal experimentation 619
  UF Experimentation on animals
      Laboratory animal experimentation
  BT **Research**
  NT **Vivisection**
  RT **Animal welfare**
Animal exploitation
  USE **Animal welfare**
Animal-facilitated therapy
  USE **Pet therapy**
Animal flight 591.1
  UF Animal flying
      Animals—Flight
  SA types of animals with the subdivision *Flight,* e.g. **Birds—Flight;** to be added as needed
  BT **Animal locomotion**
      Flight
  NT **Birds—Flight**
Animal flying
  USE **Animal flight**
Animal food 641.3
  Use for materials on human food of animal origin. Materials on the food and food habits of animals are entered under **Animals—Food.**
  UF Animals as food
      Animals, Edible
  BT **Food**
  NT **Eggs**
      Honey
      Meat
      Milk
Animal homes
  USE **Animals—Habitations**

Animal husbandry
  USE **Livestock**
Animal industry
  USE **Domestic animals**
      Livestock
Animal instinct
  USE **Instinct**
Animal intelligence 591.51
  UF Animal psychology
      Intelligence of animals
  SA types of animals with the subdivision *Psychology,* to be added as needed
  NT **Dogs—Psychology**
      Psychology of learning
  RT **Animal behavior**
      Comparative psychology
      Instinct
Animal kingdom
  USE **Zoology**
Animal language
  USE **Animal communication**
      Animal sounds
Animal liberation movement
  USE **Animal rights movements**
Animal light
  USE **Bioluminescence**
Animal locomotion 591.1
  UF Animals—Movements
      Movements of animals
  BT **Animals**
      Locomotion
  NT **Animal flight**
Animal lore
  USE **Animals—Folklore**
      Animals in literature
      Mythical animals
      Natural history
Animal luminescence
  USE **Bioluminescence**
Animal magnetism
  USE **Hypnotism**
Animal migration
  USE **Animals—Migration**
Animal oils
  USE **Oils and fats**

BT = Broader Term   NT = Narrower Term   RT = Related Term   SA = See Also   UF = Used For

Animal painting and illustration 704.9; 743; 758

Use for materials on the art of painting or drawing animals. Materials on the depiction of animals in works of art are entered under **Animals in art.** Popular materials consisting chiefly of photographs or illustrations of animals are entered under **Animals—Pictorial works.**

UF   Animal drawing

BT   **Painting**

RT   **Animals in art**

      Animals—Pictorial works

      Photography of animals

Animal parasites

USE   **Parasites**

Animal photography

USE   **Photography of animals**

Animal physiology

USE   **Zoology**

Animal pictures

USE   **Animals—Pictorial works**

Animal pounds

USE   **Animal shelters**

Animal products 338.1; 338.4

UF   Products, Animal

SA   types of animal products, to be added as needed

BT   **Commercial products**

NT   **Hides and skins**

      Ivory

      Leather

      Wool

Animal psychology

USE   **Animal intelligence**

      Comparative psychology

Animal reproduction 591.56

UF   Animals—Birth

      Animals—Reproduction

BT   **Animals**

      Reproduction

      Zoology

Animal rights 179

Use for materials on the inherent rights attributed to animals. Materials on the protection and treatment of animals are entered under **Animal welfare.**

UF   Animals' rights

      Rights of animals

RT   **Animal rights movements**

      Animal welfare

Animal rights movements 179

Use for materials on any of the politically diverse movements engaged in animal rights or animal welfare support activities.

UF   Animal liberation movement

      Animal welfare movement

      Antivivisection movement

RT   **Animal rights**

      Animal welfare

Animal sexual behavior

USE   **Sexual behavior in animals**

Animal shelters 179; 636.08

UF   Animal pounds

      Shelters, Animal

BT   **Animal welfare**

Animal signs

USE   **Animal tracks**

Animal sounds

UF   Animal language

      Animals—Sounds

BT   **Animal behavior**

NT   **Birdsongs**

RT   **Animal communication**

Animal stories

USE   **Animals—Fiction**

Animal tracks 591

UF   Animal signs

      Tracks of animals

BT   **Tracking and trailing**

Animal training

USE   **Animals—Training**

Animal welfare 179

Use for materials on the protection and treatment of animals. Materials on the inherent rights attributed to animals are entered under **Animal rights.**

UF   Abuse of animals

      Animal abuse *[Former heading]*

      Animal exploitation

      Animals, Cruelty to

      Animals—Mistreatment

      Animals—Protection

      Animals—Treatment

      Cruelty to animals

      Humane treatment of animals

      Laboratory animal welfare

      Prevention of cruelty to animals

      Protection of animals

BT = Broader Term   NT = Narrower Term   RT = Related Term   SA = See Also   UF = Used For

Animal welfare—*Continued*
- NT **Animal shelters**
- RT **Animal experimentation**
  Animal rights
  Animal rights movements

Animal welfare movement
- USE **Animal rights movements**

Animals (May subdiv. geog.) **591**

Use for descriptive and nonsystematic or nontechnical materials. Systematic or technical materials are entered under **Zoology.** Subdivisions used under this heading may be used under names of orders and classes of the animal kingdom and under names of individual species.
- UF Beasts
  Fauna
  Wild animals
- SA names of orders and classes of the animal kingdom; kinds of animals characterized by their environments; and names of individual species, to be added as needed
- NT **Animal babies**
  Animal behavior
  Animal locomotion
  Animal reproduction
  Dangerous animals
  Desert animals
  Domestic animals
  Extinct animals
  Forest animals
  Freshwater animals
  Furbearing animals
  Game and game birds
  Invertebrates
  Jungle animals
  Marine animals
  Mountain animals
  Pets
  Poisonous animals
  Prehistoric animals
  Rare animals
  Stream animals
  Swamp animals
  Vertebrates
  Wildlife
  Working animals
- RT **Zoology**

Zoos
Animals—Anatomy 591.4
- UF Anatomy, Animal
  Anatomy of animals
  Morphology
  Structural zoology
  Zoology—Anatomy
- BT **Anatomy**
- NT **Fur**

Animals and the handicapped 636.088
- UF Handicapped and animals
  Pets and the handicapped
  Service dogs
- BT **Animals—Training**
- NT **Guide dogs**
  Hearing ear dogs
  Pet therapy

Animals, Aquatic
- USE **Freshwater animals**
  Marine animals

Animals as food
- USE **Animal food**

Animals—Behavior
- USE **Animal behavior**

Animals—Birth
- USE **Animal reproduction**

Animals—Camouflage
- USE **Camouflage (Biology)**

Animals—Color 591.19; 591.57
- BT **Color**

Animals—Courtship
- USE **Animal courtship**

Animals, Cruelty to
- USE **Animal welfare**

Animals—Diseases 591.2; 636.089
- UF Diseases of animals
  Domestic animals—Diseases
- SA names of animals with the subdivision *Diseases,* to be added as needed
- BT **Diseases**
  Veterinary medicine
- NT **Cattle—Diseases**

Animals, Domestic
- USE **Domestic animals**

Animals, Edible
- USE **Animal food**

Animals, Extinct
- USE **Extinct animals**

Animals—Fiction 808.83; 813, etc.

May be used for individual works or collections of stories about animals. Materials on the theme of animals in literature are entered under **Animals in literature.**

UF   Animal stories

       Animals—Stories

SA   names of animals with the

         subdivision *Fiction,* to be

         added as needed

BT   **Fables**

       Fiction

NT   **Dogs—Fiction**

RT   **Animals in literature**

Animals—Filmography 016.591

Animals—Flight

USE **Animal flight**

Animals—Folklore 398.24

UF   Animal lore

BT   **Folklore**

NT   **Dragons**

       Monsters

RT   **Mythical animals**

Animals—Food 591.53

Use for materials on the food and food habits of animals. Materials on human food of animal origin are entered under **Animal food.**

UF   Feeding behavior in animals

SA   names of animals with the

         subdivision *Food,* to be

         added as needed

BT   **Animal behavior**

       Food

NT   **Carnivores**

       Feeds

       Food chains (Ecology)

Animals, Fossil

USE **Fossils**

Animals, Freshwater

USE **Freshwater animals**

Animals—Geographical distribution

USE **Biogeography**

Animals—Habitations 591.52

UF   Animal homes

       Habitations of animals

       Houses of animals

Animals, Habits and behavior of

USE **Animal behavior**

Animals—Hibernation

USE **Hibernation**

Animals, Imaginary

USE **Mythical animals**

Animals in art 704.9

Use for materials on the depiction of animals in works of art. Materials on the art of painting or drawing animals are entered under **Animal painting and illustration.** Materials consisting chiefly of photographs or illustrations of animals are entered under **Animals—Pictorial works.**

BT   **Art**

RT   **Animal painting and illustration**

       Animals—Pictorial works

Animals in literature 809

Use for materials on the theme of animals in literature. Poems or stories about animals are entered under **Animals— Poetry** or **Animals—Fiction.**

UF   Animal lore

SA   phrase headings of specific

         animals in literature, e.g.

         Dogs in literature; to be

         added as needed

BT   **Literature**

       Nature in literature

NT   **Birds in literature**

       Dogs in literature

RT   **Animals—Fiction**

       Animals—Poetry

Animals in motion pictures 791.43

BT   **Motion pictures**

Animals in police work 363.2; 636.088

BT   **Police**

       Working animals

Animals—Infancy

USE **Animal babies**

Animals—Language

USE **Animal communication**

Animals, Marine

USE **Marine animals**

Animals—Migration 591.52

UF   Animal migration

       Migration of animals

SA   names of animals with the

         subdivision *Migration,* to

         be added as needed

BT   **Animal behavior**

NT   **Birds—Migration**

Animals—Mistreatment

USE **Animal welfare**

Animals—Movements

USE **Animal locomotion**

Animals, Mythical

USE **Mythical animals**

BT = Broader Term   NT = Narrower Term   RT = Related Term   SA = See Also   UF = Used For

Animals—Petting zoos
USE **Petting zoos**
Animals—Photography
USE **Photography of animals**
Animals—Pictorial works 591.022; 743;
778.9

Use for popular materials consisting chiefly of photographs or illustrations of animals. Materials on the art of painting or drawing animals are entered under **Animal painting and illustration.** Materials on the depiction of animals in works of art are entered under **Animals in art.**

UF Animal pictures
BT **Pictures**
RT **Animal painting and illustration**
Animals in art
Photography of animals
Animals—Poetry 808.81; 811, etc.;
811.008, etc.

May be used for individual works or collections of poetry about animals. Materials on the theme of animals in literature are entered under **Animals in literature.**

BT **Poetry**
RT **Animals in literature**
Animals, Prehistoric
USE **Prehistoric animals**
Animals—Protection
USE **Animal welfare**
Animals, Rare
USE **Rare animals**
Animals—Reproduction
USE **Animal reproduction**
Animals' rights
USE **Animal rights**
Animals, Sea
USE **Marine animals**
Animals—Sexual behavior
USE **Sexual behavior in animals**
Animals—Sounds
USE **Animal sounds**
Animals—Stories
USE **Animals—Fiction**
Animals—Temperature
USE **Body temperature**
Animals—Training 636.088
UF Animal training
Training of animals
SA names of animals with the
subdivision *Training,* to be
added as needed

BT **Circus**
NT **Animals and the handicapped**
Dogs—Training
Horses—Training
Animals—Treatment
USE **Animal welfare**
Animals—United States 591.973
UF United States—Animals
Zoology—United States *[Former heading]*
Animals, Useful and harmful
USE **Economic zoology**
Animals, Visiting
USE **Pet therapy**
Animals—War use 355.4
UF War use of animals
BT **Working animals**
NT **Dogs—War use**
Animals, Working
USE **Working animals**
Animated cartoons
USE **Animated films**
Animated films 741.5; 791.43

May be used for individual works, collections, or materials about animated films.

UF Animated cartoons
Cartoons, Animated
Motion picture cartoons *[Former heading]*
BT **Cartoons and caricatures**
Motion pictures
RT **Animation (Cinematography)**
Animated television programs 791.45

May be used for individual works, collections, or materials about animated television programs.

UF Cartoons, Television
Television cartoons
BT **Television programs**
Animation (Cinematography) 741.5;
778.5

BT **Cinematography**
RT **Animated films**
Anniversaries
USE **Birthdays**
Holidays
Annual income guarantee
USE **Guaranteed annual income**
Annuals
USE **Almanacs**

Annuals—*Continued*
>>> **Calendars**
>>> **School yearbooks**
>>> and subjects and names of
>>> countries, cities, etc., indi-
>>> vidual persons, families,
>>> and corporate bodies with
>>> the subdivision *Periodicals,*
>>> e.g. **Engineering—**
>>> **Periodicals;** to be added as
>>> needed

Annuals (Plants) 582; 635.9
> BT **Cultivated plants**
>>> **Flower gardening**
>>> **Flowers**

Annuities 368.3
> BT **Investments**
>>> **Retirement income**
> NT **Pensions**
> RT **Life insurance**

Annulment of marriage
> USE **Marriage—Annulment**

Anointing of the sick 265
> UF Extreme unction
>>> Last rites (Sacraments)
>>> Last sacraments
>>> Unction, Extreme
> BT **Sacraments**

Anonyms
> USE **Pseudonyms**

Anorexia nervosa 616.85
> UF Self-starvation
>>> Starvation, Self-imposed
> BT **Eating disorders**

Answers to questions
> USE **Questions and answers**

Ant
> USE **Ants**

Antarctic expeditions
> USE **Antarctic regions—Exploration**

Antarctic regions 998
> UF Antarctica
> BT **Earth**
>>> **Polar regions**
> RT **South Pole**

Antarctic regions—Exploration 919.8
> UF Antarctic expeditions
>>> Polar expeditions
> SA names of expeditions, e.g.
>>> **Byrd Antarctic Expedition;**
>>> to be added as needed

> BT **Exploration**
>>> **Scientific expeditions**
> NT **Byrd Antarctic Expedition**

Antarctica
> USE **Antarctic regions**

Antenuptial contracts
> USE **Marriage contracts**

Anthems, National
> USE **National songs**

Anthologies 080; 808.8; 810.8, etc.
> Use for collections of general interest by
> more than one author not limited to a sin-
> gle literature or literary form or focused
> on a single subject.

> UF Collected papers (Anthologies)
>>> Collected works
>>> Collections (Anthologies)
>>> Collections of literature
>>> Literary collections
>>> Papers, Collected (Antholo-
>>> gies)
>>> Readings (Anthologies)
> SA names of literatures, e.g.
>>> **American literature;** and,
>>> for collections focused on a
>>> single subject by more than
>>> one author involving two
>>> or more literary forms, the
>>> subject with the subdivision
>>> *Literary collections,* e.g.
>>> **Cats—Literary collections;**
>>> to be added as needed

Anthropogeography 304.2; 572.9
> UF Geographical distribution of
>>> people
>>> Geography, Social
> BT **Anthropology**
>>> **Ethnology**
>>> **Geography**
>>> **Human ecology**
>>> **Immigration and emigration**
> NT **Environmental influence on**
>>> **humans**
> RT **Geopolitics**

Anthropology 301; 573
> UF Human race
> SA names of races and peoples,
>>> e.g. **Navajo Indians;** and
>>> names of countries, cities,
>>> etc., with the subdivision

Anthropology—*Continued*
        Race relations, to be added
            as needed
    NT Acculturation
        Anthropogeography
        Anthropometry
        Ethnopsychology
        Eugenics
        Language and languages
        National characteristics
        Physical anthropology
        Social change
    RT Civilization
        Culture
        Ethnology
        Man
Anthropology, Physical
    USE Physical anthropology
Anthropometry 573
    UF Skeletal remains
    BT Anthropology
        Ethnology
        Man
    NT Fingerprints
Anti-abortion movement
    USE Pro-life movement
Anti-Americanism
    USE United States—Foreign opin-
            ion
Anti-apartheid movement (May subdiv.
        geog.) 172; 320.5; 323.1
    BT Civil rights
        Social movements
        South Africa—Race relations
    RT Apartheid
Anti-fascist movements
    USE World War, 1939-1945—
            Underground movements
Anti-Nazi movement
    USE World War, 1939-1945—
            Underground movements
Anti-poverty programs
    USE Domestic economic assistance
Anti-Reformation
    USE Counter-Reformation
Anti-utopias
    USE Dystopias
Anti-war films
    USE War films
Anti-war poetry
    USE War poetry

Anti-war stories
    USE War stories
Antiabortion movement
    USE Pro-life movement
Antiamericanism
    USE United States—Foreign opin-
            ion
Antiballistic missiles
    USE Antimissile missiles
Antibiotics 615
    SA names of specific antibiotics,
            to be added as needed
    BT Drug therapy
    NT Penicillin
Antibusing
    USE Busing (School integration)
Anticommunist movements 322.4
    UF Underground, Anticommunist
    BT Communism
Anticorrosive paint
    USE Corrosion and anticorrosives
Antimissile missiles 358.1; 623.4
    UF A.B.M.'s
        ABMs
        Antiballistic missiles
    BT Guided missiles
Antinuclear movement (May subdiv.
        geog.) 172; 327.1; 333.79;
        355; 363.17
    UF Nuclear freeze movement
    BT Arms control
        Nuclear weapons
        Social movements
    RT Nuclear power plants—
            Environmental aspects
Antipathies
    USE Prejudices
Antipoverty programs
    USE Domestic economic assistance
Antiquarian books
    USE Rare books
Antiques (May subdiv. geog.) 745.1
    BT Antiquities
        Decoration and ornament
        Decorative arts
    NT Art objects
        Collectors and collecting

BT = Broader Term   NT = Narrower Term   RT = Related Term   SA = See Also   UF = Used For

Antiques—United States 745.10973

Use for materials about old American objects that have aesthetic or historical importance and financial value. General materials about American objects of interest to collectors, such as historical documents, relics, etc., as well as items of little intrinsic value, are entered under **Americana.**

UF   United States—Antiques

RT   **Americana**

Antiquities 930.1

Use for general materials on the relics or monuments of ancient times. Materials on the relics or monuments of an extinct city or town are entered under the name of the city or town.

UF   Archeological specimens

SA   names of extinct cities, e.g. **Delphi (Extinct city); and** names of groups of people extant in modern times and names of cities (except extinct cities), countries, regions, etc., with the subdivision *Antiquities,* e.g. **Indians of North America— Antiquities; United States— Antiquities;** etc., to be added as needed

NT   **Antiques**

      Bible—Antiquities

      Christian antiquities

      Classical antiquities

      Indians of North America— Antiquities

      Prehistoric man

RT   **Archeology**

Antiquities, Biblical

USE   **Bible—Antiquities**

Antiquities, Christian

USE   **Christian antiquities**

Antiquities, Classical

USE   **Classical antiquities**

Antiquities—Collection and preservation 069

UF   Preservation of antiquities

BT   **Collectors and collecting**

Antiquities, Ecclesiastical

USE   **Christian antiquities**

Antiquity of man

USE   **Human origins**

Antisemitism 305.892

BT   **Jews and Gentiles**

      Prejudices

NT   **Jewish holocaust (1933-1945)**

      Jews—Persecutions

Antiseptics 614.4; 617.9

BT   **Surgery**

      Therapeutics

RT   **Disinfection and disinfectants**

Antislavery

USE   **Slavery**

Antitrust law 343

UF   Trusts, Industrial—Law and legislation

BT   **Commercial law**

      Industrial trusts

Antivivisection movement

USE   **Animal rights movements**

Antiwar movements

USE   names of wars with the subdivision *Protests, demonstrations, etc.,* e.g. **World War, 1939-1945—Protests, demonstrations, etc.;** to be added as needed

Antonyms

USE   **Opposites**

      and names of languages with the subdivision *Synonyms and antonyms,* e.g. **English language—Synonyms and antonyms;** to be added as needed

Ants 595.79

UF   Ant

      Hymenoptera

BT   **Insects**

Anxiety

USE   **Fear**

      Stress (Psychology)

      Worry

Apartheid 320.5

Use for materials on the economic, political, and social policies of the government of South Africa designed to segregate racial groups in South Africa and Namibia.

UF   Separate development (Race relations)

BT   **Segregation**

      South Africa—Race relations

RT   **Anti-apartheid movement**

Apartment houses 647; 728

UF   Flats

BT = Broader Term   NT = Narrower Term   RT = Related Term   SA = See Also   UF = Used For

Apartment houses—_Continued_
    BT   **Buildings**
         Domestic architecture
         Houses
         Housing
         Landlord and tenant
    NT   **Condominiums**

Apiculture
    USE **Bees**

Apocalyptic fantasies
    USE **Fantasy fiction**
          Fantasy films
          Fantasy television programs
          Robinsonades
          Science fiction
          War films
          War stories

Apollo project 629.45
    UF   Project Apollo
    BT   **Life support systems (Space environment)**
         Orbital rendezvous (Space flight)
         Space flight to the moon

Apologetics 239
    UF   Christianity—Apologetic works
         Christianity—Evidences
         Evidences of Christianity
         Fundamental theology
    SA   individual Christian sects and religions other than Christianity with the subdivisions _Apologetic works_ and _Controversial literature,_ to be added as needed
    BT   **Theology**
    NT   **Natural theology**

Apostles 225; 920
    UF   Disciples, Twelve
    BT   **Church history—30-600, Early church**
         Christian saints

Apostles' Creed 238
    BT   **Creeds**

Apostolic Church
    USE **Church history—30-600, Early church**

Apparatus, Chemical
    USE **Chemical apparatus**

Apparatus, Electric
    USE **Electric apparatus and appliances**

Apparatus, Electronic
    USE **Electronic apparatus and appliances**

Apparatus, Scientific
    USE **Scientific apparatus and instruments**

Apparitions 133.1
    UF   Phantoms
         Specters
         Spirits
    BT   **Parapsychology**
         Superstition
    NT   **Miracles**
    RT   **Demonology**
         Ghosts
         Hallucinations and illusions
         Spiritualism
         Visions

Appearance, Personal
    USE **Personal appearance**

Apperception 153.7
    BT   **Educational psychology**
         Psychology
    NT   **Attention**
         Consciousness
         Number concept
    RT   **Perception**
         Theory of knowledge

Appetite disorders
    USE **Eating disorders**

Apple 583; 634; 641.3
    BT   **Fruit**
         Trees

Appliances, Electric
    USE **Electric apparatus and appliances**
         Electric household appliances

Appliances, Electronic
    USE **Electronic apparatus and appliances**

Applications for college
    USE **College applications**

Applications for positions 331.12; 650.14
    UF   Employment applications
         Employment references
         Job applications

BT = Broader Term   NT = Narrower Term   RT = Related Term   SA = See Also   UF = Used For

Applications for positions—*Continued*
    Letters of recommendation
    Recommendations for positions
- BT **Job hunting**
    Personnel management
- NT **Interviewing**
    Résumés (Employment)

Applied arts
- USE **Decorative arts**

Applied mechanics 620.1
    Use for materials on the application of the principles of mechanics to engineering structures other than machinery. Materials on the application of the principles of mechanics to the design, construction, and operation of machinery are entered under **Mechanical engineering.**
- UF Mechanics, Applied *[Former heading]*
- BT **Mechanics**

Applied psychology 158
- UF Industrial psychology
    Practical Psychology
    Psychology, Applied *[Former heading]*
    Psychology, Industrial
    Psychology, Practical
- SA subjects with the subdivision *Psychological aspects,* e.g. **Drugs—Psychological aspects;** to be added as needed
- BT **Psychology**
- NT **Behavior modification**
    Counseling
    Drugs—Psychological aspects
    Employee morale
    Human engineering
    Negotiation
    Pastoral psychology
    Psychological warfare
- RT **Educational psychology**
    Human relations
    Interviewing
    Social psychology

Applied science
- USE **Technology**

Apportionment (Election law) 324; 328.3; 342
- UF Legislative reapportionment

    Reapportionment (Election law)
- BT **Representative government and representation**

Appraisal
- USE **Tax assessment**
    Valuation

Appraisal of books
- USE **Book selection**
    Books and reading
    Books and reading—Best books
    Books—Reviews
    Criticism
    Literature—History and criticism

Appreciation of art
- USE **Art appreciation**

Appreciation of music
- USE **Music appreciation**

Apprentices 331.5
- BT **Children—Employment**
    Labor
    Technical education
- RT **Employees—Training**

Apprenticeship novels
- USE **Bildungsromans**

Approximate computation 372.7; 513.2
- UF Arithmetic—Estimation
    Computation, Approximate
    Estimation (Mathematics)
- BT **Numerical analysis**

April First
- USE **April Fools' Day**

April Fools' Day 394.2
- UF All Fools' Day
    April First
- BT **Holidays**

Aptitude testing
- USE **Ability—Testing**

Aquaculture 639
- UF Aquiculture
    Freshwater aquaculture
    Mariculture
    Marine aquaculture
    Ocean farming
    Sea farming
- BT **Agriculture**
    Marine resources
- NT **Fish culture**

BT = Broader Term   NT = Narrower Term   RT = Related Term   SA = See Also   UF = Used For

Aquanauts 627.092; 920
  UF Oceanauts
  BT **Undersea research stations**
      Underwater exploration
Aquarian Age movement
  USE **New Age movement**
Aquariums 597.0074; 639.3
  SA names of specific aquariums,
      to be added as needed
  BT **Freshwater biology**
      Natural history
  NT **Goldfish**
      Marine aquariums
  RT **Fish culture**
      Fishes
Aquariums, Saltwater
  USE **Marine aquariums**
Aquatic animals
  USE **Freshwater animals**
      Marine animals
Aquatic birds
  USE **Water birds**
Aquatic plants
  USE **Freshwater plants**
      Marine plants
Aquatic sports
  USE **Water sports**
Aqueducts 628.1
  UF Conduits
      Water conduits
  BT **Civil engineering**
      Hydraulic structures
      Water supply
Aquiculture
  USE **Aquaculture**
Arab architecture
  USE **Islamic architecture**
Arab civilization 306.0917; 909
  UF Civilization, Arab *[Former
      heading]*
  BT **Civilization**
Arab countries 956
    Use for materials on several Arabic-
  speaking countries. Materials on the re-
  gion consisting of northeastern Africa and
  Asia west of Afghanistan are entered un-
  der **Middle East.**
  BT **Islamic countries**
      Middle East
Arab countries—Foreign relations—
      Israel 956
  UF Arab-Israel relations

      Arab-Israeli relations
      Israel-Arab relations
      Israeli-Arab relations
  NT **Israel-Arab conflicts**
  RT **Israel—Foreign relations—**
      Arab countries
      Jewish-Arab relations
Arab countries—Politics and govern-
      ment 956
  NT **Pan-Arabism**
Arab-Israel conflicts
  USE **Israel-Arab conflicts**
Arab-Israel relations
  USE **Arab countries—Foreign**
      relations—Israel
      Israel—Foreign relations—
      Arab countries
Arab-Israel War, 1948-1949
  USE **Israel-Arab War, 1948-1949**
Arab-Israel War, 1956
  USE **Sinai Campaign, 1956**
Arab-Israel War, 1967
  USE **Israel-Arab War, 1967**
Arab-Israel War, 1973
  USE **Israel-Arab War, 1973**
Arab-Israeli conflict, 1987-
  USE **Intifada, 1987-**
Arab-Israeli conflicts
  USE **Israel-Arab conflicts**
Arab-Israeli relations
  USE **Arab countries—Foreign**
      relations—Israel
      Israel—Foreign relations—
      Arab countries
Arab-Jewish relations
  USE **Jewish-Arab relations**
Arab refugees 325
  UF Refugees, Arab *[Former head-
      ing]*
  BT **Refugees**
Arabia
  USE **Arabian Peninsula**
Arabian Peninsula 953
  UF Arabia
  BT **Peninsulas**
Arabs 305.892; 909
  SA names of specific Arab peo-
      ples, to be added as needed
  NT **Bedouins**
      Jewish-Arab relations

Arabs—*Continued*

    Moors

    Palestinian Arabs

Arabs—Palestine

    USE **Palestinian Arabs**

Arachnida

    USE **Spiders**

           Ticks

Arbitration and award 347

    Use for materials on the settlement of civil disputes by arbitration instead of a court trial.

    UF Awards (Law)

          Mediation

    BT **Commercial law**

          Courts

    RT **Litigation**

Arbitration, Industrial

    USE **Industrial arbitration**

Arbitration, International

    USE **International arbitration**

Arboriculture

    USE **Forests and forestry**

          Fruit culture

          Trees

Arc light

    USE **Electric lighting**

Arc welding

    USE **Electric welding**

Archaeology

    USE **Archeology**

Archeological specimens

    USE **Antiquities**

Archeologists 920; 930.1092

    BT **Historians**

Archeology (May subdiv. geog.) **930.1**

    Use for materials on the discipline of archeology. General materials on the relics or monuments of ancient times are entered under **Antiquities.** Materials on the relics or monuments of an extinct city or town are entered under the name of the city or town.

    UF Archaeology

          Prehistory

          Ruins

    SA names of extinct cities, e.g. **Delphi (Extinct city);** to be added as needed; and names of groups of people and of cities (except extinct cities), countries, regions, etc., with the subdivision *Antiquities,* e.g. **Indians of North America—Antiquities; United States—Antiquities;** etc., to be added as needed

    BT **Civilization**

          History

    NT **Ancient architecture**

          Bible—Antiquities

          Brasses

          Bronzes

          Burial

          Buried treasure

          Christian antiquities

          Cliff dwellers and cliff dwellings

          Ethnology

          Excavations (Archeology)

          Extinct cities

          Funeral rites and ceremonies

          Gems

          Heraldry

          Historic sites

          Inscriptions

          Mounds and mound builders

          Mummies

          Numismatics

          Obelisks

          Pottery

          Prehistoric man

          Pyramids

          Radiocarbon dating

          Religious art and symbolism

          Rock drawings, paintings, and engravings

          Stone implements

          Temples

          Tombs

    RT **Antiquities**

          Art

          Bronze Age

          Classical antiquities

          Iron Age

          Stone Age

Archeology, Biblical

    USE **Bible—Antiquities**

Archeology, Christian

    USE **Christian antiquities**

Archeology, Classical

    USE **Classical antiquities**

BT = Broader Term   NT = Narrower Term   RT = Related Term   SA = See Also   UF = Used For

Archery 799.3
  BT **Martial arts**
        Shooting
  RT **Bow and arrow**
Architects 720.92; 920
  BT **Artists**
Architectural acoustics 729; 690
  UF Acoustics
  BT **Sound**
  NT **Soundproofing**
Architectural decoration and ornament
      729
  UF Architecture—Decoration and
        ornament
        Decoration and ornament, Ar-
        chitectural *[Former heading]*
  BT **Architecture**
        Decoration and ornament
Architectural design
  USE **Architecture—Details**
Architectural designs
  USE **Architecture—Designs and
        plans**
Architectural details
  USE **Architecture—Details**
Architectural drawing 720.28
  UF Drawing, Architectural
        Plans
  BT **Drawing**
        Mechanical drawing
  NT **Architecture—Designs and
        plans**
        Architecture—Details
Architectural engineering
  USE **Building**
        Steel construction
        Strains and stresses
        Strength of materials
        Theory of structures
Architectural metalwork 721
  UF Metalwork, Architectural
  BT **Metalwork**
Architectural perspective
  USE **Perspective**
Architecture 720
    Use for materials on the design and
style of structures. Materials on the pro-
cess of construction are entered under
Building. General materials on buildings
and materials on buildings in a particular
place are entered under **Buildings.**

  UF Construction
  SA architecture of particular
        countries, e.g. **American ar-
        chitecture;** styles of archi-
        tecture, e.g. **Byzantine
        architecture;** and types of
        buildings, e.g. **Farm build-
        ings;** to be added as needed
  BT **Art**
  NT **American architecture**
        Ancient architecture
        **Architectural decoration and
        ornament**
        Asian architecture
        Baroque architecture
        Building materials
        Byzantine architecture
        Castles
        Cathedrals
        Church architecture
        Colonial architecture
        Concrete construction
        Domestic architecture
        Farm buildings
        Gothic architecture
        Greek architecture
        Historic buildings
        **Indians of North America—
        Architecture**
        Industrial buildings
        Islamic architecture
        Library architecture
        Medieval architecture
        Modern architecture
        Monuments
        Naval architecture
        Obelisks
        Palaces
        Public buildings
        Renaissance architecture
        Roman architecture
        Romanesque architecture
        School buildings
        Skyscrapers
        Spires
        Steel construction
        Strains and stresses
        Strength of materials
        Structural engineering
        Synagogues

Architecture—*Continued*
> **Temples**
> **Theaters**
> **Tombs**
> **Underground architecture**
> RT   **Building**

Architecture, American
> USE   **American architecture**

Architecture, Ancient
> USE   **Ancient architecture**

Architecture and the handicapped 720
> UF   Barrier free design
> Handicapped and architecture
> BT   **Handicapped**

Architecture, Asian
> USE   **Asian architecture**

Architecture, Baroque
> USE   **Baroque architecture**

Architecture, Byzantine
> USE   **Byzantine architecture**

Architecture, Church
> USE   **Church architecture**

Architecture, Colonial
> USE   **Colonial architecture**

Architecture—Composition, proportion, etc. 720; 729
> UF   Architecture—Proportion
> Proportion (Architecture)
> BT   **Composition (Art)**

Architecture—Conservation and restoration 690; 720.28
> UF   Architecture—Restoration
> Buildings, Restoration of
> Conservation of buildings
> Preservation of buildings
> Restoration of buildings
> RT   **Buildings—Maintenance and repair**

Architecture—Decoration and ornament
> USE   **Architectural decoration and ornament**

Architecture—Designs and plans 720.28; 729
> UF   Architectural designs
> Architecture—Plans
> Designs, Architectural
> BT   **Architectural drawing**
> NT   **Domestic architecture— Designs and plans**

Architecture—Details 721; 729
> UF   Architectural design

Architectural details
Design, Architectural
Details, Architectural
> BT   **Architectural drawing**
> NT   **Chimneys**
> **Doors**
> **Fireplaces**
> **Floors**
> **Foundations**
> **Roofs**
> **Windows**
> **Woodwork**

Architecture, Domestic
> USE   **Domestic architecture**

Architecture, Domestic—Designs and plans
> USE   **Domestic architecture— Designs and plans**

Architecture, Ecclesiastical
> USE   **Church architecture**

Architecture, Gothic
> USE   **Gothic architecture**

Architecture, Greek
> USE   **Greek architecture**

Architecture, Islamic
> USE   **Islamic architecture**

Architecture, Medieval
> USE   **Medieval architecture**

Architecture, Modern
> USE   **Modern architecture**

Architecture, Modern—1600-1799 (17th and 18th centuries)
> USE   **Modern architecture— 1600-1799 (17th and 18th centuries)**

Architecture, Modern—1800-1899 (19th century)
> USE   **Modern architecture— 1800-1899 (19th century)**

Architecture, Modern—1900-1999 (20th century)
> USE   **Modern architecture— 1900-1999 (20th century)**

Architecture, Naval
> USE   **Naval architecture**
> **Shipbuilding**

Architecture—Plans
> USE   **Architecture—Designs and plans**

Architecture—Proportion
  USE **Architecture—Composition,
      proportion, etc.**
Architecture, Renaissance
  USE **Renaissance architecture**
Architecture—Restoration
  USE **Architecture—Conservation
      and restoration**
Architecture, Roman
  USE **Roman architecture**
Architecture, Romanesque
  USE **Romanesque architecture**
Architecture, Rural
  USE **Domestic architecture
      Farm buildings**
Archives (May subdiv. geog.) **026; 027**
  UF Documents
      Government records—
        Preservation
      Historical records—
        Preservation
      Preservation of historical re-
        cords
      Public records—Preservation
      Records—Preservation
  BT **Bibliography
      Documentation
      History—Sources
      Information services**
  NT **Manuscripts**
  RT **Charters
      Libraries**
**Archives—United States 026; 027;
      353.0071**
  UF United States—Archives
Arctic expeditions
  USE **Arctic regions—Exploration**
Arctic regions 919.8; 998
  UF Far north
  BT **Earth
      Polar regions**
  NT **Northeast Passage
      Northwest Passage**
  RT **North Pole**
Arctic regions—Exploration 919.8
  UF Arctic expeditions
      Polar expeditions
  SA names of expeditions, to be
      added as needed
  BT **Exploration**

      Scientific expeditions
**Ardennes, Battle of the, 1944-1945
      940.54**
  UF Bastogne, Battle of
      Battle of the Bulge
      Bulge, Battle of the
  BT **World War, 1939-1945—
      Campaigns**
Area studies 940-990
    Use for general materials on area
  studies.
  UF Foreign area studies
  SA continents, countries, and geo-
      graphic regions with the
      subdivision *Study and
      teaching,* to be added as
      needed
  BT **Education**
  NT **Africa—Study and teaching**
Arena theater 725; 792
  UF Round stage
      Theater-in-the-round
  BT **Theater**
Argentine rummy
  USE **Canasta (Game)**
Argumentation
  USE **Debates and debating
      Logic**
Aristocracy 305.5
  BT **Political science
      Social classes
      Sociology**
  NT **Upper classes**
  RT **Nobility**
Arithmetic 513
  UF Computation (Mathematics)
  SA names of specific arithmetic
      operations, to be added as
      needed
  BT **Mathematics
      Set theory**
  NT **Average
      Calculators
      Cube root
      Fractions
      Mental arithmetic
      Multiplication
      Percentage
      Ratio and proportion
      Square root**

BT = Broader Term   NT = Narrower Term   RT = Related Term   SA = See Also   UF = Used For

Arithmetic—*Continued*
    Subtraction
  RT **Numbers**
Arithmetic, Commercial
  USE **Business mathematics**
Arithmetic—Estimation
  USE **Approximate computation**
Arithmetic, Mental
  USE **Mental arithmetic**
Arithmetic—Study and teaching 372.7;
    513.07
  NT **Counting**
    Mathematical readiness
    Number games
Arithmetical readiness
  USE **Mathematical readiness**
Armada, 1588
  USE **Spanish Armada, 1588**
Armaments
  USE **Military readiness**
    Military weapons
Armaments industries
  USE **Defense industries**
Armaments race
  USE **Arms race**
Armed forces 343; 355
  UF Armed services
  SA specific branches of the armed
      forces under names of
      countries, e.g. **United**
      States. Army; and names of
      countries, regions, and in-
      ternational organizations
      with the subdivision *Armed
      forces,* e.g. **United States—
      Armed forces; United
      Nations—Armed forces;**
      etc., to be added as needed
  BT **Military art and science**
    Military readiness
  NT **Armies**
    Military personnel
    Navies
    Voluntary military service
Armed services
  USE **Armed forces**
Armies 355.3
  UF Army
    Military forces
    Military power

  SA names of countries with the
      subhead *Army,* e.g. **United
      States. Army;** to be added
      as needed
  BT **Armed forces**
    Military personnel
    Military readiness
    Strategy
  NT **Draft**
    Soldiers
    United States. Army
    **World War, 1939-1945—
      Human resources**
  RT **Military art and science**
    Navies
    War
Armies—Medical care 355.3
  SA names of wars with the subdi-
      vision *Health aspects* or
      Medical care, to be added
      as needed
  NT **World War, 1939-1945—
      Health aspects**
    **World War, 1939-1945—
      Medical care**
  RT **Military health**
    Military medicine
Armistice Day
  USE **Veterans Day**
Armistices
  USE names of wars with the subdi-
      vision *Armistices,* e.g.
      **World War, 1939-1945—
      Armistices;** to be added as
      needed
Armor 355.8; 623.4; 739.7
    Use for materials on protective covering
  worn as a defense against weapons.
  UF Arms and armor *[Former
      heading]*
    Suits of armor
  BT **Art metalwork**
    Costume
    Military art and science
  RT **Weapons**
Armored cars (Tanks)
  USE **Military tanks**
Arms aid
  USE **Military assistance**
Arms and armor
  USE **Armor**

Arms and armor—*Continued*
    Weapons
Arms, Coats of
    USE **Heraldry**
Arms control 327.1; 341.7
    UF Disarmament
        Limitation of armament
        Non-proliferation of nuclear
          weapons
        Nuclear non-proliferation
        Nuclear test ban
    BT **International relations**
        International security
        War
    NT **Antinuclear movement**
        Arms race
    RT **International arbitration**
        Military readiness
        Peace
Arms proliferation
    USE **Arms race**
Arms race 327.1; 355
    Use for materials on the competitive in-
crease in the military power of two or
more nations or blocs.
    UF Armaments race
        Arms proliferation
        Proliferation of arms
    BT **Arms control**
        International security
    RT **Military readiness**
        Military weapons
Arms sales
    USE **Defense industries**
        Military assistance
        Military weapons
Army
    USE **Armies**
        Military art and science
        and names of countries with
          the subhead *Army,* e.g.
          United States. Army; to be
          added as needed
Army bases
    USE **Military bases**
Army desertion
    USE **Military desertion**
Army life
    USE **Soldiers**

        and names of armies with the
          subdivision *Military life,*
          e.g. **United States. Army—**
          Military life; to be added
          as needed
Army posts
    USE **Military bases**
Army schools
    USE **Military education**
Army tests
    USE **United States. Army—**
        Examinations
Army vehicles
    USE **Military vehicles**
Aromatic plant products
    USE **Essences and essential oils**
Arrow
    USE **Bow and arrow**
Art 700
    Subdivisions listed under this heading
may be used under various art media
where applicable.
    UF Iconography
    SA types of art, e.g. **Commercial**
        art; art and other subjects,
        e.g. **Art and mythology;**
        subjects and themes in art,
        e.g. **Animals in art;** and art
        of particular countries or
        regions, e.g. **Greek art;** to
        be added as needed
    BT **Civilization**
        Humanities
    NT **Aesthetics**
        African American art
        African Americans in art
        American art
        Ancient art
        Animals in art
        Architecture
        Art and society
        Art forgeries
        Art objects
        Artistic anatomy
        Artistic photography
        Artists' models
        Arts and crafts movement
        Asian art
        Baroque art
        Black art

Art—*Continued*

Blacks in art
Bronzes
Buddhist art
Byzantine art
Children in art
Christian art and symbolism
Collage
Collectors and collecting
Commercial art
Composition (Art)
Decoration and ornament
Decorative arts
Drawing
Engraving
Erotic art
Etching
Folk art
Futurism (Art)
Gems
Graphic arts
Greek art
Illumination of books and
  manuscripts
Illustration of books
Indians of North America—
  Art
Interior design
Islamic art
Medieval art
Modern art
Modern art—1800-1899 (19th
  century)
Modern art—1900-1999 (20th
  century)
Municipal art
Nude in art
Painting
Pictures
Plants in art
Portraits
Prehistoric art
Realism in art
Religious art and symbolism
Renaissance art
Rock drawings, paintings, and
  engravings
Roman art
Sculpture
Surrealism

Symbolism
Women in art
World War, 1939-1945—Art
  and the war
RT Archeology
Art, Abstract
USE Abstract art
Art, African American
USE African American art
Art, American
USE American art
Art—Analysis, interpretation, apprecia-
  tion
USE Art appreciation
Art criticism
Art—Study and teaching
Art, Ancient
USE Ancient art
Art and mythology 704.9
UF Mythology in art
BT Art and religion
Mythology
Art and religion 704.9
UF Religion and art
BT Art and society
Religion
NT Art and mythology
RT Religious art and symbolism
Art and society 701
UF Society and art
BT Art
NT Art and religion
Art patronage
Folk art
Art, Applied
USE Industrial design
Art appreciation 701
UF Appreciation of art
Art—Analysis, interpretation,
  appreciation
BT Aesthetics
Art criticism
Art, Asian
USE Asian art
Art, Baroque
USE Baroque art
Art, Black
USE Black art
Art, Buddhist
USE Buddhist art

BT = Broader Term   NT = Narrower Term   RT = Related Term   SA = See Also   UF = Used For

Art, Byzantine
   USE **Byzantine art**
Art, Christian
   USE **Christian art and symbolism**
Art collections
   USE **Art museums**
Art collections, Private
   USE names of original owners of
          private collections with the
          subdivision *Art collections,*
          to be added as needed
Art, Commercial
   USE **Commercial art**
Art—Composition
   USE **Composition (Art)**
Art, Computer
   USE **Computer art**
Art criticism 701; 709
   UF Art—Analysis, interpretation,
        appreciation
   BT **Criticism**
   NT **Art appreciation**
Art, Decorative
   USE **Decoration and ornament**
           Decorative arts
Art, Ecclesiastical
   USE **Christian art and symbolism**
Art education
   USE **Art—Study and teaching**
Art, Electronic
   USE **Computer art**
           Video art
Art, Erotic
   USE **Erotic art**
Art—Exhibitions 707.4
   BT **Exhibitions**
Art—Federal aid
   USE **Federal aid to the arts**
Art forgeries 702.8; 751.5
   UF Art objects, Forgery of
        Forgery of works of art *[For-*
        mer heading]
   BT **Art**
           Counterfeits and counterfeiting
           Forgery
Art galleries
   USE **Art museums**
Art, Geometric
   USE **Abstract art**
Art, Gothic
   USE **Gothic art**

Art, Graphic
   USE **Graphic arts**
Art, Greek
   USE **Greek art**
Art—History 709
   BT **History**
Art in advertising
   USE **Commercial art**
Art in motion
   USE **Kinetic art**
Art, Indian
   USE **Indians of North America—**
           Art
Art industries and trade
   USE **Decorative arts**
Art, Islamic
   USE **Islamic art**
Art, Kinetic
   USE **Kinetic art**
Art, Medieval
   USE **Medieval art**
Art metalwork 739; 745.56
   UF Decorative metalwork
        Metalwork, Art
   SA kinds of art metalwork, to be
        added as needed
   BT **Decorative arts**
           Metalwork
   NT **Armor**
           Brasses
           Bronzes
           Goldwork
           Jewelry
           Pewter
           Silverwork
Art, Modern
   USE **Modern art**
           Modernism (Arts)
Art, Modern—1800-1899 (19th century)
   USE **Modern art—1800-1899 (19th**
           century)
Art, Modern—1900-1999 (20th century)
   USE **Modern art—1900-1999 (20th**
           century)
Art, Municipal
   USE **Municipal art**
Art—Museums
   USE **Art museums**
Art museums 708
   UF Art collections

BT = Broader Term   NT = Narrower Term   RT = Related Term   SA = See Also   UF = Used For

Art museums—*Continued*
> Art galleries
> Art—Museums *[Former heading]*
> Collections of art, painting, etc.
> Galleries, Art
> Picture galleries

SA names of individual art museums, to be added as needed

BT **Museums**

Art, Nonobjective
USE **Abstract art**

Art objects 700; 745
> Use for general materials about decorative articles of artistic merit such as snuff boxes, brasses, pottery, needlework, glassware, etc. Materials on old decorative objects having historical or financial value are entered under **Antiques.**

UF Objets d'art

SA classes of art objects, e.g. **Furniture; Pottery;** etc., to be added as needed

BT **Antiques**
     Art
     Decoration and ornament
     Decorative arts

NT **Furniture**
     Pottery

Art objects, Forgery of
USE **Art forgeries**

Art, Organic
USE **Abstract art**

Art, Oriental
USE **Asian art**

Art patronage 700
> Use for materials on patronage of the arts by individuals or corporations. Materials on government support of the arts are entered under **Arts—Government policy** or **Federal aid to the arts.**

UF Art patrons
     Business patronage of the arts
     Corporate patronage of the arts
     Corporations—Art patronage
     Funding for the arts
     Patronage of the arts
     Private funding of the arts

BT **Art and society**

RT **Arts—Government policy**
     Federal aid to the arts

Art patrons
USE **Art patronage**

Art, Prehistoric
USE **Prehistoric art**

Art—Prices 707.5
BT **Prices**

Art, Renaissance
USE **Renaissance art**

Art robberies
USE **Art thefts**

Art, Roman
USE **Roman art**

Art, Romanesque
USE **Romanesque art**

Art schools
USE **Art—Study and teaching**

Art—Study and teaching 707
UF Art—Analysis, interpretation, appreciation
     Art education
     Art schools

Art—Technique 702.8

Art thefts 364.1
UF Art robberies
     Thefts, Art

BT **Crime**

Art, Video
USE **Video art**

Artesian wells
USE **Wells**

Arthritis 616.7
BT **Gout**
     Rheumatism

Arthur, King—Romances
USE **Arthurian romances**

Arthurian romances 398.22; 808.8; 809
> May be used for individual works, collections, or materials about Arthurian romances.

UF Arthur, King—Romances
     Knights of the Round Table

BT **Romances**

RT **Grail**

Articles of war
USE **Military law**

BT = Broader Term   NT = Narrower Term   RT = Related Term   SA = See Also   UF = Used For

Articulation (Education) 371.2

Use for materials that discuss the integration of various elements of the school system so as to provide for continuous progress by the student. This may be the adjustments and relationships between different levels (e.g. elementary and secondary schools, high school and college); the integration between subjects (e.g. humanities and social studies); or the relationship between the school's program and outside factors (e.g. church, scouts, welfare agencies).

UF   Integration in education

BT   **Education—Curricula**

     Schools—Administration

Artificial flies 688.7; 799.1

UF   Fishing flies

     Flies, Artificial *[Former heading]*

BT   **Fishing**

     Fly casting

Artificial flowers 745.594

UF   Flowers, Artificial

BT   **Decoration and ornament**

Artificial foods 641.3; 664

UF   Food, Artificial *[Former heading]*

     Synthetic foods

BT   **Food**

     Synthetic products

Artificial fuels

USE **Synthetic fuels**

Artificial heart 617.4

BT   **Artificial organs**

     Heart

Artificial insemination 636.08

Use for general materials on artificial insemination and materials specifically on the artificial insemination of livestock and other animals. Materials limited to artificial insemination in humans are entered under **Human artificial insemination.**

UF   Impregnation, Artificial

     Insemination, Artificial

BT   **Reproduction**

NT   **Human artificial insemination**

Artificial insemination, Human

USE **Human artificial insemination**

Artificial intelligence 006.3

UF   AI (Artificial intelligence)

     Electronic brains

     Intelligence, Artificial

     Machine intelligence

BT   **Bionics**

     Electronic data processing

NT   **Expert systems (Computer science)**

Artificial islands

USE **Drilling platforms**

Artificial limbs 617.5

UF   Extremities, Artificial

     Limbs, Artificial

     Prosthesis

Artificial organs 617.9

UF   Organs, Artificial

     Prosthesis

SA   names of artificial organs, e.g. **Artificial heart;** to be added as needed

NT   **Artificial heart**

Artificial reality

USE **Virtual reality**

Artificial respiration 617.1

UF   Pulmonary resuscitation

     Respiration, Artificial

     Resuscitation, Pulmonary

BT   **First aid**

Artificial satellites 629.43; 629.46

UF   Orbiting vehicles

     Satellites, Artificial

SA   satellites of particular countries, e.g. **American artificial satellites;** types of satellites; and names of specific satellites, to be added as needed

BT   **Astronautics**

NT   **American artificial satellites**

     Explorer (Artificial satellite)

     Meteorological satellites

     Soviet artificial satellites

     Space stations

RT   **Space vehicles**

Artificial satellites, American

USE **American artificial satellites**

Artificial satellites—Control systems 629.46

Artificial satellites in telecommunication 384.5; 621.382

UF   Communication satellites

     Communications relay satellites

     Global satellite communications systems

Artificial satellites in telecommunication—*Continued*
    Satellite communication systems
  SA names of specific satellites or projects, to be added as needed
  BT **Telecommunication**
  NT **Telstar project**
Artificial satellites—Launching 629.43
  UF Launching of satellites
  BT **Rockets (Aeronautics)**
Artificial satellites—Law and legislation
  USE **Space law**
Artificial satellites—Orbits 629.4
  BT **Astrodynamics**
Artificial satellites, Russian
  USE **Soviet artificial satellites**
Artificial satellites, Soviet
  USE **Soviet artificial satellites**
Artificial satellites—Tracking 629.43
  UF Tracking of satellites
Artificial silk
  USE **Rayon**
Artificial sweeteners
  USE **Sugar substitutes**
Artificial weather control
  USE **Weather control**
Artillery 355.8; 623.4
  BT **Military art and science**
  RT **Ordnance**
Artistic anatomy 704.9; 743
  UF Anatomy, Artistic *[Former heading]*
      Human anatomy in art
      Human figure in art
  BT **Anatomy**
      Art
      Drawing
      Nude in art
  NT **Figure drawing**
      Figure painting
Artistic photography 770; 779
  UF Photography—Aesthetics
      Photography, Artistic *[Former heading]*
  BT **Art**
      Photography

Artists 709.2; 920
  SA artists of particular countries, e.g. **American artists;** and names of individual artists, to be added as needed
  NT **African American artists**
      American artists
      Architects
      Black artists
      Child artists
      Engravers
      Etchers
      Illustrators
      Lithographers
      Painters
      Potters
      Sculptors
      Women artists
Artists, African American
  USE **African American artists**
Artists, American
  USE **American artists**
Artists, Black
  USE **Black artists**
Artists' materials 741.2; 751.2
  UF Drawing materials
      Painters' materials
Artists' models 702.8
  UF Models, Artists'
      Models (Persons)
  BT **Art**
Arts 700
  Use for materials on the arts in general, including the visual arts, literature, and the performing arts. Materials on the visual arts only (architecture, painting, etc.) are entered under **Art.**
  UF Arts, Fine
      Fine arts
  SA arts of particular countries, e.g. **American arts;** to be added as needed
  NT **Aesthetics**
      Allegory
      American arts
      Visual literacy
Arts, American
  USE **American arts**

BT = Broader Term   NT = Narrower Term   RT = Related Term   SA = See Also   UF = Used For

Arts and crafts movement 745

Use for materials on the movement originating in England in the nineteenth century that promoted a return to craftsmanship in the applied and decorative arts.

UF   Crafts (Arts)

BT   **Art**

      Decoration and ornament

      Decorative arts

      Industrial arts

RT   **Folk art**

      Handicraft

Arts and state

USE   **Arts—Government policy**

      Federal aid to the arts

Arts, Applied

USE   **Decorative arts**

Arts, Decorative

USE   **Decoration and ornament**

      Decorative arts

      Interior design

Arts—Federal aid

USE   **Federal aid to the arts**

Arts, Fine

USE   **Arts**

Arts—Government policy 351.85; 700

UF   Arts and state

      Funding for the arts

      State and the arts

      State encouragement of the arts

RT   **Art patronage**

      Federal aid to the arts

Arts, Graphic

USE   **Graphic arts**

Arts, Minor

USE   **Decorative arts**

Arts, Useful

USE   **Industrial arts**

      Technology

Asbestos 553.6; 620.1; 666; 691

BT   **Economic geology**

Asceticism 248.4; 291.4

BT   **Ethics**

      Religious life

NT   **Fasting**

      Sexual abstinence

Asia 950

UF   East

      Orient

SA   areas of Asia, to be added as needed

NT   **Central Asia**

      East Asia

      Middle East

      Southeast Asia

Asia, Central

USE   **Central Asia**

Asia, East

USE   **East Asia**

Asia—Politics and government 950

BT   **Politics**

Asia, Southeast

USE   **Southeast Asia**

Asian architecture 720.95

UF   Architecture, Asian *[Former heading]*

      Oriental architecture

BT   **Architecture**

NT   **Temples**

RT   **Mosques**

Asian art 709.5

UF   Art, Asian *[Former heading]*

      Art, Oriental

      Oriental art

BT   **Art**

Asian civilization 306.095; 950

UF   Civilization, Asian *[Former heading]*

      Civilization, Oriental

      Oriental civilization

BT   **Civilization**

      East and West

Asphyxiating gases

USE   **Poisonous gases**

Assassination 364.1

SA   classes of persons and names of individuals with the subdivision *Assassination,* to be added as needed

BT   **Crime**

      Homicide

      Offenses against the person

      Political crimes and offenses

NT   **Presidents—United States— Assassination**

Assault, Criminal

USE   **Offenses against the person**

Assault, Sexual

USE   **Rape**

BT = Broader Term   NT = Narrower Term   RT = Related Term   SA = See Also   UF = Used For

Assembly programs, School
  USE **School assembly programs**
Assembly, Right of
  USE **Freedom of assembly**
Assertive behavior
  USE **Assertiveness (Psychology)**
Assertiveness (Psychology) 155.2; 158.2
  UF Assertive behavior
  BT **Aggressiveness (Psychology)**
      Psychology
  RT **Self-confidence**
Assessment
  USE **Tax assessment**
Assessment, Tax
  USE **Tax assessment**
Assessments, Political
  USE **Campaign funds**
Assistance in emergencies
  USE **Helping behavior**
Assistance to developing areas
  USE **Economic assistance**
      Technical assistance
Association, Freedom of
  USE **Freedom of association**
Associations (May subdiv. geog.) **060;
      302.3; 366**
  UF Associations, institutions, etc.
      Networks (Associations, insti-
        tutions, etc.)
      Organizations
      Voluntary associations
      Voluntary organizations
  SA types of associations; subjects,
      classes or persons, ethnic
      groups, and names of indi-
      vidual persons, families,
      and corporate bodies, with
      the subdivision *Societies;*
      and names of specific asso-
      ciations, to be added as
      needed
  NT **Agriculture—Societies**
      Clubs
      Community life
      Cooperation
      Nonprofit organizations
      Social group work
      **Trade and professional associ-
        ations**
  RT **Societies**

      Voluntarism
Associations, institutions, etc.
  USE **Associations**
Associations, International
  USE **International agencies**
Asteroids 523.4
  UF Minor planets
      Planetoids
      Planets, Minor
  BT **Astronomy**
      Solar system
  RT **Planets**
Astrobiology
  USE **Life on other planets**
      Space biology
Astrodynamics 521; 629.4
  BT **Dynamics**
  NT **Artificial satellites—Orbits**
      Navigation (Astronautics)
  RT **Astronautics**
      Space flight
Astrogeology 559.9
  SA names of planets with the
      subdivision *Geology,* to be
      added as needed
  BT **Geology**
  NT **Lunar geology**
      Mars (Planet)—Geology
Astrology 133.5
  UF Hermetic art and philosophy
  BT **Astronomy**
      Divination
      Fortune telling
      Occultism
      Superstition
  NT **Horoscopes**
      Zodiac
  RT **Constellations**
      Prophecies (Occultism)
      Stars
Astronautical accidents
  USE **Astronautics—Accidents**
Astronautical communication systems
  USE **Astronautics—Communication
        systems**
Astronautical instruments 629.4
  UF Instruments, Astronautical
      Space vehicles—Instruments
  BT **Navigation (Astronautics)**
      Space optics

BT = Broader Term   NT = Narrower Term   RT = Related Term   SA = See Also   UF = Used For

Astronautical instruments—*Continued*
- RT **Astronautics—Communication systems**

Astronautics (May subdiv. geog.) **629.4**
- BT **Aeronautics**
- NT **Aerothermodynamics**
  Artificial satellites
  Interplanetary voyages
  Navigation (Astronautics)
  Outer space
  Rocketry
  Space flight
  Space flight to the moon
  Space ships
  Space stations
  Unidentified flying objects
- RT **Astrodynamics**
  Space sciences
  Space vehicles

Astronautics—Accidents 363.12; 629.4
- UF Accidents, Spacecraft
  Astronautical accidents
  Space ships—Accidents
  Space vehicles—Accidents

Astronautics and civilization 306.4
- UF Civilization and astronautics
  Outer space and civilization
  Space age
  Space power
- BT **Aeronautics and civilization**
  Civilization
- NT **Space colonies**
  Space law

Astronautics—Communication systems 629.47
- UF Astronautical communication systems
  Space communication
- BT **Interstellar communication**
  Telecommunication
- NT **Radio in astronautics**
  Television in astronautics
- RT **Astronautical instruments**

Astronautics—International cooperation 629.4
- UF International space cooperation
- BT **International cooperation**

Astronautics—Law and legislation
- USE **Space law**

Astronautics, Photography in
- USE **Space photography**

Astronautics—United States 629.40973
- UF United States—Astronautics
- NT **Project Voyager**

Astronauts 629.450092; 920
- UF Cosmonauts
  Space ships—Pilots
- BT **Air pilots**
  Space flight
- NT **Space vehicles—Piloting**

Astronauts—Clothing 629.47
- UF Pressure suits
  Space suits
- BT **Life support systems (Space environment)**

Astronauts—Nutrition 629.47
- UF Space nutrition
- BT **Nutrition**

Astronavigation
- USE **Navigation (Astronautics)**

Astronomers 520.92; 920
- BT **Scientists**

Astronomical instruments 522
- UF Instruments, Astronomical
- SA names of instruments, e.g. **Telescopes;** to be added as needed
- BT **Scientific apparatus and instruments**
  Space optics
- NT **Astronomical photography**
  Telescopes

Astronomical observatories 522
- UF Observatories, Astronomical
- RT **Astronomy**

Astronomical photography 522
- UF Astrophotography
  Photography, Astronomical
- BT **Astronomical instruments**
  Photography

Astronomical physics
- USE **Astrophysics**

Astronomy 520
- BT **Physical sciences**
  Science
  Universe
- NT **Asteroids**
  Astrology
  Astrophysics

Astronomy—*Continued*
    Bible—Astronomy
    Black holes (Astronomy)
    Chronology
    Comets
    Galaxies
    Life on other planets
    Lunar eclipses
    Meteorites
    Meteors
    Moon
    Nautical astronomy
    Outer space
    Planetariums
    Planets
    Pulsars
    Quasars
    Radio astronomy
    Seasons
    Sky
    Solar eclipses
    Solar system
    Space environment
    Spectrum analysis
    Sun
    Tides
    Zodiac
  RT Astronomical observatories
    Constellations
    Space sciences
    Stars
Astronomy—Atlases
  USE Stars—Atlases
Astronomy—Mathematics 520.1
  BT Mathematics
Astronomy, Nautical
  USE Nautical astronomy
Astrophotography
  USE Astronomical photography
Astrophysics 523.01
  UF Astronomical physics
    Physics, Astronomical
  BT Astronomy
    Physics
    Stars
  NT Black holes (Astronomy)
    Spectrum analysis
Astros (Baseball team)
  USE Houston Astros (Baseball team)

Asylum 341.4
  UF Asylum, Right of *[Former heading]*
    Political asylum
    Right of asylum
    Sanctuary (Law)
  BT International law
  NT Political refugees
    Sanctuary movement
Asylum, Right of
  USE Asylum
Asylums
  USE Institutional care
    and classes of persons with the subdivision *Institutional care,* e.g. **Blind—Institutional care; Deaf—Institutional care; Mentally ill—Institutional care;** etc., to be added as needed
At-home employment
  USE Home business
    Telecommuting
Atheism 211
  BT Religion
    Secularism
    Theology
  RT Agnosticism
    Deism
    Rationalism
    Theism
Athletes 796.092; 920
  NT African American athletes
    Black athletes
  RT Sports
Athletes, African American
  USE African American athletes
Athletes, Black
  USE Black athletes
Athletes—Drug use 362.29; 796
  BT Drugs and sports
  RT Steroids
Athletic coaching
  USE Coaching (Athletics)
Athletic medicine
  USE Sports medicine
Athletics 796
  UF College athletics
    Intercollegiate athletics

BT = Broader Term   NT = Narrower Term   RT = Related Term   SA = See Also   UF = Used For

Athletics—*Continued*
- SA   names of specific athletic activities, to be added as needed
- NT   **Boxing**
      Coaching (Athletics)
      Gymnastics
      Martial arts
      Olympic games
      Rowing
      Track athletics
      Weight lifting
      Wrestling
- RT   **Physical education**
      Sports

Atlantic cable
- USE   **Submarine cables**

Atlantic Ocean 910.9163
- BT   **Ocean**

Atlantic States 974; 975
- UF   Eastern Seaboard
      Middle Atlantic States
      South Atlantic States
- BT   **United States**

Atlas (Missile) 623.4; 629.47
- BT   **Ballistic missiles**
      Intercontinental ballistic missiles

Atlases 912

Use as a form heading for geographical atlases of world coverage. General materials about maps and their history are entered under **Maps.**
- UF   Geographical atlases
- SA   scientific and technical subjects with the subdivision *Atlases,* for materials consisting of comprehensive, often systematically arranged, collections of illustrative plates, charts, etc., usually with explanatory captions, e.g. **Human anatomy—Atlases;** and names of countries, cities, etc., with the subdivision *Maps,* e.g. **United States—Maps;** to be added as needed
- BT   **Geography**
      Maps

- NT   **Bible—Geography**
      Chicago (Ill.)—Maps
      Historical atlases
      Human anatomy—Atlases
      Stars—Atlases
      United States—Maps

Atlases, Astronomical
- USE   **Stars—Atlases**

Atlases, Historical
- USE   **Historical atlases**

Atmosphere 551.5

Use for materials on the body of air surrounding the earth. Materials on the chemical and physical properties of air are entered under **Air.**
- BT   **Air**
      Earth
- NT   **Sky**
      Upper atmosphere
- RT   **Meteorology**

Atmosphere—Pollution
- USE   **Air pollution**

Atmosphere, Upper
- USE   **Upper atmosphere**

Atmospheric greenhouse effect
- USE   **Greenhouse effect**

Atmospheric humidity
- USE   **Humidity**

Atolls
- USE   **Coral reefs and islands**

Atom smashing
- USE   **Cyclotron**

Atomic bomb 355.8; 623.4
- BT   **Bombs**
      Nuclear warfare
      Nuclear weapons
- NT   **Radioactive fallout**
- RT   **Hydrogen bomb**

Atomic bomb—Physiological effect 616.9
- RT   **Radiation—Physiological effect**

Atomic bomb—Testing 623.4

Atomic bomb victims 940.54
- UF   A-bomb victims
      Victims of atomic bombings

Atomic energy
- USE   **Nuclear energy**

Atomic industry
- USE   **Nuclear industry**

Atomic medicine
- USE   **Nuclear medicine**

BT = Broader Term   NT = Narrower Term   RT = Related Term   SA = See Also   UF = Used For

Atomic nuclei
USE **Nuclear physics**
Atomic piles
USE **Nuclear reactors**
Atomic power
USE **Nuclear energy**
Atomic power plants
USE **Nuclear power plants**
Atomic powered vehicles
USE **Nuclear propulsion**
Atomic submarines
USE **Nuclear submarines**
Atomic theory 539.7; 541.2
BT **Physical chemistry**
RT **Quantum theory**
Atomic warfare
USE **Nuclear warfare**
Atomic weapons
USE **Nuclear weapons**
Atoms 539; 541.2
BT **Physical chemistry**
NT **Cyclotron**
Electrons
Neutrons
Protons
Transmutation (Chemistry)
Atonement—Christianity 232; 234
UF Jesus Christ—Atonement
Vicarious atonement
BT **Christianity**
Jesus Christ
Sacrifice
Salvation
Atonement, Day of
USE **Yom Kippur**
Atonement—Judaism 296.3
BT **Judaism**
Atrocities 909; 930-990
BT **Crime**
Cruelty
NT **Massacres**
Persecution
Atrocities, Military
USE names of wars with the subdivision *Atrocities,* e.g. **World War, 1939-1945—Atrocities;** and names of specific atrocities, to be added as needed
Attacks by animals
USE **Animal attacks**

Attendance, School
USE **School attendance**
Attention 153.1; 153.7
UF Concentration
BT **Apperception**
Educational psychology
Memory
Psychology
Thought and thinking
NT **Listening**
Attitude (Psychology) 152.4
UF Frustration
SA classes of persons with the subdivision *Attitudes,* e.g. **Teenagers—Attitudes;** to be added as needed
BT **Emotions**
Psychology
Social psychology
NT **Conformity**
Job satisfaction
Prejudices
Racism
Sexism
Teenagers—Attitudes
RT **Public opinion**
Attorneys
USE **Lawyers**
ATVs
USE **All terrain vehicles**
Auction bridge
USE **Bridge (Game)**
Auctions 658.8
UF Sales, Auction
BT **Selling**
Audio amplifiers, Transistor
USE **Transistor amplifiers**
Audio cassettes
USE **Sound recordings**
Audiodisc players
USE **Compact disc players**
Audiotapes
USE **Sound recordings**
Audiovisual education 371.3
UF Visual instruction
SA subjects with the subdivision *Audiovisual aids,* to be added as needed
BT **Education**
NT **Audiovisual materials**

BT = Broader Term   NT = Narrower Term   RT = Related Term   SA = See Also   UF = Used For

Audiovisual education—*Continued*
> **Library education—**
> **Audiovisual aids**
> **Motion pictures in education**
> **Radio in education**
> **Television in education**

Audiovisual materials 025.17; 371.3
> UF   Multimedia materials
> Nonbook materials
> Nonprint materials
> SA   subjects with the subdivision
> *Audiovisual aids;* and names
> of specific audiovisual ma-
> terials, to be added as
> needed
> BT   **Audiovisual education**
> **Teaching—Aids and devices**
> NT   **Filmstrips**
> **Library education—**
> **Audiovisual aids**
> **Manipulative materials**
> **Motion pictures**
> **Sound recordings**
> **Videodiscs**
> **Videotapes**

Audiovisual materials centers
> USE   **Instructional materials centers**

Auditing 657
> BT   **Bookkeeping**
> RT   **Accounting**

Auricular confession
> USE   **Confession**

Aurora australis
> USE   **Auroras**

Aurora borealis
> USE   **Auroras**

Auroras 538
> UF   Aurora australis
> Aurora borealis
> Northern lights
> Polar lights
> Southern lights
> BT   **Geophysics**
> **Meteorology**

Australia 994
> May be subdivided like United States
> except for *History.*
> NT   **Australians**

Australian aborigines 305.89
> UF   Aborigines, Australian

Australians (Native people)
> BT   **Australians**

Australians 305.82; 994
> UF   Ethnology—Australia
> BT   **Australia**
> NT   **Australian aborigines**

Australians (Native people)
> USE   **Australian aborigines**

Author and publisher
> USE   **Authors and publishers**

Authoring programs for computer assisted instruction
> USE   **Computer assisted**
> **instruction—Authoring pro-**
> **grams**

Authoritarianism
> USE   **Fascism**
> **Totalitarianism**

Authors 809; 920
> UF   Writers
> SA   authors of particular coun-
> tries, e.g. **American authors;**
> types of writers, e.g. **Poets;**
> subjects and names of
> countries, cities, etc. with
> the subdivision *Bio-*
> *bibliography;* and names of
> individual authors, to be
> added as needed
> BT   **Books**
> NT   **African American authors**
> **Black authors**
> **Child authors**
> **Dramatists**
> **Historians**
> **Journalists**
> **Novelists**
> **Poets**
> **Pseudonyms**
> **Women authors**
> RT   **Literature—Bio-bibliography**
> **Literature—History and criti-**
> **cism**

Authors, African American
> USE   **African American authors**

Authors, American
> USE   **American authors**

Authors and publishers 070.5
> Use for materials on the relations be-
> tween author and publisher.

Authors and publishers—*Continued*

    UF   Author and publisher

             Publishers and authors

    BT   **Authorship**

             Contracts

             Publishers and publishing

    RT   **Copyright**

Authors, Black

    USE   **Black authors**

Authors—Correspondence 816, etc.;
      808.86; 809.6

Authors, English

    USE   **English authors**

Authors—Homes and haunts

    USE   **Literary landmarks**

Authorship 808

    Use for general materials on being or becoming an author. Materials concerning the composition of special types of literature are entered under more specific headings such as **Fiction—Technique; Biography as a literary form; Short story;** etc.

    UF   Writing (Authorship)

    BT   **Literature**

    NT   **Advertising copy**

             Authors and publishers

             Biography as a literary form

             Copyright

             Creative writing

             Drama—Technique

             Fiction—Technique

             Historiography

             Journalism

             Love stories—Technique

             Plots (Drama, fiction, etc.)

             Radio authorship

             Report writing

             Short story

             Technical writing

             Television authorship

             Versification

Authorship—Handbooks, manuals, etc.
      808

    RT   **Printing—Style manuals**

Autism 616.89; 618.92

    BT   **Child psychiatry**

Auto courts

    USE   **Hotels and motels**

Autobiographical fiction 808.83; 813,
      etc.

    May be used for individual works, collections, or materials about autobiographical fiction.

    UF   Autobiographical novels

    BT   **Biographical fiction**

    RT   **Historical fiction**

Autobiographical novels

    USE   **Autobiographical fiction**

Autobiographies 920

    Use for collections of autobiographies. Materials about autobiography as a literary form are entered under **Autobiography.**

    UF   Memoirs

             Personal narratives

    SA   ethnic groups, classes of persons, and subjects with the subdivision *Biography* or *Correspondence,* e.g. **Women—Biography; Authors—Correspondence;** etc.; and names of events and wars with the subdivision *Personal narratives,* to be added as needed

    BT   **Biography**

    NT   **United States—History— 1861-1865, Civil War— Personal narratives**

             World War, 1939-1945— Personal narratives

    RT   **Diaries**

Autobiography 809

    Use for materials on autobiography as a literary form. Collections of autobiographies are entered under **Autobiographies.**

    UF   Autobiography as a literary form

             Autobiography—History and criticism

             Autobiography—Technique

             Memoirs

    BT   **Biography as a literary form**

Autobiography as a literary form

    USE   **Autobiography**

Autobiography—History and criticism

    USE   **Autobiography**

Autobiography—Technique

    USE   **Autobiography**

Autocodes
  USE **Programming languages (Computers)**
Autographs 929.8
  BT **Biography**
       Writing
  RT **Manuscripts**
Automata
  USE **Robots**
Automated information networks
  USE **Information networks**
Automatic computers
  USE **Computers**
Automatic control
  USE **Automation**
       Cybernetics
       Electric controllers
       Servomechanisms
Automatic data processing
  USE **Electronic data processing**
Automatic drafting
  USE **Computer graphics**
Automatic drawing
  USE **Computer graphics**
Automatic information retrieval
  USE **Information systems**
Automatic programming languages
  USE **Programming languages (Computers)**
Automatic speech recognition 006.4
  UF Mechanical speech recognition
       Speech recognition, Automatic
  BT **Speech processing systems**
       Voice
Automatic teaching
  USE **Teaching machines**
Automation 629.8; 670.42
  UF Automatic control
       Computer control
       Machinery, Automatic
  SA subjects with the subdivision
       Automation, e.g. **Libraries—Automation;** to be added as
       needed
  BT **Machinery in industry**
  NT **Feedback control systems**
       Libraries—Automation
       Servomechanisms
       Systems engineering
       Telecommuting

Automobile accidents
  USE **Traffic accidents**
Automobile design
  USE **Automobiles—Design**
Automobile driver education 629.28
  UF Automobile drivers—
       Education *[Former heading]*
       Car driver education
       Driver education
  BT **Education**
Automobile drivers 629.28
  UF Automobile driving
       Automobiles—Driving
       Car drivers
       Drivers, Automobile
Automobile drivers—Education
  USE **Automobile driver education**
Automobile driving
  USE **Automobile drivers**
Automobile engines 629.25
  UF Automobiles—Engines *[Former heading]*
       Automobiles—Motors
       Car engines
  BT **Engines**
       Internal combustion engines
  RT **Diesel automobiles**
       Electric automobiles
Automobile guides
  USE **Automobile travel—Guidebooks**
Automobile industry 338.4; 388.3
  UF Automotive industry
       Car industry
       Motor vehicle industry
  BT **Industry**
  NT **Service stations**
Automobile industry—Production standards 658.5
  BT **Production standards**
Automobile insurance 368.5
  UF Car insurance
       Insurance, Automobile *[Former heading]*
       No fault automobile insurance
  BT **Insurance**
Automobile parts 629.28
  UF Automobiles—Parts *[Former heading]*
       Car parts

BT = Broader Term   NT = Narrower Term   RT = Related Term   SA = See Also   UF = Used For

Automobile parts—*Continued*
  BT **Automobiles**
Automobile pools
  USE **Car pools**
Automobile racing 796.7
  UF Automobiles—Racing
      Car racing
  SA types of automobile racing
      and names of specific races,
      to be added as needed
  BT **Racing**
  NT **Karts and karting**
Automobile repairs
  USE **Automobiles—Maintenance
      and repair**
Automobile service stations
  USE **Service stations**
Automobile styling
  USE **Automobiles—Design**
Automobile touring
  USE **Automobile travel**
Automobile transmission
  USE **Automobiles—Transmission
      devices**
Automobile travel 796.7
  UF Automobile touring
      Automobiles—Touring *[For-
      mer heading]*
      Car travel
      Motoring
  BT **Travel**
Automobile travel—Guidebooks 912
  UF Automobile guides
      Automobiles—Road guides
      [Former heading]
      Car travel—Guidebooks
  BT **Maps**
  RT **Road maps**
Automobile trucks
  USE **Trucks**
Automobiles 388.3; 629.222
  UF Cars (Automobiles)
      Motor cars
  SA names of specific makes and
      models of automobiles, e.g.
      Ford automobile; to be add-
      ed as needed
  BT **Highway transportation
      Vehicles**
  NT **Automobile parts**

Buses
Compact automobiles
Diesel automobiles
Electric automobiles
Ford automobile
Foreign automobiles
Sports cars
Trucks
Automobiles—Accidents
  USE **Traffic accidents**
Automobiles—Air conditioning 629.2
  BT **Air conditioning**
Automobiles—Brakes 629.2
  BT **Brakes**
Automobiles, Compact
  USE **Compact automobiles**
Automobiles—Conservation and resto-
      ration
  USE **Automobiles—Restoration**
Automobiles—Design 629.222
  UF Automobile design
      Automobile styling
      Automobiles—Design and
      construction *[Former head-
      ing]*
      Car design
  BT **Industrial design**
Automobiles—Design and construction
  USE **Automobiles—Design**
Automobiles, Diesel
  USE **Diesel automobiles**
Automobiles—Driving
  USE **Automobile drivers**
Automobiles, Electric
  USE **Electric automobiles**
Automobiles—Electric equipment 629.25
  UF Electric equipment of automo-
      biles
Automobiles—Engines
  USE **Automobile engines**
Automobiles, Foreign
  USE **Foreign automobiles**
Automobiles—Fuel consumption 629.28
  BT **Energy consumption
      Fuel**
Automobiles—Gearing
  USE **Automobiles—Transmission
      devices**
**Automobiles—Law and legislation
      343.09**
  BT **Law**

Automobiles—Law and legislation—
Continued
>   Legislation
RT   **Traffic regulations**
Automobiles—Maintenance and repair
>   **629.28**
UF   Automobile repairs
>   Automobiles—Repairing
>   Car maintenance
>   Car repair
BT   **Repairing**
Automobiles—Models 629.22
UF   Model cars
BT   **Machinery—Models**
Automobiles—Motors
USE **Automobile engines**
Automobiles—Parts
USE **Automobile parts**
Automobiles—Pollution control devices
>   **629.25**
UF   Pollution control devices (Mo-
>   tor vehicles)
BT   **Pollution control industry**
Automobiles—Racing
USE **Automobile racing**
Automobiles—Repairing
USE **Automobiles—Maintenance**
>   **and repair**
Automobiles—Restoration 629.28
UF   Automobiles—Conservation
>   and restoration
>   Restoration of automobiles
Automobiles—Road guides
USE **Automobile travel—**
>   **Guidebooks**
Automobiles—Touring
USE **Automobile travel**
Automobiles—Trailers
USE **Travel trailers and campers**
Automobiles—Transmission devices
>   **629.2**
UF   Automobile transmission
>   Automobiles—Gearing
>   Car transmissions
>   Transmissions, Automobile
BT   **Gearing**
Automotive industry
USE **Automobile industry**
Autosuggestion
USE **Hypnotism**

>   Mental suggestion
Autumn 508; 525
UF   Fall
BT   **Seasons**
Avant-garde churches
USE **Noninstitutional churches**
Avant-garde films
USE **Experimental films**
Avant-garde theater
USE **Experimental theater**
Avenues
USE **Streets**
Average 519.5
BT   **Arithmetic**
>   **Probabilities**
>   **Statistics**
Aviation
USE **Aeronautics**
Aviation medicine 616.9
UF   Aeronautics—Medical aspects
>   Aerospace medicine
>   Medicine, Aviation
BT   **Medicine**
NT   **Jet lag**
RT   **Space medicine**
Aviators
USE **Air pilots**
Avocations
USE **Hobbies**
Awakening, Religious
USE **Religious awakening**
Awards 001.4
UF   Competitions
>   Prizes (Rewards)
>   Rewards (Prizes, etc.) *[Former
>   heading]*
SA   types of awards and prizes
>   and names of specific
>   awards and prizes, e.g. **No-**
>   **bel Prizes;** to be added as
>   needed
NT   **Literary prizes**
>   **Nobel Prizes**
RT   **Contests**
Awards (Law)
USE **Arbitration and award**
Awards, Literary
USE **Literary prizes**
Axiology
USE **Values**

BT = Broader Term   NT = Narrower Term   RT = Related Term   SA = See Also   UF = Used For

Aztecs 972.004
    BT   **Indians of Mexico**

B-52 bomber 623.7
    BT   **Bombers**

Babies
    USE   **Infants**

Baby animals
    USE   **Animal babies**

Baby care
    USE   **Infants—Care**

Baby sitters
    USE   **Babysitters**

Baby sitting
    USE   **Babysitting**

Babysitters 649
    UF   Baby sitters *[Former heading]*
           Sitters (Babysitters)
    RT   **Babysitting**

Babysitting 649
    UF   Baby sitting
    BT   **Child care**
           Infants—Care
    RT   **Babysitters**

Bacilli
    USE   **Bacteria**
           Germ theory of disease

Back packing
    USE   **Backpacking**

Backpack cycling
    USE   **Bicycle touring**

Backpacking 796.5
    UF   Back packing
           Pack transportation
    BT   **Camping**
           Hiking

Bacon-Shakespeare controversy
    USE   **Shakespeare, William,**
           1564-1616—Authorship

Bacon's Rebellion, 1676 973.2
    BT   **United States—History—**
           1600-1775, Colonial period

Bacteria 589.9
    Use for general materials on bacteria. Materials on the science of studying bacteria are entered under **Bacteriology.**
    UF   Bacilli
           Disease germs
           Germs
           Microbes
           Prokaryotes

    BT   **Microorganisms**
           Parasites
    RT   **Bacteriology**
           Fermentation
           Fungi

Bacterial warfare
    USE   **Biological warfare**

Bacteriology 589.9
    Use for materials on the science of studying bacteria. General materials on bacteria are entered under **Bacteria.**
    SA   subjects with the subdivision
           Bacteriology, to be added
           as needed
    BT   **Communicable diseases**
           Medicine
           Microbiology
           Pathology
    NT   **Cheese—Bacteriology**
           Disinfection and disinfectants
           Immunity
           Microorganisms
    RT   **Bacteria**
           Fermentation
           Germ theory of disease

Bacteriology, Agricultural
    USE   **Agricultural bacteriology**

Badges of honor
    USE   **Decorations of honor**
           Insignia
           Medals

Bahai Faith 297
    UF   Bahaism *[Former heading]*
    BT   **Religions**

Bahaism
    USE   **Bahai Faith**

Baking 641.7
    SA   types of baked products, to be
           added as needed
    BT   **Cooking**
    NT   **Bread**
           Cake
           Pastry

Balance of nature
    USE   **Ecology**

Balance of payments 382
    BT   **International economic rela-**
           tions
    RT   **Balance of trade**

Balance of power 327.1
    UF   Power politics

Balance of power—*Continued*
  BT International relations
Balance of trade 382
  UF Trade, Balance of
  BT Commerce
      Economics
      Tariff
  RT Balance of payments
Ball bearings
  USE Bearings (Machinery)
Ball games 796.3
  SA names of games, e.g. **Baseball;**
      and names of competitions,
      to be added as needed
  BT Games
  NT Baseball
      Basketball
      Bowling
      Football
      Ping-pong
      Soccer
      Softball
      Volleyball
Ballads 808.1; 808.81; 811, etc.
    May be used for individual works, col-
  lections, or materials about ballads. Mate-
  rials on the folk tunes associated with
  these ballads, and collections that include
  both words and music are entered under
  Folk songs.
  BT Literature
      Poetry
      Songs
  RT Folk songs
Ballads, American
  USE American ballads
Ballet 792.8
    Use for musical works composed for the
  ballet and for materials about the ballet.
  Individual ballet plots or collections of
  ballet plots are entered under **Ballet—
  Stories, plots, etc.**
  UF Ballets *[Former heading]*
  BT Dancing
      Drama
      Performing arts
      Theater
  RT Pantomimes
Ballet dancers 792.8092; 920
  BT Dancers
Ballet—Stories, plots, etc. 792.8
    Use for individual ballet plots and for
  collections of ballet plots.

  RT Literature—Stories, plots, etc.
Ballet, Water
  USE Synchronized swimming
Ballets
  USE Ballet
Ballistic missile early warning system
      358.1; 621.3848
  UF BMEWS
      Early warning system, Ballistic
      missile
  BT Air defenses
      Radar defense networks
Ballistic missiles 358.1; 623.4
    Use for materials on high-altitude, high-
  speed missiles that are self-propelled and
  guided in the first stage of flight only and
  later have a natural and uncontrolled tra-
  jectory.
  UF Missiles, Ballistic
  SA types of ballistic missiles and
      names of specific missiles,
      to be added as needed
  BT Guided missiles
      Nuclear weapons
      Rockets (Aeronautics)
  NT Atlas (Missile)
      Intercontinental ballistic mis-
      siles
Balloons 629.133
  BT Airships
  RT Aeronautics
Balloons, Dirigible
  USE Airships
Ballot
  USE Elections
Ballparks
  USE Stadiums
Band music 784
  BT Instrumental music
      Military music
Bandages 616.02
  UF Bandages and bandaging *[For-
      mer heading]*
  BT First aid
Bandages and bandaging
  USE Bandages
Bandits
  USE Thieves
Bandmasters
  USE Conductors (Music)

Bands (Music) 784
- SA types of bands and names of individual bands, to be added as needed
- NT **Drum majoring**
  Instrumentation and orchestration
- RT **Conducting**
  Orchestra
  Wind instruments

Bank credit cards
- USE **Credit cards**

Bank debit cards
- USE **Debit cards**

Bank failures 332.1
- UF Failure of banks
- BT **Bankruptcy**
  Banks and banking
  Business failures

Banking
- USE **Banks and banking**

Bankruptcy 332.7; 336.3; 346
- UF Business mortality
  Failure in business
  Insolvency
- BT **Business failures**
  Commercial law
  Debtor and creditor
  Finance
- NT **Bank failures**

Banks and banking (May subdiv. geog.)
  332.1
- UF Banking
  Savings banks
- SA names of individual banks, to be added as needed
- BT **Business**
  Capital
  Commerce
  Finance
- NT **Agricultural credit**
  Bank failures
  Consumer credit
  Cooperative banks
  Debit cards
  Federal Reserve banks
  Foreign exchange
  Interest (Economics)
  Investment trusts
  Investments

  Negotiable instruments
  Savings and loan associations
- RT **Credit**
  Money
  Trust companies

Banks and banking, Cooperative
- USE **Cooperative banks**

Banks and banking—Credit cards
- USE **Credit cards**

Banks and banking—Data processing
  332.10285
- BT **Electronic data processing**

Banks and banking—United States
  332.10973
- UF United States—Banks and banking

Banned books
- USE **Books—Censorship**

Banners
- USE **Flags**

Banquets
- USE **Dining**
  Dinners

Baptism 234; 265
- UF Christening
  Immersion, Baptismal
- BT **Rites and ceremonies**
  Sacraments
  Theology
- NT **Regeneration (Theology)**

Baptists 286; 920
- BT **Christian sects**
- RT **Mennonites**

Bar
- USE **Lawyers**

Barbary corsairs
- USE **Pirates**

Barbary States
- USE **North Africa**

Barbecue cookery
- USE **Barbecue cooking**

Barbecue cooking 641.7
- UF Barbecue cookery [Former heading]
  Cooking, Barbecue
  Grill cooking
- BT **Outdoor cooking**

Barbering
- USE **Hair**

Bargaining
- USE **Negotiation**

Barns 631.2; 728
    BT   Farm buildings
Barometer
    USE Barometers
Barometers 551.5; 681
    UF   Barometer *[Former heading]*
    BT   Meteorological instruments
Baronage
    USE Nobility
Baroque architecture 724
    UF   Architecture, Baroque *[Former heading]*
    BT   Architecture
Baroque art 709.03
    UF   Art, Baroque *[Former heading]*
    BT   Art
Barrier free design
    USE Architecture and the handicapped
Barristers
    USE Lawyers
Barrooms
    USE Bars
Barrows
    USE Mounds and mound builders
Bars (May subdiv. geog.) 647.95
    Use for materials on public drinking establishments.
    UF   Barrooms
           Pubs
           Restaurants, bars, etc. *[Former heading]*
           Saloons
           Taverns
    BT   Liquor industry
    RT   Restaurants
Barter 332
    UF   Exchange, Barter
    BT   Commerce
           Economics
           Money
           Subsistence economy
           Underground economy
Basal readers 372.4; 418
    Use for readers providing controlled vocabulary in a series of books intended to be read sequentially and for materials about such readers.
    UF   English language—Basal readers

    BT   Reading materials
Baseball 796.357
    BT   Ball games
           Sports
    NT   Little League baseball
           Softball
Baseball cards 769
    BT   Sports cards
Baseball clubs 796.357
    SA   names of individual baseball clubs, to be added as needed
    NT   Houston Astros (Baseball team)
Baseball—Fiction
    USE Baseball stories
Baseball stories 808.83; 813, etc.
    May be used for individual works, collections, or materials about baseball stories.
    UF   Baseball—Fiction
    BT   Sports stories
Basements 721
    UF   Cellars
    BT   Foundations
           Underground architecture
Bases (Chemistry) 546; 661
    BT   Chemistry
Bashfulness
    USE Shyness
Basic education 370.11
    UF   Basic skills education
           Fundamental education
    BT   Education
Basic life skills
    USE Life skills
Basic rights
    USE Civil rights
           Human rights
Basic skills education
    USE Basic education
Basket making 746.41
    BT   Weaving
Basketball 796.323
    BT   Ball games
           Sports
Bastardy
    USE Illegitimacy
Bastogne, Battle of
    USE Ardennes, Battle of the, 1944-1945

Bat
  USE **Bats**
Baths 613; 615.8
  BT **Cleanliness**
      Hygiene
      Physical therapy
  RT **Hydrotherapy**
Bathyscaphe 387.2; 623.8
  BT **Oceanography—Research**
      Submersibles
Batik 746.6
  BT **Dyes and dyeing**
Baton twirling 791.6
  RT **Drum majoring**
Batrachia
  USE **Amphibians**
Bats 599.4
  UF Bat
  BT **Mammals**
Battered children
  USE **Child abuse**
Battered elderly
  USE **Elderly abuse**
Battered husbands
  USE **Husband abuse**
Battered men
  USE **Husband abuse**
Battered wives
  USE **Abused women**
Battered women
  USE **Abused women**
Batteries, Electric
  USE **Electric batteries**
      Storage batteries
Batteries, Solar
  USE **Solar batteries**
Battering of wives
  USE **Wife abuse**
Battle of the Bulge
  USE **Ardennes, Battle of the, 1944-**
      1945
Battle ships
  USE **Warships**
Battle songs
  USE **War songs**
Battles 355.4; 909; 930-990
  UF Fighting
      Sieges
  SA names of wars with the subdi-
      vision *Campaigns,* e.g.

      United States—History—
      1861-1865, Civil War—
      Campaigns; and names of
      individual battles, e.g. **Ar-**
      dennes, Battle of the, 1944-
      1945; to be added as need-
      ed
  BT **Military art and science**
      Military history
      War
  RT **Naval battles**
Battleships
  USE **Warships**
Bay of Pigs invasion
  USE **Cuba—History—1961, Inva-**
      sion
Bazaars
  USE **Fairs**
Beaches 551.4
  BT **Seashore**
Beadwork 746.5
  BT **Crocheting**
      Embroidery
      Weaving
Bearings (Machinery) 621.8
  UF Ball bearings
      Journals (Machinery)
  BT **Machinery**
  RT **Lubrication and lubricants**
Beasts
  USE **Animals**
      Domestic animals
Beat generation
  USE **Bohemianism**
Beatniks
  USE **Bohemianism**
Beautification of landscape
  USE **Landscape protection**
Beauty
  USE **Aesthetics**
Beauty parlors
  USE **Beauty shops**
Beauty, Personal
  USE **Personal appearance**
      Personal grooming
Beauty salons
  USE **Beauty shops**
Beauty shops 646.7
  UF Beauty parlors
      Beauty salons

Beauty shops—*Continued*
   NT   **Cosmetics**
Beavers 599.32
   BT   **Freshwater animals**
         Furbearing animals
Bed and breakfast accommodations
   USE **Hotels and motels**
Bedouins 305.892; 909
   BT   **Arabs**
Bedspreads 643; 746.9
   UF   Coverlets
   BT   **Interior design**
Bedtime
   UF   Getting ready for bed
   BT   **Night**
         Sleep
   NT   **Lullabies**
Bee
   USE **Bees**
Beef 641.3; 664
   BT   **Meat**
Beef cattle 636.2
   UF   Steers
   SA   names of breeds of beef cat-
         tle, to be added as needed
   BT   **Cattle**
   NT   **Hereford cattle**
Bees 595.79; 638
   UF   Apiculture
         Bee
         Hymenoptera
   BT   **Insects**
   RT   **Honey**
Begging 362.5
   UF   Mendicancy
         Panhandling
   BT   **Poor**
   RT   **Tramps**
Beginning reading materials
   USE **Easy reading materials**
Behavior
   USE **Animal behavior**
         Human behavior
Behavior, Compulsive
   USE **Compulsive behavior**
Behavior genetics 155.7
   UF   Psychogenetics
   BT   **Genetics**
         Psychology
Behavior, Helping
   USE **Helping behavior**

Behavior modification 153.8
   BT   **Applied psychology**
         Human behavior
         Psychology of learning
   NT   **Brainwashing**
         Twelve-step programs
Behavior problems (Children)
   USE **Emotionally disturbed children**
Behavior, Sexual
   USE **Sexual behavior**
Behaviorism 150.19
   Use for materials on the conception of
psychology that claims that the proper
subject matter of psychology is the objec-
tively observable actions of organisms and
not the study of mental phenomena.
   BT   **Human behavior**
         Psychology
         Psychophysiology
Beijing Massacre, 1989
   USE **China—History—1989, Tia-
         nanmen Square Incident**
Belief and doubt 121
   Use for materials on belief and doubt
from the philosophical standpoint. Materi-
als on religious belief and doubt are en-
tered under **Faith.**
   UF   Certainty
         Doubt
   BT   **Emotions**
         Philosophy
         Religion
         Theory of knowledge
   NT   **Truth**
   RT   **Agnosticism**
         Faith
         Rationalism
         Skepticism
Bell System Telstar satellite
   USE **Telstar project**
Belles lettres
   USE **Literature**
Bells 786.8
   UF   Carillons
         Chimes
         Church bells
   BT   **Musical instruments**
Belts and belting 621.8
   UF   Chain belting
   BT   **Machinery**
   RT   **Power transmission**
Beneficial insects 591.6
   UF   Economic entomology

Beneficial insects—*Continued*
      Entomology, Economic
      Helpful insects
      Insects, Injurious and benefi-
        cial *[Former heading]*
      Useful insects
  SA types of beneficial insects, e.g.
      Silkworms; to be added as
      needed
  BT **Economic zoology**
      Insects
  NT **Silkworms**
  RT **Insect pests**
Benevolent institutions
  USE **Institutional care**
Beowulf—Adaptations 829
Bequests
  USE **Gifts**
      Inheritance and succession
      Wills
Bereavement 155.9; 248.8
  UF Sympathy *[Former heading]*
  BT **Death**
  RT **Consolation**
      Grief
Bermuda Triangle 001.9
  UF Devil's Triangle
      Graveyard of the Atlantic
Berries 634
  SA names of berries, e.g. **Straw-**
      berries; to be added as
      needed, in the plural form
  BT **Fruit**
      Fruit culture
  NT **Strawberries**
Best books
  USE **Books and reading—Best**
      books
Best sellers (Books) 028; 070.5
  UF Books—Best sellers
  BT **Book industries**
      Books and reading
Betting
  USE **Gambling**
Bevel gearing
  USE **Gearing**
Beverages 613; 641.2; 641.8; 663
  UF Drinks
  SA types of beverages and names
      of specific beverages, to be
      added as needed

  BT **Diet**
      Food
  NT **Alcoholic beverages**
      Cocoa
      Coffee
      Liquors
      Tea
Bias attacks
  USE **Hate crimes**
Bias crimes
  USE **Hate crimes**
Bias (Psychology)
  USE **Prejudices**
Bible 220
    The subdivisions provided under **Bible**
may also be used with any part of the Bi-
ble, with single books of the Bible, and
with groups of books, e.g. **Bible. O.T.—
Biography; Bible. O.T. Pentateuch—
Commentaries; Bible. O.T. Psalms—
History; Bible. N.T. Gospels—Inspiration;**
etc.
  UF Holy Scriptures
      Scriptures, Holy
  BT **Ancient history**
      Hebrew literature
      Jewish literature
      Sacred books
  NT **Bible stories**
Bible and science 220.8
  UF Bible—Science
      Science and the Bible
  BT **Religion and science**
  RT **Creationism**
Bible—Animals
  USE **Bible—Natural history**
Bible—Antiquities 220.9
  UF Antiquities, Biblical
      Archeology, Biblical
      Biblical archeology
  BT **Antiquities**
      Archeology
  NT **Christian antiquities**
Bible as literature 809
  UF Bible—Language, style, etc.
      Bible—Literary character
  NT **Bible—Criticism, interpreta-**
      tion, etc.
      Bible—Parables
  RT **Religious literature**
Bible—Astronomy 220.8
  BT **Astronomy**

Bible—Biography 220.9
UF   Biblical characters
NT   **Women in the Bible**
Bible—Birds
USE   **Bible—Natural history**
Bible—Botany
USE   **Bible—Natural history**
Bible—Catechisms, question books 238
UF   Bible—Question books
BT   **Bible—Study and teaching**
      Catechisms
Bible—Chronology 220.9

Use for materials on the dates of events related in the Bible and their correlation with the dates of general history.

UF   Bible—History of biblical
        events—Chronology
      Chronology, Biblical
Bible classes
USE   **Bible—Study and teaching**
      Religious summer schools
      Sunday schools
Bible—Commentaries 220.7
UF   Bible—Interpretation
      Commentaries, Biblical
Bible—Concordances 220.4; 220.5
UF   Bible—Indexes
Bible—Criticism, interpretation, etc.
      220.6
UF   Bible—Exegesis
      Bible—Hermeneutics
      Bible—Interpretation
      Exegesis, Biblical
      Hermeneutics, Biblical
      Higher criticism
BT   **Bible as literature**
      Criticism
Bible—Dictionaries 220.3
UF   Bible—Indexes
BT   **Encyclopedias and dictionaries**
Bible—Drama
USE   **Bible plays**
Bible—Evidences, authority, etc. 220.1

Use for materials that attempt to establish the truth of statements in the Bible or the authority of its precepts. Materials on the divine inspiration of the Bible are entered under **Bible—Inspiration.**

UF   Evidences of the Bible
BT   **Bible—Inspiration**
Bible—Exegesis
USE   **Bible—Criticism, interpreta-**
      tion, etc.

Bible fiction 808.83; 813, etc.

May be used for individual works, collections, or materials about fiction in which characters and settings are taken from the Bible. Materials that retell or adapt stories from the Bible are entered under **Bible stories.**

UF   Bible—History of biblical
        events—Fiction *[Former
        heading]*
SA   names of biblical characters
        with the subdivision *Fic-
        tion,* to be added as needed
BT   **Fiction**
RT   **Bible stories**
Bible films 791.43

May be used for individual works, collections, or materials about bible films.

UF   Biblical films
      Films, Bible
BT   **Motion pictures**
RT   **Bible plays**
Bible—Flowers
USE   **Bible—Natural history**
Bible—Gardens
USE   **Bible—Natural history**
Bible—Geography 220.9
UF   Bible—Maps
      Biblical geography
      Geography, Biblical
BT   **Atlases**
      Geography
Bible—Hermeneutics
USE   **Bible—Criticism, interpreta-**
      tion, etc.
Bible—History 220.9

Use for materials on the origin, authorship, and composition of the Bible as a book. Materials dealing with historical events as described in the Bible are entered under **Bible—History of biblical events.**

Bible—History of biblical events 220.9

Use for materials on historical events as described in the Bible. Materials on the origin, authorship, and composition of the Bible as a book are entered under **Bible—History.**

UF   History, Biblical
Bible—History of biblical events—
        Chronology
USE   **Bible—Chronology**
Bible—History of biblical events—
        Fiction
USE   **Bible fiction**

Bible—Illustrations
    USE **Bible—Pictorial works**
Bible in literature 809
    Use for materials that discuss the Bible
    as a theme in literature.
    BT **Literature**
    RT **Religion in literature**
Bible in the schools
    USE **Religion in the public schools**
Bible—Indexes
    USE **Bible—Concordances**
          Bible—Dictionaries
Bible—Inspiration 220.1
    Use for materials on the divine inspira-
    tion of the Bible. Materials that attempt
    to establish the truth of statements in the
    Bible or the authority of its precepts are
    entered under **Bible—Evidence, authority,**
    etc.
    UF Inspiration, Biblical
    NT **Bible—Evidences, authority,**
          etc.
Bible—Interpretation
    USE **Bible—Commentaries**
          Bible—Criticism, interpreta-
          tion, etc.
Bible—Introductions
    USE **Bible—Study and teaching**
Bible—Language, style, etc.
    USE **Bible as literature**
Bible—Literary character
    USE **Bible as literature**
Bible—Maps
    USE **Bible—Geography**
Bible—Miracles
    USE **Miracles**
Bible. N.T. 225
    Use same subdivisions as those given
    under **Bible.** They may also be used for
    groups of books, e.g. **Bible. N.T.**
    Gospels—Inspiration; and for single
    books, e.g. **Bible. N.T. Matthew—**
    Commentaries.
    UF New Testament
Bible. N.T.—Miracles
    USE **Miracles—Christianity**
Bible—Natural history 220.8
    UF Bible—Animals
          Bible—Birds
          Bible—Botany
          Bible—Flowers
          Bible—Gardens
          Bible—Plants

Bible—Zoology
    Botany of the Bible
    Natural history, Biblical
    Nature in the bible
    Zoology of the Bible
Bible. O.T. 221
    Use same subdivisions as those given
    under **Bible.** They may also be used for
    groups of books, e.g. **Bible. O.T.**
    Pentateuch—Commentaries; and for single
    books, e.g. **Bible. O.T. Psalms—History.**
    UF Old Testament
    NT **Ten commandments**
Bible—Parables 226.8
    BT **Bible as literature**
          Parables
    NT **Jesus Christ—Parables**
Bible—Pictorial works 220.022
    UF Bible—Illustrations
    RT **Christian art and symbolism**
          Jesus Christ—Art
Bible—Plants
    USE **Bible—Natural history**
Bible plays 808.82; 812, etc.
    May be used for individual plays, collec-
    tions, or materials about dramatizations of
    biblical events.
    UF Bible—Drama [Former head-
          ing]
          Biblical plays
          Plays, Bible
    SA names of biblical characters
          with the subdivision Dra-
          ma, to be added as needed
    BT **Religious drama**
    NT **Mysteries and miracle plays**
          Passion plays
    RT **Bible films**
Bible—Prophecies 220.1
    UF Prophecies (Bible)
    NT **Jesus Christ—Prophecies**
Bible—Psychology 220.8
    UF Psychology, Biblical
Bible—Question books
    USE **Bible—Catechisms, question**
          books
Bible—Reading 220.5
Bible—Science
    USE **Bible and science**

Bible stories 220.9

Use for materials that retell or adapt stories from the Bible or for materials about Bible stories. Fiction in which characters and settings are taken from the Bible is entered under **Bible fiction.**

UF   Stories

BT   **Bible**

RT   **Bible fiction**

Bible—Study

USE   **Bible—Study and teaching**

Bible—Study and teaching 220.07

UF   Bible classes

Bible—Introductions

Bible—Study *[Former heading]*

BT   **Christian education**

Sunday schools

NT   **Bible—Catechisms, question books**

Bible—Use 220.6

Use for materials that show how the Bible is used as a guide to living, to cultivation of a spiritual life, and to problems of doctrine.

Bible—Versions 220.4; 220.5

Use for materials on the various versions and translations of the Bible.

Bible—Women

USE   **Women in the Bible**

Bible—Zoology

USE   **Bible—Natural history**

Biblical archeology

USE   **Bible—Antiquities**

Biblical characters

USE   **Bible—Biography**

Biblical films

USE   **Bible films**

Biblical geography

USE   **Bible—Geography**

Biblical plays

USE   **Bible plays**

Bibliographic control 025.3

UF   Universal bibliographic control

BT   **Documentation**

NT   **Cataloging**

Indexing

Information systems

MARC formats

Bibliographic data in machine readable form

USE   **Machine readable bibliographic data**

Bibliographic instruction 025.5

Use for materials on the instruction of readers in library use. Materials on the education of librarians are entered under **Library education.**

UF   Library instruction *[Former heading]*

Library orientation

Library skills

Library user orientation

BT   **Library services**

Bibliography 010

SA   subjects and names of persons and places with the subdivision *Bibliography,* to be added as needed

BT   **Documentation**

NT   **Agriculture—Bibliography**

Archives

Bookbinding

Classification—Books

Indexes

Indexing

Information systems

Manuscripts

Printing

Reference books

Serial publications

Shakespeare, William, 1564-1616—Bibliography

United States—Bibliography

RT   **Books**

Cataloging

Library science

Bibliography—Best books

USE   **Books and reading—Best books**

Bibliography—Bilingual books

USE   **Bilingual books**

Bibliography—Editions 016

UF   Bibliography—Reprints

Editions

Reprints

NT   **Bibliography—First editions**

Bilingual books

Paperback books

Bibliography—Editions—*Continued*
    RT   **Rare books**
Bibliography—First editions 016
    UF   Books—First editions
          First editions
    BT   **Bibliography—Editions**
    RT   **Rare books**
Bibliography—Reprints
    USE **Bibliography—Editions**
Bibliomania
    USE **Book collecting**
Bibliophily
    USE **Book collecting**
Bicentennial celebrations—United
             States—1976
    USE **American Revolution Bicenten-**
           nial, 1776-1976
Biculturalism (May subdiv. geog.) **306.4**
    Use for materials on the presence of two distinct cultures within a single country or region. Materials on the preservation of various cultures or cultural identities within a unified society are entered under **Multiculturalism**
    UF   Pluralism (Social sciences)
    BT   **Civilization**
          Culture
    RT   **Multiculturalism**
Biculturalism—United States 306.4
    UF   United States—Biculturalism
Bicycle camping
    USE **Bicycle touring**
Bicycle racing 796.6
    BT   **Cycling**
          Racing
    RT   **Bicycle touring**
          Bicycles
Bicycle touring (May subdiv. geog.)
          796.6
    UF   Backpack cycling
          Bicycle camping
          Touring, Bicycle
    BT   **Camping**
          Cycling
          Travel
    RT   **Bicycle racing**
          Bicycles
Bicycles 629.227
    UF   Bicycles and bicycling *[Former heading]*
          Bikes

    BT   **Vehicles**
    NT   **Minibikes**
          Motorcycles
          Mountain bikes
    RT   **Bicycle racing**
          Bicycle touring
          Cycling
Bicycles and bicycling
    USE **Bicycles**
          Cycling
Bicycling
    USE **Cycling**
Bicylces, All terrain
    USE **Mountain bikes**
Big band music
    USE **Dance music**
Big bang theory
    USE **Universe**
Big books 372.4
    Use as a form heading for books produced in an oversize format and intended for use in shared-reading learning experiences. May also be used for materials about big books.
    UF   Enlarged texts for shared reading
          Oversize books
          Oversized books for shared reading
          Shared reading books
    BT   **Children's literature**
          Reading materials
    RT   **Large print books**
Big foot
    USE **Sasquatch**
Bigfoot
    USE **Sasquatch**
Bigotry
    USE **Prejudices**
          Toleration
Bigotry-motivated crimes
    USE **Hate crimes**
Bikes
    USE **Bicycles**
Bikes, Mountain
    USE **Mountain bikes**
Biking
    USE **Cycling**
Bildungsromans
    May be used for individual works, collections, or materials about fiction in which the theme is the development of a character from youth to adulthood.

    BT = Broader Term   NT = Narrower Term   RT = Related Term   SA = See Also   UF = Used For

Bildungsromans—*Continued*
- UF   Apprenticeship novels
         Coming of age stories
- BT   **Fiction**

Bilingual books 002; 011

Use for materials about bilingual books. As a form heading for the bilingual materials themselves, use this heading subdivided by the languages, e.g. **Bilingual books—English-Spanish.**

- UF   Bibliography—Bilingual books
         Books—Bilingual editions
- BT   **Bibliography—Editions**
         Books

Bilingual books—English-Spanish

Use as a form heading for bilingual materials in English and Spanish.

- UF   Bilingual books—
         Spanish-English

Bilingual books—Spanish-English
- USE   **Bilingual books—**
          English-Spanish

Bilingual education 370.19; 371.97
- UF   Education, Bilingual *[Former heading]*
- BT   **Bilingualism**
         Multicultural education

Bilingualism (May subdiv. geog.) 306.4; 400
- BT   **Language and languages**
- NT   **Bilingual education**

Bilingualism—United States 306.4; 420
- UF   United States—Bilingualism

Billboards
- USE   **Signs and signboards**

Bills and notes
- USE   **Negotiable instruments**

Bills of credit
- USE   **Credit**
          Negotiable instruments
          Paper money

Bills of fare
- USE   **Menus**

Bimetallism
- USE   **Gold**
          Monetary policy
          Silver

Binary system (Mathematics) 513.5
- UF   Pair system
- BT   **Mathematics**
         Numbers

Binding of books
- USE   **Bookbinding**

Binge eating behavior
- USE   **Bulimia**

Binge-purge behavior
- USE   **Bulimia**

Bio-bibliography
- USE   subjects, ethnic groups, names of countries, cities, etc., and names of individual persons with the subdivision *Bio-bibliography,* e.g. **English literature—Bio-bibliography; United States—Bio-bibliography;** etc., to be added as needed

Bioastronautics
- USE   **Space biology**
          Space medicine

Biochemistry 574.19
- UF   Biological chemistry
         Chemistry, Biological
         Chemistry, Physiological
         Physiological chemistry *[Former heading]*
- BT   **Biology**
         Chemistry
         Medicine
- NT   **Clinical chemistry**
         Metabolism
         Molecular biology
         Nucleic acids
         Proteins
         Steroids

Bioconversion
- USE   **Biomass energy**

Biodiversity
- USE   **Biological diversity**

Bioengineering
- USE   **Agricultural engineering**

Bioethics 174
- UF   Biological ethics
         Biology—Ethics
         Biomedical ethics
         Ethics, Biological
         Life sciences ethics
- BT   **Social ethics**
- NT   **Medical ethics**

BT = Broader Term   NT = Narrower Term   RT = Related Term   SA = See Also   UF = Used For

Bioethics—*Continued*
> Transplantation of organs, tissues, etc.—Moral and religious aspects

Biofeedback training 152.1
- UF Visceral learning
- BT Feedback (Psychology)
  Mind and body
  Psychology of learning
  Psychotherapy

Biogeography 574.9
> Use for materials on the geographical distribution of animals and plants collectively or of animals only. Materials on the geographical distribution of plants are entered under **Plants—Geographical distribution.**

- UF Animals—Geographical distribution
  Distribution of animals and plants
  Geographical distribution of animals and plants
  Paleobiogeography
  Zoogeography
- SA types of plants and animals with the subdivision *Geographical distribution,* to be added as needed
- BT Ecology
  Geography
  Natural history
- NT Fishes—Geographical distribution
  Plants—Geographical distribution

Biographical dictionaries
- USE **Biography—Dictionaries**

Biographical fiction 808.83; 813, etc.
> May be used for individual works, collections, or materials about fictionalized accounts of the lives of real persons.

- UF Biographical novels
- SA names of real persons with the subdivision *Fiction,* to be added as needed
- NT **Autobiographical fiction**
  Napoleon I, Emperor of the French, 1769-1821—Fiction
- RT **Historical fiction**

Biographical films 791.43
> May be used for individual works, collections, or materials about films depicting the lives of real persons.

- BT **Motion pictures**

Biographical novels
- USE **Biographical fiction**

Biographical radio programs 791.44
> May be used for individual works, collections, or materials about radio programs recounting the lives of real persons.

- BT **Radio programs**

Biographical television programs 791.45
> May be used for individual works, collections, or materials about television programs depicting the lives of real persons.

- BT **Television programs**

Biography 920
> Use for collections of biographies not limited to one country or to one group or class of persons. Materials on the writing of biography are entered under **Biography as a literary form.**

- UF Life histories
  Memoirs
  Personal narratives
- SA subjects and names of places with the subdivision *Biography;* ethnic groups, classes of persons, and individual literary authors with the subdivision *Biography* or *Correspondence;* and names of diseases, events, and wars with the subdivision *Personal narratives,* to be added as needed
- BT **History**
- NT **Autobiographies**
  Autographs
  Celebrities
  Chicago (Ill.)—Biography
  Epitaphs
  Medicine—Biography
  Men—Biography
  Musicians—Biography
  Obituaries
  Portraits
  Religions—Biography
  Shakespeare, William, 1564-1616—Biography
  Shakespeare, William, 1564-1616—Psychology

BT = Broader Term   NT = Narrower Term   RT = Related Term   SA = See Also   UF = Used For

Biography—*Continued*
>> United States—Biography
>> United States—History—
>>> 1861-1865, Civil War—
>>> Personal narratives
>> Women—Biography
>> World War, 1939-1945—
>>> Personal narratives

RT **Genealogy**

Biography (as a literary form)
> USE **Biography as a literary form**

Biography as a literary form 809
> Use for materials on the writing of biography.

UF Biography (as a literary form)
> *[Former heading]*
> Biography—History and criticism
> Biography—Technique

BT **Authorship**
> **Literature**

NT **Autobiography**

Biography—Dictionaries 920.02
> Use for collections of biographies in dictionary form not limited to one group or class of persons.

UF Biographical dictionaries
> Dictionaries, Biographical

SA subjects, ethnic groups, classes
> of persons, and names of
> countries, cities, etc. with
> the subdivision
> *Biography—Dictionaries,* to
> be added as needed

BT **Encyclopedias and dictionaries**

NT **United States—Biography—**
> **Dictionaries**

Biography—History and criticism
> USE **Biography as a literary form**

Biography—Technique
> USE **Biography as a literary form**

Biological anthropology
> USE **Physical anthropology**

Biological chemistry
> USE **Biochemistry**

Biological clocks
> USE **Biological rhythms**

Biological diversification
> USE **Biological diversity**

Biological diversity
> Use for materials on the variety and variability among living organisms and the ecological complexes in which they occur, including ecosystem diversity, species diversity, and genetic diversity.

UF Biodiversity
> Biological diversification
> Diversity, Biological

BT **Biology**

RT **Ecology**

Biological ethics
> USE **Bioethics**

Biological oceanography
> USE **Marine biology**
> **Marine ecology**

Biological parents
> USE **Birthparents**

Biological physics
> USE **Biophysics**

Biological rhythms 574.1
> UF Biological clocks
> Biology—Periodicity
> Biorhythms

BT **Periodicity**

NT **Jet lag**

Biological warfare 358; 623.4
> UF Bacterial warfare
> Germ warfare

BT **Military art and science**
> **Tactics**

Biologists 574.092; 920
> BT **Naturalists**
> **Scientists**

Biology 574
> UF Morphology

BT **Life sciences**
> **Science**

NT **Adaptation (Biology)**
> **Anatomy**
> **Biochemistry**
> **Biological diversity**
> **Biomathematics**
> **Biophysics**
> **Botany**
> **Cells**
> **Cryobiology**
> **Death**
> **Ecology**
> **Embryology**
> **Freshwater biology**

Biology—*Continued*
>Gaia hypothesis
>Genetics
>Heredity
>Marine biology
>Microbiology
>Physiology
>Protoplasm
>Radiobiology
>Reproduction
>Sex (Biology)
>Space biology
>Symbiosis
>Variation (Biology)
>Zoology

  RT Evolution
>Life (Biology)
>Natural history

Biology—Ecology
  USE **Ecology**

Biology, Economic
  USE **Economic botany**
>**Economic zoology**

Biology—Ethics
  USE **Bioethics**

Biology, Marine
  USE **Marine biology**

Biology, Molecular
  USE **Molecular biology**

Biology—Periodicity
  USE **Biological rhythms**

Biology—Social aspects
  USE **Sociobiology**

Bioluminescence 574.19
  UF Animal light
>Animal luminescence
>Light production in animals
>Luminescence, Animal

  BT **Phosphorescence**

Biomass energy 333.95
> Use for materials on organic matter that can be converted to fuel and is therefore regarded as a potential energy source.

  UF Bioconversion
>Energy, Biomass
>Energy conversion, Microbial
>Microbial energy conversion

  SA types of matter as fuels, e.g.
>**Waste products as fuel;** to be added as needed

  BT **Energy resources**
>**Fuel**

  RT **Waste products as fuel**

Biomass energy industries 338.2; 338.4
  BT **Energy resources**

Biomathematics 574.01
  BT **Biology**
>**Mathematics**

Biomechanics
  USE **Human engineering**
>**Human locomotion**

Biomedical ethics
  USE **Bioethics**

Bionics 003
> Use for materials on the science of technological systems that function in the manner of living systems.

  BT **Biophysics**
>**Cybernetics**
>**Systems engineering**

  NT **Artificial intelligence**
>**Optical data processing**

Biophysics 574.19
  UF Biological physics
>Molecular physiology
>Physics, Biological
>Physiology, Molecular

  BT **Biology**
>**Physics**

  NT **Bionics**
>**Molecular biology**
>**Radiobiology**

Biorhythms
  USE **Biological rhythms**

Biosciences
  USE **Life sciences**

Biosociology
  USE **Sociobiology**

Biotechnology 620.8; 660
> Use for materials on the application of living organisms or their biological systems or processes to the manufacture of products.

  BT **Chemical engineering**
>**Microbiology**

  RT **Genetic engineering**

Bird
  USE **Birds**

Bird decoys (Hunting)
  USE **Decoys (Hunting)**

BT = Broader Term   NT = Narrower Term   RT = Related Term   SA = See Also   UF = Used For

Bird houses 690

Bird photography
  USE **Photography of birds**

Bird repelling devices
  USE **Scarecrows**

Bird song
  USE **Birdsongs**

Bird watching 598.07
  BT **Nature study**

Birdbanding 598.07
  UF Birds—Banding
      Birds—Marking
  BT **Wildlife conservation**

Birds (May subdiv. geog.) 598
  UF Bird
      Ornithology
  SA classes of birds, e.g. **Birds of prey**; and names of specific birds, e.g. **Canaries**; to be added as needed
  BT **Vertebrates**
      Zoology
  NT **Birds of prey**
      Cage birds
      Canaries
      Game and game birds
      Peacocks
      Robins
      State birds
      Water birds

Birds—Anatomy 598
  BT **Anatomy**

Birds, Aquatic
  USE **Water birds**

Birds—Banding
  USE **Birdbanding**

Birds—Behavior 598.251
  UF Birds—Habits and behavior
      [Former heading]

Birds—Collection and preservation 579
  BT **Collectors and collecting**
      Taxidermy
      Zoological specimens— Collection and preservation

Birds—Color 598.257
  BT **Color**

Birds' eggs
  USE **Birds—Eggs and nests**

Birds—Eggs and nests 598.256
  UF Birds' eggs
      Birds' nests
      Nests
  BT **Eggs**

Birds—Flight 598
  BT **Animal flight**

Birds—Habits and behavior
  USE **Birds—Behavior**

Birds in literature 809
  BT **Animals in literature**
      Nature in literature

Birds—Marking
  USE **Birdbanding**

Birds—Migration 598.252
  UF Migration of birds
  BT **Animals—Migration**

Birds' nests
  USE **Birds—Eggs and nests**

Birds of prey 598.9
  SA names of specific birds of prey, to be added as needed
  BT **Birds**
  NT **Eagles**

Birds—Photography
  USE **Photography of birds**

Birds—Protection 333.95; 639.9
  UF Protection of birds
  BT **Wildlife conservation**
  RT **Game protection**

Birds—Song
  USE **Birdsongs**

Birds—United States 598.2973
  UF United States—Birds

Birdsongs 598.259
  UF Bird song *[Former heading]*
      Birds—Song
  BT **Animal sounds**

Birth
  USE **Childbirth**

Birth attendants
  USE **Midwives**

Birth control 176; 350.81; 363.9; 613.9
  UF Conception—Prevention
      Contraception
      Family planning
      Fertility control
      Planned parenthood
  BT **Eugenics**
      Population
      Sexual hygiene

Birth control—*Continued*
NT **Abortion**
    Sexual abstinence
    Sterilization (Birth control)
RT **Birthrate**
    Childlessness
    Family size
    Human fertility
    Infertility
    Sexual ethics
Birth control—Moral and religious aspects 176; 241; 261.8
BT **Ethics**
Birth defects 616
UF Abnormalities, Human
    Birth injuries
    Deformities
    Human abnormalities
    Infants—Birth defects
    Malformations, Congenital
BT **Medical genetics**
    Pathology
RT **Growth disorders**
Birth injuries
USE **Birth defects**
Birth, Multiple
USE **Multiple birth**
Birth order 306.87
UF Firstborn child
    Middle child
    Oldest child
    Sibling sequence
    Youngest child
BT **Children**
    Family
Birth rate
USE **Birthrate**
Birth records
USE **Registers of births, etc.**
Birthdays 394.2
UF Anniversaries
BT **Days**
Birthparents 306.874
   Use for materials on natural, i.e. biological, parents who relinquished their children for adoption.
UF Biological parents
    Natural parents
    Parents, Biological
BT **Parent and child**

RT **Adoptees**
Birthrate 304.6
UF Birth rate
NT **Human fertility**
RT **Birth control**
    Population
Births, Registers of
USE **Registers of births, etc.**
Bison 599.73; 636.2
UF American bison
    Buffalo, American
BT **Mammals**
Black actors 791.4; 792; 920
UF Actors, Black
    Black actors and actresses
    [Former heading]
BT **Actors**
NT **African American actors**
Black actors and actresses
USE **Black actors**
Black Africa
USE **Sub-Saharan Africa**
Black Americans
USE **African Americans**
Black art 704
   Use for materials on works of art by several Black artists. Materials on Blacks depicted in works of art are entered under **Blacks in art.**
UF Art, Black
    Blacks—Art
BT **Art**
NT **African American art**
RT **Black artists**
Black art (Magic)
USE **Magic**
    Witchcraft
Black artists 709.2; 920
   Use for materials on several Black artists.
UF Artists, Black
BT **Artists**
NT **African American artists**
RT **Black art**
Black athletes 796.092; 920
UF Athletes, Black
BT **Athletes**
NT **African American athletes**
Black authors 809; 920
   Use for collections and for materials on several Black authors not limited to a single national literature or literary form.

Black authors—*Continued*

    UF   Authors, Black

    SA   individual literatures other than American literature and forms of literature with the subdivision *Black authors,* e.g. **French literature—Black authors; French poetry—Black authors;** etc., to be added as needed

    BT   **Authors**

    NT   **African American authors**

Black business people 338.092; 658.0092; 920

    UF   Business people, Black

    BT   **Blacks—Employment**
          Business people

    NT   **African American business people**

Black children 305.23

    UF   Blacks—Children
          Children, Black

    BT   **Children**

    NT   **African American children**

Black comedy (Literature)
    USE **Black humor (Literature)**

Black death
    USE **Plague**

Black folk songs
    USE **Black music**

Black folklore
    USE **Blacks—Folklore**

Black Friars
    USE **Dominicans (Religious order)**

Black Hawk War, 1832 973.5

    BT   **Indians of North America— Wars**
          United States—History— 1815-1861

Black holes (Astronomy) 523.8

    UF   Frozen stars

    BT   **Astronomy**
          Astrophysics
          Stars

Black humor (Literature) 808.7; 808.87; 813, etc.

    May be used for individual works, collections, or materials about literary works characterized by a desperate, sardonic humor intended to induce laughter as the appropriate response to the apparent meaninglessness and absurdity of existence.

    UF   Black comedy (Literature)
          Dark humor (Literature)

    BT   **Fiction**
          Literature
          Wit and humor

Black lead
    USE **Graphite**

Black librarians 020.92; 920

    UF   Librarians, Black

    BT   **Librarians**

    NT   **African American librarians**

Black literature (American)
    USE **American literature—African American authors**

Black literature (French)
    USE **French literature—Black authors**

Black magic (Witchcraft)
    USE **Magic**
          Witchcraft

Black market children
    USE **Adoption—Corrupt practices**

Black music (May subdiv. geog.) 780.089

    Use for general materials and for materials on the music of Blacks not in the United States. Materials on the music of African Americans are entered under **African American music.**

    UF   Black folk songs
          Black songs
          Blacks—Music
          Blacks—Songs and music
          [Former heading]
          Music, Black

    BT   **Music**

    NT   **African American music**

    RT   **Black musicians**

Black musicians 780.92; 920

    UF   Musicians, Black

    BT   **Musicians**

    NT   **African American musicians**

    RT   **Black music**

Black Muslims 297

    UF   Muslims, Black

Black Muslims—*Continued*
     Nation of Islam
  BT   **African Americans—Religion**
     Black nationalism
     Blacks—Religion
     Muslims—United States
Black nationalism 320.5
  UF   Black separatism
     Nationalism, Black
     Separatism, Black
  BT   **African Americans—Political
     activity**
     **African Americans—Race
     identity**
     Blacks—Political activity
     Blacks—Race identity
  NT   **Black Muslims**
Black poetry (American)
  USE **American poetry—African
     American authors**
Black poetry (French)
  USE **French poetry—Black authors**
Black power 322.4
  BT   **African Americans—Civil
     rights**
     **African Americans—Economic
     conditions**
     **African Americans—Political
     activity**
     Blacks—Civil rights
     Blacks—Economic conditions
     Blacks—Political activity
Black separatism
  USE **Black nationalism**
Black songs
  USE **Black music**
Black suffrage
  USE **Blacks—Suffrage**
Black women 305.48
  UF   Women, Black
  BT   **Women**
  NT   **African American women**
Blackboard drawing
  USE **Chalk talks**
     Crayon drawing
Blackheads (Acne)
  USE **Acne**
Blackouts, Electric power
  USE **Electric power failures**
Blackouts in war
  USE **Civil defense**

Blacks (May subdiv. geog. by regions,
     countries, etc. other than
     the U.S.) **305.896**
  Use for general materials and for mate-
  rials dealing collectively with Blacks in
  geographic areas other than the United
  States. Materials on Blacks in the United
  States are entered under **African Ameri-
  cans.**
  UF   Negroes
  SA   Blacks in various occupations
     and professions, e.g. **Black
     artists; Black librarians;**
     etc., to be added as needed
  NT   **African Americans**
Blacks—Africa 305.896; 960
  BT   **Africans**
Blacks—Art
  USE **Black art**
Blacks—Biography 920
  NT   **African Americans—Biography**
Blacks—Children
  USE **Black children**
Blacks—Civil rights 323.1; 342
  UF   Demonstrations for Black civ-
     il rights
     Freedom marches
     Marches for Black civil rights
  BT   **Blacks—Political activity**
     Civil rights
  NT   **African Americans—Civil
     rights**
     Black power
Blacks—Economic conditions 330.9
  BT   **Economic conditions**
  NT   **African Americans—Economic
     conditions**
     Black power
Blacks—Education 370.19
  BT   **Education**
  NT   **African Americans—Education**
     School integration
     Segregation in education
Blacks—Employment 331.6
  UF   Blacks—Occupations
  BT   **Discrimination in employment**
     Employment
  NT   **African Americans—
     Employment**
     Black business people
Blacks—Folklore 398
  UF   Black folklore

Blacks—Folklore—*Continued*

Folklore, Black

BT   Folklore

NT   African Americans—Folklore

Blacks—France 305.896; 944

UF   France—Blacks

Blacks—Housing 307.3; 363.5

UF   Housing, Black

BT   Housing

NT   African Americans—Housing

Blacks in art 704.9

Use for materials on Blacks depicted in works of art. Materials on African Americans depicted in works of art are entered under **African Americans in art.** Materials on the attainments of several Blacks in the area of art are entered under **Black artists.** Materials on the attainments of several African Americans in the area of art are entered under **African American artists.** Materials on works of art by several Black artists are entered under **Black art.** Materials on works of art by several African American artists are entered under **African American art.**

BT   Art

NT   African Americans in art

Blacks in literature 809

Use for materials on the theme of Blacks in works of literature. Materials on the attainments of several Blacks in the area of literature are entered under **Black authors.** Materials on works of literature by several Black authors are entered under individual literatures and forms of literature with the subdivision *Black authors,* e.g. **French literature—Black authors; French poetry—Black authors;** etc. Materials on the theme of African Americans in works of literature are entered under **African Americans in literature.** Materials on the attainments of several African Americans in the area of literature are entered under **African American authors.** Materials on works of literature by several African American authors are entered under **American literature—African American authors** and the various forms of American literature with the subdivision *African American authors,* e.g. **American poetry—African American authors.**

BT   Characters and characteristics
       in literature

NT   African Americans in litera-
       ture

Blacks in motion pictures 791.43

Use for materials on the depiction of Blacks in motion pictures. Materials on several Black actors are entered under **Black actors.** Materials discussing all aspects of Blacks' involvement in motion pictures are entered under **Blacks in the motion picture industry.**

BT   Motion pictures

NT   African Americans in motion
       pictures

Blacks in the motion picture industry
       791.43092

Use for materials on all aspects of Blacks' involvement in motion pictures. Materials on the depiction of Blacks in motion pictures are entered under **Blacks in motion pictures.**

BT   Motion picture industry

NT   African Americans in the mo-
       tion picture industry

Blacks—Integration 305.896

UF   Integration, Racial

NT   African Americans—
       Integration

       School integration

Blacks—Intellectual life 305.896

BT   Intellectual life

NT   African Americans—
       Intellectual life

Blacks—Music

USE   Black music

Blacks—Occupations

USE   Blacks—Employment

Blacks—Political activity 322.4; 324

NT   African Americans—Political
       activity

       Black nationalism

       Black power

       Blacks—Civil rights

Blacks—Race identity 305.896

UF   Negritude

BT   Race awareness

NT   African Americans—Race
       identity

       Black nationalism

Blacks—Religion 270.089; 299; 305.896

BT   Religion

NT   African Americans—Religion

       Black Muslims

Blacks—Segregation 305.896

BT   Segregation

NT   African Americans—
       Segregation

Blacks—Segregation—*Continued*
    Segregation in education
Blacks—Social conditions 305.896
  BT **Social conditions**
  NT **African Americans—Social**
      conditions
Blacks—Social life and customs
    305.896
  NT **African Americans—Social life**
      and customs
Blacks—Songs and music
  USE **Black music**
Blacks—Suffrage 324.6
  UF Black suffrage
  BT **Suffrage**
  NT **African Americans—Suffrage**
Blacks—United States
  USE **African Americans**
Blacksmithing 682
  UF Farriering
      Horseshoeing
  BT **Ironwork**
  NT **Welding**
  RT **Forging**
Blast furnaces 669
  BT **Furnaces**
      Smelting
Blast shelters
  USE **Air raid shelters**
Bleaching 667
  BT **Cleaning**
      Industrial chemistry
      Textile industry
  RT **Dyes and dyeing**
Blended family
  USE **Stepfamily**
Blessed Virgin Mary
  USE **Mary, Blessed Virgin, Saint**
Blimps
  USE **Airships**
Blind 362.4
  BT **Physically handicapped**
      Vision disorders
Blind—Books and reading 011.63;
    027.6; 028
  UF Books for the blind
      Braille books
  NT **Large print books**
      Talking books
Blind, Dogs for the
  USE **Guide dogs**

Blind—Education 371.91
  UF Education of the blind
  BT **Education**
Blind—Institutional care 362.4
  BT **Institutional care**
Blizzards 551.55
  BT **Storms**
  RT **Snow**
Block grants
  USE **Grants-in-aid**
Block printing
  USE **Color prints**
      Linoleum block printing
      Textile printing
      Wood engraving
      Woodcuts
Block signal systems
  USE **Railroads—Signaling**
Blood 591.1; 612.1
  BT **Physiology**
  NT **Blood groups**
      Blood pressure
Blood—Circulation 591.1; 612.1
  UF Circulation of the blood
  RT **Blood pressure**
      Cardiovascular system
Blood—Diseases 616.1
  UF Diseases of the blood
  SA names of blood diseases, e.g.
      Leukemia; to be added as
      needed
  NT **Leukemia**
Blood groups 612.1
  UF Rh factor
  BT **Blood**
  RT **Blood—Transfusion**
Blood pressure 612.1
  BT **Blood**
  NT **Hypertension**
  RT **Blood—Circulation**
Blood—Transfusion 615
  RT **Blood groups**
Blowing the whistle
  USE **Whistle blowing**
Blowouts, Oil well
  USE **Oil wells—Blowouts**
Blue collar workers
  USE **Labor**
      Working class
Blue prints
  USE **Blueprints**

BT = Broader Term   NT = Narrower Term   RT = Related Term   SA = See Also   UF = Used For

Blueprints 604.2; 692
UF Blue prints
BT Mechanical drawing
Blues music 781.643; 782.42164
UF Blues songs
BT African American music
Folk music—United States
Popular music
RT Jazz music
Blues songs
USE Blues music
BMEWS
USE Ballistic missile early warning
system
Board sailing
USE Windsurfing
Boarding houses
USE Hotels and motels
Boarding schools
USE Private schools
Boards of education
USE School boards
Boards of health
USE Health boards
Boards of trade
USE Chambers of commerce
Boat building
USE Boatbuilding
Boat racing 797.1
SA types of boat racing and
names of specific races, to
be added as needed
BT Boats and boating
Racing
Boatbuilding 623.8
UF Boat building
BT Boats and boating
Naval architecture
NT Yachts and yachting
RT Shipbuilding
Boating
USE Boats and boating
Boats and boating 797.1
UF Boating
BT Transportation
Water sports
NT Boat racing
Boatbuilding
Canoes and canoeing
Catamarans

Houseboats
Hydrofoil boats
Iceboats
Marinas
Motorboats
Rowing
Steamboats
Tugboats
Yachts and yachting
RT Sailing
Ships
Boats, Submarine
USE Submarines
Submersibles
Body and mind
USE Mind and body
Body building
USE Bodybuilding
Body care
USE Hygiene
Body heat
USE Body temperature
Body, Human
USE Human anatomy
Physiology
Body language 153.6; 302.2
BT Nonverbal communication
Body temperature 591.1; 612
UF Animals—Temperature
Body heat
Temperature, Animal and hu-
man
Temperature, Body
BT Diagnosis
Physiology
RT Fever
Body weight control
USE Reducing
Bodybuilding 646.7
UF Body building
Physique
BT Exercise
Physical fitness
RT Weight lifting
Boers
USE Afrikaners
Bogs
USE Marshes
Wetlands
Bohemianism 306
UF Beat generation

Bohemianism—*Continued*
    Beatniks
  BT **Counter culture**
      Manners and customs
  NT **Hippies**
Bolshevism
  USE **Communism**
Bomb shelters
  USE **Air raid shelters**
Bombers 358.4; 623.7
  SA types of bombers, e.g. **B-52 bomber;** to be added as needed
  BT **Airplanes**
      Military airplanes
  NT **B-52 bomber**
Bombs 355.8; 623.4
  Use for materials on bombs in general and those to be launched from aircraft.
  UF Aerial bombs
  SA types of bombs, e.g. **Atomic bomb;** to be added as needed
  BT **Ammunition**
      Explosives
      Ordnance
      Projectiles
  NT **Atomic bomb**
      Guided missiles
      Hydrogen bomb
      Incendiary bombs
      Neutron bomb
Bombs, Flying
  USE **Guided missiles**
Bombs, Incendiary
  USE **Incendiary bombs**
Bonds 332.63
  BT **Finance**
      Investments
      Negotiable instruments
      Securities
      Stock exchange
  NT **Junk bonds**
  RT **Public debts**
      Stocks
Bonds—Rating 332.63
  BT **Performance standards**
Bones 596; 611; 612.7
  UF Osteology
  BT **Musculoskeletal system**

  NT **Fractures**
  RT **Skeleton**
Bonsai 635.9
  UF Kamuti
  BT **Dwarf trees**
Book awards
  USE **Literary prizes**
      and names of awards, e.g. **Caldecott Medal; Newbery Medal;** etc., to be added as needed
Book buying (Libraries)
  USE **Libraries—Acquisitions**
Book catalogs 017; 025.3
  Use for materials on library catalogs in book form. Retail book catalogs and book auction catalogs and materials about such catalogs are entered under **Booksellers' catalogs.** Publishers' book catalogs and materials about such catalogs are entered under **Publishers' catalogs.**
  UF Books—Catalogs
      Catalogs, Book *[Former heading]*
      Catalogs in book form
  BT **Library catalogs**
Book collecting 002.075
  UF Bibliomania
      Bibliophily
  BT **Book selection**
      Collectors and collecting
  RT **Bookplates**
      Books
Book fairs
  USE **Book industries—Exhibitions**
Book illustration
  USE **Illustration of books**
Book industries 686
  UF Book industries and trade *[Former heading]*
      Book trade
  NT **Best sellers (Books)**
      Bookbinding
      Booksellers and bookselling
      Printing
  RT **Paper industry**
      Publishers and publishing
Book industries and trade
  USE **Book industries**
Book industries—Exhibitions 070.5074; 686.074
  UF Book fairs

BT = Broader Term   NT = Narrower Term   RT = Related Term   SA = See Also   UF = Used For

Book industries—Exhibitions—
  Continued
        Book trade—Exhibitions
        Books—Exhibitions
    RT **Printing—Exhibitions**
Book lending
    USE **Library circulation**
Book numbers, Publishers' standard
    USE **Publishers' standard book
        numbers**
Book plates
    USE **Bookplates**
Book prices
    USE **Books—Prices**
Book prizes
    USE **Literary prizes**
        and names of prizes, e.g.
        **Caldecott Medal; Newbery
        Medal;** etc., to be added as
        needed
Book rarities
    USE **Rare books**
Book reviews
    USE **Books—Reviews**
Book sales
    USE **Books—Prices**
Book selection 025.2
    Use for materials on the principles of
book appraisal and how to select books
for libraries. Lists of recommended books
are entered under **Books and reading—
Best books.**
    UF Appraisal of books
        Books—Appraisal
        Books—Selection
        Choice of books
    BT **Libraries—Acquisitions**
        **Libraries—Collection develop-
        ment**
    NT **Book collecting**
    RT **Books and reading—Best
        books**
Book trade
    USE **Book industries**
        Booksellers and bookselling
        Publishers and publishing
Book trade—Exhibitions
    USE **Book industries—Exhibitions**
Book Week, National
    USE **National Book Week**
Bookbinding 025.7; 095; 686.3
    UF Binding of books

    BT **Bibliography**
        Book industries
        Industrial arts
        Leather industry
Bookkeepers
    USE **Accountants**
Bookkeeping 657
    SA types of industries, profes-
        sions, and organizations,
        with the subdivision *Ac-
        counting,* to be added as
        needed
    BT **Business**
        Business education
        Business mathematics
    NT **Auditing**
        Corporations—Accounting
        Cost accounting
        Office equipment and supplies
    RT **Accounting**
Bookmobiles 027.4
    BT **Library extension**
Bookplates 025.7; 769.5
    UF Book plates
        Ex libris
    BT **Prints**
    RT **Book collecting**
Books 002
    NT **Authors**
        Bilingual books
        Cataloging
        Chapbooks
        **Illumination of books and
        manuscripts**
        Illustration of books
        Libraries
        Manuscripts
        Paperback books
        Rare books
        Reference books
        Textbooks
    RT **Bibliography**
        Book collecting
        Literature
        Printing
        Publishers and publishing
Books and reading 028
    Use for general materials on reading for
information and culture, advice to readers,
and surveys of reading habits.

BT = Broader Term   NT = Narrower Term   RT = Related Term   SA = See Also   UF = Used For

Books and reading—*Continued*
UF　Appraisal of books
　　　Books—Appraisal
　　　Choice of books
　　　Evaluation of literature
　　　Literature—Evaluation
　　　Reading interests
SA　names of individuals and
　　　classes of persons with the
　　　subdivision *Books and
　　　reading,* e.g. **Blind—Books
　　　and reading;** to be added as
　　　needed
BT　**Communication**
　　　Education
　　　Reading
NT　**Best sellers (Books)**
　　　Books—Reviews
　　　Libraries
　　　National Book Week
　　　Reference books
RT　**Literature**
　　　Reading materials
Books and reading—Best books 011
　　Use for lists of recommended books.
UF　Appraisal of books
　　　Best books
　　　Bibliography—Best books
　　　Books—Appraisal
　　　Choice of books
　　　Evaluation of literature
　　　Literature—Evaluation
BT　**Reference books**
RT　**Book selection**
Books and reading for children
USE　**Children—Books and reading**
Books—Appraisal
USE　**Book selection**
　　　Books and reading
　　　**Books and reading—Best
　　　books**
　　　Books—Reviews
　　　Criticism
　　　**Literature—History and criti-
　　　cism**
Books—Best sellers
USE　**Best sellers (Books)**
Books—Bilingual editions
USE　**Bilingual books**
Books—Catalogs
USE　**Book catalogs**

　　　Booksellers' catalogs
　　　Publishers' catalogs
Books—Censorship 025.2; 323.44
UF　Banned books
　　　Index librorum prohibitorum
　　　Prohibited books
BT　**Censorship**
　　　Freedom of the press
Books—Copyright
USE　**Copyright—Books**
Books—Exhibitions
USE　**Book industries—Exhibitions**
　　　Printing—Exhibitions
Books, Filmed
USE　**Film adaptations**
Books—First editions
USE　**Bibliography—First editions**
Books for children
USE　**Children's literature**
Books for sight saving
USE　**Large print books**
Books for the blind
USE　**Blind—Books and reading**
Books—Large print
USE　**Large print books**
Books, Paperback
USE　**Paperback books**
Books—Preservation
USE　**Library resources—
　　　Conservation and restoration**
Books—Prices 002.075
UF　Book prices
　　　Book sales
　　　Manuscripts—Prices
BT　**Booksellers and bookselling**
　　　Prices
Books, Rare
USE　**Rare books**
Books—Reviews 028.1; 808
UF　Appraisal of books
　　　Book reviews
　　　Books—Appraisal
　　　Evaluation of literature
　　　Literature—Evaluation
BT　**Books and reading**
　　　Criticism
Books, Sacred
USE　**Sacred books**
Books—Selection
USE　**Book selection**

Books, Talking
  USE **Talking books**
Booksellers and bookselling 070.5; 381; 658.8
  UF Book trade
  BT **Book industries**
      Sales personnel
      Selling
  NT **Books—Prices**
      Booksellers' catalogs
  RT **Publishers and publishing**
Booksellers' catalogs 017
  Use for retail book catalogs and book auction catalogs and materials about such catalogs. Materials on library catalogs in book form are entered under **Book catalogs.** Publishers' book catalogs and materials about such catalogs are entered under **Publishers' catalogs.**
  UF Books—Catalogs
      Catalogs
      Catalogs, Booksellers' *[Former heading]*
  BT **Booksellers and bookselling**
Boolean algebra 511.3
  UF Algebra, Boolean *[Former heading]*
  BT **Group theory**
      Set theory
      Symbolic logic
Boots
  USE **Shoes**
Border life
  USE **Frontier and pioneer life**
Borders (Geography)
  USE **Boundaries**
Boring 622
  Use for materials on the operation of cutting holes in earth or rock. Materials on workshop operations in metal, wood, etc., are entered under **Drilling and boring.**
  UF Drilling and boring (Earth and rocks)
      Shaft sinking
      Well boring
  BT **Hydraulic engineering**
      Mining engineering
      Tunnels
      Water supply engineering
  RT **Wells**
Boring (Metal, wood, etc.)
  USE **Drilling and boring**

Born again Christianity
  USE **Regeneration (Christianity)**
Borrowing money
  USE **Loans**
Boss rule
  USE **Political corruption**
Botanical chemistry 581.19
  UF Chemistry, Botanical
      Plant chemistry
  BT **Chemistry**
  NT **Plants—Analysis**
Botanical gardens 580.74
  SA names of individual botanical gardens, to be added as needed
  BT **Gardens**
      Parks
Botanical specimens—Collection and preservation
  USE **Plants—Collection and preservation**
Botanists 581.092; 920
  BT **Naturalists**
Botany 581
  Use for systematic or technical materials. Descriptive and nonsystematic or nontechnical materials are entered under **Plants.**
  UF Flora
      Vegetable kingdom
  BT **Biology**
      Natural history
      Nature study
      Science
  NT **Economic botany**
      Flowers
      Fossil plants
      Fruit
      Grafting
      Leaves
      Medical botany
      Photosynthesis
      Plant physiology
      Plants—Anatomy
      Popular plant names
      Seeds
      Trees
      Variation (Biology)
      Vegetables
  RT **Plants**

BT = Broader Term   NT = Narrower Term   RT = Related Term   SA = See Also   UF = Used For

Botany, Agricultural
    USE   **Economic botany**
Botany—Anatomy
    USE   **Plants—Anatomy**
Botany—Ecology
    USE   **Plants—Ecology**
Botany, Economic
    USE   **Economic botany**
Botany, Fossil
    USE   **Fossil plants**
Botany, Medical
    USE   **Medical botany**
Botany—Nomenclature
    USE   **Botany—Terminology**
          Popular plant names
Botany of the Bible
    USE   **Bible—Natural history**
Botany—Pathology
    USE   **Plant diseases**
Botany—Physiology
    USE   **Plant physiology**
Botany—Structure
    USE   **Plants—Anatomy**
Botany—Terminology 581.01
    Use for materials on the scientific names of plants. Materials on the common or vernacular names are entered under **Popular plant names.**
    UF   Botany—Nomenclature
          Plant names, Scientific
    RT   **Popular plant names**
Botany—United States
    USE   **Plants—United States**
Boulder Dam (Ariz. and Nev.)
    USE   **Hoover Dam (Ariz. and Nev.)**
Boulevards
    USE   **Streets**
Boundaries 320.1; 341.4
    UF   Borders (Geography)
          Frontiers
          Geography, Political
          Political boundaries
          Political geography
    SA   names of wars with the subdivision *Territorial questions,* and names of countries, cities, etc., with the subdivision *Boundaries,* to be added as needed
    BT   **Geography**

          International law
          International relations
    NT   **United States—Boundaries**
          World War, 1939-1945—
            Territorial questions
    RT   **Geopolitics**
Bounties
    USE   **Subsidies**
Bourgeoisie
    USE   **Middle classes**
Bow and arrow 799.2028
    UF   Arrow
          Weapons and weaponry
    RT   **Archery**
Bowed instruments
    USE   **Stringed instruments**
Bowling 794.6; 796.31
    UF   Tenpins
    BT   **Ball games**
Boxes 688.8; 745.593
    UF   Boxes, Ornamental
          Boxes, Wooden
          Containers, Box
          Crates
    BT   **Packaging**
Boxes—Collectors and collecting
          745.593
    BT   **Collectors and collecting**
Boxes, Ornamental
    USE   **Boxes**
Boxes, Wooden
    USE   **Boxes**
Boxing 796.8
    UF   Fighting
          Prize fighting
          Pugilism
          Sparring
    BT   **Athletics**
          Self-defense
Boy Scouts (May subdiv. geog.) **369.43**
    UF   Cub Scouts
    BT   **Boys' clubs**
          Scouts and scouting
Boycott
    USE   **Boycotts**
Boycotts 327.1; 331.89; 338.6; 341.5
    UF   Boycott *[Former heading]*
          Consumer boycotts
    BT   **Commerce**
          Consumers

Boycotts—*Continued*
      Passive resistance
  RT Restraint of trade
Boys 155.43; 305.23
  BT Children
  NT Fathers and sons
      Mothers and sons
  RT Teenagers
      Young men
Boys' agricultural clubs
  USE 4-H clubs
      Agriculture—Societies
      Boys' clubs
Boys' clubs 369.42
  UF Boys' agricultural clubs
      Boys—Societies
  BT Clubs
      Men—Societies
      Social settlements
      Societies
  NT 4-H clubs
      Boy Scouts
Boys—Employment
  USE Children—Employment
Boys—Societies
  USE Boys' clubs
Boys, Teenage
  USE Teenagers
Boys' towns
  USE Children—Institutional care
Brahmanism 294.5
  BT Religions
  NT Caste
  RT Hinduism
Braille books
  USE Blind—Books and reading
Brain 596; 611; 612.8
  BT Head
      Nervous system
  NT Dreams
      Memory
      Mind and body
      Phrenology
      Psychology
      Sleep
Brain damaged children 618.92
  BT Exceptional children
      Handicapped children
Brain death 616.07
  UF Irreversible coma

  BT Death
Brain—Diseases 616.8
  NT Alzheimer's disease
      Cerebral palsy
Brain opioids
  USE Endorphins
Brain storming
  USE Group problem solving
Brainwashing 153.8
    Use for materials on the forcible indoctrination of an individual or group in order to alter basic political, social, religious, or moral beliefs.
  UF Deprogramming
      Forced indoctrination
      Indoctrination, Forced
      Mind control
      Thought control
      Will
  BT Behavior modification
      Mental suggestion
      Psychological warfare
      Psychology of learning
Brakes 625.2; 629.2
  SA types of vehicles with the subdivision *Brakes,* e.g. **Automobiles—Brakes;** to be added as needed
  NT Automobiles—Brakes
Branch stores
  USE Chain stores
Brand name products 380.1; 658.8
  UF Products, Brand name
  BT Commercial products
      Manufactures
  RT Trademarks
Brass 669; 673
  BT Alloys
      Metals
  NT Brasses
Brass instruments
  USE Wind instruments
Brasses 739.5
  UF Monumental brasses
      Sepulchral brasses
  BT Archeology
      Art metalwork
      Brass
      Inscriptions
      Sculpture

Brasses—*Continued*
    Tombs
Bravery
  USE **Courage**
Brazilian literature 869
    May use same subdivisions and names
of literary forms as for **English literature.**
  BT **Latin American literature**
      Literature
  RT **Portuguese literature**
Brazing
  USE **Soldering**
Bread 641.8; 664
  BT **Baking**
      Cooking
      Food
Breadstuffs
  USE **Flour**
      Grain
      Wheat
Break dancing 793.3
  BT **Dancing**
Breakers
  USE **Ocean waves**
Breakfast cereals
  USE **Prepared cereals**
Breakfasts 642
  BT **Cooking**
      Menus
  NT **Prepared cereals**
Breast—Cancer
  USE **Breast cancer**
Breast cancer 616.99
  UF Breast—Cancer
  BT **Cancer**
      Women—Diseases
Breast feeding 649
  UF Nursing (Infant feeding)
  BT **Infants—Nutrition**
Breathing
  USE **Respiration**
Breeder reactors
  USE **Nuclear reactors**
Breeding 581.1; 631.5; 636.08
  UF Selection, Artificial
  SA types of animals with the sub-
      division *Breeding,* to be
      added as needed
  NT **Dogs—Breeding**
      Domestic animals

      Heredity
      Horses—Breeding
      Livestock—Breeding
      Mendel's law
      Plant breeding
  RT **Genetics**
Breeding behavior
  USE **Sexual behavior in animals**
Bricklaying 693
  BT **Building**
  RT **Bricks**
      Masonry
Bricks 666; 691
  BT **Building materials**
      Clay industries
  NT **Tiles**
  RT **Bricklaying**
Bridal customs
  USE **Marriage customs and rites**
Bridge (Game) 795.41
  UF Auction bridge
      Contract bridge
      Duplicate bridge
  BT **Card games**
Bridges (May subdiv. geog. by coun-
        tries, states, cities, etc., and
        by rivers) **624; 725**
  UF Suspension bridges
      Viaducts
  SA names of individual bridges,
      to be added as needed
  BT **Civil engineering**
      Transportation
  NT **Golden Gate Bridge (San**
      Francisco, Calif.)
Bridges—Chicago (Ill.) 624
  UF Chicago (Ill.)—Bridges
Bridges—Hudson River (N.Y. and N.J.)
    624
  UF Hudson River (N.Y. and
      N.J.)—Bridges
Brigands
  USE **Thieves**
Bright children
  USE **Gifted children**
British Commonwealth countries
  USE **Commonwealth countries**
British Commonwealth of Nations
  USE **Commonwealth countries**
British Dominions
  USE **Commonwealth countries**

British Empire
  USE **Great Britain—Colonies**
Broadcast journalism 070.4
  UF News broadcasting
      Radio journalism
      Radio news
      Television journalism
      Television news
  BT **Broadcasting**
      Press
  RT **Journalism**
Broadcasting 384.54
  BT **Telecommunication**
  NT **Broadcast journalism**
      Minorities in broadcasting
      Radio broadcasting
      Television broadcasting
Bronze Age 930.1
  RT **Archeology**
      Iron Age
Bronzes 739.5
  BT **Archeology**
      Art
      Art metalwork
      Decoration and ornament
      Metalwork
      Sculpture
Brothers and sisters 155.44; 306.875
  UF Siblings
      Sisters and brothers
  BT **Family**
  RT **Twins**
Brownies (Girl Scouts)
  USE **Girl Scouts**
Brownouts
  USE **Electric power failures**
Brutality
  USE **Cruelty**
Bubonic plague
  USE **Plague**
Buccaneers
  USE **Pirates**
Bucolic poetry
  USE **Pastoral poetry**
Buddhism 294.3
  BT **Religions**
  NT **Zen Buddhism**
Buddhist art 704.9
  UF Art, Buddhist *[Former heading]*

  BT **Art**
Budget (May subdiv. geog.) **351.72**
  Use for materials on government budgets or reports on governmental appropriations and expenditures. Materials on business budgets are entered under **Business budgets.** Materials on household budgets are entered under **Household budgets.** Materials on personal budgets are entered under **Personal finance.**

  SA names of countries, states, cities, government departments, agencies, etc., with the subdivision *Appropriations and expenditures,* to be added as needed
  BT **Finance**
Budget—United States 353.0072
  UF Federal budget
      United States—Budget
  NT **United States—Appropriations and expenditures**
Budgets, Business
  USE **Business budgets**
Budgets, Household
  USE **Household budgets**
Budgets, Personal
  USE **Personal finance**
Buffalo, American
  USE **Bison**
Buffing
  USE **Grinding and polishing**
Bugging, Electronic
  USE **Eavesdropping**
Building 690
  Use for materials on the process of constructing buildings and other structures. Materials on the design and style of structures are entered under **Architecture.** General materials on buildings and materials on buildings in a particular place are entered under **Buildings.**

  UF Architectural engineering
      Construction
  BT **Structural engineering**
      Technology
      Theory of structures
  NT **Bricklaying**
      Chimneys
      Concrete construction
      Doors
      Engineering
      Extraterrestrial bases

Building—*Continued*
    Floors
    Foundations
    House construction
    Masonry
    Roofs
    Sanitary engineering
    Steel construction
    Strength of materials
    Walls
    Windows
  RT Architecture
    Carpentry
    Houses

Building and earthquakes
  USE **Buildings—Earthquake effects**

Building and loan associations
  USE **Savings and loan associations**

Building, Concrete
  USE **Concrete construction**

Building contracts
  USE **Building—Contracts and specifications**

Building—Contracts and specifications 692
  UF Building contracts
    Building—Specifications
  BT **Contracts**

Building—Estimates 692

Building failures 690
  BT **Structural failures**

Building, House
  USE **House construction**

Building, Iron and steel
  USE **Steel construction**

Building materials 691
  UF Structural materials
  SA types of building materials, e.g. **Bricks**; to be added as needed
  BT **Architecture**
    Engineering
    Materials
  NT **Bricks**
    Cement
    Concrete
    Glass construction
    Reinforced concrete
    Stone
    Structural steel

    Stucco
    Terra cotta
    Tiles
    Wood
  RT **Strength of materials**

Building repair
  USE **Buildings—Maintenance and repair**

Building—Repair and reconstruction
  USE **Buildings—Maintenance and repair**

Building security
  USE **Burglary protection**

Building—Specifications
  USE **Building—Contracts and specifications**

Buildings (May subdiv. geog.) **690; 720**
    Use for general materials on buildings and, with geographic subdivisions, for materials on buildings in a particular place. Materials on the design and style of structures are entered under **Architecture**. Materials on the process of constructing buildings and other structures are entered under **Building**.

  SA types of buildings and construction, e.g. **Farm buildings**; types of institutions and names of individual institutions and corporate bodies with the subdivision *Buildings,* e.g. **Colleges and universities—Buildings**; and names of specific buildings, to be added as needed

  NT **Apartment houses**
    Colleges and universities—Buildings
    Farm buildings
    Historic buildings
    Houses
    Industrial buildings
    Prefabricated buildings
    Public buildings
    Rooms
    School buildings
    Skyscrapers

Buildings, College
  USE **Colleges and universities—Buildings**

BT = Broader Term   NT = Narrower Term   RT = Related Term   SA = See Also   UF = Used For

Buildings—Earthquake effects 693.8

Use for materials on the design and construction of buildings to withstand earthquakes.

UF Building and earthquakes
Earthquakes and building

BT **Earthquakes**

NT **Skyscrapers—Earthquake effects**

Buildings, Farm
USE **Farm buildings**

Buildings, Historic
USE **Historic buildings**

Buildings, Industrial
USE **Industrial buildings**

Buildings, Library
USE **Library architecture**

Buildings—Maintenance and repair 690

UF Building repair
Building—Repair and reconstruction
Maintenance and repair

SA types of buildings with the subdivision *Maintenance and repair,* to be added as needed

BT **Repairing**

NT **Houses—Maintenance and repair**

RT **Architecture—Conservation and restoration**

Buildings, Office
USE **Office buildings**

Buildings, Prefabricated
USE **Prefabricated buildings**

Buildings, Public
USE **Public buildings**

Buildings—Remodeling 643; 690

UF Remodeling of buildings

Buildings, Restoration of
USE **Architecture—Conservation and restoration**

Buildings, School
USE **School buildings**

Buildings—Security
USE **Burglary protection**

Built-in furniture 645; 684.1; 749

UF Furniture, Built-in

BT **Furniture**

Bulbs 584; 635.9

BT **Flower gardening**

Plants

Bulge, Battle of the
USE **Ardennes, Battle of the, 1944-1945**

Bulimarexia
USE **Bulimia**

Bulimia 616.85

UF Binge eating behavior
Binge-purge behavior
Bulimarexia
Bulimia nervosa
Gorge-purge syndrome

BT **Eating disorders**

Bulimia nervosa
USE **Bulimia**

Bulletin boards 371.3

BT **Teaching—Aids and devices**

NT **Computer bulletin boards**

Bullets
USE **Projectiles**

Bullfights 791.8

UF Fighting

BT **Sports**

Bullion
USE **Gold**
Money
Silver

Bunker Hill (Boston, Mass.), Battle of, 1775—Poetry 811

May be used for individual works, collections, or materials about poetry dealing with the Battle of Bunker Hill.

BT **Historical poetry**
Poetry

Bunnies
USE **Rabbits**

Bunny rabbits
USE **Rabbits**

Bureaucracy 302.3

BT **Political science**
Public administration

RT **Civil service**
Organizational sociology

Burglar alarms 621.389

BT **Burglary protection**
Electric apparatus and appliances

Burglars
USE **Thieves**

Burglary protection 621.389; 643

UF Building security

Burglary protection—*Continued*
>> Buildings—Security
>> Protection against burglary
>> Residential security
> SA types of protective devices,
>> e.g. **Burglar alarms;** and
>> types of buildings with the
>> subdivision *Security mea-*
>> *sures,* e.g. **Nuclear power**
>> **plants—Security measures;**
>> to be added as needed
> NT **Burglar alarms**
>> **Locks and keys**
>> **Nuclear power plants—**
>> **Security measures**

Burial 363.7; 393
> UF Burial customs
>> Burying grounds
>> Graves
>> Interment
> SA names of individual persons
>> and groups of notable indi-
>> viduals with the subdivi-
>> sion *Death and burial,* e.g.
>> **Presidents—United States—**
>> **Death and burial;** to be
>> added as needed
> BT **Archeology**
>> **Public health**
> NT **Catacombs**
>> **Cemeteries**
>> **Cryonics**
>> **Mounds and mound builders**
>> **Mummies**
>> **Tombs**
> RT **Cremation**
>> **Death**
>> **Funeral rites and ceremonies**

Burial customs
> USE **Burial**

Burial statistics
> USE **Mortality**
>> **Registers of births, etc.**
>> **Vital statistics**
>> and names of countries, cities,
>> etc., with the subdivision
>> *Statistics,* e.g. **United**
>> **States—Statistics;** to be
>> added as needed

Buried cities
> USE **Extinct cities**

Buried treasure 622; 910.4
> UF Hidden treasure
>> Sunken treasure
>> Treasure trove
> BT **Archeology**
>> **Underwater exploration**

Burn out (Psychology) 158.7
> UF Burnout syndrome
> BT **Job satisfaction**
>> **Job stress**
>> **Mental health**
>> **Motivation (Psychology)**
>> **Occupational health and safe-**
>> **ty**
>> **Stress (Psychology)**

Burnout syndrome
> USE **Burn out (Psychology)**

Bursaries
> USE **Scholarships**

Burying grounds
> USE **Burial**
>> **Cemeteries**

Buses 388.4; 629.222
> UF Motor buses
> BT **Automobiles**
>> **Highway transportation**
>> **Local transit**

Bush survival
> USE **Wilderness survival**

Business 650
> UF Trade
> BT **Commerce**
>> **Economics**
> NT **Accounting**
>> **Advertising**
>> **Banks and banking**
>> **Bookkeeping**
>> **Business budgets**
>> **Business enterprises**
>> **Business failures**
>> **Business people**
>> **Commercial law**
>> **Competition**
>> **Credit**
>> **Customer relations**
>> **Department stores**
>> **Economic conditions**
>> **Electronic spreadsheets**

Business—*Continued*
>> Entrepreneurship
>> Home business
>> Industrial efficiency
>> Instalment plan
>> Mail-order business
>> Management
>> Manufactures
>> Marketing
>> Markets
>> Merchants
>> Occupations
>> Office management
>> Profit
>> Real estate business
>> Selling
>> Small business
>> Trust companies

Business administration
> USE **Management**

Business and government
> USE **Industry—Government policy**

Business and politics 322
> UF Business—Political activity
>> Politics and business
> BT **Politics**

Business arithmetic
> USE **Business mathematics**

Business budgets 658.15
> UF Budgets, Business *[Former heading]*
> BT **Business**

Business colleges
> USE **Business schools**

Business combinations
> USE **Conglomerate corporations**
>> **Industrial trusts**

Business correspondence
> USE **Business letters**

Business cycles 338.5
> UF Business depressions
>> Cycles, Business
>> Economic cycles
>> Stabilization in industry
> SA types of business cycles, e.g. **Economic depressions;** to be added as needed
> BT **Economic conditions**
> NT **Economic depressions**
>> **Economic forecasting**

Business depressions
> USE **Business cycles**
>> **Economic conditions**
>> **Economic depressions**

Business education 650.07
> Use for materials on how to teach business and for descriptions of business operations.
> UF Business—Study and teaching
>> Clerical work—Training
>> Commercial education
>> Education, Business
>> Office work—Training
> BT **Education**
> NT **Accounting**
>> **Bookkeeping**
>> **Commercial law**
>> **Handwriting**
>> **Keyboarding (Electronics)**
>> **Secretaries**
>> **Shorthand**
>> **Typewriting**

Business English
> USE **English language—Business English**

Business enterprises (May subdiv. geog.) **338.7**
> Use for materials on business concerns as legal entities, regardless of the form of organization.
> UF Business organizations
>> Companies
>> Enterprises
>> Firms
>> Organizations, Business
> BT **Business**
>> **Commercial law**
>> **Industry**
> NT **Corporations**
>> **Minority business enterprises**
>> **New business enterprises**

Business enterprises, International
> USE **Multinational corporations**

Business enterprises, Minority
> USE **Minority business enterprises**

Business enterprises, New
> USE **New business enterprises**

Business entertaining 395; 658
> BT **Entertaining**
>> **Public relations**

Business ethics 174
> UF Ethics, Business

BT = Broader Term   NT = Narrower Term   RT = Related Term   SA = See Also   UF = Used For

Business ethics—*Continued*
- BT Ethics
- Professional ethics
- NT Competition
- Deceptive advertising
- Success

Business failures 338; 658
- UF Business mortality
- Failure in business
- BT Business
- NT Bank failures
- Bankruptcy

Business forecasting 338.5
- BT Economic forecasting
- Forecasting

Business—Information services 658.4
- BT Information services

Business—International aspects
- USE Multinational corporations

Business Japanese
- USE Japanese language—Business Japanese

Business language
- USE names of languages with unique language subdivisions, e.g. English language—Business English; Japanese language—Business Japanese; etc., to be added as needed

Business law
- USE Commercial law

Business letters 651.7
- UF Business correspondence
- Commercial correspondence
- Correspondence
- BT Letter writing
- RT English language—Business English
- Japanese language—Business Japanese

Business libraries 026
Use for materials on libraries with a subject focus on business. Materials on libraries located within companies, firms, or private businesses, covering any subject area, are entered under **Corporate libraries.**
- UF Libraries, Business
- BT Special libraries

Business machines
- USE Office equipment and supplies

Business management
- USE Management

Business math
- USE Business mathematics

Business mathematics 650.01
- UF Arithmetic, Commercial
- Business arithmetic *[Former heading]*
- Business math
- Commercial arithmetic
- Commercial mathematics
- Finance—Mathematics
- Mathematics, Business
- BT Mathematics
- NT Accounting
- Bookkeeping
- Interest (Economics)

Business mortality
- USE Bankruptcy
- Business failures

Business organizations
- USE Business enterprises

Business patronage of the arts
- USE Art patronage

Business people 338.092; 658.0092; 920
- UF Businesspeople
- BT Business
- NT African American business people
- Black business people
- Businessmen
- Businesswomen
- Capitalists and financiers
- Entrepreneurs
- Merchants
- Self-employed

Business people, African American
- USE African American business people

Business people, Black
- USE Black business people

Business—Political activity
- USE Business and politics

Business schools 650.071
- UF Business colleges
- Colleges, Business
- Schools, Business
- BT Schools

Business secrets
- USE Trade secrets

Business, Small
  USE **Small business**
Business—Study and teaching
  USE **Business education**
Businessmen 338.092; 658.0092; 920
  UF Men in business
  BT **Business people**
Businesspeople
  USE **Business people**
Businesswomen 338.092; 658.0092; 920
  UF Women in business
  BT **Business people**
       Women
Busing (School integration) 344; 370.19
  UF Antibusing
       Racial balance in schools
       School busing
       Student busing
  BT **School children—**
       Transportation
       School integration
       Segregation in education
Butter 637; 641.3
  BT **Dairy products**
  NT **Margarine**
Butter, Artificial
  USE **Margarine**
Butterflies 595.78
  UF Cocoons
       Lepidoptera
  BT **Insects**
  NT **Caterpillars**
  RT **Moths**
Buttons 646; 687
  BT **Clothing and dress**
Buy American policy
  USE **Buy national policy—United**
       States
Buy national policy (May subdiv. geog.)
    351.71; 352.1
  Use for materials on the requirement
that the government procure goods pro-
duced within the nation.
  BT **Commercial policy**
       Government purchasing
Buy national policy—United States
    353.0071
  UF Buy American policy
Buyers' guides
  USE **Consumer education**

    Shopping
Buying 351.71; 352.1; 658.7
  Use for materials on buying by govern-
ment agencies and by commercial and in-
dustrial enterprises. Materials on buying
by the consumer are entered under **Shop-
ping.**
  UF Purchasing
  BT **Management**
  NT **Government purchasing**
       Instalment plan
  RT **Shopping**
Buyouts, Corporate
  USE **Corporate mergers and acqui-
       sitions**
Buyouts, Leveraged
  USE **Leveraged buyouts**
By-products
  USE **Waste products**
Byrd Antarctic Expedition 919.8
  BT **Antarctic regions—Exploration**
Byzantine architecture 723
  UF Architecture, Byzantine *[For-
       mer heading]*
  BT **Ancient architecture**
       Architecture
       Medieval architecture
Byzantine art 709.02
  UF Art, Byzantine *[Former head-
       ing]*
  BT **Ancient art**
       Art
       Medieval art
Byzantine Empire 949.5
  UF Eastern Empire
C.A.I.
  USE **Computer assisted instruction**
C.A.T.V.
  USE **Cable television**
C.B. radio
  USE **Citizens band radio**
C.I.S.
  USE **Commonwealth of Independent
       States**
C.O.A.s
  USE **Children of alcoholics**
C.R.T.'s
  USE **Cathode ray tubes**
Cabala 135; 296.1
  UF Cabbala
       Kabbala

Cabala—*Continued*
- BT **Hebrew literature**
  Jewish literature
  Judaism
  Mysticism
  Occultism
- RT **Symbolism of numbers**

Cabbala
- USE **Cabala**

Cabinet officers 351.004; 353.04; 920
- UF Ministers of state
- NT **Prime ministers**

Cabinet work
- USE **Cabinetwork**

Cabinetwork 684.1

  Use for materials on the making and finishing of fine woodwork, such as furniture or interior details. Materials on the construction of a wooden building or the wooden portion of any building are entered under **Carpentry**.

- UF Cabinet work *[Former heading]*
- BT **Carpentry**
  Furniture
- NT **Veneers and veneering**
- RT **Woodwork**

Cabins
- USE **Log cabins and houses**

Cable codes
- USE **Cipher and telegraph codes**

Cable railroads 385; 625.5
- UF Funicular railroads
  Railroads, Cable
- BT **Railroads**
- RT **Street railroads**

Cable television 384.55
- UF C.A.T.V.
  CATV
  Community antenna television
  Pay television, Cable
  Television, Cable
- BT **Television broadcasting**
- NT **Home Box Office**

Cables 384.6; 621.319; 624.1
- BT **Power transmission**
  Rope

Cables, Submarine
- USE **Submarine cables**

Cactus 583; 635.9
- BT **Desert plants**

CAD
- USE **Computer aided design**

Cage birds 636.6
- SA names of cage birds, to be added as needed
- BT **Birds**
- NT **Canaries**

CAI
- USE **Computer assisted instruction**

Cake 641.8; 664
- BT **Baking**
  Confectionery
  Cooking
  Desserts
- RT **Pastry**

Cake decorating 641.8
- BT **Confectionery**

Calculating machines
- USE **Calculators**

Calculators 510.28; 651.8; 681

  Use for materials on present-day calculators or on calculators and mechanical computers made before 1945. Materials on modern electronic computers developed after 1945 are entered under **Computers**.

- UF Accounting machines
  Adding machines
  Calculating machines
  Pocket calculators
- BT **Arithmetic**
  Office equipment and supplies
- NT **Abacus**
  Slide rule
- RT **Computers**

Calculus 515
- UF Analysis (Mathematics)
- BT **Mathematical analysis**
  Mathematics

Caldecott Awards
- USE **Caldecott Medal**

Caldecott Medal 028.5
- UF Caldecott Awards
  Caldecott Medal books *[Former heading]*
- BT **Children's literature**
  Illustration of books
  Literary prizes

Caldecott Medal books
- USE **Caldecott Medal**

Calendars 529
- UF Annuals

Calendars—*Continued*
  BT Time
  NT Days
       Devotional calendars
       Months
       Week
  RT Almanacs
California—Gold discoveries 979.4
  UF Gold rush
Calisthenics
  USE Gymnastics
       Physical education
Calligraphy 745.6
  BT Decorative arts
       Handwriting
       Writing
Calvinism 284
  BT Reformation
  NT Predestination
  RT Congregationalism
       Puritans
Camcorders 621.388; 778.59
  UF Home video cameras
       Video cameras, Home
  BT Cameras
       Home video systems
       Video recording
  RT Amateur films
Camels 599.73; 636.2
  UF Dromedaries
  BT Desert animals
       Mammals
Cameras 681; 771.3
  SA types of cameras and names
       of individual makes of
       cameras, to be added as
       needed
  BT Photography
       Photography—Equipment and
       supplies
  NT Camcorders
       Kodak camera
       Motion picture cameras
Camouflage (Biology) 591.57
  UF Animal camouflage
       Animals—Camouflage
  BT Animal defenses
Camouflage (Military science) 355.4;
       623
  BT Military art and science

       Naval art and science
Camp cooking
  USE Outdoor cooking
Camp Fire Girls 369.47
  BT Girls' clubs
Camp sites
  USE Campgrounds
Campaign funds (May subdiv. geog.)
       324.7
  UF Assessments, Political
       Elections—Finance
       Political assessments
       Political parties—Finance
  BT Elections
       Politics
  RT Political corruption
Campaign funds—United States 324.7
  UF Elections—United States—
       Finance
       United States—Campaign
       funds
Campaign literature 324.2
    May subdivide by date and then by po-
  litical party.
  UF Political campaign literature
  BT Literature
       Politics
Campaigns, Political
  USE Politics
Campaigns, Presidential—United States
  USE Presidents—United States—
       Election
Campers and trailers
  USE Travel trailers and campers
Campgrounds 796.54
  UF Camp sites
  NT Trailer parks
  RT Camping
Camping 796.54
    Use for materials on the technique of
  camping. Materials on camps with a defi-
  nite program of activities are entered un-
  der Camps.
  BT Outdoor recreation
  NT Backpacking
       Bicycle touring
       Outdoor cooking
       Tents
       Travel trailers and campers
       Wilderness survival
  RT Campgrounds

Camping—*Continued*
    Outdoor life

Camps 796.54
    Use for materials on camps with a definite program of activities. Materials on the technique of camping are entered under **Camping**.

    UF   Summer camps

    BT   **Recreation**

Camps (Military)
    USE **Military camps**

Campus disorders
    USE **College students—Political activity**

Canada 971
    May be subdivided like United States except for *History.*

    SA   names of individual provinces, territories, or regions, to be added as needed

    NT   **Canadian Northwest**

Canada—English-French relations 305.811; 306.4

    UF   Canada—French-English relations

    NT   **Québec (Province)—History— Autonomy and independence movements**

Canada—French-English relations
    USE **Canada—English-French relations**

Canada—History—0-1763 (New France) 971.01

    UF   Canada—History—1755-1763
        New France—History

Canada—History—1755-1763
    USE **Canada—History—0-1763 (New France)**

Canada—History—1763-1791
    USE **Canada—History—1763-1867**

Canada—History—1763-1867 971.02

    UF   Canada—History—1763-1791 *[Former heading]*
        Canada—History—1791-1841
        Canada—History—1841-1867

Canada—History—1791-1841
    USE **Canada—History—1763-1867**

Canada—History—1800-1899 (19th century) 971.03-971.05

Canada—History—1812-1815, War of 1812
    USE **United States—History— 1812-1815, War of 1812**

Canada—History—1841-1867
    USE **Canada—History—1763-1867**

Canada—History—1867- 971.05

Canada—History—1867-1914 971.05

Canada—History—1900-1999 (20th century) 971.06

Canada—History—1914-1945 971.06

Canada—History—1945- 971.06

Canada, Northwest
    USE **Canadian Northwest**

Canadian Indians
    USE **Indians of North America— Canada**

Canadian Invasion, 1775-1776 973.3

    BT   **United States—History— 1775-1783, Revolution**

Canadian literature (May subdiv. geog.) 810; C810
    Use for general materials not limited to literature in a particular language or form. May use same subdivision and names of literary forms as for **English literature**; e.g. **Canadian poetry**; etc.

    BT   **Literature**

    NT   **Canadian literature (English)**
           Canadian literature (French)
           Canadian poetry

Canadian literature (English) (May subdiv. geog.) 810; C810
    May use same subdivisions and names of literary forms as for **English literature**; e.g. **Canadian poetry (English)**; etc.

    UF   English Canadian literature

    BT   **Canadian literature**

    NT   **Canadian poetry (English)**

Canadian literature (French) (May subdiv. geog.) 840; C840
    May use same subdivisions and names of literary forms as for **English literature**; e.g. **Canadian poetry (French)**; etc.

    UF   French Canadian literature *[Former heading]*
        French literature—Canada

    BT   **Canadian literature**

    NT   **Canadian poetry (French)**

Canadian Northwest 971.2
    UF   Canada, Northwest

Canadian Northwest—*Continued*

    Northwest, Canadian *[Former heading]*

  BT **Canada**

Canadian poetry (May subdiv. geog.) **811; C811**

    Use for general materials about Canadian poetry not limited to a particular language, not for individual works.

  BT **Canadian literature**

  NT **Canadian poetry (English)**

      Canadian poetry (French)

Canadian poetry (English) (May subdiv. geog.) **811; C811**

    Use for general materials about Canadian poetry in English, not for individual works.

  UF English Canadian poetry

  BT **Canadian literature (English)**

      Canadian poetry

Canadian poetry (French) (May subdiv. geog.) **841; C841**

    Use for general materials about Canadian poetry in French, not for individual works.

  UF French Canadian poetry

  BT **Canadian literature (French)**

      Canadian poetry

Canadians 305.811; 971

  NT **French Canadians**

Canals (May subdiv. geog.) **386; 627**

  SA names of individual canals, to be added as needed

  BT **Civil engineering**

      Hydraulic structures

      Transportation

      Waterways

  NT **Panama Canal**

  RT **Inland navigation**

Canaries 598.8; 636.6

  BT **Birds**

      Cage birds

Canasta (Game) 795.41

  UF Argentine rummy

  BT **Card games**

Cancer 616.99

  UF Carcinoma

      Malignant tumors

  SA types of cancer, to be added as needed

  BT **Diseases**

      Tumors

  NT **Breast cancer**

      Leukemia

      Lung cancer

Cancer—Chemotherapy 616.99

  UF Chemotherapy *[Former heading]*

  BT **Drug therapy**

Cancer—Diet therapy 616.99

  BT **Diet therapy**

Cancer—Genetic aspects 616.99

  BT **Medical genetics**

Cancer—Nursing 610.73

  BT **Nursing**

Cancer patients

  USE **Cancer—Patients**

Cancer—Patients 616.99

  UF Cancer patients

  BT **Patients**

Cancer—Surgery 616.99

  BT **Surgery**

Candles 621.32; 745.593

  BT **Lighting**

Candy

  USE **Confectionery**

Caning of chairs

  USE **Chair caning**

Cannabis

  USE **Marijuana**

Canned goods

  USE **Canning and preserving**

Cannibalism 291.3; 394

  BT **Ethnology**

      Human behavior

Canning and preserving 641.4; 664

  UF Canned goods

      Food, Canned

      Pickling

      Preserving

  SA names of foods with the subdivision *Preservation,* to be added as needed

  BT **Cooking**

      Food—Preservation

      Industrial chemistry

  NT **Fruit—Preservation**

      Vegetables—Preservation

Cannon

  USE **Ordnance**

Canoes and canoeing 797.1

  BT **Boats and boating**

BT = Broader Term   NT = Narrower Term   RT = Related Term   SA = See Also   UF = Used For

Canoes and canoeing—*Continued*
       Water sports
Canon law
    USE **Ecclesiastical law**
Canons, fugues, etc.
    USE **Fugue**
Cantatas 782.2
    Use for musical scores and for materials on the cantata as a musical form.
    BT **Choral music**
        Vocal music
Canvas embroidery
    USE **Needlepoint**
Capital 332
    BT **Economics**
        Finance
    NT **Banks and banking**
        Industrial trusts
        Interest (Economics)
        Investments
        Profit
    RT **Capitalism**
        Wealth
Capital and labor
    USE **Industrial relations**
Capital punishment (May subdiv. geog.)
        179; 364.6
    UF Abolition of capital punishment
        Death penalty
        Executions
        Hanging
    BT **Criminal law**
        Homicide
        Punishment
Capital punishment—United States
        364.6
    UF United States—Capital punishment
Capitalism 330.12
    BT **Economics**
        Labor
        Profit
    NT **Entrepreneurship**
    RT **Capital**
        Capitalists and financiers
Capitalists and financiers 332.092; 920
    UF Financiers
    BT **Business people**
    RT **Capitalism**

        Millionaires
Capitalization (Finance)
    USE **Corporations—Finance**
        Railroads—Finance
        Securities
        Valuation
Capitals (Cities)
    Use for materials on the capital cities of several countries or states.
    BT **Cities and towns**
    NT **Capitols**
Capitols 725
    BT **Capitals (Cities)**
        Public buildings
Car accidents
    USE **Traffic accidents**
Car design
    USE **Automobiles—Design**
Car driver education
    USE **Automobile driver education**
Car drivers
    USE **Automobile drivers**
Car engines
    USE **Automobile engines**
Car industry
    USE **Automobile industry**
Car insurance
    USE **Automobile insurance**
Car maintenance
    USE **Automobiles—Maintenance and repair**
Car parts
    USE **Automobile parts**
Car pools 388.4
    UF Automobile pools
        Carpools
        Ride sharing
        Van pools
    BT **Traffic engineering**
        Transportation
Car racing
    USE **Automobile racing**
Car repair
    USE **Automobiles—Maintenance and repair**
Car transmissions
    USE **Automobiles—Transmission devices**
Car travel
    USE **Automobile travel**

Car travel—Guidebooks
   USE   **Automobile travel—
          Guidebooks**
Car wheels
   USE   **Wheels**
Car wrecks
   USE   **Traffic accidents**
Carbines
   USE   **Rifles**
Carbolic acid 547; 661
   BT   **Acids**
        Chemicals
Carbon 540; 660
   BT   **Chemical elements**
   NT   **Charcoal**
        Coal
        Diamonds
        Graphite
Carbon 14 dating
   USE   **Radiocarbon dating**
Carbon dioxide greenhouse effect
   USE   **Greenhouse effect**
Carburetors 621.43
   BT   **Internal combustion engines**
Carcinoma
   USE   **Cancer**
Card catalogs 025.3
   UF   Catalogs, Card *[Former head-
         ing]*
   BT   **Library catalogs**
Card games 795.4
   UF   Cards, Playing
        Playing cards
   SA   names of card games, to be
        added as needed
   BT   **Games**
   NT   **Bridge (Game)**
        Canasta (Game)
        Card tricks
        Solitaire (Game)
        Tarot
   RT   **Gambling**
Card tricks 795.4
   BT   **Card games**
        Magic tricks
        Tricks
Cardiac diseases
   USE   **Heart diseases**
Cardiac resuscitation 616.02; 616.1
   UF   Heart resuscitation

Resuscitation, Heart
   BT   **First aid**
Cardinals 262; 920
   BT   **Catholic Church—Clergy**
Cardiovascular system 612.1
   UF   Circulatory system
        Vascular system
   BT   **Anatomy**
        Physiology
   NT   **Heart**
   RT   **Blood—Circulation**
Cards, Debit
   USE   **Debit cards**
Cards, Greeting
   USE   **Greeting cards**
Cards, Playing
   USE   **Card games**
Cards, Sports
   USE   **Sports cards**
Care and hygiene
   USE   parts of the body with the
        subdivision *Care and hy-
        giene,* e.g. **Foot—Care and
        hygiene; Skin—Care and
        hygiene;** etc., to be added
        as needed
Care givers
   USE   **Caregivers**
Care, Medical
   USE   **Medical care**
Care of children
   USE   **Child care**
Care of persons
   USE   classes of dependent persons
        with the subdivisions *Care*
        or *Home care* or *Institu-
        tional care,* e.g. **Infants—
        Care; Elderly—Home care;
        Elderly—Institutional care;
        Mentally ill—Institutional
        care;** etc., to be added as
        needed
Care of the dying
   USE   **Terminal care**
Career changes 331.7; 371.4
   UF   Changing careers
        Mid-career changes
   BT   **Age and employment**
        Vocational guidance
Career counseling
   USE   **Vocational guidance**

     BT = Broader Term   NT = Narrower Term   RT = Related Term   SA = See Also   UF = Used For

Career development
USE **Personnel management**
Vocational guidance
Career education
USE **Vocational education**
Career guidance
USE **Vocational guidance**
Careers
USE **Occupations**
Professions
Vocational guidance
Caregivers 362; 649.8

Use for materials on family and friends who on a voluntary basis provide personal home care for the elderly, ill, or handicapped.

UF Care givers
Family caregivers
BT **Voluntarism**
RT **Home care services**
Caricatures
USE **Cartoons and caricatures**
Caricatures and cartoons
USE **Cartoons and caricatures**
Carillons
USE **Bells**
Carnival (May subdiv. geog.) **394.2**

Use for materials on festivals, merrymaking, and revelry before Lent. Materials on traveling amusement enterprises, consisting of sideshows, games of chance, etc., are entered under **Carnivals.**

UF Mardi Gras
Pre-Lenten festivities
BT **Festivals**
Carnivals 394.2; 791

Use for materials on traveling amusement enterprises, consisting of sideshows, games of chance, merry-go-rounds, etc. Materials on festivals, merrymaking, and revelry before Lent are entered under **Carnival.**

UF Traveling carnivals
BT **Amusements**
Festivals
RT **Amusement parks**
Circus
Fairs
Carnivora
USE **Carnivores**
Carnivores 599.74
UF Carnivora
Carnivorous animals

Meat-eating animals
SA names of carnivorous animals, to be added as needed
BT **Animals—Food**
Mammals
Carnivorous animals
USE **Carnivores**
Carnivorous plants 583; 635.9
UF Insect-eating plants
Insectivorous plants
BT **Plants**
Carols 782.28
UF Christmas carols
Easter carols
BT **Christmas poetry**
Church music
Folk songs
Hymns
Songs
Vocal music
Carpentry 694

Use for materials on the construction of a wooden building or the wooden portion of any building. Materials on the making and finishing of fine woodwork, such as furniture or interior details, are entered under **Cabinetwork.**

NT **Cabinetwork**
Doors
Floors
Roofs
Turning
Walls
RT **Building**
Woodwork
Carpentry—Tools
USE **Carpentry tools**
Carpentry tools 694
UF Carpentry—Tools [Former heading]
SA types of carpentry tools, to be added as needed
BT **Tools**
NT **Saws**
Carpetbag rule
USE **Reconstruction (1865-1876)**
Carpets 645; 677; 746.7

Use for materials on heavy woven or felted fabrics used as floor coverings, usually covering large areas. Materials on one-piece floor coverings, such as woven fabrics, animal skins, etc., are entered under **Rugs.**

Carpets—*Continued*
  BT **Decoration and ornament**
      Interior design
      Textile industry
  RT **Rugs**
      Weaving
Carpools
  USE **Car pools**
Carriages and carts 388.3; 688.6
  UF Carts
      Coaches, Stage
      Stagecoaches
      Wagons
  BT **Vehicles**
Carriers, Aircraft
  USE **Aircraft carriers**
Cars, Armored (Tanks)
  USE **Military tanks**
Cars (Automobiles)
  USE **Automobiles**
Cartels
  USE **Industrial trusts**
Cartography
  USE **Charts**
      Map drawing
      Maps
Cartoons and caricatures 741.5
    Use for collections of pictorial humor
  and for materials about caricatures and
  cartoons.
  UF Caricatures
      Caricatures and cartoons
      Humorous pictures
      Illustrations, Humorous
      Pictures, Humorous
  SA subjects, classes of persons, or
      names of individuals with
      the subdivision *Cartoons
      and caricatures,* to be add-
      ed as needed
  BT **Pictures**
      Portraits
  NT **Animated films**
      **Computers—Cartoons and car-
      icatures**
      **World War, 1939-1945—
      Cartoons and caricatures**
  RT **Comic books, strips, etc.**
Cartoons, Animated
  USE **Animated films**

Cartoons, Television
  USE **Animated television programs**
Carts
  USE **Carriages and carts**
Carts (Midget cars)
  USE **Karts and karting**
Carving (Arts)
  USE kinds of carving, e.g. **Wood
      carving;** to be added as
      needed
Carving (Meat, etc.) 642
  BT **Dining**
      Entertaining
      Meat
Carving, Wood
  USE **Wood carving**
Case studies
  USE subjects with the subdivision
      Case studies, e.g. **Juvenile
      delinquency—Case studies;**
      to be added as needed
Case work, Social
  USE **Social case work**
Cassette books
  USE **Talking books**
Cassette recorders and recording
  USE **Magnetic recorders and re-
      cording**
Cassette tape recordings, Video
  USE **Videotapes**
Cassette tapes, Audio
  USE **Sound recordings**
Castaways
  USE **Survival after airplane acci-
      dents, shipwrecks, etc.**
Caste 294.5; 305.5; 323.3
  BT **Brahmanism**
      Hinduism
      Manners and customs
  NT **Social classes**
Casting
  USE **Founding**
      Plaster casts
Castles (May subdiv. geog.) 728.8
  UF Chateaux
  BT **Architecture**
  RT **Medieval architecture**
Casts, Plaster
  USE **Plaster casts**

Casualty insurance 368.5
>UF Insurance, Casualty *[Former heading]*
>
>BT **Insurance**
>
>NT **Accident insurance**

Cat
>USE **Cats**

CAT scan
>USE **Tomography**

Catacombs 393; 726
>BT **Burial**
>**Cemeteries**
>**Christian antiquities**
>**Christian art and symbolism**
>**Tombs**
>
>RT **Church history—30-600, Early church**

Cataloging 025.3
>May be subdivided by topic, e.g. **Cataloging—Music.**
>
>UF Cataloguing
>Libraries—Cataloging
>Library cataloging
>
>BT **Bibliographic control**
>**Books**
>**Documentation**
>**Library science**
>**Library technical processes**
>
>NT **Classification—Books**
>**International Standard Bibliographic Description**
>**Machine readable bibliographic data**
>**Subject headings**
>
>RT **Bibliography**
>**Indexing**
>**Library catalogs**

Cataloging data in machine readable form
>USE **Machine readable bibliographic data**

Cataloging—Data processing 025.3

Cataloging—Music 025.3
>UF Music—Cataloging

Catalogs
>USE **Booksellers' catalogs**
>**Library catalogs**
>**Publishers' catalogs**

and subjects with the subdivision *Catalogs,* e.g. **Motion pictures—Catalogs;** to be added as needed

Catalogs, Book
>USE **Book catalogs**

Catalogs, Booksellers'
>USE **Booksellers' catalogs**

Catalogs, Card
>USE **Card catalogs**

Catalogs, Classified
>USE **Classified catalogs**

Catalogs in book form
>USE **Book catalogs**

Catalogs, Library
>USE **Library catalogs**

Catalogs on microfilm
>USE **Library catalogs on microfilm**

Catalogs, Online
>USE **Online catalogs**

Catalogs, Publishers'
>USE **Publishers' catalogs**

Catalogs, Subject
>USE **Subject catalogs**

Catalogs, Systematic
>USE **Classified catalogs**

Cataloguing
>USE **Cataloging**

Catalysis 541.3
>BT **Physical chemistry**
>
>RT **Catalytic RNA**

Catalytic ribonucleic acid
>USE **Catalytic RNA**

Catalytic RNA 574.87
>UF Catalytic ribonucleic acid
>Ribozymes
>RNA, Catalytic
>
>BT **Enzymes**
>**RNA**
>
>RT **Catalysis**

Catamarans 797.1
>BT **Boats and boating**

Catastrophes
>USE **Disasters**

Catechisms 238; 268; 291.2
>BT **Christian education**
>**Theology—Study and teaching**
>
>NT **Bible—Catechisms, question books**
>
>RT **Creeds**

Caterers and catering
USE **Catering**
Catering 642
UF Caterers and catering *[Former heading]*
BT **Cooking**
Food service
RT **Menus**
Caterpillars 595.78
UF Cocoons
BT **Butterflies**
Moths
Cathedrals (May subdiv. geog.) **726**
SA names of individual cathedrals, to be added as needed
BT **Architecture**
Church architecture
Churches
RT **Abbeys**
Christian art and symbolism
Gothic architecture
Medieval architecture
Cathedrals—United States 726
UF United States—Cathedrals
Cathode ray tubes 537.5; 621.3815
UF C.R.T.'s
CRTs
BT **Vacuum tubes**
Catholic Church (May subdiv. geog.) **282**
UF Roman Catholic Church
SA subjects with the subdivision *Catholic Church*, e.g. **Abortion—Catholic Church**; to be added as needed
BT **Christian sects**
Christianity
NT **Abortion—Catholic Church**
Inquisition
Papacy
RT **Catholics**
Catholic Church—Charities 361.7
BT **Charities**
Catholic Church—Clergy 253
BT **Clergy**
Priests
NT **Cardinals**
Ex-priests
Catholic Church—Converts
USE **Converts to Catholicism**

Catholic Church—Foreign relations (May subdiv. geog. by appropriate political jurisdiction) **282; 327.456; 945.6**
Use for materials on the dealings and relations between the Catholic Church and political jurisdictions.
UF Catholic Church—Relations (Diplomatic) *[Former heading]*
Vatican City—Foreign relations
BT **International relations**
Catholic Church—Liturgy 264
Use for materials on the forms of prayers, rituals, and ceremonies used in the official public worship of the Catholic Church.
BT **Liturgies**
Rites and ceremonies
Catholic Church—Missions 266
BT **Christian missions**
Catholic Church—Relations 282
Use for materials on relations between the Catholic Church and other churches and religions. May subdivide by church or religion.
BT **Christianity and other religions**
Catholic Church—Relations (Diplomatic)
USE **Catholic Church—Foreign relations**
Catholic Church—United States 282
UF United States—Catholic Church
Catholic converts
USE **Converts to Catholicism**
Catholic ex-nuns
USE **Ex-nuns**
Catholic ex-priests
USE **Ex-priests**
Catholic laity
USE **Laity—Catholic Church**
Catholic literature 282; 808; 809
BT **Christian literature**
Literature
Catholic religious orders for men 271
UF Religious orders for men, Catholic *[Former heading]*
SA names of specific orders, e.g. **Jesuits**; to be added as needed

---

Catholic religious orders for men—
Continued
 BT **Religious orders for men**
 NT **Dominicans (Religious order)**
  Franciscans
  Jesuits
Catholic religious orders for women 271
 UF Religious orders for women,
  Catholic *[Former heading]*
 SA names of specific orders, to
  be added as needed
 BT **Religious orders for women**
Catholics (May subdiv. geog.) **282;**
  305.6
 NT **Converts to Catholicism**
 RT **Catholic Church**
Catholics—United States 282; 305.6
 UF United States—Catholics
Cats 599.74; 636.8
  Use for materials on domestic cats. Ma-
  terials on non-domesticated species of cats
  or domestic cats living in a wild state are
  entered under **Wild cats.**
 UF Cat
 SA names of specific breeds of
  cat, to be added as needed
 BT **Domestic animals**
  Mammals
  Pets
 NT **Kittens**
 RT **Wild cats**
Cats—Literary collections 808.8; 810.8,
  etc.
Cattle 599.73; 636.2
 UF Cows
 BT **Domestic animals**
  Livestock
 NT **Beef cattle**
  Dairy cattle
  Pastures
 RT **Dairying**
Cattle brands 636.2
Cattle—Diseases 636.2
 UF Cows—Diseases
 BT **Animals—Diseases**
  Veterinary medicine
CATV
 USE **Cable television**
Cautionary tales and verse
 USE **Fables**
  Parables

Cautionary tales and verses
 USE **Didactic fiction**
  Didactic poetry
Cave drawings 743; 759.01
 BT **Mural painting and decoration**
  Picture writing
 RT **Rock drawings, paintings, and**
  engravings
Cave dwellers 573.3; 930.1
 BT **Prehistoric man**
Caves 551.4; 796.5
 UF Grottoes
  Speleology
CB radio
 USE **Citizens band radio**
CD-I technology 004.5
 UF CDI technology
  Compact disc interactive tech-
   nology
  Interactive CD technology
 BT **Compact discs**
  Optical storage devices
CD players
 USE **Compact disc players**
CD-ROM 004.5
 UF CDROM
  Compact disc read-only mem-
   ory
 BT **Compact discs**
  Optical storage devices
CDI technology
 USE **CD-I technology**
CDROM
 USE **CD-ROM**
CDs (Compact discs)
 USE **Compact discs**
Celebrities 920
 UF Famous people
  Public figures
 SA types of celebrities, e.g. Ac-
  tors; and names of individ-
  ual celebrities, to be added
  as needed
 BT **Biography**
 NT **Actors**
Celery 635; 641.3
 BT **Vegetables**

Celibacy 248.4; 291.4

Use for materials on the renunciation of marriage for religious reasons. Materials on the virtue that moderates and regulates the sexual appetite in human beings are entered under **Chastity.** Materials on abstinence from sexual activity are entered under **Sexual abstinence.**

UF   Clerical celibacy

BT   **Clergy**
     Religious life
     Religious orders

RT   **Chastity**
     Sexual abstinence
     Single people

Cellars
  USE   **Basements**

Cello
  USE   **Violoncellos**

Cells 574.87; 581.87; 591.87

UF   Cytology

BT   **Biology**
     Physiology
     Reproduction

NT   **DNA**
     Protozoa

RT   **Embryology**
     Protoplasm

Cells, Electric
  USE   **Electric batteries**

Celtic legends 398.2

UF   Legends, Celtic *[Former heading]*

BT   **Legends**

Celtic mythology 299; 936

UF   Mythology, Celtic

BT   **Mythology**

Celts 305.891; 936.4

UF   Gaels

BT   **France—History—0-1328**
     Great Britain—History—0-1066

NT   **Druids and Druidism**

Cement 620.1; 666; 691

UF   Hydraulic cement

BT   **Adhesives**
     Building materials
     Ceramics
     Masonry
     Plaster and plastering

RT   **Concrete**

Lime (Mineral)

Cemeteries (May subdiv. geog.) **393; 718**

UF   Burying grounds
     Churchyards
     Graves
     Graveyards

SA   types of cemeteries and names of individual cemeteries, to be added as needed

BT   **Burial**
     Public health
     Sanitation

NT   **Catacombs**
     Epitaphs

RT   **Tombs**

Censorship 303.3; 363.3

Use for general materials on the limitation of freedom of expression in various fields.

SA   subjects with the subdivision *Censorship,* e.g. **Books—Censorship;** to be added as needed

BT   **Intellectual freedom**

NT   **Academic freedom**
     Books—Censorship
     Freedom of speech
     Freedom of the press
     Motion pictures—Censorship
     Television—Censorship

RT   **Freedom of information**

Census 304.6; 310; 351.81

SA   names of countries, cities, etc., with the subdivision *Census,* to be added as needed

BT   **Population**
     Statistics
     Vital statistics

NT   **United States—Census**

Centers for the performing arts 725; 790.2

SA   names of individual centers, to be added as needed

BT   **Performing arts**

NT   **Theaters**

Central Africa 967
Use for materials dealing collectively with the region of Africa that includes what are now the Central African Republic, Equatorial Guinea, Gabon, Zaire, and the Congo.
UF   Africa, Central *[Former heading]*
BT   **Africa**
NT   **French-speaking Equatorial Africa**

Central America 972.8
BT   **America**

Central American Indians
USE   **Indians of Central America**

Central Asia 958
UF   Asia, Central
BT   **Asia**

Central Asia—History 958

Central Asia—History—1991-
RT   **Former Soviet republics**

Central cities
USE   **Inner cities**

Central Europe 943
Use for materials on the area included in the basins of the Danube, Elbe and Rhine rivers.
UF   Europe, Central

Central States
USE   **Middle West**

Centralization of schools
USE   **Schools—Centralization**

Centralized processing (Libraries)
USE   **Library technical processes**

Ceramic industries 338.4
SA   types of ceramic industries, e.g. **Glass manufacture;** to be added as needed
NT   **Clay industries**
        Glass manufacture

Ceramic materials 620.1; 666; 738.1
SA   names of individual materials, e.g. **Clay;** to be added as needed
NT   **Clay**

Ceramics 666
Use for materials on the technology of fired earth products or on clay products intended for industrial use. Earthenware, chinaware, and porcelain for the table or decorative use are entered under **Pottery** or **Porcelain.**
BT   **Industrial chemistry**

NT   **Abrasives**
        Cement
        Glass
        Glazes
        Pottery
        Tiles

Cereals
USE   **Grain**

Cereals, Prepared
USE   **Prepared cereals**

Cerebral palsy 616.8
UF   Palsy, Cerebral
        Paralysis, Cerebral
        Paralysis, Spastic
        Spastic paralysis
BT   **Brain—Diseases**

Ceremonies
USE   **Etiquette**
        Manners and customs
        Rites and ceremonies

Certainty
USE   **Belief and doubt**
        Probabilities
        Truth

Certified public accountants
USE   **Accountants**

Chain belting
USE   **Belts and belting**

Chain stores 658.8
UF   Branch stores
        Stores
BT   **Retail trade**

Chair caning 684.1
UF   Caning of chairs
BT   **Handicraft**

Chairs 645; 684.1; 749
BT   **Furniture**

Chalk talks 741.2
UF   Blackboard drawing
BT   **Public speaking**

Challenger (Space shuttle) 629.44
BT   **Space shuttles**

Chamber music 785
BT   **Music**
        Orchestral music

Chamber theater
USE   **Readers' theater**

Chambers of commerce 380.106; 381.06
UF   Boards of trade
        Trade, Boards of

Chambers of commerce—*Continued*
  BT Commerce
Change of life in men
  USE Male climacteric
Change of life in women
  USE Menopause
Change of sex
  USE Transsexuality
Change, Organizational
  USE Organizational change
Change, Social
  USE Social change
Changing careers
  USE Career changes
Chanties
  USE Sea songs
Chants (Plain, Gregorian, etc.) 782.32
    Use for books of chants and for materials about chants.
  UF Gregorian chant
      Plain chant
      Plainsong
  BT Church music
Chanukah
  USE Hanukkah
Chaos (Science) 003
  UF Chaotic behavior in systems
  BT Dynamics
      Science
      System theory
Chaotic behavior in systems
  USE Chaos (Science)
Chap-books
  USE Chapbooks
Chapbooks 398
    May be used for individual works, collections, or materials about chapbooks.
  UF Chap-books
      Jestbooks
  BT Books
      Folklore
      Literature
      Pamphlets
      Periodicals
      Wit and humor
  RT Comic books, strips, etc.
Chaplains 253
  SA names of bodies or institutions having chaplains, with the subdivision *Chaplains,*

e.g. **United States. Army—Chaplains;** to be added as needed
  BT Clergy
  NT United States. Army—Chaplains
Character 155.2
  BT Personality
  NT Human behavior
  RT Temperament
Character assassination
  USE Libel and slander
Character education
  USE Moral education
Characteristics, National
  USE National characteristics
Characters and characteristics in literature 809; 810.9, etc.
  UF Literary characters
  SA names of prominent authors with the subdivision *Characters;* groups of persons in literature, and names of individual characters in literature, to be added as needed
  BT Literature
  NT African Americans in literature
      Blacks in literature
      Children in literature
      Plots (Drama, fiction, etc.)
      Shakespeare, William, 1564-1616—Characters
      Women in literature
Charades 793.2
  BT Amateur theater
      Amusements
      Literary recreations
      Riddles
Charcoal 662
  BT Carbon
      Fuel
Charitable institutions
  USE Charities
      Institutional care
      Orphanages
      and classes of persons with the subdivision *Institutional care,* e.g. **Blind—Institutional care; Deaf—**

BT = Broader Term   NT = Narrower Term   RT = Related Term   SA = See Also   UF = Used For

120

Charitable institutions—*Continued*
> **Institutional care; Mentally ill—Institutional care;** etc., to be added as needed

Charities (May subdiv. geog.) **361.7; 361.8**

Use for materials on privately supported welfare activities. Materials on tax supported welfare activities are entered under **Public welfare.** Materials on the methods employed in welfare work, public or private, are entered under **Social work.**

- UF Charitable institutions
  Endowed charities
  Homes (Institutions)
  Institutions, Charitable and philanthropic
  Philanthropy
  Poor relief
  Social welfare
  Welfare agencies
  Welfare work
- SA names of appropriate corporate bodies with the subdivision *Charities,* e.g. **Catholic Church—Charities;** and names of wars with the subdivision *Civilian relief,* e.g. **World War, 1939-1945—Civilian relief;** to be added as needed
- BT **Poverty**
  Social problems
  Social work
- NT **Catholic Church—Charities**
  Child welfare
  Disaster relief
  Food relief
  Institutional care
  Medical charities
  Orphanages
  Social settlements
  World War, 1939-1945—Civilian relief
- RT **Charity organization**
  Endowments
  Public welfare
  Voluntarism

Charities, Legal
- USE **Legal aid**

Charities, Medical
- USE **Medical charities**

Charities, Public
- USE **Public welfare**

Charity 177
- BT **Ethics**
  Virtue
- NT **Love (Theology)**

Charity organization 361
- UF **Philanthropy**
- RT **Charities**

Charlatans
- USE **Impostors and imposture**

Charms 133.4
- UF Spells
  Talismans
- BT **Demonology**
  Folklore
  Superstition
  Witchcraft

Charter flights
- USE **Airlines—Chartering**

Charters
- UF Documents
- BT **History—Sources**
- NT **Magna Carta**
- RT **Archives**
  Manuscripts

Chartography
- USE **Charts**
  Map drawing
  Maps

Charts 912
- UF Cartography
  Chartography
- RT **Maps**

Chasidism
- USE **Hasidism**

Chastity 176

Use for materials on the virtue that moderates and regulates the sexual appetite in human beings. Materials on the renunciation of marriage for religious reasons are entered under **Celibacy.** Materials on abstinence from sexual activity are entered under **Sexual abstinence.**

- BT **Ethics**
  Sexual ethics
  Virtue
- RT **Celibacy**
  Sexual abstinence

Chateaux
- USE **Castles**

Chattel mortgages
- USE **Mortgages**

BT = Broader Term   NT = Narrower Term   RT = Related Term   SA = See Also   UF = Used For

Cheating in sports
USE **Sports—Corrupt practices**
Checkers 794.2
UF Draughts
BT **Games**
Indoor games
Cheerleaders
USE **Cheerleading**
Cheerleading 371.8; 791.6
UF Cheerleaders
Cheers and cheerleading *[For-mer heading]*
BT **Student activities**
Cheers and cheerleading
USE **Cheerleading**
Cheese 637; 641.3
BT **Dairy products**
Cheese—Bacteriology 637
BT **Bacteriology**
Chemical analysis
USE **Analytical chemistry**
and names of substances with the subdivision *Analysis,* e.g. **Water—Analysis;** to be added as needed
Chemical apparatus 542
UF Apparatus, Chemical
Chemistry—Apparatus
BT **Scientific apparatus and in-struments**
Chemical elements 546
UF Elements, Chemical
SA names of chemical elements, to be added as needed
BT **Chemistry**
NT **Carbon**
Gold
Hydrogen
Iron
Mercury
Oxygen
Radium
Silver
Sulphur
Tin
Uranium
Zinc
RT **Periodic law**
Chemical engineering 660
UF Chemistry, Industrial

Chemistry, Technical
BT **Engineering**
NT **Biotechnology**
RT **Industrial chemistry**
Metallurgy
Chemical equations 540
UF Equations, Chemical
BT **Chemical reactions**
Chemical geology
USE **Geochemistry**
Chemical industries
USE **Chemical industry**
Chemical industry 338.4; 660
Use for materials about industries that produce chemicals or are based on chemi-cal processes. General materials on chemi-cals, including their manufacture, are entered under **Chemicals.**
UF Chemical industries *[Former heading]*
Chemistry, Industrial
Chemistry, Technical
SA types of industries, e.g. **Plas-tics industry;** to be added as needed
BT **Industry**
NT **Plastics industry**
RT **Chemicals**
Industrial chemistry
Chemical landfills
USE **Hazardous waste sites**
Chemical pollution
USE **Pollution**
Chemical reactions 541.3
UF Reactions, Chemical
BT **Chemistry**
NT **Chemical equations**
Chemical societies
USE **Chemistry—Societies**
Chemical technology
USE **Industrial chemistry**
Chemical warfare 358
UF Gas warfare
SA names of wars with the subdi-vision *Chemical warfare,* to be added as needed
BT **Military art and science**
War
NT **Incendiary weapons**
Poisonous gases—War use
World War, 1939-1945—Chemical warfare

BT = Broader Term   NT = Narrower Term   RT = Related Term   SA = See Also   UF = Used For

Chemicals 540; 661

> Use for general materials on chemicals, including their manufacture. Materials about industries that produce chemicals or are based on chemical processes are entered under **Chemical industry.**

- SA   types of chemicals, e.g. **Acids; Agricultural chemicals;** etc.; and names of individual chemicals, to be added as needed
- NT   **Acids**
  - **Agricultural chemicals**
  - **Alcohol**
  - **Carbolic acid**
  - **Petrochemicals**
- RT   **Chemical industry**
  - **Industrial chemistry**

Chemiculture
- USE   **Hydroponics**

Chemistry 540
- BT   **Physical sciences**
  - **Science**
- NT   **Acids**
  - **Agricultural chemistry**
  - **Alchemy**
  - **Analytical chemistry**
  - **Bases (Chemistry)**
  - **Biochemistry**
  - **Botanical chemistry**
  - **Chemical elements**
  - **Chemical reactions**
  - **Color**
  - **Combustion**
  - **Explosives**
  - **Fermentation**
  - **Fire**
  - **Geochemistry**
  - **Industrial chemistry**
  - **Inorganic chemistry**
  - **Microchemistry**
  - **Organic chemistry**
  - **Pharmaceutical chemistry**
  - **Pharmacy**
  - **Photographic chemistry**
  - **Physical chemistry**
  - **Poisons and poisoning**
  - **Space chemistry**
  - **Spectrum analysis**

Chemistry, Agricultural
- USE   **Agricultural chemistry**

Chemistry, Analytic
- USE   **Analytical chemistry**

Chemistry—Apparatus
- USE   **Chemical apparatus**

Chemistry, Biological
- USE   **Biochemistry**

Chemistry, Botanical
- USE   **Botanical chemistry**

Chemistry, Diagnostic
- USE   **Clinical chemistry**

Chemistry—Dictionaries 540.3
- BT   **Encyclopedias and dictionaries**

Chemistry—Experiments 540; 542
- BT   **Science—Experiments**

Chemistry, Industrial
- USE   **Chemical engineering**
  - **Chemical industry**
  - **Industrial chemistry**

Chemistry, Inorganic
- USE   **Inorganic chemistry**

Chemistry—Laboratory manuals 540.78

Chemistry, Medical
- USE   **Clinical chemistry**

Chemistry, Medical and pharmaceutical
- USE   **Pharmaceutical chemistry**

Chemistry of food
- USE   **Food—Analysis**
  - **Food—Composition**

Chemistry, Organic
- USE   **Organic chemistry**

Chemistry, Organic—Synthesis
- USE   **Organic chemistry—Synthesis**

Chemistry, Pharmaceutical
- USE   **Pharmaceutical chemistry**

Chemistry, Photographic
- USE   **Photographic chemistry**

Chemistry, Physical and theoretical
- USE   **Physical chemistry**

Chemistry, Physiological
- USE   **Biochemistry**

Chemistry—Problems, exercises, etc. 540.76

Chemistry—Societies 540.6
- UF   Chemical societies

Chemistry, Synthetic
- USE   **Organic chemistry—Synthesis**

Chemistry, Technical
- USE   **Chemical engineering**
  - **Chemical industry**
  - **Industrial chemistry**

BT = Broader Term   NT = Narrower Term   RT = Related Term   SA = See Also   UF = Used For

Chemistry, Textile
    USE   Textile chemistry
Chemists 540.92; 920
    BT   **Scientists**
Chemotherapy
    USE   **Cancer—Chemotherapy**
          Drug therapy
Chess 794.1
    BT   **Games**
          Indoor games
Chicago (Ill.) 917.73; 977.3
    The subdivisions under **Chicago (Ill.)**
    may be used under the name of any city.
    The subdivisions under **United States** may
    be further consulted as a guide for formu-
    lating other headings as needed.
Chicago (Ill.)—African Americans
    USE   **African Americans—Chicago**
          (Ill.)
Chicago (Ill.)—Antiquities 977.3
Chicago (Ill.)—Bibliography 015.773;
    016.9773
Chicago (Ill.)—Bio-bibliography 012
Chicago (Ill.)—Biography 920.0773
    BT   **Biography**
Chicago (Ill.)—Biography—Portraits
    920.0773
Chicago (Ill.)—Boundaries 352.0773;
    977.3
Chicago (Ill.)—Bridges
    USE   **Bridges—Chicago (Ill.)**
Chicago (Ill.)—Census 317.73
Chicago (Ill.)—City planning
    USE   **City planning—Chicago (Ill.)**
Chicago (Ill.)—Civil defense 363.3
    BT   **Civil defense**
Chicago (Ill.)—Climate 551.69773
Chicago (Ill.)—Commerce 381
Chicago (Ill.)—Description 917.73
Chicago (Ill.)—Description—
          Guidebooks
    USE   **Chicago (Ill.)—Guidebooks**
Chicago (Ill.)—Description—Maps
    USE   **Chicago (Ill.)—Maps**
Chicago (Ill.)—Description—Views
    USE   **Chicago (Ill.)—Pictorial works**
Chicago (Ill.)—Directories 917.73
    Use for lists of names and addresses.
    Lists of names without addresses are en-
    tered under **Chicago (Ill.)—Registers.**
    BT   **Directories**

RT   **Chicago (Ill.)—Registers**
Chicago (Ill.)—Directories—Telephone
    USE   **Chicago (Ill.)—Telephone di-**
          rectories
Chicago (Ill.)—Economic conditions
    330.9773
Chicago (Ill.)—Foreign population
    305.8; 325.773
Chicago (Ill.)—Government
    USE   **Chicago (Ill.)—Politics and**
          government
Chicago (Ill.)—Government publications
    USE   **Government publications—**
          Chicago (Ill.)
Chicago (Ill.)—Guidebooks 917.73
    UF   Chicago (Ill.)—Description—
          Guidebooks *[Former head-*
          ing]
Chicago (Ill.)—Historic buildings
    USE   **Historic buildings—Chicago**
          (Ill.)
Chicago (Ill.)—History 977.3
Chicago (Ill.)—History—Societies
    977.3006
Chicago (Ill.)—Industries 338.09773
    UF   Chicago (Ill.)—Manufactures
Chicago (Ill.)—Intellectual life 977.3
    BT   **Intellectual life**
Chicago (Ill.)—Manufactures
    USE   **Chicago (Ill.)—Industries**
Chicago (Ill.)—Maps 912.773
    UF   Chicago (Ill.)—Description—
          Maps
    BT   **Atlases**
          Maps
          Road maps
Chicago (Ill.)—Moral conditions 977.3
Chicago (Ill.)—Occupations 331.7
    BT   **Occupations**
Chicago (Ill.)—Officials and employees
    352.09773
    BT   **Civil service**
Chicago (Ill.)—Pictorial works 917.73
    UF   Chicago (Ill.)—Description—
          Views *[Former heading]*
          Chicago (Ill.)—Pictures
          Chicago (Ill.)—Views
    BT   **Pictures**
          Views
Chicago (Ill.)—Pictures
    USE   **Chicago (Ill.)—Pictorial works**

Chicago (Ill.)—Poetry 811; 811.008, etc.

May be used for individual works or collections of poetry about Chicago, or for materials about such poetry.

BT Poetry

Chicago (Ill.)—Politics and government 977.3

UF Chicago (Ill.)—Government

BT Municipal government
Politics

Chicago (Ill.)—Popular culture

USE Popular culture—Chicago (Ill.)

Chicago (Ill.)—Population 304.609773

BT Population

Chicago (Ill.)—Protests, demonstrations, etc.

USE Protests, demonstrations, etc.—Chicago (Ill.)

Chicago (Ill.)—Public buildings 725.09773

UF Public buildings—Chicago (Ill.)

BT City planning
Public buildings

Chicago (Ill.)—Public works 352.7

BT City planning
Public works

Chicago (Ill.)—Race relations 305.8009773

BT Race relations

Chicago (Ill.)—Registers 917.73

Use for lists of names without addresses. Lists of names that include addresses are entered under Chicago (Ill.)—Directories.

RT Chicago (Ill.)—Directories

Chicago (Ill.)—Social conditions 977.3

BT Social conditions

Chicago (Ill.)—Social life and customs 977.3

Chicago (Ill.)—Social policy 361.6; 977.3

Chicago (Ill.)—Statistics 317.73

BT Statistics

Chicago (Ill.)—Streets

USE Streets—Chicago (Ill.)

Chicago (Ill.)—Suburbs and environs 307.7609773; 977.3

BT Suburban life

NT Chicago metropolitan area (Ill.)

Chicago (Ill.)—Telephone directories 917.73

UF Chicago (Ill.)—Directories—Telephone [Former heading]

Chicago (Ill.)—Urban renewal

USE Urban renewal—Chicago (Ill.)

Chicago (Ill.)—Views

USE Chicago (Ill.)—Pictorial works

Chicago metropolitan area (Ill.) 307.7609773; 977.3

BT Chicago (Ill.)—Suburbs and environs
Metropolitan areas

Chicago metropolitan area (Ill.)—Politics and government 977.3

BT Metropolitan government

Chicanas

USE Mexican American women

Chicano literature (English)

USE American literature—Mexican American authors

Chicanos

USE Mexican Americans

Chicken pox

USE Chickenpox

Chickenpox 616.9

UF Chicken pox

BT Diseases
Viruses

Chief justices

USE Judges

Child abuse 362.7

UF Abuse of children
Battered children
Child battering
Child neglect
Children—Abuse
Children, Cruelty to
Cruelty to children

BT Child welfare
Family violence
Parent and child

NT Child sexual abuse
Juvenile prostitution

Child abuse, Sex

USE Child sexual abuse

Child and father

USE Father and child

Child and grandparent

USE Grandparent and child

Child and mother
USE **Mother and child**

Child and parent
USE **Parent and child**

Child artists 704; 709.2; 920

Use for materials on children as artists and on works of art by children.

UF   Children as artists

BT   **Artists**

Gifted children

NT   **Finger painting**

Child authors 809; 920

Use for materials on children as authors and discussions of literary works written by children. Individual literary works and collections of literary works written by children are entered under the form heading **Children's writings.**

UF   Children as authors

Children's writings—History
and criticism

BT   **Authors**

Gifted children

Child battering
USE **Child abuse**

Child birth
USE **Childbirth**

Child care 649

UF   Care of children

Children—Care

Children, Care of

NT   **Babysitting**

Child rearing

Day care centers

Infants—Care

Child care centers
USE **Day care centers**

Child custody 306.89; 346.01; 362.7

UF   Children—Custody

Custody of children

Joint custody of children

Parental custody

Shared custody

BT   **Divorce mediation**

Parent and child

NT   **Parental kidnapping**

Child development 155.4; 305.23; 612.6

UF   Child study

Children—Development

BT   **Children**

NT   **Child psychology**

Children—Growth

RT   **Child rearing**

Home instruction

Child labor
USE **Children—Employment**

Teenagers—Employment

Youth—Employment

Child molesting
USE **Child sexual abuse**

Child neglect
USE **Child abuse**

Child placing
USE **Adoption**

Foster home care

Child prostitution
USE **Juvenile prostitution**

Child psychiatry 616.89; 618.92

UF   Children—Mental health

Pediatric psychiatry

Psychiatry, Child

BT   **Psychiatry**

NT   **Autism**

Child psychology

Mentally handicapped children

Mentally ill children

Child psychology 155.4

UF   Child study

Children—Psychology

Psychology, Child

BT   **Child development**

Child psychiatry

Psychology

NT   **Children and adults**

Intelligence tests

Psychology of learning

Separation anxiety in children

RT   **Child rearing**

Educational psychology

Child raising
USE **Child rearing**

Child rearing 392; 649

Use for materials on the principles and techniques of raising children. Materials on the psychological and social interaction between parents and their minor children are entered under **Parent and child.** Materials on the skills, attributes, and attitudes needed for parenthood are entered under **Parenting.**

UF   Child raising

Children—Management

Children—Training

Child rearing—*Continued*
>Discipline of children
>Training of children
>BT **Child care**
>>**Children and adults**
>>**Parent and child**
>NT **Children's allowances**
>>**Socialization**
>>**Toilet training**
>RT **Child development**
>>**Child psychology**
>>**Home instruction**
>>**Parenting**

Child sex abuse
>USE **Child sexual abuse**

Child sexual abuse 362.7; 364.1
>UF Child abuse, Sex
>>Child molesting *[Former heading]*
>>Child sex abuse
>>Children—Molesting
>>Molesting of children
>>Sexual abuse
>BT **Child abuse**
>>**Incest**
>>**Sex crimes**
>>**Sexual harassment**

Child snatching by parents
>USE **Parental kidnapping**

Child study
>USE **Child development**
>>**Child psychology**

Child support 306.89; 346.01; 362.7
>UF Support of children
>BT **Child welfare**
>>**Desertion and nonsupport**
>>**Divorce mediation**

Child welfare 362.7
>Use for materials on the aid, support, and protection of children, by the state or by private welfare organizations.
>UF A.D.C.
>>Aid to dependent children
>>Children—Charities, protection, etc.
>>Protection of children
>BT **Charities**
>>**Public welfare**
>>**Social work**
>NT **Abandoned children**

>>**Child abuse**
>>**Child support**
>>**Children—Employment**
>>**Children—Institutional care**
>>**Day care centers**
>>**Foster home care**
>>**Unmarried fathers**
>>**Unmarried mothers**
>RT **Children's hospitals**
>>**Juvenile delinquency**
>>**Mothers' pensions**
>>**Orphanages**

Childbirth 612.6; 618.2
>UF Birth
>>Child birth
>>Labor (Childbirth)
>>Obstetrics
>NT **Midwives**
>>**Multiple birth**
>>**Natural childbirth**
>RT **Pregnancy**

Childbirth, Natural
>USE **Natural childbirth**

Childhood diseases
>USE **Children—Diseases**

Childlessness 306.85
>BT **Children**
>>**Family size**
>RT **Birth control**
>>**Human fertility**
>>**Infertility**

Children (May subdiv. geog.) **305.23**
>Use for materials on people from birth through age twelve. Materials limited to the first two years of a child's life are entered under **Infants**.
>UF Preschool children
>SA children of particular racial or ethnic groups, to be added as needed
>BT **Age**
>>**Family**
>NT **Abandoned children**
>>**Advertising and children**
>>**African American children**
>>**Birth order**
>>**Black children**
>>**Boys**
>>**Child development**
>>**Childlessness**

BT = Broader Term NT = Narrower Term RT = Related Term SA = See Also UF = Used For

Children—*Continued*
  Computers and children
  Exceptional children
  Girls
  Handicapped children
  Indians of North America—
    Children
  Infants
  Missing children
  Motion pictures and children
  Only child
  Orphans
  Play
  Runaway children
  School children
  Television and children
  World War, 1939-1945—
    Children
Children, Abandoned
  USE Abandoned children
Children, Abnormal
  USE Exceptional children
    Handicapped children
Children—Abuse
  USE Child abuse
Children, Adopted
  USE Adopted children
Children—Adoption
  USE Adoption
Children, African American
  USE African American children
Children and adults 305.23; 362.7; 649
  UF Adults and children
  BT Child psychology
  NT Child rearing
    Children and strangers
    Conflict of generations
    Grandparent and child
    Parent and child
    Teacher-student relationships
Children and advertising
  USE Advertising and children
Children and grandparents
  USE Grandparent and child
Children and motion pictures
  USE Motion pictures and children
Children and prostitution
  USE Juvenile prostitution
Children and strangers 362.7
  UF Infants and strangers

    Strangers and children
  BT Children and adults
Children and television
  USE Television and children
Children as artists
  USE Child artists
Children as authors
  USE Child authors
Children as consumers
  USE Young consumers
Children, Black
  USE Black children
Children—Books and reading 011.62;
    028.5
    Use for materials on the reading inter-
  ests of children, as well as for lists of
  books for children. Collections of works
  published for children are entered under
  Children's literature. Individual literary
  works and collections of literary works
  written by children are entered under the
  form heading **Children's writings.** Materi-
  als about works written by children and
  materials about children as authors are en-
  tered under **Child authors.**
  UF Books and reading for chil-
    dren
    Reading interests of children
Children—Care
  USE Child care
Children, Care of
  USE Child care
Children—Charities, protection, etc.
  USE Child welfare
Children—Civil rights 323.3; 342
Children—Clothing
  USE Children's clothing
Children—Costume 391
    Use for descriptive and historical mate-
  rials on children's costume among various
  nations or in the past. Materials on chil-
  dren's clothing from a practical standpoint
  are entered under **Children's clothing.**
  BT Costume
Children, Crippled
  USE Physically handicapped chil-
    dren
Children, Cruelty to
  USE Child abuse
Children—Custody
  USE Child custody
Children—Day care
  USE Day care centers
Children, Delinquent
  USE Juvenile delinquency

BT = Broader Term   NT = Narrower Term   RT = Related Term   SA = See Also   UF = Used For

Children—Development
    USE **Child development**
Children—Diseases 618.92
    UF Childhood diseases
          Children's diseases
          Diseases of children
          Medicine, Pediatric
          Pediatrics
    SA names of diseases, e.g. **Chickenpox;** to be added as needed
    BT **Diseases**
    RT **Children—Health and hygiene**
          Children's hospitals
Children—Education
    USE **Elementary education**
          Preschool education
Children, Emotionally disturbed
    USE **Emotionally disturbed children**
Children—Employment (May subdiv. geog.) **331.3**
    UF Boys—Employment
          Child labor
          Employment of children
          Girls—Employment
          Working children
    BT **Age and employment**
          Child welfare
          Compulsory education
          Labor
          Labor supply
          School attendance
          Social problems
    NT **Apprentices**
          Moneymaking projects for children
    RT **Hours of labor**
Children—Employment—United States 331.3
    UF United States—Children—Employment
Children, Exceptional
    USE **Exceptional children**
Children—Food 641.5
    UF Children's food
    BT **Children—Nutrition**
    NT **School children—Food**
Children, Gifted
    USE **Gifted children**
Children—Growth 155.4; 612.6
    BT **Child development**

Children—Health and hygiene 613
    UF Children—Hygiene
          Pediatrics
    NT **Children—Nutrition**
          Children's hospitals
          Health education
          School hygiene
          School nurses
    RT **Children—Diseases**
Children—Hospitals
    USE **Children's hospitals**
Children—Hygiene
    USE **Children—Health and hygiene**
Children, Hyperactive
    USE **Hyperactive children**
Children, Illegitimate
    USE **Illegitimacy**
Children in art 704.9
    Use for materials on children depicted in works of art. Materials on children as artists are entered under **Child artists.**
    BT **Art**
Children in literature 809
    Use for materials on the theme of children in works of literature. Individual literary works or collections of literary works written by children are entered under the form heading **Children's writings.** Materials about children as authors and about works written by children are entered under **Child authors.**
    BT **Characters and characteristics in literature**
Children—Institutional care 362.7
    UF Boys' towns
          Children's homes
    BT **Child welfare**
          Institutional care
    NT **Day care centers**
          Orphanages
          Reformatories
    RT **Foster home care**
Children—Language 155.4; 372.6
    BT **Language and languages**
Children, Latchkey
    USE **Latchkey children**
Children—Management
    USE **Child rearing**
Children—Mental health
    USE **Child psychiatry**
Children—Molesting
    USE **Child sexual abuse**

BT = Broader Term   NT = Narrower Term   RT = Related Term   SA = See Also   UF = Used For

Children—Nutrition 613.2083;
    641.1083; 649
  BT **Children—Health and hygiene**
    Nutrition
  NT **Children—Food**
Children of alcoholics 362.29
  UF Alcoholic parents
    Alcoholics' children
    C.O.A.s
    COAs
  BT **Alcoholics**
    Alcoholism
    Parent and child
  NT **Adult children of alcoholics**
Children of divorced parents 306.874;
    646.7
  BT **Divorce**
    Parent and child
    Single parent family
  RT **Part-time parenting**
Children of drug addicts 362.29
  UF Children of narcotic addicts
    Cocaine babies
    Crack babies
    Drug addicts' children
    Drug addicts' infants
  BT **Drug addiction**
    Drug addicts
    Parent and child
Children of immigrants 305.23
  UF First generation children
  BT **Immigration and emigration**
    Parent and child
Children of narcotic addicts
  USE **Children of drug addicts**
Children of single parents
  USE **Single parent family**
Children of working parents 306.874;
    362.7
  UF Working parents, Children of
  BT **Parent and child**
  NT **Latchkey children**
Children—Placing out
  USE **Adoption**
    Foster home care
Children—Psychology
  USE **Child psychology**
Children, Retarded
  USE **Mentally handicapped children**
    Slow learning children

Children—Socialization
  USE **Socialization**
Children—Surgery 617
  UF Pediatric surgery
    Surgery, Pediatric
  BT **Surgery**
Children—Training
  USE **Child rearing**
Children—United States 305.230973
  UF United States—Children
Children's allowances 332.024; 649
  UF Allowances, Children's
  BT **Child rearing**
    Money
    Personal finance
  RT **Moneymaking projects for**
    children
Children's books
  USE **Children's literature**
Children's clothing 646.4; 649
    Use for materials on children's clothing
  from a practical standpoint. Descriptive
  and historical materials on children's cos-
  tume among various nations or in the past
  are entered under **Children—Costume.**
  UF Children—Clothing
  BT **Clothing and dress**
Children's courts
  USE **Juvenile courts**
Children's day care centers
  USE **Day care centers**
Children's diseases
  USE **Children—Diseases**
Children's food
  USE **Children—Food**
Children's homes
  USE **Children—Institutional care**
Children's hospitals 362.1
  UF Children—Hospitals
  BT **Children—Health and hygiene**
    Hospitals
    Public welfare
  RT **Child welfare**
    Children—Diseases
Children's libraries 027.62
  UF Libraries and children
    Libraries, Children's
    Library services to children
  BT **School libraries**
  RT **Children's literature**
    Elementary school libraries

BT = Broader Term   NT = Narrower Term   RT = Related Term   SA = See Also   UF = Used For

Children's libraries—*Continued*
> Libraries and schools
> Young adults' library services

Children's literature 808.8; 810.8, etc.
> Use for collections of works published for children. Materials on the reading interests of children, as well as lists of books for children, are entered under **Children—Books and reading.** Individual literary works and collections of literary works written by children are entered under the form heading **Children's writings.** Materials about works written by children and materials about children as authors are entered under **Child authors.**

> UF   Books for children
>   Children's books
>   Children's stories
>   Juvenile literature
> BT   **Literature**
> NT   **Big books**
>   **Caldecott Medal**
>   **Children's plays**
>   **Children's poetry**
>   **Easy reading materials**
>   **Fairy tales**
>   **Newbery Medal**
>   **Picture books for children**
>   **Plot-your-own stories**
>   **Reading materials**
>   **Storytelling**
> RT   **Children's libraries**
>   **Libraries and schools**

Children's literature—History and criticism 809

Children's moneymaking projects
> USE   **Moneymaking projects for children**

Children's parties 395; 793.2
> BT   **Amusements**
>   **Entertaining**
>   **Parties**

Children's plays 808.82; 809.2; 812, etc.; 812.008, etc.; 812.009, etc.
> May be used for individual works, collections, or materials about plays for children.

> UF   Plays for children
>   School plays
> BT   **Amateur theater**
>   **Children's literature**
>   **Drama**

>   **Drama—Collections**
>   **Theater**

Children's poetry 808.81; 809.1; 811, etc.; 811.008, etc.; 811.009, etc.
> Use for individual poems, collections, or materials about poetry written for children. Individual works and collections of poetry written by children are entered under the form heading **Children's writings.** Materials about poetry written by children are entered under **Child authors.**

> UF   Poetry for children
> BT   **Children's literature**
>   **Poetry**
> NT   **Children's songs**
>   **Lullabies**
>   **Nonsense verses**
>   **Nursery rhymes**
>   **Tongue twisters**

Children's reading
> USE   **Reading**

Children's songs 782.42
> Use for collections of songs that contain both words and music, and for materials about songs for children. Collections of songs without the music are entered under **Children's poetry.**

> UF   Songs for children
> BT   **Children's poetry**
>   **School songbooks**
>   **Songs**
> NT   **Lullabies**
>   **Nursery rhymes**

Children's stories
> USE   **Children's literature**
>   **Fairy tales**

Children's writings 808.8; 810.8, etc.
> Use as a form heading for individual literary works or collections of literary works written by children. Materials on children as authors and discussions of literary works written by children are entered under **Child authors.** Collections of works published for children are entered under **Children's literature.**

> UF   School prose
>   School verse *[Former heading]*
> RT   **College and school journalism**

Children's writings—History and criticism
> USE   **Child authors**

Chimes
> USE   **Bells**

Chimneys 697; 721
 UF Smoke stacks
 BT **Architecture—Details**
  Building
  Heating
  Ventilation
 RT **Fireplaces**
China 951
  Use as a heading or as a geographic sub-division for materials dealing with main-land China, regardless of time period, or with the People's Republic of China, or for comprehensive materials on China including Taiwan. Materials dealing with the island of Taiwan, regardless of time period, or with the post-1948 Republic of China are entered under **Taiwan.** May be subdivided like United States except for *History.*
 UF China (People's Republic of China)
  People's Republic of China
China—History 951
China—History—1912-1949 951.04
China—History—1949- 951.05
China—History—1949-1976 951.05
China—History—1976- 951.05
China—History—1989, Tiananmen Square Incident 951.05
 UF Beijing Massacre, 1989
  Tiananmen Square Incident, China, 1989
  Tiananmen Square Massacre, China
China painting 738.1
 UF Porcelain painting
 BT **Decoration and ornament**
  Painting
  Porcelain
China (People's Republic of China)
 USE **China**
China (Porcelain)
 USE **Porcelain**
China (Republic of China, 1949-)
 USE **Taiwan**
Chinaware
 USE **Porcelain**
Chinese Americans 305.895; 973
Chinese satellite countries
 USE **Communist countries**
Chipmunks 599.32
 BT **Squirrels**
Chiropody
 USE **Podiatry**

Chiropractic 615.5
 BT **Alternative medicine**
  Massage
  Medicine
  Osteopathy
 RT **Naturopathy**
Chivalry 394
 BT **Manners and customs**
  Middle Ages
 NT **Romances**
 RT **Crusades**
  Feudalism
  Heraldry
  Knights and knighthood
  Medieval civilization
Chivalry—Romances
 USE **Romances**
Chocolate 641.3
 RT **Cocoa**
  Desserts
Choice, Freedom of
 USE **Free will and determinism**
Choice of books
 USE **Book selection**
  Books and reading
  Books and reading—Best books
Choice of college
 USE **College choice**
Choice of profession, occupation, voca-tion, etc.
 USE **Vocational guidance**
Choice (Psychology) 153.8
 BT **Psychology**
 RT **Decision making**
Choirs (Music) 782.5
 BT **Church music**
 RT **Choral conducting**
  Choral music
  Choral societies
  Singing
Cholesterol content of food
 USE **Food—Cholesterol content**
Choose-your-own story plots
 USE **Plot-your-own stories**
Choral conducting 782.5
 UF Conducting, Choral *[Former heading]*
 BT **Conducting**
 RT **Choirs (Music)**

Choral conducting—*Continued*
    Choral music
    Conductors (Music)
Choral music 782.5
  UF Music, Choral
  BT **Church music**
       Vocal music
  NT **Cantatas**
  RT **Choirs (Music)**
       Choral conducting
       Choral societies
Choral societies 782.506
  UF Singing societies
  BT **Societies**
  RT **Choirs (Music)**
       Choral music
Choral speaking 808.5
  UF Speaking choirs
       Unison speaking
  BT **Drama**
       Recitations
Christ
  USE **Jesus Christ**
Christening
  USE **Baptism**
Christian antiquities 225.9; 270; 930.1
  UF Antiquities, Christian
       Antiquities, Ecclesiastical
       Archeology, Christian
       Christian archeology
       Christians—Antiquities
       Church antiquities
       Ecclesiastical antiquities
  BT **Antiquities**
       Archeology
       Bible—Antiquities
  NT **Catacombs**
  RT **Christian art and symbolism**
       Church architecture
       Gothic architecture
Christian archeology
  USE **Christian antiquities**
Christian art and symbolism 246
  UF Art, Christian
       Art, Ecclesiastical
       Christian symbolism
       Ecclesiastical art
       Iconography
       Sacred art
  BT **Art**

       Religious art and symbolism
       Symbolism
  NT **Catacombs**
       Church architecture
       Church furniture
       Illumination of books and manuscripts
       Jesus Christ—Art
       Mary, Blessed Virgin, Saint—Art
       Symbolism of numbers
  RT **Bible—Pictorial works**
       Cathedrals
       Christian antiquities
       Gothic art
Christian biography
  USE **Christianity—Biography**
Christian civilization 200.9; 909
  UF Civilization, Christian *[Former heading]*
  BT **Christianity**
       Civilization
Christian denominations
  USE **Christian sects**
Christian devotional calendars
  USE **Devotional calendars**
Christian doctrine
  USE **Doctrinal theology**
Christian education 268
    Use for materials on the instruction of Christian religion in schools and private life. General materials on the instruction of religion in schools and private life are entered under **Religious education.** Materials on the relation of the church to education and materials on the history of the part that the church has taken in secular education are entered under **Church and education.** Materials on church supported and controlled elementary and secondary schools are entered under **Church schools.**
  UF Education, Christian
  BT **Christian life**
       Religious education
  NT **Bible—Study and teaching**
       Catechisms
  RT **Church and education**
       Fundamentalism and education
       Theology—Study and teaching
Christian ethics 241
  UF Christian moral theology
       Ethics, Christian
       Moral theology, Christian

Christian ethics—*Continued*
  BT   Ethics
  NT   Christianity and economics
       Conscience
       Sin
  RT   Christian life
Christian fasts and feasts
  USE Christian holidays
Christian holidays 263; 394.2
  UF   Christian fasts and feasts
       Christian holy days
       Fasts and feasts—Christianity
  SA   names of Christian holidays,
         e.g. Christmas; to be added
         as needed
  BT   Religious holidays
  NT   Christmas
       Easter
       Good Friday
       Lent
Christian holy days
  USE Christian holidays
Christian-Jewish relations
  USE Jewish-Christian relations
Christian life 248.4
  UF   Life, Christian
       Religious life (Christian)
  BT   Religious life
  NT   Christian education
       Conversion
       Revivals
  RT   Christian ethics
Christian literature 200
  BT   Religious literature
  NT   Catholic literature
       Devotional literature
       Early Christian literature
       Papal encyclicals
       Sermons
Christian literature—30-600, Early
  USE Early Christian literature
Christian literature, Early
  USE Early Christian literature
Christian ministry 253
  UF   Ministry, Christian *[Former
         heading]*
  BT   Ministry
Christian missionaries 266.0092; 920
  UF   Missionaries, Christian *[For-
         mer heading]*

  BT   Christian missions
Christian missions 266
  UF   Foreign missions, Christian
       Home missions, Christian
       Missions, Christian *[Former
         heading]*
  SA   names of churches, denomina-
         tions, religious orders, etc.,
         with the subdivision *Mis-
         sions,* e.g. Catholic
         Church—Missions; to be
         added as needed
  BT   Christianity
       Church history
       Church work
  NT   Catholic Church—Missions
       Christian missionaries
       Indians of North America—
         Christian missions
       Salvation Army
  RT   Evangelistic work
Christian moral theology
  USE Christian ethics
Christian names
  USE Personal names
Christian new birth
  USE Regeneration (Christianity)
Christian regeneration
  USE Regeneration (Christianity)
Christian saints 270; 920
  BT   Saints
  NT   Apostles
Christian Science 289.5
  UF   Church of Christ, Scientist
       Divine healing
       Mind cure
  BT   Christian sects
       Medicine and religion
  RT   Mental healing
       Spiritual healing
Christian sects 280
  UF   Christian denominations
       Denominations, Christian
       Sects, Christian
  SA   names of Christian sects, e.g.
         Presbyterian Church; to be
         added as needed
  BT   Christianity
       Church history
       Sects

Christian sects—*Continued*

NT   Amish
       Baptists
       Catholic Church
       Christian Science
       Church of England
       Church of Jesus Christ of
          Latter-day Saints
       Congregationalism
       Eastern churches
       Episcopal Church
       Huguenots
       Mennonites
       Moravians
       Noninstitutional churches
       Orthodox Eastern Church
       Presbyterian Church
       Protestant churches
       Puritans
       Russian Orthodox Church
       Salvation Army
       Shakers
       Society of Friends
       Unitarianism

Christian sociology 261

Use for materials on social theory from a Christian point of view. Materials on religious sociology in general are entered under **Religion and sociology.** Materials on the practical treatment of social problems from the point of view of the church are entered under **Church and social problems.**

UF   Sociology, Christian *[Former heading]*

BT   **Church and social problems**
       Religion and sociology
       Sociology

NT   **Christianity and economics**

Christian symbolism
USE   **Christian art and symbolism**

Christian unity 262.001; 270.8

Use for materials on the worldwide movement towards bringing all Christian faiths into cooperation, fellowship, and eventually one organization.

UF   Church unity
       Ecumenical movement

BT   **Church**

NT   **Community churches**
       Interfaith relations

Christianity 200

SA   names of Christian churches and sects, e.g. **Catholic Church; Huguenots;** etc.; and Christianity and other subjects, e.g. **Christianity and economics;** to be added as needed

BT   **Religions**

NT   **Atonement—Christianity**
       Catholic Church
       Christian civilization
       Christian missions
       Christian sects
       Christianity and economics
       Councils and synods
       Counter-Reformation
       Eastern churches
       Miracles—Christianity
       Protestantism
       Reformation

RT   **Church**
       God—Christianity
       Jesus Christ
       Theology

Christianity and economics 261.8

UF   Economics and Christianity

BT   **Christian ethics**
       Christian sociology
       Christianity
       Communism and religion
       Economics

RT   **Church and labor**

Christianity and evolution
USE   **Creationism**

Christianity and other religions 261.2

UF   Christianity—Relations
       Comparative religion

BT   **Religions**

NT   **Catholic Church—Relations**
       Jewish-Christian relations
       Paganism

Christianity and other religions—
       Judaism
USE   **Jewish-Christian relations**

Christianity and politics 261.7; 322

UF   Politics and Christianity

BT   **Church and state**
       Religion and politics

BT = Broader Term   NT = Narrower Term   RT = Related Term   SA = See Also   UF = Used For

Christianity and war
  USE **War and religion**
Christianity—Apologetic works
  USE **Apologetics**
Christianity—Biography 920
  UF Christian biography
       Ecclesiastical biography
       Religious biography
  BT **Religions—Biography**
Christianity—Evidences
  USE **Apologetics**
Christianity—History
  USE **Church history**
Christianity—Origin
  USE **Church history—30-600, Early
       church**
Christianity—Philosophy 201
  UF Theology—Philosophy
**Christianity—Psychology 201; 253.5;
    261.5**
  BT **Psychology**
       Psychology of religion
Christianity—Relations
  USE **Christianity and other reli-
       gions**
Christians—Antiquities
  USE **Christian antiquities**
Christians—Persecutions
  USE **Persecution**
Christmas (May subdiv. geog.) **263;
    394.2**
  BT **Christian holidays**
       Holidays
  NT **Christmas entertainments**
       Santa Claus
  RT **Jesus Christ—Nativity**
Christmas cards 741.6; 745.594
  BT **Greeting cards**
Christmas carols
  USE **Carols**
Christmas decorations 394.2; 745.594
  UF Christmas ornaments
  BT **Decoration and ornament**
  NT **Christmas trees**
Christmas—Drama
  USE **Christmas plays**
Christmas entertainments 394.2; 791
  BT **Amusements**
       Christmas
  NT **Christmas plays**

Christmas ornaments
  USE **Christmas decorations**
**Christmas plays 394.2; 792; 808.82;
    812, etc.**
  May be used for individual works, col-
  lections, or materials about Christmas
  plays.
  UF Christmas—Drama *[Former
       heading]*
       Plays, Christmas
  BT **Christmas entertainments**
       Religious drama
Christmas—Poetry
  USE **Christmas poetry**
**Christmas poetry 808.81; 811, etc.;
    811.008, etc.**
  May be used for individual works, col-
  lections, or materials about poetry about
  Christmas or associated with Christmas.
  UF Christmas—Poetry *[Former
       heading]*
  BT **Poetry**
  NT **Carols**
Christmas tree growing 635.9
  UF Growing of Christmas trees
  BT **Forests and forestry**
       Trees
  RT **Tree planting**
Christmas trees 394.2; 745.594
  BT **Christmas decorations**
       Evergreens
       Trees
Christmas—United States 394.2
  UF United States—Christmas
Christology
  USE **Jesus Christ**
Chromosome mapping
  USE **Genetic mapping**
Chromosomes 574.8
  BT **Genetics**
       Heredity
  NT **Genetic recombination**
Chronicle history (Drama)
  USE **Historical drama**
Chronicle plays
  USE **Historical drama**
Chronology 529
  Use for materials on the science that
  deals with measuring time by regular divi-
  sions and that assigns proper dates to
  events.

Chronology—*Continued*

SA subjects and groups of people with the subdivision *Chronology,* e.g. **Bible— Chronology; Indians of North America— Chronology;** etc., to be added as needed

BT **Astronomy**
 History
 Time

NT **Day**
 Indians of North America— Chronology
 Months
 Night
 Week

RT **Almanacs**

Chronology, Biblical
 USE **Bible—Chronology**

Chronology, Historical
 USE **Historical chronology**

Church 260

SA church and other subjects, e.g. **Church and education;** to be added as needed

BT **Theology**

NT **Christian unity**
 Church and education
 Church and social problems
 Church and state
 Clergy
 Ecclesiastical law
 Laity

RT **Christianity**

Church and education 261; 377

Use for materials on the relation of the church to education in general, and for materials on the history of the part that the church has taken in secular education. Materials on church supported and controlled elementary and secondary schools are entered under **Church schools.** Materials on the instruction of religion in schools and private life are entered under **Religious education,** and of Christian religion under **Christian education.**

UF **Education and church**
 Education and religion
 Religion and education

BT **Church**
 Education

NT **Fundamentalism and education**

Religion in the public schools

RT **Academic freedom**
 Christian education
 Church and state
 Theology—Study and teaching

Church and government
 USE **Church and state**

Church and labor 261.8

UF **Labor and the church**

BT **Labor**

RT **Christianity and economics**

Church and race relations 261.8

UF **Integrated churches**
 Race relations and the church

BT **Church work**

Church and social problems 261.8

Use for materials on the practical treatment of social problems from the point of view of the church. Materials on social theory from a Christian point of view are entered under **Christian sociology.** Materials on religious sociology in general are entered under **Religion and sociology.**

UF **Religion and social problems**
 Social problems and the church

BT **Church**
 Social problems

NT **Christian sociology**
 Liberation theology
 Sanctuary movement

RT **Church work**
 Religion and sociology

Church and state (May subdiv. geog.) **261.7; 322**

UF **Church and government**
 Church—Government policy *[Former heading]*
 Government and church
 Religion and state
 State and church
 State church

BT **Church**
 State, The

NT **Christianity and politics**
 Religion in the public schools

RT **Church and education**
 Ecclesiastical law
 Freedom of conscience
 Freedom of religion
 Popes—Temporal power

BT = Broader Term   NT = Narrower Term   RT = Related Term   SA = See Also   UF = Used For

Church and state—United States 322
- UF Church—Government
policy—United States *[For-
mer heading]*
United States—Church—
Government policy
Church and war
- USE **War and religion**
Church antiquities
- USE **Christian antiquities**
Church, Apostolic
- USE **Church history—30-600, Early
church**
Church architecture 726
- UF Architecture, Church
Architecture, Ecclesiastical
Ecclesiastical architecture
Religious art
- BT **Architecture**
Christian art and symbolism
- NT **Abbeys**
Cathedrals
Mosques
Spires
Temples
- RT **Christian antiquities**
Churches
Gothic architecture
Church attendance
- USE **Public worship**
Church bells
- USE **Bells**
Church councils
- USE **Councils and synods**
Church denominations
- USE **Sects**
and names of particular de-
nominations and sects, e.g.
Presbyterian Church; to be
added as needed
Church entertainments 259
- UF Church sociables
Socials
- BT **Amusements**
Church work
Church festivals
- USE **Religious holidays**
Church finance 254.8; 262.0068
- UF Finance, Church
- BT **Finance**

- NT **Tithes**
Church furniture 247; 726
- UF Ecclesiastical furniture
- BT **Christian art and symbolism**
Furniture
Church—Government policy
- USE **Church and state**
Church—Government policy—United
States
- USE **Church and state—United
States**
Church history 270
Use for materials dealing with the de-
velopment of Christianity and church or-
ganization.
- UF Christianity—History
Ecclesiastical history
History, Church
Religious history
- SA names of countries, states, etc.
with the subdivision
Church history, e.g. **United
States—Church history;** and
names of individual de-
nominations, sects, church-
es, etc. to be added as
needed
- BT **History**
- NT **Abbeys**
Christian missions
Christian sects
Councils and synods
Creeds
Martyrs
Miracles—Christianity
Papacy
Persecution
Popes
Protestant churches
Protestantism
Revivals
Sects
United States—Church history
**Church history—30-600, Early church
209; 270.1; 270.2**
- UF Apostolic Church
Christianity—Origin
Church, Apostolic
Church history—30(ca.)-600,
Early church *[Former head-
ing]*

BT = Broader Term   NT = Narrower Term   RT = Related Term   SA = See Also   UF = Used For

Church history—30-600, Early church—
  Continued
      Early church history
      Primitive Christianity
  NT **Apostles**
      Gnosticism
  RT **Catacombs**
      Early Christian literature
Church history—30(ca.)-600, Early
      church
  USE **Church history—30-600, Early
      church**
**Church history—600-1500, Middle Ages
    270.2-270.5**
  UF Medieval church history
  BT **Middle Ages**
  NT **Crusades**
      Inquisition
      Popes—Temporal power
**Church history—1500-, Modern period
    270.5-270.8**
  UF Modern church history
  RT **Counter-Reformation**
      Reformation
Church history—1517-1648, Reforma-
      tion
  USE **Reformation**
Church history—United States
  USE **United States—Church history**
Church law
  USE **Ecclesiastical law**
Church libraries 027.6
  UF Libraries, Church
      Parish libraries
  BT **Libraries**
Church music 781.71
  UF Music, Sacred
      Psalmody
      Religious music
      Sacred music
  BT **Devotional exercises**
      Music
  NT **Carols**
      Chants (Plain, Gregorian, etc.)
      Choirs (Music)
      Choral music
      Gospel music
      Liturgies
      Oratorio
      Organ music

  RT **Hymns**
Church of Christ, Scientist
  USE **Christian Science**
Church of England (May subdiv. geog.)
    283
  UF Anglican Church
      England, Church of
  BT **Christian sects**
Church of England—United States 283
    Use for materials on the Episcopal
Church in the United States prior to 1789.
Materials on the Episcopal Church in the
United States after 1789 are entered under
Episcopal Church.
  UF United States—Church of
      England
  RT **Episcopal Church**
      Puritans
**Church of Jesus Christ of Latter-day
    Saints 289.3**
  UF Latter-day Saints
      Mormon Church
  BT **Christian sects**
  RT **Mormons**
Church schools 377
    Use for materials on church supported
and controlled elementary and secondary
schools. Materials on the relation of the
church to education and on the history of
the part that the church has taken in secu-
lar education are entered under **Church
and education.** Materials on the instruc-
tion of religion in schools and private life
are entered under **Religious education,** and
of Christian religion under **Christian edu-
cation.**
  UF Denominational schools
      Nonpublic schools
      Parochial schools
      Schools, Parochial
  BT **Private schools**
      Schools
  RT **Fundamentalism and education**
Church service books
  USE **Liturgies**
Church settlements
  USE **Social settlements**
Church sociables
  USE **Church entertainments**
Church unity
  USE **Christian unity**

Church work 250
- SA church work with particular groups of persons, e.g. **Church work with the sick;** to be added as needed
- BT **Pastoral work**
- NT **Christian missions**
  Church and race relations
  Church entertainments
  Church work with the sick
  Church work with youth
  Evangelistic work
  Lay ministry
  Ministry
  Pastoral psychology
  Revivals
  Rural churches
  Sunday schools
- RT **Church and social problems**

Church work, Rural
- USE **Rural churches**

Church work with the sick 259; 362.1
- BT **Church work**
  Sick

Church work with youth 259
- BT **Church work**
  Youth

Churches (May subdiv. geog.) **726**
Use for general descriptive and historical materials on church buildings that cannot be entered under **Church architecture.**
- SA names of individual churches, e.g. **Westminster Abbey;** to be added as needed
- NT **Cathedrals**
  Westminster Abbey
- RT **Church architecture**

Churches, Avant-garde
- USE **Noninstitutional churches**

Churches, Community
- USE **Community churches**

Churches, Country
- USE **Rural churches**

Churches, Noninstitutional
- USE **Noninstitutional churches**

Churches, Rural
- USE **Rural churches**

Churches, Undenominational
- USE **Community churches**

Churches—United States 726.0973
- UF United States—Churches

Churchyards
- USE **Cemeteries**

Cicadas 595.7; 632
- UF 17 year locusts
  Locusts, Seventeen-year
  Seventeen-year locusts
- BT **Insects**

Cigarettes 679
- BT **Smoking**

Cigars 679
- BT **Smoking**

Cinema
- USE **Motion pictures**

Cinematography 778.5
Use for materials on the technical aspects of making motion pictures and their projection onto a screen. General materials on motion pictures, including motion pictures as an art form, copyrighting, distribution, editing, plots, production, etc., are entered under **Motion pictures.**
- UF Motion picture photography *[Former heading]*
  Photography—Motion pictures
- BT **Photography**
- NT **Animation (Cinematography)**
  Motion picture cameras

Cipher and telegraph codes 384.1
- UF Cable codes
  Codes, Telegraph
  Morse code
  Telegraph codes
- BT **Ciphers**
  Telegraph

Ciphers 652
- UF Codes
  Contractions
- BT **Signs and symbols**
- NT **Cipher and telegraph codes**
- RT **Abbreviations**
  Cryptography
  Writing

Ciphers (Lettering)
- USE **Monograms**

Circuits, Electric
- USE **Electric circuits**

Circulation of library materials
- USE **Library circulation**

Circulation of the blood
- USE **Blood—Circulation**

Circulatory system
- USE **Cardiovascular system**

BT = Broader Term   NT = Narrower Term   RT = Related Term   SA = See Also   UF = Used For

Circumnavigation
  USE **Voyages around the world**
Circus 791.3
  BT **Amusements**
  NT **Acrobats and acrobatics**
      Animals—Training
      Clowns
  RT **Carnivals**
CIS
  USE **Commonwealth of Independent States**
Cities and towns (May subdiv. geog.)
      307.76
    Use for general materials on cities and towns. For materials on large cities and their surrounding areas use **Metropolitan areas.** General materials on the government of cities are entered under **Municipal government.** General materials on local government other than that of cities are entered under **Local government.**
  UF Municipalities
      Towns
      Urban areas
  SA names of individual cities and towns, to be added as needed
  BT **Local government**
      Municipal government
      Sociology
  NT **Capitals (Cities)**
      City life
      Extinct cities
      Inner cities
      Markets
      Municipal art
      Parks
      Streets
      Tenement houses
      Urbanization
      Villages
  RT **Urban sociology**
Cities and towns—Civic improvement
      307.3; 352.9
  UF Civic improvement
      Municipal improvements
  NT **City planning**
      Community centers
Cities and towns—Growth 307.76
  UF Cities and towns, Movement to
      Urban development

  BT **Internal migration**
      Population
  NT **Metropolitan areas**
  RT **Urbanization**
Cities and towns—Lighting
  USE **Streets—Lighting**
Cities and towns, Movement to
  USE **Cities and towns—Growth**
       Urbanization
Cities and towns—Planning
  USE **City planning**
Cities and towns, ruined, extinct, etc.
  USE **Extinct cities**
Cities and towns—United States
      307.760973; 973
  UF United States—Cities and towns
Cities, Imaginary
  USE **Geographical myths**
Citizen participation
  USE subjects with the subdivision *Citizen participation,* e.g. **City planning—United States—Citizen participation;** to be added as needed
Citizens band radio 384.5; 621.3845
  UF C.B. radio
      CB radio
      Citizens radio service
  BT **Shortwave radio**
Citizen's defender
  USE **Ombudsman**
Citizens radio service
  USE **Citizens band radio**
Citizenship 172; 323.6
  UF Civics
      Foreigners
      Franchise
      Nationality (Citizenship)
  BT **Constitutional law**
      Political ethics
      Political science
      Social ethics
  NT **Patriotism**
      Suffrage
  RT **Aliens**
      Naturalization
Citrus fruit 634
  SA names of citrus fruits, e.g. **Orange;** to be added as needed, in the singular form

Citrus fruit—*Continued*
    BT   **Fruit**
    NT   **Lime (Fruit)**
          Orange
City and town life
    USE **City life**
City-federal relations
    USE **Federal-city relations**
City government
    USE **Municipal government**
City life 307.76
    UF   City and town life
          Town life
          Urban life
    BT   **Cities and towns**
          Urban sociology
    RT   **Community life**
City manager
    USE **Municipal government by city
           manager**
City planning (May subdiv. geog.)
          307.1; 352.9; 711
    UF   Cities and towns—Planning
          Municipal planning
          Planning, City
          Town planning
          Urban planning
    BT   **Cities and towns—Civic im-
          provement**
    NT   **Chicago (Ill.)—Public build-
          ings**
          Chicago (Ill.)—Public works
          City planning—Chicago (Ill.)
          Zoning
    RT   **Community development**
          Housing
          Municipal art
          Regional planning
          Urban renewal
**City planning—Chicago (Ill.) 307.1;
          352.9; 711**
    UF   Chicago (Ill.)—City planning
    BT   **City planning**
**City planning—United States 307.1;
          352.9; 711**
    UF   United States—City planning
**City planning—United States—Citizen
          participation 307.1**
    BT   **Social action**
City planning—Zone system
    USE **Zoning**

City-state relations
    USE **State-local relations**
City traffic 388.4
    UF   Local traffic
          Street traffic
          Traffic, City
          Urban traffic
    BT   **Streets**
          Traffic engineering
City transit
    USE **Local transit**
Civic art
    USE **Municipal art**
Civic improvement
    USE **Cities and towns—Civic im-
           provement**
Civic involvement
    USE subjects with the subdivision
           Citizen participation, e.g.
           **City planning—United
           States—Citizen participa-
           tion;** to be added as needed
Civics
    USE **Citizenship**
          Political science
          **United States—Politics and
          government**
Civil defense 363.3
    Use for general materials on civilian de-
    fenses. Materials on civilian or military
    defenses against air attack are entered un-
    der **Air defenses.**
    UF   Blackouts in war
          Civilian defense
          Defense, Civil
    SA   names of countries, cities,
          etc., with the subdivision
          Civil defense, and individu-
          al wars with the subdivi-
          sion *Evacuation of civilians,*
          to be added as needed
    BT   **Military art and science**
    NT   **Air defenses**
          Air raid shelters
          Chicago (Ill.)—Civil defense
          Rescue work
          Survival skills
          United States—Civil defense
          **World War, 1939-1945—
          Evacuation of civilians**

Civil defense—*Continued*

  RT **Disaster relief**

Civil disobedience

  USE **Passive resistance**

         Resistance to government

Civil disorders

  USE **Riots**

Civil engineering 624

  BT **Engineering**

  NT **Aqueducts**

         Bridges

         Canals

         Dams

         Drainage

         Dredging

         Excavation

         Extraterrestrial bases

         Foundations

         Harbors

         Highway engineering

         Hydraulic engineering

         Irrigation

         Lunar bases

         Marine engineering

         Masonry

         Mechanical engineering

         Military engineering

         Mining engineering

         Public works

         Railroad engineering

         Reclamation of land

         Roads

         Sanitary engineering

         Streets

         Strength of materials

         Structural engineering

         Structural steel

         Subways

         Surveying

         Tunnels

         Walls

         Water supply

         Water supply engineering

Civil government

  USE **Political science**

         United States—Politics and government

Civil law suits

  USE **Litigation**

Civil liberty

  USE **Freedom**

Civil rights (May subdiv. geog.) **323; 342**

  Use for materials on citizens' rights as established by law or protected by a constitution. Materials on the rights of persons regardless of their legal, socioeconomic, or cultural status and as recognized by the international community are entered under **Human rights.**

  UF Basic rights

         Constitutional rights

         Fundamental rights

         Rights, Civil

  SA ethnic groups and classes of persons with the subdivision *Civil rights,* to be added as needed

  BT **Constitutional law**

         Human rights

         Political science

  NT **Academic freedom**

         African Americans—Civil rights

         Anti-apartheid movement

         Blacks—Civil rights

         Due process of law

         Fair trial

         Freedom of assembly

         Freedom of association

         Freedom of information

         Freedom of movement

         Freedom of religion

         Freedom of speech

         Freedom of the press

         Right of privacy

         Women's rights

  RT **Discrimination**

         Freedom

Civil rights (International law)

  USE **Human rights**

Civil service (May subdiv. geog.) **350.6**

  Use for general materials on the history and development of public service. Materials on public personnel administration, including the duties of civil service employees, their salaries, pensions, etc., are entered under the name of the country, state, or city with the subdivision *Officials and employees.*

  UF Administration

         Employees and officials

BT = Broader Term   NT = Narrower Term   RT = Related Term   SA = See Also   UF = Used For

Civil service—*Continued*
      Government employees
      Government service
      Municipal employees
      Officials
      Tenure of office
  SA names of countries, cities,
      etc., with the subdivision
      Officials and employees, to
      be added as needed
  BT **Administrative law**
      Political science
      Public administration
  NT **Chicago (Ill.)—Officials and**
      employees
  RT **Bureaucracy**
Civil service—Examinations 351.3
  BT **Examinations**
Civil service—United States 353.006
  UF United States—Civil service
  RT **United States—Officials and**
      employees
Civil War—England
  USE **Great Britain—History—**
      1642-1660, Civil War and
      Commonwealth
Civil War—United States
  USE **United States—History—**
      1861-1865, Civil War
Civilian defense
  USE **Civil defense**
Civilian evacuation
  USE **World War, 1939-1945—**
      Evacuation of civilians
Civilization 306; 909
    Use for materials on civilization in general and on the development of social customs, art, industry, religion, etc., of several countries or peoples.
  SA names of countries, states,
      etc., with the subdivision
      Civilization, e.g. **United**
      States—Civilization; and
      the civilization of peoples
      not confined to a single
      country, e.g. **Arab civiliza-**
      tion; Western civilization;
      etc., to be added as needed
  NT **Acculturation**
      Aeronautics and civilization
      African civilization

      American civilization
      Ancient civilization
      Arab civilization
      Archeology
      Art
      Asian civilization
      Astronautics and civilization
      Biculturalism
      Christian civilization
      Education
      Greek civilization
      Industry
      Inventions
      Jewish civilization
      Learning and scholarship
      Manners and customs
      Medieval civilization
      Modern civilization
      Nonliterate folk society
      Popular culture
      Progress
      Religions
      Scandinavian civilization
      Science and civilization
      Social sciences
      Technology and civilization
      United States—Civilization
      War and civilization
      Western civilization
  RT **Anthropology**
      Culture
      Ethnology
      History
      Sociology
Civilization, African
  USE **African civilization**
Civilization, American
  USE **American civilization**
        United States—Civilization
Civilization, Ancient
  USE **Ancient civilization**
Civilization and aeronautics
  USE **Aeronautics and civilization**
Civilization and astronautics
  USE **Astronautics and civilization**
Civilization and computers
  USE **Computers and civilization**
Civilization and science
  USE **Science and civilization**

BT = Broader Term   NT = Narrower Term   RT = Related Term   SA = See Also   UF = Used For

Civilization and technology
  USE **Technology and civilization**
Civilization and war
  USE **War and civilization**
Civilization, Arab
  USE **Arab civilization**
Civilization, Asian
  USE **Asian civilization**
Civilization, Christian
  USE **Christian civilization**
Civilization, Greek
  USE **Greek civilization**
Civilization, Jewish
  USE **Jewish civilization**
Civilization, Medieval
  USE **Medieval civilization**
Civilization, Modern
  USE **Modern civilization**
Civilization, Modern—1950-
  USE **Modern civilization—1950-**
Civilization, Occidental
  USE **Western civilization**
Civilization, Oriental
  USE **Asian civilization**
Civilization, Scandinavian
  USE **Scandinavian civilization**
Civilization, Western
  USE **Western civilization**
Clairvoyance 133.8
  BT **Extrasensory perception**
      Occultism
      Parapsychology
      Spiritualism
  RT **Divination**
      Fortune telling
      Telepathy
Clans 306.85; 941.1
  UF Highland clans
      Scottish clans
  SA names of families, to be add-
      ed as needed
  BT **Family**
      Feudalism
  NT **Tartans**
Class conflict
  USE **Social conflict**
Class consciousness 305.5
  BT **Social classes**
      Social psychology
  RT **Marxism**

Class distinction
  USE **Social classes**
Class struggle
  USE **Social conflict**
Classed catalogs
  USE **Classified catalogs**
Classes (Mathematics)
  USE **Set theory**
Classical antiquities 937; 938
  UF Antiquities, Classical
      Archeology, Classical
      Classical archeology
      Greek antiquities
      Roman antiquities
  SA names of extinct cities of
      Greek and Roman antiquity
      e.g. **Delphi (Extinct city);**
      and names of groups of
      people extant in modern
      times and names of cities
      (except extinct cities), coun-
      tries, regions, etc., with the
      subdivision *Antiquities,* to
      be added as needed
  BT **Ancient art**
      Antiquities
  NT **Classical mythology**
      Great Britain—Antiquities
      Greece—Antiquities
      Greek art
      Roman art
      Rome—Antiquities
      Rome (Italy)—Antiquities
  RT **Archeology**
Classical antiquities—Dictionaries
  USE **Classical dictionaries**
Classical archeology
  USE **Classical antiquities**
Classical art
  USE **Greek art**
      Roman art
Classical biography
  USE **Greece—Biography**
      Rome—Biography
Classical dictionaries 937.003; 938.003
  UF Classical antiquities—
      Dictionaries
      Dictionaries, Classical
  BT **Ancient history**
      Encyclopedias and dictionaries

Classical education 370.11
UF Education, Classical
BT **Education**
RT **Humanism**
    Humanities
Classical geography
USE **Ancient geography**
     Greece—Historical geography
     Rome—Geography
Classical languages
USE **Greek language**
     Latin language
Classical literature 870; 880
UF Literature, Classical
BT **Literature**
RT **Greek literature**
    Latin literature
Classical music
USE **Music**
Classical mythology 292.1
UF Greek mythology
    Mythology, Classical *[Former
      heading]*
    Roman mythology
BT **Classical antiquities**
    Mythology
NT **Gods and goddesses**
Classicism 709; 809
BT **Aesthetics**
    Literature
Classification—Books 025.4
   Use same form for classification of other library materials.
UF Libraries—Classification
    Library classification
BT **Bibliography**
    Cataloging
    Documentation
    Library science
    Library technical processes
NT **Dewey Decimal Classification**
RT **Classified catalogs**
Classification, Dewey Decimal
USE **Dewey Decimal Classification**
Classified catalogs 017; 025.3
UF Catalogs, Classified *[Former
      heading]*
    Catalogs, Systematic
    Classed catalogs
BT **Library catalogs**

RT **Classification—Books**
Classroom management 371.1
BT **School discipline**
    Teaching
Clay 553.6; 666; 738.1
BT **Ceramic materials**
    Soils
NT **Modeling**
Clay industries 338.4; 666
BT **Ceramic industries**
NT **Bricks**
    Pottery
    Tiles
Clay modeling
USE **Modeling**
Cleaning 648; 667
BT **Sanitation**
NT **Bleaching**
    Cleaning compounds
    Dry cleaning
    House cleaning
    Laundry
    Street cleaning
Cleaning compounds 648; 667
BT **Cleaning**
NT **Detergents**
    Soap
Cleanliness 391; 613; 646.7
UF Messiness
    Neatness
BT **Hygiene**
    Sanitation
NT **Baths**
Clearing of land
USE **Reclamation of land**
Clearinghouses, Information
USE **Information services**
Clergy 253
UF Curates
    Ministers of the gospel
    Pastors
    Preachers
    Rectors
SA church denominations with
      the subdivision *Clergy*, e.g.
      Catholic Church—Clergy;
      to be added as needed
BT **Church**
NT **Catholic Church—Clergy**
    Celibacy

BT = Broader Term   NT = Narrower Term   RT = Related Term   SA = See Also   UF = Used For

Clergy—*Continued*
>   Chaplains
>   Ministry
>   Priests
>   Rabbis
>   Women clergy
> RT   Ordination
>   Pastoral work

Clergy—Office
> USE   Ministry

Clergy—Political activity 253; 261.7

Clerical celibacy
> USE   Celibacy

Clerical employees
> USE   Office workers

Clerical psychology
> USE   Pastoral psychology

Clerical work—Training
> USE   Business education

Clerks
> USE   Office workers

Clerks (Retail trade)
> USE   Sales personnel

Cliff dwellers and cliff dwellings 979
> BT   Archeology
>   Indians of North America

Climacteric, Female
> USE   Menopause

Climacteric, Male
> USE   Male climacteric

Climate 551.6

> Use for materials on climate as it relates to humans and to plant and animal life, including the effects of changes of climate. Materials limited to the climate of a particular region are entered under the name of the place with the subdivision *Climate.* Materials on the state of the atmosphere at a given time and place with respect to heat or cold, wetness or dryness, calm or storm, are entered under **Weather.** Scientific materials on the atmosphere, especially weather factors, are entered under **Meteorology.**

> UF   Climatology
> SA   names of countries, cities, etc., with the subdivision *Climate,* to be added as needed
> BT   Earth sciences
> NT   Forest influences
>   Greenhouse effect
>   Seasons

>   United States—Climate
> RT   Meteorology
>   Weather

Climate and forests
> USE   Forest influences

Climatology
> USE   Climate

Climbing plants 582.1; 635.9
> UF   Vines
> BT   Gardening
>   Plants

Clinical chemistry 616.07

> Use for materials on the chemical diagnosis of disease and health monitoring.

> UF   Chemistry, Diagnostic
>   Chemistry, Medical
>   Diagnostic chemistry
>   Medical chemistry
> BT   Biochemistry
>   Diagnosis

Clinical drug trials
> USE   Drugs—Testing

Clinical genetics
> USE   Medical genetics

Clinical magnetic resonance imaging
> USE   Magnetic resonance imaging

Clinical trials of drugs
> USE   Drugs—Testing

Clinics
> USE   Medical practice

Clipper ships 387.2; 623.8
> BT   Ships

Clippings (Books, newspapers, etc.) 025.17
> UF   Newspaper clippings
>   Press clippings
> BT   Newspapers

Clocks and watches 681.1
> UF   Horology
>   Watches
> BT   Time
> NT   Sundials

Clog dancing 793.3
> BT   Tap dancing

Cloisters
> USE   Convents
>   Monasteries

Clones and cloning 174; 575.1; 660
> UF   DNA cloning
> BT   Genetic engineering

BT = Broader Term   NT = Narrower Term   RT = Related Term   SA = See Also   UF = Used For

Clones and cloning—*Continued*
  NT   Molecular cloning
Cloning, Molecular
  USE Molecular cloning
Closed caption television 384.55
  BT   Deaf
        Television
Closed caption video recordings 384.55
  UF   Video recordings, Closed cap-
        tion
        Video recordings for the hear-
        ing impaired
  BT   Deaf
        Videodiscs
        Videotapes
Closed-circuit television 384.55
  UF   Television, Closed-circuit
  BT   Intercommunication systems
        Microwave communication sys-
        tems
        Television
Closed shop
  USE Open and closed shop
Cloth
  USE Fabrics
Clothes
  USE Clothing and dress
Clothiers
  USE Clothing industry
Clothing and dress 646
    Use for materials on clothing from a
practical standpoint including the art of
dress. Descriptive and historical materials
on the costume of various countries, peo-
ples, or historical periods and materials on
fancy dress and theatrical costumes are
entered under **Costume**. Materials on the
prevailing mode or style of dress are en-
tered under **Fashion**.
  UF   Clothes
        Dress
        Garments
  SA   names of articles of clothing
        and accessories, to be add-
        ed as needed
  BT   Manners and customs
  NT   Buttons
        Children's clothing
        Clothing industry
        Dress accessories
        Dressmaking
        Hats

        Hosiery
        Leather garments
        Men's clothing
        Shoes
        Tailoring
        Women's clothing
  RT   Costume
        Fashion
        Personal appearance
        Personal grooming
Clothing and dress—Dry cleaning
  USE Dry cleaning
Clothing and dress—Repairing 646.2
Clothing industry 338.4; 687
  UF   Clothiers
        Clothing trade *[Former head-
        ing]*
        Fashion industry
        Garment industry
  BT   Clothing and dress
        Industry
  NT   Fashion models
        Shoe industry
        Tailoring
Clothing, Leather
  USE Leather garments
Clothing, Men's
  USE Men's clothing
Clothing trade
  USE Clothing industry
Cloud seeding
  USE Weather control
Clouds 551.57
  BT   Meteorology
Clowns 791.3; 791.3092; 920
  BT   Circus
        Entertainers
Clubs 367
  BT   Associations
  NT   Boys' clubs
        Girls' clubs
        Men—Societies
        Scouts and scouting
        Social group work
        Women—Societies
  RT   Societies
Co-dependence
  USE Codependency
Co-dependency
  USE Codependency

Co-parenting
USE **Part-time parenting**
Coaches, Stage
USE **Carriages and carts**
Coaching
USE **Horsemanship**
Coaching (Athletics) 796.07
UF Athletic coaching
Sports coaching
SA names of sports with the sub-
division *Coaching,* to be
added as needed
BT **Athletics**
Physical education
Sports
NT **Football—Coaching**
Coal 553.2
BT **Carbon**
Economic geology
Fuel
NT **Coal gasification**
Coal liquefaction
Coal mines and mining
Coal gas
USE **Gas**
Coal gasification 665.7
UF Gasification of coal
BT **Coal**
Coal liquefaction 622
UF Liquefaction of coal
BT **Coal**
Coal miners 622; 920
BT **Miners**
Coal mines and mining 622
BT **Coal**
Mines and mineral resources
NT **Mining engineering**
Coal oil
USE **Petroleum**
Coal tar products 547.8; 661
BT **Petroleum**
RT **Gas**
Oils and fats
COAs
USE **Children of alcoholics**
Coast pilot guides
USE **Pilot guides**
Coastal signals
USE **Signals and signaling**
Coats of arms
USE **Heraldry**

Cocaine 362.29; 615
BT **Narcotics**
Psychotropic drugs
NT **Crack (Drug)**
Cocaine babies
USE **Children of drug addicts**
Cocoa 633.7; 641.3
BT **Beverages**
RT **Chocolate**
Cocoons
USE **Butterflies**
Caterpillars
Moths
Silkworms
Code deciphering
USE **Cryptography**
Code enciphering
USE **Cryptography**
Code names 423
BT **Abbreviations**
Names
NT **Acronyms**
Codependency 616.86
UF Co-dependence
Co-dependency
Codependent behavior
BT **Abnormal psychology**
Codependent behavior
USE **Codependency**
Codes
USE **Ciphers**
Codes, Penal
USE **Criminal law**
Codes, Telegraph
USE **Cipher and telegraph codes**
Coeducation 376
BT **Colleges and universities**
RT **Education**
Men—Education
Women—Education
Coffee 633.7; 641.8
BT **Beverages**
Coffee houses
USE **Coffeehouses**
Coffee shops
USE **Restaurants**

BT = Broader Term   NT = Narrower Term   RT = Related Term   SA = See Also   UF = Used For

Coffeehouses 647.95

Use for materials on public places that serve coffee and sometimes provide informal entertainment or serve as a place where small groups meet. Materials on coffee shops, that is, small inexpensive restaurants, are entered under **Restaurants.**

UF Coffee houses *[Former heading]*

BT **Restaurants**

Cog wheels

USE **Gearing**

Cognition

USE **Theory of knowledge**

Cohabitation

USE **Unmarried couples**

Coiffure

USE **Hair**

Coin collecting

USE **Coins**

Numismatics

Coinage 332.4

Use for materials on the processing and history of metal money. Lists of coins and materials about coins and coin collecting are entered under **Coins.**

NT **Counterfeits and counterfeiting**

RT **Gold**

Mints

Money

Silver

Coinage of words

USE **New words**

Coins 737.4

Use for lists of coins and materials about coins and coin collecting. Materials on coins from the point of view of art and archeology are entered under **Numismatics.** Materials on the processing of metal money are entered under **Coinage.**

UF Coin collecting

BT **Money**

RT **Numismatics**

Cold 536; 551.5; 551.6

NT **Cryobiology**

Ice

RT **Low temperatures**

Temperature

Cold (Disease) 616.2

UF Common cold

BT **Communicable diseases**

Diseases

NT **Influenza**

Cold—Physiological effect 613

BT **Cryobiology**

Cold storage 641.4; 664

BT **Food—Preservation**

Meat industry

NT **Compressed air**

RT **Refrigeration**

Cold—Therapeutic use 615.8

UF Cryotherapy

NT **Cryosurgery**

Cold war 909.82

Use for materials on the rivalry between capitalist and communist nations following World War II.

UF Power politics

BT **World politics—1945-1991**

Collaborationists

USE **Treason**

Collage 702.8; 751.4

BT **Art**

Handicraft

Collapse of structures

USE **Structural failures**

Collected papers (Anthologies)

USE **Anthologies**

Collected works

USE **Anthologies**

Literature—Collections

Storytelling—Collections

and form headings that represent collections of works of several authors, e.g. **American essays; Essays; Parodies; Short stories; etc.;** and names of literatures and literary forms with the subdivision *Collections,* e.g. **English literature—Collections; Poetry—Collections; etc.,** to be added as needed

Collectibles

USE names of events with the subdivision *Collectibles,* e.g. **American Revolution Bicentennial, 1776-1976—Collectibles;** and types of objects collected, excluding antiquities and natural objects, with the subdivision *Collectors and collecting,* e.g. **Boxes—Collectors and**

Collectibles—*Continued*
      collecting; to be added as
      needed
Collecting
  USE **Collectors and collecting**
Collecting of accounts 658.8
  UF Accounts, Collecting of
  BT **Commercial law**
      Credit
      Debtor and creditor
Collection and preservation
  USE antiquities and types of natu-
      ral objects, including ani-
      mal specimens and plant
      specimens, with the subdi-
      vision *Collection and pres-
      ervation* for materials on
      methods of collecting and
      preserving those objects, to
      be added as needed
Collection development (Libraries)
  USE **Libraries—Collection develop-
      ment**
Collections (Anthologies)
  USE **Anthologies**
Collections of art, painting, etc.
  USE **Art museums**
      and names of original owners
      of private collections with
      the subdivision *Art collec-
      tions;* and names of gal-
      leries and museums, to be
      added as needed
Collections of literature
  USE **Anthologies**
      Literature—Collections
      Storytelling—Collections
      and form headings that repre-
      sent collections of works of
      several authors, e.g. **Ameri-
      can essays; Essays; Paro-
      dies; Short stories;** etc.; and
      names of literatures and lit-
      erary forms with the subdi-
      vision *Collections,* e.g.
      **English literature—
      Collections; Poetry—
      Collections;** etc., to be add-
      ed as needed

Collections of natural specimens
  USE **Zoological specimens—
      Collection and preservation**
      and names of natural speci-
      mens with the subdivision
      Collection and preservation,
      e.g. **Birds—Collection and
      preservation;** to be added as
      needed
Collections of objects
  USE **Collectors and collecting**
      and names of events with the
      subdivision *Collectibles,* e.g.
      **American Revolution Bicen-
      tennial, 1776-1976—
      Collectibles;** and types of
      objects collected, excluding
      antiquities and natural ob-
      jects, with the subdivision
      Collectors and collecting,
      e.g. **Boxes—Collectors and
      collecting;** to be added as
      needed
Collective bargaining 331.89; 658.3
  May be subdivided by groups of profes-
sional or nonprofessional workers, e.g.
Collective bargaining—Librarians.
  UF Labor negotiations
  BT **Industrial relations**
      Labor
      Labor disputes
      Negotiation
  RT **Industrial arbitration**
      Labor contract
      Labor unions
      Participative management
      Strikes
**Collective bargaining—Librarians
  331.89**
  UF Librarians—Collective bar-
      gaining
      Libraries—Collective bargain-
      ing
Collective farms
  USE **Collective settlements**
      Cooperative agriculture
Collective labor agreements
  USE **Labor contract**
Collective security
  USE **International security**

Collective settements (May subdiv. geog.) **307.77; 335**

Use for materials on traditional, formally organized communal ventures, usually based on ideological, political, or religious affiliation. Materials on arrangements in voluntary cooperative living, usually informal, are entered under **Communal living.**

UF   Collective farms

Communal settlements

Communes

Cooperative living

SA   names of individual collective settlements, to be added as needed

BT   **Communism**

Cooperation

Socialism

RT   **Communal living**

Cooperative agriculture

Counter culture

Utopias

Collective settlements—Israel 307.77

UF   Israel—Collective settlements

Kibbutz

Collective settlements—United States 307.77

UF   United States—Collective settlements

Collectivism

USE   **Communism**

Socialism

Collectors and collecting 790.1

UF   Collecting

Collections of objects

SA   types of objects collected, excluding antiquities and natural objects, with the subdivision *Collectors and collecting,* e.g. **Postcards—Collectors and collecting;** names of original owners of private art collections with the subdivision *Art collections;* names of events with the subdivision *Collectibles,* e.g. **American Revolution Bicentennial, 1776-1976—Collectibles;** and antiquities and types of natural objects with the subdivision *Collec-*

tion and preservation, to be added as needed

BT   **Antiques**

Art

Hobbies

NT   **American Revolution Bicentennial, 1776-1976—Collectibles**

Americana

Antiquities—Collection and preservation

Birds—Collection and preservation

Book collecting

Boxes—Collectors and collecting

Plants—Collection and preservation

Stamp collecting

Zoological specimens—Collection and preservation

Collects

USE   **Prayers**

College admissions essays

USE   **College applications**

College and school drama 371.8; 792

Use for materials about college and school drama. Collections of plays for production in colleges and schools are entered under **College and school drama—Collections.**

UF   College drama

School drama

Theatricals, College

BT   **Amateur theater**

Drama

Student activities

RT   **Drama in education**

College and school drama—Collections 808.82; 812.008, etc.

UF   College plays

Plays, College

School plays

BT   **Drama—Collections**

College and school journalism 371.8

UF   College journalism

College periodicals

School journalism

School newspapers

BT   **Journalism**

Student activities

College and school journalism—
Continued
  RT **Children's writings**
College and university libraries
  USE **Academic libraries**
College applications 378.1
  UF Admissions applications
      Admissions essays
      Applications for college
      College admissions essays
      Colleges and universities—
        Applications
  RT **Colleges and universities—**
      Entrance requirements
College athletics
  USE **Athletics**
      College sports
College choice 378.1
  UF Choice of college
      Colleges and universities—
        Selection
  BT **Colleges and universities**
College costs 378.3
  UF Tuition
  BT **Colleges and universities—**
      Finance
  NT **Student aid**
      Student loan funds
College degrees
  USE **Academic degrees**
College drama
  USE **College and school drama**
College dropouts
  USE **Dropouts**
College entrance examinations
  USE **Colleges and universities—**
      Entrance examinations
College entrance requirements
  USE **Colleges and universities—**
      Entrance requirements
      and names of individual col-
      leges and universities with
      the subdivision *Entrance*
      requirements, to be added
      as needed
College fraternities
  USE **Fraternities and sororities**
College graduates 331.11; 378; 650.1
  UF Graduates, College
      University graduates

  BT **Professions**
  RT **College students**
College journalism
  USE **College and school journalism**
College life
  USE **College students**
College periodicals
  USE **College and school journalism**
College plays
  USE **College and school drama—**
      Collections
College songs
  USE **Students' songs**
College sororities
  USE **Fraternities and sororities**
College sports 371.8; 796
  UF College athletics
      Intercollegiate athletics
      Varsity sports
  SA names of specific sports, to be
      added as needed
  BT **Sports**
      Student activities
  RT **School sports**
College students 371.8; 378
  UF College life
      Colleges and universities—
        Students
      Undergraduates
      University students
  BT **Students**
  RT **College graduates**
College students, Foreign
  USE **Foreign students**
College students—Political activity
      371.8; 378
  UF Campus disorders
College students—Sexual behavior
      371.8; 378
  BT **Sexual behavior**
College teachers
  USE **Colleges and universities—**
      Faculty
      Educators
      Teachers
College yearbooks
  USE **School yearbooks**
Colleges and universities (May subdiv.
      geog.) **378**
  UF Universities

BT = Broader Term   NT = Narrower Term   RT = Related Term   SA = See Also   UF = Used For

Colleges and universities—*Continued*
SA   names of individual colleges and universities, to be added as needed
BT   **Education**
      Higher education
      Professional education
      Schools
NT   **Academic degrees**
      Academic libraries
      Coeducation
      College choice
      Commencements
      Dissertations
      Fraternities and sororities
      Free universities
      Junior colleges
      Scholarships
      Teachers colleges
      University extension

Colleges and universities—Applications
USE   **College applications**

Colleges and universities—Buildings 727
UF   Buildings, College
BT   **Buildings**

Colleges and universities—Curricula 378.1
UF   Core curriculum
BT   **Education—Curricula**

Colleges and universities—Entrance examinations 378.1
UF   College entrance examinations
      Entrance examinations for colleges
BT   **Educational tests and measurements**
      Examinations
NT   **Graduate Record Examination**
      Scholastic aptitude test

Colleges and universities—Entrance requirements 378.1
UF   College entrance requirements
      Entrance requirements for colleges and universities
SA   names of individual colleges and universities with the subdivision *Entrance requirements,* to be added as needed

BT   **Examinations**
RT   **College applications**

Colleges and universities—Faculty 378.1
UF   College teachers
      Faculty (Education)

Colleges and universities—Finance 378
UF   Tuition
NT   **College costs**
      Federal aid to education

Colleges and universities—Insignia 378.2
BT   **Insignia**

Colleges and universities, Nonformal
USE   **Free universities**

Colleges and universities—Selection
USE   **College choice**

Colleges and universities—Students
USE   **College students**

Colleges and universities—United States 378.73
UF   American colleges
      United States—Colleges and universities
      United States—Universities

Colleges, Business
USE   **Business schools**

Collies 636.7
BT   **Dogs**

Collisions, Railroad
USE   **Railroads—Accidents**

Colloids 541.3
BT   **Physical chemistry**

Colonial architecture 724
UF   Architecture, Colonial *[Former heading]*
BT   **Architecture**
RT   **Historic buildings—United States**

Colonial furniture (U.S.)
USE   **American furniture**

Colonial history (U.S.)
USE   **United States—History—1600-1775, Colonial period**

Colonialism
USE   **Colonies**
      Imperialism

Colonies 321; 325

Use for materials on general colonial policy. Materials on the policy of settling immigrants or nationals in unoccupied areas are entered under **Colonization**. Materials on migration from one country to another are entered under **Immigration and emigration**. Materials on the movement of population within a country for permanent settlement are entered under **Internal migration**.

UF   Colonialism
     Dependencies

SA   names of countries with the
     subdivisions *Colonies*, or
     Territories and possessions,
     to be added as needed

BT   **Imperialism**

NT   **Great Britain—Colonies**
     Immigration and emigration
     Land settlement
     National liberation movements
     Penal colonies
     **United States—Territories and
     possessions**

RT   **Colonization**

Colonies, Space
USE   **Space colonies**

Colonization 325

Use for materials on the policy of settling immigrants or nationals in unoccupied areas. Materials on general colonial policy are entered under **Colonies**. Materials on migration from one country to another are entered under **Immigration and emigration**. Materials on the movement of population within a country for permanent settlement are entered under **Internal migration**.

UF   Dependencies

SA   names of countries with the
     subdivision *Immigration
     and emigration*, to be add-
     ed as needed

BT   **Imperialism**
     Land settlement

NT   **Internal migration**
     Public lands
     **United States—Immigration
     and emigration**

RT   **Colonies**
     Immigration and emigration

Color 535.6; 701; 752

UF   Colour

SA   subjects with the subdivision
     Color, and names of specif-
     ic colors, to be added as
     needed

BT   **Aesthetics**
     Chemistry
     Light
     Optics
     Painting
     Photometry

NT   **Animals—Color**
     Birds—Color
     Dyes and dyeing
     Red

RT   **Pigments**

Color blindness 617.7

BT   **Color sense**
     Vision disorders

Color etchings
USE   **Color prints**

Color photography 778.6

UF   Color slides
     Photography, Color

BT   **Photography**

Color printing 686.2

Use for materials on practical printing in color. Materials on hand-colored prints or on pictures printed in color are entered under **Color prints**.

SA   types of color printing pro-
     cesses, to be added as
     needed

BT   **Printing**

NT   **Illustration of books**
     Lithography
     Silk screen printing

RT   **Color prints**

Color prints 769

Use for materials on hand-colored prints or on pictures printed in color. Materials on practical printing in color are entered under **Color printing**.

UF   Block printing
     Color etchings
     Painting—Color reproductions

SA   color prints of particular
     countries, e.g. **American col-
     or prints**; to be added as
     needed

BT   **Prints**

NT   **American color prints**

BT = Broader Term   NT = Narrower Term   RT = Related Term   SA = See Also   UF = Used For

Color prints—*Continued*
>   **Japanese color prints**
> RT **Color printing**
Color prints, American
> USE **American color prints**
Color prints, Japanese
> USE **Japanese color prints**
Color—**Psychological aspects** 152.14
> UF Psychology of color
> BT **Color sense**
>   **Psychology**
Color sense 152.14
> BT **Psychophysiology**
>   **Senses and sensation**
>   **Vision**
> NT **Color blindness**
>   **Color—Psychological aspects**
Color slides
> USE **Color photography**
>   **Slides (Photography)**
Color television 621.388
> UF Television, Color
> BT **Television**
Colorado River—Hoover Dam
> USE **Hoover Dam (Ariz. and Nev.)**
Coloring books 372.5
> UF Painting books
> BT **Picture books for children**
Colour
> USE **Color**
Columnists
> USE **Journalists**
COM catalogs
> USE **Library catalogs on microfilm**
Combinations in restraint of trade
> USE **Restraint of trade**
Combinations, Industrial
> USE **Industrial trusts**
Combustion 541.3; 621.402
> BT **Chemistry**
> NT **Fuel**
> RT **Fire**
>   **Heat**
Comedians 791; 792.2; 920
> BT **Actors**
>   **Entertainers**
> NT **Fools and jesters**
Comedies 808.82; 812, etc.
>   May be used for individual works or for collections. Materials about comedy as a literary form are entered under **Comedy**.

> UF Comic drama
>   Comic plays
>   Humorous plays
>   Slapstick comedies
> BT **Drama**
>   **Wit and humor**
> NT **Comedy films**
>   **Comedy television programs**
>   **Farces**
Comedy 792.2; 809.2
>   Use for materials on comedy as a literary form. Individual works and collections of comedies are entered under **Comedies**.
> UF Comic drama
>   Comic literature
> BT **Drama**
>   **Wit and humor**
Comedy films 791.43
>   May be used for individual works, collections, or materials about comedy films.
> UF Comic films
>   Humorous films
>   Slapstick comedies
> SA types of comedy films, e.g.
>   **Three Stooges films;** to be added as needed
> BT **Comedies**
>   **Motion pictures**
> NT **Three Stooges films**
> RT **Comedy television programs**
Comedy radio programs 791.44
>   May be used for individual works, collections, or materials about comedy radio programs.
> UF Radio comedy programs
> BT **Radio programs**
Comedy television programs 791.45
>   May be used for individual works, collections, or materials about television comedies.
> UF Comic television programs
>   Sitcoms
>   Situation comedies
>   Slapstick comedies
>   Television comedies
>   Television comedy programs
> BT **Comedies**
>   **Television programs**
> RT **Comedy films**
Comets 523.6
> BT **Astronomy**
>   **Solar system**

Comets—*Continued*
NT Halley's comet
Comic books, strips, etc. 741.5
May be used for individual works, collections, or materials about printed comic strips, i.e. groups of cartoons in narrative sequence, and books and magazines consisting of comic strips, etc.
UF Comic strips
Funnies
Humorous pictures
SA names of comic books, comic strips, and comic strip characters, to be added as needed
BT **Wit and humor**
NT **Mystery comic books, strips, etc.**
Science fiction comic books, strips, etc.
Superhero comic books, strips, etc.
Western comic books, strips, etc.
RT **Cartoons and caricatures**
Chapbooks
Comic drama
USE **Comedies**
Comedy
Comic epic literature
USE **Mock-heroic literature**
Comic films
USE **Comedy films**
Comic literature
USE **Comedy**
Parody
Satire
Comic novels
USE **Humorous fiction**
Comic opera
USE **Opera**
Operetta
Comic plays
USE **Comedies**
Comic strips
USE **Comic books, strips, etc.**
Comic television programs
USE **Comedy television programs**
Comic verse
USE **Humorous poetry**
Coming of age stories
USE **Bildungsromans**

Commandments, Ten
USE **Ten commandments**
Commencements 371.2
UF Graduation
BT **Colleges and universities**
High schools
School assembly programs
Commentaries, Biblical
USE **Bible—Commentaries**
Commerce 380.1
Use for general materials on foreign and domestic commerce. Materials limited to commerce between states are entered under **Interstate commerce.**
UF Distribution (Economics)
Exports
Imports
Trade
SA names of countries, cities, etc., with the subdivision *Commerce,* e.g. **United States—Commerce;** and names of articles of commerce, e.g. **Cotton;** to be added as needed
BT **Economics**
Finance
NT **Balance of trade**
Banks and banking
Barter
Boycotts
Business
Chambers of commerce
Commercial geography
Competition
Contracts
Cooperation
Exchange
Free trade and protection
Grocery trade
Industrial trusts
International trade
Interstate commerce
Marine insurance
Markets
Merchants
Monopolies
Multinational corporations
Prices
Profit sharing

Commerce—*Continued*

        Restraint of trade
        Retail trade
        Stock exchange
        Stocks
        Tariff
        Trade routes
        Trademarks
        United States—Commerce
  RT   Transportation

Commerce, Interstate
  USE   **Interstate commerce**

Commercial aeronautics 387.7
  UF   Aeronautics, Commercial
       [Former heading]
       Air cargo
       Air freight
       Air transport
       Commercial aviation
  BT   **Freight**
       Transportation
  NT   **Air mail service**
       Airlines
       Airplane industry

Commercial aeronautics—Hijacking
  USE   **Hijacking of airplanes**

Commercial arithmetic
  USE   **Business mathematics**

Commercial art 741.6
   Use for general materials on the application of art to business, i.e. in advertising layout, fashion design, lettering, etc.
  UF   Advertising art
       Advertising, Pictorial
       Art, Commercial
       Art in advertising
  BT   **Advertising**
       Art
       Drawing
  NT   **Fashion design**
       Posters
       Textile design

Commercial aviation
  USE   **Commercial aeronautics**

Commercial correspondence
  USE   **Business letters**

Commercial education
  USE   **Business education**

Commercial employees
  USE   **Office workers**

Commercial endeavors in space
  USE   **Space industrialization**

Commercial geography 330.9
  UF   Economic geography
       Geography, Commercial *[Former heading]*
       Geography, Economic
       World economics
  BT   **Commerce**
       Geography
  NT   **Trade routes**
  RT   **Economic conditions**

Commercial law 346
  UF   Business law
       Law, Business
       Law, Commercial
       Mercantile law
  BT   **Business**
       Business education
       Law
  NT   **Antitrust law**
       Arbitration and award
       Bankruptcy
       Business enterprises
       Collecting of accounts
       Contracts
       Corporation law
       Debtor and creditor
       Fraud
       Insider trading
       Landlord and tenant
       Mortgages
       Negotiable instruments
       Restraint of trade
       Unfair competition
  RT   **Maritime law**

Commercial mathematics
  USE   **Business mathematics**

Commercial paper
  USE   **Negotiable instruments**

Commercial photography 778
  UF   Photography, Commercial *[Former heading]*
  BT   **Photography**
  NT   **Photojournalism**

Commercial policy 380.1; 381.3; 382
   Use for general materials on the various regulations by which governments seek to protect and increase the commerce of a country, such as subsidies, tariffs, free ports, etc.

Commercial policy—*Continued*
- UF Government regulation of
commerce
Reciprocity
Trade barriers
World economics
- SA names of countries with the
subdivision *Commercial
policy,* e.g. **United States—
Commercial policy;** to be
added as needed
- BT **Economic policy**
**International economic rela-
tions**
- NT **Buy national policy**
Commercial products
Free trade and protection
Tariff
**United States—Commercial
policy**

Commercial products 338; 380.1
- UF Merchandise
Products, Commercial
- SA types of products and names
of specific products, to be
added as needed
- BT **Commercial policy**
- NT **Animal products**
Brand name products
Consumer goods
Forest products
Generic products
Manufactures
Marine resources
Raw materials
Substitute products

Commercial products recall
- USE **Product recall**

Commercial products—Safety measures
- USE **Product safety**

Commercial secrets
- USE **Trade secrets**

Commercials, Radio
- USE **Radio advertising**

Commercials, Television
- USE **Television advertising**

Commission government
- USE **Municipal government by
commission**

Commission government with city
manager
- USE **Municipal government by city
manager**

Common cold
- USE **Cold (Disease)**

Common law marriage
- USE **Unmarried couples**

Common market
- USE **European Union**

Common schools
- USE **Public schools**

Commonwealth countries 909
Use for materials dealing collectively
with the member countries of the international organization that was founded in
1931 as the British Commonwealth of Nations, changed its name to the Commonwealth of Nations in 1950, and became
known as the Commonwealth in 1969.
- UF British Commonwealth countries
British Commonwealth of Nations
British Dominions
Commonwealth of Nations
[Former heading]
Dominions, British
- RT **Great Britain—Colonies**

Commonwealth of England
- USE **Great Britain—History—
1642-1660, Civil War and
Commonwealth**

**Commonwealth of Independent States
947.085**
Use for materials specifically on the federation of independent former Soviet republics that was established in December
1991 and does not include Georgia or the
Baltic states. General materials on several
or all of the countries that emerged from
the dissolution of the Soviet Union in
1991 are entered under **Former Soviet republics.**
- UF C.I.S.
CIS
- RT **Former Soviet republics**
Russia (Republic)
Soviet Union

Commonwealth of Nations
- USE **Commonwealth countries**

Commonwealth, The
- USE **Political science**
Republics

Commonwealth, The—*Continued*
    State, The
Communal living 307.77

    Use for materials on arrangements in voluntary cooperative living, usually informal. Materials on traditional, formally organized communal ventures, usually based on ideological, political, or religious affiliation are entered under **Collective settlements.**

UF	Communal settlements
	Communes
	Cooperative housing
	Cooperative living
	Group living
RT	**Collective settlements**
	Counter culture

Communal settlements
USE	**Collective settlements**
	Communal living

Communes
USE	**Collective settlements**
	Communal living

Communicable diseases 614.4; 616.9

UF	Contagion and contagious diseases
	Contagious diseases
	Diseases, Communicable
	Diseases, Contagious
	Diseases, Infectious
	Infection and infectious diseases
	Quarantine
SA	names of communicable diseases, to be added as needed
BT	**Diseases**
	Public health
NT	**AIDS (Disease)**
	Bacteriology
	Cold (Disease)
	Disinfection and disinfectants
	Fumigation
	Germ theory of disease
	Influenza
	Insects as carriers of disease
	Plague
	Rabies
	Sexually transmitted diseases
	Vaccination
RT	**Epidemics**

    Immunity
Communicable diseases—Prevention 614.4
Communication 302.2

    Use for general materials on communication in its broadest sense, including the use of the spoken and written word, signs, symbols, or behavior.

UF	Mass communication
BT	**Sociology**
NT	**Books and reading**
	Conversation
	Cybernetics
	Deaf—Means of communication
	Information science
	Language and languages
	Language arts
	Mass media
	Nonverbal communication
	Popular culture
	Postal service
	Public speaking
	Signals and signaling
	Signs and symbols
	Telecommunication
	Writing

Communication among animals
USE	**Animal communication**

Communication arts
USE	**Language arts**

Communication satellites
USE	**Artificial satellites in telecommunication**

Communication systems
USE	subjects with the subdivision *Communication systems,* e.g. **Astronautics—Communication systems;** to be added as needed

Communication systems, Computer
USE	**Computer networks**

Communications relay satellites
USE	**Artificial satellites in telecommunication**

Communion
USE	**Lord's Supper**

Communism (May subdiv. geog.) **320.5; 321.9; 324.1; 335.43**
UF	Bolshevism

Communism—*Continued*
    Collectivism
  SA communism and other sub-
        jects, e.g. **Communism and
        literature;** to be added as
        needed
  BT **Political science**
      Totalitarianism
  NT **Anticommunist movements**
      Collective settlements
      Communism and literature
      Communism and religion
      Dialectical materialism
  RT **Marxism**
      Socialism
**Communism and literature 335.4; 809;
    810.9, etc.**
  UF Literature and communism
  BT **Communism**
      Literature
Communism and religion 261.7; 335.4
  UF Religion and communism
  BT **Communism**
      Religion
  NT **Christianity and economics**
**Communism—Soviet Union 320.5;
    335.430947; 947.084**
  UF Russian communism
      Soviet Union—Communism
**Communism—United States 320.5;
    335.43; 973**
  UF United States—Communism
Communist countries 909; 947
  UF Chinese satellite countries
      Iron curtain countries
      People's democracies
      Russian satellite countries
      Soviet bloc
Communities, Space
  USE **Space colonies**
Community and libraries
  USE **Libraries and community**
Community and school 370.19
    Use for materials on ways in which the
community at large, as distinct from gov-
ernment, may aid the school program.
  UF School and community
  BT **Community life**
  NT **Parents' and teachers' associa-
      tions**

Community antenna television
  USE **Cable television**
Community based residences
  USE **Group homes**
Community centers 374; 790.06
  UF Play centers
      Recreation centers
      School buildings as recreation
        centers
      Schools as social centers
  BT **Cities and towns—Civic im-
      provement**
      Community life
      Community organization
      Recreation
      Social problems
      Social settlements
  NT **Youth hostels**
  RT **Playgrounds**
Community chests
  USE **Fund raising**
Community churches 254
    Use for materials on local churches that
have no denominational affiliations.
  UF Churches, Community
      Churches, Undenominational
      Nondenominational churches
      Undenominational churches
      Union churches
  BT **Christian unity**
Community colleges
  USE **Junior colleges**
Community councils
  USE **Community organization**
Community development (May subdiv.
    geog.) **307.1; 361.6**
  UF Neighborhood development
  BT **Domestic economic assistance**
      Social change
      Urban renewal
  RT **Agricultural extension work**
      City planning
      Technical assistance
Community health services 362.1
  BT **Community services**
      Public health
Community history
  USE **Local history**
Community life 307
  UF Neighborhood

Community life—*Continued*
  BT Associations
  NT Community and school
      Community centers
      Community organization
      Scouts and scouting
  RT City life
Community organization 307
  UF Community councils
  BT Community life
      Social work
  NT Community centers
      Local government
  RT Urban renewal
Community schools
  USE Public schools
Community services 361.7; 361.8
  SA types of services, e.g. **Community health services**; to be added as needed
  NT Community health services
Community songbooks
  USE Songbooks
Community surveys
  USE Social surveys
Community theater
  USE Little theater movement
Compact automobiles 629.222
  UF Automobiles, Compact *[Former heading]*
      Compact cars
  SA names of specific makes and models of compact automobiles, to be added as needed
  BT Automobiles
Compact cars
  USE Compact automobiles
Compact disc interactive technology
  USE CD-I technology
Compact disc players 621.389
  UF Audiodisc players
      CD players
      Digital audio disc players
  BT Phonograph
      Sound—Recording and reproducing
Compact disc read-only memory
  USE CD-ROM

Compact discs 621.389; 780.26
    Use for materials about the compact disc format for sound recordings. General materials and materials about sound recordings that emphasize the content of the recording rather than the format are entered under **Sound recordings.**
  UF CDs (Compact discs)
      Compact disks
      Digital compact discs
      Discs, Compact
  BT Optical storage devices
      Sound recordings
  NT CD-I technology
      CD-ROM
Compact disks
  USE Compact discs
Companies
  USE Business enterprises
      Corporations
Companies, Trust
  USE Trust companies
Companion-animal partnership
  USE Pet therapy
Company libraries
  USE Corporate libraries
Company symbols
  USE Trademarks
Comparative anatomy 574.4; 591.4
  UF Anatomy, Comparative *[Former heading]*
      Morphology
  BT Anatomy
      Zoology
Comparative government 320.3
  UF Government, Comparative
  SA names of countries, cities, etc., with the subdivision *Politics and government,* e.g. **United States—Politics and government;** to be added as needed
  BT Political science
Comparative librarianship 020.9
  UF Librarianship, Comparative
  BT International education
      Library science
Comparative linguistics
  USE Linguistics
Comparative literature 809
  UF Literature, Comparative *[Former heading]*

Comparative literature—*Continued*
  BT **Literature**
Comparative philology
  USE **Linguistics**
Comparative physiology 574.1
  UF Physiology, Comparative *[Former heading]*
  BT **Physiology**
Comparative psychology 156
  UF Animal psychology
    Psychology, Comparative *[Former heading]*
  SA names of animals with the subdivision *Psychology,* e.g. **Dogs—Psychology;** to be added as needed
  BT **Zoology**
  NT **Dogs—Psychology**
    Sociobiology
  RT **Animal intelligence**
    Instinct
Comparative religion
  USE **Christianity and other religions**
    Jewish-Christian relations
    Religions
Comparison (English grammar)
  USE **English language—Comparison**
Comparison of cultures
  USE **Cross cultural studies**
Compass 538; 623.8
  UF Magnetic needle
    Mariner's compass
  BT **Magnetism**
    Navigation
Compassion
  USE **Consolation**
Compensation
  USE **Pensions**
    Wages
    Workers' compensation
Compensatory spending
  USE **Deficit financing**
Competencies, Functional
  USE **Life skills**
Competition 338.6
  BT **Business**
    Business ethics
    Commerce
    Monopolies
  RT **Industrial trusts**
Competition, International
  USE **International competition**
Competition, Unfair
  USE **Unfair competition**
Competitions
  USE **Awards**
    Contests
    and subjects with the subdivision *Competitions,* e.g. **Literature—Competitions;** to be added as needed
Composers 780.92; 920
  UF Songwriters
  SA composers of particular countries, e.g. **American composers;** to be added as needed
  BT **Musicians**
  NT **American composers**
Composers, American
  USE **American composers**
Composition (Art) 701
  UF Art—Composition
  BT **Art**
  NT **Architecture—Composition, proportion, etc.**
  RT **Painting**
Composition (Music) 781.3
  UF Music—Composition
    Musical composition
    Song writing
  BT **Music**
    Music—Theory
  NT **Counterpoint**
    Harmony
    Instrumentation and orchestration
    Musical accompaniment
    Musical form
    Popular music—Writing and publishing
Composition of natural substances
  USE natural substances of unfixed composition, such as soils, plants, animals, farm products, with the subdivision *Composition* for the results of chemical analyses of those substances, e.g.

BT = Broader Term   NT = Narrower Term   RT = Related Term   SA = See Also   UF = Used For

Composition of natural substances—
Continued

      Food—Composition; to be
added as needed

Composition (Printing)

  USE **Typesetting**

Composition (Rhetoric)

  USE **Rhetoric**

and names of languages with
the subdivision *Composition and exercises,* e.g. **English language—Composition and exercises;** to be added
as needed

Compost 631.8

  BT **Fertilizers and manures**

      Soils

  RT **Organic gardening**

Comprehensive health care organizations

  USE **Health maintenance organizations**

Compressed air 621.5

  UF Air, Compressed

      Pneumatic transmission

  BT **Cold storage**

      Foundations

      Pneumatics

      Power (Mechanics)

Compressed work week

  USE **Hours of labor**

Compulsion (Psychology)

  USE **Compulsive behavior**

Compulsive behavior 616.85

  UF Addictive behavior

      Behavior, Compulsive

      Compulsion (Psychology)

  SA types of compulsive behavior,
to be added as needed

  BT **Abnormal psychology**

  NT **Compulsive gambling**

      Exercise addiction

      Workaholism

  RT **Twelve-step programs**

Compulsive exercising

  USE **Exercise addiction**

Compulsive gambling 616.85

  UF Addiction to gambling

      Gambling, Compulsive

  BT **Compulsive behavior**

      Gambling

Compulsive working

  USE **Workaholism**

Compulsory education 379.2

  UF Compulsory school attendance

      Education, Compulsory *[Former heading]*

  BT **Education—Government policy**

  NT **Children—Employment**

      Evening and continuation schools

  RT **School attendance**

Compulsory labor

  USE **Convict labor**

      Peonage

      Slavery

Compulsory military service

  USE **Draft**

Compulsory school attendance

  USE **Compulsory education**

      School attendance

Computation, Approximate

  USE **Approximate computation**

Computation (Mathematics)

  USE **Arithmetic**

Computer aided design 620

  UF CAD

      Computer assisted design

      Drafting, Automatic

  BT **Computers**

      Design

      Engineering

Computer art 700; 760

Use for materials on works of art, mostly drawings and graphics, created or produced with the aid of digital computing or plotting devices.

  UF Art, Computer

      Art, Electronic

      Computer drawing

      Drawing, Computer

      Drawing, Electronic

      Electronic art

      Electronic drawing

  BT **Computer graphics**

      Computers

      Modern art—1900-1999 (20th century)

Computer assisted design

  USE **Computer aided design**

Computer assisted instruction 371.3

Use for materials on automated instruction in which a student interacts directly with a computer.

UF C.A.I.

CAI

Computer teaching

Computers—Educational use

Education—Automation

Education—Data processing

Teaching, Computer

Teaching—Data processing

SA subjects with the subdivision *Computer assisted instruction,* to be added as needed

BT **Electronic data processing**

Programmed instruction

NT **Mathematics—Computer assisted instruction**

Computer assisted instruction— Authoring programs 005.3; 371.3

Use for materials on computer programs that allow the user with comparatively little expertise to design customized computer programs for educational purposes.

UF Authoring programs for computer assisted instruction

Computer authoring programs

BT **Computer software**

Computer authoring programs

USE **Computer assisted instruction—Authoring programs**

Computer awareness

USE **Computer literacy**

Computer-based information systems

USE **Information systems**

Management information systems

Computer bulletin boards 004.693; 384.3

Use for works on computer services that function as a community bulletin board and allow a remote caller to dial a central calling place to enter and receive messages, or to read bulletins or notices.

UF Electronic bulletin boards

BT **Bulletin boards**

Computer networks

Electronic data processing

Electronic mail systems

Online data processing

Computer communication systems

USE **Computer networks**

Computer control

USE **Automation**

Computer crimes 364.1

UF Computer fraud

Fraud, Computer

BT **Crime**

NT **Computer viruses**

RT **Computer security**

Right of privacy

Computer drawing

USE **Computer art**

Computer fraud

USE **Computer crimes**

Computer games 794.8

Use for materials on games played on a computer.

BT **Computer software**

Electronic toys

Games

Computer graphics 006.6

Use for materials on the technique for producing line drawings, particularly engineering drawings, by the use of digital computing and plotting devices. Materials on the use of computer graphics to create artistic designs, drawings, or other works of art are entered under **Computer art.**

UF Automatic drafting

Automatic drawing

Drafting, Automatic

Drawing, Automatic

Drawing, Electronic

Electronic drawing

Graphics, Computer

BT **Electronic data processing**

NT **Computer art**

Virtual reality

Computer hardware

USE **Computer peripherals**

Computer industry (May subdiv. geog.) **338.7**

BT **Industry**

RT **Computers**

Computer input-output equipment

USE **Computer peripherals**

Computer interfaces 004.6; 621.39

Use for materials on equipment and techniques linking computers to peripheral devices or to other computers.

Computer interfaces—*Continued*
UF Interfaces, Computer
BT **Computer peripherals**
Computer jargon
USE **Computer science—
Dictionaries**
Computer keyboarding
USE **Keyboarding (Electronics)**
Computer keyboards
USE **Keyboards (Electronics)**
Computer literacy 004
Use for materials on the awareness of or knowledge about computers as well as for materials on the ability to use and understand computers, including their applications and social implications.
UF Computer awareness
Literacy, Computer
BT **Computers
Computers and civilization
Literacy**
Computer memory systems
USE **Computer storage devices**
Computer music 786.7
UF Music, Computer
BT **Music**
RT **Computer sound processing
Electronic music**
Computer networks 004.6; 384.3
Use for materials on computer systems consisting of two or more interconnected computing units.
UF Communication systems,
Computer
Computer communication systems
Data networks, Computer
Networks, Computer
Teleprocessing networks
SA names of specific computer networks, to be added as needed
BT **Data transmission systems
Electronic data processing
Information networks
Telecommunication**
NT **Computer bulletin boards
Internet (Computer network)**
Computer operating systems 005.4
UF Computers—Operating systems

Operating systems (Computers)
BT **Computer systems**
Computer peripherals 004.7; 621.39
UF Computer hardware
Computer input-output equipment
Input equipment (Computers)
Output equipment (Computers)
SA types of computer peripherals, to be added as needed
BT **Computer systems**
NT **Computer interfaces
Computer storage devices
Computer terminals
Keyboards (Electronics)
Video display terminals**
Computer program languages
USE **Programming languages (Computers)**
Computer programming
USE **Programming (Computers)**
Computer programs
USE **Computer software**
and subjects with the subdivision *Computer programs,* e.g. **Oceanography—
Computer programs;** to be added as needed
Computer science 004
Use for materials discussing collectively the disciplines that deal with the general theory and application of computers.
BT **Science**
RT **Electronic data processing**
Computer science—Dictionaries 004.03
UF Computer jargon
Computer terms
Computers—Dictionaries
Computers—Jargon
Jargon, Computer
BT **Encyclopedias and dictionaries**
Computer security 005.8
Use for materials on protecting computer hardware and software from accidental or malicious access, use, modification, disclosure, or destruction.
UF Computers—Access control
Computers—Security measures
BT **Computers**

BT = Broader Term   NT = Narrower Term   RT = Related Term   SA = See Also   UF = Used For

166

Computer security—*Continued*
RT **Computer crimes**
    Computer viruses
Computer simulation
USE **Virtual reality**
Computer software 005.3
UF Computer programs *[Former heading]*
    Programs, Computer
    Software, Computer
SA types of computer software, e.g. **Computer games; Electronic spreadsheets;** etc.; subjects with the subdivision *Computer programs,* e.g. **Oceanography—Computer programs;** and names of individual computer programs, to be added as needed.
BT **Computer systems**
NT **Computer assisted instruction—Authoring programs**
    Computer games
    Computer software industry
    Computer viruses
    Electronic spreadsheets
    Oceanography—Computer programs
    Programming languages (Computers)
    Utilities (Computer programs)
RT **Computers**
    Programming (Computers)
Computer software industry 338.4
BT **Computer software**
Computer sound processing 006.5
UF Sound processing, Computer
BT **Computers**
    Sound
RT **Computer music**
    Speech processing systems
Computer speech processing systems
USE **Speech processing systems**
Computer storage devices 004.5; 621.39
UF Computer memory systems
    Computers—Memory systems
    Computers—Storage devices

Direct access storage devices (Data processing)
    Random access memories (Data processing)
    Random access storage devices (Data processing)
    Rotating memory devices (Data processing)
    Storage devices, Computer
BT **Computer peripherals**
NT **Optical storage devices**
Computer stored cataloging data
USE **Machine readable bibliographic data**
Computer systems 004
    Use for materials on computers, their peripheral devices, and their operating systems.
BT **Electronic data processing**
NT **Computer operating systems**
    Computer peripherals
    Computer software
    Computers
Computer teaching
USE **Computer assisted instruction**
Computer terminals 004.7; 621.39
UF Terminals, Computer
BT **Computer peripherals**
NT **Video display terminals**
Computer terms
USE **Computer science—Dictionaries**
Computer utility programs
USE **Utilities (Computer programs)**
Computer viruses 005.8
UF Software viruses
    Viruses, Computer
BT **Computer crimes**
    Computer software
RT **Computer security**
Computerized tomography
USE **Tomography**
Computers 004; 338.4; 621.39
    Use for materials on modern electronic computers developed after 1945. Materials on present-day calculators and on calculating machines and mechanical computers made before 1945 are entered under **Calculators.**
UF Automatic computers
    Computers, Electronic
    Computing machines (Electronic)

Computers—*Continued*
      Electronic calculating machines
      Electronic computers
      Mechanical brains
  SA types of computers, e.g.
      Microcomputers; and names
      of specific somputers,
      e.g.**IBM 7090 (Computer);**
      to be added as needed
  BT **Computer systems**
      Cybernetics
      Electronic apparatus and appliances
  NT **Computer aided design**
      Computer art
      Computer literacy
      Computer security
      Computer sound processing
      Computers and children
      Computers and civilization
      Electronic data processing
      IBM 7090 (Computer)
      Information systems
      Microcomputers
      Minicomputers
      Portable computers
      Supercomputers
  RT **Calculators**
      Computer industry
      Computer software

Computers—Access control
  USE **Computer security**

Computers and children 004.01
  BT **Children**
      Computers

Computers and civilization 004.01;
    303.48
  UF Civilization and computers
  BT **Computers**
      Technology and civilization
  NT **Computer literacy**

Computers—Cartoons and caricatures
    338.4; 621.39; 741.5
  BT **Cartoons and caricatures**

Computers—Dictionaries
  USE **Computer science—**
      Dictionaries

Computers—Educational use
  USE **Computer assisted instruction**

Computers, Electronic
  USE **Computers**

Computers—Jargon
  USE **Computer science—**
      Dictionaries

Computers—Memory systems
  USE **Computer storage devices**

Computers—Operating systems
  USE **Computer operating systems**

Computers, Portable
  USE **Portable computers**

Computers—Programming
  USE **Programming (Computers)**

Computers—Security measures
  USE **Computer security**

Computers—Simulation programs
  USE **Virtual reality**

Computers—Storage devices
  USE **Computer storage devices**

Computers—Utility programs
  USE **Utilities (Computer programs)**

Computing machines (Electronic)
  USE **Computers**

Con artists
  USE **Swindlers and swindling**

Con game
  USE **Swindlers and swindling**

Concentration
  USE **Attention**

Concentration camps 365
  UF Internment camps
  SA names of wars with the subdivision *Prisoners and prisons;* and names of individual camps, to be added as needed
  BT **Military camps**
      Political crimes and offenses
  NT **World War, 1939-1945—**
      Prisoners and prisons
  RT **Prisoners of war**

Concept formation
  USE **Concept learning**

Concept learning 153.2; 370.15
    Use for materials on the process of discovering the distinguishing features of particular concepts and the ensuing ability to use the concepts appropriately.
  UF Concept formation
      Learning, Concept

Concept learning—*Continued*
   BT   **Concepts**
          Psychology of learning
Conception—Prevention
   USE   **Birth control**
Concepts 153.2
   SA   types of concepts and images,
          e.g. **Size and shape;** to be
          added as needed
   BT   **Perception**
   NT   **Concept learning**
          Opposites
          Size and shape
Concerto 784.18
   Use for musical scores and for materials
on the concerto as a musical form.
   UF   Concertos *[Former heading]*
   BT   **Musical form**
          Orchestral music
Concertos
   USE   **Concerto**
Concerts 780.78
   BT   **Amusements**
          Music
   RT   **Music festivals**
Conciliation, Industrial
   USE   **Industrial arbitration**
Concordances
   USE   names of individual authors,
          literary works, sacred
          works, literatures, and liter-
          ary forms, with the subdivi-
          sion *Concordances,* e.g.
          Shakespeare, William,
          1564-1616—Concordances;
          Bible—Concordances; etc.,
          to be added as needed
Concrete 691; 693
   BT   **Building materials**
          Foundations
          Masonry
          Plaster and plastering
   NT   **Reinforced concrete**
   RT   **Cement**
          Concrete construction
Concrete construction 693
   UF   Building, Concrete
          Construction, Concrete
   BT   **Architecture**
          Building

   RT   **Concrete**
Concrete—Testing 620.1
   BT   **Strength of materials**
Condemnation of land
   USE   **Eminent domain**
Condensers (Electricity) 621.31
   UF   Electric condensers
   BT   **Induction coils**
Condensers (Steam) 621.1
   BT   **Steam engines**
Condominium timesharing
   USE   **Timesharing (Real estate)**
Condominiums 346.04; 643
   BT   **Apartment houses**
   NT   **Timesharing (Real estate)**
Conduct of life 170
   Use for materials on standards of be-
havior and materials containing moral
guidance and advice to the individual.
   UF   Morals
          Personal conduct
   SA   names of vices and virtues, to
          be added as needed
   BT   **Ethics**
          Human behavior
          Life skills
   NT   **Vice**
          Virtue
Conducting 781.45
   Use for materials on orchestral conduct-
ing or a combination of orchestral and
choral conducting. Materials limited to
choral conducting are entered under **Cho-
ral conducting.**
   BT   **Music**
   NT   **Choral conducting**
   RT   **Bands (Music)**
          Conductors (Music)
          Orchestra
Conducting, Choral
   USE   **Choral conducting**
Conductors, Electric
   USE   **Electric conductors**
Conductors (Music) 784.2092; 920
   UF   Bandmasters
          Music conductors
   BT   **Musicians**
          Orchestra
   RT   **Choral conducting**
          Conducting
Conduits
   USE   **Aqueducts**

Confectionery 641.8; 664
  UF   Candy
         Sweets
  BT   **Cooking**
  NT   **Cake**
         Cake decorating
Confederacies
  USE **Federal government**
Confederate States of America 973.7
  BT   **United States—History—**
         1861-1865, Civil War
Confederation of American colonies
  USE **United States—History—**
         1783-1809
Conference calls (Teleconferencing)
  USE **Teleconferencing**
Conferences
  USE **Congresses and conventions**
Conferences, Parent-teacher
  USE **Parent-teacher conferences**
Confession 265
  UF   Auricular confession
         Forgiveness of sin
  RT   **Penance**
Confessions of faith
  USE **Creeds**
Confidence game
  USE **Swindlers and swindling**
Configuration (Psychology)
  USE **Gestalt psychology**
Confirmation 265
  BT   **Sacraments**
Conflict, Ethnic
  USE **Ethnic relations**
Conflict of cultures
  USE **Culture conflict**
Conflict of generations 306.874
  UF   Generation gap
  BT   **Children and adults**
         Human relations
         Social conflict
  RT   **Parent and child**
Conflict of interests 351.9
  BT   **Political ethics**
  NT   **Misconduct in office**
         Political corruption
Conflict, Social
  USE **Social conflict**
Conformity 153.8; 302.5; 303.3
  UF   Nonconformity

         Social conformity
  BT   **Attitude (Psychology)**
         Freedom
  RT   **Individuality**
Confucianism 181; 299
  BT   **Religions**
Congenital diseases
  USE **Medical genetics**
Conglomerate corporations 338.8
  UF   Business combinations
         Corporations, Conglomerate
         Diversified corporations
  BT   **Corporate mergers and acqui-**
         sitions
         Corporations
Congregationalism 285.8
  BT   **Christian sects**
  NT   **Unitarianism**
  RT   **Calvinism**
         Puritans
Congress (U.S.)
  USE **United States. Congress**
Congresses and conventions 060
  UF   Conferences
         Conventions (Congresses)
         International conferences
  SA   subjects with the subdivision
         Congresses, e.g. **World War,**
         1939-1945—Congresses;
         and names of specific con-
         gresses, to be added as
         needed
  BT   **Intellectual cooperation**
         International cooperation
  NT   **International organization**
         Treaties
         World War, 1939-1945—
         Congresses
Congressional investigations
  USE **Governmental investigations**
Conjuring
  USE **Magic tricks**
Conscience 170; 241
  BT   **Christian ethics**
         Duty
         Ethics
  NT   **Freedom of conscience**
Conscientious objectors 343; 355.2
  SA   names of wars with the subdi-
         vision *Conscientious objec-*
         tors, to be added as needed

BT = Broader Term   NT = Narrower Term   RT = Related Term   SA = See Also   UF = Used For

Conscientious objectors—*Continued*
- BT **Freedom of conscience**
  War and religion
- NT **World War, 1939-1945—**
  Conscientious objectors
- RT **Draft resisters**
  Pacifism

Consciousness 126; 153
- BT **Apperception**
  Mind and body
  Perception
  Psychology
- NT **Gestalt psychology**
  Individuality
  Personality
  Self
  Theory of knowledge
- RT **Subconsciousness**

Consciousness expanding drugs
- USE **Hallucinogens**

Conscription, Military
- USE **Draft**

Conservation movement
- USE **Environmental movement**

Conservation of buildings
- USE **Architecture—Conservation**
  and restoration

Conservation of energy
- USE **Energy conservation**
  Force and energy

Conservation of forests
- USE **Forests and forestry**

Conservation of natural resources 333.7;
639.9
- UF Preservation of natural re-
  sources
  Resource management
- BT **Environmental protection**
  Natural resources
- NT **Energy conservation**
  National parks and reserves
  Nature conservation
  Plant conservation
  Soil conservation
  Water conservation
  Wildlife conservation
- RT **Environmental policy**

Conservation of nature
- USE **Nature conservation**

Conservation of plants
- USE **Plant conservation**

Conservation of power resources
- USE **Energy conservation**

Conservation of the soil
- USE **Soil conservation**

Conservation of water
- USE **Water conservation**

Conservation of wildlife
- USE **Wildlife conservation**

Conservation of works of art, books,
etc.
- USE subjects with the subdivision
  Conservation and restora-
  tion, e.g. **Library**
  resources—Conservation and
  restoration; Painting—
  Conservation and restora-
  tion; etc., to be added as
  needed

Conservatism 320.5
- RT **Right and left (Political sci-**
  ence)

Conservatories, Home
- USE **Garden rooms**

Consolation 152.4; 155.9
- UF Compassion
  Solace
  Sympathy *[Former heading]*
- BT **Emotions**
  Human behavior
- RT **Bereavement**
  Grief

Consolidation and merger of corporations
- USE **Corporate mergers and acqui-**
  sitions

Consolidation of schools
- USE **Schools—Centralization**

Consortia, Library
- USE **Library cooperation**
  Library information networks

Constellations 523.8
- SA names of constellations, to be
  added as needed
- BT **Sky**
- RT **Astrology**
  Astronomy
  Stars

Constitution (U.S.)
- USE **United States—Constitution**

Constitutional history 342
- UF Constitutional law—History

Constitutional history—*Continued*
    History, Constitutional
  SA names of countries, states,
      etc., with the subdivision
      Constitutional history, to be
      added as needed
  BT **Constitutions**
      History
  NT **Democracy**
      Monarchy
      **Representative government and
      representation**
      Republics
      **United States—Constitutional
      history**
  RT **Political science**

Constitutional law 342
  Use for materials on constitutions or
constitutional law. General collections of
texts of constitutions are entered under
Constitutions. Collections of texts of state
constitutions are entered under **State con-
stitutions.**
  UF Law, Constitutional
  SA names of countries with the
      subdivision *Constitutional
      law,* e.g. **United States—
      Constitutional law;** to be
      added as needed
  BT **Law**
  NT **Citizenship**
      Civil rights
      Democracy
      Eminent domain
      Executive power
      Federal government
      Injunctions
      Legislation
      Legislative bodies
      Magna Carta
      Monarchy
      Proportional representation
      Referendum
      **Representative government and
      representation**
      Republics
      Separation of powers
      Suffrage
      **United States—Constitutional
      law**
      War and emergency powers

  RT **Administrative law**
      Constitutions
      Political science
Constitutional law—History
  USE **Constitutional history**
Constitutional rights
  USE **Civil rights**
Constitutions 342
  Use for general collections of texts of
constitutions. Collections of texts of state
constitutions are entered under **State con-
stitutions.** Materials on constitutions or
constitutional law are entered under **Con-
stitutional law.**
  SA names of corporate bodies,
      countries, states, provinces,
      etc., with the subdivision
      Constitution, e.g. **United
      States—Constitution;** to be
      added as needed
  BT **Political science**
  NT **Constitutional history**
      Equal rights amendments
      State constitutions
      United States—Constitution
  RT **Constitutional law**
      **Representative government and
      representation**
Constitutions, State
  USE **State constitutions**
Construction
  USE **Architecture**
      Building
      Engineering
Construction, Concrete
  USE **Concrete construction**
Construction, House
  USE **House construction**
Construction of roads
  USE **Roads**
Consulates
  USE **Diplomatic and consular ser-
      vice**
Consuls
  USE **Diplomats**
Consultants
  UF Advisors
  SA types of consultants, to be
      added as needed
  BT **Counseling**
  NT **Educational consultants**

Consultative management
USE **Participative management**
Consumer behavior
USE **Consumers**
Consumer boycotts
USE **Boycotts**
Consumer credit 332.7
UF Credit, Consumer
BT **Banks and banking**
Credit
Personal finance
NT **Credit cards**
Instalment plan
Personal loans
RT **Credit unions**
Consumer education 640.73

Use for materials on the selection and efficient use of consumer goods and services and on methods of educating consumers. Materials on the decision-making processes, external factors, and individual characteristics of consumers that determine their purchasing behavior are entered under **Consumers**. Materials on the economic theory of consumption are entered under **Consumption (Economics).**

UF Buyers' guides
Consumers' guides
Shoppers' guides
BT **Home economics**
RT **Consumers**
Shopping
Consumer goods 338.4

Use for materials on products that are purchased for personal or household purposes.

UF Consumer products
Goods, Consumer
Merchandise
BT **Commercial products**
Manufactures
RT **Consumption (Economics)**
Consumer loans
USE **Personal loans**
Consumer organizations
USE **Cooperative societies**
Consumer price indexes 338.5
UF Cost of living indexes
Price indexes, Consumer
BT **Cost of living**
Prices
Consumer products
USE **Consumer goods**

Consumer protection 343; 381.3

Use for materials on governmental and private activities that guard the consumer against dangers to his health, safety, or economic well-being.

UF Consumerism
BT **Industry—Government policy**
NT **Drugs—Testing**
Food adulteration and inspection
Product recall
Product safety
Consumerism
USE **Consumer protection**
Consumers 640.73; 658.8

Use for materials on the decision-making processes, external factors, and individual characteristics of consumers that determine their purchasing behavior. Materials on the selection and efficient use of consumer goods and services and on methods of educating consumers are entered under **Consumer education**. Materials on the economic theory of consumption are entered under **Consumption (Economics).**

UF Consumer behavior
NT **Boycotts**
Young consumers
RT **Consumer education**
Consumption (Economics)
Shopping
Consumers' cooperative societies
USE **Cooperative societies**
Consumers' guides
USE **Consumer education**
Consumption (Economics) 339.4

Use for materials on the economic theory of consumption. Materials on the decision-making processes, external factors, and individual characteristics of consumers that determine their purchasing behavior are entered under **Consumers**. Materials on the selection and efficient use of consumer goods and services and on methods of educating consumers are entered under **Consumer education**.

BT **Economics**
NT **Prices**
RT **Consumer goods**
Consumers
Consumption of alcoholic beverages
USE **Drinking of alcoholic beverages**
Consumption of energy
USE **Energy consumption**

Contact lenses 617.7
  BT   Eyeglasses
       Lenses
Contagion and contagious diseases
  USE   Communicable diseases
Contagious diseases
  USE   Communicable diseases
Container gardening 635.9
  BT   Gardening
  NT   Miniature gardens
  RT   Flower gardening
       House plants
       Indoor gardening
       Window gardening
Containers, Box
  USE   Boxes
Contaminated food
  USE   Food contamination
Contamination of environment
  USE   Pollution
Contemporary art
  USE   Modern art—1900-1999 (20th
        century)
Contests 001.4; 790.1
  UF   Competitions
  SA   types of contests and names
       of specific contests, e.g.
       Olympic games; and sub-
       jects with the subdivision
       Competitions or Tourna-
       ments, e.g. Literature—
       Competitions; Tennis—
       Tournaments; to be added
       as needed
  NT   Literature—Competitions
       Olympic games
       Tennis—Tournaments
  RT   Awards
Continental drift 551.1
  UF   Drifting of continents
  BT   Continents
       Geology
  RT   Plate tectonics
Continental shelf 551.4
  BT   Geology
  RT   Territorial waters
Continents 551.4
  BT   Earth
  NT   Continental drift

Continuation schools
  USE   Evening and continuation
        schools
Continuing education 374
  UF   Education, Continuing
       Lifelong education
       Permanent education
       Recurrent education
  BT   Education
  NT   Evening and continuation
       schools
  RT   Adult education
Contra-Iran Affair, 1985-1990
  USE   Iran-Contra Affair, 1985-1990
Contraband trade
  USE   Smuggling
Contraception
  USE   Birth control
Contract bridge
  USE   Bridge (Game)
Contract labor 331.5
  UF   Indentured servants
  BT   Labor
  NT   Convict labor
       Slavery
  RT   Peonage
Contractions
  USE   Abbreviations
        Ciphers
Contracts 346
  UF   Agreements
  SA   types of contracts; and sub-
       jects with the subdivision
       Contracts and specifications,
       to be added as needed
  BT   Commerce
       Commercial law
  NT   Authors and publishers
       Building—Contracts and spec-
       ifications
       Covenants
       Labor contract
       Liability (Law)
       Mortgages
       Negotiable instruments
Contrition
  USE   Penance
Control
  USE   types of control, e.g. Flood
        control; Weather control;

Control—*Continued*
etc., and animals, plants, or
crops with the subdivision
Control, e.g. **Mosquitoes—
Control;** to be added as
needed

Control of self
USE **Self-control**

Conundrums
USE **Riddles**

Convenience cooking
USE **Quick and easy cooking**

Convenience foods 641.3; 664
Use for materials on prepackaged foods
that are easy to prepare for eating.
UF Fast foods
BT **Food**

Conventions (Congresses)
USE **Congresses and conventions**

Conventions, Political
USE **Political conventions**

Convents 271; 726
UF Cloisters
Nunneries
NT **Religious orders for women**
RT **Abbeys**
Monasteries

Conversation 808.56
UF Discussion
Table talk
Talking
BT **Communication**
Language and languages
NT **Discussion groups**

Conversation in foreign languages
USE **Modern languages—
Conversations and phrases**
and names of foreign lan-
guages with the subdivision
Conversations and phrases,
e.g. **French language—
Conversations and phrases;**
to be added as needed

Conversion 248.2; 291.4
BT **Christian life**
Evangelistic work
Theology
NT **Converts**
RT **Regeneration (Theology)**

Conversion of saline water
USE **Sea water conversion**

Conversion of waste products
USE **Recycling**

Converts 248.2
Use for materials on converts from one
religion or denomination to another.
SA converts to a particular reli-
gion or denomination, e.g.
Converts to Catholicism; to
be added as needed
BT **Conversion**
NT **Converts to Catholicism**

Converts, Catholic
USE **Converts to Catholicism**

Converts to Catholicism 282
UF Catholic Church—Converts
Catholic converts *[Former
heading]*
Converts, Catholic *[Former
heading]*
BT **Catholics**
Converts

Conveying machinery 621.8
UF Conveyors
BT **Machinery**
Materials handling
RT **Hoisting machinery**

Conveyors
USE **Conveying machinery**

Convict labor 331.5; 365
UF Compulsory labor
Forced labor
Prison labor
BT **Contract labor**
Criminals
Labor
RT **Peonage**
Prisons

Convicts
USE **Criminals**
Prisoners

Cook books
USE **Cooking**

Cookbooks
USE **Cooking**

Cookery
USE **Cooking**

Cookery for the sick
USE **Cooking for the sick**

Cookery, French
USE **French cooking**

BT = Broader Term   NT = Narrower Term   RT = Related Term   SA = See Also   UF = Used For

Cookery—Natural foods
  USE   **Cooking—Natural foods**
Cookery—Ohio
  USE   **Cooking—Ohio**
Cookery—Southern States
  USE   **Cooking—Southern States**
Cookery—Vegetables
  USE   **Cooking—Vegetables**
Cooking (May subdiv. geog. by states
          or particular areas in the
          U.S., e.g. **Cooking—Ohio;**
          Cooking—Southern States;
          etc.) **641.5**

  Use for general materials on cooking
and for materials specifically on American
cooking.

  UF   Cook books
       Cookbooks
       Cookery *[Former heading]*
       Food preparation
       Gastronomy
       Recipes
  SA   types of cooking, e.g. **Micro-**
       wave cooking; cooking of
       particular countries, e.g.
       French cooking; and, for
       materials on the cooking of
       specific foods or kinds of
       food, **Cooking** with a subdi-
       vision for the food, e.g.
       Cooking—Vegetables;
       Cooking—Natural foods;
       etc., to be added as needed
  BT   **Home economics**
  NT   **Baking**
       Bread
       Breakfasts
       Cake
       Canning and preserving
       Catering
       Confectionery
       Cooking for the sick
       Desserts
       Dinners
       Eggs
       Fish as food
       Flavoring essences
       French cooking
       Herbs
       Luncheons

       Meat
       Menus
       Microwave cooking
       Outdoor cooking
       Pastry
       Quantity cooking
       Quick and easy cooking
       Salads
       Sandwiches
       Sauces
       Shellfish
       Soups
       Tea
       Vegetarian cooking
  RT   **Diet**
       Food
Cooking, Barbecue
  USE   **Barbecue cooking**
Cooking for institutions
  USE   **Food service**
Cooking for large numbers
  USE   **Quantity cooking**
Cooking for the sick 641.5
  UF   Cookery for the sick *[Former
       heading]*
       Food for invalids
       Invalid cooking
  SA   types of diets, e.g. **Salt free**
       diet; to be added as needed
  BT   **Cooking**
       Diet in disease
       Nursing
       Sick
  NT   **Diet therapy**
       Salt free diet
Cooking, French
  USE   **French cooking**
Cooking, Microwave
  USE   **Microwave cooking**
Cooking—Natural foods 641.5
  UF   Cookery—Natural foods *[For-
       mer heading]*
       Natural food cooking
  RT   **Natural foods**
Cooking—Ohio 641.59771
  UF   Cookery—Ohio *[Former head-
       ing]*
       Ohio—Cooking
Cooking, Outdoor
  USE   **Outdoor cooking**

Cooking—Southern States 641.5975
  UF Cookery—Southern States
         [Former heading]
         Southern States—Cooking
Cooking utensils
  USE **Kitchen utensils**
Cooking—Vegetables 641.6
  UF Cookery—Vegetables *[Former heading]*
  BT **Vegetables**
  RT **Salads**
        Vegetarian cooking
Cooking, Vegetarian
  USE **Vegetarian cooking**
Cooling appliances
  USE **Refrigeration**
Cooperation 334
  Use for general materials on the theory and history of cooperation and the cooperative movement. Materials dealing specifically with cooperative enterprises are entered under **Cooperative societies.**
  UF Cooperative distribution
        Distribution, Cooperative
        Rochdale system
  BT **Associations**
        Commerce
        Economics
  NT **Collective settlements**
        Cooperative agriculture
        Cooperative banks
        Cooperative societies
        International cooperation
        Labor unions
        Savings and loan associations
  RT **Profit sharing**
Cooperation, Intellectual
  USE **Intellectual cooperation**
Cooperation, International
  USE **International cooperation**
Cooperation, Library
  USE **Library cooperation**
Cooperative agriculture 334
  Use for materials on cooperation in the production and disposal of agricultural products.
  UF Agricultural cooperation
        Agriculture, Cooperative *[Former heading]*
        Collective farms
        Farmers' cooperatives

  BT **Agriculture**
        Cooperation
  RT **Collective settlements**
Cooperative banks 334
  UF Banks and banking, Cooperative *[Former heading]*
        People's banks
  BT **Banks and banking**
        Cooperation
        Cooperative societies
        Personal loans
  NT **Credit unions**
  RT **Savings and loan associations**
Cooperative building associations
  USE **Savings and loan associations**
Cooperative distribution
  USE **Cooperation**
         Cooperative societies
Cooperative housing
  USE **Communal living**
Cooperative learning 371.1
  Use for materials on the method of education that involves having students work together on projects in a structured manner.
  UF Group method in teaching
        Group teaching
        Group work in education
  BT **Education**
        Teaching
Cooperative living
  USE **Collective settlements**
         Communal living
Cooperative societies 334; 658.8
  Use for materials dealing specifically with cooperative enterprises. General materials on the theory and history of cooperation and the cooperative movement are entered under **Cooperation.**
  UF Consumer organizations
        Consumers' cooperative societies
        Cooperative distribution
        Cooperative stores
        Distribution, Cooperative
        Societies, Cooperative
        Stores
  SA types of cooperative societies, e.g. **Credit unions;** to be added as needed
  BT **Cooperation**
        Corporations

Cooperative societies—*Continued*
      Societies
  NT Cooperative banks
      Credit unions
      Savings and loan associations
Cooperative stores
  USE Cooperative societies
Coping behavior
  USE Adjustment (Psychology)
      Life skills
Copper engraving
  USE Engraving
Copperwork 673; 739.5
  BT Metalwork
Copy writing
  USE Advertising copy
Copybooks
  USE Handwriting
Copying processes and machines 686.4
  UF Duplicating processes
      Photocopying machines
      Reproduction processes
      Reprography
  SA names of specific processes,
      e.g. Xerography; to be add-
      ed as needed
  NT Xerography
Copyright 341.7; 346.04
  May be subdivided by topic, e.g.
  Copyright—Books; etc.
  UF Intellectual property
      International copyright
      Literary property
      Property, Literary
  BT Authorship
  NT Fair use (Copyright)
  RT Authors and publishers
      Publishers and publishing
Copyright—Books 341.7; 346.04
  UF Books—Copyright
Coral reefs and islands 551.4
  UF Atolls
  BT Geology
      Islands
Corals 563; 593.6
  BT Invertebrates
      Marine animals
Cordials (Liquor)
  USE Liquors

Core curriculum
  USE Colleges and universities—
      Curricula
      Education—Curricula
      and types of education and
      schools with the subdivi-
      sion *Curricula,* e.g. Library
      education—Curricula; to be
      added as needed
Corn 633.1; 633.2
  UF Maize
  BT Forage plants
      Grain
Corn—Therapeutic use 615.5
  BT Diet therapy
      Therapeutics
Coronary heart diseases
  USE Heart diseases
Corporate acquisitions
  USE Corporate mergers and acqui-
      sitions
Corporate libraries 027.6
  Use for materials on libraries located within companies, firms, or private businesses, covering any subject areas. Materials on libraries with a subject focus on business are entered under **Business libraries.**
  UF Company libraries
      Industrial libraries
      Libraries, Company
      Libraries, Corporate
      Libraries, Industrial
  BT Special libraries
Corporate mergers
  USE Corporate mergers and acqui-
      sitions
Corporate mergers and acquisitions
      338.8; 658.1
  UF Acquisition of corporations
      Buyouts, Corporate
      Consolidation and merger of
      corporations
      Corporate acquisitions
      Corporate mergers
      Corporate takeovers
      Industrial mergers
      Merger of corporations
      Takeovers, Corporate
  BT Corporations
  NT Conglomerate corporations

Corporate mergers and acquisitions—
Continued
       Leveraged buyouts
Corporate patronage of the arts
  USE **Art patronage**
Corporate symbols
  USE **Trademarks**
Corporate takeovers
  USE **Corporate mergers and acquisitions**
Corporation law 346
  UF Law, Corporation
  BT **Commercial law**
      Corporations
      Law
  NT **Public service commissions**
  RT **Industrial trusts**
      Monopolies
      Public utilities
      Restraint of trade
Corporations 338.7; 658.1
  UF Companies
  BT **Business enterprises**
      Stocks
  NT **Conglomerate corporations**
      Cooperative societies
      Corporate mergers and acquisitions
      Corporation law
      Government ownership
      Multinational corporations
      Municipal ownership
      Public service commissions
      Trust companies
  RT **Industrial trusts**
      Public utilities
Corporations—Accounting 657; 658.15
  BT **Accounting**
      Bookkeeping
Corporations—Art patronage
  USE **Art patronage**
Corporations, Conglomerate
  USE **Conglomerate corporations**
Corporations—Finance 658.15
  UF Capitalization (Finance)
Corporations, International
  USE **Multinational corporations**
Corporations, Multinational
  USE **Multinational corporations**
Corporations, Nonprofit
  USE **Nonprofit organizations**

Corpulence
  USE **Obesity**
Correctional institutions (May subdiv. geog.) **365**
  UF Penal institutions
  SA types of correctional institutions, to be added as needed
  BT **Punishment**
  NT **Halfway houses**
      Penal colonies
      Prisons
      Reformatories
Correctional services
  USE **Corrections**
Corrections 364.6
    Use for materials on the rehabilitation and treatment of offenders through parole, penal custody, and probation programs, and on the administration of such programs.
  UF Correctional services
      Criminals—Rehabilitation programs
      Penology
  BT **Administration of criminal justice**
  NT **Parole**
      Probation
      Punishment
Correspondence
  USE **Business letters**
      Letter writing
      Letters
      and ethnic groups, classes of persons, and names of individual persons and families with the subdivision *Correspondence,* e.g. **Authors—Correspondence**; to be added as needed
Correspondence schools and courses 374
  UF Home education
      Home study courses
  BT **Education**
      Technical education
      University extension
  RT **Self-instruction**
Corrosion and anticorrosives 620.1
  UF Anticorrosive paint
      Rust

Corrosion and anticorrosives—
Continued

      Rustless coatings
- BT   **Industrial chemistry**
- RT   **Paint**

Corrupt practices
- USE subjects with the subdivision
     Corrupt practices, e.g.
     Adoption—Corrupt
     practices; Sports—Corrupt
     practices; etc., to be added
     as needed

Corruption in politics
- USE **Political corruption**

Corruption in sports
- USE **Sports—Corrupt practices**

Corruption, Police
- USE **Police corruption**

Corsairs
- USE **Pirates**

Cosmetic surgery
- USE **Plastic surgery**

Cosmetics 646.7; 668
- UF   Makeup (Cosmetics)
     Toilet preparations
- BT   **Beauty shops**
     Costume
     Personal grooming
- NT   **Perfumes**
     Theatrical makeup

Cosmic chemistry
- USE **Space chemistry**

Cosmic rays 539.7
- UF   Millikan rays
- BT   **Nuclear physics**
     Radiation
     Radioactivity
     Space environment

Cosmobiology
- USE **Space biology**

Cosmochemistry
- USE **Space chemistry**

Cosmogony
- USE **Universe**

Cosmogony, Biblical
- USE **Creation**

Cosmography
- USE **Universe**

Cosmology
- USE **Universe**

Cosmology, Biblical
- USE **Creation**

Cosmonauts
- USE **Astronauts**

Cost accounting 657
- BT   **Accounting**
     Bookkeeping

Cost of living 339.4
- UF   Food, Cost of
     Household finances
     Living, Cost of
- BT   **Economics**
     Home economics
     Labor
     Social conditions
     Standard of living
- NT   **Consumer price indexes**
     Household budgets
     Subsistence economy
- RT   **Prices**
     Saving and thrift
     Wages

Cost of living indexes
- USE **Consumer price indexes**

Cost of medical care
- USE **Medical care—Costs**

Costs
- USE subjects with the subdivision
     Costs, e.g. **Medical care—**
     Costs; to be added as need-
     ed

Costume (May subdiv. geog.) 391
    Use for descriptive and historical materials on the costume of various countries, peoples, or historical periods and for materials on fancy dress and theatrical costumes. Materials on clothing from a practical standpoint, including the art of dress, are entered under **Clothing and dress.** Materials on the prevailing mode or style of dress are entered under **Fashion.**
- UF   Acting—Costume
     Fancy dress
     Style in dress
     Theatrical costume
- SA   ethnic groups and classes of
     persons with the subdivi-
     sion *Costume,* e.g. **Indians**
     of North America—
     Costume; Children—
     Costume; etc., to be added
     as needed

BT = Broader Term   NT = Narrower Term   RT = Related Term   SA = See Also   UF = Used For

Costume—*Continued*
  BT Decorative arts
      Ethnology
      Manners and customs
  NT Armor
      Children—Costume
      Cosmetics
      Fans
      Hats
      Indians of North America—
        Costume
      Jewelry
      Masks (Facial)
      Military uniforms
      Millinery
      Theatrical makeup
      Umbrellas and parasols
      Wigs
  RT Clothing and dress
      Fashion
Costume design
  USE Fashion design
Costume jewelry
  USE Jewelry
Costume, Military
  USE Military uniforms
Cottage industry
  USE Home business
Cottage industry, Electronic
  USE Telecommuting
Cotton 633.5; 677
  BT Economic botany
      Fabrics
      Fibers
      Yarn
Cotton manufacture 677
  BT Textile industry
Councils and synods 262
  UF Church councils
      Ecumenical councils
      Synods
  SA names of specific councils and
      synods, e.g. **Vatican Council
      (2nd : 1962-1965);** to be
      added as needed
  BT Christianity
      Church history
  NT Vatican Council (2nd : 1962-
      1965)

Counseling 361.3; 371.4
  Use for materials on the principles or
  practices used in various types of guidance
  work.
  UF Guidance
  SA types of counseling; and eth-
      nic groups and classes of
      persons with the subdivi-
      sion *Counseling of,* e.g.
      Employees—Counseling of;
      to be added as needed
  BT Applied psychology
      Helping behavior
      Personnel management
      Welfare work in industry
  NT Consultants
      Crisis centers
      Drug abuse counseling
      Educational counseling
      Elderly—Counseling of
      Employees—Counseling of
      Family therapy
      Health counseling
      Hotlines (Telephone counsel-
        ing)
      Marriage counseling
      Peer counseling
      School counseling
      Vocational guidance
  RT Interviewing
      Social case work
Counseling of the elderly
  USE Elderly—Counseling of
Counseling with the aged
  USE Elderly—Counseling of
Counter culture 306
  UF Alternative lifestyle
      Counterculture
      Nonconformity
      Subculture
  BT Lifestyles
      Social conditions
  NT Bohemianism
  RT Collective settlements
      Communal living
      Radicalism
Counter-Reformation 270.6
  UF Anti-Reformation
  BT Christianity
  RT Church history—1500-, Mod-
      ern period

BT = Broader Term   NT = Narrower Term   RT = Related Term   SA = See Also   UF = Used For

Counter-Reformation—*Continued*
Reformation
Counterculture
USE **Counter culture**
Counterespionage
USE **Intelligence service**
Counterfeits and counterfeiting 332;
364.1
BT **Coinage**
Crime
Forgery
Impostors and imposture
Money
Swindlers and swindling
NT **Art forgeries**
Credit card crimes
Literary forgeries
Counterintelligence
USE **Intelligence service**
Counterpoint 781.2
BT **Composition (Music)**
Music—Theory
NT **Fugue**
Counting 513.2
Use for materials on counting, including counting books. Materials on numbers, numbering, and systems of numeration are entered under **Numbers.** Materials on the conceptualization of numbers are entered under **Number concept.**
UF Counting books
BT **Arithmetic—Study and teaching**
NT **Number games**
RT **Numbers**
Counting books
USE **Counting**
Country and western music
USE **Country music**
Country churches
USE **Rural churches**
Country life (May subdiv. geog.)
307.72; 630
Use for descriptive, popular, and literary materials on living in the country. Materials on social organization and conditions in rural communities are entered under **Rural sociology.**
UF Rural life
BT **Manners and customs**
NT **Agriculture—Societies**
Farm life

Mountain life
Plantation life
RT **Outdoor life**
Rural sociology
Country life—United States 307.72; 630
UF United States—Country life
Country music 781.642
UF Country and western music
Hillbilly music
Western and country music
BT **Folk music—United States**
Popular music
RT **Cowhands—Songs**
Country schools
USE **Rural schools**
County agricultural agents 630.7
BT **Agricultural extension work**
Agriculture—Study and teaching
County government 320.8; 352
UF County officers
BT **Local government**
County libraries 027.4
UF Libraries, County
BT **Library extension**
Public libraries
Regional libraries
County officers
USE **County government**
County planning
USE **Regional planning**
Couples, Married
USE **Married people**
Coupons (Retail trade) 659
BT **Advertising**
Coups d'état
USE **Revolutions**
Courage 179
UF Bravery
Heroism
BT **Virtue**
NT **Morale**
RT **Heroes and heroines**
Courses of study
USE **Education—Curricula**
and types of education and schools with the subdivision *Curricula,* e.g. **Library education—Curricula; Colleges and universities—**

Courses of study—*Continued*
      Curricula; etc., to be added
      as needed
Court fools
  USE **Fools and jesters**
Court life
  USE **Courts and courtiers**
Court martial
  USE **Courts martial and courts of**
      inquiry
Courtesy 177; 395
  UF Manners
      Politeness
  BT **Etiquette**
      Virtue
Courtiers
  USE **Courts and courtiers**
Courting
  USE **Dating (Social customs)**
Courtroom drama
  USE **Legal drama (Films)**
      Legal drama (Radio programs)
      Legal drama (Television pro-
      grams)
Courts (May subdiv. geog.) **347**
  UF Judiciary
  BT **Law**
  NT **Arbitration and award**
      Courts martial and courts of
      inquiry
      Criminal procedure
      Jury
      Juvenile courts
  RT **Administration of justice**
      Judges
Courts and courtiers 394; 929.7
  UF Court life
      Courtiers
  BT **Manners and customs**
  NT **Fools and jesters**
      Princes and princesses
  RT **Kings, queens, rulers, etc.**
Courts martial and courts of inquiry
  343
  UF Court martial
      Military courts
  BT **Courts**
      Trials
  RT **Military law**
Courts—United States 347.73
  UF Federal courts

      United States—Courts
Courtship
  USE **Dating (Social customs)**
Courtship (Animal behavior)
  USE **Animal courtship**
Courtship of animals
  USE **Animal courtship**
Covenants 231.7
    Use for materials on religious cove-
  nants. May be subdivided by religion as
  needed. Materials on non-religious cove-
  nants are entered under **Contracts.**
  UF Agreements
  BT **Contracts**
      Theology
Covens
  USE **Witches**
Coverlets
  USE **Bedspreads**
      Quilts
Cowboys
  USE **Cowhands**
Cowgirls
  USE **Cowhands**
Cowhands 390; 636.20092; 978
  UF Cowboys
      Cowgirls
      Gauchos
  BT **Frontier and pioneer life**
      Ranch life
  RT **Rodeos**
Cowhands—Songs 782.42
  UF Cowhands—Songs and music
      [Former heading]
  BT **Music**
      Songs
  RT **Country music**
Cowhands—Songs and music
  USE **Cowhands—Songs**
Cows
  USE **Cattle**
Cows—Diseases
  USE **Cattle—Diseases**
Crabs 565; 595.3
  BT **Crustacea**
      Shellfish
Crack babies
  USE **Children of drug addicts**
Crack cocaine
  USE **Crack (Drug)**
Crack (Drug) 362.29; 615
  UF Crack cocaine

Crack (Drug)—*Continued*
- BT **Cocaine**

Cradle songs
- USE **Lullabies**

Craft festivals
- USE **Craft shows**

Craft shows 745
- UF Craft festivals
- Shows, Craft
- BT **Exhibitions**
- **Festivals**
- **Handicraft**

Crafts (Arts)
- USE **Arts and crafts movement**
- **Handicraft**

Cranes, derricks, etc. 621.8
- UF Derricks
- BT **Hoisting machinery**

Cranks
- USE **Eccentrics and eccentricities**

Crates
- USE **Boxes**

Crayon drawing 741.2
- UF Blackboard drawing
- BT **Drawing**
- RT **Pastel drawing**

Creation 213; 231.7
- UF Cosmogony, Biblical
- Cosmology, Biblical
- BT **Natural theology**
- NT **Theology**
- RT **Creationism**
- **Earth**
- **Evolution**
- **God**
- **Man**
- **Universe**

Creation (Literary, artistic, etc.) 153.3
- UF Inspiration
- BT **Genius**
- **Imagination**
- **Intellect**
- **Inventions**
- NT **Creative writing**
- RT **Creative ability**

Creation—Study and teaching 213; 231.7
- RT **Creationism**
- **Evolution—Study and teaching**
- **Fundamentalism and education**

Creationism 231.7

Use for materials on the doctrine that the universe was created by God out of nothing in the initial seven days of time and that all biological species were created rather than evolving from preexisting types through modifications in successive generations.
- UF Christianity and evolution
- Evolution and Christianity
- Fundamentalism and evolution
- Scientific creationism
- BT **Theology**
- RT **Bible and science**
- **Creation**
- **Creation—Study and teaching**
- **Evolution**
- **Evolution—Study and teaching**
- **Religion and science**

Creative ability 153.3; 701; 801
- UF Creativity
- BT **Ability**
- NT **Creative thinking**
- RT **Creation (Literary, artistic, etc.)**

Creative activities 372.5

Use for materials on activities for children that result in some form of personal expression such as painting, cooking, drama, etc.
- UF Activities curriculum
- BT **Amusements**
- **Elementary education**
- **Kindergarten**
- RT **Handicraft**

Creative movement
- USE **Movement education**

Creative thinking 153.4
- BT **Creative ability**

Creative writing 808
- UF Writing (Authorship)
- BT **Authorship**
- **Creation (Literary, artistic, etc.)**
- **Language arts**

Creativity
- USE **Creative ability**

Creature films
- USE **Horror films**

Creatures, Imaginary
- USE **Mythical animals**

BT = Broader Term   NT = Narrower Term   RT = Related Term   SA = See Also   UF = Used For

Credibility
USE **Truthfulness and falsehood**
Credit 332.7
UF Bills of credit
Letters of credit
BT **Business**
Economics
Finance
Money
NT **Agricultural credit**
Collecting of accounts
Consumer credit
Instalment plan
Loans
Mortgages
Negotiable instruments
Public debts
RT **Banks and banking**
Debtor and creditor
Credit, Agricultural
USE **Agricultural credit**
Credit card crimes 364.1
UF Credit card fraud
Fraud, Credit card
BT **Counterfeits and counterfeiting**
Fraud
Swindlers and swindling
Credit card fraud
USE **Credit card crimes**
Credit cards 332.7
UF Bank credit cards
Banks and banking—Credit
cards
BT **Consumer credit**
Credit, Consumer
USE **Consumer credit**
Credit unions 334
Use for materials on cooperative associ-
ations that make small loans to its mem-
bers at low interest rates.
BT **Cooperative banks**
Cooperative societies
Loans
Personal loans
RT **Consumer credit**
Creeds 238; 291.2
UF Confessions of faith
Faith, Confessions of
BT **Church history**
Theology

NT **Apostles' Creed**
Nicene Creed
RT **Catechisms**
Cremation 363.7; 393; 614
UF Incineration
Mortuary customs
BT **Public health**
Sanitation
RT **Burial**
Funeral rites and ceremonies
Creoles 305.84; 972.9; 976
Crests
USE **Heraldry**
Crewelwork 746.44
BT **Embroidery**
Crime (May subdiv. geog.) **364**
UF Crimes
Criminology
Felony
SA types of crimes, e.g. **Computer
crimes;** to be added as
needed
BT **Administration of criminal
justice**
Social ethics
Social problems
NT **Art thefts**
Assassination
Atrocities
Computer crimes
Counterfeits and counterfeiting
Crime prevention
Crimes without victims
Criminal law
Criminals
Drugs and crime
Drunk driving
Forgery
Fraud
Hate crimes
Homicide
Impostors and imposture
Juvenile delinquency
Lynching
Offenses against the person
Organized crime
Racketeering
Riots
Sex crimes
Smuggling

BT = Broader Term   NT = Narrower Term   RT = Related Term   SA = See Also   UF = Used For

Crime—*Continued*

        Stealing

        Swindlers and swindling

        Treason

        Victims of crime

        Vigilance committees

        War crimes

        White collar crimes

  RT **Police**

        Prisons

        Punishment

        Trials

        Vice

Crime and drugs

  USE **Drugs and crime**

Crime and narcotics

  USE **Drugs and crime**

Crime comics

  USE **Mystery comic books, strips, etc.**

Crime-drug relationship

  USE **Drugs and crime**

Crime films

  USE **Film noir**

        Gangster films

        Mystery films

Crime plays

  USE **Mystery and detective plays**

Crime prevention 364.4

  UF Prevention of crime

  BT **Crime**

  NT **Criminal psychology**

Crime programs

  USE **Mystery radio programs**

        Mystery television programs

Crime stories

  USE **Mystery fiction**

Crime syndicates

  USE **Organized crime**

        Racketeering

Crime—United States 364.973

  UF United States—Crime

Crime victims

  USE **Victims of crime**

Crimean War, 1853-1856 947

  UF Great Britain—History—1853-1856, Crimean War

        Russo-Turkish War, 1853-1856

Crimes

  USE **Crime**

Crimes against public safety

  USE **Offenses against public safety**

Crimes against the person

  USE **Offenses against the person**

Crimes, Military

  USE **Military offenses**

Crimes of hate

  USE **Hate crimes**

Crimes, Political

  USE **Political crimes and offenses**

Crimes, Sex

  USE **Sex crimes**

Crimes, White collar

  USE **White collar crimes**

Crimes without victims 364.1

  UF Non-victim crimes

        Nonvictim crimes

        Victimless crimes

  SA names of specific crimes, to be added as needed

  BT **Crime**

        Criminal law

  NT **Drug abuse**

        Gambling

        Obscenity (Law)

        Prostitution

Criminal assault

  USE **Offenses against the person**

Criminal investigation 363.2

  BT **Law enforcement**

  NT **Criminals—Identification**

        Eavesdropping

        Fingerprints

        Lie detectors and detection

        Medical jurisprudence

        Missing children

        Missing persons

        Wiretapping

  RT **Detectives**

        Police

Criminal justice, Administration of

  USE **Administration of criminal justice**

Criminal law 345

  UF Codes, Penal

        Law, Criminal

        Misdemeanors (Law)

        Penal codes

        Penal law

  SA names of crimes, e.g. **Homicide;** to be added as needed

---

BT = Broader Term   NT = Narrower Term   RT = Related Term   SA = See Also   UF = Used For

Criminal law—*Continued*
- BT   Crime
  - Law
  - Prisons
- NT   Administration of criminal justice
  - Adoption—Corrupt practices
  - Capital punishment
  - Crimes without victims
  - Homicide
  - Insanity defense
  - Jury
  - Kidnapping
  - Medical jurisprudence
  - Military offenses
  - Misconduct in office
  - Obscenity (Law)
  - Offenses against public safety
  - Offenses against the person
  - Probation
  - Prohibition
  - Trials
  - Vigilance committees
- RT   Criminal procedure
  - Punishment

Criminal procedure 345
- BT   Courts
- RT   Criminal law

Criminal psychology 364.3
- UF   Psychology, Criminal
- BT   Crime prevention
- RT   Abnormal psychology

Criminals 364.3; 364.6
- UF   Convicts
  - Delinquents
  - Reform of criminals
- BT   Crime
- NT   Convict labor
  - Gangs
  - Impostors and imposture
  - Pirates
  - Prisoners
  - Swindlers and swindling
  - Thieves

Criminals and drugs
- USE   Criminals—Drug use

Criminals and narcotics
- USE   Criminals—Drug use

Criminals—Drug use 362.2; 364.3
- UF   Criminals and drugs

Criminals and narcotics
Drugs and criminals
Narcotics and criminals
- RT   Drugs and crime

Criminals—Identification 363.2
- BT   Criminal investigation
  - Identification
- NT   Fingerprints

Criminals—Rehabilitation programs
- USE   Corrections

Criminology
- USE   Crime

Crippled children
- USE   Physically handicapped children

Crippled people
- USE   Physically handicapped

Crisis centers 361.3; 362
- UF   Crisis intervention centers
- SA   types of crisis centers, e.g. Hotlines (Telephone counseling); to be added as needed
- BT   Counseling
  - Social work
- RT   Hotlines (Telephone counseling)

Crisis counseling
- USE   Hotlines (Telephone counseling)

Crisis intervention centers
- USE   Crisis centers

Crisis intervention telephone service
- USE   Hotlines (Telephone counseling)

Crisis management 658.4
- BT   Management
  - Problem solving

Critical thinking 153.4; 160

Use for materials on thinking that is based on sound logic and the careful evaluation of all pertinent evidence.

- BT   Decision making
  - Logic
  - Problem solving
  - Reasoning
  - Thought and thinking

BT = Broader Term   NT = Narrower Term   RT = Related Term   SA = See Also   UF = Used For

Criticism 801

Use for materials on the history, principles, methods, etc., of criticism in general and of literary criticism in particular. Criticism of the work of an individual author, artist, composer, etc., is entered under that person's name as a subject; only in the case of voluminous authors is it necessary to add the subdivision *Criticism, interpretation, etc.* Criticism of a single work is entered under the name of the author, artist, or composer, followed by the title of the work.

UF   Appraisal of books
Books—Appraisal
Evaluation of literature
Literary criticism
Literature—Evaluation

SA   literature, film, and music subjects with the subdivision *History and criticism,* e.g. **English poetry—History and criticism;** to be added as needed

BT   **Aesthetics**
Literature
Literature—History and criticism
Rhetoric

NT   **Art criticism**
Bible—Criticism, interpretation, etc.
Books—Reviews
Dramatic criticism
English literature—History and criticism
English poetry—History and criticism
Music—History and criticism
Shakespeare, William, 1564-1616—Criticism, interpretation, etc.

RT   **Literary style**

Cro-Magnons 573.3

UF   Cromagnons
BT   **Prehistoric man**

Crocheting 746.43

BT   **Needlework**
NT   **Beadwork**
Lace and lace making

Crockery
USE   **Pottery**

Crocodiles 597.98

BT   **Reptiles**
RT   **Alligators**

Cromagnons
USE   **Cro-Magnons**

Crop dusting
USE   **Aeronautics in agriculture**

Crop reports
USE   **Agriculture—Statistics**

Crop rotation 631.5

UF   Crops, Rotation of
Rotation of crops
BT   **Agriculture**

Crop spraying
USE   **Aeronautics in agriculture**

Crops
USE   **Farm produce**

Crops, Rotation of
USE   **Crop rotation**

Cross cultural conflict
USE   **Culture conflict**

Cross cultural psychology
USE   **Ethnopsychology**

Cross cultural studies 155.8; 306

Use for materials on the systematic comparison of two or more cultural groups, either within the same country or in separate countries.

UF   Comparison of cultures
Intercultural studies
Transcultural studies
BT   **Culture**
Social sciences

Cross-examination
USE   **Witnesses**

Crossword puzzles 793.73

BT   **Puzzles**
Word games

Crowds 302.3

UF   Mobs
NT   **Protests, demonstrations, etc.**
Riot control
RT   **Riots**
Social psychology

Crown lands
USE   **Public lands**

CRT display terminals
USE   **Video display terminals**

CRTs
USE   **Cathode ray tubes**

Crucifixion of Christ
USE   **Jesus Christ—Crucifixion**

BT = Broader Term   NT = Narrower Term   RT = Related Term   SA = See Also   UF = Used For

Crude oil
 USE **Petroleum**
Cruelty 179
 UF Brutality
 BT **Ethics**
 NT **Atrocities**
Cruelty to animals
 USE **Animal welfare**
Cruelty to children
 USE **Child abuse**
Cruises
 USE **Ocean travel**
Crusades 909.07
 BT **Church history—600-1500,**
  Middle Ages
  Middle Ages—History
 RT **Chivalry**
Crustacea 565; 595.3
 SA names of specific crustaceans,
  e.g. **Lobsters;** to be added
  as needed
 BT **Invertebrates**
  Shellfish
 NT **Crabs**
  Lobsters
Cryobiology 574.19
 UF Freezing
  Low temperature biology
 BT **Biology**
  Cold
  Low temperatures
 NT **Cold—Physiological effect**
  Frozen embryos
Cryogenic internment
 USE **Cryonics**
Cryogenic surgery
 USE **Cryosurgery**
Cryogenics
 USE **Low temperatures**
Cryonics 621.5
 UF Cryogenic internment
  Freezing of human bodies
  Human cold storage
 BT **Burial**
Cryosurgery 617
 UF Cryogenic surgery
 BT **Cold—Therapeutic use**
  Surgery
Cryotherapy
 USE **Cold—Therapeutic use**

Cryptography 652
 UF Code deciphering
  Code enciphering
  Secret writing
 BT **Signs and symbols**
  Writing
 RT **Ciphers**
Crystal gazing
 USE **Divination**
Crystalline rocks
 USE **Rocks**
Crystallization
 USE **Crystallography**
Crystallography 548
 UF Crystallization
  Crystals
 BT **Petrology**
  Physical chemistry
  Rocks
 RT **Mineralogy**
Crystals
 USE **Crystallography**
Cub Scouts
 USE **Boy Scouts**
Cuba 972.91
  May be subdivided like United States
  except for *History.*
 BT **Islands**
Cuba—History 972.91
Cuba—History—1958-1959, Revolution
  972.9106
Cuba—History—1959- 972.9106
Cuba—History—1961, Invasion
  972.9106
 UF Bay of Pigs invasion
  Cuban invasion, 1961
  Invasion of Cuba, 1961
Cuban invasion, 1961
 USE **Cuba—History—1961, Inva-**
  sion
Cube root 513.2
 BT **Arithmetic**
Cubic measurement
 USE **Volume (Cubic content)**
Cubism 709.04; 759.06
 BT **Abstract art**
  Painting
 RT **Postimpressionism (Art)**

Cultivated plants (May subdiv. geog.)
581.6; 631.5
- UF Plants, Cultivated *[Former heading]*
- BT **Agriculture**
      Gardening
- NT **Annuals (Plants)**
      House plants
      Ornamental plants
      Perennials

Cultivated plants—United States 581.6; 631.5
- UF Plants, Cultivated—United States *[Former heading]*
      United States—Cultivated plants

Cults 291; 306.6

Use for materials on groups or movements whose beliefs or practices differ significantly from the traditional religions and are often focused upon a charismatic leader. Materials on the major world religions are entered under **Religions.** Materials on independent religious groups those teachings or practices fall within the normative bounds of the major world religions are entered under **Sects.**
- UF Religious cults
- BT **Religions**
- NT **New Age movement**
- RT **Sects**

Cultural anthropology
- USE **Ethnology**

Cultural change
- USE **Social change**

Cultural exchange programs
- USE **Exchange of persons programs**

Cultural life
- USE **Intellectual life**

Cultural pluralism
- USE **Multiculturalism**

Cultural relations 306; 341.7
- UF Intercultural relations
- BT **Intellectual cooperation**
      International cooperation
      International relations
- NT **Exchange of persons programs**

Culturally deprived
- USE **Socially handicapped**

Culturally deprived children
- USE **Socially handicapped children**

Culturally handicapped
- USE **Socially handicapped**

Culturally handicapped children
- USE **Socially handicapped children**

Culture 306; 909

Use for materials on the sum total of ways of living or thinking established by a group of human beings and transmitted from one generation to the next, including a concern for what is regarded as excellent in the arts, manners, scholarship, etc. Materials limited to the culture of individual nations are entered under names of countries with the subdivisions *Civilization; Intellectual life;* or *Social life and customs.*
- NT **Acculturation**
      Biculturalism
      Cross cultural studies
      Humanism
      Intellectual life
      Popular culture
- RT **Anthropology**
      Civilization
      Education
      Learning and scholarship
      Sociology

Culture conflict 155.8; 306; 155.8
- UF Conflict of cultures
      Cross cultural conflict
      Culture shock
      Future shock
- BT **Ethnic relations**
      Ethnopsychology
      Race relations

Culture contact
- USE **Acculturation**

Culture, Popular
- USE **Popular culture**

Culture shock
- USE **Culture conflict**

Curates
- USE **Clergy**

Curiosities and wonders 030
- UF Enigmas
      Facts, Miscellaneous
      Miscellaneous facts
      Oddities
      Trivia
      Wonders
- SA subjects with the subdivision *Miscellanea,* e.g. **Medicine—Miscellanea;** to be added as needed
- NT **Eccentrics and eccentricities**

BT = Broader Term   NT = Narrower Term   RT = Related Term   SA = See Also   UF = Used For

Curiosities and wonders—*Continued*
> Medicine—Miscellanea
> Monsters
> World records

Currency
> USE **Money**

Currency devaluation
> USE **Monetary policy**

Current events 907
> Use for materials on the study and teaching of current events. Periodicals and yearbooks devoted to the events themselves are entered under **History—Periodicals.**
> BT **Modern history—Study and teaching**

Currents, Alternating
> USE **Alternating electric currents**

Currents, Electric
> USE **Electric currents**

Currents, Ocean
> USE **Ocean currents**

Curricula (Courses of study)
> USE **Education—Curricula**
> and types of education and schools with the subdivision *Curricula,* e.g. **Library education—Curricula; Colleges and universities—Curricula;** etc., to be added as needed

Curriculum materials centers
> USE **Instructional materials centers**

Curtains
> USE **Drapery**

Custody kidnapping
> USE **Parental kidnapping**

Custody of children
> USE **Child custody**

Custom duties
> USE **Tariff**

Customer relations 658.8
> BT **Business**
> **Public relations**
> NT **Customer service**

Customer service 658.8
> UF Service, Customer
> Service (in industry)
> Services, Customer
> Technical service
> BT **Customer relations**

Customs, Social
> USE **Manners and customs**
> and names of ethnic groups, countries, cities, etc., with the subdivision *Social life and customs,* e.g. **Indians of North America—Social life and customs; Jews—Social life and customs; United States—Social life and customs;** etc., to be added as needed

Customs (Tariff)
> USE **Tariff**

Cybernetics 003
> UF Automatic control
> Mechanical brains
> BT **Communication**
> **Electronics**
> **System theory**
> NT **Bionics**
> **Computers**
> **System analysis**
> **Systems engineering**

Cycles
> USE **Periodicity**

Cycles, Business
> USE **Business cycles**

Cycles, Motor
> USE **Motorcycles**

Cycling 796.6
> UF Bicycles and bicycling *[Former heading]*
> Bicycling
> Biking
> BT **Exercise**
> **Outdoor recreation**
> **Sports**
> NT **Bicycle racing**
> **Bicycle touring**
> **Motorcycling**
> RT **Bicycles**
> **Tricycles**

Cyclones 551.55
> Use for materials on large-scale storms that involve high winds rotating around a center of low atmospheric pressure. Materials on the cyclones of the West Indies are entered under **Hurricanes.** Materials on the cyclones of the China Seas and the Philippines are entered under **Typhoons.**

BT = Broader Term   NT = Narrower Term   RT = Related Term   SA = See Also   UF = Used For

Cyclones—*Continued*
   BT   Meteorology
         Storms
         Winds
   NT   Hurricanes
         Typhoons
Cyclopedias
   USE **Encyclopedias and dictionaries**
Cyclotron 539.7
   UF   Atom smashing
         Magnetic resonance accelerator
   BT   **Atoms**
         Nuclear physics
         Transmutation (Chemistry)
Cytology
   USE **Cells**
Czech Republic 943.71
    Use for materials on this part of the former country of Czechoslovakia since its becoming independent on January 1, 1993. May be subdivided like United States except for *History.*
   RT   **Czechoslovakia**
Czechoslovakia 943.7
    Use for materials on the former country of Czechoslovakia through December 31, 1992. Materials on the two parts of the former country of Czechoslovakia, which became independent on January 1, 1993, are entered under **Czech Republic** and **Slovakia.**
   RT   **Czech Republic**
         Slovakia
Czechoslovakia—History—1918-1968 943.7
Czechoslovakia—History—1968-1989 943.704
   UF   Czechoslovakia—History—1968-, Intervention *[Former heading]*
         Russian intervention in Czechoslovakia
         Soviet intervention in Czechoslovakia
Czechoslovakia—History—1968-, Intervention
   USE **Czechoslovakia—History—1968-1989**
Czechoslovakia—History—1989-
   USE **Czechoslovakia—History—1989-1992**

Czechoslovakia—History—1989-1992 943.704
   UF   Czechoslovakia—History—1989- *[Former heading]*
D.D.T. (Insecticide) 668
   UF   DDT (Insecticide)
         Dichloro-diphenyl-trichloroethane
   BT   **Insecticides**
D Day
   USE **Normandy (France), Attack on, 1944**
D.N.A.
   USE **DNA**
Daily readings (Spiritual exercises)
   USE **Devotional calendars**
Dairies
   USE **Dairying**
Dairy cattle 636.2
   UF   Milch cattle
   SA   names of breeds of dairy cattle, to be added as needed
   BT   **Cattle**
         Dairying
   NT   **Holstein-Friesian cattle**
Dairy farming
   USE **Dairying**
Dairy products 637; 641.3
   UF   Products, Dairy
   SA   names of dairy products, to be added as needed
   NT   **Butter**
         Cheese
         Milk
   RT   **Dairying**
Dairying (May subdiv. geog.) 636.2; 637
    Use for materials on the production and marketing of milk and milk products and for general materials on dairy farming.
   UF   Dairies
         Dairy farming
   BT   **Agriculture**
         Livestock
   NT   **Dairy cattle**
         Milk
   RT   **Cattle**
         Dairy products

BT = Broader Term   NT = Narrower Term   RT = Related Term   SA = See Also   UF = Used For

Dams 627
- SA names of dams, e.g. **Hoover Dam (Ariz. and Nev.);** to be added as needed
- BT **Civil engineering**
  Flood control
  Hydraulic structures
  Irrigation
  Rivers
  Water power
  Water supply
- NT **Hoover Dam (Ariz. and Nev.)**

Dance
- USE **Dancing**

Dance music 781.5; 784.18
- UF Big band music
- BT **Dancing**
  Music
- NT **Jazz music**
  Popular music
  Rock music

Dancers 792.8092; 793.3092; 920
- SA types of dancers, e.g. **Ballet dancers;** to be added as needed
- BT **Entertainers**
- NT **Ballet dancers**

Dancing (May subdiv. geog.) **792.8; 793.3**
- UF Dance
- SA types of dances and dancing, to be added as needed
- BT **Amusements**
  Etiquette
  Performing arts
- NT **Aerobics**
  Ballet
  Break dancing
  Dance music
  Folk dancing
  Modern dance
  Tap dancing

Dancing, Aerobic
- USE **Aerobics**

Dancing—United States 792.80973; 793.30973
- UF United States—Dancing
- NT **American folk dancing**

Dangerous animals 591.6
- BT **Animals**

Wildlife
- NT **Animal attacks**
  Poisonous animals

Dangerous materials
- USE **Hazardous substances**

Dangerous occupations
- USE **Hazardous occupations**

Danish language 439.8
- May be subdivided like **English language.**
- BT **Norwegian language**
  Scandinavian languages

Danish literature 839.8
- May use same subdivisions and names of literary forms as for **English literature.**
- BT **Literature**
  Scandinavian literature

Dark Ages
- USE **Middle Ages**

Dark humor (Literature)
- USE **Black humor (Literature)**

Darkroom technique in photography
- USE **Photography—Processing**

DARPA Internet (Computer network)
- USE **Internet (Computer network)**

Darwinism
- USE **Evolution**

Data base management
- USE **Database management**

Data networks, Computer
- USE **Computer networks**

Data processing
- USE **Electronic data processing**
  Information systems
  and subjects with the subdivision *Data processing,* e.g. **Banks and banking—Data processing;** to be added as needed

Data processing, Electronic— Keyboarding
- USE **Keyboarding (Electronics)**

Data storage and retrieval systems
- USE **Information systems**

Data transmission systems 004.6; 621.38; 621.39
- UF Transmission of data
- BT **Electronic data processing**
  Telecommunication
- NT **Computer networks**

BT = Broader Term NT = Narrower Term RT = Related Term SA = See Also UF = Used For

Data transmission systems—_Continued_
> **Electronic mail systems**
> **Facsimile transmission**
> **Information networks**
> **Library information networks**
> **Teletext systems**
> **Video telephone**
> **Videotex systems**

Database management 005.74
> UF   Data base management
>   Systems, Database management
> BT   **Electronic data processing**
>   **Information systems**

Database management—Computer programs 005.75

Date etiquette
> USE   **Dating (Social customs)**

Date rape 362.88; 364.1
> UF   Acquaintance rape
>   Dating violence
> BT   **Dating (Social customs)**
>   **Rape**

Dates, Historical
> USE   **Historical chronology**

Dating, Radiocarbon
> USE   **Radiocarbon dating**

Dating (Social customs) 306.73; 392; 646.7
> UF   Courting
>   Courtship
>   Date etiquette
> BT   **Etiquette**
>   **Manners and customs**
> NT   **Date rape**
> RT   **Love**

Dating violence
> USE   **Date rape**

Daughters and fathers
> USE   **Fathers and daughters**

Daughters and mothers
> USE   **Mothers and daughters**

Day 529
> BT   **Chronology**
>   **Time**
> RT   **Night**

Day care centers 362.7
> UF   Child care centers _[Former heading]_
>   Children—Day care

     Children's day care centers
     Day nurseries
     Nurseries, Day
> BT   **Child care**
>   **Child welfare**
>   **Children—Institutional care**
> RT   **Nursery schools**

Day dreams
> USE   **Fantasy**

Day nurseries
> USE   **Day care centers**

Day of Atonement
> USE   **Yom Kippur**

Days 394.2
> UF   Days of the week
> SA   types of days and names of particular days, to be added as needed
> BT   **Calendars**
> NT   **Birthdays**
>   **Festivals**
>   **Holidays**
> RT   **Week**

Days of the week
> USE   **Days**

DDT (Insecticide)
> USE   **D.D.T. (Insecticide)**

Dead Sea scrolls 221.4; 229; 296.1
> UF   Qumran texts

Dead, Worship of the
> USE   **Ancestor worship**

Deaf 362.4
> BT   **Hearing impaired**
>   **Physically handicapped**
> NT   **Closed caption television**
>   **Closed caption video recordings**

Deaf, Dogs for
> USE   **Hearing ear dogs**

Deaf—Education 371.91
> UF   Education of the deaf
> BT   **Education**

Deaf—Institutional care 362.4
> BT   **Institutional care**

Deaf—Means of communication 362.4; 419
> Use for general materials on communication in the broadest sense by people who are deaf. Materials on language systems based on hand gestures are entered under **Sign language.**

Deaf—Means of communication—
Continued
  UF   Finger alphabet
        Lip reading
  BT   **Communication**
  NT   **Hearing ear dogs**
  RT   **Nonverbal communication**
        Sign language
Deaf—Sign language
  USE **Sign language**
Deafness 362.4; 617.8
  BT   **Ear**
  NT   **Hearing aids**
  RT   **Hearing**
Death 128; 236; 306.9
  BT   **Biology**
        Eschatology
        Life
  NT   **Bereavement**
        Brain death
        Future life
        Longevity
        Near-death experiences
        Right to die
  RT   **Burial**
        Mortality
        Terminal care
        Terminally ill
Death, Apparent
  USE **Near-death experiences**
Death masks
  USE **Masks (Sculpture)**
Death, Mercy
  USE **Euthanasia**
Death notices
  USE **Obituaries**
Death penalty
  USE **Capital punishment**
Death rate
  USE **Mortality**
        Vital statistics
Death, Right of
  USE **Right to die**
Death with dignity
  USE **Right to die**
Deaths, Registers of
  USE **Registers of births, etc.**
Debates and debating 808.53
  UF   Argumentation
        Discussion

        Speaking
  BT   **Public speaking**
        Rhetoric
  NT   **Parliamentary practice**
        Radio addresses, debates, etc.
  RT   **Discussion groups**
Debit cards 332.1
  UF   Bank debit cards
        Cards, Debit
  BT   **Banks and banking**
Debris, Space
  USE **Space debris**
Debtor and creditor 332.7; 346
     Use for economic and statistical materi-
    als about debt as well as for legal materi-
    als involving debtor and creditor.
  BT   **Commercial law**
  NT   **Bankruptcy**
        Collecting of accounts
  RT   **Credit**
Debts, Government
  USE **Public debts**
Debts, Public
  USE **Public debts**
Decalogue
  USE **Ten commandments**
Deceit
  USE **Fraud**
Decentralization of schools
  USE **Schools—Decentralization**
Deceptive advertising 343
  UF   Advertising, Fraudulent *[For-*
         mer heading]
        False advertising
        Fraudulent advertising
        Misleading advertising
        Misrepresentation in advertis-
         ing
        Truth in advertising
  BT   **Business ethics**
Decimal system 513.5
  BT   **Numbers**
  RT   **Metric system**
Decision making 153.8; 302.3; 658.4
  BT   **Game theory**
  NT   **Critical thinking**
  RT   **Choice (Psychology)**
        Problem solving
Decks (Domestic architecture)
  USE **Patios**
Declamations
  USE **Monologues**

Declamations—*Continued*
> **Recitations**

Declamations, Musical
> USE **Monologues with music**

Declaration of independence (U.S.)
> USE **United States—Declaration of independence**

Decoration and ornament 745.4
> Use for general materials on the forms and styles of decoration in various fields of fine arts or applied art and on the history of various styles of ornament. Materials limited to the decoration of houses are entered under **Interior design.**

> UF Art, Decorative
> Arts, Decorative
> Decorative art
> Decorative design
> Decorative painting
> Design, Decorative
> Ornament
> Painting, Decorative

> SA decoration and ornament of particular countries, e.g. **American decoration and ornament;** and names of particular styles of decoration and ornament, e.g. **Renaissance decoration and ornament;** to be added as needed

> BT **Art**
> **Decorative arts**

> NT **American decoration and ornament**
> **Antiques**
> **Architectural decoration and ornament**
> **Art objects**
> **Artificial flowers**
> **Arts and crafts movement**
> **Bronzes**
> **Carpets**
> **China painting**
> **Christmas decorations**
> **Decoupage**
> **Design**
> **Egg decoration**
> **Embroidery**
> **Enamel and enameling**
> **Flower arrangement**
> **Furniture**
> **Garden ornaments and furniture**
> **Gems**
> **Glass painting and staining**
> **Holiday decorations**
> **Illumination of books and manuscripts**
> **Illustration of books**
> **Interior design**
> **Ironwork**
> **Jewelry**
> **Leather work**
> **Lettering**
> **Metalwork**
> **Monograms**
> **Mosaics**
> **Mural painting and decoration**
> **Needlework**
> **Picture frames and framing**
> **Plants in art**
> **Pottery**
> **Renaissance decoration and ornament**
> **Sculpture**
> **Show windows**
> **Stencil work**
> **Stucco**
> **Table setting and decoration**
> **Tapestry**
> **Terra cotta**
> **Textile design**
> **Wood carving**

> RT **Handicraft**
> **Painting**

Decoration and ornament, American
> USE **American decoration and ornament**

Decoration and ornament, Architectural
> USE **Architectural decoration and ornament**

Decoration and ornament, Renaissance
> USE **Renaissance decoration and ornament**

Decoration Day
> USE **Memorial Day**

Decoration, Interior
> USE **Interior design**

Decorations, Holiday
> USE **Holiday decorations**

BT = Broader Term   NT = Narrower Term   RT = Related Term   SA = See Also   UF = Used For

Decorations of honor 355.1; 929.8
- UF Badges of honor
  - Emblems
- SA names of medals, to be added
  - as needed
- RT **Heraldry**
  - **Insignia**
  - **Medals**

Decorative art
- USE **Decoration and ornament**
  - **Decorative arts**

Decorative arts (May subdiv. geog.) **745**
Use for general materials on the various applied art forms having some utilitarian as well as decorative purpose, including furniture, silverware, the decoration of buildings, etc.
- UF Applied arts
  - Art, Decorative
  - Art industries and trade
  - Arts, Applied
  - Arts, Decorative
  - Arts, Minor
  - Decorative art
  - Minor arts
- SA types of decorative arts, to be added as needed
- BT **Art**
- NT **Antiques**
  - **Art metalwork**
  - **Art objects**
  - **Arts and crafts movement**
  - **Calligraphy**
  - **Costume**
  - **Decoration and ornament**
  - **Decoupage**
  - **Enamel and enameling**
  - **Fabrics**
  - **Furniture**
  - **Glassware**
  - **Interior design**
  - **Jewelry**
  - **Lacquer and lacquering**
  - **Leather work**
  - **Mosaics**
  - **Needlework**
  - **Porcelain**
  - **Pottery**
  - **Rugs**
  - **Silverware**
  - **Tapestry**
  - **Woodwork**
- RT **Folk art**
  - **Handicraft**

Decorative arts—United States 745.0973
- UF United States—Decorative arts

Decorative design
- USE **Decoration and ornament**

Decorative metalwork
- USE **Art metalwork**

Decorative painting
- USE **Decoration and ornament**

Decoupage 745.54
- BT **Decoration and ornament**
  - **Decorative arts**
  - **Paper crafts**

Decoys (Hunting) 745.593; 799.2
- UF Bird decoys (Hunting)
- BT **Hunting**
  - **Shooting**

Deduction (Logic)
- USE **Logic**

Deep diving vehicles
- USE **Submersibles**

Deep sea diving
- USE **Submarine diving**

Deep sea drilling (Petroleum)
- USE **Offshore oil well drilling**

Deep sea engineering
- USE **Ocean engineering**

Deep sea mining
- USE **Ocean mining**

Deep-sea Photography
- USE **Underwater photography**

Deep sea technology
- USE **Oceanography**

Deep sea vehicles
- USE **Submersibles**

Deep submergence vehicles
- USE **Submersibles**

Deer 599.73
- BT **Game and game birds**
- NT **Reindeer**

Defamation
- USE **Libel and slander**

Defective speech
- USE **Speech disorders**

Defective vision
- USE **Vision disorders**

Defectors 325; 327.12
  UF Defectors, Political
       Political defectors
       Turncoats
  BT **Political refugees**
Defectors, Military
  USE **Military desertion**
Defectors, Political
  USE **Defectors**
Defense, Civil
  USE **Civil defense**
Defense industries 338.4
    Use for materials on the industries pro-
  ducing the implements of war. Materials
  on the implements of war themselves are
  entered under **Ordnance** or under **Military
  weapons.**
  UF Armaments industries
       Arms sales
       Military sales
       Military supplies industry
       Munitions *[Former heading]*
  BT **Industry**
  RT **Firearms industry**
       Military readiness
       Military weapons
       Ordnance
Defense (Law)
  USE **Litigation**
Defense mechanisms (Zoology)
  USE **Animal defenses**
Defense policy
  USE **Military policy**
Defense readiness
  USE **Military readiness**
Defenses, Air
  USE **Air defenses**
Defenses, National
  USE **Industrial mobilization**
       and names of countries with
         the subdivision *Defenses,*
         e.g. **United States—
         Defenses;** to be added as
         needed
Defenses, Radar
  USE **Radar defense networks**
Deficit financing (May subdiv. geog.)
       336.3
  UF Compensatory spending
       Deficit spending
  BT **Finance**

  RT **Public debts**
Deficit spending
  USE **Deficit financing**
Defoliants
  USE **Herbicides**
Deformities
  USE **Birth defects**
Degrees, Academic
  USE **Academic degrees**
Degrees of latitude and longitude
  USE **Geodesy**
       Latitude
       Longitude
Dehydrated foods
  USE **Dried foods**
Dehydrated milk
  USE **Dried milk**
Deism 211
  BT **Religion**
       Theology
  RT **Atheism**
       Free thought
       God
       Positivism
       Rationalism
       Theism
Deities
  USE **Gods and goddesses**
Dejection
  USE **Depression (Psychology)**
Delinquency, Juvenile
  USE **Juvenile delinquency**
Delinquents
  USE **Criminals**
       Juvenile delinquency
Delphi (Ancient city)
  USE **Delphi (Extinct city)**
Delphi (Extinct city) 938
  UF Delphi (Ancient city) *[Former
         heading]*
  BT **Extinct cities—Greece**
       Greece—Antiquities
Delusions
  USE **Hallucinations and illusions**
       Superstition
       Witchcraft
Demineralization of salt water
  USE **Sea water conversion**
Democracy 321.4; 321.8
  UF Popular government

Democracy—*Continued*
    Self-government
  BT **Constitutional history**
    Constitutional law
    Political science
  NT **Freedom**
    Referendum
    Suffrage
  RT **Equality**
    Federal government
    Representative government and representation
    Republics

Democratic Party (U.S.) 324.2736
  BT **Political parties**

Demography
  USE **Population**

Demoniac possession 133.4
  RT **Devil**
    Exorcism

Demonology 133.4
  UF Evil spirits
    Spirits
  BT **Ghosts**
  NT **Charms**
  RT **Apparitions**
    Devil
    Exorcism
    Occultism
    Superstition
    Witchcraft

Demonstrations for Black civil rights
  USE **Blacks—Civil rights**

Demonstrations for Black civil rights—United States
  USE **African Americans—Civil rights**

Demonstrations (Protest)
  USE **Protests, demonstrations, etc.**

Denationalization
  USE **Privatization**

Denatured alcohol 661
  UF Alcohol, Denatured *[Former heading]*
    Alcohol, Industrial
    Industrial alcohol
  BT **Alcohol**

Denominational schools
  USE **Church schools**

Denominations, Christian
  USE **Christian sects**

Denominations, Protestant
  USE **Protestant churches**

Denominations, Religious
  USE **Sects**
    and names of particular denominations and sects, e.g. **Presbyterian Church;** to be added as needed

Dentistry 617.6
  UF Medicine, Dental
  BT **Medicine**
  RT **Teeth**

Deoxyribonucleic acid
  USE **DNA**

Department stores 658.8
  UF Stores
  BT **Business**
    Retail trade

Dependencies
  USE **Colonies**
    Colonization

Depression, Mental
  USE **Depression (Psychology)**

Depression (Psychology) 616.85
  UF Dejection
    Depression, Mental *[Former heading]*
    Depressive psychoses
    Melancholia
    Mental depression
    Mentally depressed
  BT **Abnormal psychology**
    Neuroses
  RT **Manic-depressive psychoses**

Depressions, Economic
  USE **Economic depressions**

Depressive psychoses
  USE **Depression (Psychology)**

Deprogramming
  USE **Brainwashing**

Derailments
  USE **Railroads—Accidents**

Dermatitis
  USE **Skin—Diseases**

Derricks
  USE **Cranes, derricks, etc.**

Desalination of water
  USE **Sea water conversion**

Desalting of water
  USE **Sea water conversion**

BT = Broader Term   NT = Narrower Term   RT = Related Term   SA = See Also   UF = Used For

Descent
  USE **Genealogy**
       Heredity
Description
  USE names of cities (except extinct
       cities), countries, states, and
       regions with the subdivision
       Description, e.g. **Chicago
       (Ill.)—Description; United
       States—Description;** etc.,
       for descriptive materials
       and accounts of travel,
       including the history of
       travel, in those places; and
       names of places with the
       subdivision *Geography* for
       broad geographical materi-
       als about a specific place,
       e.g. **United States—
       Geography;** etc.; also names
       of extinct cities or towns,
       without further subdivision,
       for general descriptive ma-
       terials on those places, e.g.
       Delphi (Extinct city); to be
       added as needed

Descriptive geometry 516
  UF   Geometry, Descriptive *[For-
       mer heading]*
  BT   **Geometrical drawing**
       Geometry
  NT   **Perspective**
Desegregated schools
  USE **School integration**
Desegregation
  USE **Segregation**
Desegregation in education
  USE **School integration**
Desert animals 591.52
  UF   Desert fauna
  SA   names of desert animals, e.g.
       Camels; to be added as
       needed
  BT   **Animals**
       Deserts
       Wildlife
  NT   **Camels**
Desert fauna
  USE **Desert animals**

Desert plants 581.5
  SA   names of desert plants, e.g.
       Cactus; to be added as
       needed
  BT   **Deserts**
       Plants
       Plants—Ecology
  NT   **Cactus**
Desert Shield Operation
  USE **Persian Gulf War, 1991**
Desert Storm Operation
  USE **Persian Gulf War, 1991**
Desertion
  USE **Desertion and nonsupport**
       Military desertion
       Runaway adults
**Desertion and nonsupport 306.88;
       346.01**
  UF   Abandonment of family
       Desertion
       Nonsupport
  BT   **Divorce**
       Domestic relations
  NT   **Child support**
       Runaway adults
Desertion, Military
  USE **Military desertion**
Deserts 551.4
  BT   **Physical geography**
  NT   **Desert animals**
       Desert plants
Design 745.4
  Use for materials on the theory of de-
  sign.
  SA   types of design; and subjects
       with the subdivision *Design*
       or *Design and construction,*
       to be added as needed
  BT   **Decoration and ornament**
  NT   **Computer aided design**
       Fashion design
       Garden design
       Industrial design
       Interior design
       Machine design
       Quilts—Design
       Textile design
  RT   **Pattern making**

BT = Broader Term   NT = Narrower Term   RT = Related Term   SA = See Also   UF = Used For

Design and construction
    USE   types of structures, machines,
           equipment, etc., with the
           subdivision *Design and con-*
           struction, for materials on
           their engineering and con-
           struction, e.g. **Airplanes—**
           Design and construction;
           and, for materials on meth-
           ods of designing and con-
           structing tests, types of tests
           and examinations with the
           subdivision *Design and con-*
           struction, to be added as
           needed

Design, Architectural
    USE   **Architecture—Details**

Design, Decorative
    USE   **Decoration and ornament**

Design, Industrial
    USE   **Industrial design**

Design, Interior
    USE   **Interior design**

Design, System
    USE   **System design**

Designed genetic change
    USE   **Genetic engineering**

Designer drugs 362.29; 615
    Use for materials on illicit drugs manu-
    factured by altering the molecular struc-
    ture of existing drugs to mimic the effects
    of the classical narcotics, stimulants, and
    hallucinogens.
    UF   Drugs, Designer
           Drugs of abuse, Synthetic
           Synthetic drugs of abuse
    SA   names of individual designer
           drugs, e.g. **Ice (Drug);** to be
           added as needed
    BT   **Drugs**
    NT   **Ice (Drug)**

Designs and plans
    USE   architectural and landscape
           headings with the subdivi-
           sion *Designs and plans,* for
           materials containing archi-
           tectural or landscape archi-
           tecture drawings, e.g.
           Domestic architecture—
           Designs and plans; to be
           added as needed

Designs, Architectural
    USE   **Architecture—Designs and**
           plans

Designs, Floral
    USE   **Flower arrangement**

Desktop computers
    USE   **Microcomputers**

Desktop publishing 070.5; 686.2
    Use for materials on the utilization of a
    personal computer, and writing, graphics,
    and page layout software to produce print-
    ed material for publication.
    BT   **Electronic publishing**

Desoxyribonucleic acid
    USE   **DNA**

Desserts 641.8
    SA   types of desserts and names
           of specific desserts, to be
           added as needed
    BT   **Cooking**
    NT   **Cake**
           Ice cream, ices, etc.
    RT   **Chocolate**

Destiny
    USE   **Fate and fatalism**

Destitution
    USE   **Poverty**

Destruction of Jews (1933-1945)
    USE   **Jewish holocaust (1933-1945)**

Destructive insects
    USE   **Insect pests**

Details, Architectural
    USE   **Architecture—Details**

Detective and mystery comic books,
           strips, etc.
    USE   **Mystery comic books, strips,**
           etc.

Detective and mystery films
    USE   **Mystery films**

Detective and mystery plays
    USE   **Mystery and detective plays**

Detective and mystery radio programs
    USE   **Mystery radio programs**

Detective and mystery stories
    USE   **Mystery fiction**

Detective and mystery television pro-
           grams
    USE   **Mystery television programs**

Detective comics
    USE   **Mystery comic books, strips,**
           etc.

Detective fiction
USE **Mystery fiction**
Detective stories
USE **Mystery fiction**
Detectives 351.74; 363.2; 920
RT **Criminal investigation**
Police
Secret service
Detergent pollution of rivers, lakes, etc.
USE **Water pollution**
Detergents 668
UF Detergents, Synthetic *[Former heading]*
Synthetic detergents
BT **Cleaning compounds**
RT **Soap**
Detergents, Synthetic
USE **Detergents**
Determinism and indeterminism
USE **Free will and determinism**
Deuterium oxide 546
UF Heavy water
Water—Heavy water
Devaluation of currency
USE **Monetary policy**
Developing countries 330.9

Use for comprehensive materials on those countries having relatively low per capita incomes in comparison with North American and Western European countries. This heading may be subdivided by those topical subdivisions used under countries, regions, etc., and may be used as a geographic subdivision e.g. **Education—Developing countries;** etc.

UF Fourth World
Less developed countries
Third World
Underdeveloped areas
BT **Economic conditions**
Industrialization
NT **New states**
RT **Economic assistance**
Technical assistance
Developing countries—Commerce 338.91; 382
Development
USE **Embryology**
Evolution
Growth disorders
Modernization
Development, Economic
USE **Economic development**

Deviation, Sexual
USE **Sexual deviation**
Devices (Heraldry)
USE **Heraldry**
Insignia
Devil 235
UF Satan
RT **Demoniac possession**
Demonology
Devil's Triangle
USE **Bermuda Triangle**
Devotion
USE **Prayer**
Worship
Devotional calendars 242
UF Christian devotional calendars
Daily readings (Spiritual exercises)
Devotional exercises (Daily readings)
BT **Calendars**
Devotional literature
Devotional exercises 242; 248.3

Use for general materials on acts of private prayer and private worship and for materials on religious practices other than the corporate worship of a congregation. Materials on the religious literature used as aids in devotional exercises are entered under **Devotional literature.**

UF Devotions
Family devotions
Family prayers
Theology, Devotional
BT **Worship**
NT **Church music**
Meditation
RT **Prayer**
Devotional exercises (Daily readings)
USE **Devotional calendars**
Devotional literature 242

Use for materials on the religious literature used as aids in devotional exercises. General materials on acts of private prayer and private worship and materials on religious practices other than the corporate worship of a congregation are entered under **Devotional exercises.**

BT **Christian literature**
Literature
NT **Devotional calendars**
Hymns
Liturgies

Devotional literature—*Continued*
      Meditations
Devotions
  USE **Devotional exercises**
Dewey Decimal Classification 025.4
  UF Classification, Dewey Decimal
      [Former heading]
  BT **Classification—Books**
Diagnosis 616.07
  UF Medical diagnosis
      Symptoms
  BT **Medicine**
  NT **Body temperature**
      Clinical chemistry
      Magnetic resonance imaging
      Pain
      Prenatal diagnosis
  RT **Pathology**
Diagnostic chemistry
  USE **Clinical chemistry**
Diagnostic magnetic resonance imaging
  USE **Magnetic resonance imaging**
Diagrams, Statistical
  USE **Statistics—Graphic methods**
Dialectical materialism 335.4
  UF Historical materialism
  BT **Communism**
      Socialism
  RT **Marxism**
Dialectics
  USE **Logic**
Dialects
  USE names of languages with the
      subdivision *Dialects,* e.g.
      English language—Dialects;
      to be added as needed
Diamonds 553.8
  BT **Carbon**
      Precious stones
Diaries 809; 920
  Use for collections of diaries from various countries and for materials about diaries in general.
  UF Journals (Diaries)
  SA diaries of particular countries,
      e.g. **American diaries;** and
      classes of persons, ethnic
      groups, and names of individual persons and families
      with the subdivision *Diaries;* to be added as needed

  BT **Literature**
  NT **American diaries**
  RT **Autobiographies**
Diaries, American
  USE **American diaries**
Dichloro-diphenyl-trichloroethane
  USE **D.D.T. (Insecticide)**
Dictators 321.9092; 920
  BT **Heads of state**
      Kings, queens, rulers, etc.
      Totalitarianism
Dictionaries
  USE **Encyclopedias and dictionaries**
      and names of languages and
      subjects with the subdivision *Dictionaries,* e.g. **English language—Dictionaries;**
      Biography—Dictionaries;
      etc., to be added as needed
Dictionaries, Biographical
  USE **Biography—Dictionaries**
Dictionaries, Classical
  USE **Classical dictionaries**
Dictionaries, Machine readable
  USE **Machine readable dictionaries**
Dictionaries, Multilingual
  USE **Polyglot dictionaries**
Dictionaries, Picture
  USE **Picture dictionaries**
Dictionaries, Polyglot
  USE **Polyglot dictionaries**
Didactic drama 808.82; 812, etc.
  May be used for individual works, collections, or materials about didactic drama.
  BT **Drama**
Didactic fiction 808.83; 813, etc.
  May be used for individual works, collections, or materials about didactic fiction.
  UF Cautionary tales and verses
      Moral and philosophic stories
      Morality stories
  BT **Fiction**
  RT **Fables**
      Parables
Didactic poetry 808.81; 811, etc.
  May be used for individual works, collectins, or materials about didactic poetry.
  UF Cautionary tales and verses
  BT **Poetry**

Didactic poetry—*Continued*
RT Fables
　　Parables
Dies (Metalworking) 621.9; 671.2
　BT Metalwork
Diesel automobiles 629.222
　UF Automobiles, Diesel *[Former heading]*
　　　Diesel cars
　BT **Automobiles**
　RT **Automobile engines**
Diesel cars
　USE **Diesel automobiles**
Diesel engines 621.43
　BT **Engines**
　　　Internal combustion engines
Diet 613.2
　UF Dietetics
　SA types of diets, e.g. **Salt free diet**; to be added as needed
　BT **Health**
　　　Hygiene
　NT **Beverages**
　　　Dietetic foods
　　　Eating customs
　　　Fasting
　　　Menus
　　　Salt free diet
　　　School children—Food
　　　Vegetarianism
　RT **Cooking**
　　　Digestion
　　　Food
　　　Nutrition
　　　Reducing
Diet in disease 613.2; 616.3
　UF Dieting
　SA types of diets, e.g. **Salt free diet**; to be added as needed
　BT **Therapeutics**
　NT **Cooking for the sick**
　　　Diet therapy
　　　Salt free diet
Diet—Therapeutic use
　USE **Diet therapy**
Diet therapy 615.8
　UF Diet—Therapeutic use
　　　Invalid cooking
　SA names of diseases with the subdivision *Diet therapy,*

and types of food with the subdivision *Therapeutic use,* to be added as needed
　BT **Cooking for the sick**
　　　Diet in disease
　　　Therapeutics
　NT **Cancer—Diet therapy**
　　　Corn—Therapeutic use
Dietary fiber
　USE **Food—Fiber content**
Dietetic foods 641.3; 664
　UF Food, Dietetic *[Former heading]*
　BT **Diet**
　　　Food
Dietetics
　USE **Diet**
Dieting
　USE **Diet in disease**
　　　Reducing
Diets, Reducing
　USE **Reducing**
Digestion 574.1; 612.3
　BT **Physiology**
　NT **Food**
　　　Indigestion
　RT **Diet**
　　　Nutrition
　　　Stomach
Digital audio disc players
　USE **Compact disc players**
Digital circuits
　USE **Digital electronics**
Digital compact discs
　USE **Compact discs**
Digital electronics 621.381
　UF Digital circuits
　BT **Electronics**
Dimension, Fourth
　USE **Fourth dimension**
Dining (May subdiv. geog.) 641.01
　Use for materials on dining customs and gastronomic travel. Materials on menus and recipes for dinners are entered under **Dinners.**
　UF Banquets
　　　Dinners and dining *[Former heading]*
　　　Eating
　　　Gastronomy

Dining—*Continued*
  BT Food
  NT Carving (Meat, etc.)
  RT Dinners
      Eating customs
      Entertaining
      Table etiquette

Dinners 642
  Use for materials on menus and recipes for dinners. Materials on dining customs and gastronomic travel are entered under **Dining.**
  UF Banquets
      Dinners and dining *[Former heading]*
  BT Cooking
      Menus
  RT Dining

Dinners and dining
  USE **Dining**
       Dinners

Dinosaurs 567.9
  BT Fossil reptiles
      Prehistoric animals

Dioptrics
  USE **Refraction**

Diphtheria 616.9
  BT Diseases

Diplomacy 327.2; 341.3
  SA names of countries with the subdivision *Foreign relations,* to be added as needed
  BT International relations
  NT Diplomats
      Treaties
      United States—Foreign relations
  RT Diplomatic and consular service

Diplomatic and consular service 341.3
  UF Consulates
      Embassies
      Foreign service
      Legations
  SA names of countries with the subdivision *Diplomatic and consular service,* to be added as needed
  BT International relations
  NT United States—Diplomatic and consular service

  RT Diplomacy
      Diplomats

Diplomats 327.2092; 920
  UF Ambassadors
      Consuls
      Ministers (Diplomatic agents)
  BT Diplomacy
      International relations
      Statesmen
  RT Diplomatic and consular service

Dipsomania
  USE **Alcoholism**

Diptera
  USE **Flies**
       Mosquitoes

Direct access storage devices (Data processing)
  USE **Computer storage devices**

Direct current machinery
  USE **Electric machinery—Direct current**

Direct legislation
  USE **Referendum**

Direct primaries
  USE **Primaries**

Direct selling 658.8
  BT Marketing
      Retail trade
      Selling
  NT Mail-order business
      Peddlers and peddling
      Telemarketing

Direct taxation
  USE **Income tax**
       Taxation

Direction (Motion pictures)
  USE **Motion pictures—Production and direction**

Direction sense 152.1; 796.5
  UF Orientation
      Sense of direction
  NT Left and right
  RT Hiking
      Navigation
      Orienteering

Direction (Theater)
  USE **Theater—Production and direction**

BT = Broader Term   NT = Narrower Term   RT = Related Term   SA = See Also   UF = Used For

Directories 910.25

    Use for materials about directories and for bibliographies of directories.

    SA   subjects and names of countries, cities, etc., with the subdivision *Directories,* to be added as needed

    NT   **Chicago (Ill.)—Directories**
            Junior colleges—Directories
            Ohio—Directories
            Physicians—Directories
            United States—Directories

Directories—Telephone

    USE   names of cities with the subdivision *Telephone directories,* e.g. **Chicago (Ill.)—Telephone directories;** to be added as needed

Directors and producers

    USE   directors and producers in specific media, e.g. **Motion picture producers and directors;** to be added as needed

Directory, French, 1795-1799

    USE   **France—History—1789-1799, Revolution**

Dirigible balloons

    USE   **Airships**

Disability insurance

    USE   **Accident insurance**
            Health insurance

Disability, Learning

    USE   **Learning disabilities**

Disability, Reading

    USE   **Reading disability**

Disabled

    USE   **Handicapped**

Disadvantaged

    USE   **Socially handicapped**

Disadvantaged children

    USE   **Socially handicapped children**

Disarmament

    USE   **Arms control**

Disaster preparedness

    USE   **Disaster relief**

Disaster relief 363.3

    UF   Disaster preparedness
            Emergency preparedness
            Emergency relief

    BT   **Charities**
            Public welfare

    NT   **Food relief**

    RT   **Civil defense**

Disasters 904

    UF   Catastrophes

    SA   types of disasters, to be added as needed

    NT   **Fires**
            Natural disasters
            Railroads—Accidents
            Shipwrecks

    RT   **Accidents**

Disciples, Twelve

    USE   **Apostles**

Discipline

    USE   **Punishment**

Discipline of children

    USE   **Child rearing**
            School discipline

Discipline, Self

    USE   **Self-control**

Discography

    USE   **Sound recordings**
            and subjects and names of persons with the subdivision *Discography,* e.g. **Music—Discography; Shakespeare, William, 1564-1616—Discography;** etc., for lists or catalogs of sound recordings, to be added as needed

Discount stores 381; 658.8

    UF   Stores

    BT   **Retail trade**

Discoverers

    USE   **Exploration**
            Explorers

Discoveries and exploration

    USE   **Exploration**

Discoveries (in geography)

    USE   **Exploration**

Discoveries (in science)

    USE   **Inventions**
            Patents
            Science

Discoveries, Maritime

    USE   **Exploration**

BT = Broader Term   NT = Narrower Term   RT = Related Term   SA = See Also   UF = Used For

Discrimination 177; 305

Use for general materials on discrimination by race, religion, sex, age, social status, or other factors, including reverse discrimination.

BT Ethnic relations
Human relations
Prejudices
Race relations
Social problems
Social psychology

NT Age discrimination
Discrimination in education
Discrimination in employment
Discrimination in housing
Discrimination in public accommodations
Hate crimes
Race discrimination
Sex discrimination

RT Civil rights
Minorities
Segregation
Toleration

Discrimination in education 370.19

UF Education, Discrimination in

BT Discrimination

RT Segregation in education

Discrimination in employment 331.13

UF E.E.O.
EEO
Employment discrimination
Equal employment opportunity
Equal opportunity in employment
Fair employment practice
Job discrimination
Right to work

SA national, racial, and ethnic groups and classes of persons with the subdivision *Employment,* e.g. **African Americans—Employment;** to be added as needed

BT Discrimination

NT Affirmative action programs
African Americans—Employment
Age and employment
Blacks—Employment
Equal pay for equal work
Women—Employment

Discrimination in housing 363.5

UF Fair housing
Housing, Discrimination in
Open housing
Segregation in housing

BT Discrimination
Housing

Discrimination in public accommodations 305

UF Public accommodations, Discrimination in
Segregation in public accommodations

BT Discrimination

Discrimination, Racial
USE Race discrimination

Discrimination, Sex
USE Sex discrimination

Discs, Compact
USE Compact discs

Discs, Optical
USE Optical storage devices

Discs, Sound
USE Sound recordings

Discs, Video
USE Videodiscs

Discussion
USE Conversation
Debates and debating
Negotiation

Discussion groups 374

UF Forums (Discussions)
Great books program
Group discussion
Panel discussions

BT Conversation

RT Debates and debating

Disease germs
USE Bacteria
Germ theory of disease

Disease (Pathology)
USE Pathology

Diseases 614.4; 616

UF Illness
Sickness

SA names of animals, classes of persons, and parts of the

Diseases—*Continued*

body with the subdivision *Diseases*, types of diseases, and names of specific diseases, to be added as needed

BT **Medicine**

NT **AIDS (Disease)**
Animals—Diseases
Cancer
Chickenpox
Children—Diseases
Cold (Disease)
Communicable diseases
Diphtheria
Epidemics
Heart diseases
Hyperactivity
Infants—Diseases
Influenza
Lungs—Diseases
Lyme disease
Men—Diseases
Mental illness
Occupational diseases
Pathology
Poliomyelitis
Rheumatism
Skin—Diseases
Typhoid fever
Women—Diseases

RT **Health**
Sick

Diseases and pests

USE **Agricultural bacteriology**
Agricultural pests
Fungi
Household pests
Insect pests
Parasites
Plant diseases
and names of individual pests, e.g. **Locusts;** and names of crops, etc., with the subdivision *Diseases and pests,* e.g. **Fruit— Diseases and pests;** to be added as needed

Diseases, Communicable

USE **Communicable diseases**

Diseases, Contagious

USE **Communicable diseases**

Diseases, Industrial

USE **Occupational diseases**

Diseases, Infectious

USE **Communicable diseases**

Diseases, Mental

USE **Abnormal psychology**
Mental illness

Diseases, Occupational

USE **Occupational diseases**

Diseases of animals

USE **Animals—Diseases**

Diseases of children

USE **Children—Diseases**

Diseases of occupation

USE **Occupational diseases**

Diseases of plants

USE **Plant diseases**

Diseases of the blood

USE **Blood—Diseases**

Diseases of women

USE **Women—Diseases**

Diseases—Prevention

USE **Preventive medicine**

Diseases—Treatment

USE **Therapeutics**

Diseases, Tropical

USE **Tropical medicine**

Dishes

USE **Glassware**
Porcelain
Pottery

Dishonesty

USE **Honesty**

Disinfection and disinfectants 614.4

UF Germicides

BT **Bacteriology**
Communicable diseases
Hygiene
Pharmaceutical chemistry
Public health
Sanitation

RT **Antiseptics**
Fumigation

Disney World (Fla.)

USE **Walt Disney World (Fla.)**

Disobedience

USE **Obedience**

Displaced persons

USE **Political refugees**

BT = Broader Term   NT = Narrower Term   RT = Related Term   SA = See Also   UF = Used For

Displaced persons—*Continued*
> **Refugees**
>
> and names of wars with the subdivision *Refugees,* e.g. **World War, 1939-1945— Refugees;** to be added as needed

Display terminals, Video
USE **Video display terminals**

Disposal of medical waste
USE **Medical wastes**

Disposal of refuse
USE **Refuse and refuse disposal**

Disputes, Labor
USE **Labor disputes**

Dissent 303.48; 361.2
UF Nonconformity
> Protest

BT **Freedom of conscience**
> **Freedom of religion**

Dissertations 378.2; 808
> Use for materials about academic theses and dissertations.

UF Academic dissertations
> Dissertations, Academic *[Former heading]*
> Doctoral theses
> Theses

BT **Colleges and universities**

Dissertations, Academic
USE **Dissertations**

Distillation 641.2; 663
UF Stills
BT **Analytical chemistry**
> **Industrial chemistry**
> **Technology**

NT **Essences and essential oils**
RT **Alcohol**
> **Liquors**

Distribution, Cooperative
USE **Cooperation**
> **Cooperative societies**

Distribution (Economics)
USE **Commerce**
> **Marketing**

Distribution of animals and plants
USE **Biogeography**

Distribution of wealth
USE **Economics**
> **Wealth**

District libraries
USE **Regional libraries**

District nurses
USE **Nurses**

District schools
USE **Rural schools**

Districting (in city planning)
USE **Zoning**

Diversified corporations
USE **Conglomerate corporations**

Diversity, Biological
USE **Biological diversity**

Diversity movement
USE **Multiculturalism**

Dividends
USE **Securities**
> **Stocks**

Divination 133.3
UF Crystal gazing
> Necromancy
> Soothsaying

BT **Occultism**
> **Supernatural**

NT **Astrology**
> **Dreams**
> **Fortune telling**
> **Palmistry**

RT **Clairvoyance**
> **Oracles**
> **Prophecies (Occultism)**
> **Superstition**

Divine healing
USE **Christian Science**
> **Miracles**
> **Spiritual healing**

Diving 797.2
BT **Swimming**
> **Water sports**

NT **Scuba diving**
> **Skin diving**
> **Submarine diving**

Diving, Scuba
USE **Scuba diving**

Diving, Skin
USE **Skin diving**

Diving, Submarine
USE **Submarine diving**

Divinity of Christ
USE **Jesus Christ—Divinity**

Division of powers
USE **Separation of powers**

BT = Broader Term NT = Narrower Term RT = Related Term SA = See Also UF = Used For

Divorce 173; 306.89; 346.01
    UF   Separation (Law)
    BT   **Family**
          Men—Social conditions
          Social problems
          Women—Social conditions
    NT   **Children of divorced parents**
          Desertion and nonsupport
          Divorce mediation
    RT   **Domestic relations**
          Marriage
          Marriage—Annulment
          Remarriage
Divorce counseling
    USE **Divorce mediation**
Divorce mediation 362.82
    UF   Divorce counseling
          Mediation, Divorce
    BT   **Divorce**
    NT   **Child custody**
          Child support
    RT   **Marriage counseling**
DNA 574.87
    UF   D.N.A.
          Deoxyribonucleic acid
          Desoxyribonucleic acid
    BT   **Cells**
          Heredity
          Nucleic acids
    NT   **Recombinant DNA**
DNA cloning
    USE **Clones and cloning**
          Molecular cloning
DNA fingerprinting
    USE **DNA fingerprints**
DNA Fingerprints
    USE **DNA fingerprints**
DNA fingerprints 614
    UF   DNA fingerprinting
          DNA Fingerprints *[Former heading]*
          DNA identification
          DNA profiling
          Genetic fingerprints
          Genetic profiling
    BT   **Genetics**
          Identification
          Medical jurisprudence
DNA identification
    USE **DNA fingerprints**

DNA profiling
    USE **DNA fingerprints**
Docks 386; 387.1; 627
    BT   **Hydraulic structures**
          Marinas
    RT   **Harbors**
Doctor films
    USE **Medical drama (Films)**
Doctor novels
    USE **Medical novels**
Doctor radio programs
    USE **Medical drama (Radio programs)**
Doctor television programs
    USE **Medical drama (Television programs)**
Doctoral theses
    USE **Dissertations**
Doctors
    USE **Physicians**
Doctors' degrees
    USE **Academic degrees**
Doctrinal theology 230
    UF   Christian doctrine
          Dogmatic theology
          Dogmatics
          Theology, Doctrinal *[Former heading]*
    BT   **Theology**
    NT   **Liberation theology**
          Love (Theology)
          Regeneration (Theology)
          Salvation
          Trinity
Doctrine of fairness (Broadcasting)
    USE **Fairness doctrine (Broadcasting)**
Documentaries (Motion pictures)
    USE **Documentary films**
Documentary films 070.1
    UF   Documentaries (Motion pictures)
          Nonfiction films
    BT   **Motion pictures**
Documentation 025
    SA   subjects with the subdivision *Documentation,* e.g. **Agriculture—Documentation;** to be added as needed
    BT   **Information science**

BT = Broader Term   NT = Narrower Term   RT = Related Term   SA = See Also   UF = Used For

Documentation—*Continued*
- NT **Agriculture—Documentation**
  - **Archives**
  - **Bibliographic control**
  - **Bibliography**
  - **Cataloging**
  - **Classification—Books**
  - **Information systems**
  - **Libraries**
  - **Library science**
- RT **Information services**

Documents
- USE **Archives**
  - **Charters**
  - **Government publications**

Dog
- USE **Dogs**

Dog breeding
- USE **Dogs—Breeding**

Dog guides
- USE **Guide dogs**

Dogmatic theology
- USE **Doctrinal theology**

Dogmatics
- USE **Doctrinal theology**

Dogs 599.74; 636.7
- UF Dog
- SA types of dogs, e.g. **Guide dogs;**
  and names of specific
  breeds of dogs, to be added
  as needed
- BT **Domestic animals**
  - **Mammals**
  - **Pets**
- NT **Collies**
  - **Guide dogs**
  - **Hearing ear dogs**
  - **Puppies**

Dogs—Breeding 636.7
- UF Dog breeding
- BT **Breeding**

Dogs—Fiction 808.83; 813, etc.
  May be used for individual works or
  collections of stories about dogs. Materials
  about dog stories are entered under **Dogs
  in literature.**
- BT **Animals—Fiction**

Dogs for the blind
- USE **Guide dogs**

Dogs for the deaf
- USE **Hearing ear dogs**

Dogs in literature 809
  Use for materials about poetry, fiction,
  and plays about dogs. Individual dog stories and collections of dog stories are entered under **Dogs—Fiction.**
- BT **Animals in literature**

Dogs—Psychology 636.7
- BT **Animal intelligence**
  - **Comparative psychology**
  - **Psychology**

Dogs—Training 636.7
- BT **Animals—Training**

Dogs—War use 355.4
- UF War use of dogs
- BT **Animals—War use**

Doll
- USE **Dolls**

Dollhouses 688.7
- BT **Toys**

Dolls 688.7
- UF Doll
- BT **Toys**

Domesday book 942.02
- UF Doomsday book
- BT **Great Britain—History—
  1066-1154, Norman period**

Domestic animals 636
  Use for general materials on farm ani-
  mals. Materials limited to animals as pets
  are entered under **Pets.** Materials on stock
  raising as an industry are entered under
  Livestock.
- UF Animal industry
  - Animals, Domestic
  - Beasts
  - Domestication
  - Farm animals
- SA names of domestic animals,
  e.g. **Cattle;** to be added as
  needed
- BT **Animals**
  - **Breeding**
  - **Economic zoology**
- NT **Cats**
  - **Cattle**
  - **Dogs**
  - **Pigs**
  - **Poultry**
  - **Reindeer**
  - **Sheep**
  - **Working animals**
- RT **Livestock**

BT = Broader Term   NT = Narrower Term   RT = Related Term   SA = See Also   UF = Used For

Domestic animals—*Continued*
>   Pets

Domestic animals—Diseases
>   USE **Animals—Diseases**

Domestic appliances
>   USE **Electric household appliances**
>   **Household equipment and sup-**
>   **plies**

Domestic architecture (May subdiv.
>   geog.) **728**

Use for materials on residential buildings from the standpoint of style and design. General materials on buildings in
which people live are entered under **Hous-**
es.

>   UF   Architecture, Domestic *[For-*
>   *mer heading]*
>   Architecture, Rural
>   Dwellings
>   Habitations, Human
>   Residences
>   Rural architecture
>   SA   types of residential buildings,
>   e.g. **Apartment houses;** to
>   be added as needed
>   BT   **Architecture**
>   NT   **Apartment houses**
>   **Farm buildings**
>   **House construction**
>   **Prefabricated houses**
>   **Solar homes**
>   RT   **Houses**

Domestic architecture—Designs and
>   **plans 728**

>   UF   Architecture, Domestic—
>   Designs and plans *[Former*
>   *heading]*
>   Home designs
>   House plans
>   BT   **Architecture—Designs and**
>   **plans**

Domestic arts
>   USE **Home economics**

Domestic economic assistance 338.9

>   UF   Anti-poverty programs
>   Antipoverty programs
>   Economic assistance, Domes-
>   tic *[Former heading]*
>   Poor relief
>   BT   **Economic assistance**
>   **Economic policy**

>   NT   **Community development**
>   **Government lending**
>   **Public works**
>   **Subsidies**
>   RT   **Grants-in-aid**
>   **Poverty**
>   **Unemployed**

Domestic education
>   USE **Home instruction**

Domestic finance
>   USE **Household budgets**
>   **Personal finance**

Domestic relations 346.01

>   UF   Family relations
>   BT   **Human relations**
>   NT   **Desertion and nonsupport**
>   **Grandparent and child**
>   **Parent and child**
>   **Visitation rights (Domestic re-**
>   **lations)**
>   RT   **Divorce**
>   **Family**
>   **Family life education**
>   **Marriage**

Domestic violence
>   USE **Family violence**

Domestic workers
>   USE **Household employees**

Domestication
>   USE **Domestic animals**

Dominicans
>   USE **Dominicans (Religious order)**

Dominicans (Religious order) 271

>   UF   Black Friars
>   Dominicans *[Former heading]*
>   Friars Preachers
>   Jacobins (Dominicans)
>   Mendicant orders
>   Preaching Friars
>   Saint Dominic, Order of
>   St. Dominic, Order of
>   BT   **Catholic religious orders for**
>   **men**

Dominion of the sea
>   USE **Sea power**

Dominions, British
>   USE **Commonwealth countries**

Donation of organs, tissues, etc. 362.1

>   UF   Anatomical gifts
>   Organ donation

Donation of organs, tissues, etc.—
Continued

    Tissue donation

  BT **Gifts**

  RT **Transplantation of organs, tissues, etc.**

Donations

  USE **Gifts**

Doomsday book

  USE **Domesday book**

Door to door selling

  USE **Peddlers and peddling**

Doors 721

  BT **Architecture—Details**

    Building

    Carpentry

Doping in horse racing

  USE **Drugs and sports**

Doping in sports

  USE **Drugs and sports**

Double consciousness

  USE **Multiple personality**

Double employment

  USE **Supplementary employment**

Doubt

  USE **Belief and doubt**

Down syndrome

  USE **Down's syndrome**

Down's syndrome 616.85

  UF Down syndrome

  BT **Mental retardation**

Draft 355.2

  UF Compulsory military service

    Conscription, Military

    Military draft

    Military service, Compulsory

      [Former heading]

    Military training, Universal

    Selective service

    Service, Compulsory military

    Universal military training

  BT **Armies**

    Human resources

    Military law

Draft dodgers

  USE **Draft resisters**

Draft evaders

  USE **Draft resisters**

Draft resisters 355.2

  UF Draft dodgers

    Draft evaders

    Military service,
      Compulsory—Draft resisters
      [Former heading]

  SA names of wars with the subdivision *Draft resisters,* to be added as needed

  NT **World War, 1939-1945—Draft resisters**

  RT **Conscientious objectors**

    Military desertion

Drafting, Automatic

  USE **Computer aided design**

    Computer graphics

Drafting, Mechanical

  USE **Mechanical drawing**

Dragons 398.24

  BT **Animals—Folklore**

    Folklore

    Monsters

    Mythical animals

Drainage 631.6

  Use for materials on land drainage. Materials on house drainage are entered under **House drainage.**

  UF Land drainage

  BT **Agricultural engineering**

    Civil engineering

    Hydraulic engineering

    Municipal engineering

    Reclamation of land

    Sanitary engineering

    Soils

  RT **Sewerage**

    Wetlands

Drainage, House

  USE **House drainage**

Drama 808.2; 808.82

  Use for general materials on drama, not for individual works. Materials on the history and criticism of drama as literature are entered under **Drama—History and criticism.** Materials on criticism of drama as presented on the stage are entered under **Dramatic criticism.** Materials on the presentation of plays are entered under **Acting; Amateur theater;** or **Theater—Production and direction.** Materials on how to write plays are entered under **Drama—Technique.** Collections of plays are entered under **Drama—Collections; American drama—Collections; English drama—Collections;** etc.

  UF Stage

Drama—*Continued*

SA   subjects, historical events, names of countries, cities, etc., ethnic groups, classes of persons, and names of individual persons with the subdivision *Drama,* to express the theme or subject content of individual plays or collections of plays, e.g. **Easter—Drama; United States—History— 1861-1865, Civil War— Drama; Napoleon I, Emperor of the French, 1769-1821—Drama;** etc., to be added as needed

BT   Literature

NT   Acting
American drama
Ballet
Children's plays
Choral speaking
College and school drama
Comedies
Comedy
Didactic drama
Dramatic criticism
Dramatists
Easter—Drama
English drama
Folk drama
Historical drama
Horror plays
Indians of North America— Drama
Masks (Plays)
Melodrama
Morality plays
Motion picture plays
Mystery and detective plays
Napoleon I, Emperor of the French, 1769-1821—Drama
One act plays
Opera
Pantomimes
Pastoral drama
Plots (Drama, fiction, etc.)
Puppets and puppet plays
Radio plays

Religious drama
Science fiction plays
Television plays
Tragedies
Tragedy
United States—History— 1861-1865, Civil War— Drama
United States—History— Drama

RT   Theater

Drama—Collections 808.82; 812.008, etc.

Use for collections of plays by several authors.

UF   Plays

NT   American drama—Collections
Children's plays
College and school drama— Collections
English drama—Collections

Drama—History and criticism 809.2

Use for materials on criticism of drama as a literary form. Materials on criticism of drama as presented on the stage are entered under **Dramatic criticism.**

NT   American drama—History and criticism
English drama—History and criticism

Drama in education 372.6

BT   School assembly programs

RT   Acting
Amateur theater
College and school drama

Drama—Plots

USE   **Plots (Drama, fiction, etc.)**

Drama, Religious

USE   **Religious drama**

Drama—Technique 808.2

UF   Play writing
Playwriting

BT   Authorship

NT   Motion picture plays— Technique
Radio plays—Technique
Television plays—Technique

Dramatic art

USE   **Acting**

BT = Broader Term   NT = Narrower Term   RT = Related Term   SA = See Also   UF = Used For

Dramatic criticism 792.9

    Use for materials on criticism of drama as presented on the stage. Materials on criticism of drama as a literary form are entered under **Drama—History and criticism; American drama—History and criticism;** etc.

  UF   Theater criticism

  BT   **Criticism**

        Drama

        Theater

Dramatic music

  USE **Musicals**

        Opera

        Operetta

Dramatic plots

  USE **Plots (Drama, fiction, etc.)**

Dramatists 809.2; 920

    Use for materials on the personal lives of several playwrights, not limited to a single national literature. Materials dealing with their literary work are entered under **Drama—History and criticism; English drama—History and criticism;** etc.

  UF   Playwrights

  SA   dramatists of particular countries, e.g. **American dramatists;** to be added as needed

  BT   **Authors**

        Drama

  NT   **American dramatists**

Dramatists, American

  USE **American dramatists**

Drapery 645; 684

  UF   Curtains

  BT   **Interior design**

        Upholstery

Draughts

  USE **Checkers**

Drawing 741; 743

  UF   Drawings

        Sketching

  SA   drawing of particular countries, e.g. **American drawing;** to be added as needed

  BT   **Art**

        Graphic arts

  NT   **American drawing**

        Architectural drawing

        Artistic anatomy

        Commercial art

        Crayon drawing

        Figure drawing

        Geometrical drawing

        Graphic methods

        Landscape drawing

        Map drawing

        Mechanical drawing

        Pastel drawing

        Pen drawing

        Pencil drawing

        Shades and shadows

        Topographical drawing

  RT   **Illustration of books**

        Painting

        Perspective

Drawing, American

  USE **American drawing**

Drawing, Architectural

  USE **Architectural drawing**

Drawing, Automatic

  USE **Computer graphics**

Drawing, Computer

  USE **Computer art**

Drawing, Electronic

  USE **Computer art**

        Computer graphics

Drawing materials

  USE **Artists' materials**

Drawings

  USE **Drawing**

Dreaming

  USE **Dreams**

Dreams 154.6

  UF   Dreaming

  BT   **Brain**

        Divination

        Fortune telling

        Mind and body

        Parapsychology

        Psychophysiology

        Subconsciousness

        Superstition

        Visions

  NT   **Fantasy**

  RT   **Psychoanalysis**

        Sleep

Dredging 627

  BT   **Civil engineering**

        Hydraulic engineering

Dress

  USE **Clothing and dress**

BT = Broader Term   NT = Narrower Term   RT = Related Term   SA = See Also   UF = Used For

Dress accessories 391; 646
  BT **Clothing and dress**
Dressage
  USE **Horsemanship**
Dressing of ores
  USE **Ore dressing**
Dressmaking 646.4; 687
  UF Garment making
  BT **Clothing and dress**
       Fashion
  RT **Needlework**
       Sewing
       Tailoring
Dressmaking—Patterns 646.4; 687
Dried flowers
  USE **Flower drying**
Dried foods 641.4; 664
  UF Dehydrated foods
       Food, Dehydrated
       Food, Dried *[Former heading]*
  BT **Food—Preservation**
  NT **Dried milk**
       Freeze-dried foods
Dried milk 637
  UF Dehydrated milk
       Powdered milk
  BT **Dried foods**
       Milk
Drifting of continents
  USE **Continental drift**
Drill and minor tactics 355.5
  UF Military drill
       Minor tactics
  BT **Tactics**
  RT **Military art and science**
Drill (Nonmilitary)
  USE **Marching drills**
Drilling and boring 621.9
  Use for materials on workshop opera-tions in metal, wood, etc. Materials on the operation of cutting holes in earth or rock are entered under **Boring.**
  UF Boring (Metal, wood, etc.)
  BT **Machine shop practice**
  RT **Machine tools**
Drilling and boring (Earth and rocks)
  USE **Boring**
Drilling, Oil well
  USE **Oil well drilling**
Drilling platforms 627
  UF Artificial islands

       Islands, Artificial
       Offshore structures
       Platforms, Drilling
       Structures, Offshore
  BT **Ocean engineering**
       Offshore oil well drilling
Drills, Marching
  USE **Marching drills**
Drinking age (May subdiv. geog.)
       351.76; 363.4; 613.81
  UF Minimum drinking age
  BT **Age**
       Teenagers—Alcohol use
       Youth—Alcohol use
Drinking and employees
  USE **Employees—Alcohol use**
Drinking and teenagers
  USE **Teenagers—Alcohol use**
Drinking and youth
  USE **Youth—Alcohol use**
Drinking in the workplace
  USE **Employees—Alcohol use**
Drinking of alcoholic beverages (May
       subdiv. geog.) **178; 351.76;
       363.4; 394.1; 613.81**
  Use for materials on drinking in its so-cial aspects and as a social problem.
  UF Alcohol consumption
       Alcoholic beverage consump-tion
       Consumption of alcoholic beverages
       Drinking problem
       Liquor problem
       Social drinking
  SA classes of persons and ethnic groups with the subdivision *Alcohol use,* e.g. **Employees—Alcohol use; Youth—Alcohol use;** etc., to be added as needed
  BT **Alcoholic beverages**
  NT **Drunk driving**
  RT **Alcoholism**
       Temperance
Drinking problem
  USE **Alcoholism**
       Drinking of alcoholic bever-ages
Drinks
  USE **Alcoholic beverages**

Drinks—*Continued*
>
> **Beverages**
>
> **Liquors**

Driver education
>
> USE **Automobile driver education**

Drivers, Automobile
>
> USE **Automobile drivers**

Driving under the influence of alcohol
>
> USE **Drunk driving**

Driving while intoxicated
>
> USE **Drunk driving**

Dromedaries
>
> USE **Camels**

Drop forging
>
> USE **Forging**

Dropouts 371.2
>
> UF College dropouts
>
> Elementary school dropouts
>
> High school dropouts
>
> School dropouts
>
> School withdrawals
>
> Student dropouts
>
> Teenage dropouts
>
> BT **Students**
>
> **Youth**
>
> RT **Educational counseling**
>
> **School attendance**

Droughts 551.57; 632
>
> BT **Meteorology**
>
> NT **Dust storms**
>
> RT **Rain**

Drug abuse 362.29; 613.8; 616.86

Use for general materials on the misuse of drugs, including aspirin, stimulants, sedatives, alcohol, narcotics, etc. Materials limited to addiction to hard drugs are entered under **Drug addiction.**
>
> UF Drug habit
>
> Drug misuse
>
> Drug use
>
> Drugs—Abuse
>
> Drugs—Misuse
>
> SA classes of persons with the subdivision *Drug use,* e.g. **Criminals—Drug use;** and types of drug abuse, e.g. **Alcoholism;** to be added as needed
>
> BT **Crimes without victims**
>
> **Substance abuse**
>
> NT **Alcoholism**

Drug addiction

Drug abuse counseling 362.29; 613.8
>
> UF Drug addiction counseling
>
> Drug counseling
>
> Narcotic addiction counseling
>
> BT **Counseling**
>
> NT **Drug addicts—Rehabilitation**

Drug abuse education
>
> USE **Drug education**

Drug abuse—Physiological effect
>
> USE **Drugs—Physiological effect**

Drug abuse screening
>
> USE **Drug testing**

Drug abuse—Study and teaching
>
> USE **Drug education**

Drug abuse—Testing
>
> USE **Drug testing**

Drug abusing physicians
>
> USE **Physicians—Drug use**

Drug addicted physicians
>
> USE **Physicians—Drug use**

Drug addiction 362.29; 616.86

Use for materials on addiction to hard drugs, that is, those narcotics, stimulants, synthetic drugs, etc., capable of causing severe physical or psychological dependence in most users. General materials on the misuse of drugs are entered under **Drug abuse.**
>
> UF Addiction to drugs
>
> Addiction to hard drugs
>
> Drug habit
>
> Hard drug addiction
>
> Intoxication
>
> Narcotic habit *[Former heading]*
>
> SA classes of persons with the subdivision *Drug use,* e.g. **Criminals—Drug use;** to be added as needed
>
> BT **Drug abuse**
>
> **Habit**
>
> NT **Children of drug addicts**
>
> **Drug addicts**
>
> RT **Temperance**
>
> **Twelve-step programs**

Drug addiction counseling
>
> USE **Drug abuse counseling**

Drug addiction education
>
> USE **Drug education**

Drug addicts 362.29; 616.86
>
> UF Addicts, Drug

Drug addicts—*Continued*
    Narcotic addicts
  SA classes of persons with the
       subdivision *Drug use,* e.g.
       Criminals—Drug use; to be
       added as needed
  BT **Drug addiction**
  NT **Children of drug addicts**
Drug addicts' children
  USE **Children of drug addicts**
Drug addicts' infants
  USE **Children of drug addicts**
Drug addicts—Rehabilitation 362.29;
     613.8; 616.86
  BT **Drug abuse counseling**
Drug counseling
  USE **Drug abuse counseling**
Drug-crime relationship
  USE **Drugs and crime**
Drug dealing
  USE **Drug traffic**
Drug education 362.29; 371.7; 613.8
    Use for materials on the study of drugs,
including their source, abuse, chemical
composition, and social, physical, and per-
sonal effects.
  UF Drug abuse education
       Drug abuse—Study and teach-
       ing
       Drug addiction education
  BT **Health education**
Drug habit
  USE **Drug abuse**
       Drug addiction
Drug misuse
  USE **Drug abuse**
Drug plants
  USE **Medical botany**
Drug pushers
  USE **Drug traffic**
Drug testing 344; 363.1
    Use for materials on testing to identify
personal use or misuse of drugs. Materials
on the testing of drugs for safety or effec-
tiveness are entered under **Drugs—
Testing.**
  UF Drug abuse screening
       Drug abuse—Testing
       Screening for drug abuse
       Testing for drug abuse

  SA classes of persons with the
       subdivision *Drug testing,*
       e.g. **Employees—Drug test-
       ing;** to be added as needed
  NT **Employees—Drug testing**
Drug testing in the workplace
  USE **Employees—Drug testing**
Drug therapy 615.5
  UF Chemotherapy *[Former head-
       ing]*
       Pharmacotherapy
  SA names of diseases other than
       cancer with the subdivision
       Drug therapy, e.g. **Mental
       illness—Drug therapy;** to
       be added as needed
  BT **Therapeutics**
  NT **Antibiotics**
       Cancer—Chemotherapy
       Mental illness—Drug therapy
  RT **Drugs**
       Pharmacology
Drug trade, Illicit
  USE **Drug traffic**
Drug traffic 364.1
  UF Drug dealing
       Drug pushers
       Drug trade, Illicit
       Narcotic traffic *[Former head-
       ing]*
       Smuggling of drugs
       Trafficking in drugs
       Trafficking in narcotics
  BT **Drugs and crime**
Drug use
  USE **Drug abuse**
       and classes of persons with
       the subdivision *Drug use,*
       e.g. **Criminals—Drug use;**
       Employees—Drug use;
       Teenagers—Drug use;
       Youth—Drug use; etc., to
       be added as needed
Drugs 615
  UF Pharmaceuticals
  SA classes of persons with the
       subdivision *Drug use,* e.g.
       Criminals—Drug use; types
       of drugs, e.g. **Amphet-
       amines; Hallucinogens; Nar-**

Drugs—*Continued*

cotics; **Stimulants;** etc.; and names of individual drugs, e.g. **Crack (Drug); Marijuana;** etc., to be added as needed

BT **Pharmacy**
Therapeutics

NT **Alcohol**
Designer drugs
Drugs and crime
Drugs and sports
Generic drugs
Hallucinogens
Narcotics
Nonprescription drugs
Orphan drugs
Psychotropic drugs
Steroids
Sulfonamides

RT **Drug therapy**
Materia medica
Pharmacology

Drugs—Abuse
USE **Drug abuse**

Drugs—Adulteration and analysis
USE **Pharmacology**

Drugs and crime 364.1

Use for general materials on the relationship of drugs and crime. Materials on the illicit drug trade are entered under **Drug traffic.** Materials on the use of drugs by criminals are entered under **Criminals—Drug use.**

UF Crime and drugs
Crime and narcotics
Crime-drug relationship
Drug-crime relationship
Narcotics and crime *[Former heading]*

BT **Crime**
Drugs

NT **Drug traffic**

RT **Criminals—Drug use**

Drugs and criminals
USE **Criminals—Drug use**

Drugs and employees
USE **Employees—Drug use**

Drugs and sports 617.1; 796

Use for general materials on the relationship of drugs and sports. Materials on the use of drugs by athletes are entered under **Athletes—Drug use.**

UF Doping in horse racing
Doping in sports
Sports and drugs

BT **Drugs**
Sports
Sports medicine

NT **Athletes—Drug use**

Drugs and teenagers
USE **Teenagers—Drug use**

Drugs and youth
USE **Youth—Drug use**

Drugs—Chemistry
USE **Pharmaceutical chemistry**

Drugs, Designer
USE **Designer drugs**

Drugs—Generic substitution
USE **Generic drugs**

Drugs, Hallucinogenic
USE **Hallucinogens**

Drugs in the workplace
USE **Employees—Drug use**

Drugs—Misuse
USE **Drug abuse**

Drugs, Nonprescription
USE **Nonprescription drugs**

Drugs of abuse, Synthetic
USE **Designer drugs**

Drugs, Orphan
USE **Orphan drugs**

Drugs—Physiological effect 615; 616.86

Use for materials limited to the effect of drugs on the functions of living organisms.

UF Drug abuse—Physiological effect

SA names of drugs with the subdivision *Physiological effect,* to be added as needed

BT **Pharmacology**

NT **Opium—Physiological effect**

Drugs—Psychological aspects 615; 616.86

BT **Applied psychology**

Drugs, Psychotropic
USE **Psychotropic drugs**

Drugs—Testing 363.19

Use for materials on the testing of drugs for safety or effectiveness. Materials on testing to identify the personal use or misuse or drugs are entered under **Drug testing.**

UF Clinical drug trials

Drugs—Testing—*Continued*
       Clinical trials of drugs
  BT **Consumer protection**
       Pharmacology
Druids and Druidism 299
  BT **Celts**
       Religions
Drum
  USE **Drums**
Drum majoring 784.9; 791.6
  BT **Bands (Music)**
  RT **Baton twirling**
Drums 786.9
  UF Drum *[Former heading]*
  BT **Musical instruments**
       Percussion instruments
Drunk driving 363.12; 364.1
  UF Driving under the influence of
       alcohol
       Driving while intoxicated
  BT **Crime**
       Drinking of alcoholic bever-
       ages
Drunkards
  USE **Alcoholics**
Drunkenness
  USE **Alcoholism**
       Temperance
Dry cleaning 667
  UF Clothing and dress—Dry
       cleaning
  BT **Cleaning**
Dry farming 631.5
  UF Farming, Dry
  BT **Agriculture**
       Irrigation
Dry goods
  USE **Fabrics**
Dual career family 306.85
  UF Families, Dual career
       Two-career family
       Working couples
  BT **Family**
Dual employment
  USE **Supplementary employment**
Ducks 598.4; 636.5
  BT **Poultry**
Ductless glands
  USE **Endocrine glands**

Due process of law 347
     Use for materials on the regular admin-
  istration of the law, according to which
  citizens may not be denied their legal
  rights and all laws must conform to fun-
  damental and accepted legal principles.
  Materials on legal hearings before an im-
  partial and disinterested tribunal are en-
  tered under **Fair trial.**
  UF Procedural due process
       Substantive due process
  BT **Administration of justice**
       Civil rights
  NT **Fair trial**
Dueling 179; 394
  UF Fighting
  BT **Manners and customs**
       Martial arts
Dumps, Toxic
  USE **Hazardous waste sites**
Dunes
  USE **Sand dunes**
Dungeons
  USE **Prisons**
Duplicate bridge
  USE **Bridge (Game)**
Duplicating processes
  USE **Copying processes and ma-**
       chines
Dust, Radioactive
  USE **Radioactive fallout**
Dust storms 551.55
  BT **Droughts**
       Erosion
       Storms
Dusting and spraying
  USE **Spraying and dusting**
Duties
  USE **Tariff**
       Taxation
Duty 170
  BT **Ethics**
       Human behavior
  NT **Conscience**
Dwarf trees 582.16; 635.9
  SA names of dwarf trees, e.g.
       Bonsai; to be added as
       needed
  BT **Trees**
  NT **Bonsai**
Dwarfism
  USE **Growth disorders**

BT = Broader Term   NT = Narrower Term   RT = Related Term   SA = See Also   UF = Used For

Dwellings
USE **Domestic architecture**
Houses
Housing
and ethnic groups and classes of persons with the subdivision *Dwellings,* for materials on the residential buildings of a group from the standpoint of architecture, construction, or ethnology, e.g. **Indians of North America—Dwellings;** and ethnic groups and classes of persons with the subdivision *Housing,* for materials on the social and economic aspects of providing housing for the group, e.g. **Physically handicapped—Housing;** to be added as needed

Dyes and dyeing 646; 667; 746.6
SA types of dyes and types of dyeing, to be added as needed
BT **Color**
Pigments
Textile chemistry
Textile industry
NT **Batik**
Tie dyeing
RT **Bleaching**
Dying children
USE **Terminally ill children**
Dying patients
USE **Terminally ill**
Dynamics 531
UF Kinetics
BT **Mathematics**
Mechanics
NT **Aerodynamics**
Astrodynamics
Chaos (Science)
Hydrodynamics
Kinematics
Matter
Motion
Quantum theory
Thermodynamics

RT **Force and energy**
Physics
Statics
Dynamite 662
BT **Explosives**
Dynamos
USE **Electric generators**
Dyslexia 371.91; 616.85
BT **Reading disability**
Dyspepsia
USE **Indigestion**
Dystopias 811, etc.; 813, etc.
May be used for individual works, collections, or materials about dystopias.
UF Anti-utopias
BT **Fantasy fiction**
Science fiction
RT **Utopian fiction**
E.E.C.
USE **European Union**
E.E.O.
USE **Discrimination in employment**
E-mail systems
USE **Electronic mail systems**
E.R.A.'s
USE **Equal rights amendments**
E.S.P.
USE **Extrasensory perception**
Eagles 598.9
BT **Birds of prey**
Ear 611; 612.8
BT **Head**
NT **Deafness**
RT **Hearing**
Early Christian literature 281
Use for materials about writings of early Christian authors to the time of Gregory the Great in the West and John of Damascus in the East. Collections of such writings are entered under this heading with the subdivision *Collections.*
UF Christian literature—30-600, Early
Christian literature, Early
BT **Christian literature**
Literature
Medieval literature
RT **Church history—30-600, Early church**
Latin literature
Early church history
USE **Church history—30-600, Early church**

BT = Broader Term　　NT = Narrower Term　　RT = Related Term　　SA = See Also　　UF = Used For

Early printed books
　USE **Rare books**
Early warning system, Ballistic missile
　USE **Ballistic missile early warning**
　　　　system
Earth 525; 550
　　Use for general materials on the whole
　planet. Materials limited to the structure
　and composition of the earth and the
　physical changes it has undergone and is
　still undergoing are entered under **Geolo-**
　gy.
　UF　World
　BT　**Planets**
　　　　Solar system
　NT　**Antarctic regions**
　　　　Arctic regions
　　　　Atmosphere
　　　　Continents
　　　　Earthquakes
　　　　Gaia hypothesis
　　　　Geodesy
　　　　Geography
　　　　Ice age
　　　　Latitude
　　　　Longitude
　　　　Ocean
　　　　Oceanography
　　　　Tropics
　RT　**Creation**
　　　　Earth sciences
　　　　Geology
　　　　Physical geography
　　　　Universe
Earth—Age 551.7
Earth—Chemical composition
　USE　**Geochemistry**
Earth—Crust 551.1
　NT　**Plate tectonics**
Earth, Effect of man on
　USE　**Human influence on nature**
Earth fills
　USE　**Landfills**
Earth—Internal structure 551.1
Earth—Photographs from space 778.3
　BT　**Space photography**
Earth sciences 550
　UF　Geoscience
　BT　**Physical sciences**
　　　　Science
　NT　**Climate**

　　　　Geochemistry
　　　　Geography
　　　　Geology
　　　　Geophysics
　　　　Meteorology
　　　　Oceanography
　　　　Water
　RT　**Earth**
Earth sheltered houses 690; 728
　UF　Houses, Earth sheltered
　　　　Houses, Underground
　　　　Underground houses
　BT　**House construction**
　　　　Houses
　　　　Underground architecture
Earth—Space attack and defense
　USE　**Space warfare**
Earthenware
　USE　**Pottery**
Earthquake sea waves
　USE　**Tsunamis**
Earthquakes (May subdiv. geog.) 551.2
　UF　Seismography
　　　　Seismology
　SA　types of structures subject to
　　　　earthquake forces with the
　　　　subdivision *Earthquake ef-*
　　　　fects, e.g. **Skyscrapers—**
　　　　Earthquake effects; to be
　　　　added as needed
　BT　**Earth**
　　　　Geology
　　　　Natural disasters
　　　　Physical geography
　NT　**Buildings—Earthquake effects**
　　　　Skyscrapers—Earthquake ef-
　　　　fects
Earthquakes and building
　USE　**Buildings—Earthquake effects**
Earthquakes—California 551.2
Earthquakes—United States 551.2
　UF　United States—Earthquakes
Earthwork
　USE　**Soils (Engineering)**
Earthworks (Archeology)
　USE　**Excavations (Archeology)**
Earthworks (Art) 709.04
　UF　Landscape sculpture
　　　　Site oriented art
　BT　**Modern art—1900-1999 (20th**
　　　　century)

East
  USE **Asia**
East Africa 967.6
  Use for materials dealing collectively
with the eastern region of the continent of
Africa. Although used loosely, the term is
usually used to include the areas now oc-
cupied by the countries of Burundi, Ken-
ya, Rwanda, Tanzania, Uganda, and
Somalia. Both the terms East Africa and
Eastern Africa are sometimes used to cov-
er the area extending from Sudan and
Ethiopia in the north to the Zambizi Riv-
er in the south, thereby including Malawi
and Mozambique.
  UF Africa, East *[Former heading]*
      Africa, Eastern
      Eastern Africa
  BT **Africa**
East and West 306; 909
  Use for materials on both acculturation
and cultural conflict between Asian and
Occidental civilizations.
  BT **International relations**
  NT **Asian civilization**
      Western civilization
  RT **Acculturation**
East Asia 950
  Use for materials on East Asia including
China, Japan, Korea, Taiwan, Hong Kong
and Macao.
  UF Asia, East
      East (Far East)
      Far East
      Orient
  BT **Asia**
  RT **Pacific rim**
East (Far East)
  USE **East Asia**
East Germany
  USE **Germany (East)**
East Indians 305.891; 954
  UF Indians (of India)
  RT **Hindus**
East (Near East)
  USE **Middle East**
Easter 263; 394.2
  BT **Christian holidays**
      Holy Week
  RT **Lent**
Easter carols
  USE **Carols**
Easter—Drama 808.82; 812, etc.
  May be used for individual works, col-
lections, or materials about Easter plays.

  BT **Drama**
      Religious drama
Easter egg decoration
  USE **Egg decoration**
Eastern Africa
  USE **East Africa**
Eastern churches 281
  BT **Christian sects**
      Christianity
  NT **Orthodox Eastern Church**
      Russian Orthodox Church
Eastern Empire
  USE **Byzantine Empire**
Eastern Europe 947
  UF Europe, Eastern
Eastern Europe—History 947
Eastern Europe—History—1989-
      947.085
  RT **Former Soviet republics**
Eastern Seaboard
  USE **Atlantic States**
Easy and quick cooking
  USE **Quick and easy cooking**
Easy reading materials 372.4
  UF Beginning reading materials
      Preprimers
      Preschool reading materials
      Primers
  BT **Children's literature**
      Reading materials
Eating
  USE **Dining**
Eating customs 394.1
  UF Food customs
      Food habits
  BT **Diet**
      Human behavior
      Nutrition
  NT **Table etiquette**
  RT **Dining**
Eating disorders 616.85
  UF Appetite disorders
      Ingestion disorders
  SA types of eating disorders, to
      be added as needed
  BT **Abnormal psychology**
  NT **Anorexia nervosa**
      Bulimia
Eavesdropping 363.2
  UF Bugging, Electronic

Eavesdropping—*Continued*
>Electronic bugging
>Electronic eavesdropping
>Electronic listening devices
>Listening devices
>Surveillance, Electronic

BT **Criminal investigation**
>**Right of privacy**

RT **Wiretapping**

Eccentrics and eccentricities 920

UF Cranks

BT **Curiosities and wonders**
>**Personality**

NT **Hermits**

Ecclesiastical antiquities

USE **Christian antiquities**

Ecclesiastical architecture

USE **Church architecture**

Ecclesiastical art

USE **Christian art and symbolism**

Ecclesiastical biography

USE **Christianity—Biography**

Ecclesiastical fasts and feasts

USE **Religious holidays**
>and names of specific fasts
>and feasts, e.g. **Lent; Eas-**
>**ter;** etc., to be added as
>needed

Ecclesiastical furniture

USE **Church furniture**

Ecclesiastical history

USE **Church history**

Ecclesiastical law 262.9

UF Canon law
>Church law
>Law, Ecclesiastical

BT **Church**
>**Law**

NT **Tithes**

RT **Church and state**

Ecclesiastical rites and ceremonies

USE **Rites and ceremonies**

Echo ranging

USE **Sonar**

Eclipses, Lunar

USE **Lunar eclipses**

Eclipses, Solar

USE **Solar eclipses**

Eclogues

USE **Pastoral poetry**

Ecological agriculture

USE **Organic farming**

Ecological movement

USE **Environmental movement**

Ecology 574.5

UF Balance of nature
>Biology—Ecology
>Ecosystems

SA types of ecology, e.g. **Marine**
>**ecology;** to be added as
>needed

BT **Biology**
>**Environment**

NT **Adaptation (Biology)**
>**Biogeography**
>**Environmental protection**
>**Food chains (Ecology)**
>**Gaia hypothesis**
>**Marine ecology**
>**Plants—Ecology**
>**Symbiosis**

RT **Biological diversity**

Ecology, Human

USE **Human ecology**

Ecology, Marine

USE **Marine ecology**

Ecology, Social

USE **Human ecology**

Economic aspects

USE subjects with the subdivision
>*Economic aspects,* e.g.
>**Agriculture—Economic as-**
>**pects;** to be added as need-
>ed

Economic assistance 338.91

Use for general materials on international-
al economic aid given in the form of gifts,
loans, relief grants, or technical assistance.
Materials limited to the latter are entered
under **Technical assistance.**

UF Aid to developing areas
>Assistance to developing areas
>Foreign aid program

SA economic assistance from par-
>ticular countries, e.g. **Amer-**
>**ican economic assistance;** to
>be added as needed

BT **Economic policy**
>**International cooperation**
>**International economic rela-**
>**tions**

Economic assistance—*Continued*
  NT American economic assistance
      Domestic economic assistance
      Technical assistance
      World War, 1939-1945—
        Civilian relief
  RT Developing countries
      Reconstruction (1914-1939)
      Reconstruction (1939-1951)
Economic assistance, American
  USE American economic assistance
Economic assistance, Domestic
  USE Domestic economic assistance
Economic biology
  USE Economic zoology
Economic botany 581.6
  UF Agricultural botany
      Biology, Economic
      Botany, Agricultural
      Botany, Economic *[Former
        heading]*
      Plants, Useful
  BT **Agriculture**
      Botany
  NT **Cotton**
      Edible plants
      Forage plants
      Forest products
      Grain
      Grasses
      Plant conservation
      Plant introduction
      Poisonous plants
      Weeds
Economic conditions 330.9
  Use for general materials on some or all
  of the following: natural resources, busi-
  ness, commerce, industry, labor, manufac-
  tures, financial conditions. Materials on
  the history of the economic development
  of several countries are entered under
  Economic development.
  UF Business depressions
      Economic history
      Stabilization in industry
      World economics
  SA racial and ethnic groups,
      classes of persons, and
      names of countries, cities,
      areas, etc., with the subdi-
      vision *Economic conditions,*

  e.g. **African Americans—
  Economic conditions; United
  States—Economic condi-
  tions;** etc., to be added as
  needed
  BT **Business**
      Economics
      Social conditions
      Wealth
  NT **African Americans—Economic
        conditions**
      Blacks—Economic conditions
      Business cycles
      Developing countries
      Economic policy
      Industrial revolution
      Labor supply
      Natural resources
      Quality of life
      **United States—Economic con-
        ditions**
  RT **Commercial geography**
      Economic development
Economic cycles
  USE **Business cycles**
Economic depressions 338.5
  UF Business depressions
      Depressions, Economic *[For-
        mer heading]*
      Panics, Economic
      Recessions, Economic
  BT **Business cycles**
      Economics
Economic development 338.9
  Use for materials on the theory and pol-
  icy of economic development. Materials
  restricted to a particular place are entered
  under the name of the country, city, or
  area with the subdivisions *Economic con-
  ditions; Economic policy;* or *Industries.*
  UF Development, Economic
      Economic growth
  BT **Economic policy**
      Economics
  RT **Economic conditions**
Economic entomology
  USE **Beneficial insects**
      Insect pests
Economic forecasting 338.5
  BT **Business cycles**
      Economics

Economic forecasting—*Continued*
  Forecasting
  NT Business forecasting
      Employment forecasting
Economic geography
  USE Commercial geography
Economic geology 553
  UF Geology, Economic *[Former heading]*
  SA names of geological products, e.g. **Asbestos; Gypsum;** etc., to be added as needed
  BT Geology
  NT Asbestos
      Coal
      Gypsum
      Mines and mineral resources
      Natural gas
      Ores
      Petroleum geology
      Quarries and quarrying
      Soils
      Stone
Economic growth
  USE Economic development
Economic history
  USE Economic conditions
Economic mobilization
  USE Industrial mobilization
Economic planning
  USE Economic policy
Economic policy 338.9
  Use for materials on the policy of government towards economic problems.
  UF Economic planning
      National planning
      Planning, Economic
      Planning, National
      Welfare state
      World economics
  SA names of countries and states with the subdivision *Economic policy,* and names of countries with the subdivision *Commercial policy,* to be added as needed
  BT Economic conditions
      Economics
  NT Commercial policy
      Domestic economic assistance

Economic assistance
Economic development
Fiscal policy
Free trade and protection
Government lending
Government ownership
Human resources policy
Industrial mobilization
Industrialization
International economic relations
Land reform
Monetary policy
Municipal ownership
Ohio—Economic policy
Privatization
Sanctions (International law)
Subsidies
Tariff
Technical assistance
United States—Commercial policy
United States—Economic policy
  RT Industry—Government policy
      National security
      Social policy
Economic relations, Foreign
  USE International economic relations
Economic sanctions
  USE Sanctions (International law)
Economic zones (Maritime law)
  USE Territorial waters
Economic zoology 591.6
  Use for general materials on animals injurious and beneficial to man and to agriculture, and for materials on the extermination of wild animals, venomous snakes, etc.
  UF Animals, Useful and harmful
      Biology, Economic
      Economic biology
      Zoology, Economic *[Former heading]*
  BT Zoology
  NT Agricultural pests
      Beneficial insects
      Domestic animals
      Furbearing animals
      Insect pests

Economic zoology—*Continued*
- Pest control
- Pests
- Poisonous animals
- Wildlife conservation
- Working animals

Economics 330
- UF   Distribution of wealth
- Political economy
- Production
- SA   subjects with the subdivision *Economic aspects,* e.g. **Agriculture—Economic aspects;** to be added as needed
- BT   **Social sciences**
- NT   **Agriculture—Economic aspects**
    - **Balance of trade**
    - **Barter**
    - **Business**
    - **Capital**
    - **Capitalism**
    - **Christianity and economics**
    - **Commerce**
    - **Consumption (Economics)**
    - **Cooperation**
    - **Cost of living**
    - **Credit**
    - **Economic conditions**
    - **Economic depressions**
    - **Economic development**
    - **Economic forecasting**
    - **Economic policy**
    - **Finance**
    - **Free trade and protection**
    - **Government ownership**
    - **Income**
    - **Individualism**
    - **Industrial trusts**
    - **Industry**
    - **Labor**
    - **Land use**
    - **Marxism**
    - **Money**
    - **Monopolies**
    - **Population**
    - **Prices**
    - **Profit**
    - **Property**
    - **Public debts**

- **Saving and thrift**
- **Socialism**
- **Statistics**
- **Underground economy**
- **Waste (Economics)**
- **Wealth**

Economics and Christianity
- USE   **Christianity and economics**

Economics—History 330.09; 330.1
   Use for materials describing the development of economic theories. Materials on the economic conditions and development of countries are entered under **Economic conditions.**

Economics, Medical
- USE   **Medical economics**

Economics of war
- USE   **War—Economic aspects**

Economy
- USE   **Saving and thrift**

Economy, Underground
- USE   **Underground economy**

Ecosystems
- USE   **Ecology**

Ectogenesis, Preimplantational
- USE   **Fertilization in vitro**

Ecumenical councils
- USE   **Councils and synods**

Ecumenical movement
- USE   **Christian unity**

Eddas 839
   May be used for individual works, collections, or materials about eddas.
- BT   **Old Norse literature**
    - **Poetry**
    - **Scandinavian literature**

Edible plants 581.6
- UF   Food plants
- Plants, Edible *[Former heading]*
- Plants, Useful
- BT   **Economic botany**
    - **Food**
    - **Plants**

Editions
- USE   **Bibliography—Editions**

Editors and editing
- USE   **Journalism**
    - **Journalists**
    - **Publishers and publishing**

BT = Broader Term   NT = Narrower Term   RT = Related Term   SA = See Also   UF = Used For

Education (May subdiv. geog.) **370**

Subdivisions listed under this heading may be used under other education headings where applicable.

UF Instruction
    Pedagogy

SA types of education, to be added as needed, e.g. **Vocational education;** classes of persons and social and ethnic groups with the subdivision *Education,* e.g. **Deaf—Education; African Americans—Education;** etc.; and subjects with the subdivision *Study and teaching,* e.g. **Science—Study and teaching;** to be added as needed

BT **Civilization**

NT **Adult education**
    African Americans—Education
    Area studies
    Audiovisual education
    Automobile driver education
    Basic education
    Blacks—Education
    Blind—Education
    Books and reading
    Business education
    Church and education
    Classical education
    Colleges and universities
    Continuing education
    Cooperative learning
    Correspondence schools and courses
    Deaf—Education
    Educational games
    Educational tests and measurements
    Educators
    Elementary education
    Evening and continuation schools
    Family life education
    Foreign study
    Fundamentalism and education
    Higher education
    Home instruction
    International education
    Library education
    Literacy
    Mainstreaming in education
    Men—Education
    Mentally handicapped children—Education
    Military education
    Moral education
    Multicultural education
    Nature study
    Naval education
    Outdoor education
    Physical education
    Preschool education
    Professional education
    Psychology of learning
    Religious education
    Scholarships
    Science—Study and teaching
    Secondary education
    Self-instruction
    Simulation games in education
    Socialization
    Special education
    Study skills
    Teachers
    Technical education
    Veterans—Education
    Vocational education
    Women—Education
    World War, 1939-1945—Education and the war

RT **Coeducation**
    Culture
    Learning and scholarship
    Schools
    Teaching

Education, Adult
  USE **Adult education**

Education—Aims and objectives 370.11

Education and church
  USE **Church and education**

Education and Fundamentalism
  USE **Fundamentalism and education**

Education and radio
  USE **Radio in education**

Education and religion
  USE **Church and education**

BT = Broader Term   NT = Narrower Term   RT = Related Term   SA = See Also   UF = Used For

Education and state
USE **Education—Government policy**
Education and television
USE **Television in education**
Education associations
USE **Educational associations**
Education at home
USE **Home instruction**
Education—Automation
USE **Computer assisted instruction**
Education, Bilingual
USE **Bilingual education**
Education, Business
USE **Business education**
Education, Character
USE **Moral education**
Education, Christian
USE **Christian education**
Education, Classical
USE **Classical education**
Education, Compulsory
USE **Compulsory education**
Education, Continuing
USE **Continuing education**
Education—Curricula 375
UF Core curriculum
Courses of study
Curricula (Courses of study)
Schools—Curricula
Study, Courses of
SA types of education and
schools with the subdivi-
sion *Curricula,* to be added
as needed
NT **Articulation (Education)**
**Colleges and universities—
Curricula**
Library education—Curricula
Education—Data processing
USE **Computer assisted instruction**
**Education—Developing countries
370.9172**
Education, Discrimination in
USE **Discrimination in education**
Education, Elementary
USE **Elementary education**
Education, Ethical
USE **Moral education**
Religious education
Education—Experimental methods 371.3
UF Activity schools

Experimental methods in edu-
cation
Progressive education
Teaching—Experimental
methods
SA types of experimental meth-
ods, e.g. **Nongraded schools;
Open plan schools;** etc., to
be added as needed
NT **Experimental schools
Nongraded schools
Open plan schools
Whole language**
Education—Federal aid
USE **Federal aid to education**
Education—Finance 371.2; 379.1
UF School finance
School taxes
Tuition
BT **Finance**
NT **Federal aid to education
State aid to education**
Education for librarianship
USE **Library education**
Education—Government policy 379
UF Education and state
Educational policy
State and education
NT **Compulsory education
Federal aid to education
State aid to education**
Education, Higher
USE **Higher education**
Education, Home
USE **Home instruction**
Education, Industrial
USE **Industrial arts education
Technical education**
Education—Integration
USE **School integration**
Education, Intercultural
USE **Multicultural education**
Education, International
USE **International education**
Education, Medical
USE **Medicine—Study and teaching**
Education, Military
USE **Military education**
Education, Moral
USE **Moral education**

Education, Multicultural
USE **Multicultural education**

Education, Musical
USE **Music—Study and teaching**

Education, Naval
USE **Naval education**

Education, Nonformal
USE **Free universities**

Education of adults
USE **Adult education**

Education of children
USE **Elementary education**

Education of criminals
USE **Prisoners—Education**

Education of men
USE **Men—Education**

Education of prisoners
USE **Prisoners—Education**

Education of the blind
USE **Blind—Education**

Education of the deaf
USE **Deaf—Education**

Education of veterans
USE **Veterans—Education**

Education of women
USE **Women—Education**

Education of workers
USE **Labor—Education**

Education, Outdoor
USE **Outdoor education**

Education—Personnel service
USE **Educational counseling**

Education, Physical
USE **Physical education**

Education, Preschool
USE **Preschool education**

Education, Primary
USE **Elementary education**

Education, Professional
USE **Professional education**

Education, Religious
USE **Religious education**

Education, Scientific
USE **Science—Study and teaching**

Education, Secondary
USE **Secondary education**

Education, Segregation in
USE **Segregation in education**

Education, Special
USE **Special education**

Education—State aid
USE **State aid to education**

Education—Statistics 370

Education—Study and teaching 370.7

   Use for materials on the study and teaching of education as a science. Materials limited to the methods of training teachers are entered under **Teachers—Training.** Materials on the methods of teaching are entered under **Teaching.**

   UF   Pedagogy
   NT   **Teachers colleges**
        Teachers—Training

Education, Technical
USE **Technical education**

Education, Theological
USE **Religious education**
    Theology—Study and teaching

Education—United States 370.973
   UF   United States—Education

Education, Vocational
USE **Vocational education**

Educational achievement
USE **Academic achievement**

Educational administration
USE **Schools—Administration**

Educational associations 370.6
   UF   Education associations
   BT   **Societies**
        Teachers
   NT   **Parents' and teachers' associations**

Educational consultants 370.7
   BT   **Consultants**

Educational counseling 371.4

   Use for materials on the assistance given to students by schools, colleges, or universities in the selection of a program of studies suited to their abilities, interests, future plans, and general circumstances. Materials on the assistance given to students in understanding and coping with adjustment problems are entered under **School counseling.** Materials on the activities and programs designed to help people plan, choose, and succeed in their careers are entered under **Vocational guidance.**

   UF   Academic advising
        Education—Personnel service
        Educational guidance
        Guidance counseling, Educational
        Personnel service in education
        Student guidance

Educational counseling—*Continued*

      Students—Counseling

  BT **Counseling**

  RT **Dropouts**

      School counseling

      Vocational guidance

Educational films

  USE **Libraries and motion pictures**

      Motion pictures in education

Educational freedom

  USE **Academic freedom**

Educational games 371.3

  UF Instructional games

      Instructive games

  BT **Education**

      Games

  NT **Simulation games in education**

Educational gaming

  USE **Simulation games in education**

Educational guidance

  USE **Educational counseling**

Educational measurements

  USE **Educational tests and measurements**

Educational media

  USE **Teaching—Aids and devices**

Educational media centers

  USE **Instructional materials centers**

Educational policy

  USE **Education—Government policy**

Educational psychology 370.15

  UF Psychology, Educational

  BT **Psychology**

      Teaching

  NT **Apperception**

      Attention

      Imagination

      Intelligence tests

      Listening

      Memory

      Perception

      Psychology of learning

      Thought and thinking

  RT **Applied psychology**

      Child psychology

Educational reports

  USE **School reports**

Educational simulation games

  USE **Simulation games in education**

Educational sociology 370.19

  UF Social problems in education

      Sociology, Educational

  BT **Sociology**

Educational surveys 370

  UF School surveys

  BT **Social surveys**

Educational television

  USE **Public television**

      Television in education

Educational tests and measurements 371.2

  UF Educational measurements

      Tests

  BT **Education**

      Examinations

  NT **Ability—Testing**

      Colleges and universities— Entrance examinations

      Grading and marking (Education)

  RT **Intelligence tests**

      Psychological tests

Educators 370.92; 920

  UF College teachers

      Faculty (Education)

  BT **Education**

  RT **Teachers**

Edwardian novels 813, etc.

    May be used for individual works, collections, or materials about historical novels set in the reign of Edward VII (1901-1910).

  BT **Historical fiction**

EEC

  USE **European Union**

EEO

  USE **Discrimination in employment**

Efficiency, Household

  USE **Home economics**

Efficiency, Industrial

  USE **Industrial efficiency**

Egg decoration 745.59

  UF Easter egg decoration

      Eggshell craft

  BT **Decoration and ornament**

      Handicraft

Eggs 636.5; 641

    Use for materials on animal eggs in general as well as materials on chicken eggs.

  BT **Animal food**

      Cooking

      Food

BT = Broader Term   NT = Narrower Term   RT = Related Term   SA = See Also   UF = Used For

Eggs—*Continued*

　NT　**Birds—Eggs and nests**

Eggshell craft

　USE　**Egg decoration**

Egypt 962

　　May be subdivided like United States except for *History.*

Egypt—Antiquities 932

　UF　Egyptology

Egypt—History 932; 962

　NT　**Sinai Campaign, 1956**

Egypt—History—1970- 962.05

Egyptology

　USE　**Egypt—Antiquities**

Eight-hour day

　USE　**Hours of labor**

Eighteenth century 909.7

　　Use for general materials covering progress and development during this period in one or in several countries.

　UF　1700-1799 (18th century)

　BT　**Modern history**

　NT　**Enlightenment**

Elder abuse

　USE　**Elderly abuse**

Elder care

　USE　**Elderly—Care**

Elderly (May subdiv. geog.) **155.67; 305.26**

　UF　Aged

　　　Aging persons

　　　Elderly persons

　　　Older persons

　　　Senior citizens

　SA　elderly of particular racial or ethnic groups, to be added as needed

　BT　**Age**

　　　Gerontology

　NT　**African American elderly**

　　　Aging

　　　Aging parents

　　　Elderly men

　　　Elderly women

　　　Libraries and the elderly

　　　Retirement income

　　　Social work with the elderly

　RT　**Old age**

Elderly abuse 362.6

　UF　Abuse of the elderly

　　　Abused aged

　　　Battered elderly

　　　Elder abuse

　　　Elderly—Mistreatment

　　　Elderly neglect

　　　Parent abuse

　BT　**Family violence**

Elderly and libraries

　USE　**Libraries and the elderly**

Elderly—Care 362.6

　　Use for general materials on the care of the dependent elderly.

　UF　Elder care

　NT　**Elderly—Home care**

　　　Elderly—Institutional care

　　　Elderly—Medical care

　　　Nursing homes

Elderly—Counseling of 362.6

　UF　Counseling of the elderly

　　　Counseling with the aged

　BT　**Counseling**

Elderly—Diseases 618.97

　UF　Geriatrics

　RT　**Elderly—Health and hygiene**

Elderly—Health and hygiene 618.97

　UF　Geriatrics

　RT　**Elderly—Diseases**

Elderly—Home care 362.6

　BT　**Elderly—Care**

　　　Home care services

Elderly—Housing 362.6

　UF　Housing for the elderly

　NT　**Retirement communities**

Elderly—Institutional care 362.6

　UF　Homes for the elderly

　　　Old age homes

　BT　**Elderly—Care**

Elderly—Life skills guides 362.6; 646.7

　BT　**Life skills**

　RT　**Retirement**

Elderly—Medical care 362.6; 618.97

　UF　Medical care for the elderly

　BT　**Elderly—Care**

　　　Medical care

　NT　**Medicare**

Elderly men (May subdiv. geog.) **305.26**

　UF　Aged men

　BT　**Elderly**

Elderly—Mistreatment

　USE　**Elderly abuse**

Elderly neglect

　USE　**Elderly abuse**

Elderly parents
USE **Aging parents**
Elderly persons
USE **Elderly**
Elderly—Recreation 790.084
BT **Recreation**
Elderly—Societies 367
Elderly—United States 305.260973
UF United States—Elderly
Elderly women (May subdiv. geog.)
305.26
UF Aged women
BT **Elderly**
Election (Theology)
USE **Predestination**
Electioneering
USE **Politics**
Elections (May subdiv. geog.) **324**
UF Ballot
Franchise
Polls, Election
Voting
BT **Politics**
NT **Campaign funds**
Equal time rule (Broadcasting)
Presidents—United States—
Election
Primaries
Referendum
Suffrage
Voter registration
RT **Proportional representation**
Representative government and
representation
Elections—Finance
USE **Campaign funds**
Elections, Primary
USE **Primaries**
Elections—United States 324.973
UF United States—Elections
Elections—United States—Finance
USE **Campaign funds—United**
States
Electoral college
USE **Presidents—United States—**
Election
Electric apparatus and appliances
621.3028; 643
Use for materials on small electrical ma-
chines and appliances. Materials on large
machines powered by electricity are en-
tered under **Electric machinery.**

UF Apparatus, Electric
Appliances, Electric
Electric appliances
SA names of electric apparatus
and appliances, e.g. **Burglar**
alarms; to be added as
needed
BT **Electric engineering**
Scientific apparatus and in-
struments
NT **Burglar alarms**
Electric batteries
Electric generators
Electric household appliances
Electric lamps
Induction coils
Storage batteries
Electric apparatus and appliances, Do-
mestic
USE **Electric household appliances**
Electric appliances
USE **Electric apparatus and appli-**
ances
Electric household appliances
Electric automobiles 629.222
UF Automobiles, Electric *[Former*
heading]
Electric cars
BT **Automobiles**
RT **Automobile engines**
Electric batteries 621.31
UF Batteries, Electric
Cells, Electric
BT **Electric apparatus and appli-**
ances
Electrochemistry
NT **Fuel cells**
Solar batteries
RT **Storage batteries**
Electric cars
USE **Electric automobiles**
Electric circuits 621.319
UF Circuits, Electric
BT **Electric lines**
Electricity
NT **Electronic circuits**
Electric communication
USE **Telecommunication**
Electric condensers
USE **Condensers (Electricity)**

Electric conductors 621.319
  UF Conductors, Electric
  BT **Electronics**
  NT **Semiconductors**
      Superconductors
Electric controllers 629.8
  UF Automatic control
  BT **Electric machinery**
Electric currents 537.6; 621.31
  UF Currents, Electric
  BT **Electricity**
  NT **Alternating electric currents**
      Electric measurements
      Electric transformers
Electric currents, Alternating
  USE **Alternating electric currents**
Electric distribution
  USE **Electric lines**
       Electric power distribution
Electric engineering 621.3
  UF Electrical engineering
  BT **Engineering**
      Mechanical engineering
  NT **Electric apparatus and appliances**
      Electric lighting
      Electric machinery
      Electric power distribution
      Electric railroads
      Electricity in mining
      Radio
      Telegraph
      Telephone
Electric equipment of automobiles
  USE **Automobiles—Electric equipment**
Electric eye
  USE **Photoelectric cells**
Electric generators 621.31
  UF Dynamos
      Generators, Electric
  BT **Electric apparatus and appliances**
      Electric machinery
Electric heating 621.402; 644; 697
  UF Electricity in the home
  BT **Heating**
Electric household appliances 643
  UF Appliances, Electric
      Domestic appliances

Electric apparatus and appliances, Domestic
      Electric appliances
      Electricity in the home
      Household appliances, Electric *[Former heading]*
      Labor saving devices, Household
  SA names of specific appliances, to be added as needed
  BT **Electric apparatus and appliances**
      Household equipment and supplies
Electric industries 338.4
  UF Electric utilities
      Industries, Electric
  BT **Public utilities**
Electric lamps 621.32; 645
  UF Incandescent lamps
  BT **Electric apparatus and appliances**
      Lamps
  RT **Electric lighting**
Electric light
  USE **Electric lighting**
       Photometry
       Phototherapy
Electric lighting 621.32
  UF Arc light
      Electric light
      Electricity in the home
      Light, Electric
  BT **Electric engineering**
      Electric wiring
      Lighting
  NT **Fluorescent lighting**
  RT **Electric lamps**
Electric lighting, Fluorescent
  USE **Fluorescent lighting**
Electric lines 621.319
    Use for materials on general transmission systems.
  UF Electric distribution
      Electric power transmission
      Electric transmission
      Electricity—Distribution
      Power transmission, Electric
      Transmission of power
  BT **Electric power distribution**

BT = Broader Term   NT = Narrower Term   RT = Related Term   SA = See Also   UF = Used For

Electric lines—*Continued*
  NT Electric circuits
      Electric switchgear
      Electric wiring
Electric machinery 621.31
    Use for materials on large machines
  powered by electricity. Materials on smal-
  ler machines and appliances are entered
  under **Electric apparatus and appliances.**
  BT Electric engineering
      Machinery
  NT Electric controllers
      Electric generators
      Electric motors
      Electric transformers
Electric machinery—Alternating current
        621.319
  UF Alternating current machinery
Electric machinery—Direct current
        621.319
  UF Direct current machinery
Electric measurements 621.37
  UF Measurements, Electric
  BT Electric currents
      Weights and measures
  NT Electric meters
  RT Electric testing
Electric meters 621.37
  UF Meters, Electric
  BT Electric measurements
Electric motors 621.46
  UF Induction motors
      Motors
  BT Electric machinery
  NT Electric transformers
Electric power 621.31
  BT Electricity
      Energy resources
      Power (Mechanics)
Electric power distribution 621.319
  UF Electric distribution
      Electric power transmission
      Electric transmission
      Electricity—Distribution
      Power transmission, Electric
      Rural electrification
      Transmission of power
  BT Electric engineering
      Power transmission
  NT Electric lines
      Electric wiring

Electric power failures 621.319
  UF Blackouts, Electric power
      Brownouts
      Electric power interruptions
      Power blackouts
      Power failures
Electric power in mining
  USE **Electricity in mining**
Electric power interruptions
  USE **Electric power failures**
Electric power plants 621.31
  UF Electric utilities
      Power plants, Electric
  BT Power plants
  NT Hydroelectric power plants
Electric power transmission
  USE **Electric lines**
       Electric power distribution
Electric railroads 385; 621.33; 625.1
  UF Interurban railroads
      Railroads, Electric
  BT Electric engineering
      Public utilities
      Railroads
      Transportation
  RT Railroads—Electrification
      Street railroads
Electric signs 621.32; 659.13
  UF Signs (Advertising)
      Signs, Electric
  BT Advertising
      Signs and signboards
  NT Neon tubes
Electric smelting
  USE **Electrometallurgy**
Electric switches
  USE **Electric switchgear**
Electric switchgear 621.31
  UF Electric switches
      Switches, Electric
  BT Electric lines
Electric testing 621.37
  UF Testing
  RT Electric measurements
Electric toys 688.7
  BT Toys
Electric transformers 621.31
  UF Transformers, Electric
  BT Electric currents
      Electric machinery

BT = Broader Term   NT = Narrower Term   RT = Related Term   SA = See Also   UF = Used For

Electric transformers—*Continued*
    Electric motors
Electric transmission
    USE   Electric lines
           Electric power distribution
Electric utilities
    USE   Electric industries
           Electric power plants
           Public utilities
Electric waves 537; 621.381
    UF   Hertzian waves
          Radio waves
    BT   Electricity
          Waves
    NT   Electromagnetic waves
          Microwaves
Electric welding 671.5
    UF   Arc welding
          Resistance welding
          Spot welding
          Welding, Electric
    BT   Welding
Electric wiring 621.319
    UF   Wiring, Electric
    BT   Electric lines
          Electric power distribution
    NT   Electric lighting
Electrical engineering
    USE   Electric engineering
Electricity 537; 621.3
    SA   electricity in various endeav-
         ors, e.g. **Electricity in agri-
         culture;** to be added as
         needed
    BT   Physics
    NT   Electric circuits
         Electric currents
         Electric power
         Electric waves
         Electricity in agriculture
         Electricity in mining
         Lightning
    RT   Magnetism
Electricity—Distribution
    USE   Electric lines
           Electric power distribution
Electricity in agriculture 333.79; 631.3
    UF   Electricity on the farm
          Rural electrification
    BT   Agricultural engineering

        Agricultural machinery
        Electricity
Electricity in medicine
    USE   Electrotherapeutics
Electricity in mining 622
    UF   Electric power in mining
         Mining, Electric
    BT   Electric engineering
         Electricity
    RT   Mining engineering
Electricity in the home
    USE   Electric heating
           Electric household appliances
           Electric lighting
Electricity, Medical
    USE   Electrotherapeutics
Electricity on the farm
    USE   Electricity in agriculture
Electrification of railroads
    USE   Railroads—Electrification
Electrochemistry 541.3; 547.1; 660
    BT   Industrial chemistry
         Physical chemistry
    NT   Electric batteries
         Electrometallurgy
         Electroplating
         Electrotyping
         Fuel cells
Electromagnetic waves 539.2
    UF   Waves, Electromagnetic
    BT   Electric waves
         Radiation
    NT   Gamma rays
         Heat
         Infrared radiation
         Light
         Microwaves
         Ultraviolet rays
         X rays
Electromagnetism 621.34
    BT   Magnetism
    NT   Masers
Electromagnets 621.34
    UF   Magnet winding
    BT   Magnetism
         Magnets
Electrometallurgy 669.028
    UF   Electric smelting
    BT   Electrochemistry
         Metallurgy

Electrometallurgy—*Continued*
      Smelting
  RT Electroplating
      Electrotyping
Electron microscope and microscopy
  USE **Electron microscopes**
Electron microscopes 502.8; 578; 681
  UF Electron microscope and microscopy *[Former heading]*
  BT **Microscopes**
Electron tubes
  USE **Vacuum tubes**
Electronic apparatus and appliances 621.381
  UF Apparatus, Electronic
      Appliances, Electronic
  SA names of electronic apparatus and appliances, e.g. **Computers;** to be added as needed
  BT **Electronics**
      Scientific apparatus and instruments
  NT **Computers**
      Electronic toys
      Intercommunication systems
Electronic art
  USE **Computer art**
      Video art
Electronic brains
  USE **Artificial intelligence**
Electronic bugging
  USE **Eavesdropping**
Electronic bulletin boards
  USE **Computer bulletin boards**
Electronic calculating machines
  USE **Computers**
Electronic circuits 621.319; 621.3815
  BT **Electric circuits**
      Electronics
Electronic computers
  USE **Computers**
Electronic cottage
  USE **Telecommuting**
Electronic data processing 004
  UF Automatic data processing
      Data processing
  SA subjects with the subdivision *Data processing,* e.g. **Banks and banking—Data processing;** to be added as needed

  BT **Computers**
      Information science
      Information systems
  NT **Artificial intelligence**
      Banks and banking—Data processing
      Computer assisted instruction
      Computer bulletin boards
      Computer graphics
      Computer networks
      Computer systems
      Data transmission systems
      Database management
      Expert systems (Computer science)
      Online data processing
      Optical data processing
      Programming (Computers)
      Programming languages (Computers)
      System design
  RT **Computer science**
Electronic data processing—Keyboarding
  USE **Keyboarding (Electronics)**
Electronic drawing
  USE **Computer art**
      Computer graphics
Electronic eavesdropping
  USE **Eavesdropping**
Electronic games
  USE **Electronic toys**
      Video games
Electronic listening devices
  USE **Eavesdropping**
Electronic mail systems 383; 384.3
    Use for materials on the electronic transmission of letters, messages, etc., primarily through the use of computers and computer terminals.
  UF E-mail systems
      Email systems
      Mail systems, Electronic
  BT **Data transmission systems**
      Telecommunication
  NT **Computer bulletin boards**
Electronic marketing
  USE **Telemarketing**
Electronic music 786.7
  UF Music, Electronic

BT = Broader Term   NT = Narrower Term   RT = Related Term   SA = See Also   UF = Used For

Electronic music—*Continued*
        Synthesizer music
        Tape recorder music
  BT **Music**
  RT **Computer music**
Electronic musical instruments 786.7
  UF Musical instruments, Electronic *[Former heading]*
  SA names of instruments, e.g. **Synthesizer (Musical instrument)**; to be added as needed
  BT **Musical instruments**
  NT **Synthesizers (Musical instruments)**
Electronic publishing 070.5; 686.2
  Use for materials on the process of publishing in which data are entered on a word processor or computer terminal, submitted to an editor or publisher, and made available online or offline.
  UF Online publishing
        Publishing, Electronic
  BT **Information services**
        Publishers and publishing
        Telecommunication
  NT **Desktop publishing**
        Teletext systems
Electronic speech processing systems
  USE **Speech processing systems**
Electronic spread sheets
  USE **Electronic spreadsheets**
Electronic spreadsheets 005.3
  UF Electronic spread sheets
        Spread sheets, Electronic
        Spreadsheeting, Electronic
        Spreadsheets, Electronic
  BT **Business**
        Computer software
Electronic toys 688.7
  UF Electronic games
        Games, Electronic
  BT **Electronic apparatus and appliances**
        Toys
  NT **Computer games**
        Video games
Electronics 537.5; 621.381
  BT **Engineering**
        Physics
        Technology

  NT **Amplifiers (Electronics)**
        Cybernetics
        Digital electronics
        Electric conductors
        Electronic apparatus and appliances
        Electronic circuits
        Facsimile transmission
        High-fidelity sound systems
        Microelectronics
        Semiconductors
        Superconductors
        Transistors
Electrons 539.7
  BT **Atoms**
        Particles (Nuclear physics)
Electroplating 671.7
  BT **Electrochemistry**
        Metalwork
  RT **Electrometallurgy**
Electrotherapeutics 615.8
  UF Electricity in medicine
        Electricity, Medical
        Medical electricity
  BT **Massage**
        Physical therapy
        Therapeutics
  NT **Radiotherapy**
Electrotyping 686.2
  BT **Electrochemistry**
        Printing
  RT **Electrometallurgy**
Elegiac poetry 808.81; 811, etc.
  May be used for individual works, collections, or materials about elegiac poetry.
  UF Elegies
        Lamentations
  BT **Poetry**
Elegies
  USE **Elegiac poetry**
Elementary education 372
  Use for general materials on education of children below the secondary school level.
  UF Children—Education
        Education, Elementary *[Former heading]*
        Education of children
        Education, Primary
        Grammar schools
        Primary education

Elementary education—*Continued*
  BT Education
  NT Creative activities
      Exceptional children
      Kindergarten
      Montessori method of education
      Nursery schools
      Readiness for school
Elementary particles (Physics)
  USE Particles (Nuclear physics)
Elementary school dropouts
  USE Dropouts
Elementary school libraries 027.8
  UF School libraries (Elementary school) *[Former heading]*
  BT School libraries
  RT Children's libraries
Elements, Chemical
  USE Chemical elements
Elephants 599.6
  BT Mammals
Elevators 621.8
  UF Lifts
  BT Hoisting machinery
Elite (Social sciences) (May subdiv. geog.) 305.5
  BT Leadership
      Power (Social sciences)
      Social classes
      Social groups
Elizabeth II, Queen of Great Britain, 1926- 92; B
  BT Kings, queens, rulers, etc.
Elk Mountain (Wyo.) 978.7
  BT Mountains
Elocution
  USE Public speaking
Elves
  USE Fairies
Email systems
  USE Electronic mail systems
Emancipation
  USE Freedom
Emancipation of slaves
  USE Slavery
      Slavery—United States
Emancipation of women
  USE Women's rights
Embarrassment
  USE Self-consciousness

Embassies
  USE Diplomatic and consular service
Emblems
  USE Decorations of honor
      Heraldry
      Insignia
      Mottoes
      Seals (Numismatics)
      Signs and symbols
Emblems, National
  USE National emblems
Emblems, State
  USE State emblems
Embracing
  USE Hugging
Embroidery 746.44
  SA types of embroidery, to be added as needed
  BT Decoration and ornament
      Needlework
      Sewing
  NT Beadwork
      Crewelwork
      Needlepoint
      Samplers
Embryology 574.3; 612.6
  UF Development
  BT Biology
      Zoology
  NT Fertilization in vitro
      Fetus
      Frozen embryos
      Genetics
  RT Cells
      Protoplasm
      Reproduction
Embryos, Frozen
  USE Frozen embryos
Emergencies
  USE Accidents
      First aid
Emergency assistance
  USE Helping behavior
Emergency medical technicians 610.69; 616.02
  UF Emergency paramedics
      EMTs (Medicine)
      Paramedical personnel
      Paramedics, Emergency

BT = Broader Term   NT = Narrower Term   RT = Related Term   SA = See Also   UF = Used For

Emergency medical technicians—
Continued
  BT   Allied health personnel
Emergency medicine 616.02
  BT   Medicine
Emergency paramedics
  USE Emergency medical techni-
         cians
Emergency powers
  USE War and emergency powers
Emergency preparedness
  USE Disaster relief
Emergency relief
  USE Disaster relief
Emergency survival
  USE Survival skills
Emigrants
  USE Immigrants
Emigration
  USE Immigration and emigration
Eminent domain 333.1; 343
  UF   Condemnation of land
       Expropriation
  BT   Constitutional law
       Land use
       Property
Emotional stress
  USE Stress (Psychology)
Emotionally disturbed children 155.4;
      362.2; 371.94; 618.92
  UF   Behavior problems (Children)
       Children, Emotionally dis-
         turbed
       Maladjusted children
       Problem children
  BT   Exceptional children
  NT   Mentally ill children
  RT   Juvenile delinquency
Emotions 152.4
  UF   Feelings
       Frustration
       Passions
  SA   names of emotions, to be
       added as needed
  BT   Psychology
       Psychophysiology
  NT   Attitude (Psychology)
       Belief and doubt
       Consolation
       Fanaticism

       Fear
       Grief
       Happiness
       Hope
       Horror
       Joy and sorrow
       Laughter
       Loneliness
       Love
       Pain
       Pleasure
       Prejudices
       Self-confidence
       Shyness
       Worry
Emperors
  USE Kings, queens, rulers, etc.
       Roman emperors
       and names of emperors, e.g.
         Nero, Emperor of Rome,
         37-68; to be added as need-
         ed
Empiricism 146
  UF   Experience
  BT   Philosophy
       Rationalism
       Theory of knowledge
  RT   Pragmatism
Employee absenteeism
  USE Absenteeism (Labor)
Employee benefits
  USE Nonwage payments
Employee counseling
  USE Employees—Counseling of
Employee drinking
  USE Employees—Alcohol use
Employee drug testing
  USE Employees—Drug testing
Employee health services
  USE Occupational health services
Employee morale 158.7; 658.3
  BT   Applied psychology
       Morale
       Personnel management
       Work
  NT   Job satisfaction
  RT   Absenteeism (Labor)
Employee sex in the workplace
  USE Sex in the workplace

Employees 331.11; 920

SA classes of employees, e.g. **Office workers;** and types of industries, services, establishments, or institutions, with the subdivision *Employees;* e.g. **Railroads—Employees;** to be added as needed

BT **Labor**

NT **Migrant labor**
 Office workers
 Railroads—Employees

RT **Personnel management**

Employees—Alcohol use 331.25; 658.3

UF Alcohol and employees
 Alcohol in the workplace
 Drinking and employees
 Drinking in the workplace
 Employee drinking
 Employees and alcohol

Employees and alcohol

USE **Employees—Alcohol use**

Employees and drugs

USE **Employees—Drug use**

Employees and narcotics

USE **Employees—Drug use**

Employees and officials

USE **Civil service**
 and names of countries, cities, etc., and organizations with the subdivision *Officials and employees,* e.g. **Chicago (Ill.)—Officials and employees; United Nations—Officials and employees;** etc., to be added as needed

Employees, Clerical

USE **Office workers**

Employees—Counseling of 658.3

UF Employee counseling
 Industrial counseling

BT **Counseling**

Employees—Dismissal 331.25; 658.3

BT **Job security**
 Personnel management

Employees—Drug testing 331.25; 344; 658.3

UF Drug testing in the workplace
 Employee drug testing

BT **Drug testing**

Employees—Drug use 331.25; 658.3

UF Drugs and employees
 Drugs in the workplace
 Employees and drugs
 Employees and narcotics

Employees—Rating 331.25; 658.3

BT **Performance standards**

Employees' representation in management

USE **Participative management**

Employees—Training 331.25; 658.3

Use for materials discussing on-the-job training. Materials on teaching people a skill during the educational process are entered under **Vocational education.** Materials on teaching people a skill after formal education are entered under **Occupational training.** Materials on retraining are entered under **Occupational retraining.**

UF Factories—Training departments
 Factory schools
 In-service training
 Inservice training
 Training of employees

BT **Occupational training**
 Personnel management
 Vocational education

NT **Occupational retraining**

RT **Apprentices**
 Technical education

Employer-employee relations

USE **Industrial relations**

Employers' liability

USE **Workers' compensation**

Employment 331.1

SA racial and ethnic groups and classes of persons with the subdivision *Employment,* e.g. **African Americans—Employment; Veterans—Employment;** etc., to be added as needed

BT **Labor**

NT **African Americans—Employment**
 Blacks—Employment
 Human resources
 Labor supply
 Part-time employment
 Summer employment

Employment—*Continued*
  Temporary employment
  Unemployment
  Veterans—Employment
  Women—Employment
  Youth—Employment
 RT Vocational guidance
Employment agencies 331.12
 UF Jobs
 BT **Labor**
  Labor turnover
  Personnel management
  Recruiting of employees
  Unemployment
 NT **Job hunting**
 RT **Labor supply**
Employment and age
 USE **Age and employment**
Employment applications
 USE **Applications for positions**
Employment discrimination
 USE **Discrimination in employment**
Employment forecasting 331.1
 UF Occupational forecasting
 BT **Economic forecasting**
 RT **Labor supply**
Employment guidance
 USE **Vocational guidance**
Employment management
 USE **Personnel management**
Employment of children
 USE **Children—Employment**
Employment of teenagers
 USE **Teenagers—Employment**
Employment of veterans
 USE **Veterans—Employment**
Employment of women
 USE **Women—Employment**
Employment of youth
 USE **Youth—Employment**
Employment, Part-time
 USE **Part-time employment**
Employment references
 USE **Applications for positions**
Employment security
 USE **Job security**
Employment, Supplementary
 USE **Supplementary employment**
Employment, Temporary
 USE **Temporary employment**

EMTs (Medicine)
 USE **Emergency medical technicians**
Enamel and enameling 738.4
 UF Porcelain enamels
 BT **Decoration and ornament**
  Decorative arts
Encounter groups
 USE **Group relations training**
Encyclicals, Papal
 USE **Papal encyclicals**
Encyclopedias and dictionaries 030; 031, etc.; 403; 413, etc.
 UF Cyclopedias
  Dictionaries
  Glossaries
  Subject dictionaries
 SA names of languages and subjects with the subdivision *Dictionaries,* e.g. **English language—Dictionaries; Biography—Dictionaries;** etc., to be added as needed
 BT **Reference books**
 NT **Bible—Dictionaries**
  Biography—Dictionaries
  Chemistry—Dictionaries
  Classical dictionaries
  Computer science—Dictionaries
  English language—Dictionaries
  English language—Dictionaries—French
  French language—Dictionaries—English
  Geography—Dictionaries
  History—Dictionaries
  Literature—Dictionaries
  Machine readable dictionaries
  Ohio—Biography—Dictionaries
  Picture dictionaries
  Polyglot dictionaries
  Shakespeare, William, 1564-1616—Dictionaries
  Technology—Dictionaries
End of the earth
 USE **End of the world**

End of the world 001.9; 236; 291.2; 523.1

Use for materials on the end of the world from an eschatological point of view (including Judgment Day, signs, fulfillments of prophecies, etc.) or from a scientific point of view.

UF   End of the earth
       End of the world (Astronomy)
       World, End of the

BT   **Eschatology**

End of the world (Astronomy)

USE   **End of the world**

End-of-the-world fantasies

USE   **Fantasy fiction**
       Fantasy films
       Fantasy television programs
       Robinsonades
       Science fiction
       War films
       War stories

Endangered species 333.95; 574.5

UF   Threatened species
       Vanishing species

BT   **Environmental protection**
       Nature conservation

NT   **Plant conservation**
       Wildlife conservation

RT   **Rare animals**
       Rare plants

Endocrine glands 616.4

UF   Ductless glands
       Glands, Ductless

BT   **Endocrinology**

RT   **Hormones**

Endocrinology 616.4

BT   **Medicine**

NT   **Endocrine glands**
       Hormones

Endorphins 612.8; 615

UF   Brain opioids
       Opioids, Brain

BT   **Narcotics**

Endowed charities

USE   **Charities**
       Endowments

Endowments 001.4; 361.6; 361.7

UF   Endowed charities
       Foundations (Endowments)
       Philanthropy

NT   **Scholarships**

RT   **Charities**

Endurance, Physical

USE   **Physical fitness**

Energy

USE   **Energy resources**
       Force and energy

Energy and state

USE   **Energy resources—Government policy**

Energy, Biomass

USE   **Biomass energy**

Energy conservation 333.791

UF   Conservation of energy
       Conservation of power resources
       Power resources conservation

SA   types of energy conservation, e.g. **Recycling**; to be added as needed

BT   **Conservation of natural resources**
       Energy resources

NT   **Energy resources—Government policy**
       Recycling

RT   **Energy consumption**

Energy consumption 333.79

UF   Consumption of energy

SA   subjects with the subdivision *Fuel consumption,* e.g. **Automobiles—Fuel consumption**; to be added as needed

BT   **Energy resources**

NT   **Automobiles—Fuel consumption**

RT   **Energy conservation**

Energy conversion from waste

USE   **Waste products as fuel**

Energy conversion, Microbial

USE   **Biomass energy**

Energy development 333.79

UF   Energy resources development
       Power resources development

BT   **Energy resources**

NT   **Water resources development**

Energy policy

USE   **Energy resources—Government policy**

BT = Broader Term   NT = Narrower Term   RT = Related Term   SA = See Also   UF = Used For

Energy resources 333.79

Use for materials on the available sources of mechanical power in general. Materials on the physics and engineering aspects of power are entered under **Power (Mechanics)**.

UF   Energy
       Power resources
       Power supply

BT   **Natural resources**
       Power (Mechanics)

NT   **Biomass energy**
       Biomass energy industries
       Electric power
       Energy conservation
       Energy consumption
       Energy development
       Fuel
       Ocean energy resources
       Renewable energy resources
       Solar energy
       Water power
       Wind power

Energy resources development
USE   **Energy development**

Energy resources—Government policy 333.79; 351.82

UF   Energy and state
       Energy policy
       State and energy

BT   **Energy conservation**

Energy resources, Ocean
USE   **Ocean energy resources**

Energy resources, Renewable
USE   **Renewable energy resources**

Energy technology
USE   **Power (Mechanics)**

Enforcement of law
USE   **Law enforcement**

Engineering 620

UF   Construction

SA   types of engineering, e.g.
       Chemical engineering; to be
       added as needed

BT   **Building**
       Industrial arts
       Technology

NT   **Aeronautics**
       Agricultural engineering
       Building materials
       Chemical engineering

       Civil engineering
       Computer aided design
       Electric engineering
       Electronics
       Genetic engineering
       Highway engineering
       Human engineering
       Hydraulic engineering
       Marine engineering
       Mechanical drawing
       Military engineering
       Mining engineering
       Minorities in engineering
       Municipal engineering
       Nuclear engineering
       Ocean engineering
       Railroad engineering
       Reliability (Engineering)
       Sanitary engineering
       Steam engineering
       Steel construction
       Structural engineering
       Systems engineering
       Traffic engineering
       Water supply engineering

RT   **Engineers**
       Materials
       Mechanics

Engineering drawing
USE   **Mechanical drawing**

Engineering, Genetic
USE   **Genetic engineering**

Engineering instruments 620.0028

UF   Instruments, Engineering

BT   **Scientific apparatus and instruments**

Engineering materials
USE   **Materials**

Engineering—Periodicals 620.005

BT   **Periodicals**

Engineering, Structural
USE   **Structural engineering**

Engineering—Study and teaching 620.007

BT   **Technical education**

Engineers 620.0092; 920

RT   **Engineering**
       Inventors

Engines 621.4

UF   Motors

BT = Broader Term   NT = Narrower Term   RT = Related Term   SA = See Also   UF = Used For

Engines—*Continued*

SA types of engines, e.g. **Automobile engines;** to be added as needed

BT **Machinery**

NT **Airplane engines**
Automobile engines
Diesel engines
Fire engines
Fuel
Heat engines
Internal combustion engines
Marine engines
Pumping machinery
Solar engines
Steam engines
Turbines

England 942

Use with the subdivisions *Description; Industries; Intellectual life; Social life and customs* for works limited to England.

BT **Great Britain**

England, Church of

USE **Church of England**

England—History

USE **Great Britain—History**

English as a foreign language

USE **English as a second language**

English as a second language 420.7; 428

UF English as a foreign language
English for foreigners
English language as a second language
English language—Study and teaching, Foreign
English language—Texts for foreigners

BT **English language—Study and teaching**

NT **English language—Conversations and phrases**

English authors 820.9; 920

UF Authors, English *[Former heading]*

BT **English literature**

NT **English literature—Bio-bibliography**

English Canadian literature

USE **Canadian literature (English)**

English Canadian poetry

USE **Canadian poetry (English)**

English composition

USE **English language—Composition and exercises**

English drama 822

Use for general materials about English drama, not for individual works.

BT **Drama**
English literature

NT **Morality plays**
Mysteries and miracle plays

English drama—Collections 822.008

BT **Drama—Collections**
English literature—Collections

English drama—History and criticism 822.009

BT **Drama—History and criticism**

English essays 824; 824.008

Use for collections of literary essays by several authors.

BT **English literature**
Essays

English fiction 823

May be used for collections or materials about English fiction, not for individual works.

UF Fiction, English

BT **English literature**
Fiction

English fiction—History and criticism 823.009

English for foreigners

USE **English as a second language**
English language—Conversations and phrases

English grammar

USE **English language—Grammar**

English history

USE **Great Britain—History**

English language 420

Subdivisions used under this heading may be used under other languages unless otherwise specified.

BT **Language and languages**
Modern languages

RT **Anglo-Saxon language**

English language—0-1100

USE **Anglo-Saxon language**

English language—Acronyms

USE **Acronyms**

English language—Americanisms

USE **Americanisms**

English language—Antonyms
  USE   **English language—Synonyms and antonyms**

English language as a second language
  USE   **English as a second language**

English language—Basal readers
  USE   **Basal readers**

English language—Business English 428; 808

Business English is a unique subdivision for **English language.** Use same pattern with unique subdivisions for other languages, e.g. **Japanese language—Business Japanese;** etc.

  UF   Business English
  RT   **Business letters**

English language—Comparison 425
  UF   Comparison (English grammar)
       Grammatical comparison

English language—Composition and exercises 428; 808
  UF   English composition
  RT   **Rhetoric**

English language—Conversations and phrases 428
  UF   English for foreigners
  BT   **English as a second language**

English language—Dialects 427
  NT   **Americanisms**

English language—Dictionaries 423

Dictionaries of English and another language are assigned the heading **English language—Dictionaries—[name of second language],** i.e. **English language—Dictionaries—French;** etc.

  BT   **Encyclopedias and dictionaries**
  RT   **English language—Terms and phrases**

English language—Dictionaries—French 443

Use for English-French dictionaries. French-English dictionaries are entered under **French language—Dictionaries—English.** Combined English-French and French-English dictionaries are entered under both headings.

  UF   Foreign language dictionaries
  BT   **Encyclopedias and dictionaries**
  RT   **French language—Dictionaries—English**

English language—Errors 428

English language—Etymology 422
  BT   **English language—History**

English language—Examinations 420.76
  BT   **Examinations**

English language—Foreign words and phrases 422

English language—Grammar 425
  UF   English grammar
  BT   **Grammar**
  NT   **English language—Usage**

English language—History 420.9
  BT   **History**
  NT   **English language—Etymology**

English language—Homonyms 423

English language—Idioms 428
  RT   **English language—Provincialisms**

English language—Jargon 427

English language—Old English
  USE   **Anglo-Saxon language**

English language—Orthography
  USE   **English language—Spelling**

English language—Phonetics
  USE   **English language—Pronunciation**

English language—Phrases and terms
  USE   **English language—Terms and phrases**

English language—Programmed instruction 420.7
  BT   **Programmed instruction**

English language—Pronunciation 421
  UF   English language—Phonetics
  BT   **Phonetics**
  NT   **Reading—Phonetic method**

English language—Provincialisms 427
  RT   **English language—Idioms**

English language—Punctuation
  USE   **Punctuation**

English language—Reading materials
  USE   **Reading materials**

English language—Rhetoric
  USE   **Rhetoric**

English language—Rhyme 808.1
  BT   **Rhyme**

English language—Slang 427

English language—Social aspects 420

English language—Spelling 421
  UF   English language—Orthography
  NT   **Spellers**
       Spelling reform

English language—Spelling—*Continued*
  RT   Word skills
English language—Spelling reform
  USE Spelling reform
English language—Study and teaching
      420.7
  NT   English as a second language
English language—Study and teaching,
      Foreign
  USE English as a second language
English language—Synonyms and ant-
      onyms 423
  UF   English language—Antonyms
  RT   Opposites
English language—Terms and phrases
      423; 427; 428
  Use for general lists of words and
  phrases and for lists that are applicable to
  certain situations (collective nouns, curi-
  ous expressions, etc.) rather than to specif-
  ic subjects. Lists of words and phrases
  limited to specific subjects are entered un-
  der the subject with the subdivision *Dic-
  tionaries,* e.g. **Chemistry—Dictionaries.**
  UF   English language—Phrases and
        terms
  NT   Allusions
  RT   English language—
        Dictionaries
English language—Texts for foreigners
  USE English as a second language
English language—Usage 428
  BT   English language—Grammar
English language—Versification
  USE Versification
English language—Vocabulary
  USE Vocabulary
English letters 826; 826.008
  BT   English literature
        Letters
English literature 820
  Subdivisions used under this heading
  may be used under other literatures.
  BT   Literature
  NT   English authors
        English drama
        English essays
        English fiction
        English letters
        English poetry
        English prose literature
        English satire

English speeches
English wit and humor
  RT   Anglo-Saxon literature
English literature—0-1100
  USE Anglo-Saxon literature
English literature—African authors
  USE African literature (English)
English literature—Bibliography 016.82
English literature—Bio-bibliography
      820.9
  BT   English authors
English literature—Collections 820.8
  Use for collections of English literature
  by several authors in more than one
  genre. Collections of prose are entered un-
  der **English prose literature.** Collections of
  poetry are entered under **English poetry—
  Collections.** Collections of drama are en-
  tered under **English drama—Collections.**
  BT   Literature—Collections
  NT   English drama—Collections
        English poetry—Collections
        English prose literature
English literature—Criticism
  USE English literature—History
        and criticism
English literature—Dictionaries 820.3
  BT   Literature—Dictionaries
English literature—Examinations 820.76
  BT   English literature—Study and
        teaching
English literature—History and criti-
      cism 820.9
  UF   English literature—Criticism
  BT   Criticism
        History
English literature—Indexes 016.82
English literature—Old English
  USE Anglo-Saxon literature
English literature—Outlines, syllabi,
      etc. 820.2
  BT   Literature—Outlines, syllabi,
        etc.
  RT   English literature—Study and
        teaching
English literature—Study and teaching
      820.7
  NT   English literature—
        Examinations
  RT   English literature—Outlines,
        syllabi, etc.

English newspapers 072
  BT   Newspapers

English orations
  USE English speeches

English periodicals 052
  BT   Periodicals

English poetry 821
> Use for general materials about English poetry, not for individual works.

  BT   English literature
       Poetry

English poetry—Collections 821.008
  BT   English literature—Collections
       Poetry—Collections

English poetry—History and criticism 821.009
  BT   Criticism
       Poetry—History and criticism

English prose literature 828
> Use for collections of prose writings that may include several literary forms, such as essays, fiction, orations, etc.

  UF   Prose literature, English
  BT   English literature
       English literature—Collections

English public schools 373.2; 373.42
> Use for materials on British endowed secondary schools that are open to public admission but are not financed or administered by any government body.

  UF   Public schools, Endowed (Great Britain) *[Former heading]*
       Public schools, English
  BT   Private schools

English satire 827; 827.008
  UF   Satire, English *[Former heading]*
  BT   English literature
       Satire

English speeches 825; 825.008
  UF   English orations
       Speeches, addresses, etc., English *[Former heading]*
  BT   English literature
       Speeches

English wit and humor 827; 827.008; 827.009
> Use for collections by several authors or for materials about English wit and humor. Individual works by English humorists are entered under **Wit and humor.**

  BT   English literature
       Wit and humor

Engravers 760.92; 920
  BT   Artists
  NT   Etchers

Engraving 760; 765
  UF   Copper engraving
       Engravings
       Line engraving
       Steel engraving
  SA   engraving of particular countries, e.g. **American engraving;** to be added as needed
  BT   Art
       Graphic arts
       Illustration of books
       Pictures
  NT   **American engraving**
       Gems
       Mezzotint engraving
       Photoengraving
       Wood engraving
  RT   **Etching**

Engraving, American
  USE **American engraving**

Engravings
  USE **Engraving**

Enhanced radiation weapons
  USE **Neutron weapons**

Enigmas
  USE **Curiosities and wonders**
        Riddles

Enlarged texts for shared reading
  USE **Big books**

Enlarging (Photography)
  USE **Photography—Enlarging**

Enlightenment 190; 909.7; 940.2
> Use for materials on the philosophic movement of the 18th century marked by the questioning of traditional doctrines and values, naturalistic and individualistic tendencies, and an emphasis on the empirical method in science and the free use of reason.

  BT   **Eighteenth century**
       Modern philosophy
       Rationalism

Enlistment
  USE names of armies and navies with the subdivision *Recruiting, enlistment, etc.,*

Enlistment—*Continued*

    e.g. **United States. Army—
Recruiting, enlistment, etc.;
United States. Navy—
Recruiting, enlistment, etc.;**
etc., to be added as needed

Ensemble playing
  USE **Ensembles (Music)**

Ensembles (Mathematics)
  USE **Set theory**

Ensembles (Music) 782; 784

Use for materials on small instrumental
or vocal groups and for the music written
for such groups.

  UF Ensemble playing
       Instrumental ensembles
       Musical ensembles
       Vocal ensembles
  SA kinds of vocal or instrumental
       ensembles, e.g. **Jazz ensem-
bles;** to be added as needed
  BT **Music
Musical form
Musicians**
  NT **Jazz ensembles**
  RT **Orchestra**

Ensigns
  USE **Flags**

Ensilage
  USE **Silage and silos**

Enteric fever
  USE **Typhoid fever**

Enterprises
  USE **Business enterprises**

Entertainers 791.092; 920

  SA types of entertainers and
       names of individual enter-
tainers, to be added as
needed
  NT **Actors
Clowns
Comedians
Dancers
Fools and jesters**

Entertaining 395; 642

Use for materials on hospitality and the
art of entertaining guests.

  UF Guests
       Hospitality
  BT **Etiquette
Home economics**

  NT **Business entertaining
Carving (Meat, etc.)
Children's parties
Games
Parties**
  RT **Amusements
Dining
Luncheons**

Entertainments
  USE **Amusements**

Entomology
  USE **Insects**

Entomology, Economic
  USE **Beneficial insects
Insect pests**

Entomology, Medical
  USE **Insects as carriers of disease**

Entozoa
  USE **Parasites**

Entrance examinations for colleges
  USE **Colleges and universities—
Entrance examinations**

Entrance requirements for colleges and
       universities
  USE **Colleges and universities—
Entrance requirements**
and names of individual colleges and universities with
the subdivision *Entrance
requirements,* to be added
as needed

Entrepreneurs (May subdiv. geog.) **338;
920**
  BT **Business people
Self-employed**

Entrepreneurship 338; 658.4
  BT **Business
Capitalism
Small business**

Environment 304.2; 333.7; 363.7
  SA subjects with the subdivision
       Environmental aspects, e.g.
**Nuclear power plants—
Environmental aspects;** to
be added as needed
  NT **Ecology
Environmental movement
Environmental policy
Environmental protection**

Environment—*Continued*
        Nuclear power plants—
        Environmental aspects
        Pesticides—Environmental as-
        pects
Environment and pesticides
   USE   Pesticides—Environmental as-
        pects
Environment and state
   USE   Environmental policy
Environment—Government policy
   USE   Environmental policy
Environment—Government policy—
        United States
   USE   Environmental policy—United
        States
Environment, Space
   USE   Space environment
Environmental aspects
   USE   subjects with the subdivision
        Environmental aspects, e.g.
        Nuclear power plants—
        Environmental aspects; to
        be added as needed
Environmental health 616.9
   UF   Health—Environmental as-
        pects
   SA   subjects with the subdivision
        Environmental aspects, e.g.
        Nuclear power plants—
        Environmental aspects; to
        be added as needed
   BT   Environmental influence on
        humans
        Public health
   NT   Air pollution
        Nuclear power plants—
        Environmental aspects
        Occupational health and safe-
        ty
        Pollution
        Water pollution
Environmental influence on humans
        304.2; 573
   UF   Acclimatization
        Altitude, Influence of
        Man—Influence of environ-
        ment *[Former heading]*
   BT   Adaptation (Biology)
        Anthropogeography

        Human ecology
   NT   Environmental health
        Survival skills
        Weightlessness
Environmental lobby
   USE   Environmental movement
Environmental movement 322.4; 363.7
   UF   Conservation movement
        Ecological movement
        Environmental lobby
        Environmentalism
        Green movement
   BT   Environment
        Social movements
Environmental policy (May subdiv.
        geog.) 344; 351.82; 363.7
   UF   Environment and state
        Environment—Government
        policy *[Former heading]*
        State and environment
   BT   Environment
   RT   Conservation of natural re-
        sources
        Human ecology
        Human influence on nature
Environmental policy—United States
        344; 353.0082; 363.7
   UF   American environmental poli-
        cy
        Environment—Government
        policy—United States *[For-
        mer heading]*
        United States—Environmental
        policy
Environmental pollution
   USE   Pollution
Environmental protection 344; 363.7
   UF   Environmentalism
        Protection of environment
   BT   Ecology
        Environment
   NT   Conservation of natural re-
        sources
        Endangered species
        Landscape protection
        Soil conservation
        Wildlife conservation
   RT   Pollution
Environmental radioactivity
   USE   Radioactive pollution

Environmentalism
USE **Environmental movement**
Environmental protection

Enzymes 547.7; 574.19
BT **Proteins**
NT **Catalytic RNA**
Fermentation

Eolithic period
USE **Stone Age**

Epic films 791.43
May be used for individual works, collections, or materials about epic films.
UF Film epics
BT **Motion pictures**

Epic literature 800
May be used for individual works, collections, or materials about epic literature.
BT **Literature**
NT **Epic poetry**
RT **Mock-heroic literature**

Epic poetry 808.81; 811, etc.
May be used for individual works, collections, or materials about epic poetry.
BT **Epic literature**
Narrative poetry
RT **Romances**

Epidemics 614.4
UF Pestilences
SA names of contagious diseases, e.g. **AIDS (Disease)**; to be added as needed
BT **Diseases**
Public health
NT **Plague**
RT **Communicable diseases**

Epigrams 808.88; 818, etc.
May be used for collections of epigrams and for materials about epigrams.
UF Sayings
BT **Wit and humor**
NT **Quotations**
Toasts
RT **Proverbs**

Epigraphy
USE **Inscriptions**

Epilepsy 616.8
BT **Nervous system—Diseases**

Episcopal Church 283
Use for materials on the Episcopal Church in the United States after 1789. Materials on the Episcopal Church in the United States prior to 1789 are entered under **Church of England—United States.**

UF Protestant Episcopal Church in the U.S.A.
BT **Christian sects**
RT **Church of England—United States**

Epistemology
USE **Theory of knowledge**

Epistolary fiction 813, etc.
May be used for individual works, collections, or materials about novels written in the form of a series of letters.
UF Epistolary novels
Novels in letters
BT **Fiction**

Epistolary novels
USE **Epistolary fiction**

Epistolary poetry 811, etc.
May be used for individual works, collections, or materials about epistolary verse.
UF Verse epistles
BT **Poetry**

Epitaphs 929
UF Graves
BT **Biography**
Cemeteries
Inscriptions
Tombs

Epithets
USE **Names**
Nicknames

Epizoa
USE **Parasites**

Equal employment opportunity
USE **Discrimination in employment**

Equal opportunity in employment
USE **Discrimination in employment**

Equal pay for equal work 331.2; 658.3
UF Pay equity
BT **Discrimination in employment**
Wages
Women—Employment

Equal rights amendments (May subdiv. geog.) **305.42; 323.4; 342**
UF Amendments, Equal rights
E.R.A.'s
ERAs
BT **Constitutions**
Sex discrimination

Equal time rule (Broadcasting) 324.7; 342; 343

Use for materials on the requirement that all qualified candidates for public office be granted equal broadcast time if one of the candidates is granted time.

UF   Rule of equal time (Broadcasting)

BT   **Elections**
       Radio broadcasting
       Television broadcasting
       Television in politics

RT   **Fairness doctrine (Broadcasting)**

Equality 323.42

UF   Inequality
       Social equality

BT   **Political science**
       Sociology

NT   **Individualism**

RT   **Democracy**
       Freedom

Equations, Chemical
USE   **Chemical equations**

Equestrianism
USE   **Horsemanship**

Equipment and supplies
USE   subjects with the subdivision *Equipment and supplies,* e.g. **Sports—Equipment and supplies;** to be added as needed

ERAs
USE   **Equal rights amendments**

Ergonomics
USE   **Human engineering**

Erosion 551.3

SA   types of erosion, e.g. **Soil erosion;** to be added as needed

NT   **Dust storms**
       Soil erosion

RT   **Soil conservation**

Erotic art 704.9

UF   Art, Erotic
       Sex in art

BT   **Art**
       Erotica

Erotic fiction 808.83; 813, etc.

May be used for individual works, collections, or materials about erotic fiction.

UF   Adult fiction
       Erotic novels
       Erotic stories

BT   **Erotic literature**
       Fiction

NT   **Love stories**

Erotic films 791.43

May be used for individual works, collections, or materials about erotic films.

UF   Adult films

BT   **Motion pictures**

Erotic literature 808.8; 809

UF   Literature, Erotic

BT   **Erotica**
       Literature

NT   **Erotic fiction**
       Erotic poetry

Erotic novels
USE   **Erotic fiction**

Erotic poetry 811, etc.

May be used for individual works, collections, or materials about erotic poetry.

BT   **Erotic literature**
       Poetry

RT   **Love poetry**

Erotic stories
USE   **Erotic fiction**

Erotica 704.9; 809

SA   types of erotica, e.g. **Erotic art; Erotic literature;** etc., to be added as needed

NT   **Erotic art**
       Erotic literature

RT   **Pornography**

Errors 001.9; 153.7; 165

Use for materials on errors of judgment, errors of observation, scientific errors, popular misconceptions, etc. Errors in language are entered under names of languages with the subdivision *Errors,* e.g. **English language—Errors;** etc.

UF   Fallacies
       Medical errors
       Mistakes
       Scientific errors

RT   **Superstition**

Ersatz products
USE   **Substitute products**

Erudition
USE   **Learning and scholarship**

Eruptions
USE   **Geysers**
       Volcanoes

BT = Broader Term   NT = Narrower Term   RT = Related Term   SA = See Also   UF = Used For

Escapes 365; 904
    UF   Hostage escapes
          Prison escapes
    BT   **Adventure and adventurers**
          Prisons
Eschatology 236; 291.2
    UF   Intermediate state
          Last things (Theology)
    BT   **Theology**
    NT   **Death**
          End of the world
          Future life
          Heaven
          Hell
          Immortality
          Millennium
          Purgatory
          Second Advent
Eskimos
    USE **Inuit**
ESP
    USE **Extrasensory perception**
Esperanto 499
    BT   **Universal language**
Espionage 327.12; 355.3
    UF   Spying
    SA   espionage practiced by partic-
          ular countries, e.g. **Ameri-**
          can espionage; to be added
          as needed
    BT   **Intelligence service**
          Secret service
          Subversive activities
    NT   **American espionage**
          Spies
Espionage, American
    USE **American espionage**
Espionage films
    USE **Spy films**
Espionage stories
    USE **Spy stories**
Espionage television programs
    USE **Spy television programs**
Esquimaux
    USE **Inuit**
Essay 808.4
    Use for materials on the appreciation of
the essay and on the technique of writing
essays. Collections of essays are entered
under **Essays; American essays;** etc.

    BT   **Literature**
Essays 808.84
    Use for collections of literary essays by
authors of several nationalities. Collections of literary essays by American authors are entered under **American essays;**
by English authors, under **English essays;**
etc. Essays limited to a particular subject,
by one or more authors, are entered under
that subject. Materials on the appreciation
of the essay and on the technique of writing essays are entered under **Essay.**
    BT   **Literature—Collections**
    NT   **American essays**
          English essays
Essences and essential oils 664; 668
    UF   Aromatic plant products
          Oils, Essential
          Vegetable oils
          Volatile oils
    BT   **Distillation**
          Oils and fats
    NT   **Flavoring essences**
          Perfumes
Estate planning 332.024; 343.05
    BT   **Personal finance**
    NT   **Inheritance and transfer tax**
          Insurance
    RT   **Investments**
Estate tax
    USE **Inheritance and transfer tax**
Esthetics
    USE **Aesthetics**
Estimates
    USE appropriate technical subjects
          with the subdivision *Esti-*
          mates, e.g. **Building—**
          Estimates; to be added as
          needed
Estimation (Mathematics)
    USE **Approximate computation**
Estrangement (Social psychology)
    USE **Alienation (Social psychology)**
Etchers 769.92; 920
    BT   **Artists**
          Engravers
Etching 767
    UF   Etchings
    BT   **Art**
          Pictures
    RT   **Engraving**
Etchings
    USE **Etching**

BT = Broader Term   NT = Narrower Term   RT = Related Term   SA = See Also   UF = Used For

Eternal life
USE **Future life**
Eternal punishment
USE **Hell**
Eternity 115
Use for materials on the philosophical concept of eternity. Materials on the character and form of a future life are entered under **Future life**. Materials on the question of the endless existence of the soul are entered under **Immortality**.
RT **Future life**
Ethanol
USE **Alcohol as fuel**
Ethical education
USE **Moral education**
Religious education
Ethics 170
UF Moral philosophy
Morality
Morals
Natural law
Philosophy, Moral
SA types of ethics, e.g. **Business ethics;** ethics of particular countries, e.g. **American ethics;** ethics of particular religions, e.g. **Christian ethics;** and subjects with the subdivision *Moral and religious aspects,* e.g. **Birth control—Moral and religious aspects;** to be added as needed
BT **Philosophy**
NT **American ethics**
Asceticism
Birth control—Moral and religious aspects
Business ethics
Charity
Chastity
Christian ethics
Conduct of life
Conscience
Cruelty
Duty
Free will and determinism
Good and evil
Honesty
Jewish ethics

Joy and sorrow
Justice
Loyalty
Moral education
Professional ethics
Secularism
Sin
Social ethics
Stoics
Utilitarianism
Values
Vice
Virtue
Work ethic
RT **Human behavior**
Ethics, American
USE **American ethics**
Ethics, Biological
USE **Bioethics**
Ethics, Business
USE **Business ethics**
Ethics, Christian
USE **Christian ethics**
Ethics, Jewish
USE **Jewish ethics**
Ethics, Legal
USE **Legal ethics**
Ethics, Medical
USE **Medical ethics**
Ethics, Political
USE **Political ethics**
Ethics, Professional
USE **Professional ethics**
Ethics, Sexual
USE **Sexual ethics**
Ethics, Social
USE **Social ethics**
Ethics, Work
USE **Work ethic**
Ethiopian-Italian War, 1935-1936
USE **Italo-Ethiopian War, 1935-1936**
Ethnic conflict
USE **Ethnic relations**

BT = Broader Term   NT = Narrower Term   RT = Related Term   SA = See Also   UF = Used For

Ethnic groups 305.8

Use for theoretical materials on groups of people who are bound together by common ties of ancestry and culture. Materials on several ethnic groups in a particular region or country are entered under **Ethnology** subdivided geographically. Materials on individual ethnic groups are entered under the name of the group, e.g. **Mexican Americans.**

UF   Groups, Ethnic

SA   names of individual ethnic groups, to be added as needed

BT   **Ethnology**

NT   **Ethnic relations**

      Minorities

      Race relations

Ethnic psychology

USE   **Ethnopsychology**

Ethnic relations 305.8; 323.1

UF   Conflict, Ethnic

      Ethnic conflict

      Relations among ethnic groups

SA   names of regions, countries, cities, etc., with the subdivision *Ethnic relations;* to be added as needed

BT   **Acculturation**

      Ethnic groups

      Ethnology

      Social problems

      Sociology

NT   **Culture conflict**

      Discrimination

      Multicultural education

      Multiculturalism

RT   **Minorities**

      Race relations

Ethnography

USE   **Ethnology**

Ethnology (May subdiv. geog.) **305.8; 306; 572**

Use for materials on the disciplines of ethnology and cultural anthropology, and, with appropriate geographic subdivisions, for materials on the origin, distribution, and characteristics of the elements of the population of a particular region or country. Theoretical materials on groups of people who are bound together by common ties of ancestry and culture are entered under **Ethnic groups.** Materials on individual racial or ethnic groups are entered under the name of the group, e.g. **Australian aborigines.**

UF   Aborigines

      Cultural anthropology

      Ethnography

      Geographical distribution of people

      Indigenous peoples

      Native peoples

      Races of people

      Social anthropology

SA   names of countries with the subdivision *Social life and customs,* e.g. **United States—Social life and customs;** and names of individual ethnic groups, to be added as needed

BT   **Man**

NT   **Acculturation**

      Anthropogeography

      Anthropometry

      Cannibalism

      Costume

      Ethnic groups

      Ethnic relations

      Ethnopsychology

      Folklore

      Language and languages

      Manners and customs

      Nonliterate folk society

      Nonliterate man

      Physical anthropology

      Race

      Race relations

      Sacrifice

      Semitic peoples

      Totems and totemism

      United States—Social life and customs

BT = Broader Term   NT = Narrower Term   RT = Related Term   SA = See Also   UF = Used For

Ethnology—*Continued*
RT   Anthropology
       Archeology
       Civilization
Ethnology—Australia
USE   Australians
Ethnology—United States 305.813
UF   United States—Ethnology
       United States—Peoples
SA   names of individual ethnic
       groups, to be added as
       needed
NT   Americans
       Hispanic Americans
       Indians of North America
       Mexican Americans
Ethnopsychology 155.8
UF   Cross cultural psychology
       Ethnic psychology
       Folk psychology
       National psychology
       Psychology, Ethnic
       Psychology, National
       Psychology, Racial
       Race psychology
SA   names of racial or ethnic
       groups with the subdivision
       Psychology, to be added as
       needed
BT   Anthropology
       Ethnology
       Psychology
       Sociology
NT   Culture conflict
       Indians of North America—
       Psychology
RT   National characteristics
       Social psychology
Ethyl alcohol fuel
USE   Alcohol as fuel
Etiquette 395
UF   Ceremonies
       Manners
       Politeness
       Salutations
SA   types of etiquette, e.g. **Table**
       etiquette; and names of
       countries with the subdivi-
       sion *Social life and cus-*
       toms, e.g. **United States—**

       Social life and customs; to
       be added as needed
BT   Human behavior
NT   Courtesy
       Dancing
       Dating (Social customs)
       Entertaining
       Letter writing
       Table etiquette
RT   Manners and customs
Etymology
USE   names of languages with the
       subdivision *Etymology,* e.g.
       English language—
       Etymology; to be added as
       needed
Eucharist
USE   Lord's Supper
       Mass
Eugenics 363.9; 573.2
BT   Anthropology
       Family
       Genetics
       Population
       Social problems
NT   Birth control
RT   Heredity
Europe 940
UF   Europe, Western
       Western Europe
Europe, Central
USE   Central Europe
Europe, Eastern
USE   Eastern Europe
Europe—History 940
Europe—History—0-476 936; 937
Europe—History—476-1492 940.1;
       940.2
NT   Holy Roman Empire
       Hundred Years' War, 1339-
       1453
RT   Middle Ages—History
Europe—History—1492-1789 940.2
NT   Holy Roman Empire
       Thirty Years' War, 1618-1648
Europe—History—1700-1799 (18th cen-
       tury) 940.2
Europe—History—1789-1815 940.2
UF   Napoleonic Wars
BT   Europe—History—1789-1900

BT = Broader Term   NT = Narrower Term   RT = Related Term   SA = See Also   UF = Used For

Europe—History—1789-1900 940.2

    UF   Europe—History—1800-1899
            (19th century)

    NT   **Europe—History—1789-1815**
           Europe—History—1815-1848
           Europe—History—1848-1871
           Europe—History—1871-1918

Europe—History—1800-1899 (19th century)

    USE   **Europe—History—1789-1900**

Europe—History—1815-1848 940.2

    BT   **Europe—History—1789-1900**

Europe—History—1848-1871 940.2

    BT   **Europe—History—1789-1900**

Europe—History—1871-1918 940.2

    BT   **Europe—History—1789-1900**
           Europe—History—1900-1999
           (20th century)

    NT   **World War, 1914-1918**

Europe—History—1900-1999 (20th century) 940.5

    NT   **Europe—History—1871-1918**

Europe—History—1914-1945

    USE   **Europe—History—1918-1945**

Europe—History—1918-1945 940.5

    UF   Europe—History—1914-1945
           [Former heading]

    NT   **Russo-Finnish War, 1939-1940**
           World War, 1939-1945

Europe—History—1945- 940.55

Europe—Politics and government 940

    May be subdivided by period using the same subdivisions as under **Europe—History**, e.g. **Europe—Politics and government—1789-1900.**

    NT   **European federation**

Europe, Western

    USE   **Europe**

European Common Market

    USE   **European Union**

European Community

    USE   **European Union**

European Economic Community

    USE   **European Union**

European federation 341.24; 940

    Use for general materials on the political or economic union of European countries. Materials on the corporate body formerly known as the European Economic Community and the European Community, which became known as the European Union upon ratification of the Treaty of European Union on October 29, 1993, are entered under **European Union.**

    UF   Federation of Europe
           Paneuropean federation
           United States of Europe (proposed)

    BT   **Europe—Politics and government**
           Federal government
           International organization

    NT   **European Union**

European Union 341.24; 382

    Use for materials on the corporate body formerly known as the European Economic Community and the European Community, which became known as the European Union upon ratification of the Treaty on European Union on October 29, 1993. General materials on the political or economic union of European countries are entered under **European federation.**

    UF   Common market
           E.E.C.
           EEC
           European Common Market
           European Community
           European Economic Community *[Former heading]*

    BT   **European federation**

European War, 1914-1918

    USE   **World War, 1914-1918**

European War, 1939-1945

    USE   **World War, 1939-1945**

Euthanasia 179

    UF   Death, Mercy
           Killing, Mercy
           Mercy killing

    BT   **Homicide**
           Medical ethics

    RT   **Right to die**

Evacuation of civilians

    USE   names of wars with the subdivision *Evacuation of civilians,* e.g. **World War, 1939-1945—Evacuation of civilians;** to be added as needed

---

Evaluation of literature
    USE **Books and reading**
          Books and reading—Best
            books
          Books—Reviews
          Criticism
          Literature—History and criti-
            cism
Evangelism
    USE **Evangelistic work**
Evangelism and politics
    USE **Religion and politics**
Evangelistic healing
    USE **Spiritual healing**
Evangelistic work 253
    UF Evangelism
          Revival (Religion)
    BT **Church work**
    NT **Conversion**
    RT **Christian missions**
          Revivals
Evening and continuation schools 374
    UF Continuation schools
          Evening schools
          Night schools
    BT **Compulsory education**
          Continuing education
          Education
          Public schools
          Schools
          Secondary education
          Technical education
    RT **Adult education**
Evening schools
    USE **Evening and continuation**
            schools
Evergreens 582.1; 635.9
    BT **Landscape gardening**
          Shrubs
          Trees
    NT **Christmas trees**
Everyday living skills
    USE **Life skills**
Evidences of Christianity
    USE **Apologetics**
Evidences of the Bible
    USE **Bible—Evidences, authority,**
            etc.
Evil
    USE **Good and evil**

Evil spirits
    USE **Demonology**
Evolution 573.2; 575
    UF Darwinism
          Development
          Mutation (Biology)
          Origin of species
    BT **Genetics**
          Modern philosophy
          Zoology
    NT **Life—Origin**
    RT **Biology**
          Creation
          Creationism
          Heredity
          Human origins
          Natural selection
          Religion and science
          Variation (Biology)
Evolution and Christianity
    USE **Creationism**
Evolution—Study and teaching 575.007
    RT **Creation—Study and teaching**
          Creationism
Ex libris
    USE **Bookplates**
Ex-nuns 271; 305.43; 920
    UF Catholic ex-nuns
          Former nuns
    BT **Nuns**
Ex-priests 305.33; 920
    UF Catholic ex-priests
          Former priests
    BT **Catholic Church—Clergy**
          Priests
Ex-service men
    USE **Veterans**
Ex-Soviet republics
    USE **Former Soviet republics**
Ex-Soviet states
    USE **Former Soviet republics**
Examinations 371.2
    Use for general materials, such as dis-
cussions of the value of examinations, statistics, history, etc. Materials discussing
the requirements for examinations in particular branches of study, or compilations
of questions and answers for such examinations, are entered under the subject with
the subdivision *Examinations,* e.g. **Eng-**
lish language—Examinations.
    UF Achievement tests

Examinations—*Continued*
    Objective tests
    Tests
  SA branches of study with the
      subdivision *Examinations,*
      and names of individual
      examinations, to be added
      as needed
  BT **Educational tests and mea-**
      surements
    Questions and answers
    Teaching
  NT **Civil service—Examinations**
    Colleges and universities—
      Entrance examinations
    Colleges and universities—
      Entrance requirements
    English language—
      Examinations
    Graduate Record Examination
    Music—Examinations
    Scholastic aptitude test
Examinations—Design and construction
    371.2
Excavation 624.1
  BT **Civil engineering**
    Tunnels
Excavations (Archeology) (May subdiv.
    geog.) **930.1**
  UF Earthworks (Archeology)
    Ruins
  BT **Archeology**
  RT **Extinct cities**
    Mounds and mound builders
Excavations (Archeology)—United
    States 973
  UF United States—Excavations
    (Archeology)
Exceptional children 155.45
  UF Abnormal children
    Children, Abnormal
    Children, Exceptional
  BT **Children**
    Elementary education
  NT **Brain damaged children**
    Emotionally disturbed children
    Gifted children
    Handicapped children
    Mainstreaming in education
    Slow learning children

    Wild children
Excess government property
  USE **Surplus government property**
Exchange 332.4; 332.64
  BT **Commerce**
  NT **Foreign exchange**
    Money
    Stock exchange
Exchange, Barter
  USE **Barter**
Exchange, Foreign
  USE **Foreign exchange**
Exchange of persons programs 370.19
  UF Cultural exchange programs
    Interchange of visitors
    Specialists exchange programs
    Visitors' exchange programs
  SA headings for exchange pro-
      grams for classes of per-
      sons, e.g. **Teacher exchange;**
      to be added as needed
  BT **Cultural relations**
    International cooperation
  NT **Teacher exchange**
Exchange of prisoners of war
  USE **Prisoners of war**
Exchange of teachers
  USE **Teacher exchange**
Exchange rates
  USE **Foreign exchange**
Executions
  USE **Capital punishment**
Executive ability 658.4
  UF Administrative ability
  BT **Ability**
  NT **Leadership**
  RT **Industrial efficiency**
Executive departments
  USE names of countries, states,
      etc., with the subdivision
      Executive departments, e.g.
      United States—Executive
      departments; to be added as
      needed
Executive departments—Reorganization
  USE names of countries, states,
      etc., with the subdivision
      Executive departments—
      Reorganization, e.g. **United**
      States—Executive

Executive departments—
  Reorganization—*Continued*
        departments—
        Reorganization; to be added
        as needed
Executive investigations
  USE   **Governmental investigations**
Executive power (May subdiv. geog.)
        351
  Use for materials that discuss the duties,
  rights, and abuses of the highest adminis-
  trative authority of a country, often as
  compared or contrasted with the legisla-
  tive power.
  UF   Presidents—Powers and duties
  BT   **Constitutional law**
       Political science
  NT   **Amnesty**
       Heads of state
       Monarchy
       Pardon
       Prime ministers
       Separation of powers
       War and emergency powers
  RT   **Presidents**
Executive power—United States 353
  UF   Presidents—United States—
       Power
       United States—Executive
       power
Executors and administrators 346.05
  UF   Administrators and executors
  BT   **Inheritance and succession**
  RT   **Wills**
Exegesis, Biblical
  USE   **Bible—Criticism, interpreta-
        tion, etc.**
Exercise 613.7
  SA   types of exercises and physical
       activities, to be added as
       needed
  BT   **Health**
       Hygiene
  NT   **Aerobics**
       Bodybuilding
       Cycling
       Gymnastics
       Hatha yoga
       Physical fitness
       Rowing
       Weight lifting

  RT   **Physical education**
       Reducing
Exercise addiction 616.85
  UF   Addiction to exercise
       Compulsive exercising
  BT   **Compulsive behavior**
Exercises, Aerobic
  USE   **Aerobics**
Exercises, problems, etc.
  USE   subjects with the subdivision
        Problems, exercises, etc., for
        compilations of practice
        problems or exercises for
        use in the study of a topic,
        e.g. **Chemistry—Problems,
        exercises, etc.;** to be added
        as needed
Exhaustion
  USE   **Fatigue**
Exhibitions
  UF   Exhibits
       Expositions
       Industrial exhibitions
       International exhibitions
       Trade shows
       World's fairs
  SA   subjects with the subdivision
       Exhibitions, and names of
       exhibitions, e.g. **Expo 92
       (Seville, Spain);** to be add-
       ed as needed
  NT   **Art—Exhibitions**
       Craft shows
       Expo 92 (Seville, Spain)
       Fashion shows
       Flower shows
       Printing—Exhibitions
  RT   **Fairs**
Exhibits
  USE   **Exhibitions**
Exiles
  USE   **Refugees**
Existentialism 142
  BT   **Metaphysics**
       Modern philosophy
       Phenomenology
Exobiology
  USE   **Life on other planets**
       Space biology

BT = Broader Term   NT = Narrower Term   RT = Related Term   SA = See Also   UF = Used For

Exorcism 133.4; 291.3
- BT **Superstition**
- RT **Demoniac possession**
  - **Demonology**
  - **Witchcraft**

Expanding universe
- USE **Universe**

Expeditions, Scientific
- USE **Scientific expeditions**

Experience
- USE **Empiricism**

Experiences, Near-death
- USE **Near-death experiences**

Experimental farms
- USE **Agricultural experiment stations**

Experimental films 791.43

  May be used for individual works, collections, or materials about experimental films.
- UF Avant-garde films
  - Motion pictures, Experimental
  - Personal films
  - Underground films
- BT **Motion pictures**

Experimental methods in education
- USE **Education—Experimental methods**

Experimental psychology
- USE **Psychophysiology**

Experimental schools 371

  Use for materials on schools in which new teaching methods, organizations of subject matter, educational theories, personnel practices, etc., are tested.
- UF Alternative schools
  - Free schools
  - Nonformal schools
  - Project schools
  - Schools, Nonformal
- BT **Education—Experimental methods**
  - **Schools**
- RT **Open plan schools**

Experimental theater 792
- UF Avant-garde theater
- BT **Theater**

Experimental universities
- USE **Free universities**

Experimentation on animals
- USE **Animal experimentation**

Experimentation on humans, Medical
- USE **Human experimentation in medicine**

Experiments, Scientific
- USE **Science—Experiments**

Expert systems (Computer science) 006.3
- UF Knowledge-based systems (Computer science)
  - Systems, Expert (Computer science)
- BT **Artificial intelligence**
  - **Electronic data processing**
  - **Information systems**

Exploration 910.9

  Use for materials on voyages and explorations that have advanced geographic knowledge.
- UF Discoverers
  - Discoveries and exploration
  - Discoveries (in geography) *[Former heading]*
  - Discoveries, Maritime
  - Explorations
  - Maritime discoveries
  - Navigators
- SA names of celestial bodies, continents, regions, countries, states, etc., with the subdivision *Exploration* for materials on the exploration of those areas when they were unsettled or sparsely settled and largely unknown to the world at large, e.g. **America—Exploration;** or with the subdivision *Description* for materials on later and recent travels is those areas, e.g. **United States—Description;** and names of countries, states, etc., with the subdivision *Exploring expeditions* for materials on explorations sponsored by those governments, e.g. **United States—Exploring expeditions;** to be added as needed
- BT **Adventure and adventurers**

Exploration—*Continued*
    Geography
    History
  NT **America—Exploration**
    Antarctic regions—Exploration
    Arctic regions—Exploration
    Northeast Passage
    Northwest Passage
    Outer space—Exploration
    United States—Exploration
  RT **Explorers**
    Scientific expeditions
    Voyages and travels
Exploration, Space
  USE **Outer space—Exploration**
Exploration, Submarine
  USE **Underwater exploration**
Exploration, Underwater
  USE **Underwater exploration**
Exploration—United States
  USE **United States—Exploration**
Explorations
  USE **Exploration**
    Explorers
Explorer (Artificial satellite) 629.46
  BT **Artificial satellites**
Explorers 910.92; 920
  UF Discoverers
    Explorations
    Navigators
    Voyagers
  SA names of places explored with
    the subdivision *Exploration,*
    e.g. **America—Exploration;**
    names of countries with the
    subdivisions *Description*
    and *Exploring expeditions;*
    and names of individual
    explorers, to be added as
    needed
  BT **Adventure and adventurers**
    Heroes and heroines
  NT **United States—Exploring ex-
    peditions**
  RT **Exploration**
    Travelers
    Voyages and travels
Exploring expeditions
  USE names of countries sponsoring
    exploring expeditions with

the subdivision *Exploring
expeditions,* e.g. **United
States—Exploring expedi-
tions;** etc.; and names of
expeditions, e.g. **Lewis and
Clark Expedition (1804-
1806);** to be added as need-
ed
Explosions 904
  BT **Accidents**
Explosives 363.3; 623.4; 662
  SA types of explosives and explo-
    sive devices, to be added
    as needed
  BT **Chemistry**
  NT **Ammunition**
    Bombs
    Dynamite
    Gunpowder
    Torpedoes
Expo 92 (Seville, Spain) 909.82
  UF Seville (Spain). World's Fair,
    1992
    World's Fair (1992 : Seville,
    Spain)
  BT **Exhibitions**
    Fairs
Exports
  USE **Commerce**
    Tariff
Expositions
  USE **Exhibitions**
Express highways 388.1; 625.7
  UF Freeways
    Interstate highways
    Limited access highways
    Motorways
    Parkways
    Superhighways
    Toll roads
    Turnpikes (Modern)
  BT **Roads**
    Traffic engineering
Express service 388
  BT **Railroads**
    Transportation
  NT **Pony express**
Expressionism (Art) 759.06
  BT **Painting**
  RT **Postimpressionism (Art)**

BT = Broader Term   NT = Narrower Term   RT = Related Term   SA = See Also   UF = Used For

Expropriation
  USE **Eminent domain**
Expulsion
  USE **Penal colonies**
Extended care facilities
  USE **Long-term care facilities**
Extension work, Agricultural
  USE **Agricultural extension work**
Extermination of Jews (1933-1945)
  USE **Jewish holocaust (1933-1945)**
Extermination of pests
  USE **Pest control**
External trade
  USE **International trade**
Extinct animals 560
  UF Animals, Extinct
  SA names of extinct animals, to
      be added as needed
  BT **Animals**
  NT **Mastodon**
  RT **Fossils**
      Prehistoric animals
      Rare animals
Extinct cities (May subdiv. geog.) **930**
  UF Abandoned towns
      Buried cities
      Cities and towns, ruined, ex-
      tinct, etc. *[Former heading]*
      Ruins
      Sunken cities
  SA names of extinct cities and
      towns, e.g. **Delphi (Extinct
      city);** to be added as need-
      ed
  BT **Archeology**
      Cities and towns
  NT **Ghost towns**
  RT **Excavations (Archeology)**
Extinct cities—Greece 938
  NT **Delphi (Extinct city)**
Extinct plants
  USE **Fossil plants**
Extracurricular activities
  USE **Student activities**
Extragalactic nebulae
  USE **Galaxies**
Extramarital relationships
  USE **Adultery**
Extrasensory perception 133.8
  UF E.S.P.

ESP
  BT **Parapsychology**
  NT **Clairvoyance**
      Telepathy
Extraterrestrial bases 629.44
  Use for materials on bases established
  on natural extraterrestrial bodies for spe-
  cific functions other than colonization.
  Materials on communities established in
  space or on natural extraterrestrial bodies
  are entered under **Space colonies.** Materi-
  als on manned installations orbiting in
  space for specific functions, such as servic-
  ing space ships, are entered under **Space
  stations.**
  BT **Building**
      Civil engineering
  RT **Space colonies**
Extraterrestrial beings 574.999
  UF Aliens from outer space
      Interplanetary visitors
  BT **Life on other planets**
Extraterrestrial communication
  USE **Interstellar communication**
Extraterrestrial environment
  USE **Space environment**
Extraterrestrial life
  USE **Life on other planets**
Extravehicular activity (Space flight)
      629.45
  UF Space vehicles—Extravehicular
      activity
      Space walk
      Walking in space
  BT **Space flight**
Extreme unction
  USE **Anointing of the sick**
Extremism (Political science)
  USE **Radicalism**
      **Right and left (Political sci-
      ence)**
Extremities, Artificial
  USE **Artificial limbs**
Eye 611; 612.8
  BT **Face**
      Head
  RT **Optometry**
      Vision
Eyeglasses 617.7; 681
  UF Spectacles
  SA types of eyeglasses, e.g. **Con-
      tact lenses;** to be added as
      needed

BT = Broader Term   NT = Narrower Term   RT = Related Term   SA = See Also   UF = Used For

Eyeglasses—*Continued*
  NT **Contact lenses**
F.M. radio
  USE **Radio frequency modulation**
Fables 398.2; 808.8; 811, etc.; 813, etc.
  May be used for individual works, collections, or materials about short tales intended to teach moral lessons, often with animals or inanimate objects speaking and acting like human beings, and usually with the lesson stated briefly at the end.
  UF Cautionary tales and verse
      Moral and philosophic stories
      Tales
  BT **Fiction**
      Literature
  NT **Animals—Fiction**
  RT **Allegories**
      Didactic fiction
      Didactic poetry
      Folklore
      Legends
      Parables
      Romances
Fabrics 677
  UF Cloth
      Dry goods
      Textiles
  SA types of fabrics, to be added
        as needed
  BT **Decorative arts**
  NT **Cotton**
      Linen
      Nylon
      Rayon
      Silk
      Synthetic fabrics
      Wool
Fabrics, Synthetic
  USE **Synthetic fabrics**
Face 611; 612
  BT **Head**
  NT **Eye**
      Nose
  RT **Physiognomy**
Facetiae
  USE **Anecdotes**
       Wit and humor
Facsimile transmission 384.1; 621.382
  UF Fax
      Telefax

  BT **Data transmission systems**
      Electronics
      Telecommunication
Factories 338.6; 670; 725
  UF Industrial plants
      Mill and factory buildings
      Plants, Industrial
  SA types of factories, to be added
        as needed
  BT **Industrial buildings**
  RT **Factory management**
      Mills
Factories—Management
  USE **Factory management**
Factories—Training departments
  USE **Employees—Training**
Factory and trade waste
  USE **Industrial wastes**
Factory management 658.5
  Use for materials on the technical aspects of manufacturing processes. Materials on general principles of management of industries are entered under **Management**.
  UF Factories—Management
      Production engineering
      Shop management
  BT **Management**
  NT **Job analysis**
      Motion study
      Office management
      Participative management
      Supervisors
      Time study
  RT **Factories**
      Industrial efficiency
      Industrial revolution
      Personnel management
Factory schools
  USE **Employees—Training**
Factory waste
  USE **Industrial wastes**
Factory workers
  USE **Labor**
       Working class
Facts, Miscellaneous
  USE **Curiosities and wonders**
Faculty (Education)
  USE **Colleges and universities—**
       Faculty
       Educators

Faculty (Education)—*Continued*
    Teachers
Faience
    USE **Pottery**
Failure in business
    USE **Bankruptcy**
          Business failures
Failure of banks
    USE **Bank failures**
Failure to thrive syndrome
    USE **Growth disorders**
Failures, Structural
    USE **Structural failures**
Fair employment practice
    USE **Discrimination in employment**
Fair housing
    USE **Discrimination in housing**
Fair trade
    USE **Unfair competition**
Fair trade (Tariff)
    USE **Free trade and protection**

Fair trial 345

Use for materials on legal hearings before an impartial and disinterested tribunal. Materials on the regular administration of the law, according to which citizens may not be denied their legal rights and all laws must conform to fundamental and accepted legal principles, are entered under **Due Process of law.**

    UF Right to a fair trial
    BT **Civil rights**
          Due process of law
    NT **Freedom of the press and fair trial**

Fair trial and free press
    USE **Freedom of the press and fair trial**

Fair use (Copyright) 341.7; 346.04
    BT **Copyright**

Fairies 398.21
    UF Elves
          Gnomes
          Goblins
    BT **Folklore**
          Superstition

Fairness doctrine (Broadcasting) 343.09

Use for materials on the requirement that, if one side of a controversial issue is aired, the other side must have the same opportunity.

    UF Doctrine of fairness (Broadcasting)

    BT **Radio broadcasting**
          Television broadcasting
          Television in politics
    RT **Equal time rule (Broadcasting)**

Fairs 381; 394; 607.4; 907.4

Use for general materials on public showings that suggest a variety of kinds of display and entertainment, usually in an outdoor setting, sometimes for the promotion of sales and sometimes in competition for prizes of excellence.

    UF Bazaars
          Trade fairs
          World's fairs
    SA names of fairs, e.g. **Expo 92 (Seville, Spain);** to be added as needed
    NT **Expo 92 (Seville, Spain)**
    RT **Carnivals**
          Exhibitions
          Markets

Fairy tales 398.2; 808.83; 813, etc.; 813.008, etc.

May be used for individual works, collections, or materials about short, simple narratives, often of folk origin and usually intended for children, involving fantastic forces and magical beings such as dragons, elves, fairies, goblins, witches, and wizards.

    UF Children's stories
          Stories
          Tales
    BT **Children's literature**
          Fiction
          Legends
          Literature
    RT **Fantasy fiction**
          Folklore

Faith 234

Use for materials on religious belief and doubt. Materials on belief and doubt from the philosophical standpoint are entered under **Belief and doubt.**

    UF Religious belief
    BT **Religion**
          Salvation
          Spiritual life
          Theology
    NT **Truth**
    RT **Agnosticism**
          Belief and doubt
          Skepticism

Faith, Confessions of
  USE **Creeds**
Faith cure
  USE **Spiritual healing**
Faith healing
  USE **Spiritual healing**
Faith—Psychology 200.1; 248; 253.5
  BT **Psychology**
       Psychology of religion
Faithfulness
  USE **Loyalty**
Falconry 799.2
  UF Hawking
  BT **Game and game birds**
       Hunting
Fall
  USE **Autumn**
Fallacies
  USE **Errors**
       Logic
Falling stars
  USE **Meteors**
Fallout, Radioactive
  USE **Radioactive fallout**
Fallout shelters
  USE **Air raid shelters**
False advertising
  USE **Deceptive advertising**
Falsehood
  USE **Truthfulness and falsehood**
Families, Dual career
  USE **Dual career family**
Family (May subdiv. geog.) **306.85**
> Use for materials stressing the sociological concept and structure of the family. Materials stressing the everyday life, interaction, and relationships of family members are entered under **Family life.**

  SA types of family members, e.g.
       Children; Fathers; Mothers;
       etc., to be added as needed
  BT **Human relations**
       Sociology
  NT **Birth order**
       Brothers and sisters
       Children
       Clans
       Divorce
       Dual career family
       Eugenics
       Family life

Family size
Farm family
Fathers
Grandparent and child
Husbands
Married people
Mothers
Parent and child
Single parent family
Stepfamily
Widowers
Widows
Wives
  RT **Domestic relations**
       Family reunions
       Home
       Marriage
Family budget
  USE **Household budgets**
Family caregivers
  USE **Caregivers**
Family—Counseling of
  USE **Family therapy**
Family devotions
  USE **Devotional exercises**
       Family—Religious life
Family farms 338.1; 630
  BT **Farms**
  RT **Farm family**
       Farm life
Family finance
  USE **Personal finance**
Family group therapy
  USE **Family therapy**
Family histories
  USE **Genealogy**
Family life 306.85; 392; 646.7
> Use for materials stressing the everyday life, interaction, and relationships of family members. Materials on the sociological concept and structure of the family are entered under **Family.**

  UF Family relations
       Home life
  BT **Family**
  NT **Aging parents**
Family life education 306.85; 362.82;
         372.82
  BT **Education**
  NT **Home economics**
       Marriage counseling

BT = Broader Term   NT = Narrower Term   RT = Related Term   SA = See Also   UF = Used For

Family life education—*Continued*
      Sex education
  RT **Domestic relations**
Family names
  USE **Personal names**
Family planning
  USE **Birth control**
Family prayers
  USE **Devotional exercises**
      Family—Religious life
Family psychotherapy
  USE **Family therapy**
Family relations
  USE **Domestic relations**
      Family life
Family—Religious life 249
  UF Family devotions
      Family prayers
      Family worship
  BT **Religious life**
Family reunions 394.2
  UF Reunions, Family
  RT **Family**
Family size 304.6
  BT **Family**
  NT **Childlessness**
      Only child
  RT **Birth control**
Family social work
  USE **Social case work**
Family therapy 616.89
  UF Family—Counseling of
      Family group therapy
      Family psychotherapy
      Problem families—Counseling
        of
  BT **Counseling**
      Psychotherapy
Family trees
  USE **Genealogy**
Family—United States 306.850973
Family violence 362.82
  UF Domestic violence
      Household violence
  BT **Violence**
  NT **Child abuse**
      Elderly abuse
      Husband abuse
      Wife abuse
Family worship
  USE **Family—Religious life**

Famines (May subdiv. geog.) **904**
  BT **Food supply**
      Starvation
Famines—United States 363.80973; 973
  UF United States—Famines
Famous people
  USE **Celebrities**
Fanaticism 152.4; 200.1; 303
  UF Intolerance
  BT **Emotions**
Fancy dress
  USE **Costume**
Fans 391
  BT **Costume**
Fantastic fiction
  USE **Fantasy fiction**
Fantastic films
  USE **Fantasy films**
Fantastic poetry
  USE **Fantasy poetry**
Fantastic radio programs
  USE **Fantasy radio programs**
Fantastic television programs
  USE **Fantasy television programs**
Fantasy 154.3
    Use for materials on fantasy as an aspect of psychology. Literary fantasies are entered under **Fantasy fiction.**
  UF Day dreams
  BT **Dreams**
      Imagination
  RT **Hallucinations and illusions**
Fantasy fiction 808.83; 809.3; 813, etc.
    May be used for individual works, collections, or materials about imaginative fiction with strange settings, grotesque or fanciful characters, and supernatural or impossible events or forces.
  UF Apocalyptic fantasies
      End-of-the-world fantasies
      Fantastic fiction *[Former heading]*
      Time travel (Fiction)
  BT **Fiction**
  NT **Alternative histories**
      Dystopias
      Ghost stories
      Imaginary voyages
      Utopian fiction
  RT **Fairy tales**
      Horror fiction

Fantasy fiction—*Continued*
>> Interplanetary voyages
>> Occult fiction
>> Science fiction

Fantasy films 791.43
> May be used for individual works, collections, or materials about fantasy films.
>> UF   Apocalyptic fantasies
>>> End-of-the-world fantasies
>>> Fantastic films
>>> Time travel (Fiction)
>> BT   **Motion pictures**
>> RT   **Horror films**
>>> **Science fiction films**

Fantasy poetry 808.81; 811, etc.
> May be used for individual works, collections, or materials about fantasy poetry.
>> UF   Fantastic poetry
>> BT   **Poetry**

Fantasy radio programs 791.44
> May be used for individual works, collections, or materials about fantasy radio programs.
>> UF   Fantastic radio programs
>> BT   **Radio programs**

Fantasy television programs 791.45
> May be used for individual works, collections, or materials about fantasy television programs.
>> UF   Apocalyptic fantasies
>>> End-of-the-world fantasies
>>> Fantastic television programs
>>> Time travel (Fiction)
>> BT   **Television programs**
>> RT   **Horror television programs**
>>> **Science fiction television programs**

Far East
> USE   **East Asia**

Far north
> USE   **Arctic regions**

Farces 808.82; 812, etc.
> May be used for individual works, collections, or materials about farces.
>> BT   **Comedies**

Farm animals
> USE   **Domestic animals**
>> **Livestock**

Farm buildings 631.2; 728
>> UF   Architecture, Rural
>>> Buildings, Farm
>>> Rural architecture

SA   types of farm buildings, to be added as needed
BT   **Architecture**
>> **Buildings**
>> **Domestic architecture**
NT   **Barns**

Farm credit
> USE   **Agricultural credit**

Farm crops
> USE   **Farm produce**

Farm engines
> USE   **Agricultural machinery**

Farm equipment
> USE   **Agricultural machinery**

Farm family 306.85
>> BT   **Family**
>> RT   **Family farms**
>>> **Farm life**
>>> **Rural sociology**

Farm implements
> USE   **Agricultural machinery**

Farm laborers
> USE   **Agricultural laborers**

Farm life (May subdiv. geog.) **306.3; 630**
>> UF   Rural life
>> BT   **Country life**
>>> **Farmers**
>> NT   **Ranch life**
>> RT   **Family farms**
>>> **Farm family**
>>> **Rural sociology**

Farm life—United States 306.3; 630
>> UF   United States—Farm life

Farm machinery
> USE   **Agricultural machinery**

Farm management 630
>> BT   **Farms**
>>> **Management**
>> RT   **Agriculture—Economic aspects**

Farm mechanics
> USE   **Agricultural engineering**
>> **Agricultural machinery**

Farm produce 338.1; 630; 631.5
>> UF   Agricultural products
>>> Crops
>>> Farm crops
>> SA   types of farm products, to be added as needed
>> BT   **Food**

Farm produce—*Continued*
    Raw materials
  NT **Hay**

Farm produce—Marketing 338.1
  UF Marketing of farm produce
  BT **Marketing**
       Prices
  RT **Agriculture—Economic aspects**

Farm subsidies
  USE **Agricultural subsidies**

Farm tenancy 333.5
    Use for materials on the economic and social aspects of farm tenancy. Materials on the legal aspects are entered under **Landlord and tenant.**
  UF Agriculture—Tenant farming
       Farming on shares
       Sharecropping
       Tenant farming
  BT **Farms**
       Land tenure
  RT **Landlord and tenant**

Farmers 630.92; 920
  BT **Agriculture**
  NT **Farm life**

Farmers' cooperatives
  USE **Cooperative agriculture**

Farming
  USE **Agriculture**

Farming, Dry
  USE **Dry farming**

Farming on shares
  USE **Farm tenancy**

Farming, Organic
  USE **Organic farming**

Farms 333.76; 630; 636
  BT **Land use**
       Real estate
  NT **Family farms**
       Farm management
       Farm tenancy
       Vineyards
  RT **Agriculture**

Farms, Experimental
  USE **Agricultural experiment stations**

Farriering
  USE **Blacksmithing**

Fascism (May subdiv. geog.) **320.5; 321.9; 355.6**
    Use for materials on the political philosophy, movements, or regimes that advocate a centralized autocratic government, severe economic and social regimentation, and the exaltation of nation and race over the individual. Materials on fascism in Germany during the Nazi regime are entered under **National socialism.**
  UF Authoritarianism
       Neo-fascism
       Neo-nazism
  BT **Totalitarianism**
  NT **Neo-Nazis**
  RT **National socialism**

Fascism—Germany 320.5; 943.086
  NT **National socialism**

Fascism—United States 320.5; 973.9
  UF United States—Fascism

Fashion 391
    Use for materials on the prevailing mode or style of dress. Descriptive and historical materials on the costume of particular countries, periods, or peoples and materials on fancy dress and theatrical costumes are entered under **Costume.** Materials on clothing from a practical standpoint, including the art of dress, are entered under **Clothing and dress.**
  UF Style in dress
  NT **Dressmaking**
       Tailoring
  RT **Clothing and dress**
       Costume

Fashion design 746.9
  UF Costume design
  BT **Commercial art**
       Design

Fashion industry
  USE **Clothing industry**

Fashion models 659.1; 746.9
  UF Manikins (Fashion models)
       Mannequins (Fashion models)
       Models, Fashion *[Former heading]*
       Models (Persons)
       Style manikins
  BT **Advertising**
       Clothing industry

Fashion shows 391.074; 659.1
  BT **Exhibitions**

Fashionable society
  USE **Upper classes**

Fast breeder reactors
    USE   **Nuclear reactors**
Fast foods
    USE   **Convenience foods**
Faster reading
    USE   **Rapid reading**
Fasting 178; 248.4; 291.4; 296.7
    UF   Abstinence
    BT   **Asceticism**
           Diet
    NT   **Hunger strikes**
    RT   **Hunger**
           Religious holidays
           Starvation
Fasts and feasts
    USE   **Religious holidays**
Fasts and feasts—Christianity
    USE   **Christian holidays**
Fasts and feasts—Judaism
    USE   **Jewish holidays**
Fat
    USE   **Oils and fats**
Fatally ill children
    USE   **Terminally ill children**
Fatally ill patients
    USE   **Terminally ill**
Fate and fatalism 149
    UF   Destiny
           Fortune
    BT   **Philosophy**
    NT   **Free will and determinism**
           Predestination
Father and child 306.874
    UF   Child and father
           Father-child relationship
    BT   **Parent and child**
    NT   **Fathers and daughters**
           Fathers and sons
Father-child relationship
    USE   **Father and child**
Fathers 306.8
    BT   **Family**
           Homemakers
           Men
    NT   **Teenage fathers**
           Unmarried fathers
Fathers and daughters 306.874
    UF   Daughters and fathers
    BT   **Father and child**
           Girls

Fathers and sons 306.874
    UF   Sons and fathers
    BT   **Boys**
           Father and child
Fathers, Single parent
    USE   **Single parent family**
Fatigue 152.1; 612; 613.7
    UF   Exhaustion
           Weariness
    BT   **Physiology**
    NT   **Jet lag**
    RT   **Rest**
Fatness
    USE   **Obesity**
Fats
    USE   **Oils and fats**
Fauna
    USE   **Animals**
           Zoology
Fax
    USE   **Facsimile transmission**
Fear 152.4
    UF   Anxiety
    BT   **Emotions**
    NT   **Horror**
           Phobias
           Separation anxiety in children
Feast of Dedication
    USE   **Hanukkah**
Feast of Lights
    USE   **Hanukkah**
Feasts
    USE   **Religious holidays**
Fecundity
    USE   **Fertility**
Federal aid
    USE   **Subsidies**
Federal aid to education 379.1
     Use same pattern for federal aid to other subjects.
    UF   Education—Federal aid
    BT   **Colleges and universities—**
               Finance
           Education—Finance
           Education—Government policy
           Grants-in-aid
Federal aid to libraries 021.8
    UF   Libraries—Federal aid
    BT   **Grants-in-aid**
           Libraries—Government policy

Federal aid to libraries—*Continued*
    Library finance
Federal aid to minority business enter-
    prises 338.9
  UF Minority business
        enterprises—Federal aid
  BT **Grants-in-aid**
       Minority business enterprises
       Subsidies
Federal aid to the arts 351.85
  UF Art—Federal aid
       Arts and state
       Arts—Federal aid
       Funding for the arts
       State and the arts
       State encouragement of the
         arts
  BT **Grants-in-aid**
       Subsidies
  RT **Art patronage**
       Arts—Government policy
Federal budget
  USE **Budget—United States**
Federal-city relations 351.09
  UF City-federal relations
       Federal-municipal relations
       Municipal-federal relations
       Urban-federal relations
  BT **Federal government**
       Municipal government
Federal courts
  USE **Courts—United States**
Federal debt
  USE **Public debts**
Federal debt—United States
  USE **Public debts—United States**
Federal government 321.02; 351
  UF Confederacies
       Federalism
  BT **Constitutional law**
       Political science
       Republics
  NT **European federation**
       Federal-city relations
       Federal-state relations
  RT **Democracy**
       State governments
Federal grants
  USE **Grants-in-aid**

Federal-Indian relations
  USE **Indians of North America—**
         Government relations
Federal libraries
  USE **Government libraries**
Federal-municipal relations
  USE **Federal-city relations**
Federal Republic of Germany
  USE **Germany**
       Germany (West)
Federal Reserve banks 332.1
  BT **Banks and banking**
Federal revenue sharing
  USE **Revenue sharing**
Federal spending policy
  USE **United States—Appropriations**
         and expenditures
Federal-state relations 351.09; 353.9
  UF State-federal relations
  BT **Federal government**
       State governments
Federal-state tax relations
  USE **Intergovernmental tax rela-**
         tions
Federalism
  USE **Federal government**
Federation, International
  USE **International organization**
Federation of Europe
  USE **European federation**
Feedback control systems 629.8
  BT **Automation**
  NT **Servomechanisms**
Feedback (Psychology) 153.1
  BT **Psychology of learning**
  NT **Biofeedback training**
Feeding behavior in animals
  USE **Animals—Food**
Feeds 633.2; 633.3
  UF Fodder
  SA types of feeds, e.g. **Oats;** to
       be added as needed
  BT **Animals—Food**
  NT **Forage plants**
       Oats
       Silage and silos
  RT **Grasses**
       Hay
       Root crops
Feeling
  USE **Perception**

BT = Broader Term   NT = Narrower Term   RT = Related Term   SA = See Also   UF = Used For

Feeling—*Continued*
    Touch
Feelings
  USE **Emotions**
Feet
  USE **Foot**
Felidae
  USE **Wild cats**
Fellowships
  USE **Scholarships**
Felony
  USE **Crime**
Female actors
  USE **Actresses**
Female climacteric
  USE **Menopause**
Female role
  USE **Sex role**
Feminine psychology
  USE **Women—Psychology**
Femininity of God 212; 231
  UF God—Femininity
  BT **God**
Feminism 305.42; 323.3
    Use for materials on the theory of the political and social equality of the sexes and women's perspectives on various subjects. Materials on activities aimed at obtaining equal rights and opportunities for women are entered under **Women's movement.**
  UF Feminist theory
  NT **Women—History**
  RT **Women's movement**
       Women's rights
Feminist theory
  USE **Feminism**
Fencing 796.8
  UF Fighting
  BT **Physical education**
Feral animals
  USE **Wildlife**
Feral cats
  USE **Wild cats**
Feral children
  USE **Wild children**
Fermentation 547; 660; 663
  BT **Chemistry**
       Enzymes
  NT **Yeast**
  RT **Bacteria**

       Bacteriology
       Wine and wine making
Ferns 587; 635.9
  BT **Plants**
Fertility 574.1; 591.1
    Use for general materials on fertility in animals, including humans. Materials limited to fertility in humans are entered under **Human fertility.**
  UF Fecundity
  BT **Population**
       Reproduction
  NT **Human fertility**
  RT **Infertility**
Fertility control
  USE **Birth control**
Fertility, Human
  USE **Human fertility**
Fertilization in vitro 176; 618.1; 636.089
  UF Ectogenesis, Preimplantational
       Fertilization in vitro, Human
       [Former heading]
       Fertilization, Laboratory
       Fertilization, Test tube
       In vitro fertilization
       Laboratory fertilization
       Preimplantational ectogenesis
       Test tube babies
       Test tube fertilization
  BT **Embryology**
       Genetic engineering
       Reproduction
Fertilization in vitro, Human
  USE **Fertilization in vitro**
Fertilization, Laboratory
  USE **Fertilization in vitro**
Fertilization of plants 581.1
  UF Plants—Fertilization
       Pollination
  BT **Flowers**
       Plant breeding
       Plant physiology
       Plants
  RT **Insects**
Fertilization, Test tube
  USE **Fertilization in vitro**
Fertilizers and manures 631.8; 668
  UF Manures
  BT **Agricultural chemicals**

Fertilizers and manures—*Continued*
>Soils
>NT **Compost**
>>**Lime (Mineral)**
>>**Nitrates**
>>**Phosphates**
>>**Potash**

Festivals (May subdiv. geog.) **394.2**

>Use for materials on occasions other than holidays devoted to festive community observances or to programs of cultural events. Materials on days of general exemption from work or days publicly dedicated to the commemoration of some person, event, or principle are entered under **Holidays**. Materials on religious fasts and feasts are entered under **Religious holidays**.

>UF Fiestas
>SA types of festivals and names of specific festivals, e.g. **Carnival**; to be added as needed
>BT **Days**
>>**Manners and customs**
>NT **Carnival**
>>**Carnivals**
>>**Craft shows**
>>**Film festivals**
>>**Music festivals**
>>**Parades**
>>**Powwows**
>RT **Holidays**
>>**Pageants**
>>**Religious holidays**

Festivals—Jews
>USE **Jewish holidays**

Festivals—United States 394.2
>UF United States—Festivals

Fetal death
>USE **Abortion**
>>**Miscarriage**

Fetus 574.3; 612.6
>UF Unborn child
>BT **Embryology**
>>**Reproduction**

Fetus—Growth retardation
>USE **Growth disorders**

Feudalism 321
>UF Fiefs
>>Vassals
>BT **Land tenure**

Medieval civilization
>NT **Clans**
>>**Peasantry**
>RT **Chivalry**
>>**Middle Ages**

Fever 616
>SA types of fevers, e.g. **Malaria**; to be added as needed
>BT **Pathology**
>NT **Malaria**
>>**Typhoid fever**
>RT **Body temperature**

Fiat money
>USE **Paper money**

Fiber content of food
>USE **Food—Fiber content**

Fiber glass
>USE **Glass fibers**

Fiberglass
>USE **Glass fibers**

Fibers 677
>UF Textile fibers
>NT **Cotton**
>>**Flax**
>>**Glass fibers**
>>**Hemp**
>>**Linen**
>>**Paper**
>>**Silk**
>>**Wool**

Fibers, Glass
>USE **Glass fibers**

Fiction 808.3

>Use for collections and for materials on fiction as a literary form, not for individual works.

>UF Novels
>>Stories
>SA fiction of particular national literatures, e.g. **American fiction**; and kinds of fiction, e.g. **Fantasy fiction**; to be added as needed; and any subjects provided for in the List or the names of persons or places with the subdivision *Fiction*, to be added as needed to express the themes or subject content of collections or individual works

---

BT = Broader Term   NT = Narrower Term   RT = Related Term   SA = See Also   UF = Used For

Fiction—*Continued*
- BT   Literature
- NT   Adventure fiction
       Allegories
       Allegory
       American fiction
       Animals—Fiction
       Bible fiction
       Bildungsromans
       Black humor (Literature)
       Didactic fiction
       English fiction
       Epistolary fiction
       Erotic fiction
       Fables
       Fairy tales
       Fantasy fiction
       Folklore
       Historical fiction
       Horror fiction
       Humorous fiction
       Interplanetary voyages
       Legal stories
       Legends
       Love stories
       Medical novels
       Movie novels
       Mystery fiction
       Napoleon I, Emperor of the
         French, 1769-1821—Fiction
       Occult fiction
       Pastoral fiction
       Picaresque literature
       Plot-your-own stories
       Plots (Drama, fiction, etc.)
       Radio and television novels
       Romances
       Romans à clef
       School stories
       Science fiction
       Sea stories
       Short stories
       Short story
       Slavery—United States—
         Fiction
       Sports stories
       United States—Fiction
       War stories
       Western stories

Fiction, American
- USE   American fiction

Fiction, English
- USE   English fiction

Fiction, Historical
- USE   Historical fiction

Fiction—History and criticism 809.3

Fiction—Plots
- USE   Plots (Drama, fiction, etc.)

Fiction—Technique 808.3
- BT   Authorship

Fictitious names
- USE   Pseudonyms

Fictitious places
- USE   Geographical myths

Fiddle
- USE   Violins

Fiefs
- USE   Feudalism
        Land tenure

Field athletics
- USE   Track athletics

Field hockey 796.35
- BT   Sports

Field hospitals
- USE   Military hospitals
        Military medicine

Field photography
- USE   Outdoor photography

Field trips 069; 371.3
- UF   School excursions
       School trips
- BT   Student activities

Fiestas
- USE   Festivals
        Religious holidays

Fifteenth century 909

   Use for general materials covering progress and development during this period in one or in several countries.

- UF   1400-1499 (15th century)
- BT   Middle Ages
       Renaissance

Fifth column
- USE   Subversive activities
        World War, 1939-1945—
          Collaborationists

Fighting
- USE   Battles
        Boxing

Fighting—*Continued*
>**Bullfights**
>**Dueling**
>**Fencing**
>**Gladiators**
>**Military art and science**
>**Naval art and science**
>**Self-defense**
>**Self-defense for women**
>**War**

Figure drawing 743
>UF Human figure in art
>BT **Artistic anatomy**
>**Drawing**
>RT **Figure painting**

Figure painting 757
>UF Human figure in art
>BT **Artistic anatomy**
>**Painting**
>RT **Figure drawing**
>**Portrait painting**

Figure skating
>USE **Ice skating**
>**Roller skating**

Files and filing 005.74; 025.3; 651.5
>UF Alphabetizing
>Filing systems
>BT **Office management**
>RT **Indexing**

Filing systems
>USE **Files and filing**

Filling stations
>USE **Service stations**

Fills (Earthwork)
>USE **Landfills**

Film adaptations 791.43
>May be used for individual works, collections, or materials about film adaptations of material from other media.
>UF Adaptations
>Adaptations, Film
>Books, Filmed
>Filmed books
>Films from books
>Literature—Film and video adaptations
>Motion picture adaptations
>SA individual national literatures and names of individual literary authors with the sub-

division *Film and video adaptations,* to be added as needed
>BT **Motion pictures**

Film direction
>USE **Motion pictures—Production and direction**

Film epics
>USE **Epic films**

Film festivals 791.43
>UF Motion picture festivals
>Movie festivals
>BT **Festivals**

Film industry (Motion pictures)
>USE **Motion picture industry**

Film noir 791.43
>May be used for individual works, collections, or materials about films of crime and detection photographed in somber tones and permeated by a feeling of disillusionment and pessimism.
>UF Crime films
>Films noirs
>BT **Motion pictures**
>RT **Mystery films**

Film posters 741.6; 791.43
>UF Motion picture posters
>Motion pictures—Posters
>Movie posters
>Playbills
>Posters, Film
>BT **Posters**

Film production
>USE **Motion pictures—Production and direction**

Film projectors
>USE **Projectors**

Film scripts
>USE **Motion picture plays**

Filmed books
>USE **Film adaptations**

Filmmaking
>USE **Motion pictures—Production and direction**

Filmography
>USE **Motion pictures**
>and subjects and names of individuals with the subdivision *Filmography,* e.g.
>**Animals—Filmography;**
>**Shakespeare, William,**

Filmography—*Continued*
        1564-1616—Filmography;
           etc., to be added as needed
Films
  USE **Filmstrips**
         Microfilms
         Motion pictures
Films, Amateur
  USE **Amateur films**
Films, Bible
  USE **Bible films**
Films from books
  USE **Film adaptations**
Films noirs
  USE **Film noir**
Filmscripts
  USE **Motion picture plays**
Filmstrips 371.3; 778.2
  UF Films
       Strip films
  BT **Audiovisual materials**
       Photography
  RT **Slides (Photography)**
Finance (May subdiv. geog.) 332; 336
  UF Finance, Public
       Funds
       Public finance
  SA subjects with the subdivision
       Finance, e.g. **Education—**
       Finance; to be added as
       needed
  BT **Economics**
  NT **Bankruptcy**
       Banks and banking
       Bonds
       Budget
       Capital
       Church finance
       Commerce
       Credit
       Deficit financing
       Education—Finance
       Fiscal policy
       Foreign exchange
       Government lending
       Income
       Inflation (Finance)
       Insurance
       Interest (Economics)
       Internal revenue

       Investments
       Metropolitan finance
       Money
       Municipal finance
       Paper money
       Personal finance
       Prices
       Public debts
       Securities
       Speculation
       Stock exchange
       Tariff
       Taxation
       Wealth
  RT **Monetary policy**
Finance, Church
  USE **Church finance**
Finance, Household
  USE **Household budgets**
Finance—Mathematics
  USE **Business mathematics**
Finance, Municipal
  USE **Municipal finance**
Finance, Personal
  USE **Personal finance**
Finance, Public
  USE **Finance**
Finance—United States 332.0973;
       336.73
  UF United States—Finance
Financial accounting
  USE **Accounting**
Financial aid, Student
  USE **Student aid**
Financial aid to students
  USE **Student aid**
Financial planning, Personal
  USE **Personal finance**
Financiers
  USE **Capitalists and financiers**
Finding things
  USE **Lost and found possessions**
Fine arts
  USE **Arts**
Finger alphabet
  USE **Deaf—Means of communica-**
         tion
Finger games
  USE **Finger play**
Finger marks
  USE **Fingerprints**

Finger painting 751.4
UF   Painting, Finger
BT   **Child artists**
      Painting
Finger play 796.1
UF   Finger games
BT   **Play**
Finger pressure therapy
USE   **Acupressure**
Finger prints
USE   **Fingerprints**
Fingerprints 363.2
UF   Finger marks
      Finger prints
BT   **Anthropometry**
      Criminal investigation
      Criminals—Identification
      Identification
Finishes and finishing
USE   **House painting**
      Industrial painting
      Lacquer and lacquering
      Paint
      Varnish and varnishing
      Wood finishing
Finno-Russian War, 1939-1940
USE   **Russo-Finnish War, 1939-**
      1940
Fire 536; 541.3
BT   **Chemistry**
NT   **Fires**
      Fuel
RT   **Combustion**
      Heat
Fire balls
USE   **Meteors**
Fire bombs
USE   **Incendiary bombs**
Fire departments 628.9
UF   Fire stations
RT   **Fire fighters**
Fire engines 628.9
BT   **Engines**
      Fire fighting
Fire fighters 363.37092; 920
UF   Firemen and firewomen
RT   **Fire departments**
Fire fighting 628.9
BT   **Fire prevention**
      Fires

NT   **Fire engines**
Fire insurance 368.1
UF   Insurance, Fire *[Former head-*
      ing]
BT   **Fires**
      Insurance
NT   **Fireproofing**
Fire prevention (May subdiv. geog.)
      363.37
UF   Prevention of fire
SA   types of institutions, build-
      ings, industries, and vehi-
      cles with the subdivision
      Fires and fire prevention,
      e.g. **Nuclear power plants—**
      Fires and fire prevention; to
      be added as needed
BT   **Fires**
NT   **Fire fighting**
      Fireproofing
      Nuclear power plants—Fires
      and fire prevention
Fire stations
USE   **Fire departments**
Firearms 623.4; 739.7
UF   Guns
      Small arms
SA   types of firearms, to be added
      as needed
BT   **Weapons**
NT   **Gunpowder**
      Pistols
      Rifles
      Shotguns
RT   **Ammunition**
      Shooting
Firearms—Control
USE   **Firearms—Law and legislation**
Firearms industry 338.4; 683.4
      Use for materials on the small arms in-
      dustry. Materials on heavy firearms are
      entered under **Ordnance.**
UF   Firearms industry and trade
      [Former heading]
      Firearms trade
      Gunsmithing
BT   **Weapons**
RT   **Defense industries**
Firearms industry and trade
USE   **Firearms industry**

Firearms—Law and legislation 344
  UF Firearms—Control
      Gun control
      Guns—Control
  BT **Legislation**
Firearms trade
  USE **Firearms industry**
Firemen and firewomen
  USE **Fire fighters**
Fireplaces 697; 749
  BT **Architecture—Details**
      Heating
      Space heaters
  RT **Chimneys**
Fireproofing 628.9; 693.8
  BT **Fire insurance**
      Fire prevention
Fires (May subdiv. geog.) **363.37; 904**
  SA types of institutions, build-
      ings, industries, and vehi-
      cles with the subdivision
      Fires and fire prevention,
      e.g. **Nuclear power plants—**
      Fires and fire prevention; to
      be added as needed
  BT **Accidents**
      Disasters
      Fire
  NT **Fire fighting**
      Fire insurance
      Fire prevention
      Forest fires
      Nuclear power plants—Fires
      and fire prevention
Fireworks 662
  BT **Amusements**
Firms
  USE **Business enterprises**
First aid 362.1; 616.02
  UF Emergencies
      Injuries
      Wounded, First aid to
  BT **Health self-care**
      Home accidents
      Medicine
      Nursing
      Rescue work
      Sick
  NT **Artificial respiration**
      Bandages

      Cardiac resuscitation
  RT **Accidents**
      Lifesaving
First editions
  USE **Bibliography—First editions**
First generation children
  USE **Children of immigrants**
First ladies—United States
  USE **Presidents—United States—**
      Spouses
Firstborn child
  USE **Birth order**
Fiscal policy (May subdiv. geog.) **336.3**
  BT **Economic policy**
      Finance
  RT **Monetary policy**
Fiscal policy—United States 336.73
  UF United States—Fiscal policy
Fish
  USE **Fishes**
Fish as food 641.3
  BT **Cooking**
      Fishes
      Food
  RT **Seafood**
Fish culture 639.3
  UF Fish farming
      Fish hatcheries
  BT **Aquaculture**
      Fishes
  RT **Aquariums**
Fish farming
  USE **Fish culture**
Fish hatcheries
  USE **Fish culture**
Fisheries (May subdiv. geog.) **338.3;**
      639.2
  Use for materials on the fishing indus-
try.
  UF Fishing industry
      Sea fisheries
  BT **Fishes**
      Marine resources
      Natural resources
  NT **Pearlfisheries**
      Whaling
Fisheries—United States 338.3; 639.2
  UF United States—Fisheries
Fishes (May subdiv. geog.) **597**
  UF Fish

BT = Broader Term   NT = Narrower Term   RT = Related Term   SA = See Also   UF = Used For

Fishes—*Continued*
Ichthyology
SA   names of fishes, e.g. **Salmon;**
to be added as needed
BT   **Marine animals**
Vertebrates
NT   **Fish as food**
Fish culture
Fisheries
Fishing
Salmon
Tropical fish
RT   **Aquariums**
Fishes—**Geographical distribution**
597.09
BT   **Biogeography**
Fishes—Photography
USE   **Photography of fishes**
Fishes—**United States 597.0973**
UF   United States—Fishes
Fishing (May subdiv. geog.) **799.1**
Use for materials on fishing as a sport.
Materials on fishing as an industry are en-
tered under **Fisheries.**
UF   Angling
SA   types of fishing, to be added
as needed
BT   **Fishes**
Water sports
NT   **Artificial flies**
Fly casting
Spear fishing
Trout fishing
Fishing—Equipment and supplies 799.1
UF   Fishing tackle
Fishing flies
USE   **Artificial flies**
Fishing industry
USE   **Fisheries**
Fishing tackle
USE   **Fishing—Equipment and sup-
plies**
Fishing—United States 799.10973
UF   United States—Fishing
Fitness
USE   **Physical fitness**
Five-day work week
USE   **Hours of labor**
Flags (May subdiv. geog.) **929.9**
UF   Banners

Ensigns
BT   **Heraldry**
RT   **National emblems**
Signals and signaling
Flags—United States 929.9
UF   American flag
United States—Flags
Flats
USE   **Apartment houses**
Flatware, Silver
USE   **Silverware**
Flavoring essences 664
BT   **Cooking**
Essences and essential oils
Food
Flax 633.5; 677
BT   **Fibers**
Yarn
RT   **Linen**
Flexible hours of labor
USE   **Hours of labor**
Flexitime
USE   **Hours of labor**
Flies 595.77
UF   Diptera
Fly
House flies
SA   types of flies, to be added as
needed
BT   **Household pests**
Insects as carriers of disease
Pests
NT   **Fruit flies**
Flies, Artificial
USE   **Artificial flies**
Flight 629.13
UF   Flying
BT   **Locomotion**
NT   **Animal flight**
RT   **Aeronautics**
Flight attendants 387.7
UF   Air hostesses
Air stewardesses
Air stewards
Airline hostesses
Airline stewardesses
Airline stewards
Airlines—Flight attendants
[Former heading]
Airlines—Hostesses

BT = Broader Term   NT = Narrower Term   RT = Related Term   SA = See Also   UF = Used For

Flight attendants—*Continued*
        Hostesses, Airline
        Stewardesses, Airline
        Stewards, Airline
  BT **Airlines**
Flight to the moon
  USE **Space flight to the moon**
Flight training
  USE **Aeronautics—Study and teaching**
        Airplanes—Piloting
Flights around the world
  USE **Aeronautics—Flights**
Flint implements
  USE **Stone implements**
Floating hospitals
  USE **Hospital ships**
Floats (Parades)
  USE **Parades**
Flood control 627
  UF Flood prevention
        Floods—Control *[Former heading]*
  BT **Hydraulic engineering**
  NT **Dams**
  RT **Forest influences**
Flood prevention
  USE **Flood control**
Floods (May subdiv. geog. by countries, states, cities, etc. and by rivers) **551.48; 904**
  BT **Meteorology**
        Natural disasters
        Rain
        Water
  RT **Rivers**
Floods and forests
  USE **Forest influences**
Floods—Control
  USE **Flood control**
Floors 690; 721
  BT **Architecture—Details**
        Building
        Carpentry
Flora
  USE **Botany**
        Plants
Floral decoration
  USE **Flower arrangement**
Floriculture
  USE **Flower gardening**

Florists' designs
  USE **Flower arrangement**
Flour 641.3; 664
  UF Breadstuffs
  NT **Grain**
  RT **Wheat**
Flour mills 664
  UF Grist mills
        Milling (Flour)
  BT **Mills**
Flow charts
  USE **Graphic methods**
        System analysis
Flow charts (Computer science)
  USE **Programming (Computers)**
Flowcharting
  USE **Graphic methods**
        System analysis
Flowcharting (Computer science)
  USE **Programming (Computers)**
Flower arrangement 745.92
    Use for materials on the artistic arrangement of flowers, including decoration of houses, churches, etc., with flowers.
  UF Designs, Floral
        Floral decoration
        Florists' designs
        Flowers—Arrangement
  BT **Decoration and ornament**
        Flowers
        Table setting and decoration
Flower drying 745.92
  UF Dried flowers
        Flowers, Drying *[Former heading]*
  BT **Plants—Collection and preservation**
Flower gardening 635.9
    Use for practical materials on the cultivation of flowering plants for either commercial or private purposes.
  UF Floriculture
  SA names of flowers, e.g. **Roses;** to be added as needed
  BT **Gardening**
        Horticulture
  NT **Annuals (Plants)**
        Bulbs
        Greenhouses
        House plants
        Ornamental plants

BT = Broader Term   NT = Narrower Term   RT = Related Term   SA = See Also   UF = Used For

Flower gardening—*Continued*
 Perennials
 RT Container gardening
 Flowers
 Window gardening
Flower painting and illustration 758
 UF Flowers in art
 BT Flowers
 Painting
 Plants in art
Flower shows 635.9074
 UF Flowers—Exhibitions
 BT Exhibitions
Flowers (May subdiv. geog.) 582.13
 Use for materials on the general charac-
 teristics of flowers, on the botanical study
 and classification of flowers, or on flowers
 from an artistic point of view. Materials
 limited to the cultivation of flowers are
 entered under **Flower gardening.**
 SA names of flowers, e.g. **Roses;**
 to be added as needed
 BT Botany
 Plants
 NT Annuals (Plants)
 Fertilization of plants
 Flower arrangement
 Flower painting and illustra-
 tion
 Perennials
 Roses
 State flowers
 Wild flowers
 RT Flower gardening
Flowers—Arrangement
 USE Flower arrangement
Flowers, Artificial
 USE Artificial flowers
Flowers, Drying
 USE Flower drying
Flowers—Exhibitions
 USE Flower shows
Flowers in art
 USE Flower painting and illustra-
 tion
Flowers, State
 USE State flowers
Flowers—United States 582.13
 UF United States—Flowers
Flowers, Wild
 USE Wild flowers

Flu
 USE Influenza
Fluid mechanics 532; 620.1
 Use for materials on the branch of me-
 chanics dealing with the properties of liq-
 uids or gases, either at rest or in motion.
 UF Hydromechanics
 BT Mechanics
 NT Gases
 Hydraulic engineering
 Hydraulics
 Hydrodynamics
 Hydrostatics
 Liquids
Fluorescent lighting 621.32
 UF Electric lighting, Fluorescent
 Light, Electric
 BT Electric lighting
Fluoridation of water
 USE Water fluoridation
Flute
 USE Flutes
Flutes 788.3
 UF Flute *[Former heading]*
 BT Wind instruments
Fly
 USE Flies
Fly casting 799.1
 UF Fly fishing
 BT Fishing
 NT Artificial flies
Fly fishing
 USE Fly casting
Flying
 USE Flight
Flying bombs
 USE Guided missiles
Flying saucers
 USE Unidentified flying objects
FM radio
 USE Radio frequency modulation
Foals
 USE Horses
 Ponies
Fodder
 USE Feeds
Fog 551.57
 BT Meteorology
 Water
Fog signals
 USE Signals and signaling

Foliage
USE **Leaves**
Folk art 745

Use for materials on objects of fine or decorative art produced in a peasant, popular, or naive style, often in cultural isolation and by unschooled artists or artisans.

UF Peasant art
SA folk art of particular countries or ethnic groups, e.g. **American folk art;** to be added as needed
BT **Art**
Art and society
NT **American folk art**
RT **Arts and crafts movement**
Decorative arts
Handicraft
Folk art, American
USE **American folk art**
Folk dances
USE **Folk dancing**
Folk dancing 793.3
UF Folk dances
National dances
SA folk dancing of particular countries or ethnic groups, e.g. **American folk dancing;** to be added as needed
BT **Dancing**
NT **American folk dancing**
Indians of North America—Dances
Square dancing
Folk dancing, American
USE **American folk dancing**
Folk drama 808.82; 812, etc.; 812.008, etc.

May be used for collections or materials about folk drama, not for individual works.

UF Folk plays
BT **Drama**
NT **Puppets and puppet plays**
Folk lore
USE **Folklore**
Folk medicine
USE **Traditional medicine**
Folk music (May subdiv. geog.) **781.62**
BT **Music**
Folk music—United States 781.62
UF American folk music

United States—Folk music
NT **Blues music**
Country music
Folk plays
USE **Folk drama**
Folk psychology
USE **Ethnopsychology**
Folk society, Nonliterate
USE **Nonliterate folk society**
Folk songs (May subdiv. geog. for the U.S. and Canada or for states, provinces, or regions of the U.S. and Canada) **782.42162**

Use for materials about folk songs and collections of folk songs that include both words and music. Materials about ballads and collections of ballads without music are entered under **Ballads.**

SA folk songs of particular ethnic or language groups, e.g. **French folk songs;** to be added as needed
BT **Songs**
Vocal music
NT **Carols**
French folk songs
RT **Ballads**
Folklore
National songs
Folk songs, African
USE **African songs**
Folk songs, American
USE **Folk songs—United States**
Folk songs, Black (African)
USE **African songs**
Folk songs—France
USE **French folk songs**
Folk songs, French
USE **French folk songs**
Folk songs—Ohio 782.42162009771
UF Ohio—Folk songs
Folk songs—United States 782.4216200973
UF American folk songs
Folk songs, American
United States—Folk songs
BT **American songs**
NT **Spirituals (Songs)**
Folk tales
USE **Folklore**

BT = Broader Term   NT = Narrower Term   RT = Related Term   SA = See Also   UF = Used For

Folk tales—*Continued*
>**Legends**

Folklore (May subdiv. geog.) **398; 398.2**
>Use for general materials on folklore. May also be used for individual works, collections, and materials about stories based on spoken rather than written traditions.

>UF Folk lore
>>Folk tales
>>Tales
>>Traditions

>SA topics as themes in folklore with the subdivision *Folklore,* e.g. **Plants—Folklore;** and names of ethnic or occupational groups with the subdivision *Folklore,* e.g. **Inuit—Folklore;** to be added as needed

>BT **Ethnology**
>>**Fiction**
>>**Manners and customs**

>NT **African Americans—Folklore**
>>**Animals—Folklore**
>>**Blacks—Folklore**
>>**Chapbooks**
>>**Charms**
>>**Dragons**
>>**Fairies**
>>**Ghosts**
>>**Giants**
>>**Graffiti**
>>**Grail**
>>**Indians of North America—Folklore**
>>**Inuit—Folklore**
>>**Jews—Folklore**
>>**Monsters**
>>**Nursery rhymes**
>>**Plants—Folklore**
>>**Proverbs**
>>**Sagas**
>>**Tall tales**
>>**Tongue twisters**
>>**Weather—Folklore**
>>**Witchcraft**

>RT **Fables**
>>**Fairy tales**
>>**Folk songs**
>>**Legends**

>>**Mythology**
>>**Storytelling**
>>**Superstition**

Folklore, African American
>USE **African Americans—Folklore**

Folklore, Black
>USE **Blacks—Folklore**

Folklore, Inuit
>USE **Inuit—Folklore**

Folklore, Jewish
>USE **Jews—Folklore**

Folklore, Medical
>USE **Traditional medicine**

Folklore—United States 398.0973
>UF United States—Folklore

Folkways
>USE **Manners and customs**

Food 641; 641.3; 664
>UF Gastronomy

>SA types of foods, names of specific foods, and subjects with the subdivision *Food,* to be added as needed

>BT **Digestion**
>>**Home economics**

>NT **Animal food**
>>**Animals—Food**
>>**Artificial foods**
>>**Beverages**
>>**Bread**
>>**Convenience foods**
>>**Dietetic foods**
>>**Dining**
>>**Edible plants**
>>**Eggs**
>>**Farm produce**
>>**Fish as food**
>>**Flavoring essences**
>>**Fruit**
>>**Grain**
>>**Meat**
>>**Milk**
>>**Natural foods**
>>**Nuts**
>>**Prepared cereals**
>>**School children—Food**
>>**Seafood**
>>**Shellfish**
>>**Vegetables**
>>**Vegetarianism**

BT = Broader Term   NT = Narrower Term   RT = Related Term   SA = See Also   UF = Used For

Food—*Continued*
  Vitamins
 RT Cooking
  Diet
  Grocery trade
  Nutrition
Food additives 641.3; 664
 UF Additives, Food
 BT **Food—Analysis**
  Food—Preservation
Food adulteration and inspection 363.19
 UF Adulteration of food
  Analysis of food
  Food inspection
  Inspection of food
  Pure food
 BT **Consumer protection**
  Public health
 NT **Food contamination**
  Meat inspection
  Milk supply
 RT **Food—Law and legislation**
Food allergies
 USE **Food allergy**
Food allergy 616.97
 UF Allergies, Food
  Allergy, Food
  Food allergies
 SA types of food allergies and
   specific food allergies, to be
   added as needed
 BT **Allergy**
Food—Analysis 664
 UF Analysis of food
  Chemistry of food
  Food chemistry
 BT **Industrial chemistry**
 NT **Food additives**
 RT **Food—Composition**
Food, Artificial
 USE **Artificial foods**
Food assistance programs
 USE **Food relief**
Food, Canned
 USE **Canning and preserving**
Food chains (Ecology) 574.5
 BT **Animals—Food**
  Ecology
Food chemistry
 USE **Food—Analysis**

Food—Composition
Food—Cholesterol content 641.1
 UF Cholesterol content of food
 BT **Food—Composition**
Food—Composition 641.1; 664
 UF Chemistry of food
  Food chemistry
 SA **Food—Cholesterol content;**
   and similar headings, to be
   added as needed
 NT **Food—Cholesterol content**
  Food—Fiber content
  Food—Sodium content
 RT **Food—Analysis**
Food contamination 363.19
 UF Contaminated food
 BT **Food adulteration and inspection**
  tion
Food control
 USE **Food supply**
Food, Cost of
 USE **Cost of living**
Food customs
 USE **Eating customs**
Food, Dehydrated
 USE **Dried foods**
Food, Dietetic
 USE **Dietetic foods**
Food, Dried
 USE **Dried foods**
Food—Fiber content 641.1
 UF Dietary fiber
  Fiber content of food
  Roughage
 BT **Food—Composition**
Food for invalids
 USE **Cooking for the sick**
Food for school children
 USE **School children—Food**
Food, Freeze dried
 USE **Freeze-dried foods**
Food, Frozen
 USE **Frozen foods**
Food habits
 USE **Eating customs**
Food inspection
 USE **Food adulteration and inspection**
  tion
Food—Labeling 363.19; 641.1
 UF Food labels

Food labels
USE Food—Labeling

Food—Law and legislation 344
UF Food laws
BT **Law**
Legislation
RT **Food adulteration and inspection**

Food laws
USE **Food—Law and legislation**

Food, Natural
USE **Natural foods**

Food plants
USE **Edible plants**

Food poisoning 615.9
BT **Poisons and poisoning**

Food preparation
USE **Cooking**

Food—Preservation 641.4; 664
UF Preservation of food
SA types of foods with the subdivision *Preservation,* to be added as needed
NT **Canning and preserving**
Cold storage
Dried foods
Food additives
Frozen foods
Fruit—Preservation

Food relief (May subdiv. geog.) 363.8
UF Food assistance programs
SA types of food relief, e.g.
Meals on wheels programs;
and names of wars with the subdivision *Civilian relief* or *Food supply,* to be added as needed
BT **Charities**
Disaster relief
Public welfare
Unemployed
NT **Meals on wheels programs**
World War, 1939-1945—Civilian relief
World War, 1939-1945—Food supply

Food service 642; 647.95
Use for materials on the preparation, delivery, and serving of ready-to-eat foods in large quantities outside of the home. Materials solely on the preparation of food in large quantities are entered under **Quantity cooking.**
UF Cooking for institutions
Mass feeding
Volume feeding
BT **Service industries**
NT **Catering**
Restaurants
Waiters and waitresses
RT **Quantity cooking**

Food—Sodium content 641.1
UF Sodium content of food
BT **Food—Composition**

Food supply 363.8
Use for economic materials on the availability of food. Materials on the conservation of food in wartime are entered under the name of the war with the subdivision *Food supply,* e.g. **World War, 1939-1945—Food supply.**
UF Food control
NT **Famines**
Meat industry
RT **Agriculture**

Fools and jesters 791.092; 920
UF Court fools
Jesters
BT **Comedians**
Courts and courtiers
Entertainers

Foot 611; 612
UF Feet
Toes
BT **Anatomy**

Foot—Care and hygiene 617.5
BT **Podiatry**

Football 796.332
BT **Ball games**
Sports
NT **Soccer**

Football—Coaching 796.33207
BT **Coaching (Athletics)**

Footwear
USE **Shoes**

Forage plants 633.2
SA names of forage plants, to be added as needed
BT **Economic botany**

BT = Broader Term   NT = Narrower Term   RT = Related Term   SA = See Also   UF = Used For

Forage plants—*Continued*
  Feeds
  Plants
  NT **Corn**
  Hay
  Silage and silos
  Soybean
  RT **Grasses**
  Pastures
Force and energy 531
  UF Conservation of energy
  Energy
  BT **Power (Mechanics)**
  RT **Dynamics**
  Mechanics
  Motion
  Quantum theory
Force pumps
  USE **Pumping machinery**
Forced indoctrination
  USE **Brainwashing**
Forced labor
  USE **Convict labor**
  Peonage
  Slavery
Ford automobile 629.222
  BT **Automobiles**
Forecasting 003
  UF Forecasts
  Futurology
  Predictions
  SA types of forecasting, to be
    added as needed
  NT **Business forecasting**
  Economic forecasting
  Weather forecasting
Forecasts
  USE **Forecasting**
Foreign aid program
  USE **Economic assistance**
  Military assistance
  Technical assistance
Foreign area studies
  USE **Area studies**
Foreign automobiles 629.222
  UF Automobiles, Foreign *[Former
    heading]*
  Foreign cars
  SA names of specific makes and
    models, to be added as
    needed

  BT **Automobiles**
Foreign cars
  USE **Foreign automobiles**
Foreign commerce
  USE **International trade**
Foreign economic relations
  USE **International economic rela-
    tions**
Foreign economic relations—United
    States
  USE **United States—Foreign eco-
    nomic relations**
Foreign exchange 332.4
  UF Exchange, Foreign
  Exchange rates
  International exchange
  BT **Banks and banking**
  Exchange
  Finance
  Money
  Stock exchange
Foreign investments 332.6
  UF International investment
  Investments, Foreign *[Former
    heading]*
  BT **Investments**
  Multinational corporations
Foreign language dictionaries
  USE **English language—
    Dictionaries—French
    French language—
    Dictionaries—English**
Foreign language laboratories
  USE **Language laboratories**
Foreign language phrases
  USE **Modern languages—
    Conversations and phrases**
  and names of languages with
    the subdivision *Conversa-
    tions and phrases,* e.g.
  **French language—
    Conversations and phrases;**
  and, for materials on for-
    eign words and phrases in-
    corporated into languages,
    the names of languages
    with the subdivision *For-
    eign words and phrases,* e.g.
  English language—Foreign

Foreign language phrases—*Continued*
      words and phrases; to be
      added as needed
Foreign missions, Christian
  USE **Christian missions**
Foreign opinion
  USE names of countries with the
      subdivision *Foreign opin-*
      ion, or *Foreign opinion* fur-
      ther subdivided by the
      country holding the opin-
      ion, e.g. **United States—**
      Foreign opinion; United
      States—Foreign opinion—
      France; etc., to be added as
      needed
Foreign policy
  USE names of countries with the
      subdivision *Foreign rela-*
      tions, e.g. **United States—**
      Foreign relations; to be
      added as needed
Foreign population
  USE **Immigrants**
      Immigration and emigration
      and names of countries with
      the subdivision *Immigra-*
      tion and emigration, e.g.
      United States—Immigration
      and emigration; and names
      of countries, cities, etc.,
      with the subdivision *For-*
      eign population, e.g. **United**
      States—Foreign population;
      Chicago (Ill.)—Foreign pop-
      ulation; etc., to be added as
      needed
Foreign public opinion
  USE names of countries with the
      subdivision *Foreign opin-*
      ion, or *Foreign opinion* fur-
      ther subdivided by the
      country holding the opin-
      ion, e.g. **United States—**
      Foreign opinion; United
      States—Foreign opinion—
      France; etc., to be added as
      needed
Foreign relations
  USE **International relations**

and names of countries with
      the subdivision *Foreign re-*
      lations, e.g. **United States—**
      Foreign relations; to be
      added as needed
Foreign service
  USE **Diplomatic and consular ser-**
      vice
Foreign students 370.19
  UF   College students, Foreign
      Students, Foreign *[Former*
      heading]
  BT   **Students**
Foreign study 370.19
  UF   Overseas study
      Study abroad
      Study, Foreign
      Study overseas
  BT   **Education**
Foreign trade
  USE **International trade**
Foreigners
  USE **Aliens**
      Citizenship
      Immigrants
      Naturalization
      and names of countries, cities,
      etc., with the subdivision
      Foreign population, e.g.
      United States—Foreign
      population; to be added as
      needed
Foremen and foreladies
  USE **Supervisors**
Forenames
  USE **Personal names**
Forensic medicine
  USE **Medical jurisprudence**
Foreordination
  USE **Predestination**
Forest animals 591.52
  UF   Forest fauna
  BT   **Animals**
      Wildlife
  NT   **Jungle animals**
Forest conservation
  USE **Forests and forestry**
Forest fauna
  USE **Forest animals**
Forest fires 634.9
  BT   **Fires**

Forest influences 574.5; 581.5
    UF Climate and forests
        Floods and forests
        Forests and climate
        Forests and floods
        Forests and rainfall
        Forests and water supply
        Rainfall and forests
    BT **Climate**
        Water supply
    RT **Flood control**
        Forests and forestry
        Plants—Ecology
        Rain
Forest plants 581.5
    BT **Forests and forestry**
        Plants
        Plants—Ecology
Forest products 634.9; 674
    BT **Commercial products**
        Economic botany
        Raw materials
    NT **Gums and resins**
        Lumber and lumbering
        Rubber
        Wood
Forest reserves 333.75; 719
    UF National forests
    BT **Public lands**
        Wildlife conservation
    NT **Wilderness areas**
    RT **Forests and forestry**
        National parks and reserves
Forestry
    USE **Forests and forestry**
Forests and climate
    USE **Forest influences**
Forests and floods
    USE **Forest influences**
Forests and forestry (May subdiv.
        geog.) 574.5; 634.9
    UF Arboriculture
        Conservation of forests
        Forest conservation
        Forestry
        Preservation of forests
        Timber
        Woods
    BT **Agriculture**
        Natural resources

    NT **Christmas tree growing**
        Forest plants
        Jungles
        Lumber and lumbering
        Pruning
        Rain forests
        Reforestation
        Tree planting
    RT **Forest influences**
        Forest reserves
        Trees
        Wood
Forests and forestry—United States
        574.5; 634.90973
    UF United States—Forests and
        forestry
Forests and rainfall
    USE **Forest influences**
Forests and water supply
    USE **Forest influences**
Forgery 332; 364.1
    BT **Crime**
        Fraud
        Impostors and imposture
    NT **Art forgeries**
        Counterfeits and counterfeiting
        Literary forgeries
Forgery of works of art
    USE **Art forgeries**
Forging 671.3; 682
    UF Drop forging
    BT **Metalwork**
    NT **Welding**
    RT **Blacksmithing**
        Ironwork
Forgiveness 179
    BT **Virtue**
    RT **Amnesty**
        Pardon
Forgiveness of sin
    USE **Confession**
        Penance
Form, Musical
    USE **Musical form**
Formal gardens
    USE **Gardens**
Former nuns
    USE **Ex-nuns**
Former priests
    USE **Ex-priests**

BT = Broader Term   NT = Narrower Term   RT = Related Term   SA = See Also   UF = Used For

Former Soviet republics 947.085

Use for general materials on several or all of the countries that emerged from the dissolution of the Soviet Union in 1991. Materials specifically on the federation of independent former Soviet republics that was established in 1991 and does not include Georgia or the Baltic states are entered under **Commonwealth of Independent States.**

UF Ex-Soviet republics

      Ex-Soviet states

      Former Soviet states

RT **Central Asia—History—1991-**

      Commonwealth of Independent States

      Eastern Europe—History—1989-

      Soviet Union

Former Soviet states

USE **Former Soviet republics**

Formosa

USE **Taiwan**

Formula translation (Computer language)

USE **FORTRAN (Computer language)**

Fortification 623

UF Forts

SA names of countries with the subdivision *Defenses,* to be added as needed

BT **Military art and science**

NT **United States—Defenses**

RT **Military engineering**

FORTRAN (Computer language) 005.13

UF Formula translation (Computer language)

      FORTRAN (Computer program language) *[Former heading]*

BT **Programming languages (Computers)**

FORTRAN (Computer program language)

USE **FORTRAN (Computer language)**

Forts

USE **Fortification**

Fortune

USE **Fate and fatalism**

      Probabilities

      Success

      Wealth

Fortune telling 133.3

BT **Amusements**

      Divination

      Occultism

      Prophecies (Occultism)

      Superstition

NT **Astrology**

      Dreams

      Palmistry

      Tarot

RT **Clairvoyance**

Fortunes

USE **Income**

      Wealth

Forums (Discussions)

USE **Discussion groups**

Fossil botany

USE **Fossil plants**

Fossil mammals 569

UF Mammals, Fossil *[Former heading]*

SA names of extinct mammals, to be added as needed

BT **Fossils**

      Mammals

NT **Mastodon**

Fossil plants 561

UF Botany, Fossil

      Extinct plants

      Fossil botany

      Paleobotany

      Plants, Extinct

      Plants, Fossil *[Former heading]*

BT **Botany**

      Fossils

      Plants

Fossil reptiles 567.9

UF Reptiles, Fossil *[Former heading]*

SA names of fossil reptiles, e.g. **Dinosaurs;** to be added as needed

BT **Fossils**

      Reptiles

NT **Dinosaurs**

Fossils 560

UF Animals, Fossil

Fossils—*Continued*
  Paleontology
 BT **Natural history**
   Science
   Stratigraphic geology
   Zoology
 NT **Fossil mammals**
   Fossil plants
   Fossil reptiles
   Prehistoric animals
 RT **Extinct animals**
Foster grandparents 362.7
 BT **Voluntarism**
Foster home care 362.7
 UF Child placing
   Children—Placing out
 BT **Child welfare**
 RT **Adoption**
   Children—Institutional care
   Group homes
Foundations 624.1; 721
 BT **Architecture—Details**
   Building
   Civil engineering
   Structural engineering
 NT **Basements**
   Compressed air
   Concrete
   Soils (Engineering)
 RT **Masonry**
   Walls
Foundations (Endowments)
 USE **Endowments**
Founding 671.2
 Use for materials on the melting and casting of metals.
 UF Casting
   Foundry practice
   Iron founding
   Molding (Metal)
   Moulding (Metal)
 BT **Metalwork**
 NT **Type and type founding**
 RT **Pattern making**
Foundlings
 USE **Orphans**
Foundry practice
 USE **Founding**
Four-day work week
 USE **Hours of labor**

Four-H clubs
 USE **4-H clubs**
Fourteenth century 909
 Use for general materials covering progress and development during this period in one or in several countries.
 UF 1300-1399 (14th century)
 BT **Middle Ages**
Fourth dimension 516; 530.1
 UF Dimension, Fourth
   Hyperspace
   Time travel
 BT **Mathematics**
 NT **Space and time**
Fourth of July 394.2
 UF 4th of July
   Independence Day (United States)
   July Fourth
 BT **Holidays**
   United States—History—1775-1783, Revolution
Fourth World
 USE **Developing countries**
Fractal geometry
 USE **Fractals**
Fractals 514; 516
 Use for materials on shapes or mathematical sets that have fractional, i.e. irregular, dimensions as opposed to the regular dimensions of Euclidean geometry.
 UF Fractal geometry
   Sets, Fractal
   Sets of fractional dimension
 BT **Geometry**
   Mathematical models
   Set theory
   Topology
Fractions 513.2
 BT **Arithmetic**
   Mathematics
Fractures 617.1
 BT **Bones**
   Wounds and injuries
Framing of pictures
 USE **Picture frames and framing**
France 944
 May be subdivided like United States except for *History.*
France—Blacks
 USE **Blacks—France**
France—Folk songs
 USE **French folk songs**

  BT = Broader Term NT = Narrower Term RT = Related Term SA = See Also UF = Used For

France—History 944
France—History—0-1328 944
  NT Celts
France—History—1328-1589, House of
      Valois 944
  NT Hundred Years' War, 1339-
      1453
      Saint Bartholomew's Day,
      Massacre of, 1572
France—History—1589-1789, Bourbons
      944
France—History—1789-1799, Revolu-
      tion 944.04
  UF Directory, French, 1795-1799
      French Revolution
      Napoleonic Wars
      Reign of Terror
      Revolution, French
      Terror, Reign of
  BT **Revolutions**
France—History—1799-1815 944.05
  UF Napoleonic wars
France—History—1815-1914 944.06-
      944.08
France—History—1914-1940 944.081
France—History—1940-1945, German
      occupation 944.081
  UF German occupation of France,
      1940-1945
France—History—1945-1958 944.082
France—History—1958-1969 944.083
France—History—1969- 944.083
Franchise
  USE **Citizenship**
      Elections
      Suffrage
Franciscans 271
  UF Friars Minor
      Gray Friars
      Grey Friars
      Mendicant orders
      Minorites
      Saint Francis, Order of
      St. Francis, Order of
  BT **Catholic religious orders for**
      men
Fraternities and sororities 371.8
  UF College fraternities
      College sororities
      Greek letter societies

      Sororities
  BT **Colleges and universities**
      Students—Societies
  RT **Secret societies**
Fraud 364.1
  UF Deceit
      Ripoffs
  BT **Commercial law**
      Crime
      White collar crimes
  NT **Credit card crimes**
      Forgery
  RT **Impostors and imposture**
      Swindlers and swindling
Fraud, Computer
  USE **Computer crimes**
Fraud, Credit card
  USE **Credit card crimes**
Frauds, Literary
  USE **Literary forgeries**
Fraudulent advertising
  USE **Deceptive advertising**
Free agency
  USE **Free will and determinism**
Free coinage
  USE **Monetary policy**
Free diving
  USE **Scuba diving**
      Skin diving
Free fall
  USE **Weightlessness**
Free love 176; 306.7
  BT **Sexual ethics**
Free material 371.3
  UF Giveaways
  BT **Gifts**
Free press
  USE **Freedom of the press**
Free press and fair trial
  USE **Freedom of the press and fair**
      trial
Free schools
  USE **Experimental schools**
Free speech
  USE **Freedom of speech**
Free thought 211
  BT **Freedom of conscience**
  NT **Agnosticism**
      Freedom of religion
      Skepticism

Free thought—*Continued*
  RT **Deism**
      Rationalism
Free time (Leisure)
  USE **Leisure**
Free trade and protection 382
  UF Fair trade (Tariff)
      Protection
      Tariff question—Free trade
        and protection
  BT **Commerce**
      Commercial policy
      Economic policy
      Economics
  RT **Tariff**
Free universities 378
  UF Alternative universities
      Colleges and universities,
        Nonformal
      Education, Nonformal
      Experimental universities
      Nonformal colleges and uni-
        versities
      Open universities
  BT **Colleges and universities**
Free verse 808.1
  May be used for collections or materials
about free verse, not for individual works.
  UF Vers libre
  BT **Poetry**
Free will and determinism 123
  UF Choice, Freedom of
      Determinism and indetermin-
        ism
      Free agency
      Freedom of choice
      Freedom of the will
      Indeterminism
      Liberty of the will
      Will
  BT **Ethics**
      Fate and fatalism
      Philosophy
      Predestination
Freebooters
  USE **Pirates**
Freedom 323.4
  Use for general or abstract materials on
the power or condition of acting or choos-
ing without compulsion or constraint.
  UF Civil liberty

      Emancipation
      Liberty
      Natural law
      Personal freedom
  BT **Democracy**
      Political science
  NT **Academic freedom**
      Anarchism and anarchists
      Conformity
      Freedom of assembly
      Freedom of association
      Freedom of conscience
      Freedom of movement
      Freedom of religion
      Freedom of speech
      Freedom of the press
      Intellectual freedom
      Slavery
  RT **Civil rights**
      Equality
Freedom, Academic
  USE **Academic freedom**
Freedom marches
  USE **Blacks—Civil rights**
Freedom marches—United States
  USE **African Americans—Civil
        rights**
Freedom of assembly 323.4
  UF Assembly, Right of
      Right of assembly
  BT **Civil rights**
      Freedom
  NT **Public meetings**
      Riots
  RT **Freedom of association**
      Freedom of speech
Freedom of association 323.4
  UF Association, Freedom of
      Right of association
  BT **Civil rights**
      Freedom
  RT **Freedom of assembly**
Freedom of choice
  USE **Free will and determinism**
Freedom of choice movement
  USE **Pro-choice movement**
Freedom of conscience 323.44
  UF Intolerance
      Liberty of conscience
  BT **Conscience**

Freedom of conscience—*Continued*
    Freedom
    Toleration
  NT **Conscientious objectors**
    Dissent
    Free thought
    Public opinion
  RT **Church and state**
    Freedom of religion
Freedom of information 323.44
  UF Information, Freedom of
    Right to know
  BT **Civil rights**
    Intellectual freedom
  NT **Press—Government policy**
  RT **Censorship**
    Freedom of speech
    Freedom of the press
Freedom of movement 323.4
  UF Movement, Freedom of
  BT **Civil rights**
    Freedom
Freedom of religion 261.7; 323.44
    Use for materials on the right to practice one's own religion without undue restraints.
  UF Freedom of worship
    Intolerance
    Religious freedom *[Former heading]*
    Religious liberty
  BT **Civil rights**
    Free thought
    Freedom
    Toleration
  NT **Dissent**
  RT **Church and state**
    Freedom of conscience
    Persecution
Freedom of speech 323.44
  UF Free speech *[Former heading]*
    Liberty of speech
    Speech, Freedom of
  BT **Censorship**
    Civil rights
    Freedom
    Intellectual freedom
  RT **Freedom of assembly**
    Freedom of information
    Libel and slander

Freedom of teaching
  USE **Academic freedom**
Freedom of the press 323.44
  UF Free press
    Liberty of the press
    Press censorship
  BT **Censorship**
    Civil rights
    Freedom
    Intellectual freedom
    Journalism
    Newspapers
    Periodicals
    Press
  NT **Books—Censorship**
    Freedom of the press and fair trial
  RT **Freedom of information**
    Libel and slander
Freedom of the press and fair trial 323.42; 323.44; 342
  UF Fair trial and free press
    Free press and fair trial
    Prejudicial publicity
    Trial by publicity
  BT **Fair trial**
    Freedom of the press
    Press
Freedom of the will
  USE **Free will and determinism**
Freedom of worship
  USE **Freedom of religion**
Freelancers
  USE **Self-employed**
Freemasons 366
  UF Masonic orders
    Masons (Secret order)
  BT **Secret societies**
Freeways
  USE **Express highways**
Freeze-dried foods 641.4; 664
  UF Food, Freeze dried *[Former heading]*
  BT **Dried foods**
Freezing
  USE **Cryobiology**
    Frost
    Ice
    Refrigeration
Freezing of human bodies
  USE **Cryonics**

BT = Broader Term   NT = Narrower Term   RT = Related Term   SA = See Also   UF = Used For

Freight 388

  UF   Freight and freightage *[Former heading]*

  BT   **Maritime law**
  Materials handling
  Railroads
  Transportation

  NT   **Commercial aeronautics**
  Trucking

  RT   **Railroads—Rates**

Freight and freightage
  USE   **Freight**

French and Indian War
  USE   **United States—History—1755-1763, French and Indian War**

French Canadian literature
  USE   **Canadian literature (French)**

French Canadian poetry
  USE   **Canadian poetry (French)**

French Canadians 305.811; 971
  BT   **Canadians**

French cookery
  USE   **French cooking**

French cooking 641.5944
  UF   Cookery, French *[Former heading]*
  Cooking, French
  French cookery

  BT   **Cooking**

French Equatorial Africa
  USE   **French-speaking Equatorial Africa**

French folk songs 782.4216200944
  UF   Folk songs—France
  Folk songs, French *[Former heading]*
  France—Folk songs

  BT   **Folk songs**

French foreign opinion—United States
  USE   **United States—Foreign opinion—France**

French language 440
  May be subdivided like **English language.**

  BT   **Romance languages**

French language—Conversations and phrases 448

French language—Dictionaries—English 443

  Use for French-English dictionaries. English-French dictionaries are entered under **English language—Dictionaries—French.** Combined French-English and English-French dictionaries are entered under both headings.

  UF   Foreign language dictionaries
  BT   **Encyclopedias and dictionaries**
  RT   **English language—Dictionaries—French**

French language—Reading materials 448.6

French literature 840

  May use same subdivisions and names of literary forms as for **English literature.**

  BT   **Literature**
  Romance literature
  NT   **French poetry**

French literature—Black authors 840.8; 840.9

  May be used for collections or materials about French literature by several Black authors, not for individual works.

  UF   Black literature (French)

French literature—Canada
  USE   **Canadian literature (French)**

French literature—West Indian authors
  USE   **West Indian literature (French)**

French poetry 841
  BT   **French literature**
  Poetry
  NT   **Troubadours**

French poetry—Black authors 841, etc.

  May be used for collections or materials about French poetry by several Black authors, not for individual works.

  UF   Black poetry (French)

French Revolution
  USE   **France—History—1789-1799, Revolution**

French-speaking Equatorial Africa 967

  Use for materials dealing collectively with the Central African Republic, Chad, Congo, and Gabon. The former name for the region was French Equatorial Africa.

  UF   Africa, French-speaking Equatorial *[Former heading]*
  French Equatorial Africa

  BT   **Central Africa**

BT = Broader Term   NT = Narrower Term   RT = Related Term   SA = See Also   UF = Used For

French-speaking West Africa 966

    Use for materials dealing collectively with Benin, Burkina Faso, Guinea, Ivory Coast, Mali, Mauritania, Niger, Senegal, and Togo.

  UF   Africa, French-speaking West
          [Former heading]
          French West Africa

  BT   **West Africa**

French West Africa
  USE **French-speaking West Africa**

Frequency modulation, Radio
  USE **Radio frequency modulation**

Fresco painting
  USE **Mural painting and decoration**

Freshwater animals 591.92

  UF   Animals, Aquatic
          Animals, Freshwater
          Aquatic animals
          Freshwater fauna
          Water animals

  SA   types of fresh water animals,
          e.g. **Beavers;** to be added as
          needed

  BT   **Animals**
          Freshwater biology
          Wildlife

  NT   **Beavers**

  RT   **Marine animals**

Freshwater aquaculture
  USE **Aquaculture**

Freshwater biology 574.92

  BT   **Biology**
          Natural history

  NT   **Aquariums**
          Freshwater animals
          Freshwater plants

  RT   **Marine biology**

Freshwater fauna
  USE **Freshwater animals**

Freshwater plants 581.92

  UF   Aquatic plants
          Water plants

  BT   **Freshwater biology**
          Plants

  RT   **Marine plants**

Friars Minor
  USE **Franciscans**

Friars Preachers
  USE **Dominicans (Religious order)**

Friends
  USE **Friendship**

Friends, Imaginary
  USE **Imaginary playmates**

Friends, Society of
  USE **Society of Friends**

Friendship 177

  UF   Affection
          Friends

  BT   **Human behavior**
          Social ethics

  NT   **Imaginary playmates**

  RT   **Love**

Friesian cattle
  USE **Holstein-Friesian cattle**

Fringe benefits
  USE **Nonwage payments**

Frogmen and frogwomen
  USE **Scuba diving**
          Skin diving

Frogs 597.8

  UF   Tadpoles

  BT   **Amphibians**

Frontier and pioneer life (May subdiv. geog. by state and region) **978**

  UF   Border life
          Pioneer life

  BT   **Adventure and adventurers**

  NT   **Cowhands**
          Indians of North America—Captivities
          Overland journeys to the Pacific
          Ranch life

Frontiers
  USE **Boundaries**
          and names of countries with the subdivision *Boundaries,* e.g. **United States—Boundaries;** to be added as needed

Frost 551.57

  UF   Freezing

  BT   **Meteorology**
          Water

  NT   **Ice**
          Refrigeration

Frozen animal embryos
  USE **Frozen embryos**

Frozen embryos 176; 574.3; 612.6

  UF   Animal embryos, Frozen

Frozen embryos—*Continued*

    Embryos, Frozen

    Frozen animal embryos

    Frozen human embryos

    Human embryos, Frozen

  BT **Cryobiology**

    Embryology

Frozen foods 641.4; 664

  UF Food, Frozen *[Former head-ing]*

  BT **Food—Preservation**

  NT **Ice cream, ices, etc.**

Frozen human embryos

  USE **Frozen embryos**

Frozen stars

  USE **Black holes (Astronomy)**

Fruit 634; 641.3

  Use the names of tree fruits, expressed in the singular form, for materials on the fruit or the tree or both.

  SA types of fruit, e.g. **Berries; Citrus fruit;** etc.; and names of fruits, e.g. **Apple;** to be added as needed, in the singular form for tree fruits

  BT **Botany**

    Food

  NT **Apple**

    Berries

    Citrus fruit

    Fruit culture

    Grapes

    Nuts

Fruit—Canning

  USE **Fruit—Preservation**

Fruit culture 634

  UF Arboriculture

    Orchards

  BT **Agriculture**

    Fruit

    Gardening

    Horticulture

    Trees

  NT **Berries**

    Grafting

    Nurseries (Horticulture)

    Plant propagation

    Pruning

Fruit—Diseases and pests 634

  BT **Agricultural bacteriology**

    Agricultural pests

    Insect pests

    Pests

    Plant diseases

  NT **Spraying and dusting**

Fruit flies 595.77

  BT **Flies**

Fruit—Preservation 641.4; 664

  UF Fruit—Canning

  BT **Canning and preserving**

    Food—Preservation

Frustration

  USE **Attitude (Psychology)**

    Emotions

Fuel 333.8; 662

  SA types of fuel; and subjects with the subdivision *Fuel consumption,* to be added as needed

  BT **Combustion**

    Energy resources

    Engines

    Fire

    Home economics

  NT **Alcohol as fuel**

    Automobiles—Fuel consump-tion

    Biomass energy

    Charcoal

    Coal

    Gas

    Gasoline

    Petroleum as fuel

    Synthetic fuels

    Wood

  RT **Heating**

Fuel cells 621.31

  BT **Electric batteries**

    Electrochemistry

Fuel consumption

  USE subjects with the subdivision *Fuel consumption,* e.g. **Automobiles—Fuel con-sumption;** to be added as needed

Fuel, Liquid

  USE **Petroleum as fuel**

Fuel oil

  USE **Petroleum as fuel**

BT = Broader Term   NT = Narrower Term   RT = Related Term   SA = See Also   UF = Used For

Fugue 784.18

Use for musical scores and for materials on the fugue as a musical form.

UF Canons, fugues, etc.
Fugues
Prelude and fugue
Preludes and fugues

BT **Counterpoint**
Musical form

Fugues
USE **Fugue**

Fulfillment, Self
USE **Self-realization**

Fumigation 614.4; 648

BT **Communicable diseases**
Insecticides

RT **Disinfection and disinfectants**

Functional competencies
USE **Life skills**

Functional literacy 302.2; 374

UF Occupational literacy

BT **Literacy**

Fund raising 361.7068; 658.15

UF Community chests
Money raising

RT **Gifts**

Fundamental education
USE **Basic education**

Fundamental life skills
USE **Life skills**

Fundamental rights
USE **Civil rights**
Human rights

Fundamental theology
USE **Apologetics**

Fundamentalism 273

Use for materials on the conservative interpretation of Christianity as opposed to Modernism.

UF Modernist-fundamentalist controversy

SA fundamentalism and other subjects, e.g. **Fundamentalism and education;** to be added as needed

BT **Theology**

NT **Fundamentalism and education**

RT **Modernism (Theology)**

Fundamentalism and education 377

UF Education and Fundamentalism

BT **Church and education**
Education
Fundamentalism

RT **Christian education**
Church schools
Creation—Study and teaching
Religion in the public schools

Fundamentalism and evolution
USE **Creationism**

Funding for the arts
USE **Art patronage**
Arts—Government policy
Federal aid to the arts

Funds
USE **Finance**

Funds, Scholarship
USE **Scholarships**

Funeral directors
USE **Undertakers and undertaking**

Funeral rites and ceremonies 393

UF Graves
Mortuary customs
Mourning customs

BT **Archeology**
Manners and customs
Rites and ceremonies

RT **Burial**
Cremation

Fungi 589.2

UF Diseases and pests
Mycology

BT **Agricultural pests**
Pests

NT **Molds (Fungi)**
Plant diseases

RT **Bacteria**
Mushrooms

Fungicides 632; 668

UF Germicides

BT **Pesticides**

RT **Spraying and dusting**

Funicular railroads
USE **Cable railroads**

Funnies
USE **Comic books, strips, etc.**

Fur 675; 685

BT **Animals—Anatomy**

RT **Hides and skins**

Fur-bearing animals
USE **Furbearing animals**

BT = Broader Term   NT = Narrower Term   RT = Related Term   SA = See Also   UF = Used For

Fur seals
  USE   Seals (Animals)
Fur trade 338.3
  BT   **Trapping**
Furbearing animals 591.6; 636.088; 639
  UF   Fur-bearing animals
  SA   types of furbearing animals,
      e.g. **Beavers;** to be added as
      needed
  BT   **Animals**
      Economic zoology
      Wildlife
  NT   **Beavers**
Furnaces 697
  BT   **Heating**
  NT   **Blast furnaces**
      Smelting
Furniture 645; 684.1; 749
  SA   furniture of particular coun-
      tries, e.g. **American furni-
      ture;** types of furniture, and
      names of specific articles of
      furniture, to be added as
      needed
  BT   **Art objects**
      Decoration and ornament
      Decorative arts
      Home economics
      Interior design
      Manufactures
      Woodwork
  NT   **American furniture**
      Built-in furniture
      Cabinetwork
      Chairs
      Church furniture
      Furniture finishing
      **Garden ornaments and furni-
      ture**
      **Libraries—Equipment and
      supplies**
      Mirrors
      **Schools—Equipment and sup-
      plies**
      Veneers and veneering
      Wood carving
  RT   **Upholstery**
Furniture, American
  USE   **American furniture**

Furniture, Built-in
  USE   **Built-in furniture**
Furniture, Colonial
  USE   **American furniture**
Furniture finishing 684.1; 749
  UF   Furniture—Refinishing
      Furniture—Restoration
      Refinishing furniture
  BT   **Furniture**
      Handicraft
      Wood finishing
Furniture—Refinishing
  USE   **Furniture finishing**
Furniture—Restoration
  USE   **Furniture finishing**
Future life 129; 236
      Use for materials on the character and
      form of a future existence. Materials on
      the question of the endless existence of
      the soul are entered under **Immortality.**
      Materials on the philosophical concept of
      eternity are entered under **Eternity.**
  UF   Afterlife
      Eternal life
      Intermediate state
      Life after death
      Life, Future
      Resurrection
      Retribution
  BT   **Death**
      Eschatology
  NT   **Heaven**
      Hell
      Soul
      Spiritualism
  RT   **Eternity**
      Immortality
Future shock
  USE   **Culture conflict**
Futurism (Art) 759.06
  BT   **Art**
      Painting
  NT   **Kinetic sculpture**
  RT   **Postimpressionism (Art)**
Futurology
  USE   **Forecasting**
Fuzzy logic
  USE   **Fuzzy systems**
Fuzzy systems 629.8
  UF   Fuzzy logic
      Systems, Fuzzy

BT = Broader Term   NT = Narrower Term   RT = Related Term   SA = See Also   UF = Used For

Fuzzy systems—*Continued*
    BT   **System analysis**

G.I.'s
    USE   **Soldiers—United States**
           Veterans—United States

G.R.E.
    USE   **Graduate Record Examination**

Gaels
    USE   **Celts**

Gaia concept
    USE   **Gaia hypothesis**

Gaia hypothesis 550.1; 574.01
    Use for materials on the theory formulated by James Lovelock that various terrestrial life forms can act as a unified organism regulating earth's temperature, atmospheric conditions, and other physical characteristics.
    UF   Gaia concept
           Gaia principle
           Gaia theory
           Living earth theory
    BT   **Biology**
           Earth
           Ecology
           Life (Biology)

Gaia principle
    USE   **Gaia hypothesis**

Gaia theory
    USE   **Gaia hypothesis**

Galaxies 523.1
    UF   Extragalactic nebulae
           Nebulae, Extragalactic
    BT   **Astronomy**
           Stars

Gales
    USE   **Winds**

Galleries, Art
    USE   **Art museums**

Gambling 175; 795
    UF   Betting
           Gaming
    SA   types of gambling, e.g. **Lotteries;** to be added as needed
    BT   **Crimes without victims**
           Vice
    NT   **Compulsive gambling**
           Lotteries
    RT   **Card games**
           Horse racing

Gambling, Compulsive
    USE   **Compulsive gambling**

Game and game birds 636.6
    UF   Wild fowl
    SA   names of animals and birds, e.g. **Deer; Pheasants;** etc., to be added as needed
    BT   **Animals**
           Birds
           Wildlife
    NT   **Deer**
           Falconry
           Game protection
           Pheasants
    RT   **Hunting**
           Trapping

Game preserves
    USE   **Game reserves**

Game protection 333.95; 636.9
    UF   Game wardens
           Protection of game
    BT   **Game and game birds**
           Hunting
           Wildlife conservation
    RT   **Birds—Protection**

Game reserves 333.95
    UF   Game preserves *[Former heading]*
    BT   **Hunting**
           Wildlife conservation

Game theory 519.3
    UF   Games, Theory of
           Theory of games
    BT   **Mathematical models**
           Mathematics
           Probabilities
    NT   **Decision making**
           Simulation games in education

Game wardens
    USE   **Game protection**

Games 790
    UF   Pastimes
    SA   types of games and names of individual games, to be added as needed
    BT   **Entertaining**
           Physical education
           Recreation
    NT   **Ball games**
           Card games

Games—*Continued*
>Checkers
>Chess
>Computer games
>Educational games
>Indians of North America—
>Games
>Indoor games
>Olympic games
>Singing games
>Video games
>Word games

RT Amusements
>Play
>Sports

Games, Electronic
>USE Electronic toys
>Video games

Games, Olympic
>USE Olympic games

Games, Theory of
>USE Game theory

Games, Video
>USE Video games

Gaming
>USE Gambling

Gaming, Educational
>USE Simulation games in education

Gamma rays 537.5; 539.7
>BT Electromagnetic waves
>Radiation
>X rays

Gangs (May subdiv. geog.) 302.3; 364.1
>UF Gangsters
>Street gangs
>Teenage gangs
>BT Criminals
>Juvenile delinquency
>Organized crime

Gangster films 791.43
>May be used for individual works, collections, or materials about gangster films.
>UF Crime films
>BT Motion pictures
>RT Mystery films

Gangsters
>USE Gangs

Garage sales 381
>UF Yard sales
>BT Secondhand trade

Garbage
>USE Refuse and refuse disposal

Garden design 712
>UF Gardens—Design *[Former heading]*
>BT Design
>Gardening
>RT Landscape gardening

Garden furniture
>USE Garden ornaments and furniture

Garden ornaments and furniture 717
>UF Garden furniture
>BT Decoration and ornament
>Furniture
>Gardens
>Landscape architecture
>NT Sundials

Garden pests
>USE Agricultural pests
>Insect pests
>Plant diseases

Garden rooms 643
>UF Conservatories, Home
>Home conservatories
>BT Houses
>Rooms
>RT Greenhouses

Gardening 635
>Use for materials on the practical aspects of creating gardens and cultivating flowers, fruits, vegetables, etc. Materials on the design or rearrangement of extensive gardens or estates are entered under **Landscape gardening.** Materials on the scientific and economic aspects of the cultivation of plants are entered under **Horticulture.** General materials about gardens, the history of gardens, various types of gardens, etc., are entered under **Gardens.**
>UF Planting
>BT Agriculture
>NT Climbing plants
>Container gardening
>Cultivated plants
>Flower gardening
>Fruit culture
>Garden design
>Gardening in the shade
>Gardens
>Grafting
>Greenhouses

BT = Broader Term   NT = Narrower Term   RT = Related Term   SA = See Also   UF = Used For

Gardening—*Continued*

       Grounds maintenance
       Indoor gardening
       Landscape gardening
       Nurseries (Horticulture)
       Organic gardening
       Plant propagation
       Pruning
       Vegetable gardening
       Weeds
       Window gardening
  RT **Horticulture**
       Plants

Gardening in space
  USE **Aeroponics**

Gardening in the shade 635
  UF Gardens, Shade
       Shade gardens
       Shady gardens
  BT **Gardening**

Gardening, Organic
  USE **Organic gardening**

Gardens (May subdiv. geog.) **635; 712**

    Use for general materials about gardens, the history of gardens, various types of gardens, etc. Materials on the design or re-arrangement of extensive gardens or estates are entered under **Landscape gardening**. Materials on the practical aspects of creating gardens and cultivating flowers, fruits, vegetables, etc., are entered under **Gardening**.

  UF Formal gardens
  BT **Gardening**
  NT **Botanical gardens**
       Garden ornaments and furniture
       Rock gardens

Gardens—Design
  USE **Garden design**

Gardens, Miniature
  USE **Miniature gardens**

Gardens, Shade
  USE **Gardening in the shade**

Garment industry
  USE **Clothing industry**

Garment making
  USE **Dressmaking**
       Tailoring

Garments
  USE **Clothing and dress**

Garments, Leather
  USE **Leather garments**

Gas 665.7
  UF Coal gas
       Illuminating gas
  BT **Fuel**
       Public utilities
  RT **Coal tar products**

Gas and oil engines
  USE **Internal combustion engines**

Gas companies
  USE **Public utilities**

Gas engines
  USE **Internal combustion engines**

Gas, Natural
  USE **Natural gas**

Gas stations
  USE **Service stations**

Gas turbines 621.43
  BT **Turbines**

Gas warfare
  USE **Chemical warfare**

Gases 530.4; 533
  SA names of gases, e.g. **Nitrogen;** to be added as needed
  BT **Fluid mechanics**
       Hydrostatics
       Physics
  NT **Nitrogen**
       Oxygen
       Poisonous gases
  RT **Pneumatics**

Gases, Asphyxiating and poisonous
  USE **Poisonous gases**

Gases, Poisonous
  USE **Poisonous gases**

Gasification of coal
  USE **Coal gasification**

Gasohol 662
  BT **Alcohol as fuel**

Gasoline 665.5
  BT **Fuel**
       Petroleum

Gasoline engines
  USE **Internal combustion engines**

Gastronomy
  USE **Cooking**
       Dining
       Food
       Menus

Gauchos
  USE **Cowhands**

BT = Broader Term   NT = Narrower Term   RT = Related Term   SA = See Also   UF = Used For

Gay liberation movement 305.9
    BT   Homosexuality
Gay lifestyle
    USE   Homosexuality
Gay men 305.38; 306.76
    UF   Gays, Male
           Homosexuals, Male
    BT   Men
    RT   Homosexuality
Gay men's writings 808.8; 810.8, etc.
    Use for collections of gay men's writings by more than one author and for materials about such writings.
    UF   Writings of gay men
    BT   Literature
Gay women
    USE   Lesbians
Gay women's writings
    USE   Lesbians' writings
Gays, Female
    USE   Lesbians
Gays, Male
    USE   Gay men
Gazetteers 910.3
    SA   names of countries, states, etc., with the subdivision *Gazetteers,* e.g. **United States—Gazetteers;** to be added as needed
    NT   United States—Gazetteers
    RT   Geographic names
Gearing 621.8
    UF   Bevel gearing
           Cog wheels
           Gears
           Spiral gearing
    BT   Machinery
           Power transmission
           Wheels
    NT   Automobiles—Transmission devices
    RT   Mechanical movements
Gears
    USE   Gearing
Geese 598.4; 636.5
    UF   Goose
    BT   Poultry
           Water birds
Gemini project 629.45
    UF   Project Gemini
    BT   Orbital rendezvous (Space flight)

           Space flight
Gems 736
    Use for materials on cut and polished precious stones treated from the point of view of art or antiquity. Materials on gem stones treated from a mineralogical or technological point of view are entered under **Precious stones.** Materials on gems in which the emphasis is on the setting are entered under **Jewelry.**
    UF   Jewels
    BT   Archeology
           Art
           Decoration and ornament
           Engraving
           Mineralogy
    RT   Jewelry
           Precious stones
Gemstones
    USE   Precious stones
Gender identity
    USE   Sex role
Gene mapping
    USE   Genetic mapping
Gene splicing
    USE   Genetic engineering
           Recombinant DNA
Gene therapy 616
    Use for materials on therapeutic efforts involving the replacement or supplementation of genes in order to cure diseases caused by genetic defects.
    UF   Therapy, Gene
    BT   Genetic engineering
           Therapeutics
Gene transfer
    USE   Genetic engineering
Genealogy 929
    UF   Ancestry
           Descent
           Family histories
           Family trees
           Pedigrees
    SA   names of families, e.g. **Lincoln family;** to be added as needed
    BT   History
    NT   Lincoln family
           Registers of births, etc.
           Wills
    RT   Biography
           Heraldry
Generals 355.0092; 920
    BT   Military personnel

BT = Broader Term   NT = Narrower Term   RT = Related Term   SA = See Also   UF = Used For

Generation
    USE   **Reproduction**
Generation gap
    USE   **Conflict of generations**
Generative organs
    USE   **Reproductive system**
Generators, Electric
    USE   **Electric generators**
Generic drugs 615
    UF   Drugs—Generic substitution
                [Former heading]
    BT   **Drugs**
            Generic products
Generic products 658.8
    UF   Products, Generic
    BT   **Commercial products**
            Manufactures
    NT   **Generic drugs**
Genes
    USE   **Heredity**
Genetic aspects
    USE   names of diseases with the
                subdivision *Genetic aspects,*
                e.g. **Cancer—Genetic as-**
                pects; to be added as need-
                ed
Genetic code 574.87
    BT   **Molecular biology**
Genetic counseling 616; 618
    BT   **Medical genetics**
            Prenatal diagnosis
Genetic engineering 660
    UF   Designed genetic change
            Engineering, Genetic
            Gene splicing
            Gene transfer
            Genetic intervention
            Genetic surgery
            Splicing of genes
            Transgenics
    BT   **Engineering**
            Genetic recombination
    NT   **Clones and cloning**
            Fertilization in vitro
            Gene therapy
            Molecular cloning
            Recombinant DNA
    RT   **Biotechnology**

Genetic engineering—Government policy
        351.85
Genetic engineering—Social aspects
        306.4
Genetic fingerprints
    USE   **DNA fingerprints**
Genetic intervention
    USE   **Genetic engineering**
Genetic mapping 575.1
    UF   Chromosome mapping
            Gene mapping
            Genome mapping
    BT   **Genetics**
            Heredity
Genetic profiling
    USE   **DNA fingerprints**
Genetic recombination 574.87
    UF   Recombination, Genetic
    BT   **Chromosomes**
    NT   **Genetic engineering**
            Genetic transformation
            Recombinant DNA
Genetic surgery
    USE   **Genetic engineering**
Genetic transformation 574.87
    UF   Transformation (Genetics)
    BT   **Genetic recombination**
Genetics 573.2; 575.1
    BT   **Biology**
            Embryology
            Life (Biology)
            Mendel's law
            Reproduction
    NT   **Adaptation (Biology)**
            Behavior genetics
            Chromosomes
            DNA fingerprints
            Eugenics
            Evolution
            Genetic mapping
            Medical genetics
            Natural selection
            Variation (Biology)
    RT   **Breeding**
            Heredity
Genitalia
    USE   **Reproductive system**
Genius 153.9
    UF   Talent
    BT   **Psychology**

BT = Broader Term   NT = Narrower Term   RT = Related Term   SA = See Also   UF = Used For

Genius—*Continued*
NT   Creation (Literary, artistic,
          etc.)
      Gifted children
Genome mapping
USE   Genetic mapping
Gentiles and Jews
USE   Jews and Gentiles
Geochemistry 551.9
UF   Chemical geology
      Earth—Chemical composition
      Geological chemistry
BT   Chemistry
      Earth sciences
      Petrology
      Rocks
NT   Geothermal resources
Geodesy 526
UF   Degrees of latitude and longi-
          tude
BT   Earth
      Measurement
NT   Latitude
      Longitude
RT   Surveying
Geographic names (May subdiv. geog.)
      910
UF   Names, Geographical *[Former
          heading]*
      Place names
BT   Names
RT   Gazetteers
Geographic names—United States 917.3
UF   Names, Geographical—United
          States *[Former heading]*
      United States—Geographic
          names
      United States—Names, Geo-
          graphic
Geographical atlases
USE   Atlases
Geographical distribution of animals
          and plants
USE   Biogeography
Geographical distribution of people
USE   Anthropogeography
      Ethnology
Geographical distribution of plants
USE   Plants—Geographical distribu-
          tion

Geographical myths 398.23
UF   Cities, Imaginary
      Fictitious places
      Imaginary places
      Islands, Imaginary
      Places, Imaginary
BT   Mythology
Geography 910
      Use for general materials, frequently
school materials, that describe the surface
of the earth and its interrelationship with
various peoples, animals, natural products,
and industries. Materials limited to a particular place are entered under the name
of the place with the subdivision *Geography.* General descriptive materials and
travel materials limited to a particular
place are entered under the name of the
place (except extinct cities) with the subdivision *Description.* Materials on the physical features of the earth's surface and its
atmosphere are entered under **Physical geography.**
UF   Social studies
SA   names of countries, states,
          etc., with the subdivisions
          Description and *Geography;*
          and sacred works with the
          subdivision *Geography,* e.g.
          Bible—Geography; to be
          added as needed
BT   Earth
      Earth sciences
      World history
NT   Anthropogeography
      Atlases
      Bible—Geography
      Biogeography
      Boundaries
      Commercial geography
      Exploration
      Historical geography
      Maps
      Physical geography
      Surveying
      United States—Description
      United States—Geography
      Voyages and travels
Geography, Ancient
USE   Ancient geography
Geography, Biblical
USE   Bible—Geography
Geography, Commercial
USE   Commercial geography

Geography—Dictionaries 910.3

    Use for dictionaries of geographic terms. Materials listing names and descriptions of places are entered under **Gazetteers.**

    BT   **Encyclopedias and dictionaries**

Geography, Economic
    USE   **Commercial geography**

Geography, Historical
    USE   **Historical geography**

Geography, Military
    USE   **Military geography**

Geography, Physical
    USE   **Physical geography**

Geography—Pictorial works
    USE   **Views**

Geography, Political
    USE   **Boundaries**
          Geopolitics

Geography, Social
    USE   **Anthropogeography**

Geological chemistry
    USE   **Geochemistry**

Geological physics
    USE   **Geophysics**

Geologists 551.092; 920
    BT   **Scientists**

Geology (May subdiv. geog.) **550**

    Use for materials limited to the structure and composition of the earth and the physical changes it has undergone and is still undergoing. General materials on the whole planet are entered under **Earth.**

    UF   Geoscience
    BT   **Earth sciences**
          Natural history
          Science
    NT   **Astrogeology**
          Continental drift
          Continental shelf
          Coral reefs and islands
          Earthquakes
          Economic geology
          Geysers
          Glaciers
          Mineralogy
          Mountains
          Oceanography
          Ore deposits
          Physical geography
          Stratigraphic geology
          Submarine geology

          Volcanoes
    RT   **Earth**
          Petrology
          Rocks

Geology, Dynamic
    USE   **Geophysics**

Geology, Economic
    USE   **Economic geology**

Geology, Historical
    USE   **Stratigraphic geology**

Geology, Lunar
    USE   **Lunar geology**

Geology—Maps 550.22
    BT   **Maps**

Geology—Moon
    USE   **Lunar geology**

Geology, Petroleum
    USE   **Petroleum geology**

Geology, Stratigraphic
    USE   **Stratigraphic geology**

Geology, Submarine
    USE   **Submarine geology**

Geology—United States 557.3
    UF   United States—Geology

Geometric art
    USE   **Abstract art**

Geometric patterns
    USE   **Patterns (Mathematics)**

Geometrical drawing 516; 604.2
    UF   Mathematical drawing
          Plans
    BT   **Drawing**
          Geometry
    NT   **Descriptive geometry**
          Graphic methods
          Perspective
    RT   **Mechanical drawing**

Geometry 516
    UF   Geometry, Plane
          Geometry, Solid
          Plane geometry
          Solid geometry
    BT   **Mathematics**
    NT   **Analytic geometry**
          Descriptive geometry
          Fractals
          Geometrical drawing
          Projective geometry
          Ratio and proportion
          Square

BT = Broader Term   NT = Narrower Term   RT = Related Term   SA = See Also   UF = Used For

Geometry—*Continued*
    Topology
    Trigonometry
    Volume (Cubic content)
Geometry, Analytic
  USE **Analytic geometry**
Geometry, Descriptive
  USE **Descriptive geometry**
Geometry, Plane
  USE **Geometry**
Geometry, Projective
  USE **Projective geometry**
Geometry, Solid
  USE **Geometry**
Geophysics 550
  UF Geological physics
    Geology, Dynamic
    Physics, Terrestrial
    Terrestrial physics
  BT **Earth sciences**
    Physics
  NT **Auroras**
    Oceanography
    Plate tectonics
Geopolitics 320.1; 327.101
  UF Geography, Political
    Political geography
  BT **International relations**
    Political science
  RT **Anthropogeography**
    Boundaries
    World politics
Geoscience
  USE **Earth sciences**
    Geology
Geothermal resources 333.8
  UF Natural steam energy
    Thermal waters
  SA types of geothermal resources,
    e.g. **Geysers;** to be added as
    needed
  BT **Geochemistry**
    Ocean energy resources
    Renewable energy resources
  NT **Geysers**
Geriatrics
  USE **Elderly—Diseases**
    Elderly—Health and hygiene
Germ theory
  USE **Life—Origin**

Germ theory of disease 616
  UF Bacilli
    Disease germs
    Germs
    Microbes
  BT **Communicable diseases**
  RT **Bacteriology**
Germ warfare
  USE **Biological warfare**
German Democratic Republic
  USE **Germany (East)**
German Federal Republic
  USE **Germany (West)**
German Hebrew
  USE **Yiddish language**
German language 430
    May be subdivided like **English lan-
guage.**
  BT **Language and languages**
    Modern languages
German literature 830
    May use same subdivisions and names
of literary forms as for **English literature.**
  BT **Literature**
German occupation of France, 1940-
        1945
  USE **France—History—1940-1945,
    German occupation**
German occupation of Netherlands,
        1940-1945
  USE **Netherlands—History—
    1940-1945, German occupa-
    tion**
Germany 943
    Use for materials on Germany before or
after the division of the country following
World War II and for materials on East
and West Germany discussed collectively
as occupied zones or countries. Materials
limited to the eastern part of Germany
from 1945 to 1990, the Russian occupa-
tion zone, or the German Democratic Republic, are entered under **Germany (East).**
Materials limited to the western part of
Germany from 1945 to 1990, the American, British, and French occupation zones,
or the German Federal Republic, are entered under **Germany (West).** May be
subdivided like United States except for
History.
  UF Federal Republic of Germany
  NT **Germany (East)**
    Germany (West)
Germany (Democratic Republic)
  USE **Germany (East)**

Germany (East) 943.1087

Use for materials limited to the eastern part of Germany from 1945 to 1990, the Russian occupation zone, or the German Democratic Republic. Materials on Germany before or after the division of the country following World War II and materials on East and West Germany discussed collectively as occupied zones or countries are entered under **Germany.**

UF   East Germany
       German Democratic Republic
       Germany (Democratic Republic)

BT **Germany**

Germany (Federal Republic)
USE **Germany (West)**

Germany—History 943

Germany—History—0-1517 943
NT **Holy Roman Empire**

Germany—History—1517-1740 943
NT **Holy Roman Empire**
      Thirty Years' War, 1618-1648

Germany—History—1740-1815 943
NT **Holy Roman Empire**
      Seven Years' War, 1756-1763

Germany—History—1815-1866 943

Germany—History—1848-1849, Revolution 943

Germany—History—1866-1918 943.08

Germany—History—1918-1933 943.085

Germany—History—1933-1945 943.086

Germany—History—1945-1990 943.087

Germany—History—1990- 943.087
UF Germany—History—Unification, 1990

Germany—History—Unification, 1990
USE **Germany—History—1990-**

Germany (West) 943.087

Use for materials limited to the western part of Germany from 1945 to 1990, the American, British, and French occupation zones, or the German Federal Republic. Materials on Germany before or after the division of the country following World War II and materials on East and West Germany discussed collectively as occupied zones or countries are entered under **Germany.**

UF   Federal Republic of Germany
       German Federal Republic
       Germany (Federal Republic)
       West Germany

BT **Germany**

Germicides
USE **Disinfection and disinfectants**
       Fungicides

Germination 581.1
UF Seeds—Germination
BT **Plant physiology**

Germs
USE **Bacteria**
       Germ theory of disease
       Microorganisms

Gerontology 305.26; 362.6; 612.6
BT **Social sciences**
NT **Aging**
      Elderly
      Old age

Gestalt psychology 150.19
UF Configuration (Psychology)
      Psychology, Structural
      Structural psychology
BT **Consciousness**
      Perception
      Psychology
      Senses and sensation
      Theory of knowledge

Getting ready for bed
USE **Bedtime**

Gettysburg (Pa.), Battle of, 1863 973.7
BT **United States—History—1861-1865, Civil War—Campaigns**

Geysers 551.2
UF Eruptions
      Thermal waters
BT **Geology**
      Geothermal resources
      Physical geography
      Water

Ghettoes, Inner city
USE **Inner cities**

Ghost stories 808.83; 813, etc.

May be used for individual works, collections, or materials about ghost stories.

UF Ghosts—Fiction *[Former heading]*
      Terror tales
BT **Fantasy fiction**
      Horror fiction
      Occult fiction
RT **Gothic novels**
      Mystery fiction

BT = Broader Term   NT = Narrower Term   RT = Related Term   SA = See Also   UF = Used For

Ghost towns
- UF   Abandoned towns
- BT   **Extinct cities**

Ghosts 133.1
- UF   Haunted houses
  - Phantoms
  - Poltergeists
  - Specters
  - Spirits
- BT   **Folklore**
- NT   **Demonology**
- RT   **Apparitions**
  - **Hallucinations and illusions**
  - **Parapsychology**
  - **Spiritualism**
  - **Superstition**

Ghosts—Fiction
- USE   **Ghost stories**

Giantism 612.6

Use for materials on excessive growth in humans. Materials on beings with a human form but with superhuman size or strength in folklore or imaginative literature are entered under **Giants.**
- UF   Gigantism
- BT   **Growth disorders**

Giants 398.21

Use for materials on beings with a human form but with superhuman size or strength in folklore or imaginative literature. Materials on excessive growth in humans are entered under **Giantism.**
- BT   **Folklore**
  - **Monsters**

Gift wrapping 745.54
- UF   Wrapping of gifts
- BT   **Packaging**
  - **Paper crafts**

Gifted children 155.45
- UF   Bright children
  - Children, Gifted
  - Precocious children
  - Superior children
  - Talent
- BT   **Exceptional children**
  - **Genius**
- NT   **Child artists**
  - **Child authors**

Gifts
- UF   Bequests
  - Donations
  - Philanthropy
  - Presents
- BT   **Manners and customs**
- NT   **Donation of organs, tissues, etc.**
  - **Free material**
- RT   **Fund raising**

Gigantism
- USE   **Giantism**

Gipsies
- USE   **Gypsies**

Girl Scouts (May subdiv. geog.)
   369.463
- UF   Brownies (Girl Scouts)
- BT   **Girls' clubs**
  - **Scouts and scouting**

Girls 155.43; 305.23
- BT   **Children**
- NT   **Fathers and daughters**
  - **Mothers and daughters**
- RT   **Teenagers**
  - **Young women**

Girls' agricultural clubs
- USE   **4-H clubs**
  - **Agriculture—Societies**
  - **Girls' clubs**

Girls' clubs 369.46
- UF   Girls' agricultural clubs
  - Girls—Societies and clubs
- BT   **Clubs**
  - **Social settlements**
  - **Societies**
  - **Women—Societies**
- NT   **4-H clubs**
  - **Camp Fire Girls**
  - **Girl Scouts**

Girls—Education 370.82; 376

Girls—Employment
- USE   **Children—Employment**
  - **Women—Employment**

Girls—Societies and clubs
- USE   **Girls' clubs**

Girls, Teenage
- USE   **Teenagers**

GIs
- USE   **Soldiers—United States**
  - **Veterans—United States**

Giveaways
- USE   **Free material**

Glacial epoch
- USE   **Ice age**

BT = Broader Term   NT = Narrower Term   RT = Related Term   SA = See Also   UF = Used For

Glaciers 551.3
BT Geology
Ice
Physical geography
Gladiators 796.8092; 920
UF Fighting
Gladness
USE Happiness
Glands 591.1; 611; 612.4
BT Anatomy
Physiology
Glands, Ductless
USE Endocrine glands
Glass 666
BT Ceramics
NT Glass fibers
RT Windows
Glass construction 693
BT Building materials
Glass fibers 666
UF Fiber glass
Fiberglass
Fibers, Glass
Glass, Spun
Spun glass
BT Fibers
Glass
Glass industry
USE Glass manufacture
Glass manufacture 666
UF Glass industry
BT Ceramic industries
Glass painting and staining 748.5
UF Glass, Stained
Painted glass
Stained glass
Windows, Stained glass
BT Decoration and ornament
Painting
Glass, Spun
USE Glass fibers
Glass, Stained
USE Glass painting and staining
Glassware 642; 748.2
UF Dishes
BT Decorative arts
Tableware
RT Vases
Glazes 666; 738.1
BT Ceramics

Pottery
Gliders (Aeronautics) 629.133
UF Aircraft
Sailplanes (Aeronautics)
BT Aeronautics
Airplanes
Gliding and soaring 797.5
UF Air surfing
Hang gliding
Soaring flight
BT Aeronautics
Global satellite communications sys-
tems
USE Artificial satellites in telecom-
munication
Global warming
USE Greenhouse effect
Globes 912
BT Maps
Glossaries
USE Encyclopedias and dictionaries
and names of languages or
subjects with the subdivi-
sion *Dictionaries,* e.g. Eng-
lish language—Dictionaries;
Chemistry—Dictionaries;
etc., to be added as needed
Glue 668
BT Adhesives
Glue sniffing
USE Solvent abuse
Gnomes
USE Fairies
Gnosticism 273; 299
BT Church history—30-600, Early
church
Philosophy
Religions
Go karts
USE Karts and karting
Goblins
USE Fairies
God 211; 212; 231
May subdivide by religion as needed,
e.g. God—Christianity.
NT Femininity of God
Natural theology
Rationalism
RT Creation
Deism

God—*Continued*
>> Metaphysics
>> Religion
>> Theism
>> Theology
God—Christianity 231
> NT Holy Spirit
>> Jesus Christ
>> Providence and government of God
> RT Christianity
>> Theology
>> Trinity
God—Femininity
> USE Femininity of God
Goddesses
> USE Gods and goddesses
Gods
> USE Gods and goddesses
Gods and goddesses 291; 292
> UF Deities
>> Goddesses
>> Gods
> SA names of gods and goddesses, to be added as needed
> BT Classical mythology
> RT Mythology
>> Religions
Gold 332.4; 553.4; 669
> UF Bimetallism
>> Bullion
> BT Chemical elements
>> Precious metals
> NT Gold mines and mining
>> Goldwork
> RT Coinage
>> Money
Gold articles
> USE Goldwork
Gold fish
> USE Goldfish
Gold mines and mining 622
> BT Gold
>> Mines and mineral resources
> NT Prospecting
Gold plate
> USE Plate
Gold rush
> USE California—Gold discoveries
Gold work
> USE Goldwork

Golden Gate Bridge (San Francisco, Calif.) 624; 979.4
> BT Bridges
Goldfish 597; 639.3
> UF Gold fish
> BT Aquariums
Goldsmithing
> USE Goldwork
Goldwork 739.2
> UF Gold articles
>> Gold work
>> Goldsmithing
> BT Art metalwork
>> Gold
>> Metalwork
> NT Plate
> RT Jewelry
Golf courses 796.352
> BT Grounds maintenance
Good and evil 170; 216; 241
> UF Evil
>> Wickedness
> BT Ethics
>> Philosophy
>> Theology
> NT Sin
Good Friday 263
> BT Christian holidays
>> Holy Week
>> Lent
> RT Jesus Christ—Crucifixion
Good grooming
> USE Personal grooming
Good Neighbor Policy
> USE Pan-Americanism
Goods, Consumer
> USE Consumer goods
Goose
> USE Geese
Gorge-purge syndrome
> USE Bulimia
Gospel music 781.71; 782.25
> UF Music, Gospel
>> Revivals—Music
> BT African American music
>> Church music
>> Popular music
> RT Spirituals (Songs)
Gossip 070.4; 177; 302.2
> BT Journalism

BT = Broader Term   NT = Narrower Term   RT = Related Term   SA = See Also   UF = Used For

Gossip—*Continued*
        Libel and slander
Gothic architecture 723
    UF   Architecture, Gothic *[Former heading]*
    BT   **Architecture**
    RT   **Cathedrals**
         Christian antiquities
         Church architecture
         Gothic art
Gothic art 709.02
    UF   Art, Gothic
    BT   **Medieval art**
    RT   **Christian art and symbolism**
         Gothic architecture
Gothic fiction
    USE **Gothic novels**
Gothic novels 813, etc.
    May be used for individual works, collections, or materials about novels that have a medieval setting and usually include castles and ghosts.
    UF   Gothic fiction *[Former heading]*
    BT   **Historical fiction**
         Horror fiction
         Occult fiction
    RT   **Ghost stories**
         Love stories
         Romantic suspense novels
Goths
    USE **Teutonic peoples**
Gout 616.3
    BT   **Arthritis**
         Rheumatism
Government
    USE **Political science**
         and names of countries, cities, etc., with the subdivision *Politics and government,* e.g. **United States—Politics and government;** to be added as needed
Government and business
    USE **Industry—Government policy**
Government and church
    USE **Church and state**
Government and the press
    USE **Press—Government policy**
Government buildings
    USE **Public buildings**

Government by commission
    USE **Municipal government by commission**
Government, Comparative
    USE **Comparative government**
Government debts
    USE **Public debts**
Government documents
    USE **Government publications**
Government employees
    USE **Civil service**
         and names of countries, cities, etc., and corporate bodies with the subdivision *Officials and employees,* e.g. **United States—Officials and employees; Chicago (Ill.)—Officials and employees; United Nations—Officials and employees;** etc., to be added as needed
Government health insurance
    USE **National health insurance**
Government housing
    USE **Public housing**
Government investigations
    USE **Governmental investigations**
Government lending (May subdiv. geog.) **332.7; 351.82**
    BT   **Domestic economic assistance**
         Economic policy
         Finance
         Industry—Government policy
         Loans
Government libraries 027.5
    Use for materials on special libraries maintained by government funds.
    UF   Federal libraries
         Libraries, Governmental
    BT   **Special libraries**
    NT   **National libraries**
         State libraries
Government, Local
    USE **Local government**
Government, Mandatory
    USE **Mandates**
Government, Military
    USE **Military government**
Government, Municipal
    USE **Municipal government**

BT = Broader Term   NT = Narrower Term   RT = Related Term   SA = See Also   UF = Used For

Government ownership 333.1; 338.9
    UF   Nationalization
          Public ownership
          Socialization of industry
          State ownership
    BT   **Corporations**
          Economic policy
          Economics
          Industry—Government policy
          Political science
          Socialism
    NT   **Municipal ownership**
          Railroads—Government policy
    RT   **Privatization**

Government ownership of railroads
    USE **Railroads—Government policy**

Government policy
    USE subjects with the subdivision
          Government policy, e.g.
          Homeless persons—
          Government policy;
          Industry—Government poli-
          cy; etc., to be added as
          needed

Government procurement
    USE **Government purchasing**

Government property, Surplus
    USE **Surplus government property**

Government publications (May subdiv.
    geog.) **011; 015; 025.17**
    UF   Documents
          Government documents
          Official publications
          Public documents
    BT   **Library resources**
    NT   **Government publications—**
          United States

Government publications—Chicago (Ill.)
    015.773
    UF   Chicago (Ill.)—Government
          publications *[Former head-*
          ing]

Government publications—Ohio 015.771
    UF   Ohio—Government publica-
          tions *[Former heading]*

Government publications—United States
    015.73; 025.17
    UF   United States—Government
          publications *[Former head-*
          ing]

          United States—Public docu-
          ments
    BT   **Government publications**

Government purchasing (May subdiv.
    geog.) **351.71; 352.1**
    UF   Government procurement
          Procurement, Government
          Public procurement
          Purchasing, Government
    BT   **Buying**
    NT   **Buy national policy**

Government records—Preservation
    USE **Archives**

Government regulation of commerce
    USE **Commercial policy**
          Interstate commerce
          Tariff

Government regulation of industry
    USE **Industry—Government policy**

Government regulation of railroads
    USE **Railroads—Government policy**

Government reorganization
    USE **United States—Executive**
          departments—
          Reorganization

Government, Resistance to
    USE **Resistance to government**

Government service
    USE **Civil service**

Government spending policy
    USE **United States—Appropriations**
          and expenditures

Governmental investigations (May sub-
    div. geog.) **328.3; 351.9**
    Use for materials on investigations initi-
    ated by the legislative, executive, and judi-
    cial branches of the government.
    UF   Congressional investigations
          Executive investigations
          Government investigations
          Investigations, Governmental
          Judicial investigations
          Legislative investigations
    BT   **Administration of justice**

Governmental investigations—United
    States 328.3; 353.009
    UF   United States—Governmental
          investigations

Governments in exile
    USE **World War, 1939-1945—**
          Governments in exile

BT = Broader Term   NT = Narrower Term   RT = Related Term   SA = See Also   UF = Used For

Governors (May subdiv. geog.) **351.003; 920**
    BT   **State governments**
Graal
    USE **Grail**
Grace (Theology) 234
    BT   **Salvation**
           Theology
Grade repetition
    USE **Promotion (School)**
Grade retention
    USE **Promotion (School)**
Grading and marking (Education) 371.2
    UF   Grading and marking (Students) *[Former heading]*
          Marking (Students)
          Students—Grading and marking
    BT   **Educational tests and measurements**
    NT   **Ability grouping in education**
          Promotion (School)
    RT   **School reports**
Grading and marking (Students)
    USE **Grading and marking (Education)**
Graduate record examination
    USE **Graduate Record Examination**
Graduate Record Examination 378.1
    UF   G.R.E.
          Graduate record examination *[Former heading]*
          GRE
    BT   **Colleges and universities—Entrance examinations**
          Examinations
Graduates, College
    USE **College graduates**
Graduation
    USE **Commencements**
Graffiti 080; 808.88
    BT   **Folklore**
          Inscriptions
Graft in politics
    USE **Political corruption**
Grafting 631.5
    BT   **Botany**
          Fruit culture
          Gardening
          Plant propagation

          Trees
Grail 398.22
    UF   Graal
          Holy Grail
    BT   **Folklore**
          Legends
    RT   **Arthurian romances**
Grain 633.1
    UF   Breadstuffs
          Cereals
    SA   names of cereal plants, e.g. **Corn; Wheat;** etc., to be added as needed
    BT   **Economic botany**
          Flour
          Food
    NT   **Corn**
          Wheat
Grammar 415
    SA   names of languages with the subdivision *Grammar,* to be added as needed
    NT   **English language—Grammar**
    RT   **Language and languages**
          Linguistics
Grammar schools
    USE **Elementary education**
          Public schools
Grammatical comparison
    USE **English language—Comparison**
Gramophone
    USE **Phonograph**
Grandchild and grandparent
    USE **Grandparent and child**
Grandparent and child 306.874
    Use for materials on the interaction between grandparents and their grandchildren. Materials restricted to the legal right of grandparents to visit their grandchildren are entered under **Visitation rights (Domestic relations)**.
    UF   Child and grandparent
          Children and grandparents
          Grandchild and grandparent
          Grandparent and grandchild
          Grandparenting
    BT   **Children and adults**
          Domestic relations
          Family
          Human relations

Grandparent and grandchild
USE **Grandparent and child**
Grandparenting
USE **Grandparent and child**
Grange 334
BT **Agriculture—Societies**
Granite 552; 553.5
BT **Petrology**
Rocks
Grants
USE **Subsidies**
Grants-in-aid 336.1; 351.72
Use for materials on grants of money made from a central government to a local government.
UF Block grants
Federal grants
SA federal aid to particular endeavors, e.g. **Federal aid to education;** to be added as needed
NT **Federal aid to education**
Federal aid to libraries
Federal aid to minority business enterprises
Federal aid to the arts
RT **Domestic economic assistance**
Grapes 634.8; 641.3
BT **Fruit**
RT **Vineyards**
Wine and wine making
Graph theory 511
UF Graphs, Theory of
Theory of graphs
BT **Algebra**
Mathematical analysis
Topology
Graphic arts (May subdiv. geog.) **760**
UF Art, Graphic
Arts, Graphic
SA types of graphic arts, to be added as needed
BT **Art**
NT **Drawing**
Engraving
Painting
Printing
Prints
Graphic arts, American
USE **Graphic arts—United States**

Graphic arts—United States 760.0973
UF American graphic arts
Graphic arts, American [Former heading]
United States—Graphic arts
Graphic methods 001.4; 511
UF Flow charts
Flowcharting
Graphs
BT **Drawing**
Geometrical drawing
Mechanical drawing
NT **Statistics—Graphic methods**
Graphics, Computer
USE **Computer graphics**
Graphite 553.2
UF Black lead
BT **Carbon**
Graphology 137; 155.2
Use for materials on handwriting as an expression of the writer's character. General materials on the history and art of writing and on elegant handwriting are entered under **Writing.** Practical guides are entered under **Handwriting.**
BT **Handwriting**
Writing
Graphs
USE **Graphic methods**
Graphs, Theory of
USE **Graph theory**
Grass (Drug)
USE **Marijuana**
Grasses 584; 633.2
UF Herbage
BT **Economic botany**
Lawns
NT **Grasslands**
RT **Feeds**
Forage plants
Hay
Pastures
Grasslands (May subdiv. geog.) **581.5**
BT **Grasses**
Graves
USE **Burial**
Cemeteries
Epitaphs
Funeral rites and ceremonies
Mounds and mound builders
Tombs

BT = Broader Term   NT = Narrower Term   RT = Related Term   SA = See Also   UF = Used For

Graveyard of the Atlantic
    USE **Bermuda Triangle**
Graveyards
    USE **Cemeteries**
Gravitation 521; 531
    UF Gravity
    BT **Physics**
    RT **Relativity (Physics)**
Gravity
    USE **Gravitation**
Gravity free state
    USE **Weightlessness**
Gray Friars
    USE **Franciscans**
GRE
    USE **Graduate Record Examination**
Grease
    USE **Lubrication and lubricants**
         Oils and fats
Great books program
    USE **Discussion groups**
Great Britain 941

    May be subdivided like United States
    except for *History*. For a list of subjects
    that may be used under either England or
    Great Britain, see **England.**

    NT **England**
Great Britain—Antiquities 936
    BT **Classical antiquities**
Great Britain—Colonies 325
    UF British Empire
    BT **Colonies**
         Imperialism
    RT **Commonwealth countries**
Great Britain—History 941
    UF England—History
         English history
Great Britain—History—0-1066 941.01
    NT **Anglo-Saxons**
         Celts
**Great Britain—History—1066-1154,
         Norman period 941.02**
    NT **Domesday book**
         **Hastings (East Sussex, Eng-
         land), Battle of, 1066**
         Normans
**Great Britain—History—1154-1399,
         Plantagenets 941.03**
    NT **Magna Carta**

**Great Britain—History—1399-1485,
         Lancaster and York 941.04**
    NT **Hundred Years' War, 1339-
         1453**
**Great Britain—History—1455-1485,
         War of the Roses 941.04**
    UF Wars of the Roses, 1455-1485
**Great Britain—History—1485-1603, Tu-
         dors 941.05**
    NT **Spanish Armada, 1588**
**Great Britain—History—1603-1714,
         Stuarts 941.06**
**Great Britain—History—1642-1660,
         Civil War and Common-
         wealth 941.06**
    UF Civil War—England
         Commonwealth of England
**Great Britain—History—1714-1837
         941.07**
**Great Britain—History—1800-1899
         (19th century) 941.081**
    RT **Industrial revolution**
Great Britain—History—1853-1856,
         Crimean War
    USE **Crimean War, 1853-1856**
**Great Britain—History—1900-1999
         (20th century) 941.082**
**Great Britain—History—1945-1952
         941.085**
Great Britain—History—1952- 941.085
**Great Britain—Kings, queens, rulers,
         etc. 920; 941.092**
    BT **Kings, queens, rulers, etc.**
Great Britain—Prime ministers
    USE **Prime ministers—Great Brit-
         ain**
Greece 938; 949.5

    May be subdivided like United States
    except for *History*.

Greece, Ancient
    USE **Greece—History—0-323**
Greece—Antiquities 938
    BT **Classical antiquities**
    NT **Delphi (Extinct city)**
Greece—Biography 920.038; 920.0495
    UF Classical biography
Greece—Civilization
    USE **Greek civilization**

Greece—Description 914.95

Use for descriptive materials on modern Greece, including materials for travelers. Descriptive materials on ancient Greece, including accounts by travelers in ancient times, are entered under **Greece—Description—0-323.**

UF   Greece—Description and travel *[Former heading]*

Greece—Description—0-323 913.8

Use for descriptive materials on ancient Greece including accounts by travelers of ancient times.

UF   Ancient Greece—Description

Greece—Description and geography *[Former heading]*

Greece—Description and geography

USE   **Greece—Description—0-323**

Greece—Historical geography

Greece—Description and travel

USE   **Greece—Description**

Greece—Geography 914.95

Use for materials on the geography of modern Greece. Materials on the geography of ancient Greece are entered under **Greece—Historical geography.**

NT   **Greece—Historical geography**

Greece—Historical geography 911; 913.8

UF   Classical geography

Greece—Description and geography *[Former heading]*

BT   **Ancient geography**

Greece—Geography

Historical geography

Greece—History 938; 949.5

Greece—History—0-323 938

UF   Ancient Greece

Greece, Ancient

Greece—History—323-1453 949.5

UF   Greece, Medieval

Greece—History—1453- 949.5

UF   Greece, Modern

Greece—History—1967-1974 949.507

Greece—History—1974- 949.507

Greece, Medieval

USE   **Greece—History—323-1453**

Greece, Modern

USE   **Greece—History—1453-**

Greek antiquities

USE   **Classical antiquities**

Greek architecture 722

UF   Architecture, Greek *[Former heading]*

BT   **Ancient architecture**

Architecture

Greek art 709.38; 709.495

UF   Art, Greek *[Former heading]*

Classical art

BT   **Ancient art**

Art

Classical antiquities

Greek Church

USE   **Orthodox Eastern Church**

Greek civilization 938

UF   Civilization, Greek *[Former heading]*

Greece—Civilization

BT   **Civilization**

NT   **Hellenism**

Greek language 480

Use for classical Greek. Modern Greek is entered under **Modern Greek language.** May be subdivided like **English language.**

UF   Classical languages

BT   **Language and languages**

RT   **Modern Greek language**

Greek language, Modern

USE   **Modern Greek language**

Greek letter societies

USE   **Fraternities and sororities**

Greek literature 880

May use same subdivisions and names of literary forms as for **English literature.**

BT   **Literature**

NT   **Hellenism**

RT   **Classical literature**

Greek literature, Modern

USE   **Modern Greek literature**

Greek mythology

USE   **Classical mythology**

Greek philosophy

USE   **Ancient philosophy**

Greek sculpture 730.938; 730.9495

UF   Sculpture, Greek *[Former heading]*

BT   **Sculpture**

Green movement

USE   **Environmental movement**

Greenbacks

USE   **Paper money**

Greenhouse effect 363.73; 551.5; 551.6

UF   Atmospheric greenhouse effect

Carbon dioxide greenhouse effect

Greenhouse effect—*Continued*
>Global warming
>Greenhouse effect, Atmospheric
- BT **Climate**
>**Solar radiation**

Greenhouse effect, Atmospheric
- USE **Greenhouse effect**

Greenhouses 631.5
- UF Hothouses
- BT **Flower gardening**
>**Gardening**
>**Horticulture**
- RT **Garden rooms**

Greenhouses, Window
- USE **Window gardening**

Greeting cards 741.6; 745.594
- UF Cards, Greeting
- SA types of greeting cards, to be added as needed
- NT **Christmas cards**

Gregorian chant
- USE **Chants (Plain, Gregorian, etc.)**

Grey Friars
- USE **Franciscans**

Grief 152.4; 155.9
- UF Mourning
>Sorrow
- BT **Emotions**
- RT **Bereavement**
>**Consolation**
>**Joy and sorrow**

Grievance procedures (Public administration)
- USE **Ombudsman**

Grill cooking
- USE **Barbecue cooking**

Grinding and polishing 621.9
- UF Buffing
>Polishing
- BT **Machine shop practice**
- RT **Machine tools**

Grippe
- USE **Influenza**

Grist mills
- USE **Flour mills**

Grocery trade 338.4
- BT **Commerce**
- NT **Supermarkets**
- RT **Food**

Grooming for men
- USE **Personal grooming**

Grooming for women
- USE **Personal grooming**

Grooming, Personal
- USE **Personal grooming**

Grottoes
- USE **Caves**

Ground cushion phenomena 629.3
- UF Air bearing lift
- BT **Aerodynamics**
>**Pneumatics**
- NT **Ground effect machines**

Ground effect machines 629.3
- UF Air bearing vehicles
>Air cushion vehicles
>Ground proximity machines
>Hovercraft
>Surface effect machines
- BT **Ground cushion phenomena**
- NT **Helicopters**
>**Vertically rising airplanes**

Ground proximity machines
- USE **Ground effect machines**

Grounds maintenance 712
>Use for materials on maintenance of public, industrial, and institutional grounds and large estates.
- BT **Gardening**
- NT **Golf courses**
>**Roadside improvement**

Group discussion
- USE **Discussion groups**

Group dynamics
- USE **Social groups**

Group health
- USE **Health insurance**

Group homes 362; 363.5
>Use for materials on planned housing for groups of unrelated people needing supervision.
- UF Community based residences
>Group residences
>Residential treatment centers
- BT **Institutional care**
>**Social work**
- NT **Halfway houses**
- RT **Foster home care**

Group hospitalization
- USE **Hospitalization insurance**

Group insurance 368.3

   Use for materials on group life insurance. Materials on group insurance in other fields are entered under the specific kind of insurance, e.g. **Health insurance.**

   UF   Insurance, Group *[Former heading]*

   BT   **Life insurance**

Group living

   USE   **Communal living**

Group medical practice

   USE   **Medical practice**

Group medical practice, Prepaid

   USE   **Health maintenance organizations**

Group medical service

   USE   **Health insurance**

Group method in teaching

   USE   **Cooperative learning**

Group problem solving 153.4

   UF   Brain storming

         Problem solving, Group *[Former heading]*

         Team problem solving

         Think tanks

   BT   **Problem solving**

Group relations training 302

   UF   Encounter groups

         Sensitivity training

         T groups

   BT   **Human relations**

Group residences

   USE   **Group homes**

Group teaching

   USE   **Cooperative learning**

Group theory 512

   UF   Groups, Theory of

   BT   **Algebra**

         Mathematics

         Number theory

   NT   **Boolean algebra**

Group travel

   USE   **Travel**

Group values

   USE   **Social values**

Group work in education

   USE   **Cooperative learning**

Group work, Social

   USE   **Social group work**

Grouping by ability

   USE   **Ability grouping in education**

Groups, Ethnic

   USE   **Ethnic groups**

Groups, Social

   USE   **Social groups**

Groups, Theory of

   USE   **Group theory**

Growing of Christmas trees

   USE   **Christmas tree growing**

Growth 155; 574.3; 612.6

   SA   subjects with the subdivision *Growth,* e.g. **Children— Growth; Cities and towns— Growth; Plants—Growth;** etc., to be added as needed

   BT   **Physiology**

Growth disorders 612.6

   UF   Abnormal growth

         Abnormalities, Human

         Development

         Dwarfism

         Failure to thrive syndrome

         Fetus—Growth retardation

         Human abnormalities

   BT   **Metabolism**

   NT   **Giantism**

   RT   **Birth defects**

Guaranteed annual income

   Use for materials on compensation provided by a government to anyone whose annual income falls below a specified level.

   UF   Annual income guarantee

         Guaranteed income

   BT   **Income**

Guaranteed income

   USE   **Guaranteed annual income**

Guerillas

   USE   **Guerrillas**

Guerrilla warfare 355.02; 355.4

   Use for materials on the military aspects of irregular warfare. General and historical materials are entered under **Guerrillas.**

   UF   Unconventional warfare

   BT   **Insurgency**

         Military art and science

         Tactics

         War

Guerrillas (May subdiv. geog.) 356

   Use for general and historical materials. Materials on the military aspects of irregular warfare are entered under **Guerrilla warfare.**

BT = Broader Term   NT = Narrower Term   RT = Related Term   SA = See Also   UF = Used For

Guerrillas—*Continued*
    UF   Guerillas
          Partisans
    SA   individual wars with the sub-
          division *Underground move-
          ments,* e.g. **World War,
          1939-1945—Underground
          movements;** to be added as
          needed
    RT **National liberation movements**
Guests
    USE **Entertaining**
Guidance
    USE **Counseling**
Guidance counseling, Educational
    USE **Educational counseling**
Guidance counseling, School
    USE **School counseling**
Guidance, Vocational
    USE **Vocational guidance**
Guide dogs 636.7
    UF   Blind, Dogs for the
          Dog guides
          Dogs for the blind
          Seeing eye dogs
    BT   **Animals and the handicapped
          Dogs
          Working animals**
Guide posts
    USE **Signs and signboards**
Guidebooks
    USE names of cities (except an-
          cient cities), countries,
          states, etc., with the subdi-
          vision *Guidebooks,* e.g. **Chi-
          cago (Ill.)—Guidebooks;
          United States—Guidebooks;**
          etc., to be added as needed
Guided missiles 358.1; 623.4
    UF   Bombs, Flying
          Flying bombs
          Missiles, Guided
    SA   types of missiles and names
          of specific missiles, to be
          added as needed
    BT   **Bombs
          Projectiles
          Rocketry
          Rockets (Aeronautics)**
    NT   **Antimissile missiles**

          Ballistic missiles
          Nike rocket
Guitar
    USE **Guitars**
Guitar music 787.87
    BT   **Instrumental music**
Guitars 787.87
    UF   Guitar *[Former heading]*
    BT   **Stringed instruments**
Gulf States (U.S.) 976
    BT   **United States**
Gulf War, 1991
    USE **Persian Gulf War, 1991**
Gums and resins 547.7; 668
    UF   Resins
          Rosin
    BT   **Forest products
          Industrial chemistry
          Plastics**
Gun control
    USE **Firearms—Law and legislation**
Gunning
    USE **Hunting
          Shooting**
Gunpowder 623.4
    UF   Powder, Smokeless
          Smokeless powder
    BT   **Explosives
          Firearms**
    RT   **Ammunition**
Guns
    USE **Firearms
          Ordnance
          Rifles
          Shotguns**
Guns—Control
    USE **Firearms—Law and legislation**
Gunsmithing
    USE **Firearms industry**
Gymnastics 613.7; 796.44
    UF   Calisthenics
    BT   **Athletics
          Exercise
          Sports**
    RT   **Acrobats and acrobatics
          Physical education**
Gynecology
    USE **Women—Diseases
          Women—Health and hygiene**
Gypsies 305.891
    UF   Gipsies

Gypsies—*Continued*
      Romanies
Gypsum 553.6
    UF   Plaster of paris
    BT   **Economic geology**
Gyroscope 629.135; 681
    BT   **Aeronautical instruments**
H.B.O.
    USE **Home Box Office**
H bomb
    USE **Hydrogen bomb**
H.M.O.'s
    USE **Health maintenance organiza-
            tions**
Habit 152.3
    BT   **Human behavior
          Psychology**
    NT   **Drug addiction
          Tobacco habit**
    RT   **Instinct**
Habitations, Human
    USE **Domestic architecture
           Houses
           Housing**
Habitations of animals
    USE **Animals—Habitations**
Habits of animals
    USE **Animal behavior**
Hades
    USE **Hell**
Haiku 808.1; 808.81; 811, etc.
    May be used for collections of haiku by
one or several authors or for materials
about haiku.
    BT   **Poetry**
Hair 612.7; 646.7
    Use for general materials on hair as well
for as materials on hairdressing and hair-
cutting.
    UF   Barbering
          Coiffure
          Hair and hairdressing *[Former
            heading]*
          Haircutting
          Hairdressing
          Hairstyles
          Hairstyling
    BT   **Head
          Personal grooming**
    NT   **Wigs**
Hair and hairdressing
    USE **Hair**

Haircutting
    USE **Hair**
Hairdressing
    USE **Hair**
Hairstyles
    USE **Hair**
Hairstyling
    USE **Hair**
Halftone process
    USE **Photoengraving**
Halfway houses 362; 365
    Use for materials on centers for former-
ly institutionalized individuals, such as
mental patients or drug addicts, that are
designed to facilitate their readjustment to
private life.
    BT   **Correctional institutions
          Group homes**
Halley's comet 523.6
    BT   **Comets**
Hallmarks
    UF   Marks on plate
    BT   **Plate**
Halloween 394.2
    UF   All Hallows' Eve
    BT   **Manners and customs**
**Hallucinations and illusions 616.85;
          616.89**
    UF   Delusions
          Illusions
    BT   **Abnormal psychology
          Parapsychology
          Subconsciousness
          Visions**
    NT   **Optical illusions**
    RT   **Apparitions
          Fantasy
          Ghosts
          Magic
          Magic tricks
          Personality disorders**
Hallucinogenic drugs
    USE **Hallucinogens**
Hallucinogenic plants
    USE **Hallucinogens**
Hallucinogens 615
    UF   Consciousness expanding
           drugs
          Drugs, Hallucinogenic
          Hallucinogenic drugs
          Hallucinogenic plants

Hallucinogens—*Continued*
    Plants, Hallucinogenic
  SA names of hallucinogens, to be
      added as needed
  BT **Drugs**
     Psychotropic drugs
     Stimulants
  NT **Marijuana**
Ham radio stations
  USE **Amateur radio stations**
Hand shadows
  USE **Shadow pictures**
Hand weaving
  USE **Weaving**
Handbooks, manuals, etc.
  USE general subjects with the sub-
      Zivision *Handbooks, manu-*
      als, etc., e.g. **Photography—**
      Handbooks, manuals, etc.;
      to be added as needed
Handedness
  USE **Left- and right-handedness**
Handguns
  USE **Pistols**
Handheld computers
  USE **Portable computers**
Handicapped 305.9; 362.4
  UF Disabled
  NT **Architecture and the handi-**
     capped
     Handicapped children
     Mentally handicapped
     Physically handicapped
     Sick
     Socially handicapped
     Sports for the handicapped
     Vocational guidance for the
     handicapped
Handicapped and animals
  USE **Animals and the handicapped**
Handicapped and architecture
  USE **Architecture and the handi-**
     capped
Handicapped children 362.7
  UF Abnormal children
     Children, Abnormal
  BT **Children**
     Exceptional children
     Handicapped
  NT **Brain damaged children**

     Hyperactive children
     Mainstreaming in education
     Mentally handicapped children
     Physically handicapped chil-
     dren
     Socially handicapped children
Handicraft 745.5; 746
  Use for materials on creative work done
by hand, sometimes with the aid of sim-
ple tools or machines.
  UF Crafts (Arts)
  SA types of handicrafts, to be
      addeZ as needed
  NT **Chair caning**
     Collage
     Craft shows
     Egg decoration
     Furniture finishing
     Hooked rugs
     Industrial arts
     Leather work
     Nature craft
     Paper crafts
     Picture frames and framing
     Quilting
     Weaving
  RT **Arts and crafts movement**
     Creative activities
     Decoration and ornament
     Decorative arts
     Folk art
     Hobbies
     Occupational therapy
Handling of materials
  USE **Materials handling**
Handwriting 652
  Use for practical guides on the art of
writing. General materials on the history
and art of writing and on elegant hand-
writing are entered under **Writing.** Mate-
rials on handwriting as an expression of
the writer's character are entered under
Graphology.
  UF Copybooks
     Penmanship
  BT **Business education**
  NT **Calligraphy**
     Graphology
     Writing of numerals
  RT **Writing**
Hang gliding
  USE **Gliding and soaring**

BT = Broader Term   NT = Narrower Term   RT = Related Term   SA = See Also   UF = Used For

Hanging
   USE **Capital punishment**
Hanukkah 296.4; 394.2
   UF   Chanukah
        Feast of Dedication
        Feast of Lights
        Lights, Feast of
        Maccabbees, Feast of the
   BT   **Jewish holidays**
Happening (Art)
   USE **Performance art**
Happiness 158
   UF   Gladness
   BT   **Emotions**
   RT   **Joy and sorrow**
        Pleasure
Harassment, Sexual
   USE **Sexual harassment**
Harbors (May subdiv. geog.) **386;**
        387.1; 627
   UF   Ports
   BT   **Civil engineering**
        Hydraulic structures
        Merchant marine
        Navigation
        Shipping
        Transportation
   NT   **Marinas**
        Pilots and pilotage
   RT   **Docks**
Hard drug addiction
   USE **Drug addiction**
Hard-of-hearing
   USE **Hearing impaired**
Hares
   USE **Rabbits**
Harlem Renaissance 810.9; 974.7
   UF   New Negro Movement
        Renaissance, Harlem
   BT   **African American art**
        African American music
        American literature—African
          American authors
Harmful insects
   USE **Insect pests**
Harmony 781.2
   BT   **Composition (Music)**
        Music
        Music—Theory

Harry S. Truman Library 026
   BT   **Presidents—United States—**
        Archives
Harvesting machinery 631.3
   UF   Reapers
   BT   **Agricultural machinery**
Hashish
   USE **Marijuana**
Hasidism 296.8
   UF   Chasidism
        Hassidism
   BT   **Judaism**
Hassidism
   USE **Hasidism**
Hastings (East Sussex, England), Battle
        of, 1066 941.02
   BT   **Great Britain—History—**
        1066-1154, Norman period
Hate crimes 364
   UF   Bias attacks
        Bias crimes
        Bigotry-motivated crimes
        Crimes of hate
        Prejudice-motivated crimes
   BT   **Crime**
        Discrimination
        Violence
Hatha yoga 613.7
   UF   Yoga exercises
        Yoga, Hatha
   BT   **Exercise**
        Yoga
Hats 391; 646.5; 687
   BT   **Clothing and dress**
        Costume
   RT   **Millinery**
Haunted houses
   USE **Ghosts**
Hawking
   USE **Falconry**
Hay 633.2
   SA   names of hay crops, e.g. **Al-**
        falfa; to be added as need-
        ed
   BT   **Farm produce**
        Forage plants
   NT   **Alfalfa**
   RT   **Feeds**
        Grasses
Hay fever 616.2
   BT   **Allergy**

Hazardous materials
    USE **Hazardous substances**

Hazardous occupations 331.7
    UF Dangerous occupations
         Injurious occupations
         Occupations, Dangerous *[Former heading]*
    BT **Occupations**
    RT **Labor—Accidents**
         Occupational diseases
         Occupational health and safety

Hazardous substances 363.17; 604.7
    UF Dangerous materials
         Hazardous materials
         Inflammable substances
         Toxic substances
    BT **Materials**
    NT **Hazardous wastes**
         Poisons and poisoning

Hazardous substances—Transportation 363.17; 604.7

Hazardous waste disposal
    USE **Hazardous wastes**

Hazardous waste sites 363.72; 628.4
    UF Chemical landfills
         Dumps, Toxic
         Toxic dumps
    BT **Landfills**
    NT **Love Canal Chemical Waste Landfill (Niagara Falls, N.Y.)**

Hazardous wastes 363.72
    UF Hazardous waste disposal
         Toxic wastes
         Wastes, Hazardous
    BT **Hazardous substances**
         Industrial wastes
         Refuse and refuse disposal
    RT **Medical wastes**
         Pollution

HBO
    USE **Home Box Office**

HDTV (Television)
    USE **High definition television**

Head 611; 612
    BT **Anatomy**
    NT **Brain**
         Ear
         Eye

         Face
         Hair
         Nose
         Phrenology
         Teeth

Heads of state (May subdiv. geog.) **351.003; 920**
    UF Rulers
         State, Heads of
    BT **Executive power**
         Statesmen
    NT **Dictators**
         Kings, queens, rulers, etc.
         Presidents

Healing, Mental
    USE **Mental healing**

Healing, Spiritual
    USE **Spiritual healing**

Health 613
    Use for materials on physical, mental, and social well-being. Materials on personal body care are entered under **Hygiene.**
    UF Personal health
    SA parts of the body with the subdivision *Care and hygiene,* e.g. **Foot—Care and hygiene;** and classes of persons and ethnic groups with the subdivision *Health and hygiene,* e.g. **Women—Health and hygiene;** to be added as needed
    BT **Medicine**
         Physiology
         Preventive medicine
    NT **Diet**
         Exercise
         Health education
         Health self-care
         Longevity
         Mental health
         Physical fitness
         Rest
         Sleep
    RT **Diseases**
         Holistic medicine
         Hygiene

Health and hygiene
    USE classes of persons and ethnic groups with the subdivision

---

BT = Broader Term   NT = Narrower Term   RT = Related Term   SA = See Also   UF = Used For

Health and hygiene—*Continued*
  Health and hygiene, e.g.
    Women—Health and hygiene; and parts of the body with the subdivision *Care and hygiene,* e.g.
    Foot—Care and hygiene;
    Skin—Care and hygiene;
    etc., to be added as needed
Health boards 614.06
  UF   Boards of health
       Public health boards
  BT   **Public health**
Health care
  USE   **Medical care**
Health care, Self
  USE   **Health self-care**
Health clubs
  USE   **Health resorts**
Health counseling 362.1; 613
  BT   **Counseling**
       Health education
Health education 372.3; 613.07
  UF   Health—Study and teaching
       Hygiene—Study and teaching
  BT   **Children—Health and hygiene**
       Health
       Physical education
  NT   **Drug education**
       Health counseling
       School hygiene
Health—Environmental aspects
  USE   **Environmental health**
Health foods
  USE   **Natural foods**
Health, Industrial
  USE   **Occupational health and safety**
Health insurance 368.3
  UF   Disability insurance
       Group health
       Group medical service
       Health plans, Prepaid
       Insurance, Disability
       Insurance, Health *[Former heading]*
       Insurance, Sickness
       Medical care, Prepaid
       Medical insurance
       Medical service, Prepaid

       Prepaid health plans
       Prepaid medical care
       Sickness insurance
  BT   **Insurance**
  NT   **Health maintenance organizations**
       Hospitalization insurance
       National health insurance
       Workers' compensation
Health insurance, Government
  USE   **National health insurance**
Health insurance, National
  USE   **National health insurance**
Health maintenance organizations 368.3; 610.6
  UF   Comprehensive health care organizations
       Group medical practice, Prepaid
       H.M.O.'s
       HMOs
       Prepaid group medical practice
  BT   **Health insurance**
       Medical care
Health, Mental
  USE   **Mental health**
Health plans, Prepaid
  USE   **Health insurance**
Health, Public
  USE   **Public health**
Health resorts 613
  UF   Health clubs
       Health resorts, spas, etc. *[Former heading]*
       Physical fitness centers
       Sanatoriums
       Spas
       Watering places
  BT   **Medicine**
  RT   **Hydrotherapy**
       Sick
       Summer resorts
       Winter resorts
Health resorts, spas, etc.
  USE   **Health resorts**
Health self-care 613; 616
  UF   Health care, Self
       Medical self-care

Health self-care—*Continued*
      Self-care, Health *[Former heading]*
      Self-care, Medical
      Self-examination, Medical
      Self health care
      Self-help medical care
      Self-medication
  BT **Alternative medicine**
      Health
      Medical care
  NT **First aid**
      Nutrition
      Physical fitness
  RT **Holistic medicine**
      Popular medicine
Health—Study and teaching
  USE **Health education**
Healths, Drinking of
  USE **Toasts**
Hearing 152.1; 612.8
  UF Acoustics
  BT **Senses and sensation**
      Sound
  RT **Deafness**
      Ear
      Listening
Hearing aids 617.8
  BT **Deafness**
Hearing ear dogs 636.7
  UF Deaf, Dogs for
      Dogs for the deaf
  BT **Animals and the handicapped**
      Deaf—Means of communication
      Dogs
Hearing impaired 362.4; 617.8
  UF Hard-of-hearing
      Partial hearing
      Partially hearing
  BT **Physically handicapped**
  NT **Deaf**
Heart 591.1; 611; 612.1
  BT **Cardiovascular system**
  NT **Artificial heart**
Heart attack 616.1
  UF Heart—Infarction
      Myocardial infarction
  BT **Heart diseases**
Heart disease
  USE **Heart diseases**

Heart—Diseases
  USE **Heart diseases**
Heart diseases 616.1
  UF Cardiac diseases
      Coronary heart diseases
      Heart disease
      Heart—Diseases *[Former heading]*
  BT **Diseases**
  NT **Angina pectoris**
      Heart attack
Heart—Diseases—Prevention
  USE **Heart diseases—Prevention**
Heart diseases—Prevention 616.1
  UF Heart—Diseases—Prevention *[Former heading]*
  BT **Preventive medicine**
Heart—Infarction
  USE **Heart attack**
Heart resuscitation
  USE **Cardiac resuscitation**
Heart—Surgery 617.4
  UF Open heart surgery
  BT **Surgery**
Heart—Surgery—Nursing 610.73; 617.4
  BT **Nursing**
Heart—Transplantation 617.4
  BT **Transplantation of organs, tissues, etc.**
Heat 536
  BT **Electromagnetic waves**
  NT **Steam**
      Thermometers
  RT **Combustion**
      Fire
      Temperature
      Thermodynamics
Heat—Conduction 536
Heat engines 621.4
  UF Hot air engines
  BT **Engines**
      Thermodynamics
  NT **Steam engines**
Heat insulating materials
  USE **Insulation (Heat)**
Heat pumps 621.4
  BT **Pumping machinery**
      Thermodynamics
Heat—Transmission 536
Heathenism
  USE **Paganism**

BT = Broader Term   NT = Narrower Term   RT = Related Term   SA = See Also   UF = Used For

Heating 644; 697

    SA   subjects with the subdivision *Heating and ventilation,* e.g. **Houses—Heating and ventilation;** to be added as needed

    BT   **Home economics**

    NT   **Chimneys**

           Electric heating

           Fireplaces

           Furnaces

           Hot air heating

           Hot water heating

           Houses—Heating and ventilation

           Insulation (Heat)

           Oil burners

           Radiant heating

           Solar heating

           Space heaters

           Steam heating

           Stoves

    RT   **Fuel**

           Ventilation

Heaven 236; 291.2

    UF   Paradise

    BT   **Eschatology**

           Future life

    NT   **Angels**

Heavy water

    USE **Deuterium oxide**

Hebrew language 492.4

    May be subdivided like **English language.**

    UF   Jewish language

           Jews—Language

    BT   **Language and languages**

Hebrew literature 892.4

    May use same subdivisions and names of literary forms as for **English literature.**

    UF   Jews—Literature

    BT   **Literature**

    NT   **Bible**

           Cabala

           Talmud

    RT   **Jewish literature**

Hebrews

    USE **Jews**

Heirs

    USE **Inheritance and succession**

Helicopters 387.7; 629.133

    UF   Aircraft

    BT   **Aeronautics**

           Airplanes

           Ground effect machines

Helicopters—Piloting 629.132

    BT   **Airplanes—Piloting**

Heliports 387.7

    BT   **Airports**

Helium 546

    BT   **Radioactivity**

Hell 236; 291.2

    UF   Eternal punishment

           Hades

           Retribution

    BT   **Eschatology**

           Future life

Hellenism 938; 939

    BT   **Greek civilization**

           Greek literature

Helpful insects

    USE **Beneficial insects**

Helpfulness

    USE **Helping behavior**

Helping behavior 158

    UF   Assistance in emergencies

           Behavior, Helping

           Emergency assistance

           Helpfulness

    BT   **Human behavior**

           Human relations

    NT   **Counseling**

Hemp 633.5; 677

    BT   **Fibers**

    NT   **Marijuana**

    RT   **Rope**

Heraldry 929.6

    UF   Arms, Coats of

           Coats of arms

           Crests

           Devices (Heraldry)

           Emblems

           Pedigrees

    BT   **Archeology**

           Signs and symbols

           Symbolism

    NT   **Flags**

           Insignia

           Mottoes

           Seals (Numismatics)

Heraldry—*Continued*
  RT **Chivalry**
      Decorations of honor
      Genealogy
      Knights and knighthood
      National emblems
      Nobility
Herbage
  USE **Grasses**
Herbal medicine
  USE **Medical botany**
Herbals
  USE **Herbs**
      Materia medica
      Medical botany
Herbaria
  USE **Plants—Collection and preservation**
Herbicides 632; 668
  UF Defoliants
      Plants—Effect of poisons on
      [Former heading]
      Weed killers
  SA names of herbicides, to be
      added as needed
  BT **Agricultural chemicals**
      Pesticides
  NT **Agent Orange**
  RT **Plants**
      Spraying and dusting
Herbs 581.6; 635
  UF Herbals
  BT **Cooking**
      Plants
Herbs, Medical
  USE **Medical botany**
Hereditary diseases
  USE **Medical genetics**
Hereditary succession
  USE **Inheritance and succession**
Heredity 575.1
  UF Ancestry
      Descent
      Genes
      Inheritance (Biology)
  BT **Biology**
      Breeding
  NT **Chromosomes**
      DNA
      Genetic mapping

      Variation (Biology)
  RT **Eugenics**
      Evolution
      Genetics
      Mendel's law
      Natural selection
Heredity of diseases
  USE **Medical genetics**
Hereford cattle 636.2
  BT **Beef cattle**
Hermeneutics, Biblical
  USE **Bible—Criticism, interpretation, etc.**
Hermetic art and philosophy
  USE **Alchemy**
      Astrology
      Occultism
Hermits 920
  UF Recluses
  BT **Eccentrics and eccentricities**
      Religious orders
  RT **Saints**
Heroes and heroines 920
  UF Heroines
      Heroism
  BT **Adventure and adventurers**
  NT **Explorers**
      Martyrs
      Saints
  RT **Courage**
      Mythology
Heroin 362.29; 615
  BT **Morphine**
      Narcotics
Heroines
  USE **Heroes and heroines**
      Women—Biography
      Women in the Bible
Heroism
  USE **Courage**
      Heroes and heroines
Hertzian waves
  USE **Electric waves**
Hi-fi systems
  USE **High-fidelity sound systems**
Hibernation 591.54
  UF Animals—Hibernation *[Former heading]*
      Hibernation of animals
  BT **Animal behavior**

BT = Broader Term   NT = Narrower Term   RT = Related Term   SA = See Also   UF = Used For

Hibernation of animals
  USE **Hibernation**
Hidden treasure
  USE **Buried treasure**
Hides and skins 636.088; 675
  UF Pelts
        Skins
  BT **Animal products**
  RT **Fur**
        Leather
        Tanning
Hieroglyphics 411
    Use for materials on that form of writing distinguished by stylized pictures used chiefly to represent meanings that seem arbitrary and are seldom obvious, such as the pictographic styles used in ancient Egypt, Crete, Central America, and Mexico.
  BT **Inscriptions**
        Writing
  NT **Rosetta stone inscription**
  RT **Picture writing**
High blood pressure
  USE **Hypertension**
High definition television 621.388
  UF HDTV (Television)
  BT **Television**
High-fidelity sound systems 621.389
  UF Hi-fi systems
  BT **Electronics**
        Sound—Recording and reproducing
  NT **Stereophonic sound systems**
  RT **Phonograph**
High-frequency radio
  USE **Shortwave radio**
High rise buildings
  USE **Skyscrapers**
High school dropouts
  USE **Dropouts**
High school education
  USE **Secondary education**
High school libraries 027.8
  UF Junior high school libraries
        School libraries (High school)
        [Former heading]
        Secondary school libraries
  BT **School libraries**
  RT **Young adults' library services**
High school life
  USE **High school students**

High school students 373
  UF High school life
        High schools—Students
  BT **Students**
High school yearbooks
  USE **School yearbooks**
High schools (May subdiv. geog.) 373
  UF Secondary schools
  BT **Public schools**
        Schools
  NT **Commencements**
        Junior high schools
  RT **Secondary education**
High schools, Junior
  USE **Junior high schools**
High schools, Rural
  USE **Rural schools**
High schools—Students
  USE **High school students**
High society
  USE **Upper classes**
High speed aerodynamics
  USE **Supersonic aerodynamics**
High speed aeronautics 629.132
  UF Aeronautics, High speed
  BT **Aeronautics**
  NT **Aerothermodynamics**
        Rocket planes
        Rockets (Aeronautics)
        Supersonic aerodynamics
High tech
  USE **Technology**
High technology
  USE **Technology**
High treason
  USE **Treason**
High-yield junk bonds
  USE **Junk bonds**
Higher criticism
  USE **Bible—Criticism, interpretation, etc.**
Higher education 378
    Use for general materials on education above the secondary level.
  UF Education, Higher *[Former heading]*
  BT **Education**
  NT **Adult education**
        Colleges and universities
        Junior colleges

Higher education—*Continued*
    Professional education
    Technical education
    University extension
Highjacking of airplanes
  USE **Hijacking of airplanes**
Highland clans
  USE **Clans**
Highland costume
  USE **Tartans**
Highway accidents
  USE **Traffic accidents**
Highway beautification
  USE **Roadside improvement**
Highway construction
  USE **Roads**
Highway engineering 625.7
  UF Road engineering
  BT **Civil engineering**
      Engineering
  NT **Traffic engineering**
  RT **Roads**
Highway transportation 388.3
  UF Transportation, Highway *[Former heading]*
  BT **Transportation**
  NT **Automobiles**
      Buses
      Trucks
Highwaymen
  USE **Thieves**
Highways
  USE **Roads**
Hijacking of airplanes 364.1
    Use same form for the hijacking of other modes of transportation.
  UF Air piracy
      Airlines—Hijacking
      Airplane hijacking
      Airplanes—Hijacking
      Commercial aeronautics—Hijacking
      Highjacking of airplanes
      Sky hijacking
      Skyjacking
  BT **Offenses against public safety**
Hiking 796.5
  SA types of hiking, e.g. **Backpacking**; to be added as needed

  BT **Outdoor life**
  NT **Backpacking**
      Orienteering
  RT **Direction sense**
      Walking
Hillbilly music
  USE **Country music**
Hindoos
  USE **Hindus**
Hindu philosophy 181
  UF Philosophy, Hindu *[Former heading]*
  BT **Philosophy**
  NT **Yoga**
Hinduism 294.5
  BT **Religions**
  NT **Caste**
      Vedas
      Yoga
  RT **Brahmanism**
Hindus 294.5092; 305.891
  UF Hindoos
  RT **East Indians**
Hippies (May subdiv. geog.) **306**
  UF Yippies
  BT **Bohemianism**
Hippies—United States 306
  UF United States—Hippies
Hire-purchase plan
  USE **Instalment plan**
Hispanic American literature (English)
  USE **American literature—Hispanic American authors**
Hispanic American literature (Spanish)
  USE **American literature (Spanish)**
Hispanic Americans 305.868; 973
    Use for materials on United States citizens of Latin American descent. Materials on citizens of Latin American countries are entered under **Latin Americans.**
  UF Latinos (U.S.)
  SA names of groups of U.S. citizens from specific countries, e.g. **Mexican Americans;** to be added as needed
  BT **Ethnology—United States**
  NT **Mexican Americans**
Hispano-American War, 1898
  USE **Spanish-American War, 1898**

BT = Broader Term   NT = Narrower Term   RT = Related Term   SA = See Also   UF = Used For

Historians 907; 920
  SA historians of particular coun-
       tries, e.g. **American histori-**
       ans; to be added as needed
  BT **Authors**
       Historiography
       History
  NT **American historians**
       Archeologists
Historians, American
  USE **American historians**
Historic buildings (May subdiv. geog.)
       363.6; 720.9
  UF Buildings, Historic
       Historic houses
       Houses, Historic
  SA types of historic buildings, e.g.
       Castles; Churches; Temples;
       Theaters; etc., to be added
       as needed
  BT **Architecture**
       Buildings
       Historic sites
       Monuments
  NT **Literary landmarks**
Historic buildings—Chicago (Ill.)
       720.9773; 977.3
  UF Chicago (Ill.)—Historic build-
       ings
Historic buildings—Ohio 720.9771;
       977.1
  UF Ohio—Historic buildings [For-
       mer heading]
Historic buildings—United States
       720.973; 973
  UF United States—Historic build-
       ings
  RT **Colonial architecture**
Historic houses
  USE **Historic buildings**
Historic sites (May subdiv. geog.) **363.6**
  UF Historical sites
  BT **Archeology**
       History
  NT **Historic buildings**
  RT **National monuments**
Historical atlases 911
  UF Atlases, Historical [Former
       heading]
       Historical geography—Maps

       History—Atlases
       Maps, Historical
  BT **Atlases**
  RT **Historical geography**
Historical chronology 902
  Use for materials in which events are
  arranged by date.
  UF Chronology, Historical [For-
       mer heading]
       Dates, Historical
       History—Chronology
  SA names of countries, cities,
       etc., with the subdivision
       History—Chronology, to be
       added as needed
  NT **United States—History—**
       Chronology
Historical dictionaries
  USE **History—Dictionaries**
Historical drama 808.82; 812, etc.
  May be used for individual works, col-
  lections, or materials about historical dra-
  ma.
  UF Chronicle history (Drama)
       Chronicle plays
       History plays
  BT **Drama**
  NT **Napoleon I, Emperor of the**
       French, 1769-1821—Drama
       United States—History—
       1861-1865, Civil War—
       Drama
       United States—History—
       Drama
       War films
       Western films
Historical fiction 808.83; 813, etc
  May be used for individual works, col-
  lections, or materials about fiction set dur-
  ing a time significantly prior to the time
  in which it was written.
  UF Fiction, Historical
       Historical novels
       Historical romances
  SA names of historical topics,
       events, and characters with
       the subdivision Fiction, to
       be added as needed
  BT **Fiction**
  NT **Edwardian novels**
       Gothic novels

Historical fiction—*Continued*
>> Napoleon I, Emperor of the French, 1769-1821—Fiction
>> Regency novels
>> Slavery—United States—Fiction
>> United States—History—1861-1865, Civil War—Fiction
>> War stories
>> Western stories
> RT Autobiographical fiction
>> Biographical fiction
>> History

Historical geography 911

Use for materials that discuss the extent of territory held by the states or nations at a given period of history. Materials limited to one country or region still existing in modern times are entered under the name of the place with the subdivision *Historical geography*. Materials on the geography of regions or countries of antiquity that no longer exist as such in modern times are entered under the name of the place with the subdivision *Geography*.

> UF Geography, Historical *[Former heading]*
> SA names of modern countries or regions with the subdivision *Historical geography*, e.g. **Greece—Historical geography; United States—Historical geography**; etc.; and names of ancient countries with the subdivision *Geography*, e.g. **Rome—Geography**; to be added as needed
> BT **Geography**
>> **History**
> NT **Ancient geography**
>> **Greece—Historical geography**
>> **Rome—Geography**
>> **United States—Historical geography**
> RT **Historical atlases**

Historical geography—Maps
> USE **Historical atlases**

Historical geology
> USE **Stratigraphic geology**

Historical materialism
> USE **Dialectical materialism**

Historical novels
> USE **Historical fiction**

Historical poetry 808.81; 811, etc.

May be used for individual works, collections, or materials about historical poetry.

> UF Poetry, Historical
> BT **Narrative poetry**
> NT **Bunker Hill (Boston, Mass.), Battle of, 1775—Poetry**
>> **United States—History—Poetry**

Historical records—Preservation
> USE **Archives**

Historical romances
> USE **Historical fiction**

Historical sites
> USE **Historic sites**

Historical societies
> USE **History—Societies**

Historiography 907

Use for materials limited to the study and criticism of sources of history, methods of historical research, and the writing of history. General materials on history as a science, including the principles of history, the influence of various factors on history, and the relation of the science of history to other subjects, are entered under **History**. Materials on the interpretation and meaning of history and on the course of events and their resulting consequences are entered under **History—Philosophy**.

> UF History—Criticism
>> History—Historiography
> SA subjects with the subdivision *Historiography*, to be added as needed
> BT **Authorship**
>> **History**
> NT **Historians**
>> **History—Sources**
>> **Local history**
>> **Philosophy—Historiography**
>> **United States—Historiography**
>> **United States—History—1861-1865, Civil War—Historiography**

BT = Broader Term   NT = Narrower Term   RT = Related Term   SA = See Also   UF = Used For

History 900

Use for general materials on history as a science. This includes the principles of history, the influence of various factors on history, and the relation of the science of history to other subjects. Materials on the interpretation and meaning of history and on the course of events and their resulting consequences are entered under **History—Philosophy.** Materials limited to the study and criticism of sources of history, methods of historical research, and the writing of history are entered under **Historiography.**

UF Social studies

SA countries, states, etc., with the subdivisions *Antiquities; Foreign relations; History; Politics and government;* and subjects with the subdivision *History,* or, for literature, film, and music headings, *History and criticism,* e.g. **Art—History; English literature—History and criticism;** to be added as needed

BT Humanities
   Social sciences

NT Ancient history
   Archeology
   Art—History
   Biography
   Chronology
   Church history
   Constitutional history
   English language—History
   English literature—History and criticism
   Exploration
   Genealogy
   Historians
   Historic sites
   Historical geography
   Historiography
   Local history
   Massacres
   Military history
   Modern history
   Music—History and criticism
   Naval history
   Numismatics
   Oral history

Seals (Numismatics)
   Women—History
   World history

RT **Civilization**
   Historical fiction

History, Ancient
   USE **Ancient history**

History—Atlases
   USE **Historical atlases**

History, Biblical
   USE **Bible—History of biblical events**

History—Chronology
   USE **Historical chronology**

History, Church
   USE **Church history**

History, Constitutional
   USE **Constitutional history**

History—Criticism
   USE **Historiography**

History—Dictionaries 903
   UF Historical dictionaries
   BT **Encyclopedias and dictionaries**
   NT **United States—History—Dictionaries**

History—Historiography
   USE **Historiography**

History, Local
   USE **Local history**

History, Medieval
   USE **Middle Ages—History**

History, Military
   USE **Military history**

History, Modern
   USE **Modern history**

History, Modern—1800-1899 (19th century)
   USE **Modern history—1800-1899 (19th century)**

History, Modern—1945-
   USE **Modern history—1945-**

History, Modern—1990-1999 (20th century)
   USE **Modern history—1900-1999 (20th century)**

History, Modern—Study and teaching
   USE **Modern history—Study and teaching**

History, Natural
   USE **Natural history**

BT = Broader Term   NT = Narrower Term   RT = Related Term   SA = See Also   UF = Used For

History, Naval
  USE **Naval history**
History, Oral
  USE **Oral history**
History—Periodicals 905
History—Philosophy 901
  Use for materials on the interpretation and meaning of history and on the course of events and their resulting consequences. General materials on history as a science, including the principles of history, the influences of various factors on history, and the relation of the science of history to other subjects, are entered under **History.** Materials limited to the study and criticism of the sources of history, methods of historical research, and the writing of history are entered under **Historiography.**
  UF Philosophy of history
  BT **Philosophy**
History plays
  USE **Historical drama**
History—Societies 906
  UF Historical societies
  NT **United States—History—Societies**
History—Sources 900
  Use for collections of documents, records, and other source materials upon which narrative history is based and for materials about such sources.
  SA names of countries, states, etc., with the subdivision *History—Sources,* and names of periods of history and of wars with the subdivision *Sources,* to be added as needed
  BT **Historiography**
  NT **Archives**
      Charters
      United States—History—1861-1865, Civil War—Sources
      United States—History—Sources
      World War, 1939-1945—Sources
History, Universal
  USE **World history**
Histrionics
  USE **Acting**
      Theater
Hittites 939
  BT **Ancient history**

HIV disease
  USE **AIDS (Disease)**
HMOs
  USE **Health maintenance organizations**
Hoaxes
  USE **Impostors and imposture**
Hobbies 790.1
  UF Avocations
      Recreations
  SA types of hobbies, to be added as needed
  BT **Amusements**
      Leisure
      Recreation
  NT **Collectors and collecting**
  RT **Handicraft**
Hoboes
  USE **Tramps**
Hockey 796.962
  UF Ice hockey *[Former heading]*
  BT **Winter sports**
Hogs
  USE **Pigs**
Hoisting machinery 621.8
  UF Lifts
  SA types of hoisting machinery, to be added as needed
  BT **Machinery**
  NT **Cranes, derricks, etc.**
      Elevators
  RT **Conveying machinery**
Holiday decorations 394.2; 745.5
  UF Decorations, Holiday
  BT **Decoration and ornament**
Holidays (May subdiv. geog.) **394.2**
  Use for materials on days of general exemption from work or days publicly dedicated to the commemoration of some person, event, or principle. Materials on occasions other than holidays devoted to festive community observances or to programs of cultural events are entered under **Festivals.**
  UF Anniversaries
      Legal holidays
      National holidays
  SA names of holidays, to be added as needed
  BT **Days**
      Manners and customs
  NT **April Fools' Day**

BT = Broader Term   NT = Narrower Term   RT = Related Term   SA = See Also   UF = Used For

333

Holidays—*Continued*
    Christmas
    Fourth of July
    Lincoln's Birthday
    Martin Luther King Day
    Memorial Day
    Religious holidays
    Thanksgiving Day
    Valentine's Day
    Veterans Day
  RT **Festivals**
    Vacations
Holidays, Jewish
  USE **Jewish holidays**
Holistic health
  USE **Holistic medicine**
Holistic medicine 610; 615.5
  UF Holistic health
    Humanistic medicine
    Wholistic medicine
  BT **Alternative medicine**
    Medicine
  RT **Health**
    Health self-care
    Mind and body
Holland
  USE **Netherlands**
Holocaust, Jewish (1933-1945)
  USE **Jewish holocaust (1933-1945)**
Holocaust, Jewish (1939-1945)
  USE **Jewish holocaust (1933-1945)**
Holography 774
  UF Laser photography
    Lensless photography
    Photography, Laser
    Photography, Lensless
  BT **Laser recording**
    Photography
  RT **Three dimensional photography**
Holstein-Friesian cattle 636.2
  UF Friesian cattle
  BT **Dairy cattle**
Holy communion
  USE **Lord's Supper**
Holy days
  USE **Religious holidays**
Holy Ghost
  USE **Holy Spirit**
Holy Grail
  USE **Grail**

Holy Office
  USE **Inquisition**
Holy Roman Empire 943
  BT **Europe—History—476-1492**
    Europe—History—1492-1789
    Germany—History—0-1517
    Germany—History—1517-1740
    Germany—History—1740-1815
    Middle Ages—History
Holy Scriptures
  USE **Bible**
Holy See
  USE **Papacy**
    Popes
Holy Spirit 231
  UF Holy Ghost
    Spirit, Holy
  BT **God—Christianity**
    Trinity
Holy Week 263
  BT **Lent**
  NT **Easter**
    Good Friday
Home 306.8; 640
  NT **Home economics**
  RT **Family**
    Marriage
Home accidents 363.13
  BT **Accidents**
  NT **First aid**
Home and school 371.1
  UF School and home
  RT **Parent-teacher relationships**
    Parents' and teachers' associations
Home Box Office 384.55
  UF H.B.O.
    HBO
  BT **Cable television**
    Subscription television
Home business 338.6; 658
  UF At-home employment
    Cottage industry
    Home labor
    Work at home
    Working at home
  BT **Business**
    Self-employed

BT = Broader Term   NT = Narrower Term   RT = Related Term   SA = See Also   UF = Used For

Home business—*Continued*
  Small business
  NT Telecommuting
Home buying
  USE **Houses—Buying and selling**
Home care services 362.1
  UF Home health care
      Home medical care
      Respite care
  SA classes of persons with the
      subdivision *Home care,* e.g.
      Elderly—Home care; to be
      added as needed
  BT **Medical care**
  NT **Caregivers**
      Elderly—Home care
      Home nursing
Home computers
  USE **Microcomputers**
Home conservatories
  USE **Garden rooms**
Home construction
  USE **House construction**
Home decoration
  USE **Interior design**
Home delivered meals programs
  USE **Meals on wheels programs**
Home designs
  USE **Domestic architecture—**
       Designs and plans
Home economics 640
  UF Domestic arts
      Efficiency, Household
      Homemaking
      Household management
      Housekeeping
  BT **Family life education**
      Home
  NT **Consumer education**
      Cooking
      Cost of living
      Entertaining
      Food
      Fuel
      Furniture
      Heating
      House cleaning
      Household employees
      Household equipment and sup-
        plies

  Household pests
  Interior design
  Laundry
  Mobile home living
  Moving
  Sewing
  Shopping
  Storage in the home
  Ventilation
Home economics—Accounting
  USE **Household budgets**
Home education
  USE **Correspondence schools and**
       courses
       Home instruction
       Self-instruction
Home health care
  USE **Home care services**
Home instruction 649
  UF Domestic education
      Education at home
      Education, Home
      Home education
      Home teaching
      Instruction, Home
      Teaching at home
  BT **Education**
      Teaching
  NT **Tutors and tutoring**
  RT **Child development**
      Child rearing
      Parenting
Home labor
  USE **Home business**
       Telecommuting
Home life
  USE **Family life**
Home loans
  USE **Mortgages**
Home medical care
  USE **Home care services**
Home missions, Christian
  USE **Christian missions**
Home movies
  USE **Amateur films**
Home nursing 649.8
  BT **Home care services**
      Nursing
  RT **Sick**
Home purchase
  USE **Houses—Buying and selling**

Home remodeling
USE **Houses—Remodeling**

Home repairing
USE **Houses—Maintenance and repair**

Home sharing
USE **Shared housing**

Home storage
USE **Storage in the home**

Home study courses
USE **Correspondence schools and
courses**
Self-instruction

Home teaching
USE **Home instruction**

Home video cameras
USE **Camcorders**

Home video movies
USE **Amateur films**

**Home video systems 384.55; 621.388;
778.59**
BT **Television**
NT **Camcorders**
Videotapes
RT **Video recording**

Home work (Employment)
USE **Telecommuting**

Homeless
USE **Homeless persons**
Homelessness

Homeless people
USE **Homeless persons**

Homeless people—Government policy
USE **Homeless persons—
Government policy**

Homeless persons 305.5; 362.5
UF Homeless
Homeless people *[Former
heading]*
Street people
BT **Poor**
NT **Refugees**
Runaway adults
Runaway children
Runaway teenagers
Tramps
RT **Homelessness**

**Homeless persons—Government policy
362.5**
UF Homeless people—
Government policy *[Former
heading]*

Homelessness 305.5; 362.5
UF Homeless
BT **Housing**
Poverty
Social problems
RT **Homeless persons**

Homemakers 306.85; 640
UF Househusbands
Housewives
NT **Fathers**
Mothers

Homemaking
USE **Home economics**

Homeopathy 615.5
BT **Alternative medicine**
Pharmacy

Homes
USE **Houses**

Homes for the elderly
USE **Elderly—Institutional care**

Homes (Institutions)
USE **Charities**
Institutional care
Orphanages
and classes of persons with
the subdivision *Institutional
care,* e.g. **Blind—
Institutional care;
Children—Institutional care;
Deaf—Institutional care;**
etc., to be added as needed

Homes, Mobile
USE **Mobile homes**

Homework (Employment)
USE **Telecommuting**

Homicide 364.1
UF Manslaughter
Murder *[Former heading]*
BT **Crime**
Criminal law
Offenses against the person
NT **Assassination**
Capital punishment
Euthanasia
Poisons and poisoning

BT = Broader Term   NT = Narrower Term   RT = Related Term   SA = See Also   UF = Used For

Homicide—*Continued*
　　Trials (Homicide)
　RT　Suicide
Homicide trials
　USE　Trials (Homicide)
Homo sapiens
　USE　**Man**
Homonyms
　USE　names of languages with the
　　　subdivision *Homonyms,* e.g.
　　　English language—
　　　Homonyms; to be added as
　　　needed
Homosexuality 306.76
　UF　Gay lifestyle
　BT　**Sexual behavior**
　NT　**Gay liberation movement**
　　　Lesbianism
　RT　**Gay men**
　　　Lesbians
Homosexuals, Female
　USE　**Lesbians**
Homosexuals, Male
　USE　**Gay men**
Honesty 179
　UF　Dishonesty
　BT　**Ethics**
　　　Human behavior
　RT　**Truthfulness and falsehood**
Honey 638; 641.3
　BT　**Animal food**
　RT　**Bees**
Honor system
　USE　**Student government**
Honorary degrees
　USE　**Academic degrees**
Hooked rugs 746.7
　UF　Rugs, Hooked *[Former head-ing]*
　BT　**Handicraft**
　　　Rugs
Hoover Dam (Ariz. and Nev.) 627
　UF　Boulder Dam (Ariz. and
　　　Nev.)
　　　Colorado River—Hoover
　　　Dam
　BT　**Dams**
Hope 152.4; 179; 234
　BT　**Emotions**
　　　Spiritual life

Hormones 574.19; 612.4
　BT　**Endocrinology**
　RT　**Endocrine glands**
　　　Steroids
Hornbooks 028.5; 372.4
　BT　**Reading materials**
Horology
　USE　**Clocks and watches**
　　　Sundials
　　　Time
Horoscopes 133.5
　BT　**Astrology**
Horror 152.4
　BT　**Emotions**
　　　Fear
Horror—Fiction
　USE　**Horror fiction**
Horror fiction 808.83; 809.3; 813, etc.
　　May be used for individual works, col-
　lections, or materials about horror fiction.
　UF　Horror—Fiction *[Former
　　　heading]*
　　　Horror novels
　　　Horror stories
　　　Horror tales
　　　Terror tales
　BT　**Fiction**
　NT　**Ghost stories**
　　　Gothic novels
　　　Mystery fiction
　RT　**Fantasy fiction**
　　　Occult fiction
Horror films 791.43
　　May be used for individual works, col-
　lections, or materials about horror films.
　UF　Creature films
　　　Horror movies
　　　Monster films
　SA　types of horror films, e.g.
　　　Vampire films; to be added
　　　as needed
　BT　**Motion pictures**
　NT　**Vampire films**
　RT　**Fantasy films**
Horror movies
　USE　**Horror films**
Horror novels
　USE　**Horror fiction**
Horror plays 808.82; 812, etc.
　　May be used for individual works, col-
　lections, or materials about horror plays.

Horror plays—*Continued*
    BT   **Drama**
Horror radio programs 791.44
    May be used for individual works, collections, or materials about horror radio programs.
    BT   **Radio programs**
Horror stories
    USE   **Horror fiction**
Horror tales
    USE   **Horror fiction**
Horror television programs 791.45
    May be used for individual works, collections, or materials about horror television programs.
    BT   **Television programs**
    RT   **Fantasy television programs**
Horse
    USE   **Horses**
Horse breeding
    USE   **Horses—Breeding**
Horse racing 798.4
    BT   **Racing**
    RT   **Gambling**
          Horsemanship
Horse riding
    USE   **Horsemanship**
Horseback riding
    USE   **Horsemanship**
Horsebreaking
    USE   **Horses—Training**
Horsemanship 798.2
    UF   Coaching
          Dressage
          Equestrianism
          Horse riding
          Horseback riding *[Former heading]*
          Riding
    BT   **Locomotion**
    NT   **Horses—Breeding**
          Horses—Training
    RT   **Horse racing**
          Rodeos
Horses 599.72; 636.1
    UF   Foals
          Horse
    BT   **Mammals**
    NT   **Ponies**
Horses—Breeding 636.1
    UF   Horse breeding

    BT   **Breeding**
          Horsemanship
Horses—Diseases 636.089
Horses—Training 636.1
    UF   Horsebreaking
    BT   **Animals—Training**
          Horsemanship
Horseshoeing
    USE   **Blacksmithing**
Horticulture 635
    Use for materials on the scientific and economic aspects of the cultivation of flowers, fruits, vegetables, etc. Materials on the practical aspects of creating gardens and cultivating plants are entered under **Gardening.** General materials about gardens, the history of gardens, various types of gardens, etc., are entered under **Gardens.**
    BT   **Agriculture**
          Plants
    NT   **Aeroponics**
          Flower gardening
          Fruit culture
          Greenhouses
          Hydroponics
          Landscape gardening
          Organic gardening
          Plant breeding
          Vegetable gardening
    RT   **Gardening**
Hosiery 391; 687
    UF   Stockings
    BT   **Clothing and dress**
          Textile industry
Hospices 362.1
    BT   **Hospitals**
          Social medicine
          Terminal care
Hospital libraries 027.6
    UF   Libraries, Hospital
    BT   **Libraries**
Hospital ships 362.1; 623.8
    UF   Floating hospitals
    BT   **Hospitals**
          Ships
Hospital wastes
    USE   **Medical wastes**
Hospitality
    USE   **Entertaining**
Hospitalization insurance 368.3
    UF   Group hospitalization

Hospitalization insurance—*Continued*
      Insurance, Hospitalization
      [Former heading]
  BT **Health insurance**
Hospitals (May subdiv. geog.) **362.1**
  UF Infirmaries
      Institutions, Charitable and
        philanthropic
      Sanatoriums
  SA types of hospitals and names
      of individual hospitals, to
      be added as needed
  BT **Institutional care**
      Medicine
      Public health
      Public welfare
  NT **Children's hospitals**
      Hospices
      Hospital ships
      Life support systems (Medical
        environment)
      Long-term care facilities
      Military hospitals
      Nursing homes
      Psychiatric hospitals
  RT **Medical centers**
      Medical charities
      Nursing
      Sick
Hospitals, Military
  USE **Military hospitals**
Hospitals—United States 362.1
  UF United States—Hospitals
Hostage escapes
  USE **Escapes**
Hostage negotiation
  BT **Hostages**
      Negotiation
Hostages (May subdiv. geog.) **920**
  SA hostages from a particular
      country, e.g. **American hos-**
      tages; to be added as need-
      ed
  BT **Terrorism**
  NT **American hostages**
      Hostage negotiation
Hostages, American
  USE **American hostages**
Hostages, American—Iran
  USE **American hostages—Iran**

Hostels, Youth
  USE **Youth hostels**
Hostesses, Airline
  USE **Flight attendants**
Hot air engines
  USE **Heat engines**
Hot air heating 697
  UF Warm air heating
  BT **Heating**
Hot water heating 697
  BT **Heating**
Hotels and motels (May subdiv. geog.)
      647.94; 728
      Use for materials on public accommo-
    dations, including inns, guest houses, and
    bed-and-breakfast establishments.
  UF Auto courts
      Bed and breakfast accommo-
        dations
      Boarding houses
      Hotels, motels, etc. *[Former*
        heading]
      Inns
      Lodging houses
      Motels
      Motor courts
      Rooming houses
      Tourist accommodations
  BT **Service industries**
  NT **Youth hostels**
Hotels and motels—United States
      647.9473; 728
  UF Hotels, motels, etc.—United
      States *[Former heading]*
      United States—Hotels and
      motels
Hotels, motels, etc.
  USE **Hotels and motels**
Hotels, motels, etc.—United States
  USE **Hotels and motels—United**
      States
Hothouses
  USE **Greenhouses**
Hotlines (Telephone counseling) 361.3;
      362.2
  UF Crisis counseling
      Crisis intervention telephone
        service
      Switchboard hotlines
      Telephone counseling

Hotlines (Telephone counseling)—
Continued
  BT **Counseling**
      Human relations
      Information services
      Social work
  RT **Crisis centers**
Hours of labor 331.25
  UF Alternative work schedules
      Compressed work week
      Eight-hour day
      Five-day work week
      Flexible hours of labor
      Flexitime
      Four-day work week
      Labor, Hours of
      Overtime
      Working day
      Working hours
  BT **Labor**
  NT **Absenteeism (Labor)**
      Part-time employment
  RT **Children—Employment**
House boats
  USE **Houseboats**
House buying
  USE **Houses—Buying and selling**
House cleaning 648
  BT **Cleaning**
      Home economics
      Household sanitation
House construction 690
  UF Building, House
      Construction, House
      Home construction
      Residential construction
  SA types of house construction
      and special kinds of houses,
      to be added as needed
  BT **Building**
      Domestic architecture
  NT **Earth sheltered houses**
      House painting
      Log cabins and houses
      Prefabricated houses
  RT **Houses**
House decoration
  USE **Interior design**

House drainage 690
  Use for materials on house drainage. Materials on land drainage are entered under **Drainage.**
  UF Drainage, House *[Former heading]*
  BT **Household sanitation**
  NT **Sanitary engineering**
      Sewerage
  RT **Plumbing**
House flies
  USE **Flies**
House furnishing
  USE **Interior design**
House of Representatives (U.S.)
  USE **United States. Congress. House**
House painting 698
  UF Finishes and finishing
  BT **House construction**
      Interior design
  NT **Paint**
  RT **Industrial painting**
House plans
  USE **Domestic architecture— Designs and plans**
House plants 635.9
  BT **Cultivated plants**
      Flower gardening
      Plants
      Window gardening
  RT **Container gardening**
      Indoor gardening
House purchase
  USE **Houses—Buying and selling**
House repairing
  USE **Houses—Maintenance and repair**
House sanitation
  USE **Household sanitation**
House selling
  USE **Houses—Buying and selling**
House sharing
  USE **Shared housing**
House trailers
  USE **Mobile homes**
      Travel trailers and campers
Houseboats 728.7
  UF House boats
  BT **Boats and boating**

BT = Broader Term   NT = Narrower Term   RT = Related Term   SA = See Also   UF = Used For

Household appliances
  USE **Household equipment and supplies**
Household appliances, Electric
  USE **Electric household appliances**
Household budgets 640
  UF Budgets, Household *[Former heading]*
      Domestic finance
      Family budget
      Finance, Household
      Home economics—Accounting
      Household finances
  BT **Cost of living**
      Personal finance
Household employees 640
  UF Domestic workers
      Housemaids
      Servants
  BT **Home economics**
      Labor
Household equipment and supplies 643; 683
  UF Domestic appliances
      Household appliances
      Implements, utensils, etc.
      Labor saving devices, Household
  BT **Home economics**
  NT **Electric household appliances**
      Kitchen utensils
Household finances
  USE **Cost of living**
      Household budgets
Household management
  USE **Home economics**
Household moving
  USE **Moving**
Household pests 648
  UF Diseases and pests
      Vermin
  SA types of pests, e.g. **Flies;** to be added as needed
  BT **Home economics**
      Household sanitation
      Pests
  NT **Flies**
  RT **Insect pests**
Household sanitation 648
  UF House sanitation

Sanitation, Household *[Former heading]*
  BT **Sanitation**
  NT **House cleaning**
      House drainage
      Household pests
      Laundry
      Ventilation
  RT **Plumbing**
Household utensils
  USE **Kitchen utensils**
Household violence
  USE **Family violence**
Househusbands
  USE **Homemakers**
Housekeeping
  USE **Home economics**
Housemaids
  USE **Household employees**
Houses (May subdiv. geog.) **643; 728**
    Use for general materials on buildings in which people live. Materials on residential buildings from the standpoint of style and design are entered under **Domestic architecture.**
  UF Dwellings
      Habitations, Human
      Homes
      Residences
  SA types of houses, e.g. **Earth sheltered houses;** and rooms and parts of the house, e.g. **Kitchens;** to be added as needed
  BT **Buildings**
  NT **Apartment houses**
      Earth sheltered houses
      Garden rooms
      Housing
      Kitchens
      Log cabins and houses
      Prefabricated houses
      Rooms
      Solar homes
      Tenement houses
  RT **Building**
      Domestic architecture
      House construction
Houses—Buying and selling 333.33
  UF Home buying
      Home purchase

Houses—Buying and selling—*Continued*
  House buying
  House purchase
  House selling
 BT **Real estate business**
Houses, Earth sheltered
 USE **Earth sheltered houses**
Houses—Heating and ventilation 644;
  697
 BT **Heating**
Houses, Historic
 USE **Historic buildings**
Houses, Log
 USE **Log cabins and houses**
Houses—Maintenance and repair 643
 UF Home repairing
  House repairing
 BT **Buildings—Maintenance and**
  repair
Houses of animals
 USE **Animals—Habitations**
Houses, Prefabricated
 USE **Prefabricated houses**
Houses—Remodeling 643
 UF Home remodeling
  Remodeling of houses
Houses, Underground
 USE **Earth sheltered houses**
Housewives
 USE **Homemakers**
Housing (May subdiv. geog.) 307.3;
  363.5
  Use for materials on the social and eco-
nomic aspects of housing. Materials on
the social and economic aspects of hous-
ing as it pertains to specific ethnic groups
or classes of persons are entered under
that group or class of persons with the
subdivision *Housing.* Materials on the residential buildings of ethnic groups or
classes of persons from the standpoint of
architecture, construction, or ethnology
are entered under the name of the ethnic
group or class of persons with the subdivision *Dwellings.*
 UF Dwellings
  Habitations, Human
 SA ethnic groups, classes of persons, and domestic animals
  with the subdivision *Hous-*
  ing, to be added as needed
 BT **Houses**
  Landlord and tenant

  Social problems
  Welfare work in industry
 NT **African Americans—Housing**
  Apartment houses
  Blacks—Housing
  Discrimination in housing
  Homelessness
  Mobile homes
  Physically handicapped—
   Housing
  Public housing
  Shared housing
  Timesharing (Real estate)
 RT **City planning**
  Tenement houses
Housing, African American
 USE **African Americans—Housing**
Housing, Black
 USE **Blacks—Housing**
Housing, Discrimination in
 USE **Discrimination in housing**
Housing for the elderly
 USE **Elderly—Housing**
Housing for the physically handicapped
 USE **Physically handicapped—**
   Housing
Housing loans
 USE **Mortgages**
Housing projects, Government
 USE **Public housing**
Houston Astros (Baseball team) 796.357
 UF Astros (Baseball team)
  Houston (Tex.). Baseball Club
  (National League)
 BT **Baseball clubs**
Houston (Tex.). Baseball Club (National
  League)
 USE **Houston Astros (Baseball**
   team)
Hovercraft
 USE **Ground effect machines**
How to start a business
 USE **New business enterprises**
How-to-stop-smoking programs
 USE **Smoking cessation programs**
Hudson River (N.Y. and N.J.)—Bridges
 USE **Bridges—Hudson River (N.Y.**
   and N.J.)
Hugging 158; 302.2; 395
 UF Embracing

Hugging—*Continued*
    Hugs
  BT Manners and customs
      Nonverbal communication
      Touch
Hugs
  USE Hugging
Huguenots 284
  BT Christian sects
      Reformation
  NT Saint Bartholomew's Day,
      Massacre of, 1572
Hull House
  USE Hull House (Chicago, Ill.)
Hull House (Chicago, Ill.) 361.4
  UF Hull House *[Former heading]*
  BT Social settlements
Human abnormalities
  USE Birth defects
      Growth disorders
Human anatomy 611
  UF Anatomy, Human *[Former*
      heading]
      Body, Human
      Human body
  SA names of organs and regions
      of the body, e.g. **Heart**; to
      be added as needed
  BT Anatomy
Human anatomy—Atlases 611
  BT Atlases
Human anatomy in art
  USE Artistic anatomy
      Nude in art
Human artificial insemination 176;
      346.01; 618.1
  UF Artificial insemination, Hu-
      man *[Former heading]*
  BT Artificial insemination
      Reproduction
  RT Sexual ethics
Human behavior 150; 302
  UF Behavior
      Morals
      Social behavior
  BT Character
      Psychology
      Social sciences
  NT Aggressiveness (Psychology)
      Behavior modification

      Behaviorism
      Cannibalism
      Conduct of life
      Consolation
      Duty
      Eating customs
      Etiquette
      Friendship
      Habit
      Helping behavior
      Honesty
      Lifestyles
      Love
      Patience
      Patriotism
      Sexual behavior
      Social adjustment
      Sportsmanship
      Truthfulness and falsehood
      Vice
      Virtue
  RT Ethics
      Human relations
      Life skills
Human body
  USE Human anatomy
      Physiology
Human cold storage
  USE Cryonics
Human ecology 304.2
  UF Ecology, Human
      Ecology, Social
      Social ecology
  BT Sociology
  NT Anthropogeography
      Environmental influence on
      humans
      Human influence on nature
      Population
      Social psychology
      Survival skills
  RT Environmental policy
Human embryos, Frozen
  USE Frozen embryos
Human engineering 620.8
    Use for materials on engineering design
as related to human anatomical, physio-
logical, and psychological capabilities and
limitations.
  UF Biomechanics

BT = Broader Term   NT = Narrower Term   RT = Related Term   SA = See Also   UF = Used For

Human engineering—*Continued*
    Ergonomics
  BT **Applied psychology**
      Engineering
      Industrial design
      Psychophysiology
  NT **Life support systems (Space environment)**
      Life support systems (Submarine environment)
  RT **Machine design**
Human experimentation in medicine 174
  UF Experimentation on humans, Medical
      Medical experimentation on humans
  BT **Medical ethics**
      Medicine—Research
Human fertility 304.6; 612.6; 616.6
    Use for materials on fertility in humans. General materials on fertility in animals, including humans, are entered under **Fertility.**
  UF Fertility, Human *[Former heading]*
  BT **Birthrate**
      Fertility
      Population
  NT **Infertility**
  RT **Birth control**
      Childlessness
Human figure in art
  USE **Artistic anatomy**
      Figure drawing
      Figure painting
      Nude in art
Human influence on nature 304.2; 363.7
  UF Earth, Effect of man on
      Man—Influence on nature *[Former heading]*
      Nature, Effect of man on
  BT **Human ecology**
  NT **Pollution**
  RT **Environmental policy**
Human life education
  USE **Sex education**
Human locomotion 152.3; 612.7
  UF Biomechanics
      Human mechanics
      Human movement

  BT **Locomotion**
      Physiology
  RT **Musculoskeletal system**
Human mechanics
  USE **Human locomotion**
Human movement
  USE **Human locomotion**
Human origins 573.2
  UF Antiquity of man
      Man—Antiquity
      Man—Origin *[Former heading]*
      Origin of man
  BT **Physical anthropology**
      Religion and science
  RT **Evolution**
      Prehistoric man
Human physiology
  USE **Physiology**
Human race
  USE **Anthropology**
      Man
Human records
  USE **World records**
Human relations 158; 302
    Use for materials on group behavior, social relations between persons, and problems arising from organizational and interpersonal relations.
  UF Interpersonal relations
  SA interpersonal relations between groups of persons or individuals, e.g. **Jews and Gentiles; Landlord and tenant; Parent and child;** etc., to be added as needed
  BT **Social psychology**
  NT **Conflict of generations**
      Discrimination
      Domestic relations
      Family
      Grandparent and child
      Group relations training
      Helping behavior
      Hotlines (Telephone counseling)
      Interfaith relations
      Jews and Gentiles
      Landlord and tenant
      Loneliness

BT = Broader Term   NT = Narrower Term   RT = Related Term   SA = See Also   UF = Used For

Human relations—*Continued*
        Multicultural education
        Parent and child
        Personal space
        Personnel management
        Prejudices
        Social adjustment
        Social values
        Teacher-student relationships
        Toleration
        Transactional analysis
  RT   **Applied psychology**
        Human behavior
        Life skills

Human resource management
  USE **Personnel management**

Human resources 331.11
  UF   Man power
        Manpower
  SA   names of wars with the subdi-
        vision *Human resources,* to
        be added as needed
  BT   **Employment**
  NT   **Draft**
        Unemployment
        Voluntary military service
        World War, 1939-1945—
        Human resources
  RT   **Labor supply**

Human resources development
  USE **Human resources policy**

Human resources policy 331.11
  UF   Human resources develop-
        ment
        Manpower policy
  BT   **Economic policy**
  NT   **Occupational retraining**
        Occupational training
        Vocational education
  RT   **Labor supply**

Human rights 323; 341.4
    Use for materials on the rights of per-
sons regardless of their legal, socioeconomic, or cultural status, as recognized by
the international community. Materials on
citizens' rights as established by law or
protected by a constitution are entered under **Civil rights.**
  UF   Basic rights
        Civil rights (International law)
        Fundamental rights

        Rights, Human
        Rights of man
  NT   **Civil rights**

Human survival skills
  USE **Survival skills**

Human values
  USE **Values**

Humane treatment of animals
  USE **Animal welfare**

Humanism 001.2; 880
    Use for materials on culture founded on
the study of the classics, or more narrowly
on Greek and Roman scholarship. Materials on any intellectual or philosophical
movement or set of beliefs that promotes
human values as separate and distinct
from religious doctrines are entered under
Secularism.
  BT   **Culture**
        Literature
        Philosophy
  NT   **Humanities**
  RT   **Classical education**
        Learning and scholarship
        Renaissance
        Secularism

Humanism—1900-1999 (20th century)
  USE **Secularism**

Humanism, Secular
  USE **Secularism**

Humanistic medicine
  USE **Holistic medicine**

Humanitarians
  USE **Philanthropists**

Humanities 001.3
  BT   **Humanism**
  NT   **Art**
        History
        Literature
        Music
        Philosophy
  RT   **Classical education**

Humanities and science
  USE **Science and the humanities**

Humanity, Religion of
  USE **Positivism**

Humans in space
  USE **Space flight**

Humidity 551.57
  UF   Air, Moisture of
        Atmospheric humidity
        Relative humidity

Humidity—*Continued*
   BT   Meteorology
         Weather
Humor
   USE Wit and humor
         and subjects with the subdivision *Humor,* e.g. **World War, 1939-1945—Humor;** to be added as needed
Humorists 809.7; 920
   BT   Wit and humor
Humorous fiction 808.83; 813, etc.
   May be used for individual works, collections, or materials about humorous fiction.
   UF   Comic novels
         Humorous stories *[Former heading]*
   BT   Fiction
         Wit and humor
   RT   Mock-heroic literature
Humorous films
   USE Comedy films
Humorous pictures
   USE Cartoons and caricatures
         Comic books, strips, etc.
Humorous plays
   USE Comedies
Humorous poetry 808.81; 811, etc.; 811.008, etc.
   May be used for individual works, collections, or materials about humorous poetry.
   UF   Comic verse
         Humorous verse
         Light verse
   BT   Poetry
         Wit and humor
   NT   Limericks
         Nonsense verses
Humorous stories
   USE Humorous fiction
Humorous verse
   USE Humorous poetry
Hundred Years' War, 1339-1453 944
   UF   100 years' war
   BT   Europe—History—476-1492
         France—History—1328-1589, House of Valois
         Great Britain—History—1399-1485, Lancaster and York

Hungary—History 943.9
Hungary—History—1956, Revolution 943.905
   BT   Revolutions
Hunger 363.8
   RT   Fasting
         Starvation
Hunger strikes 303.6
   UF   Strikes, Hunger
   BT   Fasting
         Nonviolence
         Passive resistance
         Protests, demonstrations, etc.
         Resistance to government
Hunting (May subdiv. geog.) 799.2
   UF   Gunning
   SA   types of hunting, to be added as needed
   NT   Decoys (Hunting)
         Falconry
         Game protection
         Game reserves
         Tracking and trailing
         Whaling
   RT   Game and game birds
         Shooting
         Trapping
Hunting, Job
   USE Job hunting
Hunting—United States 799.2973
   UF   United States—Hunting
Hurricanes (May subdiv. geog.) 551.55
   Use for cyclonic storms originating in the region of the West Indies.
   BT   Cyclones
         Storms
         Winds
   RT   Typhoons
Husband abuse 362.82
   UF   Abuse of husbands
         Battered husbands
         Battered men
         Husband battering
         Husband beating
   BT   Family violence
Husband battering
   USE Husband abuse
Husband beating
   USE Husband abuse
Husbands 306.872
   UF   Married men

Husbands—*Continued*

    Spouses
- BT   **Family**
-       **Marriage**
-       **Married people**
-       **Men**
- NT   **Widowers**

Husbands, Runaway
- USE **Runaway adults**

Hybridization
- USE **Plant breeding**

Hydraulic cement
- USE **Cement**

Hydraulic engineering 627
- BT   **Civil engineering**
-       **Engineering**
-       **Fluid mechanics**
-       **Water power**
- NT   **Boring**
-       **Drainage**
-       **Dredging**
-       **Flood control**
-       **Hydraulic structures**
-       **Hydrodynamics**
-       **Hydrostatics**
-       **Irrigation**
-       **Pumping machinery**
-       **Reclamation of land**
-       **Wells**
- RT   **Hydraulics**
-       **Rivers**
-       **Water**
-       **Water supply engineering**

Hydraulic machinery 621.2
- BT   **Machinery**
-       **Water power**
- NT   **Turbines**

Hydraulic structures 627
- SA   types of hydraulic structures,
  to be added as needed
- BT   **Hydraulic engineering**
-       **Structural engineering**
- NT   **Aqueducts**
-       **Canals**
-       **Dams**
-       **Docks**
-       **Harbors**
-       **Pipelines**
-       **Reservoirs**

Hydraulics 621.2; 627

    Use for materials on technical applications of the theory of hydrodynamics.
- UF   Water flow
- BT   **Fluid mechanics**
-       **Liquids**
-       **Mechanics**
-       **Physics**
- NT   **Hydrodynamics**
-       **Hydrostatics**
-       **Water**
-       **Water power**
- RT   **Hydraulic engineering**

Hydrodynamics 532

    Use for materials on the theory of the motion and action of fluids. Materials on the experimental investigation and technical application of this theory are entered under **Hydraulics.**
- BT   **Dynamics**
-       **Fluid mechanics**
-       **Hydraulic engineering**
-       **Hydraulics**
-       **Liquids**
-       **Mechanics**
- NT   **Hydrostatics**
-       **Viscosity**
-       **Waves**

Hydroelectric power
- USE **Water power**

Hydroelectric power plants 621.31
- UF   Power plants, Hydroelectric
- BT   **Electric power plants**
-       **Water power**
-       **Water resources development**

Hydrofoil boats 623.8
- BT   **Boats and boating**

Hydrogen 546
- BT   **Chemical elements**

Hydrogen bomb 623.4
- UF   H bomb
-       Thermonuclear bomb
- BT   **Bombs**
-       **Nuclear warfare**
-       **Nuclear weapons**
- NT   **Radioactive fallout**
- RT   **Atomic bomb**

Hydrogen nucleus
- USE **Protons**

Hydrology
- USE **Water**

Hydromechanics
   USE **Fluid mechanics**
Hydropathy
   USE **Hydrotherapy**
Hydrophobia
   USE **Rabies**
Hydroponics 631.5
   UF Agriculture, Soilless
       Chemiculture
       Plants—Soilless culture
       Soilless agriculture
       Water farming
   BT **Horticulture**
Hydrostatics 532
   BT **Fluid mechanics**
       Hydraulic engineering
       Hydraulics
       Hydrodynamics
       Liquids
       Mechanics
       Physics
       Statics
   NT **Gases**
Hydrotherapy 615.8
   UF Hydropathy
       Water cure
   BT **Physical therapy**
       Therapeutics
       Water
   RT **Baths**
       Health resorts
Hygiene 613
   UF Body care
       Personal cleanliness
       Personal hygiene
   SA parts of the body with the
       subdivision *Care and hy-*
       giene, e.g. **Foot—Care and**
       hygiene; and classes of per-
       sons and ethnic groups with
       the subdivision *Health and*
       hygiene, e.g. **Women—**
       Health and hygiene; to be
       added as needed
   BT **Cleanliness**
       Medicine
       Preventive medicine
   NT **Baths**
       Diet
       Disinfection and disinfectants

       Exercise
       Mental health
       Military health
       Personal grooming
       Rest
       School hygiene
       Sexual hygiene
       Sleep
       Ventilation
   RT **Health**
       Sanitation
Hygiene, Industrial
   USE **Occupational health and safe-**
        ty
Hygiene, Mental
   USE **Mental health**
Hygiene, Military
   USE **Military health**
Hygiene, School
   USE **School hygiene**
Hygiene, Sexual
   USE **Sexual hygiene**
Hygiene, Social
   USE **Public health**
Hygiene—Study and teaching
   USE **Health education**
Hygiene, Tropical
   USE **Tropical medicine**
Hymenoptera
   USE **Ants**
       Bees
       Wasps
Hymnology
   USE **Hymns**
Hymns 245; 264; 782.27
   Use for books of hymns and for materi-
  als on hymnology.
   UF Hymnology
       Psalmody
   BT **Devotional literature**
       Liturgies
       Poetry
       Songs
       Vocal music
   NT **Carols**
       Spirituals (Songs)
   RT **Church music**
       Religious poetry
Hyperactive children 155.4; 618.92
   UF Children, Hyperactive

Hyperactive children—*Continued*
        Hyperkinetic children
        Overactive children
  BT **Handicapped children**
  RT **Hyperactivity**
Hyperactivity 616.85; 616.92
  UF Hyperkinesia
        Overactivity
  BT **Diseases**
  RT **Hyperactive children**
Hyperkinesia
  USE **Hyperactivity**
Hyperkinetic children
  USE **Hyperactive children**
Hyperspace
  USE **Fourth dimension**
Hypertension 616.1
  UF High blood pressure
  BT **Blood pressure**
Hypnosis
  USE **Hypnotism**
Hypnotism 154.7
  UF Animal magnetism
        Autosuggestion
        Hypnosis
        Mesmerism
  BT **Mental healing**
        Psychophysiology
  RT **Mental suggestion**
        Mind and body
        Psychoanalysis
        Subconsciousness
        Suggestive therapeutics
I.B.M. 7090 (Computer)
  USE **IBM 7090 (Computer)**
I.C.B.M.
  USE **Intercontinental ballistic missiles**
I. Q. tests
  USE **Intelligence tests**
I.R.A.'s (Pensions)
  USE **Individual retirement accounts**
I.S.B.D
  USE **International Standard Bibliographic Description**
I.S.B.N.
  USE **International Standard Book Numbers**
I.S.S.N.
  USE **International Standard Serial Numbers**

IBM 7090 (Computer) 621.39
  UF I.B.M. 7090 (Computer)
  BT **Computers**
ICBM
  USE **Intercontinental ballistic missiles**
Ice 551.3
  UF Freezing
  BT **Cold**
        Frost
        Physical geography
        Water
  NT **Glaciers**
        Icebergs
Ice age 551.7
  UF Glacial epoch
  BT **Earth**
Ice boats
  USE **Iceboats**
Ice cream, ices, etc. 637; 641.8
  UF Ices
  BT **Desserts**
        Frozen foods
Ice (Drug) 362.29; 615
  BT **Designer drugs**
        Methamphetamine
Ice hockey
  USE **Hockey**
Ice manufacture
  USE **Refrigeration**
Ice skating 796.91
  UF Figure skating
        Skating
  BT **Winter sports**
Ice sports
  USE **Winter sports**
Icebergs 551.3
  BT **Ice**
        Ocean
        Physical geography
Iceboats 623.8
  UF Ice boats
  BT **Boats and boating**
Icelandic language 439
  BT **Scandinavian languages**
Icelandic language—0-1500
  USE **Old Norse language**
Icelandic literature 839
  UF Icelandic literature, Modern
  BT **Literature**

BT = Broader Term   NT = Narrower Term   RT = Related Term   SA = See Also   UF = Used For

Icelandic literature—*Continued*
Scandinavian literature
RT   Old Norse literature
Icelandic literature, Modern
USE   Icelandic literature
Ices
USE   Ice cream, ices, etc.
Ichthyology
USE   Fishes
Iconography
USE   Art
Christian art and symbolism
Portraits
Religious art and symbolism
Ideal states
USE   Utopian fiction
Utopias
Idealism 141
BT   Philosophy
Transcendentalism
RT   Materialism
Positivism
Realism
Identification
SA   subjects with the subdivision
Identification, to be added
as needed
NT   Airplanes—Identification
Criminals—Identification
DNA fingerprints
Fingerprints
Identity
USE   Individuality
Personality
Idioms
USE   names of languages with the
subdivision *Idioms,* e.g.
English language—Idioms;
to be added as needed
Idyllic poetry
USE   Pastoral poetry
Illegal aliens 323.6; 325; 342
UF   Aliens, Illegal *[Former head-
ing]*
Underground aliens
Undocumented aliens
BT   Aliens
Immigration and emigration
Underground economy
RT   Sanctuary movement

Illegitimacy 306.874; 346.01
UF   Bastardy
Children, Illegitimate
Legitimacy (Law)
BT   Social problems
NT   Unmarried fathers
Unmarried mothers
Illiteracy
USE   Literacy
Illiterate societies
USE   Nonliterate folk society
Illness
USE   Diseases
Illuminated manuscripts
USE   Illumination of books and
manuscripts
Illuminating gas
USE   Gas
Illumination
USE   Lighting
Illumination of books and manuscripts
096; 745.6
UF   Illuminated manuscripts
Manuscripts, Illuminated
Miniatures (Illumination of
books and manuscripts)
Ornamental alphabets
BT   Alphabets
Art
Books
Christian art and symbolism
Decoration and ornament
Illustration of books
Manuscripts
Medieval art
RT   Initials
Illusions
USE   Hallucinations and illusions
Optical illusions
Illustration of books 741.6
UF   Book illustration
BT   Art
Books
Color printing
Decoration and ornament
NT   Caldecott Medal
Engraving
Illumination of books and
manuscripts
Photomechanical processes

Illustration of books—*Continued*
  RT **Drawing**
      Picture books for children
Illustrations
  USE subjects with the subdivision
      Pictorial works, e.g.
      Animals—Pictorial works;
      United States—History—
      1861-1865, Civil War—
      Pictorial works; etc., to be
      added as needed
Illustrations, Humorous
  USE **Cartoons and caricatures**
Illustrators 741.6092; 920
  SA illustrators of particular coun-
      tries, e.g. **American illustra-**
      tors; to be added as needed
  BT **Artists**
  NT **American illustrators**
Illustrators, American
  USE **American illustrators**
Images, National
  USE **National characteristics**
Imaginary animals
  USE **Mythical animals**
Imaginary friends
  USE **Imaginary playmates**
Imaginary places
  USE **Geographical myths**
Imaginary playmates 155.4
  UF Friends, Imaginary
      Imaginary friends
      Invisible playmates
      Make-believe playmates
      Playmates, Imaginary
  BT **Friendship**
      Imagination
      Play
Imaginary voyages 808.83; 813, etc.
  May be used for individual works, col-
  lections, or materials about imaginary
  voyages.
  UF Space flight (Fiction)
      Subterranean voyages
      Time travel (Fiction)
      Voyages, Imaginary
      Voyages to the moon
  BT **Fantasy fiction**
      Science fiction
  NT **Robinsonades**

  RT **Interplanetary voyages**
Imagination 153.3
  BT **Educational psychology**
      Intellect
      Psychology
  NT **Creation (Literary, artistic,**
      etc.)
      Fantasy
      Imaginary playmates
Imaging, Magnetic resonance
  USE **Magnetic resonance imaging**
Immersion, Baptismal
  USE **Baptism**
Immigrants (May subdiv. geog.) **304.8**
  Use for materials on foreign-born per-
  sons who enter a country intending to be-
  come permanent residents or citizens.
  This heading may be locally subdivided
  by the names of places where immigrants
  have settled.
  UF Emigrants
      Foreign population
      Foreigners
  SA names of immigrant ethnic
      groups, e.g. **Mexican Ameri-**
      cans; and, for immigrants
      who are not citizens, the
      names of national groups
      with the appropriate subdi-
      vision for the country of
      their residence, e.g.
      Mexicans—United States;
      to be added as needed
  RT **Aliens**
      Immigration and emigration
Immigration and emigration 304.8; 325
  Use for materials on migration from
  one country to another. Materials on the
  movement of population within a country
  for permanent settlement are entered un-
  der **Internal migration.**
  UF Emigration
      Foreign population
      Migration
      Population, Foreign
  SA names of countries with the
      subdivision *Immigration*
      and emigration, e.g. **United**
      States—Immigration and
      emigration; names of coun-
      tries, cities, etc., with the
      subdivision *Foreign popula-*

BT = Broader Term   NT = Narrower Term   RT = Related Term   SA = See Also   UF = Used For

Immigration and emigration—*Continued*
tion, e.g. **United States—Foreign population;** and names of nationality groups, e.g. **Mexican Americans; Mexicans—United States;** etc., to be added as needed
BT **Colonies**
     Race relations
     Social problems
     Sociology
NT **Aliens**
     Anthropogeography
     Children of immigrants
     Illegal aliens
     Mexican Americans
     Mexicans—United States
     Naturalization
     Refugees
     United States—Foreign population
     United States—Immigration and emigration
RT **Americanization**
     Colonization
     Immigrants
Immortality 129
   Use for materials on the question of the endless existence of the soul. Materials on the character and form of a future existence are entered under **Future life.** Materials on the philosophical concept of eternity are entered under **Eternity.**
UF Life after death
BT **Eschatology**
     Soul
     Theology
RT **Future life**
Immunity 574.2; 591.2; 616.07
BT **Bacteriology**
     Pathology
     Preventive medicine
NT **Allergy**
RT **Communicable diseases**
     Vaccination
Immunization
USE **Vaccination**
Impaired vision
USE **Vision disorders**
Impeachments 351.9
BT **Administration of justice**

NT **Recall (Political science)**
Imperialism 325
UF Colonialism
SA names of countries with the subdivision *Foreign relations* or *Colonies,* to be added as needed
BT **Political science**
NT **Colonies**
     Colonization
     Great Britain—Colonies
Implements, utensils, etc.
USE **Agricultural machinery**
     Household equipment and supplies
     Stone implements
     Tools
Imports
USE **Commerce**
     Tariff
Impostors and imposture 364.1
UF Charlatans
     Hoaxes
     Pretenders
BT **Crime**
     Criminals
NT **Counterfeits and counterfeiting**
     Forgery
     Quacks and quackery
RT **Fraud**
     Swindlers and swindling
Impregnation, Artificial
USE **Artificial insemination**
Impressionism (Art) 709.03; 759.05
UF Neo-impressionism (Art)
BT **Modern art—1800-1899 (19th century)**
     Painting
RT **Postimpressionism (Art)**
Imprisonment
USE **Prisons**
In-service training
USE **Employees—Training**
     Librarians—In-service training
In vitro fertilization
USE **Fertilization in vitro**
Inaudible sound
USE **Ultrasonics**
Incandescent lamps
USE **Electric lamps**

Incas 985
BT Indians of South America
Incendiary bombs 623.4
UF Bombs, Incendiary
Fire bombs
BT Bombs
Incendiary weapons
Incendiary weapons 623.4
BT Chemical warfare
NT Incendiary bombs
Incentive (Psychology)
USE Motivation (Psychology)
Incest 306.877; 616.85
BT Sex crimes
NT Child sexual abuse
Incineration
USE Cremation
Refuse and refuse disposal
Income 331.2; 339.3
UF Fortunes
BT Economics
Finance
Property
Wealth
NT Guaranteed annual income
Retirement income
Wages
RT Profit
Income tax 336.24
UF Direct taxation
Payroll taxes
Taxation of income
BT Internal revenue
Taxation
NT Tax credits
Income, Untaxed
USE Underground economy
Indentured servants
USE Contract labor
Independence Day (United States)
USE Fourth of July
Independent schools
USE Private schools
Independent study 371.3
Use for materials on individual study that may be directed or assisted by instructional staff through periodic consultations.
BT Study skills
Tutors and tutoring
Indeterminism
USE Free will and determinism

Index librorum prohibitorum
USE Books—Censorship
Indexes 016
SA subjects with the subdivision *Indexes,* to be added as needed
BT Bibliography
NT Newspapers—Indexes
Periodicals—Indexes
Short stories—Indexes
Subject headings
Indexing 025.3
BT Bibliographic control
Bibliography
RT Cataloging
Files and filing
India rubber
USE Rubber
Indian art (North American)
USE Indians of North America—Art
Indian languages (North American)
USE Indians of North America—Languages
Indian literature (American)
USE American literature—American Indian authors
Indian literature (East Indian)
USE Indic literature
Indian literature (North American Indian)
USE Indians of North America—Literature
Indian missions
USE Indians of North America—Christian missions
Indian reservations
USE Indians of North America—Reservations
Indian women (North American)
USE Indians of North America—Women
Indians 970.004
Use for general materials on the Indians of the Western Hemisphere. May be subdivided topically like **Indians of North America.**
UF American Indians
Amerindians

Indians—*Continued*

SA names of Indian peoples and linguistic families, e.g. **Indians of Mexico; Aztecs;** etc., to be added as needed

NT **Indians of Central America**

Indians of Mexico

Indians of North America

Indians of South America

Indians of the West Indies

Indians of Canada

USE **Indians of North America— Canada**

Indians of Central America (May subdiv. geog. by countries or regions of Central America, e.g. **Indians of Central America—Guatemala.**) **972.8004**

May be subdivided topically like **Indians of North America.**

UF American Indians

Amerindians

Central American Indians

BT **Indians**

NT **Mayas**

Indians of Central America—Guatemala 972.81004

Indians (of India)

USE **East Indians**

Indians of Mexico (May subdiv. geog. by states of Mexico) **972.004**

May be subdivided topically like **Indians of North America.**

UF American Indians

Amerindians

Mexico, Indians of

BT **Indians**

NT **Aztecs**

Mayas

Indians of North America (May subdiv. geog. by Canada, its provinces or regions or by the United States, its states or regions, e.g. **Indians of North America—British Columbia; Indians of North America—Massachusetts;** etc.) **970.004**

Topical subdivisions used under this heading may also be used under the names of specific American Indian peoples and linguistic families.

UF American Indians

Amerindians

Native Americans

Native peoples

North American Indians

Pre-Columbian Americans

Precolumbian Americans

SA names of Indian peoples and linguistic families, e.g. **Navajo Indians;** to be added as needed

BT **Ethnology—United States**

Indians

NT **Cliff dwellers and cliff dwellings**

Mounds and mound builders

Navajo Indians

Indians of North America— Amusements

USE **Indians of North America— Games**

Indians of North America— Social life and customs

Indians of North America—Antiquities 970.004

BT **Antiquities**

United States—Antiquities

NT **Mounds and mound builders**

Indians of North America—Architecture 720.97; 970.004

BT **Architecture**

NT **Indians of North America— Dwellings**

Indians of North America—Art 704; 709.01

UF Art, Indian

Indian art (North American)

Indians of North America—Art—
Continued

BT   Art

Indians of North America—Canada
971.004

UF   Canadian Indians
Indians of Canada

Indians of North America—Captivities
970.004

BT   Frontier and pioneer life

Indians of North America—Children
305.23; 970.004

BT   Children

Indians of North America—Christian
missions 266

UF   Indian missions
Indians of North America—
Missions, Christian *[Former
heading]*
Missions, Indian

BT   Christian missions

Indians of North America—Chronology
970.004

BT   Chronology

Indians of North America—Civilization
and culture 970.004

Indians of North America—Claims
323.1; 970.004

UF   Indians of North America—
Land claims
Indians of North America—
Legal status, laws, etc.

Indians of North America—Costume
970.004

UF   Indians of North American—
Costume and adornment
[Former heading]

BT   Costume

Indians of North America—Customs
USE   Indians of North America—
Social life and customs

Indians of North America—Dances
793.3; 970.004

BT   Folk dancing
Indians of North America—
Religion
Indians of North America—
Social life and customs

Indians of North America—Drama 812,
etc.

May be used for individual works, collections, or materials about plays about
the Indians of North America.

BT   Drama

Indians of North America—Dwellings
728

UF   Teepees
Tepees
Tipis
Wigwams

BT   Indians of North America—
Architecture

Indians of North America—Economic
conditions 970.004

Indians of North America—Education
371.97; 970.004

UF   Indians of North America—
Schools

Indians of North America—Ethnology
305.897

Indians of North America—Fiction
808.83; 813, etc.

May be used for individual works, collections, or materials about fiction about
the Indians of North America.

Indians of North America—First contact with Europeans
970.004

BT   Indians of North America—
History

RT   Indians of North America—
Relations with early settlers

Indians of North America—Folklore
398

Use for materials about the folklore of
North American Indians. Collections of
North American Indian legends, myths,
tales, etc., are entered under **Indians of
North America—Legends**.

UF   Indians of North America—
Mythology

BT   Folklore

RT   Indians of North America—
Legends

Indians of North America—Games
790.1; 970.004

UF   Indians of North America—
Amusements
Indians of North America—
Recreations

BT = Broader Term   NT = Narrower Term   RT = Related Term   SA = See Also   UF = Used For

Indians of North America—Games—
Continued

      Indians of North America—
        Sports

BT **Games**

      **Indians of North America—
        Social life and customs**

Indians of North America—
      Government policy

USE **Indians of North America—
      Government relations**

**Indians of North America—Government
      relations 323.1; 970.004**

Use for materials on the Indian policy
of the United States government and on
relations between North American governments and the Indians of North America.

UF Federal-Indian relations

      Indians of North America—
      Government policy *[Former
      heading]*

      Indians of North America—
      Legal status, laws, etc.

RT **Indians of North America—
      Relations with early settlers**

**Indians of North America—History
      970.004**

NT **Indians of North America—
      First contact with Europe-
      ans**

      **Indians of North America—
      Relations with early settlers**

      **Indians of North America—
      Wars**

**Indians of North America—Industries
      338.4; 680; 970.004**

Indians of North America—Land
      claims

USE **Indians of North America—
      Claims**

**Indians of North America—Languages
      497**

UF Indian languages (North
      American)

SA names of individual lan-
      guages, e.g. **Navajo lan-
      guage;** to be added as
      needed

BT **Language and languages**

NT **Indians of North America—
      Sign language**

      Navajo language

Indians of North America—Legal sta-
      tus, laws, etc.

USE **Indians of North America—
      Claims**

      **Indians of North America—
      Government relations**

**Indians of North America—Legends
      398.2**

Use for collections of North American
Indian legends, myths, tales, etc. Materials
about the folklore of North American Indians are entered under **Indians of North
America—Folklore.**

UF Indians of North America—
      Mythology

      Legends, Indian

BT **Legends**

RT **Indians of North America—
      Folklore**

**Indians of North America—Literature
      897**

Use for collections or materials about
literature written in Indian languages by
several American Indians authors. Collections or materials about literature written
in English by several American Indian authors are entered under **American
literature—American Indian authors.**

UF Indian literature (North
      American Indian)

BT **Literature**

**Indians of North America—Medicine
      615.8**

BT **Medicine**

Indians of North America—Missions,
      Christian

USE **Indians of North America—
      Christian missions**

**Indians of North America—Music
      780.89**

Use for musical transcriptions or for
materials about the music of the North
American Indians.

UF Indians of North America—
      Songs and music *[Former
      heading]*

      Music, Indian

BT **Music**

Indians of North America—Mythology

USE **Indians of North America—
      Folklore**

      **Indians of North America—
      Legends**

BT = Broader Term   NT = Narrower Term   RT = Related Term   SA = See Also   UF = Used For

Indians of North America—
    Mythology—*Continued*
        Indians of North America—
        Religion
Indians of North America—Names
    929.4
Indians of North America—Origin
    970.004
Indians of North America—Poetry 811,
    etc.; 811.008, etc.; 811.009,
    etc.
    May be used for individual works, col-
    lections, or materials about poetry about
    the Indians of North America.
    BT Poetry
Indians of North America—Politics and
    government 970.004
    UF Indians of North American—
        Tribal government
    BT Politics
Indians of North America—Psychology
    155.8
    BT Ethnopsychology
        Psychology
Indians of North America—Recreations
    USE Indians of North America—
        Games
Indians of North America—Relations
    with early settlers 970.004
    BT Indians of North America—
        History
    RT Indians of North America—
        First contact with Europe-
        ans
        Indians of North America—
        Government relations
Indians of North America—Religion
    299
    UF Indians of North America—
        Mythology
        Mythology, Indian
    BT Religion
    NT Indians of North America—
        Dances
    RT Mythology
        Totems and totemism
Indians of North America—
        Reservations 333.1
    UF Indian reservations
        Reservations, Indian

Indians of North America—Rites and
    ceremonies 291.3; 970.004
    BT Rites and ceremonies
    NT Powwows
Indians of North America—Schools
    USE Indians of North America—
        Education
Indians of North America—Sign lan-
    guage 419
    BT Indians of North America—
        Languages
        Sign language
Indians of North America—Silverwork
    739.2
    BT Silverwork
Indians of North America—Social con-
    ditions 970.004
    BT Social conditions
Indians of North America—Social life
    and customs 970.004
    UF Indians of North America—
        Amusements
        Indians of North America—
        Customs
    BT Manners and customs
    NT Indians of North America—
        Dances
        Indians of North America—
        Games
        Powwows
Indians of North America—Songs and
        music
    USE Indians of North America—
        Music
Indians of North America—Sports
    USE Indians of North America—
        Games
Indians of North America—Wars
    970.004
    BT Indians of North America—
        History
    NT Black Hawk War, 1832
        King Philip's War, 1675-1676
        Pontiac's Conspiracy, 1763-
        1765
        United States—History—
        1689-1697, King William's
        War

Indians of North America—Wars—
  Continued
      **United States—History—
        1755-1763, French and In-
        dian War**
**Indians of North America—Women
        305.4; 970.004**
  UF Indian women (North Ameri-
        can)
      Native American women
      Women, Indian
  BT **Women**
**Indians of North American—Costume
        and adornment**
  USE **Indians of North America—
        Costume**
**Indians of North American—Tribal
        government**
  USE **Indians of North America—
        Politics and government**
Indians of South America (May subdiv.
        geog. by country, e.g. **Indi-
        ans of South America—
        Peru; etc.) 980**
  May be subdivided topically like **Indi-
ans of North America.**
  UF American Indians
      Amerindians
  BT **Indians**
  NT **Incas**
Indians of South America—Peru 985
Indians of the West Indies 972.9004
  May be subdivided topically like **Indi-
ans of North America.**
  UF American Indians
      Amerindians
      West Indies, Indians of the
  BT **Indians**
Indic literature 891
  UF Indian literature (East Indian)
  BT **Literature**
Indigenous peoples
  USE **Ethnology**
Indigestion 616.3
  UF Dyspepsia
  BT **Digestion**
Individual retirement accounts 332.024
  UF I.R.A.'s (Pensions)
      IRAs (Pensions)
  BT **Pensions**
      Retirement income

Individualism 141; 302.5; 330.1
  BT **Economics**
      Equality
      Political science
      Sociology
Individuality 155.2
  UF Identity
  BT **Consciousness**
      Psychology
  NT **Self**
  RT **Conformity**
      Personality
Individualized instruction 371.3
  Use for materials on the adaptation of
instruction to meet individual needs with-
in the group.
  BT **Open plan schools**
      Slow learning children
      Tutors and tutoring
Indochina 959
  Use for the area comprising Laos, Cam-
bodia, and Vietnam.
Indoctrination, Forced
  USE **Brainwashing**
Indoor games 793
  BT **Games**
  NT **Checkers**
      Chess
  RT **Amusements**
Indoor gardening 635.9
  BT **Gardening**
  NT **Miniature gardens**
      Terrariums
      Window gardening
  RT **Container gardening**
      House plants
Induction coils 537.6; 621.319
  BT **Electric apparatus and appli-
        ances**
  NT **Condensers (Electricity)**
Induction (Logic)
  USE **Logic**
Induction motors
  USE **Electric motors**
Industrial alcohol
  USE **Denatured alcohol**
Industrial arbitration 331.89
  UF Arbitration, Industrial *[Former
        heading]*
      Conciliation, Industrial
      Industrial conciliation

Industrial arbitration—*Continued*
      Labor arbitration
      Labor courts
      Labor negotiations
      Mediation, Industrial
      Trade agreements (Labor)
  BT **Industrial relations**
      Labor
      Labor disputes
      Labor unions
      Negotiation
  RT **Collective bargaining**
      Strikes

Industrial arts 600
  UF Arts, Useful
      Mechanic arts
      Trades
      Useful arts
  SA names of specific industries,
      arts, and trades; and names
      of countries, cities, etc.,
      with the subdivision *Indus-*
      tries, to be added as needed
  BT **Handicraft**
  NT **Arts and crafts movement**
      Bookbinding
      Engineering
      Industrial arts education
      Printing
      Shipbuilding
  RT **Technology**

Industrial arts education 607
  UF Education, Industrial
      Industrial education
      Industrial schools
      Manual training
  BT **Industrial arts**
      Vocational education
  RT **Technical education**

Industrial arts shops
  USE **School shops**

Industrial buildings 725
  UF Buildings, Industrial
  BT **Architecture**
      Buildings
  NT **Factories**
      Office buildings
      Skyscrapers

Industrial chemistry 660
  UF Chemical technology

      Chemistry, Industrial
      Chemistry, Technical *[Former*
      heading]
      Technical chemistry
  SA names of specific industries
      and products, e.g. **Clay in-**
      dustries; Dyes and dyeing;
      etc., to be added as needed
  BT **Chemistry**
      Technology
  NT **Alloys**
      Bleaching
      Canning and preserving
      Ceramics
      Corrosion and anticorrosives
      Distillation
      Electrochemistry
      Food—Analysis
      Gums and resins
      Synthetic products
      Tanning
      Textile chemistry
      Waste products
  RT **Chemical engineering**
      Chemical industry
      Chemicals
      Metallurgy

Industrial combinations
  USE **Industrial trusts**
Industrial conciliation
  USE **Industrial arbitration**
Industrial councils
  USE **Participative management**
Industrial counseling
  USE **Employees—Counseling of**

Industrial design 745.2
  UF Art, Applied
      Design, Industrial *[Former*
      heading]
  BT **Design**
  NT **Automobiles—Design**
      Human engineering
      Systems engineering

Industrial diseases
  USE **Occupational diseases**
Industrial disputes
  USE **Labor disputes**
Industrial drawing
  USE **Mechanical drawing**

BT = Broader Term   NT = Narrower Term   RT = Related Term   SA = See Also   UF = Used For

Industrial education
USE **Industrial arts education**
Technical education
Industrial efficiency 658

Use for materials on the various means of increasing efficiency and output in business and industries, including time and motion studies and materials on the application of psychological principles to industrial production.

UF Efficiency, Industrial *[Former heading]*
BT **Business**
Industry
Management
NT **Job analysis**
Labor productivity
Motion study
Office management
Time study
RT **Executive ability**
Factory management
Personnel management
Industrial exhibitions
USE **Exhibitions**
Industrial health
USE **Occupational health and safety**
Industrial insurance 368.3

Use for materials on insurance as carried on by companies whose agents collect the premiums from policy holders in small weekly payments.

UF Insurance, Industrial *[Former heading]*
BT **Labor**
Life insurance
Saving and thrift
Industrial libraries
USE **Corporate libraries**
Industrial management
USE **Management**
Industrial materials
USE **Materials**
Industrial mergers
USE **Corporate mergers and acquisitions**
Industrial trusts
Railroads—Consolidation
Industrial mobilization 355.2

Use for materials on industrial and labor policies and programs for defense mobilization.

UF Defenses, National
Economic mobilization
Industry and war
Mobilization, Industrial
National defenses
BT **Economic policy**
Military art and science
War—Economic aspects
RT **Military readiness**
Military weapons
Industrial organization
USE **Management**
Industrial painting 698
UF Finishes and finishing
Mechanical painting
Painting, Industrial *[Former heading]*
Painting, Mechanical
NT **Lettering**
Paint
Sign painting
Varnish and varnishing
Wood finishing
RT **House painting**
Industrial plants
USE **Factories**
Industrial psychology
USE **Applied psychology**
Industrial relations 331

Use for general materials on employer-employee relations. Materials on problems of personnel and relations from the employer's point of view are entered under **Personnel management.**

UF Capital and labor
Employer-employee relations
Labor and capital
Labor-management relations
Labor relations
BT **Labor**
Management
NT **Collective bargaining**
Industrial arbitration
Labor contract
Labor disputes
Labor unions
Participative management
Personnel management
Strikes

Industrial revolution (May subdiv. geog.) **330.9; 909.81**
UF Revolution, Industrial
SA names of countries with the subdivision *Economic conditions* or with the subdivision *Industries,* to be added as needed
BT **Economic conditions**
    Industry—History
RT **Factory management**
    Great Britain—History—1800-1899 (19th century)
    Industrialization
    Machinery in industry
    Technology and civilization

Industrial robots 629.8
UF Robots, Industrial *[Former heading]*
    Working robots
BT **Machinery in industry**
    Robotics

Industrial safety
USE **Occupational health and safety**

Industrial schools
USE **Industrial arts education**
    Technical education

Industrial secrets
USE **Trade secrets**

Industrial trusts 338.8; 658
    Use for materials on combinations in restraint of trade in which stock ownership is transferred to trustees, who in turn issue trust certificates and dividends and who attempt to achieve monopolistic control over output, prices, or markets.
UF Business combinations
    Cartels
    Combinations, Industrial
    Industrial combinations
    Industrial mergers
    Mergers, Industrial
    Trusts, Industrial *[Former heading]*
BT **Capital**
    Commerce
    Economics
NT **Antitrust law**
    Railroads—Consolidation
RT **Competition**

    Corporation law
    Corporations
    Monopolies
    Restraint of trade

Industrial uses of space
USE **Space industrialization**

Industrial wastes 363.72; 628.4
UF Factory and trade waste
    Factory waste
    Trade waste
    Waste disposal
    Wastes, Industrial
BT **Refuse and refuse disposal**
    Waste products
NT **Hazardous wastes**
RT **Pollution**
    Water pollution

Industrial workers
USE **Labor**
    Working class

Industrialization 338
    Use for general materials only. Materials on the industrialization of individual countries, regions, etc., are entered under the name of country, city, etc. with the subdivision *Industries.*
BT **Economic policy**
    Industry
NT **Developing countries**
    Space industrialization
RT **Industrial revolution**
    Modernization
    Technical assistance

Industries
USE **Industry**
    and names of industries, e.g. **Steel industry;** and names of countries, cities, etc., with the subdivision *Industries,* e.g. **United States—Industries;** to be added as needed

Industries, Electric
USE **Electric industries**

Industries, Service
USE **Service industries**

Industry 338
UF Industries
    Production
SA names of countries, cities, etc. with the subdivision *Indus-*

BT = Broader Term   NT = Narrower Term   RT = Related Term   SA = See Also   UF = Used For

Industry—*Continued*
    tries, e.g. **United States— Industries;** and names of individual industries, e.g. **Steel industry;** to be added as needed

  BT **Civilization**
        Economics
  NT **Aerospace industries**
        Automobile industry
        Business enterprises
        Chemical industry
        Clothing industry
        Computer industry
        Defense industries
        Industrial efficiency
        Industrialization
        Leather industry
        Liquor industry
        Machinery in industry
        Management
        Manufactures
        Paper industry
        Petroleum industry
        Service industries
        Steel industry
  RT **Materials**
Industry and state
  USE **Industry—Government policy**
Industry and war
  USE **Industrial mobilization**
        War—Economic aspects
Industry—Government policy (May subdiv. geog.) **338.9; 351.82**
  UF Business and government
        Government and business
        Government regulation of industry
        Industry and state
        Industry—Organization, control, etc.
        Laissez faire
        Socialization of industry
        State and industry
        State regulation of industry
  BT **Socialism**
  NT **Agriculture—Government policy**
        Consumer protection
        Government lending

        Government ownership
        Privatization
        Public interest
        Public service commissions
        Railroads—Government policy
        Subsidies
  RT **Economic policy**
Industry—Government policy—United States 338.973; 353.0082
  UF United States—Industry— Government policy
Industry—History 338.09
  NT **Industrial revolution**
Industry—Organization, control, etc.
  USE **Industry—Government policy**
Inebriates
  USE **Alcoholics**
Inequality
  USE **Equality**
Infallibility of the Pope
  USE **Popes—Infallibility**
Infant care
  USE **Infants—Care**
Infantile paralysis
  USE **Poliomyelitis**
Infants 155.42; 305.23; 362.7; 618.92
    Use for materials about children in the earliest period of life, usually the first two years only.
  UF Babies
  BT **Children**
Infants and strangers
  USE **Children and strangers**
Infants—Birth defects
  USE **Birth defects**
Infants—Care 649
  UF Baby care
        Infant care
  BT **Child care**
  NT **Babysitting**
Infants—Clothing 646; 649
Infants—Diseases 618.92
  UF Pediatrics
  BT **Diseases**
  RT **Infants—Health and hygiene**
Infants—Education
  USE **Preschool education**
Infants—Health and hygiene 613; 618.92
  UF Infants—Hygiene

Infants—Health and hygiene—
Continued
Pediatrics
RT **Infants—Diseases**
Infants—Hygiene
USE **Infants—Health and hygiene**
Infants—Nutrition 641.1; 649
NT **Breast feeding**
Infants, Sale of
USE **Adoption—Corrupt practices**
Infection and infectious diseases
USE **Communicable diseases**
Infectious wastes
USE **Medical wastes**
Infertility 616.6
Use for materials on infertility in humans and in animals.
UF Sterility in animals
Sterility in humans
RT **Birth control**
Childlessness
Fertility
Human fertility
Infidelity, Marital
USE **Adultery**
Infirmaries
USE **Hospitals**
Inflammable substances
USE **Hazardous substances**
Inflation (Finance) 332.4
BT **Finance**
NT **Paper money**
Wage-price policy
RT **Monetary policy**
Influenza 616.2
UF Flu
Grippe
BT **Cold (Disease)**
Communicable diseases
Diseases
RT **Vaccination**
Information centers
USE **Information services**
Information clearinghouses
USE **Information services**
Information, Freedom of
USE **Freedom of information**
Information networks 004.6
UF Automated information networks

Networks, Information
Telereference
SA types of information networks and names of specific networks, to be added as needed
BT **Data transmission systems**
Information services
Information systems
NT **Computer networks**
Internet (Computer network)
Library information networks
Information science 020
BT **Communication**
NT **Documentation**
Electronic data processing
Information services
Information systems
Library science
Information services 025.5
UF Clearinghouses, Information
Information centers
Information clearinghouses
SA special subjects or organizations with the subdivision *Information services*, e.g. **Business—Information services; United Nations—Information services;** etc., to be added as needed
BT **Information science**
NT **Archives**
Business—Information services
Electronic publishing
Hotlines (Telephone counseling)
Information networks
Information systems
Machine readable bibliographic data
Reference services (Libraries)
United Nations—Information services
RT **Documentation**
Libraries
Research
Information storage and retrieval systems
USE **Information systems**

BT = Broader Term   NT = Narrower Term   RT = Related Term   SA = See Also   UF = Used For

Information systems 025.04
- UF Automatic information retrieval
  - Computer-based information systems
  - Data processing
  - Data storage and retrieval systems
  - Information storage and retrieval systems *[Former heading]*
  - Punched card systems
- BT **Bibliographic control**
  - **Bibliography**
  - **Computers**
  - **Documentation**
  - **Information science**
  - **Information services**
- NT **Database management**
  - **Electronic data processing**
  - **Expert systems (Computer science)**
  - **Information networks**
  - **Machine readable bibliographic data**
  - **Management information systems**
  - **Teletext systems**
  - **Videotex systems**
- RT **Libraries—Automation**

Information systems—Management 025.04

Use for materials on the management of information systems.
- BT **Management**

Infrared radiation 535.01; 621.36
- BT **Electromagnetic waves**
  - **Radiation**

Ingestion disorders
- USE **Eating disorders**

Inhalation abuse of solvents
- USE **Solvent abuse**

Inheritance and succession 346.05
- UF Bequests
  - Heirs
  - Hereditary succession
  - Intestacy
  - Legacies
  - Succession, Intestate
- BT **Parent and child**

  Wealth
- NT **Executors and administrators**
  - **Inheritance and transfer tax**
- RT **Wills**

Inheritance and transfer tax 343.05
- UF Estate tax
  - Taxation of legacies
  - Transfer tax
- BT **Estate planning**
  - **Inheritance and succession**
  - **Internal revenue**
  - **Taxation**

Inheritance (Biology)
- USE **Heredity**

Initialisms
- USE **Acronyms**

Initials 745.6
- NT **Printing—Specimens**
- RT **Alphabets**
  - **Illumination of books and manuscripts**
  - **Lettering**
  - **Monograms**
  - **Type and type founding**

Initiative and referendum
- USE **Referendum**

Injunctions 331.89
- BT **Constitutional law**
  - **Labor unions**
- RT **Strikes**

Injuries
- USE **Accidents**
  - **First aid**
  - **Wounds and injuries**

Injurious insects
- USE **Insect pests**

Injurious occupations
- USE **Hazardous occupations**

Ink drawing
- USE **Pen drawing**

Inland navigation 386
- UF Navigation, Inland
- BT **Navigation**
  - **Shipping**
  - **Transportation**
  - **Water resources development**
  - **Waterways**
- RT **Canals**
  - **Lakes**
  - **Rivers**

Inner cities 307.76; 362.5

Use for materials on densely populated, usually deteriorating, central areas of large cities, inhabited predominantly by the poor, often of a specific ethnic group, and for materials on the social and economic problems of these areas.

UF Central cities
Ghettoes, Inner city
Inner city ghettoes
Inner city problems
BT **Cities and towns**

Inner city ghettoes
USE **Inner cities**

Inner city problems
USE **Inner cities**

Inns
USE **Hotels and motels**

Innuit
USE **Inuit**

Inoculation
USE **Vaccination**

Inorganic chemistry 546
UF Chemistry, Inorganic *[Former heading]*
BT **Chemistry**
NT **Metals**

Input equipment (Computers)
USE **Computer peripherals**

Inquisition (May subdiv. geog.) 272
UF Holy Office
BT **Church history—600-1500, Middle Ages**
Catholic Church

Insane
USE **Mentally ill**

Insane—Hospitals
USE **Mentally ill—Institutional care**
Psychiatric hospitals

Insanity
USE **Mental illness—Jurisprudence**

Insanity defense 345
UF Insanity plea
BT **Criminal law**
Mental illness—Jurisprudence

Insanity plea
USE **Insanity defense**

Inscriptions 411
UF Epigraphy
BT **Ancient history**

Archeology
NT **Brasses**
Epitaphs
Graffiti
Hieroglyphics
Seals (Numismatics)

Insect-eating plants
USE **Carnivorous plants**

Insect pests 632
UF Destructive insects
Diseases and pests
Economic entomology
Entomology, Economic
Garden pests
Harmful insects
Injurious insects
Insects, Injurious and beneficial *[Former heading]*
SA types of insect pests, e.g. **Locusts**; etc.; and types of crops, plants, trees, etc., with the subdivision *Diseases and pests,* e.g. **Fruit—Diseases and pests;** to be added as needed
BT **Economic zoology**
Insects
Parasites
Pests
NT **Fruit—Diseases and pests**
Insects as carriers of disease
Locusts
RT **Aeronautics in agriculture**
Agricultural pests
Beneficial insects
Household pests
Veterinary medicine

Insecticides 632; 668
SA names of insecticides, to be added as needed
BT **Agricultural chemicals**
Pesticides
NT **D.D.T. (Insecticide)**
Fumigation
RT **Spraying and dusting**

Insecticides—Toxicology 615.9
BT **Poisons and poisoning**

Insectivorous plants
USE **Carnivorous plants**

BT = Broader Term   NT = Narrower Term   RT = Related Term   SA = See Also   UF = Used For

Insects 595.7
UF Entomology
SA types of insects, to be added
as needed
BT **Invertebrates**
NT **Ants**
Bees
Beneficial insects
Butterflies
Cicadas
Insect pests
Moths
Wasps
RT **Fertilization of plants**
Insects as carriers of disease 614.4
UF Entomology, Medical
Medical entomology
BT **Communicable diseases**
Insect pests
NT **Flies**
Mosquitoes
RT **Lyme disease**
Insects, Injurious and beneficial
USE **Beneficial insects**
Insect pests
Insemination, Artificial
USE **Artificial insemination**
Inservice training
USE **Employees—Training**
Librarians—In-service training
Insider trading 346; 364.1
UF Securities trading, Insider
Stocks—Insider trading
BT **Commercial law**
Securities
Stock exchange
Insignia 929.9
UF Badges of honor
Devices (Heraldry)
Emblems
SA armies, navies, and other ap-
propriate subjects with the
subdivision *Insignia* or
*Medals, badges, decorations,
etc.,* to be added as needed
BT **Heraldry**
NT **Colleges and universities—
Insignia**
United States. Army—Insignia
**United States. Army—Medals,
badges, decorations, etc.**

United States. Navy—Insignia
**United States. Navy—Medals,
badges, decorations, etc.**
RT **Decorations of honor**
Medals
National emblems
Insolvency
USE **Bankruptcy**
Insomnia 616.8
UF Sleeplessness
Wakefulness
RT **Sleep**
Inspection of food
USE **Food adulteration and inspec-
tion**
Inspection of meat
USE **Meat inspection**
Inspection of schools
USE **School supervision**
Schools—Administration
Inspiration
USE **Creation (Literary, artistic,
etc.)**
Inspiration, Biblical
USE **Bible—Inspiration**
Installment plan
USE **Instalment plan**
Instalment plan 658.8
UF Hire-purchase plan
Installment plan
BT **Business**
Buying
Consumer credit
Credit
Instinct 152.3; 156
UF Animal instinct
BT **Animal behavior**
Psychology
RT **Animal intelligence**
Comparative psychology
Habit
Institutional care 361
UF Asylums
Benevolent institutions
Charitable institutions
Homes (Institutions)
SA classes of persons with the
subdivision *Institutional
care,* to be added as needed
BT **Charities**

Institutional care—*Continued*
        Medical charities
        Public welfare
  NT Blind—Institutional care
        Children—Institutional care
        Deaf—Institutional care
        Group homes
        Hospitals
        Mentally ill—Institutional
          care
        Nursing homes
        Orphanages
Institutions, Charitable and philan-
        thropic
  USE Charities
        Hospitals
Instruction
  USE Education
        Teaching
Instruction, Home
  USE Home instruction
Instructional games
  USE Educational games
Instructional materials
  USE Teaching—Aids and devices
Instructional materials centers 027.7
  UF Audiovisual materials centers
        Curriculum materials centers
        Educational media centers
        Learning resource centers
        Media centers (Education)
        Multimedia centers
        School media centers
  BT Libraries
  NT School libraries
Instructional supervision
  USE School supervision
Instructive games
  USE Educational games
Instrument flying 629.132
  BT Aeronautical instruments
        Airplanes—Piloting
Instrumental ensembles
  USE Ensembles (Music)
Instrumental music 784
  UF Music, Instrumental
  SA types of instrumental music,
        to be added as needed
  BT Music
  NT Band music

        Guitar music
        Orchestral music
        Organ music
        Piano music
  RT Musical instruments
Instrumentation and orchestration 781.3;
        784.13
  UF Orchestration
  BT Bands (Music)
        Composition (Music)
        Music
        Orchestra
  RT Musical instruments
Instruments, Aeronautical
  USE Aeronautical instruments
Instruments, Astronautical
  USE Astronautical instruments
Instruments, Astronomical
  USE Astronomical instruments
Instruments, Engineering
  USE Engineering instruments
Instruments, Measuring
  USE Measuring instruments
Instruments, Meteorological
  USE Meteorological instruments
Instruments, Musical
  USE Musical instruments
Instruments, Negotiable
  USE Negotiable instruments
Instruments, Optical
  USE Optical instruments
Instruments, Scientific
  USE Scientific apparatus and in-
        struments
Insulation (Heat) 691; 693.8
  UF Heat insulating materials
        Thermal insulation
  BT Heating
Insulation (Sound)
  USE Soundproofing
Insults
  USE Invective
Insurance 368
  UF Underwriting
  SA types of insurance, e.g. **Auto-**
        mobile insurance; to be
        added as needed
  BT Estate planning
        Finance
        Personal finance

BT = Broader Term   NT = Narrower Term   RT = Related Term   SA = See Also   UF = Used For

Insurance—*Continued*
NT   **Automobile insurance**
      Casualty insurance
      Fire insurance
      Health insurance
      Life insurance
      Malpractice insurance
      Marine insurance
      Saving and thrift
      Unemployment insurance
Insurance, Accident
  USE   **Accident insurance**
Insurance, Automobile
  USE   **Automobile insurance**
Insurance, Casualty
  USE   **Casualty insurance**
Insurance, Disability
  USE   **Accident insurance**
      Health insurance
Insurance, Fire
  USE   **Fire insurance**
Insurance, Group
  USE   **Group insurance**
Insurance, Health
  USE   **Health insurance**
Insurance, Hospitalization
  USE   **Hospitalization insurance**
Insurance, Industrial
  USE   **Industrial insurance**
Insurance, Life
  USE   **Life insurance**
Insurance, Malpractice
  USE   **Malpractice insurance**
Insurance, Marine
  USE   **Marine insurance**
Insurance, Old age
  USE   **Old age pensions**
Insurance, Professional liability
  USE   **Malpractice insurance**
Insurance, Sickness
  USE   **Health insurance**
Insurance, Social
  USE   **Social security**
Insurance, State and compulsory
  USE   **Social security**
Insurance, Unemployment
  USE   **Unemployment insurance**
Insurance, Workers'
  USE   **Social security**
Insurance, Workers' compensation
  USE   **Workers' compensation**

Insurgency (May subdiv. geog.) **322.4; 355.02**
  UF   Rebellions
  BT   **Revolutions**
  NT   **Guerrilla warfare**
      Subversive activities
      Terrorism
  RT   **Internal security**
      Resistance to government
Integrated churches
  USE   **Church and race relations**
Integrated language arts (Holistic)
  USE   **Whole language**
Integrated schools
  USE   **School integration**
Integration in education
  USE   **Articulation (Education)**
      School integration
      Segregation in education
Integration, Racial
  USE   **African Americans— Integration**
      Blacks—Integration
      Race relations
Intellect 153.4
  UF   Intelligence
      Mind
      Understanding
  BT   **Psychology**
  NT   **Creation (Literary, artistic, etc.)**
      Imagination
      Logic
      Memory
      Perception
      Reason
      Senses and sensation
  RT   **Reasoning**
      Theory of knowledge
      Thought and thinking
Intellectual cooperation 370.19
  UF   Cooperation, Intellectual
  BT   **International cooperation**
  NT   **Congresses and conventions**
      Cultural relations
  RT   **International education**
Intellectual freedom 323.44
  BT   **Freedom**
  NT   **Academic freedom**
      Censorship

BT = Broader Term   NT = Narrower Term   RT = Related Term   SA = See Also   UF = Used For

Intellectual freedom—*Continued*
> Freedom of information
> Freedom of speech
> Freedom of the press

Intellectual life 001.1
> Use for general materials on learning and scholarship, literature, the arts, etc. Materials on literature, art, music, motion pictures, etc. produced for a mass audience are entered under **Popular culture.**

> UF Cultural life

> SA classes of persons, ethnic groups, and names of countries, cities, etc., with the subdivision *Intellectual life,* to be added as needed

> BT **Culture**

> NT **African Americans— Intellectual life**
> **Blacks—Intellectual life**
> **Chicago (Ill.)—Intellectual life**
> **Learning and scholarship**
> **Ohio—Intellectual life**
> **Popular culture**
> **United States—Intellectual life**

Intellectual property
> USE **Copyright**
> **Inventions**
> **Patents**

Intellectuals (May subdiv. geog.) **305.5**
> UF Intelligentsia

> SA ethnic groups, classes of persons, and names of countries, cities, etc., with the subdivision *Intellectual life,* e.g. **African Americans— Intellectual life; United States—Intellectual life;** etc., to be added as needed

> BT **Professions**

Intelligence
> USE **Intellect**

Intelligence agents
> USE **Spies**

Intelligence, Artificial
> USE **Artificial intelligence**

Intelligence of animals
> USE **Animal intelligence**

Intelligence service (May subdiv. geog.) **327.12; 355.3**
> Use for materials on a government agency that is engaged in obtaining information, usually about an enemy, but sometimes about an ally or a neutral country, and also in blocking the attempts by foreign agents to obtain information about one's own national secrets.

> UF Counterespionage
> Counterintelligence

> BT **Public administration**
> **Research**

> NT **Espionage**

> RT **Secret service**

Intelligence service—United States 327.1273; 355.3
> UF United States—Intelligence service

Intelligence testing
> USE **Intelligence tests**

Intelligence tests
> UF I. Q. tests
> Intelligence testing
> IQ tests
> Mental tests *[Former heading]*

> BT **Child psychology**
> **Educational psychology**

> NT **Ability—Testing**

> RT **Educational tests and measurements**

Intelligentsia
> USE **Intellectuals**

Intemperance
> USE **Alcoholism**
> **Temperance**

Inter-American relations
> USE **Pan-Americanism**

Interactive CD technology
> USE **CD-I technology**

Interactive videotex
> USE **Videotex systems**

Interchange of teachers
> USE **Teacher exchange**

Interchange of visitors
> USE **Exchange of persons programs**

Intercollegiate athletics
> USE **Athletics**
> **College sports**

BT = Broader Term   NT = Narrower Term   RT = Related Term   SA = See Also   UF = Used For

Intercommunication systems 621.38;
   651.7
   UF Interoffice communication
       systems
       Loudspeakers
   BT **Electronic apparatus and appliances**
       Sound—Recording and reproducing
       Telecommunication
   NT **Closed-circuit television**
       Microwave communication systems
Intercontinental ballistic missiles 623.4
   UF I.C.B.M.
       ICBM
   SA names of specific ICBM missiles, e.g. **Atlas (Missile);** to
       be added as needed
   BT **Ballistic missiles**
   NT **Atlas (Missile)**
Intercultural education
   USE **Multicultural education**
Intercultural literature
   USE **Multicultural literature**
Intercultural relations
   USE **Cultural relations**
Intercultural studies
   USE **Cross cultural studies**
Interest centers approach to teaching
   USE **Open plan schools**
Interest (Economics) 332.8
   BT **Banks and banking**
       Business mathematics
       Capital
       Finance
       Loans
Interest groups
   USE **Lobbying**
Interfaces, Computer
   USE **Computer interfaces**
Interfaith marriage 261.8; 306.84
   UF Intermarriage, Religious *[Former heading]*
       Marriage, Mixed
       Mixed marriage
   BT **Intermarriage**
Interfaith relations 261.2; 291.1
   BT **Christian unity**
       Human relations

Intergovernmental tax relations 336.2
   UF Federal-state tax relations
       State-local tax relations
       Tax relations, Intergovernmental
       Tax sharing
   BT **Taxation**
   NT **Revenue sharing**
Interior decoration
   USE **Interior design**
Interior design 729; 747
      Use for materials on the art and techniques of planning and supervising the design and execution of architectural interiors and their furnishings.
   UF Arts, Decorative
       Decoration, Interior
       Design, Interior
       Home decoration
       House decoration
       House furnishing
       Interior decoration
   BT Art
       Decoration and ornament
       Decorative arts
       Design
       Home economics
   NT **Bedspreads**
       Carpets
       Drapery
       Furniture
       House painting
       Mural painting and decoration
       Paperhanging
       Quilts
       Rugs
       Tapestry
       Upholstery
       Wallpaper
   RT **Rooms**
Interlibrary loans
   USE **Library circulation**
Interlocking signals
   USE **Railroads—Signaling**
Intermarriage 306.84
      Use for materials that discuss collectively marriage between persons of different religions, religious denominations, races, and ethnic groups.
   UF Marriage, Mixed
       Mixed marriage

BT = Broader Term   NT = Narrower Term   RT = Related Term   SA = See Also   UF = Used For

Intermarriage—*Continued*
  BT **Marriage**
  NT **Interfaith marriage**
       Interracial marriage
Intermarriage, Racial
  USE **Interracial marriage**
Intermarriage, Religious
  USE **Interfaith marriage**
Intermediate state
  USE **Eschatology**
       Future life
Interment
  USE **Burial**
Internal combustion engines 621.43
  UF Gas and oil engines *[Former heading]*
       Gas engines
       Gasoline engines
       Oil engines
       Petroleum engines
  BT **Engines**
  NT **Automobile engines**
       Carburetors
       Diesel engines
Internal migration 304.8
    Use for materials on the movement of population within a country for permanent settlement. Materials on casual or seasonal workers who move from place to place in search of employment are entered under **Migrant labor.** Materials on migration from one country to another are entered under **Immigration and emigration.**
  UF Migration, Internal *[Former heading]*
  BT **Colonization**
       Population
  NT **Cities and towns—Growth**
  RT **Land settlement**
Internal revenue 336.2
  UF Revenue, Internal
  BT **Finance**
       Taxation
  NT **Income tax**
       Inheritance and transfer tax
Internal revenue law 343.04
  UF Law, Internal revenue
  BT **Law**
Internal security (May subdiv. geog.)
       351.74; 363.2
  UF Loyalty oaths
       Security, Internal

  RT **Insurgency**
       Subversive activities
Internal security—United States
       353.0074; 363.20973
  UF United States—Internal security
International agencies 060
  UF Associations, International
       International associations
       International organizations
  SA names of individual agencies, to be added as needad
  BT **International cooperation**
International arbitration 341.5
  UF Arbipration, International *[Former heading]*
       International mediation
       Mediation, International
  BT **International cooperation**
       International law
       International relations
       International security
       Treaties
  NT **League of Nations**
       United Nations
  RT **Arms control**
       Peace
International associations
  USE **International agencies**
International business enterprises
  USE **Multinational corporations**
International competition 337; 382; 658
  UF Competition, International
       World economics
  BT **International relations**
       International trade
  RT **War—Economic aspects**
International conferences
  USE **Congresses and conventions**
International cooperation 327.1; 341.7
    Use for general materials on international cooperative activities, with or without the participation of governments.
  UF Cooperation, International
  SA subjects with the subdivision *International cooperation,* e.g. **Astronautics— International cooperation;** to be added as needed
  BT **Cooperation**

International cooperation—*Continued*
  International law
  International relations
  NT Astronautics—International
        cooperation
      Congresses and conventions
      Cultural relations
      Economic assistance
      Exchange of persons programs
      Intellectual cooperation
      International agencies
      International arbitration
      International police
      League of Nations
      Technical assistance
      United Nations
  RT International education
      International organization
      Reconstruction (1914-1939)
      Reconstruction (1939-1951)
      Technology transfer
International copyright
  USE Copyright
International economic relations 382
  UF Economic relations, Foreign
      Foreign economic relations
  BT Economic policy
      International relations
  NT Balance of payments
      Commercial policy
      Economic assistance
      International trade
      Multinational corporations
      Sanctions (International law)
      Technical assistance
International education 370.19
  Use for materials on education for inter-
  national understanding, world citizenship,
  etc.
  UF Education, International
  BT Education
  NT Comparative librarianship
      Teacher exchange
  RT Intellectual cooperation
      International cooperation
      Multicultural education
International exchange
  USE Foreign exchange
International exhibitions
  USE Exhibitions

International federation
  USE International organization
International investment
  USE Foreign investments
International language
  USE Universal language
International law 341
  UF Law, International
      Law of nations
      Nations, Law of
      Natural law
  BT Law
  NT Aliens
      Asylum
      Boundaries
      International arbitration
      International cooperation
      Intervention (International
        law)
      Mandates
      Marine salvage
      Maritime law
      Military law
      Naturalization
      Neutrality
      Pirates
      Political refugees
      Privateering
      Sanctions (International law)
      Slave trade
      Space law
      Treaties
      War crimes
  RT International organization
      International relations
      War
International mediation
  USE International arbitration
International organization 341.2
  Use for materials on plans leading to-
  wards political organization of nations.
  UF Federation, International
      International federation
      Organization, International
      World government
      World organization
  SA names of specific organiza-
        tions, e.g. United Nations;
        to be added as needed
  BT Congresses and conventions

International organization—*Continued*
    International relations
    International security
  NT European federation
    International police
    League of Nations
    Mandates
    United Nations
  RT International cooperation
    International law
    World politics
International organizations
  USE International agencies
International police 341.7
  UF Interpol
    Police, International
  BT International cooperation
    International organization
    International relations
    International security
International politics
  USE World politics
International relations 327; 341.3

Use for materials on the theory of international relations. Historical accounts are entered under **World politics; Europe—Politics and government;** etc. Materials limited to diplomatic relations between two countries are entered under the name of each country with the subdivision *Foreign relations* further subdivided by the name of the other country, i.e. **United States—Foreign relations—Iran** and also **Iran—Foreign relations—Iran.**

  UF Foreign relations
  SA names of countries with the subdivision *Foreign relations,* to be added as needed
  NT Arms control
    Balance of power
    Boundaries
    Catholic Church—Foreign relations
    Cultural relations
    Diplomacy
    Diplomatic and consular service
    Diplomats
    East and West
    Geopolitics
    International arbitration
    International competition

International cooperation
  International economic relations
  International organization
  International police
  International security
  Mandates
  Monroe Doctrine
  Nationalism
  Neutrality
  Peace
  Political refugees
  Treaties
  United States—Foreign relations
  RT International law
    National security
    Technology transfer
    World politics
International security 327.1; 341.7
  UF Collective security
    Security, International *[Former heading]*
  BT International relations
  NT Arms control
    Arms race
    International arbitration
    International organization
    International police
    Neutrality
  RT Peace
International space cooperation
  USE Astronautics—International cooperation
International Standard Bibliographic Description 025.3
  UF I.S.B.D
    ISBD
  BT Cataloging
International Standard Book Numbers 070.5
  UF I.S.B.N.
    ISBN
  BT Publishers' standard book numbers
International Standard Serial Numbers 070.5
  UF I.S.S.N.
    ISSN
  RT Serial publications

International trade (May subdiv. geog.)
382

Use for general materials about trade among nations. Materials on foreign trade of specific countries, cities, etc., are entered under the name of the place with the subdivision *Commerce*. Materials limited to trade between two countries are entered under the name of each country with the subdivision *Commerce* further subdivided by the name of the other country, i.e. **United States—Commerce—Japan** and also **Japan—Commerce—United States.**

UF   External trade

Foreign commerce

Foreign trade

Trade, International

BT   **Commerce**

International economic relations

NT   **International competition**

Internationalism

USE   **Nationalism**

Internet (Computer network) 004.6; 384.3

UF   DARPA Internet (Computer network)

BT   **Computer networks**

Information networks

Internment camps

USE   **Concentration camps**

Interoffice communication systems

USE   **Intercommunication systems**

Interpersonal relations

USE   **Human relations**

Interplanetary communication

USE   **Interstellar communication**

Interplanetary visitors

USE   **Extraterrestrial beings**

Interplanetary voyages 629.45; 808.83; 813, etc.

Use for general materials about travel to other planets and for individual works, collections, or materials about imaginary accounts of such travels. Materials on the physics and technical details of flight beyond the earth's atmosphere are entered under **Space flight.**

UF   Interstellar travel

Outer space travel

People in space

Space travel

BT   **Astronautics**

Fiction

NT   **Outer space—Exploration**

Space ships

RT   **Fantasy fiction**

Imaginary voyages

Rockets (Aeronautics)

Science fiction

Space flight

Interplanetary warfare

USE   **Space warfare**

Interpol

USE   **International police**

Interpreting and translating

USE   **Translating and interpreting**

Interpretive dance

USE   **Modern dance**

Interracial adoption 362.7

UF   Adoption, Interracial

BT   **Adoption**

Race relations

Interracial marriage 306.84

UF   Intermarriage, Racial

Marriage, Interracial

Mixed marriage

Racial intermarriage

BT   **Intermarriage**

Interracial relations

USE   **Race relations**

Interscholastic sports

USE   **School sports**

Interstate commerce 381

Use for materials limited to commerce between states. General materials on foreign and domestic commerce are entered under **Commerce.**

UF   Commerce, Interstate

Government regulation of commerce

BT   **Commerce**

RT   **Railroads—Government policy**

Restraint of trade

Interstate highways

USE   **Express highways**

Interstellar communication 621.382

UF   Extraterrestrial communication

Interplanetary communication

Outer space—Communication

Space communication

Space telecommunication

BT   **Life on other planets**

Telecommunication

NT   **Astronautics—Communication systems**

BT = Broader Term   NT = Narrower Term   RT = Related Term   SA = See Also   UF = Used For

Interstellar communication—*Continued*
      Radio astronomy
Interstellar travel
  USE **Interplanetary voyages**
Interstellar warfare
  USE **Space warfare**
Interurban railroads
  USE **Electric railroads**
       Street railroads
Intervention (International law) 341.5
  UF Military intervention
  BT **International law**
       War
  NT **Monroe Doctrine**
  RT **Neutrality**
Interviewing 158
  BT **Applications for positions**
       Social psychology
  NT **Talk shows**
  RT **Applied psychology**
       Counseling
Interviewing (Journalism)
  USE **Journalism**
       Reporters and reporting
Interviews, Parent-teacher
  USE **Parent-teacher conferences**
Intestacy
  USE **Inheritance and succession**
Intifada, 1987- 956.9405
  UF Arab-Israeli conflict, 1987-
       Israeli-Arab conflict, 1987-
       Palestinian-Israeli conflict,
       1987-
       Palestinian uprising, 1987-
  BT **Israel-Arab conflicts**
Intolerance
  USE **Fanaticism**
       Freedom of conscience
       Freedom of religion
       Toleration
Intoxicants
  USE **Alcohol**
       Alcoholic beverages
       Liquors
       Narcotics
       Stimulants
Intoxication
  USE **Alcoholism**
       Drug addiction
       Temperance

Intuition 153.4
  BT **Philosophy**
       Psychology
       Rationalism
       Theory of knowledge
  RT **Perception**
Inuit 970.004
    Use for materials on the native peoples of the arctic regions of Alaska, Canada, and Greenland. If local usage dictates, libraries may establish **Eskimos** as a broader term than **Inuit**; and the names of other groups of Arctic peoples may be added as needed.
  UF Eskimos
       Esquimaux
       Innuit
Inuit—Folklore 398
  UF Folklore, Inuit
  BT **Folklore**
Invalid cooking
  USE **Cooking for the sick**
       Diet therapy
Invalids
  USE **Physically handicapped**
       Sick
Invasion of Cuba, 1961
  USE **Cuba—History—1961, Invasion**
Invasion of privacy
  USE **Right of privacy**
Invective 808.88
  UF Abuse, Verbal
       Insults
       Verbal abuse
  BT **Satire**
Inventions 608
  UF Discoveries (in science)
       Intellectual property
  BT **Civilization**
       Machinery
       Technology
  NT **Creation (Literary, artistic, etc.)**
       Technology transfer
  RT **Inventors**
       Patents
Inventors 609.2; 920
  RT **Engineers**
       Inventions
Inventory control 658.7
  UF Stock control

Inventory control—*Continued*
   BT   **Management**
         Retail trade
Invertebrates 592
   BT   **Animals**
         Zoology
   NT   **Corals**
         Crustacea
         Insects
         Mollusks
         Protozoa
         Shellfish
         Spiders
         Sponges
         Worms
Investigations, Governmental
   USE   **Governmental investigations**
Investment in real estate
   USE   **Real estate investment**
Investment trusts 332.63
   UF   Mutual funds
   BT   **Banks and banking**
         Trust companies
Investments 332.6
   BT   **Banks and banking**
         Capital
         Finance
   NT   **Annuities**
         Bonds
         Foreign investments
         Mortgages
         Real estate investment
         Savings and loan associations
         Securities
   RT   **Estate planning**
         Loans
         Saving and thrift
         Speculation
         Stock exchange
         Stocks
Investments, Foreign
   USE   **Foreign investments**
Invincible Armada
   USE   **Spanish Armada, 1588**
Invisible playmates
   USE   **Imaginary playmates**
IQ tests
   USE   **Intelligence tests**
Iran 935; 955
    May be subdivided like United States
    except for *History*.

   UF   Persia
Iran-Contra Affair, 1985-
   USE   **Iran-Contra Affair, 1985-1990**
Iran-Contra Affair, 1985-1990 973.927
   UF   Contra-Iran Affair, 1985-1990
         Iran-Contra Affair, 1985- *[For-
         mer heading]*
         Iran-Contra Arms Scandal,
         1985-1990
         Irangate, 1985-1990
   BT   **American military assistance**
         Political corruption
         United States—History—
         1974-1989
         United States—History—
         1989-
Iran-Contra Arms Scandal, 1985-1990
   USE   **Iran-Contra Affair, 1985-1990**
Iran—Foreign relations—United States
        327.55073
   NT   **Iran hostage crisis, 1979-1981**
Iran—History—1941-1979 955.05
Iran—History—1979- 955.05
Iran hostage crisis, 1979-1981
        327.55073; 327.73055; 955
   UF   Iranian seizure of American
         embassy
   BT   **American hostages—Iran**
         Iran—Foreign relations—
         United States
         United States—Foreign
         relations—Iran
Irangate, 1985-1990
   USE   **Iran-Contra Affair, 1985-1990**
Iranian seizure of American embassy
   USE   **Iran hostage crisis, 1979-1981**
Iraq—History—1990, Invasion of Ku-
      wait
   USE   **Kuwait—History—1990, Iraqi
         Invasion**
Iraq—History—1991, Persian Gulf War
   USE   **Persian Gulf War, 1991**
Iraq-Kuwait Crisis, 1990-1991
   USE   **Kuwait—History—1990, Iraqi
         Invasion**
         Persian Gulf War, 1991
IRAs (Pensions)
   USE   **Individual retirement accounts**
Iron 669; 672
   BT   **Chemical elements**

Iron—*Continued*
  Metals
 NT **Iron ores**
  Ironwork
  Steel
  Steel construction
Iron Age 930.1
 RT **Archeology**
  Bronze Age
Iron and steel building
 USE **Steel construction**
Iron curtain countries
 USE **Communist countries**
Iron founding
 USE **Founding**
Iron industry 338.2
 UF Iron industry and trade *[Former heading]*
  Iron trade
 NT **Ironwork**
 RT **Steel industry**
Iron industry and trade
 USE **Iron industry**
Iron ores 553.3
 BT **Iron**
  Ore deposits
  Ores
Iron trade
 USE **Iron industry**
Ironing
 USE **Laundry**
Ironwork 672; 682; 739.4
 UF Wrought iron work
 BT **Decoration and ornament**
  Iron
  Iron industry
  Metalwork
 NT **Blacksmithing**
  Welding
 RT **Forging**
Irreversible coma
 USE **Brain death**
Irrigation (May subdiv. geog.) **333.91; 627; 631.5**
 BT **Agricultural engineering**
  Civil engineering
  Hydraulic engineering
  Reservoirs
  Soils
  Water resources development

  Water supply
 NT **Dams**
  Dry farming
  Water rights
  Windmills
 RT **Reclamation of land**
Irrigation—United States 333.91; 627; 631.5
 UF United States—Irrigation
ISBD
 USE **International Standard Bibliographic Description**
ISBN
 USE **International Standard Book Numbers**
Islam 297
 Use for materials on the religion. Materials on the believers in this religion are entered under **Muslims.**
 UF Islamism
  Mohammedanism
  Moslemism
  Muhammedanism
  Muslimism
 BT **Religions**
 NT **Jewish-Islamic relations**
  Koran
  Muslims
 RT **Islamic law**
Islamic architecture 720.9
 UF Arab architecture
  Architecture, Islamic
  Moorish architecture
  Muslim architecture
  Saracenic architecture
 BT **Architecture**
 NT **Mosques**
Islamic art 709.1
 UF Art, Islamic *[Former heading]*
  Mohammedan art
  Muslim art
  Saracenic art
 BT **Art**
Islamic countries 956
 UF Moslem countries
  Muslim countries
 NT **Arab countries**
Islamic-Jewish relations
 USE **Jewish-Islamic relations**
Islamic law (May subdiv. geog.) **340.5**
 UF Law, Islamic

  BT = Broader Term NT = Narrower Term RT = Related Term SA = See Also UF = Used For

Islamic law—*Continued*
      Law, Muslim
      Muslim law
  BT **Law**
  RT **Islam**
Islamism
  USE **Islam**
Islands 551.4
  SA names of islands and groups
        of islands, to be added as
        needed
  NT **Coral reefs and islands**
      Cuba
      Islands of the Pacific
      Oceania
Islands, Artificial
  USE **Drilling platforms**
Islands, Imaginary
  USE **Geographical myths**
Islands of the Pacific 990
    Use for comprehensive materials on all
the islands of the Pacific Ocean. Materials
restricted to comprehensive treatment of
the island groups of Melanesia, Micronesia, and Polynesia are entered under **Oceania.**
  UF Pacific Islands
      Pacific Ocean Islands
  BT **Islands**
  NT **Oceania**
  RT **Pacific rim**
Isotopes 539.7; 541.3
  NT **Radioisotopes**
Israel 956.94
    May be subdivided like United States
except for *History.*
  BT **Middle East**
Israel-Arab conflicts 965.04; 956.05
    Use for materials on the conflicts between the Arab countries and Israel. Materials that discuss collectively the relations between Arabs and Jews, including religious, ethnic, and ideological relations, are entered under **Jewish-Arab relations.** Materials on relations between the religions of Judaism and Islam are entered under **Jewish-Islamic relations.**
  UF Arab-Israel conflicts
      Arab-Israeli conflicts
      Israeli-Arab conflicts
      Palestine problem, 1917-
  BT **Arab countries—Foreign**
      relations—Israel
      Israel—Foreign relations—
      Arab countries

  NT **Intifada, 1987-**
      Israel-Arab War, 1948-1949
      Israel-Arab War, 1967
      Israel-Arab War, 1973
      Lebanon—History—
        1982-1984, Israeli intervention
      Sinai Campaign, 1956
  RT **Jewish-Arab relations**
Israel-Arab relations
  USE **Arab countries—Foreign**
       relations—Israel
      Israel—Foreign relations—
      Arab countries
Israel-Arab War, 1948-1949 956.04
  UF Arab-Israel War, 1948-1949
  BT **Israel-Arab conflicts**
Israel-Arab War, 1956
  USE **Sinai Campaign, 1956**
Israel-Arab War, 1967 956.04
  UF Arab-Israel War, 1967
      Six Day War, 1967
  BT **Israel-Arab conflicts**
Israel-Arab War, 1973 956.04
  UF Arab-Israel War, 1973
      Yom Kippur War, 1973
  BT **Israel-Arab conflicts**
Israel—Collective settlements
  USE **Collective settlements—Israel**
Israel—Foreign relations—Arab countries 956
  UF Arab-Israel relations
      Arab-Israeli relations
      Israel-Arab relations
      Israeli-Arab relations
  NT **Israel-Arab conflicts**
  RT **Arab countries—Foreign**
      relations—Israel
      Jewish-Arab relations
Israeli-Arab conflict, 1987-
  USE **Intifada, 1987-**
Israeli-Arab conflicts
  USE **Israel-Arab conflicts**
Israeli-Arab relations
  USE **Arab countries—Foreign**
       relations—Israel
      Israel—Foreign relations—
      Arab countries

BT = Broader Term   NT = Narrower Term   RT = Related Term   SA = See Also   UF = Used For

Israeli intervention in Lebanon, 1982-
1984
    USE   Lebanon—History—
         1982-1984, Israeli interven-
         tion

Israelis 305.892; 920; 956.94
    BT   **Jews**

Israelites
    USE   **Jews**

ISSN
    USE   **International Standard Serial**
         Numbers

Italo-Ethiopian War, 1935-1936 963
    UF   Ethiopian-Italian War, 1935-
         1936
    BT   **Modern history—1900-1999**
         (20th century)

Italy 945
    May be subdivided like United States
    except for *History.*

Italy—History 945
Italy—History—0-1559 945
Italy—History—1559-1789 945
Italy—History—1789-1815 945
Italy—History—1815-1914 945; 945.09
Italy—History—1914-1945 945.091
Italy—History—1945-1976 945.092
Italy—History—1976- 945.092

Ivory 679
    BT   **Animal products**

Jacobins (Dominicans)
    USE   **Dominicans (Religious order)**

Jails
    USE   **Prisons**

Japan 952
    May be subdivided like United States
    except for *History.*

Japan—Commerce—United States 382
Japan—History 952
Japan—History—0-1868 952
Japan—History—1868-1945 952.03
**Japan—History—1945-1952, Allied oc-
    cupation 952.04**
    BT   **Military occupation**
         World War, 1939-1945—
         Occupied territories
Japan—History—1952- 952.04

Japanese color prints 769.952
    UF   Color prints, Japanese *[For-
         mer heading]*

    BT   **Color prints**

Japanese language 495.6
    May be subdivided like **English lan-
guage.**
    BT   **Language and languages**

**Japanese language—Business Japanese
    495.6**
    Business Japanese is a unique subdivi-
    sion for **Japanese language.**
    UF   Business Japanese
    RT   **Business letters**

Japanese paper folding
    USE   **Origami**

Jargon
    USE   subjects and names of lan-
         guages with the subdivision
         Jargon, e.g. **English
         language—Jargon;** to be
         added as needed

Jargon, Computer
    USE   **Computer science—
         Dictionaries**

Jazz ensembles 784.4
    BT   **Ensembles (Music)**

Jazz music 781.65; 782.42165
    BT   **Dance music
         Music**
    RT   **Blues music**

Jestbooks
    USE   **Chapbooks**

Jesters
    USE   **Fools and jesters**

Jesuits 271
    UF   Jesus, Society of
         Society of Jesus
    BT   **Catholic religious orders for
         men**

Jesus Christ 232
    UF   Christ
         Christology
    BT   **God—Christianity**
    NT   **Atonement—Christianity
         Lord's Supper
         Second Advent**
    RT   **Christianity**

Jesus Christ—Art 704.9
    UF   Jesus Christ—Iconography
         Jesus Christ in art
    BT   **Christian art and symbolism**
    RT   **Bible—Pictorial works**

Jesus Christ—Art—*Continued*
        Mary, Blessed Virgin, Saint—Art

Jesus Christ—Atonement
  USE **Atonement—Christianity**

Jesus Christ—Biography 232.9
  NT **Jesus Christ—Crucifixion**
       Jesus Christ—Historicity
       Jesus Christ—Nativity

Jesus Christ—Birth
  USE **Jesus Christ—Nativity**

Jesus Christ—Crucifixion 232.96
  UF Crucifixion of Christ
  BT **Jesus Christ—Biography**
  RT **Good Friday**

Jesus Christ—Divinity 232
  UF Divinity of Christ
  NT **Trinity**
       Unitarianism

Jesus Christ—Drama 808.82; 812, etc.
  May be used for individual works, collections, or materials about plays about Jesus Christ.
  NT **Passion plays**

Jesus Christ—Historicity 232.9
  BT **Jesus Christ—Biography**

Jesus Christ—Iconography
  USE **Jesus Christ—Art**

Jesus Christ in art
  USE **Jesus Christ—Art**

Jesus Christ—Last Supper
  USE **Lord's Supper**

Jesus Christ—Messiahship 232

Jesus Christ—Nativity 232.92
  UF Jesus Christ—Birth
       Nativity of Christ
  BT **Jesus Christ—Biography**
  RT **Christmas**

Jesus Christ—Parables 226.8
  BT **Bible—Parables**
       Parables

Jesus Christ—Prayers 232.9
  NT **Lord's prayer**

Jesus Christ—Prophecies 232
  BT **Bible—Prophecies**

Jesus Christ—Resurrection 232.9
  UF Resurrection

Jesus Christ—Second Advent
  USE **Second Advent**

Jesus Christ—Sermon on the mount
  USE **Sermon on the mount**

Jesus Christ—Teachings 232.9
  UF Teachings of Jesus

Jesus, Society of
  USE **Jesuits**

Jet airplanes
  USE **Jet planes**

Jet lag 616.9
  BT **Aviation medicine**
       Biological rhythms
       Fatigue

Jet planes 629.133
  UF Airplanes, Jet propelled
       Jet airplanes
       Jets (Airplanes)
  BT **Airplanes**
  NT **Short take off and landing aircraft**
       Supersonic transport planes

Jet propulsion 621.43
  BT **Airplane engines**
  RT **Rockets (Aeronautics)**

Jets (Airplanes)
  USE **Jet planes**

Jewelry 391; 739.27
  Use for general materials on jewelry and for materials on gems in which the emphasis is on the setting. Materials on cut and polished precious stones treated from the point of view of art or antiquity are entered under **Gems**. Materials on gem stones treated from the mineralogical or technological point of view are entered under **Precious stones**.
  UF Costume jewelry
       Jewels
  SA styles of jewelry and names of specific articles of jewelry, to be added as needed
  BT **Art metalwork**
       Costume
       Decoration and ornament
       Decorative arts
       Metalwork
  RT **Gems**
       Goldwork
       Silverwork

Jewels
  USE **Gems**
       Jewelry
       Precious stones

Jewish-Arab relations 956
  UF Arab-Jewish relations

BT = Broader Term   NT = Narrower Term   RT = Related Term   SA = See Also   UF = Used For

Jewish-Arab relations—*Continued*
- BT **Arabs**
    Judaism
- RT **Arab countries—Foreign relations—Israel**
    Israel-Arab conflicts
    Israel—Foreign relations—Arab countries
    Jewish-Islamic relations
    Palestinian Arabs

Jewish-Christian relations 261.2; 296.3
- UF Christian-Jewish relations
    Christianity and other religions—Judaism
    Comparative religion
    Judaism—Relations—Christianity
- BT **Christianity and other religions**
    Judaism

Jewish civilization 909
- UF Civilization, Jewish
    Jews—Civilization *[Former heading]*
- BT **Civilization**

Jewish ethics 296.3
- UF Ethics, Jewish
- BT **Ethics**

Jewish folklore
- USE **Jews—Folklore**

Jewish holidays 296.4; 394.2
- UF Fasts and feasts—Judaism *[Former heading]*
    Festivals—Jews
    Holidays, Jewish
    Jews—Festivals
- SA names of individual holidays, e.g. **Hanukkah;** to be added as needed
- BT **Judaism**
    Religious holidays
- NT **Hanukkah**
    Passover
    Yom Kippur

Jewish holocaust (1933-1945) 940.53; 943.086

Use for materials on the period of persecution and extermination of European Jews by National Socialist, or Nazi, Germany that began with Adolf Hitler's rise to power in 1933.

- UF Destruction of Jews (1933-1945)
    Extermination of Jews (1933-1945)
    Holocaust, Jewish (1933-1945) *[Former heading]*
    Holocaust, Jewish (1939-1945)
- SA names of concentration camps, to be added as needed
- BT **Antisemitism**
    Jews—Persecutions
- RT **World War, 1939-1945—Jews**

Jewish-Islamic relations 296
- UF Islamic-Jewish relations
- BT **Islam**
    Judaism
- RT **Jewish-Arab relations**

Jewish language
- USE **Hebrew language**
    Yiddish language

Jewish legends 296.1; 398.2

May be used for individual works, collections, or materials about Jewish legends.

- UF Jews—Legends
    Legends, Jewish *[Former heading]*
- BT **Legends**

Jewish literature 296; 808.8
- UF Jews—Literature
- BT **Literature**
    Religious literature
- NT **Bible**
    Cabala
    Talmud
    Yiddish literature
- RT **Hebrew literature**

Jewish religion
- USE **Judaism**

Jews (May subdiv. geog.) 305.892; 909
- UF Hebrews
    Israelites
- BT **Judaism**
- NT **Israelis**

Jews and Gentiles 305.6
- UF Gentiles and Jews
    Jews—Relations with Gentiles
- BT **Human relations**
- NT **Antisemitism**

BT = Broader Term   NT = Narrower Term   RT = Related Term   SA = See Also   UF = Used For

Jews—Antiquities 933

Jews—Civilization
   USE   **Jewish civilization**

Jews—Customs
   USE   **Jews—Social life and customs**

Jews—Economic conditions 305.892;
        330.9

Jews—Festivals
   USE   **Jewish holidays**

Jews—Folklore 398
   UF   Folklore, Jewish
          Jewish folklore
   BT   **Folklore**

Jews—Language
   USE   **Hebrew language**
          Yiddish language

Jews—Legends
   USE   **Jewish legends**

Jews—Literature
   USE   **Hebrew literature**
          Jewish literature

Jews—Persecutions 909; 933
   BT   **Antisemitism**
          Persecution
   NT   **Jewish holocaust (1933-1945)**
          World War, 1939-1945—
          Jews—Rescue

Jews—Political activity 909; 956.94

Jews—Relations with Gentiles
   USE   **Jews and Gentiles**

Jews—Religion
   USE   **Judaism**

Jews—Restoration 956.94
     Use for materials on the belief that the
   Jews, in fulfillment of Biblical prophecy,
   would some day return to Palestine.
   RT   **Zionism**

Jews—Rites and ceremonies
   USE   **Judaism—Customs and**
             practices

Jews—Ritual
   USE   **Judaism—Liturgy**

Jews—Social conditions 305.892; 909
     Use for materials relating to social con-
   ditions of the Jews themselves. Materials
   on the relation of the Jews to non-Jews
   are entered under **Jews and Gentiles.**
   BT   **Social conditions**

Jews—Social life and customs 305.892
   UF   Jews—Customs
   BT   **Manners and customs**

Job analysis 658.3
   UF   Personnel classification
   BT   **Factory management**
          Industrial efficiency
          Management
          Occupations
          Personnel management
          Wages
   NT   **Motion study**
          Time study

Job applications
   USE   **Applications for positions**

Job discrimination
   USE   **Discrimination in employment**

Job hunting 650.14
   UF   Hunting, Job
          Job searching
   BT   **Employment agencies**
          Vocational guidance
   NT   **Applications for positions**
          Résumés (Employment)

Job performance standards
   USE   **Performance standards**

Job placement guidance
   USE   **Vocational guidance**

Job résumés
   USE   **Résumés (Employment)**

Job retraining
   USE   **Occupational retraining**

Job satisfaction 650.1; 658.3
   UF   Satisfaction in work
          Work satisfaction
   BT   **Attitude (Psychology)**
          Employee morale
          Personnel management
          Work
   NT   **Burn out (Psychology)**

Job searching
   USE   **Job hunting**

Job security 331.25; 650.1; 658.3
   UF   Employment security
          Security, Job
   BT   **Personnel management**
   NT   **Employees—Dismissal**

Job sharing 331.2; 658.3
   UF   Sharing of jobs
   BT   **Part-time employment**

Job stress 158.7; 658.3
   UF   Occupational stress
          On the job stress

BT = Broader Term   NT = Narrower Term   RT = Related Term   SA = See Also   UF = Used For

Job stress—*Continued*
        Organizational stress
        Work stress
  BT **Stress (Physiology)**
        Stress (Psychology)
  NT **Burn out (Psychology)**
Job training
  USE **Occupational training**
Jobless people
  USE **Unemployed**
Joblessness
  USE **Unemployment**
Jobs
  USE **Employment agencies**
        Occupations
        Professions
Jogging 613.7
  BT **Running**
Joint custody of children
  USE **Child custody**
        Part-time parenting
Joke books
  USE **Jokes**
Jokes 808.7; 808.88; 818, etc.
    May be used for collections of jokes and
for materials about jokes.
  UF Joke books
  BT **Wit and humor**
  NT **Practical jokes**
Journalism (May subdiv. geog.) **070.4**
    Use for materials on writing for the pe-
riodical press, on the editing of such writ-
ing, or on journalism as an occupation.
Materials limited to the history, organiza-
tion, and management of newspapers are
entered under **Newspapers.**
  UF Editors and editing
        Interviewing (Journalism)
        Writing (Authorship)
  SA types of journalism, e.g. **Sci-
entific journalism;** to be
added as needed
  BT **Authorship**
        Literature
  NT **College and school journalism**
        Freedom of the press
        Gossip
        Libel and slander
        Photojournalism
        Press
        Scientific journalism
  RT **Broadcast journalism**

        Newspapers
        Periodicals
        Reporters and reporting
Journalism—Objectivity 070.4
  UF Slanted journalism
Journalism, Scientific
  USE **Scientific journalism**
Journalistic photography
  USE **Photojournalism**
Journalists 070.92; 920
  UF Columnists
        Editors and editing
  BT **Authors**
Journals
  USE **Periodicals**
Journals (Diaries)
  USE **Diaries**
Journals (Machinery)
  USE **Bearings (Machinery)**
Journeys
  USE **Voyages and travels**
        and names of cities (except
        ancient cities), countries, re-
        gions, etc., with the subdi-
        vision *Description,* e.g.
        United States—Description;
        to be added as needed
Joy and sorrow 152.4
  UF Affliction
        Sorrow
  BT **Emotions**
        Ethics
  NT **Pleasure**
  RT **Grief**
        Happiness
        Suffering
Judaeo-German
  USE **Yiddish language**
Judaism 296
  UF Jewish religion
        Jews—Religion
  SA names of Jewish sects, e.g.
        Hasidism; to be added as
        needed
  BT **Religions**
  NT **Atonement—Judaism**
        Cabala
        Hasidism
        Jewish-Arab relations
        Jewish-Christian relations

Judaism—*Continued*
>Jewish holidays
>Jewish-Islamic relations
>Jews
>Rabbis
>Sabbath
>Synagogues
>Talmud

Judaism—Customs and practices 296.4
- UF Jews—Rites and ceremonies
- BT **Rites and ceremonies**
- NT **Judaism—Liturgy**

Judaism—Liturgy 296.4
- UF Jews—Ritual
- BT **Judaism—Customs and practices**
      Liturgies

Judaism—Relations—Christianity
- USE **Jewish-Christian relations**

Judges 347; 920
- UF Chief justices
- BT **Lawyers**
- NT **Women judges**
- RT **Courts**

Judicial investigations
- USE **Governmental investigations**

Judiciary
- USE **Courts**

Judo 796.8
- BT **Physical education**
      Self-defense
      Wrestling
- NT **Karate**

Juggling 793.8
- UF Legerdemain
      Sleight of hand
- BT **Amusements**
      Tricks

July Fourth
- USE **Fourth of July**

Jungle animals 591.52
- UF Jungle fauna
- BT **Animals**
      Forest animals
      Wildlife

Jungle fauna
- USE **Jungle animals**

Jungles 634.9
>Use for materials on impenetrable thickets of second-growth vegetation replacing tropical rain forests that have been disturbed or degraded. Materials on forests of broad-leaved, mainly evergreen trees found in moist climates in the tropics, subtropics, and some parts of the temperate zones, are entered under **Rain forests.**
- UF Tropical jungles
- BT **Forests and forestry**
- RT **Rain forests**

Junior colleges 378.1
- UF Community colleges
- BT **Colleges and universities**
      Higher education

Junior colleges—Directories 378.1
- BT **Directories**

Junior high school libraries
- USE **High school libraries**

Junior high schools 373.2
- UF High schools, Junior
      Secondary schools
- BT **High schools**
      Public schools
      Schools
- RT **Secondary education**

Junk
- USE **Waste products**

Junk bonds 332.63
- UF High-yield junk bonds
- BT **Bonds**

Junk in space
- USE **Space debris**

Jurisprudence
- USE **Law**

Jurisprudence, Medical
- USE **Medical jurisprudence**

Jurists
- USE **Lawyers**

Jury 345; 347
- UF Trial by jury
- BT **Courts**
      Criminal law

Justice 340
- BT **Ethics**
      Law
      Virtue

Justice, Administration of
- USE **Administration of justice**

Juvenile courts 345
- UF Children's courts

Juvenile courts—*Continued*

- BT   Courts
- RT   Juvenile delinquency
    - Probation

Juvenile delinquency 364.3

- UF   Children, Delinquent
    - Delinquency, Juvenile
    - Delinquents
- BT   Crime
    - Social problems
- NT   Gangs
    - Juvenile prostitution
    - School violence
- RT   Child welfare
    - Emotionally disturbed children
    - Juvenile courts
    - Reformatories
    - Teenagers—Drug use
    - Youth—Drug use

Juvenile delinquency—Case studies 364.3

Juvenile literature
- USE   Children's literature

Juvenile prostitution 176; 306.74; 362.7; 363.4; 364.1

- UF   Adolescent prostitution
    - Child prostitution
    - Children and prostitution
    - Prostitution, Juvenile *[Former heading]*
    - Teenage prostitution
- BT   Child abuse
    - Juvenile delinquency
    - Prostitution

K.K.K.
- USE   Ku Klux Klan (1865-1876)
    - Ku Klux Klan (1915-)

Kabbala
- USE   Cabala

Kamuti
- USE   Bonsai

Karate 796.8

- BT   Judo
    - Self-defense

Kart racing
- USE   Karts and karting

Karting
- USE   Karts and karting

Karts and karting 796.7

Use for materials on miniature, lightweight, low-slung, four-wheeled racing or recreational motorcars that can be driven at speeds of up to 60 mph.

- UF   Carts (Midget cars)
    - Go karts
    - Kart racing
    - Karting
    - Karts (Midget cars)
    - Midget cars
- BT   Automobile racing

Karts (Midget cars)
- USE   Karts and karting

Keyboarding (Electronics) 004.7; 652.5

- UF   Computer keyboarding
    - Data processing, Electronic—Keyboarding
    - Electronic data processing—Keyboarding
    - Word processor keyboarding
- BT   Business education
    - Office practice
- RT   Typewriting

Keyboards (Electronics) 004.7

- UF   Computer keyboards
    - Word processor keyboards
- BT   Computer peripherals
    - Office equipment and supplies

Keyboards (Musical instruments) 786

- BT   Organs (Musical instruments)
    - Pianos

Keys
- USE   Locks and keys

Kibbutz
- USE   Collective settlements—Israel

Kidnapping 364.1

- UF   Abduction
- BT   Criminal law
    - Offenses against the person

Kidnapping, Parental
- USE   Parental kidnapping

Killing, Mercy
- USE   Euthanasia

Kindergarten 372.21

- BT   Elementary education
    - Schools
- NT   Creative activities
    - Montessori method of education

BT = Broader Term   NT = Narrower Term   RT = Related Term   SA = See Also   UF = Used For

Kindergarten—*Continued*
 RT Nursery schools
  Preschool education
Kinematics 531
 BT Dynamics
 NT Mechanical movements
 RT Mechanics
  Motion
Kinetic art 701; 709.04
 UF Art in motion
  Art, Kinetic
 BT Modern art—1900-1999 (20th
  century)
 NT Kinetic sculpture
Kinetic sculpture 731; 735
 UF Sculpture in motion
  Sculpture, Kinetic
 BT Futurism (Art)
  Kinetic art
  Sculpture
 NT Mobiles (Sculpture)
Kinetics
 USE Dynamics
  Motion
King, Martin Luther, holiday
 USE Martin Luther King Day
King Philip's War, 1675-1676 973.2
 UF United States—History—
  1675-1676, King Philip's
  War
 BT Indians of North America—
  Wars
  United States—History—
  1600-1775, Colonial period
King William's War, 1689-1697
 USE United States—History—
  1689-1697, King William's
  War
Kings, queens, rulers, etc. 920; 929.7
 UF Emperors
  Monarchs
  Queens
  Royalty
  Rulers
  Sovereigns
 SA names of countries with the
  subdivision *Kings, queens,
  rulers, etc.,* and names of
  individual kings, queens, or
  rulers, to be added as need-
  ed

 BT Heads of state
  Monarchy
  Political science
 NT Dictators
  Elizabeth II, Queen of Great
  Britain, 1926-
  Great Britain—Kings, queens,
  rulers, etc.
  Presidents
  Roman emperors
 RT Counts and courtiers
Kitchen gardens
 USE Vegetable gardening
Kitchen utensils 643; 683
 UF Cooking utensils
  Household utensils
  Kitchenware
  Utensils, Kitchen
 BT Household equipment and sup-
  plies
Kitchens 643
 BT Houses
  Rooms
Kitchenware
 USE Kitchen utensils
Kites 629.133; 796.1
 BT Aeronautics
Kittens 599.74; 636.8
 BT Animal babies
  Cats
Knighthood
 USE Knights and knighthood
Knights and knighthood 394; 940.1
 UF Knighthood
 BT Middle Ages
  Nobility
 RT Chivalry
  Heraldry
Knights of the Round Table
 USE Arthurian romances
Knitting 677; 746.43
 BT Needlework
Knots and splices 623.88
 UF Splicing
 BT Navigation
  Rope
Knowledge-based systems (Computer
  science)
 USE Expert systems (Computer sci-
  ence)

BT = Broader Term   NT = Narrower Term   RT = Related Term   SA = See Also   UF = Used For

Knowledge, Theory of
USE **Theory of knowledge**
Kodak camera 771.3
BT **Cameras**
Koran 297
UF Alkoran
Qur'an
BT **Islam**
Sacred books
Korea 951.9
Use for comprehensive materials on all of Korea and for materials on Korea before it was divided in 1948 into two separate republics.
NT **Korea (North)**
Korea (South)
Korea (Democratic People's Republic)
USE **Korea (North)**
Korea (North) 951.93
Use for materials on the Democratic People's Republic of Korea, established in 1948. May be subdivided like United States except for *History*.
UF Korea (Democratic People's Republic)
North Korea
BT **Korea**
Korea (Republic)
USE **Korea (South)**
Korea (South) 951.95
Use for materials on the Republic of Korea, established in 1948. May be subdivided like United States except for *History*.
UF Korea (Republic)
South Korea
BT **Korea**
Korean War, 1950-1953 951.904
BT **Modern history—1900-1999**
(20th century)
Ku Klux Klan (1865-1876) 322.4
UF K.K.K.
BT **Reconstruction (1865-1876)**
Ku Klux Klan (1915-) 322.4
UF K.K.K.
Kuwait—History—1990, Iraqi Invasion
953.67
Use for materials limited to the Iraqi invasion of Kuwait. Comprehensive materials on the subsequent war that include discussion of the Iraqi invasion as a prelude to the war are entered under **Persian Gulf War, 1991.**
UF Iraq—History—1990, Invasion of Kuwait

Iraq-Kuwait Crisis, 1990-1991
Kuwait—History—1991, Persian Gulf War
USE **Persian Gulf War, 1991**
Labor (May subdiv. geog.) **331**
Use for materials on the collective human activities involved in the production and distribution of goods and services in an economy, especially activities performed by workers for wages as distinguished from those performed by entrepreneurs for profits. Also use for general materials on workers. Materials on laborers as a social class are entered under **Working class.** Materials on the physical or mental exertion of individuals to produce or accomplish something are entered under **Work.**

UF Blue collar workers
Factory workers
Industrial workers
Labor and laboring classes
[Former heading]
Laborers
Manual workers
Skilled workers
Unskilled workers
SA types of laborers, e.g. **Agricultural laborers; Miners;** etc., to be added as needed
BT **Economics**
Social conditions
Sociology
NT **Agricultural laborers**
Apprentices
Capitalism
Children—Employment
Church and labor
Collective bargaining
Contract labor
Convict labor
Cost of living
Employees
Employment
Employment agencies
Hours of labor
Household employees
Industrial arbitration
Industrial insurance
Industrial relations
Labor supply
Labor unions
Libraries and labor

BT = Broader Term   NT = Narrower Term   RT = Related Term   SA = See Also   UF = Used For

Labor—*Continued*

    Machinery in industry
    Men—Employment
    Migrant labor
    Miners
    Occupational diseases
    Occupations
    Open and closed shop
    Part-time employment
    Peasantry
    Peonage
    Proletariat
    Slavery
    Supplementary employment
    Teenagers—Employment
    Wages
    Welfare work in industry
    Women—Employment
    Work ethic
    World War, 1939-1945—
      Human resources
    Youth—Employment
RT Labor movement
    Work
    Working class

Labor absenteeism
  USE Absenteeism (Labor)

Labor—Accidents 363.1; 658.3
  BT Accidents
  RT Hazardous occupations

Labor and capital
  USE Industrial relations

Labor and laboring classes
  USE Labor
        Working class

Labor and libraries
  USE Libraries and labor

Labor and the church
  USE Church and labor

Labor arbitration
  USE Industrial arbitration

Labor (Childbirth)
  USE Childbirth

Labor contract 331.1; 331.89
  Use for materials on agreements between employer and employee in which the latter agrees to perform work in return for compensation from the former.
  UF Collective labor agreements
        Trade agreements (Labor)
  BT Contracts

    Industrial relations
NT Open and closed shop
    Wages
RT Collective bargaining

Labor courts
  USE Industrial arbitration

Labor disputes 331.89
  UF Disputes, Labor
        Industrial disputes
  BT Industrial relations
  NT Collective bargaining
        Industrial arbitration
        Strikes

Labor—Education 331.25
  UF Education of workers

Labor force
  USE Labor supply

Labor, Hours of
  USE Hours of labor

Labor—Housing 363.5

Labor—Insurance
  USE Old age pensions
        Social security
        Unemployment insurance

Labor-management relations
  USE Industrial relations

Labor market
  USE Labor supply

Labor, Migratory
  USE Migrant labor

Labor movement 331.8
  Use for materials on the efforts of organizations and individuals to improve conditions for labor.
  BT Social movements
  RT Labor
        Labor unions

Labor negotiations
  USE Collective bargaining
        Industrial arbitration

Labor organizations
  USE Labor unions

Labor output
  USE Labor productivity

Labor participation in management
  USE Participative management

Labor productivity 331.11
  UF Labor output
        Productivity of labor

Labor productivity—*Continued*

SA types of industries, occupations, and processes with the subdivision *Labor productivity,* e.g. **Steel industry—Labor productivity**; to be added as needed

BT **Industrial efficiency**

NT **Production standards**
Steel industry—Labor productivity

RT **Machinery in industry**

Labor relations
  USE **Industrial relations**

Labor saving devices, Household
  USE **Alectric household appliances**
Household equipment and supplies

Labor supply 331.11

UF Labor force
Labor market

BT **Economic conditions**
Employment
Labor

NT **Children—Employment**
Men—Employment
Occupational retraining
Teenagers—Employment
Unemployed
Unemployment
Women—Employment
World War, 1939-1945—Human resources
Youth—Employment

RT **Employment agencies**
Employment forecasting
Human resources
Human resources policy

Labor turnover 331.12

BT **Personnel management**

NT **Employment agencies**

Labor unions (May subdiv. geog.) **331.88**

UF Labor organizations
Organized labor
Trade unions
Unions, Labor

SA types of unions and names of individual labor unions, to be added as needed

BT **Cooperation**
Industrial relations
Labor
Socialism
Societies

NT **Industrial arbitration**
Injunctions
Librarians' qnions
Open and closed shop
United Steelworkers of America

RT **Collective bargaining**
Labor movement
Strikes

Labor unions—United States
331.880973

UF American labor unions
United States—Labor unions

Labor—United Stapes 331.0973

UF United States—Labor

Laboratories, Language
  USE **Language laboratories**

Laboratories, Space
  USE **Space stations**

Laboratory animal experimentation
  USE **Animal experimentation**

Laboratory animal welfare
  USE **Animal welfare**

Laboratory fertilization
  USE **Fertilization in vitro**

Laboratory manuals
  USE scientific and technical subjects with the subdivision *Laboratory manuals,* for workbooks containing concise background information and directions for performing work, including experiments, in the laboratory, e.g. **Chemistry—Laboratory manuals**; to be added as needed

Laborers
  USE **Labor**
Working class
and names of classes of laborers, e.g. **Agricultural laborers; Miners**; etc., to be added as needed

---

Laboring class
    USE **Working class**
Laboring classes
    USE **Working class**
Lace and lace making 677; 746.2
    BT **Crocheting**
          Needlework
          Weaving
Lacquer and lacquering 667; 745.7
    UF Finishes and finishing
    BT **Decorative arts**
          Wood finishing
    RT **Varnish and varnishing**
Laissez faire
    USE **Industry—Government policy**
Laity 262
    May be subdivided by religious denomi-
nation.
    UF **Laymen**
    BT **Church**
    RT **Lay ministry**
Laity—Catholic Church 262
    UF Catholic laity
Lakes (May subdiv. geog. country and
          state) **551.48**
    SA names of lakes, to be added
          as needed
    BT **Physical geography**
          Water
          Waterways
    RT **Inland navigation**
Lakes—United States 551.48
    UF United States—Lakes
Lamaze method of childbirth
    USE **Natural childbirth**
Lambs 599.73; 636.3
    BT **Animal babies**
          Sheep
Lamentations
    USE **Elegiac poetry**
Lamps 621.32; 749
    BT **Lighting**
    NT **Electric lamps**
Land
    USE **Land use**
          Wetlands
Land drainage
    USE **Drainage**
Land question
    USE **Land tenure**

Land, Reclamation of
    USE **Reclamation of land**
Land reform (May subdiv. geog.) **333.3**
    UF Agrarian reform
          Reform, Agrarian
    BT **Economic policy**
          Land use
          Social policy
    NT **Land tenure**
    RT **Agriculture—Government poli-
          cy**
Land settlement (May subdiv. geog.)
          304.8; 325
    UF Resettlement
          Settlement of land
    BT **Colonies**
    NT **Colonization**
    RT **Internal migration**
**Land settlement—United States 304.8;
          325.73**
    UF United States—Land settle-
          ment
          Westward movement
Land surveying
    USE **Surveying**
Land tenure 333.3
    Use for general and historical materials
on systems of holding land.
    UF Agrarian question
          Fiefs
          Land question
          Tenure of land
    BT **Agriculture—Economic aspects**
          Land reform
          Land use
    NT **Farm tenancy**
          Feudalism
          Landlord and tenant
    RT **Peasantry**
          Real estate
Land use 333.73
    Use for general materials that cover
such topics as types of land, the utilization, distribution and development of
land, and the economic factors affecting
the value of land. Materials dealing only
with ownership of land are entered under
Real estate.
    UF Land
    BT **Agriculture**
          Economics
    NT **Eminent domain**

BT = Broader Term   NT = Narrower Term   RT = Related Term   SA = See Also   UF = Used For

Land use—*Continued*
>   **Farms**
>   **Land reform**
>   **Land tenure**
>   **Public lands**
>   **Real estate**
>   **Reclamation of land**
>   **Regional planning**
>   **Wetlands**

Landfills 363.72; 628.3; 628.4
>   Use for materials on places for waste disposal in which waste is buried in layers of earth in low ground.
>   UF   Earth fills
>   Fills (Earthwork)
>   Sanitary landfills
>   SA   names of landfills, to be added as needed
>   NT   **Hazardous waste sites**
>   **Love Canal Chemical Waste Landfill (Niagara Falls, N.Y.)**

Landlord and tenant 333.5; 346.04
>   Use for materials on the legal relationships between landlord and tenant.
>   UF   Tenant and landlord
>   BT   **Commercial law**
>   **Human relations**
>   **Land tenure**
>   **Real estate**
>   NT   **Apartment houses**
>   **Housing**
>   RT   **Farm tenancy**

Landmarks, Literary
>   USE   **Literary landmarks**

Landmarks, Preservation of
>   USE   **National monuments**
>   **Natural monuments**

Landscape architecture 712
>   Use for materials on modifying or arranging the features of a landscape, urban area, etc., for aesthetic or pragmatic purposes.
>   UF   Landscape design
>   NT   **Garden ornaments and furniture**
>   **Parks**
>   **Patios**
>   **Roadside improvement**
>   RT   **Landscape gardening**
>   **Landscape protection**

Landscape design
>   USE   **Landscape architecture**

Landscape drawing 743
>   BT   **Drawing**
>   RT   **Landscape painting**

Landscape gardening 712
>   Use for materials on the design or rearrangement of extensive gardens or estates.
>   UF   Planting
>   BT   **Gardening**
>   **Horticulture**
>   NT   **Evergreens**
>   **Lawns**
>   **Ornamental plants**
>   RT   **Garden design**
>   **Landscape architecture**
>   **Shrubs**
>   **Trees**

Landscape painting 758
>   BT   **Painting**
>   RT   **Landscape drawing**

Landscape protection 333.73
>   UF   Beautification of landscape
>   Natural beauty conservation
>   Preservation of natural scenery
>   Protection of natural scenery
>   Scenery
>   BT   **Environmental protection**
>   **Nature conservation**
>   NT   **Natural monuments**
>   RT   **Landscape architecture**
>   **Regional planning**

Landscape sculpture
>   USE   **Earthworks (Art)**

Language and languages 400
>   Use for general materials on the history, philosophy, origin, etc., of language. Materials on the scientific study of speech and comparative studies of language are entered under **Linguistics.**
>   UF   Philology
>   SA   names of languages or groups of cognate languages, e.g. **English language;** and classes of persons with the subdivision *Language,* e.g. **Children—Language;** to be added as needed
>   BT   **Anthropology**
>   **Communication**

BT = Broader Term   NT = Narrower Term   RT = Related Term   SA = See Also   UF = Used For

391

Language and languages—*Continued*
Ethnology

    NT   Anglo-Saxon language
          Bilingualism
          Children—Language
          Conversation
          English language
          German language
          Greek language
          Hebrew language
          Indians of North America—
              Languages
          Japanese language
          Latin language
          Linguistics
          Modern languages
          Phonetics
          Programming languages (Com-
              puters)
          Rhetoric
          Romance languages
          Russian language
          Scandinavian languages
          Semantics
          Sign language
          Sociolinguistics
          Translating and interpreting
          Universal language
          Verbal learning
          Vocabulary
          Voice
          Writing
          Yiddish language
    RT   Grammar
          Speech

Language and languages—Business lan-
          guage
    USE   names of languages with
          unique language subdivi-
          sions, e.g. **English
          language—Business English;
          Japanese language—
          Business Japanese;** etc., to
          be added as needed

Language and languages—Comparative
          philology
    USE   **Linguistics**

Language and society
    USE   **Sociolinguistics**

Language arts 372.6; 400
    UF   Communication arts
    BT   **Communication**
    NT   **Creative writing
          Literature
          Reading
          Speech
          Whole language
          Writing**

Language arts (Holistic)
    USE   **Whole language**

Language arts—Patterning 372.6
    UF   Patterns (Language arts)
          Reading—Patterning
          Writing—Patterning

Language experience approach in edu-
          cation
    USE   **Whole language**

Language games
    USE   **Literary recreations**

Language, International
    USE   **Universal language**

Language laboratories 407
    UF   Foreign language laboratories
          Laboratories, Language
    RT   **Modern languages—Study and
          teaching**

Language, Universal
    USE   **Universal language**

Languages, Modern
    USE   **Modern languages**

Languages, Modern—Conversations and
          phrases
    USE   **Modern languages—
          Conversations and phrases**

Languages—Vocabulary
    USE   **Vocabulary**

Lantern projection
    USE   **Projectors**

Lantern slides
    USE   **Slides (Photography)**

Laptop computers
    USE   **Portable computers**

Larceny
    USE   **Stealing**

Large and small
    USE   **Size and shape**

Large print books 028
    UF   Books for sight saving
          Books—Large print

Large print books—*Continued*
>> Large type books
>> Sight saving books
> BT **Blind—Books and reading**
> RT **Big books**

Large type books
> USE **Large print books**

Laser-beam recording
> USE **Laser recording**

Laser photography
> USE **Holography**

Laser recording 621.36; 621.38
> UF Laser-beam recording
>> Recording, Laser
> BT **Lasers**
> NT **Holography**
> RT **Optical storage devices**

Lasers 621.36
> UF Light amplification by stimu-
>> lated emission of radiation
>> Masers, Optical
>> Optical masers
> SA lasers in particular subjects or
>> fields of endeavor, e.g. **La-**
>> **sers in aeronautics**; to be
>> added as needed
> BT **Light**
> NT **Laser recording**
>> **Lasers in aeronautics**

Lasers in aeronautics 629.13
> BT **Aeronautics**
>> **Lasers**

Last rites (Sacraments)
> USE **Anointing of the sick**

Last sacraments
> USE **Anointing of the sick**

Last Supper
> USE **Lord's Supper**

Last things (Theology)
> USE **Eschatology**

Latchkey children 306.874; 362.7; 640
> Use for materials on children who carry
> keys to let themselves into the house on
> returning from school because the parents
> are at work.
> UF Children, Latchkey
> BT **Children of working parents**

Lateness
> USE **Punctuality**

Lathe work
> USE **Lathes**

>> Turning
Lathes 621.9
> UF Lathe work
> BT **Woodworking machinery**
> RT **Turning**

Latin America 980
> Use for materials on several or all of the
> countries of the Western Hemisphere
> south of the United States in which Span-
> ish, Portuguese, or French is the principal
> language.
> UF Spanish America
> SA names of individual Latin
>> American countries, to be
>> added as needed
> BT **America**
> NT **Pan-Americanism**

Latin America—Politics and government
980
> BT **Politics**

Latin American literature 860
> Use for materials on the French, Portu-
> guese, or Spanish literature of several Lat-
> in American countries. May use same
> subdivisions and names of literary forms
> as for **English literature.**
> UF South American literature
> SA names of individual Latin
>> American literatures, to be
>> added as needed
> BT **Literature**
> NT **Brazilian literature**
>> **Mexican literature**
> RT **Spanish literature**

Latin Americans 920; 980
> Use for materials on citizens of Latin
> American countries. Materials on United
> States citizens of Latin American descent
> are entered under **Hispanic Americans.**

Latin language 470
> May be subdivided like **English lan-**
> **guage.**
> UF Classical languages
> BT **Language and languages**
> NT **Romance languages**

Latin literature 870
> May use same subdivisions and names
> of literary forms as for **English literature.**
> UF Roman literature
> BT **Literature**
> RT **Classical literature**
>> **Early Christian literature**

Latinos (U.S.)
> USE **Hispanic Americans**

Latitude 526; 527
    UF   Degrees of latitude and longitude
    BT   **Earth**
          Geodesy
          Nautical astronomy
Latter-day Saints
    USE **Church of Jesus Christ of Latter-day Saints**
Laughter 152.4
    BT   **Emotions**
Launching of satellites
    USE **Artificial satellites—Launching**
Laundry 648
    UF   Ironing
          Washing
    BT   **Cleaning**
          Home economics
          Household sanitation
Law (May subdiv. geog.) **340**
    UF   Jurisprudence
          Laws
          Statutes
    SA   names of particular legal systems, e.g. **Islamic law;** special branches of law, e.g. **Criminal law;** and subjects with the subdivision *Law and legislation,* e.g. **Automobiles—Law and legislation;** to be added as needed
    BT   **Political science**
    NT   **Administration of justice**
          Administrative law
          Automobiles—Law and legislation
          Commercial law
          Constitutional law
          Corporation law
          Courts
          Criminal law
          Ecclesiastical law
          Food—Law and legislation
          Internal revenue law
          International law
          Islamic law
          Justice
          Law reform
          Lawyers

          Litigation
          Maritime law
          Medical jurisprudence
          Military law
          Space law
          Water rights
    RT   **Legislation**
Law, Administrative
    USE **Administrative law**
Law, Business
    USE **Commercial law**
Law, Commercial
    USE **Commercial law**
Law, Constitutional
    USE **Constitutional law**
Law, Corporation
    USE **Corporation law**
Law, Criminal
    USE **Criminal law**
Law, Ecclesiastical
    USE **Ecclesiastical law**
Law enforcement 363.2
    UF   Enforcement of law
    BT   **Administration of criminal justice**
    NT   **Criminal investigation**
          Police
Law—Fiction
    USE **Legal stories**
Law, Internal revenue
    USE **Internal revenue law**
Law, International
    USE **International law**
Law, Islamic
    USE **Islamic law**
Law, Maritime
    USE **Maritime law**
Law, Military
    USE **Military law**
Law, Muslim
    USE **Islamic law**
Law of nations
    USE **International law**
Law of the sea
    USE **Maritime law**
Law reform 340
    UF   Legal reform
    BT   **Law**
Law, Space
    USE **Space law**

Law suits
  USE   Litigation
Law—United States 349.73
  UF   United States—Law
Law—Vocational guidance 340.023
  BT   Professions
       Vocational guidance
Lawn tennis
  USE   Tennis
Lawns 635.9; 712
  BT   Landscape gardening
  NT   Grasses
Laws
  USE   Law
        Legislation
        and subjects with the subdivi-
          sion *Law and legislation,*
          e.g. **Automobiles—Law and
          legislation; Food—Law and
          legislation;** etc., to be add-
          ed as needed
Lawsuits
  USE   Litigation
Lawyers 340.092; 920
  UF   Attorneys
       Bar
       Barristers
       Jurists
       Legal profession
  BT   Law
  NT   Judges
  RT   Legal ethics
Lawyers—Fiction
  USE   Legal stories
Lay ministry 253
  UF   Volunteers in church work
  BT   Church work
  RT   Laity
Laymen
  USE   Laity
Layout and typography
  USE   Printing
LBOs (Corporations)
  USE   Leveraged buyouts
Lead poisoning 615.9
  UF   Lead—Toxicology
  BT   Occupational diseases
       Poisons and poisoning
Lead—Toxicology
  USE   Lead poisoning

Leadership 158; 303.3
  BT   Ability
       Executive ability
       Social groups
       Success
  NT   Elite (Social sciences)
League of Nations 341.22
  BT   International arbitration
       International cooperation
       International organization
       World War, 1914-1918—
         Peace
League of Nations—Mandatory system
  USE   Mandates
Learned institutions and societies
  USE   Learning and scholarship
Learned societies
  USE   Societies
Learning and scholarship 001.2
  UF   Erudition
       Learned institutions and so-
         cieties
       Scholarship
  BT   Civilization
       Intellectual life
  NT   Professional education
  RT   Culture
       Education
       Humanism
       Research
Learning, Art of
  USE   Study skills
Learning center approach to teaching
  USE   Open plan schools
Learning, Concept
  USE   Concept learning
Learning disabilities 153.1; 370.15;
          371.9; 616.85
  UF   Disability, Learning
       Learning disorders
  SA   types of learning disabilities,
         to be added as needed
  BT   Psychology of learning
       Slow learning children
  NT   Reading disability
Learning disorders
  USE   Learning disabilities
Learning, Psychology of
  USE   Psychology of learning
Learning resource centers
  USE   Instructional materials centers

Learning, Verbal
USE **Verbal learning**
Lease and rental services 333.5
UF Lease services
Rental services
BT **Service industries**
Lease services
USE **Lease and rental services**
Leather 675
BT **Animal products**
RT **Hides and skins**
Tanning
Leather clothing
USE **Leather garments**
Leather garments 391; 685
UF Clothing, Leather
Garments, Leather
Leather clothing
Skin garments
BT **Clothing and dress**
Leather work
Leather industry 338.4
UF Leather industry and trade
[Former heading]
Leather trade
BT **Industry**
NT **Bookbinding**
Shoe industry
Leather industry and trade
USE **Leather industry**
Leather trade
USE **Leather industry**
Leather work 745.53
BT **Decoration and ornament**
Decorative arts
Handicraft
NT **Leather garments**
Leaves 581.1
UF Foliage
BT **Botany**
Trees
Lebanon 956.92
May be subdivided like United States except for *History.*
Lebanon—History 956.92
Lebanon—History—1975-1976, Civil War 956.9204
Lebanon—History—1982-1984, Israeli intervention 956.05
UF Israeli intervention in Lebanon, 1982-1984

BT **Israel-Arab conflicts**
Lectures and lecturing 808.5
Use for general materials on lectures and the art of lecturing. Collections of lectures on several subjects are entered under **Speeches.** Lectures on a single subject are entered under that subject.
UF Addresses
Speaking
BT **Public speaking**
Rhetoric
Speeches
Teaching
NT **Radio addresses, debates, etc.**
Left and right 152.1
Use for children's materials on left and right as indications of location or direction. Materials on political views or attitudes are entered under **Right and left (Political science).** Materials on the physical characteristics of favoring one hand or the other are entered under **Left- and right-handedness.**
UF Right and left
BT **Direction sense**
Left- and right-handedness 152.3
UF Handedness
Right- and left-handedness
BT **Psychophysiology**
Left (Political science)
USE **Right and left (Political science)**
Legacies
USE **Inheritance and succession**
Wills
Legal aid 362.5
UF Charities, Legal
SA types of legal aid, e.g. **Legal assistance to the poor;** to be added as needed
NT **Legal assistance to the poor**
Legal assistance to the poor 362.5
UF Legal representative of the poor
Legal service for the poor
Poor—Legal assistance
BT **Legal aid**
Public welfare
Legal drama (Films) 791.43
May be used for individual works, collections, or materials about motion pictures dealing with trials or litigations.
UF Courtroom drama

Legal drama (Films)—*Continued*
>   BT   **Motion pictures**

Legal drama (Radio programs) 791.44
>   May be used for individual works, collections, or materials about radio programs dealing with trials or litigations.
>
>   UF   Courtroom drama
>   BT   **Radio programs**

Legal drama (Television programs) 791.45
>   May be used for individual works, collections, or materials about television programs dealing with trials or litigations.
>
>   UF   Courtroom drama
>   BT   **Television programs**

Legal ethics 174; 340
>   UF   Ethics, Legal
>   BT   **Professional ethics**
>   RT   **Lawyers**

Legal fiction
>   USE   **Legal stories**

Legal holidays
>   USE   **Holidays**

Legal medicine
>   USE   **Medical jurisprudence**

Legal novels
>   USE   **Legal stories**

Legal profession
>   USE   **Lawyers**

Legal reform
>   USE   **Law reform**

Legal representative of the poor
>   USE   **Legal assistance to the poor**

Legal responsibility
>   USE   **Liability (Law)**

Legal service for the poor
>   USE   **Legal assistance to the poor**

Legal stories 808.83; 813, etc.
>   May be used for individual works, collections, or materials about fiction dealing with trials or litigations.
>
>   UF   Law—Fiction
>   Lawyers—Fiction
>   Legal fiction
>   Legal novels
>   BT   **Fiction**

Legal tender
>   USE   **Paper money**

Legations
>   USE   **Diplomatic and consular service**

Legends (May subdiv. geog.) **398.2**
>   May be used for individual works, collections, or materials about tales coming down from the past, especially those relating to actual events or persons. Collections of tales written between the eleventh and fourteenth centuries and dealing with the age of chivalry or the supernatural are entered under **Romances.**
>
>   UF   Folk tales
>   Stories
>   Tales
>   Traditions
>   SA   legends of particular ethnic or religious groups, e.g. **Jewish legends;** to be added as needed
>   BT   **Fiction**
>   **Literature**
>   NT   **Celtic legends**
>   **Fairy tales**
>   **Grail**
>   **Indians of North America— Legends**
>   **Jewish legends**
>   **Mythology**
>   **Norse legends**
>   **Tall tales**
>   RT   **Fables**
>   **Folklore**
>   **Romances**
>   **Saints**

Legends, Celtic
>   USE   **Celtic legends**

Legends, Indian
>   USE   **Indians of North America— Legends**

Legends, Jewish
>   USE   **Jewish legends**

Legends, Norse
>   USE   **Norse legends**

Legends—United States 398.20973; 973
>   UF   United States—Legends

Legerdemain
>   USE   **Juggling**
>   **Magic tricks**

Legislation 328
>   Use for materials on the theory of lawmaking and descriptions of the preparation and enactment of laws.
>
>   UF   Laws

Legislation—*Continued*

    SA   subjects with the subdivision *Law and legislation,* to be added as needed

    BT   **Constitutional law**
          Political science

    NT   **Automobiles—Law and legislation**
          Firearms—Law and legislation
          Food—Law and legislation
          Legislative bodies
          Libraries—Law and legislation
          Medicine—Law and legislation
          Parliamentary practice

    RT   **Law**

Legislation, Direct
    USE   **Referendum**

Legislative bodies 328.3

Use for descriptions and histories of law making bodies, discussions of one-house legislatures, etc.

    UF   Parliaments
          Unicameral legislatures

    SA   names of individual legislative bodies, e.g. **United States. Congress;** to be added as needed

    BT   **Constitutional law**
          Legislation
          Representative government and representation

    NT   **Parliamentary practice**
          United States. Congress
          War and emergency powers

Legislative investigations
    USE   **Governmental investigations**

Legislative reapportionment
    USE   **Apportionment (Election law)**

Legitimacy (Law)
    USE   **Illegitimacy**

Leisure 790.01

    UF   Free time (Leisure)
          Leisure time

    BT   **Recreation**

    NT   **Hobbies**
          Retirement
          Time management

Leisure time
    USE   **Leisure**

LEM
    USE   **Lunar excursion module**

Lending
    USE   **Loans**

Lending of library materials
    USE   **Library circulation**

Lenses 535

    SA   types of lenses, e.g. **Contact lenses;** etc.

    NT   **Contact lenses**

Lensless photography
    USE   **Holography**

Lent 263

    BT   **Christian holidays**

    NT   **Good Friday**
          Holy Week

    RT   **Easter**

Lepidoptera
    USE   **Butterflies**
            Moths

Lesbianism 306.76

    BT   **Homosexuality**

    RT   **Lesbians**

Lesbians 305.48; 306.76

    UF   Gay women *[Former heading]*
          Gays, Female
          Homosexuals, Female

    BT   **Women**

    RT   **Homosexuality**
          Lesbianism

Lesbians' writings 808.8; 810.8, etc.

Use for collections of lesbians' writings by more than one author and for materials about such writings.

    UF   Gay women's writings
          Writings of lesbians

    BT   **Literature**

Less developed countries
    USE   **Developing countries**

Letter-sound association
    USE   **Reading—Phonetic method**

Letter writing 383; 808.6

Use for materials on composition, forms, and etiquette of correspondence. Materials limited to business correspondence are entered under **Business letters.** Collections of literary letters are entered under **Letters.**

    UF   Correspondence
          Salutations

    BT   **Etiquette**
          Literary style

BT = Broader Term   NT = Narrower Term   RT = Related Term   SA = See Also   UF = Used For

Letter writing—*Continued*
> **Rhetoric**
>> NT **Business letters**

Lettering 745.6
> UF Ornamental alphabets
> BT **Decoration and ornament**
>> **Industrial painting**
>> **Mechanical drawing**
> NT **Monograms**
> RT **Alphabets**
>> **Initials**
>> **Sign painting**

Letters 808.86
> Use for collections of literary letters. Materials on the composition, forms, and etiquette of correspondence are entered under **Letter writing.** Materials limited to business correspondence are entered under **Business letters.**
> UF Correspondence
> SA ethnic groups, classes of persons, and names of individual persons and families with the subdivision *Correspondence,* e.g. **Authors—Correspondence;** to be added as needed
> BT **Literature—Collections**
> NT **American letters**
>> **English letters**

Letters of credit
> USE **Credit**
>> **Negotiable instruments**

Letters of marque
> USE **Privateering**

Letters of recommendation
> USE **Applications for positions**

Letters of the alphabet
> USE **Alphabet**

Leukemia 616.99
> BT **Blood—Diseases**
>> **Cancer**

Levant
> USE **Middle East**

Leveraged buyouts 338.8; 658.1
> UF Buyouts, Leveraged
>> LBOs (Corporations)
>> Management buyouts
> BT **Corporate mergers and acquisitions**

Lewis and Clark Expedition (1804-1806) 973.4
> BT **United States—Exploring expeditions**
>> **United States—History—1783-1809**

Liability (Law) 346
> UF Accountability
>> Legal responsibility
>> Responsibility, Legal
> BT **Contracts**
> NT **Malpractice**

Liability, Professional
> USE **Malpractice**

Libel and slander 346.03
> UF Character assassination
>> Defamation
>> Slander (Law)
> BT **Journalism**
> NT **Gossip**
>> **Right of privacy**
> RT **Freedom of speech**
>> **Freedom of the press**

Liberalism 148; 320.5
> BT **Political science**
>> **Social sciences**
> RT **Right and left (Political science)**

Liberation movements, National
> USE **National liberation movements**

Liberation theology 261.8
> Use for materials on the Christian theological movement that argues for the total liberation of humanity and supports causes of social justice.
> UF Theology of liberation
> BT **Church and social problems**
>> **Doctrinal theology**

Liberty
> USE **Freedom**

Liberty of conscience
> USE **Freedom of conscience**

Liberty of speech
> USE **Freedom of speech**

Liberty of the press
> USE **Freedom of the press**

Liberty of the will
> USE **Free will and determinism**

Librarians 020.92; 920
> NT **African American librarians**

Librarians—*Continued*
    Black librarians
    Library technicians
  RT Libraries
Librarians, African American
  USE **African American librarians**
Librarians, Black
  USE **Black librarians**
Librarians—Collective bargaining
  USE **Collective bargaining—**
      Librarians
Librarians—Education
  USE **Library education**
Librarians—In-service training 023
  UF In-service training
     Inservice training
  BT **Library education**
Librarians—Professional ethics 174
  BT **Professional ethics**
Librarians—Rating 023
  BT **Performance standards**
Librarians—Recruiting 023
  BT **Recruiting of employees**
Librarians—Training
  USE **Library education**
Librarians' unions 331.88
  UF Library unions
  BT **Labor unions**
Librarianship
  USE **Library science**
Librarianship, Comparative
  USE **Comparative librarianship**
Libraries (May subdiv. geog.) **027**
  SA special types of libraries, e.g.
     Academic libraries; names
     of individual libraries, e.g.
     Library of Congress; li-
     braries and particular
     groups of people, e.g. **Li-**
     braries and African Ameri-
     cans; and libraries and
     other subjects, e.g. **Libraries**
     and motion pictures; to be
     added as needed
  BT **Books**
    Books and reading
    Documentation
  NT **Academic libraries**
    Church libraries
    Hospital libraries

    Instructional materials centers
    Libraries and community
    Libraries and motion pictures
    Libraries and pictures
    Library architecture
    Library catalogs
    Library cooperation
    Library of Congress
    Library resources
    Library services
    Library technical processes
    Public libraries
    School libraries
    Special libraries
  RT **Archives**
    Information services
    Librarians
Libraries—Acquisitions 025.2
  UF Acquisitions (Libraries)
     Book buying (Libraries)
     Libraries—Order department
     Library acquisitions
  BT **Libraries—Collection develop-**
     ment
    Library technical processes
  NT **Book selection**
Libraries—Administration 025.1
  UF Library administration
     Library policies
  NT **Libraries—Trustees**
    Library finance
Libraries—Advertising
  USE **Advertising—Libraries**
Libraries and African Americans 027.6
  UF African Americans and li-
     braries
     Afro-Americans and libraries
     Library services to African
     Americans
  BT **African Americans**
    Library services
Libraries and children
  USE **Children's libraries**
Libraries and community 021.2
  UF Community and libraries
  BT **Libraries**
  NT **Public relations—Libraries**
Libraries and labor 027.6
  UF Labor and libraries
     Library services to labor

Libraries and labor—*Continued*
   BT   Labor
         Library services
Libraries and motion pictures 021
   UF   Educational films
         Motion pictures and libraries
   BT   **Libraries**
         Motion pictures
         Motion pictures in education
Libraries and pictures 021
   BT   **Libraries**
         Pictures
Libraries and schools 021
   UF   Schools and libraries
   BT   **Schools**
   NT   **Libraries and students**
   RT   **Children's libraries**
         Children's literature
         School libraries
Libraries and state
   USE **Libraries—Government policy**
Libraries and students 027.62
   UF   Students and libraries
   BT   **Libraries and schools**
         Library services
         School libraries
Libraries and the elderly 027.6
   UF   Elderly and libraries
         Library services to the elderly
   BT   **Elderly**
         Library services
Libraries and young adults
   USE **Young adults' library services**
Libraries—Automation 025.04
   UF   Library automation
   SA   names of projects, formats,
         and systems, e.g. **MARC**
         formats; to be added as
         needed
   BT   **Automation**
   NT   **Machine readable bibliograph-**
         ic data
         MARC formats
   RT   **Information systems**
         Online catalogs
Libraries—Boards of trustees
   USE **Libraries—Trustees**
Libraries, Business
   USE **Business libraries**
Libraries—Cataloging
   USE **Cataloging**

Libraries—Catalogs
   USE **Library catalogs**
Libraries—Censorship 025.2
Libraries—Centralization 021.6
   UF   Library systems
Libraries, Children's
   USE• **Children's libraries**
Libraries, Church
   USE **Church libraries**
Libraries—Circulation, loans
   USE **Library circulation**
Libraries—Classification
   USE **Classification—Books**
Libraries—Collection development 025.2
   UF   Collection development (Li-
         braries)
   BT   **Library technical processes**
   NT   **Book selection**
         Libraries—Acquisitions
Libraries—Collective bargaining
   USE **Collective bargaining—**
         Librarians
Libraries, College
   USE **Academic libraries**
Libraries, Company
   USE **Corporate libraries**
Libraries—Cooperation
   USE **Library cooperation**
Libraries, Corporate
   USE **Corporate libraries**
Libraries, County
   USE **County libraries**
Libraries—Equipment and supplies 022
   UF   Library equipment and sup-
         plies
         Library supplies
   BT   **Furniture**
Libraries—Federal aid
   USE **Federal aid to libraries**
Libraries—Finance
   USE **Library finance**
Libraries—Government policy 021.8;
         351.85
   UF   Libraries and state
   NT   **Federal aid to libraries**
         State aid to libraries
Libraries, Governmental
   USE **Government libraries**
Libraries, Hospital
   USE **Hospital libraries**

Libraries, Industrial
　USE　**Corporate libraries**
Libraries—Law and legislation 344
　UF　Library laws
　　　Library legislation
　BT　**Legislation**
Libraries—Lighting 022
　BT　**Lighting**
Libraries, Music
　USE　**Music libraries**
Libraries, National
　USE　**National libraries**
Libraries—Order department
　USE　**Libraries—Acquisitions**
Libraries, Presidential
　USE　**Presidents—United States—**
　　　　Archives
Libraries, Public
　USE　**Public libraries**
Libraries—Public relations
　USE　**Public relations—Libraries**
Libraries, Regional
　USE　**Regional libraries**
Libraries, School
　USE　**School libraries**
Libraries, Special
　USE　**Special libraries**
Libraries—Special collections 026
　　　May be subdivided by subject or form,
　e.g. **Libraries—Special collections—**
　Science fiction; Libraries—Special
　collections—Videotapes; etc.
　UF　Special collections in libraries
Libraries—Standards 020
Libraries, State
　USE　**State libraries**
Libraries—State aid
　USE　**State aid to libraries**
Libraries—Statistics 020
Libraries—Technical services
　USE　**Library technical processes**
Libraries—Trustees 021.8
　UF　Libraries—Boards of trustees
　　　Library boards
　　　Library trustees
　BT　**Libraries—Administration**
Libraries—United States 027.073
　UF　United States—Libraries
Libraries, University
　USE　**Academic libraries**
Libraries, Young adults'
　USE　**Young adults' library services**

Library acquisitions
　USE　**Libraries—Acquisitions**
Library administration
　USE　**Libraries—Administration**
Library advertising
　USE　**Advertising—Libraries**
Library architecture 727
　UF　Buildings, Library
　　　Library buildings
　BT　**Architecture**
　　　Libraries
Library assistants
　USE　**Library technicians**
Library automation
　USE　**Libraries—Automation**
Library boards
　USE　**Libraries—Trustees**
Library buildings
　USE　**Library architecture**
Library cataloging
　USE　**Cataloging**
Library catalogs 017; 025.3
　UF　Catalogs
　　　Catalogs, Library
　　　Libraries—Catalogs
　SA　types of library catalogs, e.g.
　　　Online catalogs; to be add-
　　　ed as needed
　BT　**Libraries**
　NT　**Book catalogs**
　　　Card catalogs
　　　Classified catalogs
　　　Library catalogs on microfilm
　　　Online catalogs
　　　Subject catalogs
　RT　**Cataloging**
Library catalogs on microfilm 025.3
　UF　Catalogs on microfilm
　　　COM catalogs
　BT　**Library catalogs**
　　　Microfilms
Library circulation 025.6
　UF　Book lending
　　　Circulation of library materi-
　　　als
　　　Interlibrary loans
　　　Lending of library materials
　　　Libraries—Circulation, loans
　BT　**Library services**
Library classification
　USE　**Classification—Books**

Library clerks
USE **Library technicians**
Library consortia
USE **Library cooperation**
Library information networks
Library cooperation 021.6
UF Consortia, Library
Cooperation, Library
Libraries—Cooperation
Library consortia
BT **Libraries**
NT **Library information networks**
Library education 020.7
Use for materials on the education of librarians. Materials on the instruction of readers in library use are entered under **Bibliographic instruction.**
UF Education for librarianship
Librarians—Education
Librarians—Training
Library science—Study and teaching
BT **Education**
Professional education
NT **Librarians—In-service training**
Library schools
Library education—Audiovisual aids 020.7
BT **Audiovisual education**
Audiovisual materials
Library education—Curricula 020.7
BT **Education—Curricula**
Library equipment and supplies
USE **Libraries—Equipment and supplies**
Library extension 021.6
BT **Library services**
NT **Bookmobiles**
County libraries
Library finance 025.1
UF Libraries—Finance
BT **Libraries—Administration**
NT **Federal aid to libraries**
State aid to libraries
Library information networks 021.6
UF Consortia, Library
Library consortia
Library networks
Library systems
Networks, Library

BT **Data transmission systems**
Information networks
Library cooperation
Library instruction
USE **Bibliographic instruction**
Library laws
USE **Libraries—Law and legislation**
Library legislation
USE **Libraries—Law and legislation**
Library materials
USE **Library resources**
Library materials—Preservation
USE **Library resources—Conservation and restoration**
Library networks
USE **Library information networks**
Library of Congress 027.573
UF United States. Library of Congress
BT **Libraries**
Library orientation
USE **Bibliographic instruction**
Library policies
USE **Libraries—Administration**
Library processing
USE **Library technical processes**
Library reference services
USE **Reference services (Libraries)**
Library resources 025
UF Library materials
BT **Libraries**
NT **Government publications**
Library resources—Conservation and restoration 025.8
UF Books—Preservation
Library materials—Preservation
Preservation of library resources
Library schools 020.7
BT **Library education**
Library science 020
Use for general materials on the knowledge and skill necessary for the organization and administration of libraries. Materials on services offered by libraries to patrons are entered under **Library services.**
UF Librarianship
BT **Documentation**
Information science

Library science—*Continued*
  NT   Cataloging
       Classification—Books
       Comparative librarianship
       Library surveys
       Library technical processes
  RT   Bibliography
       Library services
Library science—Study and teaching
  USE   **Library education**
Library services 025.5
  Use for materials on services offered by libraries to patrons. General materials on the knowledge and skill necessary for the organization and administration of libraries are entered under **Library science.**
  UF   Reader services (Libraries)
       [Former heading]
  SA   libraries and specific types of
       users or specific activities
       for which services are pro-
       vided, e.g. **Libraries and
       the elderly;** to be added as
       needed
  BT   Libraries
  NT   Bibliographic instruction
       Libraries and African Ameri-
         cans
       Libraries and labor
       Libraries and students
       Libraries and the elderly
       Library circulation
       Library extension
       Reference services (Libraries)
       Young adults' library services
  RT   Library science
Library services to African Americans
  USE   **Libraries and African Ameri-
         cans**
Library services to children
  USE   **Children's libraries**
Library services to labor
  USE   **Libraries and labor**
Library services to teenagers
  USE   **Young adults' library services**
Library services to the elderly
  USE   **Libraries and the elderly**
Library services to young adults
  USE   **Young adults' library services**
Library skills
  USE   **Bibliographic instruction**

Library supplies
  USE   **Libraries—Equipment and
         supplies**
Library surveys 020
  BT   Library science
Library systems
  USE   **Libraries—Centralization
         Library information networks**
Library technical processes 025
  Use for materials on the activities and processes concerned with the acquisition, organization, and preparation of library materials for use.
  UF   Centralized processing (Li-
         braries)
       Libraries—Technical services
       Library processing
       Processing (Libraries)
       Technical services (Libraries)
  BT   Libraries
       Library science
  NT   Cataloging
       Classification—Books
       Libraries—Acquisitions
       Libraries—Collection develop-
         ment
Library technicians 020.92
  UF   Library assistants
       Library clerks
       Paraprofessional librarians
  BT   Librarians
       Paraprofessionals
Library trustees
  USE   **Libraries—Trustees**
Library unions
  USE   **Librarians' unions**
Library user orientation
  USE   **Bibliographic instruction**
Librettos 780; 780.26
  Use for collections of miscellaneous librettos and for materials on the history and criticism of librettos and on writing librettos. Individual librettos and collections of librettos of a specific type are entered under the specific type of libretto.
  SA   types of librettos, e.g. **Opera
         librettos;** to be added as
         needed
  NT   Opera librettos
Lie detectors and detection 363.2
  UF   Polygraph
  BT   Criminal investigation

BT = Broader Term   NT = Narrower Term   RT = Related Term   SA = See Also   UF = Used For

Lie detectors and detection—*Continued*
    Medical jurisprudence
    Truthfulness and falsehood
Life 128
  NT **Death**
Life after death
  USE **Future life**
    Immortality
Life (Biology) 577
  NT **Gaia hypothesis**
    Genetics
    Longevity
    Middle age
    Old age
    Protoplasm
    Reproduction
  RT **Biology**
Life care communities
  USE **Retirement communities**
Life, Christian
  USE **Christian life**
Life expectancy
  USE **Longevity**
Life, Future
  USE **Future life**
Life histories
  USE **Biography**
    and subjects, classes of persons, and names of countries, cities, etc., with the subdivision *Biography,* e.g. **Musicians—Biography;** to be added as needed
Life insurance 368.3
  UF Insurance, Life *[Former heading]*
  BT **Insurance**
  NT **Group insurance**
    Industrial insurance
  RT **Annuities**
    Probabilities
Life on other planets 574.999
  Use for materials on the possibility of indigenous life in outer space. Materials on the biology of humans or other earth creatures while in outer space are entered under **Space biology.**
  UF Astrobiology
    Exobiology
    Extraterrestrial life
    Planets, Life on other

  BT **Astronomy**
    Planets
    Space biology
    Universe
  NT **Extraterrestrial beings**
    Interstellar communication
Life—Origin 113
  UF Germ theory
    Origin of life
  BT **Evolution**
Life quality
  USE **Quality of life**
Life saving
  USE **Lifesaving**
Life sciences 570
  UF Biosciences
  BT **Science**
  NT **Agriculture**
    Biology
    Medicine
Life sciences ethics
  USE **Bioethics**
Life skills 158; 640
  Use for materials on skills needed by an individual to exist in modern society, including skills related to education, employment, finance, etc.
  UF Basic life skills
    Competencies, Functional
    Coping behavior
    Everyday living skills
    Functional competencies
    Fundamental life skills
    Personal life skills
    Skills, Life
  SA classes of persons with the subdivision *Life skills guides,* e.g. **Elderly—Life skills guides;** to be added as needed
  BT **Success**
  NT **Conduct of life**
    Elderly—Life skills guides
    Self-improvement
    Survival skills
  RT **Human behavior**
    Human relations
Life span prolongation
  USE **Longevity**
Life styles
  USE **Lifestyles**

BT = Broader Term   NT = Narrower Term   RT = Related Term   SA = See Also   UF = Used For

Life support systems (Medical environment) 362.1
    BT   Hospitals
          Terminal care
Life support systems (Space environment) 629.47
    BT   Human engineering
          Space medicine
    NT   Apollo project
          Astronauts—Clothing
          Lunar bases
          Space ships
Life support systems (Submarine environment) 627
    BT   Human engineering
Lifelong education
    USE Adult education
          Continuing education
Lifesaving 363.1
    UF   Life saving
    BT   Rescue work
    RT   First aid
Lifestyles 306
    Use for materials on the distinctive way of life or manner of living characteristic of individuals or groups of people.
    UF   Alternative lifestyle
          Life styles
    SA   types of lifestyles, to be added as needed
    BT   Human behavior
          Quality of life
    NT   Counter culture
          Unmarried couples
Lifts
    USE Elevators
          Hoisting machinery
Light 535
    BT   Electromagnetic waves
          Physics
    NT   Color
          Lasers
          Phosphorescence
          Refraction
    RT   Optics
          Photometry
          Radiation
          Spectrum analysis
Light amplification by stimulated emission of radiation
    USE Lasers

Light and shade
    USE Shades and shadows
Light, Electric
    USE Electric lighting
          Fluorescent lighting
          Photometry
          Phototherapy
Light production in animals
    USE Bioluminescence
Light ships
    USE Lightships
Light—Therapeutic use
    USE Phototherapy
Light verse
    USE Humorous poetry
Lighthouses 387.1; 623.89; 627
    BT   Navigation
    NT   Lightships
Lighting (May subdiv. geog.) 621.32
    UF   Illumination
    SA   subjects with the subdivision *Lighting,* to be added as needed
    NT   Candles
          Electric lighting
          Lamps
          Libraries—Lighting
          Stage lighting
          Streets—Lighting
Lightning 551.5
    BT   Electricity
          Meteorology
          Thunderstorms
Lights, Feast of
    USE Hanukkah
Lightships 623.89; 627
    UF   Light ships
    BT   Lighthouses
          Ships
Limbs, Artificial
    USE Artificial limbs
Lime
    USE Lime (Fruit)
          Lime (Mineral)
Lime (Fruit) 634
    UF   Lime
    BT   Citrus fruit
          Trees
Lime (Mineral) 631.8; 666
    UF   Lime *[Former heading]*

BT = Broader Term   NT = Narrower Term   RT = Related Term   SA = See Also   UF = Used For

Lime (Mineral)—*Continued*
  BT Fertilizers and manures
  RT Cement
Limericks 808.81; 811, etc.; 811.008, etc.
  May be used for collections of limericks by one or several authors or for materials about limericks.
  UF Rhymes
  BT Humorous poetry
  RT Nonsense verses
Limitation of armament
  USE Arms control
Limited access highways
  USE Express highways
Lincoln, Abraham, 1809-1865 92; B
  BT Presidents—United States
Lincoln Day
  USE Lincoln's Birthday
Lincoln family 920; 929
  BT Genealogy
Lincoln's Birthday 394.2
  UF Lincoln Day
  BT Holidays
Line engraving
  USE Engraving
Linear algebra 512
  UF Algebras, Linear *[Former heading]*
  BT Algebra
      Mathematical analysis
  RT Topology
Linear system theory
  USE System analysis
Linen 677
  BT Fabrics
      Fibers
  RT Flax
Linguistic science
  USE Linguistics
Linguistics 410
  Use for materials on the scientific study of speech and for comparative studies of languages. General materials on the history, philosophy, origin, etc., of languages are entered under **Language and languages.**
  UF Comparative linguistics
      Comparative philology
      Language and languages—
        Comparative philology
      Linguistic science
      Linguistics, Comparative
      Philology
      Philology, Comparative *[Former heading]*
  BT Language and languages
  NT Universal language
  RT Grammar
Linguistics, Comparative
  USE Linguistics
Linoleum block printing 761
  UF Block printing
  BT Printing
      Prints
Linotype 686.2
  BT Printing
      Type and type founding
      Typesetting
Lip reading
  USE Deaf—Means of communication
Liquefaction of coal
  USE Coal liquefaction
Liqueurs
  USE Liquors
Liquid fuel
  USE Petroleum as fuel
Liquids 532
  BT Fluid mechanics
      Physics
  NT Hydraulics
      Hydrodynamics
      Hydrostatics
Liquor industry 338.4
  BT Industry
      Liquors
  NT Bars
Liquor problem
  USE Alcoholism
      Drinking of alcoholic beverages
Liquors 663; 641.2
  UF Cordials (Liquor)
      Drinks
      Intoxicants
      Liqueurs
      Liquors and liqueurs *[Former heading]*
      Spirits, Alcoholic
  SA names of liquors and liqueurs, to be added as needed

Liquors—*Continued*
  BT **Alcohol**
      Alcoholic beverages
      Beverages
  NT **Liquor industry**
  RT **Distillation**
Liquors and liqueurs
  USE **Liquors**
Listening 153.6; 153.7
  BT **Attention**
      Educational psychology
  RT **Hearing**
Listening devices
  USE **Eavesdropping**
Literacy (May subdiv. geog.) 302.2;
     379.2
  UF Illiteracy
  BT **Education**
  NT **Computer literacy**
      Functional literacy
      Visual literacy
Literacy, Computer
  USE **Computer literacy**
Literacy, Visual
  USE **Visual literacy**
Literary awards
  USE **Literary prizes**
Literary characters
  USE **Characters and characteristics
      in literature**
Literary collections
  USE **Anthologies**
      Literature—Collections
      and names of literatures, e.g.
      American literature; and,
      for collections focused on a
      single subject by more than
      one author involving two
      or more literary forms, the
      subject with the subdivision
      Literary collections, e.g.
      Cats—Literary collections;
      to be added as needed
Literary criticism
  USE **Criticism**
      **Literature—History and criti-
      cism**
Literary forgeries 098
  UF Frauds, Literary
  BT **Counterfeits and counterfeiting**

      Forgery
Literary landmarks (May subdiv. geog.)
     809; 810.9, etc.
  UF Authors—Homes and haunts
      Landmarks, Literary
  BT **Historic buildings**
      **Literature—History and criti-
      cism**
Literary landmarks—United States
     810.9
  UF United States—Literary land-
      marks
Literary prizes 807.9
  UF Awards, Literary
      Book awards
      Book prizes
      Literary awards
      Literature—Prizes
      Prizes, Literary
  SA names of awards, e.g. **Calde-
      cott Medal;** to be added as
      needed
  BT **Awards**
  NT **Caldecott Medal**
      Literature—Competitions
      Newbery Medal
Literary property
  USE **Copyright**
Literary recreations 793.73
  UF Language games
      Recreations, Literary
  BT **Amusements**
  NT **Charades**
      Plot-your-own stories
      Riddles
      Word games
Literary style 808; 809
  UF Style, Literary *[Former head-
      ing]*
  BT **Literature**
  NT **Letter writing**
      **Literature—History and criti-
      cism**
  RT **Criticism**
      Rhetoric

Literature 800

Literatures are described by countries or geographic regions. In countries or regions with more than one major language the literature may be further qualified by the language in parentheses, e.g. **Canadian literature (French)**. There is no distinction made in subject headings between literary works in their original languages and in translations.

UF Belles lettres

SA names of national literatures, e.g. **English literature; French literature;** etc.; national literatures qualified if needed by the language in which the literature was originally written or subdivided by a sub-set of authors within the literature, e.g. **African literature (English); American literature— African American authors;** and subjects and themes in literature, e.g. **Bible in literature; Blacks in literature; African Americans in literature; Characters and characteristics in literature; Symbolism in literature;** etc., to be added as needed

BT **Humanities**
    Language arts

NT **African literature (English)**
    American literature
    Anglo-Saxon literature
    Animals in literature
    Authorship
    Ballads
    Bible in literature
    Biography as a literary form
    Black humor (Literature)
    Brazilian literature
    Campaign literature
    Canadian literature
    Catholic literature
    Chapbooks
    Characters and characteristics in literature
    Children's literature
    Classical literature
    Classicism

Communism and literature
Comparative literature
Criticism
Danish literature
Devotional literature
Diaries
Drama
Early Christian literature
English literature
Epic literature
Erotic literature
Essay
Fables
Fairy tales
Fiction
French literature
Gay men's writings
German literature
Greek literature
Hebrew literature
Humanism
Icelandic literature
Indians of North America— Literature
Indic literature
Jewish literature
Journalism
Latin American literature
Latin literature
Legends
Lesbians' writings
Literary style
Medieval literature
Mexican literature
Mock-heroic literature
Modern Greek literature
Multicultural literature
Music and literature
Nature in literature
Norwegian literature
Old Norse literature
Parody
Picaresque literature
Plots (Drama, fiction, etc.)
Poetry
Portuguese literature
Realism in literature
Religion in literature
Religious literature
Romance literature

BT = Broader Term   NT = Narrower Term   RT = Related Term   SA = See Also   UF = Used For

Russian literature
Sagas
Satire
Scandinavian literature
Short story
Soviet literature
Spanish literature
Speeches
Swedish literature
Symbolism in literature
Travel in literature
West Indian literature
(French)
Wit and humor
World War, 1939-1945—
Literature and the war
Young adults' literature
RT Books
Books and reading
Modernism (Arts)
Romanticism
Literature and communism
USE Communism and literature
Literature and music
USE Music and literature
Literature—Bio-bibliography 809
RT Authors
Literature, Classical
USE Classical literature
Literature—Collections 808.8
UF Collected works
Collections of literature
Literary collections
Literature—Selections
SA names of literatures and
names of literary forms
with the subdivision *Collec-*
tions, e.g. **English**
literature—Collections;
Poetry—Collections; etc., to
be added as needed
NT English literature—Collections
Essays
Letters
Parodies
Poetry—Collections
Quotations
Romances
Short stories

Literature, Comparative
USE Comparative literature
Literature—Competitions 807.9
BT Contests
Literary prizes
Literature—Criticism
USE Literature—History and criti-
cism
Literature—Dictionaries 803
BT Encyclopedias and dictionaries
NT English literature—
Dictionaries
RT Literature—Indexes
Literature, Erotic
USE Erotic literature
Literature—Evaluation
USE Books and reading
Books and reading—Best
books
Books—Reviews
Criticism
Literature—History and criti-
cism
Literature—Film and video adaptations
USE Film adaptations
Television adaptations
Literature—History and criticism 809
UF Appraisal of books
Books—Appraisal
Evaluation of literature
Literary criticism
Literature—Criticism
Literature—Evaluation
BT Literary style
NT Criticism
Literary landmarks
RT Authors
Literature—Indexes 016.8
RT Literature—Dictionaries
Literature, Intercultural
USE Multicultural literature
Literature, Medieval
USE Medieval literature
Literature, Multicultural
USE Multicultural literature
Literature—Outlines, syllabi, etc. 802
NT English literature—Outlines,
syllabi, etc.
Literature—Prizes
USE Literary prizes

Literature—Selections
    USE **Literature—Collections**
Literature—Stories, plots, etc. 802
    Use for collections of literary plots. Materials that analyze plots or discuss the technique of constructing plots are entered under **Plots (Drama, fiction, etc.).**
    SA types of literature and specific genres with the subdivision *Stories, plots, etc.;* to be added as needed
    RT **Ballet—Stories, plots, etc.**
        Opera—Stories, plots, etc.
Literatures of the Soviet Union
    USE **Soviet literature**
Lithographers 763.092; 920
    BT **Artists**
Lithography 686.2; 763; 764
    UF Lithoprinting
    BT **Color printing**
        Printing
        Prints
    NT **Offset printing**
Lithoprinting
    USE **Lithography**
        Offset printing
Litigation 347
    UF Actions and defenses *[Former heading]*
        Civil law suits
        Defense (Law)
        Law suits
        Lawsuits
        Personal actions (Law)
        Suing (Law)
        Suits (Law)
    BT **Law**
    NT **Witnesses**
    RT **Arbitration and award**
Littering
    USE **Refuse and refuse disposal**
Little league baseball
    USE **Little League baseball**
Little League baseball 796.357
    UF Little league baseball *[Former heading]*
    BT **Baseball**
Little theater movement 792
    UF Community theater
        Theater—Little theater movement

    BT **Amateur theater**
        Theater
Liturgies 264; 291.3
    Use for general materials on the forms of prayers, rituals, and ceremonies used in public worship, including the theological and historical study of liturgies.
    UF Church service books
        Ritual
        Service books (Liturgy)
    SA names of individual religions and denominations with the subdivision *Liturgy,* to be added as needed
    BT **Church music**
        Devotional literature
        Rites and ceremonies
        Theology
    NT **Catholic Church—Liturgy**
        Hymns
        Judaism—Liturgy
        Lord's Supper
        Mass
Live poliovirus vaccine
    USE **Poliomyelitis vaccine**
Livestock 636
    Use for materials on breeds of livestock and on stock raising as an industry. General descriptions of farm and other domestic animals are entered under **Domestic animals.**
    UF Animal husbandry
        Animal industry
        Farm animals
        Stock and stock breeding
        Stock raising
    SA types of livestock, to be added as needed
    NT **Cattle**
        Dairying
        Livestock judging
        Pigs
        Poultry
        Sheep
        Veterinary medicine
    RT **Domestic animals**
Livestock—Breeding 636.08
    BT **Breeding**
Livestock judging 636
    UF Stock judging
    BT **Livestock**

BT = Broader Term   NT = Narrower Term   RT = Related Term   SA = See Also   UF = Used For

Living, Cost of
USE Cost of living
Living earth theory
USE Gaia hypothesis
Living, Standard of
USE Standard of living
Living together
USE Unmarried couples
Living wills
USE Right to die
Livres à clef
USE Romans à clef
Lizards 597.95
BT Reptiles
Loan associations
USE Savings and loan associations
Loan funds, Student
USE Student loan funds
Loans 332.7
UF Borrowing money
Lending
BT Credit
NT Credit unions
Government lending
Interest (Economics)
Mortgages
Personal loans
Public debts
Savings and loan associations
Student aid
RT Investments
Loans, Personal
USE Personal loans
Lobbying 328.3
UF Interest groups
Lobbying and lobbyists [Former heading]
Lobbyists
PAC's
Political action committees
Pressure groups
SA names of specific lobbying and pressure groups, to be added as needed
BT Politics
RT Political corruption
Lobbying and lobbyists
USE Lobbying
Lobbyists
USE Lobbying

Lobsters 595.3
BT Crustacea
Shellfish
Local government 320.8; 352
Use for materials about local government of districts, counties, townships, etc. Materials about county government only are entered under County government. Materials about city government are entered under Municipal government.
UF Government, Local
Town meeting
Township government
BT Administrative law
Community organization
Political science
NT Cities and towns
County government
Metropolitan government
Municipal government
Public administration
State-local relations
RT Villages
Local history 907
Use for materials on the writing and compiling of local histories. Collective histories of several localities are entered under the countries, states, etc., with the subdivision *Local history,* e.g. **United States—Local history; Ohio—Local history;** etc. Individual local histories are entered under the place with the subdivision *History,* e.g. **Chicago (Ill.)—History;** etc.
UF Community history
History, Local
Regional history
SA names of countries, states, etc., with the subdivision *Local history,* to be added as needed
BT Historiography
History
Local-state relations
USE State-local relations
Local traffic
USE City traffic
Local transit (May subdiv. geog.) 388.4
Use for materials on the various modes of local public transportation.
UF City transit
Mass transit
Municipal transit
Public transit
Rapid transit

Local transit—*Continued*
  Transit systems
  Urban transportation
  BT **Traffic engineering**
    Transportation
  NT **Buses**
    Street railroads
    Subways
Localism
  USE **Sectionalism (United States)**
Localisms
  USE names of languages with the
    subdivision *Provincialisms,*
    e.g. **English language—
    Provincialisms;** to be added
    as needed
Lockouts
  USE **Strikes**
Locks and keys 683
  UF Keys
  BT **Burglary protection**
Locomotion 152.3; 388
  NT **Aeronautics**
    Animal locomotion
    Flight
    Horsemanship
    Human locomotion
    Navigation
    Transportation
    Walking
Locomotives 625.2
  BT **Machinery**
    Steam engines
Locomotives—Models 625.1
  BT **Machinery—Models**
Locusts 595.7; 632
  BT **Insect pests**
Locusts, Seventeen-year
  USE **Cicadas**
Lodging houses
  USE **Hotels and motels**
Log cabins and houses 728
  UF Cabins
    Houses, Log
  BT **House construction**
    Houses
Logarithms 513.2
  BT **Algebra**
    Mathematics—Tables
    Trigonometry—Tables

  NT **Slide rule**
Logging
  USE **Lumber and lumbering**
Logic 160
  UF Argumentation
    Deduction (Logic)
    Dialectics
    Fallacies
    Induction (Logic)
  BT **Intellect**
    Philosophy
    Science—Methodology
  NT **Critical thinking**
    Probabilities
    Symbolic logic
    Theory of knowledge
  RT **Reasoning**
    Thought and thinking
Logic, Symbolic and mathematical
  USE **Symbolic logic**
Lone Ranger films 791.43
    May be used for individual works, col-
    lections, or materials about Lone Ranger
    films.
  BT **Western films**
Loneliness 155.9; 158
  UF Social isolation
    Solitude
  BT **Emotions**
    Human relations
Long distance running
  USE **Marathon running**
Long distance swimming
  USE **Marathon swimming**
Long life
  USE **Longevity**
Long-term care facilities 362.1
  UF Extended care facilities
  BT **Hospitals**
    Medical care
  NT **Nursing homes**
Longevity 612.6; 613
  UF Life expectancy
    Life span prolongation
    Long life
  BT **Age**
    Death
    Health
    Life (Biology)
  NT **Aging**

BT = Broader Term   NT = Narrower Term   RT = Related Term   SA = See Also   UF = Used For

Longevity—*Continued*
    RT   **Middle age**
          Old age
Longitude 526; 527
    UF Degrees of latitude and longitude
    BT   **Earth**
          Geodesy
          Nautical astronomy
Looking glasses
    USE **Mirrors**
Looms 677; 746.1
    BT   **Weaving**
Loran 621.384
    BT   **Navigation**
Lord's Day
    USE **Sabbath**
Lord's prayer 226.9; 242
    BT   **Jesus Christ—Prayers**
Lord's Supper 232.9; 264
    UF Communion
          Eucharist
          Holy communion
          Jesus Christ—Last Supper
          Last Supper
    BT   **Jesus Christ**
          Liturgies
          Rites and ceremonies
          Sacraments
    RT   **Mass**
Losing things
    USE **Lost and found possessions**
Lost and found possessions 330.1
    UF Finding things
          Losing things
          Lost pets
          Possessions, Lost and found
    BT   **Property**
Lost children
    USE **Missing children**
Lost pets
    USE **Lost and found possessions**
Lotteries 336.1
    BT   **Gambling**
Loudspeakers
    USE **Intercommunication systems**
Louisiana Purchase 973.4; 976.3
    BT   **United States—History—1783-1809**
Love 152.4; 177; 306.7
    UF Affection

    BT   **Emotions**
          Human behavior
    NT   **Marriage**
    RT   **Dating (Social customs)**
          Friendship
Love Canal Chemical Waste Landfill (Niagara Falls, N.Y.) 363.72
    BT   **Hazardous waste sites**
          Landfills
Love poetry 808.81; 811, etc.
    May be used for individual works, collections, or materials about love poetry.
    BT   **Poetry**
    RT   **Erotic poetry**
Love stories 808.83; 813, etc.
    May be used for individual works, collections, or materials about love stories.
    UF Romance novels
          Romances (Love stories)
          Romantic fiction
          Romantic stories
    BT   **Fiction**
    RT   **Erotic fiction**
          Gothic novels
          Romantic suspense novels
Love stories—Technique 808.3
    BT   **Authorship**
Love (Theology) 231
    BT   **Charity**
          Doctrinal theology
Low income housing
    USE **Public housing**
Low sodium diet
    USE **Salt free diet**
Low temperature biology
    USE **Cryobiology**
Low temperatures 536; 621.5
    UF Cryogenics
          Temperatures, Low
    BT   **Temperature**
    NT   **Cryobiology**
    RT   **Cold**
          Refrigeration
Loyalists, American
    USE **American Loyalists**
Loyalty 172
    UF Faithfulness
    BT   **Ethics**
          Virtue

BT = Broader Term   NT = Narrower Term   RT = Related Term   SA = See Also   UF = Used For

Loyalty—*Continued*
    NT   **Patriotism**
Loyalty oaths
    USE   **Internal security**
Lubrication and lubricants 621.8
    UF   Grease
    BT   **Machinery**
    RT   **Bearings (Machinery)**
         Oils and fats
Lullabies 782.42
    UF   Cradle songs
         Slumber songs
    BT   **Bedtime**
         Children's poetry
         Children's songs
         Songs
Lumber and lumbering 634.9; 674
    Use for general materials on lumber and for materials on the felling of trees and the preparation of lumber.
    UF   Logging
         Timber
         Woods
    BT   **Forest products**
         Forests and forestry
         Trees
         Wood
Luminescence
    USE   **Phosphorescence**
Luminescence, Animal
    USE   **Bioluminescence**
Lunar bases 629.45
    UF   Moon bases
    BT   **Civil engineering**
         Life support systems (Space environment)
Lunar cars
    USE   **Moon cars**
Lunar eclipses 523.3
    UF   Eclipses, Lunar *[Former heading]*
         Moon—Eclipses
    BT   **Astronomy**
Lunar excursion module 629.45
    UF   LEM
         Lunar module
    BT   **Space vehicles**
Lunar expeditions
    USE   **Space flight to the moon**
Lunar exploration
    USE   **Moon—Exploration**

Lunar geology 559.9
    UF   Geology, Lunar
         Geology—Moon
         Moon—Geology
    BT   **Astrogeology**
    NT   **Lunar petrology**
         Lunar soil
Lunar module
    USE   **Lunar excursion module**
Lunar petrology 552; 552.0999
    UF   Lunar rocks
         Moon rocks
         Rocks, Moon
    BT   **Lunar geology**
         Petrology
Lunar photography 778.3
    UF   Moon photography
    BT   **Space photography**
    NT   **Moon—Photographs**
Lunar probes 629.43
    UF   Moon probes
    SA   names of specific lunar probe projects, to be added as needed
    BT   **Space probes**
    NT   **Project Ranger**
Lunar rocks
    USE   **Lunar petrology**
Lunar rover vehicles
    USE   **Moon cars**
Lunar soil 523.3; 552.0999; 631.4
    UF   Moon soil
         Soils, Lunar
    BT   **Lunar geology**
    RT   **Moon—Surface**
Lunar surface
    USE   **Moon—Surface**
Lunar surface radio communication
    USE   **Radio in astronautics**
Lunar surface vehicles
    USE   **Moon cars**
Luncheons 642
    BT   **Cooking**
         Menus
    RT   **Entertaining**
Lunchrooms
    USE   **Restaurants**
Lung cancer 616.99
    UF   Lungs—Cancer
    BT   **Cancer**

Lung cancer—*Continued*
      Lungs—Diseases
Lungs 611; 612.2
  BT **Respiratory system**
  NT **Respiration**
Lungs—Cancer
  USE **Lung cancer**
Lungs—Diseases 616.2
  SA names of lung diseases, to be
      added as needed
  BT **Diseases**
  NT **Lung cancer**
      Pneumonia
      Tuberculosis
Lying
  USE **Truthfulness and falsehood**
Lyme disease 616.9
  BT **Diseases**
  RT **Insects as carriers of disease**
      Ticks
Lymphatic system 596; 612.4; 616.4
  BT **Physiology**
Lynching 364.1
  BT **Crime**
  RT **Vigilance committees**
Lyric drama
  USE **Opera**
Lyricists 782.0092; 920
  UF Songwriters
  BT **Poets**
M.I.A.'s
  USE **Missing in action**
Maccabbees, Feast of the
  USE **Hanukkah**
Machine design 621.8
  UF Machinery—Construction
      Machinery—Design and con-
      struction *[Former heading]*
  SA types of machines, equipment,
      etc., with the subdivision
      Design and construction,
      e.g. **Airplanes—Design and**
      construction; to be added as
      needed
  BT **Design**
      Machinery
  NT **Human engineering**
      Machinery—Models
Machine intelligence
  USE **Artificial intelligence**

Machine language
  USE **Programming languages (Com-**
      puters)
Machine readable bibliographic data
      025.3
  UF Bibliographic data in machine
      readable form
      Cataloging data in machine
      readable form
      Computer stored cataloging
      data
  SA names of projects, formats,
      and systems, e.g. **MARC**
      formats; to be added as
      needed
  BT **Cataloging**
      Information services
      Information systems
      Libraries—Automation
  NT **MARC formats**
Machine readable catalog system
  USE **MARC formats**
Machine readable dictionaries 423, etc.
  UF Dictionaries, Machine read-
      able
  BT **Encyclopedias and dictionaries**
Machine shop practice 670.42
  UF Shop practice
  NT **Drilling and boring**
      Grinding and polishing
Machine shops 670.42
  UF Shops, Machine
Machine tools 621.9
  SA types of machine tools, to be
      added as needed
  BT **Machinery**
      Tools
  NT **Planing machines**
  RT **Drilling and boring**
      Grinding and polishing
Machine translating
  USE **Translating and interpreting**
Machinery 621.8
  UF Machines
  BT **Manufactures**
      Mechanical engineering
      Power (Mechanics)
      Technology
      Tools
  NT **Agricultural machinery**

Machinery—*Continued*

   Bearings (Machinery)
   Belts and belting
   Conveying machinery
   Electric machinery
   Engines
   Gearing
   Hoisting machinery
   Hydraulic machinery
   Invantions
   Locomotives
   Lubrication and lubricants
   Machine design
   Machine tools
   Mechanical drawing
   Metalworking machinery
   Simple machines
   Steam engines
   Woodworking machinery
 RT **Mechanics**
   Mills
   Power transmission

Machinery, Automatic
 USE **Automation**

Machinery—Construction
 USE **Machine design**

Machinery—Design and construction
 USE **Machine design**

Machinery—Drawing
 USE **Mechanical drawing**

Machinery in industry 338

 Use for materials on the social and economic aspects of mechanization in the industrial world, the machine age, etc.

 BT **Industry**
   Labor
   Technology and civilization
 NT **Automation**
   Industrial robots
 RT **Industrial revolution**
   Labor productivity

Machinery—Models 621.8
 UF Mechanical models
   Models, Mechanical
 BT **Machine design**
 NT **Airplanes—Models**
   Automobiles—Models
   Locomotives—Models
   Motorboats—Models
   Railroads—Models

   Ships—Models

Machines
 USE **Machinery**

Machines, Simple
 USE **Simple machines**

Made-for-TV movies
 USE **Television movies**

Madonna
 USE **Mary, Blessed Virgin, Saint**

Magazines
 USE **Periodicals**

Maghreb
 USE **North Africa**

Magic 133.4

 Use for materials on charms, spells, etc., believed to have supernatural power. Materials on types of entertainment involving illusionistic tricks are entered under **Magic tricks.**

 UF Black art (Magic)
   Black magic (Witchcraft)
   Necromancy
   Sorcery
   Spells
 BT **Occultism**
 NT **Symbolism of numbers**
 RT **Hallucinations and illusions**
   Magic tricks
   Witchcraft

Magic tricks 793.8
 UF Conjuring
   Legerdemain
   Prestidigitation
   Sleight of hand
 BT **Amusements**
   Tricks
 NT **Card tricks**
 RT **Hallucinations and illusions**
   Magic
   Occultism

Magna Carta 342; 942.03
 BT **Charters**
   Constitutional law
   Great Britain—History—
    1154-1399, Plantagenets

Magnet schools 370.19; 371.9

 Use for materials on schools offering special courses not available in the regular school curriculum and designed to attract students without reference to the usual attendance zone rules, often as an aid to voluntary school desegregation.

Magnet schools—*Continued*
  UF   Schools, Magnet
  BT   **Public schools**
       School integration
       Schools
Magnet winding
  USE **Electromagnets**
Magnetic needle
  USE **Compass**
**Magnetic recorders and recording
       621.382**

    Use for general materials on audio, computer, and video recording on a magnetizable medium.

  UF   Cassette recorders and recording
       Recorders, Tape
       Tape recorders
  RT   **Optical storage devices**
       Sound—Recording and reproducing
       Video recording
Magnetic resonance accelerator
  USE **Cyclotron**
Magnetic resonance imaging 616.07
  UF   Clinical magnetic resonance imaging
       Diagnostic magnetic resonance imaging
       Imaging, Magnetic resonance
       NMR imaging
       Nuclear magnetic resonance imaging
  BT   **Diagnosis**
Magnetism 538
  BT   **Physics**
  NT   **Compass**
       Electromagnetism
       Electromagnets
       Magnets
  RT   **Electricity**
Magnets 538; 621.34
  BT   **Magnetism**
  NT   **Electromagnets**
Mail-order business 658.8; 659.13
  BT   **Business**
       Direct selling
       Selling
Mail service
  USE **Postal service**

Mail systems, Electronic
  USE **Electronic mail systems**
Mainstreaming in education 371.9
  BT   **Education**
       Exceptional children
       Handicapped children
  RT   **Special education**
Maintenance and repair
  USE **Buildings—Maintenance and repair**
       and types of buildings, machines, and instruments, etc., with the subdivision *Maintenance and repair,* e.g. **Automobiles—Maintenance and repair;** to be added as needed
Maize
  USE **Corn**
Make-believe playmates
  USE **Imaginary playmates**
Makeup (Cosmetics)
  USE **Cosmetics**
Makeup, Theatrical
  USE **Theatrical makeup**
Making-choices stories
  USE **Plot-your-own stories**
Maladjusted children
  USE **Emotionally disturbed children**
Maladjustment (Psychology)
  USE **Adjustment (Psychology)**
Malaria 616.9
  UF   Ague
  BT   **Fever**
Male actors
  USE **Men actors**
Male change of life
  USE **Male climacteric**
Male climacteric 612.6
  UF   Change of life in men
       Climacteric, Male *[Former heading]*
       Male change of life
       Male menopause
       Menopause, Male
  BT   **Aging**
Male menopause
  USE **Male climacteric**
Male role
  USE **Sex role**

Malfeasance in office
USE **Misconduct in office**
Malformations, Congenital
USE **Birth defects**
Malignant tumors
USE **Cancer**
Malls, Shopping
USE **Shopping centers and malls**
Malnutrition 362.1; 616.3
    BT **Nutrition**
    RT **Starvation**
Malpractice 346.03
    UF Liability, Professional
        Professional liability
        Professions—Tort liability
        Tort liability of professions
    SA types of professional person-
        nel with the subdivision
        Malpractice, to be added as
        needed
    BT **Liability (Law)**
    NT **Physicians—Malpractice**
Malpractice insurance 368.5
    UF Insurance, Malpractice *[For-*
        mer heading]
        Insurance, Professional liabili-
        ty
        Professional liability insurance
    BT **Insurance**
Mammals 599
    SA groups of mammals, e.g. **Car-**
        nivores; Marine mammals;
        Primates; etc.; and names
        of mammals, e.g. **Bats;** to
        be added as needed
    BT **Vertebrates**
        Zoology
    NT **Bats**
        Bison
        Camels
        Carnivores
        Cats
        Dogs
        Elephants
        Fossil mammals
        Horses
        Marine mammals
        Mice
        Primates
        Rabbits

        Squirrels
        Wild cats
Mammals, Fossil
USE **Fossil mammals**
Mammals, Marine
USE **Marine mammals**
Man 572; 573
    Use for materials on the human species
or on the human race in general.
    UF Homo sapiens
        Human race
    BT **Primates**
    NT **Anthropometry**
        Ethnology
    RT **Anthropology**
        Creation
Man—Antiquity
USE **Human origins**
Man in space
USE **Space flight**
Man—Influence of environment
USE **Environmental influence on**
        humans
Man—Influence on nature
USE **Human influence on nature**
Man, Nonliterate
USE **Nonliterate man**
Man—Origin
USE **Human origins**
Man power
USE **Human resources**
Man, Prehistoric
USE **Prehistoric man**
Man, Primitive
USE **Nonliterate man**
Man (Theology) 218; 233
    BT **Theology**
    NT **Soul**
Management 658
    Use for materials on the theory of man-
agement and on the application of man-
agement principles to business and
industry.
    UF Administration
        Business administration
        Business management
        Industrial management *[For-*
        mer heading]
        Industrial organization
        Management science
        Management, Scientific

Management—*Continued*

    Organization and management

    Scientific management

SA   types of management, e.g. **Office management;** types of businesses and industries, types of industrial plants and processes, and names of individual corporate bodies, with the subdivision *Management,* e.g. **Information systems—Management;** and types of government agencies and special activities, types of institutions, and names of individual institutions with the subdivision *Administration,* e.g. **Libraries—Administration; Schools—Administration;** etc., to be added as needed

BT   **Business**

     Industry

NT   **Buying**

     Crisis management

     Factory management

     Farm management

     Industrial efficiency

     Industrial relations

     Information systems— Management

     Inventory control

     Job analysis

     Marketing

     Materials handling

     Natural resources— Management

     Occupational health and safety

     Office management

     Organizational change

     Personnel management

     Production standards

     Sales management

     Time management

     Welfare work in industry

Management buyouts

USE **Leveraged buyouts**

Management—Employee participation

USE **Participative management**

Management information systems 658.4

UF   Computer-based information systems

     MIS (Information systems)

BT   **Information systems**

Management, Sales

USE **Sales management**

Management science

USE **Management**

Management, Scientific

USE **Management**

Managers

USE **Supervisors**

Mandates 321

UF   Government, Mandatory

     League of Nations— Mandatory system

BT   **International law**

     International organization

     International relations

     World War, 1914-1918— Territorial questions

Mania

USE **Manic-depressive psychoses**

Manic depression

USE **Manic-depressive psychoses**

Manic-depressive psychoses 616.89

UF   Mania

     Manic depression

     Melancholia

BT   **Mental illness**

RT   **Depression (Psychology)**

Manikins (Fashion models)

USE **Fashion models**

Manipulative materials 371.3078

Use for works on educational materials designed to be handled or touched by students as well as for the materials themselves.

UF   Tactile materials

BT   **Audiovisual materials**

     Teaching—Aids and devices

RT   **Patterns (Mathematics)**

     Perception

Manned space flight

USE **Space flight**

Manned space flight—Rescue work

USE **Space rescue operations**

Manned undersea research stations

USE **Undersea research stations**

Mannequins (Fashion models)

USE **Fashion models**

Manners
  USE **Courtesy**
          Etiquette
Manners and customs 390
  UF Ceremonies
        Customs, Social
        Folkways
        Social customs
        Social life and customs
        Traditions
  SA ethnic groups and names of
        countries, cities, etc., with
        the subdivision *Social life*
        and customs, to be added
        as needed
  BT **Civilization**
        Ethnology
  NT **Bohemianism**
        Caste
        Chivalry
        Clothing and dress
        Costume
        Country life
        Courts and courtiers
        Dating (Social customs)
        Dueling
        Festivals
        Folklore
        Funeral rites and ceremonies
        Gifts
        Halloween
        Holidays
        Hugging
        Indians of North America—
          Social life and customs
        Jews—Social life and customs
        Marriage customs and rites
        Popular culture
        Travel
        United States—Social life and
          customs
  RT **Etiquette**
        Rites and ceremonies
Manpower
  USE **Human resources**
Manpower policy
  USE **Human resources policy**
Manslaughter
  USE **Homicide**

Manual training
  USE **Industrial arts education**
Manual workers
  USE **Labor**
          Working class
Manufactures 338.4; 670
  SA types of industries; names of
        manufactured articles; and
        names of countries, cities,
        etc., with the subdivision
        Industries, e.g. **Chicago**
        (Ill.)—Industries; to be add-
        ed as needed
  BT **Business**
        Commercial products
        Industry
        Technology
  NT **Brand name products**
        Consumer goods
        Furniture
        Generic products
        Machinery
        Mills
        Papermaking
        Patents
        Prices
        Trademarks
        Waste products
Manufactures—Defects
  USE **Product recall**
Manufactures recall
  USE **Product recall**
Manufacturing in space
  USE **Space industrialization**
Manures
  USE **Fertilizers and manures**
Manuscripts 091
  BT **Archives**
        Bibliography
        Books
  NT **Illumination of books and**
          manuscripts
  RT **Autographs**
        Charters
Manuscripts, Illuminated
  USE **Illumination of books and**
          manuscripts
Manuscripts—Prices
  USE **Books—Prices**

Map drawing 526.022
- UF Cartography
- Chartography
- Plans
- BT **Drawing**
- RT **Topographical drawing**

Maple sugar 641.3; 664
- BT **Sugar**

Maps 912

Use for general materials about maps and their history. Materials on the methods of map making and the mapping of areas are entered under **Map drawing.** Geographical atlases of world coverage are entered under **Atlases.**

- UF Cartography
- Chartography
- Plans
- SA types of maps, e.g. **Road maps;** subjects with the subdivision *Maps,* e.g. **Geology—Maps;** and names of countries, cities, etc., with the subdivision *Maps,* to be added as needed
- BT **Geography**
- NT **Atlases**
- **Automobile travel— Guidebooks**
- **Chicago (Ill.)—Maps**
- **Geology—Maps**
- **Globes**
- **Moon—Maps**
- **Road maps**
- **United States—Maps**
- **World War, 1939-1945— Maps**
- RT **Charts**

Maps, Historical
- USE **Historical atlases**

Maps, Military
- USE **Military geography**

Maps, Road
- USE **Road maps**

Marathon running 796.42
- UF Long distance running
- BT **Running**

Marathon swimming 797.2
- UF Long distance swimming
- BT **Swimming**

Marble 553.5
- BT **Petrology**

Stone

MARC formats 025.3
- UF Machine readable catalog system
- MARC project
- MARC system *[Former heading]*
- Project MARC
- BT **Bibliographic control**
- **Libraries—Automation**
- **Machine readable bibliographic data**

MARC project
- USE **MARC formats**

MARC system
- USE **MARC formats**

Marches (Demonstrations)
- USE **Protests, demonstrations, etc.**

Marches (Exercises)
- USE **Marching drills**

Marches for Black civil rights
- USE **Blacks—Civil rights**

Marches for Black civil rights—United States
- USE **African Americans—Civil rights**

Marches (Music) 783.18
- BT **Military music**

Marching
- USE **Marching drills**

Marching drills 613.7
- UF Drill (Nonmilitary) *[Former heading]*
- Drills, Marching
- Marches (Exercises)
- Marching
- BT **Physical education**

Mardi Gras
- USE **Carnival**

Margarine 641.3; 664
- UF Butter, Artificial
- Oleomargarine
- BT **Butter**

Mariculture
- USE **Aquaculture**

Marihuana
- USE **Marijuana**

Marijuana 362.29; 613.8; 615; 633.7
- UF Cannabis
- Grass (Drug)

BT = Broader Term   NT = Narrower Term   RT = Related Term   SA = See Also   UF = Used For

Marijuana—*Continued*
    Hashish
    Marihuana
    Pot (Drug)
  BT **Hallucinogens**
    Hemp
    Narcotics
    Smoking
Marinas 387.1
  UF Yacht basins
  BT **Boats and boating**
    Harbors
    Yachts and yachting
  NT **Docks**
Marine animals 591.92
  UF Animals, Aquatic
    Animals, Marine
    Animals, Sea
    Aquatic animals
    Marine fauna
    Marine zoology
    Sea animals
    Water animals
  BT **Animals**
    Marine biology
    Wildlife
  NT **Corals**
    Fishes
    Marine mammals
  RT **Freshwater animals**
Marine aquaculture
  USE **Aquaculture**
Marine aquariums 597.0074; 599.5;
    639.3
  UF Aquariums, Saltwater
    Oceanariums
    Salt water aquariums
    Sea water aquariums
  SA names of specific marine
    aquariums, to be added as
    needed
  BT **Aquariums**
  NT **Marineland (Fla.)**
Marine architecture
  USE **Naval architecture**
    Shipbuilding
Marine biology 574.92
  UF Biological oceanography
    Biology, Marine
    Ocean life

  BT **Biology**
    Natural history
    Oceanography
    Underwater exploration
  NT **Marine animals**
    Marine ecology
    Marine plants
    Marine resources
    Ocean bottom
  RT **Freshwater biology**
Marine disasters
  USE **Shipwrecks**
Marine ecology 574.5
  UF Biological oceanography
    Ecology, Marine
  BT **Ecology**
    Marine biology
Marine engineering 623.8
    Use for materials on engineering as applied to ships and their machinery.
  UF Naval engineering
  BT **Civil engineering**
    Engineering
    Mechanical engineering
    Naval architecture
    Naval art and science
    Steam navigation
Marine engines 623.8
  BT **Engines**
    Shipbuilding
    Steam engines
Marine fauna
  USE **Marine animals**
Marine flora
  USE **Marine plants**
Marine geology
  USE **Submarine geology**
Marine insurance 368.2
  UF Insurance, Marine *[Former*
    heading]
  BT **Commerce**
    Insurance
    Maritime law
    Merchant marine
    Shipping
Marine law
  USE **Maritime law**
Marine mammals 599.5
  UF Mammals, Marine *[Former*
    heading]

Marine mammals—*Continued*
- SA   names of marine mammals,
to be added as needed
- BT   **Mammals**
      Marine animals
- NT   **Seals (Animals)**
      Whales

Marine mineral resources 333.8; 553
- UF   Mineral resources, Marine
      Ocean mineral resources
- BT   **Marine resources**
      Mines and mineral resources
      Ocean bottom
      Ocean engineering
- NT   **Ocean mining**
- RT   **Ocean energy resources**

Marine painting 758
- UF   Sea in art
      Seascapes
      Ships in art
- BT   **Painting**

Marine plants 581.92
- UF   Aquatic plants
      Marine flora
      Water plants
- BT   **Marine biology**
- NT   **Algae**
- RT   **Freshwater plants**

Marine pollution 363.73
- UF   Ocean pollution
      Offshore water pollution
      Sea pollution
- BT   **Oceanography**
      Pollution
      Water pollution
- NT   **Oil spills**
- RT   **Oil pollution of water**

Marine resources 333.91; 574.92
- UF   Ocean—Economic aspects
      Ocean resources
      Resources, Marine
      Sea resources
- BT   **Commercial products**
      Marine biology
      Natural resources
      Oceanography
- NT   **Aquaculture**
      Fisheries
      Marine mineral resources
      Ocean energy resources

      Ocean engineering
      Seafood

Marine salvage 387.5; 627
- UF   Salvage, Marine
      Ship salvage
- BT   **International law**
      Maritime law
      Salvage
- RT   **Shipwrecks**

Marine transportation
- USE   **Shipping**

Marine zoology
- USE   **Marine animals**

**Marineland (Fla.) 597.0074; 599.5;
      639.3**
- BT   **Marine aquariums**

Mariners
- USE   **Sailors**

Mariner's compass
- USE   **Compass**

Marionettes
- USE   **Puppets and puppet plays**

Marital counseling
- USE   **Marriage counseling**

Marital infidelity
- USE   **Adultery**

Maritime discoveries
- USE   **Exploration**

Maritime law 341.7; 343.09
- UF   Law, Maritime
      Law of the sea
      Marine law
      Merchant marine—Law and
        legislation
      Naval law
      Navigation—Law and legisla-
        tion
      Sea laws
- BT   **International law**
      Law
      Shipping
- NT   **Freight**
      Marine insurance
      Marine salvage
      Merchant marine
      Pirates
- RT   **Commercial law**
      Territorial waters

Market gardening
- USE   **Vegetable gardening**

Market surveys 658.8
  BT **Advertising**
  RT **Public opinion polls**
Marketing 380.1; 658.8
    Use for materials on the principles and methods involved in the distribution of merchandise from producer to consumer.
  UF Distribution (Economics)
       Merchandising
  SA subjects with the subdivision *Marketing,* to be added as needed
  BT **Business**
       Management
  NT **Direct selling**
       Farm produce—Marketing
       Sales management
       Telemarketing
  RT **Advertising**
       Selling
Marketing (Home economics)
  USE **Shopping**
Marketing of farm produce
  USE **Farm produce—Marketing**
Markets (May subdiv. geog.) **380.1; 658.8**
  BT **Business**
       Cities and towns
       Commerce
  RT **Fairs**
Marking (Students)
  USE **Grading and marking (Education)**
Marks on plate
  USE **Hallmarks**
Marks, Potters'
  USE **Pottery—Marks**
Marriage 173; 306.81; 346.01
  UF Matrimony
  BT **Love**
       Sacraments
  NT **Husbands**
       Intermarriage
       Marriage contracts
       Marriage counseling
       Married people
       Remarriage
       Weddings
       Wives
  RT **Divorce**

       Domestic relations
       Family
       Home
Marriage—Annulment 262.9; 346.01
  UF Annulment of marriage
  RT **Divorce**
Marriage contracts 306.81; 346.01
  UF Antenuptial contracts
       Premarital contracts
       Prenuptial contracts
  BT **Marriage**
Marriage counseling 362.82
  UF Marital counseling
       Premarital counseling
  BT **Counseling**
       Family life education
       Marriage
  RT **Divorce mediation**
Marriage customs and rites 392
  UF Bridal customs
  BT **Manners and customs**
       Rites and ceremonies
       Weddings
Marriage, Interracial
  USE **Interracial marriage**
Marriage, Mixed
  USE **Interfaith marriage**
       Intermarriage
Marriage, Open ended
  USE **Unmarried couples**
Marriage registers
  USE **Registers of births, etc.**
Marriage statistics
  USE **Vital statistics**
Married men
  USE **Husbands**
Married people 306.872
  UF Couples, Married
       Married persons
  BT **Family**
       Marriage
  NT **Husbands**
       Wives
Married persons
  USE **Married people**
Married women
  USE **Wives**
Mars (Planet) 523.4
  BT **Planets**
  NT **Mars probes**

Mars (Planet)—Exploration 629.43
  BT Planets—Exploration
Mars (Planet)—Geology 559.9
  BT Astrogeology
Mars (Planet)—Photographs 523.4;
      778.3
Mars probes 629.43
  UF Martian probes
  BT Mars (Planet)
       Space probes
Marshall Plan
  USE Reconstruction (1939-1951)
Marshes 333.91; 574.5
  UF Bogs
       Swamps
  BT Wetlands
  NT Swamp animals
Martial arts 796.8
  BT Athletics
  NT Archery
       Dueling
  RT Self-defense
       Self-defense for women
Martian probes
  USE Mars probes
Martin Luther King Day 394.2
  UF King, Martin Luther, holiday
  BT Holidays
Martyrs 272.092; 920
  BT Church history
       Heroes and heroines
  RT Persecution
       Saints
Marxian theory
  USE Marxism
Marxism 335.4
    Use for materials on the system of economic and political thought developed by Karl Marx, Friedrich Engels, or their followers.
  UF Marxian theory
       Marxist theory
  BT Economics
       Philosophy
       Political science
       Sociology
  RT Class consciousness
       Communism
       Dialectical materialism
       Socialism
Marxist theory
  USE Marxism

Mary, Blessed Virgin, Saint 232.91
  UF Blessed Virgin Mary
       Madonna
       Virgin Mary
  BT Saints
Mary, Blessed Virgin, Saint—Art 704.9
  BT Christian art and symbolism
  RT Jesus Christ—Art
Masculine psychology
  USE Men—Psychology
Masers 621.381
  UF Microwave amplification by stimulated emission of radiation
  BT Amplifiers (Electronics)
       Electromagnetism
       Microwaves
Masers, Optical
  USE Lasers
Masks (Facial) 391
  BT Costume
Masks (Plays) 808.82; 812, etc.
    May be used for individual works, collections, or materials about masks.
  UF Masques (Plays)
  BT Drama
       Pageants
       Theater
Masks (Sculpture) 731
  UF Death masks
  BT Sculpture
Masonic orders
  USE Freemasons
Masonry 693
  BT Building
       Civil engineering
       Stone
  NT Cement
       Concrete
       Plaster and plastering
       Stonecutting
  RT Bricklaying
       Foundations
       Walls
Masons (Secret order)
  USE Freemasons
Masques (Plays)
  USE Masks (Plays)
Mass 264
  UF Eucharist

Mass—*Continued*
  BT **Liturgies**
  RT **Lord's Supper**
Mass communication
  USE **Communication**
       Mass media
       Telecommunication
Mass culture
  USE **Popular culture**
Mass feeding
  USE **Food service**
Mass media 302.23
  UF Mass communication
      Media
  BT **Communication**
  NT **Motion pictures**
      Newspapers
      Periodicals
      Radio broadcasting
      Television broadcasting
  RT **Popular culture**
Mass psychology
  USE **Social psychology**
Mass spectra
  USE **Mass spectrometry**
Mass spectrometry 543; 547.3
  UF Mass spectra
      Mass spectrum analysis
  BT **Spectrum analysis**
Mass spectrum analysis
  USE **Mass spectrometry**
Mass transit
  USE **Local transit**
Massacres (May subdiv. geog.) **179;**
      904
  SA names of individual massa-
      cres, e.g. **Saint Bartholo-**
      mew's Day, Massacre of,
      1572; to be added as need-
      ed
  BT **Atrocities**
      History
      Persecution
  NT **Saint Bartholomew's Day,**
      Massacre of, 1572
Massage 615.8; 646.7
  BT **Physical therapy**
  NT **Acupressure**
      Chiropractic
      Electrotherapeutics

  RT **Osteopathy**
Mastodon 569
  BT **Extinct animals**
      Fossil mammals
Mate selection in animals
  USE **Animal courtship**
Materia medica 615
  UF Herbals
      Pharmacopoeias
  SA classes of drugs and names of
      individual drugs, to be add-
      ed as needed
  BT **Medicine**
      Pharmaceutical chemistry
      Therapeutics
  NT **Anesthetics**
      Narcotics
      Pharmacology
  RT **Drugs**
      Pharmacy
Materialism 146
  BT **Philosophy**
      Positivism
  RT **Idealism**
      Realism
Materials 620.1
    Use for comprehensive discussions of
  materials in engineering and industry.
  UF Engineering materials
      Industrial materials
      Strategic materials
  SA types of materials, e.g. **Build-**
      ing materials; Hazardous
      substances; etc.; and scien-
      tific and technical disci-
      plines and types of
      equipment and construction
      with the subdivision *Mate-*
      rials, to be added as need-
      ed
  NT **Airplanes—Materials**
      Building materials
      Hazardous substances
      Raw materials
      Strength of materials
  RT **Engineering**
      Industry
Materials handling 388; 658.7
  UF Handling of materials
      Mechanical handling

BT = Broader Term   NT = Narrower Term   RT = Related Term   SA = See Also   UF = Used For

Materials handling—*Continued*
  BT **Management**
  NT **Conveying machinery**
      Freight
  RT **Trucks**
Materials, Strength of
  USE **Strength of materials**
Maternity
  USE **Mothers**
Mathematical analysis 515
  UF Analysis (Mathematics)
  NT **Algebra**
      Calculus
      Graph theory
      Linear algebra
      Numerical analysis
      Programming (Computers)
Mathematical drawing
  USE **Geometrical drawing**
       Mechanical drawing
Mathematical logic
  USE **Symbolic logic**
Mathematical models 511
  UF Models, Mathematical
  SA subjects with the subdivision
      Mathematical models, to be
      added as needed
  NT **Fractals**
      Game theory
      Pollution—Mathematical mod-
      els
      Programming (Computers)
      System analysis
Mathematical notation 510
   Use for materials on the system of
  graphic symbols used in mathematics as
  well as for materials on the process or
  method of setting these down.
  UF Mathematical symbols
      Mathematics—Notation
      Mathematics—Symbols
      Notation, Mathematical
      Symbols, Mathematical
  RT **Mathematics**
Mathematical readiness 372.7
  UF Arithmetical readiness
      Mathematics readiness
      Number readiness
      Readiness for mathematics
  BT **Arithmetic—Study and teach-**
      ing

Mathematics—Study and
  teaching
Mathematical recreations 793.7
  UF Recreations, Mathematical
  BT **Amusements**
      Puzzles
      Scientific recreations
  NT **Number games**
Mathematical sequences
  USE **Sequences (Mathematics)**
Mathematical sets
  USE **Set theory**
Mathematical symbols
  USE **Mathematical notation**
Mathematicians 510.92; 920
  BT **Scientists**
Mathematics 510
  SA subjects with the subdivision
      Mathematics, e.g. **Astrono-**
      my—Mathematics; to be
      added as needed
  BT **Science**
  NT **Algebra**
      Arithmetic
      Astronomy—Mathematics
      Binary system (Mathematics)
      Biomathematics
      Business mathematics
      Calculus
      Dynamics
      Fourth dimension
      Fractions
      Game theory
      Geometry
      Group theory
      Measurement
      Number theory
      Patterns (Mathematics)
      Probabilities
      Sequences (Mathematics)
      Set theory
      Symbolic logic
      Trigonometry
  RT **Mathematical notation**
Mathematics, Business
  USE **Business mathematics**
Mathematics—Computer assisted in-
  struction 372.7; 510.7
  BT **Computer assisted instruction**

BT = Broader Term   NT = Narrower Term   RT = Related Term   SA = See Also   UF = Used For

Mathematics—Notation
  USE **Mathematical notation**
Mathematics readiness
  USE **Mathematical readiness**
Mathematics—Study and teaching
            372.7; 510.7
  NT **Mathematical readiness**
Mathematics—Symbols
  USE **Mathematical notation**
Mathematics—Tables 510
  UF Ready reckoners
  NT **Logarithms**
        Trigonometry—Tables
Mating behavior
  USE **Animal courtship**
        Sexual behavior in animals
Matrimony
  USE **Marriage**
Matter 117; 530
  BT **Dynamics**
        Physics
Mausoleums
  USE **Tombs**
Maxims
  USE **Proverbs**
Mayas 972.004
  BT **Indians of Central America**
        Indians of Mexico
Meal planning
  USE **Menus**
        Nutrition
Meals
  USE types of meals, e.g. **Break-**
        fasts; Dinners; etc., to be
        added as needed
Meals for school children
  USE **School children—Food**
Meals on wheels programs 362
    Use for materials on programs that de-
  liver meals to the homebound.
  UF Home delivered meals pro-
        grams
  BT **Food relief**
Measurement 389; 530.8
  UF Mensuration
        Metrology
  SA subjects with the subdivision
        Measurement, e.g. **Air**
        pollution—Measurement; to
        be added as needed

  BT **Mathematics**
  NT **Air pollution—Measurement**
        Geodesy
        Measuring instruments
        Surveying
        Volume (Cubic content)
  RT **Weights and measures**
Measurements, Electric
  USE **Electric measurements**
Measures
  USE **Weights and measures**
Measuring instruments 389; 681
  UF Instruments, Measuring
  BT **Measurement**
        Weights and measures
Meat 641.3; 664
  SA types of meat, to be added as
        needed
  BT **Animal food**
        Cooking
        Food
  NT **Beef**
        Carving (Meat, etc.)
Meat-eating animals
  USE **Carnivores**
Meat industry 338.1
  UF Meat industry and trade *[For-*
        mer heading]
        Meat packing industry
        Meat trade
        Packing industry
        Stockyards
  BT **Food supply**
  NT **Cold storage**
        Meat inspection
Meat industry and trade
  USE **Meat industry**
Meat inspection 363.19
  UF Inspection of meat
  BT **Food adulteration and inspec-**
        tion
        Meat industry
        Public health
Meat packing industry
  USE **Meat industry**
Meat trade
  USE **Meat industry**
Mechanic arts
  USE **Industrial arts**
Mechanical brains
  USE **Computers**

BT = Broader Term   NT = Narrower Term   RT = Related Term   SA = See Also   UF = Used For

Mechanical brains—*Continued*
    Cybernetics
Mechanical drawing 604.2
    UF   Drafting, Mechanical
          Engineering drawing
          Industrial drawing
          Machinery—Drawing
          Mathematical drawing
          Plans
          Structural drafting
    BT   **Drawing**
          Engineering
          Machinery
          Pattern making
    NT   **Architectural drawing**
          Blueprints
          Graphic methods
          Lettering
    RT   **Geometrical drawing**
Mechanical engineering 621
    Use for materials on the application of the principles of mechanics to the design, construction, and operation of machnery. Materials on the application of the principles of mechanics to engineering structures other than machinery are entered under **Applied mechanics.**
    BT   **Civil engineering**
    NT   **Electric engineering**
          Machinery
          Marine engineering
          Mechanical movements
          Power (Mechanics)
          Power transmission
          Robotics
    RT   **Steam engineering**
Mechanical handling
    USE **Materials handling**
Mechanical models
    USE **Machinery—Models**
Mechanical movements 531
    UF   Mechanisms (Machinery)
    BT   **Kinematics**
          Mechanical engineering
          Mechanics
          Motion
    NT   **Robots**
          Simple machines
    RT   **Gearing**
Mechanical musical instruments 786.6
    UF   Musical instruments, Mechanical *[Former heading]*

    SA   names of instruments, e.g. **Music box;** to be added as needed
    BT   **Musical instruments**
    NT   **Music boxes**
Mechanical painting
    USE **Industrial painting**
Mechanical speech recognition
    USE **Automatic speech recognition**
Mechanical translating
    USE **Translating and interpreting**
Mechanics 530; 531
    BT   **Physics**
    NT   **Applied mechanics**
          Dynamics
          Fluid mechanics
          Hydraulics
          Hydrodynamics
          Hydrostatics
          Mechanical movements
          Power (Mechanics)
          Simple machines
          Statics
          Steam engines
          Strains and stresses
          Strength of materials
          Vibration
          Viscosity
          Wave mechanics
    RT   **Engineering**
          Force and energy
          Kinematics
          Machinery
          Motion
Mechanics, Applied
    USE **Applied mechanics**
Mechanics (Persons) 920
Mechanisms (Machinery)
    USE **Mechanical movements**
Medallions
    USE **Medals**
Medals 355.1; 737
    UF   Badges of honor
          Medallions
    SA   names of military services and other appropriate subjects with the subdivision *Medals, badges, decorations, etc.,* to be added as needed

---

Medals—*Continued*
   NT   **United States. Army—Medals,**
         badges, decorations, etc.
         United States. Navy—Medals,
         badges, decorations, etc.
   RT   **Decorations of honor**
         Insignia
         Numismatics
Media
   USE **Mass media**
Media centers (Education)
   USE **Instructional materials centers**
Mediation
   USE **Arbitration and award**
Mediation, Divorce
   USE **Divorce mediation**
Mediation, Industrial
   USE **Industrial arbitration**
Mediation, International
   USE **International arbitration**
Medicaid 368.4
   UF   Medical care for the poor
         Medical care, State
   BT   **National health insurance**
         Poor—Medical care
Medical appointments and schedules
   USE **Medical practice**
Medical botany 581.6
   UF   Botany, Medical *[Former*
         heading]
         Drug plants
         Herbal medicine
         Herbals
         Herbs, Medical
         Medicinal plants
         Plants, Medicinal
   BT   **Botany**
         Medicine
         Pharmacy
Medical care (May subdiv. geog.) **362.1**
   UF   Care, Medical
         Health care
         Medical service
   SA   classes of people with the
         subdivision *Medical care,*
         e.g. **Elderly—Medical care;**
         to be added as needed
   BT   **Public health**
   NT   **Elderly—Medical care**
         Health maintenance organiza-
         tions

         Health self-care
         Home care services
         Long-term care facilities
         Medical charities
         Occupational health services
         Sports medicine
         Terminal care
Medical care—Costs 362.1
   UF   Cost of medical care
         Medical service, Cost of
         Medicine—Cost of medical
         care
   BT   **Medical economics**
Medical care for the elderly
   USE **Elderly—Medical care**
         Medicare
Medical care for the poor
   USE **Medicaid**
         Poor—Medical care
Medical care—Moral and religious as-
         pects
   USE **Medical ethics**
Medical care, Prepaid
   USE **Health insurance**
Medical care—Social aspects
   USE **Social medicine**
Medical care, State
   USE **Medicaid**
         Medicare
Medical centers 362.1
   NT   **Medicine—Study and teaching**
   RT   **Hospitals**
Medical charities 362.1
   UF   Charities, Medical *[Former*
         heading]
         Socialized medicine
   BT   **Charities**
         Medical care
         Public health
   NT   **Institutional care**
   RT   **Hospitals**
Medical chemistry
   USE **Clinical chemistry**
Medical colleges
   USE **Medicine—Study and teaching**
Medical consultation
   USE **Medical practice**
Medical diagnosis
   USE **Diagnosis**

Medical drama (Films) 791.43

May be used for individual works, collections, or materials about medical films.

UF   Doctor films

BT   **Motion pictures**

Medical drama (Radio programs) 791.44

May be used for individual works, collections, or materials about medical radio programs.

UF   Doctor radio programs

BT   **Radio programs**

Medical drama (Television programs) 791.45

May be used for individual works, collections, or materials about medical television programs.

UF   Doctor television programs

BT   **Television programs**

Medical economics 338.4

Use for comprehensive materials on the economic aspects of medical service from the point of view of both the practitioner and the public. Materials on special aspects of medical economics are entered under specific headings, e.g. **Medical care—Costs;** etc.

UF   Economics, Medical

NT   **Medical care—Costs**

Medical education

USE   **Medicine—Study and teaching**

Medical electricity

USE   **Electrotherapeutics**

Medical entomology

USE   **Insects as carriers of disease**

Medical errors

USE   **Errors**

       Physicians—Malpractice

Medical ethics 174

UF   Ethics, Medical

       Medical care—Moral and religious aspects

       Medicine—Moral and religious aspects

BT   **Bioethics**

       Professional ethics

NT   **Euthanasia**

       Human experimentation in medicine

       Physicians—Malpractice

       Right to die

RT   **Social medicine**

Medical experimentation on humans

USE   **Human experimentation in medicine**

Medical folklore

USE   **Traditional medicine**

Medical genetics 616

UF   Clinical genetics

       Congenital diseases

       Hereditary diseases

       Heredity of diseases

SA   names of diseases with the subdivision *Genetic aspects,* to be added as needed

BT   **Genetics**

       Pathology

NT   **Birth defects**

       Cancer—Genetic aspects

       Genetic counseling

Medical insurance

USE   **Health insurance**

Medical insurance, National

USE   **National health insurance**

Medical jurisprudence 614

Use for materials on the application of medical knowledge to questions of law. Materials that include laws affecting medicine and the medical profession, or discussion of those laws, are entered under **Medicine—Law and legislation.**

UF   Forensic medicine

       Jurisprudence, Medical

       Legal medicine

       Medicine, Legal

SA   subjects with the subdivision *Jurisprudence,* e.g. **Mental illness—Jurisprudence;** to be added as needed

BT   **Criminal investigation**

       Criminal law

       Law

       State medicine

NT   **DNA fingerprints**

       Lie detectors and detection

       Mental illness—Jurisprudence

       Poisons and poisoning

       Suicide

RT   **Medicine—Law and legislation**

Medical law and legislation

USE   **Medicine—Law and legislation**

Medical malpractice
  USE   classes of persons in the med-
          ical field with the subdivi-
          sion *Malpractice,* e.g.
          Physicians—Malpractice; to
          be added as needed
Medical missions 362.1
  UF   Missions, Medical *[Former
          heading]*
  BT   **Medicine**
Medical novels 813, etc.
  May be used for individual works, col-
  lections, or materials about novels with a
  medical setting.
  UF   Doctor novels
  BT   **Fiction**
Medical offices
  USE   **Medical practice**
Medical partnership
  USE   **Medical practice**
Medical photography 621.36; 778.3
  UF   Photography, Medical *[Former
          heading]*
  BT   **Photography**
          **Photography—Scientific appli-
          cations**
Medical practice 610.6
  UF   Clinics
          Group medical practice
          Medical appointments and
            schedules
          Medical consultation
          Medical offices
          Medical partnership
          Medical profession
          Medicine—Practice *[Former
            heading]*
  BT   **Medicine**
Medical profession
  USE   **Medical practice**
          Medicine
          Physicians
          Surgeons
Medical research
  USE   **Medicine—Research**
Medical schools
  USE   **Medicine—Study and teaching**
Medical self-care
  USE   **Health self-care**
Medical service
  USE   **Medical care**

Medical service, Cost of
  USE   **Medical care—Costs**
Medical service, Prepaid
  USE   **Health insurance**
Medical sociology
  USE   **Social medicine**
Medical technologists 610.69
  BT   **Allied health personnel**
Medical technology 610.28
  BT   **Medicine**
Medical transplantation
  USE   **Transplantation of organs, tis-
          sues, etc.**
Medical waste disposal
  USE   **Medical wastes**
Medical wastes 363.72
  UF   Disposal of medical waste
          Hospital wastes
          Infectious wastes
          Medical waste disposal
          Waste disposal
          Wastes, Medical
  BT   **Refuse and refuse disposal**
  RT   **Hazardous wastes**
Medicare 368.4
  UF   Medical care for the elderly
          Medical care, State
  BT   **Elderly—Medical care**
          National health insurance
Medicinal chemistry
  USE   **Pharmaceutical chemistry**
Medicinal plants
  USE   **Medical botany**
Medicine (May subdiv. geog.) **610**
  UF   Medical profession
  SA   types of medicine, e.g. **Sports
          medicine;** and names of dis-
          eases and groups of dis-
          eases, e.g. **AIDS (Disease);
          Fever; Nervous system—
          Diseases;** etc., to be added
          as needed
  BT   **Life sciences
          Therapeutics**
  NT   **Alternative medicine
          Anatomy
          Aviation medicine
          Bacteriology
          Biochemistry
          Chiropractic**

BT = Broader Term   NT = Narrower Term   RT = Related Term   SA = See Also   UF = Used For

Medicine—*Continued*
    Dentistry
    Diagnosis
    Diseases
    Emergency medicine
    Endocrinology
    First aid
    Health
    Health resorts
    Holistic medicine
    Hospitals
    Hygiene
    Indians of North America—Medicine
    Materia medica
    Medical botany
    Medical missions
    Medical practice
    Medical technology
    Medicine and religion
    Military medicine
    Mind and body
    Nuclear medicine
    Nursing
    Pharmacology
    Pharmacy
    Physiology
    Podiatry
    Popular medicine
    Preventive medicine
    Psychiatry
    Psychosomatic medicine
    Quacks and quackery
    Social medicine
    Space medicine
    Sports medicine
    State medicine
    Submarine medicine
    Surgery
    Traditional medicine
    Tropical medicine
    Veterinary medicine
 RT **Pathology**
    Physicians
Medicine and religion 261.5; 615.8
 UF Religion and medicine
 BT **Medicine**
    Religion
 NT **Christian Science**
    Spiritual healing

Medicine, Atomic
 USE **Nuclear medicine**
Medicine, Aviation
 USE **Aviation medicine**
Medicine—Biography 610.92; 920
 BT **Biography**
Medicine—Cost of medical care
 USE **Medical care—Costs**
Medicine, Dental
 USE **Dentistry**
    Teeth—Diseases
Medicine—Law and legislation 344
    Use for materials on laws relating to medicine and the medical profession and for collections of such laws. Materials on the application of medical knowledge to questions of law are entered under **Medical jurisprudence.**
 UF Medical law and legislation
 BT **Legislation**
 NT **Physicians—Malpractice**
    Right to die
 RT **Medical jurisprudence**
Medicine, Legal
 USE **Medical jurisprudence**
Medicine, Military
 USE **Military medicine**
Medicine—Miscellanea 610.2
 BT **Curiosities and wonders**
Medicine—Moral and religious aspects
 USE **Medical ethics**
Medicine, Nuclear
 USE **Nuclear medicine**
Medicine, Pediatric
 USE **Children—Diseases**
Medicine—Physiological effect
 USE **Pharmacology**
Medicine, Popular
 USE **Popular medicine**
Medicine—Practice
 USE **Medical practice**
Medicine, Preventive
 USE **Preventive medicine**
Medicine, Psychosomatic
 USE **Psychosomatic medicine**
Medicine—Research 610.7
 UF Medical research
 BT **Research**
 NT **Human experimentation in medicine**
Medicine, Social
 USE **Social medicine**

BT = Broader Term   NT = Narrower Term   RT = Related Term   SA = See Also   UF = Used For

Medicine—Social aspects
  USE **Social medicine**
Medicine, State
  USE **State medicine**
Medicine—Study and teaching 610.7
  UF Education, Medical
      Medical colleges
      Medical education
      Medical schools
  BT **Medical centers**
      Professional education
Medicine, Submarine
  USE **Submarine medicine**
Medicine, Tropical
  USE **Tropical medicine**
Medicine—United States 610.973
  UF United States—Medicine
Medieval architecture 723
  UF Architecture, Medieval *[Former heading]*
  BT **Architecture**
      Middle Ages
  NT **Byzantine architecture**
      Romanesque architecture
  RT **Castles**
      Cathedrals
Medieval art 709.02
  UF Art, Medieval *[Former heading]*
      Religious art
  BT **Art**
      Medieval civilization
      Middle Ages
  NT **Byzantine art**
      Gothic art
      Illumination of books and manuscripts
      Romanesque art
Medieval church history
  USE **Church history—600-1500, Middle Ages**
Medieval civilization 909.07
  UF Civilization, Medieval *[Former heading]*
  BT **Civilization**
      Middle Ages—History
  NT **Feudalism**
      Medieval art
      Monasticism
  RT **Chivalry**

Middle Ages
Medieval history
  USE **Middle Ages—History**
Medieval literature 809
  May use same subdivisions as for **Literature.**
  UF Literature, Medieval *[Former heading]*
  BT **Literature**
      Middle Ages
  NT **Early Christian literature**
      Old Norse literature
Medieval philosophy 189
  UF Philosophy, Medieval *[Former heading]*
  BT **Middle Ages**
      Philosophy
Meditation 158; 291.4; 296.7
  Use for materials on the act or process of meditating.
  BT **Devotional exercises**
      Spiritual life
  NT **Transcendental meditation**
  RT **Meditations**
Meditations 242; 291.4; 296.7
  Use as a form heading for actual discourses written to express the author's reflections or to serve as a guide to contemplation.
  BT **Devotional literature**
      Prayers
  RT **Meditation**
Meetings, Public
  USE **Public meetings**
Melancholia
  USE **Depression (Psychology)**
      Manic-depressive psychoses
Melodrama 808.82; 812, etc.
  May be used for individual works, collections, or materials about melodrama.
  BT **Drama**
Memoirs
  USE **Autobiographies**
      Autobiography
      Biography
Memorial Day 394.2
  UF Decoration Day
  BT **Holidays**
Memory 153.1
  UF Mnemonics
  BT **Brain**

Memory—*Continued*
    Educational psychology
    Intellect
    Psychology
    Psychophysiology
    Thought and thinking
  NT Attention
    Psychology of learning
Men (May subdiv. geog.) 305.31
  NT Fathers
    Gay men
    Husbands
    Single men
    Widowers
    Young men
Men actors 791.4; 792; 920
    Use for materials on male actors that emphasize their identity as men. General materials on persons of the acting profession, whether male or female, are entered under **Actors.**
  UF Actors, Male
    Male actors
  BT Actors
Men—Biography 920
  BT Biography
Men—Clothing
  USE Men's clothing
Men—Clubs
  USE Men—Societies
Men—Diseases 616.0081
  BT Diseases
Men—Education 370.81
  UF Education of men
  BT Education
  RT Coeducation
Men—Employment 331.11
  BT Labor
    Labor supply
Men in business
  USE Businessmen
Men—Psychology 155.3
  UF Masculine psychology
  BT Psychology
Men, Single
  USE Single men
Men—Social conditions 305.32
  NT Divorce
    Men—Societies
    Men's movement
Men—Societies 367
  UF Men—Clubs

    Men's clubs
    Men's organizations
  BT Clubs
    Men—Social conditions
    Societies
  NT Boys' clubs
Mendel's law 575.1
  BT Breeding
    Variation (Biology)
  NT Genetics
  RT Heredity
Mendicancy
  USE Begging
Mendicant orders
  USE Dominicans (Religious order)
    Franciscans
Mennonites 289.7
  BT Christian sects
  NT Amish
  RT Baptists
Menopause 612.6; 618.1
  UF Change of life in women
    Climacteric, Female
    Female climacteric
  BT Aging
Menopause, Male
  USE Male climacteric
Men's clothing 646; 687
  UF Clothing, Men's
    Men—Clothing
  BT Clothing and dress
Men's clubs
  USE Men—Societies
Men's liberation movement
  USE Men's movement
Men's movement 305.32
  UF Men's liberation movement
    [Former heading]
  BT Men—Social conditions
Men's organizations
  USE Men—Societies
Menstruation 612.6
  BT Reproduction
  NT Premenstrual syndrome
Mensuration
  USE Measurement
Mental arithmetic 513
  UF Arithmetic, Mental *[Former heading]*
    Oral arithmetic

Mental arithmetic—*Continued*

  BT   **Arithmetic**

Mental deficiency
  USE **Mental retardation**

Mental depression
  USE **Depression (Psychology)**

Mental diseases
  USE **Abnormal psychology**
        Mental illness

Mental healing 615.8

    Use for materials on psychic or psycho-
logical means to treat illness. Materials on
the use of faith, prayer, or religious means
to treat illness are entered under **Spiritual
healing.**

  UF   Healing, Mental
        Mind cure
        Psychic healing

  BT   **Alternative medicine**

  NT   **Hypnotism**

  RT   **Christian Science**
        Mental suggestion
        Mind and body
        Psychotherapy
        Spiritual healing
        Subconsciousness
        Suggestive therapeutics

Mental health 362.2

  UF   Health, Mental
        Hygiene, Mental
        Mental hygiene

  BT   **Health**
        Hygiene

  NT   **Abnormal psychology**
        Burn out (Psychology)
        Mental retardation
        Occupational therapy
        Psychophysiology
        Stress (Psychology)
        Worry

  RT   **Mental illness**
        Mind and body
        Psychiatry

Mental hospitals
  USE **Mentally ill—Institutional
           care**
        Psychiatric hospitals

Mental hygiene
  USE **Mental health**

Mental illness 362.2; 616.89

    Use for popular materials and materials
on regional or social aspects of mental disorders. Materials on clinical aspects of
mental disorders, including therapy, are
entered under **Psychiatry.** Systematic descriptions of mental disorders are entered
under **Abnormal psychology.**

  UF   Diseases, Mental
        Mental diseases
        Psychoses

  SA   names of specific illnesses,
        e.g. **Manic-depressive psy-
        choses;** to be added as
        needed

  BT   **Abnormal psychology**
        Diseases

  NT   **Manic-depressive psychoses**
        Mental retardation
        Multiple personality

  RT   **Mental health**
        Personality disorders
        Psychiatry

Mental illness—Drug therapy 616.89

  BT   **Drug therapy**

Mental illness—Jurisprudence 344

    Use for materials on the legal aspects of
mental disorders.

  UF   Insanity

  BT   **Medical jurisprudence**

  NT   **Insanity defense**

Mental institutions
  USE **Mentally ill—Institutional
           care**

Mental retardation 362.3; 616.85

  UF   Mental deficiency

  BT   **Mental health**
        Mental illness

  NT   **Down's syndrome**

  RT   **Mentally handicapped**

Mental stress
  USE **Stress (Psychology)**

Mental suggestion 131; 154.7; 615.8

  UF   Autosuggestion
        Suggestion, Mental

  BT   **Mind and body**
        Parapsychology
        Subconsciousness

  NT   **Brainwashing**

  RT   **Hypnotism**
        Mental healing
        Suggestive therapeutics

Mental telepathy
  USE **Telepathy**
Mental tests
  USE **Intelligence tests**
         Psychological tests
Mentally depressed
  USE **Depression (Psychology)**
Mentally deranged
  USE **Mentally ill**
**Mentally handicapped 305.9; 362.2;
     362.3**
  UF Mentally retarded
  BT **Handicapped**
  NT **Mentally handicapped children**
  RT **Mental retardation**
**Mentally handicapped children 155.45;
     362.2; 362.3**
  UF Children, Retarded
         Mentally retarded children
         Retarded children
  BT **Child psychiatry**
         Handicapped children
         Mentally handicapped
  NT **Mentally ill children**
  RT **Slow learning children**
**Mentally handicapped children—
     Education 371.92**
  BT **Education**
         Special education
Mentally ill 362.2; 616.89
  UF Insane
         Mentally deranged
         Psychotics
  BT **Psychiatry**
  NT **Mentally ill children**
**Mentally ill children 155.4; 362.2;
     616.89**
  UF Psychotic children
  BT **Child psychiatry**
         Emotionally disturbed children
         Mentally handicapped children
         Mentally ill
Mentally ill—Institutional care 362.2
  UF Insane—Hospitals
         Mental hospitals
         Mental institutions
  BT **Institutional care**
  NT **Psychiatric hospitals**
Mentally retarded
  USE **Mentally handicapped**

Mentally retarded children
  USE **Mentally handicapped children**
Menus 642
  UF Bills of fare
         Gastronomy
         Meal planning
  BT **Cooking**
         Diet
  NT **Breakfasts**
         Dinners
         Luncheons
  RT **Catering**
Mercantile law
  USE **Commercial law**
Mercantile marine
  USE **Merchant marine**
Mercenary soldiers 355.3
  UF Mercenary troops
         Soldiers of fortune
  BT **Military personnel**
         Soldiers
Mercenary troops
  USE **Mercenary soldiers**
Merchandise
  USE **Commercial products**
         Consumer goods
Merchandising
  USE **Marketing**
         Retail trade
Merchant marine (May subdiv. geog.)
     387.5
  UF Mercantile marine
  BT **Maritime law**
         Sailors
         Ships
         Transportation
  NT **Harbors**
         Marine insurance
  RT **Shipping**
Merchant marine—Law and legislation
  USE **Maritime law**
**Merchant marine—United States
     387.50973**
  UF United States—Merchant ma-
         rine
Merchants 380.1092; 920
  BT **Business**
         Business people
         Commerce
Mercury 546; 669
  UF Quicksilver

Mercury—*Continued*
   BT   **Chemical elements**
         Metals
Mercy killing
   USE **Euthanasia**
Merger of corporations
   USE **Corporate mergers and acqui-
          sitions**
Mergers, Industrial
   USE **Industrial trusts**
          Railroads—Consolidation
Mermaids and mermen 398.21
   BT   **Mythical animals**
Mesmerism
   USE **Hypnotism**
Messages to Congress
   USE **Presidents—United States—
          Messages**
Messiness
   USE **Cleanliness**
Metabolism 574.1
   BT   **Biochemistry**
   NT   **Growth disorders**
   RT   **Nutrition**
Metal work
   USE **Metalwork**
Metallography 669
     Use for materials on the science of met-
al structures and alloys, especially the
study of such structures with the micro-
scope. Materials on the process of extract-
ing metals from their ores, refining them,
and preparing them for use, are entered
under **Metallurgy.**
   UF   Analysis, Microscopic
         Micrographic analysis
         Microscopic analysis
   BT   **Metals**
   RT   **Microscopes**
Metallurgy 669
     Use for materials on the process of ex-
tracting metals from their ores, refining
them, and preparing them for use. Materials on the science of metal structures and
alloys, especially the study of such structures with the microscope, are entered under **Metallography.**
   BT   **Ores**
   NT   **Electrometallurgy**
         Metals
   RT   **Alloys**
         Chemical engineering
         Industrial chemistry

     Smelting
Metals 669
   SA   types of metals, to be added
         as needed
   BT   **Inorganic chemistry**
         Metallurgy
         Ores
   NT   **Alloys**
         Aluminum
         Brass
         Iron
         Mercury
         Metallography
         Pewter
         Precious metals
         Soldering
         Tin
         Zinc
   RT   **Metalwork**
Metals, Transmutation of
   USE **Alchemy**
          Transmutation (Chemistry)
Metalwork 671; 739
   UF   Metal work
   BT   **Decoration and ornament**
   NT   **Architectural metalwork**
         Art metalwork
         Bronzes
         Copperwork
         Dies (Metalworking)
         Electroplating
         Forging
         Founding
         Goldwork
         Ironwork
         Jewelry
         Plate metalwork
         Sheet metalwork
         Silverwork
         Soldering
         Steel
         Tinwork
         Welding
   RT   **Metals**
         Metalworking machinery
Metalwork, Architectural
   USE **Architectural metalwork**
Metalwork, Art
   USE **Art metalwork**

Metalworking machinery 621.9
  BT Machinery
  RT Metalwork
Metamorphic rocks
  USE Rocks
Metaphysics 110
  BT Philosophy
  NT Existentialism
      Space and time
      Theory of knowledge
      Universe
  RT God
Meteorites 523.5
  BT Astronomy
      Meteors
Meteorological instruments 551.5
  UF Instruments, Meteorological
  SA names of meteorological in-
      struments, to be added as
      needed
  BT Scientific apparatus and in-
      struments
  NT Barometers
      Thermometers
Meteorological observatories
  USE Meteorology—Observatories
Meteorological satellites 551.5
  UF Weather satellites
  SA names of satellites, e.g. Tiros
      (Meteorological satellite);
      etc.
  BT Artificial satellites
  NT Tiros (Meteorological satellite)
Meteorology 551.5
    Use for scientific materials on the atmo-
sphere, especially weather factors. Materi-
als on climate as it relates to humans and
to plant and animal life, including the ef-
fects of changes of climate, are entered un-
der Climate. Materials on the state of the
atmosphere at a given time and place with
respect to heat or cold, wetness or dry-
ness, calm or storm, are entered under
Weather.
  BT Earth sciences
  NT Air
      Auroras
      Clouds
      Cyclones
      Droughts
      Floods
      Fog

      Frost
      Humidity
      Lightning
      Rain
      Rainbow
      Seasons
      Snow
      Solar radiation
      Storms
      Sunspots
      Thunderstorms
      Tornadoes
      Weather control
      Weather—Folklore
      Weather forecasting
      Winds
  RT Atmosphere
      Climate
      Weather
Meteorology in aeronautics 629.132
  UF Aeronautics, Meteorology in
  BT Aeronautics
      Weather forecasting
Meteorology—Observatories 551.5028
  UF Meteorological observatories
      Observatories, Meteorological
      Weather stations
Meteorology—Tables 551.5
  UF Meteorology—Tables, etc.
      [Former heading]
Meteorology—Tables, etc.
  USE Meteorology—Tables
Meteors 523.5
  UF Falling stars
      Fire balls
      Shooting stars
      Stars, Falling
  BT Astronomy
      Solar system
      Stars
  NT Meteorites
Meter
  USE Musical meter and rhythm
      Versification
Meters, Electric
  USE Electric meters
Meth (Drug)
  USE Methamphetamine
Methamphetamine 362.29; 615
  UF Meth (Drug)

Methamphetamine—*Continued*
> Speed (Drug)
> BT **Amphetamines**
> NT **Ice (Drug)**

Method of study
> USE **Study skills**

Methodology
> USE subjects with the subdivision
> *Methodology,* e.g. **Science—**
> **Methodology;** to be added
> as needed

Metric system 389; 530.8
> BT **Weights and measures**
> RT **Decimal system**

Metrical romances
> USE **Romances**

Metrology
> USE **Measurement**
> **Weights and measures**

Metropolitan areas 307.76
> UF Suburban areas
> Urban areas
> SA names of metropolitan areas,
> e.g. **Chicago metropolitan**
> **area (Ill.);** to be added as
> needed
> BT **Cities and towns—Growth**
> NT **Chicago metropolitan area**
> **(Ill.)**
> **Urban renewal**

Metropolitan finance 336
> BT **Finance**
> **Municipal finance**

Metropolitan government 320.8; 352
> SA names of metropolitan areas
> with the subdivision *Poli-*
> *tics and government,* to be
> added as needed
> BT **Local government**
> NT **Chicago metropolitan area**
> **(Ill.)—Politics and govern-**
> **ment**
> RT **Municipal government**

Metropolitan planning
> USE **Regional planning**

Mexican American literature (English)
> USE **American literature—Mexican**
> **American authors**

Mexican American women 305.868
> UF Chicanas

Mexican Americans—Women
> Women, Mexican American
> BT **Mexican Americans**
> **Women**

Mexican Americans 305.868; 973
> Use for materials on American citizens
> of Mexican descent. Materials on nonciti-
> zens from Mexico are entered under
> **Mexicans—United States.** Use these same
> patterns for other ethnic groups in the
> U.S. and other countries.
> UF Chicanos
> BT **Ethnology—United States**
> **Hispanic Americans**
> **Immigration and emigration**
> **Minorities**
> **United States—Foreign popu-**
> **lation**
> **United States—Immigration**
> **and emigration**
> NT **Mexican American women**
> RT **Mexicans—United States**

Mexican Americans—Women
> USE **Mexican American women**

Mexican literature 860; M860
> May use same subdivisions and names
> of literary forms as for **English literature.**
> BT **Latin American literature**
> **Literature**

Mexican War, 1846-1848 973.6
> UF United States—History—
> 1845-1848, War with Mexi-
> co *[Former heading]*
> BT **United States—History—**
> **1815-1861**

Mexicans (May subdiv. geog.) **305.868;**
> **920; 972**

Mexicans—United States 305.868
> Use for materials on noncitizens from
> Mexico. Materials on American citizens of
> Mexican descent are entered under **Mexi-**
> **can Americans.** Use these same patterns
> for other ethnic groups in the U.S. and
> other countries.
> BT **Aliens**
> **Immigration and emigration**
> **Minorities**
> **United States—Foreign popu-**
> **lation**
> **United States—Immigration**
> **and emigration**
> RT **Mexican Americans**

Mexico, Indians of
> USE **Indians of Mexico**

BT = Broader Term   NT = Narrower Term   RT = Related Term   SA = See Also   UF = Used For

Mexico—Presidents
USE **Presidents—Mexico**
Mezzotint engraving 766
BT **Engraving**
MIA's
USE **Missing in action**
Mice 599.32; 636.088
UF Mouse
BT **Mammals**
Microbes
USE **Bacteria**
Germ theory of disease
Microorganisms
Viruses
Microbial energy conversion
USE **Biomass energy**
Microbiology 576
SA subjects with the subdivision
Microbiology, to be added
as needed
BT **Biology**
NT **Air—Microbiology**
Bacteriology
Biotechnology
RT **Microorganisms**
Microscopes
Microchemistry 540
BT **Chemistry**
RT **Microscopes**
Microcomputers 004.16; 621.39
Use for materials on small, usually
desktop-sized computers that have a self-
contained central processing unit.
UF Desktop computers
Home computers
PC computers
Personal computers
BT **Computers**
NT **Microprocessors**
Portable computers
Microelectronics 621.381
UF Microminiature electronic
equipment
Microminiaturization (Elec-
tronics)
BT **Electronics**
Semiconductors
Microfilming
USE **Microphotography**
Microfilms 302.23; 686.4
UF Films

BT **Microforms**
NT **Library catalogs on microfilm**
Microforms 302.23; 686.4
UF Micropublications
SA types of microforms, to be
added as needed
BT **Microphotography**
NT **Microfilms**
Micrographic analysis
USE **Metallography**
Microscopes
Microminiature electronic equipment
USE **Microelectronics**
Microminiaturization (Electronics)
USE **Microelectronics**
Microorganisms 576
UF Germs
Microbes
Microscopic organisms
NT **Bacteria**
Protozoa
Viruses
RT **Bacteriology**
Microbiology
Microscopes
Microphotography 686.4
Use for materials on the photographing
of objects of any size upon a microscopic
or on a very small scale.
UF Microfilming
BT **Photography**
NT **Microforms**
Microprocessors 004.16
Use for materials on the central process-
ing units of microcomputers.
BT **Microcomputers**
Micropublications
USE **Microforms**
Microscope and microscopy
USE **Microscopes**
Microscopes 502.8; 578; 681
UF Analysis, Microscopic
Micrographic analysis
Microscope and microscopy
[Former heading]
Microscopic analysis
BT **Optical instruments**
NT **Electron microscopes**
RT **Metallography**
Microbiology
Microchemistry

Microscopes—*Continued*
    Microorganisms
Microscopic analysis
  USE **Metallography**
    Microscopes
Microscopic organisms
  USE **Microorganisms**
Microwave amplification by stimulated
        emission of radiation
  USE **Masers**
Microwave communication systems
     621.381
  BT **Intercommunication systems**
    Shortwave radio
    Telecommunication
  NT **Closed-circuit television**
Microwave cookery
  USE **Microwave cooking**
Microwave cooking 641.5
  UF Cooking, Microwave
    Microwave cookery *[Former
      heading]*
  BT **Cooking**
Microwaves 537.5
  BT **Electric waves**
    Electromagnetic waves
    Shortwave radio
  NT **Masers**
Mid-career changes
  USE **Career changes**
Middle age 305.24
  BT **Age**
    Life (Biology)
  NT **Age and employment**
    Aging
  RT **Longevity**
    Middle aged persons
Middle aged men (May subdiv. geog.)
     305.24
  BT **Middle aged persons**
Middle aged persons (May subdiv.
     geog.) **305.24**
  BT **Age**
  NT **Middle aged men**
    Middle aged women
  RT **Middle age**
Middle aged women (May subdiv.
     geog.)
  BT **Middle aged persons**
Middle Ages 909.07; 940.1
  UF Dark Ages

  BT **World history**
  NT **Chivalry**
    **Church history—600-1500,
      Middle Ages**
    Fifteenth century
    Fourteenth century
    Knights and knighthood
    Medieval architecture
    Medieval art
    Medieval literature
    Medieval philosophy
    Thirteenth century
  RT **Feudalism**
    Medieval civilization
    Renaissance
Middle Ages—History 909.07; 940.1
  UF History, Medieval
    Medieval history
  BT **World history**
  NT **Crusades**
    Holy Roman Empire
    Medieval civilization
    Monasticism
  RT **Europe—History—476-1492**
Middle Atlantic States
  USE **Atlantic States**
Middle child
  USE **Birth order**
Middle classes 305.5
  UF Bourgeoisie
    Middle-income class
  BT **Social classes**
Middle East 956
    Use for materials on the region consist-
    ing of northeastern Africa and Asia west
    of Afghanistan. Materials on several Arab-
    speaking countries are entered under **Arab
    countries.**
  UF East (Near East)
    Levant
    Near East
    Orient
  BT **Asia**
  NT **Arab countries**
    Israel
Middle East—Strategic aspects 956
  BT **Military geography**
    Strategy
Middle East War, 1991
  USE **Persian Gulf War, 1991**
Middle-income class
  USE **Middle classes**

Middle West 977
    UF   Central States
          Midwest
          North Central States
    BT   **Mississippi River Valley**
          United States
    RT   **Old Northwest**
Mideast War, 1991
    USE **Persian Gulf War, 1991**
Midget cars
    USE **Karts and karting**
Midwest
    USE **Middle West**
Midwifery
    USE **Midwives**
Midwives 618.2
    UF   Birth attendants
          Midwifery
          Nurse widwives
          Traditional birth attendants
    BT   **Childbirth**
          Natural childbirth
          Nurses
Migrant labor 331.5; 362.85
    Use for materials on casual or seasonal workers who move from place to place in search of employment. Materials on the movement of population within a country for permanent settlement are entered under **Internal migration.**
    UF   Labor, Migratory
          Migratory workers
    BT   **Employees**
          Labor
    RT   **Agricultural laborers**
Migration
    USE **Immigration and emigration**
Migration, Internal
    USE **Internal migration**
Migration of animals
    USE **Animals—Migration**
Migration of birds
    USE **Birds—Migration**
Migratory workers
    USE **Migrant labor**
Milch cattle
    USE **Dairy cattle**
Military aeronautics 358.4
    UF   Aeronautics, Military *[Former heading]*
          Aeronautics, Naval

          Air raid defensive measures
          Air warfare
          Naval aeronautics
    SA   names of wars with the subdivision *Aerial operations,* e.g. **World War, 1939-1945— Aerial operations;** to be added as needed
    BT   **Aeronautics**
          Military art and science
          War
    NT   **Aerial reconnaissance**
          Air bases
          Air defenses
          Air power
          Aircraft carriers
          Military airplanes
          Parachute troops
          World War, 1939-1945— Aerial operations
Military aid
    USE **Military assistance**
Military air bases
    USE **Air bases**
Military airplanes 623.7
    UF   Air warfare
          Airplanes, Military *[Former heading]*
          Airplanes, Naval
          Naval airplanes
    SA   types of military airplanes and specific makes of military airplanes, to be added as needed
    BT   **Military aeronautics**
    NT   **Bombers**
Military art and science 355
    UF   Army
          Fighting
          Military power
          Military science
    NT   **Armed forces**
          Armor
          Artillery
          Battles
          Biological warfare
          Camouflage (Military science)
          Chemical warfare
          Civil defense
          Fortification

Military art and science—*Continued*
    Guerrilla warfare
    Industrial mobilization
    Military aeronautics
    Military camps
    Militany hospitals
    Military transportation
    Ordnance
    Psychological warfare
    Signals and signaling
    Tactics
    Veterans
  RT **Armies**
    Drill and minor tactics
    Military personnel
    Naval art and science
    Strategy
    War
    Weapons
Military art and science—Study and
       teaching
  USE **Military education**
Military assistance 355
  UF Arms aid
    Arms sales
    Foreign aid program
    Military aid
    Military sales
    Mutual defense assistance pro-
      gram
  SA military assistance from par-
    ticular countries, e.g. **Amer-
    ican military assistance;** to
    be added as needed
  BT **Military policy**
  NT **American military assistance**
Military assistance, American
  USE **American military assistance**
Military atrocities
  USE names of wars with the subdi-
    vision *Atrocities,* e.g. **World
    War, 1939-1945—Atrocities;**
    and names of specific
    atrocities, to be added as
    needed
Military bases 355.7
  UF Army bases
    Army posts
    Military facilities
    Military installations

Military posts *[Former head-
    ing]*
    Military stations
Military biography
  USE names of armies and navies
    with the subdivision *Biog-
    raphy,* e.g. **United States.
    Army—Biography; United
    States. Navy—Biography;**
    etc., to be added as needed
Military camps 355.7
  UF Camps (Military) *[Former
    heading]*
  BT **Military art and science**
  NT **Concentration camps**
Military costume
  USE **Military uniforms**
Military courts
  USE **Courts martial and courts of
    inquiry**
Military crimas
  USE **Military offenses**
Military desertion (May subdiv. geog.)
       343; 355.1
  UF Army desertion
    Defectors, Military
    Desertion
    Desertion, Military *[Former
    heading]*
  SA names of wars with the subdi-
    vision *Desertions,* to be
    added as needed
  BT **Military offenses**
  NT **World War, 1939-1945—
    Desertions**
  RT **Draft resisters**
Military desertion—United States 343
  UF United States. Army—
    Desertions
Military draft
  USE **Draft**
Military drill
  USE **Drill and minor tactics**
Military education 355.007; 355.5
  UF Army schools
    Education, Military
    Military art and science—
    Study and teaching
    Military training
    Schools, Military

Military education—*Continued*
  SA names of military schools, e.g.
      **United States Military
      Academy**; to be added as
      needed
  BT **Education**
  NT **Military training camps**
Military engineering 623
  SA names of wars with the subdi-
      vision *Engineering and con-
      struction,* to be added as
      needed
  BT **Civil engineering
      Engineering**
  NT **World War, 1939-1945—
      Engineering and construc-
      tion**
  RT **Fortification**
Military facilities
  USE **Military bases**
Military forces
  USE **Armies
      Navies**
      and names of countries with
      the subdivision *Armed
      forces,* e.g. **United States—
      Armed forces**; to be added
      as needed
Military geography 355.4
  UF Geography, Military
      Maps, Military
      Military maps
  SA areas of the world with the
      subdivision *Strategic as-
      pects,* to be added as need-
      ed
  NT **Middle East—Strategic as-
      pects**
Military government (May subdiv.
      geog.) **341.6; 355.4**
  UF Government, Military
  BT **Military occupation
      Public administration**
Military health 613.6
  UF Hygiene, Military
      Soldiers—Hygiene
  SA names of wars with the subdi-
      vision *Health aspects* or
      Medical care, to be added
      as needed

  BT **Hygiene
      Sanitation**
  NT **World War, 1939-1945—
      Health aspects
      World War, 1939-1945—
      Medical care**
  RT **Armies—Medical care
      Military medicine**
Military history 355.009
  UF History, Military
      Wars
  SA names of countries with the
      subhead *Army* or the subdi-
      vision *Military history,* e.g.
      **United States. Army; Unit-
      ed States—Military history;**
      and names of wars, battles,
      sieges, etc., to be added as
      needed
  BT **History**
  NT **Battles
      Military policy
      United States. Army
      United States—Military histo-
      ry**
  RT **Naval history**
Military hospitals 355.7
  UF Field hospitals
      Hospitals, Military *[Former
      heading]*
      Veterans—Hospitals
  SA names of wars with the subdi-
      vision *Medical care,* to be
      added as needed
  BT **Hospitals
      Military art and science
      Military medicine**
  NT **World War, 1939-1945—
      Medical care**
  RT **Veterans**
Military installations
  USE **Military bases**
Military intervention
  USE **Intervention (International
      law)**
Military law 343
  UF Articles of war
      Law, Military
      War, Articles of
  BT **International law**

Military law—*Continued*
    Law
    War
  NT **Draft**
    Military offenses
    Veterans—Legal status, laws, etc.
  RT **Courts martial and courts of inquiry**
Military life
  USE **Military personnel**
    and names of countries with the subdivision *Armed forces* or the subheads *Army* or *Navy;* etc., with the subdivision *Military life,* e.g. **United States—Armed forces—Military life; United States. Army—Military life;** etc., to be added as needed
Military maps
  USE **Military geography**
Military medicine 616.9
  UF Field hospitals
    Medicine, Military *[Former heading]*
  SA names of wars with the subdivision *Medical care,* to be added as needed
  BT **Medicine**
  NT **Military hospitals**
    World War, 1939-1945—Medical care
  RT **Armies—Medical care**
    Military health
Military motorization
  USE **Military transportation**
Military music 781.5
  UF Music, Military
  SA names of wars with the subdivision *Songs,* to be added as needed
  BT **Music**
  NT **Band music**
    Marches (Music)
    World War, 1939-1945—Songs
Military occupation 341.6; 355.4
  UF Occupation, Military

    Occupied territory
  SA names of occupied countries with the subdivision *History—1940-1945, German occupation;* or *History—1945-, Allied occupation,* to be added as needed
  NT **Japan—History—1945-1952, Allied occupation**
    Military government
    Netherlands—History—1940-1945, German occupation
    World War, 1939-1945—Occupied territories
Military offenses (May subdiv. geog.) **343; 355.1**
  UF Crimes, Military
    Military crimes
    Naval offenses
    Offenses, Military
  SA names of military offenses, e.g. **Military desertion;** to be added as needed
  BT **Criminal law**
    Military law
  NT **Military desertion**
Military offenses—United States 343; 355.1
  UF United States. Army—Crimes and misdemeanors
    United States—Military offenses
Military pensions 331.25
  UF Naval pensions
    Pensions, Military *[Former heading]*
    Pensions, Naval
    War pensions
  BT **Pensions**
  RT **Veterans**
Military personnel (May subdiv. geog.) **355.3**
  UF Military life
    Servicemen
    Servicewomen
  SA names of countries with the subdivision *Armed forces* or the subheads *Army* or

---

Military personnel—*Continued*

    Navy, etc., with the subdivision *Military life,* e.g. **United States—Armed forces—Military life; United States. Army—Military life;** etc., to be added as needed

  BT **Armed forces**
       War

  NT **Admirals**
       Armies
       Generals
       Mercenary soldiers
       Navies
       Sailors
       Soldiers
       United States—Armed forces—Military life
       United States. Army—Military life

  RT **Military art and science**
       Veterans

Military personnel missing in action
  USE **Missing in action**

Military personnel—United States
  355.30973
  UF United States—Military personnel

Military policy 355
  UF Defense policy
  SA names of countries with the subdivision *Military policy,* e.g. **United States—Military policy;** etc.
  BT **Military history**
  NT **Military assistance**
       Military readiness
       United States—Military policy
  RT **National security**

Military posts
  USE **Military bases**

Military power
  USE **Armies**
       Military art and science
       Navies
       Sea power

Military preparedness
  USE **Military readiness**

Military readiness 355

    Use for materials on military strength, including military personnel, munitions, natural resources, and industrial war potential. Materials on the implements of war are entered under **Ordnance** or **Military weapons.** Materials on the industries producing them are entered under **Defense industries.** Materials on the armaments of a particular country are entered under the name of the country with the subdivision *Defenses,* e.g. **United States—Defenses;** etc.

  UF Armaments *[Former heading]*
       Defense readiness
       Military preparedness
       National defenses
  BT **Military policy**
  NT **Armed forces**
       Armies
       Navies
  RT **Arms control**
       Arms race
       Defense industries
       Industrial mobilization

Military sales
  USE **Defense industries**
       Military assistance

Military science
  USE **Military art and science**

Military service, Compulsory
  USE **Draft**

Military service, Compulsory—Draft resisters
  USE **Draft resisters**

Military service, Voluntary
  USE **Voluntary military service**

Military signaling
  USE **Signals and signaling**

Military stations
  USE **Military bases**

Military strategy
  USE **Strategy**

Military supplies industry
  USE **Defense industries**

Military tactics
  USE **Tactics**

Military tanks 358; 623.7
  UF Armored cars (Tanks)
       Cars, Armored (Tanks)
       Tanks (Military science) *[Former heading]*
  BT **Military vehicles**

Military training
  USE **Military education**
Military training camps 355.7
  UF Students' military training
        camps
      Training camps, Military
  BT **Military education**
Military training, Universal
  USE **Draft**
Military transportation 355.8
  UF Military motorization
      Motorization, Military
      Transportation, Military *[For-
        mer heading]*
  BT **Military art and science**
      Transportation
  NT **Military vehicles**
Military uniforms 355.1; 355.8
  UF Costume, Military
      Military costume
      Naval uniforms
      Uniforms, Military *[Former
        heading]*
      Uniforms, Naval
  BT **Costume**
      Tailoring
Military vehicles 355.8
  UF Army vehicles
      Vehicles, Military *[Former
        heading]*
  BT **Military transportation**
      Vehicles
  NT **Military tanks**
Military weapons 355.8; 623.4
  UF Armaments *[Former heading]*
      Arms sales
      Munitions *[Former heading]*
      Weapons and weaponry
  SA names of wars with the subdi-
        vision *Equipment and sup-
        plies,* to be added as
        needed
  BT **War**
      Weapons
  NT **Nuclear weapons**
      Space weapons
      **World War, 1939-1945—
        Equipment and supplies**
  RT **Arms race**
      Defense industries

Industrial mobilization
Ordnance
Militia
  USE names of countries and states
        with the subdivision *Mili-
        tia,* e.g. **United States—
        Militia;** to be added as
        needed
Milk 637; 641.3
  BT **Animal food**
      Dairy products
      Dairying
      Food
  NT **Dried milk**
Milk—Analysis 637; 641.3
Milk supply 338.1
  BT **Food adulteration and inspec-
        tion**
      Public health
Mill and factory buildings
  USE **Factories**
Millenarianism
  USE **Millennium**
Millennialism
  USE **Millennium**
Millennium 236
  UF Millenarianism
      Millennialism
  BT **Eschatology**
  RT **Second Advent**
Millikan rays
  USE **Cosmic rays**
Millinery 646.5; 687
  BT **Costume**
  RT **Hats**
Milling (Flour)
  USE **Flour mills**
Millionaires 920
  BT **Wealth**
  RT **Capitalists and financiers**
Mills 670.42
  UF Mills and millwork *[Former
        heading]*
  SA types of mills, to be added as
        needed
  BT **Manufactures**
      Technology
  NT **Flour mills**
  RT **Factories**
      Machinery

BT = Broader Term   NT = Narrower Term   RT = Related Term   SA = See Also   UF = Used For

Mills and millwork
  USE **Mills**
Mime 792.3
  BT **Acting**
  RT **Pantomimes**
Mind
  USE **Intellect**
       Psychology
Mind and body 128; 150
  UF Body and mind
       Mind cure
  BT **Brain**
       Medicine
       Parapsychology
       Philosophy
  NT **Abnormal psychology**
       Biofeedback training
       Consciousness
       Dreams
       Mental suggestion
       Psychosomatic medicine
       Sleep
       Spiritual healing
       Temperament
  RT **Holistic medicine**
       Hypnotism
       Mental healing
       Mental health
       Phrenology
       Psychoanalysis
       Psychophysiology
       Subconsciousness
Mind control
  USE **Brainwashing**
Mind cure
  USE **Christian Science**
       Mental healing
       Mind and body
Mind reading
  USE **Telepathy**
Mine surveying 622.028
  BT **Mining engineering**
       Prospecting
       Surveying
Mineral industries
  USE **Mines and mineral resources**
Mineral lands
  USE **Mines and mineral resources**
Mineral resources
  USE **Mines and mineral resources**

Mineral resources, Marine
  USE **Marine mineral resources**
Mineralogy 549
  UF Minerals
  SA names of minerals, e.g.
       Quartz; to be added as
       needed
  BT **Geology**
       Natural history
       Ores
       Rocks
  NT **Gems**
       Phosphorescence
       Precious stones
       Quartz
  RT **Crystallography**
       Mines and mineral resources
       Petrology
Minerals
  USE **Mineralogy**
       Mines and mineral resources
       and names of minerals, e.g.
       Quartz; to be added as
       needed
Miners 622.092; 920
  SA types of miners, to be added
       as needed
  BT **Labor**
  NT **Coal miners**
Mines and mineral resources (May sub-
       div. geog.) **333.8; 338.2**
       Use for general descriptive materials
       and for technical and economic materials
       on mining, metallurgy, and minerals of
       economic value.
  UF Mineral industries
       Mineral lands
       Mineral resources
       Minerals
       Mining
  SA types of mines and mining,
       e.g. **Coal mines and mining;**
       to be added as needed
  BT **Economic geology**
       Natural resources
       Ores
       Raw materials
  NT **Coal mines and mining**
       Gold mines and mining
       Marine mineral resources

BT = Broader Term   NT = Narrower Term   RT = Related Term   SA = See Also   UF = Used For

Mines and mineral resources—
Continued
> **Mining engineering**
> **Precious metals**
> **Prospecting**
> **Silver mines and mining**
- RT **Mineralogy**

Mines and mineral resources—United States 333.8; 338.2
- UF United States—Mines and mineral resources

Miniature computers
- USE **Minicomputers**

Miniature gardens 635.9
- UF Gardens, Miniature *[Former heading]*
  Tray gardens
- BT **Container gardening**
  Indoor gardening
- RT **Terrariums**

Miniature objects
- USE names of miniature objects, e.g. **Dollhouses; Miniature gardens; Models and model making; Toys;** etc.; and names of objects with the subdivision *Models,* e.g. **Airplanes—Models;** to be added as needed

Miniature painting 751.7; 757
- UF Miniatures (Portraits)
- BT **Painting**
- RT **Portrait painting**

Miniatures (Illumination of books and manuscripts)
- USE **Illumination of books and manuscripts**

Miniatures (Portraits)
- USE **Miniature painting**

Minibikes 629.227
- BT **Bicycles**
  Motorcycles

Minicomputers 004.16; 621.39
Use for materials on computers larger than microcomputers but smaller than mainframes.
- UF Miniature computers
- BT **Computers**

Minimum drinking age
- USE **Drinking age**

Minimum wage 331.2
- UF Wages—Minimum wage *[Former heading]*
- BT **Wages**

Mining
- USE **Mines and mineral resources**
  Mining engineering

Mining, Electric
- USE **Electricity in mining**

Mining engineering 622
- UF Mining
- BT **Civil engineering**
  Coal mines and mining
  Engineering
  Mines and mineral resources
- NT **Boring**
  Mine surveying
  Ocean mining
- RT **Electricity in mining**

Mining, Ocean
- USE **Ocean mining**

Ministers (Diplomatic agents)
- USE **Diplomats**

Ministers of state
- USE **Cabinet officers**

Ministers of the gospel
- USE **Clergy**

Ministry 253
- UF Clergy—Office
- SA ministries of particular religious, e.g. **Christian ministry;** to be added as needed
- BT **Church work**
  Clergy
  Pastoral work
- NT **Christian ministry**

Ministry, Christian
- USE **Christian ministry**

Minor arts
- USE **Decorative arts**

Minor planets
- USE **Asteroids**

Minor tactics
- USE **Drill and minor tactics**

Minorites
- USE **Franciscans**

Minorities 305.8; 323.1
- UF Minority groups
- SA names of peoples living within a country, state, or city

---

BT = Broader Term   NT = Narrower Term   RT = Related Term   SA = See Also   UF = Used For

Minorities—*Continued*
dominated by another nationality, e.g. **Mexican Americans; Mexicans— United States;** etc.; names of countries with the subdivisions *Foreign population* and *Race relations;* and minorities in various industries and fields of endeavor, e.g., **Minorities in broadcasting;** to be added as needed

BT **Ethnic groups**
NT **Mexican Americans**
　　 Mexicans—United States
　　 Minorities in broadcasting
　　 Minority business enterprises
　　 Race relations
　　 United States—Foreign population
　　 United States—Race relations
RT **Discrimination**
　　 Ethnic relations
　　 Nationalism
　　 Segregation

Minorities in broadcasting 384.5; 791.4
UF Minority groups in broadcasting
BT **Broadcasting**
　　 Minorities

Minorities in engineering 620
UF Minority groups in engineering
BT **Engineering**

Minority business enterprises 338.6
UF Business enterprises, Minority
　　 Minority businesses
　　 Minority-owned business enterprises
BT **Business enterprises**
　　 Minorities
NT **Federal aid to minority business enterprises**

Minority business enterprises—Federal aid
USE **Federal aid to minority business enterprises**

Minority businesses
USE **Minority business enterprises**

Minority groups
USE **Minorities**

Minority groups in broadcasting
USE **Minorities in broadcasting**

Minority groups in engineering
USE **Minorities in engineering**

Minority-owned business enterprises
USE **Minority business enterprises**

Minstrels 791.092; 920
BT **Poets**
NT **Troubadours**

Mints 332.4
BT **Money**
RT **Coinage**

Miracle plays
USE **Mysteries and miracle plays**

Miracles 231.7
UF Bible—Miracles
　　 Divine healing
BT **Apparitions**
　　 Spiritual healing
RT **Shrines**
　　 Supernatural

Miracles—Christianity 231.7
UF Bible. N.T.—Miracles
BT **Christianity**
　　 Church history

Mirrors 748.8
UF Looking glasses
BT **Furniture**

MIS (Information systems)
USE **Management information systems**

Miscarriage 618.3
UF Abortion, Spontaneous
　　 Fetal death
　　 Spontaneous abortion
BT **Pregnancy**

Miscellanea
USE subjects with the subdivision *Miscellanea,* e.g. **Medicine—Miscellanea;** to be added as needed

Miscellaneous facts
USE **Curiosities and wonders**

Misconduct in office 351.9; 364.1
UF Malfeasance in office
　　 Official misconduct
SA names of specific incidents and offenses, to be added as needed

---

BT = Broader Term　　NT = Narrower Term　　RT = Related Term　　SA = See Also　　UF = Used For

Misconduct in office—*Continued*
  BT **Conflict of interests**
      Criminal law
  NT **Police corruption**
      Watergate Affair, 1972-1974
  RT **Political corruption**
Misdemeanors (Law)
  USE **Criminal law**
Misleading advertising
  USE **Deceptive advertising**
Misrepresentation in advertising
  USE **Deceptive advertising**
Missiles, Ballistic
  USE **Ballistic missiles**
Missiles, Guided
  USE **Guided missiles**
Missing children 362.82; 363.2
  UF Lost children
  BT **Children**
      Criminal investigation
      Missing persons
  NT **Runaway children**
Missing in action
  UF M.I.A.'s
      MIA's
      Military personnel missing in
         action
  SA names of wars with the subdi-
      vision *Missing in action,* to
      be added as needed
  BT **Prisoners of war**
      Soldiers
  NT **World War, 1939-1945—**
      Missing in action
Missing persons (May subdiv. geog.)
    363.2
  BT **Criminal investigation**
  NT **Missing children**
      Runaway adults
      Runaway teenagers
Missionaries, Christian
  USE **Christian missionaries**
Missions, Christian
  USE **Christian missions**
Missions, Indian
  USE **Indians of North America—**
      Christian missions
Missions, Medical
  USE **Medical missions**
Mississippi River Valley 977
  UF Mississippi Valley

  BT **United States**
  NT **Middle West**
Mississippi River Valley—History 977
  UF New France—History
Mississippi Valley
  USE **Mississippi River Valley**
Mistakes
  USE **Errors**
Mixed marriage
  USE **Interfaith marriage**
      Intermarriage
      Interracial marriage
Mnemonics
  USE **Memory**
Mobile home living 643; 728.7
  BT **Home economics**
      Mobile homes
  NT **Van life**
Mobile home parks 647
  BT **Trailer parks**
Mobile homes 643; 728.7
    Use for materials on stationary trans-
    portable structures designed for year-
    round living. Materials on structures
    mounted upon a truck or towed by a
    truck or automobile for the purpose of
    temporary dwelling or cargo hauling are
    entered under **Travel trailers and campers.**
  UF Homes, Mobile
      House trailers
      Trailers, Home
  BT **Housing**
  NT **Mobile home living**
  RT **Travel trailers and campers**
Mobiles (Sculpture) 731
  BT **Kinetic sculpture**
      Sculpture
Mobilization, Industrial
  USE **Industrial mobilization**
Mobs
  USE **Crowds**
      Riots
Mock epic literature
  USE **Mock-heroic literature**
Mock-heroic literature 800
    May be used for individual works, col-
    lections, or materials about mock-heroic
    literature.
  UF Comic epic literature
      Mock epic literature
  BT **Literature**
      Wit and humor

BT = Broader Term   NT = Narrower Term   RT = Related Term   SA = See Also   UF = Used For

Mock-heroic literature—*Continued*
   RT   **Epic literature**
        Humorous fiction
Model airplanes
   USE   **Airplanes—Models**
Model cars
   USE   **Automobiles—Models**
Model making
   USE   **Models and model making**
Modeling 731.4; 738.1
   UF   Clay modeling
   BT   **Clay**
        Sculpture
   NT   **Soap sculpture**
   RT   **Sculpture—Technique**
Modelmaking
   USE   **Models and model making**
Models
   USE   **Models and model making**
        and names of objects with the
        subdivision *Models,* e.g.
        Airplanes—Models; to be
        added as needed
Models and model making 688
   UF   Model making
        Modelmaking
        Models
        Models and modelmaking
   SA   names of objects with the
        subdivision *Models,* to be
        added as needed
   NT   **Airplanes—Models**
        Pattern making
        Ships—Models
Models and modelmaking
   USE   **Models and model making**
Models, Artists'
   USE   **Artists' models**
Models, Fashion
   USE   **Fashion models**
Models, Mathematical
   USE   **Mathematical models**
Models, Mechanical
   USE   **Machinery—Models**
Models (Persons)
   USE   **Artists' models**
        Fashion models
Modern architecture 724
   UF   Architecture, Modern *[Former
        heading]*

   BT   **Architecture**
**Modern architecture—1600-1799 (17th
      and 18th centuries) 724**
   UF   Architecture, Modern—
        1600-1799 (17th and 18th
        centuries) *[Former heading]*
**Modern architecture—1800-1899 (19th
      century) 724**
   UF   Architecture, Modern—
        1800-1899 (19th century)
        [Former heading]
**Modern architecture—1900-1999 (20th
      century) 724**
   UF   Architecture, Modern—
        1900-1999 (20th century)
        [Former heading]
Modern art 709.03; 709.04
   UF   Art, Modern *[Former heading]*
   BT   **Art**
   RT   **Modernism (Arts)**
**Modern art—1800-1899 (19th century)
      709.03**
   UF   Art, Modern—1800-1899
        (19th century) *[Former
        heading]*
   BT   **Art**
   NT   **Impressionism (Art)**
        Postimpressionism (Art)
**Modern art—1900-1999 (20th century)
      709.04**
   UF   Art, Modern—1900-1999
        (20th century) *[Former
        heading]*
        Contemporary art
   SA   types of modern art, to be
        added as needed
   BT   **Art**
   NT   **Abstract art**
        Computer art
        Earthworks (Art)
        Kinetic art
        Performance art
        Postimpressionism (Art)
        Video art
Modern church history
   USE   **Church history—1500- , Mod-
        ern period**
Modern civilization 306.09; 909
     Use for materials covering the period af-
   ter 1453.

Modern civilization—*Continued*
UF Civilization, Modern *[Former heading]*
BT **Civilization**
NT **Renaissance**
RT **Modern history**
Modern civilization—1950- 306.09; 909.82
UF Civilization, Modern—1950- *[Former heading]*
Modern dance 792.8
UF Interpretive dance
BT **Dancing**
Modern Greek language 489
May be subdivided like **English language.**
UF Greek language, Modern *[Former heading]*
Romaic language
BT **Modern languages**
RT **Greek language**
Modern Greek literature 889
May use same subdivisions and names of literary forms as for **English literature.**
UF Greek literature, Modern *[Former heading]*
Neo-Greek literature
Romaic literature
BT **Literature**
Modern history 909.08
Use for materials covering the period after 1453.
UF History, Modern *[Former heading]*
BT **History**
World history
NT **Eighteenth century**
Reformation
Renaissance
Seventeenth century
RT **Modern civilization**
Modern history—1800-1899 (19th century) 909.81
UF History, Modern—1800-1899 (19th century) *[Former heading]*
NT **Nineteenth century**
Modern history—1900-1999 (20th century) 909.82
UF History, Modern—1990-1999 (20th century) *[Former heading]*

NT **Italo-Ethiopian War, 1935-1936**
Korean War, 1950-1953
Twentieth century
World War, 1914-1918
World War, 1939-1945
Modern history—1945- 909.82
UF History, Modern—1945- *[Former heading]*
Modern history—Study and teaching 907
UF History, Modern—Study and teaching *[Former heading]*
NT **Current events**
Modern languages 410
Use for materials dealing collectively with living literary languages. May be subdivided like **English language.**
UF Languages, Modern *[Former heading]*
BT **Language and languages**
NT **English language**
German language
Modern Greek language
Romance languages
Russian language
Scandinavian languages
Modern languages—Conversations and phrases 418
UF Conversation in foreign languages
Foreign language phrases
Languages, Modern—Conversations and phrases *[Former heading]*
Modern languages—Study and teaching 418
RT **Language laboratories**
Modern painting 759.06
UF Painting, Modern *[Former heading]*
BT **Painting**
Modern painting—1800-1899 (19th century) 759.05
UF Painting, Modern—1800-1899 (19th century) *[Former heading]*

Modern painting—1900-1999 (20th century) 759.06
UF   Painting, Modern—1900-1999 (20th century) *[Former heading]*
Modern philosophy 190
UF   Philosophy, Modern *[Former heading]*
BT   **Philosophy**
NT   **Enlightenment**
       Evolution
       Existentialism
       Phenomenology
Modern sculpture 735
UF   Sculpture, Modern *[Former heading]*
BT   **Sculpture**
Modern sculpture—1900-1999 (20th century) 735
UF   Sculpture, Modern—1900-1999 (20th century) *[Former heading]*
Modernism
USE   **Modernism (Arts)**
         Modernism (Theology)
Modernism (Aesthetics)
USE   **Modernism (Arts)**
Modernism (Art)
USE   **Modernism (Arts)**
Modernism (Arts) 700.1
   Use for materials on the philosophy and practice of the arts since the nineteenth century characterized by a self-conscious break with the past and a search for new forms of expression.
UF   Art, Modern
       Modernism
       Modernism (Aesthetics)
       Modernism (Art)
       Modernism (Literature)
BT   **Aesthetics**
RT   **Literature**
       Modern art
       Postmodernism
Modernism (Literature)
USE   **Modernism (Arts)**
Modernism (Theology) 230; 273
   Use for materials on the movement in the Christian churches that applies modern critical methods to biblical study and the history of dogma, and emphasizes the spiritual and ethical side of religion over historic dogmas and creeds.

UF   Modernism *[Former heading]*
       Modernist-fundamentalist controversy
BT   **Theology**
RT   **Fundamentalism**
Modernist-fundamentalist controversy
USE   **Fundamentalism**
         Modernism (Theology)
Modernization 303.44
   Use for materials on the process of change in a society or social institution in which the most recent styles, ideas, or usages are acquired or adapted.
UF   Development
BT   **Social change**
RT   **Industrialization**
Mohammedan art
USE   **Islamic art**
Mohammedanism
USE   **Islam**
Mohammedans
USE   **Muslims**
Mold (Fungi)
USE   **Molds (Fungi)**
Molding (Metal)
USE   **Founding**
Molds (Botany)
USE   **Molds (Fungi)**
Molds (Fungi) 589.2
UF   Mold (Fungi)
       Molds (Botany) *[Former heading]*
BT   **Fungi**
Molecular biochemistry
USE   **Molecular biology**
Molecular biology 574.8
UF   Biology, Molecular
       Molecular biochemistry
       Molecular biophysics
BT   **Biochemistry**
       Biophysics
NT   **Genetic code**
Molecular biophysics
USE   **Molecular biology**
Molecular cloning 174; 574.87
UF   Cloning, Molecular
       DNA cloning
BT   **Clones and cloning**
       Genetic engineering
Molecular physiology
USE   **Biophysics**

Molecules 539; 541.2
  BT **Physical chemistry**
Molesting of children
  USE **Child sexual abuse**
Mollusks 594
    Use for materials on mollusks and for systematic and comprehensive materials on shells. Popular materials on shells and shell collecting are entered under **Shells.**
  BT **Invertebrates**
       Shellfish
  NT **Shells**
Monarchs
  USE **Kings, queens, rulers, etc.**
Monarchy 321; 321.8
  UF Sovereigns
  BT **Constitutional history**
       Constitutional law
       Executive power
       Political science
  NT **Kings, queens, rulers, etc.**
Monasteries (May subdiv. geog.) 726
  UF Cloisters
  RT **Abbeys**
       Convents
       Monasticism
Monastic orders
  USE **Religious orders**
Monasticism 255; 271
  BT **Medieval civilization**
       Middle Ages—History
  NT **Religious orders**
  RT **Monasteries**
       Religious life
Monetary policy (May subdiv. geog.) 332.4
  UF Bimetallism
       Currency devaluation
       Devaluation of currency
       Free coinage
  BT **Economic policy**
  RT **Finance**
       Fiscal policy
       Inflation (Finance)
       Money
Monetary policy—United States 332.4
  UF United States—Monetary policy
Money 332.4
    Use for materials on currency as a medium of exchange or measure of value.

  UF Bullion
       Currency
       Specie
       Standard of value
  BT **Economics**
       Exchange
       Finance
  NT **Barter**
       Children's allowances
       Coins
       Counterfeits and counterfeiting
       Credit
       Foreign exchange
       Mints
       Paper money
  RT **Banks and banking**
       Coinage
       Gold
       Monetary policy
       Silver
       Wealth
Money, Paper
  USE **Paper money**
Money raising
  USE **Fund raising**
Moneymaking projects for children 332.024; 650.1
  UF Children's moneymaking projects
  BT **Children—Employment**
  RT **Children's allowances**
Monkeys 599.8
  BT **Primates**
Monkeys—Behavior 599.8
  UF Monkeys—Habits and behavior *[Former heading]*
  BT **Animal behavior**
Monkeys—Habits and behavior
  USE **Monkeys—Behavior**
Monks 255; 271
  BT **Religious orders for men**
Monograms 745.6
  UF Ciphers (Lettering)
  BT **Alphabets**
       Decoration and ornament
       Lettering
  RT **Initials**

Monologues 808.85; 815, etc.

May be used for individual works, collections, or materials about monologues. Monologues with incidental musical background and musical works in which spoken language is an integral part are entered under **Monologues with music.**

UF   Declamations

       Narrations

BT   **Recitations**

RT   **Monologues with music**

Monologues with music 808.85; 815, etc.; 782.2

Use for musical scores and for materials about monologues with incidental musical background and musical works in which spoken language is an integral part. Individual monologues without music, collections, and materials about monologues without music are entered under **Monologues.**

UF   Declamations, Musical

       Narration with music

       Recitations with music

BT   **Recitations**

RT   **Monologues**

Monopolies 338.8

BT   **Commerce**

       Economics

NT   **Railroads—Consolidation**

RT   **Competition**

       Corporation law

       Industrial trusts

       Restraint of trade

Monorail railroads 385; 625.1

UF   Railroads, Single rail

       Single rail railroads

BT   **Railroads**

Monroe Doctrine 327.73

BT   **International relations**

       Intervention (International law)

       Pan-Americanism

       United States—Foreign relations

Monster films

USE   **Horror films**

Monsters 001.9; 398.2

Use for materials on legendary animals combining features of human and animal form or having the forms of various animals in combination. Materials on human abnormalities are entered under either **Birth defects** or **Growth disorders.**

BT   **Animals—Folklore**

       Curiosities and wonders

       Folklore

       Mythology

NT   **Dragons**

       Giants

       Sasquatch

       Yeti

Montessori method of education 371.3

BT   **Elementary education**

       Kindergarten

       Teaching

Months 529

SA   names of the months, to be added as needed

BT   **Calendars**

       Chronology

Monumental brasses

USE   **Brasses**

Monuments (May subdiv. geog.) **725**

UF   Statues

BT   **Architecture**

       Sculpture

NT   **Historic buildings**

       National monuments

       Obelisks

       Pyramids

       Tombs

Monuments, National

USE   **National monuments**

Monuments, Natural

USE   **Natural monuments**

Moon 523.3

BT   **Astronomy**

       Solar system

NT   **Tides**

Moon bases

USE   **Lunar bases**

Moon cars 629.2

UF   Lunar cars

       Lunar rover vehicles

       Lunar surface vehicles

BT   **Vehicles**

Moon—Eclipses

USE   **Lunar eclipses**

Moon—Exploration 629.45

UF   Lunar exploration

BT   **Space flight to the moon**

Moon—Geology

USE   **Lunar geology**

Moon (in religion, folklore, etc.)

USE   **Moon worship**

Moon—Maps 523.3022
  BT Maps
Moon—Photographs 523.3; 778.3
  BT Lunar photography
Moon—Photographs from space 523.2;
      778.3
  BT Space photography
Moon photography
  USE Lunar photography
Moon probes
  USE Lunar probes
Moon rocks
  USE Lunar petrology
Moon soil
  USE Lunar soil
Moon—Surface 523.3
  UF Lunar surface
  RT Lunar soil
Moon, Voyages to
  USE Space flight to the moon
Moon worship 291.2
  UF Moon (in religion, folklore,
        etc.)
  BT Religion
Moonlighting
  USE Supplementary employment
Moorish architecture
  USE Islamic architecture
Moors 305.892; 909
  BT Arabs
Moral and philosophic stories
  USE Didactic fiction
        Fables
        Parables
Moral and religious aspects
  USE subjects with the subdivision
        Moral and religious aspects,
        e.g. Birth control—Moral
        and religious aspects; to be
        added as needed
Moral conditions 301; 306; 900
  UF Morals
  SA names of countries, cities,
        etc., with the subdivision
        Moral conditions, to be
        added as needed
  BT Social conditions
  NT United States—Moral condi-
        tions
Moral education 370.11
  UF Character education

Education, Character
Education, Ethical
Education, Moral
Ethical education
  BT Education
      Ethics
  RT Religious education
Moral philosophy
  USE Ethics
Moral theology, Christian
  USE Christian ethics
Morale 152.4
  SA types of morale, e.g. Employee
        morale; to be added as
        needed
  BT Courage
  NT Employee morale
      Psychological warfare
Moralities
  USE Morality plays
Morality
  USE Ethics
Morality plays 792.1; 808.82; 812, etc.
    May be used for individual works, col-
    lections, or materials about plays in which
    the chief characters are personifications of
    abstract qualities.
  UF Moralities
  BT Drama
      English drama
      Religious drama
      Theater
  RT Mysteries and miracle plays
Morality stories
  USE Didactic fiction
Morality tales
  USE Parables
Morals
  USE Conduct of life
      Ethics
      Human behavior
      Moral conditions
Moravians 284
  UF United Brethren
  BT Christian sects
Mormon Church
  USE Church of Jesus Christ of
        Latter-day Saints
Mormons 289.3
  RT Church of Jesus Christ of
        Latter-day Saints

BT = Broader Term   NT = Narrower Term   RT = Related Term   SA = See Also   UF = Used For

Morphine 362.29; 615
BT   Narcotics
NT   Heroin
RT   Opium
Morphology
USE   Anatomy
       Animals—Anatomy
       Biology
       Comparative anatomy
       Plants—Anatomy
Morse code
USE   Cipher and telegraph codes
Mortality 304.6
UF   Burial statistics
     Death rate
     Mortuary statistics
BT   Population
     Vital statistics
RT   Death
Mortar 666; 691
BT   Adhesives
     Plaster and plastering
Mortgage loans
USE   Mortgages
Mortgages 332.63; 332.7
UF   Chattel mortgages
     Home loans
     Housing loans
     Mortgage loans
BT   Commercial law
     Contracts
     Credit
     Investments
     Loans
     Personal loans
     Real estate
     Securities
NT   Agricultural credit
Morticians
USE   Undertakers and undertaking
Mortuary customs
USE   Cremation
     Funeral rites and ceremonies
Mortuary statistics
USE   Mortality
     Vital statistics
Mosaics 729; 738.5; 748.5
BT   Decoration and ornament
     Decorative arts
RT   Mural painting and decoration

Moslem countries
USE   Islamic countries
Moslemism
USE   Islam
Moslems
USE   Muslims
Mosques 726
BT   Church architecture
     Islamic architecture
     Temples
RT   Asian architecture
Mosquitoes 595.77
UF   Diptera
BT   Insects as carriers of disease
Mosquitoes—Control 595.77; 614.4
BT   Pest control
Mosses 588
BT   Plants
Motels
USE   Hotels and motels
Mother and child 306.874
UF   Child and mother
     Mother-child relationship
BT   Parent and child
NT   Mothers and daughters
     Mothers and sons
Mother-child relationship
USE   Mother and child
Mothers 306.874
UF   Maternity
BT   Family
     Homemakers
     Women
NT   Surrogate mothers
     Teenage mothers
     Unmarried mothers
Mothers and daughters 305.4; 306.874
UF   Daughters and mothers
BT   Girls
     Mother and child
Mothers and sons 306.874
UF   Sons and mothers
BT   Boys
     Mother and child
Mothers' pensions 362.82
BT   Pensions
RT   Child welfare
Mothers, Single parent
USE   Single parent family
Moths 595.78
UF   Cocoons

BT = Broader Term   NT = Narrower Term   RT = Related Term   SA = See Also   UF = Used For

Moths—*Continued*
> Lepidoptera
- BT **Insects**
- NT **Caterpillars**
  Silkworms
- RT **Butterflies**

Motion 531
- UF Kinetics
- BT **Dynamics**
- NT **Mechanical movements**
  Speed
- RT **Force and energy**
  Kinematics
  Mechanics

Motion picture actors
- USE **Actors**

Motion picture adaptations
- USE **Film adaptations**

Motion picture cameras 778.5
- UF Movie cameras
- BT **Cameras**
  Cinematography
- RT **Amateur films**

Motion picture cartoons
- USE **Animated films**

Motion picture direction
- USE **Motion pictures—Production and direction**

Motion picture festivals
- USE **Film festivals**

Motion picture industry (May subdiv. geog.) **384; 791.43**
- UF Film industry (Motion pictures)
- NT **African Americans in the motion picture industry**
  Blacks in the motion picture industry
  Motion picture producers and directors
  Women in the motion picture industry
- RT **Motion pictures**

Motion picture musicals
- USE **Musical films**

Motion picture photography
- USE **Cinematography**

Motion picture plays 808.82; 812, etc.
> May be used for individual works, collections, or materials about motion picture plays.

- UF Film scripts
  Filmscripts
  Photoplays
  Scenarios
  Screen plays
  Screenplays
- BT **Drama**

Motion picture plays—Technique 808.2
- UF Motion pictures—Play writing
  Play writing
  Playwriting
- BT **Drama—Technique**

Motion picture posters
- USE **Film posters**

Motion picture producers and directors 791.43; 920
- UF Producers and directors
- BT **Motion picture industry**

Motion picture production
- USE **Motion pictures—Production and direction**

Motion picture projectors
- USE **Projectors**

Motion picture serials 791.43
> May be used for individual works, collections, or materials about motion picture serials.

- BT **Motion pictures**

Motion pictures (May subdiv. geog.) **384; 791.43**
> Use for general materials on motion pictures themselves, including motion pictures as an art form, copyrighting, distribution, editing, plots, production, etc. Materials on the technical aspects of making motion pictures and their projection onto a screen are entered under **Cinematography.** For materials on motion pictures produced by the motion picture industry of an individual country or on the motion pictures shown in a country, subdivide geographically, e.g. **Motion pictures—United States.**

- UF Cinema
  Filmography
  Films
  Movies
  Moving pictures
  Talking pictures
- SA types of motion pictures, e.g. **Documentary films; Horror films;** etc.; motion pictures and particular groups of persons, e.g., **Motion pic-**

Motion pictures—*Continued*

tures and children; motion
pictures as used in various
industries or fields of endeavor, e.g. **Motion pictures
in education;** and names of
individual motion pictures,
to be added as needed

BT   **Amusements**
    Audiovisual materials
    Mass media

NT   **Adventure films**
    **African Americans in motion
      pictures**
    Amateur films
    Animals in motion pictures
    Animated films
    Bible films
    Biographical films
    Blacks in motion pictures
    Comedy films
    Documentary films
    Epic films
    Erotic films
    Experimental films
    Fantasy films
    Film adaptations
    Film noir
    Gangster films
    Horror films
    Legal drama (Films)
    Libraries and motion pictures
    Medical drama (Films)
    Motion picture serials
    Motion pictures and children
    Motion pictures in education
    Musical films
    Mystery films
    Science fiction films
    Sherlock Holmes films
    Short films
    Silent films
    Sports drama (Films)
    Spy films
    Star Wars films
    Television movies
    Three Stooges films
    Vampire films
    War films
    Western films

    Women in motion pictures
    **World War, 1939-1945—
      Motion pictures and the
      war**

RT   **Motion picture industry**

Motion pictures, Amateur
USE   **Amateur films**

Motion pictures, American
USE   **Motion pictures—United
      States**

**Motion pictures and children 305.23;
    649; 791.43**

Use for materials on the effect of motion pictures on children and youth.

UF   Children and motion pictures
BT   **Children**
    Motion pictures

Motion pictures and libraries
USE   **Libraries and motion pictures**

**Motion pictures—Biography 791.43092;
    920**

Motion pictures—Catalogs 016.79143

Motion pictures—Censorship 791.43
BT   **Censorship**

Motion pictures, Experimental
USE   **Experimental films**

**Motion pictures in education 371.3;
    791.43**

UF   Educational films
BT   **Audiovisual education**
    Motion pictures
    Teaching—Aids and devices
NT   **Libraries and motion pictures**

**Motion pictures—Moral and religious
    aspects 791.43**

Motion pictures—Play writing
USE   **Motion picture plays—
      Technique**

Motion pictures—Posters
USE   **Film posters**

**Motion pictures—Production and direc-
    tion 384; 791.43**

UF   Direction (Motion pictures)
    Film direction
    Film production
    Filmmaking
    Motion picture direction
    Motion picture production

Motion pictures—Television adapta-
    tions
USE   **Television adaptations**

Motion pictures—United States
791.430973

Use for materials on motion pictures produced by the motion picture industry of the United States or on motion pictures shown in the United States.

UF   American films
American motion pictures
Motion pictures, American

Motion study 658.5

BT   **Factory management**
Industrial efficiency
Job analysis
Personnel management
Production standards

RT   **Time study**

Motivation (Psychology) 153.8

UF   Incentive (Psychology)

BT   **Psychology**

NT   **Burn out (Psychology)**
Wishes

Motor boats
USE   **Motorboats**

Motor buses
USE   **Buses**

Motor cars
USE   **Automobiles**

Motor coordination
USE   **Movement education**

Motor courts
USE   **Hotels and motels**

Motor cycles
USE   **Motorcycles**

Motor trucks
USE   **Trucks**

Motor vehicle industry
USE   **Automobile industry**

Motorboats 623.8

UF   Motor boats
Outboard motorboats
Power boats

BT   **Boats and boating**

Motorboats—Models 623.8

BT   **Machinery—Models**

Motorcycles 629.227

UF   Cycles, Motor
Motor cycles

SA   specific makes and models of motorcycles, to be added as needed

BT   **Bicycles**

NT   **Minibikes**

RT   **Motorcycling**

Motorcycling 796.7

BT   **Cycling**

RT   **Motorcycles**

Motoring
USE   **Automobile travel**

Motorization, Military
USE   **Military transportation**

Motors
USE   **Electric motors**
Engines

Motorways
USE   **Express highways**

Mottoes 808.88; 818.008, etc.; 929.8

May be used for collections of mottoes and for materials about mottoes.

UF   Emblems

BT   **Heraldry**

RT   **National emblems**

Moulding (Metal)
USE   **Founding**

Mound-builders
USE   **Mounds and mound builders**

Mounds and mound builders 930.1;
970.004

UF   Barrows
Graves
Mound-builders

BT   **Archeology**
Burial
Indians of North America
Indians of North America—
Antiquities
Tombs

RT   **Excavations (Archeology)**

Mountain animals 591.909

UF   Alpine animals *[Former heading]*
Alpine fauna
Mountain fauna

BT   **Animals**
Wildlife

Mountain bicycles
USE   **Mountain bikes**

Mountain bikes 629.227

UF   All terrain bicycles
Bicylces, All terrain
Bikes, Mountain

Mountain bikes—*Continued*
    Mountain bicycles
  BT **All terrain vehicles**
      Bicycles
Mountain climbing
  USE **Mountaineering**
Mountain fauna
  USE **Mountain animals**
Mountain flora
  USE **Mountain plants**
Mountain life 307.72
  BT **Country life**
Mountain plants 581.909; 635.9
  UF Alpine flora
      Alpine plants *[Former heading]*
      Mountain flora
  BT **Plants**
      Plants—Ecology
Mountaineering 796.5
  UF Mountain climbing
      Rock climbing
  BT **Mountains**
      Outdoor life
Mountains (May subdiv. geog.) **551.4**
  SA names of mountain ranges
      and of individual moun-
      tains, to be added as need-
      ed
  BT **Geology**
      Physical geography
  NT **Elk Mountain (Wyo.)**
      Mountaineering
      Rocky Mountains
      Volcanoes
Mourning
  USE **Grief**
Mourning customs
  USE **Funeral rites and ceremonies**
Mouse
  USE **Mice**
Movable books
  USE **Toy and movable books**
Movement education 152.3; 153.7; 372.86
  UF Creative movement
      Motor coordination
  BT **Physical education**
Movement, Freedom of
  USE **Freedom of movement**

Movements of animals
  USE **Animal locomotion**
Movie cameras
  USE **Motion picture cameras**
Movie festivals
  USE **Film festivals**
Movie novelizations
  USE **Movie novels**
Movie novels 813, etc.
    May be used for individual works, col-
    lections, or materials about novels based
    on movies.
  UF Movie novelizations
      Movie tie-ins
  BT **Fiction**
  RT **Radio and television novels**
Movie posters
  USE **Film posters**
Movie tie-ins
  USE **Movie novels**
Movies
  USE **Motion pictures**
Moving 648
    Use for materials on changing the loca-
    tion of possessions, household, office, etc.
  UF Household moving
      Moving, household *[Former heading]*
  BT **Home economics**
Moving, household
  USE **Moving**
Moving pictures
  USE **Motion pictures**
Muhammedanism
  USE **Islam**
Muhammedans
  USE **Muslims**
Multiage grouping
  USE **Nongraded schools**
Multicultural education 370.19
    Use for materials on the attempt to
    eradicate racial and religious prejudices
    through the study of various races, creeds,
    and immigrant cultures.
  UF Education, Intercultural
      Education, Multicultural
      Intercultural education *[For-
        mer heading]*
  BT **Acculturation**
      Education
      Ethnic relations

Multicultural education—*Continued*
> Human relations
> Multiculturalism
> Race relations

NT   **Bilingual education**

RT   **International education**
> **Multicultural literature**

Multicultural literature 808.8

Use for collections that bring together literatures of various cultures for the purpose of illustrating racial, religious, or ethnic diversity.

UF   Intercultural literature
> Literature, Intercultural
> Literature, Multicultural

BT   **Literature**
> **Multiculturalism**

RT   **Multicultural education**

Multiculturalism (May subdiv. geog.)
> **306.4**

Use for materials on the preservation of various cultures or cultural identities within a unified society. Materials on the presence of two distinct cultures within a single country or region are entered under **Biculturalism.**

UF   Cultural pluralism
> Diversity movement
> Pluralism (Social sciences)

BT   **Ethnic relations**
> **Race relations**

NT   **Multicultural education**
> **Multicultural literature**

RT   **Biculturalism**

Multilingual dictionaries

USE   **Polyglot dictionaries**

Multilingual glossaries, phrase books,
> etc.

USE   **Polyglot dictionaries**

Multimedia centers

USE   **Instructional materials centers**

Multimedia materials

USE   **Audiovisual materials**

Multinational corporations 338.8; 658

UF   Business enterprises, International
> Business—International aspects
> Corporations, International
> Corporations, Multinational
> International business enterprises *[Former heading]*

BT   **Commerce**
> **Corporations**
> **International economic relations**

NT   **Foreign investments**

Multiple birth 618.2

UF   Birth, Multiple *[Former heading]*

SA   types of multiple births, e.g. **Twins;** to be added as needed

BT   **Childbirth**

NT   **Twins**

Multiple personalities

USE   **Multiple personality**

Multiple personality 616.85

UF   Double consciousness
> Multiple personalities
> Personality, Multiple
> Split personality

BT   **Abnormal psychology**
> **Mental illness**
> **Personality disorders**
> **Psychology**

Multiple plot stories

USE   **Plot-your-own stories**

Multiplication 513.2

BT   **Arithmetic**

Mummies 393

BT   **Archeology**
> **Burial**

Municipal administration

USE   **Municipal government**

Municipal art 711

UF   Art, Municipal *[Former heading]*
> Civic art
> Municipal improvements

BT   **Art**
> **Cities and towns**

RT   **City planning**

Municipal employees

USE   **Civil service**
> **Municipal government**
> and names of cities with the subdivision *Officials and employees,* e.g. **Chicago (Ill.)—Officials and employees;** to be added as needed

Municipal engineering 628

BT   **Engineering**

BT = Broader Term   NT = Narrower Term   RT = Related Term   SA = See Also   UF = Used For

Municipal engineering—*Continued*
    Public works
  NT **Drainage**
    Refuse and refuse disposal
    Sewerage
    Street cleaning
    Water supply
  RT **Sanitary engineering**
Municipal-federal relations
  USE **Federal-city relations**
Municipal finance 336; 352.1
  UF Finance, Municipal
  BT **Finance**
    Municipal government
  NT **Metropolitan finance**
Municipal government (May subdiv. geog.) **320.8; 352**

Use for materials on the government of cities in general and, when subdivided by country, state, or region, for general consideration of municipal government in those places. Materials on the government of individual cities, towns, or metropolitan areas are entered under the name of the city, town, or area with the subdivision *Politics and government.*

  UF City government
    Government, Municipal
    Municipal administration
    Municipal employees
    Municipalities
  SA names of cities with the subdivision *Politics and government,* to be added as needed
  BT **Local government**
    Political science
  NT **Chicago (Ill.)—Politics and government**
    Cities and towns
    Federal-city relations
    Municipal finance
    Municipal government by city manager
    Municipal government by commission
    Public administration
    State-local relations
  RT **Metropolitan government**
Municipal government by city manager 320.8; 352
  UF City manager

    Commission government with city manager
  BT **Municipal government**
Municipal government by commission 320.8; 352
  UF Commission government
    Government by commission
  BT **Municipal government**
Municipal government—United States 320.8; 352.073
  UF United States—Municipal government
Municipal improvements
  USE **Cities and towns—Civic improvement**
    Municipal art
    and names of cities with the subdivision *Public works,* e.g. **Chicago (Ill.)—Public works;** to be added as needed
Municipal ownership 338.9; 352
  UF Public ownership
  BT **Corporations**
    Economic policy
    Government ownership
Municipal planning
  USE **City planning**
Municipal transit
  USE **Local transit**
Municipalities
  USE **Cities and towns**
    Municipal government
Munitions
  USE **Defense industries**
    Military weapons
Muppets
  USE **Puppets and puppet plays**
Mural painting and decoration 729; 751.7
  UF Fresco painting
    Wall decoration
    Wall painting
  BT **Decoration and ornament**
    Interior design
    Painting
    Walls
  NT **Cave drawings**
    Rock drawings, paintings, and engravings

BT = Broader Term   NT = Narrower Term   RT = Related Term   SA = See Also   UF = Used For

Mural painting and decoration—
Continued
  RT Mosaics
Murder
  USE Homicide
Murder mysteries
  USE Mystery and detective plays
       Mystery fiction
       Mystery films
       Mystery radio programs
       Mystery television programs
Murder trials
  USE Trials (Homicide)
Muscles 611; 612.7
  BT **Musculoskeletal system**
Muscular system
  USE **Musculoskeletal system**
Musculoskeletal system 611; 612.7
  UF Muscular system
  BT **Anatomy**
       Physiology
  NT **Bones**
       Muscles
       Skeleton
  RT **Human locomotion**
Museums (May subdiv. geog.) **069; 708**
  SA appropriate subjects and
      names of wars and of cor-
      porate bodies with the sub-
      division *Museums,* e.g.
      World War, 1939-1945—
      Museums; and names of in-
      dividual galleries and muse-
      ums, to be added as
      needed
  NT **Art museums**
       Museums and schools
       World War, 1939-1945—
       Museums
Museums and schools 069
  UF Schools and museums
  BT **Museums**
       Schools
Museums—Ohio 708.171
  UF Ohio—Museums
Museums—United States 708.13
  UF United States—Museums
Mushrooms 589.2; 635
  UF Toadstools
  BT **Plants**

  RT **Fungi**
Music 780
  UF Classical music
  SA music of particular countries,
      e.g. **American music;** types
      of music, e.g. **Vocal music;**
      subjects, classes of persons,
      and names of persons, cor-
      porate bodies, places, or
      wars, with the subdivision
      Songs for collections or in-
      dividual songs about the
      topic or entity named, e.g.
      Surfing—Songs; and ethnic
      groups with the subdivision
      Music for music of the
      group, e.g. **Indians of North**
      America—Music; to be
      added as needed
  BT **Humanities**
  NT **African American music**
       American music
       Black music
       Chamber music
       Church music
       Composition (Music)
       Computer music
       Concerts
       Conducting
       Cowhands—Songs
       Dance music
       Electronic music
       Ensembles (Music)
       Folk music
       Harmony
       Indians of North America—
        Music
       Instrumental music
       Instrumentation and orchestra-
        tion
       Jazz music
       Military music
       Music and literature
       Musical notation
       Musicians
       Orchestral music
       Organ music
       Piano music
       Popular music
       Radio and music

Music—*Continued*
>> Rock music
>> Singing
>> Sound
>> Violin music
>> Vocal music
> RT Romanticism

Music—Acoustics and physics 781.2
> UF Acoustics
> BT Music—Theory
>> Physics
> RT Sound

Music, African American
> USE African American music

Music, American
> USE American music

Music—Analysis, appreciation
> USE Music appreciation
>> Music—History and criticism

Music and literature 780
> UF Literature and music
>> Music and poetry
>> Poetry and music
> BT Literature
>> Music

Music and poetry
> USE Music and literature

Music and radio
> USE Radio and music

Music—Anecdotes 780
> UF Music—Anecdotes, facetiae,
>> satire, etc. [Former heading]
> BT Anecdotes

Music—Anecdotes, facetiae, satire, etc.
> USE Music—Anecdotes
>> Music—Humor

Music appreciation 781.1
> UF Appreciation of music
>> Music—Analysis, appreciation
>> [Former heading]
>> Musical appreciation
> BT Music—Study and teaching
> RT Music—History and criticism

Music, Black
> USE Black music

Music box
> USE Music boxes

Music boxes 786.6
> UF Music box [Former heading]
> BT Mechanical musical instru-
>> ments

Music—Cataloging
> USE Cataloging—Music

Music, Choral
> USE Choral music

Music—Composition
> USE Composition (Music)

Music, Computer
> USE Computer music

Music conductors
> USE Conductors (Music)

Music—Discography 016.78

Music education
> USE Music—Study and teaching

Music, Electronic
> USE Electronic music

Music—Examinations 780.76
> UF Music—Examinations, ques-
>> tions, etc. [Former heading]
> BT Examinations

Music—Examinations, questions, etc.
> USE Music—Examinations

Music festivals 780.79
> UF Musical festivals
> BT Festivals
> RT Concerts

Music, Gospel
> USE Gospel music

Music—History and criticism 780.9
> UF Music—Analysis, appreciation
>> Musical criticism
> BT Criticism
>> History
> RT Music appreciation

Music—Humor 780
> UF Music—Anecdotes, facetiae,
>> satire, etc. [Former heading]
> BT Wit and humor

Music, Indian
> USE Indians of North America—
>> Music

Music, Influence of
> USE Music—Psychological aspects

Music—Instruction and study
> USE Music—Study and teaching

Music, Instrumental
> USE Instrumental music

Music libraries 026
> UF Libraries, Music
> BT Special libraries

Music, Military
> USE Military music

BT = Broader Term   NT = Narrower Term   RT = Related Term   SA = See Also   UF = Used For

Music—Notation
USE **Musical notation**
Music, Popular (Songs, etc.)
USE **Popular music**
Music—Psychological aspects 781
UF Music, Influence of
Psychology of music
BT **Psychology**
Music, Rock
USE **Rock music**
Music, Sacred
USE **Church music**
Music—Study and teaching 780.7
UF Education, Musical
Music education
Music—Instruction and study
Musical education
Musical instruction
School music
NT **Music appreciation**
Music—Theory 781
NT **Composition (Music)**
Counterpoint
Harmony
Music—Acoustics and physics
Musical form
Musical meter and rhythm
Music videos 384.55; 778.59
May be used for individual works, collections, or materials about music videos.
UF Videos, Music
BT **Television programs**
Videodiscs
Videotapes
Music, Vocal
USE **Vocal music**
Musical ability 780.7
UF Musical talent
Talent
BT **Ability**
Musical accompaniment 781.47
UF Accompaniment, Musical
BT **Composition (Music)**
Musical appreciation
USE **Music appreciation**
Musical comedies
USE **Musicals**
Musical composition
USE **Composition (Music)**
Musical criticism
USE **Music—History and criticism**

Musical education
USE **Music—Study and teaching**
Musical ensembles
USE **Ensembles (Music)**
Musical festivals
USE **Music festivals**
Musical films 791.43
May be used for individual works, collections, or materials about musical films.
UF Motion picture musicals
Musicals (Motion pictures)
BT **Motion pictures**
RT **Musicals**
Musical form 784.18
UF Form, Musical
SA names of musical forms expressed in the singular, to be used both for musical scores and for materials about the musical form, e.g. **Concerto**; to be added as needed
BT **Composition (Music)**
Music—Theory
NT **Concerto**
Ensembles (Music)
Fugue
Opera
Operetta
Oratorio
Sonata
Suite (Music)
Symphony
Musical instruction
USE **Music—Study and teaching**
Musical instruments 784.19
UF Instruments, Musical
SA kinds of instruments, e.g. **Percussion instruments**; and names of specific musical instruments, to be added as needed
NT **Bells**
Drums
Electronic musical instruments
Mechanical musical instruments
Orchestra
Organs (Musical instruments)
Percussion instruments

Musical instruments—*Continued*
    Stringed instruments
    Tuning
    Wind instruments
  RT **Instrumental music**
    Instrumentation and orchestration
Musical instruments, Electronic
  USE **Electronic musical instruments**
Musical instruments, Mechanical
  USE **Mechanical musical instruments**
Musical meter and rhythm 781.2
  UF Meter
  BT **Music—Theory**
    Rhythm
Musical notation 780.1
  UF Music—Notation
    Notation, Music
  BT **Music**
Musical revues, comedies, etc.
  USE **Musicals**
Musical talent
  USE **Musical ability**
Musicals 782.1; 792.6
  Use for scores and for materials about musical comedies and revues.
  UF Dramatic music
    Musical comedies
    Musical revues, comedies, etc.
    [Former heading]
  BT **Theater**
  RT **Musical films**
    Operetta
Musicals (Motion pictures)
  USE **Musical films**
Musicians 780.92; 920
  SA musicians of particular countries, e.g. **American musicians;** types of musicians; and names of individual musicians, to be added as needed
  BT **Music**
  NT **African American musicians**
    American musicians
    Black musicians
    Composers
    Conductors (Music)
    Ensembles (Music)

    Organists
    Pianists
    Singers
    Violinists, violoncellists, etc.
Musicians, African American
  USE **African American musicians**
Musicians, American
  USE **American musicians**
Musicians—Biography 780.92; 920
  BT **Biography**
Musicians, Black
  USE **Black musicians**
Musicians—Portraits 780.92
  BT **Portraits**
Muslim architecture
  USE **Islamic architecture**
Muslim art
  USE **Islamic art**
Muslim countries
  USE **Islamic countries**
Muslim law
  USE **Islamic law**
Muslimism
  USE **Islam**
Muslims (May subdiv. geog.) **297**
  UF Mohammedans
    Moslems
    Muhammedans
    Mussulmans
  BT **Islam**
Muslims, Black
  USE **Black Muslims**
Muslims—United States 297.0973
  UF United States—Muslims
  NT **Black Muslims**
Mussulmans
  USE **Muslims**
Mutation (Biology)
  USE **Evolution**
    Variation (Biology)
Mutual defense assistance program
  USE **Military assistance**
Mutual funds
  USE **Investment trusts**
Mutualism (Biology)
  USE **Symbiosis**
Mycology
  USE **Fungi**
Myocardial infarction
  USE **Heart attack**

BT = Broader Term   NT = Narrower Term   RT = Related Term   SA = See Also   UF = Used For

Myotherapy
  USE **Acupressure**
Mysteries
  USE **Mysteries and miracle plays**
      Mystery and detective plays
      Mystery fiction
      Mystery films
      Mystery radio programs
      Mystery television programs
Mysteries and miracle plays 792.1;
      808.82; 822, etc.
  May be used for individual plays, collections, or materials about medieval plays depicting the life of Jesus or legends of the saints.
  UF Miracle plays
      Mysteries
      Mystery plays
  BT **Bible plays**
      English drama
      Pageants
      Religious drama
      Theater
  NT **Passion plays**
  RT **Morality plays**
Mystery and detective comics
  USE **Mystery comic books, strips,**
      etc.
Mystery and detective films
  USE **Mystery films**
Mystery and detective plays 808.82;
      812, etc.
  May be used for individual works, collections, or materials about mystery and detective dramas.
  UF Crime plays
      Detective and mystery plays
      Murder mysteries
      Mysteries
      Mystery plays
      Private eye stories
      Whodunits
  BT **Drama**
Mystery and detective radio programs
  USE **Mystery radio programs**
Mystery and detective stories
  USE **Mystery fiction**
Mystery and detective television programs
  USE **Mystery television programs**

Mystery comic books, strips, etc. 741.5
  May be used for individual works, collections, or materials about mystery and detective comics.
  UF Crime comics
      Detective and mystery comic
        books, strips, etc.
      Detective comics
      Mystery and detective comics
  BT **Comic books, strips, etc.**
Mystery fiction 808.83; 813, etc.
  May be used for individual works, collections, or materials about mystery fiction.
  UF Crime stories
      Detective and mystery stories
      Detective fiction
      Detective stories
      Murder mysteries
      Mysteries
      Mystery and detective stories
        [Former heading]
      Mystery stories
      Private eye stories
      Suspense novels
      Whodunits
  BT **Fiction**
  RT **Ghost stories**
      Horror fiction
      Romantic suspense novels
      Spy stories
Mystery films 791.43
  May be used for individual works, collections, or materials about mystery and detective films.
  UF Crime films
      Detective and mystery films
      Murder mysteries
      Mysteries
      Mystery and detective films
      Private eye stories
      Suspense films
      Whodunits
  SA particular kinds of detective
        and mystery films, e.g.
      Sherlock Holmes films; to
        be added as needed
  BT **Motion pictures**
  NT **Sherlock Holmes films**
  RT **Film noir**
      Gangster films

Mystery films—*Continued*
      Spy films
Mystery plays
  USE **Mysteries and miracle plays**
         Mystery and detective plays
Mystery radio programs
  May be used for individual works, collections, or materials about mystery and detective radio programs.
  UF Crime programs
         Detective and mystery radio programs
         Murder mysteries
         Mysteries
         Mystery and detective radio programs
         Private eye stories
         Suspense programs
         Whodunits
  BT **Radio programs**
Mystery stories
  USE **Mystery fiction**
Mystery television programs 791.45
  May be used for individual works, collections, or materials about mystery and detective television programs.
  UF Crime programs
         Detective and mystery television programs
         Murder mysteries
         Mysteries
         Mystery and detective television programs
         Private eye stories
         Suspense programs
         Whodunits
  BT **Television programs**
  RT **Spy television programs**
Mysticism 149; 248.2
  BT **Philosophy**
      Religion
      Theology
  NT **Cabala**
      Religious art and symbolism
      Symbolism of numbers
      Theosophy
  RT **Spiritual life**
Mythical animals 398.24
  UF Animal lore
         Animals, Imaginary
         Animals, Mythical *[Former heading]*

         Creatures, Imaginary
         Imaginary animals
  SA types of mythical animals, to be added as needed
  BT **Mythology**
  NT **Dragons**
      Mermaids and mermen
      Sasquatch
      Yeti
  RT **Animals—Folklore**
Mythology 291.1
  UF Myths
  SA mythology of particular national or ethnic groups or of particular geographic areas, e.g. **Celtic mythology;** to be added as needed
  BT **Legends**
      Religion
      Religions
  NT **Art and mythology**
      Celtic mythology
      Classical mythology
      Geographical myths
      Monsters
      Mythical animals
      Symbolism
      Totems and totemism
  RT **Folklore**
      Gods and goddesses
      Heroes and heroines
      Indians of North America— Religion
Mythology, Celtic
  USE **Celtic mythology**
Mythology, Classical
  USE **Classical mythology**
Mythology in art
  USE **Art and mythology**
Mythology, Indian
  USE **Indians of North America— Religion**
Myths
  USE **Mythology**
N.A.T.O.
  USE **North Atlantic Treaty Organization**
Names 929.4
  UF Epithets
         Nomenclature

BT = Broader Term   NT = Narrower Term   RT = Related Term   SA = See Also   UF = Used For

Names—*Continued*
>
> Proper names
> Terminology
> SA types of names, e.g. **Geographic names;** to be added as needed
> NT **Code names**
> **Geographic names**
> **Personal names**
> **Pseudonyms**

Names, Fictitious
> USE **Pseudonyms**

Names, Geographical
> USE **Geographic names**

Names, Geographical—United States
> USE **Geographic names—United States**

Names, Personal
> USE **Personal names**

Names, Personal—Scottish
> USE **Scottish personal names**

Names—Pronunciation 421
> UF Pronunciation

Napoleon I, Emperor of the French, 1769-1821—Drama
> **808.82; 812, etc.**
> May be used for individual works, collections, or materials about plays about Napoleon.
> UF Napoleon in fiction, drama, poetry, etc.
> BT **Drama**
> **Historical drama**

Napoleon I, Emperor of the French, 1769-1821—Fiction 813, etc.
> May be used for individual works, collections, or materials about fiction about Napoleon.
> UF Napoleon in fiction, drama, poetry, etc.
> BT **Biographical fiction**
> **Fiction**
> **Historical fiction**

Napoleon I, Emperor of the French, 1769-1821—Poetry
> **808.81; 811, etc.**
> May be used for individual works, collections, or materials about poetry about Napoleon.
> UF Napoleon in fiction, drama, poetry, etc.

> BT **Poetry**

Napoleon in fiction, drama, poetry, etc.
> USE **Napoleon I, Emperor of the French, 1769-1821—Drama**
> **Napoleon I, Emperor of the French, 1769-1821—Fiction**
> **Napoleon I, Emperor of the French, 1769-1821—Poetry**

Napoleonic Wars
> USE **Europe—History—1789-1815**
> **France—History—1789-1799, Revolution**
> **France—History—1799-1815**

Narcotic addiction counseling
> USE **Drug abuse counseling**

Narcotic addicts
> USE **Drug addicts**

Narcotic habit
> USE **Drug addiction**

Narcotic traffic
> USE **Drug traffic**

Narcotics 178; 394.1; 615
> UF Intoxicants
> Opiates
> Soporifics
> SA names of specific narcotics, to be added as needed
> BT **Drugs**
> **Materia medica**
> **Therapeutics**
> NT **Cocaine**
> **Endorphins**
> **Heroin**
> **Marijuana**
> **Morphine**
> **Opium**
> RT **Stimulants**

Narcotics and crime
> USE **Drugs and crime**

Narcotics and criminals
> USE **Criminals—Drug use**

Narcotics and teenagers
> USE **Teenagers—Drug use**

Narcotics and youth
> USE **Youth—Drug use**

Narration with music
> USE **Monologues with music**

Narrations
> USE **Monologues**
> **Recitations**

Narrative poetry 808.81; 811, etc.

May be used for individual works, collections, or materials about narrative poetry. Rhyming stories for very young children are entered under the form heading **Stories in rhyme.**

BT   **Poetry**

NT   **Epic poetry**

     Historical poetry

     Stories in rhyme

Nation of Islam

USE **Black Muslims**

National anthems

USE **National songs**

National book week

USE **National Book Week**

National Book Week 021.7

UF   Book Week, National

     National book week *[Former heading]*

BT   **Books and reading**

National characteristics

UF   Characteristics, National

     Images, National

     National images

     National psychology

     Psychology, National

SA   national characteristics of particular countries, e.g. **American national characteristics;** to be added as needed

BT   **Anthropology**

     Nationalism

     Social psychology

NT   **American national characteristics**

RT   **Ethnopsychology**

National characteristics, American

USE **American national characteristics**

National consciousness

USE **Nationalism**

National dances

USE **Folk dancing**

National debts

USE **Public debts**

National defenses

USE **Industrial mobilization**

     Military readiness

and names of countries with the subdivision *Defenses,*

e.g. **United States—Defenses;** to be added as needed

National emblems (May subdiv. geog.) **929.9**

UF   Emblems, National

     National symbols

SA   types of national emblems and national symbols, e.g. **Flags;** to be added as needed

BT   **Signs and symbols**

RT   **Flags**

     Heraldry

     Insignia

     Mottoes

     Seals (Numismatics)

     State emblems

National forests

USE **Forest reserves**

National Guard (U.S.)

USE **United States. National Guard**

National health insurance (May subdiv. geog.) **362.1; 368.4**

UF   Government health insurance

     Health insurance, Government

     Health insurance, National

     Medical insurance, National

     National health service

     Socialized medicine

BT   **Health insurance**

NT   **Medicaid**

     Medicare

RT   **State medicine**

National health service

USE **National health insurance**

     State medicine

National holidays

USE **Holidays**

and names of national holidays, e.g. **Memorial Day;** to be added as needed

National hymns

USE **National songs**

National images

USE **National characteristics**

National interest

USE **Public interest**

National landmarks

USE **National monuments**

National liberation movements (May
　　　subdiv. geog. except U.S.)
　　　320.5
　UF　Liberation movements, Na-
　　　tional
　SA　names of individual liberation
　　　movements, to be added as
　　　needed
　BT　**Colonies**
　　　Nationalism
　　　Revolutions
　RT　**Guerrillas**
National libraries 027.5
　Use for materials on libraries main-
　tained by government funds that serve a
　country as a whole, particularly in collect-
　ing and preserving that country's publica-
　tions.
　UF　Libraries, National
　SA　names of individual national
　　　libraries, to be added as
　　　needed
　BT　**Government libraries**
National monuments 917.3
　Use for materials on monuments, such
　as historic sites or geographic areas, that
　are owned and maintained in the public
　interest by the federal government.
　UF　Landmarks, Preservation of
　　　Monuments, National
　　　National landmarks
　SA　names of individual national
　　　monuments, to be added as
　　　needed
　BT　**Monuments**
　　　National parks and reserves
　RT　**Historic sites**
　　　Natural monuments
National parks and reserves (May sub-
　　　div. geog.) **338.78; 363.6;**
　　　719
　SA　names of individual national
　　　parks, to be added as need-
　　　ed
　BT　**Conservation of natural re-
　　　sources**
　　　Parks
　　　Public lands
　　　Wildlife conservation
　NT　**National monuments**
　　　Natural monuments
　　　Wilderness areas

　RT　**Forest reserves**
**National parks and reserves—United
　　　States 719; 917.3**
　UF　United States—National parks
　　　and reserves
　NT　**Yosemite National Park
　　　(Calif.)**
National planning
　USE　**Economic policy**
　　　Social policy
　　　and names of countries with
　　　the subdivision *Economic
　　　policy* or *Social policy,* e.g.
　　　**United States—Economic
　　　policy; United States—
　　　Social policy;** etc.; and sub-
　　　jects with the subdivision
　　　Government policy, e.g.
　　　**Homeless persons—
　　　Government policy;** to be
　　　added as needed
National psychology
　USE　**Ethnopsychology**
　　　National characteristics
National resources
　USE　**Natural resources**
　　　and names of countries with
　　　the subdivision *Economic
　　　conditions,* e.g. **United
　　　States—Economic condi-
　　　tions;** to be added as need-
　　　ed
National security 355
　SA　names of countries with the
　　　subdivision *National securi-
　　　ty,* to be added as needed
　NT　**United States—National se-
　　　curity**
　RT　**Economic policy**
　　　International relations
　　　Military policy
National socialism 320.5; 335.6
　Use for materials limited to fascism in
　Germany during the Nazi regime.
　UF　Nazism
　BT　**Fascism—Germany**
　　　Totalitarianism
　　　**World War, 1939-1945—
　　　Causes**
　RT　**Fascism**

BT = Broader Term　　NT = Narrower Term　　RT = Related Term　　SA = See Also　　UF = Used For

National socialism—*Continued*
      Neo-Nazis
      Socialism
National songs (May subdiv. geog.)
      782.42
  UF Anthems, National
      National anthems
      National hymns
      Patriotic songs
      Songs, National
  BT **Songs**
  NT **War songs**
  RT **Folk songs**
      Patriotic poetry
National songs, American
  USE **National songs—United States**
National songs—United States 782.42
  UF American national songs
      National songs, American
      [Former heading]
      United States—National songs
  BT **American songs**
National symbols
  USE **National emblems**
Nationalism (May subdiv. geog.) **320.5**
  UF Internationalism
      National consciousness
      Regionalism
  BT **International relations**
      Political science
  NT **National characteristics**
      National liberation movements
  RT **Minorities**
      Patriotism
Nationalism, Black
  USE **Black nationalism**
Nationalism—United States 320.5
Nationalist China
  USE **Taiwan**
Nationality (Citizenship)
  USE **Citizenship**
Nationalization
  USE **Government ownership**
Nationalization of railroads
  USE **Railroads—Government policy**
Nations, Law of
  USE **International law**
Native American women
  USE **Indians of North America—
      Women**

Native Americans
  USE **Indians of North America**
Native peoples
  USE **Ethnology**
      Indians of North America
Nativity of Christ
  USE **Jesus Christ—Nativity**
NATO
  USE **North Atlantic Treaty Organization**
Natural beauty conservation
  USE **Landscape protection**
Natural Bridge (Va.) 975.5
  BT **Natural monuments**
Natural childbirth 618.4
  UF Childbirth, Natural
      Lamaze method of childbirth
  BT **Childbirth**
  NT **Midwives**
Natural disasters (May subdiv. geog.)
      904
  SA types of natural disasters, to
      be added as needed
  BT **Disasters**
  NT **Earthquakes**
      Floods
      Storms
      Tsunamis
Natural disasters—United States 973
  UF United States—Natural disasters
Natural food cooking
  USE **Cooking—Natural foods**
Natural foods 641.3
  UF Food, Natural *[Former heading]*
      Health foods
      Organically grown foods
  BT **Food**
  RT **Cooking—Natural foods**
Natural gardening
  USE **Organic gardening**
Natural gas 553.2; 665.7
  UF Gas, Natural
  BT **Economic geology**
Natural history (May subdiv. geog.) **508**
    Use for popular materials describing animals, plants, minerals, and nature in general. Materials on the study of animals and plants, especially by amateurs, are entered under **Nature study.**

Natural history—*Continued*
    UF   Animal lore
          History, Natural
    BT   **Science**
    NT   **Aquariums**
          Biogeography
          Botany
          Fossils
          Freshwater biology
          Geology
          Marine biology
          Mineralogy
          Zoology
    RT   **Biology**
Natural history, Biblical
    USE **Bible—Natural history**
Natural history—Outdoor guides
    USE **Nature study**
Natural history—United States 508.73
    UF   United States—Natural history
Natural law
    USE **Ethics**
          Freedom
          International law
Natural monuments (May subdiv. geog.) **719**
    Use for general materials on natural objects of historic or scientific interest such as caves, cliffs, and natural bridges.
    UF   Landmarks, Preservation of
          Monuments, Natural
          Preservation of natural scenery
          Protection of natural scenery
    SA   names of individual natural monuments, to be added as needed
    BT   **Landscape protection**
          National parks and reserves
          Nature conservation
    NT   **Natural Bridge (Va.)**
          Wilderness areas
    RT   **National monuments**
Natural monuments—United States 719; 917.3
    UF   United States—Natural monuments
Natural parents
    USE **Birthparents**

Natural pesticides 668
    BT   **Pesticides**
Natural religion
    USE **Natural theology**
Natural resources (May subdiv. geog.) **333.7**
    UF   National resources
          Resources, Natural
    SA   types of natural resources, to be added as needed
    BT   **Economic conditions**
    NT   **Conservation of natural resources**
          Energy resources
          Fisheries
          Forests and forestry
          Marine resources
          Mines and mineral resources
          Water resources development
    RT   **Public lands**
Natural resources—Management 333.7
    BT   **Management**
Natural resources—United States 333.7
    UF   United States—Natural resources
    NT   **United States—Economic conditions**
Natural selection 575.01
    UF   Selection, Natural
          Survival of the fittest
    BT   **Genetics**
          Variation (Biology)
    RT   **Evolution**
          Heredity
Natural steam energy
    USE **Geothermal resources**
Natural theology 210
    Use for materials on the knowledge of God's existence obtained by observing the visible processes of nature.
    UF   Natural religion
          Theology, Natural
    BT   **Apologetics**
          God
          Religion
          Theology
    NT   **Creation**
    RT   **Religion and science**
Natural therapy
    USE **Naturopathy**

BT = Broader Term   NT = Narrower Term   RT = Related Term   SA = See Also   UF = Used For

Naturalism in art
  USE **Realism in art**
Naturalism in literature
  USE **Realism in literature**
Naturalists 508.092; 920
  SA   types of naturalists, e.g. **Botanists**; to be added as needed
  BT   **Scientists**
  NT   **Biologists**
       Botanists
Naturalization 323.6
  UF   Foreigners
  BT   **Immigration and emigration**
       International law
       Suffrage
  RT   **Aliens**
       Americanization
       Citizenship
Nature conservation 333.7
  UF   Conservation of nature
       Nature protection
       Preservation of natural scenery
       Protection of natural scenery
  BT   **Conservation of natural resources**
  NT   **Endangered species**
       Landscape protection
       Natural monuments
       Plant conservation
       Wildlife conservation
Nature craft 745.5
  Use for materials on crafts using objects found in nature, such as leaves, shells, etc.
  UF   Naturecraft
  BT   **Handicraft**
Nature, Effect of man on
  USE **Human influence on nature**
Nature in literature 809
  BT   **Literature**
  NT   **Animals in literature**
       Birds in literature
       Nature poetry
Nature in poetry
  USE **Nature poetry**
Nature in the bible
  USE **Bible—Natural history**
Nature photography 778.9
  UF   Photography of nature

  SA   photography of particular subjects in nature, e.g. **Photography of birds**; to be added as needed
  BT   **Nature study**
       Photography
  NT   **Photography of animals**
       Photography of birds
       Photography of fishes
       Photography of plants
  RT   **Outdoor photography**
Nature—Poetry
  USE **Nature poetry**
Nature poetry 809.1; 811, etc.
  May be used for individual works or collections of nature poetry and for materials about the theme of nature in poetry.
  UF   Nature in poetry
       Nature—Poetry
  BT   **Nature in literature**
       Poetry
Nature protection
  USE **Nature conservation**
Nature study (May subdiv. geog.) 372.3; 508
  Use for materials on the study of animals and plants, especially by amateurs. Popular materials describing animals, plants, minerals, and nature in general are entered under **Natural history.**
  UF   Natural history—Outdoor guides
  BT   **Education**
       Science—Study and teaching
  NT   **Bird watching**
       Botany
       Nature photography
       Zoology
  RT   **Animal behavior**
       Outdoor education
       Outdoor life
Nature study—United States 508.73
  UF   United States—Nature study
Naturecraft
  USE **Nature craft**
Naturopathy 615.5
  UF   Natural therapy
  BT   **Alternative medicine**
       Therapeutics
  RT   **Chiropractic**
Nautical almanacs 528
  BT   **Almanacs**

BT = Broader Term   NT = Narrower Term   RT = Related Term   SA = See Also   UF = Used For

Nautical almanacs—*Continued*
    Navigation
Nautical astronomy 527
    UF   Astronomy, Nautical
    BT   **Astronomy**
    NT   **Latitude**
          Longitude
    RT   **Navigation**
          Time
Navaho Indians
    USE **Navajo Indians**
Navaho language
    USE **Navajo language**
Navajo Indians 970.004
    UF   Navaho Indians
    BT   **Indians of North America**
Navajo language 497
    UF   Navaho language
    BT   **Indians of North America—**
          Languages
Naval administration
    USE **Naval art and science**
          and names of countries with
          the subhead *Navy,* e.g.
          United States. Navy; to be
          added as needed
Naval aeronautics
    USE **Military aeronautics**
Naval air bases
    USE **Air bases**
Naval airplanes
    USE **Military airplanes**
Naval architecture 623.8
    UF   Architecture, Naval
          Marine architecture
    BT   **Architecture**
    NT   **Boatbuilding**
          Marine engineering
          Ships
          Steamboats
          Warships
    RT   **Shipbuilding**
Naval art and science 359
    UF   Fighting
          Naval administration
          Naval science
          Naval warfare
          Navy
    BT   **War**
    NT   **Camouflage (Military science)**

          Marine engineering
          Navy yards and naval stations
          Privateering
          Sailors
          Sea power
          Shipbuilding
          Signals and signaling
          Submarine warfare
          Torpedoes
          Warships
    RT   **Military art and science**
          Navies
          Navigation
          Strategy
Naval art and science—Study and
       teaching
    USE **Naval education**
Naval bases
    USE **Navy yards and naval stations**
Naval battles 359.4; 904
    UF   Naval warfare
    SA   names of countries with the
          subdivision *Naval history;*
          names of wars with the
          subdivision *Naval opera-*
          tions, and names of specific
          naval battles, to be added
          as needed
    BT   **Sea power**
    NT   **United States—Naval history**
          World War, 1939-1945—
          Naval operations
    RT   **Battles**
          Naval history
Naval biography
    USE names of navies with the sub-
          division *Biography,* e.g.
          United States. Navy—
          Biography; to be added as
          needed
Naval education 359.5
    UF   Education, Naval
          Naval art and science—Study
          and teaching
          Naval schools
    BT   **Education**
Naval engineering
    USE **Marine engineering**
Naval history 359.409
    UF   History, Naval

Naval history—*Continued*
>Wars
>>SA   names of countries with the
>>>subhead *Navy* or the subdi-
>>>vision *Naval history,* to be
>>>added as needed
>>BT   **History**
>>NT   **Pirates**
>>>**Privateering**
>>>**United States—Naval history**
>>>**United States. Navy**
>>RT   **Military history**
>>>**Naval battles**
>>>**Sea power**

Naval law
>USE   **Maritime law**

Naval offenses
>USE   **Military offenses**

Naval pensions
>USE   **Military pensions**

Naval personnel
>USE   **Sailors**

Naval power
>USE   **Sea power**

Naval schools
>USE   **Naval education**

Naval science
>USE   **Naval art and science**

Naval shipyards
>USE   **Navy yards and naval stations**

Naval signaling
>USE   **Signals and signaling**

Naval strategy
>USE   **Strategy**

Naval uniforms
>USE   **Military uniforms**

Naval warfare
>USE   **Naval art and science**
>>**Naval battles**
>>**Submarine warfare**
>>and names of wars with the
>>subdivision *Naval opera-*
>>*tions,* e.g. **World War,**
>>**1939-1945—Naval opera-**
>>**tions**; to be added as need-
>>ed

Navies 359.3
>UF   **Military forces**
>>**Military power**
>>**Navy**

SA   names of countries with the
>subhead *Navy,* e.g. **United**
>**States. Navy;** to be added
>as needed
BT   **Armed forces**
>**Military personnel**
>**Military readiness**
>**Ships**
>**War**
NT   **Admirals**
>**Sailors**
>**United States. Navy**
RT   **Armies**
>**Naval art and science**
>**Sea power**
>**Warships**

Navigation 623.89; 629.04
>UF   **Seamanship**
>BT   **Locomotion**
>>**Oceanography**
>>**Ships**
>NT   **Compass**
>>**Harbors**
>>**Inland navigation**
>>**Knots and splices**
>>**Lighthouses**
>>**Loran**
>>**Nautical almanacs**
>>**Ocean currents**
>>**Orienteering**
>>**Pilot guides**
>>**Radar**
>>**Shipwrecks**
>>**Signals and signaling**
>>**Tides**
>>**Winds**
>RT   **Direction sense**
>>**Nautical astronomy**
>>**Naval art and science**
>>**Pilots and pilotage**
>>**Sailing**
>>**Steam navigation**

Navigation, Aerial
>USE   **Navigation (Aeronautics)**

Navigation (Aeronautics) 629.132
>UF   **Aerial navigation**
>>**Aeronautics—Navigation**
>>**Air navigation**
>>**Navigation, Aerial**
>BT   **Aeronautics**

BT = Broader Term   NT = Narrower Term   RT = Related Term   SA = See Also   UF = Used For

Navigation (Aeronautics)—*Continued*
  NT **Airplanes—Piloting**
      Radio in aeronautics
Navigation (Astronautics) 629.45
  UF Astronavigation
      Space navigation
  BT **Astrodynamics**
      Astronautics
  NT **Astronautical instruments**
      Radio in astronautics
      Space vehicles—Piloting
  RT **Space flight**
Navigation, Inland
  USE **Inland navigation**
Navigation—Law and legislation
  USE **Maritime law**
Navigation, Steam
  USE **Steam navigation**
Navigators
  USE **Exploration**
      Explorers
      Sailors
Navy
  USE **Naval art and science**
      Navies
      Sea power
      and names of countries with
        the subhead *Navy,* e.g.
        United States. Navy; to be
        added as needed
Navy Sealab project
  USE **Sealab project**
Navy yards and naval stations 359.7
  UF Naval bases
      Naval shipyards
  BT **Naval art and science**
Nazism
  USE **National socialism**
Near-death experiences 133.9; 155.9
  Use for materials on the paranormal experiences of those who have survived near death or apparent death.
  UF Death, Apparent
      Experiences, Near-death
  BT **Death**
  RT **Parapsychology**
Near East
  USE **Middle East**
Neatness
  USE **Cleanliness**
Nebulae, Extragalactic
  USE **Galaxies**

Necrologies
  USE **Obituaries**
Necromancy
  USE **Divination**
      Magic
      Witchcraft
Needlepoint 746.44
  UF Canvas embroidery
  BT **Embroidery**
      Needlework
Needlework 746.4
  SA types of needlework, to be
        added as needed
  BT **Decoration and ornament**
      Decorative arts
  NT **Crocheting**
      Embroidery
      Knitting
      Lace and lace making
      Needlepoint
      Samplers
      Tapestry
  RT **Dressmaking**
      Sewing
Negotiable instruments 332.7
  UF Bills and notes
      Bills of credit
      Commercial paper
      Instruments, Negotiable
      Letters of credit
  BT **Banks and banking**
      Commercial law
      Contracts
      Credit
  NT **Bonds**
Negotiation 158; 302.3
  UF Bargaining
      Discussion
  BT **Applied psychology**
  NT **Collective bargaining**
      Hostage negotiation
      Industrial arbitration
Negritude
  USE **Blacks—Race identity**
Negroes
  USE **African Americans**
      Blacks
Neighborhood
  USE **Community life**
Neighborhood centers
  USE **Social settlements**

BT = Broader Term   NT = Narrower Term   RT = Related Term   SA = See Also   UF = Used For

Neighborhood development
USE **Community development**
Neighborhood schools
USE **Public schools**
Neo-fascism
USE **Fascism**
Neo-Greek literature
USE **Modern Greek literature**
Neo-impressionism (Art)
USE **Impressionism (Art)**
Neo-Latin languages
USE **Romance languages**
Neo-Nazis 320.5
Use for materials on political groups whose social beliefs or political agendas are reminiscent of those of Hitler's Nazis.
BT **Fascism**
RT **National socialism**
Neo-nazism
USE **Fascism**
Neolithic period
USE **Stone Age**
Neon tubes 621.32
BT **Electric signs**
Nero, Emperor of Rome, 37-68 92; B
BT **Roman emperors**
Nerves 611; 612.8
BT **Nervous system**
Nerves—Diseases
USE **Nervous system—Diseases**
Nervous breakdown
USE **Neurasthenia**
Nervous exhaustion
USE **Neurasthenia**
Nervous prostration
USE **Neurasthenia**
Nervous system 611; 612.8
UF Neurology
BT **Anatomy**
Physiology
NT **Abnormal psychology**
Brain
Nerves
Psychophysiology
Nervous system—Diseases 616.8
UF Nerves—Diseases
Neuropathology
NT **Epilepsy**
Neurasthenia
Nests
USE **Birds—Eggs and nests**

Netherlands 949.2
May be subdivided like United States except for *History*.
UF Holland
Netherlands—History 949.2
Netherlands—History—1940-1945, German occupation 949.207
UF German occupation of Netherlands, 1940-1945
BT **Military occupation**
World War, 1939-1945—Occupied territories
Network theory
USE **System analysis**
Networks (Associations, institutions, etc.)
USE **Associations**
Networks, Computer
USE **Computer networks**
Networks, Information
USE **Information networks**
Networks, Library
USE **Library information networks**
Neurasthenia 616.85
UF Nervous breakdown
Nervous exhaustion
Nervous prostration
BT **Nervous system—Diseases**
Neurology
USE **Nervous system**
Neuropathology
USE **Nervous system—Diseases**
Neuroses 616.85
BT **Abnormal psychology**
NT **Depression (Psychology)**
Phobias
Psychosomatic medicine
Neutrality 327.1; 341.6
UF Nonalignment
SA names of countries with the subdivision *Neutrality*, to be added as needed
BT **International law**
International relations
International security
NT **United States—Neutrality**
RT **Intervention (International law)**
Neutron bomb 623.4
UF Neutron bombs *[Former heading]*

Neutron bomb—*Continued*
  BT **Bombs**
      Neutron weapons
Neutron bombs
  USE **Neutron bomb**
Neutron weapons 623.4
  UF Enhanced radiation weapons
      Weapons, Enhanced radiation
      Weapons, Neutron
  BT **Nuclear weapons**
  NT **Neutron bomb**
Neutrons 539.7
  BT **Atoms**
      Particles (Nuclear physics)
New Age movement 131; 133; 291; 299
      Use for materials on any of various
      post-1970 cults and organizations that in-
      corporate Eastern or Native American re-
      ligions, occult beliefs and practices,
      mysticism, or meditation techniques in an
      attempt to enhance consciousness and de-
      velop human potential.
  UF Aquarian Age movement
  BT **Cults**
      Occultism
      Social movements
New birth (Theology)
  USE **Regeneration (Theology)**
New business enterprises 338.7
  UF Business enterprises, New
      How to start a business
      Starting a business
  BT **Business enterprises**
New England 974
  BT **United States**
New France—History
  USE **Canada—History—0-1763
      (New France)**
      **Mississippi River Valley—
      History**
New left
  USE **Right and left (Political sci-
      ence)**
New nations
  USE **New states**
New Negro Movement
  USE **Harlem Renaissance**
New states 321
  UF New nations
      States, New *[Former heading]*
  BT **Developing countries**
New Testament
  USE **Bible. N.T.**

New words 417; 427, etc.
  UF Coinage of words
      Words, New *[Former heading]*
  BT **Vocabulary**
New York (N.Y.)—Streets
  USE **Streets—New York (N.Y.)**
Newbery Award
  USE **Newbery Medal**
Newbery Medal 028.5
  UF Newbery Award
      Newbery Medal books *[For-
      mer heading]*
      Newbery Prize books
  BT **Children's literature**
      Literary prizes
Newbery Medal books
  USE **Newbery Medal**
Newbery Prize books
  USE **Newbery Medal**
News agencies 070.4
  UF News services
      Wire agencies
  BT **Press**
News broadcasting
  USE **Broadcast journalism**
News photography
  USE **Photojournalism**
News services
  USE **News agencies**
Newspaper advertising 659.13
      Use for materials on advertising in
      newspapers. Materials on the advertising
      of newspapers are entered under
      Advertising—Newspapers.
  UF Advertising, Newspaper
  BT **Newspapers**
Newspaper clippings
  USE **Clippings (Books, newspapers,
      etc.)**
Newspaper work
  USE **Reporters and reporting**
Newspapers 070
      Use for materials limited to the history,
      organization, and management of newspa-
      pers. Materials on writing for the periodi-
      cal press, on the editing of such writing,
      and on journalism as an occupation, are
      entered under **Journalism.**

Newspapers—*Continued*

SA   newspapers of particular countries, e.g. **American newspapers; English newspapers;** etc.; and names of individual newspapers, to be added as needed

BT   **Mass media**
       Serial publications

NT   **American newspapers**
       Clippings (Books, newspapers, etc.)
       English newspapers
       Freedom of the press
       Newspaper advertising
       Reporters and reporting

RT   **Journalism**
       Periodicals
       Press

Newspapers—Advertising
USE   **Advertising—Newspapers**

Newspapers—Indexes 070.1
BT   **Indexes**

Nicene Creed 238
BT   **Creeds**

Nicknames 929.4
UF   Epithets
       Sobriquets
       Soubriquets
BT   **Personal names**

Night 529
BT   **Chronology**
       Time
NT   **Bedtime**
RT   **Day**

Night schools
USE   **Evening and continuation schools**

Nike rocket 623.4
BT   **Guided missiles**

Nineteenth century 909.81

Use for general materials covering progress and development during this period in one or in several countries.

UF   1800-1899 (19th century)
BT   **Modern history—1800-1899 (19th century)**

Nitrates 553.6
BT   **Fertilizers and manures**

Nitrogen 546; 665
BT   **Gases**

NMR imaging
USE   **Magnetic resonance imaging**

No fault automobile insurance
USE   **Automobile insurance**

Nobel prizes
USE   **Nobel Prizes**

Nobel Prizes 001.4; 807.9
UF   Nobel prizes *[Former heading]*
BT   **Awards**

Nobility 305.5; 929.7
UF   Baronage
       Peerage
BT   **Social classes**
NT   **Knights and knighthood**
RT   **Aristocracy**
       Heraldry

Noise 363.7
SA   subjects with the subdivision *Noise,* to be added as needed
BT   **Public health**
       Sound
NT   **Airplanes—Noise**

Noise pollution 363.7
SA   subjects with the subdivision *Noise,* to be added as needed
BT   **Pollution**
NT   **Airplanes—Noise**

Nomads 304.2; 306.08
UF   Pastoral peoples
BT   **Nonliterate folk society**

Nomenclature
USE   **Names**
       and scientific and technical subjects with the subdivision *Terminology,* e.g. **Botany—Terminology;** to be added as needed

Nomination of presidents
USE   **Presidents—United States—Nomination**

Non-proliferation of nuclear weapons
USE   **Arms control**

Non-promotion (School)
USE   **Promotion (School)**

Non-victim crimes
USE   **Crimes without victims**

Non-wage payments
USE   **Nonwage payments**

BT = Broader Term   NT = Narrower Term   RT = Related Term   SA = See Also   UF = Used For

Nonalignment
　　USE　**Neutrality**
Nonbook materials
　　USE　**Audiovisual materials**
Noncitizens
　　USE　**Aliens**
Nonconformity
　　USE　**Conformity**
　　　　　Counter culture
　　　　　Dissent
Nondenominational churches
　　USE　**Community churches**
Nonfamily households
　　USE　**Shared housing**
Nonfiction films
　　USE　**Documentary films**
Nonformal colleges and universities
　　USE　**Free universities**
Nonformal schools
　　USE　**Experimental schools**
Nonfossil fuels
　　USE　**Synthetic fuels**
Nongraded schools 371.2
　　UF　Multiage grouping
　　　　　Schools, Nongraded
　　　　　Schools, Ungraded
　　　　　Ungraded schools
　　BT　**Ability grouping in education**
　　　　　Education—Experimental
　　　　　　methods
Noninstitutional churches 289.9
　　UF　Avant-garde churches
　　　　　Churches, Avant-garde
　　　　　Churches, Noninstitutional
　　BT　**Christian sects**
Nonlinguistic communication
　　USE　**Nonverbal communication**
Nonliterate folk society 306; 305.8
　　UF　Folk society, Nonliterate
　　　　　Illiterate societies
　　　　　Preliterate society
　　　　　Primitive society
　　　　　Society, Nonliterate folk *[For-*
　　　　　　mer heading]
　　　　　Society, Primitive
　　BT　**Civilization**
　　　　　Ethnology
　　　　　Sociology
　　NT　**Nomads**
　　　　　Nonliterate man

Nonliterate man 306
　　UF　Man, Nonliterate *[Former*
　　　　　　heading]
　　　　　Man, Primitive
　　　　　Preliterate man
　　　　　Primitive man
　　BT　**Ethnology**
　　　　　Nonliterate folk society
Nonmarital relations
　　USE　**Unmarried couples**
Nonnationals
　　USE　**Aliens**
Nonnutritive sweeteners
　　USE　**Sugar substitutes**
Nonobjective art
　　USE　**Abstract art**
Nonprescription drugs 615
　　UF　Drugs, Nonprescription *[For-*
　　　　　　mer heading]
　　　　　Over-the-counter drugs
　　　　　Patent medicines
　　BT　**Drugs**
Nonprint materials
　　USE　**Audiovisual materials**
Nonprofit corporations
　　USE　**Nonprofit organizations**
Nonprofit organizations 346; 658
　　UF　Corporations, Nonprofit
　　　　　Nonprofit corporations
　　　　　Nonprofit sector
　　　　　Nonprofits
　　　　　Not-for-profit organizations
　　　　　Organizations, Nonprofit
　　BT　**Associations**
Nonprofit sector
　　USE　**Nonprofit organizations**
Nonprofitable drugs
　　USE　**Orphan drugs**
Nonprofits
　　USE　**Nonprofit organizations**
Nonpublic schools
　　USE　**Church schools**
　　　　　Private schools
Nonsense verses 808.81; 811, etc.;
　　　　　811.008, etc.
　　May be used for individual works, col-
　　lections, or materials about nonsense
　　verse.
　　UF　Rhymes
　　BT　**Children's poetry**

BT = Broader Term　　NT = Narrower Term　　RT = Related Term　　SA = See Also　　UF = Used For

Nonsense verses—*Continued*
      Humorous poetry
      Wit and humor
  NT Tongue twisters
  RT Limericks
Nonsupport
  USE **Desertion and nonsupport**
Nonverbal communication 302.2
  UF Nonlinguistic communication
  SA types of nonverbal communi-
      cation, e.g. **Body language;**
      to be added as needed
  BT **Communication**
  NT **Body language**
      Hugging
      Personal space
  RT **Deaf—Means of communica-
      tion**
Nonvictim crimes
  USE **Crimes without victims**
Nonviolence 179; 303.6
  NT **Hunger strikes**
  RT **Pacifism**
      Passive resistance
Nonviolent noncooperation
  USE **Passive resistance**
Nonwage payments 331.25
  UF Employee benefits
      Fringe benefits
      Non-wage payments
  BT **Wages**
Nonword stories
  USE **Stories without words**
Nordic peoples
  USE **Teutonic peoples**
Normal schools
  USE **Teachers colleges**
**Normandy (France), Attack on, 1944
      940.54**
  UF D Day
  BT **World War, 1939-1945—
      Campaigns**
Normans 941.02
  BT **Great Britain—History—
      1066-1154, Norman period**
  RT **Vikings**
Norse languages
  USE **Old Norse language
      Scandinavian languages**

Norse legends 398.2
  UF Legends, Norse *[Former head-
      ing]*
  BT **Legends**
Norse literature
  USE **Old Norse literature
      Scandinavian literature**
Norsemen
  USE **Vikings**
North Africa 961
    Use for materials dealing collectively
  with Morocco, Algeria, Tunisia, and Lib-
  ya.
  UF Africa, North *[Former head-
      ing]*
      Barbary States
      Maghreb
  BT **Africa**
North America 970
  BT **America**
  NT **Pacific Northwest**
North American Indians
  USE **Indians of North America**
**North Atlantic Treaty Organization
      341.7**
  UF N.A.T.O.
      NATO
North Central States
  USE **Middle West**
North Korea
  USE **Korea (North)**
North Pole 910.9163; 998
  BT **Polar regions**
  RT **Arctic regions**
Northeast Africa 960
    Use for materials dealing collectively
  with Sudan, Ethiopia, Somalia, and Dji-
  bouti.
  UF Africa, Northeast *[Former
      heading]*
  BT **Africa**
Northeast Passage 998
  BT **Arctic regions
      Exploration
      Voyages and travels**
Northern lights
  USE **Auroras**
Northmen
  USE **Vikings**

Northwest Africa 964

Use for materials dealing collectively with the area extending eastward from Morocco, Western Sahara, and Mauritania to include Libya and Chad. Northwest Africa includes the political entities of Morocco, Western Sahara, Mauritania, Algeria, Mali, Tunisia, Libya, Niger, and Chad.

UF   Africa, Northwest *[Former heading]*

BT   **Africa**

Northwest, Canadian

USE   **Canadian Northwest**

Northwest coast of North America

USE   **Northwest Coast of North America**

Northwest Coast of North America 979.5

UF   Northwest coast of North America *[Former heading]*
Northwest, Pacific coast
Pacific Northwest coast

Northwest, Old

USE   **Old Northwest**

Northwest, Pacific

USE   **Pacific Northwest**

Northwest, Pacific coast

USE   **Northwest Coast of North America**

Northwest Passage 971.9

BT   **America—Exploration**
Arctic regions
Exploration
Voyages and travels

Northwest Territory

USE   **Old Northwest**

Norwegian language 439.8

May be subdivided like **English language.**

BT   **Scandinavian languages**

NT   **Danish language**

Norwegian language—0-1350

USE   **Old Norse language**

Norwegian literature 839.8

May use same subdivisions and names of literary forms as for **English literature.**

BT   **Literature**
Scandinavian literature

Nose 611; 612.2

BT   **Face**
Head

RT   **Smell**

Not-for-profit organizations

USE   **Nonprofit organizations**

Notation, Mathematical

USE   **Mathematical notation**

Notation, Music

USE   **Musical notation**

Novelists 809.3; 920

SA   novelists of particular countries, e.g. **American novelists;** and names of individual novelists, to be added as needed

BT   **Authors**

NT   **American novelists**

Novelists, American

USE   **American novelists**

Novels

USE   **Fiction**

Novels in letters

USE   **Epistolary fiction**

Novels—Plots

USE   **Plots (Drama, fiction, etc.)**

Nuclear bomb shelters

USE   **Air raid shelters**

Nuclear energy 333.792; 539.7

UF   Atomic energy
Atomic power
Nuclear power

BT   **Nuclear physics**

NT   **Nuclear engineering**
Nuclear industry
Nuclear propulsion
Nuclear reactors

RT   **Nuclear power plants**

Nuclear engineering 621.48

BT   **Engineering**
Nuclear energy
Nuclear physics

NT   **Nuclear reactors**
Radioactive waste disposal
Radioisotopes

Nuclear freeze movement

USE   **Antinuclear movement**

Nuclear industry 333.792

UF   Atomic industry

BT   **Nuclear energy**

Nuclear magnetic resonance imaging

USE   **Magnetic resonance imaging**

Nuclear medicine 616.07

UF   Atomic medicine

Nuclear medicine—*Continued*
    Medicine, Atomic
    Medicine, Nuclear
  BT **Medicine**
  RT **Radiation—Physiological effect**
Nuclear non-proliferation
  USE **Arms control**
Nuclear particles
  USE **Particles (Nuclear physics)**
Nuclear physics 539.7
  UF Atomic nuclei
    Physics, Nuclear
  BT **Physics**
  NT **Cosmic rays**
    Cyclotron
    Nuclear energy
    Nuclear engineering
    Nuclear reactors
    Particles (Nuclear physics)
    Radiobiology
    Transmutation (Chemistry)
  RT **Physical chemistry**
    Radioactivity
Nuclear pollution
  USE **Radioactive pollution**
Nuclear power
  USE **Nuclear energy**
Nuclear power plants 621.48
  UF Atomic power plants
    Power plants, Atomic
  BT **Power plants**
  RT **Nuclear energy**
Nuclear power plants--Environmental
    aspects 333.792; 621.48
  BT **Environment**
    Environmental health
  NT **Radioactive waste disposal**
  RT **Antinuclear movement**
Nuclear power plants—Fires and fire
    prevention 363.37; 621.48
  BT **Fire prevention**
    Fires
Nuclear power plants—Security mea-
    sures 621.48
  BT **Burglary protection**
Nuclear propulsion 621.48
  UF Atomic powered vehicles
  SA specific applications of nuclear
    propulsion, e.g. **Nuclear**
    submarines; to be added as
    needed

  BT **Nuclear energy**
  NT **Nuclear submarines**
  RT **Nuclear reactors**
Nuclear reactors 621.48
  UF Atomic piles
    Breeder reactors
    Fast breeder reactors
    Reactors (Nuclear physics)
  BT **Nuclear energy**
    Nuclear engineering
    Nuclear physics
  RT **Nuclear propulsion**
Nuclear submarines 623.8
  UF Atomic submarines
    Submarines, Nuclear
  BT **Nuclear propulsion**
    Submarines
Nuclear test ban
  USE **Arms control**
Nuclear warfare 355.02
  UF Atomic warfare
  BT **War**
  NT **Atomic bomb**
    Hydrogen bomb
  RT **Nuclear weapons**
Nuclear waste disposal
  USE **Radioactive waste disposal**
Nuclear weapons 355.8; 623.4
  UF Atomic weapons
    Weapons, Atomic
    Weapons, Nuclear
  SA names of specific nuclear
    weapons, e.g. **Atomic bomb;**
    to be added as needed
  BT **Military weapons**
    Ordnance
  NT **Antinuclear movement**
    Atomic bomb
    Ballistic missiles
    Hydrogen bomb
    Neutron weapons
  RT **Nuclear warfare**
Nucleic acids 547.7; 574.87
  UF Polynucleotides
  BT **Biochemistry**
  NT **DNA**
    RNA
Nucleons
  USE **Particles (Nuclear physics)**
Nude in art 704.9
  UF Human anatomy in art

BT = Broader Term   NT = Narrower Term   RT = Related Term   SA = See Also   UF = Used For

Nude in art—*Continued*

Human figure in art

BT Art

NT Artistic anatomy

Number concept 119; 155.4; 372.7

Use for materials on the apperception and conceptualization of numbers. Materials on numbers, numbering, and systems of numeration are entered under **Numbers**. Materials on counting, including counting books, are entered under **Counting.**

BT Apperception

Psychology

RT Numbers

Number games 793.7

BT Arithmetic—Study and teaching

Counting

Mathematical recreations

Number patterns

USE Patterns (Mathematics)

Number readiness

USE Mathematical readiness

Number symbolism

USE Symbolism of numbers

Number systems

USE Numbers

Number theory 512

Use for materials on that branch of mathematics that involves the study of integers and their relation to one another.

UF Numbers, Theory of

Theory of numbers

BT Algebra

Mathematics

Set theory

NT Group theory

RT Numbers

Numbers 119; 513

Use for materials on numbers, numbering, and systems of numeration. Materials on the conceptualization of numbers are entered under **Number concept.** Materials on counting, including counting books, are entered under **Counting.** Materials on the graphic representation of numbers are entered under **Numerals.**

UF Number systems

Numeration *[Former heading]*

SA names of individual numbers, e.g. **Three (The number);** and systems of numeration, e.g. **Decimal system;** to be added an needed

NT Binary system (Mathematics)

Decimal system

Three (The number)

RT Arithmetic

Counting

Number concept

Number theory

Numerals

Symbolism of numbers

Numbers, Theory of

USE Number theory

Numeral formation

USE Writing of numerals

Numeral writing

USE Writing of numerals

Numerals 513

Use for materials on the graphic representation of numbers.

SA types of numerals, e.g. **Roman numerals;** to be added as needed

NT Roman numerals

Writing of numerals

RT Numbers

Numerals, Writing of

USE Writing of numerals

Numeration

USE Numbers

Numerical analysis 515

BT Mathematical analysis

NT Approximate computation

Numerical sequences

USE Sequences (Mathematics)

Numerology

USE Symbolism of numbers

Numismatics 737

Use for materials on coins, paper money, medals, and tokens considered as works of art, as historical specimens, or as aids to the study of history, archeology, etc.

UF Coin collecting

BT Ancient history

Archeology

History

NT Seals (Numismatics)

RT Coins

Medals

Nunneries

USE Convents

Nuns 255; 271; 920

UF Sisters (Religious)

BT = Broader Term   NT = Narrower Term   RT = Related Term   SA = See Also   UF = Used For

Nuns—*Continued*
 BT **Religious orders for women**
   Women
 NT **Ex-nuns**
Nurse clinicians
 USE **Nurse practitioners**
Nurse practitioners 610.73092; 920
 UF Nurse clinicians
 BT **Allied health personnel**
   Nurses
Nurse widwives
 USE **Midwives**
Nurseries, Day
 USE **Day care centers**
Nurseries (Horticulture) 631.5; 635
 BT **Fruit culture**
   Gardening
   Trees
 NT **Plant propagation**
Nursery rhymes 398.8

 May be used for collections of nursery rhymes or for materials about nursery rhymes.

 UF Poetry for children
   Rhymes
 BT **Children's poetry**
   Children's songs
   Folklore
Nursery schools 372.21
 BT **Elementary education**
   Schools
 RT **Day care centers**
   Kindergarten
   Preschool education
Nurses 610.73092; 920
 UF District nurses
   Trained nurses
 SA types of nurses, to be added
   as needed
 NT **Midwives**
   Nurse practitioners
   Practical nurses
   School nurses
Nursing 610.73; 649.8
 SA types of nursing, e.g. **Home
   nursing;** and diseases and
   medical procedures with the
   subdivision *Nursing,* to be
   added as needed
 BT **Medicine**

   Therapeutics
 NT **Cancer—Nursing**
   Cooking for the sick
   First aid
   Heart—Surgery—Nursing
   Home nursing
   Practical nursing
 RT **Hospitals**
   Sick
Nursing homes 362.1
 BT **Elderly—Care**
   Hospitals
   Institutional care
   Long-term care facilities
Nursing (Infant feeding)
 USE **Breast feeding**
Nutrition 641.1
 UF Meal planning
 SA subjects and classes of persons
   with the subdivision *Nutri-
   tion,* e.g. **Children—
   Nutrition;** to be added as
   needed
 BT **Health self-care**
   Physiology
   Therapeutics
 NT **Astronauts—Nutrition**
   Children—Nutrition
   Eating customs
   Malnutrition
   Plants—Nutrition
   Vitamins
 RT **Diet**
   Digestion
   Food
   Metabolism
Nuts 582.13; 634

 Use the names of specific kinds of nuts, expressed in the singular form, for materials on the nut or the tree or both.

 SA types of nuts, e.g. **Pecan;** to
   be added as needed, in the
   singular form
 BT **Food**
   Fruit
   Seeds
   Trees
 NT **Pecan**
Nylon 677
 BT **Fabrics**

Nylon—*Continued*
    Synthetic fabrics
Oak 583
  BT **Trees**
      Wood
Oats 633.1
  BT **Feeds**
Obedience 179
  UF Disobedience
  BT **Virtue**
Obelisks 721
  BT **Archeology**
      Architecture
      Monuments
      Pyramids
Obesity 613.2; 616.3
  UF Corpulence
      Fatness
      Overweight
Obituaries 920
  UF Death notices
      Necrologies
  BT **Biography**
Objective tests
  USE **Examinations**
Objets d'art
  USE **Art objects**
Obscene materials
  USE **Pornography**
Obscenity (Law) 344; 345
  BT **Crimes without victims**
      Criminal law
      Pornography
Observatories, Astronomical
  USE **Astronomical observatories**
Observatories, Meteorological
  USE **Meteorology—Observatories**
Obstetrics
  USE **Childbirth**
Occidental civilization
  USE **Western civilization**
Occult fiction 808.83; 813, etc.
    May be used for individual works, collections, or materials about fiction dealing with supernatural powers.
  BT **Fiction**
  NT **Ghost stories**
      Gothic novels
      Horror fiction
  RT **Fantasy fiction**
Occult sciences
  USE **Occultism**

Occult, The
  USE **Occultism**
Occultism 133
  UF Hermetic art and philosophy
      Occult sciences *[Former heading]*
      Occult, The
      Sorcery
  BT **Religions**
      Supernatural
  NT **Alchemy**
      Astrology
      Cabala
      Clairvoyance
      Divination
      Fortune telling
      New Age movement
      Oracles
      Palmistry
      Prophecies (Occultism)
      Spiritualism
      Witchcraft
  RT **Demonology**
      Magic
      Magic tricks
      Parapsychology
      Superstition
Occupation, Military
  USE **Military occupation**
Occupational crimes
  USE **White collar crimes**
Occupational diseases 616.9
  UF Diseases, Industrial
      Diseases, Occupational
      Diseases of occupation
      Industrial diseases
      Occupations—Diseases
  SA names of occupational diseases, to be added as needed
  BT **Diseases**
      Labor
      Occupational health and safety
      Public health
  NT **Lead poisoning**
      Occupational health services
      Workers' compensation
  RT **Hazardous occupations**

BT = Broader Term   NT = Narrower Term   RT = Related Term   SA = See Also   UF = Used For

Occupational forecasting
   USE **Employment forecasting**

Occupational guidance
   USE **Vocational guidance**

Occupational health and safety 363.11; 658.3
   UF Health, Industrial
        Hygiene, Industrial
        Industrial health
        Industrial safety
        Safety, Industrial
   BT **Environmental health**
        Management
        Public health
   NT **Burn out (Psychology)**
        Occupational diseases
   RT **Hazardous occupations**

Occupational health services 362.1; 613.6; 658.3
   Use for materials on health services for employees, usually provided at the place of work.
   UF Employee health services
   BT **Medical care**
        Occupational diseases

Occupational literacy
   USE **Functional literacy**

Occupational retraining 331.25
   UF Job retraining
        Retraining, Occupational
   BT **Employees—Training**
        Human resources policy
        Labor supply
        Occupational training
        Technical education
        Unemployed
        Vocational education

Occupational stress
   USE **Job stress**

Occupational therapy 615.8
   BT **Mental health**
        Physical therapy
        Physically handicapped— Rehabilitation
        Therapeutics
   RT **Handicraft**

Occupational training 331.25; 374
   Use for materials on teaching people a skill after formal education. Materials on teaching a skill during the educational process are entered under **Vocational education.** Materials discussing on-the-job training are entered under **Employees— Training.** Materials on retraining are entered under **Occupational retraining.**
   UF Job training
        Training, Occupational
        Training, Vocational
        Vocational training
   BT **Human resources policy**
        Technical education
        Vocational education
   NT **Employees—Training**
        Occupational retraining

Occupations 331.7
   Use for descriptions and lists of occupations.
   UF Careers
        Jobs
        Trades
        Vocations
   SA names of countries, cities, etc., with the subdivision *Occupations,* and names of specific occupations, to be added as needed
   BT **Business**
        Labor
   NT **Chicago (Ill.)—Occupations**
        Hazardous occupations
        Job analysis
        Paraprofessionals
        United States—Occupations
   RT **Professions**
        Vocational guidance

Occupations, Dangerous
   USE **Hazardous occupations**

Occupations—Diseases
   USE **Occupational diseases**

Occupied territory
   USE **Military occupation**

Ocean 551.46
   UF Oceans
        Sea
   SA names of oceans and seas, to be added as needed
   BT **Earth**
        Physical geography

Ocean—*Continued*
    Water
  NT **Atlantic Ocean**
    Icebergs
    Oceanography
    Seashore
Ocean bottom 551.46
  UF Ocean floor
    Sea bed
  BT **Marine biology**
    Oceanography
    Submarine geology
  NT **Marine mineral resources**
Ocean cables
  USE **Submarine cables**
Ocean currents 551.47
  UF Currents, Ocean
  BT **Navigation**
    Oceanography
    Physical geography
Ocean—Economic aspects
  USE **Marine resources**
    Shipping
Ocean energy resources 333.91
  UF Energy resources, Ocean
  BT **Energy resources**
    Marine resources
    Ocean engineering
  NT **Geothermal resources**
  RT **Marine mineral resources**
Ocean engineering 627
  Use for materials on engineering beneath the surface of the ocean.
  UF Deep sea engineering
    Submarine engineering
    Undersea engineering
  BT **Engineering**
    Marine resources
    Oceanography
  NT **Drilling platforms**
    Marine mineral resources
    Ocean energy resources
    Ocean mining
    Offshore oil well drilling
Ocean farming
  USE **Aquaculture**
Ocean floor
  USE **Ocean bottom**
Ocean life
  USE **Marine biology**

Ocean mineral resources
  USE **Marine mineral resources**
Ocean mining 622
  UF Deep sea mining
    Mining, Ocean
  BT **Marine mineral resources**
    Mining engineering
    Ocean engineering
Ocean pollution
  USE **Marine pollution**
Ocean resources
  USE **Marine resources**
Ocean routes
  USE **Trade routes**
Ocean transportation
  USE **Shipping**
Ocean travel 910.4
  UF Cruises
    Sea travel
  BT **Transportation**
    Travel
    Voyages and travels
  NT **Ships**
    Steamboats
    Yachts and yachting
Ocean waves 551.47
  UF Breakers
    Sea waves
    Surf
    Swell
    Tidal waves
  BT **Oceanography**
    Waves
  NT **Tsunamis**
Oceanariums
  USE **Marine aquariums**
Oceanauts
  USE **Aquanauts**
Oceania 995
  Use for comprehensive materials on the lands and area of the central and southern Pacific Ocean, including Micronesia, Melanesia, and Polynesia. Comprehensive works on all the islands of the Pacific Ocean are entered under **Islands of the Pacific.**
  UF South Pacific region
    South Sea Islands
    South Seas
    Southwest Pacific region
  BT **Islands**

BT = Broader Term   NT = Narrower Term   RT = Related Term   SA = See Also   UF = Used For

Oceania—*Continued*
     Islands of the Pacific
Oceanographic research
  USE **Oceanography—Research**
Oceanographic submersibles
  USE **Submersibles**
Oceanography (May subdiv. geog. area,
      e.g. **Oceanography—Atlantic
      Ocean;** etc.) **551.46**
  UF Deep sea technology
      Oceanology
      Undersea technology
  BT **Earth**
      Earth sciences
      Geology
      Geophysics
      Ocean
  NT **Marine biology**
      Marine pollution
      Marine resources
      Navigation
      Ocean bottom
      Ocean currents
      Ocean engineering
      Ocean waves
      Submarine geology
      Tides
Oceanography—Atlantic Ocean 551.46
Oceanography—Computer programs
     551.46
  BT **Computer software**
Oceanography—Research 551.46
  UF Oceanographic research
  NT **Bathyscaphe**
      Skin diving
      Submarine diving
      Submersibles
      Undersea research stations
      Underwater exploration
Oceanology
  USE **Oceanography**
Oceans
  USE **Ocean**
Oddities
  USE **Curiosities and wonders**
Offenses against public safety 364.1
  UF Crimes against public safety
      Public safety, Crimes against
  SA names of specific offenses, e.g.
      Hijacking of airplanes; to
      be added as needed

  BT **Criminal law**
  NT **Hijacking of airplanes**
      Riots
      Sabotage
Offenses against the person 364.1
  UF Abuse of persons
      Assault, Criminal
      Crimes against the person
      Criminal assault
      Persons, Crimes against
  SA names of specific offenses, to
      be added as needed
  BT **Crime**
      Criminal law
  NT **Assassination**
      Homicide
      Kidnapping
      Rape
Offenses, Military
  USE **Military offenses**
Office buildings (May subdiv. geog.)
     725
  UF Buildings, Office
  BT **Industrial buildings**
  NT **Skyscrapers**
Office employees
  USE **Office workers**
Office equipment and supplies 651
  UF Business machines
      Office machines
      Office supplies
  SA types of office equipment and
      supplies, to be added as
      needed
  BT **Bookkeeping**
      Office management
  NT **Calculators**
      Keyboards (Electronics)
      Typewriters
Office machines
  USE **Office equipment and supplies**
Office management 651.3
  UF Office procedures
  BT **Business**
      Factory management
      Industrial efficiency
      Management
  NT **Files and filing**
      Office equipment and supplies
      Office practice

Office management—*Continued*
    Secretaries
    Word processing
  RT Personnel management
Office practice 651.3
  UF Secretarial practice
  BT **Office management**
  NT **Keyboarding (Electronics)**
    Shorthand
    Typewriting
    Word processing
  RT **Office workers**
Office procedures
  USE **Office management**
Office romance
  USE **Sex in the workplace**
Office supplies
  USE **Office equipment and supplies**
Office work—Training
  USE **Business education**
Office workers 331.7; 651.3
  UF Clerical employees
    Clerks
    Commercial employees
    Employees, Clerical
    Office employees *[Former heading]*
  BT **Employees**
  RT **Office practice**
Official misconduct
  USE **Misconduct in office**
Official publications
  USE **Government publications**
Officials
  USE **Civil service**
    and names of countries, cities, etc., and corporate bodies with the subdivision *Officials and employees,* e.g. **United States—Officials and employees; Chicago (Ill.)—Officials and employees; United Nations—Officials and employees;** etc., to be added as needed
Offset printing 686.2
  UF Lithoprinting
    Printing, Offset
  BT **Lithography**
    Printing

Offshore oil industry 338.2
  UF Oil industry, Offshore
    Petroleum industry, Offshore
  BT **Petroleum industry**
  NT **Offshore oil well drilling**
Offshore oil well drilling 622
  UF Deep sea drilling (Petroleum)
    Oil well drilling, Offshore
    Oil well drilling, Submarine *[Former heading]*
    Submarine oil well drilling
    Underwater drilling (Petroleum)
  BT **Ocean engineering**
    Offshore oil industry
    Oil well drilling
  NT **Drilling platforms**
Offshore structures
  USE **Drilling platforms**
Offshore water pollution
  USE **Marine pollution**
Ohio 977.1
    The subdivisions under **Ohio** may be used under the name of any state of the United States or province of Canada. The subdivisions under **United States** may be further consulted as a guide for formulating other headings as needed.
Ohio—African Americans
  USE **African Americans—Ohio**
Ohio—Antiquities 977.1
Ohio—Bibliography 015.771; 016.9771
Ohio—Bio-bibliography 012
Ohio—Biography 920.0771
Ohio—Biography—Dictionaries 920.0771
  BT **Encyclopedias and dictionaries**
Ohio—Biography—Portraits 920.0771
Ohio—Boundaries 977.1
Ohio—Census 317.71
Ohio—Church history 277.71
Ohio—Civilization 977.1
Ohio—Climate 551.69771
Ohio—Commerce 381
Ohio—Constitution 342.771
  BT **State constitutions**
Ohio—Constitutional history 342.771
Ohio—Cooking
  USE **Cooking—Ohio**
Ohio—Description 917.71
  UF Ohio—Description and travel *[Former heading]*

Ohio—Description—*Continued*
    Ohio—Travel
Ohio—Description and travel
  USE **Ohio—Description**
Ohio—Description—Guidebooks
  USE **Ohio—Guidebooks**
Ohio—Description—Views
  USE **Ohio—Pictorial works**
Ohio—Directories 917.710025
    Use for lists of names and addresses. Lists of names without addresses are entered under **Ohio—Registers.**
  BT **Directories**
  RT **Ohio—Registers**
Ohio—Economic conditions 330.9771
Ohio—Economic policy 338.9771
  BT **Economic policy**
Ohio—Executive departments 353.9771
Ohio—Folk songs
  USE **Folk songs—Ohio**
Ohio—Foreign population 325.771
Ohio—Gazetteers 917.71
Ohio—Government publications
  USE **Government publications—Ohio**
Ohio—Guidebooks 917.7104
  UF Ohio—Description—Guidebooks *[Former heading]*
Ohio—Historic buildings
  USE **Historic buildings—Ohio**
Ohio—History 977.1
Ohio—History, Local
  USE **Ohio—Local history**
Ohio—History—Societies 977.106
Ohio—History—Sources 977.1
Ohio—Industries 338.09771
  UF Ohio—Manufactures
Ohio—Intellectual life 977.1
  BT **Intellectual life**
Ohio—Local history 977.1
  UF Ohio—History, Local *[Former heading]*
Ohio—Manufactures
  USE **Ohio—Industries**
Ohio—Maps 912.771
Ohio—Militia 355.3
Ohio—Moral conditions 977.1
Ohio—Museums
  USE **Museums—Ohio**

Ohio—Occupations 331.7
Ohio—Officials and employees 353.9771004
Ohio—Pictorial works 917.710022
  UF Ohio—Description—Views *[Former heading]*
Ohio—Politics and government 977.1
  BT **State governments**
Ohio—Population 304.609771
Ohio—Public buildings 725.09771
  UF Public buildings—Ohio
  BT **Public buildings**
Ohio—Public lands
  USE **Public lands—Ohio**
Ohio—Public works 353.97710086
Ohio—Race relations 305.8009771
Ohio—Registers 917.710025
    Use for lists of names without addresses. Lists of names that include addresses are entered under **Ohio—Directories.**
  RT **Ohio—Directories**
Ohio—Religion 277.71
Ohio—Rural conditions 307.7209771
Ohio—Social conditions 977.1
Ohio—Social life and customs 977.1
Ohio—Social policy 361.6; 977.1
Ohio—Statistics 317.71
Ohio—Travel
  USE **Ohio—Description**
Oil
  USE **Oils and fats**
      Petroleum
Oil burners 697
  BT **Heating**
      Petroleum as fuel
Oil engines
  USE **Internal combustion engines**
Oil fuel
  USE **Petroleum as fuel**
Oil industry
  USE **Petroleum industry**
Oil industry, Offshore
  USE **Offshore oil industry**
Oil painting
  USE **Painting**
Oil pollution of rivers, harbors, etc.
  USE **Oil pollution of water**
Oil pollution of water 363.73; 628.1
  UF Oil pollution of rivers, harbors, etc. *[Former heading]*

Oil pollution of water—*Continued*
  Petroleum pollution of water
  Water—Oil pollution
  BT **Water pollution**
  RT **Marine pollution**
    Oil spills
Oil spills 363.73
  BT **Marine pollution**
  RT **Oil pollution of water**
Oil well drilling 622
  UF Drilling, Oil well
    Petroleum—Well boring
    Well drilling, Oil
  BT **Petroleum industry**
  NT **Offshore oil well drilling**
    Oil wells—Blowouts
  RT **Oil wells**
Oil well drilling, Offshore
  USE **Offshore oil well drilling**
Oil well drilling, Submarine
  USE **Offshore oil well drilling**
Oil wells 622
  BT **Petroleum industry**
  RT **Oil well drilling**
Oil wells—Blowouts 622
  UF Blowouts, Oil well
  BT **Oil well drilling**
Oils and fats 665
  UF Animal oils
    Fat
    Fats
    Grease
    Oil
    Vegetable oils
  NT **Essences and essential oils**
    Petroleum
  RT **Coal tar products**
    Lubrication and lubricants
Oils, Essential
  USE **Essences and essential oils**
Old age 305.26
  BT **Age**
    Gerontology
    Life (Biology)
  NT **Age and employment**
    Aging
    Retirement
  RT **Elderly**
    Longevity
Old age homes
  USE **Elderly—Institutional care**

Old age pensions 331.25; 368.4
  UF Insurance, Old age
    Labor—Insurance
  BT **Pensions**
    Retirement income
    Saving and thrift
    Social security
Old English language
  USE **Anglo-Saxon language**
Old English literature
  USE **Anglo-Saxon literature**
Old Icelandic language
  USE **Old Norse language**
Old Norse language 439
  UF Icelandic language—0-1500
    Norse languages
    Norwegian language—0-1350
    Old Icelandic language
    Old Norwegian language
  BT **Scandinavian languages**
Old Norse literature 839
  UF Norse literature
  BT **Literature**
    Medieval literature
  NT **Eddas**
    Sagas
  RT **Icelandic literature**
    Scandinavian literature
Old Northwest 977
  Use for materials on the region between the Ohio and Mississippi rivers and the Great Lakes.
  UF Northwest, Old
    Northwest Territory
  BT **United States**
  RT **Middle West**
Old Norwegian language
  USE **Old Norse language**
Old Southwest 976
  Use for materials on that section of the United States that comprised the southwestern part before the cessions of land from Mexico following the Mexican War. It included Louisiana, Texas, Arkansas, Tennessee, Kentucky and Missouri.
  UF Southwest, Old
  BT **United States**
Old Testament
  USE **Bible. O.T.**
Older persons
  USE **Elderly**
Oldest child
  USE **Birth order**

BT = Broader Term   NT = Narrower Term   RT = Related Term   SA = See Also   UF = Used For

Oleomargarine
USE **Margarine**
Olympic games 796.48; 796.98
　UF　Games, Olympic
　BT　**Athletics**
　　　Contests
　　　Games
　　　Sports
　NT　**Special Olympics**
Olympics, Special
USE **Special Olympics**
Ombudsman (May subdiv. geog.) **328.3;**
　　　342; 351.9
　UF　Citizen's defender
　　　Grievance procedures (Public
　　　administration)
　BT　**Administrative law**
　　　Public interest
On the job stress
USE **Job stress**
One act plays 808.82; 812, etc.
　　May be used for individual works, col-
　　lections, or materials about one-act plays.
　UF　Plays
　　　Short plays
　BT　**Amateur theater**
　　　Drama
One parent family
USE **Single parent family**
Online catalogs 025.3
　UF　Catalogs, Online *[Former
　　　heading]*
　　　Online public access catalogs
　　　OPACs (Online public access
　　　catalogs)
　BT　**Library catalogs**
　RT　**Libraries—Automation**
Online data processing 004
　BT　**Electronic data processing**
　NT　**Computer bulletin boards**
Online public access catalogs
USE **Online catalogs**
Online publishing
USE **Electronic publishing**
Online reference services
USE **Reference services (Libraries)**
Only child 155.44; 306.874
　UF　Single child
　BT　**Children**
　　　Family size

OPACs (Online public access catalogs)
USE **Online catalogs**
Opaque projectors
USE **Projectors**
Open and closed shop 331.88
　UF　Closed shop
　　　Right to work
　　　Union shop
　BT　**Labor**
　　　Labor contract
　　　Labor unions
Open classroom approach to teaching
USE **Open plan schools**
Open education
USE **Open plan schools**
Open ended marriage
USE **Unmarried couples**
Open heart surgery
USE **Heart—Surgery**
Open housing
USE **Discrimination in housing**
Open plan schools 371.2
　　Use for materials on schools without in-
　　terior walls.
　UF　Interest centers approach to
　　　teaching
　　　Learning center approach to
　　　teaching
　　　Open classroom approach to
　　　teaching
　　　Open education
　BT　**Education—Experimental
　　　methods**
　NT　**Individualized instruction**
　RT　**Experimental schools**
Open universities
USE **Free universities**
Opera (May subdiv. geog.) **782.1; 792.5**
　　Use for musical scores and for materials
　　about the opera.
　UF　Comic opera
　　　Dramatic music
　　　Lyric drama
　　　Operas *[Former heading]*
　BT　**Drama**
　　　Musical form
　　　Performing arts
　　　Vocal music
　NT　**Operetta**
Opera librettos 782.1026
　　Use for individual opera librettos and
　　for collections of opera librettos.

Opera librettos—*Continued*
  UF   Operas—Librettos *[Former heading]*
  BT   **Librettos**
  RT   **Opera—Stories, plots, etc.**
Opera—Stories, plots, etc. 782.1026
    Use for individual opera plots and for collections of opera plots.
  RT   **Literature—Stories, plots, etc.**
        Opera librettos
Operas
  USE   **Opera**
Operas—Librettos
  USE   **Opera librettos**
Operating systems (Computers)
  USE   **Computer operating systems**
Operation Desert Shield
  USE   **Persian Gulf War, 1991**
Operation Desert Storm
  USE   **Persian Gulf War, 1991**
Operations research 658.5
  BT   **Research**
        System theory
  RT   **Systems engineering**
Operations, Surgical
  USE   **Surgery**
Operetta 782.1; 792.5
    Use for musical scores and for materials on the operetta as a musical form.
  UF   Comic opera
        Dramatic music
        Operettas
  BT   **Musical form**
        Opera
        Vocal music
  RT   **Musicals**
Operettas
  USE   **Operetta**
Opiates
  USE   **Narcotics**
Opinion polls
  USE   **Public opinion polls**
Opinion, Public
  USE   **Public opinion**
Opioids, Brain
  USE   **Endorphins**
Opium 615
  BT   **Narcotics**
  RT   **Morphine**
Opium—Physiological effect 615
  BT   **Drugs—Physiological effect**

Opposites 153.2
  UF   Antonyms
        Polarity
  BT   **Concepts**
  RT   **English language—Synonyms and antonyms**
Optical data processing 006.4; 621.36; 621.39; 651.8
  UF   Visual data processing
  BT   **Bionics**
        Electronic data processing
Optical discs
  USE   **Optical storage devices**
Optical illusions 152.14
  UF   Illusions
  BT   **Hallucinations and illusions**
        Psychophysiology
        Vision
Optical instruments 681
  UF   Instruments, Optical
  BT   **Scientific apparatus and instruments**
  NT   **Microscopes**
        Telescopes
  RT   **Optics**
        Space optics
Optical masers
  USE   **Lasers**
Optical storage devices 004.5; 621.39
    Use for materials on data storage devices in which audio, video, or digital data are optically encoded.
  UF   Discs, Optical
        Optical discs
  BT   **Computer storage devices**
        Optics
  NT   **CD-I technology**
        CD-ROM
        Compact discs
        Videodiscs
  RT   **Laser recording**
        Magnetic recorders and recording
        Sound—Recording and reproducing
Optics 535; 621.36
  BT   **Physics**
  NT   **Color**
        Optical storage devices
        Perspective

Optics—*Continued*
>Phosphorescence
>Radiation
>Refraction
>Space optics
>Spectrum analysis
>Vision

>RT Light
>>Optical instruments
>>Photometry

Optometry 617.7
>RT Eye

Oracles 133.3
>BT Occultism
>RT Divination
>>Prophecies (Occultism)

Oral arithmetic
>USE Mental arithmetic

Oral history 907

>Use for materials on recording oral recollections of places, events, etc., from persons drawing on their own life experiences. Oral histories that focus on a particular subject are entered under that subject.

>UF History, Oral
>BT History

Oral interpretation
>USE Recitations

Orange 634 ; 641.3
>BT Citrus fruit
>>Trees

Orations
>USE Speeches

Oratorio 782.23

>Use for musical scores and for materials on the oratorio as a musical form.

>UF Oratorios *[Former heading]*
>BT Church music
>>Musical form
>>Vocal music

Oratorios
>USE Oratorio

Oratory
>USE Public speaking

Orbital debris
>USE Space debris

Orbital laboratories
>USE Space stations

Orbital rendezvous (Space flight) 629.45
>UF Rendezvous in space
>>Space orbital rendezvous

>SA names of projects, e.g. **Apollo project; Gemini project;** etc.; and names of specific space ships, to be added as needed
>BT Space flight
>>Space ships
>>Space stations
>NT Apollo project
>>Gemini project

Orbiting vehicles
>USE Artificial satellites
>>Space stations

Orchards
>USE Fruit culture

Orchestra 784.2
>SA types of orchestras, to be added as needed
>BT Musical instruments
>NT Conductors (Music)
>>Instrumentation and orchestration
>>Orchestral music
>RT Bands (Music)
>>Conducting
>>Ensembles (Music)

Orchestral music 784.2
>SA types of orchestral music, e.g. **Symphony;** to be added as needed
>BT Instrumental music
>>Music
>>Orchestra
>NT Chamber music
>>Concerto
>>Quintets
>>String orchestra music
>>Suite (Music)
>>Symphonic poems
>>Symphony

Orchestration
>USE Instrumentation and orchestration

Orders, Monastic
>USE Religious orders

Ordination 262; 265
>BT Rites and ceremonies
>>Sacraments
>NT Ordination of women
>RT Clergy

BT = Broader Term   NT = Narrower Term   RT = Related Term   SA = See Also   UF = Used For

Ordination of women 262
  UF   Women—Ordination
  BT   **Ordination**
  RT   **Women clergy**
Ordnance 355.8; 623.4
  Use for materials on military supplies including weapons, ammunition, and vehicles, and the task of procuring, testing, storing, and issuing such supplies.
  UF   Cannon
       Guns
  SA   types of military ordnance, e.g. **Bombs;** and names of armies with the subdivision *Ordnance,* e.g. **United States. Army—Ordnance;** to be added as needed
  BT   **Military art and science**
  NT   **Ammunition**
       Bombs
       Nuclear weapons
       United States. Army— Ordnance
  RT   **Artillery**
       Defense industries
       Military weapons
       Projectiles
Ore deposits 553
  SA   types of ores, e.g. **Iron ores;** to be added as needed
  BT   **Geology**
  NT   **Iron ores**
  RT   **Ores**
Ore dressing 622
  UF   Dressing of ores
  BT   **Smelting**
Oregon country
  USE   **Pacific Northwest**
Oregon Trail 978
  BT   **Overland journeys to the Pacific**
       United States
Ores 553
  SA   types of ores, e.g. **Iron ores;** to be added as needed
  BT   **Economic geology**
  NT   **Iron ores**
       Metallurgy
       Metals
       Mineralogy

  Mines and mineral resources
  RT   **Ore deposits**
Organ
  USE   **Organs (Musical instruments)**
Organ donation
  USE   **Donation of organs, tissues, etc.**
Organ music 786.5
  BT   **Church music**
       Instrumental music
       Music
Organ preservation (Anatomy)
  USE   **Preservation of organs, tissues, etc.**
Organ transplantation
  USE   **Transplantation of organs, tissues, etc.**
Organic agriculture
  USE   **Organic farming**
Organic art
  USE   **Abstract art**
Organic chemistry 547
  UF   Chemistry, Organic *[Former heading]*
  BT   **Chemistry**
Organic chemistry—Synthesis 547
  UF   Chemistry, Organic—Synthesis *[Former heading]*
       Chemistry, Synthetic
       Synthetic chemistry
  NT   **Polymers**
       Synthetic products
  RT   **Plastics**
Organic farming 631.5
  UF   Ecological agriculture
       Farming, Organic
       Organic agriculture
       Organiculture *[Former heading]*
  BT   **Agriculture**
Organic gardening 635
  UF   Gardening, Organic
       Natural gardening
       Organiculture *[Former heading]*
  BT   **Gardening**
       Horticulture
  RT   **Compost**
Organic waste as fuel
  USE   **Waste products as fuel**

BT = Broader Term   NT = Narrower Term   RT = Related Term   SA = See Also   UF = Used For

Organically grown foods
  USE **Natural foods**
Organiculture
  USE **Organic farming**
          Organic gardening
Organists 786.5092; 920
  BT **Musicians**
Organization and management
  USE **Management**
Organization development
  USE **Organizational change**
Organization, International
  USE **International organization**
Organization (Sociology)
  USE **Organizational sociology**
Organization theory
  USE **Organizational sociology**
Organizational change 338.7; 658.4
  UF Change, Organizational
          Organization development
          Organizational development
          Organizational innovation
  BT **Management**
Organizational development
  USE **Organizational change**
Organizational innovation
  USE **Organizational change**
Organizational sociology 302.3
  UF Organization (Sociology)
          Organization theory
          Sociology of organizations
  BT **Sociology**
  RT **Bureaucracy**
Organizational stress
  USE **Job stress**
Organizations
  USE **Associations**
Organizations, Business
  USE **Business enterprises**
Organizations, Nonprofit
  USE **Nonprofit organizations**
Organized crime 364.1
  UF Crime syndicates
  SA types of organized crime, e.g.
          Racketeering; to be added
          as needed
  BT **Crime**
  NT **Gangs**
          Racketeering
Organized labor
  USE **Labor unions**

Organs (Anatomy)—Preservation
  USE **Preservation of organs, tissues, etc.**
Organs, Artificial
  USE **Artificial organs**
Organs (Musical instruments) 786.5
  UF Organ *[Former heading]*
          Pipe organs
  BT **Musical instruments**
  NT **Keyboards (Musical instruments)**
Orient
  USE **Asia**
          East Asia
          Middle East
Oriental architecture
  USE **Asian architecture**
Oriental art
  USE **Asian art**
Oriental civilization
  USE **Asian civilization**
Oriental rugs 746.7
  UF Rugs, Oriental *[Former heading]*
  SA types of Oriental rugs, to be
          added as needed
  BT **Rugs**
Orientation
  USE **Direction sense**
Orienteering 796.5
    Use for materials on the cross-country sport in which competitors using maps and compasses proceed on foot to checkpoints through unknown terrain.
  BT **Hiking**
          Navigation
          Racing
          Running
          Sports
  RT **Direction sense**
Origami 736
  UF Japanese paper folding
          Paper folding, Japanese
  BT **Paper crafts**
Origin of life
  USE **Life—Origin**
Origin of man
  USE **Human origins**
Origin of species
  USE **Evolution**
Ornament
  USE **Decoration and ornament**

BT = Broader Term   NT = Narrower Term   RT = Related Term   SA = See Also   UF = Used For

Ornamental alphabets
  USE **Illumination of books and**
       manuscripts
       Lettering
Ornamental plants 635.9; 715
  UF Plants, Ornamental *[Former*
      heading]
  BT **Cultivated plants**
      Flower gardening
      Landscape gardening
  RT **Shrubs**
Ornithology
  USE **Birds**
Orphan drugs 615
    Use for materials on drugs that appear
  to be useful for the treatment of rare dis-
  orders but owing to their limited commer-
  cial value have difficulty in finding
  funding for research and marketing.
  UF Drugs, Orphan
      Nonprofitable drugs
  BT **Drugs**
Orphanages (May subdiv. geog.) **362.7**
  UF Charitable institutions
      Homes (Institutions)
  BT **Charities**
      Children—Institutional care
      Institutional care
      Public welfare
  RT **Child welfare**
Orphans 362.7
  UF Foundlings
  BT **Children**
  RT **Abandoned children**
      Adopted children
Orthodox Eastern Church 281.9
  UF Greek Church
  BT **Christian sects**
      Eastern churches
Orthodox Eastern Church, Russian
  USE **Russian Orthodox Church**
Orthography
  USE **Spelling reform**
       and names of languages with
       the subdivision *Spelling,*
       e.g. **English language—**
       Spelling; to be added as
       needed
Orthopedic surgery
  USE **Orthopedics**
Orthopedics 617.3
  UF Orthopedic surgery

Surgery, Orthopedic
  BT **Surgery**
  RT **Physically handicapped**
Osteology
  USE **Bones**
Osteopathy 610; 615.5
  BT **Alternative medicine**
  NT **Chiropractic**
  RT **Massage**
Ostrogoths
  USE **Teutonic peoples**
Out-of-doors education
  USE **Outdoor education**
Out-of-work people
  USE **Unemployed**
Outboard motorboats
  USE **Motorboats**
Outdoor cookery
  USE **Outdoor cooking**
Outdoor cooking 641.5
  UF Camp cooking
      Cooking, Outdoor
      Outdoor cookery *[Former*
      heading]
  BT **Camping**
      Cooking
  NT **Barbecue cooking**
Outdoor education 371.3
  UF Education, Outdoor
      Out-of-doors education
  BT **Education**
  RT **Nature study**
      Outdoor life
Outdoor life 796.5
  UF Rural life
  SA types of outdoor life, educa-
      tion, or activities, to be
      added as needed
  NT **Hiking**
      Mountaineering
      Wilderness survival
  RT **Camping**
      Country life
      Nature study
      Outdoor education
      Sports
Outdoor photography 778.7
  UF Field photography
      Photography, Outdoor
  BT **Photography**

BT = Broader Term   NT = Narrower Term   RT = Related Term   SA = See Also   UF = Used For

Outdoor photography—_Continued_
   RT   **Nature photography**
Outdoor recreation 796
   SA   types of outdoor recreation,
          e.g. **Camping;** to be added
          as needed
   BT   **Recreation**
   NT   **Camping**
          Cycling
          Parks
          Recreational vehicles
          Roller skating
Outdoor survival
   USE   **Wilderness survival**
Outer space 523.1
   UF   Space, Outer
   BT   **Astronautics**
          Astronomy
          Space sciences
   NT   **Space environment**
          Space warfare
Outer space and civilization
   USE   **Astronautics and civilization**
Outer space—Colonies
   USE   **Space colonies**
Outer space—Communication
   USE   **Interstellar communication**
Outer space—Exploration 629.4
   UF   Exploration, Space
          Space exploration (Astronau-
          tics)
          Space research
   BT   **Exploration**
          Interplanetary voyages
          Space flight
   NT   **Planets—Exploration**
          Space probes
Outer space—Pollution
   USE   **Space debris**
Outer space travel
   USE   **Interplanetary voyages**
Outlaws
   USE   **Thieves**
Outlines, syllabi, etc.
   USE   subjects with the subdivision
          Outlines, syllabi, etc., e.g.
          English literature—
          Outlines, syllabi, etc.; to be
          added as needed
Output equipment (Computers)
   USE   **Computer peripherals**

Output standards
   USE   **Production standards**
Over-the-counter drugs
   USE   **Nonprescription drugs**
Overactive children
   USE   **Hyperactive children**
Overactivity
   USE   **Hyperactivity**
Overland journeys to the Pacific 978
     Use for materials on the pioneers' cross-
  ing of the American continent toward the
  Pacific by foot, horseback, wagon, etc.
   UF   Transcontinental journeys
          (American continent)
   BT   **Frontier and pioneer life**
          Voyages and travels
   NT   **Oregon Trail**
   RT   **West (U.S.)—Exploration**
Overseas study
   USE   **Foreign study**
Oversize books
   USE   **Big books**
Oversized books for shared reading
   USE   **Big books**
Overtime
   USE   **Hours of labor**
          Wages
Overweight
   USE   **Obesity**
Ownership
   USE   **Property**
Oxyacetylene welding
   USE   **Welding**
Oxygen 546; 547; 665.8
   BT   **Chemical elements**
          Gases
   NT   **Ozone**
Oysters, Pearl
   USE   **Pearlfisheries**
Ozone 665.8
   BT   **Oxygen**
Ozone layer 363.73; 551.5
   UF   Ozonosphere
          Stratospheric ozone
   BT   **Stratosphere**
Ozonosphere
   USE   **Ozone layer**
P.O.W.'s
   USE   **Prisoners of war**
P.T.A.'s
   USE   **Parents' and teachers' associa-**
          tions

     BT = Broader Term   **NT = Narrower Term**   **RT = Related Term**   **SA = See Also**   **UF = Used For**

Pacific cable
USE **Submarine cables**
Pacific Islands
USE **Islands of the Pacific**
Pacific Northwest 979.5
Use for materials on the old Oregon country, comprising the present states of Oregon, Washington, and Idaho, parts of Montana and Wyoming, and the province of British Columbia.
UF Northwest, Pacific
Oregon country
BT **North America**
United States
West (U.S.)
Pacific Northwest coast
USE **Northwest Coast of North America**
Pacific Ocean Islands
USE **Islands of the Pacific**
Pacific rim 330.99; 910.9182
Use for materials on the periphery of the Pacific Ocean, especially as a region of interdependent economies.
RT **East Asia**
Islands of the Pacific
Pacific States 979
BT **West (U.S.)**
Pacifism 174; 303.6
UF Peace movements
BT **Peace**
War and religion
RT **Conscientious objectors**
Nonviolence
Pack transportation
USE **Backpacking**
Packaged houses
USE **Prefabricated houses**
Packaging 658.5; 658.7; 658.8
SA types of packaging and packaging materials, to be added as needed
BT **Advertising**
Retail trade
NT **Aluminum foil**
Boxes
Gift wrapping
Packing industry
USE **Meat industry**
PAC's
USE **Lobbying**
Paganism 291; 292
UF Heathenism

BT **Christianity and other religions**
Religions
Pageants 394; 791.6
BT **Acting**
NT **Masks (Plays)**
Mysteries and miracle plays
Parades
RT **Festivals**
Pain 152.1; 612.8
BT **Diagnosis**
Emotions
Psychophysiology
Senses and sensation
NT **Anesthetics**
RT **Pleasure**
Suffering
Paint 645; 667
UF Finishes and finishing
BT **House painting**
Industrial painting
RT **Corrosion and anticorrosives**
Pigments
Paint sniffing
USE **Solvent abuse**
Painted glass
USE **Glass painting and staining**
Painters 759; 920
SA painters of particular countries, e.g. **American painters**; and names of individual painters, to be added as needed
BT **Artists**
NT **American painters**
Painters, American
USE **American painters**
Painters' materials
USE **Artists' materials**
Painting 750
UF Oil painting
Paintings
SA painting of particular countries, e.g. **American painting**; and types of painting, e.g. **Landscape painting**; to be added as needed
BT **Art**
Graphic arts
NT **American painting**

Painting—*Continued*

      Animal painting and illustration

      China painting

      Color

      Cubism

      Expressionism (Art)

      Figure painting

      Finger painting

      Flower painting and illustration

      Futurism (Art)

      Glass painting and staining

      Impressionism (Art)

      Landscape painting

      Marine painting

      Miniature painting

      Modern painting

      Mural painting and decoration

      Perspective

      Portrait painting

      Postimpressionism (Art)

      Scene painting

      Stencil work

      Textile painting

      Watercolor painting

  RT **Composition (Art)**

      Decoration and ornament

      Drawing

      Pictures

Painting, Abstract

  USE **Abstract art**

Painting, American

  USE **American painting**

Painting books

  USE **Coloring books**

Painting—Color reproductions

  USE **Color prints**

Painting—Conservation and restoration 751.6

Painting, Decorative

  USE **Decoration and ornament**

Painting, Finger

  USE **Finger painting**

Painting, Industrial

  USE **Industrial painting**

Painting, Mechanical

  USE **Industrial painting**

Painting, Modern

  USE **Modern painting**

Painting, Modern—1800-1899 (19th century)

  USE **Modern painting—1800-1899 (19th century)**

Painting, Modern—1900-1999 (20th century)

  USE **Modern painting—1900-1999 (20th century)**

Painting, Religious

  USE **Religious art and symbolism**

Painting, Romanesque

  USE **Romanesque painting**

Painting—Technique 751.4

Paintings

  USE **Painting**

Pair system

  USE **Binary system (Mathematics)**

Palaces (May subdiv. geog.) **728.8**

  BT **Architecture**

Paleobiogeography

  USE **Biogeography**

Paleobotany

  USE **Fossil plants**

Paleolithic period

  USE **Stone Age**

Paleontology

  USE **Fossils**

Palestine problem, 1917-

  USE **Israel-Arab conflicts**

Palestinian Arabs 305.892; 956.94

  UF Arabs—Palestine

      Palestinians

  BT **Arabs**

  RT **Jewish-Arab relations**

Palestinian-Israeli conflict, 1987-

  USE **Intifada, 1987-**

Palestinian uprising, 1987-

  USE **Intifada, 1987-**

Palestinians

  USE **Palestinian Arabs**

Palmistry 133.6

  BT **Divination**

      Fortune telling

      Occultism

Palsy, Cerebral

  USE **Cerebral palsy**

Pamphlets 025.17

  UF Street literature

  BT **Press**

  NT **Chapbooks**

BT = Broader Term   NT = Narrower Term   RT = Related Term   SA = See Also   UF = Used For

Pan-Africanism 320.5; 327

Use for materials on the advocacy of either political alliance or close economic, cultural, and military cooperation among the countries of Africa.

UF African relations

BT **Africa**

Pan-Americanism 320.5; 327

Use for materials on the advocacy of either political alliance or close economic, cultural, and military cooperation among the countries of North and South America.

UF Good Neighbor Policy

Inter-American relations

BT **Latin America**

NT **Monroe Doctrine**

RT **America—Politics and government**

Pan-Arabism 320.5

Use for materials on the advocacy of either political alliance or close economic, cultural, and military cooperation among the Arab countries.

UF Panarabism *[Former heading]*

BT **Arab countries—Politics and government**

Panama Canal 972.87

BT **Canals**

Panarabism

USE **Pan-Arabism**

Panel discussions

USE **Discussion groups**

Panel heating

USE **Radiant heating**

Paneuropean federation

USE **European federation**

Panhandling

USE **Begging**

Panics, Economic

USE **Economic depressions**

Pantomimes 792.3

BT **Acting**

Amateur theater

Drama

Theater

NT **Shadow pantomimes and plays**

RT **Ballet**

Mime

Papacy 262

UF Holy See

BT **Catholic Church**

Church history

RT **Popes**

Papal encyclicals 262.9

UF Encyclicals, Papal *[Former heading]*

BT **Christian literature**

Paper 676

BT **Fibers**

NT **Papermaking**

Paper airplanes

USE **Airplanes—Models**

Paper bound books

USE **Paperback books**

Paper crafts 745.54

UF Paper folding

Paper sculpture

Paper work

Papier-mâché

SA types of paper crafts, to be added as needed

BT **Handicraft**

NT **Decoupage**

Gift wrapping

Origami

RT **Papermaking**

Paper folding

USE **Paper crafts**

Paper folding, Japanese

USE **Origami**

Paper hanging

USE **Paperhanging**

Paper industry 338.4

Use for materials on the business of making and selling paper. Materials on the technology and craft of making paper are entered under **Papermaking.**

UF Paper making and trade *[Former heading]*

Paper trade

Papermaking industry

BT **Industry**

RT **Book industries**

Paper making

USE **Papermaking**

Paper making and trade

USE **Paper industry**

Paper manufacture

USE **Papermaking**

Paper money 332.4

UF Bills of credit

Fiat money

Paper money—*Continued*
>> Greenbacks
>> Legal tender
>> Money, Paper
> BT **Finance**
>> **Inflation (Finance)**
>> **Money**

Paper sculpture
> USE **Paper crafts**

Paper trade
> USE **Paper industry**

Paper work
> USE **Paper crafts**

Paperback books 070.5
> UF Books, Paperback
>> Paper bound books
> BT **Bibliography—Editions**
>> **Books**
>> **Publishers and publishing**

Paperhanging 698
> UF Paper hanging *[Former heading]*
> BT **Interior design**
> RT **Wallpaper**

Papermaking 676

Use for materials on the technology and craft of making paper. Materials on the business of making and selling paper are entered under **Paper industry.**

> UF Paper making
>> Paper manufacture
> BT **Manufactures**
>> **Paper**
> RT **Paper crafts**

Papermaking industry
> USE **Paper industry**

Papers, Collected (Anthologies)
> USE **Anthologies**

Papier-mâché
> USE **Paper crafts**

Parables 808

May be used for individual works, collections, or matierals about parables.

> UF Cautionary tales and verse
>> Moral and philosophic stories
>> Morality tales
> NT **Bible—Parables**
>> **Jesus Christ—Parables**
> RT **Allegories**
>> **Didactic fiction**
>> **Didactic poetry**
>> Fables

Parachute troops 356
> UF Paratroops
> SA names of armies with the subdivision *Parachute troops,* e.g. **United States. Army—Parachute troops;** to be added as needed
> BT **Military aeronautics**
>> **Parachutes**
> NT **United States. Army—Parachute troops**

Parachutes 629.134
> BT **Aeronautics**
> NT **Parachute troops**

Parades 791.6
> UF Floats (Parades)
>> Pomp
>> Processions
> BT **Festivals**
>> **Pageants**

Paradise
> USE **Heaven**

Paralysis, Anterior spinal
> USE **Poliomyelitis**

Paralysis, Cerebral
> USE **Cerebral palsy**

Paralysis, Infantile
> USE **Poliomyelitis**

Paralysis, Spastic
> USE **Cerebral palsy**

Paramedical personnel
> USE **Allied health personnel**
>> **Emergency medical technicians**

Paramedics, Emergency
> USE **Emergency medical technicians**

Paranormal phenomena
> USE **Parapsychology**

Paraphilia
> USE **Sexual deviation**

Paraprofessional librarians
> USE **Library technicians**

Paraprofessionals 331.7
> UF Paraprofessions and paraprofessionals *[Former heading]*

Paraprofessionals—*Continued*
  SA types of paraprofessional per-
       sonnel, e.g. **Library techni-**
       cians; to be added as
       needed
  BT **Occupations**
       Professions
       Vocational guidance
  NT **Library technicians**
Paraprofessions and paraprofessionals
  USE **Paraprofessionals**
Parapsychology 133
  Use for materials on investigations of
phenomena that appear to be contrary to
physical laws and beyond the normal
sense perceptions.
  UF Paranormal phenomena
       Psi (Parapsychology)
       Psychic phenomena
       Psychical research *[Former*
       heading]
  BT **Psychology**
       Research
       Supernatural
  NT **Apparitions**
       Clairvoyance
       Dreams
       Extrasensory perception
       Hallucinations and illusions
       Mental suggestion
       Mind and body
       Near-death experiences
       Psychokinesis
       Subconsciousness
       Telepathy
       Visions
  RT **Ghosts**
       Occultism
       Spiritualism
Parasites 574.5; 581.5; 591.52
  UF Animal parasites
       Diseases and pests
       Entozoa
       Epizoa
  BT **Pests**
  NT **Bacteria**
       Insect pests
       Ticks
  RT **Symbiosis**
Parasols
  USE **Umbrellas and parasols**

Paratroops
  USE **Parachute troops**
Parcel post
  USE **Postal service**
Pardon 364.6
  BT **Administration of criminal**
       justice
       Executive power
  RT **Amnesty**
       Forgiveness
Parent abuse
  USE **Elderly abuse**
Parent and child 306.874
  Use for materials on the psychological
and social interaction between parents and
their minor children. Materials on the
skills, attributes and attitudes needed for
parenthood are entered under **Parenting.**
Materials on the principles and techniques
of raising children are entered under **Child**
rearing. Materials restricted to the legal
right of parents to visit their children in
situations of separation, divorce, etc., are
entered under **Visitation rights (Domestic**
relations).
  UF Child and parent
  BT **Children and adults**
       Domestic relations
       Family
       Human relations
  NT **Adoption**
       Adult children of alcoholics
       Birthparents
       Child abuse
       Child custody
       Child rearing
       Children of alcoholics
       Children of divorced parents
       Children of drug addicts
       Children of immigrants
       Children of working parents
       Father and child
       Inheritance and succession
       Mother and child
       Parenting
  RT **Conflict of generations**
Parent-teacher associations
  USE **Parents' and teachers' associa-**
       tions
Parent-teacher conferences 371.1
  UF Conferences, Parent-teacher
       Interviews, Parent-teacher
       Teacher-parent conferences

Parent-teacher conferences—*Continued*
 BT **Parent-teacher relationships**
Parent-teacher relationships 371.1
 UF Parents and teachers
  Teacher-parent relationships
  Teachers and parents
 NT **Parent-teacher conferences**
  Parents' and teachers' associations
 RT **Home and school**
Parental behavior
 USE **Parenting**
Parental custody
 USE **Child custody**
Parental kidnapping 362.82; 364.1
 UF Child snatching by parents
  Custody kidnapping
  Kidnapping, Parental *[Former heading]*
 BT **Child custody**
Parenting 306.874; 649
  Use for materials on the skills, attributes and attitudes needed for parenthood. Materials on the psychological and social interaction between parents and their minor children are entered under **Parent and child**. Materials on the principles and techniques of raising children are entered under **Child rearing**.
 UF Parental behavior
 BT **Parent and child**
 NT **Part-time parenting**
 RT **Child rearing**
  Home instruction
Parenting, Part-time
 USE **Part-time parenting**
Parents, Aging
 USE **Aging parents**
Parents and teachers
 USE **Parent-teacher relationships**
Parents' and teachers' associations 370.19
 UF P.T.A.'s
  Parent-teacher associations
  PTAs
 BT **Community and school**
  Educational associations
  Parent-teacher relationships
  Societies
 RT **Home and school**
Parents, Biological
 USE **Birthparents**

Parents, Single
 USE **Single parent family**
Parents, Teenage
 USE **Teenage fathers**
  Teenage mothers
Parents, Unmarried
 USE **Unmarried fathers**
  Unmarried mothers
Parents without partners
 USE **Single parent family**
Parish libraries
 USE **Church libraries**
Parish registers
 USE **Registers of births, etc.**
Parks (May subdiv. geog.) **363.6; 712**
 BT **Cities and towns**
  Landscape architecture
  Outdoor recreation
 NT **Amusement parks**
  Botanical gardens
  National parks and reserves
  Zoos
 RT **Playgrounds**
Parks—United States 363.6; 712; 917.3
 UF United States—Parks
Parkways
 USE **Express highways**
Parliamentary government
 USE **Representative government and representation**
Parliamentary practice 060.4
 UF Rules of order
 BT **Debates and debating**
  Legislation
  Legislative bodies
  Public meetings
Parliaments
 USE **Legislative bodies**
Parochial schools
 USE **Church schools**
Parodies 808.87; 817, etc.; 817.008, etc.
  Use for collections of parodies. Materials on the literary form of parody, that is, satirical or humorous imitation of a serious piece of literature, are entered under **Parody**.
 UF Travesties
 SA names of prominent authors with the subdivision *Parodies, travesties, etc.*, e.g. **Shakespeare, William,**

Parodies—*Continued*
       1564-1616—Parodies,
       travesties, etc.; to be added
       as needed
  BT   **Literature—Collections**

Parody 808.7
  Use for materials about the literary form of parody, that is, satirical or humorous imitation of a serious piece of literature. Collections of parodies are entered under **Parodies.**
  UF   Comic literature
  BT   **Literature**
       Satire
       Wit and humor

Parole 364.6
  BT   **Administration of criminal**
       justice
       Corrections
       Punishment
       Social case work
  RT   **Probation**

Part-time employment 331.25
  UF   Alternative work schedules
       Employment, Part-time
  BT   **Employment**
       Hours of labor
       Labor
  NT   **Job sharing**
       Supplementary employment

Part-time parenting 306.874; 649
  Use for materials on parenting skills for separated, divorced, or surrogate parents who live apart from their children and spend less than full time with them.
  UF   Co-parenting
       Joint custody of children
       Parenting, Part-time *[Former heading]*
       Shared parenting
       Single parents
  BT   **Parenting**
  NT   **Single parent family**
  RT   **Children of divorced parents**

Partial hearing
  USE **Hearing impaired**

Partially hearing
  USE **Hearing impaired**

Participative management 331.89; 658.3
  UF   Consultative management
       Employees' representation in
       management

       Industrial councils
       Labor participation in management
       Management—Employee participation *[Former heading]*
       Workers' participation in management
       Workshop councils
  BT   **Factory management**
       Industrial relations
       Personnel management
  RT   **Collective bargaining**

Particles (Nuclear physics) 539.7
  UF   Elementary particles (Physics)
       Nuclear particles
       Nucleons
  SA   names of particles, to be added as needed
  BT   **Nuclear physics**
  NT   **Electrons**
       Neutrons
       Protons
       Quarks

Parties 793.2
  SA   types of parties, to be added as needed
  BT   **Entertaining**
  NT   **Children's parties**
       Showers (Parties)

Parties, Political
  USE **Political parties**

Partisans
  USE **Guerrillas**

Partita
  USE **Suite (Music)**

Passion plays 792.1; 808.82; 822, etc.
  May be used for individual plays, collections, or materials about medieval plays depicting the Passion of Christ.
  BT   **Bible plays**
       Jesus Christ—Drama
       Mysteries and miracle plays
       Religious drama
       Theater

Passions
  USE **Emotions**

Passive resistance 303.6; 322.4
  UF   Civil disobedience
       Nonviolent noncooperation
  BT   **Resistance to government**

BT = Broader Term   NT = Narrower Term   RT = Related Term   SA = See Also   UF = Used For

Passive resistance—*Continued*
  NT **Boycotts**
        Hunger strikes
  RT **Nonviolence**
Passover 296.4; 394.2
  UF Pesach
  BT **Jewish holidays**
Pastel drawing 741.2
  BT **Drawing**
  RT **Crayon drawing**
Pastimes
  USE **Amusements**
        Games
        Recreation
Pastoral drama 808.82; 812, etc.
    May be used for individual works, collections, or materials about pastoral drama.
  UF Rural comedies
  BT **Drama**
Pastoral fiction 808.83; 813, etc.
    May be used for individual works, collections, or materials about novels or short stories with a rural setting and a tone of romantic nostalgia.
  UF Pastoral romances
        Rural comedies
  BT **Fiction**
Pastoral peoples
  USE **Nomads**
Pastoral poetry 808.81; 811, etc.
    May be used for individual works, collections, or materials about pastoral poetry.
  UF Bucolic poetry
        Eclogues
        Idyllic poetry
        Rural poetry
  BT **Poetry**
Pastoral psychiatry
  USE **Pastoral psychology**
Pastoral psychology 253.5
    Use for materials on the application of psychology and psychiatry by the clergy to the spiritual problems of individuals.
  UF Clerical psychology
        Pastoral psychiatry
        Psychology, Pastoral *[Former heading]*
        Psychology, Religious
  BT **Applied psychology**
        Church work

        Pastoral work
        Psychology of religion
Pastoral romances
  USE **Pastoral fiction**
Pastoral theology
  USE **Pastoral work**
Pastoral work 253
  UF Pastoral theology
        Theology, Pastoral
  BT **Church work**
  NT **Ministry**
        Pastoral psychology
        Preaching
  RT **Clergy**
Pastors
  USE **Clergy**
        Priests
Pastry 641.8
  BT **Baking**
        Cooking
  RT **Cake**
Pastures 333.74
  BT **Agriculture**
        Cattle
  RT **Forage plants**
        Grasses
Patchwork quilts
  USE **Quilts**
Patent medicines
  USE **Nonprescription drugs**
Patents 608
  UF Discoveries (in science)
        Intellectual property
  BT **Manufactures**
  RT **Inventions**
        Trademarks
Pathological botany
  USE **Plant diseases**
Pathological psychology
  USE **Abnormal psychology**
Pathology 616.07
  UF Disease (Pathology)
  BT **Diseases**
  NT **Bacteriology**
        Birth defects
        Fever
        Immunity
        Medical genetics
        Therapeutics
  RT **Diagnosis**

BT = Broader Term   NT = Narrower Term   RT = Related Term   SA = See Also   UF = Used For

Pathology—*Continued*
      Medicine
      Preventive medicine
Pathology, Vegetable
  USE **Plant diseases**
Patience 179
  BT **Human behavior**
      Virtue
Patience (Game)
  USE **Solitaire (Game)**
Patients 362.1
  SA types of diseases with the
      subdivision *Patients,* e.g.
      Cancer—Patients; and indi-
      vidual organs or regions of
      the body with the subdivi-
      sions *Surgery—Patients,* or
      Transplantation—Patients,
      to be added as needed
  NT **Cancer—Patients**
  RT **Sick**
Patios 643
  UF Decks (Domestic architecture)
  BT **Landscape architecture**
Patriotic poetry 808.81; 811, etc.;
      811.008, etc.
  May be used for individual works, col-
  lections, or materials about patriotic poet-
  ry.
  BT **Poetry**
  RT **National songs**
Patriotic songs
  USE **National songs**
Patriotism 172
  BT **Citizenship**
      Human behavior
      Loyalty
  RT **Nationalism**
Patronage of the arts
  USE **Art patronage**
Pattern making 671.2
  BT **Models and model making**
  NT **Mechanical drawing**
  RT **Design**
      Founding
Patterns for crafts
  USE subjects with the subdivision
      Patterns, e.g. **Dressmak-**
      ing—Patterns; to be added
      as needed

Patterns (Language arts)
  USE **Language arts—Patterning**
Patterns (Mathematics) 372.7
  UF Geometric patterns
      Number patterns
  BT **Mathematics**
  RT **Manipulative materials**
Pauperism
  USE **Poverty**
Pavements 625.8
  RT **Roads**
      Streets
Pay equity
  USE **Equal pay for equal work**
Pay television, Cable
  USE **Cable television**
Pay television, Subscription
  USE **Subscription television**
Payroll taxes
  USE **Income tax**
      Unemployment insurance
PC computers
  USE **Microcomputers**
Peace 172; 327.1; 341.7
  SA names of wars with the subdi-
      vision *Peace,* to be added
      as needed
  BT **International relations**
  NT **Pacifism**
      World War, 1939-1945—
        Peace
  RT **Arms control**
      International arbitration
      International security
      War
Peace keeping forces
  USE **United Nations—Armed forces**
Peace movements
  USE **Pacifism**
Peacocks 598.6
  UF Peafowl
      Peahens
  BT **Birds**
Peafowl
  USE **Peacocks**
Peahens
  USE **Peacocks**
Pearl Harbor (Oahu, Hawaii), Attack
      on, 1941 940.54
  BT **World War, 1939-1945—**
      Campaigns

BT = Broader Term   NT = Narrower Term   RT = Related Term   SA = See Also   UF = Used For

Pearlfisheries 338.3; 639
    UF   Oysters, Pearl
    BT   Fisheries
Peasant art
    USE Folk art
Peasantry (May subdiv. geog.) 305.5;
        307.72
    BT   Feudalism
        Labor
    RT   Agricultural laborers
        Land tenure
        Rural sociology
Pecan 583; 634
    BT   Nuts
        Trees
Pedagogy
    USE Education
        Education—Study and teach-
          ing
        Teaching
Peddlers and peddling 658.8
    UF   Door to door selling
    BT   Direct selling
        Sales personnel
Pediatric psychiatry
    USE Child psychiatry
Pediatric surgery
    USE Children—Surgery
Pediatrics
    USE Children—Diseases
        Children—Health and hygiene
        Infants—Diseases
        Infants—Health and hygiene
Pedigrees
    USE Genealogy
        Heraldry
Peer counseling 158; 361.3
    UF   Peer counseling in rehabilita-
          tion
        Peer counseling of students
        Peer group counseling
        Rehabilitation peer counseling
        Student to student counseling
    BT   Counseling
Peer counseling in rehabilitation
    USE Peer counseling
Peer counseling of students
    USE Peer counseling
Peer group counseling
    USE Peer counseling

Peer group influence
    USE Peer pressure
Peer pressure 303.3; 364.2
    UF   Peer group influence
    BT   Socialization
Peerage
    USE Nobility
Pelts
    USE Hides and skins
Pen drawing 741.2
    UF   Ink drawing
    BT   Drawing
Pen names
    USE Pseudonyms
Penal codes
    USE Criminal law
Penal colonies 365
    UF   Expulsion
        Transportation of criminals
    BT   Colonies
        Correctional institutions
Penal institutions
    USE Correctional institutions
        Prisons
        Reformatories
Penal law
    USE Criminal law
Penal reform
    USE Prison reform
Penance 265
    UF   Contrition
        Forgiveness of sin
        Reconciliation, Sacrament of
        Sacrament of Reconciliation
    BT   Sacraments
    RT   Confession
Pencil drawing 741.2
    BT   Drawing
Penicillin 615
    BT   Antibiotics
Peninsulas (May subdiv. geog.) 551.4
    SA   names of peninsulas, to be
          added as needed
    NT   Arabian Peninsula
Penitentiaries
    USE Prisons
Penmanship
    USE Handwriting
Pennsylvania Dutch 974.8
    UF   Pennsylvania Germans

Pennsylvania Germans
    USE **Pennsylvania Dutch**
Penology
    USE **Corrections**
           Punishment
Pensions 331.25; 350.5; 351.5
    UF Compensation
    BT **Annuities**
          Retirement income
    NT **Individual retirement accounts**
          Military pensions
          Mothers' pensions
          Old age pensions
          Social security
Pensions, Military
    USE **Military pensions**
Pensions, Naval
    USE **Military pensions**
Peonage 306.3; 331.5
    UF Compulsory labor
          Forced labor
          Servitude
    BT **Labor**
    RT **Contract labor**
          Convict labor
          Slavery
People in space
    USE **Interplanetary voyages**
          Space flight
People's banks
    USE **Cooperative banks**
People's democracies
    USE **Communist countries**
People's Republic of China
    USE **China**
Pep pills
    USE **Amphetamines**
Percentage 513.2
    BT **Arithmetic**
Perception 152.1; 153.7
    UF Feeling
    SA types of concepts and images,
          e.g. **Size and shape;** to be
          added as needed
    BT **Educational psychology**
          Intellect
          Psychology
          Theory of knowledge
          Thought and thinking
    NT **Concepts**

          Consciousness
          Gestalt psychology
          Size and shape
    RT **Apperception**
          Intuition
          Manipulative materials
Percussion instruments 786.8
    SA names of percussion instru-
          ments, e.g. **Drums;** to be
          added as needed
    BT **Musical instruments**
    NT **Drums**
          Pianos
Perennials 635.9
    BT **Cultivated plants**
          Flower gardening
          Flowers
Perfectionism (Personality trait) 155.2
    UF Self-expectations, Perfectionist
    BT **Personality**
Performance art 700
    Use for materials on live performances
by artists, drawing on literature, theater,
music, film, etc., and combining elements
of the various arts in untraditional ways.
    UF Happening (Art)
    BT **Modern art—1900-1999 (20th**
          century)
          Performing arts
Performance standards 658.5
    UF Job performance standards
          Rating
          Work performance standards
    SA subjects and classes of persons
          with the subdivision *Rat-*
          ing, e.g. **Bonds—Rating;**
          Employees—Rating; etc., to
          be added as needed
    NT **Bonds—Rating**
          Employees—Rating
          Librarians—Rating
Performing arts 790.2
    UF Show business
    SA specific art forms performed
          on stage or screen, to be
          added as needed
    NT **Ballet**
          Centers for the performing
          arts
          Dancing

    BT = Broader Term   NT = Narrower Term   RT = Related Term   SA = See Also   UF = Used For

Performing arts—*Continued*
    Opera
    Performance art
    Theater
Perfumes 391; 668
  BT Cosmetics
      Essences and essential oils
Periodic law 541.2
  BT Physical chemistry
  RT Chemical elements
Periodicals 050
  UF Journals
      Magazines
  SA periodicals of particular countries, e.g. **American periodicals**; subjects with the subdivision *Periodicals,* e.g. **Engineering—Periodicals;** and names of individual periodicals, to be added as needed
  BT Mass media
      Serial publications
  NT American periodicals
      Chapbooks
      Engineering—Periodicals
      English periodicals
      Freedom of the press
  RT Journalism
      Newspapers
      Press
Periodicals—Indexes 050
  BT Indexes
Periodicity 574.1
  UF Cycles
  NT Biological rhythms
  RT Rhythm
      Time
Permanent education
  USE Continuing education
Persecution 272
  UF Christians—Persecutions
  BT Atrocities
      Church history
  NT Jews—Persecutions
      Massacres
  RT Freedom of religion
      Martyrs
Persia
  USE Iran

Persian Gulf War, 1991 956.7044
  Use for comprehensive materials on the war. Materials limited to the Iraqi invasion of Kuwait are entered under **Kuwait—History—1990, Iraqi Invasion.**
  UF Desert Shield Operation
      Desert Storm Operation
      Gulf War, 1991
      Iraq—History—1991, Persian Gulf War
      Iraq-Kuwait Crisis, 1990-1991
      Kuwait—History—1991, Persian Gulf War
      Middle East War, 1991
      Mideast War, 1991
      Operation Desert Shield
      Operation Desert Storm
      United States—History—1991, Persian Gulf War
Personal actions (Law)
  USE Litigation
Personal appearance 391
  UF Appearance, Personal
      Beauty, Personal
      Physical appearance
      Self image
  NT Personal grooming
  RT Clothing and dress
Personal cleanliness
  USE Hygiene
Personal computers
  USE Microcomputers
Personal conduct
  USE Conduct of life
Personal development
  USE Personality
      Self-improvement
      Success
Personal films
  USE Amateur films
      Experimental films
Personal finance 332.024
  UF Budgets, Personal
      Domestic finance
      Family finance
      Finance, Personal *[Former heading]*
      Financial planning, Personal
  BT Finance
  NT Children's allowances

BT = Broader Term   NT = Narrower Term   RT = Related Term   SA = See Also   UF = Used For

Personal finance—*Continued*
    Consumer credit
    Estate planning
    Household budgets
    Insurance
    Saving and thrift
Personal freedom
  USE **Freedom**
Personal grooming 646.7
  UF Beauty, Personal
    Good grooming
    Grooming for men
    Grooming for women
    Grooming, Personal *[Former heading]*
  BT **Hygiene**
    Personal appearance
  NT **Cosmetics**
    Hair
  RT **Clothing and dress**
Personal growth
  USE **Self-improvement**
Personal health
  USE **Health**
Personal hygiene
  USE **Hygiene**
Personal life skills
  USE **Life skills**
Personal loans 332.7
  Use for materials on loans to individuals for personal rather than business uses.
  UF Consumer loans
    Loans, Personal
    Small loans
  BT **Consumer credit**
    Loans
  NT **Cooperative banks**
    Credit unions
    Mortgages
    Savings and loan associations
Personal names (May subdiv. geog.)
    929.4
  UF Christian names
    Family names
    Forenames
    Names, Personal *[Former heading]*
    Surnames
  SA personal names of particular national or ethnic origins

regardless of the place where they are found, e.g. **Scottish personal names;** to be added as needed
  BT **Names**
  NT **Nicknames**
    Pseudonyms
    Scottish personal names
Personal names, Scottish
  USE **Scottish personal names**
Personal names—United States
    929.40973
  UF American personal names
    United States—Names, Personal
    United States—Personal names
Personal narratives
  USE **Autobiographies**
    Biography
and subjects with the subdivision *Biography* or *Correspondence;* and, for collective or individual eyewitness reports or autobiographical accounts of diseases, events, and wars, the names of these diseases, events, and wars with the subdivision *Personal narratives,* e.g. **World War, 1939-1945—Personal narratives;** to be added as needed
Personal space 153.6; 302.2
  Use for materials on the sense of physical space required for psychological comfort.
  UF Space, Personal
  BT **Human relations**
    Nonverbal communication
    Space and time
Personal time management
  USE **Time management**
Personality 155.2
  UF Identity
    Personal development
  BT **Consciousness**
    Psychology
  NT **Character**

BT = Broader Term   NT = Narrower Term   RT = Related Term   SA = See Also   UF = Used For

Personality—*Continued*
      Eccentrics and eccentricities
      Perfectionism (Personality
        trait)
      Self
  RT **Individuality**
      Soul
Personality disorders 616.85
  BT **Abnormal psychology**
  NT **Multiple personality**
  RT **Hallucinations and illusions**
      Mental illness
Personality, Multiple
  USE **Multiple personality**
Personnel administration
  USE **Personnel management**
Personnel classification
  USE **Job analysis**
Personnel management 658.3
  Use for materials on problems of personnel in factories, business, etc., hiring and dismissing employees, and general questions of the relationship between officials and employees.
  UF Career development
      Employment management
      Human resource management
      Personnel administration
      Supervision of employees
  BT **Human relations**
      Industrial relations
      Management
  NT **Absenteeism (Labor)**
      Affirmative action programs
      Applications for positions
      Counseling
      Employee morale
      Employees—Dismissal
      Employees—Training
      Employment agencies
      Job analysis
      Job satisfaction
      Job security
      Labor turnover
      Motion study
      Participative management
      Recruiting of employees
      Supervisors
      Time study
  RT **Employees**
      Factory management

      Industrial efficiency
      Office management
Personnel service in education
  USE **Educational counseling**
Persons, Care of
  USE classes of dependent persons with the subdivisions *Care* or *Home care* or *Institutional care,* e.g. **Infants—Care; Elderly—Home care; Mentally ill—Institutional care;** etc., to be added as needed
Persons, Crimes against
  USE **Offenses against the person**
Perspective 701
  UF Architectural perspective
  BT **Descriptive geometry**
      Geometrical drawing
      Optics
      Painting
  RT **Drawing**
Persuasion (Rhetoric)
  USE **Public speaking**
      Rhetoric
Perversion, Sexual
  USE **Sexual deviation**
Pesach
  USE **Passover**
Pest control 363.7; 628.9; 632
  UF Extermination of pests
      Pest extermination
      Pests—Biological control *[Former heading]*
      Pests—Control *[Former heading]*
      Pests—Extermination
  SA types of pests with the subdivision *Control,* e.g. **Mosquitoes—Control;** to be added as needed
  BT **Agricultural pests**
      Economic zoology
      Pests
  NT **Mosquitoes—Control**
      Pesticides
Pest extermination
  USE **Pest control**
Pesticide pollution
  USE **Pesticides—Environmental aspects**

BT = Broader Term   NT = Narrower Term   RT = Related Term   SA = See Also   UF = Used For

Pesticides 632; 668
- BT   **Agricultural chemicals**
  - **Pest control**
  - **Poisons and poisoning**
- NT   **Fungicides**
  - **Herbicides**
  - **Insecticides**
  - **Natural pesticides**

Pesticides and wildlife 574.5
- UF   Wildlife and pesticides
- BT   **Pesticides—Environmental aspects**
  - **Wildlife conservation**

Pesticides—Environmental aspects 363.7; 632
- UF   Environment and pesticides
  - Pesticide pollution
- BT   **Environment**
  - **Pollution**
- NT   **Pesticides and wildlife**

Pestilences
- USE   **Epidemics**

Pests 574.6; 632
> Use for materials on detrimental or annoying animals or organisms.
- UF   Vermin
- SA   types of pests, e.g. **Agricultural pests; Flies;** etc., and names of crops, trees, etc., with the subdivision *Diseases and pests,* e.g. **Fruit—Diseases and pests;** to be added as needed
- BT   **Economic zoology**
- NT   **Agricultural pests**
  - **Flies**
  - **Fruit—Diseases and pests**
  - **Fungi**
  - **Household pests**
  - **Insect pests**
  - **Parasites**
  - **Pest control**

Pests—Biological control
- USE   **Pest control**

Pests—Control
- USE   **Pest control**

Pests—Extermination
- USE   **Pest control**

Pet-facilitated psychotherapy
- USE   **Pet therapy**

Pet therapy 615.8
- UF   Animal-facilitated therapy
  - Animals, Visiting
  - Companion-animal partnership
  - Pet-facilitated psychotherapy
  - Visiting animals
- BT   **Animals and the handicapped**
  - **Therapeutics**

Petrochemicals 661
- UF   Petroleum chemicals
- BT   **Chemicals**

Petroglyphs
- USE   **Rock drawings, paintings, and engravings**

Petroleum (May subdiv. geog.) **553.2; 665.5**
- UF   Coal oil
  - Crude oil
  - Oil
- BT   **Oils and fats**
- NT   **Coal tar products**
  - **Gasoline**
- RT   **Petroleum geology**

Petroleum as fuel 338.4; 665.5
- UF   Fuel, Liquid
  - Fuel oil
  - Liquid fuel
  - Oil fuel
- BT   **Fuel**
- NT   **Oil burners**

Petroleum chemicals
- USE   **Petrochemicals**

Petroleum engines
- USE   **Internal combustion engines**

Petroleum geology 553.2
- UF   Geology, Petroleum
- BT   **Economic geology**
  - **Prospecting**
- RT   **Petroleum**

Petroleum industry 338.2
- UF   Oil industry
  - Petroleum industry and trade *[Former heading]*
  - Petroleum trade
- BT   **Industry**
- NT   **Offshore oil industry**
  - **Oil well drilling**
  - **Oil wells**
  - **Service stations**

BT = Broader Term   NT = Narrower Term   RT = Related Term   SA = See Also   UF = Used For

Petroleum industry and trade
USE **Petroleum industry**
Petroleum industry, Offshore
USE **Offshore oil industry**
Petroleum—Pipelines
USE **Petroleum pipelines**
Petroleum pipelines 338.2; 665.5
UF Petroleum—Pipelines *[Former heading]*
Pipelines, Petroleum
BT **Pipelines**
Petroleum pollution of water
USE **Oil pollution of water**
Petroleum trade
USE **Petroleum industry**
Petroleum—United States 553.2; 665.5
UF United States—Petroleum
Petroleum—Well boring
USE **Oil well drilling**
Petrology 552
SA varieties of rocks, e.g. **Granite**; to be added as needed
BT **Science**
NT **Crystallography**
Geochemistry
Granite
Lunar petrology
Marble
RT **Geology**
Mineralogy
Rocks
Stone
Pets 636.088
SA names of animals, to be added as needed
BT **Animals**
NT **Cats**
Dogs
RT **Domestic animals**
Pets and the handicapped
USE **Animals and the handicapped**
Petting zoos 590.74
UF Animals—Petting zoos
BT **Zoos**
Pewter 673; 739.5
BT **Alloys**
Art metalwork
Metals
Phantoms
USE **Apparitions**

Ghosts
Pharmaceutical chemistry 615
UF Chemistry, Medical and pharmaceutical *[Former heading]*
Chemistry, Pharmaceutical
Drugs—Chemistry
Medicinal chemistry
BT **Chemistry**
NT **Disinfection and disinfectants**
Materia medica
RT **Pharmacy**
Therapeutics
Pharmaceuticals
USE **Drugs**
Pharmacodynamics
USE **Pharmacology**
Pharmacology 615
Use for materials on the action and properties of drugs in general. For materials limited to the effect of drugs on the functions of living organisms, use **Drugs—Physiological effect.**
UF Drugs—Adulteration and analysis *[Former heading]*
Medicine—Physiological effect
Pharmacodynamics
BT **Materia medica**
Medicine
NT **Drugs—Physiological effect**
Drugs—Testing
RT **Drug therapy**
Drugs
Pharmacy
Pharmacopoeias
USE **Materia medica**
Pharmacotherapy
USE **Drug therapy**
Pharmacy 615
Use for materials on the art or practice of preparing, preserving, and dispensing drugs.
BT **Chemistry**
Medicine
NT **Drugs**
Homeopathy
Medical botany
RT **Materia medica**
Pharmaceutical chemistry
Pharmacology
Pheasants 598.6; 636.5
BT **Game and game birds**

BT = Broader Term   NT = Narrower Term   RT = Related Term   SA = See Also   UF = Used For

Phenomenology 142
    BT   Modern philosophy
    NT   Existentialism
Philanthropists 361.7092; 920
    UF   Altruists
         Humanitarians
Philanthropy
    USE Charities
         Charity organization
         Endowments
         Gifts
         Social work
Philately
    USE Stamp collecting
Philology
    USE Language and languages
         Linguistics
Philology, Comparative
    USE Linguistics
Philosophers 180; 190; 920
    SA   philosophers of particular
         countries, e.g. **American
         philosophers;** to be added
         as needed
    NT   **American philosophers**
    RT   **Philosophy**
Philosophers, American
    USE **American philosophers**
Philosophers' stone
    USE **Alchemy**
Philosophy 100
    SA   philosophy of particular coun-
         tries, e.g. **American philoso-
         phy;** and subjects with the
         subdivision *Philosophy,* e.g.
         History—Philosophy; to be
         added as needed
    BT   **Humanities**
    NT   **American philosophy**
         Ancient philosophy
         Belief and doubt
         Empiricism
         Ethics
         Fate and fatalism
         Free will and determinism
         Gnosticism
         Good and evil
         Hindu philosophy
         History—Philosophy
         Humanism

Idealism
Intuition
Logic
Marxism
Materialism
Medieval philosophy
Metaphysics
Mind and body
Modern philosophy
Mysticism
Philosophy and religion
Positivism
Pragmatism
Psychology
Rationalism
Realism
Reality
Skepticism
Soul
Theism
Theory of knowledge
Transcendentalism
Truth
Universe
    RT   **Philosophers**
Philosophy, American
    USE **American philosophy**
Philosophy, Ancient
    USE **Ancient philosophy**
Philosophy and religion 210; 291
    UF   Religion and philosophy
    BT   **Philosophy**
         Religion
    RT   **Religion—Philosophy**
Philosophy, Greek
    USE **Ancient philosophy**
Philosophy, Hindu
    USE **Hindu philosophy**
Philosophy—Historiography 109
    BT   **Historiography**
Philosophy, Medieval
    USE **Medieval philosophy**
Philosophy, Modern
    USE **Modern philosophy**
Philosophy, Moral
    USE **Ethics**
Philosophy of history
    USE **History—Philosophy**
Philosophy of religion
    USE **Religion—Philosophy**

Philosophy, Roman
USE **Ancient philosophy**
Phobias 616.85
BT **Fear**
Neuroses
Phonetic spelling
USE **Spelling reform**
Phonetics 414
UF Phonics
Phonology
SA names of languages with the
subdivision *Pronunciation,*
to be added as needed
BT **Language and languages**
Sound
NT **English language—**
Pronunciation
RT **Reading—Phonetic method**
Speech
Voice
Phonics
USE **Phonetics**
Reading—Phonetic method
Phonograph 621.389
UF Gramophone
BT **Sound—Recording and repro-**
ducing
NT **Compact disc players**
RT **High-fidelity sound systems**
Phonograph records
USE **Sound recordings**
Phonology
USE **Phonetics**
and names of languages with
the subdivision *Pronuncia-*
tion, e.g. **English lan-**
guage—Pronunciation; to be
added as needed
Phosphates 546; 553.6; 631.8
BT **Fertilizers and manures**
Phosphorescence 535; 574.19
UF Luminescence
BT **Light**
Mineralogy
Optics
Radiation
Radioactivity
NT **Bioluminescence**
Photo journalism
USE **Photojournalism**

Photocopying machines
USE **Copying processes and ma-**
chines
Photoelectric cells 537.5; 621.3815
UF Electric eye
Photoengraving 686.2
UF Halftone process
BT **Engraving**
RT **Photomechanical processes**
Photographic chemistry 771
Use for materials on the chemical pro-
cesses employed in photography.
UF Chemistry, Photographic
BT **Chemistry**
NT **Photography—Processing**
Photographic film
USE **Photography—Film**
Photographic slides
USE **Slides (Photography)**
Photographic supplies
USE **Photography—Equipment and**
supplies
Photography 770
SA kinds of photography, e.g.
Portrait photography; and
photography of particular
subjects, e.g. **Photography**
of birds; to be added as
needed
NT **Aerial photography**
Artistic photography
Astronomical photography
Cameras
Cinematography
Color photography
Commercial photography
Filmstrips
Holography
Medical photography
Microphotography
Nature photography
Outdoor photography
Photojournalism
Photomechanical processes
Portrait photography
Slides (Photography)
Space photography
Telephotography
Three dimensional photogra-
phy

Photography—*Continued*
        Underwater photography
Photography, Aerial
    USE **Aerial photography**
Photography—Aesthetics
    USE **Artistic photography**
Photography, Artistic
    USE **Artistic photography**
Photography, Astronomical
    USE **Astronomical photography**
Photography, Color
    USE **Color photography**
Photography, Commercial
    USE **Commercial photography**
Photography—Darkroom technique
    USE **Photography—Processing**
Photography—Developing and developers 771
    BT **Photography—Processing**
Photography—Enlarging 771
    UF Enlarging (Photography)
Photography—Equipment and supplies 771
    UF Photographic supplies
    NT **Cameras**
Photography—Film 771
    UF Photographic film
Photography—Handbooks, manuals, etc. 770.2
Photography in astronautics
    USE **Space photography**
Photography, Journalistic
    USE **Photojournalism**
Photography, Laser
    USE **Holography**
Photography, Lensless
    USE **Holography**
Photography—Lighting 771; 778.7
Photography, Medical
    USE **Medical photography**
Photography—Motion pictures
    USE **Cinematography**
Photography of animals 778.9
    Use for materials on the technique and accounts of photographing animals. Materials consisting of photographs and pictures of animals are entered under **Animals—Pictorial works.**
    UF Animal photography
        Animals—Photography
    BT **Nature photography**

    RT **Animal painting and illustration**
        Animals—Pictorial works
Photography of birds 778.9
    UF Bird photography
        Birds—Photography
    BT **Nature photography**
Photography of fishes 778.9
    UF Fishes—Photography
    BT **Nature photography**
Photography of nature
    USE **Nature photography**
Photography of plants 778.9
    UF Plants—Photography
    BT **Nature photography**
Photography, Outdoor
    USE **Outdoor photography**
Photography—Portraits
    USE **Portrait photography**
Photography—Printing processes 771
    BT **Photography—Processing**
Photography—Processing 771
    UF Darkroom technique in photography
        Photography—Darkroom technique
    SA names of special techniques, e.g. **Photography— Developing and developers; Photography—Printing processes;** etc., to be added as needed
    BT **Photographic chemistry**
    NT **Photography—Developing and developers**
        Photography—Printing processes
Photography—Retouching 771
    UF Retouching (Photography)
Photography—Scientific applications 778.3
    SA specific applications, e.g. **Medical photography;** to be added as needed
    NT **Medical photography**
        Space photography
Photography, Space
    USE **Space photography**
Photography, Stereoscopic
    USE **Three dimensional photography**

BT = Broader Term   NT = Narrower Term   RT = Related Term   SA = See Also   UF = Used For

Photography, Underwater
USE **Underwater photography**
Photojournalism 070.4; 779
UF Journalistic photography
News photography
Photo journalism
Photography, Journalistic
[Former heading]
BT **Commercial photography**
Journalism
Photography
Photomechanical processes 686.2
SA types of photomechanical pro-
cesses, e.g. **Photoengraving;**
to be added as needed
BT **Illustration of books**
Photography
RT **Photoengraving**
Photometry 535
UF Electric light
Light, Electric
NT **Color**
RT **Light**
Optics
Photoplays
USE **Motion picture plays**
Photosynthesis 581.1
BT **Botany**
Phototherapy 615.8
UF Electric light
Light, Electric
Light—Therapeutic use
BT **Physical therapy**
Therapeutics
RT **Radiotherapy**
Ultraviolet rays
Photovoltaic power generation 621.31
UF Solar cells
BT **Solar energy**
NT **Solar batteries**
Phrenology 139
BT **Brain**
Head
Psychology
RT **Mind and body**
Physiognomy
Physical anthropology 573
UF Anthropology, Physical
Biological anthropology
Somatology

BT **Anthropology**
Ethnology
NT **Human origins**
Physical appearance
USE **Personal appearance**
Physical chemistry 541
UF Chemistry, Physical and theo-
retical *[Former heading]*
Theoretical chemistry
BT **Chemistry**
Physics
NT **Atomic theory**
Atoms
Catalysis
Colloids
Crystallography
Electrochemistry
Molecules
Periodic law
Polymers
Radiochemistry
Solids
Thermodynamics
RT **Nuclear physics**
Quantum theory
Physical culture
USE **Physical education**
Physical education 613.7; 796.07
UF Calisthenics
Education, Physical
Physical culture
Physical training
SA names of sports and types of
physical exercise, to be
added as needed
BT **Education**
NT **Coaching (Athletics)**
Fencing
Games
Health education
Judo
Marching drills
Movement education
Physical fitness
Posture
RT **Athletics**
Exercise
Gymnastics
Sports

BT = Broader Term   NT = Narrower Term   RT = Related Term   SA = See Also   UF = Used For

Physical education—Medical aspects
  USE **Sports medicine**
Physical fitness 613.7
  UF Endurance, Physical
      Fitness
      Physical stamina
      Stamina, Physical
  BT **Exercise**
      Health
      Health self-care
      Physical education
  NT **Bodybuilding**
Physical fitness centers
  USE **Health resorts**
Physical geography (May subdiv. geog.)
      910

Use for materials on the physical features of the earth's surface and its atmosphere. General materials, frequently school materials, describing the surface of the earth and its interrelationship with various peoples, animals, natural products, and industries are entered under **Geography.**

  UF Geography, Physical
      Physiography
  BT **Geography**
      Geology
  NT **Deserts**
      Earthquakes
      Geysers
      Glaciers
      Ice
      Icebergs
      Lakes
      Mountains
      Ocean
      Ocean currents
      Rivers
      Tides
      Volcanoes
      Winds
  RT **Earth**
Physical geography—United States
      917.3
  UF United States—Physical geography
Physical sciences 500.2
  BT **Science**
  NT **Astronomy**
      Chemistry
      Earth sciences

Physics
Physical stamina
  USE **Physical fitness**
Physical therapy 615.8

Use for general materials on the treatment of disability, injury, or disease through exercise, heat, water, body manipulation, massage, etc.

  UF Physiotherapy
  SA types of physical therapy, to
      be added as needed
  BT **Therapeutics**
  NT **Baths**
      Electrotherapeutics
      Hydrotherapy
      Massage
      Occupational therapy
      Phototherapy
      Radiotherapy
Physical training
  USE **Physical education**
Physically handicapped 362.4
  UF Crippled people
      Invalids
  SA types of physically handicapped persons, e.g. **Blind; Deaf;** etc., to be added as needed
  BT **Handicapped**
  NT **Blind**
      Deaf
      Hearing impaired
      Physically handicapped children
  RT **Orthopedics**
Physically handicapped children 155.45; 362.4; 362.7
  UF Children, Crippled
      Crippled children
  BT **Handicapped children**
      Physically handicapped
Physically handicapped—Housing 362.4
  UF Housing for the physically handicapped
  BT **Housing**
Physically handicapped—Rehabilitation 362.4
  NT **Occupational therapy**
Physicians 610.69; 920
  UF Doctors

BT = Broader Term   NT = Narrower Term   RT = Related Term   SA = See Also   UF = Used For

Physicians—*Continued*
  Medical profession
 SA types of medical specialists, to
   be added as needed
 NT **Radiologists**
  Surgeons
  Women physicians
 RT **Medicine**
Physicians—Directories 610.69
 BT **Directories**
Physicians—Drug use 362.29; 610.69
 UF Drug abusing physicians
  Drug addicted physicians
Physicians—Malpractice 346.03
 UF Medical errors
  Physicians—Tort liability
 BT **Malpractice**
  Medical ethics
  **Medicine—Law and legisla-
   tion**
Physicians—Tort liability
 USE **Physicians—Malpractice**
Physicists 530.092; 920
 BT **Scientists**
Physics 530
 BT **Physical sciences**
  Science
 NT **Astrophysics**
  Biophysics
  Electricity
  Electronics
  Gases
  Geophysics
  Gravitation
  Hydraulics
  Hydrostatics
  Light
  Liquids
  Magnetism
  Matter
  Mechanics
  Music—Acoustics and physics
  Nuclear physics
  Optics
  Physical chemistry
  Pneumatics
  Quantum theory
  Radiation
  Radioactivity
  Relativity (Physics)

  Solids
  Sound
  Statics
  Thermodynamics
  Weights and measures
 RT **Dynamics**
Physics, Astronomical
 USE **Astrophysics**
Physics, Biological
 USE **Biophysics**
Physics, Nuclear
 USE **Nuclear physics**
Physics, Terrestrial
 USE **Geophysics**
Physiognomy 138
 BT **Psychology**
 RT **Face**
  Phrenology
Physiography
 USE **Physical geography**
Physiological chemistry
 USE **Biochemistry**
Physiological effect
 USE subjects with the subdivision
   Physiological effect, e.g.
   **Alcohol—Physiological ef-
   fect; Opium—Physiological
   effect;** etc., to be added as
   needed
Physiological psychology
 USE **Psychophysiology**
Physiological stress
 USE **Stress (Physiology)**
Physiology 574.1; 612
  Use for general materials on physiology
 and for materials on human physiology.
 Physiology of other animals and of plants
 are entered under the appropriate heading
 with the subdivision *Physiology.*
 UF Body, Human
  Human body
  Human physiology
 SA names of organs and regions
   of the body, e.g. **Heart;** and
   types of plants and ani-
   mals, classes of persons,
   and parts of the body with
   the subdivision *Physiology,*
   to be added as needed
 BT **Biology**
  Medicine

Physiology—*Continued*
>   Science
> NT Blood
>   Body temperature
>   Cardiovascular system
>   Cells
>   Comparative physiology
>   Digestion
>   Fatigue
>   Glands
>   Growth
>   Health
>   Human locomotion
>   Lymphatic system
>   Musculoskeletal system
>   Nervous system
>   Nutrition
>   Psychophysiology
>   Reproduction
>   Reproductive system
>   Respiration
>   Respiratory system
>   Senses and sensation
>   Skin
>   Stress (Physiology)
> RT Anatomy

Physiology, Comparative
> USE Comparative physiology

Physiology, Molecular
> USE Biophysics

Physiology of plants
> USE Plant physiology

Physiotherapy
> USE Physical therapy

Physique
> USE Bodybuilding

Phytogeography
> USE Plants—Geographical distribution

Pianists 786.2092; 920
> BT Musicians

Piano
> USE Pianos

Piano music 786.2
> BT Instrumental music
>   Music

Piano—Tuning
> USE Pianos—Tuning

Pianos 786.2
> UF Piano [Former heading]

> BT Percussion instruments
> NT Keyboards (Musical instruments)

Pianos—Tuning 786.2
> UF Piano—Tuning [Former heading]
> BT Tuning

Picaresque literature 800
>   May be used for individual works, collections, or materials about episodic accounts of the adventures of an engagingly roguish hero.
> UF Picaresque novels
> BT Fiction
>   Literature

Picaresque novels
> USE Picaresque literature

Picketing
> USE Strikes

Pickling
> USE Canning and preserving

Pickup campers
> USE Travel trailers and campers

Pictographs
> USE Picture writing

Pictorial works
> USE Pictures
>   and subjects, names of cities, states, and countries, and named entities, such as individual parks, structures, etc., with the subdivision *Pictorial works,* e.g. **Animals—Pictorial works; United States—History— 1861-1865, Civil War— Pictorial works; Chicago (Ill.)—Pictorial works; United States—Pictorial works; Yosemite National Park (Calif.)—Pictorial works;** etc.; also names of persons or groups of persons with, as appropriate, the subdivisions *Cartoons and caricatures; Pictorial works;* or *Portraits;* to be added as needed

Picture books for children
> BT Children's literature

Picture books for children—*Continued*
  NT   **Coloring books**
        Stories without words
        Toy and movable books
  RT   **Illustration of books**
Picture books for children, Wordless
  USE **Stories without words**
Picture dictionaries 413; 423, etc.
  UF   Dictionaries, Picture
        Word books
  BT   **Encyclopedias and dictionaries**
Picture frames and framing 684; 749
  UF   Framing of pictures
  BT   **Decoration and ornament**
        Handicraft
Picture galleries
  USE **Art museums**
Picture postcards
  USE **Postcards**
Picture posters
  USE **Posters**
Picture telephone
  USE **Video telephone**
Picture writing 411
    Use for materials on the recording of events or the expression of messages by pictures representing actions or facts.
  UF   Pictographs
  BT   **Writing**
  NT   **Cave drawings**
        Rock drawings, paintings, and engravings
  RT   **Hieroglyphics**
Pictures 025.17; 760
    Use for general materials on the study and use of pictures and for miscellaneous collections of pictures.
  UF   Pictorial works
  SA   subjects, names of cities, states, and countries, and named entities, such as individual parks, structures, etc., with the subdivision *Pictorial works;* and groups and classes of persons and names of individuals with, as appropriate, the subdivision *Cartoons and caricatures; Pictorial works;* or *Portraits;* to be added as needed

  BT   **Art**
  NT   **Animals—Pictorial works**
        Cartoons and caricatures
        Chicago (Ill.)—Pictorial works
        Engraving
        Etching
        Libraries and pictures
        Portraits
        United States—History— 1861-1865, Civil War— Pictorial works
        United States—Pictorial works
        Yosemite National Park (Calif.)—Pictorial works
  RT   **Painting**
Pictures, Humorous
  USE **Cartoons and caricatures**
Pigments 547.8; 667; 751.2
  NT   **Dyes and dyeing**
  RT   **Color**
        Paint
Pigs 599.73; 636.4
  UF   Hogs
        Swine
  BT   **Domestic animals**
        Livestock
Pilgrims and pilgrimages 248.4
  BT   **Voyages and travels**
  RT   **Saints**
        Shrines
Pilgrims (New England colonists) 974.4
  BT   **Puritans**
        United States—History— 1600-1775, Colonial period
Pilot guides 623.89
  UF   Coast pilot guides
  BT   **Navigation**
        Pilots and pilotage
Piloting (Aeronautics)
  USE types of aircraft with the subdivision *Piloting,* e.g. **Airplanes—Piloting;** to be added as needed
Piloting (Astronautics)
  USE **Space vehicles—Piloting**
Piloting (Ships)
  USE **Pilots and pilotage**
Pilots, Airplane
  USE **Air pilots**

Pilots and pilotage 623.89
    UF   Piloting (Ships)
          Pilots, Ship
          Ship pilots
    BT   **Harbors**
          Sailors
    NT   **Pilot guides**
    RT   **Navigation**
Pilots, Ship
    USE **Pilots and pilotage**
Pimples (Acne)
    USE **Acne**
Ping-pong 796.34
    UF   Table tennis
    BT   **Ball games**
Pioneer life
    USE **Frontier and pioneer life**
Pipe fitting 696
    UF   Steam fitting
    RT   **Plumbing**
Pipe lines
    USE **Pipelines**
Pipe organs
    USE **Organs (Musical instruments)**
Pipelines 388.5; 621.8
    UF   Pipe lines
    SA   types of pipelines, to be add-
          ed as needed
    BT   **Hydraulic structures**
          Transportation
    NT   **Petroleum pipelines**
Pipelines, Petroleum
    USE **Petroleum pipelines**
Pipes, Tobacco
    USE **Tobacco pipes**
Pirates 364.1; 910.4
    UF   Barbary corsairs
          Buccaneers
          Corsairs
          Freebooters
    BT   **Criminals**
          International law
          Maritime law
          Naval history
    NT   **Privateering**
          United States—History—
          1801-1805, Tripolitan War
Pistols 683.4
    UF   Handguns
    BT   **Firearms**

Place names
    USE **Geographic names**
Places, Imaginary
    USE **Geographical myths**
Places of retirement
    USE **Retirement communities**
Plague 616.9
    UF   Black death
          Bubonic plague
    BT   **Communicable diseases**
          Epidemics
Plain chant
    USE **Chants (Plain, Gregorian, etc.)**
Plainsong
    USE **Chants (Plain, Gregorian, etc.)**
Plane geometry
    USE **Geometry**
Plane trigonometry
    USE **Trigonometry**
Planetariums 520.74
    BT   **Astronomy**
Planetoids
    USE **Asteroids**
Planets 523.4
    SA   names of planets, e.g. **Saturn**
          (Planet); to be added as
          needed
    BT   **Astronomy**
          Solar system
    NT   **Earth**
          Life on other planets
          Mars (Planet)
          Saturn (Planet)
    RT   **Asteroids**
          Stars
Planets—Exploration 523.4
    SA   names of planets with the
          subdivision *Exploration,* to
          be added as needed
    BT   **Outer space—Exploration**
    NT   **Mars (Planet)—Exploration**
Planets, Life on other
    USE **Life on other planets**
Planets, Minor
    USE **Asteroids**
Planing machines 621.9
    BT   **Machine tools**
Planned parenthood
    USE **Birth control**
Planning, City
    USE **City planning**

BT = Broader Term   NT = Narrower Term   RT = Related Term   SA = See Also   UF = Used For

Planning, Economic
  USE **Economic policy**
        and names of countries,
        states, etc., with the subdi-
        vision *Economic policy,* e.g.
        United States—Economic
        policy; to be added as
        needed
Planning, National
  USE **Economic policy**
        Social policy
        and names of countries with
        the subdivision *Economic*
        policy or *Social policy,* e.g.
        United States—Economic
        policy; United States—
        Social policy; etc.; and sub-
        jects with the subdivision
        Government policy, e.g.
        Homeless persons—
        Government policy; to be
        added as needed
Planning, Regional
  USE **Regional planning**
Plans
  USE **Architectural drawing**
        Geometrical drawing
        Map drawing
        Maps
        Mechanical drawing
Plant anatomy
  USE **Plants—Anatomy**
Plant breeding 581.1; 631.5
    Use for materials on attempts to pro-
  duce new or improved varieties of plants
  through controlled reproduction. Materials
  on the continuance or multiplication of
  plants by successive production are en-
  tered under **Plant propagation.**
  UF Hybridization
  BT **Agriculture**
        Breeding
        Horticulture
  NT **Fertilization of plants**
  RT **Plant propagation**
Plant chemistry
  USE **Botanical chemistry**
        Plants—Analysis
Plant conservation 333.95; 639.9
  UF Conservation of plants
        Plants—Conservation

Protection of plants
      Wild flowers—Conservation
  BT **Conservation of natural re-**
        sources
        Economic botany
        Endangered species
        Nature conservation
  NT **Scarecrows**
  RT **Rare plants**
Plant diseases 581.2; 632
  UF Botany—Pathology
        Diseases and pests
        Diseases of plants
        Garden pests
        Pathological botany
        Pathology, Vegetable
        Plant pathology
        Plants—Diseases *[Former*
          heading]
        Vegetable pathology
  SA names of crops, etc., with the
        subdivision *Diseases and*
        pests, to be added as need-
        ed
  BT **Agricultural pests**
        Fungi
  NT **Fruit—Diseases and pests**
Plant distribution
  USE **Plants—Geographical distribu-**
        tion
Plant introduction 581.5; 631.5
  UF Acclimatization
  BT **Economic botany**
Plant lore
  USE **Plants—Folklore**
Plant names, Popular
  USE **Popular plant names**
Plant names, Scientific
  USE **Botany—Terminology**
Plant nutrition
  USE **Plants—Nutrition**
Plant pathology
  USE **Plant diseases**
Plant physiology 581.1
  UF Botany—Physiology
        Physiology of plants
  BT **Botany**
  NT **Fertilization of plants**
        Germination
        Plants—Growth

BT = Broader Term   NT = Narrower Term   RT = Related Term   SA = See Also   UF = Used For

Plant physiology—*Continued*
   Plants—Nutrition
Plant propagation 581.1; 631.5
   Use for materials on the continuance or multiplication of plants by successive production. Materials on attempts to produce new or improved varieties of plants through controlled reproduction are entered under **Plant breeding.**
   UF   Plants—Propagation
        Propagation of plants
   BT   **Fruit culture**
        Gardening
        Nurseries (Horticulture)
   NT   **Grafting**
        Seeds
   RT   **Plant breeding**
Plantation life 307.72
   BT   **Country life**
Planting
   USE **Agriculture**
        Gardening
        Landscape gardening
        Tree planting
Plants (May subdiv. geog.) **581**
   Use for descriptive and nonsystematic or nontechnical materials. Systematic or technical materials are entered under **Botany.** Subdivisions used under this heading may be used under names of orders and classes of the plant kingdom and under names of individual species.
   UF   Flora
        Vegetable kingdom
   SA   types of plants characterized by their physical characteristics, environment, or use, e.g. **Climbing plants; Desert plants; Forage plants;** etc.; and names of botanical categories of plants, e.g. **Ferns;** to be added as needed
   NT   **Bulbs**
        Carnivorous plants
        Climbing plants
        Desert plants
        Edible plants
        Ferns
        Fertilization of plants
        Flowers
        Forage plants
        Forest plants
        Fossil plants

Freshwater plants
Herbs
Horticulture
House plants
Mosses
Mountain plants
Mushrooms
Poisonous plants
Popular plant names
Rare plants
Seeds
Shrubs
Trees
Vegetables
Weeds
   RT   **Botany**
        Gardening
        Herbicides
Plants—Analysis 581.19
   UF   Plant chemistry
        Plants—Chemical analysis
   BT   **Botanical chemistry**
Plants—Anatomy 581.4
   UF   Anatomy of plants
        Anatomy, Vegetable
        Botany—Anatomy *[Former heading]*
        Botany—Structure
        Morphology
        Plant anatomy
        Structural botany
        Vegetable anatomy
   BT   **Anatomy**
        Botany
Plants—Chemical analysis
   USE **Plants—Analysis**
Plants—Collection and preservation 579
   UF   Botanical specimens—Collection and preservation
        Herbaria
        Preservation of botanical specimens
        Specimens, Preservation of
   BT   **Collectors and collecting**
   NT   **Flower drying**
Plants—Conservation
   USE **Plant conservation**
Plants, Cultivated
   USE **Cultivated plants**

Plants, Cultivated—United States
   USE **Cultivated plants—United States**

Plants—Diseases
   USE **Plant diseases**

Plants—Ecology 581.5
   UF Botany—Ecology *[Former heading]*
   BT **Ecology**
   NT **Desert plants**
       Forest plants
       Mountain plants
   RT **Forest influences**
       Symbiosis

Plants, Edible
   USE **Edible plants**

Plants—Effect of poisons on
   USE **Herbicides**

Plants, Extinct
   USE **Fossil plants**

Plants—Fertilization
   USE **Fertilization of plants**

Plants—Folklore 398.24
   UF Plant lore
   BT **Folklore**
       Popular plant names

Plants, Fossil
   USE **Fossil plants**

Plants—Geographical distribution 581.9
   UF Geographical distribution of plants
       Phytogeography
       Plant distribution
   SA types of plants with the subdivision *Geographical distribution,* to be added as needed
   BT **Biogeography**

Plants—Growth 581.3
   BT **Plant physiology**

Plants, Hallucinogenic
   USE **Hallucinogens**

Plants in art 704.9
   BT **Art**
       Decoration and ornament
   NT **Flower painting and illustration**

Plants, Industrial
   USE **Factories**

Plants, Medicinal
   USE **Medical botany**

Plants—Nutrition 581.1; 631.5
   UF Plant nutrition
   BT **Nutrition**
       Plant physiology

Plants, Ornamental
   USE **Ornamental plants**

Plants—Photography
   USE **Photography of plants**

Plants, Poisonous
   USE **Poisonous plants**

Plants—Propagation
   USE **Plant propagation**

Plants—Soilless culture
   USE **Aeroponics**
       Hydroponics

Plants—United States 581.973
   UF Botany—United States *[Former heading]*
       United States—Plants

Plants, Useful
   USE **Economic botany**
       Edible plants

Plaster and plastering 693
   UF Plastering
   BT **Masonry**
   NT **Cement**
       Concrete
       Mortar
       Stucco

Plaster casts 731.4
   UF Casting
       Casts, Plaster
   BT **Sculpture**

Plaster of paris
   USE **Gypsum**

Plastering
   USE **Plaster and plastering**

Plastic industries
   USE **Plastics industry**

Plastic materials
   USE **Plastics**

Plastic surgery 617.9
   UF Cosmetic surgery
       Surgery, Cosmetic
       Surgery, Plastic *[Former heading]*
   BT **Surgery**
       Transplantation of organs, tissues, etc.

Plastics 668.4
   UF Plastic materials

BT = Broader Term   NT = Narrower Term   RT = Related Term   SA = See Also   UF = Used For

Plastics—*Continued*
- SA names of specific plastics, to be added as needed
- BT **Polymers**
- NT **Gums and resins**
  Synthetic rubber
- RT **Organic chemistry—Synthesis**
  Plastics industry
  Synthetic products

Plastics industry 338.4; 668.4
- UF Plastic industries
  Plastics trade
- BT **Chemical industry**
- RT **Plastics**

Plastics trade
- USE **Plastics industry**

Plate 739.2
- UF Gold plate
  Silver plate
- BT **Goldwork**
  Silverwork
- NT **Hallmarks**
  Sheffield plate

Plate metalwork 671.8
- BT **Metalwork**
  Sheet metalwork

Plate tectonics 551.1
- BT **Earth—Crust**
  Geophysics
- RT **Continental drift**
  Submarine geology

Platforms, Drilling
- USE **Drilling platforms**

Play 790
- BT **Children**
- NT **Finger play**
  Imaginary playmates
  Sports
- RT **Amusements**
  Games
  Recreation

Play centers
- USE **Community centers**
  Playgrounds

Play direction (Theater)
- USE **Theater—Production and direction**

Play production
- USE **Amateur theater**
  Theater—Production and direction

Play writing
- USE **Drama—Technique**
  Motion picture plays—Technique
  Radio plays—Technique
  Television plays—Technique

Playbills
- USE **Film posters**

Playgrounds 796.06
- UF Play centers
  Public playgrounds
  School playgrounds
- BT **Recreation**
  Sports facilities
- RT **Community centers**
  Parks

Playhouses
- USE **Theaters**

Playing cards
- USE **Card games**

Playmates, Imaginary
- USE **Imaginary playmates**

Plays
- USE **Drama—Collections**
  One act plays

Plays, Bible
- USE **Bible plays**

Plays, Christmas
- USE **Christmas plays**

Plays, College
- USE **College and school drama—Collections**

Plays for children
- USE **Children's plays**

Playwrights
- USE **Dramatists**

Playwriting
- USE **Drama—Technique**
  Motion picture plays—Technique
  Radio plays—Technique
  Television plays—Technique

Pleasure 152.4
- BT **Emotions**
  Joy and sorrow
  Senses and sensation
- RT **Happiness**
  Pain

Plot-your-own stories 808.3; 813, etc.
- UF Choose-your-own story plots

BT = Broader Term   NT = Narrower Term   RT = Related Term   SA = See Also   UF = Used For

Plot-your-own stories—*Continued*
    Making-choices stories
    Multiple plot stories
    Which-way stories
  BT **Children's literature**
      Fiction
      Literary recreations

Plots (Drama, fiction, etc.) 808
    Use for materials that analyze plots or discuss the technique of constructing plots. Collections of plots of a specific literary or musical form are entered under that form with the subdivision *Stories, plots, etc.* Collections of literary plots are entered under **Literature—Stories, plots, etc.**

  UF Drama—Plots
      Dramatic plots
      Fiction—Plots
      Novels—Plots
      Scenarios
  SA national literatures and literary or musical forms with the subdivision *Stories, plots, etc.,* e.g. **Ballet—Stories, plots, etc.; Opera—Stories, plots, etc.;** to be added as needed
  BT **Authorship**
      Characters and characteristics in literature
      Drama
      Fiction
      Literature

Plows 631.3
  BT **Agricultural machinery**

Plumbing 696
  NT **Sanitary engineering**
      Sewerage
      Soldering
  RT **House drainage**
      Household sanitation
      Pipe fitting

Pluralism (Social sciences)
  USE **Biculturalism**
       Multiculturalism

Plywood 674
  BT **Wood**

PMS (Gynecology)
  USE **Premenstrual syndrome**

Pneumatic transmission
  USE **Compressed air**

Pneumatics 533; 621.5
  BT **Physics**
  NT **Aerodynamics**
      Compressed air
      Ground cushion phenomena
      Sound
  RT **Gases**

Pneumonia 616.2
  BT **Lungs—Diseases**

Pocket calculators
  USE **Calculators**

Podiatry 617.5
  UF Chiropody
  BT **Medicine**
  NT **Foot—Care and hygiene**

Poetics 808.1
    Use for materials on the art and technique of poetry. General materials on the appreciation, philosophy, etc. of poetry are entered under **Poetry.**
  UF Poetry—Technique
  BT **Poetry**
  NT **Rhyme**
      Rhythm
      Versification

Poetry 809.1
    Use for general materials on poetry, not for individual works. Materials on the history and criticism of poetry from more than one literature are entered under **Poetry—History and criticism.** Materials on the art and technique of poetry are entered under **Poetics.** Collections of poetry are entered under **Poetry—Collections; English poetry—Collections;** etc.
  UF Poetry—Philosophy
  SA types of poetry, e.g. **Haiku;** and subjects, historical events, names of places, ethnic groups, classes of persons, and names of individual persons with the subdivision *Poetry,* to express the theme or subject content of individual works or collections of poetry, e.g. **Animals—Poetry; Bunker Hill (Boston, Mass.), Battle of, 1775—Poetry; Napoleon I, Emperor of the French, 1769-1821—Poetry;** etc., to be added as needed
  BT **Aesthetics**

Poetry—*Continued*
    Literature
  NT American poetry
      Animals—Poetry
      Ballads
      Bunker Hill (Boston, Mass.),
        Battle of, 1775—Poetry
      Chicago (Ill.)—Poetry
      Children's poetry
      Christmas poetry
      Didactic poetry
      Eddas
      Elegiac poetry
      English poetry
      Epistolary poetry
      Erotic poetry
      Fantasy poetry
      Free verse
      French poetry
      Haiku
      Humorous poetry
      Hymns
      Indians of North America—
        Poetry
      Love poetry
      Napoleon I, Emperor of the
        French, 1769-1821—Poetry
      Narrative poetry
      Nature poetry
      Pastoral poetry
      Patriotic poetry
      Poetics
      Religious poetry
      Science fiction poetry
      Sea poetry
      Songs
      United States—History—
        Poetry
      War poetry
Poetry and music
  USE Music and literature
Poetry—Collections 808.81; 811.08, etc.
  UF Poetry—Selections
      Rhymes
  BT Literature—Collections
  NT American poetry—Collections
      English poetry—Collections
Poetry for children
  USE Children's poetry
      Nursery rhymes

Poetry, Historical
  USE Historical poetry
Poetry—History and criticism 809.1
  NT American poetry—History and
      criticism
      English poetry—History and
      criticism
Poetry—Philosophy
  USE Poetry
Poetry—Selections
  USE Poetry—Collections
Poetry—Technique
  USE Poetics
Poets 809.1; 920
    Use for materials on the personal lives
of several poets, not limited to a single
national literature. Materials about their
literary productions are entered under
**Poetry—History and criticism; English
poetry—History and criticism;** etc.
  SA poets of particular countries,
      e.g. **American poets;** to be
      added as needed
  BT Authors
  NT American poets
      Lyricists
      Minstrels
      Troubadours
Poets, American
  USE American poets
Point Four program
  USE Reconstruction (1939-1951)
Poison ivy 583
  BT Poisonous plants
Poisonous animals 591.6
  SA names of poisonous animals,
      e.g. **Rattlesnakes;** to be
      added as needed
  BT Animals
      Dangerous animals
      Economic zoology
      Poisons and poisoning
  NT Rattlesnakes
Poisonous gases 363.7; 363.17
  UF Asphyxiating gases
      Gases, Asphyxiating and poi-
      sonous
      Gases, Poisonous
  BT Gases
      Poisons and poisoning
  NT Radon

BT = Broader Term   NT = Narrower Term   RT = Related Term   SA = See Also   UF = Used For

Poisonous gases—War use 623.4
    BT   Chemical warfare
    NT   World War, 1914-1918—Gas
          warfare
Poisonous plants 581.6
    UF   Plants, Poisonous
          Toxic plants
    SA   names of poisonous plants,
          e.g. **Poison ivy;** to be added
          as needed
    BT   **Economic botany**
          Plants
          Poisons and poisoning
    NT   **Poison ivy**
Poisonous substances
    USE **Poisons and poisoning**
Poisons and poisoning 363.17; 615.9
    UF   Poisonous substances
          Toxic substances
          Toxicology
    SA   individual poisons, to be add-
          ed as needed; and, for the
          influence of particular sub-
          stances on humans and ani-
          mals, names of poisonous
          substances with the subdivi-
          sion *Toxicology,* e.g.
          Insecticides—Toxicology; to
          be added as needed
    BT   **Accidents**
          Chemistry
          Hazardous substances
          Homicide
          Medical jurisprudence
    NT   **Food poisoning**
          Insecticides—Toxicology
          Lead poisoning
          Pesticides
          Poisonous animals
          Poisonous gases
          Poisonous plants
Polar expeditions
    USE **Antarctic regions—Exploration**
          Arctic regions—Exploration
          Scientific expeditions
Polar lights
    USE **Auroras**
Polar regions 998
    Use for materials on both the Antarctic
    and Arctic regions.

    NT   **Antarctic regions**
          Arctic regions
          North Pole
          South Pole
Polarity
    USE **Opposites**
Police (May subdiv. geog.) **363.2**
    Use for materials on the police forces or
    on police personnel in general. Materials
    limited to women as police officers are en-
    tered under **Policewomen.**
    UF   Police officers
          Policemen
    BT   **Administration of criminal**
           justice
          Law enforcement
    NT   **Animals in police work**
          Police brutality
          Police corruption
          Policewomen
          Secret service
          State police
    RT   **Crime**
          Criminal investigation
          Detectives
Police brutality (May subdiv. geog.)
          363.2
    UF   Police—Complaints against
          [Former heading]
          Police cruelty
          Police repression
          Police violence
    BT   **Police**
Police—Complaints against
    USE **Police brutality**
          Police corruption
Police—Corrupt practices
    USE **Police corruption**
Police corruption (May subdiv. geog.)
          363.2
    UF   Corruption, Police
          Police—Complaints against
          [Former heading]
          Police—Corrupt practices
          [Former heading]
    BT   **Misconduct in office**
          Police
Police cruelty
    USE **Police brutality**
Police, International
    USE **International police**

Police officers
USE **Police**
Police repression
USE **Police brutality**
Police, State
USE **State police**
Police—United States 363.20973
UF United States—Police
Police violence
USE **Police brutality**
Policemen
USE **Police**
Policewomen 363.2
UF Women police officers
BT **Police**
Women
Polio
USE **Poliomyelitis**
Poliomyelitis 616.8
UF Infantile paralysis
Paralysis, Anterior spinal
Paralysis, Infantile
Polio
Spinal paralysis, Anterior
BT **Diseases**
Poliomyelitis vaccine 614.4; 615
UF Live poliovirus vaccine
Sabin vaccine
Salk vaccine
BT **Vaccination**
Polishing
USE **Grinding and polishing**
Politeness
USE **Courtesy**
Etiquette
Political action committees
USE **Lobbying**
Political assessments
USE **Campaign funds**
Political asylum
USE **Asylum**
Political behavior
USE **Political psychology**
Political boundaries
USE **Boundaries**
Political campaign literature
USE **Campaign literature**
Political campaigns
USE **Politics**
Political conventions 324.5
UF Conventions, Political

BT **Political science**
Politics
NT **Primaries**
RT **Political parties**
Political corruption 324; 351.9; 352
UF Boss rule
Corruption in politics *[Former
heading]*
Graft in politics
Political scandals
Politics—Corrupt practices
Spoils system
SA names of specific incidents,
e.g. **Watergate Affair, 1972-
1974**; to be added as need-
ed
BT **Conflict of interests**
Political crimes and offenses
Political ethics
Politics
NT **Iran-Contra Affair, 1985-1990**
Watergate Affair, 1972-1974
Whistle blowing
RT **Campaign funds**
Lobbying
Misconduct in office
Political crimes and offenses 364.1
UF Crimes, Political
Sedition
BT **Political ethics**
Subversive activities
NT **Anarchism and anarchists**
Assassination
Concentration camps
Political corruption
Political prisoners
Resistance to government
Terrorism
Treason
Political defectors
USE **Defectors**
Political economy
USE **Economics**
Political ethics 172
UF Ethics, Political
BT **Political science**
Politics
Social ethics
NT **Citizenship**
Conflict of interests

BT = Broader Term   NT = Narrower Term   RT = Related Term   SA = See Also   UF = Used For

Political ethics—*Continued*
  Political corruption
  Political crimes and offenses
  Resistance to government
Political extremism
  USE **Radicalism**
Political geography
  USE **Boundaries**
    Geopolitics
Political participation
  USE **Politics**
    and classes of persons with
      the subdivision *Political ac-
      tivity,* e.g. **College stu-
      dents—Political activity;
      Women—Political activity;**
      etc., to be added as needed
Political parties (May subdiv. geog.)
  324.2
  UF Parties, Political
  SA names of parties, to be added
      as needed
  BT **Political science**
      Politics
  NT **Democratic Party (U.S.)**
      Republican Party (U.S.)
      **Right and left (Political sci-
      ence)**
      **Third parties (United States
      politics)**
  RT **Political conventions**
Political parties—Finance
  USE **Campaign funds**
Political prisoners 365
  UF Prisoners, Political
  BT **Political crimes and offenses**
      Prisoners
Political psychology 302
  UF Political behavior
      Politics—Psychological aspects
      Psychology, Political
  BT **Political science**
      Psychology
      Social psychology
  NT **Propaganda**
      Public opinion
Political refugees 325
  UF Displaced persons
      Refugees, Political *[Former
      heading]*

  SA names of wars with the subdi-
      vision *Refugees,* to be add-
      ed as needed
  BT **Asylum**
      International law
      International relations
      Refugees
  NT **Defectors**
      **World War, 1939-1945—
      Refugees**
Political scandals
  USE **Political corruption**
Political science 320
  Use for materials on the science of poli-
  tics. Materials on the various aspects of
  practical politics, such as electioneering,
  political machines, etc., are entered under
  Politics. Materials on the political process-
  es of particular regions, countries, cities,
  etc., are entered under the place names
  with the subdivision *Politics and govern-
  ment,* e.g. **United States—Politics and
  government;** etc.
  UF Administration
      Civics
      Civil government
      Commonwealth, The
      Government
  SA names of countries, cities,
      etc., with the subdivision
      Politics and government,
      e.g. **United States—Politics
      and government;** to be add-
      ed as needed
  BT **Social sciences**
  NT **Anarchism and anarchists**
      Aristocracy
      Bureaucracy
      Citizenship
      Civil rights
      Civil service
      Communism
      Comparative government
      Constitutions
      Democracy
      Equality
      Executive power
      Federal government
      Freedom
      Geopolitics
      Government ownership
      Imperialism

Political science—*Continued*
    Individualism
    Kings, queens, rulers, etc.
    Law
    Legislation
    Liberalism
    Local government
    Marxism
    Monarchy
    Municipal government
    Nationalism
    Political conventions
    Political ethics
    Political parties
    Political psychology
    Power (Social sciences)
    Public administration
    Radicalism
    Representative government and
      representation
    Republics
    Resistance to government
    Revolutions
    Right and left (Political science)
    Separation of powers
    Social contract
    Socialism
    State constitutions
    State governments
    State rights
    Suffrage
    Taxation
    Totalitarianism
    United States—Politics and
      government
    Utopias
    World politics
  RT Constitutional history
    Constitutional law
    Politics
    State, The
Political violence
  USE Sabotage
    Terrorism
Politicians (May subdiv. geog.)
    324.2092; 920
  BT Statesmen
  NT Women politicians

Politicians, American
  USE Politicians—United States
Politicians—United States 324.2092;
    920
  UF American politicians
    Politicians, American
    United States—Politicians
Politics 324.7
    Use for materials on the various aspects of practical politics, such as electioneering, political machines, etc. Materials on the science of politics are entered under **Political science.**
  UF Campaigns, Political
    Electioneering
    Political campaigns
    Political participation
    Politics, Practical *[Former heading]*
    Practical politics
  SA names of continents, areas, countries, cities, etc., and native peoples, with the subdivision *Politics and government;* and classes of persons with the subdivision *Political activity,* e.g. **College students—Political activity;** to be added as needed
  BT Political parties
  NT Asia—Politics and government
    Business and politics
    Campaign funds
    Campaign literature
    Chicago (Ill.)—Politics and government
    Elections
    Indians of North America—Politics and government
    Latin America—Politics and government
    Lobbying
    Political conventions
    Political corruption
    Political ethics
    Primaries
    Religion and politics
    Television in politics
    United States—Politics and government

Politics—*Continued*
        Women—Political activity
    RT   **Political science**
Politics and business
    USE   **Business and politics**
Politics and Christianity
    USE   **Christianity and politics**
Politics and religion
    USE   **Religion and politics**
Politics and students
    USE   **Students—Political activity**
Politics—Corrupt practices
    USE   **Political corruption**
Politics, Practical
    USE   **Politics**
Politics—Psychological aspects
    USE   **Political psychology**
Pollination
    USE   **Fertilization of plants**
Polls, Election
    USE   **Elections**
Polls, Public opinion
    USE   **Public opinion polls**
Pollution 304.2; 363.73
    UF   Chemical pollution
           Contamination of environ-
              ment
           Environmental pollution
    SA   types of pollution, e.g. **Air
           pollution;** to be added as
           needed
    BT   **Environmental health**
           Human influence on nature
           Public health
           Sanitary engineering
           Sanitation
    NT   **Air pollution**
           Marine pollution
           Noise pollution
           **Pesticides—Environmental as-
             pects**
           Pollution control industry
           Radioactive pollution
           Space debris
           Water pollution
    RT   **Environmental protection**
           Hazardous wastes
           Industrial wastes
           Refuse and refuse disposal
Pollution control
    USE   **Pollution control industry**

Pollution control devices (Motor vehi-
           cles)
    USE   **Automobiles—Pollution con-
             trol devices**
Pollution control industry 338.4; 363.73
    UF   Pollution control
           Pollution—Prevention
    BT   **Pollution**
    NT   **Automobiles—Pollution con-
             trol devices**
           Recycling
    RT   **Refuse and refuse disposal**
**Pollution—Mathematical models 304.2;
           363.73**
    BT   **Mathematical models**
Pollution of air
    USE   **Air pollution**
Pollution of water
    USE   **Water pollution**
Pollution—Prevention
    USE   **Pollution control industry**
Pollution, Radioactive
    USE   **Radioactive pollution**
Pollution, Space
    USE   **Space debris**
Poltergeists
    USE   **Ghosts**
Polyglot dictionaries 413
    UF   Dictionaries, Multilingual
           Dictionaries, Polyglot
           Multilingual dictionaries
           Multilingual glossaries, phrase
             books, etc.
           Polyglot glossaries, phrase
             books, etc.
    BT   **Encyclopedias and dictionaries**
Polyglot glossaries, phrase books, etc.
    USE   **Polyglot dictionaries**
Polygraph
    USE   **Lie detectors and detection**
Polymers 541.3; 547.7; 668.9
    UF   Polymers and polymerization
           [Former heading]
    SA   types of polymers, e.g. **Plas-
           tics;** to be added as needed
    BT   **Organic chemistry—Synthesis**
           Physical chemistry
    NT   **Plastics**
Polymers and polymerization
    USE   **Polymers**

Polynucleotides
USE **Nucleic acids**
Pomp
USE **Parades**
Ponds 551.48
BT **Water**
Ponies 636.1
UF Foals
BT **Horses**
Pontiac's Conspiracy, 1763-1765 973.2
BT **Indians of North America—
Wars
United States—History—
1600-1775, Colonial period
United States—History—
1755-1763, French and In-
dian War**
Pony express 383
BT **Express service
Postal service**
Pools
USE **Swimming pools**
Poor (May subdiv. geog.) **305.5; 362.5**
BT **Poverty
Public welfare**
NT **Begging
Homeless persons
Tramps
Unemployed**
Poor—Legal assistance
USE **Legal assistance to the poor**
Poor—Medical care 362.6; 368.4
UF Medical care for the poor
NT **Medicaid**
Poor relief
USE **Charities
Domestic economic assistance
Public welfare**
Pop culture
USE **Popular culture**
Pop-up books
USE **Toy and movable books**
Popes 262; 920
UF Holy See
BT **Church history**
RT **Papacy**
Popes—Infallibility 262
UF Infallibility of the Pope
Popes—Temporal power 262
UF Temporal power of the Pope

BT **Church history—600-1500,
Middle Ages**
RT **Church and state**
Popes—Voyages and travels 262
BT **Voyages and travels**
Popular arts
USE **Popular culture**
Popular culture (May subdiv. geog.)
306.4
Use for materials on literature, art, mu-
sic, motion pictures, etc. produced for a
mass audience. General materials on
learning and scholarship, literature, the
arts, etc. are entered under **Intellectual
life.**
UF Culture, Popular
Mass culture
Pop culture
Popular arts
BT **Civilization
Communication
Culture
Intellectual life
Manners and customs
Recreation**
RT **Mass media**
Popular culture—Chicago (Ill.) 977.3
UF Chicago (Ill.)—Popular culture
[Former heading]
Popular culture—United States 973
UF United States—Popular cul-
ture *[Former heading]*
NT **Americana**
Popular government
USE **Democracy**
Popular medicine 616.02
Use for medical books written for the
layman.
UF Medicine, Popular *[Former
heading]*
BT **Medicine**
NT **Traditional medicine**
RT **Health self-care**
Popular music 781.64; 782.42164
UF Music, Popular (Songs, etc.)
[Former heading]
Popular songs
Songs, Popular
SA types of popular music, to be
added as needed
BT **Dance music**

Popular music—*Continued*
  Music
  Songs
  NT   **Blues music**
       Country music
       Gospel music
       Rap music
       Rock music
Popular music—**Writing and publishing**
       070.5; 781.3
  UF   Song writing
  BT   **Composition (Music)**
Popular plant names 581
  Use for materials on the common or vernacular names of plants. Materials on the scientific names are entered under **Botany**—**Terminology**.
  UF   Botany—Nomenclature
       Plant names, Popular *[Former heading]*
  BT   **Plants**
  NT   **Plants**—**Folklore**
  RT   **Botany**
       Botany—**Terminology**
Popular songs
  USE   **Popular music**
Popularity 158
  BT   **Social psychology**
Population 304.6; 363.9
  UF   Demography
  SA   names of countries, cities, etc., with the subdivision *Population,* to be added as needed
  BT   **Economics**
       Human ecology
       Sociology
       Vital statistics
  NT   **Birth control**
       Census
       Chicago (Ill.)—**Population**
       Cities and towns—**Growth**
       Eugenics
       Fertility
       Human fertility
       Internal migration
       Mortality
       United States—**Population**
  RT   **Birthrate**
Population, Foreign
  USE   **Immigration and emigration**

and names of countries with the subdivision *Immigration and emigration,* e.g. **United States**—**Immigration and emigration;** and names of countries, cities, etc., with the subdivision *Foreign population,* e.g. **United States**—**Foreign population; Chicago (Ill.)**—**Foreign population;** etc., to be added as needed
Porcelain 738.2
  Use for materials on chinaware and porcelain for the table or decorative use. Materials on the technology of fired earthen products or on clay products intended for industrial use are entered under **Ceramics.**
  UF   China (Porcelain)
       Chinaware
       Dishes
  SA   types of porcelain, to be added as needed
  BT   **Decorative arts**
       Pottery
  NT   **China painting**
Porcelain enamels
  USE   **Enamel and enameling**
Porcelain painting
  USE   **China painting**
Pornography 176; 363.4
  UF   Obscene materials
  BT   **Obscenity (Law)**
  RT   **Erotica**
Portable computers 004.16
  UF   Computers, Portable
       Handheld computers
       Laptop computers
  BT   **Computers**
       Microcomputers
Portrait painting 757
  UF   Portraiture
  BT   **Painting**
       Portraits
  RT   **Figure painting**
       Miniature painting
Portrait photography 778.9; 779
  UF   Photography—Portraits *[Former heading]*
       Portraiture
  BT   **Photography**

Portrait photography—*Continued*
    Portraits
Portraits 704.9; 757
    UF   Iconography
    SA   headings for collective and in-
          dividual biography, classes
          of persons, and names of
          individuals with the subdi-
          vision *Portraits,* to be add-
          ed as needed
    BT   **Art**
          Biography
          Pictures
    NT   **Cartoons and caricatures**
          Musicians—Portraits
          Portrait painting
          Portrait photography
          Shakespeare, William,
            1564-1616—Portraits
          United States—Biography—
            Portraits
Portraiture
    USE **Portrait painting**
           Portrait photography
Ports
    USE **Harbors**
Portuguese literature 869
    BT   **Literature**
          Romance literature
    RT   **Brazilian literature**
Position analysis
    USE **Topology**
Positivism 146
    UF   Humanity, Religion of
          Religion of humanity
    BT   **Philosophy**
          Rationalism
    NT   **Materialism**
          Pragmatism
    RT   **Agnosticism**
          Deism
          Idealism
          Realism
Possessions, Lost and found
    USE **Lost and found possessions**
Post cards
    USE **Postcards**
Post-impressionism
    USE **Postimpressionism (Art)**
Post-modernism
    USE **Postmodernism**

Post office
    USE **Postal service**
Postage stamp collecting
    USE **Stamp collecting**
Postage stamps 383; 769.56
    UF   Stamps, Postage
    RT   **Stamp collecting**
Postage stamps—Collectors and collect-
           ing
    USE **Stamp collecting**
Postal cards
    USE **Postcards**
Postal delivery code
    USE **Zip code**
Postal service (May subdiv. geog.) **383;**
           351.0087
    UF   Mail service
          Parcel post
          Post office
    BT   **Communication**
          Transportation
    NT   **Air mail service**
          Pony express
          Zip code
Postal service—United States 353.0087;
           383
    UF   United States—Mail
          United States—Postal service
Postcards 383; 741.6
    UF   Picture postcards
          Post cards
          Postal cards
Postcards—Collectors and collecting
           790.1
Posters 741.6
    UF   Advertising, Pictorial
          Picture posters
    SA   types of posters, e.g. **Film**
           posters; to be added as
           needed
    BT   **Advertising**
          Commercial art
    NT   **Film posters**
    RT   **Signs and signboards**
Posters, Film
    USE **Film posters**
Postimpressionism (Art) 709.03
    UF   Post-impressionism
    BT   **Modern art—1800-1899 (19th**
          century)

BT = Broader Term   NT = Narrower Term   RT = Related Term   SA = See Also   UF = Used For

Postimpressionism (Art)—*Continued*

> Modern art—1900-1999 (20th
> century)
> Painting

RT Cubism
> Expressionism (Art)
> Futurism (Art)
> Impressionism (Art)
> Surrealism

Postmodernism 190; 700.1

UF Post-modernism

BT Aesthetics

RT Modernism (Arts)

Posture 613.7

BT Physical education

Pot (Drug)

USE Marijuana

Potash 631.8; 668

BT Fertilizers and manures

Potatoes 635; 641.3

BT Vegetables

Potters 738.092; 920

BT Artists

Potters' marks

USE Pottery—Marks

Pottery 666; 738

> Use for materials on pottery for the ta-
> ble or for decorative use. Materials on the
> technology of fired earthen products or on
> clay products intended for industrial use
> are entered under **Ceramics.**

UF Crockery
> Dishes
> Earthenware
> Faience
> Stoneware

SA types of pottery and pottery
> of particular countries, e.g.
> **American pottery;** to be
> added as needed

BT Archeology
> Art objects
> Ceramics
> Clay industries
> Decoration and ornament
> Decorative arts
> Tableware

NT American pottery
> Glazes
> Porcelain
> Terra cotta

> Tiles

RT Vases

Pottery, American

USE American pottery

Pottery—Marks 738

UF Marks, Potters'
> Potters' marks

Poultry 598.6; 636.5

SA types of domesticated birds,
> e.g. **Ducks;** to be added as
> needed

BT Domestic animals
> Livestock

NT Ducks
> Geese
> Turkeys

Poverty 305.5; 362.5

UF Destitution
> Pauperism

SA names of countries with the
> subdivisions *Economic con-*
> *ditions* and *Social condi-*
> *tions,* to be added as
> needed

BT Wealth

NT Charities
> Homelessness
> Poor
> Public welfare
> United States—Economic con-
> ditions
> United States—Social condi-
> tions

RT Domestic economic assistance
> Subsistence economy

Powder, Smokeless

USE Gunpowder

Powdered milk

USE Dried milk

Power blackouts

USE Electric power failures

Power boats

USE Motorboats

Power failures

USE Electric power failures

Power (Mechanics) 531; 621

> Use for materials on the physics and en-
> gineering aspects of power. Materials on
> the available sources of mechanical power
> in general are entered under **Energy re-**
> **sources.**

BT = Broader Term   NT = Narrower Term   RT = Related Term   SA = See Also   UF = Used For

Power (Mechanics)—*Continued*
    UF   Energy technology
    BT   **Mechanical engineering**
          Mechanics
    NT   **Compressed air**
          Electric power
          Energy resources
          Force and energy
          Machinery
          Power transmission
          Steam
          Water power
          Wind power

Power plants 621.4
    UF   Power stations
    SA   types of power plants, to be
          added as needed
    NT   **Electric power plants**
          Nuclear power plants
          Steam power plants

Power plants, Atomic
    USE **Nuclear power plants**
Power plants, Electric
    USE **Electric power plants**
Power plants, Hydroelectric
    USE **Hydroelectric power plants**
Power plants, Steam
    USE **Steam power plants**
Power politics
    USE **Balance of power**
          Cold war
Power resources
    USE **Energy resources**
Power resources conservation
    USE **Energy conservation**
Power resources development
    USE **Energy development**
Power (Social sciences) 303.3
    BT   **Political science**
    NT   **Elite (Social sciences)**
Power stations
    USE **Power plants**
Power supply
    USE **Energy resources**
Power tools 621.9
    BT   **Tools**
Power transmission 621.8
    UF   Transmission of power
    BT   **Mechanical engineering**
          Power (Mechanics)

    NT   **Cables**
          Electric power distribution
          Gearing
    RT   **Belts and belting**
          Machinery
Power transmission, Electric
    USE **Electric lines**
          Electric power distribution
Powerlifting
    USE **Weight lifting**
Powers, Separation of
    USE **Separation of powers**
POWs
    USE **Prisoners of war**
Powwows 291.3; 394.2; 970.004
    BT   **Festivals**
          Indians of North America—
            Rites and ceremonies
          Indians of North America—
            Social life and customs
Practical jokes 818, etc.
    UF   Pranks
    BT   **Jokes**
          Wit and humor
Practical nurses 610.73; 920
    BT   **Nurses**
Practical nursing 610.73; 649.8
    BT   **Nursing**
Practical politics
    USE **Politics**
Practical Psychology
    USE **Applied psychology**
Practice teaching
    USE **Student teaching**
Pragmatism 144
    BT   **Philosophy**
          Positivism
          Realism
          Theory of knowledge
    RT   **Empiricism**
          Reality
          Truth
          Utilitarianism
Pranks
    USE **Practical jokes**
Prayer 242
    UF   Devotion
    BT   **Worship**
    RT   **Devotional exercises**
          Prayers

Prayers 242; 264
    UF   Collects
           Theology, Devotional
    NT   **Meditations**
    RT   **Prayer**
Prayers in the public schools
    USE   **Religion in the public schools**
Pre-Columbian Americans
    USE   **Indians of North America**
Pre-Lenten festivities
    USE   **Carnival**
Preachers
    USE   **Clergy**
Preaching 251
    UF   Speaking
    BT   **Pastoral work**
           Public speaking
           Rhetoric
    RT   **Sermons**
Preaching Friars
    USE   **Dominicans (Religious order)**
Precious metals 553.4; 669
    BT   **Metals**
           Mines and mineral resources
    NT   **Gold**
           Silver
Precious stones 553.8
    Use for mineralogical or technological materials on gem stones. Materials on cut and polished precious stones treated from the point of view of art or antiquity are entered under **Gems.** Materials on gems in which the emphasis is on the setting are entered under **Jewelry.**
    UF   Gemstones
           Jewels
           Stones, Precious
    SA   names of precious stones, to be added as needed
    BT   **Mineralogy**
    NT   **Diamonds**
    RT   **Gems**
Precipitation forecasting
    USE   **Weather forecasting**
Precipitation (Meteorology)
    USE   **Rain**
           Snow
Precocious children
    USE   **Gifted children**
Precolumbian Americans
    USE   **Indians of North America**
Predestination 234
    UF   Election (Theology)

           Foreordination
    BT   **Calvinism**
           Fate and fatalism
           Theology
    NT   **Free will and determinism**
Predictions
    USE   **Forecasting**
           Prophecies (Occultism)
Prefabricated buildings 693
    UF   Buildings, Prefabricated *[Former heading]*
    BT   **Buildings**
    NT   **Prefabricated houses**
Prefabricated houses 693; 728
    UF   Houses, Prefabricated
           Packaged houses
    BT   **Domestic architecture**
           House construction
           Houses
           Prefabricated buildings
Pregnancy 599; 612.6; 618.2
    BT   **Reproduction**
    NT   **Miscarriage**
           Prenatal care
           Teenage pregnancy
    RT   **Childbirth**
Pregnancy, Adolescent
    USE   **Teenage pregnancy**
Pregnancy, Teenage
    USE   **Teenage pregnancy**
Pregnancy, Termination of
    USE   **Abortion**
Prehistoric animals 560
    UF   Animals, Prehistoric
    BT   **Animals**
           Fossils
    NT   **Dinosaurs**
    RT   **Extinct animals**
Prehistoric art 709.01
    UF   Art, Prehistoric *[Former heading]*
    BT   **Art**
    NT   **Rock drawings, paintings, and engravings**
Prehistoric man 573.3
    UF   Man, Prehistoric *[Former heading]*
           Prehistory
    SA   names of prehistoric peoples, e.g. **Cro-Magnons;** etc.; and

---

Prehistoric man—*Continued*
>   names of countries, cities,
>   etc., with the subdivision
>   *Antiquities,* e.g. **United
>   States—Antiquities;** to be
>   added as needed
- BT **Ancient civilization**
     Antiquities
     Archeology
- NT **Cave dwellers**
     Cro-Magnons
- RT **Human origins**

Prehistory
- USE **Archeology**
     Prehistoric man
>   and names of countries, cities,
>   etc., with the subdivision
>   *Antiquities,* e.g. **United
>   States—Antiquities;** to be
>   added as needed

Preimplantational ectogenesis
- USE **Fertilization in vitro**

Prejudgments
- USE **Prejudices**

Prejudice
- USE **Prejudices**

Prejudice-motivated crimes
- USE **Hate crimes**

Prejudices 152.4; 177; 303.3
- UF Antipathies
     Bias (Psychology)
     Bigotry
     Prejudgments
     Prejudice
- SA types of prejudice, to be add-
     ed as needed
- BT **Attitude (Psychology)**
     Emotions
     Human relations
- NT **Antisemitism**
     Discrimination
     Racism
     Sexism

Prejudicial publicity
- USE **Freedom of the press and fair
     trial**

Preliterate man
- USE **Nonliterate man**

Preliterate society
- USE **Nonliterate folk society**

Prelude and fugue
- USE **Fugue**

Preludes and fugues
- USE **Fugue**

Premarital contracts
- USE **Marriage contracts**

Premarital counseling
- USE **Marriage counseling**

Premenstrual syndrome 618.1
- UF PMS (Gynecology)
     Premenstrual tension
     Tension, Premenstrual
- BT **Menstruation**

Premenstrual tension
- USE **Premenstrual syndrome**

Premiers
- USE **Prime ministers**

Prenatal care 618.2
- BT **Pregnancy**

Prenatal diagnosis 618.3
- BT **Diagnosis**
- NT **Amniocentesis**
     Genetic counseling

Prenuptial contracts
- USE **Marriage contracts**

Prepaid group medical practice
- USE **Health maintenance organiza-
     tions**

Prepaid health plans
- USE **Health insurance**

Prepaid medical care
- USE **Health insurance**

Prepared cereals 641.3; 664
- UF Breakfast cereals
     Cereals, Prepared *[Former
     heading]*
- BT **Breakfasts**
     Food

Preprimers
- USE **Easy reading materials**

Presbyterian Church 285
- BT **Christian sects**

Preschool children
- USE **Children**

Preschool education 372.21
- UF Children—Education
     Education, Preschool *[Former
     heading]*
     Infants—Education
- BT **Education**

BT = Broader Term   NT = Narrower Term   RT = Related Term   SA = See Also   UF = Used For

Preschool education—*Continued*
 NT **Readiness for school**
 RT **Kindergarten**
  Nursery schools
Preschool reading materials
 USE **Easy reading materials**
Presents
 USE **Gifts**
Preservation of antiquities
 USE **Antiquities—Collection and preservation**
Preservation of botanical specimens
 USE **Plants—Collection and preservation**
Preservation of buildings
 USE **Architecture—Conservation and restoration**
Preservation of food
 USE **Food—Preservation**
Preservation of forests
 USE **Forests and forestry**
Preservation of historical records
 USE **Archives**
Preservation of library resources
 USE **Library resources—Conservation and restoration**
Preservation of natural resources
 USE **Conservation of natural resources**
Preservation of natural scenery
 USE **Landscape protection**
  Natural monuments
  Nature conservation
  Wilderness areas
Preservation of organs, tissues, etc.
  617.9
 UF Organ preservation (Anatomy)
  Organs (Anatomy)—Preservation
 RT **Transplantation of organs, tissues, etc.**
Preservation of specimens
 USE **Taxidermy**
Preservation of wildlife
 USE **Wildlife conservation**
Preservation of wood
 USE **Wood—Preservation**
Preservation of works of art
 USE subjects with the subdivision
  Conservation and restora-

tion, e.g. **Painting—Conservation and restoration;** to be added as needed
Preservation of zoological specimens
 USE **Zoological specimens—Collection and preservation**
Preserving
 USE **Canning and preserving**
Presidential aides
 USE **Presidents—United States—Staff**
Presidential campaigns—United States
 USE **Presidents—United States—Election**
Presidential libraries
 USE **Presidents—United States—Archives**
Presidents (May subdiv. geog.) **351.003; 920**
 SA names of presidents, to be added as needed
 BT **Heads of state**
  Kings, queens, rulers, etc.
 NT **Presidents—United States**
  Vice-presidents
 RT **Executive power**
Presidents—Mexico 920; 972
 UF Mexico—Presidents
Presidents—Powers and duties
 USE **Executive power**
Presidents—United States 353.03; 920
 When applicable, the subdivisions under this heading may be used under names of presidents, prime ministers, and other rulers.
 UF United States—Presidents
 SA names of presidents, to be added as needed
 BT **Presidents**
Presidents—United States—Appointment 353.03
Presidents—United States—Archives 026
 UF Libraries, Presidential
  Presidential libraries
  Presidents—United States—Libraries
 SA names of individual libraries, to be added as needed
 NT **Harry S. Truman Library**

Presidents—United States—
Assassination 364.1; 973
BT Assassination
Presidents—United States—
Death and burial

Presidents—United States—Burial
USE Presidents—United States—
Death and burial

Presidents—United States—Children
920

Presidents—United States—Death and
burial 393; 973
UF Presidents—United States—
Burial
Presidents—United States—
Funeral and memorial ser-
vices [Former heading]
Presidents—United States—
Memorial services
NT Presidents—United States—
Assassination

Presidents—United States—Election
324.973
May further subdivide by date.
UF Campaigns, Presidential—
United States
Electoral college
Presidential campaigns—
United States
BT Elections

Presidents—United States—Family 920

Presidents—United States—Fathers 920

Presidents—United States—Friends and
associates 920

Presidents—United States—Funeral and
memorial services
USE Presidents—United States—
Death and burial

Presidents—United States—Health
353.03; 920
UF Presidents—United States—
Illness

Presidents—United States—Homes 728

Presidents—United States—Illness
USE Presidents—United States—
Health

Presidents—United States—
Impeachment 353.009;
353.03

Presidents—United States—Inability
USE Presidents—United States—
Succession

Presidents—United States—Inaugural
addresses 353.03
BT Presidents—United States—
Inauguration
Speeches

Presidents—United States—
Inauguration 353.03
NT Presidents—United States—
Inaugural addresses

Presidents—United States—Libraries
USE Presidents—United States—
Archives

Presidents—United States—Medals
353.03

Presidents—United States—Memorial
services
USE Presidents—United States—
Death and burial

Presidents—United States—Messages
353.03
UF Messages to Congress
Presidents—United States—
State of the Union message
State of the Union messages

Presidents—United States—Mothers
920

Presidents—United States—Nomination
324.50973
UF Nomination of presidents

Presidents—United States—Portraits
973

Presidents—United States—Power
USE Executive power—United
States

Presidents—United States—Press relations 070.4; 353.03

Presidents—United States—Protection
353.03

Presidents—United States—Quotations
818
BT Quotations

Presents—United States—Relations
with Congress 328.73;
353.03
Presidents—United States—Religion
920
Presidents—United States—Resignation
353.03
Presidents—United States—Sports 920
Presidents—United States—Spouses
920
   UF   First ladies—United States
         Presidents' wives—United
         States
         Wives of presidents—United
         States
Presidents—United States—Staff 353.03
   UF   Presidential aides
   BT   United States—Executive de-
         partments
Presidents—United States—State of the
         Union message
   USE   Presidents—United States—
         Messages
Presidents—United States—Succession
342; 353.03
   UF   Presidents—United States—
         Inability
Presidents—United States—Tombs
917.3
Presidents—United States—Voyages
and travels 353.03; 910
Presidents' wives—United States
   USE   Presidents—United States—
         Spouses
Press 070
   BT   Journalism
         Propaganda
         Public opinion
         Publicity
   NT   Alternative press
         Broadcast journalism
         Freedom of the press
         Freedom of the press and fair
         trial
         News agencies
         Pamphlets
   RT   Newspapers
         Periodicals
Press, Alternative
   USE   Alternative press

Press and government
   USE   Press—Government policy
Press censorship
   USE   Freedom of the press
Press clippings
   USE   Clippings (Books, newspapers,
         etc.)
Press—Government policy 323.44
   UF   Government and the press
         Press and government
   BT   Freedom of information
Press, Underground
   USE   Alternative press
Press working of metal
   USE   Sheet metalwork
Pressure groups
   USE   Lobbying
Pressure suits
   USE   Astronauts—Clothing
Prestidigitation
   USE   Magic tricks
Pretenders
   USE   Impostors and imposture
Prevention of accidents
   USE   Accidents—Prevention
Prevention of crime
   USE   Crime prevention
Prevention of cruelty to animals
   USE   Animal welfare
Prevention of disease
   USE   Preventive medicine
         and names of diseases and
         medical conditions with the
         subdivision *Prevention,* e.g.
         AIDS (Disease)—
         Prevention; to be added as
         needed
Prevention of fire
   USE   Fire prevention
Prevention of smoke
   USE   Smoke prevention
Preventive medicine 613
   UF   Diseases—Prevention
         Medicine, Preventive *[Former
         heading]*
         Prevention of disease
   SA   names of diseases with the
         subdivision *Prevention,* to
         be added as needed
   BT   Medicine

BT = Broader Term   NT = Narrower Term   RT = Related Term   SA = See Also   UF = Used For

Preventive medicine—*Continued*
- NT **Health**
   Heart diseases—Prevention
   Hygiene
   Immunity
   Vaccination
- RT **Pathology**
   Public health

Price controls
- USE **Wage-price policy**

Price indexes, Consumer
- USE **Consumer price indexes**

Price-wage policy
- USE **Wage-price policy**

Prices 338.5
- SA subjects with the subdivision
   Prices, e.g. **Art—Prices;** to
   be added as needed
- BT **Commerce**
   Consumption (Economics)
   Economics
   Finance
   Manufactures
- NT **Art—Prices**
   Books—Prices
   Consumer price indexes
   Farm produce—Marketing
   Wage-price policy
- RT **Cost of living**
   Wages

Priests 253; 253.092; 920
- UF Pastors
- SA names of church denomina-
   tions with the subdivision
   Clergy, e.g. **Catholic
   Church—Clergy;** to be add-
   ed as needed
- BT **Clergy**
- NT **Catholic Church—Clergy**
   Ex-priests

Primaries 324.5
- UF Direct primaries
   Elections, Primary
- BT **Elections**
   Political conventions
   Politics

Primary education
- USE **Elementary education**

Primates 599.8
- SA types of primates, e.g. **Mon-
   keys;** to be added as need-
   ed
- BT **Mammals**
- NT **Man**
   Monkeys

Primates—Behavior 599.8
- UF Primates—Habits and behav-
   ior *[Former heading]*
- BT **Animal behavior**

Primates—Habits and behavior
- USE **Primates—Behavior**

Prime ministers (May subdiv. geog.)
   351.003; 920
- UF Premiers
- BT **Cabinet officers**
   Executive power

Prime ministers—Great Britain
   351.003; 920
- UF Great Britain—Prime ministers

Primers
- USE **Easy reading materials**

Primitive Christianity
- USE **Church history—30-600, Early
   church**

Primitive man
- USE **Nonliterate man**

Primitive society
- USE **Nonliterate folk society**

Princes and princesses 920
- UF Royalty
- BT **Courts and courtiers**

Printing 686.2
- UF Layout and typography
   Typography
- SA types of printing processes, to
   be added as needed
- BT **Bibliography**
   Book industries
   Graphic arts
   Industrial arts
   Publishers and publishing
- NT **Advertising layout and typog-
   raphy**
   Color printing
   Electrotyping
   Linoleum block printing
   Linotype

BT = Broader Term   NT = Narrower Term   RT = Related Term   SA = See Also   UF = Used For

Printing—*Continued*
    Lithography
    Offset printing
    Proofreading
    Textile printing
    Type and type founding
    Typesetting
  RT Books
    Prints
Printing—Exhibitions 686.2074
  UF Books—Exhibitions
  BT Exhibitions
  RT Book industries—Exhibitions
Printing, Offset
  USE Offset printing
Printing—Specimens 686.2
  UF Type specimens
  BT Advertising
    Initials
  RT Type and type founding
Printing—Style manuals 686.02
  UF Style manuals
  RT Authorship—Handbooks, manuals, etc.
Printing, Textile
  USE Textile printing
Prints 769
  SA prints of particular countries, e.g. **American prints**; to be added as needed
  BT Graphic arts
  NT American prints
    Bookplates
    Color prints
    Linoleum block printing
    Lithography
    Woodcuts
  RT Printing
Prints, American
  USE American prints
Prison escapes
  USE Escapes
Prison labor
  USE Convict labor
Prison reform 365
  UF Penal reform
  BT Social problems
Prison schools
  USE Prisoners—Education
Prisoners 365
  UF Convicts

  BT Criminals
    Prisons
  NT Political prisoners
Prisoners—Education 365
  UF Education of criminals
    Education of prisoners
    Prison schools
  BT Adult education
    Prisons
Prisoners of war 341.6; 355.7
  UF Exchange of prisoners of war
    P.O.W.'s
    POWs
  SA prisoners of war from particular countries, e.g. **American prisoners of war;** and names of wars with the subdivision *Prisoners and prisons,* to be added as needed
  NT American prisoners of war
    Missing in action
    World War, 1939-1945—Prisoners and prisons
  RT Concentration camps
Prisoners of war, American
  USE American prisoners of war
Prisoners, Political
  USE Political prisoners
Prisons (May subdiv. geog.) 365
  UF Dungeons
    Imprisonment
    Jails
    Penal institutions
    Penitentiaries
  SA types of prisons and names of individual prisons, to be added as needed
  BT Administration of criminal justice
    Correctional institutions
    Punishment
  NT Criminal law
    Escapes
    Prisoners
    Prisoners—Education
    Probation
    Reformatories
  RT Convict labor
    Crime

BT = Broader Term   NT = Narrower Term   RT = Related Term   SA = See Also   UF = Used For

Prisons—United States 365
  UF   United States—Prisons
Privacy, Right of
  USE   **Right of privacy**
Private art collections
  USE   names of original owners of
        private collections with the
        subdivision *Art collections,*
        to be added as needed
Private eye stories
  USE   **Mystery and detective plays**
        Mystery fiction
        Mystery films
        Mystery radio programs
        Mystery television programs
Private funding of the arts
  USE   **Art patronage**
Private schools 371; 373.2
  UF   Boarding schools
        Independent schools
        Nonpublic schools
  BT   **Schools**
  NT   **Church schools**
        English public schools
Private theater
  USE   **Amateur theater**
Privateering 341
  UF   Letters of marque
  BT   **International law**
        Naval art and science
        Naval history
        Pirates
Privatisation
  USE   **Privatization**
Privatization 338.9
     Use for materials on the transfer of pub-
  lic assets and service functions to the pri-
  vate sector.
  UF   Denationalization
        Privatisation
  BT   **Economic policy**
        Industry—Government policy
  RT   **Government ownership**
Prize fighting
  USE   **Boxing**
Prizes, Literary
  USE   **Literary prizes**
Prizes (Rewards)
  USE   **Awards**
Pro-abortion movement
  USE   **Pro-choice movement**

Pro-choice movement 179; 363.4
  UF   Abortion rights movement
        Freedom of choice movement
        Pro-abortion movement
        Right to choose movement
  BT   **Abortion—Moral and religious**
        aspects
        Social movements
        Women's rights
Pro-life movement 179; 363.4
  UF   Anti-abortion movement
        Antiabortion movement
        Right-to-life movement (Anti-
        abortion movement)
  BT   **Abortion—Moral and religious**
        aspects
        Social movements
        Women's rights
Probabilities 519.2
  UF   Certainty
        Fortune
        Statistical inference
  BT   **Algebra**
        Logic
        Mathematics
        Statistics
  NT   **Average**
        Game theory
        Reliability (Engineering)
        Sampling (Statistics)
  RT   **Life insurance**
Probation 364.6
  UF   Reform of criminals
        Suspended sentence
  BT   **Corrections**
        Criminal law
        Prisons
        Punishment
        Reformatories
        Social case work
  RT   **Juvenile courts**
        Parole
Probes, Space
  USE   **Space probes**
Problem children
  USE   **Emotionally disturbed children**
Problem drinking
  USE   **Alcoholism**
Problem families—Counseling of
  USE   **Family therapy**

Problem solving 153.4; 510.76
- UF   Solution achievement
- BT   **Psychology**
- NT   **Crisis management**
       Critical thinking
       Group problem solving
- RT   **Decision making**

Problem solving, Group
- USE   **Group problem solving**

Problems, exercises, etc.
- USE   subjects with the subdivision *Problems, exercises, etc.,* for compilations of practice problems or exercises for use in the study of a topic, e.g. **Chemistry—Problems, exercises, etc.;** to be added as needed

Procedural due process
- USE   **Due process of law**

Processing (Libraries)
- USE   **Library technical processes**

Processions
- USE   **Parades**

Procurement, Government
- USE   **Government purchasing**

Producers and directors
- USE   **Motion picture producers and directors**

Product recall 658.5
- UF   Commercial products recall
       Manufactures—Defects
       Manufactures recall
       Recall of products
- BT   **Consumer protection**

Product safety 363.19; 658.5
- UF   Commercial products—Safety measures
- BT   **Consumer protection**

Production
- USE   **Economics**
       Industry

Production engineering
- USE   **Factory management**

Production standards 658.5
  Use for materials on the unit time value for the accomplishment of a work task as determined by work measurement techniques.
- UF   Output standards
       Standards of output
       Time production standards
       Work standards
- SA   types of industries and processes with the subdivision *Production standards,* e.g. **Automobile industry—Production standards;** to be added as needed
- BT   **Labor productivity**
       Management
- NT   **Automobile industry—Production standards**
       Motion study
       Time study

Productivity of labor
- USE   **Labor productivity**

Products, Animal
- USE   **Animal products**

Products, Brand name
- USE   **Brand name products**

Products, Commercial
- USE   **Commercial products**

Products, Dairy
- USE   **Dairy products**

Products, Generic
- USE   **Generic products**

Products, Waste
- USE   **Waste products**

Professional associations
- USE   **Trade and professional associations**

Professional education 378.1
- UF   Education, Professional
- SA   names of professions with the subdivision *Study and teaching,* e.g. to be added as needed
- BT   **Education**
       Higher education
       Learning and scholarship
- NT   **Colleges and universities**
       Library education
       Medicine—Study and teaching
- RT   **Technical education**
       Vocational education

Professional ethics 174
- UF   Ethics, Professional
- SA   names of professions and types of professional per-

Professional ethics—*Continued*
    sonnel with the subdivision
    Professional ethics, e.g.
    Librarians—Professional
    ethics; to be added as
    needed
  BT **Ethics**
  NT **Business ethics**
      Legal ethics
      Librarians—Professional eth-
      ics
      Medical ethics
Professional liability
  USE **Malpractice**
Professional liability insurance
  USE **Malpractice insurance**
Professional sports 796
  SA names of specific sports, to be
      added as needed
  BT **Sports**
Professions 331.7
  UF Careers
      Jobs
      Vocations
  SA names of professions with the
      subdivision *Vocational*
      guidance, e.g. **Law—**
      Vocational guidance; to be
      added as needed
  BT **Self-employed**
  NT **College graduates**
      Intellectuals
      Law—Vocational guidance
      Paraprofessionals
  RT **Occupations**
      Vocational guidance
Professions—Tort liability
  USE **Malpractice**
Professors
  USE **Teachers**
Profit 338.5; 658.15
  BT **Business**
      Capital
      Economics
      Wealth
  NT **Capitalism**
  RT **Income**
Profit sharing 658.3; 331.2
  BT **Commerce**
      Wages

  RT **Cooperation**
Programmed instruction 371.3
  UF Programmed textbooks
  SA subjects with the subdivision
      Programmed instruction, to
      be added as needed
  BT **Teaching—Aids and devices**
  NT **Computer assisted instruction**
      English language—
      Programmed instruction
      Teaching machines
Programmed textbooks
  USE **Programmed instruction**
Programming (Computers) 005.1
  UF Computer programming
      Computers—Programming
      Flow charts (Computer sci-
      ence)
      Flowcharting (Computer sci-
      ence)
  SA subjects with the subdivision
      Computer programs, to be
      added as needed
  BT **Electronic data processing**
      Mathematical analysis
      Mathematical models
  NT **Programming languages (Com-**
      puters)
  RT **Computer software**
Programming languages (Computers)
    005.13
  UF Autocodes
      Automatic programming lan-
      guages
      Computer program languages
      Machine language
  SA names of specific languages,
      e.g. **FORTRAN (Computer**
      language); to be added as
      needed
  BT **Computer software**
      Electronic data processing
      Language and languages
      Programming (Computers)
  NT **FORTRAN (Computer lan-**
      guage)
Programs, Computer
  USE **Computer software**
Programs, Radio
  USE **Radio programs**

Programs, School assembly
    USE **School assembly programs**
Programs, Television
    USE **Television programs**
Programs, Twelve-step
    USE **Twelve-step programs**
Programs, Utility (Computer programs)
    USE **Utilities (Computer programs)**
Progress 303.44
    BT **Civilization**
    NT **Science and civilization**
Progressive education
    USE **Education—Experimental
           methods**
Prohibited books
    USE **Books—Censorship**
Prohibition 344
    Use for materials on the legal prohibi-
    tion of liquor traffic and liquor manufac-
    ture.
    BT **Criminal law**
    RT **Temperance**
Project Apollo
    USE **Apollo project**
Project Gemini
    USE **Gemini project**
Project MARC
    USE **MARC formats**
Project method in teaching 371.3
    BT **Teaching**
Project Ranger 629.43
    UF Ranger project
    BT **Lunar probes**
Project schools
    USE **Experimental schools**
Project Sealab
    USE **Sealab project**
Project Telstar
    USE **Telstar project**
Project Voyager 629.43
    UF Voyager project
    BT **Astronautics—United States**
Projectiles 623.4
    UF Bullets
          Shells (Projectiles)
    NT **Ammunition**
          Bombs
          Guided missiles
          Rockets (Aeronautics)
    RT **Ordnance**

Projective geometry 516
    UF Geometry, Projective *[Former
           heading]*
    BT **Geometry**
Projectors 778.2
    UF Film projectors
          Lantern projection
          Motion picture projectors
          Opaque projectors
          Slide projectors
Projects, Science
    USE **Science projects**
Prokaryotes
    USE **Bacteria**
Proletariat 305.5
    BT **Labor**
          Socialism
          Working class
Proliferation of arms
    USE **Arms race**
Promotion in school
    USE **Promotion (School)**
Promotion (School) 371.2
    UF Grade repetition
          Grade retention
          Non-promotion (School)
          Promotion in school
          Retention, Grade
          School grade retention
          School promotion
          Student promotion
    BT **Grading and marking (Educa-
           tion)**
Promptness
    USE **Punctuality**
Pronunciation
    USE **Names—Pronunciation**
          and names of languages with
          the subdivision *Pronuncia-
          tion,* e.g. **English lan-
          guage—Pronunciation;** to be
          added as needed
Proofreading 070.5; 686.2
    BT **Printing**
Propaganda 303.3; 327.1
    SA propaganda of particular
          countries, e.g. **American
          propaganda;** to be added as
          needed
    BT **Political psychology**

Propaganda—*Continued*
  Public opinion
 NT American propaganda
  Press
  Psychological warfare
  World War, 1939-1945—
   Propaganda
 RT Advertising
  Publicity
Propaganda, American
 USE American propaganda
Propagation of plants
 USE Plant propagation
Propellers, Aerial
 USE Aerial propellers
Proper names
 USE Names
Property 330.1
 UF Ownership
 BT Economics
 NT Airspace law
  Eminent domain
  Income
  Lost and found possessions
  Real estate
  Surplus government property
 RT Wealth
Property, Literary
 USE Copyright
Property, Real
 USE Real estate
Property tax—Assessment
 USE Tax assessment
Prophecies (Bible)
 USE Bible—Prophecies
Prophecies (Occult sciences)
 USE Prophecies (Occultism)
Prophecies (Occultism) 133.3
 UF Predictions
  Prophecies (Occult sciences)
   [Former heading]
 BT Occultism
  Supernatural
 NT Fortune telling
 RT Astrology
  Divination
  Oracles
Prophets 221.9; 920
 RT Saints

Proportion (Architecture)
 USE Architecture—Composition,
   proportion, etc.
Proportional representation 328.3
 UF Representation, Proportional
 BT Constitutional law
  Representative government and
   representation
 RT Elections
Prose literature, American
 USE American prose literature
Prose literature, English
 USE English prose literature
Prosody
 USE Versification
Prospecting 622
 BT Gold mines and mining
  Mines and mineral resources
  Silver mines and mining
 NT Mine surveying
  Petroleum geology
Prosthesis
 USE Artificial limbs
  Artificial organs
Prostitution 176; 306.74; 363.4; 364.1
 BT Crimes without victims
  Sexual ethics
  Social problems
  Vice
  Women—Social conditions
 NT Juvenile prostitution
Prostitution, Juvenile
 USE Juvenile prostitution
Protection
 USE Free trade and protection
Protection against burglary
 USE Burglary protection
Protection of animals
 USE Animal welfare
Protection of birds
 USE Birds—Protection
Protection of children
 USE Child welfare
Protection of environment
 USE Environmental protection
Protection of game
 USE Game protection
Protection of natural scenery
 USE Landscape protection
  Natural monuments

BT = Broader Term NT = Narrower Term RT = Related Term SA = See Also UF = Used For

Protection of natural scenery—
Continued
  Nature conservation
  Wilderness areas
Protection of plants
  USE **Plant conservation**
Protection of wildlife
  USE **Wildlife conservation**
Proteins 547.7; 574.19
  BT **Biochemistry**
  NT **Enzymes**
Protest
  USE **Dissent**
Protest marches and rallies
  USE **Protests, demonstrations, etc.**
Protest movements (War)
  USE names of wars with the subdivision *Protests, demonstrations, etc.,* e.g. **World War, 1939-1945—Protests, demonstrations, etc.;** to be added as needed

Protestant churches 280
  Use for materials on Protestant denominations treated collectively. Works on Protestant church buildings are entered under **Churches.**
  UF **Denominations, Protestant**
      Protestant denominations
  SA names of Protestant churches, e.g. **Presbyterian Church;** to be added as needed
  BT **Christian sects**
      Church history
  RT **Protestantism**
Protestant denominations
  USE **Protestant churches**
Protestant Episcopal Church in the U.S.A.
  USE **Episcopal Church**
Protestant Reformation
  USE **Reformation**
Protestant work ethic
  USE **Work ethic**
Protestantism 280
  BT **Christianity**
      Church history
  RT **Protestant churches**
      Reformation

Protests, demonstrations, etc. (May subdiv. geog.) 322.4; 361.2
  Use for materials on public gatherings, marches, etc., organized for nonviolent protest even though incidental disturbances or rioting may occur.
  UF **Demonstrations (Protest)**
      Marches (Demonstrations)
      Protest marches and rallies
      Public demonstrations
      Rallies (Protest)
  SA names of specific wars or other objects of protest with the subdivision *Protests, demonstrations, etc.,* to be added as needed
  BT **Crowds**
      Public meetings
  NT **Hunger strikes**
      World War, 1939-1945—Protests, demonstrations, etc.
      Youth movement
  RT **Riots**
Protests, demonstrations, etc.—Chicago (Ill.) 322.409773
  UF **Chicago (Ill.)—Protests, demonstrations, etc.**
Protests, demonstrations, etc.—United States 322.40973; 361.2
  UF **United States—Protests, demonstrations, etc.**
Protons 539.7
  UF **Hydrogen nucleus**
  BT **Atoms**
      Particles (Nuclear physics)
Protoplasm 574.87
  BT **Biology**
      Life (Biology)
  RT **Cells**
      Embryology
Protozoa 593.1
  BT **Cells**
      Invertebrates
      Microorganisms
Proverbs 398.9
  UF **Adages**
      Maxims
      Sayings
  BT **Folklore**

BT = Broader Term   NT = Narrower Term   RT = Related Term   SA = See Also   UF = Used For

Proverbs—*Continued*
    Quotations
  RT   **Epigrams**
Providence and government of God 214;
    231
  BT   **God—Christianity**
     Theology
Provincialism
  USE **Sectionalism (United States)**
Provincialisms
  USE names of languages with the
      subdivision *Provincialisms,*
      e.g. **English language—**
      Provincialisms; to be added
      as needed
Pruning 631.5
  BT   **Forests and forestry**
     Fruit culture
     Gardening
     Trees
Psalmody
  USE **Church music**
     Hymns
Pseudonyms 929.4
  UF   Anonyms
     Fictitious names
     Names, Fictitious
     Pen names
  BT   **Authors**
     Names
     Personal names
Psi (Parapsychology)
  USE **Parapsychology**
Psychiatric hospitals 362.2
  UF   Insane—Hospitals
     Mental hospitals
  BT   **Hospitals**
     Mentally ill—Institutional
     care
Psychiatrists 920; 926
  UF   Psychopathologists
  BT   **Psychologists**
Psychiatry 616.89
    Use for materials on clinical aspects of
mental disorders, including therapy. Popu-
lar materials and materials on regional or
social aspects of mental disorders are en-
tered under **Mental illness.** Systematic de-
scriptions of mental disorders are entered
under **Abnormal psychology.**
  BT   **Medicine**

  NT   **Adolescent psychiatry**
     Child psychiatry
     Mentally ill
     Psychotherapy
  RT   **Abnormal psychology**
     Mental health
     Mental illness
Psychiatry, Adolescent
  USE **Adolescent psychiatry**
Psychiatry, Child
  USE **Child psychiatry**
Psychic healing
  USE **Mental healing**
Psychic phenomena
  USE **Parapsychology**
Psychical research
  USE **Parapsychology**
Psychoactive drugs
  USE **Psychotropic drugs**
Psychoanalysis 150.19; 616.89
  BT   **Psychology**
  NT   **Psychosomatic medicine**
  RT   **Abnormal psychology**
     Dreams
     Hypnotism
     Mind and body
     Subconsciousness
Psychogenetics
  USE **Behavior genetics**
Psychokinesis 133.8
  UF   Telekinesis
  BT   **Parapsychology**
     Spiritualism
Psychological aspects
  USE subjects with the subdivision
      Psychological aspects, e.g.
      Drugs—Psychological as-
      pects; World War,
      1939-1945—Psychological
      aspects; etc., to be added as
      needed
Psychological stress
  USE **Stress (Psychology)**
Psychological tests
  UF   Mental tests *[Former heading]*
  BT   **Psychology**
  NT   **Ability—Testing**
  RT   **Educational tests and mea-**
     surements

Psychological warfare 355.3

Use for materials on methods used to undermine the morale of the civilian population and the military forces of an enemy country.

UF   War of nerves

SA   names of wars with the subdivision *Psychological aspects,* to be added as needed

BT   **Applied psychology**
       Military art and science
       Morale
       Propaganda
       War

NT   **Brainwashing**
       World War, 1939-1945—Psychological aspects

Psychologists 150.92; 920

NT   **Psychiatrists**

RT   **Psychology**

Psychologists, School

USE   **School psychologists**

Psychology 150

UF   Mind

SA   religions, theological topics, titles of individual sacred works, types of animals, classes of persons, ethnic groups, and names of individual persons, including individual literary authors, with the subdivision *Psychology,* to be added as needed; and subjects with the subdivision *Psychological aspects* for materials on the influence of particular situations, conditions, activities, environments, or objects on the mental condition or personality of the individual, e.g. **Color—Psychological aspects**; to be added as needed

BT   **Brain**
       Philosophy
       Soul

NT   **Adjustment (Psychology)**
       Adolescent psychology
       Aggressiveness (Psychology)
       Apperception
       Applied psychology
       Assertiveness (Psychology)
       Attention
       Attitude (Psychology)
       Behavior genetics
       Behaviorism
       Child psychology
       Choice (Psychology)
       Christianity—Psychology
       Color—Psychological aspects
       Consciousness
       Dogs—Psychology
       Educational psychology
       Emotions
       Ethnopsychology
       Faith—Psychology
       Genius
       Gestalt psychology
       Habit
       Human behavior
       Imagination
       Indians of North America—Psychology
       Individuality
       Instinct
       Intellect
       Intuition
       Memory
       Men—Psychology
       Motivation (Psychology)
       Multiple personality
       Music—Psychological aspects
       Number concept
       Parapsychology
       Perception
       Personality
       Phrenology
       Physiognomy
       Political psychology
       Problem solving
       Psychoanalysis
       Psychological tests
       Psychology of religion
       Psychophysiology
       Reasoning
       Self-acceptance
       Self-consciousness
       Self-control
       Self-esteem

BT = Broader Term   NT = Narrower Term   RT = Related Term   SA = See Also   UF = Used For

Psychology—*Continued*
    Self-perception
    Self-realization
    Senses and sensation
    Shakespeare, William,
      1564-1616—Psychology
    Social psychology
    Stress (Psychology)
    Subconsciousness
    Temperament
    Thought and thinking
    Values
    Women—Psychology
  RT **Psychologists**
Psychology, Abnormal
  USE **Abnormal psychology**
Psychology, Adolescent
  USE **Adolescent psychology**
Psychology and religion
  USE **Psychology of religion**
Psychology, Applied
  USE **Applied psychology**
Psychology, Biblical
  USE **Bible—Psychology**
Psychology, Child
  USE **Child psychology**
Psychology, Comparative
  USE **Comparative psychology**
Psychology, Criminal
  USE **Criminal psychology**
Psychology, Educational
  USE **Educational psychology**
Psychology, Ethnic
  USE **Ethnopsychology**
Psychology, Experimental
  USE **Psychophysiology**
Psychology, Industrial
  USE **Applied psychology**
Psychology, Medical
  USE **Abnormal psychology**
Psychology, National
  USE **Ethnopsychology**
      National characteristics
Psychology of color
  USE **Color—Psychological aspects**
Psychology of learning 153.1
  UF Learning, Psychology of *[For-*
      mer heading]
  BT **Animal intelligence**
      Child psychology

      Education
      Educational psychology
      Memory
  NT **Behavior modification**
      Biofeedback training
      Brainwashing
      Concept learning
      Feedback (Psychology)
      Learning disabilities
      Reading comprehension
      Verbal learning
Psychology of music
  USE **Music—Psychological aspects**
Psychology of religion 200.1; 253.5
  UF Psychology and religion
      Psychology, Religious *[Former*
        heading]
      Religion and psychology
      Religious psychology
  SA titles of individual sacred
      works and names of reli-
      gions or religious topics
      with the subdivision *Psy-*
      chology, to be added as
      needed
  BT **Psychology**
      Religion
  NT **Christianity—Psychology**
      Faith—Psychology
      Pastoral psychology
Psychology, Pastoral
  USE **Pastoral psychology**
Psychology, Pathological
  USE **Abnormal psychology**
Psychology, Physiological
  USE **Psychophysiology**
Psychology, Political
  USE **Political psychology**
Psychology, Practical
  USE **Applied psychology**
Psychology, Racial
  USE **Ethnopsychology**
Psychology, Religious
  USE **Pastoral psychology**
      Psychology of religion
Psychology, Social
  USE **Social psychology**
Psychology, Structural
  USE **Gestalt psychology**
Psychopathologists
  USE **Psychiatrists**

    BT = Broader Term   NT = Narrower Term   RT = Related Term   SA = See Also   UF = Used For

Psychopathology
USE **Abnormal psychology**
Psychopathy
USE **Abnormal psychology**
Psychopharmaceuticals
USE **Psychotropic drugs**
Psychophysics
USE **Psychophysiology**
Psychophysiology 152
Use for materials on the relationship between psychological and physiological processes.
UF Experimental psychology
Physiological psychology
Psychology, Experimental
Psychology, Physiological
[Former heading]
Psychophysics
BT **Mental health**
Nervous system
Physiology
Psychology
NT **Behaviorism**
Color sense
Dreams
Emotions
Human engineering
Hypnotism
Left- and right-handedness
Memory
Optical illusions
Pain
Senses and sensation
Sleep
Temperament
RT **Mind and body**
Psychoses
USE **Mental illness**
Psychosomatic medicine 616.08
UF Medicine, Psychosomatic
[Former heading]
BT **Abnormal psychology**
Medicine
Mind and body
Neuroses
Psychoanalysis
Psychotherapy 616.89
UF Therapy, Psychological
BT **Psychiatry**
Therapeutics

NT **Biofeedback training**
Family therapy
Sex therapy
Transactional analysis
RT **Mental healing**
Suggestive therapeutics
Psychotic children
USE **Mentally ill children**
Psychotics
USE **Mentally ill**
Psychotropic drugs 615
Use for general materials on the group of drugs that act on the central nervous system to affect behavior, mental activity, or perception, including the antipsychotic drugs, antidepressants, hallucinogenic agents, and tranquilizers
UF Drugs, Psychotropic
Psychoactive drugs
Psychopharmaceuticals
SA types of drugs and names of individual drugs, to be added as needed
BT **Drugs**
NT **Cocaine**
Hallucinogens
PTAs
USE **Parents' and teachers' associations**
Public accommodations, Discrimination in
USE **Discrimination in public accommodations**
Public administration 350
Use for general materials on the principles and techniques involved in the conduct of public business. Materials limited to the governmental process of individual countries, states, cities, etc., are entered under the name of the place with the subdivision *Politics and government.*
UF Administration
SA names of countries, states, cities, etc., with the subdivision *Politics and government,* to be added as needed
BT **Local government**
Municipal government
Political science
NT **Bureaucracy**
Civil service
Intelligence service

BT = Broader Term   NT = Narrower Term   RT = Related Term   SA = See Also   UF = Used For

Public administration—*Continued*
       Military government
       United States—Politics and
       government
  RT   Administrative law
Public assistance
  USE Public welfare
Public buildings 350.86; 725

Use for materials on buildings owned by the public and maintained at public expense, such as government office buildings, public libraries, public schools, etc. Materials on buildings that are privately owned and maintained and are open to the public for business or entertainment are entered under **Buildings** or under the specific type of building.

  UF   Buildings, Public
       Government buildings
  SA   names of cities, states, etc.,
       with the subdivision *Public
       buildings,* e.g. **Chicago
       (Ill.)—Public buildings;**
       names of countries with the
       subdivision *Public buildings*
       for that government's public buildings located within
       the country, as well as for
       embassies, consulates, and
       other public buildings of
       that country in foreign locations, e.g. **United
       States—Public buildings;**
       and names of individual
       public buildings; to be added as needed
  BT   **Architecture**
       Buildings
       Public works
  NT   **Capitols**
       Chicago (Ill.)—Public buildings
       Ohio—Public buildings
       United States—Public buildings
Public buildings, American
  USE **United States—Public buildings**
Public buildings—Chicago (Ill.)
  USE **Chicago (Ill.)—Public buildings**
Public buildings—Ohio
  USE **Ohio—Public buildings**

Public buildings—United States
  USE **United States—Public buildings**
Public charities
  USE **Public welfare**
Public debts (May subdiv. geog.) **336.3**

Use for materials on government debts.

  UF   Debts, Government
       Debts, Public *[Former heading]*
       Federal debt
       Government debts
       National debts
       State debts
       War debts
  SA   names of wars with the subdivision *Finance,* to be added
       as needed
  BT   **Credit**
       Economics
       Finance
       Loans
  NT   **World War, 1939-1945—Finance**
  RT   **Bonds**
       Deficit financing
Public debts—United States 336.3
  UF   Federal debt—United States
       United States—Public debts
Public demonstrations
  USE **Protests, demonstrations, etc.**
Public documents
  USE **Government publications**
Public domain
  USE **Public lands**
Public figures
  USE **Celebrities**
Public finance
  USE **Finance**
Public health (May subdiv. geog.)
        362.1; 614
  UF   Health, Public
       Hygiene, Social
       Public hygiene
       Social hygiene
  BT   **Social problems**
       State medicine
  NT   **Burial**
       Cemeteries
       Communicable diseases

Public health—*Continued*
  Community health services
  Cremation
  Disinfection and disinfectants
  Environmental health
  Epidemics
  Food adulteration and inspection
  Health boards
  Hospitals
  Meat inspection
  Medical care
  Medical charities
  Milk supply
  Noise
  Occupational diseases
  Occupational health and safety
  Pollution
  Refuse and refuse disposal
  Sanitary engineering
  School hygiene
  Sewage disposal
  Social medicine
  Street cleaning
  Vaccination
  Water pollution
  Water supply
 RT Preventive medicine
  Sanitation
Public health boards
 USE Health boards
Public health—United States
  362.10973; 614
 UF United States—Public health
Public housing (May subdiv. geog.)
  363.5
 UF Government housing
  Housing projects, Government
  Low income housing
 BT Housing
Public hygiene
 USE Public health
Public interest 172; 320.01; 344
 UF National interest
 BT Industry—Government policy
  State, The
 NT Ombudsman
  Whistle blowing

Public lands (May subdiv. geog.) 333.1
 UF Crown lands
  Public domain
 BT Colonization
  Land use
 NT Forest reserves
  National parks and reserves
 RT Natural resources
Public lands—Ohio 333.109771
 UF Ohio—Public lands *[Former heading]*
Public lands—United States 333.10973
 UF United States—Public lands *[Former heading]*
Public libraries (May subdiv. geog.) 027.4
 UF Libraries, Public
 BT Libraries
 NT County libraries
  Regional libraries
Public meetings 302.3
 UF Meetings, Public
 BT Freedom of assembly
 NT Parliamentary practice
  Protests, demonstrations, etc.
Public opinion 303.3
 UF Opinion, Public
 SA subjects with the subdivision *Public opinion,* e.g. **World War, 1939-1945—Public opinion;** and names of countries with the subdivision *Foreign opinion* for materials dealing with foreign public opinion about the country, e.g. **United States—Foreign opinion;** to be added as needed
 BT Freedom of conscience
  Political psychology
 NT Press
  Propaganda
  Public opinion polls
  Publicity
  United States—Foreign opinion
  World War, 1939-1945—Public opinion
 RT Attitude (Psychology)
  Public relations

BT = Broader Term NT = Narrower Term RT = Related Term SA = See Also UF = Used For

Public opinion polls 303.3
- UF   Opinion polls
      Polls, Public opinion
      Straw votes
- BT   **Public opinion**
- RT   **Market surveys**

Public ownership
- USE   **Government ownership**
      Municipal ownership

Public playgrounds
- USE   **Playgrounds**

Public procurement
- USE   **Government purchasing**

Public records—Preservation
- USE   **Archives**

Public relations 659.2

May be subdivided by topic, e.g. **Public relations—Libraries**; etc.
- NT   **Business entertaining**
      Customer relations
- RT   **Advertising**
      Public opinion
      Publicity

Public relations—Libraries 021.7
- UF   Libraries—Public relations
- BT   **Libraries and community**

Public safety, Crimes against
- USE   **Offenses against public safety**

Public schools (May subdiv. geog.) **371**

Use for materials on preschool, elementary, and secondary schools supported by state and local government. Materials on British endowed secondary schools that are open to public admission but are not financed or administered by any government body are entered under **English public schools.**
- UF   Common schools
      Community schools
      Grammar schools
      Neighborhood schools
- BT   **Schools**
- NT   **Evening and continuation schools**
      High schools
      Junior high schools
      Magnet schools
      Rural schools
      Summer schools

Public schools and religion
- USE   **Religion in the public schools**

Public schools, Endowed (Great Britain)
- USE   **English public schools**

Public schools, English
- USE   **English public schools**

Public schools—United States 371; 379.73
- UF   United States—Public schools

Public service commissions 350

Use for materials on bodies appointed to regulate or control public utilities.
- UF   Public utility commissions
- BT   **Corporation law**
      Corporations
      Industry—Government policy

Public service corporations
- USE   **Public utilities**

Public shelters
- USE   **Air raid shelters**

Public speaking 808.5
- UF   Elocution
      Oratory
      Persuasion (Rhetoric)
      Speaking
- BT   **Communication**
- NT   **Acting**
      Chalk talks
      Debates and debating
      Lectures and lecturing
      Preaching
- RT   **Voice**

Public television 384.55

Use for materials on non-commercial television, publicly owned and operated, that presents educational, cultural, and public service programs.
- UF   Educational television
      Television, Public
- BT   **Television broadcasting**

Public transit
- USE   **Local transit**

Public utilities 343.09; 351.87; 363.6
- UF   Electric utilities
      Gas companies
      Public service corporations
      Utilities, Public
- NT   **Electric industries**
      Electric railroads
      Gas
      Railroads
      Railroads—Government policy
      Street railroads
      Telegraph
      Telephone

Public utilities—*Continued*
　　Water supply
　RT　**Corporation law**
　　Corporations
Public utility commissions
　USE　**Public service commissions**
Public welfare 361.6

Use for materials on tax-supported welfare activities. Materials on privately supported welfare activities are entered under **Charities**. Materials on the methods employed in welfare work, public or private, are entered under **Social work.**

　UF　Charities, Public
　　Poor relief
　　Public assistance
　　Public charities
　　Relief, Public
　　Social welfare
　　Welfare state
　　Welfare work
　BT　**Poverty**
　　Social work
　NT　**Child welfare**
　　Children's hospitals
　　Disaster relief
　　Food relief
　　Hospitals
　　Institutional care
　　Legal assistance to the poor
　　Orphanages
　　Poor
　　Social medicine
　RT　**Charities**
Public works 350.86; 363
　SA　names of countries, cities,
　　etc., with the subdivision
　　Public works, to be added
　　as needed
　BT　**Civil engineering**
　　Domestic economic assistance
　NT　**Chicago (Ill.)—Public works**
　　Municipal engineering
　　Public buildings
　　United States—Public works
Public worship 264
　UF　Church attendance
　BT　**Worship**
Publicity 659
　BT　**Public opinion**
　NT　**Press**

　RT　**Advertising**
　　Propaganda
　　Public relations
Publishers and authors
　USE　**Authors and publishers**
Publishers and publishing 070.5
　UF　Book trade
　　Editors and editing
　　Publishing
　NT　**Authors and publishers**
　　Electronic publishing
　　Paperback books
　　Printing
　　Publishers' catalogs
　　Publishers' standard book
　　numbers
　　Serial publications
　RT　**Book industries**
　　Books
　　Booksellers and bookselling
　　Copyright
Publishers' catalogs 015

Use for catalogs produced by publishers and for materials about such catalogs. Retail book catalogs and book auction catalogs and materials about such catalogs are entered under **Booksellers' catalogs.**

　UF　Books—Catalogs
　　Catalogs
　　Catalogs, Publishers' *[Former heading]*
　BT　**Publishers and publishing**
Publishers' standard book numbers
　　070.5
　UF　Book numbers, Publishers'
　　standard
　　Standard book numbers
　BT　**Publishers and publishing**
　NT　**International Standard Book**
　　Numbers
Publishing
　USE　**Publishers and publishing**
Publishing, Electronic
　USE　**Electronic publishing**
Pubs
　USE　**Bars**
Pugilism
　USE　**Boxing**
Pulmonary resuscitation
　USE　**Artificial respiration**
Pulsars 523.8
　UF　Pulsating radio sources

Pulsars—*Continued*
    BT **Astronomy**
Pulsating radio sources
    USE **Pulsars**
Pumping iron
    USE **Weight lifting**
Pumping machinery 621.6
    UF Force pumps
        Pumps
        Steam pumps
    SA types of pumping machinery,
          e.g. **Heat pumps;** to be add-
          ed as needed
    BT **Engines**
        Hydraulic engineering
    NT **Heat pumps**
Pumps
    USE **Pumping machinery**
Punch and Judy
    USE **Puppets and puppet plays**
Punched card systems
    USE **Information systems**
Punctuality
    UF Lateness
        Promptness
        Tardiness
    BT **Time**
        Virtue
Punctuation 411; 421, etc.
    UF English language—Punctuation
    BT **Rhetoric**
Punishment 364.6
    UF Discipline
        Penology
    BT **Administration of criminal**
          justice
        Corrections
    NT **Capital punishment**
        Correctional institutions
        Parole
        Prisons
        Probation
        Reformatories
    RT **Crime**
        Criminal law
Punishment in schools
    USE **School discipline**
Puns 808.88; 818, etc.
    May be used for collections of puns or
  for materials about puns.

    UF Puns and punning *[Former*
        heading]
    BT **Wit and humor**
Puns and punning
    USE **Puns**
Pupil-teacher relationships
    USE **Teacher-student relationships**
Puppets and puppet plays 791.5
    UF Marionettes
        Muppets
        Punch and Judy
    BT **Drama**
        Folk drama
        Theater
    NT **Shadow pantomimes and plays**
Puppies 599.74; 636.7
    BT **Animal babies**
        Dogs
Purchase tax
    USE **Sales tax**
Purchasing
    USE **Buying**
        Shopping
Purchasing, Government
    USE **Government purchasing**
Pure food
    USE **Food adulteration and inspec-**
          tion
Purgatory 236; 291.2
    BT **Eschatology**
Purification of water
    USE **Water purification**
Puritans 285; 920
    BT **Christian sects**
        United States—History—
          1600-1775, Colonial period
    NT **Pilgrims (New England colo-**
          nists)
    RT **Calvinism**
        Church of England—United
          States
        Congregationalism
Puzzles 793.73
    BT **Amusements**
    NT **Crossword puzzles**
        Mathematical recreations
    RT **Riddles**
Pyramids 722; 909
    BT **Ancient architecture**
        Archeology

BT = Broader Term   NT = Narrower Term   RT = Related Term   SA = See Also   UF = Used For

Pyramids—*Continued*
>Monuments
>NT Obelisks

Quacks and quackery 615.8
>BT Impostors and imposture
>Medicine
>Swindlers and swindling

Quakers
>USE Society of Friends

Qualitative analysis
>USE Analytical chemistry

Quality control 519.8; 658.5
>SA specific industries with the subdivision *Quality control,* to be added as needed
>BT Reliability (Engineering)
>Sampling (Statistics)
>NT Steel industry—Quality control

Quality of life 303.3
>Use for materials on the objective standards and subjective attitudes by which individuals and groups assess their life situations.
>UF Life quality
>BT Economic conditions
>Social conditions
>NT Lifestyles
>Standard of living
>RT Social values

Quantitative analysis
>USE Analytical chemistry

Quantity cookery
>USE Quantity cooking

Quantity cooking 641.5
>Use for general materials solely on the preparation of food in large quantities. For materials on the preparation, delivery, and serving of ready-to-eat foods in large quantities outside of the home, use **Food service.**
>UF Cooking for large numbers
>Quantity cookery *[Former heading]*
>BT Cooking
>RT Food service

Quantum mechanics
>USE Quantum theory

Quantum theory 530.1
>UF Quantum mechanics
>BT Dynamics
>Physics

>NT Wave mechanics
>RT Atomic theory
>Force and energy
>Physical chemistry
>Radiation
>Relativity (Physics)
>Thermodynamics

Quarantine
>USE Communicable diseases

Quarks 539.7
>BT Particles (Nuclear physics)

Quarries and quarrying 622
>UF Stone quarries
>BT Economic geology
>RT Stone

Quartz 549
>UF Rock crystal
>BT Mineralogy

Quasars 523.1
>UF Quasi-stellar radio sources
>BT Astronomy
>Radio astronomy

Quasi-stellar radio sources
>USE Quasars

Québec (Province) 971.4
Québec (Province)—History 971.4
Québec (Province)—History—Autonomy and independence movements 971.4
>UF Québec (Province)—Separatist movement
>Separatist movement in Québec (Province)
>BT Canada—English-French relations

Québec (Province)—Separatist movement
>USE Québec (Province)—History—Autonomy and independence movements

Queens
>USE Kings, queens, rulers, etc.

Queries
>USE Questions and answers

Questions and answers 793.73

Use for collections of informal quizzes on various subjects. Informal quizzes on a particular subject are entered under the subject with the subdivision *Miscellanea.* Materials on formal examinations are entered under **Examinations.** Examination questions on a particular subject are entered under the subject with the subdivision *Examinations,* e.g. **Music— Examinations.** Compilations of practice problems or exercises for use in the study of a topic are entered under the topic with the subdivision *Problems, exercises, etc.,* e.g. **Chemistry—Problems, exercises, etc.**

- UF   Answers to questions
  - Queries
  - Quizzes
  - Trivia
- SA   subjects with the subdivision *Miscellanea,* e.g. **Medicine—Miscellanea;** to be added as needed
- NT   **Examinations**

Quick and easy cookery
- USE   **Quick and easy cooking**

Quick and easy cooking 641.5

Use for materials containing recipes or cooking techniques emphasizing economy of preparation time and the use of readily available ingredients.

- UF   Convenience cooking
  - Easy and quick cooking
  - Quick and easy cookery *[Former heading]*
  - Quick-meal cooking
  - Time saving cooking
- BT   **Cooking**

Quick-meal cooking
- USE   **Quick and easy cooking**

Quicksilver
- USE   **Mercury**

Quilt designing
- USE   **Quilts—Design**

Quilting 746.46
- BT   **Handicraft**

Qrilts 746.46
- UF   Coverlets
  - Patchwork quilts
- BT   **Interior design**

Quilts—Design 746.46
- UF   Quilt designing
- BT   **Design**

Quintets 785
- BT   **Orchestral music**

Quislings
- USE   **World War, 1939-1945— Collaborationists**

Quit-smoking programs
- USE   **Smoking cessation programs**

Quizzes
- USE   **Questions and answers**

Qumran texts
- USE   **Dead Sea scrolls**

Quotations 080; 808.88
- UF   Sayings
- SA   subjects, classes of persons, ethnic groups, and names of individuals with the subdivision *Quotations,* to be added as needed
- BT   **Epigrams**
  - **Literature—Collections**
- NT   **Presidents—United States— Quotations**
  - **Proverbs**

Qur'an
- USE   **Koran**

R.V.'s
- USE   **Recreational vehicles**

Rabbis 296.6; 920
- BT   **Clergy**
  - **Judaism**

Rabbits 599.32; 636
- UF   Bunnies
  - Bunny rabbits
  - Hares
- BT   **Mammals**

Rabies 616.9; 636.089
- UF   Hydrophobia
- BT   **Communicable diseases**

Race 572
- BT   **Ethnology**

Race awareness 305.8
- UF   Race identity
  - Racial identity
- SA   names of racial groups with the subdivision *Race identity,* to be added as needed
- BT   **Race relations**
- NT   **African Americans—Race identity**
  - **Blacks—Race identity**
  - **Racism**

Race discrimination 305.8

Use for materials on the restriction or denial of rights, privileges, or choice because of race. Materials on prejudicial attitudes about particular groups because of their race are entered under **Racism.**

UF   Discrimination, Racial
      Racial discrimination

SA   types of discrimination, e.g.
      Discrimination in education;
      to be added as needed

BT   **Discrimination**
      Race relations
      Racism
      Social problems

Race identity

USE   **Race awareness**
      and names of racial groups
      with the subdivision *Race*
      identity, e.g. **Blacks—Race**
      identity; African
      Americans—Race identity;
      etc., to be added as needed

Race prejudice

USE   **Racism**

Race problems

USE   **Race relations**

Race psychology

USE   **Ethnopsychology**

Race relations 305.8

Use for materials on the contact and interaction between racial groups.

UF   Integration, Racial
      Interracial relations
      Race problems

SA   names of countries, cities,
      etc., with the subdivision
      Race relations, to be added
      as needed

BT   **Acculturation**
      Ethnic groups
      Ethnology
      Minorities
      Social problems
      Sociology

NT   **Chicago (Ill.)—Race relations**
      Culture conflict
      Discrimination
      Immigration and emigration
      Interracial adoption
      Multicultural education

      Multiculturalism
      Race awareness
      Race discrimination
      Racism
      South Africa—Race relations
      United States—Race relations
      White supremacy movements

RT   **Ethnic relations**

Race relations and the church

USE   **Church and race relations**

Races of people

USE   **Ethnology**

Racial balance in schools

USE   **Busing (School integration)**
      School integration
      Segregation in education

Racial bias

USE   **Racism**

Racial discrimination

USE   **Race discrimination**

Racial identity

USE   **Race awareness**

Racial intermarriage

USE   **Interracial marriage**

Racing 796

SA   types of racing, to be added
      as needed

BT   **Sports**

NT   **Airplane racing**
      Automobile racing
      Bicycle racing
      Boat racing
      Horse racing
      Orienteering
      Soap box derbies

RT   **Running**

Racism 305.8; 320.5

Use for materials on prejudicial attitudes about particular groups because of their race. Materials on the restriction or denial of rights, privileges, or choice because of race are entered under **Race discrimination.**

UF   Race prejudice
      Racial bias

BT   **Attitude (Psychology)**
      Prejudices
      Race awareness
      Race relations

NT   **Race discrimination**
      White supremacy movements

BT = Broader Term   NT = Narrower Term   RT = Related Term   SA = See Also   UF = Used For

Racketeering 364.1
UF Crime syndicates
BT **Crime**
      Organized crime

Radar 621.3848
BT **Navigation**
      Radio
      Remote sensing

Radar defense networks 623
UF Defenses, Radar
BT **Air defenses**
NT **Ballistic missile early warning system**

Radiant heating 697
UF Panel heating
BT **Heating**

Radiation 539.2
BT **Optics**
      Physics
      Waves
NT **Cosmic rays**
      Electromagnetic waves
      Gamma rays
      Infrared radiation
      Phosphorescence
      Radioactivity
      Radium
      Sound
      Spectrum analysis
      Ultraviolet rays
      X rays
RT **Light**
      Quantum theory

Radiation biology
USE **Radiobiology**

Radiation—Physiological effect 612
RT **Atomic bomb—Physiological effect**
      Nuclear medicine

Radiation—Safety measures 363.1; 612

Radiation, Solar
USE **Solar radiation**

Radiation therapy
USE **Radiotherapy**

Radicalism (May subdiv. geog.) **320.5**
    Use for materials on extremist social and political movements of the right or the left.
UF Extremism (Political science)
      Political extremism

      Radicals and radicalism *[Former heading]*
BT **Political science**
      Revolutions
      Right and left (Political science)
RT **Counter culture**

Radicals and radicalism
USE **Radicalism**

Radio 621.384
UF Wireless
SA radio and other subjects, e.g. **Radio and music;** and radio in various industries or fields of endeavor, e.g. **Radio in aeronautics;** to be added as needed
BT **Electric engineering**
      Telecommunication
NT **Radar**
      Radio and music
      Radio in aeronautics
      Radio in astronautics
      Radio in education
      Shortwave radio

Radio addresses, debates, etc. 384.54; 808.5; 808.85
UF Radio lectures
BT **Debates and debating**
      Lectures and lecturing
      Radio broadcasting
      Radio scripts

Radio advertising 659.14
UF Advertising, Radio
      Commercials, Radio
      Radio commercials
BT **Advertising**
      Radio broadcasting

Radio and music 780; 781.5
UF Music and radio
BT **Music**
      Radio

Radio and television novels 813, etc.
    May be used for individual works, collections, or materials about novels based on radio or television programs.
UF Radio novels
      Television novels
BT **Fiction**
RT **Movie novels**

Radio apparatus industry
USE **Radio supplies industry**
Radio astronomy 522
SA names of celestial radio
sources, e.g. **Quasars;** to be
added as needed
BT **Astronomy**
Interstellar communication
NT **Quasars**
Radio authorship 808
UF Radio script writing
Radio writing
BT **Authorship**
Radio broadcasting
NT **Radio plays—Technique**
RT **Radio scripts**
Radio broadcasting 384.54
UF Radio industry
BT **Broadcasting**
Mass media
NT **Equal time rule (Broadcasting)**
Fairness doctrine (Broadcasting)
Radio addresses, debates, etc.
Radio advertising
Radio authorship
Radio programs
Radio stations
Radio chemistry
USE **Radiochemistry**
Radio comedy programs
USE **Comedy radio programs**
Radio commercials
USE **Radio advertising**
Radio drama
USE **Radio plays**
Radio—Equipment and supplies
621.384028
BT **Radio supplies industry**
NT **Radio—Receivers and reception**
Radio equipment industry
USE **Radio supplies industry**
Radio frequency modulation 621.384
UF F.M. radio
FM radio
Frequency modulation, Radio
NT **Shortwave radio**
Radio in aeronautics 629.135
BT **Aeronautics**

Navigation (Aeronautics)
Radio
Radio in astronautics 629.4
UF Lunar surface radio communication
BT **Astronautics—Communication systems**
Navigation (Astronautics)
Radio
Radio in education 371.3
UF Education and radio
BT **Audiovisual education**
Radio
Teaching—Aids and devices
Radio industry
USE **Radio broadcasting**
Radio industry and trade
USE **Radio supplies industry**
Radio journalism
USE **Broadcast journalism**
Radio lectures
USE **Radio addresses, debates, etc.**
Radio news
USE **Broadcast journalism**
Radio novels
USE **Radio and television novels**
Radio operators 621.3841
Radio plays 808.82; 812, etc.
May be used for individual works, collections, or materials about radio plays. Works on how to write radio plays are entered under **Radio plays—Technique.**
UF Radio drama
Scenarios
BT **Drama**
Radio programs
NT **Soap operas**
RT **Radio scripts**
Radio plays—Technique 808.2
UF Play writing
Playwriting
BT **Drama—Technique**
Radio authorship
RT **Television plays—Technique**
Radio programs 384.54
May be used for individual works, collections, or materials about radio programs.
UF Programs, Radio
SA types of programs and names
of specific programs, to be
added as needed

BT = Broader Term   NT = Narrower Term   RT = Related Term   SA = See Also   UF = Used For

Radio programs—*Continued*
    BT   **Radio broadcasting**
    NT   **Adventure radio programs**
           Biographical radio programs
           Comedy radio programs
           Fantasy radio programs
           Horror radio programs
           Legal drama (Radio programs)
           Medical drama (Radio programs)
           Mystery radio programs
           Radio plays
           Radio serials
           Science fiction radio programs
           Sports drama (Radio programs)
           Spy radio programs
           Talk shows
           Variety shows (Radio programs)
           War radio programs
           Westerns (Radio programs)
    RT   **Radio scripts**
Radio—Receivers and reception 621.384
    UF   Radio reception
           Radios
    BT   **Radio—Equipment and supplies**
Radio reception
    USE **Radio—Receivers and reception**
Radio—Repairing 621.384
    UF   Radio servicing
    BT   **Repairing**
Radio script writing
    USE **Radio authorship**
Radio scripts 791.44; 808.8; 818, etc.
    May be used for individual works, collections, or materials about radio scripts.
    NT   **Radio addresses, debates, etc.**
    RT   **Radio authorship**
           Radio plays
           Radio programs
Radio serials 791.44
    May be used for individual works, collections, or materials about radio serials.
    BT   **Radio programs**
    RT   **Soap operas**
Radio servicing
    USE **Radio—Repairing**

Radio, Shortwave
    USE **Shortwave radio**
Radio stations 384.54
    SA   names of specific radio stations, to be added as needed
    BT   **Radio broadcasting**
Radio stations, Amateur
    USE **Amateur radio stations**
Radio supplies industry 338.4
    UF   Radio apparatus industry
           Radio equipment industry
           Radio industry and trade
           [Former heading]
    BT   **Radio—Equipment and supplies**
Radio waves
    USE **Electric waves**
Radio writing
    USE **Radio authorship**
Radioactive fallout 539.7
    UF   Dust, Radioactive
           Fallout, Radioactive
    BT   **Atomic bomb**
           Hydrogen bomb
           Radioactive pollution
Radioactive isotopes
    USE **Radioisotopes**
Radioactive pollution 363.17; 363.73; 621.48
    UF   Environmental radioactivity
           Nuclear pollution
           Pollution, Radioactive
    BT   **Pollution**
           Radioactivity
    NT   **Radioactive fallout**
    RT   **Radioactive waste disposal**
Radioactive substances
    USE **Radioactivity**
Radioactive waste disposal 363.72; 621.48
    UF   Nuclear waste disposal
           Waste disposal
    BT   **Nuclear engineering**
           Nuclear power plants—Environmental aspects
           Radioactivity
           Refuse and refuse disposal
    RT   **Radioactive pollution**
Radioactivity 539.7
    UF   Radioactive substances

Radioactivity—*Continued*
  BT **Physics**
       Radiation
  NT **Cosmic rays**
       Helium
       Phosphorescence
       Radioactive pollution
       Radioactive waste disposal
       Radiobiology
       Radiochemistry
       Radiotherapy
       Transmutation (Chemistry)
  RT **Nuclear physics**
       Radium
       Radon
       Uranium

Radiobiology 574.19
  UF Radiation biology
  BT **Biology**
       Biophysics
       Nuclear physics
       Radioactivity

Radiocarbon dating 539.7
  UF Carbon 14 dating
       Dating, Radiocarbon
  BT **Archeology**

Radiochemistry 541.3
  UF Radio chemistry
  BT **Physical chemistry**
       Radioactivity

Radiography
  USE **X rays**

Radioisotopes 621.48
  UF Radioactive isotopes
  BT **Isotopes**
       Nuclear engineering

Radiologists 920
  UF Roentgenologists
  BT **Physicians**
       Radiotherapy
       X rays

Radios
  USE **Radio—Receivers and reception**

Radiotherapy 615.8
  UF Radiation therapy
  BT **Electrotherapeutics**
       Physical therapy
       Radioactivity
       Therapeutics

  NT **Radiologists**
  RT **Phototherapy**
       Radium
       Ultraviolet rays
       X rays

Radium 546; 661; 669
  BT **Chemical elements**
       Radiation
  RT **Radioactivity**
       Radiotherapy

Radium emanation
  USE **Radon**

Radon 363.73; 546
  UF Radium emanation
  BT **Poisonous gases**
  RT **Radioactivity**

Railroad accidents
  USE **Railroads—Accidents**

Railroad construction
  USE **Railroad engineering**

Railroad engineering 625.1
  UF Railroad construction
  BT **Civil engineering**
       Engineering
       Railroads

Railroad fares
  USE **Railroads—Rates**

Railroad mergers
  USE **Railroads—Consolidation**

Railroad rates
  USE **Railroads—Rates**

Railroad workers
  USE **Railroads—Employees**

Railroads (May subdiv. geog.) **385; 625.1**
  UF Railways
       Trains
  SA names of individual railroads, to be added as needed
  BT **Public utilities**
       Transportation
  NT **Cable railroads**
       Electric railroads
       Express service
       Freight
       Monorail railroads
       Railroad engineering
       Street railroads
       Subways

Railroads—Accidents 363.12
  UF Collisions, Railroad

Railroads—Accidents—*Continued*
    Derailments
    Railroad accidents
    Train wrecks
  BT **Accidents**
    Disasters
  NT **Railroads—Safety appliances**
    Railroads—Signaling
Railroads and state
  USE **Railroads—Government policy**
Railroads, Cable
  USE **Cable railroads**
Railroads—Consolidation 338.8
  UF Industrial mergers
    Mergers, Industrial
    Railroad mergers
  BT **Industrial trusts**
    Monopolies
Railroads, Electric
  USE **Electric railroads**
Railroads—Electrification 621.33
  UF Electrification of railroads
  RT **Electric railroads**
Railroads—Employees 331.7
  UF Railroad workers
  BT **Employees**
Railroads—Fares
  USE **Railroads—Rates**
Railroads—Finance 385
  UF Capitalization (Finance)
  NT **Railroads—Rates**
    Railroads—Statistics
Railroads—Government ownership
  USE **Railroads—Government policy**
Railroads—Government policy 351.87
  UF Government ownership of
     railroads
    Government regulation of
     railroads
    Nationalization of railroads
    Railroads and state
    Railroads—Government own-
     ership
    Railroads, Nationalization of
    State and railroads
    State ownership of railroads
  BT **Government ownership**
    Industry—Government policy
    Public utilities
  NT **Railroads—Rates**

  RT **Interstate commerce**
Railroads—Models 625.1
  BT **Machinery—Models**
Railroads, Nationalization of
  USE **Railroads—Government policy**
Railroads—Rates 385
  UF Railroad fares
    Railroad rates
    Railroads—Fares
    Rebates (Railroads)
  BT **Railroads—Finance**
    Railroads—Government policy
  RT **Freight**
Railroads—Safety appliances 625.10028
  BT **Accidents—Prevention**
    Railroads—Accidents
    Safety appliances
  NT **Railroads—Signaling**
Railroads—Signaling 625.1
  UF Block signal systems
    Interlocking signals
  BT **Railroads—Accidents**
    Railroads—Safety appliances
    Signals and signaling
Railroads, Single rail
  USE **Monorail railroads**
Railroads—Statistics 385
  BT **Railroads—Finance**
Railroads, Street
  USE **Street railroads**
Railroads, Underground
  USE **Subways**
Railways
  USE **Railroads**
Rain 551.57
  UF Precipitation (Meteorology)
    Rain and rainfall *[Former
     heading]*
    Rainfall
  BT **Meteorology**
    Water
    Weather
  NT **Acid rain**
    Floods
  RT **Droughts**
    Forest influences
    Storms
Rain, Acid
  USE **Acid rain**
Rain and rainfall
  USE **Rain**

BT = Broader Term   NT = Narrower Term   RT = Related Term   SA = See Also   UF = Used For

Rain forests (May subdiv. geog.) **574.5; 634.9**

Use for materials on forests of broad-leaved, mainly evergreen trees found in moist climates in the tropics, subtropics, and some parts of the temperate zones. Materials on impenetrable thickets of second-growth vegetation replacing tropical rain forests that have been disturbed or degraded are entered under **Jungles.**

UF   Rainforests

       Tropical rain forests

BT   **Forests and forestry**

RT   **Jungles**

Rain making

USE   **Weather control**

Rainbow 551.5

BT   **Meteorology**

RT   **Refraction**

Rainfall

USE   **Rain**

Rainfall and forests

USE   **Forest influences**

Rainforests

USE   **Rain forests**

Rallies (Protest)

USE   **Protests, demonstrations, etc.**

Ranch life 307.72; 636

BT   **Farm life**

       Frontier and pioneer life

NT   **Cowhands**

Random access memories (Data processing)

USE   **Computer storage devices**

Random access storage devices (Data processing)

USE   **Computer storage devices**

Random sampling

USE   **Sampling (Statistics)**

Ranger project

USE   **Project Ranger**

Rank

USE   **Social classes**

Rap music 782.42164

UF   Rap songs

       Rapping (Music)

BT   **African American music**

       Popular music

Rap songs

USE   **Rap music**

Rape 364.1

UF   Assault, Sexual

       Sexual assault

BT   **Offenses against the person**

       Sex crimes

NT   **Date rape**

Rapid reading 372.4; 418

UF   Accelerated reading

       Faster reading

       Speed reading

BT   **Reading**

Rapid transit

USE   **Local transit**

Rapping (Music)

USE   **Rap music**

Rare animals 591.52

UF   Animals, Rare

SA   names of specific animals, e.g. **Bison;** to be added as needed

BT   **Animals**

       Wildlife

RT   **Endangered species**

       Extinct animals

       Wildlife conservation

Rare books 090

UF   Antiquarian books

       Book rarities

       Books, Rare

       Early printed books

BT   **Books**

RT   **Bibliography—Editions**

       Bibliography—First editions

Rare plants 581.5

BT   **Plants**

RT   **Endangered species**

       Plant conservation

Rating

USE   **Performance standards**

       and subjects and classes of persons with the subdivision *Rating,* e.g. **Bonds— Rating; Employees—Rating;** etc., to be added as needed

Ratio and proportion 513.2

BT   **Arithmetic**

       Geometry

Rationalism 149; 211

BT   **God**

       Philosophy

       Religion

       Secularism

BT = Broader Term   NT = Narrower Term   RT = Related Term   SA = See Also   UF = Used For

Rationalism—*Continued*
Theory of knowledge
- NT Empiricism
  Enlightenment
  Intuition
  Positivism
  Reason
  Skepticism
  Theism
- RT Agnosticism
  Atheism
  Belief and doubt
  Deism
  Free thought
  Realism

Rattlesnakes 597.96
- BT Poisonous animals
  Snakes

Raw materials 333.7
- BT Commercial products
  Materials
- NT Farm produce
  Forest products
  Mines and mineral resources

Rayon 677
- UF Acetate silk
  Artificial silk
  Silk, Artificial
- BT Fabrics
  Synthetic fabrics

Rays, Roentgen
- USE X rays

Rays, Ultra-violet
- USE Ultraviolet rays

Reaction (Political science)
- USE Right and left (Political science)

Reactions, Chemical
- USE Chemical reactions

Reactors (Nuclear physics)
- USE Nuclear reactors

Reader services (Libraries)
- USE Library services

Readers
- USE Reading materials

Readers' theater 792
Use for materials on the dramatic reading of plays before an audience.
- UF Chamber theater
  Story theater

- BT Amateur theater
  Theater

Readiness for mathematics
- USE Mathematical readiness

Readiness for reading
- USE Reading readiness

Readiness for school 372
Use for materials on the prerequisite abilities, such as degree of psychosocial maturity, previous experience, cognition, physical abilities, etc., to learning in a school setting.
- UF School readiness
- BT Elementary education
  Preschool education

Reading 372.4; 418
Use for materials on methods of teaching reading and for general materials on the art of reading. Materials on teaching slow readers are entered under **Reading—Remedial teaching**. Materials on the cultural or informational aspects of reading and general discussions of books are entered under **Books and reading**.
- UF Children's reading
  Reading—Study and teaching
- BT Language arts
- NT Books and reading
  Rapid reading
  Reading comprehension
  Reading disability
  Reading—Phonetic method
  Reading readiness
  Whole language
  Word skills

Reading clinics
- USE Reading—Remedial teaching

Reading comprehension 372.4
- BT Psychology of learning
  Reading
  Verbal learning

Reading disability 371.91
- UF Disability, Reading
  Reading retardation
  Retarded readers
- SA names of specific reading disabilities, e.g. **Dyslexia;** to be added as needed
- BT Learning disabilities
  Reading
- NT Dyslexia

Reading interests
- USE Books and reading

BT = Broader Term   NT = Narrower Term   RT = Related Term   SA = See Also   UF = Used For

Reading interests of children
USE **Children—Books and reading**
Reading materials 372.4; 418

Use for materials in English intended to be used in teaching reading or language skills. Such materials in other languages are entered under the language with the subdivision *Reading materials,* e.g. **French language—Reading materials.**

UF English language—Reading materials
Readers
BT **Children's literature**
NT **Basal readers**
Big books
Easy reading materials
Hornbooks
Recitations
RT **Books and reading**
Reading—Patterning
USE **Language arts—Patterning**
Reading—Phonetic method 372.4
UF Letter-sound association
Phonics
BT **English language—Pronunciation**
Reading
RT **Phonetics**
Reading readiness 372.4
UF Readiness for reading
BT **Reading**
Reading—Remedial teaching 372.4
UF Reading clinics
Remedial reading
Reading retardation
USE **Reading disability**
Reading—Study and teaching
USE **Reading**
Readings and recitations
USE **Recitations**
Readings (Anthologies)
USE **Anthologies**
Ready reckoners
USE **Mathematics—Tables**
Real estate 333.3

Use for materials on land and buildings considered as property. Materials on the buying and selling of real property are entered under **Real estate business.** General materials on land apart from the aspect of ownership are entered under **Land use.**

UF Property, Real
Real property

Realty
BT **Land use**
Property
NT **Farms**
Landlord and tenant
Mortgages
Real estate business
Real estate investment
RT **Land tenure**
Real estate business 333.33; 346.04

Use for materials limited to the buying and selling of real property. General materials on land and buildings considered as property are entered under **Real estate.**

BT **Business**
Real estate
NT **Houses—Buying and selling**
Real estate investment 332.63
UF Investment in real estate
Real property investment
BT **Investments**
Real estate
Speculation
Real estate investment—Taxation 343.05
BT **Taxation**
Real estate timesharing
USE **Timesharing (Real estate)**
Real property
USE **Real estate**
Real property investment
USE **Real estate investment**
Real property tax—Assessment
USE **Tax assessment**
Realism 149
BT **Philosophy**
NT **Pragmatism**
RT **Idealism**
Materialism
Positivism
Rationalism
Realism in art 709
UF Naturalism in art
BT **Art**
Realism in literature 809
UF Naturalism in literature
BT **Literature**
RT **Romanticism**
Reality 111
BT **Philosophy**

Reality—*Continued*
Truth
NT   **Virtual reality**
RT   **Pragmatism**
      Theory of knowledge
Realty
USE   **Real estate**
Reapers
USE   **Harvesting machinery**
Reapportionment (Election law)
USE   **Apportionment (Election law)**
Reason 128; 160
BT   **Intellect**
      Rationalism
NT   **Reasoning**
Reasoning 153.4; 160
BT   **Psychology**
      Reason
      Thought and thinking
NT   **Critical thinking**
RT   **Intellect**
      Logic
Rebates (Railroads)
USE   **Railroads—Rates**
Rebellions
USE   **Insurgency**
      Revolutions
Rebels (Social psychology)
USE   **Alienation (Social psychology)**
Rebirth
USE   **Regeneration (Theology)**
      Reincarnation
Rebuses
USE   **Riddles**
Recall of products
USE   **Product recall**
Recall (Political science) 324.6
BT   **Impeachments**
      Representative government and representation
Recessions, Economic
USE   **Economic depressions**
Recipes
USE   **Cooking**
Reciprocity
USE   **Commercial policy**
Recitations 808.85
    Use for collections of material written or selected for oral presentation and for materials about recitation.

UF   Declamations
      Narrations
      Oral interpretation
      Readings and recitations *[Former heading]*
      Speakers (Recitation books)
BT   **Reading materials**
      School assembly programs
NT   **Choral speaking**
      Monologues
      Monologues with music
Recitations with music
USE   **Monologues with music**
Reclamation of land 627; 631.6
    Use for general materials on reclamation, including drainage and irrigation.
UF   Clearing of land
      Land, Reclamation of
BT   **Agriculture**
      Civil engineering
      Hydraulic engineering
      Land use
      Soils
NT   **Drainage**
RT   **Irrigation**
      Wetlands
Recluses
USE   **Hermits**
Recombinant DNA 574.87
UF   Gene splicing
BT   **DNA**
      Genetic engineering
      Genetic recombination
Recombination, Genetic
USE   **Genetic recombination**
Recommendations for positions
USE   **Applications for positions**
Reconciliation, Sacrament of
USE   **Penance**
Reconnaissance, Aerial
USE   **Aerial reconnaissance**
Reconstruction (1865-1876) 973.8
UF   Carpetbag rule
      United States—History—1861-1865, Civil War—Reconstruction
BT   **United States—History—1865-1898**
NT   **Ku Klux Klan (1865-1876)**

Reconstruction (1914-1939) 940.3
   UF   World War, 1914-1918—
          Reconstruction
   NT   **Veterans—Education**
          Veterans—Employment
   RT   **Economic assistance**
          International cooperation
          World War, 1914-1918—
          Economic aspects

Reconstruction (1939-1951) (May sub-
     div. geog. except U.S.)
     940.53
   UF   Marshall Plan
          Point Four program
          World War, 1939-1945—
          Reconstruction
   NT   **Veterans—Education**
          Veterans—Employment
          World War, 1939-1945—
          Civilian relief
          World War, 1939-1945—
          Reparations
   RT   **Economic assistance**
          International cooperation
          World War, 1939-1945—
          Economic aspects

Recorders, Tape
   USE   **Magnetic recorders and re-**
          cording

Recording, Laser
   USE   **Laser recording**

Recordings, Sound
   USE   **Sound recordings**

Records, Human
   USE   **World records**

Records of achievement
   USE   **World records**

Records of births, etc.
   USE   **Registers of births, etc.**
          Vital statistics

Records, Phonograph
   USE   **Sound recordings**

Records—Preservation
   USE   **Archives**

Records, Sports
   USE   **Sports records**

Records, World
   USE   **World records**

Recovery of space vehicles
   USE   **Space vehicles—Recovery**

Recovery of waste products
   USE   **Recycling**

Recreation (May subdiv. geog.) 790
     Use for materials on the psychological
   and social aspects of recreation and for
   materials on organized recreational proj-
   ects.
   UF   Pastimes
          Relaxation
   SA   classes of persons with the
          subdivision *Recreation,* e.g.
          Elderly—Recreation; to be
          added as needed
   BT   **Leisure**
   NT   **Camps**
          Community centers
          Elderly—Recreation
          Games
          Hobbies
          Outdoor recreation
          Playgrounds
          Popular culture
          Sports
          Summer resorts
          Vacations
          Winter resorts
   RT   **Amusements**
          Play
          Sports facilities

Recreation centers
   USE   **Community centers**

Recreational vehicles 629.226
   UF   R.V.'s
          RVs
          Vehicles, Recreational
   SA   types of recreational vehicles,
          e.g. **Travel trailers and**
          campers; to be added as
          needed
   BT   **Outdoor recreation**
          Vehicles
   NT   **Travel trailers and campers**

Recreations
   USE   **Hobbies**

Recreations, Literary
   USE   **Literary recreations**

Recreations, Mathematical
   USE   **Mathematical recreations**

Recreations, Scientific
   USE   **Scientific recreations**

Recruiting and enlistment
  USE   names of armies and navies
         with the subdivision *Re-
         cruiting, enlistment, etc.,*
         e.g. **United States. Army—
         Recruiting, enlistment, etc.;
         United States. Navy—
         Recruiting, enlistment, etc.;**
         etc., to be added as needed
Recruiting of employees 658.3
  SA   names of occupations and
         professions with the subdi-
         vision *Recruiting,* e.g.
         Librarians—Recruiting; to
         be added as needed
  BT   **Personnel management**
  NT   **Employment agencies**
         Librarians—Recruiting
Rectors
  USE   **Clergy**
Recurrent education
  USE   **Continuing education**
Recycling 628.4
  Use for materials on the recovery and
  processing of waste paper, cans, bottles,
  etc. Materials on the recycling or reuse of
  a specific waste products are entered un-
  der that product with the subdivision *Re-
  cycling.*
  UF   Conversion of waste products
         Recovery of waste products
         Recycling (Waste, etc.) *[For-
         mer heading]*
         Reuse of waste
         Utilization of waste
         Waste products—Recycling
         Waste reclamation
  SA   subjects with the subdivision
         Recycling, e.g. **Aluminum—
         Recycling;** to be added as
         needed
  BT   **Energy conservation**
         Pollution control industry
         Salvage
  NT   **Aluminum—Recycling**
  RT   **Refuse and refuse disposal**
         Waste products
Recycling (Waste, etc.)
  USE   **Recycling**
Red 535.6; 752
  BT   **Color**

Redemption
  USE   **Salvation**
Reducing 613.2
  UF   Body weight control
         Dieting
         Diets, Reducing
         Weight control
  RT   **Diet**
         Exercise
Reference books 028.7
  Use for materials about reference books.
  Reference books themselves are entered
  under **Encyclopedias and dictionaries;** or
  under the appropriate subjects with the
  subdivisions *Dictionaries; Bibliography;*
  etc., as needed.
  BT   **Bibliography**
         Books
         Books and reading
  NT   **Books and reading—Best
         books**
         Encyclopedias and dictionaries
Reference services (Libraries) 025.5
  Use for materials on activities designed
  to make information available to library
  users, including direct personal assistance.
  UF   Library reference services
         Online reference services
         Reference work (Libraries)
  BT   **Information services**
         Library services
Reference work (Libraries)
  USE   **Reference services (Libraries)**
Referendum 328.2
  UF   Direct legislation
         Initiative and referendum
         Legislation, Direct
  BT   **Constitutional law**
         Democracy
         Elections
Refinishing furniture
  USE   **Furniture finishing**
Reforestation 333.75; 634.9
  BT   **Forests and forestry**
  RT   **Tree planting**
Reform, Agrarian
  USE   **Land reform**
Reform of criminals
  USE   **Criminals**
         Probation
         Reformatories
Reform schools
  USE   **Reformatories**

Reform, Social
USE **Social problems**
Reformation 270.6
UF Church history—1517-1648,
Reformation
Protestant Reformation
SA names of religious sects, e.g.
Huguenots; to be added as
needed
BT **Christianity**
Modern history
NT **Calvinism**
Huguenots
RT **Church history—1500-, Mod-
ern period**
Counter-Reformation
Protestantism
Sixteenth century
Reformatories 365
UF Penal institutions
Reform of criminals
Reform schools
BT **Children—Institutional care**
Correctional institutions
Prisons
Punishment
NT **Probation**
RT **Juvenile delinquency**
Reformers 920
Use for materials about political, social,
or religious reformers.
Refraction 535
UF Dioptrics
BT **Light**
Optics
RT **Rainbow**
Refrigeration 621.5
UF Cooling appliances
Freezing
Ice manufacture
Refrigeration and refrigerating
machinery *[Former heading]*
Refrigerators
BT **Frost**
RT **Air conditioning**
Cold storage
Low temperatures
Refrigeration and refrigerating machine-
ry
USE **Refrigeration**

Refrigerators
USE **Refrigeration**
Refugees 325; 341.4
UF Displaced persons
Exiles
SA refugees of particular coun-
tries, geographic regions, or
ethnic groups, e.g. **Vietnam-
ese refugees; Arab refugees;**
to be added as needed
BT **Aliens**
Homeless persons
Immigration and emigration
NT **Arab refugees**
Political refugees
Vietnamese refugees
RT **Sanctuary movement**
Refugees, Arab
USE **Arab refugees**
Refugees, Political
USE **Political refugees**
Refugees, Vietnamese
USE **Vietnamese refugees**
Refuges, Wildlife
USE **Wildlife refuges**
**Refuse and refuse disposal 363.72;
628.4**
UF Disposal of refuse
Garbage
Incineration
Littering
Solid waste disposal
Waste disposal
BT **Municipal engineering**
Public health
Sanitary engineering
Sanitation
NT **Hazardous wastes**
Industrial wastes
Medical wastes
Radioactive waste disposal
Sewage disposal
RT **Pollution**
Pollution control industry
Recycling
Salvage
Street cleaning
Waste products
Water pollution

Regattas
USE **Rowing**
     Yachts and yachting
Regency novels 813, etc.
  May be used for individual works, col-
lections, or materials about historical nov-
els set during the period when the future
George IV acted as Regent for George III
(1811-1820).
BT **Historical fiction**
Regeneration (Christianity) 234; 248.2
UF Born again Christianity
     Christian new birth
     Christian regeneration
BT **Regeneration (Theology)**
Regeneration (Theology) 234
UF New birth (Theology)
     Rebirth
BT **Baptism**
     Doctrinal theology
NT **Regeneration (Christianity)**
RT **Conversion**
     Salvation
Regional history
USE **Local history**
Regional libraries 027.4
  Use for materials on public libraries
serving a group of communities, several
counties, or other regions.
UF District libraries
     Libraries, Regional
BT **Public libraries**
NT **County libraries**
Regional planning (May subdiv. geog.)
     307.1; 711
UF County planning
     Metropolitan planning
     Planning, Regional
     State planning
BT **Land use**
RT **City planning**
     Landscape protection
Regionalism
USE **Nationalism**
     Sectionalism (United States)
Registers of births, etc. 929
UF Birth records
     Births, Registers of
     Burial statistics
     Deaths, Registers of
     Marriage registers

     Parish registers
     Records of births, etc.
     Vital records
BT **Genealogy**
NT **Wills**
RT **Vital statistics**
Registers of persons
USE names of countries, cities,
     etc., and names of colleges,
     universities, etc., with the
     subdivision *Registers,* e.g.
     United States—Registers;
     United States Military
     Academy—Registers; etc.,
     to be added as needed
Registration of voters
USE **Voter registration**
Rehabilitation
USE classes of persons with the
     subdivision *Rehabilitation,*
     e.g. **Drug addicts—**
     Rehabilitation; Physically
     handicapped—
     Rehabilitation; etc., to be
     added as needed
Rehabilitation peer counseling
USE **Peer counseling**
Reign of Terror
USE **France—History—1789-1799,**
     Revolution
Reincarnation 129
UF Rebirth
BT **Theosophy**
RT **Soul**
Reindeer 599.73; 636.2
BT **Deer**
     Domestic animals
Reinforced concrete 691
BT **Building materials**
     Concrete
Relations among ethnic groups
USE **Ethnic relations**
Relative humidity
USE **Humidity**
Relativity (Physics) 530.1
BT **Physics**
RT **Gravitation**
     Quantum theory
     Space and time
Relaxation
USE **Recreation**

BT = Broader Term   NT = Narrower Term   RT = Related Term   SA = See Also   UF = Used For

Relaxation—*Continued*
>> Rest

Reliability (Engineering) 620
>> UF Reliability of equipment
>> Systems reliability
>> Testing
>> BT **Engineering**
>> **Probabilities**
>> **Systems engineering**
>> NT **Quality control**
>> **Structural failures**

Reliability of equipment
>> USE **Reliability (Engineering)**

Relief, Public
>> USE **Public welfare**

Religion 200
>> SA names of peoples, ethnic
>> groups, countries, states,
>> etc., with the subdivision
>> *Religion,* e.g. **Indians of**
>> **North America—Religion;**
>> **Blacks—Religion; African**
>> **Americans—Religion; Unit-**
>> **ed States—Religion;** etc., to
>> be added as needed
>> NT **African Americans—Religion**
>> **Agnosticism**
>> **Ancestor worship**
>> **Art and religion**
>> **Atheism**
>> **Belief and doubt**
>> **Blacks—Religion**
>> **Communism and religion**
>> **Deism**
>> **Faith**
>> **Indians of North America—**
>> **Religion**
>> **Medicine and religion**
>> **Moon worship**
>> **Mysticism**
>> **Mythology**
>> **Natural theology**
>> **Philosophy and religion**
>> **Psychology of religion**
>> **Rationalism**
>> **Religion and politics**
>> **Religion and sociology**
>> **Religion in literature**
>> **Religious awakening**
>> **Religious education**

>> **Religious life**
>> **Revelation**
>> **Sacrifice**
>> **Sun worship**
>> **Supernatural**
>> **Superstition**
>> **Theism**
>> **United States—Religion**
>> **Visions**
>> **War and religion**
>> **Worship**
>> RT **God**
>> **Religions**
>> **Theology**

Religion and art
>> USE **Art and religion**

Religion and communism
>> USE **Communism and religion**

Religion and education
>> USE **Church and education**

Religion and literature
>> USE **Religion in literature**

Religion and medicine
>> USE **Medicine and religion**

Religion and philosophy
>> USE **Philosophy and religion**

Religion and politics 261.7; 322
>> UF Evangelism and politics
>> Politics and religion
>> BT **Politics**
>> **Religion**
>> NT **Christianity and politics**

Religion and psychology
>> USE **Psychology of religion**

Religion and science 215; 261.5
>> UF Science and religion
>> BT **Theology**
>> NT **Bible and science**
>> **Human origins**
>> RT **Creationism**
>> **Evolution**
>> **Natural theology**
>> **Science**

Religion and social problems
>> USE **Church and social problems**

Religion and society
>> USE **Religion and sociology**

Religion and sociology 306.6

Use for materials on religious sociology in general. Materials on the sociology of Christian denominations and on social theory from a Christian point of view are entered under **Christian sociology.** Materials on the practical treatment of social problems from the point of view of the church are entered under **Church and social problems.**

UF   Religion and society
      Religious sociology
      Society and religion
      Sociology and religion
      Sociology of religion

BT   **Religion**
      Sociology

NT   **Christian sociology**

RT   **Church and social problems**

Religion and state

USE   **Church and state**

Religion and war

USE   **War and religion**

Religion in literature 809

UF   Religion and literature

BT   **Literature**
      Religion

RT   **Bible in literature**

Religion in the public schools 377

UF   Bible in the schools
      Prayers in the public schools
      Public schools and religion
      Schools—Prayers

BT   **Church and education**
      Church and state
      Religious education

RT   **Fundamentalism and education**

Religion of humanity

USE   **Positivism**

Religion—Philosophy 200.1

UF   Philosophy of religion

RT   **Philosophy and religion**

Religion—Study and teaching

USE   **Religious education**
      Theology—Study and teaching

Religions 200

Use for materials on the major world religions. Materials on independent religious groups whose teachings or practices fall within the normative bounds of the major world religions are entered under **Sects.** Materials on groups or movements whose beliefs or practices differ significantly from the traditional religions, often focused upon a charismatic leader, are entered under **Cults.**

UF   Comparative religion

SA   names of religions and of
      sects within the major
      world religions, to be added
      as needed

BT   **Civilization**

NT   **Bahai Faith**
      Brahmanism
      Buddhism
      Christianity
      Christianity and other religions
      Confucianism
      Cults
      Druids and Druidism
      Gnosticism
      Hinduism
      Islam
      Judaism
      Mythology
      Occultism
      Paganism
      Sects
      Shinto
      Taoism
      Theosophy

RT   **Gods and goddesses**
      Religion

Religions—Biography 200.92; 920

UF   Religious biography

SA   names of religions with the
      subdivision *Biography,* to
      be added as needed

BT   **Biography**

NT   **Christianity—Biography**

Religious art

USE   **Church architecture**
      Medieval art
      Religious art and symbolism

Religious art and symbolism 704.9

UF   Iconography

Religious art and symbolism—
Continued

> Painting, Religious
> Religious art
> Religious painting
> Religious symbolism
> Sacred art
> Sculpture, Religious

BT **Archeology**
    Art
    Mysticism
    Symbolism

NT **Christian art and symbolism**

RT **Art and religion**

Religious awakening 200; 269

Use for materials on a renewal of interest in religion.

UF Awakening, Religious
    Revival (Religion)

BT **Religion**

Religious belief
USE **Faith**

Religious biography
USE **Christianity—Biography**
    Religions—Biography

Religious ceremonies
USE **Rites and ceremonies**

Religious cults
USE **Cults**

Religious denominations
USE **Sects**
    and names of particular denominations and sects, e.g.
    Presbyterian Church; to be added as needed

Religious drama 792.1; 808.82; 812, etc.

May be used for collections or materials about religious drama, not for individual works.

UF Drama, Religious

BT **Drama**
    Religious literature

NT **Bible plays**
    Christmas plays
    Easter—Drama
    Morality plays
    Mysteries and miracle plays
    Passion plays

Religious education 268; 377

Use for materials on the instruction of religion in schools and private life. Materials limited to the instruction of Christian religion in schools and private life are entered under **Christian education.** Materials on the relation of the church to education and on the history of the part that the church has taken in secular education are entered under **Church and education.** Materials on church supported and controlled elementary and secondary schools are entered under **Church schools.**

UF Education, Ethical
    Education, Religious
    Education, Theological
    Ethical education
    Religion—Study and teaching

BT **Education**
    Religion

NT **Christian education**
    Religion in the public schools
    Sunday schools

RT **Moral education**
    Theology—Study and teaching

Religious festivals
USE **Religious holidays**

Religious freedom
USE **Freedom of religion**

Religious history
USE **Church history**

Religious holidays 263; 394.2

Use for materials on religious holidays in general. Materials on secular holidays are entered under **Holidays.** Materials on secular festivals other than holidays are entered under **Festivals.**

UF Church festivals
    Ecclesiastical fasts and feasts
    Fasts and feasts *[Former heading]*
    Feasts
    Fiestas
    Holy days
    Religious festivals

SA holidays of particular religions, e.g. **Jewish holidays**; and names of specific religious holidays, e.g. **Christmas**; to be added as needed

BT **Holidays**
    Rites and ceremonies

NT **Christian holidays**
    Jewish holidays

Religious holidays—*Continued*
>> **Thanksgiving Day**
> RT **Fasting**
>> **Festivals**

Religious liberty
> USE **Freedom of religion**

Religious life 248.4; 291.4
> Use for materials that describe or promote personal or community religious and devotional life.
> SA groups and classes of persons with the subdivision *Religious life,* to be added as needed
> BT **Religion**
> NT **Asceticism**
>> **Celibacy**
>> **Christian life**
>> **Family—Religious life**
>> **Teenagers—Religious life**
>> **Youth—Religious life**
> RT **Monasticism**
>> **Religious orders**
>> **Spiritual life**

Religious life (Christian)
> USE **Christian life**

Religious literature 800
> SA literatures of particular religions or denominations, e.g. **Catholic literature;** to be added as needed
> BT **Literature**
> NT **Christian literature**
>> **Jewish literature**
>> **Religious drama**
>> **Religious poetry**
>> **Sacred books**
> RT **Bible as literature**

Religious music
> USE **Church music**

Religious orders 255; 271
> UF Monastic orders
>> Orders, Monastic
> BT **Monasticism**
> NT **Celibacy**
>> **Hermits**
>> **Religious orders for men**
>> **Religious orders for women**
> RT **Religious life**

Religious orders for men 255; 271
> SA religious orders of particular religions or denominations and names of specific orders, to be added as needed
> BT **Religious orders**
> NT **Catholic religious orders for men**
>> **Monks**

Religious orders for men, Catholic
> USE **Catholic religious orders for men**

Religious orders for women 255; 271
> UF Sisterhoods
> SA religious orders of particular religions or denominations and names of specific orders, to be added as needed.
> BT **Convents**
>> **Religious orders**
> NT **Catholic religious orders for women**
>> **Nuns**

Religious orders for women, Catholic
> USE **Catholic religious orders for women**

Religious painting
> USE **Religious art and symbolism**

Religious poetry 808.81; 811, etc.; 811.008, etc.
> May be used for collections or materials about religious poetry, not for individual works.
> BT **Poetry**
>> **Religious literature**
> RT **Hymns**

Religious psychology
> USE **Psychology of religion**

Religious sociology
> USE **Religion and sociology**

Religious summer schools 268; 377
> UF Bible classes
>> Summer schools, Religious *[Former heading]*
>> Vacation church schools
>> Vacation schools, Religious
> BT **Schools**
>> **Summer schools**

Religious symbolism
> USE **Religious art and symbolism**

BT = Broader Term   NT = Narrower Term   RT = Related Term   SA = See Also   UF = Used For

Remarriage 306.84
  BT Marriage
  RT Divorce
Remedial reading
  USE **Reading—Remedial teaching**
Remodeling of buildings
  USE **Buildings—Remodeling**
Remodeling of houses
  USE **Houses—Remodeling**
Remote sensing 621.36
  UF Sensing, Remote
      Terrain sensing, Remote
  BT Aerial photography
  NT Aerial reconnaissance
      Radar
  RT Space optics
Renaissance 940.2
  UF Revival of letters
  BT Modern civilization
      Modern history
  NT Fifteenth century
      Renaissance architecture
      Renaissance art
      Sixteenth century
  RT Humanism
      Middle Ages
Renaissance architecture 724
  UF Architecture, Renaissance
      [Former heading]
  BT Architecture
      Renaissance
Renaissance art 709.02
  UF Art, Renaissance *[Former heading]*
  BT Art
      Renaissance
Renaissance decoration and ornament 745.4
  UF Decoration and ornament, Renaissance
  BT Decoration and ornament
Renaissance, Harlem
  USE **Harlem Renaissance**
Rendezvous in space
  USE **Orbital rendezvous (Space flight)**
Renewable energy resources 333.79
  UF Alternate energy resources
      Alternative energy resources
      Energy resources, Renewable

  SA types of renewable resources, to be added as needed
  BT Energy resources
  NT Geothermal resources
      Solar energy
      Water power
      Wind power
Rental services
  USE **Lease and rental services**
Reorganization of administrative agencies
  USE **United States—Executive departments—Reorganization**
Repairing 620
  SA names of machines, instruments, etc., that require maintenance with the subdivision *Maintenance and repair,* e.g. **Automobiles—Maintenance and repair;** and names of subjects that need no maintenance with the subdivision *Repairing,* e.g. **Radio—Repairing;** to be added as needed
  NT Automobiles—Maintenance and repair
      Buildings—Maintenance and repair
      Radio—Repairing
Reparations (World War, 1939-1945)
  USE **World War, 1939-1945—Reparations**
Report writing 808
  UF Reports—Preparation
      Research paper writing
      Term paper writing
  BT Authorship
  NT School reports
Reporters and reporting 070.4
  UF Interviewing (Journalism)
      Newspaper work
  BT Newspapers
  RT Journalism
Reports—Preparation
  USE **Report writing**
Reports, Teachers'
  USE **School reports**

Representation
   USE **Representative government and representation**

Representation, Proportional
   USE **Proportional representation**

Representative government and representation 321.8
   UF Parliamentary government
         Representation
         Self-government
   BT **Constitutional history**
         Constitutional law
         Political science
   NT **Apportionment (Election law)**
         Legislative bodies
         Proportional representation
         Recall (Political science)
   RT **Constitutions**
         Democracy
         Elections
         Republics
         Suffrage

Representatives, House of (U.S.)
   USE **United States. Congress. House**

Reprints
   USE **Bibliography—Editions**

Reproduction 574.1; 612.6
   UF Generation
   BT **Biology**
         Life (Biology)
         Physiology
   NT **Animal reproduction**
         Artificial insemination
         Cells
         Fertility
         Fertilization in vitro
         Fetus
         Genetics
         Human artificial insemination
         Menstruation
         Pregnancy
   RT **Embryology**
         Reproductive system
         Sex (Biology)

Reproduction processes
   USE **Copying processes and machines**

Reproductive behavior
   USE **Sexual behavior in animals**

Reproductive organs
   USE **Reproductive system**

Reproductive system 574.1; 611; 612.6
   UF Generative organs
         Genitalia
         Reproductive organs
         Sex organs
   BT **Anatomy**
         Physiology
         Sex (Biology)
   NT **Transsexuality**
   RT **Reproduction**

Reprography
   USE **Copying processes and machines**

Reptiles 597.9
   BT **Vertebrates**
   NT **Alligators**
         Crocodiles
         Fossil reptiles
         Lizards
         Snakes
         Turtles

Reptiles, Fossil
   USE **Fossil reptiles**

Republic of China, 1949-
   USE **Taiwan**

Republic of South Africa
   USE **South Africa**

Republican Party (U.S.) 324.2734
   BT **Political parties**

Republics 321.8
   UF Commonwealth, The
   BT **Constitutional history**
         Constitutional law
         Political science
   NT **Federal government**
   RT **Democracy**
         Representative government and representation

Rescue of Jews, 1939-1945
   USE **World War, 1939-1945—Jews—Rescue**

Rescue operations, Space
   USE **Space rescue operations**

Rescue work 363.3
   UF Search and rescue operations
   BT **Civil defense**
   NT **First aid**
         Lifesaving

BT = Broader Term   NT = Narrower Term   RT = Related Term   SA = See Also   UF = Used For

Rescue work—*Continued*
    Space rescue operations
Research 001.4
    UF Research and development
    SA subjects with the subdivision
        Research, to be added as
        needed
    NT **Agriculture—Research**
        Animal experimentation
        Intelligence service
        Medicine—Research
        Operations research
        Parapsychology
    RT **Information services**
        Learning and scholarship
Research and development
    USE **Research**
Research paper writing
    USE **Report writing**
Reservations, Indian
    USE **Indians of North America—**
        Reservations
Reservoirs 627; 628.1
    BT **Hydraulic structures**
    NT **Irrigation**
    RT **Water supply**
Resettlement
    USE **Land settlement**
Residences
    USE **Domestic architecture**
        Houses
Residential construction
    USE **House construction**
Residential security
    USE **Burglary protection**
Residential treatment centers
    USE **Group homes**
Resins
    USE **Gums and resins**
Resistance of materials
    USE **Strength of materials**
Resistance to government 322.4
    UF Civil disobedience
        Government, Resistance to
        [Former heading]
    BT **Political crimes and offenses**
        Political ethics
        Political science
    NT **Hunger strikes**
        Passive resistance

    RT **Insurgency**
        Revolutions
Resistance welding
    USE **Electric welding**
Resorts
    USE types of resorts, e.g. **Health**
        resorts; Summer resorts;
        Winter resorts; etc., to be
        added as needed
Resource management
    USE **Conservation of natural re-**
        sources
Resources, Marine
    USE **Marine resources**
Resources, Natural
    USE **Natural resources**
Respiration 574.1; 612.2
    UF Breathing
    BT **Lungs**
        Physiology
    NT **Aerobics**
        Respiratory system
Respiration, Artificial
    USE **Artificial respiration**
Respiratory organs
    USE **Respiratory system**
Respiratory system 591.1; 611; 612.2
    UF Respiratory organs
    BT **Anatomy**
        Physiology
        Respiration
    NT **Lungs**
Respite care
    USE **Home care services**
Responsibility, Legal
    USE **Liability (Law)**
Rest 613.7
    UF Relaxation
    BT **Health**
        Hygiene
    NT **Sleep**
    RT **Fatigue**
Restaurants (May subdiv. geog.) 647.95
    UF Coffee shops
        Lunchrooms
        Restaurants, bars, etc. *[For-*
        mer heading]
        Tea rooms
        Tearooms
    SA types of restaurants, to be
        added as needed

Restaurants—*Continued*
  BT Food service
  NT Coffeehouses
  RT Bars
Restaurants, bars, etc.
  USE Bars
       Restaurants
Restoration of automobiles
  USE Automobiles—Restoration
Restoration of buildings
  USE Architecture—Conservation
       and restoration
Restoration of works of art
  USE subjects with the subdivision
       Conservation and restora-
       tion, e.g. Painting—
       Conservation and restora-
       tion; to be added as needed
Restraint of trade 338.6
  UF Combinations in restraint of
      trade
      Restrictive trade practices
      Trade, Restraint of
  BT Commerce
      Commercial law
  RT Boycotts
      Corporation law
      Industrial trusts
      Interstate commerce
      Monopolies
      Unfair competition
Restrictive trade practices
  USE Restraint of trade
Résumés (Employment) 650.14; 808
  UF Job résumés
  BT Applications for positions
      Job hunting
Resurrection
  USE Jesus Christ—Resurrection
       Future life
Resuscitation, Heart
  USE Cardiac resuscitation
Resuscitation, Pulmonary
  USE Artificial respiration
Retail sales tax
  USE Sales tax
Retail trade 381; 658.8
  UF Merchandising
      Stores
  BT Commerce

  NT Advertising
      Chain stores
      Department stores
      Direct selling
      Discount stores
      Inventory control
      Packaging
      Sales personnel
      Selling
      Shopping centers and malls
      Supermarkets
Retarded children
  USE Mentally handicapped children
       Slow learning children
Retarded readers
  USE Reading disability
Retention, Grade
  USE Promotion (School)
Retirement 305.26; 306.3
  BT Leisure
      Old age
  RT Elderly—Life skills guides
Retirement communities 307.7
  UF Life care communities
      Places of retirement
      Retirement places
  BT Elderly—Housing
Retirement income 331.25; 351.5; 368.4
  BT Elderly
      Income
  NT Annuities
      Individual retirement accounts
      Old age pensions
      Pensions
Retirement places
  USE Retirement communities
Retouching (Photography)
  USE Photography—Retouching
Retraining, Occupational
  USE Occupational retraining
Retribution
  USE Future life
       Hell
Reunions, Family
  USE Family reunions
Reusable space vehicles
  USE Space shuttles
Reuse of waste
  USE Recycling
Revelation 231.7
  BT Religion

BT = Broader Term   NT = Narrower Term   RT = Related Term   SA = See Also   UF = Used For

Revelation—*Continued*
      Supernatural
      Theology
Revenue
  USE **Tariff**
       Taxation
Revenue, Internal
  USE **Internal revenue**
Revenue sharing 336.1
     Use for materials on the practice of re-turning a percentage of federal tax money to state and local governments for locally directed and controlled public service programs.
  UF Federal revenue sharing
       Tax sharing
  BT **Intergovernmental tax rela-tions**
Reviews
  USE subjects with the subdivision *Reviews,* e.g. **Books—Reviews;** to be added as needed
Revival of letters
  USE **Renaissance**
Revival (Religion)
  USE **Evangelistic work**
       Religious awakening
       Revivals
Revivals 269
  UF Revival (Religion)
  BT **Christian life**
       Church history
       Church work
  RT **Evangelistic work**
Revivals—Music
  USE **Gospel music**
Revolution, American
  USE **United States—History—1775-1783, Revolution**
Revolution, French
  USE **France—History—1789-1799, Revolution**
Revolution, Industrial
  USE **Industrial revolution**
Revolution, Russian
  USE **Soviet Union—History—1917-1921, Revolution**
Revolutions 303.6
  UF Coups d'état
       Rebellions

      Sedition
  SA names of countries with the subdivision *History—[dates], Revolution,* e.g. **France—History—1789-1799, Revolution;** to be added as needed
  BT **Political science**
  NT **France—History—1789-1799, Revolution**
       Hungary—History—1956, Revolution
       Insurgency
       National liberation movements
       Radicalism
       Soviet Union—History—1917-1921, Revolution
       United States—History—1775-1783, Revolution
  RT **Resistance to government**
Rewards (Prizes, etc.)
  USE **Awards**
Rh factor
  USE **Blood groups**
Rhetoric 808
  UF Composition (Rhetoric)
       English language—Rhetoric
       Persuasion (Rhetoric)
       Speaking
  SA names of languages with the subdivision *Composition and exercises,* e.g. **English language—Composition and exercises;** to be added as needed
  BT **Language and languages**
  NT **Criticism**
       Debates and debating
       Lectures and lecturing
       Letter writing
       Preaching
       Punctuation
       Satire
  RT **English language—Composition and exercises**
       Literary style
Rheumatism 616.7
  BT **Diseases**
  NT **Arthritis**
       Gout

BT = Broader Term   NT = Narrower Term   RT = Related Term   SA = See Also   UF = Used For

Rhyme 808.1
  SA names of languages with the subdivision *Rhyme,* to be added as needed
  BT Poetics
      Versification
  NT English language—Rhyme
      Stories in rhyme
Rhymes
  USE Limericks
      Nonsense verses
      Nursery rhymes
      Poetry—Collections
Rhythm 808.1
  BT Aesthetics
      Poetics
  NT Musical meter and rhythm
      Versification
  RT Periodicity
Ribonucleic acid
  USE RNA
Ribose nucleic acid
  USE RNA
Ribozymes
  USE Catalytic RNA
Riches
  USE Wealth
Riddles 398.6; 793.73; 818, etc.
  Use for collections of riddles considered as folklore, as games, or as literary exercises, by one or several authors, and for materials about riddles.
  UF Conundrums
      Enigmas
      Rebuses
  BT Amusements
      Literary recreations
  NT Charades
  RT Puzzles
Ride sharing
  USE Car pools
Riding
  USE Horsemanship
Rifles 683.4
  UF Carbines
      Guns
  BT Firearms
Right and left
  USE Left and right
Right- and left-handedness
  USE Left- and right-handedness

Right and left (Political science) 320.5
  Use for general materials on political views or attitudes, i.e. conservative, traditional, liberal, radical, etc. Materials on the physical characteristics of favoring one hand or the other are entered under **Left- and right-handedness.** Materials on left and right as indications of location or direction are entered under **Left and right.**
  UF Extremism (Political science)
      Left (Political science)
      New left
      Reaction (Political science)
      Right (Political science)
  BT Political parties
      Political science
  NT Radicalism
  RT Conservatism
      Liberalism
Right of assembly
  USE Freedom of assembly
Right of association
  USE Freedom of association
Right of asylum
  USE Asylum
Right of privacy 323.44
  UF Invasion of privacy
      Privacy, Right of *[Former heading]*
  BT Civil rights
      Libel and slander
  NT Eavesdropping
      Trade secrets
      Wiretapping
  RT Computer crimes
Right (Political science)
  USE Right and left (Political science)
Right to a fair trial
  USE Fair trial
Right to choose movement
  USE Pro-choice movement
Right to die 179
  UF Death, Right of
      Death with dignity
      Living wills
      Wills, Living
  BT Death
      Medical ethics
      Medicine—Law and legislation
  RT Euthanasia

BT = Broader Term   NT = Narrower Term   RT = Related Term   SA = See Also   UF = Used For

Right to die—*Continued*
> **Suicide**

Right to know
> USE **Freedom of information**

Right-to-life movement (Anti-abortion
> movement)
> USE **Pro-life movement**

Right to work
> USE **Discrimination in employment**
> **Open and closed shop**

Rights, Civil
> USE **Civil rights**

Rights, Human
> USE **Human rights**

Rights of animals
> USE **Animal rights**

Rights of man
> USE **Human rights**

Rights of women
> USE **Women's rights**

Riot control 303.6
> UF Riots—Control *[Former head-
> ing]*
> BT **Crowds**

Riots (May subdiv. geog.) **303.6**
> UF Civil disorders
> Mobs
> SA names of institutions with the
> subdivision *Riots;* and
> names of specific riots, to
> be added as needed
> BT **Crime**
> **Freedom of assembly**
> **Offenses against public safety**
> RT **Crowds**
> **Protests, demonstrations, etc.**

Riots—Control
> USE **Riot control**

Ripoffs
> USE **Fraud**

Rites and ceremonies (May subdiv.
> geog.) **390**
> UF Ceremonies
> Ecclesiastical rites and cere-
> monies
> Religious ceremonies
> Ritual
> Traditions
> SA classes of persons and ethnic
> groups with the subdivision

Rites and ceremonies, e.g.
> **Indians of North America—
> Rites and ceremonies; etc.;**
> and names of individual re-
> ligions and denominations
> with the subdivisions *Litur-
> gy* and *Customs and
> practices,* e.g. **Catholic
> Church—Liturgy;
> Judaism—Customs and
> practices;** etc., to be added
> as needed
> NT **Baptism**
> **Catholic Church—Liturgy**
> **Funeral rites and ceremonies**
> **Indians of North America—
> Rites and ceremonies**
> **Judaism—Customs and
> practices**
> **Liturgies**
> **Lord's Supper**
> **Marriage customs and rites**
> **Ordination**
> **Religious holidays**
> **Sacraments**
> **Secret societies**
> RT **Manners and customs**

Ritual
> USE **Liturgies**
> **Rites and ceremonies**

River animals
> USE **Stream animals**

River pollution
> USE **Water pollution**

Rivers 551.48
> SA names of rivers, to be added
> as needed
> BT **Physical geography**
> **Water**
> **Waterways**
> NT **Dams**
> **Stream animals**
> **Water power**
> **Water rights**
> RT **Floods**
> **Hydraulic engineering**
> **Inland navigation**

RNA 574.87
> UF Ribonucleic acid *[Former
> heading]*

RNA—*Continued*
      Ribose nucleic acid
  BT **Nucleic acids**
  NT **Catalytic RNA**
RNA, Catalytic
  USE **Catalytic RNA**
Road construction
  USE **Roads**
Road engineering
  USE **Highway engineering**
Road maps 912
  UF Maps, Road
      Roads—Maps
  SA names of countries, areas,
      states, cities, etc., with the
      subdivision *Maps,* to be
      added as needed
  BT **Maps**
  NT **Chicago (Ill.)—Maps**
      United States—Maps
  RT **Automobile travel—**
      Guidebooks
Road signs
  USE **Signs and signboards**
Roads 388.1; 625.7
  UF Construction of roads
      Highway construction
      Highways
      Road construction
      Thoroughfares
  BT **Civil engineering**
      Transportation
  NT **Express highways**
      Roadside improvement
      Soils (Engineering)
      Street cleaning
  RT **Highway engineering**
      Pavements
      Streets
Roads—Maps
  USE **Road maps**
Roadside improvement 713
  UF Highway beautification
  BT **Grounds maintenance**
      Landscape architecture
      Roads
Robbers and outlaws
  USE **Thieves**
Robins 598.8
  BT **Birds**

Robinsonades 808.83; 813, etc.
  May be used for individual works, collections, or materials about fictional works describing a character's survival without the aid of civilization, as on a desert island.
  UF Apocalyptic fantasies
      End-of-the-world fantasies
  BT **Adventure fiction**
      Imaginary voyages
Robotics 629.8
  Use for materials on the construction, maintenance, and automatic operation of robots.
  BT **Mechanical engineering**
  NT **Industrial robots**
      Robots
Robots 629.8
  Use for materials on completely self-controlled electronic, electric, or mechanical devices that perform functions ordinarily ascribed to human beings or that operate with what appears to be almost human intelligence.
  UF Androids
      Automata
  BT **Mechanical movements**
      Robotics
Robots, Industrial
  USE **Industrial robots**
Rochdale system
  USE **Cooperation**
Rock and roll music
  USE **Rock music**
Rock climbing
  USE **Mountaineering**
Rock crystal
  USE **Quartz**
Rock drawings, paintings, and engravings 759.01
  UF Petroglyphs
      Rock engravings
      Rock paintings
  BT **Archeology**
      Art
      Mural painting and decoration
      Picture writing
      Prehistoric art
  RT **Cave drawings**
Rock engravings
  USE **Rock drawings, paintings, and engravings**
Rock gardens 635.9
  BT **Gardens**

BT = Broader Term   NT = Narrower Term   RT = Related Term   SA = See Also   UF = Used For

Rock music 781.66; 782.42166
 UF Music, Rock
   Rock and roll music
 BT **Dance music**
   Music
   Popular music
Rock paintings
 USE **Rock drawings, paintings, and**
    engravings
Rock tombs
 USE **Tombs**
Rocket airplanes
 USE **Rocket planes**
Rocket flight
 USE **Space flight**
Rocket planes 629.133
 UF Airplanes, Rocket propelled
   Rocket airplanes
 SA names of rocket planes, e.g.
   X-15 (Rocket aircraft); to
   be added as needed
 BT **High speed aeronautics**
   Space ships
 NT **X-15 (Rocket aircraft)**
Rocketry 621.43
 BT **Aeronautics**
   Astronautics
 NT **Guided missiles**
   Rockets (Aeronautics)
   Space ships
   Space vehicles
Rockets (Aeronautics) 629.133
 UF Aerial rockets
 SA types of rockets and missiles
   and names of specific rock-
   ets and missiles, to be add-
   ed as needed
 BT **Aeronautics**
   High speed aeronautics
   Projectiles
   Rocketry
 NT **Artificial satellites—Launching**
   Ballistic missiles
   Guided missiles
 RT **Interplanetary voyages**
   Jet propulsion
Rocks 552
 UF Crystalline rocks
   Metamorphic rocks
 SA varieties of rock, e.g. **Granite;**
   to be added as needed

 NT **Crystallography**
   Geochemistry
   Granite
   Mineralogy
 RT **Geology**
   Petrology
   Stone
Rocks, Moon
 USE **Lunar petrology**
Rocky Mountains 978
 BT **Mountains**
Rodeos 791.8
 BT **Sports**
 RT **Cowhands**
   Horsemanship
Roentgen rays
 USE **X rays**
Roentgenologists
 USE **Radiologists**
Role conflict 302.5
  Use for materials on the conflict within
  one person who is being called upon to
  fulfill two or more competing roles.
 BT **Social conflict**
   Social role
 NT **Sex role**
Role playing 302
 BT **Social role**
Role, Social
 USE **Social role**
Roller skating 796.2
 UF Figure skating
   Skating
 BT **Outdoor recreation**
Romaic language
 USE **Modern Greek language**
Romaic literature
 USE **Modern Greek literature**
Roman antiquities
 USE **Classical antiquities**
   Rome—Antiquities
   Rome (Italy)—Antiquities
Roman architecture 722
 UF Architecture, Roman *[Former*
    heading]
 BT **Ancient architecture**
   Architecture
Roman art 709.37
 UF Art, Roman *[Former heading]*
   Classical art

BT = Broader Term NT = Narrower Term RT = Related Term SA = See Also UF = Used For

596

Roman art—*Continued*
- BT Ancient art
  - Art
  - Classical antiquities

Roman Catholic Church
- USE Catholic Church

Roman emperors 920
- UF Emperors
  - Sovereigns
- SA names of Roman emperors, e.g. **Nero, Emperor of Rome, 37-68**; to be added as needed
- BT Kings, queens, rulers, etc.
- NT Nero, Emperor of Rome, 37-68

Roman Empire
- USE Rome

Roman literature
- USE Latin literature

Roman mythology
- USE Classical mythology

Roman numerals 513
- BT Numerals

Roman philosophy
- USE Ancient philosophy

Romance languages 440
- UF Neo-Latin languages
- SA names of languages belonging to the Romance group, e.g. **French language**; to be added as needed
- BT Language and languages
  - Latin language
  - Modern languages
- NT French language
  - Spanish language

Romance literature 840
- SA names of literatures belonging to the Romance group, e.g. **French literature**; to be added as needed
- BT Literature
- NT French literature
  - Portuguese literature
  - Spanish literature

Romance novels
- USE Love stories

Romances 808.8; 821, etc.; 823, etc.

May be used for individual works, collections, or materials about medieval tales dealing with the age of chivalry or the supernatural. They may be either in verse or in prose and may or may not have a basis in fact. Contemporary romance novels are entered under **Love stories** or **Romantic suspense novels.**
- UF Chivalry—Romances
  - Metrical romances
  - Stories
- SA names of historic persons with the subdivision *Romances,* to be added as needed
- BT **Chivalry**
  - **Fiction**
  - **Literature—Collections**
- NT **Arthurian romances**
- RT **Epic poetry**
  - **Fables**
  - **Legends**

Romances (Love stories)
- USE Love stories

Romanesque architecture 723
- UF Architecture, Romanesque *[Former heading]*
- BT **Architecture**
  - **Medieval architecture**

Romanesque art 709.02
- UF Art, Romanesque *[Former heading]*
- BT **Medieval art**
- NT **Romanesque painting**

Romanesque painting 759.02
- UF Painting, Romanesque *[Former heading]*
- BT **Romanesque art**

Romanies
- USE Gypsies

Romans à clef 808.83; 813, etc.

May be used for individual works, collections, or materials about novels in which fictional characters and events can be readily identified with real persons and events.
- UF Livres à clef
- BT **Fiction**

Romantic fiction
- USE Love stories

Romantic stories
- USE Love stories

Romantic suspense novels 813, etc.

May be used for individual works, collections, or materials about modern romantic suspense novels. Medieval tales are entered under **Romances.**

UF   Suspense novels

BT   **Adventure fiction**

RT   **Gothic novels**

      Love stories

      Mystery fiction

      Spy stories

Romanticism 141; 709.03; 809

BT   **Aesthetics**

RT   **Literature**

      Music

      Realism in literature

Rome 937

Use for materials about the city of Rome in antiquity or about the Roman Empire. Materials on the modern city of Rome are entered under **Rome (Italy).** Materials on the ruins and remains of ancient Rome, the city and its environs, are entered under **Rome (Italy)—Antiquities.** Materials on Roman antiquities in several countries are entered under **Rome—Antiquities.** Materials on Roman antiquities limited to one modern country are entered under the country with the subdivision *Antiquities.*

UF   Roman Empire

Rome—Antiquities 937

Use for materials on Roman antiquities in several countries. Materials on Roman antiquities limited to one modern country are entered under the country with the subdivision *Antiquities.* Materials on the ruins and remains of ancient Rome, the city and its environs, are entered under **Rome (Italy)—Antiquities.**

UF   Roman antiquities

BT   **Classical antiquities**

Rome—Biography 920.037

UF   Classical biography

Rome—Description 913.7; 937

Use for descriptive materials on the Roman Empire including accounts by travelers of ancient times.

UF   Rome—Description and geography *[Former heading]*

Rome—Description and geography

USE   **Rome—Description**

       Rome—Geography

Rome—Geography 913.7

Use for geographic materials on ancient Rome.

UF   Classical geography

Rome—Description and geography *[Former heading]*

BT   **Ancient geography**

      Historical geography

Rome—History 937

Rome (Italy) 945

Use for materials on the modern city of Rome. Materials about the city of Rome in antiquity or about the Roman Empire are entered under **Rome.**

Rome (Italy)—Antiquities 937

Use for materials on the ruins and remains of ancient Rome, the city and its environs. Materials on Roman antiquities in several countries are entered under **Rome—Antiquities.** Materials on Roman antiquities limited to one modern country are entered under the country with the subdivision *Antiquities.*

UF   Roman antiquities

BT   **Classical antiquities**

Rome (Italy)—Description 914.5

Rome (Italy)—History 945

Roofs 690; 695; 721

BT   **Architecture—Details**

      Building

      Carpentry

Rooming houses

USE   **Hotels and motels**

Rooms 643; 645

SA   types of rooms, to be added as needed

BT   **Buildings**

      Houses

NT   **Garden rooms**

      Kitchens

RT   **Interior design**

Root crops 633; 635

BT   **Vegetables**

RT   **Feeds**

Rope 623.88; 677

NT   **Cables**

      Knots and splices

RT   **Hemp**

Roses 583; 635.9

BT   **Flowers**

Rosetta stone inscription 493

BT   **Hieroglyphics**

Rosin

USE   **Gums and resins**

Rotating memory devices (Data processing)

USE   **Computer storage devices**

Rotation of crops
USE **Crop rotation**
Roughage
USE **Food—Fiber content**
Round stage
USE **Arena theater**
Routes of trade
USE **Trade routes**
Routines, Utility (Computer programs)
USE **Utilities (Computer programs)**
Rowing 797.1
UF Regattas
Sculling
BT **Athletics**
Boats and boating
Exercise
Sports
Water sports
Royalty
USE **Kings, queens, rulers, etc.**
Princes and princesses
Rubber 678
UF India rubber
BT **Forest products**
Rubber, Artificial
USE **Synthetic rubber**
Rubber sheet geometry
USE **Topology**
Rubber, Synthetic
USE **Synthetic rubber**
Rubber tires
USE **Tires**
Rugs 645; 677; 746.7
Use for materials on one-piece floor coverings, such as woven fabrics, animal skins, etc. Materials on heavy woven or felted fabrics used as floor coverings, usually covering large areas, are entered under **Carpets.**
BT **Decorative arts**
Interior design
NT **Hooked rugs**
Oriental rugs
RT **Carpets**
Rugs, Hooked
USE **Hooked rugs**
Rugs, Oriental
USE **Oriental rugs**
Ruins
USE **Archeology**
Excavations (Archeology)

Extinct cities
and names of extinct cities, e.g. **Delphi (Extinct city);** and names of countries, regions, cities (except extinct cities), etc., with the subdivision *Antiquities,* e.g. **Greece—Antiquities;** to be added as needed
Rule of equal time (Broadcasting)
USE **Equal time rule (Broadcasting)**
Rulers
USE **Heads of state**
Kings, queens, rulers, etc.
and names of individual rulers, to be added as needed
Rules of order
USE **Parliamentary practice**
Runaway adults 173; 306.88
UF Adults, Runaway
Desertion
Husbands, Runaway
Wives, Runaway
BT **Desertion and nonsupport**
Homeless persons
Missing persons
Runaway children 362.7
BT **Children**
Homeless persons
Missing children
Runaway teenagers 362.7
BT **Homeless persons**
Missing persons
Teenagers
Running 796.42
BT **Track athletics**
NT **Jogging**
Marathon running
Orienteering
RT **Racing**
Rural architecture
USE **Domestic architecture**
Farm buildings
Rural churches 254
UF Church work, Rural
Churches, Country
Churches, Rural
Country churches
BT **Church work**

Rural comedies
　USE　**Pastoral drama**
　　　　Pastoral fiction
Rural conditions
　USE　names of countries, states,
　　　　etc., with the subdivision
　　　　Rural conditions, e.g. **Unit-**
　　　　ed States—Rural conditions;
　　　　Ohio—Rural conditions;
　　　　etc., to be added as needed
Rural credit
　USE　**Agricultural credit**
Rural electrification
　USE　**Electric power distribution**
　　　　Electricity in agriculture
Rural high schools
　USE　**Rural schools**
Rural life
　USE　**Country life**
　　　　Farm life
　　　　Outdoor life
Rural poetry
　USE　**Pastoral poetry**
Rural schools 371
　UF　Country schools
　　　　District schools
　　　　High schools, Rural
　　　　Rural high schools
　BT　**Public schools**
　　　　Schools
Rural sociology 307.72
　　Use for materials on the discipline of rural sociology and the theory of social organization in rural areas. Materials on the rural conditions of particular regions, countries, cities, etc., are entered under the place with the subdivision *Rural conditions.* Descriptive, popular, and literary materials on living in the country are entered under **Country life.**
　UF　Sociology, Rural *[Former*
　　　　heading]
　SA　names of countries, states,
　　　　etc., with the subdivision
　　　　Rural conditions, to be add-
　　　　ed as needed
　BT　**Sociology**
　NT　**United States—Rural condi-**
　　　　tions
　　　　Urbanization
　RT　**Country life**
　　　　Farm family

Farm life
Peasantry
Russia 947
　　Use for materials on Russia (including the Russian Empire) prior to 1917. Materials on the Union of Soviet Socialist Republics from its inception in 1917 until its dissolution in December 1991 are entered under **Soviet Union.** Materials on the independent republic of Russia since its establishment in December 1991 are entered under **Russia (Republic).**
　UF　Russian Empire
　RT　**Russia (Republic)**
　　　　Soviet Union
Russia (Federation)
　USE　**Russia (Republic)**
Russia—History 947
　　Use for materials on the history of Russia and the Russian empire before 1917.
Russia—History—1905, Revolution
　　　　947.08
　UF　Soviet Union—History—1905,
　　　　Revolution *[Former head-*
　　　　ing]
Russia (Republic) 947.085
　　Use for materials on the independent republic, established in December 1991. Materials on Russia and the Russian Empire before 1917 are entered under **Russia.** Materials on the Union of Soviet Socialist Republics between 1917 and 1991 are entered under **Soviet Union.**
　UF　Russia (Federation)
　RT　**Commonwealth of Independent**
　　　　States
　　　　Russia
　　　　Soviet Union
Russian Church
　USE　**Russian Orthodox Church**
Russian communism
　USE　**Communism—Soviet Union**
Russian Empire
　USE　**Russia**
Russian intervention in Czechoslovakia
　USE　**Czechoslovakia—History—**
　　　　1968-1989
Russian language 491.7
　　May be subdivided like **English lan-**
guage.
　BT　**Language and languages**
　　　　Modern languages

Russian literature 891.7

Use for materials on literature in the Russian language. Materials on several of the literatures of the Soviet Union are entered under **Soviet literature.** May use same subdivisions and names of literary forms as for **English literature.**

BT   Literature

RT   Soviet literature

Russian Orthodox Church 281.9

UF   Orthodox Eastern Church, Russian *[Former heading]*

Russian Church

BT   Christian sects

Eastern churches

Russian revolution

USE   **Soviet Union—History— 1917-1921, Revolution**

Russian satellite countries

USE   **Communist countries**

Russians (May subdiv. geog.) **920; 947**

Use for materials on the dominant Slavic-speaking ethnic group of Russia. Materials on the citizens of the Soviet Union between 1917 and 1991, not limited to a single national or linguistic group, are entered under **Soviets (People).**

BT   Soviet Union

Russo-Finnish War, 1939-1940 948.9703

UF   Finno-Russian War, 1939-1940

Soviet Union—History—1939-1940, War with Finland

BT   Europe—History—1918-1945

Russo-Turkish War, 1853-1856

USE   **Crimean War, 1853-1856**

Rust

USE   **Corrosion and anticorrosives**

Rustless coatings

USE   **Corrosion and anticorrosives**

RVs

USE   **Recreational vehicles**

S.A.T.

USE   **Scholastic aptitude test**

S.S.T.'s

USE   **Supersonic transport planes**

Sabbath 263; 296.4

UF   Lord's Day

BT   Judaism

Sabin vaccine

USE   **Poliomyelitis vaccine**

Sabotage 331.89; 364.1

UF   Political violence

BT   Offenses against public safety

Strikes

Subversive activities

Terrorism

Sacrament of Reconciliation

USE   Penance

Sacraments 234; 265

BT   Rites and ceremonies

Theology

NT   Anointing of the sick

Baptism

Confirmation

Lord's Supper

Marriage

Ordination

Penance

Sacred art

USE   Christian art and symbolism

Religious art and symbolism

Sacred books 291.8

UF   Books, Sacred

SA   names of sacred books, to be added as needed

BT   Religious literature

NT   Bible

Koran

Vedas

Sacred music

USE   Church music

Sacred numbers

USE   Symbolism of numbers

Sacrifice 291.3

BT   Ethnology

Religion

Theology

Worship

NT   Atonement—Christianity

Safe sex in AIDS prevention 613.9; 616.97

Use for materials on sexual activities in which measures are taken to reduce the risk of passing on or contracting AIDS.

BT   AIDS (Disease)—Prevention

Sexual hygiene

Safety appliances 363.19; 620.8

UF   Safety devices

Safety equipment

Safety appliances—*Continued*
  SA subjects with the subdivision
      Safety appliances, to be
      added as needed
  NT **Railroads—Safety appliances**
  RT **Accidents—Prevention**
Safety devices
  USE **Safety appliances**
Safety education 363.1; 371.7
  BT **Accidents—Prevention**
Safety equipment
  USE **Safety appliances**
Safety, Industrial
  USE **Occupational health and safe-
       ty**
Safety measures
  USE **Accidents—Prevention**
      and subjects with the subdivi-
      sion *Safety measures,* e.g.
      **Aeronautics—Safety mea-
      sures;** to be added as need-
      ed
Sagas 398.22; 839
  BT **Folklore**
      Literature
      Old Norse literature
      Scandinavian literature
Sailboarding
  USE **Windsurfing**
Sailing 623.88; 797.1
  BT **Ships**
      Water sports
  NT **Windsurfing**
  RT **Boats and boating**
      Navigation
      Yachts and yachting
Sailors 387.5092; 623.88092; 920
  UF Mariners
      Naval personnel
      Navigators
      Sailors' life
      Sea life
      Seamen
  SA names of navies, e.g. **United
      States. Navy;** to be added
      as needed
  BT **Military personnel**
      Naval art and science
      Navies
  NT **Merchant marine**

Pilots and pilotage
      United States. Navy
  RT **Seafaring life**
Sailors' life
  USE **Sailors**
      Seafaring life
Sailors' song
  USE **Sea songs**
Sailplanes (Aeronautics)
  USE **Gliders (Aeronautics)**
**Saint Bartholomew's Day, Massacre of,
      1572 944**
  UF St. Bartholomew's Day, Mas-
      sacre of, 1572
  BT **France—History—1328-1589,
      House of Valois**
      Huguenots
      Massacres
Saint Dominic, Order of
  USE **Dominicans (Religious order)**
Saint Francis, Order of
  USE **Franciscans**
Saint Valentine's Day
  USE **Valentine's Day**
Saints 235; 920
  SA saints of particular religions,
      e.g. **Christian saints;** and
      names of individual saints,
      to be added as needed
  BT **Heroes and heroines**
  NT **Christian saints**
      Mary, Blessed Virgin, Saint
  RT **Hermits**
      Legends
      Martyrs
      Pilgrims and pilgrimages
      Prophets
      Shrines
Salads 641.8
  BT **Cooking**
  RT **Cooking—Vegetables**
Salamanders 597.6
  BT **Amphibians**
Salaries
  USE **Wages**
Sale of infants
  USE **Adoption—Corrupt practices**
Sales, Auction
  USE **Auctions**
Sales management 658.8
  UF Management, Sales

Sales management—*Continued*
  BT   **Management**
       Marketing
       Selling
Sales personnel 381.092; 658.85
  UF   Agents, Sales
       Clerks (Retail trade)
       Salesmen
       Saleswomen
       Traveling sales personnel
  BT   **Retail trade**
  NT   **Booksellers and bookselling**
       Peddlers and peddling
Sales tax 336.2
  UF   Purchase tax
       Retail sales tax
       Taxation of sales
  BT   **Taxation**
Salesmanship
  USE **Selling**
Salesmen
  USE **Sales personnel**
Saleswomen
  USE **Sales personnel**
Saline water
  USE **Sea water**
Salk vaccine
  USE **Poliomyelitis vaccine**
Salmon 597
  BT   **Fishes**
Saloons
  USE **Bars**
Salt free diet 613.2
  UF   Low sodium diet
  BT   **Cooking for the sick**
       Diet
       Diet in disease
Salt water
  USE **Sea water**
Salt water aquariums
  USE **Marine aquariums**
Salutations
  USE **Etiquette**
       Letter writing
Salvage 627; 628.4
     Use for materials on the recovery of
  equipment, parts, cargo, merchandise,
  structures, or waste.
  UF   Salvage (Waste, etc.) *[Former
          heading]*

       Utilization of waste
       Waste reclamation
  NT   **Marine salvage**
       Recycling
       Waste products as fuel
  RT   **Refuse and refuse disposal**
Salvage, Marine
  USE **Marine salvage**
Salvage (Waste, etc.)
  USE **Salvage**
Salvation 234
  UF   Redemption
  BT   **Doctrinal theology**
  NT   **Atonement—Christianity**
       Faith
       Grace (Theology)
       Sanctification
  RT   **Regeneration (Theology)**
Salvation Army 287.9
  BT   **Christian missions**
       Christian sects
Samplers 746.3
  BT   **Embroidery**
       Needlework
Sampling (Statistics) 519.5
  UF   Random sampling
  BT   **Probabilities**
       Statistics
  NT   **Quality control**
Sanatoriums
  USE **Health resorts**
       Hospitals
Sanctification 234
  BT   **Salvation**
       Spiritual life
       Theology
Sanctions (International law) 341.5
  UF   Economic sanctions
  BT   **Economic policy**
       **International economic rela-
          tions**
       International law
Sanctuaries, Wildlife
  USE **Wildlife refuges**
Sanctuary (Law)
  USE **Asylum**
Sanctuary movement 261.8
     Use for materials on any network of re-
  ligious congregations or churches that
  shelter refugees or illegal aliens.

Sanctuary movement—*Continued*
   UF   Sanctuary movement (Refugee
           aid) *[Former heading]*
   BT   **Asylum**
          Church and social problems
          Social movements
   RT   **Illegal aliens**
          Refugees
Sanctuary movement (Refugee aid)
   USE **Sanctuary movement**
Sand dunes 551.3
   UF   Dunes
   BT   **Seashore**
Sandwiches 641.8
   BT   **Cooking**
Sanitary affairs
   USE **Sanitary engineering**
          Sanitation
Sanitary engineering 628
   UF   Sanitary affairs
   BT   **Building**
          Civil engineering
          Engineering
          House drainage
          Plumbing
          Public health
   NT   **Drainage**
          Pollution
          Refuse and refuse disposal
          Sewerage
          Soils—Bacteriology
          Street cleaning
          Water supply
   RT   **Municipal engineering**
          Sanitation
Sanitary landfills
   USE **Landfills**
Sanitation 363.72; 648
   UF   Sanitary affairs
   BT   **Cleanliness**
   NT   **Cemeteries**
          Cleaning
          Cremation
          Disinfection and disinfectants
          Household sanitation
          Military health
          Pollution
          Refuse and refuse disposal
          School hygiene
          Smoke prevention

          Ventilation
          Water purification
          Water supply
          World War, 1939-1945—
            Health aspects
   RT   **Hygiene**
          Public health
          Sanitary engineering
Sanitation, Household
   USE **Household sanitation**
Santa Claus 394.2
   BT   **Christmas**
Saracenic architecture
   USE **Islamic architecture**
Saracenic art
   USE **Islamic art**
Sasquatch 001.9
   UF   Big foot
          Bigfoot
   BT   **Monsters**
          Mythical animals
SAT
   USE **Scholastic aptitude test**
Satan
   USE **Devil**
Satellite communication systems
   USE **Artificial satellites in telecom-
         munication**
Satellites, Artificial
   USE **Artificial satellites**
Satire 808.7; 808.87
   UF   Comic literature
   SA   satire of particular countries,
          e.g. **American satire**; to be
          added as needed
   BT   **Literature**
          Rhetoric
          Wit and humor
   NT   **American satire**
          English satire
          Invective
          Parody
Satire, American
   USE **American satire**
Satire, English
   USE **English satire**
Satisfaction in work
   USE **Job satisfaction**
Saturn (Planet) 523.4
   BT   **Planets**

Saucers, Flying
USE   Unidentified flying objects
Sauces 641.8
BT   Cooking
Saving and thrift 332.024
UF   Economy
Thrift
BT   Economics
Insurance
Personal finance
Success
NT   Industrial insurance
Old age pensions
Savings and loan associations
RT   Cost of living
Investments
Savings and loan associations 332.3
UF   Building and loan associations
Cooperative building associa-
tions
Loan associations
BT   Banks and banking
Cooperation
Cooperative societies
Investments
Loans
Personal loans
Saving and thrift
RT   Cooperative banks
Savings banks
USE   Banks and banking
Saws 621.9
BT   Carpentry tools
Tools
Saxons
USE   Anglo-Saxons
Teutonic peoples
Sayings
USE   Epigrams
Proverbs
Quotations
Scandinavian civilization 948
UF   Civilization, Scandinavian
[Former heading]
BT   Civilization
Scandinavian languages 439
UF   Norse languages
BT   Language and languages
Modern languages
NT   Danish language

Icelandic language
Norwegian language
Old Norse language
Swedish language
Scandinavian literature 839.7; 839.8
UF   Norse literature
BT   Literature
NT   Danish literature
Eddas
Icelandic literature
Norwegian literature
Sagas
Swedish literature
RT   Old Norse literature
Scandinavians 920; 948
Use for materials on the people of Scan-
dinavia since the tenth century. Materials
on earlier Scandinavians are entered under
Vikings.
NT   Vikings
Scarecrows 632
UF   Bird repelling devices
BT   Plant conservation
Scenarios
USE   Motion picture plays
Plots (Drama, fiction, etc.)
Radio plays
Television plays
Scene painting 751.7
BT   Painting
Theaters—Stage setting and
scenery
Scenery
USE   Landscape protection
Views
and names of cities, states,
and countries, and named
entities, such as individual
parks, structures, etc., with
the subdivision *Pictorial
works,* e.g. **Chicago (Ill.)—
Pictorial works; United
States—Pictorial works; Yo-
semite National Park
(Calif.)—Pictorial works**
etc., to be added as needed
Scenery (Stage)
USE   Theaters—Stage setting and
scenery
Scepticism
USE   Skepticism

Scholarship
 USE **Learning and scholarship**
Scholarship funds
 USE **Scholarships**
Scholarships 371.2; 378.3
 UF Bursaries
  Fellowships
  Funds, Scholarship
  Scholarship funds
  Scholarships, fellowships, etc.
  [Former heading]
 SA fields of study, ethnic groups,
  and classes of persons with
  the subdivision *Scholar-*
  ships, fellowships, etc., to be
  added as needed
 BT **Colleges and universities**
  Education
  Endowments
  Student aid
 RT **Student loan funds**
Scholarships, fellowships, etc.
 USE **Scholarships**
Scholastic achievement
 USE **Academic achievement**
Scholastic aptitude test 378.1
 UF S.A.T.
  SAT
 BT **Colleges and universities—**
  Entrance examinations
  Examinations
School administration and organization
 USE **Schools—Administration**
School age fathers
 USE **Teenage fathers**
School age mothers
 USE **Teenage mothers**
School and community
 USE **Community and school**
School and home
 USE **Home and school**
School architecture
 USE **School buildings**
School assembly programs 371.8
 UF Assembly programs, School
  Programs, School assembly
  School entertainments
  Schools—Exercises and recre-
  ations
  Schools—Opening exercises

 BT **Student activities**
 NT **Commencements**
  Drama in education
  Recitations
School athletics
 USE **School sports**
School attendance 371.2
 UF Absence from school
  Absenteeism (School)
  Attendance, School
  Compulsory school attendance
  School enrollment
  Truancy (Schools)
 NT **Children—Employment**
 RT **Compulsory education**
  Dropouts
School boards 379.1
 UF Boards of education
 BT **Schools—Administration**
School books
 USE **Textbooks**
School buildings 371.6; 727
 UF Buildings, School
  School architecture
  School houses
  Schoolhouses
 BT **Architecture**
  Buildings
  Schools
School buildings as recreation centers
 USE **Community centers**
School busing
 USE **Busing (School integration)**
  School children—
  Transportation
School children 155.42; 305.23
 BT **Children**
  Students
School children—Food 371.7
 UF Food for school children
  Meals for school children
  School lunches
 BT **Children—Food**
  Diet
  Food
School children—Transportation 371.8
 UF School busing
 BT **Transportation**
 NT **Busing (School integration)**
School clubs
 USE **Students—Societies**

School counseling 371.4

Use for materials on the assistance given to students by schools, colleges, or universities in understanding and coping with adjustment problems. Materials on the assistance given to students in the selection of a program of studies are entered under **Educational counseling.**

UF Guidance counseling, School

BT **Counseling**

RT **Educational counseling**
School psychologists

School desegregation

USE **School integration**

School discipline 371.5

UF Discipline of children
Punishment in schools

BT **Schools—Administration**
Teaching

NT **Classroom management**
Student government

School drama

USE **College and school drama**

School dropouts

USE **Dropouts**

School enrollment

USE **School attendance**

School entertainments

USE **School assembly programs**

School excursions

USE **Field trips**

School fiction

USE **School stories**

School finance

USE **Education—Finance**

School furniture

USE **Schools—Equipment and supplies**

School grade retention

USE **Promotion (School)**

School houses

USE **School buildings**

School hygiene 371.7

UF Hygiene, School

BT **Children—Health and hygiene**
Health education
Hygiene
Public health
Sanitation

School inspection

USE **School supervision**

Schools—Administration

School integration 370.19

UF Desegregated schools
Desegregation in education
Education—Integration
Integrated schools
Integration in education
Racial balance in schools
School desegregation

BT **African Americans—Education**
African Americans—Integration
Blacks—Education
Blacks—Integration

NT **Busing (School integration)**
Magnet schools

RT **Segregation in education**

School journalism

USE **College and school journalism**

School libraries 027.8

UF Libraries, School

BT **Instructional materials centers**
Libraries

NT **Children's libraries**
Elementary school libraries
High school libraries
Libraries and students

RT **Libraries and schools**

School libraries (Elementary school)

USE **Elementary school libraries**

School libraries (High school)

USE **High school libraries**

School life

USE **Students**

School lunches

USE **School children—Food**

School management and organization

USE **Schools—Administration**

School media centers

USE **Instructional materials centers**

School music

USE **Music—Study and teaching**
School songbooks
Singing

School newspapers

USE **College and school journalism**

School nurses 371.7

BT **Children—Health and hygiene**
Nurses

School organization

USE **Schools—Administration**

BT = Broader Term   NT = Narrower Term   RT = Related Term   SA = See Also   UF = Used For

School playgrounds
USE **Playgrounds**
School plays
USE **Children's plays**
College and school drama—
Collections
School principals
USE **School superintendents and**
principals
School promotion
USE **Promotion (School)**
School prose
USE **Children's writings**
School psychologists 371.4
UF Psychologists, School
RT **School counseling**
School readiness
USE **Readiness for school**
School reports 371.2
UF Educational reports
Reports, Teachers'
Teachers' reports
BT **Report writing**
RT **Grading and marking (Educa-**
tion)
School science projects
USE **Science projects**
School shops 373.2
UF Industrial arts shops
BT **Technical education**
School songbooks 782.42
UF School music
Songbooks, School
BT **Songbooks**
Songs
NT **Children's songs**
School sports 371.8
UF Interscholastic sports
School athletics
BT **Sports**
Student activities
RT **College sports**
School stories 808.83; 813, etc.
May be used for individual works, col-
lections, or materials about school stories.
UF School fiction
Schools—Fiction
BT **Fiction**
School superintendents and principals
371.2
UF School principals

Superintendents of schools
BT **Schools—Administration**
RT **School supervision**
School supervision 371.1
Use for materials on the supervision of
instruction. Materials on the management
and organization of schools and on the
administrative duties of educators are en-
tered under **Schools—Administration.**
UF Inspection of schools
Instructional supervision
School inspection
Supervision of schools
BT **Schools—Administration**
Teaching
RT **School superintendents and**
principals
School surveys
USE **Educational surveys**
School taxes
USE **Education—Finance**
School teaching
USE **Teaching**
School trips
USE **Field trips**
School vandalism
USE **School violence**
School verse
USE **Children's writings**
School violence 371.5
UF School vandalism
Student violence
BT **Juvenile delinquency**
Violence
School withdrawals
USE **Dropouts**
School yearbooks 371.8
UF Annuals
College yearbooks
High school yearbooks
Senior yearbooks
Student yearbooks
Students—Yearbooks
Yearbooks, Student
BT **Serial publications**
Schoolboy fathers
USE **Teenage fathers**
Schoolgirl mothers
USE **Teenage mothers**
Schoolhouses
USE **School buildings**

Schools (May subdiv. geog.) 371
　SA　types of schools, e.g. **Church
　　　schools; Rural schools;** etc.;
　　　subjects with the subdivi-
　　　sion *Study and teaching,*
　　　e.g. **Medicine—Study and
　　　teaching;** and names of in-
　　　dividual schools, to be add-
　　　ed as needed
　NT　**Business schools**
　　　Church schools
　　　Colleges and universities
　　　**Evening and continuation
　　　schools**
　　　Experimental schools
　　　High schools
　　　Junior high schools
　　　Kindergarten
　　　Libraries and schools
　　　Magnet schools
　　　Museums and schools
　　　Nursery schools
　　　Private schools
　　　Public schools
　　　Religious summer schools
　　　Rural schools
　　　School buildings
　　　Summer schools
　RT　**Education**
Schools—Administration 371.2
　Use for materials on the management
and organization of schools and on the
administrative duties of educators. Materi-
als on the supervision of instruction are
entered under **School supervision.**
　UF　Educational administration
　　　Inspection of schools
　　　School administration and or-
　　　ganization
　　　School inspection
　　　School management and orga-
　　　nization
　　　School organization
　　　Schools—Management and or-
　　　ganization
　NT　**Articulation (Education)**
　　　School boards
　　　School discipline
　　　**School superintendents and
　　　principals**
　　　School supervision

　　　Schools—Centralization
　　　Schools—Decentralization
　　　Student government
　　　Teaching
Schools and libraries
　USE　**Libraries and schools**
Schools and museums
　USE　**Museums and schools**
Schools as social centers
　USE　**Community centers**
Schools, Business
　USE　**Business schools**
Schools—Centralization 379.1
　UF　Centralization of schools
　　　Consolidation of schools
　BT　**Schools—Administration**
Schools—Curricula
　USE　**Education—Curricula**
　　　and types of education and
　　　schools with the subdivi-
　　　sion *Curricula,* e.g. **Library
　　　education—Curricula; Col-
　　　leges and universities—
　　　Curricula;** etc., to be added
　　　as needed
Schools—Decentralization 379.1
　UF　Decentralization of schools
　BT　**Schools—Administration**
Schools—Equipment and supplies 371.6
　UF　School furniture
　BT　**Furniture**
Schools—Exercises and recreations
　USE　**School assembly programs**
Schools—Fiction
　USE　**School stories**
Schools, Magnet
　USE　**Magnet schools**
Schools—Management and organization
　USE　**Schools—Administration**
Schools, Military
　USE　**Military education**
Schools, Nonformal
　USE　**Experimental schools**
Schools, Nongraded
　USE　**Nongraded schools**
Schools—Opening exercises
　USE　**School assembly programs**
Schools, Parochial
　USE　**Church schools**
Schools—Prayers
　USE　**Religion in the public schools**

Schools, Ungraded
USE **Nongraded schools**
Schools—United States 371
UF United States—Schools
Science (May subdiv. geog.) **500**
UF Discoveries (in science)
NT **Astronomy**
Biology
Botany
Chaos (Science)
Chemistry
Computer science
Earth sciences
Fossils
Geology
Life sciences
Mathematics
Natural history
Petrology
Physical sciences
Physics
Physiology
Space sciences
System theory
Zoology
RT **Religion and science**
Scientific apparatus and instruments
Scientists
Science and civilization 306.4
UF Civilization and science
Science and society
BT **Civilization**
Progress
Science and religion
USE **Religion and science**
Science and society
USE **Science and civilization**
Science and space
USE **Space sciences**
Science and state
USE **Science—Government policy**
Science and the Bible
USE **Bible and science**
Science and the humanities 001.3
UF Humanities and science
Science exhibition projects
USE **Science projects**
Science—Exhibitions 507.4
UF Science fairs

NT **Science projects**
Science experiments
USE **Science—Experiments**
Science—Experiments 507
UF Experiments, Scientific
Science experiments
Scientific experiments
SA particular branches of science
with the subdivision *Experiments,* e.g. **Chemistry—Experiments;** to be added
as needed
NT **Chemistry—Experiments**
Science projects
Science fair projects
USE **Science projects**
Science fairs
USE **Science—Exhibitions**
Science fiction 808.83; 813, etc.
May be used for individual works, collections, or materials about fiction based on imagined developments in science and technology.
UF Apocalyptic fantasies
End-of-the-world fantasies
Space flight (Fiction)
Time travel (Fiction)
BT **Adventure fiction**
Fiction
NT **Dystopias**
Imaginary voyages
Utopian fiction
RT **Fantasy fiction**
Interplanetary voyages
**Science fiction comic books, strips, etc.
741.5**
May be used for individual works, collections, or materials about science fiction comics.
BT **Comic books, strips, etc.**
Science fiction films 791.43
May be used for individual works, collections, or materials about science fiction films.
SA particular kinds of science fiction films, e.g. **Star Wars films;** to be added as needed
BT **Motion pictures**
NT **Star Wars films**
RT **Fantasy films**

BT = Broader Term   NT = Narrower Term   RT = Related Term   SA = See Also   UF = Used For

Science fiction plays 808.82; 812, etc.

> May be used for individual works, collections, or materials about science fiction plays.

UF   Time travel (Fiction)

BT   **Drama**

Science fiction poetry 808.81; 811, etc.

> May be used for individual works, collections, or materials about science fiction poetry.

BT   **Poetry**

Science fiction radio programs 791.44

> May be used for individual works, collections, or materials about science fiction radio programs.

UF   Time travel (Fiction)

BT   **Radio programs**

Science fiction television programs 791.45

> May be used for individual works, collections, or materials about science fiction television programs.

UF   Time travel (Fiction)

BT   **Television programs**

RT   **Fantasy television programs**

Science—Government policy 351.85

UF   Science and state

Science policy

State and science

Science journalism

USE   **Scientific journalism**

Science—Methodology 501

NT   **Logic**

Science policy

USE   **Science—Government policy**

Science projects 507.8

UF   Projects, Science

School science projects

Science exhibition projects

Science fair projects

BT   **Science—Exhibitions**

RT   **Science—Experiments**

Science—Societies 506

UF   Scientific societies

Science—Study and teaching 507

UF   Education, Scientific

Scientific education

BT   **Education**

Teaching

NT   **Nature study**

Science—United States 509.73

UF   American science

United States—Science

Scientific apparatus and instruments 502.8

UF   Apparatus, Scientific

Instruments, Scientific

Scientific instruments

SA   types of instruments, e.g. **Aeronautical instruments;** and names of specific instruments, to be added as needed

NT   **Aeronautical instruments**

Astronomical instruments

Chemical apparatus

Electric apparatus and appliances

Electronic apparatus and appliances

Engineering instruments

Meteorological instruments

Optical instruments

RT   **Science**

Scientific creationism

USE   **Creationism**

Scientific education

USE   **Science—Study and teaching**

Scientific errors

USE   **Errors**

Scientific expeditions 508

UF   Expeditions, Scientific

Polar expeditions

SA   names of regions explored with the subdivision *Exploration* for materials on scientific expeditions to regions that are unsettled or sparsely settled and largely unknown to the world at large, e.g. **Antarctic regions—Explorations;** names of countries, states, etc., with the subdivision *Exploring expeditions* for materials on explorations sponsored by those governments; and names of expeditions, to be added as needed

BT   **Voyages and travels**

NT   **Antarctic regions—Exploration**

Scientific expeditions—*Continued*
          Arctic regions—Exploration
    RT   **Exploration**
Scientific experiments
    USE   **Science—Experiments**
Scientific instruments
    USE   **Scientific apparatus and instruments**
Scientific journalism 070.4
    UF   Journalism, Scientific *[Former heading]*
          Science journalism
    BT   **Journalism**
Scientific management
    USE   **Management**
Scientific method
    USE   subjects with the subdivision *Methodology,* e.g. **Science—Methodology;** to be added as needed
Scientific recreations 793.8
    UF   Recreations, Scientific
    BT   **Amusements**
    NT   **Mathematical recreations**
Scientific societies
    USE   **Science—Societies**
Scientific writing
    USE   **Technical writing**
Scientists 509.2; 920
    SA   types of scientists and names of individual scientists, to be added as needed
    NT   **Astronomers**
          Biologists
          Chemists
          Geologists
          Mathematicians
          Naturalists
          Physicists
    RT   **Science**
Scottish clans
    USE   **Clans**
Scottish personal names 929.4
    UF   Names, Personal—Scottish *[Former heading]*
          Personal names, Scottish *[Former heading]*
    BT   **Personal names**
Scottish tartans
    USE   **Tartans**

Scouts and scouting 369.4
    BT   **Clubs**
          Community life
    NT   **Boy Scouts**
          Girl Scouts
Screen plays
    USE   **Motion picture plays**
Screen printing
    USE   **Silk screen printing**
Screening for drug abuse
    USE   **Drug testing**
Screenplays
    USE   **Motion picture plays**
          Television scripts
Scriptures, Holy
    USE   **Bible**
Scuba diving 797.2
    Use for materials on free diving with the aid of a self-contained underwater breathing apparatus. Materials on free diving with mask, fins, and snorkel are entered under **Skin diving.**
    UF   Diving, Scuba
          Free diving
          Frogmen and frogwomen
    BT   **Diving**
          Submarine diving
    RT   **Skin diving**
Sculling
    USE   **Rowing**
Sculptors 730.92; 920
    SA   sculptors of particular countries, e.g. **American sculptors;** to be added as needed
    BT   **Artists**
    NT   **American sculptors**
Sculptors, American
    USE   **American sculptors**
Sculpture 730
    UF   Statues
    SA   sculpture of particular countries, e.g. **Greek sculpture;** and specific types of sculpture, to be added as needed
    BT   **Art**
          Decoration and ornament
    NT   **American sculpture**
          Brasses
          Bronzes
          Greek sculpture
          Kinetic sculpture

Sculpture—*Continued*
>> Masks (Sculpture)
>> Mobiles (Sculpture)
>> Modeling
>> Modern sculpture
>> Monuments
>> Plaster casts
>> Soap sculpture
>> Wood carving

Sculpture, American
> USE American sculpture

Sculpture, Greek
> USE Greek sculpture

Sculpture in motion
> USE Kinetic sculpture

Sculpture, Kinetic
> USE Kinetic sculpture

Sculpture, Modern
> USE Modern sculpture

Sculpture, Modern—1900-1999 (20th century)
> USE Modern sculpture—1900-1999 (20th century)

Sculpture, Religious
> USE Religious art and symbolism

Sculpture—Technique 731.4
> RT Modeling

SDI (Ballistic missile defense system)
> USE Strategic Defense Initiative

Sea
> USE Ocean

Sea animals
> USE Marine animals

Sea bed
> USE Ocean bottom

Sea farming
> USE Aquaculture

Sea fisheries
> USE Fisheries

Sea food
> USE Seafood

Sea in art
> USE Marine painting

Sea laboratories
> USE Undersea research stations

Sea laws
> USE Maritime law

Sea life
> USE Sailors
>> Seafaring life

and names of countries with the subhead *Navy,* e.g. **United States. Navy;** to be added as needed

Sea lions
> USE Seals (Animals)

Sea mosses
> USE Algae

Sea poetry 808.81; 811, etc.; 811.008, etc.

> May be used for individual works, collections, or materials about poetry about the sea.

> BT Poetry
> NT Sea songs

Sea pollution
> USE Marine pollution

Sea power 359
> UF Dominion of the sea
>> Military power
>> Naval power
>> Navy
> SA names of countries with the subhead *Navy* or the subdivision *Naval history,* e.g. **United States. Navy; United States—Naval history;** etc., to be added as needed
> BT Naval art and science
> NT Naval battles
>> United States. Navy
>> Warships
> RT Naval history
>> Navies

Sea resources
> USE Marine resources

Sea routes
> USE Trade routes

Sea shells
> USE Shells

Sea-shore
> USE Seashore

Sea songs 782.42
> UF Chanties
>> Sailors' song
> BT Sea poetry
>> Songs

Sea stories 808.83; 813, etc.

> May be used for individual works, collections, or materials about sea stories.

> BT Adventure and adventurers

BT = Broader Term   NT = Narrower Term   RT = Related Term   SA = See Also   UF = Used For

Sea stories—*Continued*
      Adventure fiction
      Fiction
Sea transportation
  USE **Shipping**
Sea travel
  USE **Ocean travel**
Sea water 551.46
  UF Saline water
      Salt water
  BT **Water**
Sea water aquariums
  USE **Marine aquariums**
Sea water conversion 628.1
  UF Conversion of saline water
      Demineralization of salt water
      Desalination of water
      Desalting of water
  BT **Water purification**
Sea waves
  USE **Ocean waves**
Seafaring life 910.4
  UF Sailors' life
      Sea life
  BT **Adventure and adventurers**
      Voyages and travels
  RT **Sailors**
Seafood 641.3
  UF Sea food
  SA names of marine fish, shell-
      fish, etc., used as food, to
      be added as needed
  BT **Food**
      Marine resources
  RT **Fish as food**
Sealab project 551.46
  UF Navy Sealab project
      Project Sealab
      United States. Navy—Sealab
      project
  BT **Undersea research stations**
Seals (Animals) 599.74
  UF Fur seals
      Sea lions
  BT **Marine mammals**
Seals (Numismatics) 737; 929.8
  UF Emblems
      Signets
  BT **Heraldry**
      History

      Inscriptions
      Numismatics
  RT **National emblems**
Seamanship
  USE **Navigation**
Seamen
  USE **Sailors**
Search and rescue operations
  USE **Rescue work**
Seascapes
  USE **Marine painting**
Seashore 551.4
  UF Sea-shore
  BT **Ocean**
  NT **Beaches**
      Sand dunes
Seasons 508; 525
  SA names of the seasons, to be
      added as needed
  BT **Astronomy**
      Climate
      Meteorology
  NT **Autumn**
Seaweeds
  USE **Algae**
Secession
  USE **State rights**
      United States—History—
        1861-1865, Civil War—
        Causes
Second Advent 236
  UF Jesus Christ—Second Advent
      Second coming of Christ
  BT **Eschatology**
      Jesus Christ
  RT **Millennium**
Second coming of Christ
  USE **Second Advent**
Second hand trade
  USE **Secondhand trade**
Second job
  USE **Supplementary employment**
Secondary education 373
  Use for materials on those levels of edu-
cation higher than elementary and lower
than college or university.
  UF Education, Secondary *[Former
       heading]*
      High school education
      Secondary schools

BT = Broader Term   NT = Narrower Term   RT = Related Term   SA = See Also   UF = Used For

Secondary education—*Continued*
- BT **Education**
- NT **Adult education**
  Evening and continuation schools
- RT **High schools**
  Junior high schools

Secondary employment
- USE **Supplementary employment**

Secondary school libraries
- USE **High school libraries**

Secondary schools
- USE **High schools**
  Junior high schools
  Secondary education

Secondhand trade 381
- UF Second hand trade
  Used merchandise
- SA types of secondhand trade, e.g. **Garage sales;** to be added as needed
- BT **Selling**
- NT **Garage sales**

Secret service (May subdiv. geog.) **327.12; 355.3**

Use for materials on governmental service of a secret nature.
- SA names of wars with the subdivision *Secret service,* to be added as needed
- BT **Police**
- NT **Espionage**
  World War, 1939-1945— Secret service
- RT **Detectives**
  Intelligence service
  Spies

Secret service—United States 353.0074
- UF United States—Secret service

Secret societies 366; 371.8
- SA names of secret societies, e.g. **Freemasons;** to be added as needed
- BT **Rites and ceremonies**
  Societies
- NT **Freemasons**
- RT **Fraternities and sororities**

Secret writing
- USE **Cryptography**

Secretarial practice
- USE **Office practice**

Secretaries 651.3
- BT **Business education**
  Office management

Secrets, Trade
- USE **Trade secrets**

Sectionalism (U.S.)
- USE **Sectionalism (United States)**

Sectionalism (United States) 917.3; 973
- UF Localism
  Provincialism
  Regionalism
  Sectionalism (U.S.) *[Former heading]*

Sects 280; 291.9; 296.8

Use for materials on independent religious groups whose teachings or practices fall within the normative bounds of the major world religions. Materials on the major world religions are entered under **Religions.** Materials on groups or movements whose beliefs or practices differ significantly from the traditional religions, often focused upon a charismatic leader, are entered under **Cults.**
- UF Church denominations
  Denominations, Religious
  Religious denominations
- SA names of churches and sects within the major world religions, e.g. **Presbyterian Church; Hasidim;** etc., to be added as needed
- BT **Church history**
  Religions
- NT **Christian sects**
- RT **Cults**

Sects, Christian
- USE **Christian sects**

Secular humanism
- USE **Secularism**

Secularism 211

Use for materials on any intellectual or philosophical movement or set of beliefs that promotes human values as separate and distinct from religious doctrines.
- UF Humanism—1900-1999 (20th century) *[Former heading]*
  Humanism, Secular
  Secular humanism
- BT **Ethics**
  Theology
  Utilitarianism
- NT **Atheism**

BT = Broader Term   NT = Narrower Term   RT = Related Term   SA = See Also   UF = Used For

Secularism—*Continued*
>Rationalism
RT Humanism
Securities 332.63
>UF Capitalization (Finance)
>Dividends
>SA types of securities, to be added as needed
>BT Finance
>Investments
>Stock exchange
>NT Bonds
>Insider trading
>Mortgages
>Stocks
Securities exchange
>USE Stock exchange
Securities trading, Insider
>USE Insider trading
Security, Internal
>USE Internal security
Security, International
>USE International security
Security, Job
>USE Job security
Security measures
>USE subjects with the subdivision *Security measures*, e.g. Nuclear power plants—Security measures; to be added as needed
Security, Social
>USE Social security
Sedition
>USE Political crimes and offenses
>Revolutions
Seeds 582
>BT Botany
>Plant propagation
>Plants
>NT Nuts
Seeds—Germination
>USE Germination
Seeing eye dogs
>USE Guide dogs
Segregation 305.8
>UF Desegregation
>SA racial and ethnic groups and classes of persons with the subdivision *Segregation*, e.g.

African Americans—Segregation; to be added as needed
>NT African Americans—Segregation
>Apartheid
>Blacks—Segregation
>RT Discrimination
>Minorities
Segregation in education 370.19
>UF Education, Segregation in
>Integration in education
>Racial balance in schools
>BT African Americans—Education
>African Americans—Segregation
>Blacks—Education
>Blacks—Segregation
>NT Busing (School integration)
>RT Discrimination in education
>School integration
Segregation in housing
>USE Discrimination in housing
Segregation in public accommodations
>USE Discrimination in public accommodations
Seismic sea waves
>USE Tsunamis
Seismography
>USE Earthquakes
Seismology
>USE Earthquakes
Selection, Artificial
>USE Breeding
Selection, Natural
>USE Natural selection
Selective service
>USE Draft
Self 126; 155.2
>BT Consciousness
>Individuality
>Personality
Self-acceptance 155.2
>UF Self-love (Psychology)
>BT Psychology
>RT Self-confidence
>Self-esteem
>Self-perception
Self-actualization
>USE Self-realization

Self-assurance
    USE   **Self-confidence**
            Self-reliance
Self-awareness
    USE   **Self-perception**
Self-care, Health
    USE   **Health self-care**
Self-care, Medical
    USE   **Health self-care**
Self-concept
    USE   **Self-perception**
Self-confidence 155.2
    UF   Self-assurance
    BT   **Emotions**
    RT   **Assertiveness (Psychology)**
            Self-acceptance
            Self-consciousness
            Self-esteem
            Self-reliance
Self-consciousness 155.2
    UF   Embarrassment
    BT   **Psychology**
    RT   **Self-confidence**
            Self-esteem
            Self-perception
Self-control 153.8
    UF   Control of self
            Discipline, Self
            Self-discipline
            Self-mastery
            Will power
            Willpower
    BT   **Psychology**
Self-culture
    USE   **Self-improvement**
            Self-instruction
Self-defense 613.6; 796.8
    UF   Fighting
    NT   **Boxing**
            Judo
            Karate
            Self-defense for women
    RT   **Martial arts**
Self-defense for women 613.6; 796.8
    UF   Fighting
            Women—Self-defense
            Women's self-defense
    BT   **Self-defense**
    RT   **Martial arts**
Self-defense in animals
    USE   **Animal defenses**

Self-development
    USE   **Self-improvement**
            Self-instruction
Self-discipline
    USE   **Self-control**
Self-education
    USE   **Self-instruction**
Self-employed 331.12
    UF   Freelancers
    BT   **Business people**
            Entrepreneurs
    NT   **Home business**
            Professions
            Small business
Self-employed women 331.4
    UF   Women, Self-employed
    BT   **Women—Employment**
Self-esteem 155.2
    UF   Self-love (Psychology)
            Self-respect *[Former heading]*
    BT   **Psychology**
    RT   **Self-acceptance**
            Self-confidence
            Self-consciousness
            Self-perception
Self-examination, Medical
    USE   **Health self-care**
Self-expectations, Perfectionist
    USE   **Perfectionism (Personality**
               trait)
Self-fulfillment
    USE   **Self-realization**
Self-government
    USE   **Democracy**
            Representative government and
               representation
Self-government (in education)
    USE   **Student government**
Self health care
    USE   **Health self-care**
Self-help medical care
    USE   **Health self-care**
Self-help programs
    USE   **Twelve-step programs**
Self image
    USE   **Personal appearance**
Self-improvement 158
    UF   Personal development
            Personal growth
            Self-culture *[Former heading]*

Self-improvement—*Continued*
      Self-development
  BT **Life skills**
  RT **Self-instruction**
Self-instruction 371.3; 374
  UF Home education
      Home study courses
      Self-culture *[Former heading]*
      Self-development
      Self-education
      Teach yourself courses
  SA names of subjects with the
      subdivision *Programmed in-
      struction,* e.g. **English
      language—Programmed in-
      struction;** to be added as
      needed
  BT **Education**
      Study skills
  RT **Correspondence schools and
      courses**
      Self-improvement
Self-love (Psychology)
  USE **Self-acceptance**
      Self-esteem
Self-mastery
  USE **Self-control**
Self-medication
  USE **Health self-care**
Self-perception 155.2
  UF Self-awareness
      Self-concept
  BT **Psychology**
  RT **Self-acceptance**
      Self-consciousness
      Self-esteem
Self-protection in animals
  USE **Animal defenses**
Self-realization 155.2; 158
  UF Fulfillment, Self
      Self-actualization
      Self-fulfillment
  BT **Psychology**
  RT **Success**
Self-reliance 179
  UF Self-assurance
  RT **Self-confidence**
      Survival skills
Self-respect
  USE **Self-esteem**

Self-starvation
  USE **Anorexia nervosa**
Selling 380.1; 658.8
  UF Salesmanship
  BT **Business**
      Retail trade
  NT **Auctions**
      Booksellers and bookselling
      Direct selling
      Mail-order business
      Sales management
      Secondhand trade
  RT **Advertising**
      Marketing
Selling of infants
  USE **Adoption—Corrupt practices**
Semantics 121; 302.2; 401
    Use for materials on the historical and
  psychological study of meanings in lan-
  guage and changes in those meanings.
  BT **Language and languages**
  NT **Semiotics**
Semiconductors 621.3815
  BT **Electric conductors**
      Electronics
  NT **Microelectronics**
      Transistors
Semiotics 302.2; 401
    Use for materials on the relationship be-
  tween signs and symbols and whatever it
  is they stand for.
  BT **Semantics**
  NT **Visual literacy**
  RT **Signs and symbols**
Semitic peoples 305.892
  BT **Ethnology**
Senate (U.S.)
  USE **United States. Congress. Sen-
      ate**
Senescence
  USE **Aging**
Senior citizens
  USE **Elderly**
Senior yearbooks
  USE **School yearbooks**
Sense of direction
  USE **Direction sense**
Senses and sensation 152.1; 612.8
  BT **Intellect**
      Physiology
      Psychology

BT = Broader Term   NT = Narrower Term   RT = Related Term   SA = See Also   UF = Used For

Senses and sensation—*Continued*

Psychophysiology
Theory of knowledge
NT Color sense
Gestalt psychology
Hearing
Pain
Pleasure
Smell
Taste
Touch
Vision

Sensing, Remote
USE **Remote sensing**
Sensitivity training
USE **Group relations training**
Separate development (Race relations)
USE **Apartheid**

Separation anxiety in children 155.4
BT **Child psychology**
Fear
Stress (Psychology)

Separation (Law)
USE **Divorce**

Separation of powers (May subdiv. geog.) **320.4; 342**
UF Division of powers
Powers, Separation of
BT **Constitutional law**
Executive power
Political science

Separation of powers—United States 320.473
UF United States—Separation of powers

Separatism, Black
USE **Black nationalism**
Separatist movement in Québec (Province)
USE **Québec (Province)—History—Autonomy and independence movements**

Sepulchers
USE **Tombs**
Sepulchral brasses
USE **Brasses**

Sequences (Mathematics) 510
UF Mathematical sequences
Numerical sequences
BT **Algebra**

Mathematics
Serial publications 050
Use for general materials on publications in any medium issued in successive parts bearing numerical or chronological designations and intended to be continued indefinitely.
BT **Bibliography**
Publishers and publishing
NT **Almanacs**
Newspapers
Periodicals
School yearbooks
RT **International Standard Serial Numbers**

Serigraphy
USE **Silk screen printing**
Sermon on the mount 226.9
UF Jesus Christ—Sermon on the mount

Sermons 251; 252
BT **Christian literature**
RT **Preaching**

Serpents
USE **Snakes**
Servants
USE **Household employees**
Service books (Liturgy)
USE **Liturgies**
Service, Compulsory military
USE **Draft**
Service, Customer
USE **Customer service**
Service dogs
USE **Animals and the handicapped**
Service (in industry)
USE **Customer service**

Service industries 338.4
UF Industries, Service
SA individual service industries, to be added as needed
BT **Industry**
NT **Food service**
Hotels and motels
Lease and rental services
Undertakers and undertaking

Service stations 629.28
UF Automobile service stations
[Former heading]
Filling stations
Gas stations

BT = Broader Term NT = Narrower Term RT = Related Term SA = See Also UF = Used For

Service stations—*Continued*
  BT   **Automobile industry**
        Petroleum industry
Servicemen
  USE **Military personnel**
Services, Customer
  USE **Customer service**
Servicewomen
  USE **Military personnel**
Servitude
  USE **Peonage**
        Slavery
Servomechanisms 629.8
  UF Automatic control
  BT   **Automation**
        Feedback control systems
Set theory 511.3
  UF Aggregates
        Classes (Mathematics)
        Ensembles (Mathematics)
        Mathematical sets
        Sets (Mathematics)
  BT   **Mathematics**
  NT   **Arithmetic**
        Boolean algebra
        Fractals
        Number theory
        Topology
  RT   **Symbolic logic**
Sets, Fractal
  USE **Fractals**
Sets (Mathematics)
  USE **Set theory**
Sets of fractional dimension
  USE **Fractals**
Settlement of land
  USE **Land settlement**
Settlements, Social
  USE **Social settlements**
Seven Years' War, 1756-1763 940.2
  BT   **Germany—History—**
         1740-1815
Seventeen-year locusts
  USE **Cicadas**
Seventeenth century 909
  Use for general materials covering progress and development during this period in one or in several countries.
  UF 1600-1699 (17th century)
  BT   **Modern history**
Seville (Spain). World's Fair, 1992
  USE **Expo 92 (Seville, Spain)**

Sewage disposal 628.3
  UF Waste disposal
  BT   **Public health**
        Refuse and refuse disposal
  RT   **Water pollution**
Sewerage 628
  UF Sewers
  BT   **House drainage**
        Municipal engineering
        Plumbing
        Sanitary engineering
  RT   **Drainage**
Sewers
  USE **Sewerage**
Sewing 646.2
  BT   **Home economics**
  NT   **Embroidery**
  RT   **Dressmaking**
        Needlework
Sex
  USE **Sexual behavior**
Sex bias
  USE **Sexism**
Sex (Biology) 574.3; 612.6
  Use for materials on the physiological traits that distinguish the males and females of a species. Materials on sexuality and sexual behavior are entered under **Sexual behavior.**
  BT   **Biology**
  NT   **Androgyny**
        Reproductive system
        Sexual disorders
  RT   **Reproduction**
        Sexual behavior
Sex change
  USE **Transsexuality**
Sex crimes 364.1
  UF Crimes, Sex
        Sexual abuse
        Sexual crimes
  SA   types of sex crimes, to be
        added as needed
  BT   **Crime**
        Sexual behavior
  NT   **Child sexual abuse**
        Incest
        Rape
Sex customs
  USE **Sexual behavior**
Sex differences (Psychology) 155.3
  NT   **Sex role**

Sex differences (Psychology)—
Continued
  RT **Androgyny**
       Sex discrimination
       Sexual behavior

Sex discrimination 305.3

Use for materials on the restriction or denial of rights, privileges, or choice because of one's sex. Materials on prejudicial attitudes toward people because of their sex are entered under **Sexism.**

  UF Discrimination, Sex
  BT **Discrimination**
       Sexism
  NT **Equal rights amendments**
       Women's rights
  RT **Sex differences (Psychology)**

Sex disorders
  USE **Sexual disorders**

Sex education 372.3; 613.907; 649
  UF Human life education
       Sex instruction
  BT **Family life education**
  RT **Sexual hygiene**

Sex in art
  USE **Erotic art**

Sex in business
  USE **Sex in the workplace**

Sex in the office
  USE **Sex in the workplace**

Sex in the workplace 306.7; 658
  UF Employee sex in the workplace
       Office romance
       Sex in business
       Sex in the office
  BT **Sexual behavior**
       Work
  RT **Sexual harassment**

Sex instruction
  USE **Sex education**

Sex organs
  USE **Reproductive system**

Sex (Psychology)
  USE **Sexual behavior**

Sex role 305.3

Use for materials on the patterns of attitudes and behavior that are regarded as appropriate to one sex rather than the other.

  UF Female role
       Gender identity

       Male role
  BT **Role conflict**
       Sex differences (Psychology)
       Social role
  NT **Sexism**
       Transsexuality
  RT **Androgyny**

Sex therapy 616.6; 616.85
  BT **Psychotherapy**
  RT **Sexual disorders**

Sexism 305.3

Use for materials on prejudicial attitudes toward people because of their sex. Materials on the restriction or denial of rights, privileges, or choice because of one's sex are entered under **Sex discrimination.**

  UF Sex bias
  BT **Attitude (Psychology)**
       Prejudices
       Sex role
       Sexual behavior
  NT **Sex discrimination**

Sexual abstinence 176; 306.73

Use for materials on abstinence from sexual activity. Materials on the virtue that moderates and regulates the sexual appetite in human beings are entered under **Chastity.** Materials on the renunciation of marriage for religious reasons are entered under **Celibacy.**

  UF Abstinence, Sexual
  BT **Asceticism**
       Sexual behavior
  RT **Birth control**
       Celibacy
       Chastity

Sexual abuse
  USE **Child sexual abuse**
        Sex crimes
        Sexual harassment

Sexual assault
  USE **Rape**

Sexual behavior 155.3

Use for materials on sexuality or sexual behavior. Materials on the physiological traits that distinguish the males and females of a species are entered under **Sex (Biology).**

  UF Behavior, Sexual
       Sex
       Sex customs
       Sex (Psychology)
       Sexuality

BT = Broader Term   NT = Narrower Term   RT = Related Term   SA = See Also   UF = Used For

Sexual behavior—*Continued*
  SA   social groups and classes of persons with the subdivision *Sexual behavior,* e.g. **College students—Sexual behavior;** to be added as needed
  BT   **Human behavior**
  NT   **Androgyny**
       College students—Sexual behavior
       Homosexuality
       Sex crimes
       Sex in the workplace
       Sexism
       Sexual abstinence
       Sexual behavior in animals
       Sexual deviation
       Sexual harassment
  RT   **Sex (Biology)**
       Sex differences (Psychology)
       Sexual disorders
       Sexual ethics

Sexual behavior in animals 591.56
  UF   Animal sexual behavior
       Animals—Sexual behavior
       Breeding behavior
       Mating behavior
       Reproductive behavior
  BT   **Animal behavior**
       Sexual behavior
  NT   **Animal courtship**

Sexual crimes
  USE **Sex crimes**

Sexual deviation 306.7; 616.85
  UF   Deviation, Sexual
       Paraphilia
       Perversion, Sexual
       Sexual perversion
  BT   **Sexual behavior**
       Sexual disorders

Sexual disorders 616.6; 616.85
  UF   Sex disorders
  BT   **Sex (Biology)**
  NT   **Sexual deviation**
  RT   **Sex therapy**
       Sexual behavior

Sexual ethics 176
  UF   Ethics, Sexual
  BT   **Social ethics**

  NT   **Adultery**
       Chastity
       Free love
       Prostitution
       Sexual hygiene
       Unmarried couples
  RT   **Birth control**
       Human artificial insemination
       Sexual behavior

Sexual harassment 331.13; 344; 370.19
    Use for materials on unsolicited and unwelcome sexual behavior that interferes with study, work, or everyday activities and creates an intimidating or offensive environment.
  UF   Harassment, Sexual
       Sexual abuse
  SA   types of sexual harassment, to be added as needed
  BT   **Sexual behavior**
  NT   **Child sexual abuse**
  RT   **Sex in the workplace**

Sexual hygiene 613.9
  UF   Hygiene, Sexual
       Social hygiene
  BT   **Hygiene**
       Sexual ethics
  NT   **Birth control**
       Safe sex in AIDS prevention
  RT   **AIDS (Disease)—Prevention**
       Sex education
       Sexually transmitted diseases

Sexual perversion
  USE **Sexual deviation**

Sexuality
  USE **Sexual behavior**

Sexually transmitted diseases 616.95
  UF   V.D.
       VD
       Venereal diseases *[Former heading]*
  SA   names of sexually transmitted diseases, to be added as needed
  BT   **Communicable diseases**
  NT   **AIDS (Disease)**
       Syphilis
  RT   **Sexual hygiene**

Shade gardens
  USE **Gardening in the shade**

Shades and shadows 741.2
  UF   Light and shade

BT = Broader Term   NT = Narrower Term   RT = Related Term   SA = See Also   UF = Used For

Shades and shadows—*Continued*
    Shadows
    BT **Drawing**
Shadow pantomimes and plays 791.5
    BT **Amateur theater**
          Pantomimes
          Puppets and puppet plays
          Shadow pictures
          Theater
Shadow pictures 793
    UF Hand shadows
          Shadowplay
    BT **Amusements**
    NT **Shadow pantomimes and plays**
Shadowplay
    USE **Shadow pictures**
Shadows
    USE **Shades and shadows**
Shady gardens
    USE **Gardening in the shade**
Shaft sinking
    USE **Boring**
Shakers 289
    BT **Christian sects**
Shakespeare, William, 1564-1616 822.3

When applicable, the subdivisions provided with this heading may be used for other voluminous authors, e.g. **Dante; Goethe;** etc. These headings are to be used for materials about Shakespeare and about his writings. The texts of his plays, etc., are not given subject headings.

Shakespeare, William, 1564-1616—
          Adaptations 822.3

May be used for individual works, collections, or materials about adaptations of Shakespeare's works for other media.

    UF Shakespeare, William,
          1564-1616—Paraphrases
Shakespeare, William, 1564-1616—
          Anniversaries 822.3
Shakespeare, William, 1564-1616—
          Authorship 822.3
    UF Bacon-Shakespeare controversy
Shakespeare, William, 1564-1616—
          Bibliography 016.8223
    BT **Bibliography**
Shakespeare, William, 1564-1616—
          Biography 92; B
    BT **Biography**
    NT **Shakespeare, William,**
          1564-1616—Psychology

Shakespeare, William, 1564-1616—
          Biography—Psychology
    USE **Shakespeare, William,**
          1564-1616—Psychology

Shakespeare, William, 1564-1616—
          Characters 822.3

    BT **Characters and characteristics**
          in literature

Shakespeare, William, 1564-1616—
          Comedies 822.3

Use for criticism, etc., of the comedies, not for the texts of the plays.

Shakespeare, William, 1564-1616—
          Concordances 822.303

    UF Shakespeare, William,
          1564-1616—Indexes

    BT **Shakespeare, William,**
          1564-1616—Dictionaries

Shakespeare, William, 1564-1616—
          Contemporary England
          822.3; 942.05

    UF Shakespeare's England

Shakespeare, William, 1564-1616—
          Criticism, interpretation,
          etc. 822.3

Use for criticism of the works in general; criticism of the comedies is entered under **Shakespeare, William, 1564-1616—Comedies;** criticism of the tragedies under **Shakespeare, William, 1564-1616—Tragedies;** criticism of an individual play is entered under **Shakespeare, William, 1564-1616,** followed by the title of the play. Materials limited to criticism of the sonnets are entered under **Shakespeare, William, 1564-1616—Sonnets.**

    UF Shakespeare, William,
          1564-1616—Psychological
          studies

    BT **Criticism**

Shakespeare, William, 1564-1616—
          Dictionaries 822.303

    UF Shakespeare, William,
          1564-1616—Indexes

    BT **Encyclopedias and dictionaries**

    NT **Shakespeare, William,**
          1564-1616—Concordances

BT = Broader Term   NT = Narrower Term   RT = Related Term   SA = See Also   UF = Used For

Shakespeare, William, 1564-1616—
Discography 016.8223

Shakespeare, William, 1564-1616—
Dramatic production
822.3

UF   Shakespeare, William,
1564-1616—Stage setting
and scenery

Shakespeare, William, 1564-1616—
Filmography 016.8223

Shakespeare, William, 1564-1616—
Histories 822.3

Use for criticism, etc., of the histories,
not for the texts of the plays.

Shakespeare, William, 1564-1616—
Indexes

USE   Shakespeare, William,
1564-1616—Concordances
Shakespeare, William,
1564-1616—Dictionaries

Shakespeare, William, 1564-1616—
Influence 822.3

Use for materials on Shakespeare's influence on national literatures, literary
movements, or specific persons.

Shakespeare, William, 1564-1616—
Knowledge 822.3

Use for materials on Shakespeare's
knowledge or treatment of specific subjects. May be subdivided by subject, e.g.
**Shakespeare, William, 1564-1616—
Knowledge—Animals;** etc.

Shakespeare, William, 1564-1616—
Paraphrases

USE   Shakespeare, William,
1564-1616—Adaptations

Shakespeare, William, 1564-1616—
Parodies, travesties, etc.
822.3

Shakespeare, William, 1564-1616—
Portraits 822.3022

BT   Portraits

Shakespeare, William, 1564-1616—
Psychological studies

USE   Shakespeare, William,
1564-1616—Criticism, interpretation, etc.
Shakespeare, William,
1564-1616—Psychology

Shakespeare, William, 1564-1616—
Psychology 92; B

UF   Shakespeare, William,
1564-1616—Biography—
Psychology *[Former head-
ing]*
Shakespeare, William,
1564-1616—Psychological
studies

BT   Biography
Psychology
Shakespeare, William,
1564-1616—Biography

Shakespeare, William, 1564-1616—
Quotations 822.3

Shakespeare, William, 1564-1616—
Religion and ethics 822.3

Shakespeare, William, 1564-1616—
Sonnets 822.3

Use for criticism, etc., of the sonnets,
not for the texts of the sonnets.

Shakespeare, William, 1564-1616—
Stage history 792; 822.3

BT   Theater

Shakespeare, William, 1564-1616—Stage
setting and scenery

USE   Shakespeare, William,
1564-1616—Dramatic pro-
duction

Shakespeare, William, 1564-1616—Style

USE   Shakespeare, William,
1564-1616—Technique

Shakespeare, William, 1564-1616—
Technique 822.3

UF   Shakespeare, William,
1564-1616—Style

Shakespeare, William, 1564-1616—
Tragedies 822.3

Use for criticism, etc., of the tragedies,
not for the texts of the plays

Shakespeare's England

USE   Shakespeare, William,
1564-1616—Contemporary
England

Shape

USE   **Size and shape**

Shapes

USE   names of geometric shapes,
e.g. **Square;** to be added as
needed

BT = Broader Term   NT = Narrower Term   RT = Related Term   SA = See Also   UF = Used For

Sharecropping
   USE **Farm tenancy**
Shared custody
   USE **Child custody**
Shared housing 363.5
   Use for materials on two or more single, unrelated adults who live together.
   UF Home sharing
        House sharing
        Nonfamily households
   BT **Housing**
   NT **Unmarried couples**
Shared parenting
   USE **Part-time parenting**
Shared reading books
   USE **Big books**
Shares of stock
   USE **Stocks**
Sharing of jobs
   USE **Job sharing**
Sheep 599.73; 636.3
   BT **Domestic animals**
        Livestock
   NT **Lambs**
Sheet metalwork 671.8
   UF Press working of metal
   BT **Metalwork**
   NT **Plate metalwork**
Sheffield plate 739.2
   BT **Plate**
Shellfish 594; 595.3; 641.3
   BT **Cooking**
        Food
        Invertebrates
   NT **Crabs**
        Crustacea
        Lobsters
        Mollusks
Shells 594
   Use for popular materials on seashells and shell collecting. Systematic and comprehensive materials on shells are entered under **Mollusks.**
   UF Sea shells
   BT **Mollusks**
Shells (Projectiles)
   USE **Projectiles**
Shelterbelts
   USE **Windbreaks**
Shelters, Air raid
   USE **Air raid shelters**

Shelters, Animal
   USE **Animal shelters**
Sherlock Holmes films 791.43
   May be used for individual works, collections, or materials about Sherlock Holmes films.
   BT **Motion pictures**
        Mystery films
Shinto 299
   BT **Religions**
   RT **Ancestor worship**
Ship building
   USE **Shipbuilding**
Ship models
   USE **Ships—Models**
Ship pilots
   USE **Pilots and pilotage**
Ship salvage
   USE **Marine salvage**
Shipbuilding 623.8
   UF Architecture, Naval
        Marine architecture
        Ship building
        Ships—Construction
   BT **Industrial arts**
        Naval art and science
   NT **Marine engines**
        Ships—Models
        Steamboats
   RT **Boatbuilding**
        Naval architecture
        Ships
Shipping (May subdiv. geog.) **387.5**
   UF Marine transportation
        Ocean—Economic aspects
        Ocean transportation
        Sea transportation
        Water transportation
   BT **Transportation**
   NT **Harbors**
        Inland navigation
        Marine insurance
        Maritime law
        Territorial waters
   RT **Merchant marine**
Shipping—United States 387.00973
   UF United States—Shipping
Ships 387.2; 623.8
   UF Vessels (Ships)
   SA types of ships and vessels, to be added as needed

Ships—*Continued*
    BT   **Naval architecture**
          Ocean travel
    NT   **Clipper ships**
          Hospital ships
          Lightships
          Merchant marine
          Navies
          Navigation
          Sailing
          Steamboats
          Submarines
          Warships
          Yachts and yachting
    RT   **Boats and boating**
          Shipbuilding

Ships—Construction
    USE **Shipbuilding**

Ships in art
    USE **Marine painting**

Ships—**Models** 623.8
    UF   Ship models
    BT   **Machinery**—**Models**
          Models and model making
          Shipbuilding

Shipwrecks 363.12; 910.4
    UF   Marine disasters
          Wrecks
    SA   names of wrecked ships, to be
          added as needed
    BT   **Accidents**
          Adventure and adventurers
          Disasters
          Navigation
          Voyages and travels
    NT   **Survival after airplane acci-**
          dents, shipwrecks, etc.
    RT   **Marine salvage**

Shoe industry 338.4; 685
    BT   **Clothing industry**
          Leather industry
          Shoes

Shoes 391; 646; 685
    UF   Boots
          Footwear
    BT   **Clothing and dress**
    NT   **Shoe industry**

Shooting 799.3
    Use for materials on the use of firearms.
Materials on shooting game are entered
under **Hunting**.

    UF   Gunning
    NT   **Archery**
          Decoys (Hunting)
    RT   **Firearms**
          Hunting

Shooting stars
    USE **Meteors**

Shop management
    USE **Factory management**

Shop practice
    USE **Machine shop practice**

Shop windows
    USE **Show windows**

Shoplifting 364.1
    BT   **Stealing**

Shoppers' guides
    USE **Consumer education**
          Shopping

Shopping 381; 640.73
    Use for materials on buying by the con-
sumer. Materials on buying by government agencies and by commercial and
industrial enterprises are entered under
Buying.
    UF   Buyers' guides
          Marketing (Home economics)
          Purchasing
          Shoppers' guides
    BT   **Home economics**
    RT   **Buying**
          Consumer education
          Consumers

Shopping centers and malls 658.8
    UF   Malls, Shopping
          Shopping malls
    BT   **Retail trade**

Shopping malls
    USE **Shopping centers and malls**

Shops, Machine
    USE **Machine shops**

Short films 791.43
    May be used for individual works, col-
lections, or materials about short films.
    BT   **Motion pictures**

Short plays
    USE **One act plays**

Short stories 808.83; 813, etc.
    Use for collections of short stories by
one author or by several authors. Materials on the short story as a literary form
and on the technique of writing short stories are entered under **Short story.**

Short stories—*Continued*
   UF   Stories
   BT   **Fiction**
          Literature—Collections
Short stories—Indexes 016.80883
   BT   **Indexes**
Short story 808.3
   Use for materials on the short story as a literary form and on the technique of writing short stories. Collections of stories are entered under **Short stories.**
   BT   **Authorship**
          Fiction
          Literature
   RT   **Storytelling**
Short take off and landing aircraft 629.133
   UF   STOL aircraft
   BT   **Jet planes**
Shorthand 653
   UF   Stenography
   BT   **Business education**
          Office practice
          Writing
   RT   **Abbreviations**
Shortwave radio 621.3841
   UF   High-frequency radio
          Radio, Shortwave *[Former heading]*
          UHF radio
          Ultrahigh frequency radio
          Very high frequency radio
          VHF radio
   BT   **Radio**
          Radio frequency modulation
   NT   **Amateur radio stations**
          Citizens band radio
          Microwave communication systems
          Microwaves
Shotguns 683.4
   UF   Guns
   BT   **Firearms**
Show business
   USE   **Performing arts**
Show windows 659.1
   UF   Shop windows
          Window dressing
   BT   **Advertising**
          Decoration and ornament
          Windows

Showers (Parties) 793.2
   BT   **Parties**
Shows, Craft
   USE   **Craft shows**
Shrines (May subdiv. geog.) **263; 291.3; 726**
   NT   **Tombs**
   RT   **Miracles**
          Pilgrims and pilgrimages
          Saints
Shrubs 582.1; 635.9
   BT   **Plants**
          Trees
   NT   **Evergreens**
   RT   **Landscape gardening**
          Ornamental plants
Shuttles, Space
   USE   **Space shuttles**
Shyness 155.2
   UF   Bashfulness *[Former heading]*
   BT   **Emotions**
Sibling sequence
   USE   **Birth order**
Siblings
   USE   **Brothers and sisters**
Sick 362.1
   UF   Invalids
   BT   **Handicapped**
   NT   **Church work with the sick**
          Cooking for the sick
          First aid
          Terminally ill
   RT   **Diseases**
          Health resorts
          Home nursing
          Hospitals
          Nursing
          Patients
Sickness
   USE   **Diseases**
Sickness insurance
   USE   **Health insurance**
Sieges
   USE   **Battles**
Sight
   USE   **Vision**
Sight saving books
   USE   **Large print books**
Sign boards
   USE   **Signs and signboards**

BT = Broader Term   NT = Narrower Term   RT = Related Term   SA = See Also   UF = Used For

Sign language 419
- UF   Deaf—Sign language
- BT   **Language and languages**
- NT   **Indians of North America— Sign language**
- RT   Deaf—Means of communication
  - Signs and symbols

Sign painting 667
- BT   **Advertising**
  - **Industrial painting**
- NT   **Alphabets**
- RT   **Lettering**
  - **Signs and signboards**

Signals and signaling 388; 621.382
- UF   Coastal signals
  - Fog signals
  - Military signaling
  - Naval signaling
- BT   **Communication**
  - **Military art and science**
  - **Naval art and science**
  - **Navigation**
  - **Signs and symbols**
- NT   **Railroads—Signaling**
  - **Sonar**
- RT   **Flags**

Signboards
- USE   **Signs and signboards**

Signets
- USE   **Seals (Numismatics)**

Signs (Advertising)
- USE   **Electric signs**
  - **Signs and signboards**

Signs and signboards 659.13
- UF   Billboards
  - Guide posts
  - Road signs
  - Sign boards
  - Signboards
  - Signs (Advertising)
- BT   **Advertising**
- NT   **Electric signs**
- RT   **Posters**
  - **Sign painting**

Signs and symbols 302.2; 419
- UF   Emblems
  - Symbols
- BT   **Communication**
- NT   **Ciphers**

-     **Cryptography**
  - **Heraldry**
  - **National emblems**
  - **Signals and signaling**
  - **State emblems**
- RT   **Abbreviations**
  - **Semiotics**
  - **Sign language**
  - **Symbolism**

Signs and symbols in literature
- USE   **Symbolism in literature**

Signs, Electric
- USE   **Electric signs**

Silage and silos 633.2
- UF   Ensilage
  - Silos
- BT   **Feeds**
  - **Forage plants**

Silent films 791.43
> May be used for individual works, collections, or materials about films made before the development of films with sound.
- UF   Silent motion pictures
- BT   **Motion pictures**

Silent motion pictures
- USE   **Silent films**

Silk 677
- BT   **Fabrics**
  - **Fibers**
- RT   **Silkworms**

Silk, Artificial
- USE   **Rayon**

Silk screen printing 764
- UF   Screen printing
  - Serigraphy
- BT   **Color printing**
  - **Stencil work**
- RT   **Textile printing**

Silkworms 595.7; 638
- UF   Cocoons
- BT   **Beneficial insects**
  - **Moths**
- RT   **Silk**

Silos
- USE   **Silage and silos**

Silver 332.4; 669
- UF   Bimetallism
  - Bullion
- BT   **Chemical elements**

BT = Broader Term   NT = Narrower Term   RT = Related Term   SA = See Also   UF = Used For

Silver—*Continued*
Precious metals
NT   Silverware
Silverwork
RT   Coinage
Money

Silver articles
USE   Silverwork

Silver mines and mining 622
BT   Mines and mineral resources
NT   Prospecting

Silver plate
USE   **Plate**
Silverware

Silver work
USE   Silverwork

Silversmithing
USE   Silverwork

Silverware 642; 739.2
UF   Flatware, Silver
Silver plate
BT   **Decorative arts**
Silver
Silverwork
Tableware

Silverwork 739.2
UF   Silver articles
Silver work
Silversmithing
BT   **Art metalwork**
Metalwork
Silver
NT   **Indians of North America—Silverwork**
Plate
Silverware
RT   Jewelry

Simple machines 621.8
UF   Machines, Simple
SA   types of simple machines, e.g. **Wheels;** to be added as needed
BT   **Machinery**
Mechanical movements
Mechanics
NT   **Wheels**

Simulation games in education 371.3
UF   Educational gaming
Educational simulation games
Gaming, Educational

BT   **Education**
Educational games
Game theory

Sin 241; 291.5
BT   **Christian ethics**
Ethics
Good and evil
Theology

Sinai Campaign, 1956 956.04
UF   Anglo-French intervention in Egypt, 1956
Arab-Israel War, 1956
Israel-Arab War, 1956
BT   **Egypt—History**
Israel-Arab conflicts

Singers 782.0092; 920
BT   **Musicians**

Singing 782; 783
UF   School music
Vocal culture
Voice culture
BT   **Music**
NT   **Songbooks**
RT   **Choirs (Music)**
Vocal music
Voice

Singing games 796.1
BT   **Games**

Singing societies
USE   **Choral societies**

Single child
USE   **Only child**

Single men 155.6; 305.38
UF   Men, Single
Unmarried men
BT   **Men**
Single people
NT   **Widowers**

Single parent family 306.85
Use for materials on households in which a parent living without a partner is rearing children. Materials on parents who were not married at the time of the birth of their children are entered under **Unmarried fathers; Unmarried mothers.**
UF   Children of single parents
Fathers, Single parent
Mothers, Single parent
One parent family
Parents, Single
Parents without partners

BT = Broader Term   NT = Narrower Term   RT = Related Term   SA = See Also   UF = Used For

Single parent family—*Continued*
   Single parents
 BT **Family**
   Part-time parenting
 NT **Children of divorced parents**
 RT **Unmarried fathers**
   Unmarried mothers
   Widowers
   Widows
Single parents
 USE **Part-time parenting**
   Single parent family
Single people 155.6; 305.9
 UF Unmarried people
 NT **Single men**
   Single women
   Unmarried couples
 RT **Celibacy**
Single rail railroads
 USE **Monorail railroads**
Single women 155.6; 305.48
 UF Unmarried women
   Women, Single
 BT **Single people**
   Women
 NT **Widows**
Sirius 523.8
 BT **Stars**
Sisterhoods
 USE **Religious orders for women**
Sisters and brothers
 USE **Brothers and sisters**
Sisters (Religious)
 USE **Nuns**
Sit-down strikes
 USE **Strikes**
Sitcoms
 USE **Comedy television programs**
Site oriented art
 USE **Earthworks (Art)**
Sitters (Babysitters)
 USE **Babysitters**
Situation comedies
 USE **Comedy television programs**
Six Day War, 1967
 USE **Israel-Arab War, 1967**
Sixteenth century 909
 Use for general materials covering progress and development during this period in one or in several countries.

 UF 1500-1599 (16th century)
 BT **Renaissance**
 RT **Reformation**
Size and shape 516
 UF Large and small
   Shape
   Small and large
 SA names of geometric shapes,
    e.g. **Square;** to be added as
    needed
 BT **Concepts**
   Perception
 NT **Square**
Skating
 USE **Ice skating**
   Roller skating
Skeletal remains
 USE **Anthropometry**
Skeleton 591.4; 611
 Use for materials on the human or animal skeleton.
 BT **Musculoskeletal system**
 RT **Bones**
Skepticism 149; 186; 211
 UF Scepticism
   Unbelief
 BT **Free thought**
   Philosophy
   Rationalism
 RT **Agnosticism**
   Belief and doubt
   Faith
   Truth
Sketching
 USE **Drawing**
Skidoos
 USE **Snowmobiles**
Skiing 796.93
 UF Skiing, Snow
   Skis and skiing *[Former heading]*
 BT **Winter sports**
Skiing, Snow
 USE **Skiing**
Skiing, Water
 USE **Water skiing**
Skilled workers
 USE **Labor**
   Working class
Skills, Life
 USE **Life skills**

  BT = Broader Term NT = Narrower Term RT = Related Term SA = See Also UF = Used For

630

Skin 611; 612.7
   BT   **Anatomy**
         Physiology
Skin care
   USE   **Skin—Care and hygiene**
Skin—Care and hygiene 616.5; 646.7
   UF   Skin care
Skin—Diseases 616.5
   UF   Dermatitis
   SA   names of skin diseases, to be
         added as needed
   BT   **Diseases**
   NT   **Acne**
Skin diving 797.2
     Use for materials on free diving with
mask, fins, and snorkel. Materials on free
diving with the aid of a self-contained un-
derwater breathing apparatus are entered
under **Scuba diving.**
   UF   Diving, Skin
         Free diving
         Frogmen and frogwomen
         Snorkeling
         Underwater swimming
   BT   **Diving**
         Oceanography—Research
         Submarine diving
         Water sports
   NT   **Undersea research stations**
   RT   **Scuba diving**
         Underwater exploration
Skin garments
   USE   **Leather garments**
Skinheads
   USE   **White supremacy movements**
Skins
   USE   **Hides and skins**
Skis and skiing
   USE   **Skiing**
Skits 791
   BT   **Amusements**
         Theater
Sky 520; 551.5
   BT   **Astronomy**
         Atmosphere
   NT   **Constellations**
Sky diving
   USE   **Skydiving**
Sky hijacking
   USE   **Hijacking of airplanes**
Sky laboratories
   USE   **Space stations**

Skydiving 797.5
   UF   Sky diving
   BT   **Aeronautical sports**
Skyjacking
   USE   **Hijacking of airplanes**
Skyscrapers 690; 720
   UF   High rise buildings
   BT   **Architecture**
         Buildings
         Industrial buildings
         Office buildings
         Steel construction
Skyscrapers—Earthquake effects 690;
        725
   BT   **Buildings—Earthquake effects**
         Earthquakes
Slander (Law)
   USE   **Libel and slander**
Slang
   USE   names of languages with the
         subdivision *Slang*, e.g. **Eng-**
         lish language—Slang; to be
         added as needed
Slanted journalism
   USE   **Journalism—Objectivity**
Slapstick comedies
   USE   **Comedies**
         Comedy films
         Comedy television programs
Slave trade 341; 345; 380.1
   BT   **International law**
         Slavery
         Slavery—United States
Slavery (May subdiv. geog.) 177; 306.3;
        326; 342
   UF   Abolition of slavery
         Antislavery
         Compulsory labor
         Emancipation of slaves
         Forced labor
         Servitude
   BT   **Contract labor**
         Freedom
         Labor
         Sociology
   NT   **Slave trade**
         Slaves
   RT   **Peonage**
Slavery—United States 306.3; 326.0973
   UF   Emancipation of slaves

Slavery—United States—*Continued*
BT   United States—History—
     1861-1865, Civil War
NT   Abolitionists
     Slave trade
     State rights
RT   African Americans
     Southern States—History
     Underground railroad
Slavery—United States—Fiction 808.83;
     813, etc.

    May be used for individual works, collections, or materials about fiction dealing with slavery in the United States.
BT   Fiction
     Historical fiction
Slaves (May subdiv. geog.) 305.5
BT   Slavery
Sledding 796.9
UF   Sledges
     Sleds and sledding *[Former heading]*
     Sleighs
BT   Winter sports
Sledges
USE   Sledding
Sleds and sledding
USE   Sledding
Sleep 154.6; 612.8; 613.7
BT   Brain
     Health
     Hygiene
     Mind and body
     Psychophysiology
     Rest
     Subconsciousness
NT   Bedtime
RT   Dreams
     Insomnia
Sleeplessness
USE   Insomnia
Sleighs
USE   Sledding
Sleight of hand
USE   Juggling
     Magic tricks
Slide projectors
USE   Projectors
Slide rule 510.28
BT   Calculators

Logarithms
Slides (Photography) 778.2
UF   Color slides
     Lantern slides
     Photographic slides
BT   Photography
RT   Filmstrips
Slovakia 943.73
    May be subdivided like United States except for *History.*
RT   Czechoslovakia
Slow learning children 155.4; 371.92
    Use for materials on children with less than average intelligence and slow social development.
UF   Children, Retarded
     Retarded children
BT   Exceptional children
NT   Individualized instruction
     Learning disabilities
RT   Mentally handicapped children
Slum clearance
USE   Urban renewal
Slumber songs
USE   Lullabies
Small and large
USE   Size and shape
Small arms
USE   Firearms
Small business 338.6; 658.02
    Use for materials on small independent business enterprises.
UF   Business, Small
BT   Business
     Self-employed
NT   Entrepreneurship
     Home business
Small loans
USE   Personal loans
Smell 152.1
BT   Senses and sensation
RT   Nose
Smelting 669
BT   Furnaces
NT   Blast furnaces
     Electrometallurgy
     Ore dressing
RT   Metallurgy
Smoke-ending programs
USE   Smoking cessation programs
Smoke prevention 363.73; 628.5
UF   Prevention of smoke

Smoke prevention—*Continued*
    BT   **Sanitation**
Smoke stacks
    USE **Chimneys**
Smokeless powder
    USE **Gunpowder**
Smoking 178; 613.85
    NT   **Cigarettes**
          Cigars
          Marijuana
          Tobacco habit
          Tobacco pipes
    RT   **Tobacco**
Smoking cessation programs 613.85
    UF   How-to-stop-smoking pro-
          grams
          Quit-smoking programs
          Smoke-ending programs
    BT   **Tobacco habit**
Smuggling 364.1
    UF   Contraband trade
    BT   **Crime**
          Tariff
Smuggling of drugs
    USE **Drug traffic**
Snakes 597.96
    UF   Serpents
          Vipers
    SA   types of snakes, e.g. **Rattle-**
          snakes; to be added as
          needed
    BT   **Reptiles**
    NT   **Rattlesnakes**
Snorkeling
    USE **Skin diving**
Snow 551.57
    UF   Precipitation (Meteorology)
    BT   **Meteorology**
          Water
          Weather
    RT   **Blizzards**
          Storms
Snowmobiles 629.22; 796.94
    UF   Skidoos
    BT   **All terrain vehicles**
Soap 668
    BT   **Cleaning compounds**
    RT   **Detergents**
Soap box derbies 796.6
    BT   **Racing**

Soap carving
    USE **Soap sculpture**
Soap operas 791.44; 791.45
    May be used for individual works, col-
    lections, or materials about soap operas.
    BT   **Radio plays**
          Television plays
    RT   **Radio serials**
          Television serials
Soap sculpture 736
    UF   Soap carving
    BT   **Modeling**
          Sculpture
Soaring flight
    USE **Gliding and soaring**
Sobriquets
    USE **Nicknames**
Soccer 796.334
    BT   **Ball games**
          Football
          Sports
Social action 361.2
    UF   Action, Social
          Activism, Social
    SA   subjects with the subdivision
          Citizen participation, e.g.
          City planning—United
          States—Citizen participa-
          tion; to be added as needed
    BT   **Social policy**
          Social problems
    NT   **City planning—United**
          States—Citizen participation
    RT   **Social work**
Social adjustment 158; 303.3
    UF   Adjustment, Social
    BT   **Human behavior**
          Human relations
          Social psychology
    NT   **Socially handicapped**
Social alienation
    USE **Alienation (Social psychology)**
Social anthropology
    USE **Ethnology**
Social aspects
    USE subjects with the subdivision
          Social aspects, e.g. **Genetic**
          engineering—Social aspects;
          to be added as needed
Social behavior
    USE **Human behavior**

Social case work 361.3
- UF   Case work, Social
  - Family social work
- BT   **Social work**
- NT   **Parole**
  - **Probation**
- RT   **Counseling**

Social change 303.4; 909
- UF   Change, Social
  - Cultural change
  - Social evolution
- BT   **Anthropology**
  - **Social sciences**
  - **Sociology**
- NT   **Community development**
  - **Modernization**
  - **Urbanization**

Social classes 305.5; 323.3
- UF   Class distinction
  - Rank
  - Social distinctions
- BT   **Caste**
  - **Sociology**
- NT   **Aristocracy**
  - **Class consciousness**
  - **Elite (Social sciences)**
  - **Middle classes**
  - **Nobility**
  - **Upper classes**
  - **Working class**

Social compact
- USE   **Social contract**

Social conditions 306.09; 909

Use for materials on the social aspects of several of the following topics: labor, poverty, education, health, housing, recreation, moral conditions.
- UF   Social history
- SA   racial and ethnic groups, classes of persons, and names of countries, cities, etc., with the subdivision *Social conditions,* to be added as needed
- BT   **Social ethics**
  - **Sociology**
- NT   **African Americans—Social conditions**
  - **Blacks—Social conditions**
  - **Chicago (Ill.)—Social conditions**

- **Cost of living**
- **Counter culture**
- **Economic conditions**
- **Indians of North America— Social conditions**
- **Jews—Social conditions**
- **Labor**
- **Moral conditions**
- **Quality of life**
- **Social movements**
- **Social problems**
- **Social surveys**
- **Standard of living**
- **United States—Social conditions**
- **Urbanization**

Social conflict 303.6
- UF   Class conflict
  - Class struggle
  - Conflict, Social
- BT   **Social psychology**
  - **Sociology**
- NT   **Conflict of generations**
  - **Role conflict**

Social conformity
- USE   **Conformity**

Social contract 320.01; 320.1
- UF   Social compact
- BT   **Political science**
  - **Sociology**

Social customs
- USE   **Manners and customs**
  - and names of ethnic groups, countries, cities, etc., with the subdivision *Social life and customs,* e.g. **Indians of North America—Social life and customs; Jews—Social life and customs; United States—Social life and customs;** etc., to be added as needed

Social democracy
- USE   **Socialism**

Social distinctions
- USE   **Social classes**

Social drinking
- USE   **Drinking of alcoholic beverages**

BT = Broader Term   NT = Narrower Term   RT = Related Term   SA = See Also   UF = Used For

Social ecology
  USE **Human ecology**
Social equality
  USE **Equality**
Social ethics 170
  UF Ethics, Social
  BT **Ethics**
  NT **Bioethics**
      Citizenship
      Crime
      Friendship
      Political ethics
      Sexual ethics
      Social conditions
  RT **Social problems**
Social evolution
  USE **Social change**
Social group work 361.4; 362
  UF Group work, Social
  BT **Associations**
      Clubs
      Social work
Social groups 302.3; 305
  UF Group dynamics
      Groups, Social
  BT **Sociology**
  NT **Elite (Social sciences)**
      Leadership
      Social psychology
      Social values
Social history
  USE **Social conditions**
Social hygiene
  USE **Public health**
      Sexual hygiene
Social insurance
  USE **Social security**
Social isolation
  USE **Loneliness**
Social learning
  USE **Socialization**
Social life and customs
  USE **Manners and customs**
      and names of ethnic groups,
      countries, cities, etc., with
      the subdivision *Social life
      and customs,* e.g. **Indians of
      North America—Social life
      and customs; Jews—Social
      life and customs; United**

**States—Social life and cus-
toms;** etc., to be added as
needed
Social medicine (May subdiv. geog.)
      306.4; 362.1
  Use for materials on the study of social,
  genetic, and environmental influences on
  human disease and disability, as well as
  the promotion of health measures to pro-
  tect both the individual and the commu-
  nity.
  UF Medical care—Social aspects
      Medical sociology
      Medicine, Social
      Medicine—Social aspects
  BT **Medicine**
      Public health
      Public welfare
      Sociology
  NT **Hospices**
  RT **Medical ethics**
Social movements 303.4
  SA individual social movements,
      e.g. **Environmental move-
      ment;** to be added as need-
      ed
  BT **Social conditions**
      Social problems
      Social psychology
  NT **Anti-apartheid movement**
      Antinuclear movement
      Environmental movement
      Labor movement
      New Age movement
      Pro-choice movement
      Pro-life movement
      Sanctuary movement
      Survivalism
      White supremacy movements
Social planning
  USE **Social policy**
Social policy 361.6
  UF National planning
      Planning, National
      Social planning
      State planning
  SA names of countries, cities,
      etc., with the subdivision
      Social policy, to be added
      as needed
  NT **Land reform**

BT = Broader Term   NT = Narrower Term   RT = Related Term   SA = See Also   UF = Used For

Social policy—*Continued*
    Social action
    United States—Social policy
  RT Economic policy
Social problems 361.1
  UF Reform, Social
    Social reform
    Social welfare
  BT Social conditions
    Sociology
  NT Charities
    Children—Employment
    Church and social problems
    Community centers
    Crime
    Discrimination
    Divorce
    Ethnic relations
    Eugenics
    Homelessness
    Housing
    Illegitimacy
    Immigration and emigration
    Juvenile delinquency
    Prison reform
    Prostitution
    Public health
    Race discrimination
    Race relations
    Social action
    Social movements
    Social surveys
    Standard of living
    Substance abuse
    Suicide
    Unemployment
  RT Social ethics
Social problems and the church
  USE Church and social problems
Social problems in education
  USE Educational sociology
Social psychology 302
  UF Mass psychology
    Psychology, Social
  BT Human ecology
    Psychology
    Social groups
    Sociology
  NT Alienation (Social psychology)
    Attitude (Psychology)

    Class consciousness
    Discrimination
    Human relations
    Interviewing
    National characteristics
    Political psychology
    Popularity
    Social adjustment
    Social conflict
    Social movements
    Social role
    Violence
  RT Applied psychology
    Crowds
    Ethnopsychology
Social reform
  USE Social problems
Social role 302
  UF Role, Social
  BT Social psychology
  NT Role conflict
    Role playing
    Sex role
Social sciences 300
  Use for general and comprehensive materials dealing with the various branches of the social sciences, such as sociology, political science, economics, etc.
  UF Social studies
  BT Civilization
  NT Cross cultural studies
    Economics
    Gerontology
    History
    Human behavior
    Liberalism
    Political science
    Social change
    Social surveys
    Sociology
Social security 362; 368.4
  UF Insurance, Social
    Insurance, State and compulsory
    Insurance, Workers'
    Labor—Insurance
    Security, Social
    Social insurance
    State and insurance
  BT Pensions

BT = Broader Term   NT = Narrower Term   RT = Related Term   SA = See Also   UF = Used For

Social security—*Continued*

   NT   **Old age pensions**

          Workers' compensation

Social service

   USE **Social work**

Social settlements 361.7; 362.5

   UF Church settlements

         Neighborhood centers

         Settlements, Social

   SA names of settlements, e.g.

         Hull House; to be added as

         needed

   BT **Charities**

         Social work

         Welfare work in industry

   NT **Boys' clubs**

         Community centers

         Girls' clubs

         Hull House (Chicago, Ill.)

Social studies

   USE **Geography**

          History

          Social sciences

Social surveys (May subdiv. geog.) **301**

   Use for materials on the methods employed in conducting surveys of social and economic conditions of communities and also for surveys of individual regions or cities. In the latter case a second heading may be used for the name of a region or city followed by the subdivision *Social conditions.*

   UF Community surveys

   BT **Social conditions**

         Social problems

         Social sciences

   NT **Educational surveys**

Social surveys—United States 301

   UF United States—Social surveys

Social values 303.3

   Use for materials on the principles and standards of human interaction within a particular group.

   UF Group values

   BT **Human relations**

         Social groups

         Values

   RT **Quality of life**

Social welfare

   USE **Charities**

          Public welfare

          Social problems

Social work

Social work 361.3

   Use for materials on the methods employed in welfare work, public or private. Materials on privately supported welfare activities are entered under **Charities.** Materials on tax-supported welfare activities are entered under **Public welfare.**

   UF Philanthropy

         Social service

         Social welfare

         Welfare work

   SA social work with particular

         groups of people, e.g. **Social**

         work and the elderly; to be

         added as needed

   NT **Charities**

         Child welfare

         Community organization

         Crisis centers

         Group homes

         Hotlines (Telephone counseling)

         Public welfare

         Social case work

         Social group work

         Social settlements

         Social work with the elderly

         Welfare work in industry

   RT **Social action**

Social work with the elderly 362.6

   BT **Elderly**

         Social work

Socialism (May subdiv. geog.) **320.5; 335**

   UF Collectivism

         Social democracy

   BT **Economics**

         Political science

   NT **Collective settlements**

         Dialectical materialism

         Government ownership

         Industry—Government policy

         Labor unions

         Proletariat

         Utopias

   RT **Communism**

         Marxism

         National socialism

Socialism—United States 320.5; 335.00973

   UF United States—Socialism

Socialization 303.3

Use for materials on the process by which individuals acquire group values and learn to function effectively in society.

UF   Children—Socialization

Social learning

BT   **Acculturation**

Child rearing

Education

Sociology

NT   **Americanization**

Peer pressure

Socialization of industry

USE   **Government ownership**

Industry—Government policy

Socialized medicine

USE   **Medical charities**

National health insurance

State medicine

Socially handicapped 362

UF   Culturally deprived

Culturally handicapped

Disadvantaged

Underprivileged

BT   **Handicapped**

Social adjustment

NT   **Socially handicapped children**

Socially handicapped children 362.7

UF   Culturally deprived children

Culturally handicapped children

Disadvantaged children

Underprivileged children

BT   **Handicapped children**

Socially handicapped

Socials

USE   **Church entertainments**

Societies 060

UF   Learned societies

SA   types of societies, e.g. **Choral societies**; subjects with the subdivision *Societies,* e.g. **Agriculture—Societies;** and names of individual societies, to be added as needed

NT   **Agriculture—Societies**

Boys' clubs

Choral societies

Cooperative societies

Educational associations

Girls' clubs

Labor unions

Men—Societies

Parents' and teachers' associations

Secret societies

Women—Societies

RT   **Associations**

Clubs

Societies, Cooperative

USE   **Cooperative societies**

Society and art

USE   **Art and society**

Society and language

USE   **Sociolinguistics**

Society and religion

USE   **Religion and sociology**

Society, Nonliterate folk

USE   **Nonliterate folk society**

Society of Friends 289.6

UF   Friends, Society of

Quakers

BT   **Christian sects**

Society of Jesus

USE   **Jesuits**

Society, Primitive

USE   **Nonliterate folk society**

Society, Upper

USE   **Upper classes**

Sociobiology 304.5; 574.5

Use for materials on the biological basis of social behavior, especially as transmitted genetically.

UF   Biology—Social aspects

Biosociology

BT   **Comparative psychology**

Sociology

Sociolinguistics 306.4

Use for materials on the study of the social aspects of language, particularly linguistic behavior as determined by sociocultural factors.

UF   Language and society

Society and language

Sociology and language

BT   **Language and languages**

Sociology

Sociology 301

Use for systematic studies on the structure of society. General materials on sociology, political science, economics, etc., are entered under **Social sciences.**

Sociology—*Continued*

    SA   sociology of particular religions, e.g. **Christian sociology; to be added as needed**

    BT   **Social sciences**

    NT   **Aristocracy**
           Christian sociology
           Cities and towns
           Communication
           Educational sociology
           Equality
           Ethnic relations
           Ethnopsychology
           Family
           Human ecology
           Immigration and emigration
           Individualism
           Labor
           Marxism
           Nonliterate folk society
           Organizational sociology
           Population
           Race relations
           Religion and sociology
           Rural sociology
           Slavery
           Social change
           Social classes
           Social conditions
           Social conflict
           Social contract
           Social groups
           Social medicine
           Social problems
           Social psychology
           Socialization
           Sociobiology
           Sociolinguistics
           Urban sociology

    RT   **Civilization**
           Culture

Sociology and language
    USE **Sociolinguistics**

Sociology and religion
    USE **Religion and sociology**

Sociology, Christian
    USE **Christian sociology**

Sociology, Educational
    USE **Educational sociology**

Sociology of organizations
    USE **Organizational sociology**

Sociology of religion
    USE **Religion and sociology**

Sociology, Rural
    USE **Rural sociology**

Sociology, Urban
    USE **Urban sociology**

Sodium content of food
    USE **Food—Sodium content**

Softball 796.357
    BT   **Ball games**
           Baseball

Software, Computer
    USE **Computer software**

Software viruses
    USE **Computer viruses**

Soil conservation 631.4
    UF   Conservation of the soil
    BT   **Conservation of natural resources**
           Environmental protection
    RT   **Erosion**
           Soil erosion

Soil erosion 631.4
    UF   Top soil loss
    BT   **Erosion**
    RT   **Soil conservation**

Soil fertility
    USE **Soils**

Soil mechanics
    USE **Soils (Engineering)**

Soilless agriculture
    USE **Aeroponics**
           Hydroponics

Soils 631.4
    UF   Soil fertility
    BT   **Agriculture**
           Economic geology
    NT   **Clay**
           Compost
           Drainage
           Fertilizers and manures
           Irrigation
           Reclamation of land
           Soils (Engineering)
    RT   **Agricultural chemistry**

Soils—Bacteriology 631.4
    BT   **Sanitary engineering**
    RT   **Agricultural bacteriology**

Soils (Engineering) 620.1
- UF   Earthwork
-      Soil mechanics
- BT   **Foundations**
-      **Roads**
-      **Soils**
-      **Structural engineering**

Soils, Lunar
- USE   **Lunar soil**

Solace
- USE   **Consolation**

Solar batteries 621.31
- UF   Batteries, Solar
-      Solar cells
-      Sun powered batteries
- BT   **Electric batteries**
-      **Photovoltaic power generation**
-      **Solar radiation**

Solar cells
- USE   **Photovoltaic power generation**
-       **Solar batteries**

Solar eclipses 523.7
- UF   Eclipses, Solar *[Former heading]*
-      Sun—Eclipses
- BT   **Astronomy**

Solar energy 333.792; 621.47
- UF   Solar power
- BT   **Energy resources**
-      **Renewable energy resources**
-      **Solar radiation**
-      **Sun**
- NT   **Photovoltaic power generation**
-      **Solar engines**
-      **Solar heating**

Solar engines 621.47
- BT   **Engines**
-      **Solar energy**

Solar heat
- USE   **Solar heating**

Solar heating 621.47; 697
- UF   Solar heat
- SA   types of solar heating applications, e.g. **Solar homes;** to be added as needed
- BT   **Heating**
-      **Solar energy**
- NT   **Solar homes**

Solar homes 697; 728
- BT   **Domestic architecture**
-      **Houses**
-      **Solar heating**

Solar physics
- USE   **Sun**

Solar power
- USE   **Solar energy**

Solar radiation 523.7; 621.47
- UF   Radiation, Solar
-      Sun—Radiation
- BT   **Meteorology**
-      **Space environment**
- NT   **Greenhouse effect**
-      **Solar batteries**
-      **Solar energy**
-      **Sunspots**

Solar system 523.2
- SA   names of planets, e.g. **Saturn (Planet);** to be added as needed
- BT   **Astronomy**
-      **Stars**
- NT   **Asteroids**
-      **Comets**
-      **Earth**
-      **Meteors**
-      **Moon**
-      **Planets**
-      **Sun**

Solder and soldering
- USE   **Soldering**

Soldering 671.5
- UF   Brazing
-      Solder and soldering *[Former heading]*
- BT   **Metals**
-      **Metalwork**
-      **Plumbing**
- RT   **Welding**

Soldiers (May subdiv. geog.) 355.0092; 920
- UF   Army life
-      Soldiers' life
- SA   names of countries with the subdivision *Army—Military life,* to be added as needed
- BT   **Armies**
-      **Military personnel**
- NT   **Mercenary soldiers**
-      **Missing in action**

Soldiers—*Continued*
        United States. Army—
          Military life
  RT **Veterans**
Soldiers' handbooks
  USE **United States. Army—**
          Handbooks, manuals, etc.
Soldiers—Hygiena
  USE **Military health**
Soldiers' life
  USE **Soldiers**
       and names of countries with
       the subdivision *Army—*
       Military life, e.g. **United**
       States. Army—Military life;
       to be added as needed
Soldiers of fortune
  USE **Mercenary soldiers**
Soldiers' songs
  USE **War songs**
Soldiers—United States 355.0092; 920
  UF G.I.'s
       GIs
       United States—Soldiers
Solid geometry
  USE **Geometry**
Solid waste disposal
  USE **Refuse and refuse disposal**
Solids 530.4; 531; 541
  BT **Physical chemistry**
       Physics
Solitaire (Game) 795.4
  UF Patience (Game)
  BT **Card games**
Solitude
  USE **Loneliness**
Solution achievement
  USE **Problem solving**
Solvent abuse 362.29
  UF Aerosol sniffing
       Glue sniffing
       Inhalation abuse of solvents
       Paint sniffing
  BT **Substance abuse**
Somatology
  USE **Physical anthropology**
Sonar 621.389
  UF Echo ranging
       Sound navigation
  BT **Signals and signaling**

Sonata 784.18
  Use for musical scores and for materials on the sonata as a musical form.
  UF Sonatas *[Former heading]*
  BT **Musical form**
Sonatas
  USE **Sonata**
Song books
  USE **Songbooks**
Song writing
  USE **Composition (Music)**
       Popular music—Writing and
         publishing
Songbooks 782.42
  Use for general collections of songs intended for home, school, or community singing, largely secular in content, arranged principally for mixed voices and scored on two staves. Similar collections of sacred songs are entered under **Hymns.**
  UF Community songbooks
       Song books
  BT **Singing**
       Songs
  NT **School songbooks**
Songbooks, School
  USE **School songbooks**
Songs 782.42
  Use for collections of songs that include both words and music, and for materials about songs. Collections of songs that contain the words but not the music are entered under **Poetry—Collections.**
  SA types of songs, e.g. **Children's Songs;** songs of particular countries, e.g. **American songs;** subjects, classes of persons, and names of persons, corporate bodies, places, or wars, with the subdivision *Songs,* for collections or individual songs about the topic or entity named, e.g. **Cowhands—Songs; Surfing—Songs; United States Military Academy—Songs; World War, 1939-1945—Songs;** etc.; and names of individual songs, to be added as needed
  BT **Poetry**
       Vocal music

Songs—*Continued*
NT   **African songs**
     American songs
     Ballads
     Carols
     Children's songs
     Cowhands—Songs
     Folk songs
     Hymns
     Lullabies
     National songs
     Popular music
     School songbooks
     Sea songs
     Songbooks
     Spirituals (Songs)
     State songs
     Students' songs
     Surfing—Songs
     War songs

Songs, African
USE **African songs**
Songs, African American
USE **African American music**
Songs, American
USE **American songs**
Songs and music
USE subjects, classes of persons, and names of persons, corporate bodies, places, or wars, with the subdivision *Songs,* for collections or individual songs about the topic or entity named, e.g. **Cowhands—Songs; Surfing—Songs; United States Military Academy—Songs; World War, 1939-1945—Songs;** and ethnic groups with the subdivision *Music* for music of the group, e.g. **Indians of North America—Music;** to be added as needed
Songs for children
USE **Children's songs**
Songs, National
USE **National songs**
Songs, Popular
USE **Popular music**

Songwriters
USE **Composers**
     Lyricists
Sons and fathers
USE **Fathers and sons**
Sons and mothers
USE **Mothers and sons**
Soothsaying
USE **Divination**
Soporifics
USE **Narcotics**
Sorcery
USE **Magic**
     Occultism
     Witchcraft
Sororities
USE **Fraternities and sororities**
Sorrow
USE **Grief**
     Joy and sorrow
Soubriquets
USE **Nicknames**
Soul 128; 233
UF Spirit
BT **Future life**
     Man (Theology)
     Philosophy
NT **Immortality**
     Psychology
     Spiritual life
RT **Personality**
     Reincarnation
Sound 534; 620.2
UF Acoustics
BT **Music**
     Physics
     Pneumatics
     Radiation
NT **Architectural acoustics**
     Computer sound processing
     Hearing
     Noise
     Phonetics
     Sound effects
     Soundproofing
     Sounds
     Ultrasonics
     Vibration
RT **Music—Acoustics and physics**
Sound effects 534; 620.2
BT **Sound**

Sound insulation
USE **Soundproofing**
Sound navigation
USE **Sonar**
Sound processing, Computer
USE **Computer sound processing**
Sound recording
USE **Sound—Recording and repro-
ducing**
Sound—Recording and reproducing
621.389
Use for materials on the equipment or
the process by which sound is recorded.
Materials on sound recordings that em-
phasize the content of the recording rather
than the equipment, process, or format are
entered under **Sound recordings.** Materials
about the format are entered under the
format, e.g. **Compact discs.**
UF Sound recording
SA methods of recording, e.g.
**Magnetic recorders and re-
cording;** to be added as
needed
BT **Phonograph**
NT **Compact disc players**
High-fidelity sound systems
Intercommunication systems
Stereophonic sound systems
RT **Magnetic recorders and re-
cording**
Optical storage devices
Sound recordings
Sound recordings 621.389; 780.26
Use for general materials and for mate-
rials on sound recordings that emphasize
the content of the recording rather than
the format. Materials about the format are
entered under the format, e.g. **Compact
discs.** Materials about the equipment or
the process by which sound is recorded
are entered under **Sound—Recording and
reproducing.**
UF Audio cassettes
Audiotapes
Cassette tapes, Audio
Discography
Discs, Sound
Phonograph records
Recordings, Sound
Records, Phonograph
Tape recordings, Audio
SA types of sound recordings, e.g.
Compact discs; to be added
as needed

BT **Audiovisual materials**
NT **Compact discs**
Talking books
RT **Sound—Recording and repro-
ducing**
Sound waves 534; 620.2
BT **Vibration**
Waves
NT **Ultrasonic waves**
Soundproofing 620.2; 693.8
UF Insulation (Sound)
Sound insulation
BT **Architectural acoustics**
Sound
Sounds 534; 620.2
BT **Sound**
Soups 641.8
BT **Cooking**
South Africa 968
Use for materials on the Republic of
South Africa.
UF Africa, South
Republic of South Africa
Union of South Africa
BT **Africa**
Southern Africa
South Africa—History 968
**South Africa—Race relations
305.800968; 968**
BT **Race relations**
NT **Anti-apartheid movement**
Apartheid
South African Dutch
USE **Afrikaners**
South Africans, Afrikaans-speaking
USE **Afrikaners**
South America 980
BT **America**
South American literature
USE **Latin American literature**
South Atlantic States
USE **Atlantic States**
South Korea
USE **Korea (South)**
South Pacific region
USE **Oceania**
South Pole 998
BT **Polar regions**
RT **Antarctic regions**
South Sea Islands
USE **Oceania**

South Seas
USE **Oceania**

South (U.S.)
USE **Southern States**

Southeast Asia 959
Use for materials on Southeast Asia including Burma, Thailand, Malaysia, Singapore, Indonesia, Vietnam, Cambodia, Laos, and the Philippines.
UF Asia, Southeast
BT **Asia**

Southern Africa 968
Use for materials dealing collectively with the area south of the countries of Zaire and Tanzania. Southern Africa includes the political entities of Angola, Botswana, Comoros, Lesotho, Madagascar, Malawi, Mozambique, Namibia, South Africa, Swaziland, Zambia, and Zimbabwe. Materials on the Republic of South Africa are entered under **South Africa.**
UF Africa, Southern *[Former heading]*
BT **Africa**
NT **South Africa**

Southern lights
USE **Auroras**

Southern literature
USE **American literature—Southern States**

Southern States 975
UF South (U.S.)
BT **United States**

Southern States—African Americans
USE **African Americans—Southern States**

Southern States—Cooking
USE **Cooking—Southern States**

Southern States—History 975
BT **United States—History**
RT **Slavery—United States**

Southwest, New
USE **Southwestern States**

Southwest, Old
USE **Old Southwest**

Southwest Pacific region
USE **Oceania**

Southwestern States 979
Use for materials on that part of the United States that corresponds roughly with the old Spanish province of New Mexico, including the present Arizona, New Mexico, southern Colorado, Utah, Nevada, and California.

UF Southwest, New
BT **United States**

Sovereigns
USE **Kings, queens, rulers, etc.**
       Monarchy
       Roman emperors

Soviet artificial satellites 629.43; 629.46
UF Artificial satellites, Russian
       [Former heading]
       Artificial satellites, Soviet
       [Former heading]
       Sputniks
BT **Artificial satellites**

Soviet bloc
USE **Communist countries**

Soviet intervention in Czechoslovakia
USE **Czechoslovakia—History—1968-1989**

Soviet literature 890
Use for materials on several of the literatures of the Soviet Union. Materials on the individual literatures of the republics that made up the Soviet Union are entered with the appropriate adjective, e.g. **Russian literature;** etc.

UF Literatures of the Soviet Union
       Soviet Union—Literatures
       [Former heading]
BT **Literature**
RT **Russian literature**

Soviet people
USE **Soviets (People)**

Soviet Union 947.084; 947.085

Use for materials on the Union of Soviet Socialist Republics between 1917 and 1991. Materials on Russia or the Russian empire before 1917 are entered under **Russia.** Materials on the independent republic of Russia since its establishment in December 1991 are entered under **Russia (Republic).** Materials on several or all of the countries that emerged from the dissolution of the Soviet Union in 1991 are entered under **Former Soviet republics.** Material specifically on the federation of former Soviet republics that was established in December 1991 and does not include Georgia or the Baltic states are entered under **Commonwealth of Independent States.** The Baltic states and the other republics of the former Soviet Union are: Armenia; Azerbaijan; Belarus; Estonia; Georgia (Republic); Kazakhstan; Kyrgyzstan; Latvia; Lithuania; Moldova; Tajikistan; Turkmenistan; Ukraine; and Uzbekistan; to be added as needed. The adjective **Soviet** is used to refer to the Soviet Union as a whole between 1917 and 1991, e.g. **Soviet artificial satellites.** Materials on the citizens of the Soviet Union between 1917 and 1991 are entered under **Soviets (People).** Materials on topics pertaining to individual republics, nationalities, or ethnic groups of the former Soviet Union are to be added as needed with the appropriate qualifier, e.g., **Russians; Russian language;** etc.

UF   U.S.S.R.
      Union of Soviet Socialist Republics
      USSR

NT   **Russians**
      Soviets (People)

RT   **Commonwealth of Independent States**
      Former Soviet republics
      Russia
      Russia (Republic)

Soviet Union—Communism
USE **Communism—Soviet Union**

Soviet Union—History 947.084; 947.085
UF   Soviet Union—History—1917-
      [Former heading]

Soviet Union—History—1905, Revolution
USE **Russia—History—1905, Revolution**

Soviet Union—History—1917-
USE **Soviet Union—History**

Soviet Union—History—1917-1921, Revolution 947.084
UF   Revolution, Russian

      Russian revolution
BT   **Revolutions**

Soviet Union—History—1917-1925 947.084

Soviet Union—History—1925-1953 947.084

Soviet Union—History—1939-1940, War with Finland
USE **Russo-Finnish War, 1939-1940**

Soviet Union—History—1953-
USE **Soviet Union—History—1953-1991**

Soviet Union—History—1953-1985 947.085

Soviet Union—History—1953-1991 947.085
UF   Soviet Union—History—1953-
      [Former heading]

Soviet Union—History—1985-
USE **Soviet Union—History—1985-1991**

Soviet Union—History—1985-1991 947.085
UF   Soviet Union—History—1985-
      [Former heading]

Soviet Union—Literatures
USE **Soviet literature**

Soviets (People) 947.084

Use for materials on the citizens of the Soviet Union between 1917 and 1991, not limited to a single national or ethnic group. Materials on the individual ethnic groups of the former Soviet Union are entered under the name for the ethnic group, e.g. **Russians;** etc.

UF   Soviet people
BT   **Soviet Union**

Soybean 633.3
BT   **Forage plants**

Space age
USE **Astronautics and civilization**

Space and time 115
UF   Time and space
BT   **Fourth dimension**
      Metaphysics
      Space sciences
      Time
NT   **Personal space**
RT   **Relativity (Physics)**

Space-based weapons
USE **Space weapons**

Space biology 574.19; 612

Use for materials on the biology of humans or other earth creatures while in outer space. Materials on the possibility of indigenous life in outer space are entered under **Life on other planets.**

UF   Astrobiology
      Bioastronautics
      Cosmobiology
      Exobiology

BT   **Biology**
      Space sciences

NT   **Life on other planets**
      Space medicine

Space chemistry 523

UF   Cosmic chemistry
      Cosmochemistry

BT   **Chemistry**

Space colonies 629.44; 999

Use for materials on communities established in space or on natural extraterrestrial bodies. Materials on bases established on natural extraterrestrial bodies for specific functions other than colonization are entered under **Extraterrestrial bases.** Materials on manned installations orbiting in space for specific functions, such as servicing space ships, are entered under **Space stations.**

UF   Colonies, Space
      Communities, Space
      Outer space—Colonies

BT   **Astronautics and civilization**

RT   **Extraterrestrial bases**

Space commercialization

USE   **Space industrialization**

Space communication

USE   **Astronautics—Communication systems**
      Interstellar communication

Space craft

USE   **Space vehicles**

Space debris 629.4

UF   Debris, Space
      Junk in space
      Orbital debris
      Outer space—Pollution
      Pollution, Space
      Space pollution

BT   **Pollution**
      Space environment

Space environment 629.4

UF   Environment, Space

      Extraterrestrial environment
      Space weather

BT   **Astronomy**
      Outer space

NT   **Cosmic rays**
      Solar radiation
      Space debris

Space exploration (Astronautics)

USE   **Outer space—Exploration**

Space flight 629.4

Use for materials on the physics and technical details of flight beyond the earth's atmosphere. General materials and imaginary accounts of travel to other planets are entered under **Interplanetary voyages.**

UF   Humans in space
      Man in space
      Manned space flight
      People in space
      Rocket flight
      Space flight, Manned
      Space travel

SA   names of projects, e.g. **Gemini project;** and space flight to particular places, e.g. **Space flight to the moon;** to be added as needed

BT   **Aeronautics—Flights**
      Astronautics

NT   **Astronauts**
      Extravehicular activity (Space flight)
      Gemini project
      Orbital rendezvous (Space flight)
      Outer space—Exploration
      Space flight to the moon

RT   **Astrodynamics**
      Interplanetary voyages
      Navigation (Astronautics)
      Space medicine
      Space ships

Space flight (Fiction)

USE   **Imaginary voyages**
      Science fiction

Space flight—Law and legislation

USE   **Space law**

Space flight, Manned

USE   **Space flight**

Space flight to the moon 629.45

UF   Flight to the moon

BT = Broader Term   NT = Narrower Term   RT = Related Term   SA = See Also   UF = Used For

Space flight to the moon—*Continued*
Lunar expeditions
Moon, Voyages to
Voyages to the moon
BT **Astronautics**
Space flight
NT **Apollo project**
Moon—Exploration
Space gardening
USE **Aeroponics**
Space heaters 644; 697
BT **Heating**
NT **Fireplaces**
Stoves
Space industrial processing
USE **Space industrialization**
Space industrialization 629.44
UF Commercial endeavors in
space
Industrial uses of space
Manufacturing in space
Space commercialization
Space industrial processing
Space manufacturing
Space stations—Industrial ap-
plications
BT **Industrialization**
Space laboratories
USE **Space stations**
Space law 341.4
UF Aerospace law
Artificial satellites—Law and
legislation
Astronautics—Law and legis-
lation
Law, Space
Space flight—Law and legisla-
tion
Space stations—Law and leg-
islation
BT **Astronautics and civilization**
International law
Law
Space manufacturing
USE **Space industrialization**
Space medicine 616.9
UF Aerospace medicine
Bioastronautics
BT **Medicine**
Space biology

Space sciences
NT **Life support systems (Space
environment)**
Weightlessness
RT **Aviation medicine**
Space flight
Space navigation
USE **Navigation (Astronautics)**
Space nutrition
USE **Astronauts—Nutrition**
Space optics 535
BT **Optics**
Space sciences
NT **Astronautical instruments**
Astronomical instruments
RT **Optical instruments**
Remote sensing
Space orbital rendezvous
USE **Orbital rendezvous (Space
flight)**
Space, Outer
USE **Outer space**
Space, Personal
USE **Personal space**
Space photography 778.3
UF Astronautics, Photography in
Photography in astronautics
Photography, Space
SA objects with the subdivision
Photographs from space,
e.g. **Earth—Photographs
from space;** to be added as
needed
BT **Photography**
**Photography—Scientific appli-
cations**
NT **Earth—Photographs from
space**
Lunar photography
**Moon—Photographs from
space**
Space platforms
USE **Space stations**
Space pollution
USE **Space debris**
Space power
USE **Astronautics and civilization**
Space probes 629.43
Use for materials on space exploration
by remote control from earth.

Space probes—*Continued*

UF Probes, Space

SA types of probes, e.g. **Lunar probes; Mars probes;** etc.; and names of space vehicles and space projects, e.g. **Project Voyager;** to be added as needed

BT **Outer space—Exploration**
   Space vehicles

NT **Lunar probes**
   Mars probes

Space rescue operations 629.45

UF Manned space flight—Rescue work
   Rescue operations, Space
   Space ships—Rescue work

BT **Rescue work**

Space research

USE **Outer space—Exploration**
   Space sciences

Space rockets

USE **Space vehicles**

Space sciences 500.5

Use for general materials and for scientific results of space exploration and scientific applications of space flight.

UF Science and space
   Space research

BT **Science**

NT **Outer space**
   Space and time
   Space biology
   Space medicine
   Space optics

RT **Astronautics**
   Astronomy

Space sciences—International cooperation 500.5

Space ships 629.45

Use for materials limited to space vehicles with people on board. Comprehensive materials on spacecraft are entered under **Space vehicles.**

BT **Astronautics**
   Life support systems (Space environment)
   Rocketry
   Space vehicles

NT **Orbital rendezvous (Space flight)**

   Rocket planes

RT **Interplanetary voyages**
   Space flight

Space ships—Accidents

USE **Astronautics—Accidents**

Space ships—Pilots

USE **Astronauts**

Space ships—Rescue work

USE **Space rescue operations**

Space shuttles 629.44

Use for materials on reusable vehicles that transport equipment and personnel in space.

UF Reusable space vehicles
   Shuttles, Space
   Space vehicles, Reusable

SA names of individual space shuttles, to be added as needed

BT **Space vehicles**

NT **Challenger (Space shuttle)**

Space stations 629.44

Use for materials on manned installations orbiting in space for specific functions, such as servicing space ships. Materials on bases established on natural extraterrestrial bodies for specific functions other than colonization are entered under **Extraterrestrial bases.** Materials on communities established in space or on natural extraterrestrial bodies are entered under **Space colonies.**

UF Laboratories, Space
   Orbital laboratories
   Orbiting vehicles
   Sky laboratories
   Space laboratories
   Space platforms

BT **Artificial satellites**
   Astronautics
   Space vehicles

NT **Orbital rendezvous (Space flight)**

Space stations—Industrial applications

USE **Space industrialization**

Space stations—Law and legislation

USE **Space law**

Space suits

USE **Astronauts—Clothing**

Space telecommunication

USE **Interstellar communication**

Space television

USE **Television in astronautics**

BT = Broader Term NT = Narrower Term RT = Related Term SA = See Also UF = Used For

Space travel
USE **Interplanetary voyages**
Space flight
Space vehicles 629.47
Use for comprehensive materials on spacecraft. Materials limited to space vehicles with people on board are entered under **Space ships.**
UF Space craft
Space rockets
Spacecraft
BT **Rocketry**
NT **Lunar excursion module**
Space probes
Space ships
Space shuttles
Space stations
RT **Artificial satellites**
Astronautics
Space vehicles—Accidents
USE **Astronautics—Accidents**
Space vehicles—Extravehicular activity
USE **Extravehicular activity (Space flight)**
Space vehicles—Guidance systems 629.47
Space vehicles—Instruments
USE **Astronautical instruments**
Space vehicles—Piloting 629.45
UF Piloting (Astronautics)
BT **Astronauts**
Navigation (Astronautics)
Space vehicles—Propulsion systems 629.47
Space vehicles—Recovery 629.4
UF Recovery of space vehicles
Space vehicles, Reusable
USE **Space shuttles**
Space vehicles—Thermodynamics 629.47
BT **Thermodynamics**
Space vehicles—Tracking 629.4
UF Tracking of satellites
Space walk
USE **Extravehicular activity (Space flight)**
Space warfare 358
Use for materials on interplanetary warfare, attacks on earth from outer space, and warfare among the nations of earth in outer space.

UF Earth—Space attack and defense
Interplanetary warfare
Interstellar warfare
Space wars
War, Space
Warfare, Space
BT **Outer space**
NT **Space weapons**
Strategic Defense Initiative
Space wars
USE **Space warfare**
Space weapons 358
UF Space-based weapons
Star Wars weapons
Weapons, Space
BT **Military weapons**
Space warfare
RT **Strategic Defense Initiative**
Space weather
USE **Space environment**
Spacecraft
USE **Space vehicles**
Spain 946
May be subdivided like United States except for *History.*
Spain—History 946
NT **Spanish Armada, 1588**
Spain—History—1898, War of 1898
USE **Spanish-American War, 1898**
Spain—History—1936-1939, Civil War 946.081
Spain—History—1939-1975 946.082
Spain—History—1975- 946.083
Spanish America
USE **Latin America**
Spanish American literature
USE **American literature (Spanish)**
Spanish-American War, 1898 973.8
UF American-Spanish War, 1898
Hispano-American War, 1898
Spain—History—1898, War of 1898
United States—History—1898, War of 1898 *[Former heading]*
BT **United States—History—1865-1898**
United States—History—1898-1919

Spanish Armada, 1588 942.05; 946
    UF   Armada, 1588 *[Former heading]*
           Invincible Armada
    BT   **Great Britain—History—**
          1485-1603, Tudors
          Spain—History
Spanish language 460
    May be subdivided like **English language.**
    BT   **Romance languages**
Spanish literature 860
    May use same subdivisions and names of literary forms as for **English literature.**
    BT   **Literature**
          Romance literature
    RT   **Latin American literature**
Spanish literature—Hispanic American authors
    USE   **American literature (Spanish)**
Sparring
    USE   **Boxing**
Spas
    USE   **Health resorts**
Spastic paralysis
    USE   **Cerebral palsy**
Speakers (Recitation books)
    USE   **Recitations**
Speaking
    USE   **Debates and debating**
          Lectures and lecturing
          Preaching
          Public speaking
          Rhetoric
          Voice
Speaking choirs
    USE   **Choral speaking**
Spear fishing 799.1
    BT   **Fishing**
Special collections in libraries
    USE   **Libraries—Special collections**
Special education 371.9
    UF   Education, Special
    SA   classes of exceptional children with the subdivision *Education,* to be added as needed
    BT   **Education**
    NT   **Mentally handicapped children—Education**
    RT   **Mainstreaming in education**

Special libraries 026; 027.6
    Use for materials on libraries covering specialized subjects, containing special format materials, or serving a specialized clientele.
    UF   Libraries, Special
    SA   types of special libraries, e.g. **Business libraries;** to be added as needed
    BT   **Libraries**
    NT   **Business libraries**
          Corporate libraries
          Government libraries
          Music libraries
Special Olympics 796.087
    UF   Olympics, Special
    BT   **Olympic games**
          Sports for the handicapped
Specialists exchange programs
    USE   **Exchange of persons programs**
Specie
    USE   **Money**
Specimens, Preservation of
    USE   **Plants—Collection and preservation**
          Taxidermy
          Zoological specimens— Collection and preservation
          and types of natural specimens with the subdivision *Collection and preservation,* e.g. **Birds—Collection and preservation;** to be added as needed
Spectacles
    USE   **Eyeglasses**
Specters
    USE   **Apparitions**
          Ghosts
Spectra
    USE   **Spectrum analysis**
Spectrochemical analysis
    USE   **Spectrum analysis**
Spectrochemistry
    USE   **Spectrum analysis**
Spectroscopy
    USE   **Spectrum analysis**
Spectrum analysis 535.8
    UF   Analysis, Spectrum
          Spectra

BT = Broader Term   NT = Narrower Term   RT = Related Term   SA = See Also   UF = Used For

Spectrum analysis—*Continued*
>Spectrochemical analysis
>Spectrochemistry
>Spectroscopy
>BT **Astronomy**
>**Astrophysics**
>**Chemistry**
>**Optics**
>**Radiation**
>NT **Mass spectrometry**
>RT **Light**

Speculation 332.64
>BT **Finance**
>NT **Real estate investment**
>RT **Investments**
>**Stock exchange**

Speech 302.2; 372.6; 410; 612.7
>BT **Language arts**
>NT **Speech disorders**
>**Speech processing systems**
>**Speech therapy**
>RT **Language and languages**
>**Phonetics**
>**Voice**

Speech correction
>USE **Speech therapy**

Speech disorders 616.85
>UF Defective speech
>Speech pathology
>Stammering
>Stuttering
>BT **Speech**

Speech, Freedom of
>USE **Freedom of speech**

Speech pathology
>USE **Speech disorders**

Speech processing systems 006.5
>UF Computer speech processing systems
>Electronic speech processing systems
>Speech scramblers
>Speech synthesis
>BT **Speech**
>**Telecommunication**
>NT **Automatic speech recognition**
>RT **Computer sound processing**

Speech recognition, Automatic
>USE **Automatic speech recognition**

Speech scramblers
>USE **Speech processing systems**

Speech synthesis
>USE **Speech processing systems**

Speech therapy 616.85
>UF Speech correction
>BT **Speech**

Speeches 808.85; 815.008, etc.
>UF Addresses
>Orations
>Speeches, addresses, etc. *[Former heading]*
>SA speeches of particular countries, e.g. **American speeches**; to be added as needed
>BT **Literature**
>NT **After dinner speeches**
>**American speeches**
>**English speeches**
>**Lectures and lecturing**
>**Presidents—United States—Inaugural addresses**
>**Toasts**

Speeches, addresses, etc.
>USE **Speeches**

Speeches, addresses, etc., American
>USE **American speeches**

Speeches, addresses, etc., English
>USE **English speeches**

Speed 531
>UF Velocity
>BT **Motion**

Speed (Drug)
>USE **Methamphetamine**

Speed reading
>USE **Rapid reading**

Speed, Supersonic
>USE **Supersonic aerodynamics**

Speleology
>USE **Caves**

Spellers 418; 428.1, etc.
>BT **English language—Spelling**

Spelling
>USE names of languages with the subdivision *Spelling,* e.g. **English language—Spelling;** to be added as needed

Spelling reform 418; 428.1, etc.
>UF English language—Spelling reform
>Orthography
>Phonetic spelling

Spelling reform—*Continued*
   BT   **English language—Spelling**
Spells
   USE **Charms**
          Magic
Spherical trigonometry
   USE **Trigonometry**
Spices 641.3
   SA   names of spices, to be added
          as needed
Spiders 595.4
   UF   Arachnida
   BT   **Invertebrates**
Spies 327.12; 355.3
   UF   Intelligence agents
          Spying
   BT   **Espionage**
          Subversive activities
   RT   **Secret service**
Spinal paralysis, Anterior
   USE **Poliomyelitis**
Spinning 677; 746.1
   BT   **Textile industry**
Spiral gearing
   USE **Gearing**
Spires 721
   UF   Steeples
   BT   **Architecture**
          Church architecture
Spirit
   USE **Soul**
Spirit, Holy
   USE **Holy Spirit**
Spiritism
   USE **Spiritualism**
Spirits
   USE **Angels**
          Apparitions
          Demonology
          Ghosts
          Spiritualism
          Witchcraft
Spirits, Alcoholic
   USE **Liquors**
Spiritual healing 615.8
   Use for materials on the use of faith, prayer, or other religious means to treat illness. Materials on psychic or psychological means to treat illness are entered under **Mental healing.**
   UF   Divine healing

          Evangelistic healing
          Faith cure
          Faith healing
          Healing, Spiritual
   BT   **Medicine and religion**
          Mind and body
   NT   **Miracles**
   RT   **Christian Science**
          Mental healing
          Subconsciousness
          Suggestive therapeutics
Spiritual life 248
   Use for materials on spiritual practices and on the relationship that individuals may attain with the sacred.
   BT   **Soul**
          Theology
   NT   **Faith**
          Hope
          Meditation
          Sanctification
   RT   **Mysticism**
          Religious life
Spiritualism 133.9
   UF   Spiritism
          Spirits
   BT   **Future life**
          Occultism
          Supernatural
   NT   **Clairvoyance**
          Psychokinesis
   RT   **Apparitions**
          Ghosts
          Parapsychology
Spirituals (Songs) 782.25
   BT   **American songs**
          Folk songs—United States
          Hymns
          Songs
   RT   **African American music**
          Gospel music
Splicing
   USE **Knots and splices**
Splicing of genes
   USE **Genetic engineering**
Split personality
   USE **Multiple personality**
Spoils system
   USE **Political corruption**
Sponges 593.4
   BT   **Invertebrates**

Spontaneous abortion
USE **Miscarriage**
Sport cars
USE **Sports cars**
Sports (May subdiv. geog.) **796**
SA types of sports and names of
sports competitions, to be
added as needed
BT **Play**
Recreation
NT **Aeronautical sports**
Baseball
Basketball
Bullfights
Coaching (Athletics)
College sports
Cycling
Drugs and sports
Field hockey
Football
Gymnastics
Olympic games
Orienteering
Professional sports
Racing
Rodeos
Rowing
School sports
Soccer
Sports cards
Sports records
Sportsmanship
Tennis
Track athletics
Water sports
Winter sports
RT **Amusements**
Athletes
Athletics
Games
Outdoor life
Physical education
Sports facilities
Sports and drugs
USE **Drugs and sports**
Sports cards 769
UF Cards, Sports
SA types of cards for specific
sports, e.g. **Baseball cards;**
to be added as needed

BT **Sports**
NT **Baseball cards**
Sports cars 629.222
UF Sport cars
SA names of specific sports cars,
to be added as needed
BT **Automobiles**
Sports coaching
USE **Coaching (Athletics)**
Sports—Corrupt practices 796
UF Cheating in sports
Corruption in sports
Sports scandals
Sports drama (Films) 791.43
May be used for individual works, col-
lections, or materials about sports drama
on film.
BT **Motion pictures**
Sports drama (Radio programs) 791.44
May be used for individual works, col-
lections, or materials about sports drama
on the radio.
BT **Radio programs**
**Sports drama (Television programs)
791.45**
May be used for individual works, col-
lections, or materials about sports drama
on television.
BT **Television programs**
**Sports—Equipment and supplies
796.028**
Sports facilities 796.06
SA types of sports facilities, to be
added as needed
NT **Playgrounds**
Stadiums
Swimming pools
RT **Recreation**
Sports
Sports—Fiction
USE **Sports stories**
Sports for the handicapped 796.01
BT **Handicapped**
NT **Special Olympics**
Sports—Medical aspects
USE **Sports medicine**
Sports medicine 613.7; 617.1
UF Athletic medicine
Physical education—Medical
aspects
Sports—Medical aspects

BT = Broader Term   NT = Narrower Term   RT = Related Term   SA = See Also   UF = Used For

Sports medicine—*Continued*
   BT   Medical care
        Medicine
   NT   Drugs and sports
Sports records 796
   Use for materials on top performances or achievements.
   UF   Records, Sports
   BT   Sports
   RT   Sports—Statistics
        World records
Sports scandals
   USE   Sports—Corrupt practices
Sports—Statistics 796
   SA   names of individual sports with the subdivision *Statistics,* to be added as needed
   RT   Sports records
Sports stories 808.83; 813, etc.
   May be used for individual works, collections, or materials about sports stories.
   UF   Sports—Fiction
   SA   particular kinds of sports stories, e.g. **Baseball stories;** to be added as needed
   BT   Fiction
   NT   Baseball stories
Sportsmanship 175
   BT   Human behavior
        Sports
Spot welding
   USE   Electric welding
Spouses
   USE   Husbands
        Wives
Spraying and dusting 632
   UF   Dusting and spraying
   BT   Agricultural pests
        Fruit—Diseases and pests
   NT   Aeronautics in agriculture
   RT   Fungicides
        Herbicides
        Insecticides
Spread sheets, Electronic
   USE   Electronic spreadsheets
Spreadsheeting, Electronic
   USE   Electronic spreadsheets
Spreadsheets, Electronic
   USE   Electronic spreadsheets
Spun glass
   USE   Glass fibers

Sputniks
   USE   Soviet artificial satellites
Spy films 791.43
   May be used for individual works, collections, or materials about spy films.
   UF   Espionage films
        Suspense films
   BT   Motion pictures
   RT   Mystery films
Spy novels
   USE   Spy stories
Spy radio programs 791.44
   May be used for individual works, collections, or materials about spy radio programs.
   UF   Suspense programs
   BT   Radio programs
Spy stories 808.83; 813, etc.
   May be used for individual works, collections, or materials about spy stories.
   UF   Espionage stories
        Spy novels
   BT   Adventure fiction
   RT   Mystery fiction
        Romantic suspense novels
Spy television programs 791.45
   May be used for individual works, collection, or materials about spy television programs.
   UF   Espionage television programs
        Suspense programs
   BT   Television programs
   RT   Mystery television programs
Spying
   USE   Espionage
        Spies
Square 516
   BT   Geometry
        Size and shape
Square dancing 793.3
   BT   Folk dancing
Square root 513.2
   BT   Arithmetic
Squirrels 599.32
   BT   Mammals
   NT   Chipmunks
SSTs
   USE   Supersonic transport planes
St. Bartholomew's Day, Massacre of, 1572
   USE   Saint Bartholomew's Day, Massacre of, 1572

BT = Broader Term   NT = Narrower Term   RT = Related Term   SA = See Also   UF = Used For

St. Dominic, Order of
USE **Dominicans (Religious order)**
St. Francis, Order of
USE **Franciscans**
St. Valentine's Day
USE **Valentine's Day**
Stabilization in industry
USE **Business cycles**
Economic conditions
Stadia
USE **Stadiums**
Stadiums 796.06
UF Ballparks
Stadia
BT **Sports facilities**
Stage
USE **Acting**
Actors
Drama
Theater
Stage lighting 792
UF Television—Stage lighting
Theaters—Stage lighting
BT **Lighting**
Stage scenery
USE **Theaters—Stage setting and
scenery**
Stage setting
USE **Theaters—Stage setting and
scenery**
Stagecoaches
USE **Carriages and carts**
Stained glass
USE **Glass painting and staining**
Stamina, Physical
USE **Physical fitness**
Stammering
USE **Speech disorders**
Stamp collecting 769.56
Use for materials on the collecting, buy-
ing, and selling of postage stamps.
UF Philately
Postage stamp collecting
Postage stamps—Collectors
and collecting *[Former
heading]*
BT **Collectors and collecting**
RT **Postage stamps**
Stamps, Postage
USE **Postage stamps**

Standard book numbers
USE **Publishers' standard book
numbers**
Standard of living 339.4
UF Living, Standard of
BT **Quality of life**
Social conditions
Social problems
Wealth
NT **Cost of living**
Standard of value
USE **Money**
Standard time
USE **Time**
Standards of output
USE **Production standards**
Star Wars (Ballistic missile defense sys-
tem)
USE **Strategic Defense Initiative**
Star Wars films 791.43
May be used for individual works, col-
lections, or materials about Star Wars
films.
BT **Motion pictures**
Science fiction films
Star Wars weapons
USE **Space weapons**
Stars 523.8
SA names of constellations and of
individual stars, e.g. **Sirius;**
to be added as needed
NT **Astrophysics**
Black holes (Astronomy)
Galaxies
Meteors
Sirius
Solar system
Supernovas
RT **Astrology**
Astronomy
Constellations
Planets
Stars—Atlases 523.8022
UF Astronomy—Atlases
Atlases, Astronomical
BT **Atlases**
Stars, Falling
USE **Meteors**
Starting a business
USE **New business enterprises**

Starvation 363.8
- NT   **Famines**
- RT   **Fasting**
       Hunger
       Malnutrition

Starvation, Self-imposed
- USE   **Anorexia nervosa**

State aid to education 379
- UF   Education—State aid
- BT   **Education—Finance**
       Education—Government policy

State aid to libraries 021.8
- UF   Libraries—State aid
- BT   **Libraries—Government policy**
       Library finance

State and agriculture
- USE   **Agricultural subsidies**
       Agriculture—Government policy

State and church
- USE   **Church and state**

State and education
- USE   **Education—Government policy**

State and energy
- USE   **Energy resources—Government policy**

State and environment
- USE   **Environmental policy**

State and industry
- USE   **Industry—Government policy**

State and insurance
- USE   **Social security**

State and railroads
- USE   **Railroads—Government policy**

State and science
- USE   **Science—Government policy**

State and the arts
- USE   **Arts—Government policy**
       Federal aid to the arts

State birds 598
- BT   **Birds**
       State emblems

State church
- USE   **Church and state**

State constitutions 342
- UF   Constitutions, State *[Former heading]*
- SA   names of states with the subdivision *Constitution,* to be added as needed

- BT   **Constitutions**
       Political science
- NT   **Ohio—Constitution**
- RT   **State governments**

State debts
- USE   **Public debts**

State emblems (May subdiv. geog.) **929.9**
- UF   Emblems, State
       State symbols
- SA   types of state emblems and state symbols, e.g. **State birds; State flowers;** to be added as needed
- BT   **Signs and symbols**
- NT   **State birds**
       State flowers
- RT   **National emblems**

State encouragement of the arts
- USE   **Arts—Government policy**
       Federal aid to the arts

State-federal relations
- USE   **Federal-state relations**

State flowers 582.13
- UF   Flowers, State
- BT   **Flowers**
       State emblems

State governments 353.9

Use for general materials on state government. Materials on the government of a particular state are entered under the name of the state with the subdivision *Politics and government.*

- UF   United States—State governments
- SA   names of states with the subdivision *Politics and government,* to be added as needed
- BT   **Political science**
- NT   **Federal-state relations**
       Governors
       Ohio—Politics and government
       State-local relations
- RT   **Federal government**
       State constitutions

State, Heads of
- USE   **Heads of state**

BT = Broader Term   NT = Narrower Term   RT = Related Term   SA = See Also   UF = Used For

State libraries 027.5

Use for materials on government libraries, maintained by state funds, that preserve state records and publications for use by state officials and residents.

UF   Libraries, State

BT   **Government libraries**

State-local relations 342 ; 351.09

UF   City-state relations

      Local-state relations

BT   **Local government**

      Municipal government

      State governments

State-local tax relations

USE **Intergovernmental tax relations**

State medicine 362.1; 368.4; 614

Use for general materials on the relations of the state to medicine, public health, medical legislation, examinations of physicians by state boards, etc.

UF   Medicine, State *[Former heading]*

      National health service

      Socialized medicine

BT   **Medicine**

NT   **Medical jurisprudence**

      Public health

RT   **National health insurance**

State of the Union messages

USE **Presidents—United States—Messages**

State ownership

USE **Government ownership**

State ownership of railroads

USE **Railroads—Government policy**

State planning

USE **Regional planning**

      Social policy

      and names of states with the subdivision *Economic policy* or *Social policy,* e.g.

      Ohio—Economic policy;

      Ohio—Social policy; etc., to be added as needed

State police 351.74

UF   Police, State *[Former heading]*

BT   **Police**

State regulation of industry

USE **Industry—Government policy**

State rights 321.02; 342

UF   Secession

      States' rights

BT   **Political science**

      Slavery—United States

State songs 782.42

BT   **Songs**

State symbols

USE **State emblems**

State, The 320.1

UF   Administration

      Commonwealth, The

      Welfare state

NT   **Church and state**

      Public interest

RT   **Political science**

States, New

USE **New states**

States' rights

USE **State rights**

Statesmen (May subdiv. geog.) **920**

NT   **Diplomats**

      Heads of state

      Politicians

Statics 531

BT   **Mechanics**

      Physics

NT   **Hydrostatics**

      Strains and stresses

RT   **Dynamics**

Statistical inference

USE **Probabilities**

Statistics 001.4; 310

Use for materials on the theory and methods of statistics.

SA   subjects and names of countries, cities, etc., with the subdivision *Statistics,* to be added as needed

BT   **Economics**

NT   **Agriculture—Statistics**

      Average

      Census

      Chicago (Ill.)—Statistics

      Probabilities

      Sampling (Statistics)

      United States—Statistics

      Vital statistics

Statistics—Graphic methods 001.4

UF   Diagrams, Statistical

BT   **Graphic methods**

Statues

USE **Monuments**

Statues—*Continued*
   Sculpture
Statutes
 USE Law
Stealing 364.1
 UF Larceny
   Theft
 BT Crime
 NT Shoplifting
 RT Thieves
Steam 536; 621.1
 BT Heat
   Power (Mechanics)
   Water
 RT Steam engineering
Steam engineering 621.1
 BT Engineering
 NT Steam engines
   Steam navigation
   Steam power plants
 RT Mechanical engineering
   Steam
Steam engines 621.1
 BT Engines
   Heat engines
   Machinery
   Mechanics
   Steam engineering
 NT Condensers (Steam)
   Locomotives
   Marine engines
   Steam turbines
Steam fitting
 USE Pipe fitting
Steam heating 697
 BT Heating
Steam navigation 387; 623.8
 UF Navigation, Steam
 BT Steam engineering
   Transportation
 NT Marine engineering
   Steam turbines
 RT Navigation
   Steamboats
Steam power plants 621.1
 UF Power plants, Steam
 BT Power plants
   Steam engineering
Steam pumps
 USE Pumping machinery

Steam turbines 621.1
 BT Steam engines
   Steam navigation
   Turbines
Steamboats 387.2; 623.8
 UF Steamships
 BT Boats and boating
   Naval architecture
   Ocean travel
   Shipbuilding
   Ships
 RT Steam navigation
Steamships
 USE Steamboats
Steel 669; 672
 BT Iron
   Metalwork
 NT Steel construction
   Structural steel
Steel construction 693
 UF Architectural engineering
   Building, Iron and steel *[For-*
     mer heading]
   Iron and steel building
 BT Architecture
   Building
   Engineering
   Iron
   Steel
 NT Skyscrapers
 RT Strength of materials
   Structural steel
   Theory of structures
Steel engraving
 USE Engraving
Steel industry 338.4; 672
 UF Steel industry and trade *[For-*
     mer heading]
   Steel trade
 BT Industry
 RT Iron industry
Steel industry and trade
 USE Steel industry
Steel industry—Labor productivity 338.4
 BT Labor productivity
Steel industry—Quality control 338.4;
   672
 BT Quality control
Steel, Structural
 USE Structural steel

BT = Broader Term NT = Narrower Term RT = Related Term SA = See Also UF = Used For

658

Steel trade
  USE **Steel industry**
Steeples
  USE **Spires**
Steers
  USE **Beef cattle**
Stencil work 686.2; 745.7
  BT **Decoration and ornament**
      Painting
  NT **Silk screen printing**
Stenography
  USE **Shorthand**
Step-family
  USE **Stepfamily**
Stepfamilies
  USE **Stepfamily**
Stepfamily 306.85
  UF Blended family
      Step-family
      Stepfamilies
  BT **Family**
Stereo photography
  USE **Three dimensional photography**
Stereo sound systems
  USE **Stereophonic sound systems**
Stereophonic sound systems 621.389
  UF Stereo sound systems
  BT **High-fidelity sound systems**
      Sound—Recording and reproducing
Stereophotography
  USE **Three dimensional photography**
Stereoscopic photography
  USE **Three dimensional photography**
Sterility in animals
  USE **Infertility**
Sterility in humans
  USE **Infertility**
Sterilization (Birth control) 363.9; 613.9
  BT **Birth control**
  NT **Vasectomy**
Steroids 574.19; 612
  UF Anabolic steroids
  BT **Biochemistry**
      Drugs
  RT **Athletes—Drug use**
      Hormones

Stewardesses, Airline
  USE **Flight attendants**
Stewards, Airline
  USE **Flight attendants**
Stills
  USE **Distillation**
Stimulants 613.8; 615
  UF Intoxicants
  SA types of stimulants, e.g. **Amphetamines;** and names of individual stimulants, to be added as needed
  BT **Therapeutics**
  NT **Amphetamines**
      Hallucinogens
  RT **Narcotics**
Stock and stock breeding
  USE **Livestock**
Stock control
  USE **Inventory control**
Stock exchange 332.64
  UF Securities exchange
      Stock market
  BT **Commerce**
      Exchange
      Finance
  NT **Bonds**
      Foreign exchange
      Insider trading
      Securities
      Wall Street (New York, N.Y.)
  RT **Investments**
      Speculation
      Stocks
Stock judging
  USE **Livestock judging**
Stock market
  USE **Stock exchange**
Stock raising
  USE **Livestock**
Stockings
  USE **Hosiery**
Stocks 332.63
  UF Dividends
      Shares of stock
  BT **Commerce**
      Securities
  NT **Corporations**
  RT **Bonds**
      Investments

BT = Broader Term   NT = Narrower Term   RT = Related Term   SA = See Also   UF = Used For

Stocks—*Continued*
        Stock exchange
Stocks—Insider trading
    USE **Insider trading**
Stockyards
    USE **Meat industry**
Stoics 188
    BT **Ancient philosophy**
          Ethics
STOL aircraft
    USE **Short take off and landing aircraft**
Stomach 612.3
    BT **Anatomy**
    RT **Digestion**
Stone 553.5; 693
    SA types of stone, e.g. **Marble**; to be added as needed
    BT **Building materials**
          Economic geology
    NT **Marble**
          Masonry
          Stonecutting
    RT **Petrology**
          Quarries and quarrying
          Rocks
Stone Age 930.1
    UF Eolithic period
          Neolithic period
          Paleolithic period
    NT **Stone implements**
    RT **Archeology**
Stone-cutting
    USE **Stonecutting**
Stone implements 930.1
    UF Flint implements
          Implements, utensils, etc.
    BT **Archeology**
          Stone Age
Stone quarries
    USE **Quarries and quarrying**
Stonecutting 693
    UF Stone-cutting
    BT **Masonry**
          Stone
Stones, Precious
    USE **Precious stones**
Stoneware
    USE **Pottery**
Storage batteries 621.31
    UF Batteries, Electric

    BT **Electric apparatus and appliances**
    RT **Electric batteries**
Storage devices, Computer
    USE **Computer storage devices**
Storage in the home 648
    UF Home storage
    BT **Home economics**
Stores
    USE **Chain stores**
          Cooperative societies
          Department stores
          Discount stores
          Retail trade
          Supermarkets
Stories
    USE **Anecdotes**
          Bible stories
          Fairy tales
          Fiction
          Legends
          Romances
          Short stories
          Stories in rhyme
          Stories without words
          Storytelling
          and for collections of plots, **Literature—Stories, plots, etc.**; and literary and musical forms with the subdivision *Stories, plots, etc.,* e.g. **Ballet—Stories, plots, etc.; Opera—Stories, plots, etc.;** etc., to be added as needed
Stories in rhyme 811, etc.; 813, etc.
    Use as a form heading for rhyming stories for very young children. Narrative poetry and materials about narrative poetry for older children and for adults are entered under **Narrative poetry.**
    UF Stories
    BT **Narrative poetry**
          Rhyme
Stories without words
    UF Nonword stories
          Picture books for children, Wordless
          Stories
          Wordless stories
    BT **Picture books for children**

Storms (May subdiv. geog.) **551.55**
  SA types of storms, to be added
      as needed
  BT **Meteorology**
      Natural disasters
      Weather
  NT **Blizzards**
      Cyclones
      Dust storms
      Hurricanes
      Thunderstorms
      Tornadoes
      Typhoons
  RT **Rain**
      Snow
      Winds
Story theater
  USE **Readers' theater**
Storytelling 027.62; 372.64
  UF Stories
  BT **Children's literature**
  RT **Folklore**
      Short story
Storytelling—Collections 808.85
  Use for collections of stories compiled
primarily for oral presentation.
  UF Collected works
      Collections of literature
Stoves 697
  BT **Heating**
      Space heaters
Strain (Psychology)
  USE **Stress (Psychology)**
Strains and stresses 531; 620.1; 624.1
  UF Architectural engineering
      Stresses
  BT **Architecture**
      Mechanics
      Statics
      Theory of structures
  RT **Strength of materials**
Strangers and children
  USE **Children and strangers**
Strategic Defense Initiative 358.1
  UF SDI (Ballistic missile defense
      system)
      Star Wars (Ballistic missile
      defense system)
  BT **Space warfare**
      United States—Defenses

      United States—Military policy
  RT **Space weapons**
Strategic materials
  USE **Materials**
Strategy 355.4
  UF Military strategy
      Naval strategy
  SA countries and areas of the
      world with the subdivision
      Strategic aspects, e.g. **Mid-**
      dle East—Strategic aspects;
      to be added as needed
  BT **War**
  NT **Armies**
      Middle East—Strategic as-
      pects
      Tactics
  RT **Military art and science**
      Naval art and science
Stratigraphic geology 551.7
  UF Geology, Historical
      Geology, Stratigraphic *[For-*
      mer heading]
      Historical geology
  BT **Geology**
  NT **Fossils**
Stratosphere 551.5
  BT **Upper atmosphere**
  NT **Ozone layer**
Stratospheric ozone
  USE **Ozone layer**
Straw votes
  USE **Public opinion polls**
Strawberries 634
  BT **Berries**
Stream animals 591.52
  UF River animals
      Stream fauna
  BT **Animals**
      Rivers
      Wildlife
Stream fauna
  USE **Stream animals**
Streamlining
  USE **Aerodynamics**
Street cars
  USE **Street railroads**
Street cleaning 363.72; 628.4
  BT **Cleaning**
      Municipal engineering

Street cleaning—*Continued*
>> Public health
>> Roads
>> Sanitary engineering
>> Streets
> RT **Refuse and refuse disposal**

Street gangs
> USE **Gangs**

Street lighting
> USE **Streets—Lighting**

Street literature
> USE **Pamphlets**

Street people
> USE **Homeless persons**

Street railroads 388.4; 625.6
> UF Interurban railroads
>> Railroads, Street
>> Street cars
>> Trams
>> Trolley cars
> BT **Local transit**
>> **Public utilities**
>> **Railroads**
>> **Transportation**
> NT **Subways**
> RT **Cable railroads**
>> **Electric railroads**

Street traffic
> USE **City traffic**
>> **Traffic engineering**
>> **Traffic regulations**

Streets (May subdiv. geog.) 388.4; 625.7
> UF Alleys
>> Avenues
>> Boulevards
>> Thoroughfares
> BT **Cities and towns**
>> **Civil engineering**
>> **Transportation**
> NT **City traffic**
>> **Street cleaning**
> RT **Pavements**
>> **Roads**

Streets—Chicago (Ill.) 977.3
> UF Chicago (Ill.)—Streets

Streets—Lighting 628.9
> UF Cities and towns—Lighting
>> Street lighting
> BT **Lighting**

Streets—New York (N.Y.) 974.7
> UF New York (N.Y.)—Streets
> RT **Wall Street (New York, N.Y.)**

Strength of materials 620.1
> UF Architectural engineering
>> Materials, Strength of
>> Resistance of materials
>> Testing
> SA specific materials with the subdivision *Testing,* e.g. **Concrete—Testing;** to be added as needed
> BT **Architecture**
>> **Building**
>> **Civil engineering**
>> **Materials**
>> **Mechanics**
>> **Theory of structures**
> NT **Concrete—Testing**
> RT **Building materials**
>> **Steel construction**
>> **Strains and stresses**

Strength training
> USE **Weight lifting**

Stress (Physiology) 612; 616.8
> UF Physiological stress
>> Tension (Physiology)
> BT **Adaptation (Biology)**
>> **Physiology**
> NT **Job stress**

Stress (Psychology) 155.9; 616.89
> UF Anxiety
>> Emotional stress
>> Mental stress
>> Psychological stress
>> Strain (Psychology)
>> Tension (Psychology)
> BT **Mental health**
>> **Psychology**
> NT **Burn out (Psychology)**
>> **Job stress**
>> **Separation anxiety in children**

Stresses
> USE **Strains and stresses**

Strikes (May subdiv. geog.) 331.89
> May also subdivide by industry or occupation and then geographically.
> UF Lockouts
>> Picketing
>> Sit-down strikes

Strikes—*Continued*
Strikes and lockouts *[Former heading]*
Work stoppages
BT **Industrial relations**
Labor disputes
NT **Sabotage**
RT **Collective bargaining**
Industrial arbitration
Injunctions
Labor unions
Strikes and lockouts
USE **Strikes**
Strikes and lockouts—Automobile industry—United States
USE **Strikes—Automobile industry—United States**
Strikes and lockouts—United States
USE **Strikes—United States**
Strikes—Automobile industry—United States 331.89
UF Strikes and lockouts—Automobile industry—United States *[Former heading]*
Strikes, Hunger
USE **Hunger strikes**
Strikes—United States 331.89
UF Strikes and lockouts—United States *[Former heading]*
United States—Strikes
United States—Strikes and lockouts
String orchestra music 784.7
BT **Orchestral music**
Stringed instruments 787
UF Bowed instruments
SA names of stringed instruments, to be added as needed
BT **Musical instruments**
NT **Guitars**
Violins
Violoncellos
Strip films
USE **Filmstrips**
Structural botany
USE **Plants—Anatomy**
Structural drafting
USE **Mechanical drawing**

Structural engineering 624.1
UF Engineering, Structural
BT **Architecture**
Civil engineering
Engineering
NT **Building**
Foundations
Hydraulic structures
Soils (Engineering)
RT **Theory of structures**
Structural failures 624.1
UF Collapse of structures
Failures, Structural
SA types of structural failures, e.g. **Building failures;** to be added as needed
BT **Reliability (Engineering)**
NT **Building failures**
Structural materials
USE **Building materials**
Structural psychology
USE **Gestalt psychology**
Structural steel 691
UF Steel, Structural *[Former heading]*
BT **Building materials**
Civil engineering
Steel
RT **Steel construction**
Structural zoology
USE **Animals—Anatomy**
Structures, Offshore
USE **Drilling platforms**
Structures, Theory of
USE **Theory of structures**
Stucco 693
BT **Building materials**
Decoration and ornament
Plaster and plastering
Student activities 371.8
UF Extracurricular activities
NT **After school programs**
Cheerleading
College and school drama
College and school journalism
College sports
Field trips
School assembly programs
School sports
Student aid 371.2; 378.3
UF Financial aid, Student

BT = Broader Term   NT = Narrower Term   RT = Related Term   SA = See Also   UF = Used For

Student aid—*Continued*
　　　　Financial aid to students
　　　　Student financial aid
　　　　Student financial assistance
　　BT　**College costs**
　　　　Loans
　　NT　**Scholarships**
　　　　Student loan funds
Student busing
　　USE　**Busing (School integration)**
Student clubs
　　USE　**Students—Societies**
Student councils
　　USE　**Student government**
Student customs
　　USE　**Student life**
Student dropouts
　　USE　**Dropouts**
Student evaluation of teachers 371.1
　　UF　Student rating of teachers
　　　　Teachers, Student rating of
　　BT　**Teacher-student relationships**
Student financial aid
　　USE　**Student aid**
Student financial assistance
　　USE　**Student aid**
Student government 371.5
　　UF　Honor system
　　　　Self-government (in education)
　　　　　[Former heading]
　　　　Student councils
　　　　Student self-government
　　BT　**School discipline**
　　　　Schools—Administration
Student guidance
　　USE　**Educational counseling**
Student life 371.8
　　UF　Student customs
　　BT　**Students**
Student loan funds 371.2; 378.3
　　UF　Loan funds, Student
　　BT　**College costs**
　　　　Student aid
　　RT　**Scholarships**
Student movement
　　USE　**Youth movement**
Student promotion
　　USE　**Promotion (School)**
Student protests, demonstrations, etc.
　　USE　**Students—Political activity**

　　　　Youth movement
Student rating of teachers
　　USE　**Student evaluation of teachers**
Student revolt
　　USE　**Students—Political activity**
　　　　Youth movement
Student self-government
　　USE　**Student government**
Student societies
　　USE　**Students—Societies**
Student songs
　　USE　**Students' songs**
Student-teacher interaction
　　USE　**Teacher-student relationships**
Student teaching 371.1
　　UF　Practice teaching
　　　　Teachers—Practice teaching
　　BT　**Teachers—Training**
　　　　Teaching
Student to student counseling
　　USE　**Peer counseling**
Student violence
　　USE　**School violence**
Student yearbooks
　　USE　**School yearbooks**
Students (May subdiv. geog.) **371.8**
　　UF　School life
　　SA　types of students, e.g. **College**
　　　　students; to be added as
　　　　needed
　　NT　**College students**
　　　　Dropouts
　　　　Foreign students
　　　　High school students
　　　　School children
　　　　Student life
Students and libraries
　　USE　**Libraries and students**
Students—Counseling
　　USE　**Educational counseling**
Students, Foreign
　　USE　**Foreign students**
Students—Grading and marking
　　USE　**Grading and marking (Educa-**
　　　　tion)
Students' military training camps
　　USE　**Military training camps**
Students—Political activity 324; 371.8
　　UF　Politics and students
　　　　Student protests, demonstra-
　　　　tions, etc.

Students—Political activity—*Continued*
    Student revolt
  BT **Youth movement**
Students—Societies 371.8
  UF School clubs
       Student clubs
       Student societies
  NT **Fraternities and sororities**
Students' songs 782.42
  UF College songs
       Student songs
  BT **Songs**
  NT **United States Military**
       Academy—Songs
Students—United States 371.8
  UF United States—Students
Students—Yearbooks
  USE **School yearbooks**
Study abroad
  USE **Foreign study**
Study, Courses of
  USE **Education—Curricula**
       and types of education and
       schools with the subdivi-
       sion *Curricula,* e.g. **Library**
       education—Curricula; Col-
       leges and universities—
       Curricula; etc., to be added
       as needed
Study, Foreign
  USE **Foreign study**
Study, Method of
  USE **Study skills**
Study overseas
  USE **Foreign study**
Study skills 371.3
  UF Learning, Art of
       Method of study
       Study, Method of *[Former*
       heading]
       Study strategies
  SA subjects with the subdivision
       Study and teaching, e.g.
       Art—Study and teaching; to
       be added as needed
  BT **Education**
       Teaching
  NT **Independent study**
       Self-instruction
Study strategies
  USE **Study skills**

Stunt flying 797.5
  UF Aerobatic flying
       Aerobatics
  BT **Airplanes—Piloting**
Stunt men
  USE **Stunt performers**
Stunt men and women
  USE **Stunt performers**
Stunt performers 791.4
  UF Stunt men
       Stunt men and women *[For-*
       mer heading]
  BT **Actors**
Stuttering
  USE **Speech disorders**
Style in dress
  USE **Costume**
       Fashion
Style, Literary
  USE **Literary style**
Style manikins
  USE **Fashion models**
Style manuals
  USE **Printing—Style manuals**
Sub-Saharan Africa 960
  UF Africa, Sub-Saharan *[Former*
       heading]
       Black Africa
  BT **Africa**
Subconsciousness 127; 154.2
  BT **Parapsychology**
       Psychology
  NT **Dreams**
       Hallucinations and illusions
       Mental suggestion
       Sleep
  RT **Consciousness**
       Hypnotism
       Mental healing
       Mind and body
       Psychoanalysis
       Spiritual healing
       Telepathy
Subculture
  USE **Counter culture**
Subgravity state
  USE **Weightlessness**
Subject catalogs 016; 017
  UF Catalogs, Subject *[Former*
       heading]

Subject catalogs—*Continued*
  BT **Library catalogs**
  NT **Subject headings**
Subject dictionaries
  USE **Encyclopedias and dictionaries**
Subject headings 025.4
  UF Thesauri
  BT **Cataloging**
      Indexes
      Subject catalogs
Submarine boats
  USE **Submarines**
      Submersibles
Submarine cables 384.1; 384.6
  UF Atlantic cable
      Cables, Submarine *[Former heading]*
      Ocean cables
      Pacific cable
      Submarine telegraph
      Telegraph, Submarine
  BT **Telecommunication**
      Telegraph
Submarine diving 627
  UF Deep sea diving
      Diving, Submarine *[Former heading]*
  BT **Diving**
      Oceanography—Research
  NT **Scuba diving**
      Skin diving
  RT **Underwater exploration**
Submarine engineering
  USE **Ocean engineering**
Submarine exploration
  USE **Underwater exploration**
Submarine geology 551.46
  UF Geology, Submarine
      Marine geology
      Underwater geology
  BT **Geology**
      Oceanography
  NT **Ocean bottom**
  RT **Plate tectonics**
Submarine medicine 616.9
  UF Medicine, Submarine
      Underwater medicine
      Underwater physiology
  BT **Medicine**
Submarine oil well drilling
  USE **Offshore oil well drilling**

Submarine photography
  USE **Underwater photography**
Submarine research stations
  USE **Undersea research stations**
Submarine telegraph
  USE **Submarine cables**
Submarine vehicles
  USE **Submersibles**
Submarine warfare 359.4
  UF Naval warfare
      Warfare, Submarine
  BT **Naval art and science**
      War
  NT **Submarines**
      Torpedoes
      World War, 1939-1945—Naval operations—Submarine
Submarines 359.3; 623.8
  Use for materials on submarines only. Materials on other underwater craft are entered under **Submersibles.**
  UF Boats, Submarine
      Submarine boats
      U boats
  BT **Ships**
      Submarine warfare
      Submersibles
      Warships
  NT **Nuclear submarines**
Submarines, Nuclear
  USE **Nuclear submarines**
Submersibles 623.8
  UF Boats, Submarine
      Deep diving vehicles
      Deep sea vehicles
      Deep submergence vehicles
      Oceanographic submersibles
      Submarine boats
      Submarine vehicles
      Undersea vehicles
      Underwater exploration devices
  SA types of submersibles, to be added as needed
  BT **Oceanography—Research**
      Underwater exploration
  NT **Bathyscaphe**
      Submarines
      Undersea research stations

Subscription television 384.55
- UF Pay television, Subscription Television, Subscription
- BT **Television broadcasting**
- NT **Home Box Office**

Subsidies 338.9
- UF Bounties
   Federal aid
   Grants
   Subventions
- SA kinds of subsidies, e.g. **Agricultural subsidies;** and federal aid to specific endeavors, e.g. **Federal aid to the arts;** to be added as needed
- BT **Domestic economic assistance**
   Economic policy
   Industry—Government policy
- NT **Agricultural subsidies**
   Federal aid to minority business enterprises
   Federal aid to the arts

Subsidies, Agricultural
- USE **Agricultural subsidies**

Subsidies, Farm
- USE **Agricultural subsidies**

Subsistence economy 330.9
- BT **Cost of living**
- NT **Barter**
- RT **Poverty**

Substance abuse 362.29; 616.86
- UF Abuse of substances
   Addiction
   Addiction to substances
   Addictive behavior
- BT **Social problems**
- NT **Alcoholism**
   Drug abuse
   Solvent abuse
   Tobacco habit
- RT **Twelve-step programs**

Substantive due process
- USE **Due process of law**

Substitute products
- UF Ersatz products
- SA types of substitute products, e.g. **Sugar substitutes;** to be added as needed
- BT **Commercial products**

- NT **Sugar substitutes**
- RT **Synthetic products**
   Waste products

Subterranean voyages
- USE **Imaginary voyages**

Subtraction 513.2
- BT **Arithmetic**

Suburban areas
- USE **Metropolitan areas**

Suburban life 307.74
- SA names of cities with the subdivision *Suburbs and environs,* to be added as needed
- NT **Chicago (Ill.)—Suburbs and environs**

Subventions
- USE **Subsidies**

Subversive activities 322.4; 327.12
- UF Fifth column
- BT **Insurgency**
- NT **Espionage**
   Political crimes and offenses
   Sabotage
   Spies
   Terrorism
- RT **Internal security**

Subways 388.4; 625.4
- UF Railroads, Underground
   Underground railroads
- BT **Civil engineering**
   Local transit
   Railroads
   Street railroads
   Transportation
   Tunnels

Success 158; 646.7
- UF Fortune
   Personal development
- BT **Business ethics**
   Wealth
- NT **Academic achievement**
   Leadership
   Life skills
   Saving and thrift
- RT **Ability**
   Self-realization

Succession, Intestate
- USE **Inheritance and succession**

Suffering 128; 152.1; 214
- UF Affliction

Suffering—*Continued*
   RT   Joy and sorrow
         Pain
Suffrage 324.6
   UF Franchise
         Voting
   SA ethnic groups and classes of
         persons with the subdivi-
         sion *Suffrage,* to be added
         as needed
   BT **Citizenship**
         Constitutional law
         Democracy
         Elections
         Political science
   NT **African Americans—Suffrage**
         Blacks—Suffrage
         Naturalization
         Voter registration
         Women—Suffrage
   RT **Representative government and**
         representation
Suffragettes
   USE **Women—Suffrage**
Suffragists
   USE **Women—Suffrage**
Sugar 641.3; 664
   SA types of sugar, to be added as
         needed
   NT **Maple sugar**
         Syrups
Sugar substitutes 641.3; 664
   UF Artificial sweeteners
         Nonnutritive sweeteners
   BT **Substitute products**
Suggestion, Mental
   USE **Mental suggestion**
Suggestive therapeutics 615.8
   UF Therapeutics, Suggestive *[For-
         mer heading]*
   BT **Therapeutics**
   RT **Hypnotism**
         Mental healing
         Mental suggestion
         Psychotherapy
         Spiritual healing
Suicide 179; 362.2
   BT **Medical jurisprudence**
         Social problems
   RT **Homicide**

         Right to die
Suing (Law)
   USE **Litigation**
Suite (Music) 784.18
      Use for musical scores and for materials
   on the suite as a musical form.
   UF Partita
         Suites *[Former heading]*
   BT **Musical form**
         Orchestral music
Suites
   USE **Suite (Music)**
Suits (Law)
   USE **Litigation**
Suits of armor
   USE **Armor**
Sulfa drugs
   USE **Sulfonamides**
Sulfonamides 615
   UF Sulfa drugs
   BT **Drugs**
Sulfur
   USE **Sulphur**
Sulphur 546; 553.6; 661
   UF Sulfur
   BT **Chemical elements**
Summer camps
   USE **Camps**
Summer employment 331.1
   BT **Employment**
   RT **Teenagers—Employment**
         Youth—Employment
Summer resorts 613; 790
   BT **Recreation**
   RT **Health resorts**
Summer schools 371.2
   UF Vacation schools
   BT **Public schools**
         Schools
   NT **Religious summer schools**
Summer schools, Religious
   USE **Religious summer schools**
Sun 523.7
   UF Solar physics
   BT **Astronomy**
         Solar system
   NT **Solar energy**
         Sunspots
Sun-dials
   USE **Sundials**
Sun—Eclipses
   USE **Solar eclipses**

     BT = Broader Term   NT = Narrower Term   RT = Related Term   SA = See Also   UF = Used For

Sun (in religion, folklore, etc.)
USE **Sun worship**
Sun powered batteries
USE **Solar batteries**
Sun—Radiation
USE **Solar radiation**
Sun-spots
USE **Sunspots**
Sun worship 291.2
UF Sun (in religion, folklore, etc.)
BT **Religion**
Sunday schools 268
UF Bible classes
BT **Church work**
Religious education
NT **Bible—Study and teaching**
Sundials 681.1
UF Horology
Sun-dials
BT **Clocks and watches**
Garden ornaments and furniture
Time
Sunken cities
USE **Extinct cities**
Sunken treasure
USE **Buried treasure**
Sunspots 523.7
UF Sun-spots
BT **Meteorology**
Solar radiation
Sun
Super markets
USE **Supermarkets**
Supercomputers 004.1
Use for materials on extraordinarily powerful computers.
BT **Computers**
Superconducting materials
USE **Superconductors**
Superconductive devices
USE **Superconductors**
Superconductors 537.6; 621.3
UF Superconducting materials
Superconductive devices
BT **Electric conductors**
Electronics
Superhero comic books, strips, etc. 741.5
May be used for individual works, collections, or materials about superhero comics.

BT **Comic books, strips, etc.**
Superhero films 791.43
May be used for individual works, collections, or materials about superhero films.
SA films with particular superheroes, e.g. **Superman films;** to be added as needed
BT **Adventure films**
NT **Superman films**
Superhero radio programs 791.44
May be used for individual works, collections, or materials about superhero radio programs.
BT **Adventure radio programs**
Superhero television programs 791.45
May be used for individual works, collections, or materials about superhero television programs.
BT **Adventure television programs**
Superhighways
USE **Express highways**
Superintendents of schools
USE **School superintendents and principals**
Superior children
USE **Gifted children**
Superman films 791.43
May be used for individual works, collections, or materials about Superman films.
BT **Superhero films**
Supermarkets 658.8
UF Stores
Super markets
BT **Grocery trade**
Retail trade
Supernatural 133; 398.2
BT **Religion**
NT **Divination**
Occultism
Parapsychology
Prophecies (Occultism)
Revelation
Spiritualism
Superstition
RT **Miracles**
Supernovae
USE **Supernovas**
Supernovas 523.8
UF Supernovae

Supernovas—*Continued*
  BT **Stars**
Supersonic aerodynamics 629.132
  UF Aerodynamics, Supersonic
      [Former heading]
      High speed aerodynamics
      Speed, Supersonic
  BT **High speed aeronautics**
  NT **Aerothermodynamics**
Supersonic airliners
  USE **Supersonic transport planes**
Supersonic transport planes 629.133
  UF S.S.T.'s
      SSTs
      Supersonic airliners
  BT **Jet planes**
Supersonic waves
  USE **Ultrasonic waves**
Supersonics
  USE **Ultrasonics**
Superstition 001.9; 398
  UF Delusions
      Traditions
  BT **Religion**
      Supernatural
  NT **Alchemy**
      Apparitions
      Astrology
      Charms
      Dreams
      Exorcism
      Fairies
      Fortune telling
      Vampires
      Witchcraft
  RT **Demonology**
      Divination
      Errors
      Folklore
      Ghosts
      Occultism
Supervision of employees
  USE **Personnel management**
Supervision of schools
  USE **School supervision**
Supervisors 331.7; 658.3
  UF Foremen and foreladies
      Managers
  BT **Factory management**
      Personnel management

Supplementary employment 331.1
  UF Double employment
      Dual employment
      Employment, Supplementary
      Moonlighting
      Second job
      Secondary employment
  BT **Labor**
      Part-time employment
Support of children
  USE **Child support**
Supreme Court—United States
  USE **United States. Supreme Court**
Surf
  USE **Ocean waves**
Surf riding
  USE **Surfing**
Surface effect machines
  USE **Ground effect machines**
Surfing 797.3
  UF Surf riding
  BT **Water sports**
Surfing—Songs 782.42
  UF Surfing—Songs and music
      [Former heading]
  BT **Songs**
Surfing—Songs and music
  USE **Surfing—Songs**
Surgeons 610.69; 617.092; 920
  UF Medical profession
  BT **Physicians**
Surgery 617
  UF Operations, Surgical
  SA classes of persons, names of
      diseases, and names of or-
      gans and regions of the
      body with the subdivision
      Surgery, to be added as
      needed
  BT **Medicine**
  NT **Anesthetics**
      Antiseptics
      Cancer—Surgery
      Children—Surgery
      Cryosurgery
      Heart—Surgery
      Orthopedics
      Plastic surgery
      **Transplantation of organs, tis-
      sues, etc.**

BT = Broader Term   NT = Narrower Term   RT = Related Term   SA = See Also   UF = Used For

Surgery—*Continued*
    Vivisection
Surgery, Cosmetic
  USE **Plastic surgery**
Surgery, Orthopedic
  USE **Orthopedics**
Surgery, Pediatric
  USE **Children—Surgery**
Surgery, Plastic
  USE **Plastic surgery**
Surgical transplantation
  USE **Transplantation of organs, tissues, etc.**
Surnames
  USE **Personal names**
Surplus government property 351.71; 353.0071
  UF Excess government property
      Government property, Surplus
  BT **Property**
Surrealism 709.04; 759.06
  BT **Art**
  RT **Postimpressionism (Art)**
Surrogate mothers 176; 306.874; 346
  BT **Mothers**
Surveillance, Electronic
  USE **Eavesdropping**
Surveying 526.9
  UF Land surveying
  BT **Civil engineering**
      Geography
      Measurement
  NT **Mine surveying**
      Topographical drawing
  RT **Geodesy**
Surveys
  USE types of surveys, e.g. **Educational surveys; Library surveys; Social surveys;** etc., to be added as needed
Survival (after airplane accidents, shipwrecks, etc.)
  USE **Survival after airplane accidents, shipwrecks, etc.**
Survival after airplane accidents, shipwrecks, etc. 613.6
  UF Castaways
      Survival (after airplane accidents, shipwrecks, etc.)
      [Former heading]
  BT **Aeronautics—Accidents**
      Shipwrecks
  RT **Wilderness survival**
Survival of the fittest
  USE **Natural selection**
Survival skills 613.6
  Use for materials on skills needed to survive in a hazardous environment, usually stressing self-reliance and economic self-sufficiency.
  UF Emergency survival
      Human survival skills
  SA types of survival, e.g. **Wilderness survival;** to be added as needed
  BT **Civil defense**
      Environmental influence on humans
      Human ecology
      Life skills
  NT **Wilderness survival**
  RT **Self-reliance**
Survivalism 320.5; 613.6
  UF Survivalist movements
  BT **Social movements**
Survivalist movements
  USE **Survivalism**
Suspended sentence
  USE **Probation**
Suspense films
  USE **Adventure films**
      Mystery films
      Spy films
Suspense novels
  USE **Adventure fiction**
      Mystery fiction
      Romantic suspense novels
Suspense programs
  USE **Mystery radio programs**
      Mystery television programs
      Spy radio programs
      Spy television programs
Suspension bridges
  USE **Bridges**
Swamp animals 591.52
  UF Swamp fauna
  BT **Animals**
      Marshes
      Wildlife
Swamp fauna
  USE **Swamp animals**

Swamps
　USE　**Marshes**
　　　　Wetlands
Swashbucklers
　USE　**Adventure fiction**
　　　　Adventure films
Swedish language 439.7
　　May be subdivided like **English language.**
　BT　**Scandinavian languages**
Swedish literature 839.7
　　May use same subdivisions and names of literary forms as for **English literature.**
　BT　**Literature**
　　　　Scandinavian literature
Sweets
　USE　**Confectionery**
Swell
　USE　**Ocean waves**
Swimming 797.2
　BT　**Water sports**
　NT　**Diving**
　　　　Marathon swimming
　　　　Synchronized swimming
Swimming pools 690; 725; 797.2
　UF　Pools
　BT　**Sports facilities**
Swindlers and swindling 364.1
　UF　Con artists
　　　　Con game
　　　　Confidence game
　BT　**Crime**
　　　　Criminals
　NT　**Counterfeits and counterfeiting**
　　　　Credit card crimes
　　　　Quacks and quackery
　RT　**Fraud**
　　　　Impostors and imposture
Swine
　USE　**Pigs**
Switchboard hotlines
　USE　**Hotlines (Telephone counseling)**
Switches, Electric
　USE　**Electric switchgear**
Symbiosis 574.5
　UF　Mutualism (Biology)
　BT　**Biology**
　　　　Ecology
　RT　**Parasites**

Plants—Ecology
Symbolic logic 511.3
　UF　Logic, Symbolic and mathematical [Former heading]
　　　　Mathematical logic
　BT　**Logic**
　　　　Mathematics
　NT　**Boolean algebra**
　RT　**Set theory**
Symbolic numbers
　USE　**Symbolism of numbers**
Symbolism 291.3; 704.9
　SA　types of symbolism in religions, e.g. **Christian art and symbolism; Religious art and symbolism;** and symbolism in particular subjects, e.g. **Symbolism in literature;** to be added as needed
　BT　**Art**
　　　　Mythology
　NT　**Christian art and symbolism**
　　　　Heraldry
　　　　Religious art and symbolism
　　　　Symbolism in literature
　　　　Symbolism of numbers
　RT　**Signs and symbols**
Symbolism in literature 809
　UF　Signs and symbols in literature
　BT　**Literature**
　　　　Symbolism
　RT　**Allegory**
Symbolism of numbers 133.3
　UF　Number symbolism
　　　　Numerology
　　　　Sacred numbers
　　　　Symbolic numbers
　BT　**Christian art and symbolism**
　　　　Magic
　　　　Mysticism
　　　　Symbolism
　RT　**Cabala**
　　　　Numbers
Symbols
　USE　**Abbreviations**
　　　　Signs and symbols
Symbols, Mathematical
　USE　**Mathematical notation**

Sympathy
USE **Bereavement**
Consolation
Symphonic poems 784.2
BT **Orchestral music**
Symphonies
USE **Symphony**
Symphony 784.18; 784.2
Use for musical scores and for materials on the symphony as a musical form.
UF Symphonies *[Former heading]*
BT **Musical form**
Orchestral music
Symptoms
USE **Diagnosis**
Synagogues (May subdiv. geog.) **291.6; 726**
BT **Architecture**
Judaism
Synchronized swimming 797.2
UF Ballet, Water
Water ballet
BT **Swimming**
Synfuels
USE **Synthetic fuels**
Synods
USE **Councils and synods**
Synonyms
USE names of languages with the subdivision *Synonyms and antonyms,* e.g. **English language—Synonyms and antonyms;** to be added as needed
Synthesizer music
USE **Electronic music**
Synthesizer (Musical instrument)
USE **Synthesizers (Musical instruments)**
Synthesizers (Musical instruments) 786.7
UF Synthesizer (Musical instrument) *[Former heading]*
BT **Electronic musical instruments**
Synthetic chemistry
USE **Organic chemistry—Synthesis**
Synthetic detergents
USE **Detergents**
Synthetic drugs of abuse
USE **Designer drugs**

Synthetic fabrics 677
UF Fabrics, Synthetic
SA names of synthetic fabrics, to be added as needed
BT **Fabrics**
Synthetic products
NT **Nylon**
Rayon
Synthetic foods
USE **Artificial foods**
Synthetic fuels 662
UF Artificial fuels
Nonfossil fuels
Synfuels
BT **Fuel**
Synthetic products
Synthetic products 670
SA types of synthetic products and names of specific products, to be added as needed
BT **Industrial chemistry**
Organic chemistry—Synthesis
NT **Artificial foods**
Synthetic fabrics
Synthetic fuels
Synthetic rubber
RT **Plastics**
Substitute products
Synthetic rubber 678
UF Rubber, Artificial *[Former heading]*
Rubber, Synthetic
BT **Plastics**
Synthetic products
Syphilis 616.95
BT **Sexually transmitted diseases**
Syrups 641.3
BT **Sugar**
System analysis 003; 004.2; 658.4
UF Flow charts
Flowcharting
Linear system theory
Network theory
Systems analysis
BT **Cybernetics**
Mathematical models
System theory
NT **Fuzzy systems**
System design
Systems engineering

BT = Broader Term   NT = Narrower Term   RT = Related Term   SA = See Also   UF = Used For

System design 003; 004.2; 621.39
   UF   Design, System
          Systems design
   BT   **Electronic data processing**
          System analysis
System engineering
   USE **Systems engineering**
System theory 003
   UF   Systems, Theory of
          Theory of systems
   BT   **Science**
   NT   **Chaos (Science)**
          Cybernetics
          Operations research
          System analysis
          Systems engineering
Systems analysis
   USE **System analysis**
Systems, Database management
   USE **Database management**
Systems design
   USE **System design**
Systems engineering 620
   UF   System engineering
   BT   **Automation**
          Cybernetics
          Engineering
          Industrial design
          System analysis
          System theory
   NT   **Bionics**
          Reliability (Engineering)
   RT   **Operations research**
Systems, Expert (Computer science)
   USE **Expert systems (Computer science)**
Systems, Fuzzy
   USE **Fuzzy systems**
Systems reliability
   USE **Reliability (Engineering)**
Systems, Theory of
   USE **System theory**
T groups
   USE **Group relations training**
T.I.R.O.S. (Meteorological satellite)
   USE **Tiros (Meteorological satellite)**
T.V.
   USE **Television**
Table decoration
   USE **Table setting and decoration**

Table etiquette 395
   BT   **Eating customs**
          Etiquette
   RT   **Dining**
Table setting and decoration 642
   UF   Table decoration
   BT   **Decoration and ornament**
   NT   **Flower arrangement**
          Tableware
Table talk
   USE **Conversation**
Table tennis
   USE **Ping-pong**
Tables (Systematic lists)
   USE scientific and economic subjects with the subdivision *Tables*, e.g. **Trigonometry—Tables**; to be added as needed
Tableware 642
   BT   **Table setting and decoration**
   NT   **Glassware**
          Pottery
          Silverware
Tactics 355.4
   UF   Military tactics
   BT   **Military art and science**
          Strategy
   NT   **Biological warfare**
          Drill and minor tactics
          Guerrilla warfare
Tactile materials
   USE **Manipulative materials**
Tadpoles
   USE **Frogs**
Tailoring 646.4; 687
   UF   Garment making
   BT   **Clothing and dress**
          Clothing industry
          Fashion
   NT   **Military uniforms**
   RT   **Dressmaking**
Taiwan 951.24
   Use for materials dealing with the island of Taiwan, regardless of time period, or with the post-1948 Republic of China. Materials dealing with mainland China, regardless of time period, or with the People's Republic of China and comprehensive materials on China including Taiwan are entered under **China.** May be subdivided like United States except for *History.*

Taiwan—*Continued*

> UF China (Republic of China, 1949-)
> Formosa
> Nationalist China
> Republic of China, 1949-

Takeovers, Corporate

> USE **Corporate mergers and acquisitions**

Talent

> USE **Genius**
> **Gifted children**
> **Musical ability**

Tales

> USE **Fables**
> **Fairy tales**
> **Folklore**
> **Legends**

Talismans

> USE **Charms**

Talk shows 791.44; 791.45

> May be used for individual works, collections, or materials about talk shows.

> BT **Interviewing**
> **Radio programs**
> **Television programs**

Talking

> USE **Conversation**

Talking books 011; 027.6

> UF Books, Talking
> Cassette books

> BT **Blind—Books and reading**
> **Sound recordings**

Talking pictures

> USE **Motion pictures**

Tall tales 398.2; 808.83; 813, etc.

> May be used for individual works, collections, or materials about tall tales.

> BT **Folklore**
> **Legends**
> **Wit and humor**

Talmud 296.1

> BT **Hebrew literature**
> **Jewish literature**
> **Judaism**

Tanks (Military science)

> USE **Military tanks**

Tanning 675

> BT **Industrial chemistry**
> RT **Hides and skins**

> Leather

Taoism 299

> BT **Religions**

Tap dancing 792.7

> BT **Dancing**
> NT **Clog dancing**

Tape recorder music

> USE **Electronic music**

Tape recorders

> USE **Magnetic recorders and recording**

Tape recordings, Audio

> USE **Sound recordings**

Tape recordings, Video

> USE **Videotapes**

Tapestry 677; 746.3

> BT **Decoration and ornament**
> **Decorative arts**
> **Interior design**
> **Needlework**

Tardiness

> USE **Punctuality**

Tariff (May subdiv. geog.) **336.2; 382**

> UF Custom duties
> Customs (Tariff)
> Duties
> Exports
> Government regulation of commerce
> Imports
> Revenue

> BT **Commerce**
> **Commercial policy**
> **Economic policy**
> **Finance**
> **Taxation**

> NT **Balance of trade**
> **Smuggling**

> RT **Free trade and protection**

Tariff question—Free trade and protection

> USE **Free trade and protection**

Tariff—United States 336.2; 382

> UF United States—Tariff

Tarot 133.3; 795.4

> Use for materials on the cards and the game.

> BT **Card games**
> **Fortune telling**

Tartans 391; 929.6

> UF Highland costume

Tartans—*Continued*
>Scottish tartans

BT   **Clans**

Taste 152.1

BT   **Senses and sensation**

Taste (Aesthetics)

USE   **Aesthetics**

Taverns

USE   **Bars**

Tax assessment 336.2

>Use for general materials on the valuation of property for determining tax liability. Materials on the assessment of property for tax purposes in a particular place are entered under **Taxation** followed by the appropriate geographical subdivision.

UF   Appraisal
>Assessment *[Former heading]*
>Assessment, Tax
>Property tax—Assessment
>Real property tax—
> Assessment

BT   **Taxation**
>**Valuation**

Tax credits 336.2

BT   **Income tax**

Tax relations, Intergovernmental

USE   **Intergovernmental tax relations**

Tax sharing

USE   **Intergovernmental tax relations**
>**Revenue sharing**

Taxation (May subdiv. geog.) **336.2**

UF   Direct taxation
>Duties
>Revenue
>Taxes

SA   subjects with the subdivision *Taxation,* e.g. **Real estate investment—Taxation;** to be added as needed

BT   **Finance**
>**Political science**

NT   **Income tax**
>**Inheritance and transfer tax**
>**Intergovernmental tax relations**
>**Internal revenue**
>**Real estate investment—Taxation**

>**Sales tax**
>**Tariff**
>**Tax assessment**
>**Tithes**

Taxation of income

USE   **Income tax**

Taxation of legacies

USE   **Inheritance and transfer tax**

Taxation of sales

USE   **Sales tax**

Taxation—United States 336.200973

UF   United States—Taxation

Taxes

USE   **Taxation**

Taxidermy 579

UF   Preservation of specimens
>Specimens, Preservation of

SA   types of specimens with the subdivision *Collection and preservation,* to be added as needed

NT   **Birds—Collection and preservation**

RT   **Zoological specimens—Collection and preservation**

Tea 633.7; 641.8; 642

>Use for materials on the beverage or on the meal.

UF   Afternoon teas

BT   **Beverages**
>**Cooking**

Tea rooms

USE   **Restaurants**

Teach yourself courses

USE   **Self-instruction**

Teacher exchange 370.19

UF   Exchange of teachers
>Interchange of teachers
>Teachers, Exchange of
>Teachers, Interchange of *[Former heading]*

BT   **Exchange of persons programs**
>**International education**

Teacher-parent conferences

USE   **Parent-teacher conferences**

Teacher-parent relationships

USE   **Parent-teacher relationships**

Teacher-student relationships 371.1; 378.1

UF   Pupil-teacher relationships

Teacher-student relationships—
Continued
     Student-teacher interaction
  BT **Children and adults**
      Human relations
      Teaching
  NT **Student evaluation of teachers**
Teacher training
  USE **Teachers colleges**
      Teachers—Training
Teachers 371.1; 920
  UF College teachers
      Faculty (Education)
      Professors
  BT **Education**
  NT **Educational associations**
      Teaching
  RT **Educators**
Teachers and parents
  USE **Parent-teacher relationships**
Teachers colleges 378.1
    Use for general and historical materials about teachers colleges. Materials on their educational functions are entered under **Teachers—Training.**
  UF Normal schools
      Teacher training
      Training colleges for teachers
  SA names of teachers colleges, to
      be added as needed
  BT **Colleges and universities**
      Education—Study and teaching
  RT **Teachers—Training**
Teachers, Exchange of
  USE **Teacher exchange**
Teachers' institutes
  USE **Teachers' workshops**
Teachers, Interchange of
  USE **Teacher exchange**
Teachers—Practice teaching
  USE **Student teaching**
Teachers' reports
  USE **School reports**
Teachers, Student rating of
  USE **Student evaluation of teachers**
Teachers—Training 371.1
    Use for materials on the history and methods of training teachers, including the educational functions of teachers colleges. Materials on the study of education as a science are entered under **Education—Study and teaching.**

  UF Teacher training
  BT **Education—Study and teaching**
      Teaching
  NT **Student teaching**
      Teachers' workshops
  RT **Teachers colleges**
Teachers' workshops 371.1
  UF Teachers' institutes
      Workshops, Teachers'
  BT **Teachers—Training**
Teaching 371.1
    Use for materials on the art and method of teaching.
  UF Instruction
      Pedagogy
      School teaching
  SA subjects with the subdivision
      Study and teaching, e.g.
      Science—Study and teaching; to be added as needed
  BT **Schools—Administration**
      Teachers
  NT **Classroom management**
      Cooperative learning
      Educational psychology
      Examinations
      Home instruction
      Lectures and lecturing
      Montessori method of education
      Project method in teaching
      School discipline
      School supervision
      Science—Study and teaching
      Student teaching
      Study skills
      Teacher-student relationships
      Teachers—Training
      Teaching teams
      Tutors and tutoring
  RT **Education**
Teaching—Aids and devices 371.3
  UF Educational media
      Instructional materials
      Teaching materials
  NT **Audiovisual materials**
      Bulletin boards
      Manipulative materials
      Motion pictures in education

BT = Broader Term   NT = Narrower Term   RT = Related Term   SA = See Also   UF = Used For

Teaching—Aids and devices—*Continued*
      Programmed instruction
      Radio in education
      Teaching machines
      Television in education
Teaching at home
    USE **Home instruction**
Teaching, Computer
    USE **Computer assisted instruction**
Teaching—Data processing
    USE **Computer assisted instruction**
Teaching—Experimental methods
    USE **Education—Experimental**
          methods
Teaching, Freedom of
    USE **Academic freedom**
Teaching machines 371.3
    UF Automatic teaching
        Tutorial machines
    BT **Programmed instruction**
        Teaching—Aids and devices
Teaching materials
    USE **Teaching—Aids and devices**
Teaching teams 371.1
    UF Team teaching
    BT **Teaching**
Teachings of Jesus
    USE **Jesus Christ—Teachings**
Team problem solving
    USE **Group problem solving**
Team teaching
    USE **Teaching teams**
Tearooms
    USE **Restaurants**
Technical assistance 338.91; 361.6
    UF Aid to developing areas
        Assistance to developing areas
        Foreign aid program
    SA technical assistance from par-
        ticular countries, e.g. **Amer-**
        ican technical assistance; to
        be added as needed
    BT **Economic assistance**
        Economic policy
        International cooperation
        International economic rela-
        tions
    NT **American technical assistance**
    RT **Community development**
        Developing countries

        Industrialization
Technical assistance, American
    USE **American technical assistance**
Technical chemistry
    USE **Industrial chemistry**
Technical education 370.11; 373.2; 374
    UF Education, Industrial
        Education, Technical
        Industrial education
        Industrial schools
        Technical schools
        Trade schools
    SA technical subjects with the
        subdivision *Study and*
        teaching, e.g. **Engineering—**
        Study and teaching; to be
        added as needed
    BT **Education**
        Higher education
        Technology
    NT **Apprentices**
        Correspondence schools and
        courses
        Engineering—Study and
        teaching
        Evening and continuation
        schools
        Occupational retraining
        Occupational training
        School shops
    RT **Employees—Training**
        Industrial arts education
        Professional education
        Vocational education
Technical schools
    USE **Technical education**
Technical service
    USE **Customer service**
Technical services (Libraries)
    USE **Library technical processes**
Technical terms
    USE **Technology—Dictionaries**
Technical writing 808
    UF Scientific writing
    BT **Authorship**
        Technology—Language
Technique
    USE subjects with the subdivision
        Technique, e.g. **Fiction—**
        Technique; Love stories—

BT = Broader Term   NT = Narrower Term   RT = Related Term   SA = See Also   UF = Used For

Technique—*Continued*
    Technique; Painting—
    Technique; etc., to be add-
    ed as needed
Technological transfer
  USE **Technology transfer**
Technology 600
  UF Applied science
      Arts, Useful
      High tech
      High technology
      Useful arts
  SA technology and other subjects,
      e.g. **Technology and civiliza-**
      tion; to be added as needed
  NT **Building**
      Distillation
      Electronics
      Engineering
      Industrial chemistry
      Inventions
      Machinery
      Manufactures
      Mills
      Technical education
      Technology and civilization
      Technology transfer
  RT **Industrial arts**
Technology and civilization 303.4
  UF Civilization and technology
  BT **Civilization**
      Technology
  NT **Computers and civilization**
      Machinery in industry
  RT **Industrial revolution**
Technology—Dictionaries 603
  UF Technical terms
  BT **Encyclopedias and dictionaries**
Technology—Language 601; 603
  NT **Technical writing**
Technology transfer (May subdiv. geog.)
    338.9
  May be subdivided by the region or
country receiving the technology or by the
region or country transferring the technol-
ogy. Where applicable use both headings
thus subdivided.
  UF Technological transfer
      Transfer of technology
  BT **Inventions**
      Technology

  RT **International cooperation**
      International relations
Teen age
  USE **Adolescence**
Teen-agers
  USE **Teenagers**
Teenage consumers
  USE **Young consumers**
Teenage drinking
  USE **Teenagers—Alcohol use**
Teenage dropouts
  USE **Dropouts**
Teenage fathers 305.23; 362.7
  Use for materials focusing on fathers
who are teenagers. Materials on fathers
who at the time of childbirth were not
married to the child's mother are entered
under **Unmarried fathers.** Materials focus-
ing on fathers rearing children without a
partner in the household are entered un-
der **Single parent family.**
  UF Adolescent fathers
      Parents, Teenage
      School age fathers
      Schoolboy fathers
      Teenage parents
  BT **Fathers**
Teenage gangs
  USE **Gangs**
Teenage mothers 305.23; 362.7; 362.83
  Use for materials focusing on mothers
who are teenagers. Materials on mothers
who at the time of giving birth were not
married to the child's father are entered
under **Unmarried mothers.** Materials fo-
cusing on mothers rearing children with-
out a partner in the household are entered
under **Single parent family.**
  UF Adolescent mothers *[Former*
      heading]
      Parents, Teenage
      School age mothers
      Schoolgirl mothers
      Teenage parents
  BT **Mothers**
  RT **Teenage pregnancy**
Teenage parents
  USE **Teenage fathers**
      Teenage mothers
Teenage pregnancy 362.7; 618.2
  UF Adolescent pregnancy
      Pregnancy, Adolescent *[For-*
      mer heading]
      Pregnancy, Teenage

Teenage pregnancy—*Continued*
 BT **Pregnancy**
 RT **Teenage mothers**
Teenage prostitution
 USE **Juvenile prostitution**
Teenagers (May subdiv. geog.) 305.23
 Use for materials about teen youth. Materials on the time of life extending from thirteen to twenty-five years, as well as on people in that general age range, are entered under **Youth.** Materials limited to people in the general age range of eighteen through twenty-five years of age are entered under **Young men** or **Young women.** Materials on the process or state of growing up are entered under **Adolescence.**
 UF Adolescents
  Boys, Teenage
  Girls, Teenage
  Teen-agers
  Teens
 BT **Age**
  Youth
 NT **Runaway teenagers**
 RT **Boys**
  Girls
Teenagers—Alcohol use 362.29; 613.81; 616.86
 UF Alcohol and teenagers
  Drinking and teenagers
  Teenage drinking
  Teenagers and alcohol
 NT **Drinking age**
Teenagers and alcohol
 USE **Teenagers—Alcohol use**
Teenagers and drugs
 USE **Teenagers—Drug use**
Teenagers and narcotics
 USE **Teenagers—Drug use**
Teenagers—Attitudes 155.5; 305.23
 BT **Attitude (Psychology)**
Teenagers—Development
 USE **Adolescence**
Teenagers—Drug use 362.29; 613.8; 616.86
 UF Drugs and teenagers
  Narcotics and teenagers
  Teenagers and drugs
  Teenagers and narcotics
 BT **Youth—Drug use**
 RT **Juvenile delinquency**
Teenagers—Employment 331.3
 UF Child labor

Employment of teenagers
 BT **Age and employment**
  Labor
  Labor supply
  Youth—Employment
 RT **Summer employment**
Teenagers' library services
 USE **Young adults' library services**
Teenagers—Literature
 USE **Young adults' literature**
Teenagers, Psychiatry of
 USE **Adolescent psychiatry**
Teenagers—Psychology
 USE **Adolescent psychology**
Teenagers—Religious life 248.8
 BT **Religious life**
  Youth—Religious life
Teenagers—United States 305.23
 UF American teenagers
  United States—Teenagers
 BT **Youth—United States**
Teens
 USE **Teenagers**
Teepees
 USE **Indians of North America—Dwellings**
Teeth 611; 612.3; 617.6
 UF Anatomy, Dental
 BT **Head**
 RT **Dentistry**
Teeth—Diseases 617.6
 UF Medicine, Dental
 RT **Water fluoridation**
Telecommunication 384; 621.382
 UF Electric communication
  Mass communication
 SA subjects with the subdivision *Communication systems,* e.g. **Astronautics—Communication systems;** to be added as needed
 BT **Communication**
 NT **Artificial satellites in telecommunication**
  Astronautics—Communication systems
  Broadcasting
  Computer networks
  Data transmission systems
  Electronic mail systems

BT = Broader Term NT = Narrower Term RT = Related Term SA = See Also UF = Used For

Telecommunication—*Continued*
>   Electronic publishing
>   Facsimile transmission
>   Intercommunication systems
>   Interstellar communication
>   Microwave communication systems
>   Radio
>   Speech processing systems
>   Submarine cables
>   Telecommuting
>   Telegraph
>   Telephone
>   Television

Telecommuting 331.25
> Use for materials on employment at home with computers, word processors, etc., connected to a central work site, permitting employees to substitute telecommunications for transportation.

> UF   Alternate work sites
>   At-home employment
>   Cottage industry, Electronic
>   Electronic cottage
>   Home labor
>   Home work (Employment)
>   Homework (Employment)
>   Work at home
>   Working at home

> BT   **Automation**
>   **Home business**
>   **Telecommunication**

Teleconferencing 384; 658.4
> UF   Conference calls (Teleconferencing)
>   Telephone—Conference calls
> BT   **Telephone**

Telefax
> USE   **Facsimile transmission**

Telegraph 384.1; 621.383
> BT   **Electric engineering**
>   **Public utilities**
>   **Telecommunication**
> NT   **Cipher and telegraph codes**
>   **Submarine cables**

Telegraph codes
> USE   **Cipher and telegraph codes**

Telegraph, Submarine
> USE   **Submarine cables**

Telekinesis
> USE   **Psychokinesis**

Telemarketing 381; 658.8
> Use for materials on the use of electronic media as a form of marketing that bypasses retail outlets in the advertising and selling of goods.

> UF   Electronic marketing
> BT   **Direct selling**
>   **Marketing**

Telepathy 133.8
> UF   Mental telepathy
>   Mind reading *[Former heading]*
>   Thought transference
> BT   **Extrasensory perception**
>   **Parapsychology**
> RT   **Clairvoyance**
>   **Subconsciousness**

Telephone 384.6; 621.385
> BT   **Electric engineering**
>   **Public utilities**
>   **Telecommunication**
> NT   **Teleconferencing**
>   **Video telephone**

Telephone—Conference calls
> USE   **Teleconferencing**

Telephone counseling
> USE   **Hotlines (Telephone counseling)**

Telephone directories
> USE   names of cities with the subdivision *Telephone directories,* e.g. **Chicago (Ill.)—Telephone directories;** to be added as needed

Telephotography 778.3
> BT   **Photography**

Teleprocessing networks
> USE   **Computer networks**

Telereference
> USE   **Information networks**
>   **Teletext systems**
>   **Videotex systems**

Telescope
> USE   **Telescopes**

Telescopes 522; 681
> UF   Telescope *[Former heading]*
> BT   **Astronomical instruments**
>   **Optical instruments**

BT = Broader Term   NT = Narrower Term   RT = Related Term   SA = See Also   UF = Used For

Teletext systems 004.692; 384.3

Use for materials on the one-way transmission of computer-based data, such as weather forecasts or stock quotations, from a central source to a television set.

UF   Telereference

BT   **Data transmission systems**
Electronic publishing
Information systems
Television broadcasting

RT   **Videotex systems**

Television 302.23; 384.55; 621.388

UF   T.V.
TV

SA   television and particular groups of people, e.g. **Television and children;** and television in various industries or fields of endeavor, e.g. **Television in education;** to be added as needed

BT   **Telecommunication**

NT   **Closed caption television**
Closed-circuit television
Color television
High definition television
Home video systems
Television and children
Television and youth
Television broadcasting
Television in astronautics
Television in education
Video art
Video telephone

RT   **Videodiscs**
Videotapes

Television actors
USE   **Actors**

Television adaptations 791.45

May be used for individual works, collections, or materials about television adaptations of material from other media.

UF   Adaptations
Adaptations, Television
Literature—Film and video adaptations
Motion pictures—Television adaptations

SA   individual national literatures and individual literary authors with the subdivision

Film and video adaptations, to be added as needed

BT   **Television plays**
Television programs
Television scripts

Television advertising 659.14

UF   Advertising, Television
Commercials, Television
Television commercials

BT   **Advertising**
Television broadcasting

Television and children 305.23; 384.55; 791.45

Use for materials on the effect of television on children.

UF   Children and television

BT   **Children**
Television

Television and infrared observation satellite
USE   **Tiros (Meteorological satellite)**

Television and youth 305.23; 384.55; 791.45

UF   Youth and television

BT   **Television**
Youth

Television apparatus industry
USE   **Television supplies industry**

Television authorship 808

UF   Television writing

BT   **Authorship**

NT   **Television plays—Technique**

Television broadcasting 384.55

UF   Television industry

BT   **Broadcasting**
Mass media
Television

NT   **Cable television**
Equal time rule (Broadcasting)
Fairness doctrine (Broadcasting)
Public television
Subscription television
Teletext systems
Television advertising
Television in politics
Television programs
Television scripts
Television stations
Videotex systems

Television broadcasting—*Continued*
RT   Video recording
Television broadcasting—Vocational
        guidance 384.55
BT   Vocational guidance
Television, Cable
USE   Cable television
Television cartoons
USE   Animated television programs
Television—Censorship 384.55
BT   Censorship
Television, Closed-circuit
USE   Closed-circuit television
Television, Color
USE   Color television
Television comedies
USE   Comedy television programs
Television comedy programs
USE   Comedy television programs
Television commercials
USE   Television advertising
Television drama
USE   Television plays
Television—Equipment and supplies
        621.388
NT   Television—Receivers and re-
        ception
        Television supplies industry
        Videodisc players
RT   Video recording
Television equipment industry
USE   Television supplies industry
Television films
USE   Television movies
Television games
USE   Video games
Television in astronautics 621.388;
        629.47
UF   Space television
        Television, Space
BT   Astronautics—Communication
        systems
        Television
Television in education 371.3
UF   Education and television
        Educational television
BT   Audiovisual education
        Teaching—Aids and devices
        Television
Television in politics 324.7
BT   Politics

Television broadcasting
NT   Equal time rule (Broadcasting)
        Fairness doctrine (Broadcast-
        ing)
Television industry
USE   Television broadcasting
        Television supplies industry
Television journalism
USE   Broadcast journalism
Television movies 791.45
    May be used for individual works, col-
    lections, or materials about television
    movies.
UF   Made-for-TV movies
        Television films
BT   Motion pictures
        Television programs
Television news
USE   Broadcast journalism
Television novels
USE   Radio and television novels
Television plays 808.82; 812, etc.
    May be used for individual works, col-
    lections, or materials about television
    plays. Materials on how to write television
    plays are entered under Television plays—
    Technique.
UF   Scenarios
        Television drama
BT   Drama
        Television programs
NT   Soap operas
        Television adaptations
RT   Television scripts
Television plays—Technique 808.2
UF   Play writing
        Playwriting
BT   Drama—Technique
        Television authorship
RT   Radio plays—Technique
Television—Production and direction
        384.55; 791.45
Television programs 791.45
    May be used for individual works, col-
    lections, or materials about television pro-
    grams.
UF   Programs, Television
SA   types of television programs
        and names of specific pro-
        grams, to be added as
        needed
BT   Television broadcasting

BT = Broader Term   NT = Narrower Term   RT = Related Term   SA = See Also   UF = Used For

Television programs—*Continued*
NT　Adventure television programs
　　Animated television programs
　　Biographical television programs
　　Comedy television programs
　　Fantasy television programs
　　Horror television programs
　　Legal drama (Television programs)
　　Medical drama (Television programs)
　　Music videos
　　Mystery television programs
　　Science fiction television programs
　　Sports drama (Television programs)
　　Spy television programs
　　Talk shows
　　Television adaptations
　　Television movies
　　Television plays
　　Television serials
　　Variety shows (Television programs)
　　War television programs
　　Westerns (Television programs)
RT　Television scripts
Television, Public
USE　Public television
Television—Receivers and reception 621.388
UF　Television reception
　　Television sets
BT　Television—Equipment and supplies
NT　Video games
Television reception
USE　Television—Receivers and reception
Television—Repairing 621.388
Television scripts 791.45; 808.8; 818, etc.
　　May be used for individual works, collections, or materials about television scripts.
UF　Screenplays
BT　Television broadcasting

NT　Television adaptations
RT　Television plays
　　Television programs
Television serials 791.45
　　May be used for individual works, collections, or materials about television serials.
BT　Television programs
RT　Soap operas
Television sets
USE　Television—Receivers and reception
Television, Space
USE　Television in astronautics
Television—Stage lighting
USE　Stage lighting
Television stations 384.55
BT　Television broadcasting
Television, Subscription
USE　Subscription television
Television supplies industry 338.4; 384.55
UF　Television apparatus industry
　　Television equipment industry
　　Television industry
BT　Television—Equipment and supplies
Television writing
USE　Television authorship
Telstar project 621.382
UF　Bell System Telstar satellite
　　Project Telstar
BT　Artificial satellites in telecommunication
Temperament 155.2
BT　Mind and body
　　Psychology
　　Psychophysiology
RT　Character
Temperance 178; 241; 613.81
　　Use for general materials on the temperance question and the temperance movement.
UF　Abstinence
　　Drunkenness
　　Intemperance
　　Intoxication
　　Total abstinence
BT　Virtue
NT　Alcohol—Physiological effect
RT　Alcoholism

BT = Broader Term　NT = Narrower Term　RT = Related Term　SA = See Also　UF = Used For

Temperance—*Continued*
> Drinking of alcoholic beverages
> Drug addiction
> Prohibition

Temperature 536
  NT Low temperatures
  RT Cold
> Heat
> Thermometers

Temperature, Animal and human
  USE **Body temperature**
Temperature, Body
  USE **Body temperature**
Temperatures, Low
  USE **Low temperatures**

Temples (May subdiv. geog.) **291.3; 726**
  BT **Ancient architecture**
> Archeology
> Architecture
> Asian architecture
> Church architecture
  NT **Mosques**

Temporal power of the Pope
  USE **Popes—Temporal power**

Temporary employment 331.25
  UF Employment, Temporary
  BT **Employment**

Ten commandments 222
  UF Commandments, Ten
> Decalogue
  BT **Bible. O.T.**

Tenant and landlord
  USE **Landlord and tenant**
Tenant farming
  USE **Farm tenancy**

Tenement houses 363.5
  BT **Cities and towns**
> Houses
  RT **Housing**

Tennis 796.342
  UF Lawn tennis
  BT **Sports**

Tennis—Tournaments 796.342
  BT **Contests**

Tenpins
  USE **Bowling**
Tension (Physiology)
  USE **Stress (Physiology)**
Tension, Premenstrual
  USE **Premenstrual syndrome**

Tension (Psychology)
  USE **Stress (Psychology)**

Tents 796.54
  BT **Camping**

Tenure of land
  USE **Land tenure**
Tenure of office
  USE **Civil service**
Tepees
  USE **Indians of North America— Dwellings**

Term paper writing
  USE **Report writing**

Terminal care 362.1; 649.8
  UF Care of the dying
  BT **Medical care**
  NT **Hospices**
> Life support systems (Medical environment)
> **Terminally ill**
  RT **Death**

Terminally ill 362.1; 649.8
  UF Dying patients
> Fatally ill patients
  BT **Sick**
> Terminal care
  NT **Terminally ill children**
  RT **Death**

Terminally ill children 362.1; 649.8
  UF Dying children
> Fatally ill children
  BT **Terminally ill**

Terminals, Computer
  USE **Computer terminals**
Termination of pregnancy
  USE **Abortion**
Terminology
  USE **Names**
> and subjects with the subdivision *Terminology,* e.g.
> **Botany—Terminology;** to be added as needed

Terns 598.3
  BT **Water birds**

Terra cotta 620.1; 691
  BT **Building materials**
> **Decoration and ornament**
> **Pottery**

Terrain sensing, Remote
  USE **Remote sensing**

BT = Broader Term   NT = Narrower Term   RT = Related Term   SA = See Also   UF = Used For

Terrapins
USE **Turtles**
Terrariums 635.9
UF Vivariums
BT **Indoor gardening**
RT **Miniature gardens**
Terrestrial physics
USE **Geophysics**
Territorial waters (May subdiv. geog.)
341.4
UF 3 mile limit
200 mile limit
Economic zones (Maritime
law)
Three mile limit
Two hundred mile limit
BT **Shipping**
RT **Continental shelf**
Maritime law
Territorial waters—United States 341.4
UF United States—Territorial wa-
ters
Terror, Reign of
USE **France—History—1789-1799,**
Revolution
Terror tales
USE **Ghost stories**
Horror fiction
Terrorism (May subdiv. geog.) 303.6
UF Political violence
BT **Insurgency**
Political crimes and offenses
Subversive activities
NT **Hostages**
Sabotage
RT **Anarchism and anarchists**
Terrorism—United States 303.6; 322.4
UF United States—Terrorism
Test pilots
USE **Air pilots**
Airplanes—Testing
Test tube babies
USE **Fertilization in vitro**
Test tube fertilization
USE **Fertilization in vitro**
Testing
USE **Electric testing**
Reliability (Engineering)
Strength of materials

and things tested with the
subdivision *Testing,* e.g.
Ability—Testing; Air-
planes—Testing; Con-
crete—Testing; etc; and
classes of persons with the
subdivision *Drug testing,*
e.g. **Employees—Drug test-**
ing; to be added as needed
Testing for drug abuse
USE **Drug testing**
Tests
USE **Educational tests and mea-**
surements
Examinations
Teutonic peoples 305.83
UF Goths
Nordic peoples
Ostrogoths
Saxons
Visigoths
NT **Anglo-Saxons**
Textbooks 371.3
Use for materials about textbooks. Text-
books themselves are entered under the
subject only, e.g. **Arithmetic; Geography;**
etc.
UF School books
BT **Books**
Textile chemistry 677
UF Chemistry, Textile
BT **Industrial chemistry**
Textile industry
NT **Dyes and dyeing**
Textile design 746
BT **Commercial art**
Decoration and ornament
Design
NT **Textile painting**
RT **Textile printing**
Textile fibers
USE **Fibers**
Textile industry 338.4; 677
SA names of articles manufac-
tured, e.g **Carpets; Hosiery;**
etc., to be added as needed
NT **Bleaching**
Carpets
Cotton manufacture
Dyes and dyeing

Textile industry—*Continued*
    Hosiery
    Spinning
    Textile chemistry
    Textile printing
    Yarn
  RT Weaving
Textile painting 746.6
  BT Painting
    Textile design
Textile printing 746.6
  UF Block printing
    Printing, Textile
  BT Printing
    Textile industry
  RT Silk screen printing
    Textile design
Textiles
  USE Fabrics
Thanksgiving Day 394.2
  BT Holidays
    Religious holidays
Theater (May subdiv. geog.) 792
    Use for materials on drama as acted on the stage and on the historical, moral, and religious aspects of the theater. Materials on drama as a literary form are entered under **Drama; American drama; English drama;** etc. Materials on theater buildings are entered under **Theaters.**
  UF Histrionics
    Stage
  SA names of wars with the subdivision *Theater and the war,* to be added as needed
  BT Amusements
    Performing arts
  NT Amateur theater
    Arena theater
    Ballet
    Children's plays
    Dramatic criticism
    Experimental theater
    Little theater movement
    Masks (Plays)
    Morality plays
    Musicals
    Mysteries and miracle plays
    Pantomimes
    Passion plays
    Puppets and puppet plays

    Readers' theater
    Shadow pantomimes and plays
    Shakespeare, William, 1564-1616—Stage history
    Skits
    Theaters
    Vaudeville
    World War, 1939-1945—Theater and the war
  RT Acting
    Actors
    Drama
Theater, Amateur
  USE Amateur theater
Theater criticism
  USE Dramatic criticism
Theater-in-the-round
  USE Arena theater
Theater—Little theater movement
  USE Little theater movement
Theater—Production and direction 792
  UF Direction (Theater)
    Play direction (Theater)
    Play production
Theater—United States 792.0973
  UF United States—Theater
Theaters (May subdiv. geog.) 725
    Use for materials on theater buildings, their architecture, technical fixtures, decoration, etc. Materials on drama as a literary form are entered under **Drama.** Materials on drama as acted on the stage are entered under **Theater.**
  UF Playhouses
  SA types of theaters, to be added as needed
  BT Architecture
    Centers for the performing arts
    Theater
Theaters—Stage lighting
  USE Stage lighting
Theaters—Stage setting and scenery 792
  UF Scenery (Stage)
    Stage scenery
    Stage setting
    Theatrical scenery
  NT Scene painting
Theatrical costume
  USE Costume

BT = Broader Term   NT = Narrower Term   RT = Related Term   SA = See Also   UF = Used For

Theatrical makeup 791.43; 791.45; 792
  UF Makeup, Theatrical *[Former*
       heading]
  BT Cosmetics
       Costume
Theatrical scenery
  USE Theaters—Stage setting and
        scenery
Theatricals, College
  USE College and school drama
Theft
  USE Stealing
Thefts, Art
  USE Art thefts
Theism 211
  BT Philosophy
       Rationalism
       Religion
       Theology
  RT Atheism
       Deism
       God
Theme parks
  USE Amusement parks
Theological education
  USE Theology—Study and teaching
Theology 230; 291.2
  BT Creation
  NT Apologetics
       Atheism
       Baptism
       Church
       Conversion
       Covenants
       Creationism
       Creeds
       Deism
       Doctrinal theology
       Eschatology
       Faith
       Fundamentalism
       Good and evil
       Grace (Theology)
       Immortality
       Liturgies
       Man (Theology)
       Modernism (Theology)
       Mysticism
       Natural theology
       Predestination

       Providence and government of
        God
       Religion and science
       Revelation
       Sacraments
       Sacrifice
       Sanctification
       Secularism
       Sin
       Spiritual life
       Theism
       Worship
  RT Christianity
       God
       God—Christianity
       Religion
Theology, Devotional
  USE Devotional exercises
        Prayers
Theology, Doctrinal
  USE Doctrinal theology
Theology, Natural
  USE Natural theology
Theology of liberation
  USE Liberation theology
Theology, Pastoral
  USE Pastoral work
Theology—Philosophy
  USE Christianity—Philosophy
Theology—Study and teaching 230.07;
        291.2
  UF Education, Theological
       Religion—Study and teaching
       Theological education
  NT Catechisms
  RT Christian education
       Church and education
       Religious education
Theoretical chemistry
  USE Physical chemistry
Theory of games
  USE Game theory
Theory of graphs
  USE Graph theory
Theory of knowledge 001.01; 121
    Use for materials on the origin, nature,
  methods, and limits of human knowledge.
  UF Cognition
       Epistemology
       Knowledge, Theory of *[For-*
        mer heading]

Theory of knowledge—*Continued*
Understanding
BT **Consciousness**
Logic
Metaphysics
Philosophy
NT **Belief and doubt**
Empiricism
Gestalt psychology
Intuition
Perception
Pragmatism
Rationalism
Senses and sensation
RT **Apperception**
Intellect
Reality
Truth
Theory of numbers
USE **Number theory**
Theory of structures 624
UF Architectural engineering
Structures, Theory of *[Former heading]*
NT **Building**
Strains and stresses
Strength of materials
RT **Steel construction**
Structural engineering
Theory of systems
USE **System theory**
Theosophy 299
BT **Mysticism**
Religions
NT **Reincarnation**
Yoga
Therapeutic systems
USE **Alternative medicine**
Therapeutics 615.5
UF Diseases—Treatment
Therapy
Treatment of diseases
SA types of therapies; names of diseases and groups of diseases with the subdivision *Treatment,* e.g. **AIDS (Disease)—Treatment**; names of foods with the subdivision *Therapeutic use,* e.g. **Corn—Therapeutic use;**

and types of drugs and names of specific drugs, to be added as needed
BT **Medicine**
Pathology
NT **Aids (Disease)—Treatment**
Antiseptics
Corn—Therapeutic use
Diet in disease
Diet therapy
Drug therapy
Drugs
Electrotherapeutics
Gene therapy
Hydrotherapy
Materia medica
Narcotics
Naturopathy
Nursing
Nutrition
Occupational therapy
Pet therapy
Phototherapy
Physical therapy
Psychotherapy
Radiotherapy
Stimulants
Suggestive therapeutics
RT **Pharmaceutical chemistry**
Therapeutics, Suggestive
USE **Suggestive therapeutics**
Therapy
USE **Therapeutics**
Therapy, Gene
USE **Gene therapy**
Therapy, Psychological
USE **Psychotherapy**
Thermal insulation
USE **Insulation (Heat)**
Thermal waters
USE **Geothermal resources**
Geysers
Thermoaerodynamics
USE **Aerothermodynamics**
Thermodynamics 536
SA subjects with the subdivision *Thermodynamics,* e.g. **Space vehicles—Thermodynamics;** to be added as needed
BT **Dynamics**

BT = Broader Term   NT = Narrower Term   RT = Related Term   SA = See Also   UF = Used For

Thermodynamics—*Continued*
    Physical chemistry
    Physics
  NT **Aerothermodynamics**
    Heat pumps
    Space vehicles—
      Thermodynamics
  RT **Heat**
    Heat engines
    Quantum theory
Thermometers 536
  UF Thermometry
  BT **Heat**
    Meteorological instruments
  RT **Temperature**
Thermometry
  USE **Thermometers**
Thermonuclear bomb
  USE **Hydrogen bomb**
Thesauri
  USE **Subject headings**
    and names of languages with
    the subdivision *Synonyms*
    and antonyms, e.g. **English**
    language—Synonyms and
    antonyms; to be added as
    needed
Theses
  USE **Dissertations**
Thieves 364.3
  UF Bandits
    Brigands
    Burglars
    Highwaymen
    Outlaws
    Robbers and outlaws *[Former
      heading]*
  BT **Criminals**
  RT **Stealing**
Think tanks
  USE **Group problem solving**
Thinking
  USE **Thought and thinking**
Third parties (U.S. politics)
  USE **Third parties (United States**
    politics)
Third parties (United States politics)
  324.273
  UF Third parties (U.S. politics)
    [Former heading]

  BT **Political parties**
    United States—Politics and
      government
Third World
  USE **Developing countries**
Third World War
  USE **World War III**
Thirteenth century 909
    Use for general materials covering prog-
    ress and development during this period
    in one or in several countries.
  UF 1200-1299 (13th century)
  BT **Middle Ages**
Thirty Years' War, 1618-1648 909.08;
  940.2
  BT **Europe—History—1492-1789**
    Germany—History—
      1517-1740
Thoroughfares
  USE **Roads**
    Streets
Thought and thinking 153.4
  UF Thinking
  BT **Educational psychology**
    Psychology
  NT **Attention**
    Critical thinking
    Memory
    Perception
    Reasoning
  RT **Intellect**
    Logic
Thought control
  USE **Brainwashing**
Thought transference
  USE **Telepathy**
Threatened species
  USE **Endangered species**
Three dimensional computer graphics
  USE **Virtual reality**
Three dimensional photography 778.4
  UF 3-D photography
    3D photography
    Photography, Stereoscopic
      [Former heading]
    Stereo photography
    Stereophotography
    Stereoscopic photography
  BT **Photography**
  RT **Holography**

Three mile limit
　USE　**Territorial waters**
Three Stooges films 791.43
　　May be used for individual works, col-
　lections, or materials about Three Stooges
　films.
　BT　**Comedy films**
　　　Motion pictures
Three (The number) 513
　BT　**Numbers**
Thrift
　USE　**Saving and thrift**
Thrillers
　USE　**Adventure fiction**
　　　Adventure films
Throat 611; 612; 617.5
　BT　**Anatomy**
　NT　**Voice**
Thunderstorms 551.55
　BT　**Meteorology**
　　　Storms
　NT　**Lightning**
Tiananmen Square Incident, China,
　　　1989
　USE　**China—History—1989, Tia-**
　　　nanmen Square Incident
Tiananmen Square Massacre, China
　USE　**China—History—1989, Tia-**
　　　nanmen Square Incident
Ticks 595.4
　UF　Arachnida
　BT　**Parasites**
　RT　**Lyme disease**
Tidal waves
　USE　**Ocean waves**
Tidal waves, Seismic
　USE　**Tsunamis**
Tides 551.47
　BT　**Astronomy**
　　　Moon
　　　Navigation
　　　Oceanography
　　　Physical geography
Tie dyeing 746.6
　BT　**Dyes and dyeing**
Tiles 666; 693; 738.6
　BT　**Bricks**
　　　Building materials
　　　Ceramics
　　　Clay industries

　　　Pottery
Timber
　USE　**Forests and forestry**
　　　Lumber and lumbering
　　　Trees
　　　Wood
Time 529
　UF　Horology
　　　Standard time
　NT　**Calendars**
　　　Chronology
　　　Clocks and watches
　　　Day
　　　Night
　　　Punctuality
　　　Space and time
　　　Sundials
　RT　**Nautical astronomy**
　　　Periodicity
Time and space
　USE　**Space and time**
Time management 640; 650.1
　UF　Allocation of time
　　　Personal time management
　　　Time—Organization
　　　Time, Use of
　　　Use of time
　BT　**Leisure**
　　　Management
Time—Organization
　USE　**Time management**
Time production standards
　USE　**Production standards**
Time saving cooking
　USE　**Quick and easy cooking**
Time sharing (Real estate)
　USE　**Timesharing (Real estate)**
Time study 658.5
　BT　**Factory management**
　　　Industrial efficiency
　　　Job analysis
　　　Personnel management
　　　Production standards
　RT　**Motion study**
Time travel
　USE　**Fourth dimension**
Time travel (Fiction)
　USE　**Fantasy fiction**
　　　Fantasy films
　　　Fantasy television programs

Time travel (Fiction)—*Continued*
  Imaginary voyages
  Science fiction
  Science fiction plays
  Science fiction radio programs
  Science fiction television programs
Time, Use of
 USE Time management
Timesharing (Real estate) 333.3; 333.5;
  643
 UF Condominium timesharing
  Real estate timesharing
  Time sharing (Real estate)
  Vacation home timesharing
 BT Condominiums
  Housing
Tin 669
 BT Chemical elements
  Metals
Tinsmithing
 USE Tinwork
Tinwork 673
 UF Tinsmithing
 BT Metalwork
Tipis
 USE Indians of North America—
  Dwellings
Tires 678
 UF Rubber tires
 BT Wheels
Tiros (Meteorological satellite) 551.5
 UF T.I.R.O.S. (Meteorological satellite)
  Television and infrared observation satellite
 BT Meteorological satellites
Tissue donation
 USE Donation of organs, tissues, etc.
Tissues—Transplantation
 USE Transplantation of organs, tissues, etc.
Tithes 254.8
 BT Church finance
  Ecclesiastical law
  Taxation
Toadstools
 USE Mushrooms
Toasts 808.5; 808.85
 UF Healths, Drinking of

 BT Epigrams
  Speeches
 RT After dinner speeches
Tobacco 633.7
 RT Smoking
Tobacco habit 178; 613.85; 616.86
 UF Addiction to tobacco
 BT Habit
  Smoking
  Substance abuse
 NT Smoking cessation programs
Tobacco pipes 688
 UF Pipes, Tobacco
 BT Smoking
Toes
 USE Foot
Toilet preparations
 USE Cosmetics
Toilet training 649
 UF Training, Toilet
 BT Child rearing
Toleration 179; 323
 UF Bigotry
  Intolerance
 BT Human relations
 NT Academic freedom
  Freedom of conscience
  Freedom of religion
 RT Discrimination
Toll roads
 USE Express highways
Tombs (May subdiv. geog.) 726
 UF Graves
  Mausoleums
  Rock tombs
  Sepulchers
  Vaults (Sepulchral)
 BT Archeology
  Architecture
  Burial
  Monuments
  Shrines
 NT Brasses
  Catacombs
  Epitaphs
  Mounds and mound builders
 RT Cemeteries
Tomography 616.07; 621.36
 UF CAT scan
  Computerized tomography

Tomography—*Continued*
BT X rays
Tongue twisters 398.8
BT **Children's poetry**
Folklore
Nonsense verses
Tools 621.9
UF Implements, utensils, etc.
SA types of tools, to be added as needed
NT **Agricultural machinery**
Carpentry tools
Machine tools
Machinery
Power tools
Saws
Weapons
Top soil loss
USE **Soil erosion**
Topographical drawing 526.022
BT **Drawing**
Surveying
RT **Map drawing**
Topology 514
UF Analysis situs
Position analysis
Rubber sheet geometry
BT **Geometry**
Set theory
NT **Fractals**
Graph theory
RT **Linear algebra**
Tories, American
USE **American Loyalists**
Tornadoes (May subdiv. geog.) **551.55**
UF Twisters (Tornadoes)
BT **Meteorology**
Storms
Winds
Torpedoes 623.4
BT **Explosives**
Naval art and science
Submarine warfare
Tort liability of professions
USE **Malpractice**
Tortoises
USE **Turtles**
Total abstinence
USE **Temperance**
Totalitarianism 321.9
UF Authoritarianism

BT **Political science**
NT **Communism**
Dictators
Fascism
National socialism
Totem poles 299; 730.89
BT **Totems and totemism**
Totems and totemism 299
BT **Ethnology**
Mythology
NT **Totem poles**
RT **Indians of North America—Religion**
Touch 152.1; 612
UF Feeling
BT **Senses and sensation**
NT **Hugging**
Touring, Bicycle
USE **Bicycle touring**
Tourism
USE **Tourist trade**
Tourist accommodations
USE **Hotels and motels**
Youth hostels
Tourist trade 338.4
UF Tourism
Tourists
RT **Travel**
Tourists
USE **Tourist trade**
Travelers
Tournaments
USE subjects with the subdivision *Tournaments*, e.g. **Tennis—Tournaments**; to be added as needed
Town life
USE **City life**
Town meeting
USE **Local government**
Town planning
USE **City planning**
Towns
USE **Cities and towns**
Township government
USE **Local government**
Toxic dumps
USE **Hazardous waste sites**
Toxic plants
USE **Poisonous plants**

Toxic substances
  USE **Hazardous substances**
       Poisons and poisoning
Toxic wastes
  USE **Hazardous wastes**
Toxicology
  USE **Poisons and poisoning**
Toy and movable books
  UF Movable books
       Pop-up books
  BT **Picture books for children**
Toys 688.7; 790.1
  SA types of toys, to be added as
       needed
  BT **Amusements**
  NT **Dollhouses**
       Dolls
       Electric toys
       Electronic toys
Track and field
  USE **Track athletics**
Track athletics 796.42
  UF Field athletics
       Track and field
  SA names of specific track sports,
       to be added as needed
  BT **Athletics**
       Sports
  NT **Running**
Tracking and trailing 799.2
  UF Trailing
  BT **Hunting**
  NT **Animal tracks**
  RT **Animal behavior**
Tracking of satellites
  USE **Artificial satellites—Tracking**
       Space vehicles—Tracking
Tracks of animals
  USE **Animal tracks**
Traction engines
  USE **Tractors**
Tractors 629.225; 631.3
  UF Traction engines
  BT **Agricultural machinery**
Trade
  USE **Business**
       Commerce
Trade agreements (Labor)
  USE **Industrial arbitration**
       Labor contract

**Trade and professional associations
       380.1; 650**
  Use for materials on business or profes-
sional organizations whose aim is the pro-
tection or advancement of their common
interests without regard to the relations of
employer and employee.
  UF Professional associations
  BT **Associations**
Trade, Balance of
  USE **Balance of trade**
Trade barriers
  USE **Commercial policy**
Trade, Boards of
  USE **Chambers of commerce**
Trade fairs
  USE **Fairs**
Trade, International
  USE **International trade**
Trade marks
  USE **Trademarks**
Trade, Restraint of
  USE **Restraint of trade**
Trade routes 387
  UF Ocean routes
       Routes of trade
       Sea routes
  BT **Commerce**
       Commercial geography
       Transportation
Trade schools
  USE **Technical education**
Trade secrets 346.04; 658.4
  UF Business secrets
       Commercial secrets
       Industrial secrets
       Secrets, Trade
  BT **Right of privacy**
       Unfair competition
Trade shows
  USE **Exhibitions**
Trade unions
  USE **Labor unions**
Trade waste
  USE **Industrial wastes**
       Waste products
Trademarks 346.04; 929.9
  UF Company symbols
       Corporate symbols
       Trade marks
  BT **Commerce**

BT = Broader Term   NT = Narrower Term   RT = Related Term   SA = See Also   UF = Used For

Trademarks—*Continued*
    Manufactures
  RT **Brand name products**
    Patents
Trades
  USE **Industrial arts**
    Occupations
Traditional birth attendants
  USE **Midwives**
Traditional medicine (May subdiv.
    geog.) **615.8**
  UF Folk medicine *[Former head-
    ing]*
    Folklore, Medical
    Medical folklore
  SA ethnic groups and groups of
    American Indians with the
    subdivision *Medicine,* e.g.
    **Indians of North America—
    Medicine;** to be added as
    needed
  BT **Medicine**
    Popular medicine
Traditions
  USE **Folklore**
    Legends
    Manners and customs
    Rites and ceremonies
    Superstition
Traffic accidents 363.12
  UF Automobile accidents
    Automobiles—Accidents
    Car accidents
    Car wrecks
    Highway accidents
  BT **Accidents**
  RT **Traffic regulations**
Traffic, City
  USE **City traffic**
Traffic control
  USE **Traffic engineering**
Traffic engineering 388.4
  Use for materials on the planning of the
flow of traffic and related topics, largely as
they concern street transportation in cities
and metropolitan areas.
  UF Street traffic
    Traffic control
    Traffic regulation
  BT **Engineering**
    Highway engineering

    Transportation
  NT **Car pools**
    City traffic
    Express highways
    Local transit
    Traffic regulations
Traffic regulation
  USE **Traffic engineering**
Traffic regulations 388.4
  UF Street traffic
  BT **Traffic engineering**
    Transportation
  RT **Automobiles—Law and legis-
    lation**
    Traffic accidents
Trafficking in drugs
  USE **Drug traffic**
Trafficking in narcotics
  USE **Drug traffic**
Tragedies 808.82; 812, etc.
  May be used for individual works or for
collections. Materials about tragedy as a
literary form are entered under **Tragedy.**
  BT **Drama**
Tragedy 792.1; 809.2
  Use for materials on tragedy as a liter-
ary form. Individual works and collections
of tragedies are entered under **Tragedies.**
  BT **Drama**
Trailer parks 796.54
  BT **Campgrounds**
  NT **Mobile home parks**
Trailers
  USE **Travel trailers and campers**
Trailers, Home
  USE **Mobile homes**
Trailing
  USE **Tracking and trailing**
Train wrecks
  USE **Railroads—Accidents**
Trained nurses
  USE **Nurses**
Training camps, Military
  USE **Military training camps**
Training colleges for teachers
  USE **Teachers colleges**
Training, Occupational
  USE **Occupational training**
Training of animals
  USE **Animals—Training**
Training of children
  USE **Child rearing**

Training of employees
USE **Employees—Training**
Training, Toilet
USE **Toilet training**
Training, Vocational
USE **Occupational training**
Trains
USE **Railroads**
Tramps 305.5

    Use for materials on persons who travel about from place to place living on occasional jobs or gifts of money and food.

UF Hoboes
      Vagabonds
      Vagrants
BT **Homeless persons**
      Poor
RT **Begging**
      Unemployed
Trams
USE **Street railroads**
Transactional analysis 158
BT **Human relations**
      Psychotherapy
Transatlantic flights
USE **Aeronautics—Flights**
Transcendental meditation 158
BT **Meditation**
Transcendentalism 141
BT **Philosophy**
RT **Idealism**
Transcontinental journeys (American continent)
USE **Overland journeys to the Pacific**
Transcultural studies
USE **Cross cultural studies**
Transexuality
USE **Transsexuality**
Transfer of technology
USE **Technology transfer**
Transfer tax
USE **Inheritance and transfer tax**
Transformation (Genetics)
USE **Genetic transformation**
Transformers, Electric
USE **Electric transformers**
Transgenics
USE **Genetic engineering**
Transistor amplifiers 621.3815
UF Amplifiers, Transistor

      Audio amplifiers, Transistor
      Transistor audio amplifiers
BT **Amplifiers (Electronics)**
      Transistors
Transistor audio amplifiers
USE **Transistor amplifiers**
Transistors 621.3815
BT **Electronics**
      Semiconductors
NT **Transistor amplifiers**
Transit systems
USE **Local transit**
Translating and interpreting 418
UF Interpreting and translating
      Machine translating
      Mechanical translating
BT **Language and languages**
Transmission of data
USE **Data transmission systems**
Transmission of power
USE **Electric lines**
      Electric power distribution
      Power transmission
Transmissions, Automobile
USE **Automobiles—Transmission devices**
Transmutation (Chemistry) 539.7

    Use for materials on the transmutation of metals in nuclear physics. Materials on medieval attempts to change base metals into gold are entered under **Alchemy.**

UF Metals, Transmutation of
      Transmutation of metals
BT **Atoms**
      Nuclear physics
      Radioactivity
NT **Cyclotron**
RT **Alchemy**
Transmutation of metals
USE **Alchemy**
      Transmutation (Chemistry)
Transplantation of organs, tissues, etc. 617.9
UF Medical transplantation
      Organ transplantation
      Surgical transplantation
      Tissues—Transplantation
SA names of organs of the body with the subdivision *Transplantation,* to be added as needed

---

Transplantation of organs, tissues, etc.—*Continued*
  BT **Surgery**
  NT **Heart—Transplantation**
       Plastic surgery
  RT **Donation of organs, tissues, etc.**
       Preservation of organs, tissues, etc.

Transplantation of organs, tissues, etc.—Moral and religious aspects 174
  BT **Bioethics**

Transportation 388
  SA subjects, classes of person, and names of wars with the subdivision *Transportation,* to be added as needed
  BT **Locomotion**
  NT **Boats and boating**
       Bridges
       Canals
       Car pools
       Commercial aeronautics
       Electric railroads
       Express service
       Freight
       Harbors
       Highway transportation
       Inland navigation
       Local transit
       Merchant marine
       Military transportation
       Ocean travel
       Pipelines
       Postal service
       Railroads
       Roads
       School children—Transportation
       Shipping
       Steam navigation
       Street railroads
       Streets
       Subways
       Trade routes
       Traffic engineering
       Traffic regulations
       Trucking
       Vehicles
       Waterways
       World War, 1939-1945—Transportation
  RT **Commerce**

Transportation, Highway
  USE **Highway transportation**
Transportation, Military
  USE **Military transportation**
Transportation of criminals
  USE **Penal colonies**

Transsexuality 305.3; 616.85
  UF Change of sex
       Sex change
       Transexuality
  BT **Reproductive system**
       Sex role

Trapping 639
  NT **Fur trade**
  RT **Game and game birds**
       Hunting

Travel 910
  Use for materials on the art and enjoyment of travel and advice for travelers. Descriptions of actual voyages are entered under **Voyages and travels** or under the name of a place with the subdivision *Description.* An account of an extinct city or town by a traveler in ancient times is entered under the name of the extinct city or town, without further subdivision, e.g. **Delphi (Extinct city).**
  UF Group travel
  SA names of cities (except extinct cities), countries, states, etc., with the subdivision *Description,* e.g. **United States—Description;** to be added as needed
  BT **Manners and customs**
  NT **Automobile travel**
       Bicycle touring
       Ocean travel
       Travel in literature
       United States—Description
       Voyages around the world
  RT **Tourist trade**
       Voyages and travels

Travel books
  USE **Travel in literature**
        Voyages and travels
        Voyages around the world

BT = Broader Term   NT = Narrower Term   RT = Related Term   SA = See Also   UF = Used For

Travel books—*Continued*
    and names of continents,
    countries, cities, etc., with
    the subdivision *Description,*
    to be added as needed

Travel in literature 809
    Use for materials about travel writing
and about the theme of travel in literature. Collections and accounts of voyages
and travels not limited to a single place
are entered under **Voyages and travels.** Accounts of voyages and travels limited to a
single place are entered under the name of
the place with the subdivision *Description.*

  UF   Travel books
        Voyages and travels in litera-
          ture
  BT   **Literature**
        Travel
  RT   **Voyages and travels**

Travel trailers and campers 629.226;
    796.7
    Use for materials on structures mounted
upon a truck or towed by a truck or automobile for the purpose of temporary
dwelling or cargo hauling. Materials on
stationary transportable structures designed for year-round living are entered
under **Mobile homes.**

  UF   Automobiles—Trailers *[For-*
          mer heading]
        Campers and trailers
        House trailers
        Pickup campers
        Trailers
  BT   **Camping**
        Recreational vehicles
  NT   **Vans**
  RT   **Mobile homes**

avelers 910.92; 920
  UF   Tourists
        Voyagers
  SA   travelers from particular coun-
          tries, e.g. **American travel-**
          ers; to be added as needed
  BT   **Voyages and travels**
  NT   **American travelers**
  RT   **Explorers**

velers, American
  ISE **American travelers**
reling carnivals
  SE **Carnivals**
eling sales personnel
  SE **Sales personnel**

Travels
  USE   **Voyages and travels**
        and names of cities (except
          extinct cities), countries,
          states, etc., with the subdi-
          vision *Description,* e.g.
          United States—Description;
          and names of extinct
          cities or towns, without fur-
          ther subdivision, for ac-
          counts of those places by
          travelers in ancient times,
          e.g. **Delphi (Extinct city);** to
          be added as needed

Travesties
  USE **Parodies**
Tray gardens
  USE **Miniature gardens**

Treason 364.1
  UF   Collaborationists
        High treason
  BT   **Crime**
        Political crimes and offenses

Treasure trove
  USE **Buried treasure**

Treaties 341; 341.3
  SA   names of countries with the
          subdivision *Foreign*
          relations—Treaties, and
          names of wars with the
          subdivision *Treaties,* to be
          added as needed
  BT   **Congresses and conventions**
        Diplomacy
        International law
        International relations
  NT   **International arbitration**
        United States—Foreign
          relations—Treaties
        World War, 1939-1945—
          Treaties

Treatment of diseases
  USE **Therapeutics**

Tree planting 635.9
  UF   Planting
  BT   **Forests and forestry**
  NT   **Windbreaks**
  RT   **Christmas tree growing**
        Reforestation
        Trees

    BT = Broader Term   NT = Narrower Term   RT = Related Term   SA = See Also   UF = Used For

Trees (May subdiv. geog.) **582.16; 635.9**
    UF   Arboriculture
          Timber
    SA   names of trees, e.g. **Oak;** to
          be added as needed, in the
          singular form
    BT   **Botany**
          Plants
    NT   **Apple**
          Christmas tree growing
          Christmas trees
          Dwarf trees
          Evergreens
          Fruit culture
          Grafting
          Leaves
          Lime (Fruit)
          Lumber and lumbering
          Nurseries (Horticulture)
          Nuts
          Oak
          Orange
          Pecan
          Pruning
          Shrubs
          Wood
    RT   **Forests and forestry**
          Landscape gardening
          Tree planting
Trees—United States **582.160973**
    UF   United States—Trees
Trent Affair, 1861 973.7
    BT   **United States—History—**
          1861-1865, Civil War
Trial by jury
    USE **Jury**
Trial by publicity
    USE **Freedom of the press and fair**
          trial
Trial marriage
    USE **Unmarried couples**
Trials 345; 347
    May be qualified by topic, e.g. **Trials**
(Homicide).
    BT   **Criminal law**
    NT   **Courts martial and courts of**
          inquiry
          Trials (Homicide)
          War crime trials
          Witnesses

    RT   **Crime**
Trials (Homicide) 345
    UF   Homicide trials
          Murder trials
          Trials (Murder) *[Former head-*
          ing]
    BT   **Homicide**
          Trials
Trials (Murder)
    USE **Trials (Homicide)**
Tricks 793.5
    SA   types of tricks, to be added as
          needed
    BT   **Amusements**
    NT   **Card tricks**
          Juggling
          Magic tricks
Tricycles 629.227; 796.6
    UF   Trikes
    BT   **Vehicles**
    RT   **Cycling**
Trigonometry 516.24
    UF   Plane trigonometry
          Spherical trigonometry
    BT   **Geometry**
          Mathematics
Trigonometry—Tables 516.24
    UF   Trigonometry—Tables, etc.
          [Former heading]
    BT   **Mathematics—Tables**
    NT   **Logarithms**
Trigonometry—Tables, etc.
    USE **Trigonometry—Tables**
Trikes
    USE **Tricycles**
Trinity 231
    BT   **Doctrinal theology**
    NT   **Holy Spirit**
    RT   **God—Christianity**
          Jesus Christ—Divinity
Tripoline War
    USE **United States—History—**
          1801-1805, Tripolitan War
Trivia
    USE **Curiosities and wonders**
          Questions and answers
Trolley cars
    USE **Street railroads**
Tropical diseases
    USE **Tropical medicine**

Tropical fish 597; 639.3
  BT Fishes
Tropical jungles
  USE Jungles
Tropical medicine 614
  UF Diseases, Tropical
      Hygiene, Tropical
      Medicine, Tropical
      Tropical diseases
  SA names of tropical diseases,
      e.g. **Yellow fever;** to be add-
      ed as needed
  BT **Medicine**
  NT **Yellow fever**
Tropical rain forests
  USE **Rain forests**
Tropics 910.913
  SA subjects with the subdivision
      Tropics, to be added as
      needed
  BT **Earth**
  NT **Agriculture—Tropics**
Troubadours 849.1; 920
  BT **French poetry**
      Minstrels
      Poets
Trout fishing 799.1
  BT **Fishing**
Truancy (Schools)
  USE **School attendance**
Truck farming
  USE **Vegetable gardening**
Truck freight
  USE **Trucking**
Trucking 388.3
  UF Truck freight
  BT **Freight**
      Transportation
Trucks 629.224
  UF Automobile trucks
      Motor trucks
  SA types of trucks and names of
      specific makes and models,
      to be added as needed
  BT **Automobiles**
      Highway transportation
  RT **Materials handling**
Trust companies 332.2
  UF Companies, Trust
  BT **Business**

      Corporations
  NT **Investment trusts**
  RT **Banks and banking**
Trusts, Industrial
  USE **Industrial trusts**
Trusts, Industrial—Law and legislation
  USE **Antitrust law**
Truth 121
  UF Certainty
  BT **Belief and doubt**
      Faith
      Philosophy
  NT **Agnosticism**
      Reality
      Truthfulness and falsehood
  RT **Pragmatism**
      Skepticism
      Theory of knowledge
Truth in advertising
  USE **Deceptive advertising**
Truthfulness and falsehood 177
  UF Credibility
      Falsehood
      Lying
      Untruth
  BT **Human behavior**
      Truth
  NT **Lie detectors and detection**
  RT **Honesty**
Tsunamis 551.47
      Use for materials on unusually large sea
      waves generated by earthquakes or under-
      sea volcanic eruptions.
  UF Earthquake sea waves
      Seismic sea waves
      Tidal waves, Seismic
  BT **Natural disasters**
      Ocean waves
Tuberculosis 362.1; 616.9
  BT **Lungs—Diseases**
Tugboats 623.8
  BT **Boats and boating**
Tuition
  USE **College costs**
      Colleges and universities—
      Finance
      Education—Finance
Tumbling 796.47
  BT **Acrobats and acrobatics**
Tumors 616.99
  NT **Cancer**

Tuning 784.192
SA names of instruments with the subdivision *Tuning,* to be added as needed

BT **Musical instruments**

NT **Pianos—Tuning**

Tunnels 388; 624.1
BT **Civil engineering**

NT **Boring**
     Excavation
     Subways

Turbines 621.406
BT **Engines**
     Hydraulic machinery

NT **Gas turbines**
     Steam turbines

Turkeys 598.6; 636.5
BT **Poultry**

Turncoats
USE **Defectors**

Turning 621.9
UF Lathe work
     Wood turning

BT **Carpentry**

RT **Lathes**
     Woodwork

Turnpikes (Modern)
USE **Express highways**

Turtles 597.92
UF Terrapins
     Tortoises

BT **Reptiles**

Tutorial machines
USE **Teaching machines**

Tutors and tutoring 371.3
Use for materials on instruction provided to an individual or small group by a professional teacher, peer, or individual with appropriate training or experience.

BT **Home instruction**
     Teaching

NT **Independent study**
     Individualized instruction

TV
USE **Television**

Twelve-step programs 158; 291.4; 362.29
Use for materials on self-help programs to resolve personal problems which are based on the twelve-step, group approach of Alcoholics Anonymous. Materials on specific twelve-step programs are entered under the name of the individual organization.

UF Programs, Twelve-step
     Self-help programs
     Twelve steps (Self-help)

BT **Behavior modification**

RT **Alcoholism**
     Compulsive behavior
     Drug addiction
     Substance abuse

Twelve steps (Self-help)
USE **Twelve-step programs**

Twentieth century 909.82
Use for general materials covering progress and development during this period in one or in several countries.

UF 1900-1999 (20th century)

BT **Modern history—1900-1999 (20th century)**

Twenty-first century 909.83
UF 2000-2099 (21st century)

Twins 155.44; 306.875
BT **Multiple birth**

RT **Brothers and sisters**

Twisters (Tornadoes)
USE **Tornadoes**

Two-career family
USE **Dual career family**

Two hundred mile limit
USE **Territorial waters**

Type and type founding 686.2
BT **Founding**
     Printing

NT **Advertising layout and typography**
     Linotype

RT **Initials**
     Printing—Specimens
     Typesetting

Type-setting
USE **Typesetting**

Type specimens
USE **Printing—Specimens**

Typesetting 686.2
UF Composition (Printing)

Typesetting—*Continued*
> Type-setting
>> BT **Printing**
>> NT **Linotype**
>> RT **Type and type founding**

Typewriters 652.3; 681
> BT **Office equipment and supplies**

Typewriting 652.3
> BT **Business education**
>> **Office practice**
>> **Writing**
> RT **Keyboarding (Electronics)**

Typhoid fever 616.9
> UF Enteric fever
> BT **Diseases**
>> **Fever**

Typhoons 551.55
> Use for cyclonic storms originating in the region of the China Seas and the Philippines.
>> BT **Cyclones**
>>> **Storms**
>>> **Winds**
>> RT **Hurricanes**

Typography
> USE **Printing**

U boats
> USE **Submarines**

U.F.O.'s
> USE **Unidentified flying objects**

U.N.
> USE **United Nations**

U.S.
> USE **United States**

U.S.A.
> USE **United States**

U.S.M.A.
> USE **United States Military Academy**

U.S.S.R.
> USE **Soviet Union**

UFOs
> USE **Unidentified flying objects**

UHF radio
> USE **Shortwave radio**

Ultrahigh frequency radio
> USE **Shortwave radio**

Ultrasonic waves 534.5
> UF Supersonic waves
>> Waves, Ultrasonic

> BT **Sound waves**
>> **Ultrasonics**

Ultrasonics 534.5
> UF Inaudible sound
>> Supersonics
> BT **Sound**
> NT **Ultrasonic waves**

Ultraviolet rays 535.01; 621.36
> UF Rays, Ultra-violet
> BT **Electromagnetic waves**
>> **Radiation**
> RT **Phototherapy**
>> **Radiotherapy**

Umbrellas and parasols 391; 685
> UF Parasols
> BT **Costume**

UN
> USE **United Nations**

Unbelief
> USE **Skepticism**

Unborn child
> USE **Fetus**

Unconventional warfare
> USE **Guerrilla warfare**

Unction, Extreme
> USE **Anointing of the sick**

Undenominational churches
> USE **Community churches**

Under water exploration
> USE **Underwater exploration**

Underdeveloped areas
> USE **Developing countries**

Undergraduates
> USE **College students**

Underground aliens
> USE **Illegal aliens**

Underground, Anticommunist
> USE **Anticommunist movements**

Underground architecture 624.1; 690; 720
> UF Underground design
> BT **Architecture**
> NT **Basements**
>> **Earth sheltered houses**

Underground design
> USE **Underground architecture**

Underground economy 381
> UF Economy, Underground
>> Income, Untaxed
> BT **Economics**

BT = Broader Term   NT = Narrower Term   RT = Related Term   SA = See Also   UF = Used For

Underground economy—*Continued*
  NT Barter
      Illegal aliens
Underground films
  USE Experimental films
Underground houses
  USE Earth sheltered houses
Underground literature
  USE Alternative press
Underground movements (World War,
      1939-1945)
  USE World War, 1939-1945—
        Underground movements
Underground press
  USE Alternative press
Underground railroad 326
  RT Slavery—United States
Underground railroads
  USE Subways
Underprivileged
  USE Socially handicapped
Underprivileged children
  USE Socially handicapped children
Undersea engineering
  USE Ocean engineering
Undersea exploration
  USE Underwater exploration
Undersea research habitats
  USE Undersea research stations
Undersea research stations 551.46
  UF Manned undersea research
        stations
      Sea laboratories
      Submarine research stations
      Undersea research habitats
      Underwater research stations
  SA names of special research
        projects and stations, e.g.
        Sealab project; to be added
        as needed
  BT Oceanography—Research
      Skin diving
      Submersibles
      Underwater exploration
  NT Aquanauts
      Sealab project
Undersea technology
  USE Oceanography
Undersea vehicles
  USE Submersibles

Understanding
  USE Intellect
      Theory of knowledge
Undertakers and undertaking 363.7; 393
  UF Funeral directors
      Morticians
  BT Service industries
Underwater drilling (Petroleum)
  USE Offshore oil well drilling
Underwater exploration 551.46; 627
  UF Exploration, Submarine
      Exploration, Underwater
      Submarine exploration
      Under water exploration
      Undersea exploration
  BT Adventure and adventurers
      Oceanography—Research
  NT Aquanauts
      Buried treasure
      Marine biology
      Submersibles
      Undersea research stations
  RT Skin diving
      Submarine diving
Underwater exploration devices
  USE Submersibles
Underwater geology
  USE Submarine geology
Underwater medicine
  USE Submarine medicine
Underwater photography 778.7
  UF Deep-sea Photography
      Photography, Underwater
      Submarine photography
  BT Photography
Underwater physiology
  USE Submarine medicine
Underwater research stations
  USE Undersea research stations
Underwater swimming
  USE Skin diving
Underwriting
  USE Insurance
Undocumented aliens
  USE Illegal aliens
Unemployed 331.13
  UF Jobless people
      Out-of-work people
  BT Labor supply
      Poor

BT = Broader Term   NT = Narrower Term   RT = Related Term   SA = See Also   UF = Used For

Unemployed—*Continued*
    Unemployment
NT **Food relief**
    Occupational retraining
RT **Domestic economic assistance**
    Tramps
Unemployment 331.13
UF Joblessness
BT **Employment**
    Human resources
    Labor supply
    Social problems
NT **Employment agencies**
    Unemployed
Unemployment insurance 368.4
UF Insurance, Unemployment
    [Former heading]
    Labor—Insurance
    Payroll taxes
BT **Insurance**
Unfair competition 338.6
UF Competition, Unfair *[Former heading]*
    Fair trade
    Unfair trade practices
BT **Commercial law**
NT **Trade secrets**
RT **Restraint of trade**
Unfair trade practices
USE **Unfair competition**
Ungraded schools
USE **Nongraded schools**
Unicameral legislatures
USE **Legislative bodies**
Unidentified flying objects 001.9
UF Flying saucers
    Saucers, Flying
    U.F.O.'s
    UFOs
BT **Aeronautics**
    Astronautics
Uniforms, Military
USE **Military uniforms**
Uniforms, Naval
USE **Military uniforms**
Union churches
USE **Community churches**
Union of South Africa
USE **South Africa**
Union of Soviet Socialist Republics
USE **Soviet Union**

Union shop
USE **Open and closed shop**
Unions, Labor
USE **Labor unions**
Unisexuality
USE **Androgyny**
Unison speaking
USE **Choral speaking**
Unitarianism 289.1
BT **Christian sects**
    Congregationalism
RT **Jesus Christ—Divinity**
United Brethren
USE **Moravians**
United Nations 341.23
UF U.N.
    UN
BT **International arbitration**
    International cooperation
    International organization
United Nations—Armed forces 341.23
UF Peace keeping forces
United Nations—Finance 341.23
United Nations—Information services 341.23
BT **Information services**
United Nations—Officials and employees 341.23
United States 973
    The subdivisions under **United States**, with the exception of the period divisions of history, may be used under the name of any country or region. For subdivisions that may be used under names of states and cities see **Ohio**; and **Chicago (Ill.)**. Corporate entries, that is, those official bodies that may be used as author entries and as subjects, are included in the List only when they have been used as examples or as references, or when they are subdivided by subject. Other corporate entries may be added as needed. Corporate entries are distinguished by the use of a period between parts instead of a dash, e.g. **United States. Army**.
UF U.S.
    U.S.A.
    US
    USA
SA regions of the United States and groups of states, e.g. **New England; Southern States**; etc., to be added as needed

---

BT = Broader Term   NT = Narrower Term   RT = Related Term   SA = See Also   UF = Used For

United States—*Continued*

NT   Americans
      Atlantic States
      Gulf States (U.S.)
      Middle West
      Mississippi River Valley
      New England
      Old Northwest
      Old Southwest
      Oregon Trail
      Pacific Northwest
      Southern States
      Southwestern States
      West (U.S.)

United States—Agriculture
  USE   **Agriculture—United States**

United States—Air pollution
  USE   **Air pollution—United States**

United States—Animals
  USE   **Animals—United States**

United States—Antiques
  USE   **Antiques—United States**

United States—Antiquities 973

NT   **Indians of North America— Antiquities**

United States—Appropriations and expenditures 353.0072

  UF   Federal spending policy
        Government spending policy
  BT   **Budget—United States**

United States—Architecture
  USE   **American architecture**

United States—Archives
  USE   **Archives—United States**

United States—Armed forces 355.009783

  SA   official names and branches of the armed forces, e.g. **United States. Army; United States. Navy;** etc., to be added as needed

  NT   **United States. Army**
       United States. Navy

United States—Armed forces—Military life 355.10973

  BT   **Military personnel**

United States. Army 355.00973

Subdivisions used under this subject may be used under armies of other countries.

BT   **Armies**
      Military history
      United States—Armed forces

NT   **United States Military Academy**

United States. Army—Appointments and retirements 355.1

  UF   United States. Army— Retirements

United States. Army—Biography 920

United States. Army—Chaplains 355.3; 920

  BT   **Chaplains**

United States. Army—Crimes and misdemeanors
  USE   **Military offenses—United States**

United States. Army—Demobilization 355.2

United States. Army—Desertions
  USE   **Military desertion—United States**

United States. Army—Enlistment
  USE   **United States. Army— Recruiting, enlistment, etc.**

United States. Army—Examinations 355.1

  UF   Army tests

United States. Army—Handbooks, manuals, etc. 355

  UF   Soldiers' handbooks
       United States. Army— Officers' handbooks
       United States. Army— Soldiers' handbooks

United States. Army—Insignia 355.1
  BT   **Insignia**

United States. Army—Medals, badges, decorations, etc. 355.1

  BT   **Insignia**
      Medals

United States. Army—Military life 355.1

  BT   **Military personnel**
      Soldiers

United States. Army—Music
  USE   **United States. Army—Songs**

BT = Broader Term   NT = Narrower Term   RT = Related Term   SA = See Also   UF = Used For

United States. Army—Officers 355.3
United States. Army—Officers' handbooks
    USE   **United States. Army—**
        Handbooks, manuals, etc.
United States. Army—Ordnance 355.8
    UF   United States. Army—
        Ordnance and ordnance
        stores *[Former heading]*
    BT   **Ordnance**
United States. Army—Ordnance and
    ordnance stores
    USE   **United States. Army—**
        Ordnance
United States. Army—Parachute troops
356
    UF   United States—Parachute
        troops
    BT   **Parachute troops**
United States. Army—Recruiting, enlistment, etc. 355.2
    UF   United States. Army—
        Enlistment
United States. Army—Retirements
    USE   **United States. Army—**
        Appointments and retirements
United States. Army—Soldiers' handbooks
    USE   **United States. Army—**
        Handbooks, manuals, etc.
United States. Army—Songs 782.42
    UF   United States. Army—Music
        United States. Army—Songs
        and music *[Former heading]*
United States. Army—Songs and music
    USE   **United States. Army—Songs**
United States—Art
    USE   **American art**
United States—Artificial satellites
    USE   **American artificial satellites**
United States—Artists
    USE   **American artists**
United States—Astronautics
    USE   **Astronautics—United States**
United States—Atlases
    USE   **United States—Maps**
United States—Authors
    USE   **American authors**

United States—Ballads
    USE   **American ballads**
United States—Banks and banking
    USE   **Banks and banking—United**
        States
United States—Bibliography 015.73;
    016.973
    BT   **Bibliography**
United States—Bicentennial celebrations
    USE   **American Revolution Bicentennial, 1776-1976**
United States—Biculturalism
    USE   **Biculturalism—United States**
United States—Bilingualism
    USE   **Bilingualism—United States**
United States—Bio-bibliography 012
United States—Biography 920.073
    BT   **Biography**
United States—Biography—Dictionaries
920.073
    BT   **Biography—Dictionaries**
United States—Biography—Portraits
920.073
    UF   United States—History—
        Portraits
    BT   **Portraits**
United States—Birds
    USE   **Birds—United States**
United States—Boundaries 973
    BT   **Boundaries**
United States—Budget
    USE   **Budget—United States**
United States—Campaign funds
    USE   **Campaign funds—United**
        States
United States—Capital punishment
    USE   **Capital punishment—United**
        States
United States—Cathedrals
    USE   **Cathedrals—United States**
United States—Catholic Church
    USE   **Catholic Church—United**
        States
United States—Catholics
    USE   **Catholics—United States**
United States—Census 317.3; 353.0081
    BT   **Census**
United States—Centennial celebrations,
    etc. 353.0085
    NT   **American Revolution Bicentennial, 1776-1976**

United States—Children
USE **Children—United States**
United States—Children—Employment
USE **Children—Employment—
United States**
United States—Christmas
USE **Christmas—United States**
United States—Church—Government
policy
USE **Church and state—United
States**
United States—Church history 277.3
UF Church history—United States
United States—Religious his-
tory
BT **Church history**
RT **United States—Religion**
United States—Church of England
USE **Church of England—United
States**
United States—Churches
USE **Churches—United States**
United States—Cities and towns
USE **Cities and towns—United
States**
United States—City planning
USE **City planning—United States**
United States—Civil defense 363.3
BT **Civil defense**
United States—Civil service
USE **Civil service—United States**
United States—Civilization 973
UF Civilization, American
BT **Civilization**
NT **Americana**
**United States—Civilization—1960-1970
973.92**
**United States—Civilization—1970-
973.92**
**United States—Civilization—Foreign in-
fluences 973**
United States—Climate 551.6973
BT **Climate
Weather**
United States—Collective settlements
USE **Collective settlements—United
States**
United States—Colleges and universi-
ties
USE **Colleges and universities—
United States**

United States—Colonies
USE **United States—Territories and
possessions**
**United States—Commerce 380.1;
382.0973**
BT **Commerce**
United States—Commerce—Japan 382
**United States—Commercial policy
380.1; 381.3; 382**
BT **Commercial policy
Economic policy**
United States—Communism
USE **Communism—United States**
United States—Composers
USE **American composers**
United States. Congress 328.73
UF Congress (U.S.)
BT **Legislative bodies**
United States. Congress. House 328.73
UF House of Representatives
(U.S.)
Representatives, House of
(U.S.)
United States. Congress. Senate 328.73
UF Senate (U.S.)
**United States—Constitution 342.73;
973.3**
UF American Constitution
Constitution (U.S.)
BT **Constitutions**
**United States—Constitutional history
342.73**
BT **Constitutional history
United States—History**
RT **United States—History—
1783-1809**
**United States—Constitutional law
342.73**
BT **Constitutional law**
United States—Consular service
USE **United States—Diplomatic
and consular service**
United States—Country life
USE **Country life—United States**
United States—Courts
USE **Courts—United States**
United States—Crime
USE **Crime—United States**
United States—Cultivated plants
USE **Cultivated plants—United
States**

United States—Dancing
USE **Dancing—United States**
United States—Declaration of independence 973.3
UF Declaration of independence (U.S.)
United States—Decoration and ornament
USE **American decoration and ornament**
United States—Decorative arts
USE **Decorative arts—United States**
United States—Defenses 355.4
BT **Fortification**
NT **Strategic Defense Initiative**
United States—Description 917.3
UF United States—Description and travel *[Former heading]*
United States—Travel
BT **Geography**
Travel
Voyages and travels
United States—Description and travel
USE **United States—Description**
United States—Description—Guidebooks
USE **United States—Guidebooks**
United States—Description—Maps
USE **United States—Maps**
United States—Description—Views
USE **United States—Pictorial works**
United States—Diplomatic and consular service 327.73; 353.0089
UF United States—Consular service
BT **Diplomatic and consular service**
United States—Diplomatic and consular service—Buildings
USE **United States—Public buildings**
United States—Directories 917.30025
Use for lists of names and addresses. Lists of names without addresses are entered under **United States—Registers**.
BT **Directories**
RT **United States—Registers**
United States—Dramatists
USE **American dramatists**

United States—Drawing
USE **American drawing**
United States—Earthquakes
USE **Earthquakes—United States**
United States—Economic assistance
USE **American economic assistance**
United States—Economic conditions 330.973
May be subdivided by period using the subdivisions under **United States—History**, e.g. **United States—Economic conditions—1600-1775, Colonial period.**
UF United States—History, Economic
United States—Natural resources
BT **Economic conditions**
Natural resources—United States
Poverty
United States—Economic policy 338.973
BT **Economic policy**
United States—Education
USE **Education—United States**
United States—Elderly
USE **Elderly—United States**
United States—Elections
USE **Elections—United States**
United States—Emigration
USE **United States—Immigration and emigration**
United States—Employees
USE **United States—Officials and employees**
United States—Engraving
USE **American engraving**
United States—Environmental policy
USE **Environmental policy—United States**
United States—Ethics
USE **American ethics**
United States—Ethnology
USE **Ethnology—United States**
United States—European War, 1914-1918
USE **World War, 1914-1918—United States**
United States—Excavations (Archeology)
USE **Excavations (Archeology)—United States**

United States—Executive departments
353.03

  NT **Presidents—United States—
      Staff**

**United States—Executive departments—
Reorganization 353.03**

  UF Administrative agencies—
      Reorganization
      Government reorganization
      Reorganization of administra-
      tive agencies

United States—Executive power

  USE **Executive power—United
      States**

United States—Exploration 973

  UF Exploration—United States

  BT **America—Exploration
      Exploration**

  NT **West (U.S.)—Exploration**

**United States—Exploring expeditions
910.973; 973**

Use for materials on exploring expeditions sponsored by the United States. Materials on early exploration of a particular
place are entered under the name of the
place with the subdivision *Exploration.*

  UF American exploring expedi-
      tions

  SA names of expeditions, e.g.
      **Lewis and Clark Expedition
      (1804-1806);** to be added as
      needed

  BT **Explorers**

  NT **Lewis and Clark Expedition
      (1804-1806)**

United States—Famines

  USE **Famines—United States**

United States—Farm life

  USE **Farm life—United States**

United States—Fascism

  USE **Fascism—United States**

United States—Festivals

  USE **Festivals—United States**

United States—Fiction 808.83; 813, etc.

  BT **Fiction**

United States—Finance

  USE **Finance—United States**

United States—Fiscal policy

  USE **Fiscal policy—United States**

United States—Fisheries

  USE **Fisheries—United States**

United States—Fishes

  USE **Fishes—United States**

United States—Fishing

  USE **Fishing—United States**

United States—Flags

  USE **Flags—United States**

United States—Flowers

  USE **Flowers—United States**

United States—Folk art

  USE **American folk art**

United States—Folk dancing

  USE **American folk dancing**

United States—Folk music

  USE **Folk music—United States**

United States—Folk songs

  USE **Folk songs—United States**

United States—Folklore

  USE **Folklore—United States**

**United States—Foreign economic rela-
tions 337.73**

  UF Foreign economic relations—
      United States

United States—Foreign opinion (May
subdiv. geog.) **303.3; 973**

Use for materials on foreign public
opinion about the United States. May be
further subdivided by the country holding
the opinion, e.g. **United States—Foreign
opinion—France.**

  UF Anti-Americanism
      Antiamericanism
      United States—Foreign public
      opinion

  BT **Public opinion**

**United States—Foreign opinion—France
303.3; 973**

Use for materials on French public
opinion about the United States.

  UF French foreign opinion—
      United States
      United States—Foreign opin-
      ion, French *[Former head-
      ing]*
      United States—Foreign public
      opinion, French

United States—Foreign opinion, French

  USE **United States—Foreign
      opinion—France**

United States—Foreign policy

  USE **United States—Foreign rela-
      tions**

United States—Foreign population
325.73
SA ethnic groups from particular
countries, e.g. **Mexican
Americans;** and citizens of
other countries with the
subdivision *United States,*
e.g. **Mexicans—United
States;** to be added as
needed
BT **Americanization
Immigration and emigration
Minorities**
NT **Mexican Americans
Mexicans—United States**
RT **United States—Immigration
and emigration**
United States—Foreign public opinion
USE **United States—Foreign opin-
ion**
United States—Foreign public opinion,
French
USE **United States—Foreign
opinion—France**
United States—Foreign relations (May
subdiv. geog.) **327.73**
When further subdividing geographical-
ly, provide an additional subject entry
with the two places in reversed positions,
i.e. **United States—Foreign relations—
Iran** and also **Iran—Foreign relations—
United States.**
UF United States—Foreign policy
BT **Diplomacy
International relations
World politics**
NT **Monroe Doctrine**
RT **United States—Neutrality**
**United States—Foreign relations—Iran
327.73055**
NT **Iran hostage crisis, 1979-1981**
**United States—Foreign relations—
Treaties 327.73; 341.3**
UF United States—Treaties
BT **Treaties**
United States—Forests and forestry
USE **Forests and forestry—United
States**
United States—Furniture
USE **American furniture**
United States—Gazetteers 917.3003
BT **Gazetteers**

United States—Geographic names
USE **Geographic names—United
States**
United States—Geography 917.3
BT **Geography**
United States—Geology
USE **Geology—United States**
United States—Government
USE **United States—Politics and
government**
United States—Government buildings
USE **United States—Public build-
ings**
United States—Government employees
USE **United States—Officials and
employees**
United States—Government publica-
tions
USE **Government publications—
United States**
United States—Governmental investiga-
tions
USE **Governmental investigations—
United States**
United States—Graphic arts
USE **Graphic arts—United States**
United States—Guidebooks 917.304
UF United States—Description—
Guidebooks *[Former head-
ing]*
United States—Hippies
USE **Hippies—United States**
United States—Historians
USE **American historians**
United States—Historic buildings
USE **Historic buildings—United
States**
**United States—Historical geography
911**
BT **Historical geography**
**United States—Historical geography—
Maps 911**
BT **United States—Maps**
United States—Historiography 973.07
UF United States—History—
Historiography *[Former
heading]*
BT **Historiography**
United States—History 973
UF American history

United States—History—*Continued*

NT **Americana**
 Southern States—History
 United States—Constitutional history
 West (U.S.)—History

United States—History—1600-1775, Colonial period 973.2

Use for materials on American history from the earliest permanent English settlements on the Atlantic coast up to the American Revolution. Materials on the period of discovery are entered under **United States—Exploration.**

UF American colonies
 Colonial history (U.S.)

NT **Bacon's Rebellion, 1676**
 King Philip's War, 1675-1676
 Pilgrims (New England colonists)
 Pontiac's Conspiracy, 1763-1765
 Puritans
 United States—History—1689-1697, King William's War
 United States—History—1755-1763, French and Indian War

United States—History—1675-1676, King Philip's War

USE **King Philip's War, 1675-1676**

United States—History—1689-1697, King William's War 973.2

UF King William's War, 1689-1697

BT **Indians of North America—Wars**
 United States—History—1600-1775, Colonial period

United States—History—1755-1763, French and Indian War 973.2

UF French and Indian War

BT **Indians of North America—Wars**
 United States—History—1600-1775, Colonial period

NT **Pontiac's Conspiracy, 1763-1765**

United States—History—1775-1783, Revolution 973.3

May be subdivided like **United States—History—1861-1865, Civil War.**

UF American Revolution
 Revolution, American
 War of the American Revolution

BT **Revolutions**

NT **American Loyalists**
 Canadian Invasion, 1775-1776
 Fourth of July

United States—History—1775-1783, Revolution—Centennial celebrations, etc.

USE **American Revolution Bicentennial, 1776-1976**

United States—History—1783-1809 973.3; 973.4

UF Confederation of American colonies

NT **Lewis and Clark Expedition (1804-1806)**
 Louisiana Purchase

RT **United States—Constitutional history**

United States—History—1783-1865 973.3-973.7

United States—History—1801-1805, Tripolitan War 973.4

UF Tripoline War

BT **Pirates**

United States—History—1812-1815, War of 1812 973.5

UF Canada—History—1812-1815, War of 1812
 War of 1812

United States—History—1815-1861 973.5; 973.6

NT **Black Hawk War, 1832**
 Mexican War, 1846-1848

United States—History—1845-1848, War with Mexico

USE **Mexican War, 1846-1848**

United States—History—1861-1865, Civil War 973.7

UF American Civil War
 Civil War—United States
 War of Secession (U.S.)

NT **Confederate States of America**

United States—History—1861-1865,
Civil War—*Continued*

Slavery—United States

Trent Affair, 1861

United States—History—1861-1865,
Civil War—Biography 920;
973.7092

United States—History—1861-1865,
Civil War—Campaigns
973.7

SA names of battles, e.g. **Gettysburg (Pa.), Battle of, 1863;**
to be added as needed

NT Gettysburg (Pa.), Battle of,
1863

United States—History—1861-1865,
Civil War—Causes 973.7

UF Secession

United States—History—1861-1865,
Civil War—Centennial celebrations, etc. 973.7

United States—History—1861-1865,
Civil War—Drama 808.82;
812, etc.

May be used for individual works, collections, or materials about plays dealing with the Civil War.

BT Drama

Historical drama

United States—History—1861-1865,
Civil War—Fiction 808.83;
813, etc.

May be used for individual works, collections, or materials about fiction dealing with the Civil War.

BT Historical fiction

United States—History—1861-1865,
Civil War—Health aspects
973.7

United States—History—1861-1865,
Civil War—Historiography
973.7

BT Historiography

United States—History—1861-1865,
Civil War—Medical care
973.7

United States—History—1861-1865,
Civil War—Naval operations 973.7

United States—History—1861-1865,
Civil War—Personal narratives 973.7

Use for collective or individual eyewitness reports or autobiographical accounts of the war in general. Accounts limited to a specific topic are entered under that topic.

BT Autobiographies

Biography

United States—History—1861-1865,
Civil War—Pictorial works
973.7022

BT Pictures

United States—History—1861-1865,
Civil War—Prisoners and
prisons 973.7

United States—History—1861-1865,
Civil War—
Reconstruction

USE Reconstruction (1865-1876)

United States—History—1861-1865,
Civil War—Sources 973.7

BT History—Sources

United States—History—1865-1898
973.8

NT Reconstruction (1865-1876)
Spanish-American War, 1898

United States—History—1898-1919
973.9; 973.91

NT Spanish-American War, 1898

United States—History—1898, War of
1898

USE Spanish-American War, 1898

United States—History—1900-1999
(20th century) 973.9

United States—History—1914-1918, European War

USE World War, 1914-1918—
United States

United States—History—1914-1918,
World War

USE World War, 1914-1918—
United States

BT = Broader Term   NT = Narrower Term   RT = Related Term   SA = See Also   UF = Used For

United States—History—1919-1933
973.91

United States—History—1933-1945
973.917

United States—History—1939-1945,
World War
USE **World War, 1939-1945—
United States**

United States—History—1945- 973.92

United States—History—1945-1953
973.918

United States—History—1953-1961
973.921

United States—History—1961-1974
973.922-973.924
NT **Vietnam War, 1961-1975
Watergate Affair, 1972-1974**

United States—History—1974-1989
973.925-973.927
NT **Iran-Contra Affair, 1985-1990**

United States—History—1989- 973.928
NT **Iran-Contra Affair, 1985-1990**

United States—History—1991, Persian
Gulf War
USE **Persian Gulf War, 1991**

United States—History—Bibliography
016.973

United States—History—Chronology
973
BT **Historical chronology**

United States—History—Dictionaries
973.03
BT **History—Dictionaries**

United States—History—Drama 808.82;
812, etc.
May be used for individual works, collections, or materials about plays dealing
with American history.
BT **Drama
Historical drama**

United States—History, Economic
USE **United States—Economic conditions**

United States—History—Examinations
973.076
UF United States—History—
Examinations, questions,
etc. *[Former heading]*
RT United States—History—
Study and teaching

United States—History—Examinations,
questions, etc.
USE **United States—History—
Examinations**

United States—History—Fiction 808.83;
813, etc.
May be used for individual works, collections, or materials about fiction dealing
with American history.

United States—History—Historiography
USE **United States—Historiography**

United States—History, Local
USE **United States—Local history**

United States—History, Military
USE **United States—Military history**

United States—History, Naval
USE **United States—Naval history**

United States—History—Outlines, syl-
labi, etc. 973.02
BT **United States—History—
Study and teaching**

United States—History—Periodicals
973.05

United States—History—Poetry 808.81;
811, etc.; 811.008, etc.
May be used for individual works, collections, or materials about poetry dealing
with American history.
BT **Historical poetry
Poetry**

United States—History, Political
USE **United States—Politics and
government**

United States—History—Portraits
USE **United States—Biography—
Portraits**

United States—History—Societies
973.06
BT **History—Societies**

United States—History—Sources 973
BT **History—Sources**

United States—History—Study and
teaching 973.07
NT **United States—History—
Outlines, syllabi, etc.**
RT **United States—History—
Examinations**

United States—Hospitals
USE **Hospitals—United States**

United States—Hostages
USE **American hostages**

United States—Hotels and motels
USE **Hotels and motels—United States**
United States—Hunting
USE **Hunting—United States**
United States—Illustrators
USE **American illustrators**
United States—Immigration and emigration 325; 325.73
    UF   United States—Emigration
    SA   names of nationality groups, e.g. **Mexican Americans; Mexicans—United States;** to be added as needed
    BT   **Americanization**
         Colonization
         Immigration and emigration
    NT   **Mexican Americans**
         Mexicans—United States
    RT   **United States—Foreign population**
United States—Industries 338.0973; 658; 670
    UF   United States—Manufactures
United States—Industry—Government policy
USE **Industry—Government policy—United States**
United States—Insular possessions
USE **United States—Territories and possessions**
United States—Intellectual life 973
    BT   **Intellectual life**
United States—Intelligence service
USE **Intelligence service—United States**
United States—Internal security
USE **Internal security—United States**
United States—Irrigation
USE **Irrigation—United States**
United States—Labor
USE **Labor—United States**
United States—Labor unions
USE **Labor unions—United States**
United States—Lakes
USE **Lakes—United States**
United States—Land settlement
USE **Land settlement—United States**

United States—Law
USE **Law—United States**
United States—Legends
USE **Legends—United States**
United States—Libraries
USE **Libraries—United States**
United States. Library of Congress
USE **Library of Congress**
United States—Literary landmarks
USE **Literary landmarks—United States**
United States—Literature
USE **American literature**
United States—Local history 973
    UF   United States—History, Local *[Former heading]*
United States—Mail
USE **Postal service—United States**
United States—Manners and customs
USE **United States—Social life and customs**
United States—Manufactures
USE **United States—Industries**
United States—Maps 912.73
    UF   United States—Atlases
         United States—Description—Maps
    BT   **Atlases**
         Maps
         Road maps
    NT   **United States—Historical geography—Maps**
United States—Medicine
USE **Medicine—United States**
United States—Merchant marine
USE **Merchant marine—United States**
United States Military Academy 355.0071
    UF   U.S.M.A.
         USMA
         West Point (Military academy)
    BT   **United States. Army**
United States Military Academy— Songs 782.42
    UF   United States Military Academy—Songs and music *[Former heading]*
    BT   **Students' songs**

BT = Broader Term   NT = Narrower Term   RT = Related Term   SA = See Also   UF = Used For

United States Military Academy—Songs
and music
  USE **United States Military
Academy—Songs**
**United States—Military history
355.00973; 973**
  UF United States—History, Military *[Former heading]*
  BT **Military history**
United States—Military offenses
  USE **Military offenses—United
States**
United States—Military personnel
  USE **Military personnel—United
States**
United States—Military policy 355
  BT **Military policy**
  NT **Strategic Defense Initiative**
United States—Militia 355.3
  NT **United States. National Guard**
United States—Mines and mineral resources
  USE **Mines and mineral
resources—United States**
United States—Monetary policy
  USE **Monetary policy—United
States**
United States—Moral conditions 973
  BT **Moral conditions**
United States—Municipal government
  USE **Municipal government—
United States**
United States—Museums
  USE **Museums—United States**
United States—Music
  USE **American music**
United States—Musicians
  USE **American musicians**
United States—Muslims
  USE **Muslims—United States**
United States—Names, Geographic
  USE **Geographic names—United
States**
United States—Names, Personal
  USE **Personal names—United
States**
United States—National characteristics
  USE **American national characteristics**
United States. National Guard 355.3
  UF National Guard (U.S.)

  BT **United States—Militia**
United States—National parks and reserves
  USE **National parks and reserves—
United States**
United States—National security 355
  BT **National security**
United States—National songs
  USE **National songs—United States**
United States—Natural disasters
  USE **Natural disasters—United
States**
United States—Natural history
  USE **Natural history—United
States**
United States—Natural monuments
  USE **Natural monuments—United
States**
United States—Natural resources
  USE **Natural resources—United
States**
      United States—Economic conditions
United States—Nature study
  USE **Nature study—United States**
United States—Naval history 359.00973
  UF United States—History, Naval
[Former heading]
  BT **Naval battles**
      Naval history
United States. Navy 359
  Subdivisions used under this subject may be used under navies of other countries.
  BT **Naval history**
      Navies
      Sailors
      Sea power
      United States—Armed forces
      Warships
United States. Navy—Biography 920
United States. Navy—Enlistment
  USE **United States. Navy—
Recruiting, enlistment, etc.**
United States. Navy—Handbooks, manuals, etc. 359
  UF United States. Navy—
Officers' handbooks
United States. Navy—Insignia 359.1
  BT **Insignia**

United States. Navy—Medals, badges, decorations, etc. 359.1
  BT Insignia
      Medals
United States. Navy—Officers 359.3
United States. Navy—Officers' handbooks
  USE United States. Navy—Handbooks, manuals, etc.
United States. Navy—Recruiting, enlistment, etc. 359.2
  UF United States. Navy—Enlistment
United States. Navy—Sealab project
  USE Sealab project
United States—Neutrality 327.73
  BT Neutrality
  RT United States—Foreign relations
United States—Novelists
  USE American novelists
United States—Occupations 331.7
  BT Occupations
United States of Europe (proposed)
  USE European federation
United States—Officials and employees 353.001
  UF United States—Employees
      United States—Government employees
  RT Civil service—United States
United States—Painters
  USE American painters
United States—Painting
  USE American painting
United States—Parachute troops
  USE United States. Army—Parachute troops
United States—Parks
  USE Parks—United States
United States—Peoples
  USE Ethnology—United States
United States—Personal names
  USE Personal names—United States
United States—Petroleum
  USE Petroleum—United States
United States—Philosophers
  USE American philosophers
United States—Philosophy
  USE American philosophy

United States—Physical geography
  USE Physical geography—United States
United States—Pictorial works 917.30022
  UF United States—Description—Views [Former heading]
  BT Pictures
      Views
United States—Plants
  USE Plants—United States
United States—Poets
  USE American poets
United States—Police
  USE Police—United States
United States—Politicians
  USE Politicians—United States
United States—Politics and government 973
  May be subdivided by period using the subdivisions under United States—History, e.g. United States—Politics and government—1600-1775, Colonial period.
  UF American government
      American politics
      Civics
      Civil government
      United States—Government
      United States—History, Political
  BT Political science
      Politics
      Public administration
  NT Third parties (United States politics)
United States—Popular culture
  USE Popular culture—United States
United States—Population 304.60973
  BT Population
United States—Postal service
  USE Postal service—United States
United States—Pottery
  USE American pottery
United States—Presidents
  USE Presidents—United States
United States—Prints
  USE American prints
United States—Prisons
  USE Prisons—United States
United States—Propaganda
  USE American propaganda

United States—Protests, demonstrations, etc.
USE **Protests, demonstrations,**
etc.—United States
United States—Public buildings
353.0086; 725.0973

Use for materials on U.S. federal government buildings located in or outside of
the United States, as well as for materials
on U.S embassy or consulate buildings
abroad.

UF Public buildings, American
Public buildings—United
States
United States—Diplomatic
and consular service—
Buildings
United States—Government
buildings
BT **Public buildings**
United States—Public debts
USE **Public debts—United States**
United States—Public documents
USE **Government publications—**
United States
United States—Public health
USE **Public health—United States**
United States—Public lands
USE **Public lands—United States**
United States—Public schools
USE **Public schools—United States**
United States—Public works 353.0086;
363.0973
BT **Public works**
United States—Race relations
305.800973
BT **Minorities**
Race relations
United States—Registers 917.30025

Use for lists of names without addresses. Lists of names that include addresses
are entered under **United States—**
Directories.

RT **United States—Directories**
United States—Religion 200.973; 277.3
BT **Religion**
RT **United States—Church history**
United States—Religious history
USE **United States—Church history**
United States—Rural conditions
307.720973
BT **Rural sociology**

United States—Schools
USE **Schools—United States**
United States—Science
USE **Science—United States**
United States—Sculptors
USE **American sculptors**
United States—Sculpture
USE **American sculpture**
United States—Secret service
USE **Secret service—United States**
United States—Separation of powers
USE **Separation of powers—United**
States
United States—Shipping
USE **Shipping—United States**
United States—Social conditions 973
BT **Poverty**
Social conditions
United States—Social life and customs
973
UF United States—Manners and
customs
BT **Ethnology**
Manners and customs
United States—Social policy 361.6; 973
BT **Social policy**
United States—Social surveys
USE **Social surveys—United States**
United States—Socialism
USE **Socialism—United States**
United States—Soldiers
USE **Soldiers—United States**
United States—Songs
USE **American songs**
United States—State governments
USE **State governments**
United States—Statistics 317.3
BT **Statistics**
United States—Strikes
USE **Strikes—United States**
United States—Strikes and lockouts
USE **Strikes—United States**
United States—Students
USE **Students—United States**
United States. Supreme Court 347.73
UF Supreme Court—United
States
United States. Supreme Court—
Biography 920
United States—Tariff
USE **Tariff—United States**

United States—Taxation
USE **Taxation—United States**
United States—Technical assistance
USE **American technical assistance**
United States—Teenagers
USE **Teenagers—United States**
**United States—Territorial expansion
973**
UF Westward movement
United States—Territorial waters
USE **Territorial waters—United
States**
**United States—Territories and posses-
sions 325; 973**
UF United States—Colonies *[For-
mer heading]*
United States—Insular posses-
sions
BT **Colonies**
United States—Terrorism
USE **Terrorism—United States**
United States—Theater
USE **Theater—United States**
United States—Travel
USE **United States—Description**
United States—Travelers
USE **American travelers**
United States—Treaties
USE **United States—Foreign
relations—Treaties**
United States—Trees
USE **Trees—United States**
United States—Universities
USE **Colleges and universities—
United States**
United States—Urban renewal
USE **Urban renewal—United States**
United States—Veterans
USE **Veterans—United States**
United States—Vice-presidents
USE **Vice-presidents—United States**
United States—Women
USE **Women—United States**
United States—World War, 1914-1918
USE **World War, 1914-1918—
United States**
United States—World War, 1939-1945
USE **World War, 1939-1945—
United States**
United States—Youth
USE **Youth—United States**

United Steelworkers of America 331.88
BT **Labor unions**
Universal bibliographic control
USE **Bibliographic control**
Universal history
USE **World history**
Universal language 401
UF International language
Language, International
Language, Universal *[Former
heading]*
World language
BT **Language and languages**
Linguistics
NT **Esperanto**
Universal military training
USE **Draft**
Universe 113; 523.1
UF Big bang theory
Cosmogony
Cosmography
Cosmology
Expanding universe
BT **Metaphysics**
Philosophy
NT **Astronomy**
Life on other planets
RT **Creation**
Earth
Universities
USE **Colleges and universities**
University degrees
USE **Academic degrees**
University extension 378.1
BT **Colleges and universities**
Higher education
NT **Adult education**
**Correspondence schools and
courses**
University graduates
USE **College graduates**
University libraries
USE **Academic libraries**
University students
USE **College students**
Unmarried couples 306.7
UF Cohabitation
Common law marriage
Living together
Marriage, Open ended

Unmarried couples—*Continued*
　　Nonmarital relations
　　Open ended marriage
　　Trial marriage
　　Unmarried people
　BT　**Lifestyles**
　　　Sexual ethics
　　　Shared housing
　　　Single people
Unmarried fathers 306.85; 362.82
　　Use for materials on fathers who at the time of childbirth were not married to the child's mother. Materials on fathers rearing children without a partner in the household are entered under **Single parent family**. Materials on fathers who are teenagers are entered under **Teenage fathers.**
　UF　Parents, Unmarried
　　　Unwed fathers
　BT　**Child welfare**
　　　Fathers
　　　Illegitimacy
　RT　**Single parent family**
Unmarried men
　USE　**Single men**
Unmarried mothers 306.85; 362.83
　　Use for materials on mothers who at the time of giving birth were not married to the child's father. Materials on mothers rearing children without a partner in the household are entered under **Single parent family**. Materials on mothers who are teenagers are entered under **Teenage mothers.**
　UF　Parents, Unmarried
　　　Unwed mothers
　BT　**Child welfare**
　　　Illegitimacy
　　　Mothers
　RT　**Single parent family**
Unmarried people
　USE　**Single people**
　　　Unmarried couples
Unmarried women
　USE　**Single women**
Unskilled workers
　USE　**Labor**
　　　Working class
Untruth
　USE　**Truthfulness and falsehood**
Unwed fathers
　USE　**Unmarried fathers**
Unwed mothers
　USE　**Unmarried mothers**

Upholstery 684.1; 747
　BT　**Interior design**
　NT　**Drapery**
　RT　**Furniture**
Upper atmosphere 551.5
　UF　Atmosphere, Upper *[Former heading]*
　BT　**Atmosphere**
　NT　**Stratosphere**
Upper classes 305.5
　UF　Fashionable society
　　　High society
　　　Society, Upper
　BT　**Aristocracy**
　　　Social classes
Uranium 669
　BT　**Chemical elements**
　RT　**Radioactivity**
Urban areas
　USE　**Cities and towns**
　　　Metropolitan areas
Urban development
　USE　**Cities and towns—Growth**
　　　Urbanization
Urban-federal relations
　USE　**Federal-city relations**
Urban life
　USE　**City life**
Urban planning
　USE　**City planning**
Urban renewal (May subdiv. geog.) **307.3**
　　Use for materials on urban redevelopment and the economic, sociological, and political factors involved. Materials on the architectural and engineering aspects of urban redevelopment are entered under **City planning.**
　UF　Slum clearance
　BT　**Metropolitan areas**
　　　Urban sociology
　NT　**Community development**
　RT　**City planning**
　　　Community organization
Urban renewal—Chicago (Ill.) 307.3
　UF　Chicago (Ill.)—Urban renewal
Urban renewal—United States 307.3
　UF　United States—Urban renewal
Urban sociology 307.76
　UF　Sociology, Urban *[Former heading]*

BT = Broader Term　　NT = Narrower Term　　RT = Related Term　　SA = See Also　　UF = Used For

Urban sociology—*Continued*
- BT **Sociology**
- NT **City life**
  Urban renewal
  Urbanization
- RT **Cities and towns**

Urban traffic
- USE **City traffic**

Urban transportation
- USE **Local transit**

Urbanization (May subdiv. geog.)
307.76

Use for materials on the process by which town and communities acquire urban characteristics.
- UF Cities and towns, Movement to
  Urban development
- BT **Cities and towns**
  Rural sociology
  Social change
  Social conditions
  Urban sociology
- RT **Cities and towns—Growth**

US
- USE **United States**

USA
- USE **United States**

Use of time
- USE **Time management**

Used merchandise
- USE **Secondhand trade**

Useful arts
- USE **Industrial arts**
  Technology

Useful insects
- USE **Beneficial insects**

USMA
- USE **United States Military Academy**

USSR
- USE **Soviet Union**

Utensils, Kitchen
- USE **Kitchen utensils**

Utilitarianism 144
- BT **Ethics**
- NT **Secularism**
- RT **Pragmatism**

Utilities (Computer programs) 005.4

Use for materials on software used to perform standard computer system operations such as sorting data, searching for viruses, copying data from one file to another, etc.
- UF Computer utility programs
  Computers—Utility programs
  Programs, Utility (Computer programs)
  Routines, Utility (Computer programs)
  Utility programs (Computer programs)
  Utility routines (Computer programs)
- BT **Computer software**

Utilities, Public
- USE **Public utilities**

Utility programs (Computer programs)
- USE **Utilities (Computer programs)**

Utility routines (Computer programs)
- USE **Utilities (Computer programs)**

Utilization of waste
- USE **Recycling**
  Salvage

Utopian fiction 813, etc.

May be used for individual works, collections, or materials about imaginative accounts of ideal societies. Theoretical materials about ideal societies and accounts of practical attempts to create such societies are entered under **Utopias.**
- UF Ideal states
  Utopian literature
- BT **Fantasy fiction**
  Science fiction
- RT **Dystopias**
  Utopias

Utopian literature
- USE **Utopian fiction**
  Utopias

Utopias 321; 335

Use for theoretical materials on ideal societies and for accounts of practical attempts to create such societies. Imaginative accounts of ideal societies are entered under **Utopian fiction.**
- UF Ideal states
  Utopian literature
- BT **Political science**
  Socialism
- RT **Collective settlements**

Utopias—*Continued*
>> **Utopian fiction**

V.C.R.'s
>> USE **Video recording**

V.D.
>> USE **Sexually transmitted diseases**

V.T.O.L.'s
>> USE **Vertically rising airplanes**

Vacation church schools
>> USE **Religious summer schools**

Vacation home timesharing
>> USE **Timesharing (Real estate)**

Vacation schools
>> USE **Summer schools**

Vacation schools, Religious
>> USE **Religious summer schools**

Vacations 331.25; 658.3
>> BT **Recreation**
>> RT **Holidays**

Vaccination 614.4
>> UF Immunization
>> Inoculation
>> BT **Communicable diseases**
>> **Preventive medicine**
>> **Public health**
>> NT **Poliomyelitis vaccine**
>> RT **Immunity**
>> **Influenza**

Vacuum tubes 537.5; 621.3815
>> UF Electron tubes
>> BT **X rays**
>> NT **Cathode ray tubes**

Vagabonds
>> USE **Tramps**

Vagrants
>> USE **Tramps**

Valentine's Day 394.2
>> UF Saint Valentine's Day
>> St. Valentine's Day
>> BT **Holidays**

Valuation 338.5
>> Use for general materials on the appraisal of property. Materials on valuation of particular types of property are entered under the type of property, e.g. **Real estate.** Materials on valuation for taxing purposes are entered under **Tax assessment.**
>> UF Appraisal
>> Capitalization (Finance)
>> NT **Tax assessment**

Values 121; 170; 303.3
>> Use for materials on moral and aesthetic values.
>> UF Axiology
>> Human values
>> Worth
>> BT **Aesthetics**
>> **Ethics**
>> **Psychology**
>> NT **Social values**

Vampire films 791.43
>> May be used for individual works, collections, or materials about vampire films.
>> UF Vampires in motion pictures
>> BT **Horror films**
>> **Motion pictures**

Vampires 398.21
>> BT **Superstition**

Vampires in motion pictures
>> USE **Vampire films**

Van life 796.7
>> UF Vanning
>> Vans—Social aspects
>> BT **Mobile home living**
>> **Vans**

Van pools
>> USE **Car pools**

Vanishing species
>> USE **Endangered species**

Vanning
>> USE **Van life**

Vans 728.7
>> BT **Travel trailers and campers**
>> NT **Van life**

Vans—Social aspects
>> USE **Van life**

Variation (Biology) 575.2
>> UF Mutation (Biology)
>> BT **Biology**
>> **Botany**
>> **Genetics**
>> **Heredity**
>> **Zoology**
>> NT **Adaptation (Biology)**
>> **Mendel's law**
>> **Natural selection**
>> RT **Evolution**

Variety shows (Radio programs) 791.44
>> May be used for individual works, collections, or materials about variety shows on the radio.

BT = Broader Term   NT = Narrower Term   RT = Related Term   SA = See Also   UF = Used For

Variety shows (Radio programs)—
Continued
   BT   **Radio programs**
Variety shows (Television programs)
   791.45
     May be used for individual works, collections, or materials about variety shows on television.
   BT   **Television programs**
Varnish and varnishing 667; 698
   UF   Finishes and finishing
   BT   **Industrial painting**
         Wood finishing
   RT   **Lacquer and lacquering**
Varsity sports
   USE   **College sports**
Vascular system
   USE   **Cardiovascular system**
Vasectomy 613.9
   BT   **Sterilization (Birth control)**
Vases 731; 738
   RT   **Glassware**
         Pottery
Vassals
   USE   **Feudalism**
Vatican City 945.6
     Use for materials on the independent papal state of Vatican City in Rome.
Vatican City—Foreign relations
   USE   **Catholic Church—Foreign relations**
Vatican Council (2nd : 1962-1965) 262
   BT   **Councils and synods**
Vaudeville 792.7
   BT   **Amusements**
         Theater
Vaults (Sepulchral)
   USE   **Tombs**
VCRs
   USE   **Video recording**
VD
   USE   **Sexually transmitted diseases**
VDTs
   USE   **Video display terminals**
Vedas 294.5
   BT   **Hinduism**
         Sacred books
Vegetable anatomy
   USE   **Plants—Anatomy**
Vegetable gardening 635
   UF   Kitchen gardens

       Market gardening
       Truck farming
   BT   **Gardening**
         Horticulture
   RT   **Vegetables**
Vegetable kingdom
   USE   **Botany**
         Plants
Vegetable oils
   USE   **Essences and essential oils**
         Oils and fats
Vegetable pathology
   USE   **Plant diseases**
Vegetables 635; 641.3
   SA   names of vegetables, to be added as needed
   BT   **Botany**
         Food
         Plants
   NT   **Celery**
         Cooking—Vegetables
         Potatoes
         Root crops
         Vegetarianism
   RT   **Vegetable gardening**
Vegetables—Canning
   USE   **Vegetables—Preservation**
Vegetables—Preservation 641.4
   UF   Vegetables—Canning
   BT   **Canning and preserving**
Vegetarian cookery
   USE   **Vegetarian cooking**
Vegetarian cooking 641.5
   UF   Cooking, Vegetarian
       Vegetarian cookery *[Former heading]*
   BT   **Cooking**
   RT   **Cooking—Vegetables**
Vegetarianism 613.2
   BT   **Diet**
         Food
         Vegetables
Vehicles 388; 629.2
   SA   types of vehicles and names of specific makes and models of vehicles, to be added as needed
   BT   **Transportation**
   NT   **All terrain vehicles**
         Automobiles

Vehicles—*Continued*
>> **Bicycles**
>> **Carriages and carts**
>> **Military vehicles**
>> **Moon cars**
>> **Recreational vehicles**
>> **Tricycles**

Vehicles, Military
> USE **Military vehicles**

Vehicles, Recreational
> USE **Recreational vehicles**

Velocity
> USE **Speed**

Veneers and veneering 674; 698
> BT **Cabinetwork**
>> **Furniture**

Venereal diseases
> USE **Sexually transmitted diseases**

Ventilation 697.9
> BT **Air**
>> **Home economics**
>> **Household sanitation**
>> **Hygiene**
>> **Sanitation**
> NT **Chimneys**
> RT **Air conditioning**
>> **Heating**

Ventriloquism 793.8
> BT **Amusements**
>> **Voice**

Verbal abuse
> USE **Invective**

Verbal learning 153.1; 370.15

Use for materials on the process of learning and understanding written or spoken language, ranging from learning to associate two nonsense syllables to solving problems presented in verbal terms.

> UF **Learning, Verbal**
> BT **Language and languages**
>> **Psychology of learning**
> NT **Reading comprehension**

Vermin
> USE **Household pests**
>> **Pests**

Vers libre
> USE **Free verse**

Verse epistles
> USE **Epistolary poetry**

Versification 808.1
> UF **English language—Versification**

Meter
Prosody
> BT **Authorship**
>> **Poetics**
>> **Rhythm**
> NT **Rhyme**

Vertebrates 596
> BT **Animals**
>> **Zoology**
> NT **Amphibians**
>> **Birds**
>> **Fishes**
>> **Mammals**
>> **Reptiles**

Vertical take off airplanes
> USE **Vertically rising airplanes**

Vertically rising airplanes 629.133
> UF **Airplanes, Vertically rising**
>> **V.T.O.L.'s**
>> **Vertical take off airplanes**
>> **VTOLs**
> BT **Airplanes**
>> **Ground effect machines**

Very high frequency radio
> USE **Shortwave radio**

Vessels (Ships)
> USE **Ships**

Veterans (May subdiv. geog.) **305.9; 351.81; 362.86; 920**
> UF **Ex-service men**
>> **War veterans**
> BT **Military art and science**
> RT **Military hospitals**
>> **Military pensions**
>> **Military personnel**
>> **Soldiers**

Veterans Day 394.2
> UF **Armistice Day**
> BT **Holidays**

Veterans—Education 362.86
> UF **Education of veterans**
> BT **Education**
>> **Reconstruction (1914-1939)**
>> **Reconstruction (1939-1951)**

Veterans—Employment 331.5
> UF **Employment of veterans**
> BT **Employment**
>> **Reconstruction (1914-1939)**
>> **Reconstruction (1939-1951)**

Veterans—Hospitals
> USE **Military hospitals**

BT = Broader Term   NT = Narrower Term   RT = Related Term   SA = See Also   UF = Used For

Veterans—Legal status, laws, etc. 343
  BT Military law
Veterans—United States 353.0081; 920
  UF G.I.'s
       GIs
       United States—Veterans
Veterinary medicine 636.089
  SA types of animals with the sub-
       division *Diseases,* to be
       added asn needed
  BT Livestock
       Medicine
  NT Animals—Diseases
       Cattle—Diseases
  RT Insect pests
VHF radio
  USE Shortwave radio
Viaducts
  USE Bridges
Vibration 531; 620.3
  BT Mechanics
       Sound
  NT Sound waves
       Waves
Vicarious atonement
  USE Atonement—Christianity
Vice 170
  UF Vices
  SA names of vices, to be added
       as needed
  BT Conduct of life
       Ethics
       Human behavior
  NT Gambling
       Prostitution
  RT Crime
Vice-presidents (May subdiv. geog.)
      351.003; 920
  BT Presidents
Vice-presidents—United States 353.03;
      920
  UF United States—Vice-presidents
Vices
  USE Vice
Victimless crimes
  USE Crimes without victims
Victims of atomic bombings
  USE Atomic bomb victims
Victims of crime 362.88; 364.1
  UF Crime victims

  BT Crime
  NT Abused women
Video art 700; 791.45
  Use for materials on works of art creat-
  ed with the use of television and video re-
  cording technology.
  UF Art, Electronic
       Art, Video
       Electronic art
  BT Modern art—1900-1999 (20th
       century)
       Television
       Video recording
Video cameras, Home
  USE Camcorders
Video cassette recorders and recording
  USE Video recording
Video cassettes
  USE Videotapes
Video disc players
  USE Videodisc players
Video discs
  USE Videodiscs
Video display terminals 004.7
  UF CRT display terminals
       Display terminals, Video
       VDTs
  BT Computer peripherals
       Computer terminals
Video games 688.7; 794.8
  Use for materials on electronic games
  played by means of images on a video
  screen.
  UF Electronic games
       Games, Electronic
       Games, Video
       Television games
  SA types of video games and
       names of individual games,
       to be added as needed
  BT Electronic toys
       Games
       Television—Receivers and re-
       ception
Video recording 384.55; 621.388; 778.59
  Use for materials on the process and the
  equipment by which video or video and
  audio materials are recorded.
  UF V.C.R.'s
       VCRs
       Video cassette recorders and
       recording

Video recording—*Continued*
> Videorecorders
> Videotape recorders and recording *[Former heading]*
>> NT   **Camcorders**
>> **Video art**
>> **Videodiscs**
>> **Videotapes**
>> RT   **Home video systems**
>> **Magnetic recorders and recording**
>> **Television broadcasting**
>> **Television—Equipment and supplies**

Video recordings
> USE   **Videodiscs**
> **Videotapes**

Video recordings, Closed caption
> USE   **Closed caption video recordings**

Video recordings for the hearing impaired
> USE   **Closed caption video recordings**

Video tapes
> USE   **Videotapes**

Video telephone 384.6; 621.386
> UF   Picture telephone
> Videophone
> BT   **Data transmission systems**
> **Telephone**
> **Television**

Videocassettes
> USE   **Videotapes**

Videodisc players 384.55; 621.388
> Use for materials on the equipment that plays back pictures and sound from prerecorded discs.
> UF   Video disc players
> BT   **Television—Equipment and supplies**

Videodiscs 384.55; 621.388
> Use for materials on plastic discs that play back optically encoded, prerecorded sound and pictures through a television receiver.
> UF   Discs, Video
> Video discs
> Video recordings
> BT   **Audiovisual materials**
> **Optical storage devices**

Video recording
> NT   **Closed caption video recordings**
> **Music videos**
> RT   **Television**

Videophone
> USE   **Video telephone**

Videorecorders
> USE   **Video recording**

Videos, Music
> USE   **Music videos**

Videotape recorders and recording
> USE   **Video recording**

Videotapes 384.55; 778.59
> Use for materials dealing with magnetic tapes on which video or video and audio material is recorded.
> UF   Cassette tape recordings, Video
> Tape recordings, Video
> Video cassettes
> Video recordings
> Video tapes
> Videocassettes
> BT   **Audiovisual materials**
> **Home video systems**
> **Video recording**
> NT   **Closed caption video recordings**
> **Music videos**
> RT   **Television**

Videotex systems 004.69; 384.3
> Use for materials on the transmission of computer-based data from a central source to a television set or personal computer allowing for two-way interactions, such as with home shopping or home banking.
> UF   Interactive videotex
> Telereference
> Viewdata systems
> BT   **Data transmission systems**
> **Information systems**
> **Television broadcasting**
> RT   **Teletext systems**

Vietnam War, 1961-1975 959.704
> May use appropriate subdivisions under **World War, 1939-1945.**
> UF   Vietnamese War, 1961-1975
> BT   **United States—History—1961-1974**

Vietnamese refugees 325
> UF   Refugees, Vietnamese *[Former heading]*

Vietnamese refugees—*Continued*
   BT **Refugees**
Vietnamese War, 1961-1975
   USE **Vietnam War, 1961-1975**
Viewdata systems
   USE **Videotex systems**
Views 910.22
    Use for collections of pictures of many places.
   UF Geography—Pictorial works
         Scenery
   SA names of cities, states, and countries, and of named entities, such as individual parks, structures, etc., with the subdivision *Pictorial works,* to be added as needed
   NT **Chicago (Ill.)—Pictorial works**
         United States—Pictorial works
         Yosemite National Park (Calif.)—Pictorial works
Vigilance committees 364.1; 364.4
   UF Vigilantes
   BT **Crime**
         Criminal law
   RT **Lynching**
Vigilantes
   USE **Vigilance committees**
Vikings 948
    Use for materials on early Scandinavian people. Materials on the people since the tenth century are entered under **Scandinavians.**
   UF Norsemen
         Northmen
   BT **Scandinavians**
   RT **Normans**
Villages 307.76
   BT **Cities and towns**
   RT **Local government**
Vines
   USE **Climbing plants**
Vineyards (May subdiv. geog.) **634.8**
   BT **Farms**
   RT **Grapes**
         Wine and wine making
Violence 303.6
   SA types of violence, to be added as needed

   BT **Aggressiveness (Psychology)**
         Social psychology
   NT **Family violence**
         Hate crimes
         School violence
Violin
   USE **Violins**
Violin music 787.2
   BT **Music**
Violinists, violoncellists, etc. 787.2092; 920
   UF Violoncellists
   BT **Musicians**
Violins 787.2
   UF Fiddle
         Violin *[Former heading]*
   BT **Stringed instruments**
Violoncellists
   USE **Violinists, violoncellists, etc.**
Violoncello
   USE **Violoncellos**
Violoncellos 787.4
   UF Cello
         Violoncello *[Former heading]*
   BT **Stringed instruments**
Vipers
   USE **Snakes**
Virgin Mary
   USE **Mary, Blessed Virgin, Saint**
Virtual reality 003
   UF Artificial reality
         Computer simulation
         Computers—Simulation programs
         Three dimensional computer graphics
   BT **Reality**
   RT **Computer graphics**
Virtue 170
   UF Virtues
   SA names of virtues, to be added as needed
   BT **Conduct of life**
         Ethics
         Human behavior
   NT **Charity**
         Chastity
         Courage
         Courtesy
         Forgiveness

Virtue—*Continued*
>>> Justice
>>> Loyalty
>>> Obedience
>>> Patience
>>> Punctuality
>>> Temperance

Virtues
>> USE **Virtue**

Viruses 576
>> UF Microbes
>> BT **Microorganisms**
>> NT **Chickenpox**

Viruses, Computer
>> USE **Computer viruses**

Visceral learning
>> USE **Biofeedback training**

Viscosity 532; 620.1
>> BT **Hydrodynamics**
>>> **Mechanics**

Visigoths
>> USE **Teutonic peoples**

Vision 152.14; 591.1; 612.8; 617.7
>> UF Sight
>> BT **Optics**
>>> **Senses and sensation**
>> NT **Color sense**
>>> **Optical illusions**
>>> **Vision disorders**
>> RT **Eye**

Vision disorders 362.4; 617.7
>> UF Defective vision
>>> Impaired vision
>>> Visual handicaps
>>> Visual impairments
>> BT **Vision**
>> NT **Blind**
>>> **Color blindness**

Visions 133.8
>> BT **Parapsychology**
>>> **Religion**
>> NT **Dreams**
>>> **Hallucinations and illusions**
>> RT **Apparitions**

Visitation rights (Domestic relations) 306.8
> Use for materials on the legal right of parents or grandparents to visit their children or grandchildren in situations of separation, divorce, etc.
>> BT **Domestic relations**

Visiting animals
>> USE **Pet therapy**

Visitors' exchange programs
>> USE **Exchange of persons programs**

Visual data processing
>> USE **Optical data processing**

Visual handicaps
>> USE **Vision disorders**

Visual impairments
>> USE **Vision disorders**

Visual instruction
>> USE **Audiovisual education**

Visual literacy 153; 707
> Use for materials on the ability to interpret and evaluate visual objects and symbols, such as television, motion pictures, art works, etc.
>> UF Literacy, Visual
>> BT **Arts**
>>> **Literacy**
>>> **Semiotics**

Vital records
>> USE **Registers of births, etc.**

Vital statistics 304.6; 310
>> UF Burial statistics
>>> Death rate
>>> Marriage statistics
>>> Mortuary statistics
>>> Records of births, etc.
>> BT **Statistics**
>> NT **Census**
>>> **Mortality**
>>> **Population**
>> RT **Registers of births, etc.**

Vitamins 574.19; 615; 641.1
>> BT **Food**
>>> **Nutrition**

Vivariums
>> USE **Terrariums**

Vivisection 179
>> BT **Animal experimentation**
>>> **Surgery**

Vocabulary 418; 428, etc.
>> UF English language—Vocabulary
>>> Languages—Vocabulary
>>> Words
>> BT **Language and languages**
>> NT **New words**

Vocal culture
>> USE **Singing**

Vocal culture—*Continued*
> **Voice**

Vocal ensembles
  USE **Ensembles (Music)**

Vocal music 782
  UF Music, Vocal
  BT **Music**
  NT **Cantatas**
  Carols
  Choral music
  Folk songs
  Hymns
  Opera
  Operetta
  Oratorio
  Songs
  RT **Singing**

Vocation, Choice of
  USE **Vocational guidance**

Vocational education 370.11; 373.246; 374

Use for materials on teaching a skill during the educational process. Materials on teaching people a skill after formal education are entered under **Occupational training.** Materials discussing on-the-job training are entered under **Employees—Training.** Materials on retraining are entered under **Occupational retraining.**

  UF Career education
  Education, Vocational
  SA names of industries, professions, etc., with the subdivision *Study and teaching,* e.g. **Agriculture—Study and teaching;** to be added as needed
  BT **Education**
  Human resources policy
  NT **Agriculture—Study and teaching**
  Employees—Training
  Industrial arts education
  Occupational retraining
  Occupational training
  Vocational guidance
  RT **Professional education**
  Technical education

Vocational guidance 331.7; 371.4

Use for materials on the activities and programs designed to help people plan, choose, and succeed in their careers. Materials on the assistance given to students by schools, colleges, or universities in the selection of a program of studies suited to their abilities, interests, future plans, and general circumstances are entered under **Educational counseling.**

  UF Career counseling
  Career development
  Career guidance
  Careers
  Choice of profession, occupation, vocation, etc.
  Employment guidance
  Guidance, Vocational
  Job placement guidance
  Occupational guidance
  Vocation, Choice of
  SA vocational guidance for particular classes of persons, e.g. **Vocational guidance for the handicapped;** and fields of knowledge, corporate bodies, military services, and industries and trades with the subdivision *Vocational guidance,* to be added as needed
  BT **Counseling**
  Vocational education
  NT **Career changes**
  Job hunting
  Law—Vocational guidance
  Paraprofessionals
  Television broadcasting—Vocational guidance
  Vocational guidance for the handicapped
  RT **Educational counseling**
  Employment
  Occupations
  Professions

Vocational guidance for the handicapped 371.4
  BT **Handicapped**
  Vocational guidance

Vocational training
  USE **Occupational training**

BT = Broader Term   NT = Narrower Term   RT = Related Term   SA = See Also   UF = Used For

Vocations
USE **Occupations**
Professions
Voice 783
UF Speaking
Vocal culture
Voice culture
BT **Language and languages**
Throat
NT **Automatic speech recognition**
Ventriloquism
RT **Phonetics**
Public speaking
Singing
Speech
Voice culture
USE **Singing**
Voice
Volatile oils
USE **Essences and essential oils**
Volcanoes (May subdiv. geog.) **551.2**
UF Eruptions
SA names of volcanoes, to be
added as needed
BT **Geology**
Mountains
Physical geography
Volleyball 796.325
BT **Ball games**
Volume (Cubic content) 389; 530.8
UF Cubic measurement
BT **Geometry**
Measurement
Weights and measures
Volume feeding
USE **Food service**
Voluntarism 361.3
UF Volunteer work
Volunteering
Volunteerism
Volunteers
SA names of volunteer programs,
e.g. **Meals on wheels pro-
grams;** to be added as
needed
NT **Caregivers**
Foster grandparents
RT **Associations**
Charities
Voluntary associations
USE **Associations**

Voluntary military service 355.2
UF Military service, Voluntary
[Former heading]
Volunteer military service
BT **Armed forces**
Human resources
Voluntary organizations
USE **Associations**
Volunteer military service
USE **Voluntary military service**
Volunteer work
USE **Voluntarism**
Volunteering
USE **Voluntarism**
Volunteerism
USE **Voluntarism**
Volunteers
USE **Voluntarism**
Volunteers in church work
USE **Lay ministry**
Voter registration 324.6
UF Registration of voters
BT **Elections**
Suffrage
Voting
USE **Elections**
Suffrage
Voyager project
USE **Project Voyager**
Voyagers
USE **Explorers**
Travelers
Voyages and travels 910.4
Use for collections of travel writings
and for accounts of voyages and travels
not limited to a single place. Materials
about travel writing and about the theme
of travel in literature are entered under
Travel in literature.
UF Journeys
Travel books
Travels
SA names of cities (except extinct
cities), countries, continents,
etc., with the subdivision
Description; names of re-
gions, e.g. **Antarctic regions;**
names of individual ships;
classes of persons and individuals with the subdivi-
sion *Voyages and travels,*

BT = Broader Term   NT = Narrower Term   RT = Related Term   SA = See Also   UF = Used For

Voyages and travels—*Continued*
    e.g. **Popes—Voyages and
    travels;** names of countries
    with the subdivision *Ex-
    ploring expeditions;* and
    names of places that were
    unsettled or sparsely settled
    and largely unknown to the
    world at large at the time
    of exploration, with the
    subdivision *Exploration,*
    e.g. **America—Exploration;**
    to be added as needed
  BT **Geography**
  NT **Aeronautics—Flights**
      Northeast Passage
      Northwest Passage
      Ocean travel
      **Overland journeys to the Pa-
      cific**
      Pilgrims and pilgrimages
      Popes—Voyages and travels
      Scientific expeditions
      Seafaring life
      Shipwrecks
      Travelers
      United States—Description
      Voyages around the world
      Whaling
      Yachts and yachting
  RT **Adventure and adventurers**
      Exploration
      Explorers
      Travel
      Travel in literature
Voyages and travels in literature
  USE **Travel in literature**
Voyages around the world 910.4
  UF Circumnavigation
      Travel books
  BT **Travel**
      Voyages and travels
Voyages, Imaginary
  USE **Imaginary voyages**
Voyages to the moon
  USE **Imaginary voyages**
      Space flight to the moon
VTOLs
  USE **Vertically rising airplanes**

Wage-price controls
  USE **Wage-price policy**
Wage-price policy 331.2
  UF Price controls
      Price-wage policy
      Wage-price controls
  BT **Inflation (Finance)**
      Prices
      Wages
Wages 331.2; 658.3
  UF Compensation
      Overtime
      Salaries
  BT **Income**
      Labor
      Labor contract
  NT **Equal pay for equal work**
      Job analysis
      Minimum wage
      Nonwage payments
      Profit sharing
      Wage-price policy
  RT **Cost of living**
      Prices
Wages—Minimum wage
  USE **Minimum wage**
Wagons
  USE **Carriages and carts**
Waiters and waitresses 642
  UF Waitresses
  BT **Food service**
Waitresses
  USE **Waiters and waitresses**
Wakefulness
  USE **Insomnia**
Walking 796.5
  BT **Locomotion**
  RT **Hiking**
Walking in space
  USE **Extravehicular activity (Space
        flight)**
Wall decoration
  USE **Mural painting and decoration**
Wall painting
  USE **Mural painting and decoration**
Wall Street (New York, N.Y.) 332.6
    Use for materials on the activities of
    Wall Street as a financial district. Histori-
    cal and descriptive materials on Wall
    Street as a street are entered under
    Streets—New York (N.Y.).

Wall Street (New York, N.Y.)—
Continued
   BT   Stock exchange
   RT   Streets—New York (N.Y.)

Wallpaper 676; 747
   BT   Interior design
   RT   Paperhanging

Walls 690; 721
   BT   Building
        Carpentry
        Civil engineering
   NT   Mural painting and decoration
   RT   Foundations
        Masonry

Walt Disney World (Fla.) 791.06
   UF   Disney World (Fla.)
   BT   Amusement parks

War 172; 303.6; 355.02
   UF   Fighting
        Wars
   SA   names of wars, battles, etc.,
          e.g. **United States—**
          History—1861-1865, Civil
          War; Gettysburg (Pa.), Bat-
          tle of, 1863; and war and
          other subjects, e.g. **War and**
          religion; to be added as
          needed
   NT   Arms control
        Battles
        Chemical warfare
        Guerrilla warfare
        Intervention (International
          law)
        Military aeronautics
        Military law
        Military personnel
        Military weapons
        Naval art and science
        Navies
        Nuclear warfare
        Psychological warfare
        Strategy
        Submarine warfare
        War and civilization
        War and emergency powers
        War and religion
        War crimes
        World War III
   RT   Armies

        International law
        Military art and science
        Peace

War and civilization 172; 303.4
   UF   Civilization and war
   BT   Civilization
        War

War and emergency powers 342
   UF   Emergency powers
        War powers
   BT   Constitutional law
        Executive power
        Legislative bodies
        War

War and industry
   USE   **War—Economic aspects**

War and religion 291.1; 261.8
   UF   Christianity and war
        Church and war
        Religion and war
   BT   Religion
        War
   NT   Conscientious objectors
        Pacifism
        World War, 1939-1945—
          Moral and religious aspects

War, Articles of
   USE   **Military law**

War crime trials 341.6
   BT   Trials

War crimes (May subdiv. geog.) 341.6;
          364.1
   SA   names of wars with the subdi-
          vision *Atrocities,* e.g. **World**
          War, 1939-1945—Atrocities;
          and names of specific
          atrocities, to be added as
          needed
   BT   Crime
        International law
        War

War debts
   USE   **Public debts**
        and names of wars with the
        subdivision *Finance,* e.g.
        World War, 1939-1945—
        Finance; to be added as
        needed

BT = Broader Term   NT = Narrower Term   RT = Related Term   SA = See Also   UF = Used For

War—Economic aspects 303.6

Use for materials discussing the economic causes of war and the effect of war on industry and trade.

UF Economics of war
Industry and war
War and industry

SA names of wars with the subdivision *Economic aspects,* to be added as needed

NT **Industrial mobilization**
World War, 1939-1945—Economic aspects
World War, 1939-1945—Human resources

RT **International competition**

War films 791.43

May be used for individual works, collections, or materials about war films in general, not limited to a particular war.

UF Anti-war films
Apocalyptic fantasies
End-of-the-world fantasies

SA names of individual wars with the subdivision *Motion pictures and the war;* e.g. **World War, 1939-1945—Motion pictures and the war;** to be added as needed

BT **Historical drama**
Motion pictures

NT **World War, 1939-1945—Motion pictures and the war**

War of 1812

USE **United States—History—1812-1815, War of 1812**

War of 1914

USE **World War, 1914-1918**

War of 1939-1945

USE **World War, 1939-1945**

War of nerves

USE **Psychological warfare**

War of Secession (U.S.)

USE **United States—History—1861-1865, Civil War**

War of the American Revolution

USE **United States—History—1775-1783, Revolution**

War pensions

USE **Military pensions**

War poetry 808.81; 811, etc.; 811.008, etc.

May be used for individual works or collections of war poetry, or for materials about war poetry in general, not confined to a particular war.

UF Anti-war poetry

SA names of wars with the subdivision *Poetry,* to be added as needed

BT **Poetry**

NT **World War, 1939-1945—Poetry**

RT **War songs**

War powers

USE **War and emergency powers**

War protest movements

USE names of wars with the subdivision *Protests, demonstrations, etc.,* e.g. **World War, 1939-1945—Protests, demonstrations, etc.;** to be added as needed

War radio programs 791.44

May be used for individual works, collections, or materials about war radio programs.

BT **Radio programs**

War ships

USE **Warships**

War songs 782.42

UF Battle songs
Soldiers' songs

BT **National songs**
Songs

NT **World War, 1939-1945—Songs**

RT **War poetry**

War, Space

USE **Space warfare**

War stories 808.83; 813, etc.

May be used for individual works, collections, or materials about war stories.

UF Anti-war stories
Apocalyptic fantasies
End-of-the-world fantasies

BT **Fiction**
Historical fiction

War television programs 791.45

May be used for individual works, collections, or materials about war television programs.

BT = Broader Term   NT = Narrower Term   RT = Related Term   SA = See Also   UF = Used For

War television programs—*Continued*
  BT   **Television programs**
War use of animals
  USE **Animals—War use**
War use of dogs
  USE **Dogs—War use**
War veterans
  USE **Veterans**
War work
  USE names of wars with the subdivision *War work,* e.g.
      World War, 1939-1945— War work; to be added as needed
Warfare, Space
  USE **Space warfare**
Warfare, Submarine
  USE **Submarine warfare**
Warm air heating
  USE **Hot air heating**
Wars
  USE **Military history**
      Naval history
      War
      and names of wars, e.g. **World War, 1939-1945;** to be added as needed
Wars of the Roses, 1455-1485
  USE **Great Britain—History— 1455-1485, War of the Roses**
Warships 359.8; 623.8
  UF Battle ships
      Battleships
      War ships
  SA names of countries with the subhead *Navy,* e.g. **United States. Navy;** and names of individual warships, to be added as needed
  BT   **Naval architecture**
      Naval art and science
      Sea power
      Ships
  NT **Aircraft carriers**
      Submarines
      United States. Navy
  RT **Navies**
Washing
  USE **Laundry**

Wasps 595.79
  UF Hymenoptera
  BT   **Insects**
Waste as fuel
  USE **Waste products as fuel**
Waste disposal
  USE **Industrial wastes**
      Medical wastes
      Radioactive waste disposal
      Refuse and refuse disposal
      Sewage disposal
      Waste products
Waste (Economics) 339.4
  BT   **Economics**
Waste products 628.4
  UF By-products
      Junk
      Products, Waste
      Trade waste
      Waste disposal
  BT   **Industrial chemistry**
      Manufactures
  NT **Industrial wastes**
  RT **Recycling**
      Refuse and refuse disposal
      Substitute products
Waste products as fuel 333.79; 662
  UF Energy conversion from waste
      Organic waste as fuel
      Waste as fuel
  BT   **Salvage**
  RT **Biomass energy**
Waste products—Recycling
  USE **Recycling**
Waste reclamation
  USE **Recycling**
      Salvage
Wastes, Hazardous
  USE **Hazardous wastes**
Wastes, Industrial
  USE **Industrial wastes**
Wastes, Medical
  USE **Medical wastes**
Watches
  USE **Clocks and watches**
Water 551.4; 553.7
  UF Hydrology
  BT   **Earth sciences**
      Hydraulics
  NT **Floods**

BT = Broader Term   NT = Narrower Term   RT = Related Term   SA = See Also   UF = Used For

Water—*Continued*
 Fog
 Frost
 Geysers
 Hydrotherapy
 Ice
 Lakes
 Ocean
 Ponds
 Rain
 Rivers
 Sea water
 Snow
 Steam
 RT **Hydraulic engineering**
Water—Analysis 546; 628.1
 BT **Analytical chemistry**
 RT **Water pollution**
Water animals
 USE **Freshwater animals**
  Marine animals
Water ballet
 USE **Synchronized swimming**
Water birds 598.29
 UF Aquatic birds
  Birds, Aquatic
  Water fowl
  Wild fowl
 SA types of water birds, to be
  added as needed
 BT **Birds**
 NT **Geese**
  Terns
Water color painting
 USE **Watercolor painting**
Water colors
 USE **Watercolor painting**
Water conduits
 USE **Aqueducts**
Water conservation 333.91
 UF Conservation of water
 BT **Conservation of natural re-
  sources**
 RT **Water supply**
Water cure
 USE **Hydrotherapy**
Water farming
 USE **Hydroponics**
Water flow
 USE **Hydraulics**

Water—Fluoridation
 USE **Water fluoridation**
Water fluoridation 628.1
 UF Fluoridation of water
  Water—Fluoridation *[Former
  heading]*
 BT **Water supply**
 RT **Teeth—Diseases**
Water fowl
 USE **Water birds**
Water—Heavy water
 USE **Deuterium oxide**
Water—Oil pollution
 USE **Oil pollution of water**
Water plants
 USE **Freshwater plants**
  Marine plants
Water pollution 363.73; 628.1
 UF Detergent pollution of rivers,
  lakes, etc. *[Former heading]*
  Pollution of water
  River pollution
 SA types of pollution, e.g. **Oil
  pollution of water;** to be
  added as needed
 BT **Environmental health**
  Pollution
  Public health
 NT **Acid rain**
  Marine pollution
  Oil pollution of water
 RT **Industrial wastes**
  Refuse and refuse disposal
  Sewage disposal
  Water—Analysis
  Water supply
Water power 333.9; 621.2
 UF Hydroelectric power
 BT **Energy resources**
  Hydraulics
  Power (Mechanics)
  Renewable energy resources
  Rivers
  Water resources development
 NT **Dams**
  Hydraulic engineering
  Hydraulic machinery
  Hydroelectric power plants
Water—Purification
 USE **Water purification**

Water purification 628.1
UF Purification of water
Water—Purification *[Former heading]*
BT **Sanitation**
Water supply
NT **Sea water conversion**
Water resources development 333.91
BT **Energy development**
Natural resources
NT **Hydroelectric power plants**
Inland navigation
Irrigation
Water power
Water supply
Water rights 333.91; 346.04
BT **Irrigation**
Law
Rivers
Water skiing 797.3
UF Skiing, Water
BT **Water sports**
Water sports 797
UF Aquatic sports
SA names of water sports, to be added as needed
BT **Sports**
NT **Boats and boating**
Canoes and canoeing
Diving
Fishing
Rowing
Sailing
Skin diving
Surfing
Swimming
Water skiing
Yachts and yachting
Water supply (May subdiv. geog.) 363.6; 628.1
UF Waterworks
BT **Civil engineering**
Municipal engineering
Public health
Public utilities
Sanitary engineering
Sanitation
Water resources development
NT **Aqueducts**
Dams

Forest influences
Irrigation
Water fluoridation
Water purification
RT **Reservoirs**
Water conservation
Water pollution
Wells
Water supply engineering 628.1
BT **Civil engineering**
Engineering
NT **Boring**
RT **Hydraulic engineering**
Water transportation
USE **Shipping**
Watercolor painting 751.42
UF Water color painting
Water colors
Watercolors
BT **Painting**
Watercolors
USE **Watercolor painting**
Watergate Affair, 1972-1974 353.009; 973.924
BT **Misconduct in office**
Political corruption
United States—History—1961-1974
Watering places
USE **Health resorts**
Waterways 386
Use for general materials on rivers, lakes, and canals as highways for transportation or commerce.
BT **Transportation**
NT **Canals**
Inland navigation
Lakes
Rivers
Waterworks
USE **Water supply**
Wave mechanics 530.1
BT **Mechanics**
Quantum theory
Waves
Waves 530.1; 551.47
BT **Hydrodynamics**
Vibration
NT **Electric waves**
Ocean waves

BT = Broader Term   NT = Narrower Term   RT = Related Term   SA = See Also   UF = Used For

Waves—*Continued*
    Radiation
    Sound waves
    Wave mechanics
Waves, Electromagnetic
  USE **Electromagnetic waves**
Waves, Ultrasonic
  USE **Ultrasonic waves**
Wealth 330.1
  UF Distribution of wealth
      Fortune
      Fortunes
      Riches
  BT **Economics**
      Finance
  NT **Economic conditions**
      Income
      Inheritance and succession
      Millionaires
      Poverty
      Profit
      Standard of living
      Success
  RT **Capital**
      Money
      Property
Weaponry
  USE **Weapons**
Weapons 355.8; 623.4
  UF Arms and armor *[Former heading]*
      Weaponry
  BT **Tools**
  NT **Firearms**
      Firearms industry
      Military weapons
  RT **Armor**
      Military art and science
Weapons and weaponry
  USE **Bow and arrow**
      Military weapons
Weapons, Atomic
  USE **Nuclear weapons**
Weapons, Enhanced radiation
  USE **Neutron weapons**
Weapons, Neutron
  USE **Neutron weapons**
Weapons, Nuclear
  USE **Nuclear weapons**
Weapons, Space
  USE **Space weapons**

Weariness
  USE **Fatigue**
Weather 551.6
    Use for materials on the state of the atmosphere at a given time and place with respect to heat or cold, wetness or dryness, calm or storm. Scientific materials on the atmosphere, especially weather factors, are entered under **Meteorology.** Materials on climate as it relates to humans and to plant and animal life, including the effects of changes of climate, are entered under **Climate.**
  SA names of countries, cities, etc., with the subdivision *Climate,* to be added as needed
  NT **Humidity**
      Rain
      Snow
      Storms
      United States—Climate
      Weather control
      Weather forecasting
      Winds
  RT **Climate**
      Meteorology
Weather control 551.68
  UF Artificial weather control
      Cloud seeding
      Rain making
      Weather modification
  BT **Meteorology**
      Weather
Weather—Folklore 398.26
  UF Weather lore
  BT **Folklore**
      Meteorology
      Weather forecasting
Weather forecasting 551.6
  UF Precipitation forecasting
  BT **Forecasting**
      Meteorology
      Weather
  NT **Meteorology in aeronautics**
      Weather—Folklore
Weather lore
  USE **Weather—Folklore**
Weather modification
  USE **Weather control**
Weather satellites
  USE **Meteorological satellites**

Weather stations
USE   Meteorology—Observatories
Weaving 677; 746.1; 746.41
UF   Hand weaving
SA   names of woven articles, e.g.
      Carpets; to be added as
      needed
BT   **Handicraft**
NT   **Basket making**
      Beadwork
      Lace and lace making
      Looms
RT   **Carpets**
      Textile industry
Weddings 392
BT   **Marriage**
NT   **Marriage customs and rites**
Weed killers
USE   **Herbicides**
Weeds 632
BT   **Agricultural pests**
      Economic botany
      Gardening
      Plants
Week 529
BT   **Calendars**
      Chronology
RT   **Days**
Weight control
USE   **Reducing**
Weight lifting 796.41; 613.7
UF   Powerlifting
      Pumping iron
      Strength training
      Weight training
      Weightlifting
BT   **Athletics**
      Exercise
RT   **Bodybuilding**
Weight training
USE   **Weight lifting**
Weightlessness 531
UF   Free fall
      Gravity free state
      Subgravity state
      Zero gravity
BT   **Environmental influence on**
      humans
      Space medicine
Weightlifting
USE   **Weight lifting**

Weights and measures 389; 530.8
UF   Measures
      Metrology
BT   **Physics**
NT   **Electric measurements**
      Measuring instruments
      Metric system
      Volume (Cubic content)
RT   **Measurement**
Welding 671.5
UF   Oxyacetylene welding
BT   **Blacksmithing**
      Forging
      Ironwork
      Metalwork
NT   **Electric welding**
RT   **Soldering**
Welding, Electric
USE   **Electric welding**
Welfare agencies
USE   **Charities**
Welfare state
USE   **Economic policy**
      Public welfare
      State, The
Welfare work
USE   **Charities**
      Public welfare
      Social work
Welfare work in industry 658.3
BT   **Labor**
      Management
      Social work
NT   **Counseling**
      Housing
      Social settlements
Well boring
USE   **Boring**
Well drilling, Oil
USE   **Oil well drilling**
Wells 551.49; 628.1
UF   Artesian wells
BT   **Hydraulic engineering**
RT   **Boring**
      Water supply

West Africa 966

Use for materials dealing collectively with the southern half of the western bulge of the African continent. The area is defined on the north by the Sahara and on the south and west by the Atlantic Ocean. The term is used loosely, but includes Benin, Burkina Faso, Cameroon, Gambia, Ghana, Guinea, Guinea-Bissau, Ivory Coast, Liberia, Nigeria, Senegal, Sierra Leone, and Togo. Sometimes, additional countries of the Sahel (Mali, Mauritania, and Niger) are also included.

UF Africa, West *[Former heading]*
BT **Africa**
NT **French-speaking West Africa**

West Germany

USE **Germany (West)**

West Indian literature (French) 840

Use for collections and for materials on West Indian literature written originally in French.

UF French literature—West Indian authors
BT **Literature**

West Indies, Indians of the

USE **Indians of the West Indies**

West Point (Military academy)

USE **United States Military Academy**

West (U.S.) 978

Use for the region west of the Mississippi River.

UF Western States
SA names of individual states in this region, to be added as needed
BT **United States**
NT **Pacific Northwest**
  Pacific States

West (U.S.)—Exploration 978

BT **United States—Exploration**
RT **Overland journeys to the Pacific**

West (U.S.)—History

UF Westward movement
BT **United States—History**

Western and country music

USE **Country music**

Western civilization 306.09; 909

Use for materials on the culture and society stemming from the Greco-Roman traditions of the occident rather than those of Islam, India, or the Far East.

UF Civilization, Occidental *[Former heading]*

Civilization, Western
Occidental civilization
BT **Civilization**
  East and West

Western comic books, strips, etc. 741.5

May be used for individual works, collections, or materials about Western comics.

BT **Comic books, strips, etc.**

Western Europe

USE **Europe**

Western films 791.43

May be used for individual works, collections, or materials about Western films.

UF Westerns
SA particular kinds of Western films, e.g. **Lone Ranger films;** to be added as needed
BT **Adventure films**
  Historical drama
  Motion pictures
NT **Lone Ranger films**

Western States

USE **West (U.S.)**

Western stories 808.83; 813, etc.

May be used for individual works, collections, or materials about post-19th-century fiction set in the 19th-century American West.

UF Westerns
BT **Adventure fiction**
  Fiction
  Historical fiction

Westerns

USE **Western films**
  Western stories
  Westerns (Radio programs)
  Westerns (Television programs)

Westerns (Radio programs) 791.44

May be used for individual works, collections, or materials about Westerns on the radio.

UF Westerns
BT **Radio programs**

Westerns (Television programs) 791.45

May be used for individual works, collections, or materials about Western on television.

UF Westerns
BT **Television programs**

Westminster Abbey 726

BT **Abbeys**

BT = Broader Term NT = Narrower Term RT = Related Term SA = See Also UF = Used For

738

Westminster Abbey—*Continued*
  Churches
Westward movement
  USE **Land settlement—United States**
      United States—Territorial expansion
      West (U.S.)—History
Wetlands
  UF Bogs
      Land
      Swamps
  SA types of wetlands, e.g. **Marshes;** to be added as needed
  BT **Land use**
  NT **Marshes**
  RT **Drainage**
      Reclamation of land
Whales 599.5
  BT **Marine mammals**
Whaling 639.2
  BT **Fisheries**
      Hunting
      Voyages and travels
Wheat 633.1
  UF Breadstuffs
  BT **Grain**
  RT **Flour**
Wheels 621.8; 629.2
  UF Car wheels
  BT **Simple machines**
  NT **Gearing**
      Tires
Which-way stories
  USE **Plot-your-own stories**
Whistle blowing 174; 351.9; 342
    Use for materials on the practice of calling public attention to corruption, mismanagement, or waste in government, business, the military, etc.
  UF Blowing the whistle
      Whistleblowing
  BT **Political corruption**
      Public interest
Whistleblowing
  USE **Whistle blowing**
White collar crimes 364.1
    Use for comprehensive materials on crimes such as fraud, embezzlement, stealing of company property, etc., committed by business persons and professionals in the course of their work.

  UF Crimes, White collar
      Occupational crimes
  BT **Crime**
  NT **Fraud**
White supremacist movements
  USE **White supremacy movements**
White supremacy movements 320.5
  UF Skinheads
      White supremacist movements
  BT **Race relations**
      Racism
      Social movements
Whittling
  USE **Wood carving**
Whodunits
  USE **Mystery and detective plays**
      Mystery fiction
      Mystery films
      Mystery radio programs
      Mystery television programs
Whole language 372.6
    Use for materials on the integration of listening, speaking, writing, and reading skills in meaningful situations in which children participate actively.
  UF Integrated language arts (Holistic)
      Language arts (Holistic)
      Language experience approach in education
  BT **Education—Experimental methods**
      Language arts
      Reading
      Writing
Wholistic medicine
  USE **Holistic medicine**
Wica
  USE **Witchcraft**
Wicca
  USE **Witchcraft**
Wickedness
  USE **Good and evil**
Widowers 305.38; 306.88
  BT **Family**
      Husbands
      Men
      Single men
  RT **Single parent family**
Widows 305.48; 306.88
  BT **Family**

BT = Broader Term   NT = Narrower Term   RT = Related Term   SA = See Also   UF = Used For

Widows—*Continued*
>>Single women
>>Wives
>>Women
>RT Single parent family

Wife abuse 362.82
>UF Abuse of wives
>>Battering of wives
>>Wife battering
>>Wife beating
>BT **Family violence**
>RT **Abused women**

Wife battering
>USE **Wife abuse**

Wife beating
>USE **Wife abuse**

Wigs 391
>BT **Costume**
>>**Hair**

Wigwams
>USE **Indians of North America— Dwellings**

Wild animals
>USE **Animals**
>>**Wildlife**

Wild cats 599.74; 636.8
>Use for materials on non-domesticated species of cats or domestic cats living in a wild state. Materials on domestic cats are entered under **Cats.**
>UF Felidae
>>Feral cats
>>Wildcats
>SA types of wild cats, to be added as needed.
>BT **Mammals**
>RT **Cats**

Wild children 155.45
>Use for materials on children who have been raised by animals or have lived their formative years in the wild without contact with human society
>UF Feral children *[Former heading]*
>>Wolf children
>BT **Exceptional children**

Wild flowers 582.13
>UF Flowers, Wild
>>Wildflowers
>BT **Flowers**

Wild flowers—Conservation
>USE **Plant conservation**

Wild fowl
>USE **Game and game birds**
>>**Water birds**

Wildcats
>USE **Wild cats**

Wilderness areas 333.78
>UF Preservation of natural scenery
>>Protection of natural scenery
>BT **Forest reserves**
>>**National parks and reserves**
>>**Natural monuments**

Wilderness survival 613.6; 796.5
>UF Bush survival
>>Outdoor survival
>BT **Camping**
>>**Outdoor life**
>>**Survival skills**
>RT **Survival after airplane accidents, shipwrecks, etc.**

Wildflowers
>USE **Wild flowers**

Wildlife (May subdiv. geog.) 333.95; 639
>Use for materials on wild animals in their natural environment, especially mammals, birds, and fishes that are hunted for sport or food.
>UF Feral animals
>>Wild animals
>SA types of wildlife, e.g. **Desert animals**; to be added as needed
>BT **Animals**
>NT **Dangerous animals**
>>**Desert animals**
>>**Forest animals**
>>**Freshwater animals**
>>**Furbearing animals**
>>**Game and game birds**
>>**Jungle animals**
>>**Marine animals**
>>**Mountain animals**
>>**Rare animals**
>>**Stream animals**
>>**Swamp animals**

Wildlife and pesticides
>USE **Pesticides and wildlife**

Wildlife conservation 639.9
>UF Conservation of wildlife

Wildlife conservation—*Continued*
    Preservation of wildlife
    Protection of wildlife
  BT **Conservation of natural resources**
      sources
    Economic zoology
    Endangered species
    Environmental protection
    Nature conservation
  NT **Birdbanding**
    Birds—Protection
    Forest reserves
    Game protection
    Game reserves
    National parks and reserves
    Pesticides and wildlife
    Wildlife refuges
  RT **Rare animals**
Wildlife refuges 639.9
  UF Refuges, Wildlife
    Sanctuaries, Wildlife
    Wildlife sanctuaries
  SA names of specific refuges, to
      be added as needed
  BT **Wildlife conservation**
Wildlife sanctuaries
  USE **Wildlife refuges**
Will
  USE **Brainwashing**
    Free will and determinism
Will power
  USE **Self-control**
Willpower
  USE **Self-control**
Wills 346.05
  UF Bequests
    Legacies
  BT **Genealogy**
    Registers of births, etc.
  RT **Executors and administrators**
    Inheritance and succession
Wills, Living
  USE **Right to die**
Wind
  USE **Winds**
Wind instruments 788
  UF Brass instruments
    Woodwind instruments
  SA names of wind instruments,
      to be added as needed

  BT **Musical instruments**
  NT **Flutes**
  RT **Bands (Music)**
Wind power 333.9; 621.4
  BT **Energy resources**
    Power (Mechanics)
    Renewable energy resources
  RT **Windmills**
Windbreaks 634.9
  UF Shelterbelts
  BT **Tree planting**
Windmills 621.4
  BT **Irrigation**
  RT **Wind power**
Window dressing
  USE **Show windows**
Window gardening 635.9
  UF Greenhouses, Window
    Window greenhouses
    Windowbox gardening
    Windowsill gardening
  BT **Gardening**
    Indoor gardening
  NT **House plants**
  RT **Container gardening**
    Flower gardening
Window greenhouses
  USE **Window gardening**
Windowbox gardening
  USE **Window gardening**
Windows 721
  BT **Architecture—Details**
    Building
  NT **Show windows**
  RT **Glass**
Windows, Stained glass
  USE **Glass painting and staining**
Windowsill gardening
  USE **Window gardening**
Winds 551.5
  UF Gales
    Wind
  BT **Meteorology**
    Navigation
    Physical geography
    Weather
  NT **Cyclones**
    Hurricanes
    Tornadoes
    Typhoons

BT = Broader Term   NT = Narrower Term   RT = Related Term   SA = See Also   UF = Used For

Winds—*Continued*
  RT Storms
Windsurfing 797.3
  UF Board sailing
      Sailboarding
  BT **Sailing**
Wine and wine making (May subdiv.
      geog.) **641.2; 663**
  BT **Alcoholic beverages**
  RT **Fermentation**
      Grapes
      Vineyards
Winter resorts 613; 796.9
  BT **Recreation**
  RT **Health resorts**
Winter sports 796.9
  UF Ice sports
  SA names of winter sports, to be
      added as needed
  BT **Sports**
  NT **Hockey**
      Ice skating
      Skiing
      Sledding
Wire agencies
  USE **News agencies**
Wireless
  USE **Radio**
Wiretapping 363.2
  BT **Criminal investigation**
      Right of privacy
  RT **Eavesdropping**
Wiring, Electric
  USE **Electric wiring**
Wishes 153.8
  BT **Motivation (Psychology)**
Wit and humor 808.87; 817, etc.
    May be used for individual works, col-
  lections, or materials about wit and hu-
  mor.
  UF Facetiae
      Humor
  SA wit and humor of particular
      countries, e.g. **American wit
      and humor;** and subjects
      with the subdivision *Hu-
      mor,* e.g. **Music—Humor;**
      to be added as needed
  BT **Literature**
  NT **American wit and humor**

Black humor (Literature)
Chapbooks
Comedies
Comedy
Comic books, strips, etc.
English wit and humor
Epigrams
Humorists
Humorous fiction
Humorous poetry
Jokes
Mock-heroic literature
Music—Humor
Nonsense verses
Parody
Practical jokes
Puns
Satire
Tall tales
**World War, 1939-1945—
      Humor**
  RT **Anecdotes**
Witchcraft 133.4
  UF Black art (Magic)
      Black magic (Witchcraft)
      Delusions
      Necromancy
      Sorcery
      Spirits
      Wica
      Wicca
      Wizardry
  BT **Folklore**
      Occultism
      Superstition
  NT **Charms**
      Witches
  RT **Demonology**
      Exorcism
      Magic
Witches 133.4
  UF Covens
  BT **Witchcraft**
Witnesses 345; 347
  UF Cross-examination
  BT **Litigation**
      Trials
Wives 306.872
    Use for materials on wives in general
  and for materials on the legal status of
  married women.

Wives—*Continued*
    UF   Married women *[Former heading]*
           Spouses
    BT   Family
           Marriage
           Married people
           Women
    NT   Widows

Wives of presidents—United States
    USE Presidents—United States—Spouses

Wives, Runaway
    USE Runaway adults

Wizardry
    USE Witchcraft

Wolf children
    USE Wild children

Woman
    USE Women

Women (May subdiv. geog.) **305.4**
    UF   Woman
    SA   women of particular racial or ethnic groups, e.g. **Mexican American women;** and women in various occupations and professions, e.g. **Women artists; Policewomen; Women in the motion picture industry;** etc., to be added as needed
    NT   Abused women
           African American women
           Black women
           Businesswomen
           Indians of North America—Women
           Lesbians
           Mexican American women
           Mothers
           Nuns
           Policewomen
           Single women
           Widows
           Wives
           Women air pilots
           Women artists
           Women authors
           Women clergy

           Women in the motion picture industry
           Women judges
           Women physicians
           World War, 1939-1945—Women
           Young women

Women actors
    USE Actresses

Women, African American
    USE African American women

Women air pilots **629.13092; 920**
    BT   Air pilots
           Women

Women artists **709.2; 920**
    Use for materials on the attainments of several women in the area of art.
    BT   Artists
           Women

Women authors **809; 920**
    Use for collections and for materials on the attainments of several women authors not limited to a single national literature or literary form.
    SA   literary forms and national literatures with the subdivision *Women authors,* e.g. **American literature—Women authors;** to be added as needed
    BT   Authors
           Women
    NT   American literature—Women authors

Women—Biography **920**
    UF   Heroines
    BT   Biography

Women, Black
    USE Black women

Women—Civil rights
    USE Women's rights

Women clergy **253**
    BT   Clergy
           Women
    RT   Ordination of women

Women—Clothing
    USE Women's clothing

Women—Clubs
    USE Women—Societies

Women—Diseases **616.0082; 618.1**
    UF   Diseases of women

Women—Diseases—*Continued*
      Gynecology
  BT **Diseases**
  NT **Breast cancer**
  RT **Women—Health and hygiene**
Women—Dress
  USE **Women's clothing**
Women—Education 376
  UF Education of women
  BT **Education**
  RT **Coeducation**
Women—Emancipation
  USE **Women's rights**
Women—Employment 331.4
  UF Employment of women
      Girls—Employment
      Women—Occupations
      Working women
  SA women in various occupations and professions, e.g. **Women artists; Policewomen; Women in the motion picture industry**; etc., to be added as needed
  BT **Discrimination in employment**
      Employment
      Labor
      Labor supply
  NT **Equal pay for equal work**
      Self-employed women
Women—Enfranchisement
  USE **Women—Suffrage**
Women—Equal rights
  USE **Women's rights**
Women—Health and hygiene 613
  UF Gynecology
      Women—Hygiene
  RT **Women—Diseases**
Women—History 305.409
  Use for comprehensive materials on the history of women, their socio-economic, political, and legal position, their participation in historical events, and their contributions to society. Materials dealing specifically with women's social condition and status, including historical discussions of the same, are entered under **Women—Social conditions.**
  BT **Feminism**
      History
Women—Hygiene
  USE **Women—Health and hygiene**

Women in art 704.9
  Use for materials on women depicted in works of art. Materials on the attainments of several women in the area of art are entered under **Women artists.**
  BT **Art**
Women in business
  USE **Businesswomen**
Women in literature 809
  Use for materials on the theme of women in works of literature. Collections and materials on several women authors not limited to a single national literature or literary form are entered under **Women authors.**
  BT **Characters and characteristics in literature**
Women in motion pictures 791.43
  Use for materials discussing the portrayal of women in motion pictures. Materials discussing all aspects of women's involvement in motion pictures are entered under **Women in the motion picture industry.**
  BT **Motion pictures**
Women in the Bible 220.8
  UF Bible—Women
      Heroines
  BT **Bible—Biography**
Women in the motion picture industry 791.43
  Use for materials discussing all aspects of women's involvement in motion pictures. Materials discussing the portrayal of women in motion pictures are entered under **Women in motion pictures.**
  BT **Motion picture industry**
      Women
Women, Indian
  USE **Indians of North America—Women**
Women judges 347; 920
  BT **Judges**
      Women
Women, Mexican American
  USE **Mexican American women**
Women—Occupations
  USE **Women—Employment**
Women—Ordination
  USE **Ordination of women**
Women physicians 610.69; 920
  BT **Physicians**
      Women
Women police officers
  USE **Policewomen**

Women—Political activity 324
  BT Politics
  NT Women politicians
Women politicians 324.2092; 920
  BT Politicians
       Women—Political activity
Women—Psychology 155.3
  UF Feminine psychology
  BT Psychology
Women—Self-defense
  USE Self-defense for women
Women, Self-employed
  USE Self-employed women
Women, Single
  USE Single women
Women—Social conditions 305.42
  Use for materials dealing specifically with women's social condition and status, including historical discussions of the same. Comprehensive materials on the history of women are entered under **Women—History.**
  NT Divorce
       Prostitution
       Women—Societies
       Women's movement
Women—Societies 367
  UF Women—Clubs
       Women's clubs
       Women's organizations
  BT Clubs
       Societies
       Women—Social conditions
  NT Girls' clubs
Women—Suffrage 324.6
  UF Suffragettes
       Suffragists
       Women—Enfranchisement
  BT Suffrage
  RT Women's rights
Women—United States 305.40973
  UF United States—Women
Women's clothing 646
  UF Women—Clothing
       Women—Dress
  BT Clothing and dress
Women's clubs
  USE Women—Societies
Women's liberation movement
  USE Women's movement

Women's movement 305.42; 323.3
  Use for materials on activities aimed at obtaining equal rights and opportunities for women. Materials on the theory of the political and social equality of the sexes and women's perspectives on various subjects are entered under **Feminism.**
  UF Women's liberation movement
  BT Women—Social conditions
       Women's rights
  RT Feminism
Women's organizations
  USE Women—Societies
Women's rights 323.3; 342
  UF Emancipation of women
       Rights of women
       Women—Civil rights *[Former heading]*
       Women—Emancipation
       Women—Equal rights
  BT Civil rights
       Sex discrimination
  NT Pro-choice movement
       Pro-life movement
       Women's movement
  RT Feminism
       Women—Suffrage
Women's self-defense
  USE Self-defense for women
Wonders
  USE Curiosities and wonders
Wood 620.1; 674
  Use for materials on the various types of wood, their chemical and physical properties, and how they are used.
  UF Timber
       Woods
  SA types of wood, e.g. **Oak;** to be added as needed
  BT Building materials
       Forest products
       Fuel
       Trees
  NT Lumber and lumbering
       Oak
       Plywood
       Woodwork
  RT Forests and forestry
Wood block printing
  USE Wood engraving
       Woodcuts

BT = Broader Term   NT = Narrower Term   RT = Related Term   SA = See Also   UF = Used For

Wood carving 731.4; 736
    UF   Carving, Wood
          Whittling
    BT   **Decoration and ornament**
          Furniture
          Sculpture
          Woodwork
Wood engraving 761
    UF   Block printing
          Wood block printing
    BT   **Engraving**
Wood finishing 698
    UF   Finishes and finishing
    BT   **Industrial painting**
    NT   **Furniture finishing**
          Lacquer and lacquering
          Varnish and varnishing
Wood—Preservation 674
    UF   Preservation of wood
Wood turning
    USE **Turning**
Woodcuts 761
    UF   Block printing
          Wood block printing
    BT   **Prints**
Woods
    USE **Forests and forestry**
          Lumber and lumbering
          Wood
Woodwind instruments
    USE **Wind instruments**
Woodwork 684
    BT   **Architecture—Details**
          Decorative arts
          Wood
    NT   **Furniture**
          Wood carving
    RT   **Cabinetwork**
          Carpentry
          Turning
Woodworking machinery 621.9; 684
    SA   types of woodworking ma-
          chines, to be added as
          needed
    BT   **Machinery**
    NT   **Lathes**
Wool 677
    BT   **Animal products**
          Fabrics
          Fibers

    RT   **Yarn**
Word books
    USE **Picture dictionaries**
Word building
    USE **Word skills**
Word games 793.73
    SA   types of word games, e.g.
          Crossword puzzles; to be
          added as needed
    BT   **Games**
          Literary recreations
    NT   **Crossword puzzles**
Word processing 652.5
    BT   **Office management**
          Office practice
Word processor keyboarding
    USE **Keyboarding (Electronics)**
Word processor keyboards
    USE **Keyboards (Electronics)**
Word skills 372.4; 418
    Use for educational materials on conso-
nants, blends, vowels, prefixes and suffix-
es, digraphs, syllables, root words,
rhyming, and alphabet, etc.
    UF   Word building
          Words
    BT   **Reading**
    RT   **English language—Spelling**
Wordless stories
    USE **Stories without words**
Words
    USE **Vocabulary**
          Word skills
Words, New
    USE **New words**
Work 158.7; 306.3
    Use for materials on the physical or
mental exertion of individuals to produce
or accomplish something. Materials on the
collective human activities involved in the
production and distribution of goods and
services in an economy, as well as materials on the group of workers who render
these services for wages, are entered under
Labor.
    NT   **Employee morale**
          Job satisfaction
          Sex in the workplace
          Work ethic
    RT   **Labor**
Work addiction
    USE **Workaholism**
Work at home
    USE **Home business**

BT = Broader Term   NT = Narrower Term   RT = Related Term   SA = See Also   UF = Used For

Work at home—*Continued*
> **Telecommuting**

Work ethic 174
> UF   Ethics, Work
>   Protestant work ethic
>   Work ethics *[Former heading]*
>   Work, Ethics of
>   Work ethos
> BT   **Ethics**
>   **Labor**
>   **Work**

Work ethics
> USE   **Work ethic**

Work, Ethics of
> USE   **Work ethic**

Work ethos
> USE   **Work ethic**

Work performance standards
> USE   **Performance standards**

Work satisfaction
> USE   **Job satisfaction**

Work standards
> USE   **Production standards**

Work stoppages
> USE   **Strikes**

Work stress
> USE   **Job stress**

Workaholic syndrome
> USE   **Workaholism**

Workaholism 155.2; 616.85
> UF   Addiction to work
>   Compulsive working
>   Work addiction
>   Workaholic syndrome
>   Working, Compulsive
> BT   **Compulsive behavior**

Workers' compensation 368.4
> UF   Compensation
>   Employers' liability
>   Insurance, Workers' compensation
>   Workmen's compensation
> BT   **Accident insurance**
>   **Health insurance**
>   **Occupational diseases**
>   **Social security**

Workers' participation in management
> USE   **Participative management**

Working animals 636.088
> UF   Animals, Working

SA   animals in specific working situations, to be added as needed
> BT   **Animals**
>   **Domestic animals**
>   **Economic zoology**
> NT   **Animals in police work**
>   **Animals—War use**
>   **Guide dogs**

Working at home
> USE   **Home business**
>   **Telecommuting**

Working children
> USE   **Children—Employment**

Working class 305.5
> Use for materials on the social class composed of persons who work for wages, usually in manual labor.
> UF   Blue collar workers
>   Factory workers
>   Industrial workers
>   Labor and laboring classes
>   *[Former heading]*
>   Laborers
>   Laboring class
>   Laboring classes
>   Manual workers
>   Skilled workers
>   Unskilled workers
>   Working classes
> BT   **Social classes**
> NT   **Proletariat**
> RT   **Labor**

Working classes
> USE   **Working class**

Working, Compulsive
> USE   **Workaholism**

Working couples
> USE   **Dual career family**

Working day
> USE   **Hours of labor**

Working hours
> USE   **Hours of labor**

Working parents, Children of
> USE   **Children of working parents**

Working robots
> USE   **Industrial robots**

Working women
> USE   **Women—Employment**

Workmen's compensation
> USE   **Workers' compensation**

BT = Broader Term   NT = Narrower Term   RT = Related Term   SA = See Also   UF = Used For

Workshop councils
　USE　**Participative management**
Workshops, Teachers'
　USE　**Teachers' workshops**
World
　USE　**Earth**
World economics
　USE　**Commercial geography**
　　　Commercial policy
　　　Economic conditions
　　　Economic policy
　　　International competition
World, End of the
　USE　**End of the world**
World government
　USE　**International organization**
World history 909
　UF　History, Universal
　　　Universal history
　BT　**History**
　NT　**Ancient history**
　　　Geography
　　　Middle Ages
　　　Middle Ages—History
　　　Modern history
World language
　USE　**Universal language**
World organization
　USE　**International organization**
World politics 909
　　Use for historical accounts of interna-
　tional political affairs. Materials on the
　theory of international relations are en-
　tered under **International relations.**
　UF　International politics
　SA　names of countries with the
　　　subdivisions *Foreign rela-*
　　　tions and *Politics and gov-*
　　　ernment, to be added as
　　　needed
　BT　**Political science**
　NT　**United States—Foreign rela-**
　　　tions
　　　World War, 1914-1918
　　　World War, 1939-1945
　　　World War III
　RT　**Geopolitics**
　　　International organization
　　　International relations
World politics—1945-1965 909.82
World politics—1945-1991 909.82
　NT　**Cold war**

World politics—1965- 909.82
World records 030
　UF　Human records
　　　Records, Human
　　　Records of achievement
　　　Records, World
　　　World's records
　BT　**Curiosities and wonders**
　RT　**Sports records**
World War I
　USE　**World War, 1914-1918**
World War II
　USE　**World War, 1939-1945**
World War, 1914-1918 (May subdiv.
　　　geog.) **940.3; 940.4**
　May be subdivided like **World War,
1939-1945.**
　UF　European War, 1914-1918
　　　War of 1914
　　　World War I
　BT　**Europe—History—1871-1918**
　　　Modern history—1900-1999
　　　(20th century)
　　　World politics
World War, 1914-1918—Economic as-
　　　pects 940.3
　RT　**Reconstruction (1914-1939)**
World War, 1914-1918—Gas warfare
　　　940.4
　BT　**Poisonous gases—War use**
World War, 1914-1918—Peace 940.3
　NT　**League of Nations**
World War, 1914-1918—Reconstruction
　USE　**Reconstruction (1914-1939)**
World War, 1914-1918—Territorial
　　　questions 940.3
　NT　**Mandates**
World War, 1914-1918—United States
　　　940.3; 940.4; 973.91
　UF　United States—European War,
　　　1914-1918
　　　United States—History—
　　　1914-1918, European War
　　　United States—History—
　　　1914-1918, World War
　　　United States—World War,
　　　1914-1918
World War, 1939-1945 (May subdiv.
　　　geog.) **940.53; 940.54**
　Subdivisions used under this heading
　may be used under other wars.

World War, 1939-1945—*Continued*

   UF   European War, 1939-1945
          War of 1939-1945
          World War II

   SA   names of battles, campaigns, sieges, etc., e.g. **Ardennes, Battle of the, 1944-1945; Pearl Harbor (Oahu, Hawaii), Attack on, 1941**; etc., to be added as needed

   BT   **Europe—History—1918-1945**
          Modern history—1900-1999 (20th century)
          World politics

World War, 1939-1945—Aerial operations 940.54

   UF   World War, 1939-1945—Battles, sieges, etc.

   BT   **Military aeronautics**

World War, 1939-1945—African Americans 940.53; 940.54

World War, 1939-1945—Amphibious operations 940.54

   BT   **World War, 1939-1945—Naval operations**

World War, 1939-1945—Antiwar movements

   USE   **World War, 1939-1945—Protests, demonstrations, etc.**

World War, 1939-1945—Armistices 940.53

World War, 1939-1945—Arms

   USE   **World War, 1939-1945—Equipment and supplies**

World War, 1939-1945—Art and the war 940.53

   UF   World War, 1939-1945—Iconography
          World War, 1939-1945, in art

   BT   **Art**

World War, 1939-1945—Atrocities 940.54

   SA   names of specific atrocities and crimes, to be added as needed

World War, 1939-1945—Battles, sieges, etc.

   USE   **World War, 1939-1945—Aerial operations**

World War, 1939-1945—Campaigns

World War, 1939-1945—Naval operations

World War, 1939-1945—Biography 920

World War, 1939-1945—Blockades 940.54

World War, 1939-1945—Campaigns (May subdiv. geog.) **940.54**

   UF   World War, 1939-1945—Battles, sieges, etc.

   SA   names of battles, campaigns, sieges, etc., **Ardennes, Battle of the, 1944-1945;** to be added as needed

   NT   **Ardennes, Battle of the, 1944-1945**
          Normandy (France), Attack on, 1944
          Pearl Harbor (Oahu, Hawaii), Attack on, 1941

World War, 1939-1945—Cartoons and caricatures 940.53

   UF   World War, 1939-1945—Humor, caricatures, etc. *[Former heading]*

   BT   **Cartoons and caricatures**

World War, 1939-1945—Causes 940.53

   NT   **National socialism**

World War, 1939-1945—Censorship 940.54

World War, 1939-1945—Charities

   USE   **World War, 1939-1945—Civilian relief**
             World War, 1939-1945—War work

World War, 1939-1945—Chemical warfare 940.54

   BT   **Chemical warfare**

World War, 1939-1945—Children 940.53

   BT   **Children**

World War, 1939-1945—Civilian evacuation

   USE   **World War, 1939-1945—Evacuation of civilians**

World War, 1939-1945—Civilian relief 940.54

   UF   World War, 1939-1945—Charities

World War, 1939-1945—Civilian
relief—*Continued*
   BT   Charities
        Economic assistance
        Food relief
        Reconstruction (1939-1951)
        World War, 1939-1945—Food
          supply
        World War, 1939-1945—
          Medical care
        World War, 1939-1945—War
          work
   RT   World War, 1939-1945—
          Refugees
World War, 1939-1945—
          Collaborationists 940.53
   UF   Fifth column
        Quislings
   BT   World War, 1939-1945—
          Occupied territories
World War, 1939-1945—Congresses
        940.53
   BT   Congresses and conventions
World War, 1939-1945—Conscientious
        objectors 940.53
   BT   Conscientious objectors
        World War, 1939-1945—
          Protests, demonstrations,
          etc.
   NT   World War, 1939-1945—Draft
          resisters
World War, 1939-1945—
          Correspondents
   USE World War, 1939-1945—
          Journalists
World War, 1939-1945—Desertions
        940.54
   BT   Military desertion
World War, 1939-1945—Destruction
        and pillage 940.54
World War, 1939-1945—Diplomatic
        history 940.53
   NT   World War, 1939-1945—
          Governments in exile
World War, 1939-1945—Displaced per-
        sons
   USE World War, 1939-1945—
          Refugees
World War, 1939-1945—Draft resisters
        940.54
   BT   Draft resisters

World War, 1939-1945—
        Conscientious objectors
World War, 1939-1945—Economic as-
        pects 940.53
      Use for materials on the economic
causes of the war and the effect of the war
on commerce and industry.
   BT   War—Economic aspects
   NT   World War, 1939-1945—
          Finance
        World War, 1939-1945—
          Human resources
        World War, 1939-1945—
          Reparations
   RT   Reconstruction (1939-1951)
World War, 1939-1945—Education and
        the war 940.53
   BT   Education
World War, 1939-1945—Engineering
        and construction 940.54
   BT   Military engineering
World War, 1939-1945—Equipment and
        supplies 940.54
   UF   World War, 1939-1945—Arms
        World War, 1939-1945—
          Military supplies
        World War, 1939-1945—
          Military weapons
        World War, 1939-1945—
          Ordnance
        World War, 1939-1945—
          Supplies
        World War, 1939-1945—
          Weapons
   BT   Military weapons
World War, 1939-1945—Evacuation of
        civilians 940.54
   UF   Civilian evacuation
        World War, 1939-1945—
          Civilian evacuation
   BT   Civil defense
        World War, 1939-1945—
          Refugees
World War, 1939-1945—Fiction 808.83;
        813, etc.
      May be used for individual works, col-
lections, or materials about fiction dealing
with the Second World War.

World War, 1939-1945—Finance 940.53

Use for materials on the cost and financing of the war, including war debts, and the effect of the war on financial systems, including inflation.

BT Public debts

World War, 1939-1945—
Economic aspects

World War, 1939-1945—Food question

USE **World War, 1939-1945—Food supply**

World War, 1939-1945—Food supply 940.53

UF World War, 1939-1945—Food question

BT **Food relief**

NT **World War, 1939-1945—Civilian relief**

World War, 1939-1945—Forced repatriation 940.53

BT **World War, 1939-1945—Prisoners and prisons**

RT **World War, 1939-1945—Refugees**

World War, 1939-1945—Governments in exile 940.53

UF Governments in exile

BT **World War, 1939-1945—Diplomatic history**

World War, 1939-1945—Guerrillas

USE **World War, 1939-1945—Underground movements**

World War, 1939-1945—Health aspects 940.54

BT **Armies—Medical care**
Military health
Sanitation

World War, 1939-1945—Hospitals

USE **World War, 1939-1945—Medical care**

World War, 1939-1945—Human resources 940.54

BT **Armies**
Human resources
Labor
Labor supply
War—Economic aspects
World War, 1939-1945—Economic aspects

World War, 1939-1945—Humor 940.53

UF World War, 1939-1945—
Humor, caricatures, etc.
[Former heading]

BT **Wit and humor**

World War, 1939-1945—Humor, caricatures, etc.

USE **World War, 1939-1945—Cartoons and caricatures**
World War, 1939-1945—Humor

World War, 1939-1945—Iconography

USE **World War, 1939-1945—Art and the war**

World War, 1939-1945, in art

USE **World War, 1939-1945—Art and the war**

World War, 1939-1945, in literature

USE **World War, 1939-1945—Literature and the war**

World War, 1939-1945, in motion pictures

USE **World War, 1939-1945—Motion pictures and the war**

World War, 1939-1945—Influence 940.53

World War, 1939-1945—Jews 940.53

RT **Jewish holocaust (1933-1945)**

World War, 1939-1945—Jews—Rescue 940.54

UF Rescue of Jews, 1939-1945

BT **Jews—Persecutions**

World War, 1939-1945—Journalists 940.54

UF World War, 1939-1945—Correspondents
World War, 1939-1945—War correspondents

World War, 1939-1945—Literature and the war 809; 810, etc.; 940.53

UF World War, 1939-1945, in literature

BT **Literature**

World War, 1939-1945—Maps 940.53022

BT **Maps**

World War, 1939-1945—Medical care
940.54

UF   World War, 1939-1945—
Hospitals

BT   **Armies—Medical care**
Military health
Military hospitals
Military medicine

NT   **World War, 1939-1945—**
Civilian relief

World War, 1939-1945—Military supplies

USE   **World War, 1939-1945—**
Equipment and supplies

World War, 1939-1945—Military weapons

USE   **World War, 1939-1945—**
Equipment and supplies

World War, 1939-1945—Missing in action 940.54

BT   **Missing in action**
World War, 1939-1945—
Prisoners and prisons

World War, 1939-1945—Moral and religious aspects 940.53;
940.54

UF   World War, 1939-1945—
Religious aspects

BT   **War and religion**

World War, 1939-1945—Motion pictures and the war 791.43;
940.53

    May be used for individual works, collections, or materials about films dealing with the Second World War.

UF   World War, 1939-1945, in
motion pictures

BT   **Motion pictures**
War films

World War, 1939-1945—Museums
940.54

BT   **Museums**

World War, 1939-1945—Naval operations 940.54

UF   World War, 1939-1945—
Battles, sieges, etc.

BT   **Naval battles**

NT   **World War, 1939-1945—**
Amphibious operations

World War, 1939-1945—Naval
operations—Submarine
940.54

UF   World War, 1939-1945—
Submarine operations

BT   **Submarine warfare**

World War, 1939-1945—Occupied territories 940.54

Use for general treatment of the subject.

SA   names of countries with the
subdivision *History—1940-*
1945, German occupa-
tion, e.g. **Netherlands—**
History—1940-1945, Ger-
man occupation; or with
the subdivision *History—*
1945- , Allied occupa-
tion, e.g. **Japan—History—**
1945-1952, Allied occu-
pation; to be added as
needed

BT   **Military occupation**
World War, 1939-1945—
Territorial questions

NT   **Japan—History—1945-1952,**
Allied occupation
Netherlands—History—
1940-1945, German occupa-
tion
World War, 1939-1945—
Collaborationists
World War, 1939-1945—
Underground movements

World War, 1939-1945—Ordnance

USE   **World War, 1939-1945—**
Equipment and supplies

World War, 1939-1945—Peace 940.53

BT   **Peace**

World War, 1939-1945—Personal narratives 940.53; 940.54

Use for collective or individual eyewitness reports or autobiographical accounts of the war in general. Accounts limited to a specific topic are entered under that topic.

BT   **Autobiographies**
Biography

World War, 1939-1945—Pictorial works
940.53022

World War, 1939-1945—Poetry 808.81;
811, etc.; 811.008, etc.

May be used for individual works, collections, or materials about poetry dealing
with the Second World War.

BT   War poetry

World War, 1939-1945—Prisoners and
prisons 940.54

BT   Concentration camps
Prisoners of war

NT   World War, 1939-1945—
Forced repatriation
World War, 1939-1945—
Missing in action

World War, 1939-1945—Propaganda
940.54

BT   Propaganda

World War, 1939-1945—Protests, demonstrations, etc. 940.53

UF   World War, 1939-1945—
Antiwar movements

BT   Protests, demonstrations, etc.

NT   World War, 1939-1945—
Conscientious objectors

World War, 1939-1945—Psychological
aspects 940.53

BT   Psychological warfare

World War, 1939-1945—Public opinion
940.53

BT   Public opinion

World War, 1939-1945—Railroads
USE   World War, 1939-1945—
Transportation

World War, 1939-1945—Reconstruction
USE   Reconstruction (1939-1951)

World War, 1939-1945—Refugees
940.53

UF   World War, 1939-1945—
Displaced persons

BT   Political refugees

NT   World War, 1939-1945—
Evacuation of civilians

RT   World War, 1939-1945—
Civilian relief
World War, 1939-1945—
Forced repatriation

World War, 1939-1945—Regimental
histories 940.54

World War, 1939-1945—Religious aspects

USE   World War, 1939-1945—
Moral and religious aspects

World War, 1939-1945—Reparations
940.53

UF   Reparations (World War,
1939-1945)

BT   Reconstruction (1939-1951)
World War, 1939-1945—
Economic aspects

World War, 1939-1945—Resistance
movements

USE   World War, 1939-1945—
Underground movements

World War, 1939-1945—Secret service
940.54

BT   Secret service

World War, 1939-1945—Social aspects
940.53

World War, 1939-1945—Social work
USE   World War, 1939-1945—War
work

World War, 1939-1945—Songs 782.42

UF   World War, 1939-1945—
Songs and music [Former
heading]

BT   Military music
War songs

World War, 1939-1945—Songs and music

USE   World War, 1939-1945—
Songs

World War, 1939-1945—Sources 940.53

BT   History—Sources

World War, 1939-1945—Submarine operations

USE   World War, 1939-1945—
Naval operations—
Submarine

World War, 1939-1945—Supplies
USE   World War, 1939-1945—
Equipment and supplies

World War, 1939-1945—Territorial
questions 940.53

BT   Boundaries

NT   World War, 1939-1945—
Occupied territories

BT = Broader Term   NT = Narrower Term   RT = Related Term   SA = See Also   UF = Used For

World War, 1939-1945—Theater and
  the war 792; 940.53
 BT Theater
World War, 1939-1945—Transportation
  940.54
 UF World War, 1939-1945—
   Railroads
 BT Transportation
World War, 1939-1945—Treaties
  940.53
 BT Treaties
World War, 1939-1945—Underground
  movements 940.54
 UF Anti-fascist movements
   Anti-Nazi movement
   Underground movements
   (World War, 1939-1945)
   World War, 1939-1945—
   Guerrillas
   World War, 1939-1945—
   Resistance movements
 BT World War, 1939-1945—
   Occupied territories
World War, 1939-1945—United States
  940.53; 940.54; 973.917
 UF United States—History—
   1939-1945, World War
   United States—World War,
   1939-1945
World War, 1939-1945—War corre-
  spondents
 USE World War, 1939-1945—
   Journalists
World War, 1939-1945—War work
  940.53
 UF World War, 1939-1945—
   Charities
   World War, 1939-1945—
   Social work
 NT World War, 1939-1945—
   Civilian relief
World War, 1939-1945—Weapons
 USE World War, 1939-1945—
   Equipment and supplies
World War, 1939-1945—Women 940.54
 BT Women
World War III 355
 UF Third World War
 BT War
   World politics

World's Fair (1992 : Seville, Spain)
 USE Expo 92 (Seville, Spain)
World's fairs
 USE Exhibitions
   Fairs
World's records
 USE World records
Worms 595.1
 BT Invertebrates
Worry 152.4
 UF Anxiety
 BT Emotions
   Mental health
Worship 248.3; 264; 291.3
 UF Devotion
 BT Religion
   Theology
 NT Devotional exercises
   Prayer
   Public worship
   Sacrifice
Worship of the dead
 USE Ancestor worship
Worth
 USE Values
Wounded, First aid to
 USE First aid
Wounds and injuries 617.1
 UF Injuries
 BT Accidents
 NT Fractures
Wrapping of gifts
 USE Gift wrapping
Wrecks
 USE Shipwrecks
   and subjects with the subdivi-
   sion *Accidents,* e.g. **Rail-**
   roads—Accidents; to be
   added as needed
Wrestling 796.8
 BT Athletics
 NT Judo
Writers
 USE Authors
Writing 411
  Use for general materials on the history
 and art of writing and on elegant hand-
 writing. Practical guides are entered under
 Handwriting. Materials on handwriting as
 an expression of the writer's character are
 entered under **Graphology.**

Writing—*Continued*
- BT **Communication**
  Language and languages
  Language arts
- NT **Abbreviations**
  Autographs
  Calligraphy
  Cryptography
  Graphology
  Hieroglyphics
  Picture writing
  Shorthand
  Typewriting
  Whole language
  Writing of numerals
- RT **Alphabet**
  Ciphers
  Handwriting

Writing (Authorship)
- USE **Authorship**
  Creative writing
  Journalism

Writing of numerals 513
- UF Numeral formation
  Numeral writing
  Numerals, Writing of
- BT **Handwriting**
  Numerals
  Writing

Writing—Patterning
- USE **Language arts—Patterning**

Writings of gay men
- USE **Gay men's writings**

Writings of lesbians
- USE **Lesbians' writings**

Wrought iron work
- USE **Ironwork**

X-15 (Rocket aircraft) 629.133
- BT **Rocket planes**

X rays 539.7
- UF Radiography
  Rays, Roentgen
  Roentgen rays
- BT **Electromagnetic waves**
  Radiation
- NT **Gamma rays**
  Radiologists
  Tomography
  Vacuum tubes
- RT **Radiotherapy**

Xerography 686.4
- BT **Copying processes and machines**

Yacht basins
- USE **Marinas**

Yachts and yachting 797.1
- UF Regattas
- BT **Boatbuilding**
  Boats and boating
  Ocean travel
  Ships
  Voyages and travels
  Water sports
- NT **Marinas**
- RT **Sailing**

Yard sales
- USE **Garage sales**

Yarn 677
- BT **Textile industry**
- NT **Cotton**
  Flax
- RT **Wool**

Yearbooks
- USE subjects with the subdivision *Periodicals,* e.g. **Engineering—Periodicals;** to be added as needed

Yearbooks, Student
- USE **School yearbooks**

Yeast 641.3
- BT **Fermentation**

Yellow fever 616.9
- BT **Tropical medicine**

Yeti 001.9
- UF Abominable snowman
- BT **Monsters**
  Mythical animals

Yiddish language 437
  May be subdivided like **English language.**
- UF German Hebrew
  Jewish language
  Jews—Language
  Judaeo-German
- BT **Language and languages**

Yiddish literature 839
  May use same subdivisions and names of literary forms as for **English literature.**
- BT **Jewish literature**

Yippies
- USE **Hippies**

Yoga 181; 613.7
  BT Hindu philosophy
      Hinduism
      Theosophy
  NT Hatha yoga
Yoga exercises
  USE Hatha yoga
Yoga, Hatha
  USE Hatha yoga
Yom Kippur 296.4
  UF Atonement, Day of
      Day of Atonement
  BT Jewish holidays
Yom Kippur War, 1973
  USE Israel-Arab War, 1973
Yoruba (African people) 305.896
  BT Africans
Yosemite National Park (Calif.) 719;
      979.4
  BT National parks and reserves—
      United States
Yosemite National Park (Calif.)—
      Pictorial works 979.4
  BT Pictures
      Views
Young adults' library services 027.62
  UF Libraries and young adults
      Libraries, Young adults'
      Library services to teenagers
      Library services to young
        adults
      Teenagers' library services
      Young people's libraries
  BT Library services
  RT Children's libraries
      High school libraries
      Young adults' literature
Young adults' literature 028.5; 808.8;
      810.8, etc.; 809
  UF Teenagers—Literature
  BT Literature
  RT Young adults' library services
Young consumers 640.73; 658.8
  UF Children as consumers
      Teenage consumers
      Youth market
  BT Consumers

Young men 305.23; 305.31
    Use for materials on men in the general
  age range of eighteen through twenty-five
  years. Materials on the time of life between thirteen and twenty-five, as well as
  on people in that greater age range are en-
  tered under Youth.
  BT Men
      Youth
  RT Boys
Young people
  USE Youth
Young people's libraries
  USE Young adults' library services
Young persons
  USE Youth
Young women 305.4; 305.23
    Use for materials on women in the gen-
  eral age range of eighteen through twenty-
  five years. Materials on the time of life
  between thirteen and twenty-five, as well
  as on people in that greater age range are
  entered under Youth.
  BT Women
      Youth
  RT Girls
Youngest child
  USE Birth order
Youth (May subdiv. geog.) 305.23
    Use for materials on the time of life be-
  tween thirteen and twenty-five years, as
  well as on people in this general age range.
  Materials limited to teen youth are entered under Teenagers. Materials limited
  to people in the general age range of eighteen through twenty-five years of age are
  entered under Young men or Young wom-
  en. Materials on the process or state of
  growing up are entered under Adolescence.
  UF Young people
      Young persons
  SA youth of particular racial or
        ethnic groups, to be added
        as needed
  BT Age
  NT Adolescence
      African American youth
      Church work with youth
      Dropouts
      Teenagers
      Television and youth
      Young men
      Young women
Youth—Alcohol use 613.81; 616.86
  UF Alcohol and youth

Youth—Alcohol use—*Continued*
    Drinking and youth
  NT **Drinking age**
Youth and drugs
  USE **Youth—Drug use**
Youth and narcotics
  USE **Youth—Drug use**
Youth and television
  USE **Television and youth**
Youth—Drug use 613.8; 616.86
  UF Drugs and youth
      Narcotics and youth
      Youth and drugs
      Youth and narcotics
  NT **Teenagers—Drug use**
  RT **Juvenile delinquency**
Youth—Employment 331.3
  UF Child labor
      Employment of youth
  BT **Age and employment**
      Employment
      Labor
      Labor supply
  NT **Teenagers—Employment**
  RT **Summer employment**
Youth hostels 647.94
  UF Hostels, Youth
      Tourist accommodations
  BT **Community centers**
      Hotels and motels
Youth market
  USE **Young consumers**
Youth movement (May subdiv. geog.)
    322.4
  UF Student movement
      Student protests, demonstra-
        tions, etc.
      Student revolt
  BT **Protests, demonstrations, etc.**
  NT **Students—Political activity**
Youth—Religious life 248.8; 268
  BT **Religious life**
  NT **Teenagers—Religious life**
Youth—United States 305.230973
  UF American youth
      United States—Youth
  NT **Teenagers—United States**
Zen Buddhism 294.3
  BT **Buddhism**
Zeppelins
  USE **Airships**

Zero gravity
  USE **Weightlessness**
Zinc 669
  BT **Chemical elements**
      Metals
Zionism 320.5
  UF Zionist movement
  RT **Jews—Restoration**
Zionist movement
  USE **Zionism**
Zip code (May subdiv. geog.) 383
  UF Postal delivery code
  BT **Postal service**
Zodiac 133.5; 523
  BT **Astrology**
      Astronomy
Zoning 346.04; 352.9
  UF City planning—Zone system
      Districting (in city planning)
  BT **City planning**
Zoogeography
  USE **Biogeography**
Zoological gardens
  USE **Zoos**
Zoological specimens—Collection and
    preservation 579
  UF Collections of natural speci-
      mens
      Preservation of zoological
      specimens
      Specimens, Preservation of
  SA names of specimens with the
      subdivision *Collection and
      preservation,* e.g. **Birds—
      Collection and preservation;**
      to be added as needed
  BT **Collectors and collecting**
  NT **Birds—Collection and preser-
      vation**
  RT **Taxidermy**
Zoology 591
  Use for systematic or technical materi-
als. Descriptive and nonsystematic or non-
technical materials are entered under
Animals.
  UF Animal kingdom
      Animal physiology
      Fauna
  SA names of divisions, classes,
      etc., of the animal king-

BT = Broader Term   NT = Narrower Term   RT = Related Term   SA = See Also   UF = Used For

Zoology—*Continued*

    dom, e.g. **Invertebrates; Vertebrates; Birds; Mammals;** etc.; and names of animals, to be added as needed

BT **Biology**
    Natural history
    Nature study
    Science

NT **Animal behavior**
    Animal reproduction
    Birds
    Comparative anatomy
    Comparative psychology
    Economic zoology
    Embryology
    Evolution
    Fossils
    Invertebrates
    Mammals

    Variation (Biology)
    Vertebrates

RT **Animals**
    Zoos

Zoology—Anatomy
  USE **Animals—Anatomy**

Zoology, Economic
  USE **Economic zoology**

Zoology of the Bible
  USE **Bible—Natural history**

Zoology—United States
  USE **Animals—United States**

Zoos 590.74

  UF Zoological gardens

  SA names of individual zoos, to be added as needed

  BT **Parks**

  NT **Petting zoos**

  RT **Animals**
      Zoology